U.S. GOLF COURSE DIRECTORY

Your Resource Guide to America's 16,431 Golf Destinations

18th Edition

www.golfyellowpages.com

U.S. Golf Course Directory: Your Resource Guide to America's 16,431 Golf Destinations, 18th Edition from Golf Yellow Pages

Copyright © 2012 by Sellbox Inc., All Rights Reserved.
ISBN-13: 978-1481917322 (print edition)
Also available in eBook edition

Published by SellBox Inc. 7668 El Camino Real, Ste 104-333, Carlsbad, CA 92009

an eBook Agency
Sellbox.com

Cover design by Yolanda Zuniga

This book is intended to provide accurate information with regards to its subject matter, however, in times of rapid change, ensuring all information provided is entirely accurate and up-to-date at all times is not always possible. Therefore, the author and publisher accept no responsibility for inaccuracies or omissions and specifically disclaim any liability, loss or risk, personal, professional or otherwise, which may be incurred as a consequence, directly or indirectly, of the use and/or application of any of the contents of this book.

Volume Discounts

Books may be purchased at volume discounts by contacting the publisher: 760-942-4227 | www.golfyellowpages.com

CONTENTS

First published in 1994, the U.S. Golf Course Directory from Golf Yellow Pages is the most comprehensive resource of its kind.

Volume Discounts... ii
About the Listings... iv
Index to Course Listings by State... 1

U.S. Golf Course Distribution by State

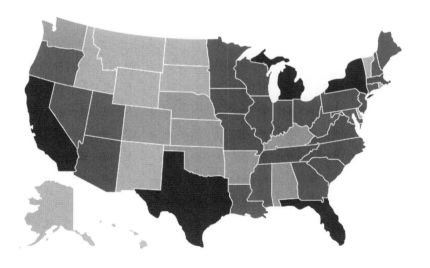

States	Range
5	800+
9	400 - 799
7	300 - 399
8	200 - 299
10	100 - 199
11	< 100

About the listings:

- Some golf course facilities may manage more than one course (i.e. "north course", "south course"). There is a pro shop for every course listed in this book.
- Can find it? Try looking under "The", "Country Club of", etc.

Inside this 18th edition you will find:

- Golf courses organized alphabetically by state.
- Telephone number, city and number of holes for each destination.
- Website addresses for 12,416 golf course destinations.
- All U.S. golf course destinations are included: Public, Private, Semi-Private and Resort. Also included are Municipal, Military and University golf courses.

Correcting Information:

Course contact information can change. If you come across information that is no longer accurate we would appreciate it if you let us know so we can correct it in the next edition. Use the handy contact form found at www.GolfYellowPages.com.

Mailing Lists:

Visit www.ContactGolfCourses.com or call us for more information: (760) 942-4227 or (800) 864-2754.

Golf Yellow Pages, 18th Edition

ALABAMA

Alabama................1	Kentucky..............83	North Dakota..........158
Alaska..................4	Louisiana..............86	Ohio...................160
Arizona.................4	Maine..................88	Oklahoma..............171
Arkansas................9	Maryland...............91	Oregon.................173
California..............12	Massachusetts.........93	Pennsylvania...........176
Colorado...............26	Michigan...............99	Rhode Island...........187
Connecticut............30	Minnesota.............111	South Carolina.........187
Delaware...............32	Mississippi............118	South Dakota..........193
District of Columbia...33	Missouri...............120	Tennessee.............194
Florida.................33	Montana...............125	Texas..................198
Georgia................49	Nebraska..............126	Utah...................210
Hawaii.................55	Nevada................129	Vermont...............212
Idaho..................57	New Hampshire.......131	Virginia................213
Illinois.................58	New Jersey............132	Washington............218
Indiana................68	New Mexico...........137	West Virginia..........222
Iowa...................74	New York..............138	Wisconsin.............224
Kansas.................79	North Carolina........150	Wyoming..............231

ALABAMA

Albertville G&CC, *Albertville*.....................18 [V] 256-878-4403
Aliceville CC, *Aliceville*..........................9 [V] 205-367-7868
Alpine Bay Resort, *Alpine*......................18 [R] 256-268-2920
Altadena Valley G&CC, *Birmingham*..........18 [V] 205-967-5324
   avccgolf.org
Andalusia CC, *Andalusia*.......................18 [V] 334-222-5282
Anniston CC, *Anniston*.........................18 [V] 256-237-8412
   annistoncc.com
Anniston Muni GC, *Anniston*....................9 [M] 256-231-7631
Arrowhead CC, *Montgomery*...................18 [V] 334-272-7188
   arrowheadcountryclub.net
Athens G&CC, *Athens*............................9 [P] 256-232-0809
Atmore CC, *Atmore*..............................9 [V] 251-368-4486
Auburn Links At Mill Creek, *Auburn*...........18 [P] 334-887-5151
   auburnlinks.com
Auburn Univ Club At Yarbrough Farms, *Auburn*. 18 [N] 334-821-8381
   aucyf.com
Azalea City GC, *Mobile*.........................18 [M] 251-208-5150
   cityofmobile.org
Ballantrae GC, *Pelham*..........................18 [S] 205-620-4653
   ballantraegolf.com
Bear Branch GC, *Jasper*..........................9 [R] 205-522-9237
Becky Peirce Muni GC, *Huntsville*.............18 [M] 256-880-1151
   huntsvillemuni.com
Bent Brook GC, *Bessemer*......................27 [P] 205-424-2368
   bentbrook.com
Blackberry Trail GC, *Florence*..................18 [M] 256-740-8825
   florenceal.org
Boaz GC, *Boaz*..................................18 [P] 256-593-5501
Bonnie Crest CC, *Montgomery*................18 [V] 334-272-9316
   bonniecrestcountryclub.com
Briarmeade GC, *Glencoe*.......................18 [V] 256-492-1150
   briarmeadegolf.com
Broken Arrow GC, *Scottsboro*..................18 [P] 256-582-9888
   brokenarrowgolf.com
Brookside GC, *Arab*.............................18 [P] 256-586-5765
Brundidge GC, *Brundidge*.......................9 [V] 334-735-3680
Burningtree CC, *Decatur*.......................18 [V] 256-355-5982
   btcountryclub.com

Cahaba Shoals CC, *Centreville*.................18 [S] 205-926-9323
Cane Creek GC, *Anniston*......................18 [M] 256-820-9174
   canecreekgolf.com
Canebrake GC, *Athens*.........................18 [S] 256-232-2412
   canebrakeclub.com
Capitol Hill GC, *Prattville*......................54 [S] 334-285-1114
   rtjgolf.com
Capstone GC, *Brookwood*.....................18 [V] 205-462-0590
   capstoneclub.com
Castle Pines CC, *Gardendale*..................18 [P] 205-631-3140
   castlepinesllc.com
CC of Birmingham, *Birmingham*...............36 [V] 205-879-4611
   ccbham.org
CC of Brewton, *Brewton*.......................18 [S] 251-867-3408
CC of Mobile, *Mobile*...........................27 [V] 251-342-5138
   ccofmobile.com
CC of Tuscaloosa, *Tuscaloosa*..................18 [V] 205-759-5535
Cedar Creek Golf, *Bessemer*...................18 [S] 205-424-8450
Cedar Ridge GC, *Decatur*......................18 [P] 256-353-4653
   cedarridgegolfdecatur.com
Cherokee CC, *Centre*..........................18 [S] 256-927-5070
Cherokee Ridge CC, *Union Grove*..............18 [V] 256-498-5305
   cherokeeridge.com
Chesley Oaks GC, *Cullman*.....................18 [P] 256-796-9808
Choctaw CC, *Butler*.............................9 [V] 205-459-2529
Chriswood CC, *Athens*.........................18 [P] 256-232-9759
Cider Ridge GC, *Oxford*........................18 [P] 256-831-7222
   ciderridgegolf.com
Clanton CC, *Clanton*............................9 [V] 205-755-0415
Clay County GC, *Ashland*.......................9 [S] 256-354-2814
Cloudmont Ski & Golf Resort, *Mentone*.........9 [R] 256-634-4344
   cloudmont.com
Colonial GC, *Meridianville*.....................18 [P] 256-828-0431
Coosa Pines GC, *Childersburg*.................18 [P] 256-378-5529
   coosapinesgolfclub.com
Cottonwood GC, *Montgomery*................18 [P] 334-281-3344
   cottonwoodgolfclub.com
Craft Farms Golf Resort, *Gulf Shores*...........36 [R] 251-968-7500
   craftfarms.com
Craig GC, *Selma*..................................9 [P] 334-872-4451
   craigcomplex.com

[S] = SEMI-PRIVATE   [V] = PRIVATE   [U] = UNIVERSITY   [N] = UNIVERSITY-PRIVATE

ALABAMA

Golf Yellow Pages, 18th Edition

Course	City	Holes	Type	Phone
Crenshaw County Rec Club,	Luverne	9	[V]	334-335-5404
Cullman Muni GC,	Hanceville	18	[M]	256-739-2386
cullmanrecreation.org				
Cumberland Lake CC,	Pinson	18	[S]	205-680-4653
cumberlandlakegolf.com				
Curry GC,	Jasper	9	[P]	205-221-5678
Cypress Lakes G&CC,	Muscle Shoals	18	[S]	256-381-1232
clgcc.com				
Cypress Tree GC,	Montgomery	36	[A]	334-953-2209
cypresstreegolf.com				
De Soto CC,	Fort Payne	9	[V]	256-845-2571
Decatur CC,	Decatur	18	[V]	256-353-3039
decaturcountryclub.org				
Deer Run GC,	Moulton	18	[M]	256-974-7384
Deer Valley Links,	Chelsea	9	[P]	205-678-2292
Deerfield CC,	Chatom	18	[S]	251-847-2056
Demopolis CC,	Demopolis	18	[V]	334-289-0880
demopoliscountryclub.com				
Dogwood Hills GC,	Flat Rock	18	[P]	256-632-3634
dogwoodhillsgolfresortandgardens.com				
Dogwood Hills GC,	Brewton	9	[M]	251-809-1750
cityofbrewton.org				
Dothan CC,	Dothan	18	[V]	334-792-8255
dothancountryclub.com				
Dothan National GC & Hotel,	Dothan	18	[R]	334-677-3321
dngch.com				
Eagle Point GC,	Birmingham	18	[P]	205-991-9070
eaglepointgolfclub.com				
Elba CC,	Elba	9	[V]	334-897-6600
Emerald Mountain GC,	Wetumpka	18	[S]	334-514-8082
emeraldmountaingolfclub.com				
Enterprise CC,	Enterprise	18	[V]	334-347-2726
enterprisecountryclub.com				
Eufaula CC,	Eufaula	18	[V]	334-687-2007
Evans Barnes GC,	Andalusia	9	[U]	334-222-8400
Evergreen GC,	Evergreen	9	[P]	251-578-5214
FarmLinks GC,	Sylacauga	18	[R]	256-403-4653
farmlinks.com				
Fayette CC,	Fayette	9	[V]	205-932-4079
Florence G&CC,	Florence	18	[V]	256-766-1427
florencegolfandcountryclub.com				
Fox Run GC,	Meridianville	18	[P]	256-828-7564
foxrun-golf.com				
Frank House Muni GC,	Bessemer	18	[M]	205-424-9540
Gadsden CC,	Gadsden	18	[V]	256-546-2011
gadsdengolfshop.com				
Gateway Park Exec GC,	Montgomery	9	[M]	334-284-7920
playmontgomerygolf.com				
Glenlakes GC,	Foley	27	[P]	251-955-1220
glenlakesgolf.com				
Goose Pond Colony GC,	Scottsboro	18	[P]	256-574-5353
goosepond.org				
Goose Pond Plantation GC,	Scottsboro	18	[P]	256-259-0101
goosepond.org				
Grand National GC,	Opelika	54	[P]	334-749-9011
rtjgolf.com				
Grayson Valley CC,	Birmingham	18	[V]	205-854-2382
graysonvalleycc.com				
Green Briar GC,	Morris	18	[S]	205-647-2680
Green Hill GC,	Dothan	18	[P]	334-792-3597
golfgreenhilll.com				
Greene County GC,	Eutaw	9	[M]	205-372-4144
Greenville CC,	Greenville	9	[V]	334-382-8312
Greystone G&CC - Founders,	Birmingham	18	[V]	205-986-5125
greystonecc.com				
Greystone G&CC - Legacy,	Birmingham	18	[V]	205-986-5160
greystonecc.com				
Gulf Links Exec GC,	Foley	18	[P]	251-970-1444
Gulf Pines GC,	Mobile	18	[U]	251-431-6413
brookleycenter.com				
Gulf St Park GC,	Gulf Shores	18	[M]	251-948-4653
alaparkgolf.itgo.com				
Gunters Landing,	Guntersville	18	[S]	256-582-3000
gunterslanding.com				
Haleyville CC,	Haleyville	18	[V]	205-486-3906
Hatchett Creek GC,	Goodwater	9	[P]	256-839-5612
Headland CC,	Headland	9	[P]	334-693-2324
headlandcountryclub.org				
Heatherwood CC,	Birmingham	18	[V]	205-991-7474
diamondclubs.com				
Heritage GC,	Oneonta	18	[P]	205-274-2390
heritagegolftwinoaks.com				
Heron Lakes CC,	Mobile	18	[V]	251-666-7070
Hidden Meadows GC,	Northport	18	[P]	205-339-3673
Hidden Valley GC,	Bryant	18	[P]	256-495-9608
High Pointe GC,	Eight Mile	9	[M]	251-452-6531
thecityofprichard.org				
Highland Oaks GC,	Dothan	36	[P]	334-712-2820
rtjgolf.com				
Highland Park GC,	Birmingham	18	[P]	205-322-1902
highlandparkgolf.com				
Holly Hills CC,	Bay Minette	9	[V]	251-937-8230
Hoover CC,	Birmingham	18	[V]	205-822-5707
hoovercountryclub.org				
Horse Creek GC,	Dora	18	[M]	205-648-1499
horsecreekgolf.com				
Huntsville CC,	Huntsville	18	[V]	256-859-3110
hcc1925.com				
Indian Hills CC,	Tuscaloosa	18	[V]	205-349-1504
Indian Oaks GC,	Anniston	18	[S]	256-820-4030
golfindianoaks.com				
Indian Pines GC,	Auburn	18	[M]	334-821-0880
Inverness CC,	Birmingham	18	[V]	205-991-8610
invernesscc.com				
Isle Dauphine Club GC,	Dauphin Island	18	[P]	251-861-2433
dipoa.com				
Jackson Links GC,	Jackson	9	[P]	251-246-9993
Joe Wheeler St Park GC,	Rogersville	18	[M]	256-247-9308
alapark.com/JoeWheeler				
Kiva Dunes GC,	Gulf Shores	18	[R]	251-540-7000
kivadunes.com				
Lagoon Park GC,	Montgomery	18	[M]	334-271-7000
playmontgomerygolf.com				
Lake Forest Y&CC,	Daphne	27	[V]	251-626-9324
lakeforestpoa.com				
Lake Guntersville St Park GC,	Guntersville	18	[S]	256-571-5458
guntersvillestatepark.com				
Lake Point Resort St Park GC,	Eufaula	18	[R]	334-687-6677
alaparkgolf.itgo.com				
Lake Winds GC,	Jacksons Gap	18	[M]	256-825-9860
lakewindsgolf.net				
Lakeview CC,	Greensboro	18	[S]	334-624-8654
Lakeview CC,	Mc Calla	9	[S]	205-477-6125
Lakewood GC,	Point Clear	36	[R]	251-990-6312
lakewoodatthegrand.com				
Lakewood GC,	Phenix City	18	[M]	334-291-4726

[A] = MILITARY [M] = MUNICIPAL [P] = PUBLIC [R] = RESORT

ALABAMA

Golf Yellow Pages, 18th Edition

LilMole Run GC, *Mentone* .... 18 [P] 256-634-4159
Limestone Springs GC, *Oneonta* .... 18 [S] 205-274-4653
  limestonesprings.com
Linden CC, *Linden* .... 18 [V] 334-295-8678
Livingston CC, *Livingston* .... 9 [V] 205-652-9931
Magnolia GC, *Montgomery* .... 18 [S] 334-288-3310
Magnolia Grove GC, *Mobile* .... 54 [M] 251-645-0075
  rtjgolf.com
Magnolia Meadows GC, *Columbiana* ..... 18 [P] 205-670-0031
  magnoliameadows.com
Magnolia Springs Golf, *Foley* .... 9 [R] 251-965-4653
  magnoliaspringsgolf.com
Marcum GC, *Empire* .... 18 [S] 205-647-3377
Marion Military Institute GC, *Marion* ...... 9 [U] 334-683-2178
  marionmilitary.edu
Meadowlake GC, *Theodore* .... 9 [P] 251-401-0274
  meadowlakegc.com
Mill Creek GC, *Citronelle* .... 18 [M] 251-866-7881
Montevallo GC, *Montevallo* .... 18 [S] 205-665-8057
Montgomery CC, *Montgomery* .... 18 [V] 334-264-7198
  montgomerycountryclub.com
Moores Mill GC, *Auburn* .... 18 [P] 334-826-8989
  mooresmillclub.com
Mountain Brook Club, *Birmingham* .... 18 [V] 205-871-3769
  mountainbrookclub.org
Mountain View GC, *Graysville* .... 27 [P] 205-674-8362
Musgrove CC, *Jasper* .... 18 [V] 205-221-7902
  musgrovecc.com
NorthRiver Yacht Club, *Tuscaloosa* .... 18 [V] 205-343-4508
  northriveryc.com
Oak Hill CC, *Sulligent* .... 9 [V] 662-574-9534
Oak Mt St Park GC, *Pelham* .... 18 [M] 205-620-2522
  alaparkgolf.itgo.com
Occidental Chemical Co GC, *Sheffield* .... 9 [V] 256-389-2301
Ol Colony G Complex, *Tuscaloosa* .... 18 [P] 205-562-3201
  tcpara.org
Old Overton Club, *Vestavia Hills* .... 18 [V] 205-972-9001
Old Pine GC, *Andalusia* .... 9 [P] 334-222-3242
Opp CC, *Opp* .... 9 [V] 334-493-4342
Orange Beach Golf Ctr, *Orange Beach* ... 9 [M] 251-981-4653
  cityoforangebeach.com
Ozark CC, *Ozark* .... 18 [S] 334-774-2615
Pell City CC, *Pell City* .... 9 [V] 205-338-2066
Peninsula G&RC, *Gulf Shores* .... 27 [S] 251-968-8009
  peninsulagolfclub.com
Pikeville CC, *Guin* .... 18 [V] 205-921-9577
Pine Harbor G&RC, *Pell City* .... 18 [V] 205-338-4354
Pine Hill CC, *Anniston* .... 18 [S] 256-237-2633
  pinehill-countryclub.com
Pine Tree CC, *Birmingham* .... 18 [V] 205-956-1599
  ptccalabama.com
Pineview CC, *Thomasville* .... 9 [V] 334-636-5938
Plantation GC, *Hayden* .... 18 [P] 205-559-8200
  plantationgolfal.com
Point Mallard GC, *Decatur* .... 18 [M] 256-341-4925
  pointmallardpark.com
Prattville CC, *Prattville* .... 18 [V] 334-365-4497
  prattvillecountryclub.com
Quail Creek GC, *Fairhope* .... 18 [M] 251-990-0240
  cofairhope.com
Quail Creek Golf Resort & Conf Ctr, *Hartselle* ...... 18 [R] 256-784-5033
  quailcreek.com

Quail Walk CC, *Wetumpka* .... 18 [V] 334-567-5014
  quailwalkcountryclub.com
Rainsville G&CC, *Rainsville* .... 9 [S] 256-638-8846
Red Eagle GC, *Eufaula* .... 18 [R] 334-687-8003
Redmont Rec Club GC, *Red Bay* .... 18 [S] 256-356-8070
River Oaks G&CC, *Leeds* .... 18 [P] 205-699-4851
River Oaks GC, *Geneva* .... 9 [P] 334-684-6190
River Trace GC, *Gadsden* .... 18 [V] 256-546-8821
Riverbend GC, *Cordova* .... 18 [P] 205-648-4393
Riverchase CC, *Birmingham* .... 18 [V] 205-988-8111
  riverchasecc.com
Riverside CC, *Lanett* .... 9 [V] 334-644-4503
  theriversidecountryclub.com
Roanoke CC, *Roanoke* .... 9 [P] 334-863-6416
Rock Creek GC, *Fairhope* .... 18 [S] 251-928-4223
  rockcreekgolf.com
Roebuck Muni GC, *Birmingham* .... 18 [M] 205-836-7318
Roland Cooper St Park GC, *Camden* ..... 9 [M] 334-682-4838
  alaparkgolf.itgo.com
Rolling Hills GC, *Valley* .... 9 [P] 334-749-1972
Ross Bridge Golf Resort, *Birmingham* .... 18 [R] 205-949-3185
  rossbridgeresort.com
Roundabout Plantation, *Cowarts* .... 18 [P] 334-793-3300
  roundaboutgolf.com
RTJGT At Oxmoor Valley, *Birmingham* ... 54 [P] 205-942-1177
  rtjgolf.com
Saugahatchee CC, *Opelika* .... 18 [V] 334-749-3441
  saugahatcheecountryclub.com
Scottsboro G&CC, *Scottsboro* .... 9 [V] 256-574-1356
Selma CC, *Selma* .... 18 [V] 334-874-6907
  selmacc.com
Shoal Creek, *Shoal Creek* .... 27 [V] 205-991-9000
  shoalcreekclub.com
Silver King GC, *Irvington* .... 18 [S] 251-824-9660
  silverkinggolf.com
Silver Ridge GC, *Horton* .... 18 [P] 256-593-4055
Silver Wings GC, *Fort Rucker* .... 27 [A] 334-598-2449
  rucker.army.mil
Soldiers Creek GC At Woerner Preserve, *Elberta* .. 18 [R] 251-986-8633
  soldierscreekgolf.com
Southern Gayles Golf Community, *Athens* .... 18 [P] 256-232-9888
  southerngayles.com
Spring Creek GC, *Tuscumbia* .... 9 [M] 256-386-5670
Spring Hill College GC, *Mobile* .... 18 [U] 251-380-4655
  shc.edu
Steelwood CC, *Loxley* .... 18 [V] 251-964-4800
  steelwood.us
StillWaters G&CC, *Dadeville* .... 36 [R] 256-825-1353
  stillwatersgolf.com
Stoney Brook GC, *Jacksonville* .... 18 [P] 256-435-3114
Stoney Mountain GC, *Guntersville* .... 18 [P] 256-582-2598
Sumter CC, *York* .... 9 [V] 205-392-9911
Sunset Landing GC, *Huntsville* .... 18 [P] 256-464-5050
  sunsetlanding.itgo.com
Sylacauga CC, *Sylacauga* .... 18 [V] 256-249-8084
Talladega Muni GC, *Talladega* .... 9 [M] 256-362-8151
Tallapoosa Lakes GC, *Montgomery* .... 36 [P] 334-260-4900
  tlakesgolf.com
Tartan Pines GC, *Enterprise* .... 18 [P] 334-393-8000
  tartanpines.com
Tennessee Valley CC, *Tuscumbia* .... 9 [V] 256-383-3689
Terrapin Hills CC, *Fort Payne* .... 18 [V] 256-845-4624

[S] = SEMI-PRIVATE   [V] = PRIVATE   [U] = UNIVERSITY   [N] = UNIVERSITY-PRIVATE

ALABAMA

Golf Yellow Pages, 18th Edition

Terri Pines CC, *Cullman* .... 18 [V] 256-739-0720
  terripines.com
The GC of the Wharf, *Gulf Shores*................... 18 [R] 251-968-7366
  thewharfal.com
The Knolls CC, *Reform*...................................... 9 [V] 205-375-2173
The Ledges CC, *Huntsville* .... 18 [V] 256-883-4191
  theledges.com
The Links At Redstone, *Huntsville*..................27 [A] 256-883-7977
  redstonemwr.com
The Links At Tuscaloosa, *Tuscaloosa*.............18 [P] 205-247-9990
  lindseymanagement.com
The Meadows GC, *Harpersville*........................18 [P] 205-672-7529
The Pines GC, *Millbrook* ....18 [M] 334-285-7529
  cityofmillbrook.org
The Ravine GC, *Demopolis* ....18 [M] 334-289-1414
  ravinegolfcourse.com
The RTJGT At Cambrian Ridge, *Greenville*............36 [P] 334-382-9787
  rtjgolf.com
The RTJGT at Hampton Cove, *Owens Cross Roads* 54 [P] 256-551-1818
  rtjgolf.com
The RTJGT At Silver Lake, *Glencoe* ....36 [P] 256-892-3268
  rtjgolf.com
The Shoals GC, *Muscle Shoals* ....36 [P] 256-446-5111
  rtjgolf.com
Timber Ridge GC, *Talladega*.............................18 [P] 256-362-0346
TimberCreek GC, *Spanish Fort*..........................27 [P] 251-621-9900
  golftimbercreek.com
Timberline GC, *Calera*.......................................18 [S] 205-668-7888
  timberlinegc.com
Trojan Oaks GC, *Troy* .... 9 [U] 334-670-3377
  troy.edu
Troy CC, *Troy* .... 18 [V] 334-566-1169
  troycountryclub.org
Trussville CC, *Trussville*....................................18 [P] 205-655-2095
  trussvillecountryclub.com
Turtle Point Y&CC, *Killen* .... 18 [V] 256-757-2155
  tpycc.org
Twin Bridges GC, *Gadsden* ....18 [M] 256-549-4866
  twinbridgesgolf.com
Twin Lakes GC, *Arab* ....18 [P] 256-586-3269
  playtwinlakes.com
Twin Pines GC, *Russellville* .... 18 [P] 256-332-4191
Union Springs CC, *Union Springs*....................... 9 [P] 334-738-5015
Valley Grande GC, *Valley Grande*.....................18 [P] 334-877-4433
  valleygrandegolfcourse.com
Valley Hill CC, *Huntsville* .... 27 [V] 256-883-7620
  vhcc.com
Valley Landing GC, *Courtland* ....18 [M] 256-637-8735
Vanity Fair G&TC, *Monroeville*......................... 18 [P] 251-575-4700
Vestavia CC, *Birmingham*................................. 27 [V] 205-822-8300
  vestaviacc.com
West Side Golf Ctr, *Birmingham*........................ 9 [P] 205-923-2979
Whippoorwill GC, *Altoona* ....18 [P] 205-466-7003
Whispering Pines GC, *Oneonta* ....18 [P] 205-625-3435
White Oak GC, *Greenville* ....18 [P] 334-383-1909
Willow Brook Golf Corp, *Albertville*..................18 [P] 205-878-6766
Willow Point G&CC, *Alexander City* .... 18 [P] 256-212-1409
  willowpoint.com
Wills Creek CC, *Attalla*.....................................18 [S] 256-538-7811
Woodland Forrest CC, *Tuscaloosa*....................18 [V] 205-556-1232
  wfcc.net
Woodward G&CC, *Bessemer*............................18 [V] 205-424-5500

Wynlakes G&CC, *Montgomery*......................... 18 [V] 334-279-0297
  wynlakes.com

ALASKA

Anchorage GC, *Anchorage* ....18 [P] 907-522-3363
  anchoragegolfcourse.com
Bear Valley GC, *Kodiak*.. 9 [A] 907-486-9793
Birch Ridge GC, *Soldotna* .... 9 [R] 907-262-5270
  birchridgegolf.com
Bird Homestead GC, *Soldotna*............................ 9 [P] 907-260-4653
  alaska-golf.com
Black Diamond GC, *Healy* .... 9 [P] 907-683-4653
  blackdiamondgolf.com
Chena Bend GC, *Fort Wainwright*..................18 [A] 907-353-6223
Cottonwood CC, *Nikiski*....................................... 9 [R] 907-776-8745
  cottonwoodcountryclub.com
Eagleglen GC, *Elmendorf AFB* ....18 [A] 907-552-3821
  elmendorfservices.com
Fairbanks GC, *Fairbanks*..................................... 9 [P] 907-479-6555
  fairbanksgolfassociation.org
Fireweed Meadows GC, *Anchor Point*............... 9 [P] 907-226-2582
Kachemak Bay Lynx Par 3 Golf, *Homer*............... 9 [P] 907-235-0606
  lynxgolfbnb.com
Kenai GC, *Kenai* .... 18 [P] 907-283-7500
  kenaigolfcourse.com
Mendenhall GC, *Juneau*....................................... 9 [P] 907-789-1221
  home.gci.net/~hakari/mendenhall_golf/golf.html
Moose Run GC, *Fort Richardson* ....36 [A] 907-428-0056
  mooserungolfcourse.com
Mount Fairweather GC, *Gustavus* .... 9 [P] 907-697-2214
  gustavus.com
Muskeg Meadows GC, *Wrangell*........................ 9 [P] 907-874-4653
  wrangellalaskagolf.com
North Star GC, *Fairbanks*..................................18 [S] 907-457-4653
  northstargolf.com
Palmer GC, *Palmer*...18 [M] 907-745-4653
Russian Jack GC, *Anchorage*.............................. 9 [M] 907-343-6992
  muni.org
Sea Mountain GC, *Sitka* ....9 [P] 907-747-5663
  seamountaingolf.com
Settlers Bay GC, *Wasilla*...................................18 [P] 907-376-5466
  settlersbay.org
Sleepy Hollow GC, *Wasilla*................................. 9 [P] 907-376-5948
Tanglewood Lakes GC, *Anchorage* ....9 [P] 907-345-4600
  alaskagolflinks.com/blakesmith
Valley of the Eagles Golf Links & DR, *Haines* ....9 [P] 907-766-2401
  hainesgolf.com

ARIZONA

3 Parks Fairways, *Florence* .... 9 [V] 520-868-0110
Adobe Dam Family Golf Ctr, *Glendale*..............9 [P] 623-581-2800
  adobedamfamilygolfcenter.com
Aguila GC, *Laveen* ....27 [M] 602-534-6116
  phoenix.gov/golf
Ahwatukee CC, *Phoenix*...................................18 [S] 480-893-1161
  ahwatukeegc.com
Ajo CC, *Ajo*.. 9 [S] 520-387-5011
AllGolf At Rio Salado, *Tempe*............................9 [P] 480-990-1233
  allgolf.com
Alpine CC, *Alpine* .... 9 [P] 928-339-4944
Alta Mesa GC, *Mesa*..18 [V] 480-827-9411
  altamesagolf.com

4   [A] = MILITARY   [M] = MUNICIPAL   [P] = PUBLIC   [R] = RESORT

Golf Yellow Pages, 18th Edition — ARIZONA

Name	Location	Holes	Type	Phone
Ancala CC	Scottsdale	18	[R]	480-391-1000
ancalacc.com				
Antelope Hills GC	Prescott	36	[M]	928-776-7888
antelopehillsgolf.com				
Anthem G&CC	Anthem	36	[V]	623-742-6210
anthemarizona.com				
Apache Creek GC	Apache Junction	18	[P]	480-982-2677
apachecreekgolfclub.com				
Apache Stronghold GC	San Carlos	18	[R]	928-475-7800
apachegoldcasinoresort.com				
Apache Sun GC	Queen Creek	9	[P]	480-987-9065
apachesungolfclub.com				
Apache Wells CC	Mesa	18	[S]	480-830-4725
apachewellsgolfclub.com				
Arizona Biltmore G&CC	Phoenix	36	[R]	602-955-9655
azbiltmoregc.com				
Arizona CC	Phoenix	18	[V]	480-889-1529
azcountryclub.com				
Arizona City GC	Arizona City	18	[S]	520-466-5327
myazcitygolf.com				
Arizona Golf Resort & CCtr	Mesa	18	[R]	480-832-1661
azgolfresort.com				
Arizona Grand Resort GC	Phoenix	18	[R]	602-431-6480
arizonagrandresort.com				
Arizona National GC	Tucson	18	[P]	520-749-3636
arizonanationalgolfclub.com				
Arizona Traditions GC	Surprise	18	[P]	623-584-4000
arizonatraditionsgolfclub.com				
Arrowhead CC	Glendale	18	[V]	623-561-9600
arrowheadccaz.com				
Arroyo Dunes GC	Yuma	18	[M]	928-726-8350
ci.yuma.az.us				
Aspen Valley GC	Flagstaff	18	[V]	928-527-4653
aspenvalleygolf.com				
ASU Karsten GC	Tempe	18	[U]	480-921-8070
asukarsten.com				
Augusta Ranch GC	Mesa	18	[P]	480-354-1234
augustaranchgolf.com				
BC Ranch GC	Rimrock	18	[R]	928-567-4487
Bear Creek G Complex	Chandler	36	[P]	480-883-8200
bearcreekaz.com				
Bellaire GC	Glendale	18	[P]	602-978-0330
bellairgolf.com				
Bison G&CC	Show Low	18	[S]	928-537-4564
bisongolf.net				
Blackstone CC	Peoria	18	[V]	623-707-8700
blackstonecountryclub.com				
Bougainvillea GC	Laveen	18	[P]	602-237-4567
bvgolf.net				
Briarwood CC	Sun City West	18	[V]	623-584-5301
briarwoodcc.com				
Bridgewater Links	Lake Havasu City	9	[R]	928-855-4777
londonbridgeresort.com				
Butterfield GC	Wellton	18	[M]	928-785-4834
Camelback GC	Scottsdale	36	[R]	480-948-1700
camelbackinn.com				
Canoa Hills GC	Green Valley	18	[S]	520-648-1880
canoahillsgolfclub.com				
Canoa Ranch GC	Green Valley	18	[P]	520-393-1966
canoaranchgolfcourse.com				
Canyon Mesa CC	Sedona	9	[P]	928-284-0036
Cave Creek Muni GC	Phoenix	18	[M]	602-866-8076
phoenix.gov/golf				
CC of Green Valley	Green Valley	18	[V]	520-625-8831
countryclubofgreenvalley.com				
Cerbat Cliffs GC	Kingman	18	[M]	928-753-6593
cityofkingman.gov				
Chaparral G&CC	Bullhead City	9	[S]	928-758-6330
bhcgolf.com				
Cimarron GC	Surprise	18	[S]	623-975-5654
grandinfo.com				
Club West GC	Phoenix	18	[P]	480-460-4400
clubwestgolf.com				
Cobre Valley CC	Miami	9	[S]	928-473-2542
Cocopah RV & Golf Resort	Yuma	18	[R]	928-343-1663
cocopahrv.com				
Coldwater GC	Avondale	18	[P]	623-932-9000
coldwatergolfclub.com				
Concho Valley CC	Concho	18	[P]	928-337-4644
Continental CC	Flagstaff	18	[P]	928-527-7997
continentalflagstaff.com				
Continental GC	Scottsdale	18	[P]	480-941-1047
continentalgc.com				
Copper Canyon GC	Buckeye	18	[P]	928-252-6783
coppercanyongolfclub.com				
Coronado GC	Scottsdale	9	[P]	480-947-8364
coronadogolfscottsdale.com				
Corte Bella GC	Sun City West	18	[V]	623-556-8951
cortebellagolfclub.com				
Cottonwood CC	Sun Lakes	18	[V]	480-895-9449
cottonwoodpaloverde.com				
Coyote Lakes GC	Surprise	18	[P]	623-566-2323
coyotelakesgolfclub.com				
Crooked Tree GC	Tucson	18	[P]	520-744-3322
crookedtreegolfcourse.net				
Dave White Muni GC	Casa Grande	18	[M]	520-836-9216
casagrandeaz.gov				
Deer Valley GC	Sun City West	18	[V]	623-544-6016
rcscw.com				
Del Lago GC	Vail	18	[P]	520-647-1100
dellagogolf.com				
Desert Canyon GC	Fountain Hills	18	[P]	480-837-1173
desertcanyongolf.com				
Desert Forest GC	Carefree	18	[V]	480-488-4589
desertforestgolfclub.com				
Desert Highlands GC	Scottsdale	18	[V]	480-585-7444
deserthighlandsscottsdale.com				
Desert Hills GC	Yuma	18	[M]	928-344-4653
deserthillsgc.com				
Desert Hills GC of Green Valley	Green Valley	18	[V]	520-625-5090
deserthillsgolfclub.org				
Desert Lakes GC	Fort Mohave	18	[R]	928-768-1000
desertlakesgc.com				
Desert Mirage GC	Glendale	9	[P]	623-772-0110
desertmiragegolf.com				
Desert Mountain Club	Scottsdale	54	[V]	480-595-4880
desertmountain.com				
Desert Mountain Club - Apache	Scottsdale	18	[V]	480-488-1362
desertmountain.com				
Desert Mountain Club - Outlaw	Scottsdale	18	[V]	480-488-1362
desertmountain.com				
Desert Mountain Club - Renegade	Scottsdale	18	[V]	480-488-1362
desertmountain.com				
Desert Sands GC	Mesa	18	[S]	480-832-0210
desertsandsgc.com				
Desert Springs GC	Surprise	18	[S]	623-546-7401
grandinfo.com				

[S] = SEMI-PRIVATE   [V] = PRIVATE   [U] = UNIVERSITY   [N] = UNIVERSITY-PRIVATE

ARIZONA — Golf Yellow Pages, 18th Edition

Desert Trails, *Sun City West* .... 18 [V]   623-544-6017
  rcscw.com
Dobson Ranch Muni GC, *Mesa* .... 18 [M]   480-644-2291
  dobsonranchgolfcourse.com
Dorado CC, *Tucson* .... 18 [P]   520-885-6751
  doradogolf.com
Douglas Golf & Social Club, *Douglas* .... 18 [M]   520-364-1588
Dove Valley Ranch, *Cave Creek* .... 18 [P]   480-473-1444
  dovevalleyranch.com
Dreamland Villa GC, *Mesa* .... 9 [P]   480-985-6591
  sunlandsprings.com
Eagle Mountain GC, *Fountain Hills* .... 18 [P]   480-816-1234
  eaglemtn.com
Eagles Nest at Pebble Creek, *Goodyear* ..... 18 [P]   623-935-6750
Echo Mesa GC, *Sun City West* .... 18 [V]   623-544-6014
  rcscw.com
El Conquistador CC, *Tucson* .... 36 [R]   520-544-5000
  elconquistadorcc.com
El Rio G&CC, *Mohave Valley* .... 18 [P]   928-577-0123
  elriocountryclub.com
El Rio GC, *Tucson* .... 18 [M]   520-791-4229
  tucsoncitygolf.com
Elephant Rocks at Williams, *Williams* .... 18 [M]   928-635-4935
  elephant-rocks.com
Emerald Canyon GC, *Parker* .... 18 [M]   928-667-3366
  emeraldcanyongolf.com
Encanterra CC, *Queen Creek* .... 18 [V]   480-677-8000
  encanterragolf.com
Encanto 18 GC, *Phoenix* .... 18 [M]   602-253-3963
  phoenix.gov/golf
Encanto Nine GC, *Phoenix* .... 9 [M]   602-262-6870
  phoenix.gov/golf
Estrella Mountain GC, *Goodyear* .... 18 [M]   623-932-3714
  estrella-golf.com
Falcon Dunes GC At Luke AFB, *Waddell* .... 18 [A]   623-535-9334
  lukeevents.com
Falcon GC, *Litchfield Park* .... 18 [P]   623-935-7800
  falcongolfclub.com
Fiesta Lakes GC, *Mesa* .... 9 [P]   480-969-0377
FireRock CC, *Fountain Hills* .... 18 [P]   480-836-8000
  firerockcc.com
Flagstaff Ranch GC, *Flagstaff* .... 18 [V]   928-213-9066
  flagstaffranch.com
Foothills Exec GC, *Yuma* .... 9 [P]   928-342-9090
  lasbarrancasgolf.com
Foothills Par 3 GC, *Yuma* .... 9 [P]   928-342-9090
  lasbarrancasgolf.com
Forest Highlands GC, *Flagstaff* .... 36 [V]   928-525-9000
  fhgc.com
Fortuna de Oro RV Park GC, *Yuma* .... 9 [R]   928-342-4766
  fortunadeoro.com
Forty Niner G&CC, *Tucson* .... 18 [P]   520-749-4001
  fortyninercc.com
Fountain of the Sun CC, *Mesa* .... 18 [V]   480-986-3128
  fountainofthesun.org
Francisco Grande Resort & GC, *Casa Grande* ... 18 [R]   520-836-6444
  franciscogrande.com
Fred Enke GC, *Tucson* .... 18 [P]   520-791-2539
  tucsoncitygolf.com
Gainey Ranch GC, *Scottsdale* .... 27 [V]   480-951-0022
  gaineyranchcc.com
General William Blanchard GC, *Tucson* .... 18 [A]   520-228-3734
Glen Lakes GC, *Glendale* .... 9 [M]   623-939-7541
  playglenlakesgolf.com

Gold Canyon Golf Resort, *Gold Canyon* .... 36 [R]   480-982-9090
  gcgr.com
Gold Canyon RV Ranch, *Gold Canyon* .... 9 [R]   480-982-5800
  robertsresorts.com
Grande Valley Ranch GC, *Grande Valley* ..... 18 [P]   520-466-7734
  gvrgolfclub.com
Grandview GC, *Sun City West* .... 18 [V]   623-544-6013
  suncitywestgolf.com
Granite Falls GC, *Surprise* .... 36 [S]   623-546-7575
  grandinfo.com
Grayhawk GC, *Scottsdale* .... 36 [P]   480-502-1800
  grayhawkgolf.com
Great Eagle GC, *Surprise* .... 18 [R]   623-584-6000
Greenfield Lakes GC, *Gilbert* .... 18 [S]   480-503-0500
  greenfieldlakesgolfcourse.com
Greenlee CC, *Duncan* .... 9 [V]   928-687-1099
Hassayampa GC, *Prescott* .... 18 [V]   928-445-0009
  hassayampagolf.com
Havasu Island GC, *Lake Havasu City* .... 18 [P]   928-855-5585
Haven GC, *Green Valley* .... 27 [P]   520-625-4281
  havengolf.com
Hayden Muni GC, *Hayden* .... 9 [M]   520-356-7801
Heritage Highlands At Dove Mountain, *Marana* . 18 [S]   520-579-7000
  heritagehighlands.com
Hidden Cove GC, *Holbrook* .... 9 [M]   928-524-3097
  hiddencovegolf.com
Hillcrest GC, *Sun City West* .... 18 [P]   623-584-1500
  hillcrestgolfclub.com
Ironwood GC, *Chandler* .... 18 [P]   480-895-0614
  sunlakesofarizona.com
Ironwood GC, *Yuma* .... 9 [P]   928-343-1466
Juniper Ridge RV Resort, *Show Low* .... 9 [R]   928-537-7873
  juniperridgeresort.com
Kearny GC, *Kearny* .... 9 [P]   520-363-7441
Ken McDonald GC, *Tempe* .... 18 [M]   480-350-5250
  tempegolf.net
Kino Springs CC, *Nogales* .... 18 [P]   520-287-8701
  kinospringsgc.com
Kokopelli GC, *Gilbert* .... 18 [R]   480-926-3589
  kokopelligc.com
Lake Powell National GC, *Page* .... 27 [M]   928-645-2023
  golflakepowell.com
Las Barrancas GC, *Yuma* .... 18 [P]   928-342-7130
  lasbarrancasgolf.com
Las Colinas GC, *Queen Creek* .... 18 [P]   480-987-3633
  lascolinasgolfclub.com
Las Sendas GC, *Mesa* .... 18 [P]   480-396-4000
  lassendas.com
Laughlin Ranch GC, *Bullhead City* .... 18 [P]   928-754-1243
  laughlinranch.com
Legend Trail GC, *Scottsdale* .... 18 [P]   480-488-7434
  legendtrailgc.com
Leisure World CC, *Mesa* .... 36 [V]   480-634-4370
  leisureworldarizona.com
London Bridge GC, *Lake Havasu City* .... 36 [P]   928-855-2719
  londonbridgegc.com
Lone Tree GC, *Chandler* .... 18 [P]   480-219-0831
  lonetreegolf18.com
Longbow GC, *Mesa* .... 18 [P]   480-807-5400
  longbowgolf.com
Los Caballeros GC, *Wickenburg* .... 18 [R]   928-684-2704
  loscaballerosgolf.com

[A] = MILITARY   [M] = MUNICIPAL   [P] = PUBLIC   [R] = RESORT

Golf Yellow Pages, 18th Edition — ARIZONA

Los Lagos GC, *Fort Mohave*	18 [R]	928-768-7778	
loslagoslinks.com			
Maryvale GC, *Phoenix*	18 [M]	623-846-4022	
phoenix.gov/golf			
McCormick Ranch GC, *Scottsdale*	36 [R]	480-948-0260	
mccormickranchgolf.com			
Mesa CC, *Mesa*	18 [V]	480-964-1797	
mesacountryclub.com			
Mesa Del Sol GC, *Yuma*	18 [P]	928-342-1283	
mesadelsolgolf.com			
Mesa View GC, *Bagdad*	9 [P]	928-633-2818	
Mirabel GC, *Scottsdale*	18 [V]	480-437-1500	
mirabel.com			
Mission Royale GC, *Casa Grande*	18 [P]	520-876-5335	
missionroyalegolfclub.com			
Moon Valley CC, *Phoenix*	36 [V]	602-942-1278	
moonvalleycc.com			
Mountain Brook GC, *Gold Canyon*	18 [P]	480-671-1000	
mountainbrookgolf.com			
Mountain Shadows Exec GC, *Paradise Valley*	18 [R]	480-905-8999	
mountainshadowsgolfclub.com			
Mountain View GC, *Fort Huachuca*	18 [A]	520-533-7088	
MountainView CC, *Tucson*	18 [P]	520-818-1100	
Mt Graham Muni GC, *Safford*	18 [M]	928-348-3140	
mtgrahamgolfcourse.com			
Oakcreek CC, *Sedona*	18 [S]	928-284-1660	
oakcreekcountryclub.com			
Oakwood GC, *Sun Lakes*	27 [S]	480-895-1159	
sunlakesofarizona.com			
Oasis GC, *Florence*	18 [P]	480-888-8890	
Ocotillo Golf Resort, *Chandler*	27 [R]	480-917-6660	
ocotillogolf.com			
Omni Tucson National Golf Resort & Spa, *Tucson*	36 [R]	520-575-7540	
tucsonnational.com			
Oro Valley CC, *Tucson*	18 [V]	520-297-1121	
orovalleycountryclub.com			
Painted Mountain GC, *Mesa*	27 [P]	480-832-0156	
paintedmountaingolf.com			
Palm Creek Golf & RV Resort, *Casa Grande*	18 [P]	480-421-7000	
palmcreekgolf.com			
Palm Valley GC, *Goodyear*	36 [P]	623-935-2500	
palmvalleygolf.com			
PalmBrook CC, *Sun City*	18 [V]	623-977-8383	
palmbrookgolf.com			
Palms GC Oasis Resort, *Littlefield*	18 [R]	702-346-5232	
oasisresort.com			
Palo Duro Creek GC, *Nogales*	18 [P]	520-761-4394	
innatsanignacio.com/palodurogc.htm			
Palo Verde CC, *Sun Lakes*	18 [V]	480-895-0300	
cottonwoodpaloverde.com			
Palo Verde GC, *Phoenix*	9 [M]	602-249-9930	
phoenix.gov/golf			
Papago GC, *Phoenix*	18 [M]	602-275-8428	
papagogolfcourse.net			
Paradise Peak West, *Phoenix*	9 [V]	480-515-2043	
theparadisepeakwest.com			
Paradise Valley CC, *Paradise Valley*	18 [V]	602-952-7232	
paradisevalleycc.com			
Paradise Valley Park GC, *Phoenix*	18 [P]	602-992-7190	
Pavilion Lakes GC, *Scottsdale*	18 [P]	480-948-3370	
Payson GC, *Payson*	18 [P]	928-474-2273	
Pebblebrook GC, *Sun City West*	18 [V]	623-544-6010	
rcscw.info			
Peoria Pines Golf & Restaurant, *Peoria*	18 [P]	623-972-1364	
peoriapines.com			
Phoenix CC, *Phoenix*	18 [V]	602-263-5208	
phoenixcc.org			
Pine Canyon Club, *Flagstaff*	18 [V]	928-779-5800	
pinecanyon.net			
Pine Meadows CC, *Overgaard*	9 [P]	928-535-4220	
Pine Shadows GC, *Cottonwood*	9 [P]	928-634-1093	
pineshadowsgolfcourse.com			
Pinetop CC, *Pinetop*	18 [V]	928-369-2461	
pinetopcc.com			
Pinetop Lakes G&CC, *Pinetop*	18 [P]	928-369-4531	
pinetoplakesgolf.com			
Pinewood CC, *Munds Park*	18 [V]	928-286-1110	
pinewoodcountryclubaz.com			
Pinnacle Peak CC, *Scottsdale*	18 [V]	480-585-0385	
pp-cc.org			
Poco Diablo Resort, *Sedona*	9 [P]	928-282-7333	
radisson.com/sedonaaz			
Pointe GC on Lookout Mountain, *Phoenix*	18 [R]	602-866-6356	
pointehilton.com			
Poston Butte GC, *Florence*	18 [P]	520-723-1880	
postonbuttegc.com			
Prescott G&CC, *Dewey*	18 [S]	928-772-8984	
prescottgolf.net			
Prescott Lakes GC, *Prescott*	18 [V]	928-443-3500	
prescottlakesgolf.com			
Pueblo Del Sol CC, *Sierra Vista*	18 [V]	520-378-6444	
pdscountryclub.com			
Pueblo El Mirage GC, *El Mirage*	18 [P]	623-583-0425	
pemgolf.com			
Pusch Ridge GC, *Tucson*	9 [R]	520-544-1770	
hiltonelconquistador.com			
Quail Canyon GC, *Tucson*	18 [P]	520-887-6161	
quailcanyongolf.com			
Quail Creek CC, *Green Valley*	27 [P]	520-393-5802	
robson.com			
Quail Run GC, *Sun City*	9 [V]	623-876-3035	
sunaz.com			
Quail Wood Greens GC, *Dewey*	18 [P]	928-772-0130	
Queen Valley GC, *Queen Valley*	18 [S]	480-463-2214	
queenvalleygolfcourse.com			
Quintero G&CC, *Peoria*	36 [P]	928-501-1500	
quinterogolf.com			
Rancho Manana GC, *Cave Creek*	18 [S]	480-488-0398	
ranchomanana.com			
Randolph Park GC, *Tucson*	36 [M]	520-791-4161	
tucsoncitygolf.com			
Raven GC At South Mountain, *Phoenix*	18 [P]	602-243-3636	
theravensouthmountain.com			
Raven GC At Verrado, *Buckeye*	18 [R]	623-215-3443	
ravenatverrado.com			
Red Mountain Ranch CC, *Mesa*	18 [V]	480-985-0285	
rmrcc.com			
Rio Rico Resort & CC, *Rio Rico*	18 [R]	520-281-8567	
hhandr.com/golf.php			
Rio Verde CC, *Rio Verde*	36 [V]	480-471-9420	
rioverdecc.com			
Riverview GC, *Bullhead City*	9 [P]	928-763-9707	
riverviewrvresort.com			
Riverview GC, *Mesa*	9 [M]	480-644-3515	
riverviewgolfcourse.com			
Roadhaven GC, *Apache Junction*	9 [V]	480-982-4653	
roadhaven.com			

[S] = SEMI-PRIVATE [V] = PRIVATE [U] = UNIVERSITY [N] = UNIVERSITY-PRIVATE

ARIZONA — Golf Yellow Pages, 18th Edition

Robson Ranch GC, *Eloy* .... 18 [P] 520-426-3333
  robsonranch.com
Rolling Hills GC, *Tucson* .... 18 [V] 520-298-2401
Rolling Hills GC, *Tempe* .... 18 [M] 480-350-5275
  tempegolf.net
Royal Palms GC, *Mesa* .... 9 [P] 480-964-1709
Saddlebrooke GC, *Tucson* .... 27 [V] 520-825-2505
  saddlebrooke.org
SaddleBrooke Ranch GC, *Oracle* .... 18 [P] 520-818-6403
  robson.com
San Ignacio GC, *Green Valley* .... 18 [P] 520-648-3468
  sanignaciogolfclub.com
San Manuel CC, *San Manuel* .... 9 [P] 520-385-2224
San Marcos Golf Resort, *Chandler* .... 18 [R] 480-963-3358
  sanmarcosresort.com
San Pedro GC, *Benson* .... 18 [P] 520-586-7888
  sanpedrogolf.com
Sanctuary GC At WestWorld, *Scottsdale* ... 18 [P] 480-502-8200
  sanctuarygolf.com
Santa Rita GC, *Corona de Tucson* .... 18 [P] 520-762-5620
  santaritagolf.com
Scottsdale Shadows, *Scottsdale* .... 9 [V] 480-994-0433
  scottsdaleshadowsarizona.com
Scottsdale Silverado GC, *Scottsdale* .... 18 [P] 480-778-0100
  scottsdalesilveradogolfclub.com
Sedona Golf Resort, *Sedona* .... 18 [R] 928-284-9355
  sedonagolfresort.com
Seven Canyons, *Sedona* .... 18 [R] 928-203-2001
  sevencanyons.com
Seville G&CC, *Gilbert* .... 18 [V] 480-722-8100
  clubcorp.com
Shadow Mt CC, *Pearce* .... 18 [S] 520-826-3412
  shadowmountaingolfcourse.com
Shalimar GC, *Tempe* .... 9 [S] 480-838-0488
  shalimarcountryclub.com
Silver Creek GC, *Show Low* .... 18 [S] 928-537-2744
  silvercreekgolfclub.com
Silverbell GC, *Tucson* .... 18 [M] 520-791-5235
  tucsoncitygolf.com
Skyline CC, *Tucson* .... 18 [V] 520-299-1111
  skylinecountryclub.com
Snowflake Muni GC, *Snowflake* .... 27 [M] 928-536-7233
  ci.snowflake.az.us
Southern Dunes GC, *Maricopa* .... 18 [P] 520-568-2000
  golfsoutherndunes.com
Springfield Golf Resort, *Chandler* .... 18 [R] 480-895-5759
Stardust GC, *Sun City West* .... 18 [V] 623-544-6012
  rcscw.com
Starfire At Scottsdale CC, *Scottsdale* ..... 27 [P] 480-948-6000
  starfiregolfclub.com
Starr Pass GC, *Tucson* .... 27 [R] 520-670-0406
  jwmarriottstarrpass.com
Stone Canyon Club, *Tucson* .... 18 [V] 520-219-1500
  stonecanyon.com
Stonecreek GC, *Phoenix* .... 18 [R] 602-953-9111
  stonecreekgc.com
StoneRidge GC, *Prescott Valley* .... 18 [P] 928-772-6500
  stoneridgegolf.com
Sun City CC, *Sun City* .... 18 [S] 623-933-1353
  suncitycountryclub.org
Sun City Lakes West & East, *Sun City* ... 36 [V] 623-876-3020
  sunaz.com
Sun City North GC, *Sun City* .... 18 [V] 623-876-3010
  sunaz.com

Sun City Riverview GC, *Sun City* .... 18 [V] 623-561-4600
  sunaz.com
Sun City South GC, *Sun City* .... 18 [V] 623-876-3015
  sunaz.com
Sun City Vistoso GC, *Tucson* .... 18 [V] 520-825-3110
  suncity-vistoso.com
Sun City Willow Creek Willow Brook, *Sun City* ... 36 [V] 623-876-3033
  sunaz.com
Sun Lakes CC, *Chandler* .... 18 [V] 480-895-9274
  sunlakescountryclub.com
Sun Village, *Surprise* .... 18 [R] 623-584-5774
  sunvillage.org
SunBird GC, *Chandler* .... 18 [R] 480-883-0820
Sundance GC, *Buckeye* .... 18 [P] 623-328-0400
  sundancegolfaz.com
Sunland Springs Village, *Mesa* .... 27 [P] 480-984-4209
  sunlandsprings.com
Sunland Village East GC, *Mesa* .... 18 [S] 480-986-4079
Sunland Village GC, *Mesa* .... 18 [P] 480-832-3691
  sunlandvillage.webs.com
SunRidge Canyon GC, *Fountain Hills* ... 18 [P] 480-837-5100
  sunridgegolf.com
Superstition Mountain Club, *Apache Junction* ... 36 [V] 480-983-3200
  superstitionmountain.com
Superstition Springs GC, *Mesa* .... 18 [R] 480-985-5622
  superstitionspringsgc.com
Talking Rock GC, *Prescott* .... 18 [V] 928-858-7000
  talkingrock.info
Talking Stick GC, *Scottsdale* .... 36 [P] 480-860-2221
  talkingstickgolfclub.com
Tatum Ranch GC, *Cave Creek* .... 18 [V] 480-585-2399
  tatumranchgc.com
Terravita, *Scottsdale* .... 18 [V] 480-488-7962
  terravitagolfclub.com
The 500 Club at Adobe Dam, *Glendale* ... 27 [S] 623-492-9500
  the500club.com
The Boulders Resort GC, *Carefree* .... 36 [R] 480-488-9028
  thebouldersclub.com
The CC At DC Ranch, *Scottsdale* .... 18 [V] 480-342-7210
  ccdcranch.com
The Duke At Rancho El Dorado GC, *Maricopa* ... 18 [P] 480-844-1100
  thedukegolf.com
The Estancia Club, *Scottsdale* .... 18 [V] 480-473-4400
  estanciaclub.com
The First Tee of Phoenix, *Phoenix* .... 9 [P] 602-305-7655
  thefirstteephoenix.org
The Foothills GC, *Phoenix* .... 18 [S] 480-460-4653
  thefoothillsgc.com
The Gallery GC, *Marana* .... 36 [V] 520-744-4700
  gallerygolf.com
The GC At Chaparral Pines, *Payson* ...... 18 [V] 928-472-1430
  chaparralpines.com
The GC At Johnson Ranch, *Queen Creek* ... 18 [P] 480-987-9800
  johnsonranch.com
The GC at Vistoso, *Tucson* .... 18 [V] 520-797-7900
  vistosogolf.com
The GC of Estrella, *Goodyear* .... 18 [P] 623-386-2600
  estrellagolf.com
The GC Scottsdale, *Scottsdale* .... 18 [V] 480-443-8868
  thegolfclubscottsdale.com
The Lakes at Ahwatukee, *Phoenix* .... 18 [P] 480-893-3004
The Legacy Golf Resort, *Phoenix* .... 18 [R] 602-305-5550
  legacygolfresort.com

[A] = MILITARY   [M] = MUNICIPAL   [P] = PUBLIC   [R] = RESORT

Golf Yellow Pages, 18th Edition

ARKANSAS

The Legend at Arrowhead, *Glendale* .... 18 [R]	623-561-1902
legendatarrowhead.com	
The Links At Coyote Wash, *Wellton* .... 18 [P]	928-785-9180
glencurtisinc.com	
The Links GC At Queen Creek, *Queen Creek* .... 18 [P]	480-987-1910
linksqueencreekgolfclub.com	
The Lodge At Ventana Canyon, *Tucson* .... 36 [R]	520-577-1400
thelodgeatventanacanyon.com	
The Orange Tree Golf Resort, *Scottsdale* .... 18 [R]	480-948-3730
orangetree.com	
The Phoenician, *Scottsdale* .... 27 [R]	480-423-2450
thephoenician.com	
The Pines GC At Marana, *Tucson* .... 18 [P]	520-744-7443
playthepines.com	
The Preserve, *Tucson* .... 18 [P]	520-825-9022
robson.com	
The Refuge G&CC, *Lake Havasu City* .... 18 [P]	928-764-1404
refugecountryclub.com	
The Rim GC, *Payson* .... 18 [V]	928-472-1480
therimgolfclub.com	
The Ritz Carlton GC, *Dove Mountain, Marana* ..... 27 [R]	520-572-3500
thegolfclubdovemountain.com	
The Silverleaf Club, *Scottsdale* .... 18 [V]	480-515-3210
silverleafclub.com	
The Westin Kierland Resort & Spa, *Scottsdale* ..... 27 [R]	480-922-9283
kierlandgolf.com	
The Westin La Paloma Resort & Spa, *Tucson* .... 27 [R]	520-299-1500
lapalomacc.com	
Tierra Grande GC, *Casa Grande* .... 9 [P]	520-723-9717
tierragrandegolf.com	
Toka Sticks GC, *Mesa* .... 18 [P]	480-988-9405
tokasticksgolf.com	
Tonto Verde GC, *Rio Verde* .... 36 [S]	480-471-2710
tontoverde.org	
Torreon GC, *Show Low* .... 36 [V]	928-532-4653
torreon.com	
Torres Blancas GC, *Green Valley* .... 18 [P]	520-625-5200
torresblancasgolf.com	
TPC Scottsdale, *Scottsdale* .... 36 [R]	480-585-4334
tpc.com	
Trail Ridge GC, *Sun City West* .... 18 [V]	623-544-6015
rcscw.com	
Trilogy GC At Power Ranch, *Gilbert* .... 18 [P]	480-988-0004
trilogygolfclub.com/powerranch	
Trilogy GC At Vistancia, *Peoria* .... 18 [R]	623-328-5100
trilogygolfclub.com	
Troon CC, *Scottsdale* .... 18 [V]	480-585-4310
trooncc.com	
Troon North GC, *Scottsdale* .... 36 [P]	480-585-5300
troonnorthgolf.com	
Tubac Golf Resort, *Tubac* .... 27 [R]	520-398-2211
tubacgolfresort.com	
Tucson CC, *Tucson* .... 18 [V]	520-298-2381
tucsoncountryclub.com	
Tucson Estates GC, *Tucson* .... 18 [V]	520-883-5566
tucsonestates.com	
Turquoise Hills Family Golf Ctr, *Benson* .... 18 [P]	520-586-2585
turquoisehills.com	
Turquoise Valley Golf RV Park, *Naco* .... 18 [R]	520-432-3091
turquoisevalley.com	
Tuscany Falls At Pebble Creek, *Goodyear* ...... 27 [P]	623-536-2491
robson.com	
Twin Lakes G&CC, *Willcox* .... 9 [M]	520-384-2720
willcoxazgolf.com	
Union Hills CC, *Sun City* .... 18 [V]	623-974-5888
unionhillscc.com	
Valle Vista GC, *Kingman* .... 18 [S]	928-757-8744
myvallevista.org	
Verde Santa Fe GC, *Cornville* .... 18 [P]	928-634-5454
verdesantafe.com	
Viewpoint Golf Resort, *Mesa* .... 27 [R]	480-373-8715
viewpointgolfresort.com	
Villa De Paz GC, *Phoenix* .... 18 [P]	623-877-1171
villadepazgolf.com	
Vista Verde GC, *Rio Verde* .... 18 [S]	480-471-2710
theverdes.com	
Vistal GC, *Phoenix* .... 18 [P]	602-305-7755
vistalgolfclub.com	
Voyager RV Resort & GC, *Tucson* .... 9 [R]	520-574-5700
voyagerrv.com	
We Ko Pa GC, *Fort McDowell* .... 36 [R]	480-836-9000
wekopa.com	
Westbrook Village Lakes Course, *Peoria* ...... 18 [S]	623-566-3439
westbrookvillagegolfclub.org	
Westbrook Village Vista Course, *Peoria* .... 18 [S]	623-566-1633
wbvgc.com	
Western Skies GC, *Gilbert* .... 18 [P]	480-545-8542
westernskiesgolf.com	
Whirlwind GC at Wild Horse Pass, *Chandler* ... 36 [R]	480-940-1500
whirlwindgolf.com	
Whisper Rock GC, *Scottsdale* .... 36 [V]	480-575-8700
whisperrockgolf.com	
White Mountain CC, *Pinetop* .... 18 [V]	928-367-4357
wmccpinetop.com	
Wickenburg CC, *Wickenburg* .... 18 [P]	928-684-2011
wickenburggolf.com	
Wigwam G&CC, *Litchfield Park* .... 54 [R]	623-935-9414
wigwamresort.com	
Wildfire GC, *Phoenix* .... 36 [S]	480-473-0205
wildfiregolf.com	
Willow Springs GC, *Mohave Valley* .... 9 [P]	928-768-4414
Yuma G&CC, *Yuma* .... 18 [V]	928-726-1104
ygcc.org	

ARKANSAS

Alotian GC, *Roland* .... 18 [V]	501-379-2568
Balboa-Hot Springs Vg, *Hot Springs Village* .... 18 [V]	501-922-1504
hsvgolf.com	
Bald Knob CC, *Bald Knob* .... 9 [P]	501-724-3537
Batesville CC, *Batesville* .... 9 [P]	870-793-2525
Batesville Muni GC, *Batesville* .... 9 [M]	870-698-2431
Bella Vista CC, *Bella Vista* .... 27 [V]	479-855-5070
bellavistapoa.com	
Bella Vista CC, *Bella Vista* .... 36 [V]	479-855-5070
bellavistapoa.com	
Bella Vista CC - Branchwood, *Bella Vista* ...... 9 [V]	479-855-5070
bellavistapoa.com	
Bella Vista CC - Country Club, *Bella Vista* .... 18 [V]	479-855-5070
bellavistapoa.com	
Bella Vista CC - Highlands, *Bella Vista* .... 18 [V]	479-855-5070
bellavistapoa.com	
Bella Vista CC - Scottsdale, *Bella Vista* .... 18 [V]	479-855-5070
bellavistapoa.com	
Belvedere GC, *Hot Springs Nat Pk* .... 18 [P]	501-321-3591
belvederegolfclubar.com	
Ben Geren Regional Park GC, *Fort Smith* ..... 27 [M]	479-646-5301
sebastiancountyonline.com	

[S] = SEMI-PRIVATE   [V] = PRIVATE   [U] = UNIVERSITY   [N] = UNIVERSITY-PRIVATE

ARKANSAS
Golf Yellow Pages, 18th Edition

Course	Holes	Type	Phone
Big Creek G&CC, *Mountain Home*	18	[S]	870-425-8815
bigcreekgolf.com			
Big Lake CC, *Manila*	9	[P]	870-561-9988
Big Sugar GC, *Pea Ridge*	18	[P]	479-451-9550
bigsugargolfclub.com			
Blessings GC, *Fayetteville*	18	[V]	479-444-6330
Blytheville CC, *Blytheville*	18	[V]	870-763-7821
blythevillecc.com			
Brinkley CC, *Brinkley*	9	[V]	870-734-2967
Brookland Hills GC, *Brookland*	18	[P]	870-932-3253
Brush Creek GC, *Springdale*	9	[P]	479-750-0606
Bunker Hill GC, *Houston*	18	[P]	501-759-1200
Burns Park GC, *North Little Rock*	36	[M]	501-791-8587
Caddo Creek GC, *Bismarck*	9	[P]	501-865-3666
Camden CC, *Camden*	18	[V]	870-836-8414
Camp Robinson GC, *North Little Rock*	9	[P]	501-753-8877
Carroll County GC, *Berryville*	9	[S]	870-423-3280
CC of Little Rock, *Little Rock*	18	[V]	501-663-4189
cclr1902.org			
Cedar Glade GC, *Horseshoe Bend*	9	[R]	870-670-5141
hillhigh.com			
Cedars CC, *Van Buren*	9	[S]	479-474-2412
Centennial Valley GC, *Conway*	18	[V]	501-513-2522
lindseymanagement.com			
Chamberlyne CC, *Danville*	18	[P]	479-495-4100
chamberlynecountryclub.com			
Chenal CC, *Little Rock*	36	[V]	501-821-7500
chenalcc.com			
Cherokee Creek GC, *Booneville*	18	[P]	479-675-5858
cherokeecreekgolf.com			
Cherokee Village North Course, *Cherokee Village*	18	[V]	870-257-3430
Cherokee Village South Course, *Cherokee Village*	18	[V]	870-257-2555
Clarksville CC, *Clarksville*	9	[S]	479-754-3026
Conway CC, *Conway*	18	[V]	501-329-9887
conwaycountryclub.com			
Coopers Hawk, *Melbourne*	18	[P]	870-368-3280
coopershawkgolf.com			
Coronado-Hot Springs Vg, *Hot Springs Village*	18	[V]	501-922-2355
hsvgolf.com			
Cortez-Hot Springs Vg, *Hot Springs Village*	18	[V]	501-922-1590
hsvgolf.com			
Crowleys Ridge CC, *Wynne*	9	[V]	870-238-9918
Cypress Creek CC, *Augusta*	9	[V]	870-347-3211
Dawn Hill CC, *Siloam Springs*	18	[R]	479-524-4838
De Gray St Park GC, *Bismarck*	18	[R]	501-865-2807
degray.com			
De Queen Country C&Lodge, *De Queen*	9	[V]	870-642-8800
dqcountryclub.com			
De Soto - Hot Springs Village, *Hot Springs Village*	18	[V]	501-922-0001
hsvpoa.org			
Deer Run GC LRAFB, *Little Rock AFB*	18	[A]	501-987-6825
lrafbservices.org			
Deer Trails GC, *Barling*	9	[A]	479-478-6971
Delta CC, *Mc Gehee*	9	[V]	870-222-6622
Diamante G&CC, *Hot Springs Village*	18	[R]	501-922-4191
diamanteclub.com			
Diamond Hills CC, *Diamond City*	18	[S]	870-422-7613
Diamondhead G&CC, *Hot Springs*	18	[P]	501-262-3734
diamondheadcommunity.com			
Eagle Crest GC, *Alma*	18	[P]	479-632-8857
golfeaglecrest.com			
Eagle Hill G&AC, *Little Rock*	18	[V]	501-455-8848
El Dorado G&CC, *El Dorado*	18	[V]	870-863-7380
eldocountryclub.com			
Emerald Park GC, *North Little Rock*	9	[M]	501-244-8500
emeraldparkgolfacademy.com			
England CC, *England*	9	[V]	501-842-2781
Fayetteville CC, *Fayetteville*	18	[V]	479-442-5112
fayettevillecc.com			
Fianna Hills CC, *Fort Smith*	18	[V]	479-646-5134
fiannahillscountryclub.com			
Fordyce CC, *Fordyce*	9	[V]	870-352-2264
Forrest City CC, *Forrest City*	18	[V]	870-633-3380
forrestcitycc.com			
Fort Smith CC, *Fort Smith*	9	[P]	479-783-4653
Fox Hills GC, *Paragould*	9	[P]	870-236-7847
Foxwood GC, *Jacksonville*	18	[S]	501-982-7508
Galla Creek GC, *Pottsville*	18	[S]	479-890-6653
GC At Valley View, *Farmington*	18	[P]	479-267-1096
vvgolfclub.com			
Glenwood CC, *Glenwood*	18	[P]	870-356-4422
glenwoodcountryclub.com			
Golf of Castle Valley, *Mabelvale*	18	[P]	501-562-1814
golfofcastlevalley.com			
Granada-Hot Springs Vg, *Hot Springs Village*	18	[V]	501-922-3095
hsvgolf.com			
Grand Prairie CC, *Hazen*	9	[S]	870-255-3043
Greystone CC, *Cabot*	36	[S]	501-941-4441
golfgreystonecc.com			
Harbor Oaks GC, *Pine Bluff*	18	[P]	870-541-9010
harboroaksgolf.com			
Hardscrabble CC, *Fort Smith*	18	[V]	479-783-3731
hardscrabblecc.com			
Harrison CC, *Harrison*	18	[S]	870-741-2443
Helena CC, *West Helena*	18	[V]	870-572-2877
Hickory Creek GC, *Jacksonville*	18	[P]	501-988-4257
Highland GC, *Camden*	9	[P]	870-574-9080
Hindman GC, *Little Rock*	18	[M]	501-565-6450
littlerock.org			
Holiday Island GC, *Holiday Island*	27	[V]	479-253-9511
holidayislandark.org			
Hope CC, *Hope*	18	[V]	870-777-8182
Hot Springs CC, *Hot Springs*	36	[R]	501-624-2661
hotspringscc.com			
Hurricane G&CC, *Bryant*	18	[V]	501-847-2609
hurricanegolfcc.com			
Indian Hills CC, *Fairfield Bay*	18	[V]	501-884-3852
Isabella GC-Hot Springs Vg, *Hot Springs Village*	27	[V]	501-922-5505
hsvgolf.com			
Jaycee Memorial GC, *Pine Bluff*	9	[M]	870-536-5241
Jonesboro CC, *Jonesboro*	18	[V]	870-932-2410
jcclub.com			
Lake Village CC, *Lake Village*	9	[P]	870-265-3146
Lakeside GC, *Hot Springs*	9	[P]	501-262-1826
Lakeside Par 3, *Fayetteville*	9	[P]	479-442-7748
Lakeview GC, *Hot Springs*	9	[P]	501-262-0050
Links At Bentonville G&AC, *Bentonville*	9	[P]	479-271-0163
lindseymanagement.com			
Links At Jonesboro, *Jonesboro*	9	[P]	870-932-2578
Links at Texarkana, *Texarkana*	9	[P]	870-773-6154
Lions Club Muni GC, *El Dorado*	18	[M]	870-881-4180
Lions Den GC, *Dardanelle*	18	[S]	479-229-4162
Little Creek Rec Club, *Ratcliff*	9	[P]	479-635-5551
Little River CC, *Winthrop*	9	[V]	870-381-7408
Longhills GC, *Benton*	18	[P]	501-316-3000

[A] = MILITARY [M] = MUNICIPAL [P] = PUBLIC [R] = RESORT

Golf Yellow Pages, 18th Edition — ARKANSAS

Course	Holes	Type	Phone
Lonoke GC, *Lonoke*	18	[P]	501-676-0542
Lost Creek GC, *Heber Springs*	18	[S]	501-362-2582
lostcreekgc.com			
Lost Mine GC, *Silver Hill*	9	[P]	870-448-3478
Lost Springs G&AC, *Rogers*	18	[V]	479-631-9988
lostspringsgolfac.com			
Magellan-Hot Springs Vg, *Hot Springs Village*	18	[V]	501-922-4497
hsvgolf.com			
Magic Hills Public GC, *Hot Springs*	9	[P]	501-620-4567
Magnolia CC, *Magnolia*	18	[V]	870-234-6484
Malvern CC, *Malvern*	18	[V]	501-337-1482
Marianna CC, *Marianna*	9	[V]	870-295-5270
Marion G&AC, *Marion*	18	[V]	870-739-6305
lindseymanagement.com			
Maumelle G&CC, *Maumelle*	18	[V]	501-851-3700
maumellecc.com			
Meadowbrook CC, *West Memphis*	18	[V]	870-735-6767
meadowbrookcountryclub.org			
Meadowbrook G&CC, *Magazine*	18	[P]	479-963-8025
Mena GC, *Mena*	9	[P]	479-243-0699
Millwood Landing Golf & RV Resort, *Ashdown*	18	[R]	870-222-0469
millwoodlandinggolfresort.com			
Monticello CC, *Monticello*	9	[V]	870-367-0384
monticellocc.com			
Morrilton G&CC, *Morrilton*	18	[V]	501-354-0324
Mountain Ranch GC, *Fairfield Bay*	18	[R]	501-884-3400
tboxgolf.net			
Nashville CC, *Nashville*	18	[V]	870-845-9992
Newport CC, *Newport*	18	[V]	870-523-8904
Oak Hills CC, *De Witt*	9	[V]	870-946-3891
Oakridge GC, *Huntsville*	9	[S]	479-738-6401
Osceola GC, *Osceola*	9	[M]	891-563-2462
Ouachita G&CC, *Mena*	9	[P]	479-394-5382
Ozark Rec Assoc Club, *Ozark*	9	[S]	479-667-2908
Paradise Valley Ath Club, *Fayetteville*	18	[V]	479-521-5841
paradisegolfac.com			
Paragould CC, *Paragould*	18	[V]	870-239-2328
paragouldcc.com			
Persimmon Ridge GC, *Greenbrier*	9	[P]	501-679-5423
persimmonridgegolfcourse.com			
Pine Bluff CC, *Pine Bluff*	18	[V]	501-535-3180
pinebluffcc.com			
Pine Haven GC, *White Hall*	9	[A]	870-540-3028
Pine Hills G&TC, *Louann*	9	[V]	870-725-2371
Pine Hills GC, *Mountain View*	9	[P]	870-269-5777
Pine Valley GC, *North Little Rock*	18	[P]	501-835-3424
myspace.com/pinevalleygolfcourse			
Pines GC, *Clarendon*	9	[P]	870-462-8374
Pinnacle CC, *Rogers*	18	[V]	479-273-0500
pinnaclecc.com			
Pleasant Valley CC, *Little Rock*	27	[V]	501-225-2234
pleasantvalleycountryclub.net			
Ponce De Leon-Hot Spring Vg, *Hot Springs Village*	18	[V]	501-922-4250
hsvgolf.com			
Prairie CC, *Crossett*	9	[V]	870-364-2456
Prairie Creek CC, *Rogers*	18	[S]	479-925-2414
realark.com/pc			
Prescott CC, *Prescott*	9	[V]	870-887-5341
Razorback Park GC, *Fayetteville*	18	[P]	479-443-5862
razorbackpark.com			
Rebsamen Park GC, *Little Rock*	27	[M]	501-666-7965
littlerock.org			
Red Apple Inn & CC, *Heber Springs*	18	[R]	501-362-3131
redappleinn.com			
Red Martin CC, *Gurdon*	9	[V]	870-353-9981
Red River GC, *Clinton*	9	[P]	501-745-8774
Ridgecrest CC, *Forrest City*	9	[V]	870-633-9863
RidgePointe CC, *Jonesboro*	18	[V]	870-931-5000
ridgepointecountryclub.com			
River Valley GC, *Alma*	18	[P]	479-997-1188
Rivercliff GC, *Bull Shoals*	18	[P]	870-445-4800
rivercliffgolf.com			
Riverland CC, *Heber Springs*	9	[P]	501-362-7541
Riverlawn CC, *Osceola*	9	[S]	870-563-5083
Rolling Hills CC, *Pocahontas*	18	[S]	870-892-3323
rollinghillscountryclub.com			
Rolling Hills CC, *Cabot*	18	[V]	501-843-5231
Russellville CC, *Russellville*	18	[V]	479-968-2660
golfrcc.com			
Sage Meadows GC, *Jonesboro*	18	[P]	870-932-4420
sagemeadows.com			
Searcy CC, *Searcy*	18	[V]	501-268-8577
searcycountryclub.com			
Shadow Valley CC, *Rogers*	18	[V]	479-203-0000
shadowvalleyinfo.com			
Sheridan GC, *Sheridan*	9	[V]	870-942-2688
Siloam Spring CC, *Siloam Springs*	9	[P]	479-524-4269
Silver Springs CC, *Benton*	18	[P]	501-315-1843
South Haven GC, *Texarkana*	18	[P]	870-774-5771
Southern Fairways, *Ashdown*	18	[P]	870-898-5649
Springdale CC, *Springdale*	18	[V]	479-751-5185
springdalecc.com			
Stonebridge Meadows GC, *Fayetteville*	18	[P]	479-571-3673
stonebridgemeadows.com			
StoneLinks GC, *North Little Rock*	18	[R]	501-945-0945
stonelinks.net			
Stuttgart CC, *Stuttgart*	18	[V]	870-673-8421
stuttgartcountryclub.com			
Sugar Creek CC, *Piggott*	9	[P]	870-598-3546
Tannenbaum GC, *Drasco*	18	[P]	501-362-5577
tboxgolf.net			
Texarkana CC, *Texarkana*	18	[V]	870-772-8221
texarkanacc.com			
The CC of Arkansas, *Maumelle*	18	[P]	501-851-0095
countryclubofarkansas.com			
The Course At Eagle Mountain, *Batesville*	18	[S]	870-612-8000
thecourseateaglemountain.com			
The Course at River Oaks, *Searcy*	18	[S]	501-279-4653
The Course At Turkey Mountain, *Horseshoe Bend*	18	[S]	870-670-5252
turkeymtngc.com			
The Creeks GC LLC, *Cave Springs*	18	[P]	479-248-1000
creeksgolf.com			
The First Tee of Central Arkansas, *Little Rock*	18	[P]	501-562-4653
thefirsttteear.org			
The First Tee of Fort Smith, *Fort Smith*	9	[P]	479-648-9833
thefirstteefortsmith.org			
The Greens at North Hills, *Sherwood*	18	[S]	501-833-3790
thegreensatnorthhills.net			
The Greens At Nutters Chapel, *Conway*	18	[P]	501-329-5867
lindseymanagement.com			
The Greens on Blossom Way, *Rogers*	9	[P]	479-631-1811
lindseymanagement.com			
The Links at Cadron Valley G&CC, *Conway*	9	[P]	501-336-0909
lindseymanagement.com			
The Links At Fayetteville, *Fayetteville*	9	[S]	479-966-4330

[S] = SEMI-PRIVATE   [V] = PRIVATE   [U] = UNIVERSITY   [N] = UNIVERSITY-PRIVATE

ARKANSAS

Name	Holes	Type	Phone
The Links At Harrison, *Harrison*	9	[P]	870-365-3621
lindseymanagement.com			
The Links at Lowell, *Lowell*	9	[P]	479-770-6066
lindseymanagement.com			
The Links at Sherwood, *Sherwood*	9	[P]	501-833-8010
lindseymanagement.com			
The Links At Springdale, *Springdale*	9	[P]	479-750-0216
lindseymanagement.com			
The Links At the Rock, *North Little Rock*	9	[S]	501-812-5020
lindseymanagement.com			
The Links of Fort Smith, *Fort Smith*	9	[P]	479-648-9691
Three Rivers CC, *Marked Tree*	9	[P]	870-358-3385
Thunder Bayou Golf Links, *Blytheville*	18	[M]	870-532-2621
Thunderbird CC, *Heber Springs*	9	[S]	501-362-5200
Trumann CC, *Trumann*	9	[V]	870-483-7627
Turtle Pointe GC, *Arkadelphia*	18	[P]	870-246-6642
turtlepointe.com			
Twin Lakes GC, *Mountain Home*	18	[S]	870-425-2028
tlga.org			
Vache Grasse CC, *Greenwood*	18	[S]	479-996-4191
Victory Lake GC, *Corning*	9	[M]	870-857-6378
Village Creek Golf, *Newport*	18	[V]	870-523-9676
Waldron CC, *Waldron*	9	[S]	479-637-4374
Walnut Lake CC, *Pickens*	9	[V]	870-382-4388
Walnut Ridge CC, *Walnut Ridge*	9	[P]	870-886-9816
War Memorial GC, *Little Rock*	18	[M]	501-663-0854
littlerock.org			
Warren CC, *Warren*	9	[V]	870-226-9935
West Helena Muni GC, *Lexa*	9	[M]	870-572-1490

CALIFORNIA

Name	Holes	Type	Phone
3 Par At Four Points, *San Diego*	9	[R]	858-277-8888
sd4points.com			
Adams Springs GC, *Loch Lomond*	9	[P]	707-928-9992
adamsspringsgolfcourse.com			
Admiral Baker GC, *San Diego*	36	[A]	619-556-5520
mwrtoday.com			
Adobe Creek GC, *Petaluma*	18	[P]	707-765-3000
adobecreek.com			
Aetna Springs GC, *Pope Valley*	9	[V]	707-967-6282
aetnasprings.com			
Airways GC, *Fresno*	18	[M]	559-291-6254
airways-golf.com			
Alhambra GC, *Alhambra*	18	[S]	626-570-5059
alhambragolf.com			
Aliso Creek Inn & GC, *Laguna Beach*	9	[R]	949-499-1919
alisocreekinn.com			
Aliso Viejo CC, *Aliso Viejo*	18	[V]	949-598-9200
alisogolf.com			
Allens GC, *Redding*	9	[P]	530-241-5055
Almaden G&CC, *San Jose*	18	[V]	408-268-3959
almadengcc.org			
Alondra Park GC, *Lawndale*	36	[M]	310-217-9916
lacountyparks.org			
Alta Sierra CC, *Grass Valley*	18	[S]	530-273-2010
altasierracc.com			
Alta Vista CC, *Placentia*	18	[V]	714-528-1103
altavistacc.com			
Altadena GC, *Altadena*	9	[P]	626-797-8441
dcgolf.info			
Anaheim Hills GC, *Anaheim*	18	[P]	714-998-3041
playanaheimgolf.com			
Ancil Hoffman GC, *Carmichael*	18	[M]	916-482-3813
golfancilhoffman.com			
Andalusia CC at Coral Mountain, *La Quinta*	18	[R]	760-777-1050
andalusiaatcoralmountain.com			
Angeles National GC, *Sunland*	18	[P]	818-951-8771
angelesnational.com			
Annandale GC, *Pasadena*	18	[V]	626-796-6125
annandalegolf.com			
Antelope Green GC, *Antelope*	18	[P]	916-334-5764
antelopegreensgolf.com			
Antelope Valley CC, *Palmdale*	18	[V]	661-947-3400
antelopevalleycc.com			
Apple Mountain Golf Resort, *Camino*	18	[R]	530-647-7400
applemountaingolfresort.com			
Apple Valley CC, *Apple Valley*	18	[P]	760-242-3125
applevalleycountryclub.com			
Arbuckle GC, *Arbuckle*	9	[S]	530-476-2470
Arcadia GC, *Arcadia*	18	[P]	626-443-9367
arcadia.americangolf.com			
Arrowhead CC, *San Bernardino*	18	[V]	909-882-1638
arrowheadcc.org			
Arrowhead GC, *Alturas*	9	[P]	530-233-3404
Arrowood GC, *Oceanside*	18	[P]	760-967-8400
arrowoodgolf.com			
Arroyo Fairways Mobile Home Club, *Hemet*	9	[R]	909-927-1610
Arroyo Seco GC, *South Pasadena*	18	[M]	323-255-1506
arroyoseco.com			
Arroyo Trabuco GC, *Mission Viejo*	18	[P]	949-305-5100
arroyotrabuco.com			
Ashwood GC, *Apple Valley*	27	[P]	760-240-1800
ashwoodgolf.com			
Auburn Lake Trails GC, *Cool*	9	[V]	530-885-6526
auburnlaketrails.org			
Auburn Valley GC, *Auburn*	18	[V]	530-269-1837
auburnvalleygc.com			
Aviara GC, *Carlsbad*	18	[R]	760-603-6900
golfaviara.com			
Avila Beach Golf Resort, *Avila Beach*	18	[R]	805-595-4000
avilabeachresort.com			
Avondale GC, *Palm Desert*	18	[V]	760-345-2727
avondalegolfclub.com			
Azusa Greens CC, *Azusa*	18	[P]	626-969-1727
azusagreenscc.com			
Bailey Creek GC, *Lake Almanor*	18	[R]	530-259-4653
baileycreek.com			
Bakersfield CC, *Bakersfield*	18	[V]	661-871-4121
bakersfieldcountryclub.com			
Balboa Park GC, *San Diego*	27	[M]	619-239-1660
balboapark.americangolf.com			
Barbara Worth Golf Resort, *Holtville*	18	[R]	760-356-5842
bwgolfresort.com			
Barona Creek GC, *Lakeside*	18	[R]	619-387-7018
barona.com			
Bartley Cavanaugh GC, *Sacramento*	18	[M]	916-665-2020
bartleycavanaugh.com			
Bass Lake GC, *Rescue*	18	[P]	530-677-4653
basslakegolfcourse.com			
Bayonet Black Horse GC, *Seaside*	36	[M]	831-899-7271
bayonetblackhorse.com			
Baywood G&CC, *Arcata*	18	[V]	707-822-3688
baywoodgcc.com			
Bear Creek G&CC, *Murrieta*	18	[V]	951-677-8631
bearcreekgc.com			

[A] = MILITARY [M] = MUNICIPAL [P] = PUBLIC [R] = RESORT

CALIFORNIA

Beau Pre GC, *McKinleyville*.................................18 [S]   707-839-3412
  beaupregc.com
Bel Air CC, *Los Angeles*...........................18 [V]   310-472-9563
  bel-aircc.org
Bel Air Greens, *Palm Springs*.........................9 [S]   760-322-6062
Bella Collina Towne & GC, *San Clemente*............ 27 [V]   949-498-6604
  bellacollinagolf.com
Belmont CC, *Fresno*.............................18 [V]   559-251-5076
  belmontcountryclub.net
Benbow Valley Resort GC, *Garberville*...................9 [R]   707-923-2777
  benbowinn.com
Bennett Valley GC, *Santa Rosa*........................18 [M]   707-528-3673
  bennettvalleygolf.com
Bermuda Dunes CC, *Bermuda Dunes*................. 27 [V]   760-360-2481
  bermudadunescc.org
Bernardo Heights CC, *San Diego*......................18 [V]   858-487-4022
  bhcc.net
Bidwell Park GC, *Chico*............................18 [M]   530-891-8417
  bidwellpark.americangolf.com
Big Bear Mountain Ski & Golf Resort, *Big Bear Lake*9 [R]   909-585-8002
  bigbearmountainresorts.com
Big Canyon CC, *Newport Beach*......................18 [V]   949-644-5404
  bigcanyoncc.org
Bighorn GC, *Palm Desert*............................. 36 [V]   760-341-4653
  bighorngolf.com
Bijou GC, *South Lake Tahoe*.........................9 [M]   530-542-6097
Bing Maloney GC, *Sacramento*........................27 [M]   916-808-2283
  bingmaloney.com
Birch Hills GC, *Brea*..........................18 [P]   714-990-0201
  birchhillsgolf.com
Birnam Wood GC, *Santa Barbara*...................... 18 [V]   805-969-0919
  bwgc.net
Bishop CC, *Bishop*.........................18 [P]   760-873-5828
  bishopcountryclub.com
Bixby Village GC, *Long Beach*........................9 [V]   562-498-7003
Black Gold GC, *Yorba Linda*...........................18 [M]   714-961-0060
  blackgoldgolf.com
Black Oak GC, *Auburn*..........................9 [P]   530-878-1900
Blackberry Farm GC, *Cupertino*......................9 [M]   408-253-9200
  blackberryfarm.org
Blackhawk CC - Falls, *Danville*...................... 18 [V]   925-736-6550
  blackhawkcc.org
Blackhawk CC - Lakeside, *Danville*..................... 18 [V]   925-736-6550
  blackhawkcc.org
BlackLake Resort GC, *Nipomo*........................27 [R]   805-343-1214
  blacklake.com
Blue Rock Springs GC, *Vallejo*..........................36 [M]   707-643-8476
  bluerockspringsgolf.com
Blythe Muni GC, *Blythe*...........................18 [M]   760-922-7272
  cityofblythe.ca.gov
Bolado Park GC, *Tres Pinos*..............................9 [P]   831-628-9995
Bonita GC, *Bonita*............................ 18 [S]   619-267-1103
  bonitagolfclub.com
Borrego Springs Resort & CC, *Borrego Springs*.....27 [R]   760-767-3330
  borregospringsresort.com
Boulder Creek G&CC, *Boulder Creek*.................18 [R]   831-338-2121
  bouldercreekgolf.com
Boundary Oak GC, *Walnut Creek*.........................18 [M]   925-934-6212
  playboundaryoak.com
Bradshaw Ranch GC, *Sacramento*....................9 [P]   916-363-6549
  bradshawranchgolf.com
Braemar CC, *Tarzana*............................... 36 [V]   818-344-5172
  braemarclub.com

Brea Creek GC, *Brea*..............................9 [P]   714-529-3003
  golfbrea.com
Brentwood CC, *Los Angeles*............................ 18 [V]   310-451-8011
  brentwoodcc.net
Brentwood GC, *Brentwood*...........................27 [P]   925-516-3400
  thegolfclubatbrentwood.com
Brookside GC, *Stockton*................................ 18 [V]   209-956-6200
  brooksidegolf.net
Brookside GC, *Pasadena*.............................36 [M]   626-585-3598
  brookside.americangolf.com
Brooktrails GC, *Willits*....................................9 [M]   707-459-6761
  brooktrailslodge.com
Buchanan Fields GC, *Concord*..........................9 [P]   925-682-1846
Buckingham G&CC, *Kelseyville*.........................9 [P]   707-279-4863
  buckinghamgolf.com
Buena Vista GC, *Taft*...................................18 [M]   661-398-9720
  bvgolfcourse.com
Buenaventura GC, *Ventura*...........................18 [S]   805-677-6772
  buenaventuragolf.com
Burlingame CC, *Hillsborough*............................ 18 [V]   650-343-1843
Butte Creek GC, *Chico*................................... 18 [V]   530-343-8292
  buttecreekcountryclub.com
Calabasas G&CC, *Calabasas*............................... 18 [V]   818-222-8111
  calabasasgolf.com
Caliente Springs RV Park, *Desert Hot Springs*........ 9 [R]   760-329-8400
  calientesprings.com
California CC, *Whittier*................................... 18 [V]   626-968-4222
  golfccc.com
California City Muni Par 3 GC, *California City*......18 [M]   760-373-7165
California GC of San Francisco, *South San Francisco*18 [V]650-589-0144
  calclub.org
California Golf & Art CC, *Sun City*.................18 [P]   951-679-1182
  calgolfandart.com
California Oaks GC, *Murrieta*..........................18 [R]   951-677-2221
  californiaoaksgc.com
Calimesa CC, *Calimesa*.................................18 [P]   909-795-2488
  calimesacountryclub.com
Callippe Preserve GC, *Pleasanton*.................18 [M]   925-426-6666
  playcallippe.com
Camarillo Springs GC, *Camarillo*........................18 [P]   805-484-1075
  camarillospringsgolf.com
Cameron Park CC, *Cameron Park*...................... 18 [V]   530-672-9840
  cameronparkcc.com
Camino Heights GC, *Camino*......................9 [P]   530-644-0190
  historichwy49.com/chtwo.html
Campers Inn GC, *Dunnigan*.......................... 9 [R]   530-724-3350
  campersinnrv.com
Campus Commons GC, *Sacramento*....................9 [P]   916-922-5861
  campuscommonsgolf.com
Candlewood CC, *Whittier*.............................. 18 [V]   562-941-5310
  candlewoodcc.com
Canyon Crest CC, *Riverside*......................... 18 [V]   951-274-7906
  canyoncrestcc.com
Canyon Estates, *Palm Springs*..................... 9 [V]   760-327-1346
Canyon Lake CC, *Canyon Lake*........................ 18 [V]   951-246-1782
  canyonlakepoa.com
Canyon Lakes CC, *San Ramon*.......................18 [P]   925-735-6511
  canyonlakesgolfclub.com
Canyon Oaks CC, *Chico*.............................. 18 [V]   530-343-2582
  canyonoaks.americangolf.com
Carlton Oaks CC, *Santee*...............................18 [P]   619-448-4242
  carltonoaksgolf.com
Carmel Mountain Ranch CC, *San Diego*...............18 [S]   858-487-9224
  clubcmr.com

[S] = SEMI-PRIVATE   [V] = PRIVATE   [U] = UNIVERSITY   [N] = UNIVERSITY-PRIVATE

CALIFORNIA
Golf Yellow Pages, 18th Edition

Carmel Valley Ranch GC, *Carmel* .... 18 [R] 831-626-2510
  premierclubcvr.com
Casserly Par 3 GC, *Watsonville*.............................. 9 [P] 831-724-1654
Casta del Sol GC, *Mission Viejo*...........................18 [P] 949-470-4996
  castadelsol.americangolf.com
Castle Creek CC, *Escondido*.................................18 [P] 760-749-2422
  castlecreekcc.com
Castle Oaks GC, *Ione* ....18 [P] 209-274-0167
  castleoaksgolf.com
Castlewood CC, *Pleasanton*................................ 36 [V] 925-846-5151
  castlewoodcc.org
Catalina Island GC, *Avalon*................................... 9 [R] 310-510-0533
  visitcatalinaisland.com
Cathedral Canyon G&TC, *Cathedral City*...............27 [P] 760-328-6571
  cathedral-canyon.com
Catta Verdera CC At Twelve Bridges, *Lincoln*........ 18 [V] 916-645-7200
  cattaverdera.com
Center City GC, *Oceanside* ....18 [P] 760-433-8590
  centercitygolf.com
Cerritos Iron Wood Nine, *Cerritos* .... 9 [M] 562-916-8400
  ci.cerritos.ca.us
Chalk Mountain GC, *Atascadero*..........................18 [M] 805-466-8848
  chalkmountaingolf.com
Champions Club At the Retreat, *Corona* ....18 [P] 951-277-0562
  championsclubretreat.com
Chaparral CC, *Palm Desert* .... 18 [V] 760-340-1501
Chardonnay GC, *American Canyon* ....27 [S] 707-257-1900
  chardonnaygolfclub.com
Cherry Island GC, *Elverta* ....18 [M] 916-991-7293
  golfcherryisland.com
Chester Washington GC, *Los Angeles*...................18 [M] 323-756-6975
  lacountyparks.org
Chevy Chase CC, *Glendale* .... 9 [V] 818-246-5566
  chevychasecc.com
China Lake CC, *Ridgecrest*...................................18 [A] 760-939-2990
Chuck Corica G Complex, *Alameda*.....................45 [M] 510-747-7824
  golfinalameda.com
Chula Vista Muni GC, *Bonita* ....18 [M] 619-479-4141
  chulavista.americangolf.com
Churn Creek GC, *Redding* ....9 [P] 530-222-6353
  ccgagolfredding.com
Cimarron Golf Resort, *Cathedral City*...................36 [R] 760-770-6060
  cimarrongolf.com
Cinnabar Hills GC, *San Jose*.................................27 [P] 408-323-5200
  cinnabarhills.com
Claremont CC, *Oakland*....................................... 18 [V] 510-653-6789
  claremontcountryclub.org
Claremont GC, *Claremont*..................................... 9 [U] 909-624-2748
  claremontgolf.com
Classic Club, *Palm Desert* ....18 [P] 760-601-3600
  classicclubgolf.com
Cold Springs G&CC, *Placerville* .... 18 [V] 530-622-4567
  clubconnectweb.com
Colina Park GC, *San Diego*..................................18 [M] 619-582-4704
  prokidsonline.org
Colonial CC, *Hemet* .... 18 [V] 951-925-2664
  colonialcountryclub.com
Colton GC, *Colton*..18 [P] 909-877-1712
  coltongolf.com
Colusa G&CC, *Colusa* .... 9 [S] 530-458-5577
Compton Par 3 GC, *Compton* ....9 [P] 562-633-6721
Contra Costa CC, *Pleasant Hill* .... 18 [V] 925-798-7135
  contracostacc.com

Copper River CC, *Fresno* .... 18 [V] 559-434-5255
  copperrivercountryclub.com
CordeValle GC, *San Martin* ....18 [R] 408-695-4590
  cordevalle.com
Cordova GC, *Sacramento*.....................................18 [M] 916-362-1196
  cordovagc.com
Coronado Muni GC, *Coronado* ....18 [M] 619-435-3121
  golfcoronado.com
Corral De Tierra CC, *Salinas* .... 18 [V] 831-484-1325
  corraldetierracc.com
Costa Mesa CC, *Costa Mesa* ....36 [P] 714-540-7500
  costamesacountryclub.com
Coto De Caza GC, *Coto de Caza*.......................... 36 [V] 949-858-4100
  coto-de-caza.com
Cottonwood GC, *El Cajon* ....36 [P] 619-442-9891
  cottonwoodgolf.com
Cottonwood Golf Ctr, *Moreno Valley*......................9 [M] 951-413-3290
Coyote Creek GC, *Morgan Hill*..............................36 [P] 408-463-1800
  coyotecreekgolf.com
Coyote Hills GC, *Fullerton*....................................18 [R] 714-672-6800
  coyotehillsgc.com
Coyote Moon GC, *Truckee*....................................18 [P] 530-587-0886
  coyotemoongolf.com
Coyote Run GC, *Beale AFB*...................................18 [A] 530-788-0192
  bealeservices.com
Creekside GC, *Modesto* ....18 [M] 209-571-5123
  modestogov.com/prnd/recreation/golf/
Creekside GC, *Ontario*..9 [M] 909-947-1981
Cresta Verde GC, *Corona*.....................................18 [P] 951-737-2255
  golfcrestaverde.com
CrossCreek GC, *Temecula*....................................18 [P] 951-506-3402
  crosscreekgolfclub.com
Crow Canyon CC, *Danville* .... 18 [V] 925-735-5700
  crow-canyon.com
Crystal Springs GC, *Burlingame* ....18 [P] 650-342-4188
  playcrystalsprings.com
Crystalaire CC, *Llano* .... 18 [V] 661-944-2111
  crystalairecc.com
Cypress Lakes GC, *Vacaville*................................18 [A] 707-448-7186
  travisfss.com
Cypress Point Club, *Pebble Beach* .... 18 [V] 831-624-2223
  cypresspointclub.org
Cypress Ridge, *Arroyo Grande* ....18 [P] 805-474-7979
  cypressridge.com
Dad Miller GC, *Anaheim*......................................18 [M] 714-765-3481
  playanaheimgolf.com
Dairy Creek GC, *San Luis Obispo* ....18 [M] 805-782-8060
  slocountyparks.com
DarkHorse GC, *Auburn*...18 [P] 530-269-7900
  darkhorsegolf.com
Date Palm CC, *Cathedral City*...............................18 [P] 760-328-1315
David L Baker Memorial GC, *Fountain Valley*......18 [M] 714-418-2152
  davidlbakergc.com
Davis Muni GC, *Davis* ....18 [M] 530-756-4010
  davisgolfcourse.com
De Anza Desert CC, *Borrego Springs* .... 18 [V] 760-767-5577
  deanzacountryclub.com
De Laveaga GC, *Santa Cruz* ....18 [M] 831-423-7212
  delaveagagolf.com
DeBell GC, *Burbank* ....27 [M] 818-845-0022
  debellgolf.com
Deep Cliff GC, *Cupertino*......................................18 [P] 408-253-5357
  playdeepcliff.com

14   [A] = MILITARY   [M] = MUNICIPAL   [P] = PUBLIC   [R] = RESORT

CALIFORNIA

Deer Ridge CC, *Brentwood* .... 18 [P]   925-516-6600
deerridgecc.com
Del Mar CC, *Rancho Santa Fe* .... 18 [V]   858-759-5500
delmarcountryclub.com
Del Monte GC, *Monterey* .... 18 [R]   831-373-2700
pebblebeach.com
Del Norte GC, *Crescent City* .... 9 [P]   707-458-3214
Del Paso CC, *Sacramento* .... 18 [V]   916-483-0401
delpasocountryclub.com
Del Rio CC, *Modesto* .... 27 [V]   209-341-2414
delriocountryclub.com
Del Rio CC, *Brawley* .... 18 [S]   760-344-0085
delriocc.com
Delano GC, *Delano* .... 9 [M]   661-725-7527
cityofdelano.org
Delta View GC, *Pittsburg* .... 18 [M]   925-252-4080
deltaviewgolfcourse.com
Desert Aire GC, *Palmdale* .... 9 [P]   661-538-0370
desertairegolfcourse.net
Desert Crest CC, *Desert Hot Springs* .... 9 [P]   760-329-8711
Desert Dunes GC, *Desert Hot Springs* ...... 18 [R]   760-251-5366
desertdunesgolf.com
Desert Falls CC, *Palm Desert* .... 18 [S]   760-340-5646
desert-falls.com
Desert Horizons CC, *Indian Wells* .... 18 [V]   760-340-4646
deserthorizonscc.com
Desert Island G&CC, *Rancho Mirage* .... 18 [V]   760-328-0841
digcc.com
Desert Princess CC, *Cathedral City* .... 27 [R]   760-322-2280
desertprincesscc.com
Desert Trails GC & Resort, *El Centro* .... 9 [V]   760-353-4653
deserttrailsrv.com
Desert Willow Golf Resort, *Palm Desert* .... 36 [P]   760-346-0015
desertwillow.com
Desert Winds GC, *Twentynine Palms* .... 18 [A]   760-830-6132
mccs29palms.com
Diablo CC, *Diablo* .... 18 [V]   925-837-9233
diablocc.com
Diablo Creek GC, *Concord* .... 18 [M]   925-686-6262
diablocreekgc.com
Diablo Grande G&CC, *Patterson* .... 36 [P]   209-892-4653
golfdiablogrande.com
Diablo Hills GC, *Walnut Creek* .... 9 [P]   925-939-7372
diablohillsgc.com
Diamond Bar GC, *Diamond Bar* .... 18 [M]   909-861-8282
diamondbargolf.com
Diamond Mountain GC, *Susanville* .... 18 [P]   530-257-2520
diamondmountaingolf.com
Diamond Oaks Muni GC, *Roseville* .... 18 [M]   916-783-4947
roseville.ca.us
Diamond Valley CC, *Hemet* .... 18 [P]   951-767-0828
Discovery Bay CC, *Discovery Bay* .... 18 [V]   925-634-0704
dbgcc.com
Dominguez Hills GC, *Carson* .... 18 [P]   310-719-1942
domhills.americangolf.com
Dos Lagos GC, *Corona* .... 18 [R]   951-277-8787
doslagosgolf.com
Doubletree Golf Resort, *San Diego* .... 18 [R]   858-485-4145
palmergolf.com
Dove Canyon CC, *Dove Canyon* .... 18 [V]   949-858-2800
dovecanyonclub.com
Dry Creek Ranch GC, *Galt* .... 18 [P]   209-745-2330
dcrgc.com

Dryden Park GC, *Modesto* .... 18 [M]   209-577-5359
modestogov.com/prnd/recreation/golf/
Dublin Ranch GC, *Dublin* .... 18 [P]   925-556-7040
dublinranchgolf.com
Eagle Crest GC, *Escondido* .... 18 [S]   760-737-9762
eaglecrestgc.com
Eagle Falls GC, *Indio* .... 18 [R]   760-238-5633
eaglefallsgolf.com
Eagle Glen GC, *Corona* .... 18 [P]   951-272-4653
eagleglengc.com
Eagle Ridge GC, *Gilroy* .... 18 [P]   408-846-4531
eagleridgegc.com
Eagle Springs G&CC, *Friant* .... 18 [P]   559-325-8900
eaglespringsgc.com
Eagle Vines Vineyards & GC, *American Canyon* .... 18 [P]   707-257-4470
eaglevinesgolfclub.com
Eastlake CC, *Chula Vista* .... 18 [R]   619-482-5757
eastlakecountryclub.com
Eaton Canyon GC, *Pasadena* .... 9 [M]   626-794-6773
dcgolf.info
Echo Hills GC, *Hemet* .... 9 [P]   951-652-2203
echohillsgolfcourse.com
El Caballero CC, *Tarzana* .... 18 [V]   818-654-3092
elcaballerocc.com
El Camino CC, *Oceanside* .... 18 [V]   760-757-2100
elcaminoclub.com
El Cariso GC, *Sylmar* .... 18 [M]   818-367-6157
lacountyparks.org
El Dorado Park GC, *Long Beach* .... 18 [M]   562-430-5411
eldoradopark.americangolf.com
El Macero CC, *El Macero* .... 18 [V]   530-753-5621
elmacerocc.org
El Niguel CC, *Laguna Niguel* .... 18 [V]   949-496-5767
elniguelcc.com
El Prado GC, *Chino* .... 36 [P]   909-597-1751
elpradogolfcourses.com
El Rancho Verde Royal Vista GC, *Rialto* .... 18 [P]   909-875-5346
pacificgolfenterprises.com
El Toro GC, *Irvine* .... 18 [P]   949-726-2577
Eldorado CC, *Indian Wells* .... 18 [V]   760-346-8081
eldoradocc.org
Elkhorn CC, *Stockton* .... 18 [V]   209-477-0252
elkhorncc.com
Elkins Ranch GC, *Fillmore* .... 18 [P]   805-524-1121
elkinsranchgc.com
Emerald Desert Golf & RV Resort, *Palm Desert* ..... 9 [R]   760-345-4770
emeralddesert.com
Emerald Hills GC, *Redwood City* .... 9 [S]   650-368-7820
emeraldhillslodge.com
Emerald Isle GC, *Oceanside* .... 18 [P]   760-721-4700
emeraldislegolf.net
Emerald Lakes GC, *Elk Grove* .... 9 [M]   916-685-4653
yourcsd.com
Empire Lakes GC, *Rancho Cucamonga* ..... 18 [P]   909-481-6663
empirelakes.com
Empire Ranch GC, *Folsom* .... 18 [P]   916-817-8100
empireranchgolfclub.com
Encina Royale GC, *Goleta* .... 9 [S]   805-964-4797
Encinitas Ranch GC, *Encinitas* .... 18 [M]   760-944-1936
jcgolf.com
Escalon GC, *Escalon* .... 9 [P]   209-838-1277
Escena GC Palm Springs, *Palm Springs* .... 18 [R]   760-778-2737
escenagolf.com

[S] = SEMI-PRIVATE   [V] = PRIVATE   [U] = UNIVERSITY   [N] = UNIVERSITY-PRIVATE

CALIFORNIA
Golf Yellow Pages, 18th Edition

Escondido CC, *Escondido*.................................. 18 [V] 760-746-4212
  escondidocc.com
Eureka GC, *Eureka*...................................... 18 [P] 707-443-4808
  playeureka.com
Exeter GC, *Exeter*.. 9 [P] 559-592-4783
Fairbanks Ranch CC, *Rancho Sante Fe*................ 27 [V] 858-259-8819
  fairbanksranch.com
Fairgrounds GC, *Santa Rosa*.......................... 9 [P] 707-284-3520
  fairgroundgolfcourse.com
Fairmount Park GC, *Riverside*....................... 9 [M] 951-682-2202
  riversideca.gov/park_rec/facilities.asp
Fall River Valley G&CC, *Fall River Mills*............ 18 [P] 530-336-5555
  fallrivergolf.com
Fallbrook GC, *Fallbrook*............................. 18 [P] 760-728-8434
  fallbrookgolf.com
Feather River Park Resort, *Blairsden*................ 9 [R] 530-836-2328
  featherriverparkresort.com
Fig Garden GC, *Fresno*............................... 18 [S] 559-439-2928
  figgardengolf.com
Foothills Golf Ctr, *Sacramento*...................... 9 [M] 916-725-3399
  foothillgolfcenter.com
Ford Park GC, *Bell Gardens*.......................... 9 [M] 562-927-8811
Fore Bay GC, *Santa Nella*............................ 9 [M] 209-826-3637
  forebaygolfcourse.com
Forest Lake GC, *Acampo*.............................. 18 [P] 209-369-5451
Forest Meadows GC, *Murphys*.......................... 18 [P] 209-728-3439
  forestmeadowsgolf.com
Fort Washington G&CC, *Fresno*....................... 18 [V] 559-434-9120
  fortwashingtoncc.org
Fountaingrove G&AC, *Santa Rosa*..................... 18 [P] 707-521-3214
  fountaingrovegolf.com
Foxtail GC, *Rohnert Park*............................ 36 [R] 707-584-7766
  playfoxtail.com
Franklin Canyon GC, *Hercules*....................... 18 [P] 510-799-6191
  franklincanyon.americangolf.com
Fremont Park GC, *Fremont*........................... 9 [P] 510-790-1919
  fremontparkgolf.com
French Camp RV Park & GC, *Manteca*.................. 9 [R] 209-234-3030
  frenchcamp.com
Friendly Hills CC, *Whittier*......................... 18 [V] 562-698-0331
  friendlyhillscc.com
Friendly Valley GC, *Newhall*......................... 9 [V] 661-252-3223
Fullerton GC, *Fullerton*............................. 18 [M] 714-578-9201
  fullerton.americangolf.com
Furnace Creek Ranch, *Death Valley*.................. 18 [R] 760-786-2301
  furnacecreekresort.com
Gavilan GC, *Gilroy*................................... 9 [U] 408-846-4920
  gavilangolf.com
GC At Boulder Ridge, *San Jose*...................... 18 [V] 408-323-9900
  boulderridgegolf.com
GC at Rancho California, *Murrieta*.................. 18 [P] 951-677-7446
  thegolfclubatranchocalifornia.com
GC At Rio Vista, *Rio Vista*.......................... 18 [P] 707-374-2900
  thegolfclubatriovista.com
GC At Terra Lago, *Indio*............................. 36 [R] 760-775-2000
  golfclub-terralago.com
General Old GC, *Riverside*........................... 18 [M] 951-697-6690
Gilroy GC, *Gilroy*.................................... 9 [P] 408-848-0490
  gilroygolfcourse.com
Glen Annie GC, *Goleta*............................... 18 [P] 805-968-6400
  glenanniegolf.com
Glendora CC, *Glendora*............................... 18 [V] 626-335-4501

Gleneagles International GC, *San Francisco*......... 9 [M] 415-587-2425
  gleneaglesgolfsf.com
Glenn G&CC, *Willows*................................. 9 [P] 530-934-9918
Glenoaks GC & Learning Ctr, *Glendora*............... 9 [M] 626-335-7565
  glenoaksglc.com
Gold Hills GC, *Redding*.............................. 18 [P] 530-246-7867
  goldhillsgolf.com
Golden Era GC Community Ctr, *San Jacinto*.......... 9 [V] 951-654-0130
Golden Gate GC, *San Francisco*...................... 9 [M] 415-751-8987
  goldengateparkgolf.com
Goose Creek GC, *Mira Loma*.......................... 18 [P] 951-735-3982
  golfgoosecreek.com
Graeagle Meadows GC, *Graeagle*...................... 18 [R] 530-836-2323
  playgraeagle.com
Granite Bay GC, *Granite Bay*........................ 18 [V] 916-791-5379
  granitebayclub.com
Grayson Woods GC, *Pleasant Hill*.................... 9 [P] 925-935-7277
  golfgraysonwoods.com
Green Hills CC, *Millbrae*............................ 18 [V] 650-648-9951
  greenhillscc.com
Green River GC, *Corona*.............................. 36 [P] 951-737-7393
  playgreenriver.com
Green Tree GC, *Victorville*.......................... 18 [M] 760-245-4860
  ci.victorville.ca.us
Green Tree GC, *Vacaville*............................ 27 [P] 707-448-1420
  greentreegolfclub.com
Green Valley CC, *Fairfield*.......................... 18 [V] 707-864-1101
  greenvalleycc.com
Greenhorn Creek Resort, *Angels Camp*................ 18 [R] 209-736-8111
  greenhorncreek.com
Grizzly Ranch GC, *Portola*........................... 18 [V] 530-832-4200
  grizzlyranch.com
Hacienda GC, *La Habra Heights*...................... 18 [V] 562-694-1081
  haciendagolfclub.com
Haggin Oaks G Complex, *Sacramento*.................. 36 [P] 916-808-2525
  hagginoaks.com
Half Moon Bay Golf Links, *Half Moon Bay*............ 36 [R] 650-726-4438
  hmbgolflinks.com
Hanks Par 3 & DR, *Fresno*............................ 9 [P] 559-252-7077
Hanks Woodlake Ranch Golf, *Woodlake*................ 18 [P] 559-564-1503
Hansen Dam GC, *Pacoima*.............................. 18 [M] 818-899-2200
  laparks.com
Harbor Park GC, *Wilmington*......................... 9 [M] 310-549-4953
  laparks.org
Harding & Wilson Muni GC, *Los Angeles*.............. 36 [M] 323-664-2255
  griffithparkgolfshop.com
Harding Park Muni GC, *San Francisco*................ 27 [M] 415-664-4690
  harding-park.com
Healdsburg GC at Taymen Park, *Healdsburg*........... 9 [M] 707-433-4275
  healdsburggolfclub.com
Heartwell GC, *Long Beach*............................ 18 [M] 562-421-8855
  heartwell.americangolf.com
Hemet GC, *Hemet*..................................... 18 [P] 951-926-4653
  hemetgolfclub.com
Hemet West Mobile Estates, *Hemet*................... 9 [V] 951-925-2575
  hemetwest.com
Heritage Palms GC, *Indio*............................ 18 [P] 760-772-7334
  heritagepalms.org
Hesperia G&CC, *Hesperia*............................. 18 [P] 760-244-9301
  hesperiagolf.com
Hidden Oaks GC, *Santa Barbara*...................... 9 [P] 805-967-3493
  hiddenoaksgolfsb.net
Hidden Springs CC, *Desert Hot Springs*.............. 9 [P] 760-288-4653
  cal-am.com

[A] = MILITARY   [M] = MUNICIPAL   [P] = PUBLIC   [R] = RESORT

CALIFORNIA

Hidden Valley GC, *Norco* ....18 [P] 951-737-1010
 hiddenvalleygolf.com
Hidden Valley Lake G&CC, *Hidden Valley Lake* .....18 [S] 707-987-3035
 hvla.com
Hiddenbrooke GC, *Vallejo* ....18 [S] 707-558-1140
 hiddenbrookegolf.com
Highland Palms Mobil Homes, *Homeland*............9 [V] 951-926-3952
Highland Springs Village GC, *Cherry Valley* ....9 [V] 951-845-3060
Hillcrest CC, *Los Angeles*......................18 [V] 310-300-6130
 hcc-la.com
Horse Thief G&CC, *Tehachapi* ....18 [R] 661-823-8571
 horsethiefcountryclub.com
Hunter Ranch GC, *Paso Robles* ....18 [P] 805-237-7444
 hunterranchgolf.com
Hyatt Newport Back Bay GC, *Newport Beach* ....9 [R] 949-644-1700
Indian Camp GC, *Tulelake* ....9 [P] 530-667-2922
 indiancampgolfcourse.com
Indian Canyons-North Course, *Palm Springs*.......18 [P] 760-833-8700
 indianyonsgolf.com
Indian Canyons-South Course, *Palm Springs*.......18 [P] 760-833-8700
 indianyonsgolf.com
Indian Creek CC, *Loomis*.........................9 [P] 916-652-5546
 indiancreekgolfcourse.com
Indian Hills CC, *Riverside*......................18 [P] 951-360-2090
 indianhillsgolf.com
Indian Palms CC & Resort, *Indio*..................27 [R] 760-347-2326
 indianpalms.com
Indian Ridge CC, *Palm Desert*.................... 36 [V] 760-772-7272
 indianridgecc.com
Indian Springs GC, *Indio* ....27 [V] 760-200-8988
 indianspringsgc.com
Indian Valley GC, *Novato* ....18 [P] 415-897-1118
 ivgc.com
Indian Wells CC, *Indian Wells* .... 36 [V] 760-345-2561
 indianwellsclub.com
Indian Wells Golf Resort, *Indian Wells*.............36 [R] 760-346-4653
 indianwellsgolfresort.com
Indio GC, *Indio*................................18 [M] 760-347-9156
Industry Hills-Pacific Palms Conf, *City of Industry*36 [R] 626-810-4653
 ihgolfclub.com
Ironwood CC, *Palm Desert*.................... 36 [V] 760-766-1062
 ironwoodcountryclub.com
Ivey Ranch CC, *Thousand Palms* ....9 [S] 760-343-2013
 iveyranchcountryclub.com
J B GC, *Farmington* ....9 [P] 209-886-5670
Jack Tone Golf, *Ripon* ....18 [P] 209-599-2973
 jacktonegolf.net
Javiers Fresno West G&CC, *Kerman* ....18 [P] 559-846-8655
Joe Mortara Muni GC, *Vallejo*....................9 [M] 707-642-5146
Jurupa Hills CC, *Riverside*......................18 [A] 951-685-7214
 jurupahills.net
Kern River GC, *Bakersfield*......................18 [M] 661-872-5128
 kernrivergolf.com
Kern Valley G&CC, *Kernville*..................... 9 [R] 760-376-2828
 kernvalley.com/news/kvgolf.htm
King City GC, *King City*.........................9 [M] 831-385-4546
Kings CC, *Hanford* ....18 [V] 559-582-0740
Kings River G&CC, *Kingsburg* .... 18 [V] 559-897-5661
 krgcc.com
Kings Valley GC, *Crescent City*...................9 [P] 707-464-2886
Knollwood GC, *Granada Hills* ....18 [M] 818-363-8161
 knollwoodgc.com

La Canada Flintridge CC, *La Canada* ....18 [V] 818-790-0611
 lcfcc.net
La Contenta GC, *Valley Springs*.......................18 [R] 209-772-1081
 lacontentagolf.com
La Costa Resort & Spa, *Carlsbad*......................36 [R] 760-438-9111
 lacosta.com
La Cumbre CC, *Santa Barbara* .... 18 [V] 805-687-2421
 lacumbrecc.org
La Jolla Beach & Tennis Club, *La Jolla*..................9 [V] 858-551-4653
 ljbtc.com
La Jolla CC, *La Jolla*................................ 18 [V] 858-454-2505
 lajollacc.com
La Mirada GC, *La Mirada*..........................18 [M] 562-943-7123
 lamirada.americangolf.com
La Purisima GC, *Lompoc*............................18 [P] 805-735-8395
 lapurisimagolf.com
La Quinta CC, *La Quinta* .... 18 [V] 760-564-4151
 lqcc.org
La Quinta GC Citrus, *La Quinta* ....18 [R] 760-564-7620
 laquintaresort.com
La Quinta Resort GC, *La Quinta* ....36 [R] 760-564-7610
 laquintaresort.com
La Rinconada CC, *Los Gatos*......................... 18 [V] 408-395-4220
 larinconadacc.com
Laguna Lake GC, *San Luis Obispo* ....9 [M] 805-781-7309
 ci.san-luis-obispo.ca.us/parksandrecreation/golf.asp
Laguna Seca Golf Ranch, *Monterey* ....18 [P] 831-373-3701
 lagunasecagolf.com
Laguna Woods Village GC, *Laguna Woods*.......... 36 [V] 949-597-4336
 thelagunawoodsvillage.com
Lahontan GC, *Truckee* .... 27 [V] 530-550-2424
 lahontangolf.com
Lake Almanor CC, *Westwood* ....9 [S] 530-259-2868
 lakealmanorcountryclub.org
Lake Almanor West GC, *Chester* ....9 [P] 530-259-4555
 lakealmanorwest.org
Lake Arrowhead CC, *Lake Arrowhead*................. 18 [V] 909-337-2441
 lakearrowheadcc.com
Lake Chabot GC, *Oakland*..........................27 [M] 510-351-5812
 lakechabotgolf.com
Lake Don Pedro G&CC, *La Grange*..................18 [R] 209-852-0404
 lakedonpedrogolf.com
Lake Elizabeth Golf & Ranch Club, *Lake Hughes*..18 [S] 661-347-0792
 legrc.com
Lake Forest Golf & Practice Ctr, *Lake Forest* ....9 [P] 949-859-1455
 lakeforest.americangolf.com
Lake Merced GC, *Daly City*......................... 18 [V] 650-755-2239
 lmgc.org
Lake of the Pines CC, *Auburn* .... 18 [V] 530-268-8337
 lop.org
Lake Oroville G&CC, *Oroville*........................9 [P] 530-589-0777
 logncc.com
Lake Redding GC, *Redding*..........................9 [P] 530-243-5531
 golfredding.com
Lake San Marcos CC (North Course), *San Marcos*.18 [R] 760-744-1310
 lakesanmarcosresort.com
Lake San Marcos Exec GC (South Course),
 San Marcos.....................................9 [R] 760-744-1310
 lakesanmarcosresort.com
Lake Shastina Golf Resort, *Weed* ....27 [R] 530-938-3201
 lakeshastinagolf.com
Lake Tahoe GC, *South Lake Tahoe*.................18 [R] 530-577-0788
 laketahoegc.com
Lake Tamarisk GC, *Desert Center*....................9 [M] 760-227-3203

[S] = SEMI-PRIVATE   [V] = PRIVATE   [U] = UNIVERSITY   [N] = UNIVERSITY-PRIVATE

CALIFORNIA — Golf Yellow Pages, 18th Edition

- Lake Wildwood GC, *Penn Valley* .... 18 [V] 530-432-1163
  lakewildwood.net
- Lakes At El Segundo, *El Segundo* .... 9 [P] 310-322-0202
  golfthelakes.com
- Lakeside GC, *Burbank* .... 18 [V] 818-984-0601
  lakesidegolfclub.com
- Lakeview GC, *Hanford* .... 9 [P] 559-583-7888
- Lakewood CC & Tennis Ctr, *Lakewood* .... 18 [V] 562-429-9711
  lakewood.americangolf.com
- Lancaster Golf Ctr, *Lancaster* .... 9 [P] 661-726-3131
- Las Posas CC, *Camarillo* .... 18 [V] 805-388-2901
  lasposascc.com
- Las Positas GC, *Livermore* .... 27 [M] 925-455-7820
  laspositasgolfcourse.com
- Lava Creek GC, *Paradise* .... 9 [P] 530-872-4653
- Leisure Village GC, *Camarillo* .... 18 [V] 805-484-2861
- Leisure World Seal Beach GC, *Seal Beach* .... 9 [V] 562-431-6586
  lwsb.com
- Lemoore Muni GC, *Lemoore* .... 18 [M] 559-924-9658
  lemooregolfcourse.com
- Likely Place RV & Golf Resort, *Likely* .... 18 [R] 530-233-4466
  likelyplace.com
- Lincoln Park GC, *San Francisco* .... 18 [M] 415-221-9911
  playlincolngolf.com
- Lindero CC, *Agoura Hills* .... 9 [P] 818-889-1158
  linderocc.com
- Lindsay GC, *Lindsay* .... 9 [P] 559-562-5544
- Links At Summerly, *Lake Elsinore* .... 18 [P] 951-674-3900
  linksatsummerly.com
- Little River Inn G&TC, *Little River* .... 9 [R] 707-937-5667
  littleriverinn.com
- Lockeford Springs GC, *Lodi* .... 18 [P] 209-333-6275
  lockefordsprings.com
- Lomas Santa Fe CC, *Solana Beach* .... 18 [V] 858-755-6768
  lomassantafecc.americangolf.com
- Lomas Santa Fe Exec GC, *Solana Beach* .... 18 [P] 858-755-0195
  lomasexec.americangolf.com
- Lone Tree GC, *Antioch* .... 18 [M] 925-706-4220
  lonetreegolfcourse.com
- Los Altos G&CC, *Los Altos* .... 18 [V] 650-947-3100
  lagcc.org
- Los Amigos Country GC, *Downey* .... 18 [M] 562-869-0302
  lacountyparks.org
- Los Angeles CC, *Los Angeles* .... 36 [V] 310-276-6104
  thelacc.org
- Los Angeles Royal Vista GC, *Walnut* .... 27 [P] 909-595-7441
  larv.com
- Los Arroyos GC, *Sonoma* .... 9 [P] 707-938-8835
- Los Coyotes GC, *Buena Park* .... 27 [V] 714-994-7788
  loscoyotescc.com
- Los Feliz Muni GC, *Los Angeles* .... 9 [P] 323-663-7758
  laparks.org
- Los Lagos GC, *San Jose* .... 18 [M] 408-361-0250
  playloslagos.com
- Los Robles Greens GC, *Thousand Oaks* .... 18 [P] 805-495-6421
  losroblesgreens.com
- Los Serranos CC, *Chino Hills* .... 36 [P] 909-597-1711
  losserranoscountryclub.com
- Los Verdes GC, *Rancho Palos Verdes* .... 18 [P] 310-377-7888
  losverdes.americangolf.com
- Lost Canyons GC, *Simi Valley* .... 36 [P] 805-522-4653
  lostcanyons.com

- Mace Meadow G&CC, *Pioneer* .... 18 [P] 209-295-7020
  macemeadow.com
- Madera G&CC, *Madera* .... 18 [V] 559-674-2682
  maderacountryclub.com
- Madera GC, *Madera* .... 18 [M] 559-675-3504
  maderagolf.com
- Maderas GC, *Poway* .... 18 [P] 858-451-8100
  maderasgolf.com
- Maggie Hathaway GC, *Los Angeles* .... 9 [M] 323-755-6285
  lacountyparks.org
- Malibu CC, *Malibu* .... 18 [P] 818-889-6680
  malibucountryclub.net
- Mallard Lake Golf Ctr, *Yuba City* .... 9 [P] 530-674-0475
- Manhattan Beach GC, *Manhattan Beach* .... 9 [R] 310-939-1465
  marriottgolf.com
- Manteca Park GC, *Manteca* .... 18 [M] 209-825-2500
  ci.manteca.ca.us/golf
- Marbella CC, *San Juan Capistrano* .... 18 [V] 949-248-3700
  marbellacc.net
- Mare Island GC, *Vallejo* .... 18 [S] 707-562-4653
  mareislandgolfclub.com
- Marin CC, *Novato* .... 18 [V] 415-382-6701
  marincountryclub.com
- Marine Memorial GC, *Camp Pendleton* .... 27 [A] 760-725-4390
  mccscp.com
- Mariners Point Golf Links, *Foster City* .... 9 [P] 650-573-7888
  marinerspoint.com
- Marrakesh CC, *Palm Desert* .... 18 [V] 760-568-2660
  marrakeshcountryclub.com
- Marriott Desert Springs Resort, *Palm Desert* .... 36 [R] 760-862-1540
  desertspringsresort.com
- Marshall Canyon GC, *La Verne* .... 18 [M] 909-593-8211
  marshallcanyon.com
- Marshallia Ranch GC Vandenberg AFB,
  Vandenberg AFB .... 18 [A] 805-734-1333
  30svs.com
- Martis Camp Club, *Truckee* .... 18 [V] 530-550-2990
  martiscamp.com
- Mather GC, *Mather* .... 18 [M] 916-364-4354
  playmather.com
- Mayacama GC, *Santa Rosa* .... 18 [V] 707-569-2900
  mayacama.com
- McCloud GC, *McCloud* .... 9 [P] 530-964-2535
- McInnis Park Golf Ctr, *San Rafael* .... 9 [P] 415-492-1800
  mcinnisparkgolfcenter.com
- Meadow Club, *Fairfax* .... 18 [V] 415-456-9393
  meadowclub.org
- Meadow Lake GC, *Escondido* .... 18 [S] 760-749-1620
  meadowlakegolfclub.com
- Meadowlark GC, *Huntington Beach* .... 18 [M] 714-846-1364
  meadowlarkgc.com
- Meadowmont GC, *Arnold* .... 9 [P] 209-795-1313
  meadowmontgolf.com
- Meadowood Napa Valley, *St Helena* .... 9 [R] 707-963-3646
  meadowood.com
- Menifee Lakes CC, *Menifee* .... 36 [S] 951-672-4824
  menifee-lakes.com
- Menlo CC, *Woodside* .... 18 [V] 650-366-9910
  menlocc.com
- Merced G&CC, *Merced* .... 18 [V] 209-722-3357
  mercedgolfandcountryclub.com
- Mesa Verde CC, *Costa Mesa* .... 18 [V] 714-549-0522
  mesaverdecc.com

[A] = MILITARY   [M] = MUNICIPAL   [P] = PUBLIC   [R] = RESORT

Golf Yellow Pages, 18th Edition — CALIFORNIA

Mesquite CC HOA, *Palm Springs* .... 18 [R] 760-323-9377
mcchoa.com
Metropolitan Golf Links, *Oakland* .... 18 [P] 510-569-5555
playmetro.com
Micke Grove Golf Links, *Lodi* .... 18 [M] 209-369-4410
mickegrove.com
Mile Square GC, *Fountain Valley* .... 36 [P] 714-545-7106
milesquaregolfcourse.com
Mill Valley GC, *Mill Valley* .... 9 [S] 415-388-9982
mvgolf.com
Mira Vista G&CC, *El Cerrito* .... 18 [V] 510-237-7045
miravista.org
Miramar Memorial GC, *San Diego* .... 18 [A] 858-577-1719
mccsmiramar.com/golfcourse.html
Mission Bay Golf Resort, *San Diego* .... 18 [R] 858-581-7880
sandiego.gov/park-and-recreation/golf
Mission Hills CC, *Rancho Mirage* .... 54 [V] 760-324-9400
missionhills.com
Mission Hills GC, *Rancho Mirage* .... 18 [R] 760-328-3198
westinmissionhillsgolf.com
Mission Hills GC, *North Hills* .... 9 [P] 818-892-3019
Mission Hills of Hayward GC, *Hayward* .... 9 [M] 510-888-0200
haywardrec.org
Mission Lakes CC, *Desert Hot Springs* .... 18 [S] 760-329-8061
missionlakescountryclub.com
Mission Trails GC, *San Diego* .... 18 [M] 619-460-5400
missiontrails.americangolf.com
Mission Viejo CC, *Mission Viejo* .... 18 [V] 949-582-1550
missionviejocc.com
Modesto Muni GC, *Modesto* .... 9 [P] 209-577-5360
modestogov.com/prnd/recreation/golf/
Monarch Bay GC, *San Leandro* .... 27 [M] 510-895-2162
monarchbay.americangolf.com
Monarch Beach GL, *Monarch Beach* .... 18 [R] 949-240-8447
monarchbeachgolf.com
Monarch Dunes GC, *Nipomo* .... 30 [P] 805-343-9459
monarchdunesgolf.com
Montebello GC, *Montebello* .... 18 [M] 323-887-4565
bad link
Montecito CC, *Santa Barbara* .... 18 [V] 805-969-0800
montecitocc.com
Monterey CC, *Palm Desert* .... 27 [V] 760-568-9311
montereycc.com
Monterey Park GC, *Monterey Park* .... 9 [M] 323-266-4632
Monterey Peninsula CC, *Pebble Beach* .... 36 [V] 831-373-1556
mpccpb.org
Monterey Pines GC, *Monterey* .... 18 [A] 831-656-2167
mwrtoday.com
Montesoro Golf & Social Club, *Borrego Springs* .. 18 [V] 760-767-5000
montesoro.com
Moorpark CC, *Moorpark* .... 27 [S] 805-532-2834
moorparkgolf.com
Moraga CC, *Moraga* .... 18 [V] 925-376-2200
moragacc.com
Moreno Valley Ranch GC, *Moreno Valley* .... 27 [P] 951-924-4444
theranchatmorenovalley.com
Morgan Creek G&CC, *Roseville* .... 18 [V] 916-786-4653
morgancreekclub.com
Morgan Run Resort & Club, *Rancho Santa Fe* ... 27 [R] 858-756-2471
morganrun.com
Morongo GC At Tukwet Canyon, *Beaumont* .... 36 [P] 951-845-0014
tukwetcanyon.com
Morro Bay GC, *Morro Bay* .... 18 [M] 805-782-8060
slocountyparks.com

Motorcoach CC, *Indio* .... 9 [R] 760-863-0789
motorcoachcc.com
Mount Huff GC, *Crescent Mills* .... 9 [P] 530-284-6204
Mount Shasta Resort, *Mt Shasta* .... 18 [R] 530-926-3052
mountshastaresort.com
Mount St Helena GC, *Calistoga* .... 9 [M] 707-942-9966
Mountain Meadows GC, *Pomona* .... 18 [P] 909-623-3704
mountainmeadows.americangolf.com
Mountain Springs GC, *Sonora* .... 18 [P] 209-532-1000
mountainspringsgolf.com
Mountain Valley Golf Ctr, *Woodland* .... 9 [P] 530-669-7324
Mountain View CC, *La Quinta* .... 18 [V] 760-771-4311
mountainviewcc.info
Mountain View GC, *Santa Paula* .... 18 [S] 805-525-1571
mountainviewgc.com
Mountain Vista GC-Sun City Palm Desert,
Palm Desert .... 36 [S] 760-200-2200
scpdca.com
MountainGate CC, *Los Angeles* .... 27 [V] 310-476-6215
mtngatecc.com
Mt Whitney GC, *Lone Pine* .... 9 [P] 760-876-5795
mtwhitneygolfclub.com
Mt Woodson GC, *Ramona* .... 18 [S] 760-788-3555
mtwoodsongc.com
Muroc Lake GC, *Edwards AFB* .... 18 [A] 661-275-7888
Nakoma Golf Resort, *Clio* .... 18 [R] 530-832-5067
nakomagolfresort.com
Napa GC At Kennedy Park, *Napa* .... 18 [M] 707-255-4333
playnapa.com
Napa Valley CC, *Napa* .... 18 [V] 707-252-1111
napavalleycc.com
National City GC, *National City* .... 9 [M] 619-474-1400
nationalcity.americangolf.com
Navy GC, *Cypress* .... 27 [A] 714-889-1576
navygc.com
Nevada County CC, *Grass Valley* .... 9 [S] 530-273-6436
New Horizons GC, *Torrance* .... 9 [V] 310-325-3080
Newport Beach GC, *Newport Beach* .... 18 [P] 949-852-8681
npbgolf.com
North GC, *Sun City* .... 18 [S] 951-679-5111
northgolfcourse.net
North Kern GC, *Bakersfield* .... 18 [M] 661-399-0347
northkerngolf.com
North Ranch CC, *Westlake Village* .... 27 [V] 805-496-1995
northranchcc.com
North Ridge CC, *Fair Oaks* .... 18 [V] 916-967-5716
northridgegolf.com
Northstar At Tahoe GC, *Truckee* .... 18 [R] 530-562-2490
northstarattahoe.com
Northwood GC, *Monte Rio* .... 9 [P] 707-865-1116
northwoodgolf.com
Norwalk GC, *Norwalk* .... 9 [M] 562-921-6500
Oak Creek GC, *Red Bluff* .... 9 [P] 530-529-0674
Oak Creek GC, *Irvine* .... 18 [P] 949-653-5300
oakcreekgolfclub.com
Oak Quarry GC, *Riverside* .... 18 [P] 951-685-1440
oakquarry.com
Oak Tree CC, *Tehachapi* .... 9 [V] 661-821-5144
Oak Valley GC, *Beaumont* .... 18 [P] 951-769-7200
oakvalleygolf.com
Oakdale G&CC, *Oakdale* .... 18 [V] 209-847-2924
oakdalegcc.org

[S] = SEMI-PRIVATE   [V] = PRIVATE   [U] = UNIVERSITY   [N] = UNIVERSITY-PRIVATE

CALIFORNIA
Golf Yellow Pages, 18th Edition

Oakhurst CC, *Clayton* .... 18 [V] 925-672-9739
oakhurstcc.com
Oakmont CC, *Glendale* .... 18 [V] 818-542-4292
oakmontcc.com
Oakmont GC - East, *Santa Rosa* .... 18 [V] 707-538-2454
oakmontgc.com
Oakmont GC - West, *Santa Rosa* .... 18 [P] 707-539-0415
oakmontgc.com
Oakmoore GC, *Stockton* .... 9 [V] 209-601-4883
oakmooregolfcourse.com
Oaks North GC, *San Diego* .... 27 [S] 858-487-3021
jcgolf.com
Oasis CC, *Palm Desert* .... 18 [P] 760-345-2715
theoasiscountryclub.com
Ocean Hills CC, *Oceanside* .... 18 [V] 760-758-8772
oceanhillscountryclub.com
Ocean Meadows GC, *Goleta* .... 9 [P] 805-968-6814
oceanmeadowsgolfclub.com
Oceanside GC, *Oceanside* .... 18 [P] 760-433-1360
playoceansidegolf.com
ODonnell GC, *Palm Springs* .... 9 [P] 760-325-2259
odonnellgolfclub.com
Ojai Valley Inn & Spa, *Ojai* .... 18 [R] 805-646-2420
ojairesort.com
Old Brockway GC, *Kings Beach* .... 9 [P] 530-546-9909
oldbrockway.com
Old Greenwood GC, *Truckee* .... 18 [P] 530-550-7010
oldgreenwood.com
Old Ranch CC, *Seal Beach* .... 18 [V] 562-596-4425
oldranch.com
Old River GC, *Banta* .... 18 [P] 209-830-8585
oldrivergolf.com
Olivas Links GC, *Ventura* .... 18 [S] 805-677-6770
olivaslinks.com
Orinda CC, *Orinda* .... 18 [V] 925-254-0811
orindacc.org
Outdoor Resort Indio, *Indio* .... 18 [R] 760-775-7255
orindio.com
Outdoor Resorts Palm Springs, *Cathedral City*..... 18 [R] 760-324-8638
orps.com
Ozzie Osborns Par 3 GC, *Santa Paula* .... 9 [P] 805-933-4457
Pacific Grove GC, *Pacific Grove* .... 18 [M] 831-648-5775
ci.pg.ca.us
Pajaro Valley GC, *Royal Oaks* .... 18 [P] 831-724-3851
pajarovalleygolf.com
Pala Mesa Resort, *Fallbrook* .... 18 [R] 760-731-6803
palamesa.com
Palacio Del Mar GC, *San Diego* .... 9 [V] 858-792-4641
Palm Desert CC, *Palm Desert* .... 27 [P] 760-345-2525
pdccgolf.com
Palm Desert Greens CC, *Palm Desert* .... 18 [P] 760-346-2941
pdgcc.org
Palm Desert Resort CC, *Palm Desert* .... 18 [R] 760-345-2791
theresorter.com
Palm Lake GC, *Pomona* .... 9 [P] 909-629-2852
Palm Royale CC, *La Quinta* .... 18 [P] 760-345-9701
Palm Valley CC, *Palm Desert* .... 36 [P] 760-345-2737
palmvalley-cc.com
Palo Alto GC, *Palo Alto* .... 18 [M] 650-856-0881
bradlozaresgolfshop.com
Palo Alto Hills G&CC, *Palo Alto* .... 18 [V] 650-948-2320
pahgcc.com
Palo Cedro GC, *Palo Cedro* .... 9 [V] 530-547-3012

Palos Verdes GC, *Palos Verdes Estates* .... 18 [V] 310-375-2533
pvgec.com
Palos Verdes Shores GC, *San Pedro* .... 9 [V] 310-547-4403
Panorama Village GC, *Hemet* .... 9 [V] 951-658-1832
Paradise Knolls GC, *Riverside* .... 18 [P] 951-685-7034
paradiseknolls.americangolf.com
Paradise Pines GC, *Magalia* .... 9 [P] 530-873-1111
paradisepinesgolfcourse.com
Paradise Valley GC, *Fairfield* .... 18 [M] 707-426-1600
fairfieldgolf.com
Pasadera G&CC, *Monterey* .... 18 [V] 831-647-2400
pasadera.com
Pasatiempo GC, *Santa Cruz* .... 18 [S] 831-459-9169
pasatiempo.com
Paso Robles GC, *Paso Robles* .... 18 [P] 805-238-4710
centralcoast.com/pasoroblesgolfclub
Pauma Valley CC, *Pauma Valley* .... 18 [V] 760-742-3721
paumavalleycc.com
Peach Tree G&CC, *Marysville* .... 18 [V] 530-743-1897
peachtreecountryclub.com
Peacock Gap CC & Spa, *San Rafael* .... 18 [V] 415-453-4940
peacockgapgc.com
Pebble Beach Golf Links, *Pebble Beach* ....27 [R] 831-624-3811
pebblebeach.com
Peninsula G&CC, *San Mateo* .... 18 [V] 650-638-2239
thepgcc.org
Penmar GC, *Venice* .... 9 [M] 310-396-6228
laparks.org
Petaluma G&CC, *Petaluma* .... 9 [V] 707-762-7041
petalumagolfandcountryclub.com
PGA West Private GC, *La Quinta* .... 54 [V] 760-564-3914
pgawest.com
PGA West Resort - Norman Course, *La Quinta* ..... 18 [R] 760-564-3900
pgawest.com
PGA West Stadium Clubhouse, *La Quinta* .... 36 [R] 760-564-7101
pgawest.com
Pheasant Run GC, *Chowchilla* .... 18 [P] 559-665-3411
pheasantrungolfclub.com
Phoenix Lake GC, *Sonora* .... 9 [P] 209-532-0111
phoenixlakegolf.com
Pico Rivera Muni GC, *Pico Rivera* .... 9 [M] 562-692-9933
Pine Meadows Public GC, *Martinez* .... 9 [P] 925-228-2881
Pine Mountain Club, *Pine Mt Club* .... 9 [V] 661-242-3734
pinemountainclub.net
Pine Mountain Lake CC, *Groveland* .... 18 [R] 209-962-8620
pinemountainlake.com
Pismo State Beach GC, *Grover Beach* .... 9 [M] 805-481-5215
pismogolf.com
Plantation GC, *Indio* .... 18 [V] 760-775-3688
theplantationgc.com
Pleasanton Golf Ctr, *Pleasanton* .... 9 [P] 925-462-4653
pleasantongolfcenter.com
Plumas Lake G&CC, *Olivehurst* .... 18 [S] 530-742-3201
plumaslake.com
Plumas Pines Golf Resort, *Blairsden* .... 18 [R] 530-836-1420
plumaspinesgolf.com
Ponderosa GC, *Truckee* .... 9 [P] 530-587-3501
ponderosagolfclub.com
Poplar Creek GC, *San Mateo* .... 18 [M] 650-522-4653
poplarcreekgolf.com
Poppy Hills GC, *Pebble Beach* .... 18 [P] 831-622-8239
poppyhillsgolf.com
Poppy Ridge GC, *Livermore* .... 27 [P] 925-456-8202
poppyridgegolf.com

[A] = MILITARY [M] = MUNICIPAL [P] = PUBLIC [R] = RESORT

Golf Yellow Pages, 18th Edition — CALIFORNIA

Porter Valley CC, *Northridge* .... 18 [V] 818-368-2919
   portervalley.com
Porterville GC, *Porterville* .... 9 [M] 559-784-9468
Portola CC, *Palm Desert* .... 18 [V] 760-568-1592
   portolacc.com
Presidio GC, *San Francisco* .... 18 [P] 415-561-4670
   presidiogolf.com
Presidio Hills GC, *San Diego* .... 18 [P] 619-295-9476
   presidiohillsgolf.com
Primm Valley GC, *Nipton* .... 36 [P] 702-679-5510
   primmvalleyresorts.com
Pruneridge GC, *Santa Clara* .... 9 [P] 408-248-4424
   pruneridgegolfclub.com
Quail Lodge GC, *Carmel* .... 18 [R] 831-620-8808
   quaillodge.com
Quail Ranch GC, *Moreno Valley* .... 18 [R] 951-654-2727
   pacificgolfenterprises.com
Quail Valley CC, *Grass Valley* .... 9 [P] 530-274-1340
Rancho Bernardo Inn GC, *San Diego* .... 18 [R] 858-675-8470
   jcgolf.com
Rancho Canada GC, *Carmel* .... 36 [S] 831-624-0111
   ranchocanada.com
Rancho Carlsbad GC, *Carlsbad* .... 18 [P] 760-438-1772
   ranchocarlsbadgolf.com
Rancho Casa Blanca, *Indio* .... 18 [R] 760-775-7116
   rcboa.com
Rancho Del Pueblo GC, *San Jose* .... 9 [M] 408-347-0990
   ranchodelpueblo.com
Rancho Del Rey GC, *Atwater* .... 18 [P] 209-358-7131
   ranchordr.com
Rancho Duarte GC, *Duarte* .... 9 [P] 626-357-9981
Rancho La Quinta GC, *La Quinta* .... 36 [V] 760-777-7799
   rancholaquinta.com
Rancho Las Palmas CC, *Rancho Mirage* .... 27 [R] 760-568-2727
   rancholaspalmas.com/golf
Rancho Maria GC, *Santa Maria* .... 18 [P] 805-937-2019
   ranchomariagolf.com
Rancho Mirage CC, *Rancho Mirage* .... 18 [S] 760-324-4711
   ranchomiragegolf.com
Rancho Monserate CC & Homeowners Assoc,
   Fallbrook .... 9 [V] 760-728-2316
   ranchomonserate.com
Rancho Murieta CC, *Rancho Murieta* .... 36 [V] 916-354-2400
   ranchomurietacc.com
Rancho Park GC, *Los Angeles* .... 27 [M] 310-839-9812
   rpgc.org
Rancho San Joaquin GC, *Irvine* .... 18 [P] 949-786-5522
   rsj.americangolf.com
Rancho San Marcos GC, *Santa Barbara* .... 18 [P] 805-683-6534
   rsm1804.com
Rancho Santa Fe GC, *Rancho Santa Fe* .... 18 [V] 858-756-1182
   rsfgolfclub.com
Rancho Sierra GC, *Lancaster* .... 9 [P] 661-946-1080
   ranchosierragolf.com
Rancho Solano GC, *Fairfield* .... 18 [M] 707-429-4653
   fairfieldgolf.com
Rancho Vista GC, *Palmdale* .... 18 [P] 661-272-9903
   ranchovistagolfcourse.com
Raspberry Hills GC, *Auburn* .... 9 [P] 530-878-7818
   razberryhill.com
Recreation Park GC 18, *Long Beach* .... 18 [M] 562-494-4424
   recpark18.americangolf.com
Recreation Park GC 9, *Long Beach* .... 9 [M] 562-438-4012
   recpark9.americangolf.com

Red Hill CC, *Rancho Cucamonga* .... 18 [V] 909-982-4559
   redhillcc.com
RedHawk GC, *Temecula* .... 18 [P] 951-302-3850
   redhawkgolfcourse.com
Redlands CC, *Redlands* .... 18 [V] 909-793-1295
   redlandscountryclub.com
Redwood Empire G&CC, *Fortuna* .... 18 [V] 707-725-5194
Reidy Creek GC, *Escondido* .... 18 [M] 760-740-2450
   jcgolf.com
Resort At Pelican Hill, *Newport Coast* .... 36 [R] 949-467-6800
   pelicanhill.com
Resort At Squaw Creek, *Olympic Valley* .... 18 [R] 530-581-6637
   squawcreek.com
Richmond CC, *Richmond* .... 18 [V] 510-232-1080
   richmondcc.com
Ridge Creek GC, *Dinuba* .... 18 [M] 559-591-2254
   golfridgecreek.com
Ridgemark G&CC, *Hollister* .... 36 [R] 831-637-8151
   ridgemark.com
Rio Bend RV & Golf Resort, *El Centro* .... 9 [R] 760-352-6638
   riobendrvgolfresort.com
Rio Bravo CC, *Bakersfield* .... 18 [V] 661-871-4772
   riobravocountryclub.com
Rio Hondo GC, *Downey* .... 18 [M] 562-927-2329
   downeyca.org
River Bend G&CC, *Redding* .... 9 [V] 530-246-9077
   golfredding.com
River Course at Alisal, *Solvang* .... 18 [P] 805-688-6042
   rivercourse.com
River Creek GC, *Ahwahnee* .... 9 [S] 559-683-5600
   rivercreekgolfcourse.com
River Island CC, *Porterville* .... 18 [V] 559-784-9425
   riverislandcc.net
River Oaks GC, *Paso Robles* .... 9 [P] 805-226-2096
   riveroaksgolfcourse.com
River Oaks GC, *Nicolaus* .... 18 [S] 916-488-4653
   riveroaksgolfclub.net
River Oaks GC, *Ceres* .... 18 [P] 209-537-4653
River Park Golf Ctr, *Fresno* .... 9 [P] 559-448-9467
   riverparkgolf.com
River Ridge GC, *Oxnard* .... 36 [M] 805-983-4653
   riverridge-golfclub.com
River View GC, *Santa Ana* .... 18 [P] 714-543-1115
   riverviewgolf.com
Riverbend GC, *Madera* .... 18 [R] 559-432-3020
   riverbendgolfclub.com
Rivers Edge GC, *Needles* .... 18 [M] 760-326-3931
   golfneedlesca.com
Riverside GC, *Riverside* .... 18 [P] 951-682-3748
   riverside-golf-club.com
Riverside GC, *Fresno* .... 18 [M] 559-275-5900
   playriverside.com
Riverview G&CC, *Redding* .... 18 [V] 530-224-2255
   riverviewgolf.net
Riverwalk GC, *San Diego* .... 27 [P] 619-296-4653
   riverwalkgc.com
Riviera CC, *Pacific Palisades* .... 18 [V] 310-454-6591
   rccla.com
Riviera Hills G&CC, *Kelseyville* .... 15 [S] 707-277-7575
Road Runner G&CC, *Borrego Springs* .... 18 [R] 760-767-5373
   roadrunnerclub.com
Roadrunner Dunes GC, *Twentynine Palms* ..... 9 [P] 760-367-5770
   roadrunnerdunes.com

[S] = SEMI-PRIVATE [V] = PRIVATE [U] = UNIVERSITY [N] = UNIVERSITY-PRIVATE

CALIFORNIA
Golf Yellow Pages, 18th Edition

Rob Roy GC, *Cobb* .... 9 [R] 707-928-5276
robroygc.com
Robinson Ranch, *Canyon Country* .... 36 [P] 661-252-7666
robinsonranchgolf.com
Roddy Ranch GC, *Antioch* .... 18 [P] 925-978-4653
roddyranch.com
Rolling Greens GC, *Granite Bay* .... 9 [P] 916-797-9986
rollinggreens.com
Rolling Hills CC, *Rolling Hills Estates* .... 18 [V] 310-326-4343
rollinghillscc.com
Roosevelt Muni GC, *Los Angeles* .... 9 [M] 323-665-2011
laparks.org
Rooster Run GC, *Petaluma* .... 18 [P] 707-778-1211
roosterrun.com
Rossmoor GC, *Walnut Creek* .... 27 [V] 925-933-2607
rossmoor.com
Round Hill CC, *Alamo* .... 18 [V] 925-934-8211
rhcountryclub.com
Ruby Hill GC, *Pleasanton* .... 18 [V] 925-417-5840
rubyhill.com
Rustic Canyon GC, *Moorpark* .... 18 [P] 805-530-0221
rusticcanyongolfcourse.com
Saddle Creek GC, *Copperopolis* .... 18 [S] 209-785-3700
saddlecreek.com
Sail Ho GC, *San Diego* .... 9 [P] 619-222-4653
sailhogolf.com
Salinas Fairways GC, *Salinas* .... 18 [M] 831-758-4653
salinasfairways.com
Salinas G&CC, *Salinas* .... 18 [V] 831-449-6617
salinascountryclub.com
Salt Creek GC, *Chula Vista* .... 18 [P] 619-482-4666
saltcreekgc.com
San Bernardino GC, *San Bernardino* .... 18 [P] 909-825-1670
sanbernardinogolfclub.com
San Clemente Muni GC, *San Clemente* .... 18 [M] 949-361-8380
sanclementegc.com
San Diego CC, *Chula Vista* .... 18 [V] 619-422-8895
sandiegocountryclub.org
San Diego Naval Station GC, *San Diego* .... 9 [A] 619-556-7502
mwrtoday.com
San Dimas Canyon GC, *San Dimas* .... 18 [P] 909-599-2313
sandimas.americangolf.com
San Francisco GC, *San Francisco* .... 18 [V] 415-469-4122
San Gabriel CC, *San Gabriel* .... 18 [V] 626-287-9671
sangabrielcc.com
San Geronimo GC, *San Geronimo* .... 18 [P] 415-488-4030
sangeronimogc.com
San Joaquin CC, *Fresno* .... 18 [V] 559-439-3359
sjcc.cc
San Jose CC, *San Jose* .... 18 [V] 408-258-4901
sanjosecountryclub.org
San Jose Muni GC, *San Jose* .... 18 [M] 408-441-4653
sjmuni.com
San Juan Hills CC, *San Juan Capistrano* .... 18 [P] 949-493-1167
sanjuanhillsgolf.com
San Juan Oaks GC, *Hollister* .... 18 [P] 831-636-6113
sanjuanoaks.com
San Luis Obispo CC, *San Luis Obispo* .... 18 [P] 805-543-3400
sanluisobispocountryclub.com
San Luis Rey Downs Golf Resort, *Bonsall* .... 18 [R] 760-758-3762
slrd.com
San Ramon GC, *San Ramon* .... 18 [P] 925-828-6100
sanramongolfclub.net

San Simeon Pines Resort, *Cambria* .... 9 [R] 805-927-4648
sspines.com
San Vicente Inn & GC, *Ramona* .... 18 [R] 760-789-3477
sanvicenteresort.com
Sandpiper GC, *Santa Barbara* .... 18 [P] 805-968-1541
sandpipergolf.com
Sands RV & Golf Resort, *Desert Hot Springs* .... 9 [R] 760-251-1030
sandsrvresort.com
Santa Ana CC, *Santa Ana* .... 18 [V] 714-556-3000
santaanacc.org
Santa Anita GC, *Arcadia* .... 18 [M] 626-447-7156
lacountyparks.com
Santa Barbara GC, *Santa Barbara* .... 18 [M] 805-687-7087
sbgolf.com
Santa Clara G&TC, *Santa Clara* .... 18 [M] 408-980-9515
santaclara.americangolf.com
Santa Maria CC, *Santa Maria* .... 18 [V] 805-937-2027
santamariacc.com
Santa Rosa CC, *Palm Desert* .... 18 [V] 760-568-5717
santarosaccpd.com
Santa Rosa G&CC, *Santa Rosa* .... 18 [V] 707-546-6617
santarosagolf.com
Santa Teresa GC, *San Jose* .... 27 [M] 408-225-2650
santateresagolf.com
Saratoga CC, *Saratoga* .... 9 [V] 408-253-5494
saratogacc.com
Saticoy CC, *Somis* .... 18 [V] 805-485-4956
saticoycountryclub.com
Saticoy Regional GC, *Ventura* .... 9 [M] 805-647-6678
saticoy.americangolf.com
Scholl Canyon GC, *Glendale* .... 18 [M] 818-243-4100
schollcanyon.americangolf.com
Sea Aire Park GC, *Torrance* .... 9 [M] 310-543-4653
Sea N Air GC, *San Diego* .... 18 [A] 619-545-9659
mwrtoday.com
Sea Pines Golf Resort, *Los Osos* .... 9 [R] 805-528-5252
seapinesgolfresort.com
SeaBee (CBC) GC of Port Hueneme, *Port Hueneme* 18 [A] 805-982-2620
scga.org/clubs/cbcgc
SeaCliff CC, *Huntington Beach* .... 18 [V] 714-536-7575
seacliffcc.net
Seascape GC, *Aptos* .... 18 [R] 831-688-3213
seascapegc.com
Sebastopol GC, *Sebastopol* .... 9 [P] 707-823-9852
Selma Valley GC, *Selma* .... 18 [P] 559-896-2424
Sepulveda Golf, *Encino* .... 36 [M] 818-995-1170
golf.lacity.org
Sequoia Woods CC, *Arnold* .... 18 [V] 209-795-2141
sequoiawoods.com
Sequoyah CC, *Oakland* .... 18 [V] 510-632-2900
sequoyahcc.com
Serrano CC, *El Dorado Hills* .... 18 [V] 916-933-5716
serranogolf.com
Seven Hills GC, *Hemet* .... 18 [P] 951-925-4815
Seven Lakes CC, *Palm Springs* .... 18 [V] 760-328-9774
7lakescountryclub.com
Seven Oaks GC, *Bakersfield* .... 27 [V] 661-664-6474
sevenoakscountryclub.com
Sevillano Links, *Corning* .... 18 [P] 530-528-4600
sevillanolinks.com
Shadow Hills GC, *Indio* .... 27 [P] 760-200-3375
shadowhillsgolfclub.com
Shadow Lakes GC, *Brentwood* .... 18 [P] 925-516-2837
shadowlakesgolf.com

22   [A] = MILITARY   [M] = MUNICIPAL   [P] = PUBLIC   [R] = RESORT

Golf Yellow Pages, 18th Edition — CALIFORNIA

Shadow Mountain GC, *Palm Desert* .... 18 [V] 760-346-8242
    shadowmountaingc.com
Shadow Ridge Golf Resort, *Palm Desert*............18 [R] 760-674-2700
    golfshadowridge.com
Shadowridge CC, *Vista*.................................... 18 [V] 760-727-7706
    shadowridgecc.com
Shady Canyon GC, *Irvine*................................ 18 [V] 949-856-7000
    shadycanyongolfclub.com
Shandin Hills GC, *San Bernardino* ....18 [M] 909-886-0669
    shandinhillsgolf.com
Sharon Heights G&CC, *Menlo Park* .... 18 [V] 650-854-6429
    shgcc.com
Sharp Park GC, *Pacifica* ....18 [M] 650-359-3380
    sharpparkgc.com
Shasta Valley CC, *Montague*............................9 [P] 530-842-2302
Shelter Cove GC, *Whitethorn*...........................9 [P] 707-986-1464
    sheltercove-ca.us
Sherwood CC, *Thousand Oaks*........................ 18 [V] 805-496-3036
    sherwoodcc.us
Sherwood Forest GC, *Sanger*..........................18 [P] 559-787-2611
    sherwoodforestgolfclub.com
Sherwood Lake Club, *Westlake Village*............... 18 [V] 805-497-3037
    sherwoodlakeclub.com
Shorecliffs GC, *San Clemente*.........................18 [P] 949-492-1177
    pacificgolfenterprises.com
Shoreline Golf Links, *Mountain View* ....18 [M] 650-903-4653
    ci.mtnview.ca.us
Sierra La Verne CC, *La Verne* .... 18 [V] 909-596-2100
    sierralavernecc.com
Sierra Lakes GC, *Fontana* ....18 [P] 909-350-2500
    sierralakes.com
Sierra Meadows CC, *Ahwahnee*........................18 [R] 559-642-1343
    sierrameadows.com
Sierra Star GC, *Mammoth Lakes* ....18 [R] 760-924-4653
    mammothmountain.com
Sierra View CC, *Roseville* .... 18 [V] 916-782-3741
    sierraviewcc.org
Silver Creek Valley CC, *San Jose*...................... 18 [V] 408-239-5775
    scvcc.com
Silver Lakes Assoc, *Helendale*...........................27 [R] 760-245-7435
    silverlakesassociation.com
Silverado Resort & Spa, *Napa* ....36 [R] 707-257-0200
    silveradogolfresort.com
SilverRock Resort, *La Quinta*...............................18 [R] 760-777-8884
    silverrock.org
Simi Hills GC, *Simi Valley* ....18 [M] 805-522-0803
    simihillsgolf.com
Sinaloa GC, *Simi Valley* ....9 [P] 805-581-2662
    sinaloapark.com
Skyline Ranch CC, *Valley Center*.......................... 9 [P] 760-749-3233
Skylinks At Long Beach GC, *Long Beach* ....18 [M] 562-421-3388
    skylinks.americangolf.com
Skywest GC, *Hayward*.....................................18 [M] 510-317-2300
    haywardrec.org
Snowcreek Resort GC, *Mammoth Lakes* .... 9 [R] 760-934-6633
    snowcreek.com
Sonoma GC, *Sonoma* .... 18 [V] 707-996-0300
    sonomagolfclub.com
Soule Park GC, *Ojai* ....18 [M] 805-646-5633
    soulepark.com
South Gate Muni Par 3 GC, *South Gate*...............9 [M] 323-357-9613
    sogate.org
South Hills GC, *West Covina*........................... 18 [V] 626-339-1231
    southhillscountryclub.org

Spanish Hills G&CC, *Camarillo*........................ 18 [V] 805-389-1644
    spanishhillscc.com
Spring Creek G&CC, *Ripon*............................. 18 [V] 209-599-3258
    springcreekcc.com
Spring Hills GC, *Watsonville*...............................18 [P] 831-724-1404
    springhillsgolf.com
Spring Valley GC, *Milpitas* ....18 [M] 408-262-1722
    springvalleygolfcourse.com
Spring Valley Lake CC, *Victorville*.................... 18 [V] 760-245-7921
    spring-valley-lake.com
Springs At Borrego GC, *Borrego Springs* .... 9 [R] 760-767-0004
    springsatborrego.com
Springtown GC, *Livermore* ....9 [M] 925-455-5695
    ci.livermore.ca.us/maintenance/golf.html
Spyglass Hill GC, *Pebble Beach*......................... 18 [S] 831-625-8563
    pebblebeach.com
St Stanislaus GC, *Modesto*................................9 [P] 209-538-2828
Stanford Univ GC, *Palo Alto*............................. 18 [N] 650-724-0944
    stanfordgolfcourse.com
Steele Canyon GC, *Jamul* ....27 [S] 619-441-6900
    steelecanyon.com
Sterling Hills GC, *Camarillo*.............................18 [V] 805-604-1234
    sterlinghillsgolf.com
Stevinson Ranch GC, *Stevinson* ....18 [P] 209-664-6450
    stevinsonranch.com
Stockdale CC, *Bakersfield* .... 18 [V] 661-832-0587
    stockdalecountryclub.com
Stockton G&CC, *Stockton* .... 18 [V] 209-466-4313
    stocktongolfcc.com
Stone Eagle GC, *Palm Desert*.......................... 18 [V] 760-773-6223
    stoneeagleclub.com
StoneRidge GC, *Poway*................................... 18 [V] 858-487-2138
    stoneridgeclub.com
StoneTree GC, *Novato* .... 18 [S] 415-209-6090
    stonetreegolf.com
Strawberry Farms GC, *Irvine*............................18 [P] 949-551-1811
    sf-golf.com
Summitpointe GC, *Milpitas* ....18 [P] 408-262-8813
    summitpointe.americangolf.com
Sun Lakes CC, *Banning* .... 18 [S] 951-845-2135
    sunlakesgolf.com
Sun Lakes CC Exec, *Banning* .... 18 [V] 951-769-8444
    sunlakesgolf.com
Sun Valley Fairways, *La Mesa*............................9 [P] 619-466-6102
    sunvalleygolfclub.com
Suncrest CC, *Palm Desert* ....9 [P] 760-340-2467
Sundale CC, *Bakersfield* .... 18 [V] 661-831-5224
    sundalecountryclub.com
Sunken Gardens Muni GC, *Sunnyvale* ....9 [M] 408-739-6588
    sunnyvale.ca.gov
Sunnyside CC, *Fresno*..................................... 18 [V] 559-255-6871
    sunnyside-cc.com
Sunnyvale GC, *Sunnyvale* ....18 [M] 408-738-3666
    sunnyvale.ca.gov
Sunol Valley GC, *Sunol*....................................36 [P] 925-862-0414
    sunolvalley.com
Sunrise CC, *Rancho Mirage*............................. 18 [V] 760-328-1139
    sunrisecountryclub.com
Sunrise GC, *Citrus Heights* .... 9 [V] 916-764-8282
Sunset Hills CC, *Thousand Oaks*...................... 18 [V] 805-495-6484
    sunsethillsclub.com
Sunset Hills G&CC, *Chico* ....9 [P] 530-342-4600
Sunset Ridge GC, *Santa Maria* ....9 [P] 805-347-1070

[S] = SEMI-PRIVATE   [V] = PRIVATE   [U] = UNIVERSITY   [N] = UNIVERSITY-PRIVATE

CALIFORNIA — Golf Yellow Pages, 18th Edition

Sunset Whitney CC, *Rocklin* .... 18 [P] 916-624-2610
sunsetwhitney.com
Swallows Nest CC, *Sacramento* .... 9 [V] 916-920-4680
swallowsnestcountryclub.com
Swenson Park GC, *Stockton* .... 27 [M] 209-937-7360
playstocktongolf.com
Sycamore Canyon GC, *Arvin* .... 18 [P] 661-854-3163
sycamorecanyongc.com
Sycuan Resort, *El Cajon* .... 54 [R] 619-442-0364
sycuanresort.com
Table Mountain GC, *Oroville* .... 18 [M] 530-533-3922
tablemountaingolf.com
Tahoe City GC, *Tahoe City* .... 9 [P] 530-583-1516
tahoecitygolf.com
Tahoe Donner GC, *Truckee* .... 18 [R] 530-587-9443
tahoedonner.com
Tahoe Paradise GC, *South Lake Tahoe* ... 18 [P] 530-577-2121
tahoeparadisegc.com
Tahquitz Creek Golf Resort, *Palm Springs* .. 36 [P] 760-328-1005
tahquitzgolfresort.com
Talega GC, *San Clemente* .... 18 [P] 949-369-6226
talegagolfclub.com
Tamarisk CC, *Rancho Mirage* .... 18 [V] 760-328-2141
tamariskcountryclub.com
Teal Bend GC, *Sacramento* .... 18 [P] 916-922-5209
clubcorpgolf.com
Tecolote Canyon GC, *San Diego* .... 18 [P] 858-279-1600
tecolotecanyon.americangolf.com
Tees & Trees, *Barstow* .... 9 [A] 760-577-6431
Tehama GC, *Carmel* .... 18 [V] 831-622-2200
tehamagolfclub.com
Temecula Creek Inn, *Temecula* .... 27 [R] 951-676-2405
jcgolf.com
The Alisal Guest Ranch & Resort, *Solvang* .. 18 [R] 805-688-4215
alisal.com
The Bethel Island GC, *Bethel Island* .... 18 [P] 925-684-2654
bethelislandgolf.com
The Bridges At Rancho Santa Fe, *Rancho Santa Fe* 18 [V] 858-756-8700
thebridgesrsf.com
The Bridges GC At Gale Ranch, *San Ramon* .. 18 [P] 925-735-4253
thebridgesgolf.com
The CC At Soboba Springs, *San Jacinto* ... 18 [S] 951-654-9354
sobobaspringscc.com
The CC of Rancho Bernardo, *San Diego* .. 18 [V] 858-487-1134
ccofrb.com
The Club At Morningside, *Rancho Mirage* .. 18 [V] 760-321-1555
clubatmorningside.org
The Club At Shenandoah Springs, *Thousand Palms* 27 [S] 760-343-3669
theclubatshenandoahsprings.com
The Course At Wente Vineyards, *Livermore* .. 18 [P] 925-456-2475
wentegolf.com
The Crosby At Rancho Santa Fe, *San Diego* .. 18 [V] 858-756-6310
thecrosbyclub.com
The Crossings at Carlsbad, *Carlsbad* .... 18 [M] 760-444-1800
thecrossingsatcarlsbad.com
The Farms GC, *Rancho Santa Fe* .... 18 [P] 858-756-5585
thefarmsgolfclub.com
The GC at Glen Ivy, *Corona* .... 18 [S] 951-277-7900
glenivygolf.com
The GC at Grays Crossing, *Truckee* .... 18 [P] 530-550-5800
grayscrossinggolf.com
The GC at La Quinta, *La Quinta* .... 18 [P] 760-771-0707
thegolfclubsofcalifornia.com

The GC at Moffett Field, *Mountain View* .. 18 [S] 650-603-8026
moffettgolf.com
The GC at Westridge, *La Habra* .... 18 [P] 562-690-4200
thegolfclubsofcalifornia.com
The GC of California, *Fallbrook* .... 18 [V] 760-451-3700
thegolfclubsofcalifornia.com
The GC Tierra Oaks, *Redding* .... 18 [V] 530-275-0795
tierraoaksgc.com
The Golf Center at Palm Desert, *Palm Desert* .. 9 [M] 760-779-1877
The Grand GC, *San Diego* .... 18 [R] 858-792-6200
thegrandgolfclub.com
The Hideaway GC, *La Quinta* .... 36 [V] 760-777-7400
hideawaygolfclub.com
The Inn & Links at Spanish Bay, *Pebble Beach* .. 18 [R] 831-647-7500
pebblebeach.com
The Institute LLC, *Morgan Hill* .... 18 [V] 408-782-7101
The Journey At Pechanga, *Temecula* ..... 18 [R] 951-770-4653
journeyatpechanga.com
The Lakes CC, *Palm Desert* .... 27 [V] 760-568-4321
thelakescc.com
The Legends GC, *Temecula* .... 18 [S] 951-694-9998
thelegendsgc.com
The Lincoln Hills GC, *Lincoln* .... 36 [P] 916-543-9200
lincolnhillsgolfclub.com
The Links At Riverlakes Ranch, *Bakersfield* .. 18 [P] 661-587-5465
riverlakesgc.com
The Links At Terranea, *Rancho Palos Verdes* .. 9 [R] 310-265-2755
terranea.com
The Links At Victoria Park, *Carson* .... 18 [M] 310-323-4174
linksatvictoria.com
The Links At Vista Del Hombre, *Paso Robles* .. 18 [P] 805-227-4567
linkscourseatpasorobles.com
The Madison Club, *La Quinta* .... 18 [V] 760-391-4500
madisonclubca.com
The New Links At Bodega Harbour, *Bodega Bay* .18 [R] 707-875-3538
bodegaharbourgolf.com
The Newport Beach CC, *Newport Beach* .. 18 [V] 949-644-9680
newportbeachcc.com
The Olympic Club, *Daly City* .... 45 [V] 415-404-4333
olyclub.com
The Palms GC, *La Quinta* .... 18 [V] 760-771-2606
thepalmsgc.org
The Preserve GC, *Carmel* .... 18 [V] 831-626-8200
santaluciapreserve.com
The Quarry at LaQuinta, *La Quinta* .... 18 [V] 760-777-1100
quarryinfo.com
The Ranch GC, *San Jose* .... 18 [P] 408-270-0557
theranchgc.com
The Reserve at Spanos Park, *Stockton* ... 18 [S] 209-477-4653
thereserve.americangolf.com
The Reserve Club, *Indian Wells* .... 18 [V] 760-674-2240
thereserveclub.com
The Ridge GC, *Auburn* .... 18 [P] 530-888-7888
ridgegc.com
The Santaluz Club, *San Diego* .... 18 [V] 858-759-3131
santaluz.com
The Sea Ranch Golf Links, *Sea Ranch* ..... 18 [R] 707-785-2468
888searanch.com
The Springs CC, *Rancho Mirage* .... 18 [V] 760-324-8292
springsclub.com
The Timilick Club, *Truckee* .... 18 [V] 530-582-6964
timilick.com
The Tuscan Ridge Club, *Paradise* .... 18 [S] 530-624-7006
tuscanridgeclub.com

24 [A] = MILITARY   [M] = MUNICIPAL   [P] = PUBLIC   [R] = RESORT

Golf Yellow Pages, 18th Edition — CALIFORNIA

Course	City	Holes	Type	Phone
The Vineyard at Escondido,	Escondido	18	[M]	760-735-9545
vineyardatescondido.com				
The Vineyards GC,	Coachella	9	[S]	760-863-1936
thenewvineyards.com				
The Vintage Club,	Indian Wells	36	[V]	760-862-2076
vintageclubsales.com				
The Westin Mission Hills Resort & Spa,				
	Rancho Mirage	18	[R]	760-770-2908
troongolf.com				
The Windsor GC,	Windsor	18	[P]	707-838-7888
windsorgolf.com				
Three Rivers GC,	Three Rivers	9	[P]	559-561-3133
Thunderbird CC,	Rancho Mirage	18	[V]	760-328-2161
thunderbirdcc.org				
Tierra Del Sol GC,	California City	18	[M]	760-373-2384
Tierra Rejada GC,	Moorpark	18	[P]	805-531-9300
tierrarejadagolf.com				
Tijeras Creek GC,	Rancho Santa Marg	18	[P]	949-589-9793
tijerascreek.com				
Tilden Park GC,	Berkeley	18	[M]	510-848-7373
tildenparkgc.americangolf.com				
Timber Creek GC At Sun City Roseville,	Roseville	27	[P]	916-774-3851
timbercreekgc.com				
Torrey Pines GC,	La Jolla	36	[M]	858-452-3226
torreypinesgolfcourse.com				
Toscana CC,	Indian Wells	36	[V]	760-404-1457
toscanacc.com				
Town Park Villas GC,	San Diego	9	[P]	858-558-7273
TPC San Francisco Bay At Stonebrae,	Hayward	18	[S]	510-728-7878
tpcstonebrae.com				
TPC Valencia,	Valencia	18	[S]	661-288-1995
tpcvalencia.com				
Tracy G&CC,	Tracy	18	[V]	209-835-9463
tracycountryclub.com				
Tradition GC,	La Quinta	27	[V]	760-564-1067
traditiongolfclub.net				
Trinitas GC,	Valley Springs	18	[R]	209-887-9150
trinitasgolf.com				
Trinity Alps GC,	Weaverville	9	[P]	530-623-6209
trinityalpsgolf.com				
Trona GC,	Trona	9	[P]	760-372-5159
Trump National GC, Los Angeles,				
	Rancho Palos Verdes	18	[R]	310-303-3240
trumpnationallosangeles.com				
Tucker Oaks GC,	Redding	9	[P]	530-365-3350
Tulare GC,	Tulare	18	[P]	559-686-5300
Turkey Creek GC,	Lincoln	18	[P]	916-434-9100
plantationoaksgolf.com				
Turlock G&CC,	Turlock	18	[V]	209-634-4976
turlockcountryclub.com				
Tustin Ranch GC,	Tustin	18	[P]	714-730-1611
tustinranchgolf.com				
Twain Harte GC,	Twain Harte	9	[P]	209-586-3131
twainhartegolf.com				
Twin Creeks GC,	Salinas	9	[P]	831-442-6922
thefirstteemc.org				
Twin Lakes GC,	Goleta	9	[P]	805-964-1414
twinlakesgolf.com				
Twin Oaks GC,	San Marcos	18	[P]	760-591-4653
jcgolf.com				
Ukiah Muni GC,	Ukiah	18	[M]	707-467-2832
ukiahgolf.com				
Upland Hills CC,	Upland	18	[S]	909-946-4711
golfuhcc.com				
Valencia CC,	Valencia	18	[V]	661-254-4401
valenciagolfclub.com				
Valley Club of Montecito,	Santa Barbara	18	[V]	805-969-4681
valleyclub.org				
Valley Gardens GC,	Scotts Valley	9	[P]	831-438-3058
valleygardensgolf.com				
Valley Hi CC,	Elk Grove	18	[V]	916-423-2170
valleyhicc.com				
Valley Oaks GC,	Visalia	27	[M]	559-651-1441
playvalleyoaks.com				
Valley Rose GC,	Wasco	18	[P]	661-758-8301
valleyrosegolf.com				
Van Buren Golf Ctr,	Riverside	18	[M]	951-688-2563
vanburengolf.com				
Van Buskirk Muni GC,	Stockton	18	[M]	209-937-7357
playstocktongolf.com				
Van Nuys GC,	Van Nuys	27	[P]	818-785-8871
Vellano CC,	Chino Hills	18	[S]	909-597-2801
experiencevellano.com				
Venetian Gardens GC,	Stockton	9	[V]	209-477-3871
Verdugo Hills GC,	Tujunga	18	[P]	818-352-3161
Via Verde CC,	San Dimas	18	[V]	909-599-8486
viaverdecountryclub.com				
Victoria Club,	Riverside	18	[V]	951-683-5323
victoriaclub.com				
Village CC,	Lompoc	18	[V]	805-733-3537
villagecc.net				
Villages G&CC,	San Jose	27	[V]	408-274-3220
thevillagesgcc.com				
Vineyard Knolls GC,	Napa	9	[V]	707-226-8184
vineyardknolls.com				
Vintners GC,	Yountville	9	[P]	707-944-1992
vintnersgolfclub.com				
Virginia CC,	Long Beach	18	[V]	562-427-0924
vcc1909.org				
Visalia CC,	Visalia	18	[V]	559-734-1458
visaliacc.net				
Vista Valencia GC,	Valencia	27	[P]	661-253-1870
vistavalencia.americangolf.com				
Vista Valley CC,	Vista	18	[V]	760-758-5275
vistavalley.com				
Warner Springs Ranch,	Warner Springs	18	[R]	760-782-4200
warnersprings.com				
Washoe Creek GC,	Cotati	18	[S]	707-792-7700
Wawona Hotel GC,	Yosemite Nat Park	9	[R]	209-375-6572
yosemitepark.com				
Weddington G&TC,	Studio City	9	[P]	818-761-3250
weddingtongolfandtennis.com				
Weed GC,	Weed	9	[P]	530-938-9971
weedgolfclub.com				
Welk Resort San Diego,	Escondido	36	[R]	760-749-3225
welkgolf.com				
Westchester GC,	Los Angeles	18	[P]	310-649-9173
westchester.americangolf.com				
Western Hills G&CC,	Chino Hills	18	[V]	714-528-6400
Westlake GC,	Westlake Village	18	[P]	818-889-0770
Westwinds GC,	Victorville	9	[M]	760-243-1936
ci.victorville.ca.us				
Whispering Lakes GC,	Ontario	18	[M]	909-923-3673
Whitehawk Ranch GC,	Clio	18	[R]	530-836-0394
golfwhitehawk.com				
Whitney Oaks GC,	Rocklin	18	[P]	916-632-8333
whitneyoaksgolf.com				

[S] = SEMI-PRIVATE   [V] = PRIVATE   [U] = UNIVERSITY   [N] = UNIVERSITY-PRIVATE

CALIFORNIA

Whittier Mobile CC, *Whittier*................................. 9 [V] 562-692-2755
Whittier Narrows GC, *Rosemead*....................27 [M] 626-288-1044
  whittiernarrowsgc.com
Wikiup GC, *Santa Rosa*..................................9 [P] 707-546-8787
Wilcox Oaks GC, *Red Bluff*............................. 18 [V] 530-527-7087
  wilcoxoaksgolfclub.com
Wild Wings GC, *Woodland* ....9 [P] 530-661-4720
  wildwingsgolf.com
WildHawk GC, *Sacramento* ....18 [M] 916-688-4653
  wildhawkgolf.com
Wildhorse GC, *Davis* ....18 [P] 530-753-4900
  wildhorsegolfclub.com
Wildwood Mobile CC, *Hacienda Heights*.............. 9 [V] 626-968-2338
William Land GC, *Sacramento* ....9 [M] 916-277-1207
  thefirstteesacramento.org
Willow Creek G&CC, *Willow Creek* ....9 [S] 530-629-2977
Willow Park GC, *Castro Valley*.....................18 [M] 510-537-8989
Willowbrook GC, *Lakeside*...............................9 [P] 619-561-1061
  willowbrookgolfcourse.com
Willowick Muni GC, *Santa Ana* ....18 [M] 714-554-0672
  willowickgolf.com
Wilshire CC, *Los Angeles*............................. 18 [V] 323-934-1121
  wilshirecountryclub.com
Winchester CC, *Meadow Vista*...................18 [P] 530-878-9585
  winchestercountryclub.com
Wood Ranch GC, *Simi Valley* .... 18 [V] 805-527-9663
  woodranch.americangolf.com
Woodbridge G&CC, *Woodbridge* .... 27 [V] 209-369-2371
  woodbridgegcc.com
Woodcreek GC, *Roseville*...........................18 [M] 916-771-4662
  roseville.ca.us
Woodhaven CC, *Palm Desert*......................18 [R] 760-345-7513
  woodhavencc.net
Woodland Hills CC, *Woodland Hills* .... 18 [V] 818-347-1511
  woodlandhillscc.org
Woodley Lakes GC, *Van Nuys* ....18 [M] 818-787-8163
  laparks.org
Woods Valley GC, *Valley Center* ....18 [P] 760-751-3007
  woodsvalleygolfclub.com
Yocha Dehe GC, *Brooks* ....18 [R] 530-796-4653
  yocha-de-hegolfclub.com
Yolo Fliers Club, *Woodland* .... 18 [V] 530-662-0281
  yolofliers.org
Yorba Linda CC, *Yorba Linda*..................... 18 [V] 714-779-2461
  yorbalinda.americangolf.com
Yosemite Lakes Park GC, *Coarsegold* .... 9 [V] 559-642-2562
  yloa.org
Yucaipa Valley GC, *Yucaipa* ....18 [P] 909-790-6522
  yucaipavalleygolf.com
Zaca Creek GC, *Buellton* ....9 [P] 805-688-2575
  zacacreekgolfcourseandlearningcenter.com

COLORADO

Adams Mountain CC, *Eagle*..................... 18 [V] 970-328-2326
  adamsribranch.com
Adobe Creek National GC, *Fruita*.......................27 [P] 970-858-0521
  adobecreekgolf.com
Antelope Hills GC, *Bennett*.....................18 [P] 303-644-5992
  antelopehillsgolfcourse.com
Antler Creek GC, *Peyton* ....18 [P] 719-494-1900
  antlercreekgolf.com
Applewood GC, *Golden*........................18 [P] 303-279-3003
  applewoodgc.com

Arrowhead GC, *Littleton* ....18 [R] 303-973-9614
  arrowheadcolorado.com
Aspen G&TC, *Aspen* ....18 [M] 970-925-2145
  aspengolf.com
Aspen Glen Club, *Carbondale*............... 18 [V] 970-704-1988
  aspen-glen.com
Aurora Hills GC, *Aurora* ....18 [M] 303-364-6111
  golfaurora.com
Ballyneal Golf & Hunt Club, *Holyoke* .... 18 [V] 970-854-5900
  ballyneal.com
Battlement Mesa GC, *Parachute* ....18 [P] 970-285-7274
  battlementmesagolf.com
Bear Creek GC, *Denver* .... 18 [V] 303-980-8700
  bearcreekgolfclub.net
Beaver Creek GC, *Beaver Creek*........................18 [R] 970-754-5775
  beavercreek.com
Bella Rosa GC, *Frederick* ....9 [M] 303-678-2940
  bellarosagolf.com
Black Canyon GC At Montrose, *Montrose*............18 [P] 970-249-4653
  blackcanyongolfclub.com
Bookcliff CC, *Grand Junction* .... 18 [V] 970-242-9053
  bookcliffcc.com
Boomerang Links, *Greeley* ....18 [M] 970-351-8934
  greeleygov.com/golf
Boulder CC, *Boulder*................................ 27 [V] 303-530-4600
  bouldercc.org
Breckenridge GC, *Breckenridge* ....27 [M] 970-453-9104
  breckenridgegolfclub.com
Brightwater Club, *Gypsum*............................. 18 [V] 970-777-1700
  brightwatervailvalley.com
Broken Tee Englewood, *Englewood* ....27 [M] 303-762-2670
  brokenteegolf.com
Buffalo Run GC, *Commerce City* ....18 [M] 303-289-1500
  buffalorungolfcourse.com
Bunker Hill CC, *Brush*.............................9 [S] 970-842-5470
Canongate at Blackstone CC, *Aurora* .... 18 [V] 303-680-0245
  canongatecolorado.com
Castle Pines GC, *Castle Rock* .... 18 [V] 303-688-6000
  ccatcastlepines.com
Catamount Ranch & Club, *Steamboat Springs*.... 18 [V] 970-871-9200
  catamountranchclub.com
Cattail Creek GC, *Loveland* ....9 [M] 970-663-5310
  golfloveland.com
Cattails GC, *Alamosa*........................18 [M] 719-589-9515
  alamosacattails.com
CC of Colorado, *Colorado Springs*....................... 18 [V] 719-538-4080
  ccofcolorado.com
CC of the Rockies, *Edwards* .... 18 [V] 970-926-3021
  countrycluboftherockies.com
Cedar Ridges GC, *Rangely* ....9 [M] 970-675-8403
  westernrioblanco.org
Centre Hills Par 3 GC, *Aurora* ....9 [M] 303-326-8674
  golfaurora.com
Challenger GC, *Crestone*...........................9 [P] 719-256-4856
Cherokee Ridge GC, *Colorado Springs*..................18 [P] 719-597-2637
  cherokeeridgegolfcourse.com
Cherry Creek GC, *Denver*................................ 18 [V] 303-597-0300
  cherrycreekcountryclub.com
Cherry Hills CC, *Englewood* .... 27 [V] 303-350-5220
  chcc.com
Cheyenne Shadows GC At Fort Carson, *Fort Carson* 18 [P] 719-526-4122
  mwrfortcarson.com
Chipeta GC At Orchard Mesa, *Grand Junction*......18 [P] 970-245-7177
  chipetagolf.com

[A] = MILITARY   [M] = MUNICIPAL   [P] = PUBLIC   [R] = RESORT

COLORADO

City Park GC, *Denver* .... 18 [M] 303-295-2096
 cityofdenvergolf.com
City Park Nine GC, *Fort Collins* .... 9 [M] 970-221-6650
 fcgov.com/golf
Club at Cordillera - Mountain, *Edwards* .... 18 [R] 970-926-5117
 cordillera-vail.com
Club at Cordillera - Summit, *Edwards* .... 18 [R] 970-926-5300
 cordillera-vail.com
Club at Cordillera - Valley, *Edwards* .... 18 [V] 970-926-5950
 cordillera-vail.com
Club At Pradera, *Parker* .... 18 [V] 303-607-5700
 theclubatpradera.com
Coal Creek GC, *Louisville* .... 18 [P] 303-666-7888
 coalcreekgolf.com
Collegiate Peaks GC, *Buena Vista* .... 9 [P] 719-395-8189
 collegiatepeaksgolf.com
Collindale GC, *Fort Collins* .... 18 [M] 970-221-6651
 fcgov.com/golf
Colorado GC, *Parker* .... 27 [V] 303-840-5400
 coloradogolfclub.com
Colorado National GC, *Erie* .... 18 [P] 303-926-1723
 coloradonationalgolfclub.com
Colorado Springs CC, *Colorado Springs* .... 18 [V] 719-473-1782
 cscountryclub.com
Columbine CC, *Littleton* .... 27 [V] 303-794-6333
 columbinecountryclub.com
CommonGround GC, *Aurora* .... 27 [P] 303-340-1520
 commongroundgc.com
Conquistador GC, *Cortez* .... 18 [M] 970-565-9208
 cityofcortez.com
Copper Creek GC, *Copper Mountain* .... 18 [R] 970-968-3333
 coppercolorado.com
Cornerstone Colorado GC, *Montrose* .... 18 [V] 970-650-2000
 cornerstonecolorado.com
Cottonwood Links GC, *Fowler* .... 9 [S] 719-263-4500
 fowlercolorado.com
Cougar Canyon Golf Links, *Trinidad* .... 18 [R] 719-422-7015
 cougarcanyonliving.com
Coyote Creek GC, *Fort Lupton* .... 18 [M] 303-857-6152
 fortlupton.org
Dalton Ranch GC, *Durango* .... 18 [S] 970-247-7921
 daltonranch.com
Deer Creek GC At Meadow Ranch, *Littleton* .... 18 [S] 303-978-1800
 deercreekgolfclub.net
DeerCreek Village GC, *Cedaredge* .... 18 [M] 970-856-7781
 deercreekvillage-golf.com
Denver CC, *Denver* .... 18 [V] 303-733-2441
 denvercc.net
Desert Hawk At Pueblo West, *Pueblo West* .... 18 [M] 719-547-2280
 deserthawkgolfcourse.com
Devils Thumb GC, *Delta* .... 18 [M] 970-874-6262
 devilsthumbgolfclub.com
Dos Rios GC, *Gunnison* .... 18 [S] 970-641-1482
 dosriosgolf.net
Eagle Ranch GC, *Eagle* .... 18 [P] 970-328-2882
 eagleranchgolf.com
Eagle Springs GC, *Wolcott* .... 18 [V] 970-926-4404
 eaglesprings.org
Eagle Trace GC, *Broomfield* .... 18 [P] 303-466-3322
 eagletracegolfclub.com
Eagle Vail GC, *Avon* .... 27 [P] 970-949-5267
 eaglevailgolfclub.com
Eaton CC, *Eaton* .... 18 [V] 970-454-2587
 eatoncountryclub.com

Eisenhower GC, *USAFA Academy* .... 36 [A] 719-333-2606
 eisenhowergolfclub.com
Elmwood GC, *Pueblo* .... 27 [M] 719-561-4946
 pueblocitygolf.com
Emerald Greens GC at Windsor Gardens, *Denver* ... 9 [P] 303-366-3133
 windsorgardensdenver.org
Estes Park GC, *Estes Park* .... 18 [M] 970-586-8146
 golfestes.com
Evergreen GC, *Evergreen* .... 18 [M] 303-674-6351
 evergreengc.com
F & H GC, *Haxtun* .... 9 [P] 970-774-6362
 fandhgolf.com
Family Sports Center GC, *Englewood* .... 9 [M] 303-649-1115
 ssprd.org
Fitzsimons GC, *Aurora* .... 18 [M] 303-364-8125
 golfaurora.com
Flatirons GC, *Boulder* .... 18 [M] 303-442-7851
 flatironsgolf.com
Foothills GC, *Denver* .... 36 [M] 303-409-2400
 foothillsgolf.org
Fort Collins CC, *Fort Collins* .... 18 [V] 970-482-9988
 fcgolf.org
Fort Morgan Muni GC, *Fort Morgan* .... 18 [M] 970-867-5990
 cityoffortmorgan.com
Fossil Trace GC, *Golden* .... 18 [M] 303-277-8750
 fossiltrace.com
Four Mile Ranch GC, *Canon City* .... 18 [S] 719-275-5400
 fourmileranch.com
Fox Acres CC, *Red Feather Lakes* .... 18 [V] 970-881-2191
 foxacres.com
Fox Hill CC, *Longmont* .... 18 [V] 303-772-0246
 foxhillcc.com
Fox Hollow At Lakewood, *Lakewood* .... 27 [M] 303-986-7888
 lakewoodgolf.org
Garden of the Gods Club, *Colorado Springs* .... 27 [V] 719-636-2520
 gardenofthegodsclub.com
GC at Cordillera - Short Course, *Edwards* .... 9 [R] 970-926-5550
 cordillera-vail.com
GC At Heather Ridge, *Aurora* .... 18 [P] 303-755-3660
 golfclubatheatherridge.com
Glacier Club at Tamarron, *Durango* .... 27 [V] 970-375-8300
 theglacierclub.com
Gleneagle GC, *Colorado Springs* .... 18 [S] 719-488-0900
 gleneaglegolfclub.com
Glenmoor CC, *Cherry Hills Village* .... 18 [V] 303-781-3000
 glenmoorcc.org
Glenwood Springs GC, *Glenwood Springs* .... 9 [P] 970-945-7086
 glenwoodgolf.com
Grand Elk Ranch & Club, *Granby* .... 18 [R] 970-887-9122
 grandelk.com
Grand Lake GC, *Grand Lake* .... 18 [M] 970-627-8008
 grandlakerecreation.com
Grandote Peaks GC, *La Veta* .... 18 [R] 719-742-3391
 grandotepeaks.com
Greeley CC, *Greeley* .... 18 [V] 970-353-2431
 greeleycc.org
Green Gables CC, *Denver* .... 18 [V] 303-985-4433
 greengablescc.com
Green Valley Ranch GC, *Denver* .... 27 [S] 303-371-3131
 gvrgolf.com
Greenway Park GC, *Broomfield* .... 9 [P] 303-466-3729
 gwphoa.org
Gypsum Creek GC, *Gypsum* .... 18 [P] 970-524-6200
 gypsumcreekgolf.com

[S] = SEMI-PRIVATE   [V] = PRIVATE   [U] = UNIVERSITY   [N] = UNIVERSITY-PRIVATE

COLORADO

Golf Yellow Pages, 18th Edition

Harmony GC, *Timnath* .... 18 [V]   970-482-4653
  harmonyclub.info
Harvard Gulch Par3 GC, *Denver* ....9 [M]   303-698-4078
  cityofdenvergolf.com
Haymaker GC, *Steamboat Springs* ....18 [M]   970-870-1846
  haymakergolf.com
Haystack Mountain GC, *Longmont* ....9 [P]   303-530-1400
  golfhaystack.com
Headwaters GC At Granby Ranch, *Granby* ....18 [R]   970-887-2709
  granbyranch.com
Heather Gardens GC, *Aurora* ....9 [P]   303-751-2390
  heathergardens.org
Heritage Eagle Bend G&CC, *Aurora* .... 18 [S]   303-400-6700
  heritageeaglebend.com
Heritage GC At Westmoor, *Westminster* ....18 [M]   303-469-2974
  golfwestminster.com
Heritage Todd Creek GC, *Thornton* .... 18 [S]   303-655-1779
  heritagetoddcreekgolf.com
Highland Hills GC, *Greeley* ....18 [P]   970-330-7327
  greeleygov.com/golf
Highland Meadows GC, *Windsor* ....18 [P]   970-204-4653
  highlandmeadowsgolfcourse.com
Highlands Ranch GC, *Highlands Ranch* .... 18 [S]   303-471-0000
  highlandsranchgolf.com
Hillcrest GC, *Durango* ....18 [M]   970-247-1499
  golfhillcrest.com
Hiwan GC, *Evergreen* .... 18 [V]   303-674-3369
  hiwan.com
Hollydot GC, *Colorado City* ....27 [M]   719-676-3341
  hollydotgolf.com
Holyoke GC, *Holyoke* ....9 [P]   970-854-3200
Hugo GC, *Hugo* ....9 [P]   719-743-2492
Hunters Run GC, *Ignacio* ....9 [P]   970-884-9785
Hyland Hills GC, *Westminster* ....45 [M]   303-428-6526
  golfhylandhills.com
Indian Hills GC, *Yuma* ....9 [P]   970-848-2812
Indian Peaks GC, *Lafayette* ....18 [P]   303-666-4706
  indianpeaksgolf.com
Indian Tree GC, *Arvada* ....27 [M]   303-403-2542
  indiantree.apexprd.org
Inverness GC, *Englewood* ....18 [R]   303-397-7878
  invernesshotel.com
Ironbridge GC, *Glenwood Springs* .... 18 [S]   970-384-0630
  ironbridgeclub.com
Kennedy GC, *Aurora* ....36 [M]   720-865-0720
  cityofdenvergolf.com
Keystone Ranch GC, *Keystone* ....18 [R]   970-496-4250
  golfkeystone.com
Kings Deer GC, *Monument* ....18 [P]   719-481-1518
  kingsdeergolfclub.com
La Junta Muni GC, *La Junta* ....9 [M]   719-384-7133
Lake Arbor GC, *Arvada* ....18 [M]   720-898-7360
  lakearborgolf.com
Lake Estes GC, *Estes Park* ....9 [M]   970-586-8176
  golfestes.com
Lake Valley GC, *Longmont* ....18 [V]   303-444-2114
  lakevalley.com
Lakewood CC, *Lakewood* ....18 [V]   303-233-4614
  lakewoodcountryclub.net
Lakota Canyon Ranch GC, *New Castle* ....18 [P]   970-984-9700
  lakotacanyonranch.com
Las Animas GC, *Las Animas* ....9 [P]   719-456-2511

Legacy Ridge GC, *Westminster* ....18 [M]   303-438-8997
  golfwestminster.com
Lincoln Park GC, *Grand Junction* ....9 [M]   970-242-6394
  golfgrandjunction.net
Link N Greens GC, *Fort Collins* ....18 [P]   970-221-4818
Links At Cobble Creek, *Montrose* ....18 [P]   970-240-9542
  cobblecreek.com
Littleton G&TC, *Littleton* ....18 [M]   303-794-5838
  littletongov.org/parks
Lone Tree GC & Hotel, *Littleton* ....18 [M]   303-799-9940
  lonetreegolfclubandhotel.com
Mad Russian GC, *Milliken* ....18 [P]   970-587-5157
  madrussiangolf.com
Mariana Butte GC, *Loveland* ....18 [M]   970-667-8308
  golfloveland.com
Maroon Creek Club, *Aspen* .... 18 [V]   970-920-4080
  mccaspen.com
Meadow Hills GC, *Aurora* ....18 [M]   303-690-2500
  golfaurora.com
Meeker GC, *Meeker* ....9 [P]   970-878-5642
Meridian GC, *Englewood* .... 18 [V]   303-799-4043
  meridiangolfclub.com
Monte Vista CC, *Monte Vista* ....9 [M]   719-852-4906
  monte-vistagolfclub.com
Monument Hill CC, *Monument* .... 18 [V]   719-481-2272
  monumenthillcc.com
Mossland Memorial GC, *Flagler* ....9 [P]   719-765-4659
Mount Massive GC, *Leadville* ....9 [P]   719-486-2176
  mtmassivegolf.com
Mountain Meadows GC, *Red Feather Lakes* ....9 [P]   970-881-2631
Mountain Vista Greens GC, *Fort Collins* ....9 [P]   970-482-4847
  mountainvistagreens.com
Murphy Creek GC, *Aurora* ....18 [M]   303-361-7300
  golfaurora.com
Northeastern 18, *Sterling* .... 18 [S]   970-521-6889
  northeastern18.com
Omni Interlocken Resort GC, *Broomfield* ....27 [R]   303-464-9000
  omniinterlockengolfclub.com
Overland GC, *Denver* ....18 [M]   303-777-7331
  overlandgolfcourse.com
Pagosa Springs GC, *Pagosa Springs* ....27 [R]   970-731-4755
  golfpagosa.com
Park Hill GC, *Denver* ....18 [P]   303-333-5411
  parkhillgc.com
Patty Jewett GC, *Colorado Springs* ....27 [M]   719-385-6934
  springsgov.com
Pelican Lakes G&CC, *Windsor* .... 27 [S]   970-674-0930
  watervalley.com
Perry Park CC, *Larkspur* .... 18 [V]   303-681-3186
  perryparkcc.com
Pine Creek GC, *Colorado Springs* ....18 [P]   719-594-9999
  pinecreekgc.com
Pinehurst CC, *Denver* .... 27 [V]   303-985-1551
  pinehurstcountryclub.com
Pinery CC, *Parker* .... 27 [V]   303-841-2850
  thepineryсс.com
Plainsman GC, *Kirk* ....9 [P]   970-358-4321
Plum Creek G&CC, *Castle Rock* .... 18 [V]   303-688-2612
  plumcreekgolfandcc.com
Pole Creek GC, *Tabernash* ....27 [M]   970-887-9195
  polecreekgolf.com
Prairie Pines GC, *Burlington* ....9 [P]   719-346-8207

[A] = MILITARY   [M] = MUNICIPAL   [P] = PUBLIC   [R] = RESORT

Golf Yellow Pages, 18th Edition — COLORADO

Course	Location	Holes	Type	Phone
Ptarmigan CC,	Fort Collins	18	[V]	970-226-6600
ptarmigancc.com				
Pueblo CC,	Pueblo	18	[V]	719-543-4844
pueblocountryclub.com				
Quint Valley GC,	Byers	9	[P]	303-822-5509
Raccoon Creek GC,	Littleton	18	[P]	303-973-4653
raccooncreek.com				
Ranch at Roaring Fork GC,	Carbondale	9	[P]	970-963-4410
ranchatroaringfork.com				
Raven GC At Three Peaks,	Silverthorne	18	[S]	970-262-3636
ravenatthreepeaks.com				
Red Hawk Ridge GC,	Castle Rock	18	[M]	720-733-3500
redhawkridge.com				
Red Rocks CC,	Morrison	18	[V]	303-697-4438
redrockscountryclub.org				
Red Sky Ranch & GC (Guest Clubhouse),	Wolcott	36	[R]	970-754-8425
redskygolfclub.com				
Red Sky Ranch & GC (Member Clubhouse),	Wolcott	36	[R]	970-754-8425
redskygolfclub.com				
Rifle Creek GC,	Rifle	18	[P]	970-625-1093
riflecreekgc.com				
Rio Grande Club,	South Fork	18	[R]	719-873-1995
theriograndeclub.com				
River Valley Ranch GC,	Carbondale	18	[P]	970-963-3625
rvrgolf.com				
Riverdale GC,	Brighton	36	[M]	303-659-6700
riverdalegolf.com				
Riverview GC,	Sterling	18	[M]	970-522-3035
Rocky Ford GC,	Rocky Ford	9	[M]	719-254-7528
golfcolorado.com				
Rolling Hills CC,	Golden	18	[V]	303-279-3334
rhillscc.com				
Rollingstone Ranch GC,	Steamboat Springs	18	[R]	970-879-1391
rollingstoneranchgolf.com				
Saddle Rock GC,	Aurora	18	[M]	303-699-3939
golfaurora.com				
Saddleback GC,	Longmont	18	[P]	303-833-5000
saddlebackgolf.com				
Salida GC,	Salida	9	[P]	719-539-1060
salidagolfclub.com				
Sanctuary,	Sedalia	18	[V]	303-224-2860
sanctuarygolfcourse.com				
Sand Creek GC at World Golf,	Colorado Springs	9	[P]	719-597-5489
worldgolfsandcreek.com				
Sedgewick County GC,	Julesburg	9	[P]	970-474-3574
Shadow Hills GC,	Canon City	18	[P]	719-275-0603
golfshadowhills.com				
Shining Mountain GC,	Woodland Park	18	[S]	719-687-7587
shiningmountaingolfclub.com				
Silver Spruce GC,	Colorado Springs	18	[A]	719-556-7414
21svs.com				
Smoky River GC,	Cheyenne Wells	9	[P]	719-767-5021
Sonnenalp GC,	Edwards	18	[R]	970-477-5371
sonnenalpgolfclub.com				
South Forty GC & DR,	Cortez	9	[P]	970-565-3501
South Suburban GC,	Centennial	27	[M]	303-770-5508
ssprd.org				
Southglenn CC,	Littleton	9	[V]	303-798-1656
southglenncc.com				
SouthRidge GC,	Fort Collins	18	[M]	970-416-2828
golfsouthridge.com				
Spreading Antlers GC,	Lamar	9	[M]	719-336-5274
Spring Valley GC,	Elizabeth	18	[P]	303-646-4240
springvalleygolf.com				
Springfield GC,	Springfield	9	[P]	719-523-6236
Springhill GC,	Aurora	18	[M]	303-739-6854
golfaurora.com				
Springs Ranch GC,	Colorado Springs	18	[P]	719-573-4863
springsranchgolfclub.com				
St Andrews at Westcliffe,	Westcliffe	9	[P]	719-783-9410
Steamboat GC,	Steamboat Springs	9	[S]	970-879-4295
steamboatgolfclub.com				
Stoney Creek GC,	Arvada	9	[P]	303-431-9268
stoneycreekgc.com				
Stratton GC,	Stratton	9	[P]	719-348-5412
Sumo Golf Village,	Florence	18	[S]	719-784-4653
Sunset GC,	Longmont	9	[M]	303-651-8466
golflongmont.com				
Tamarack GC,	Limon	9	[M]	719-775-9461
tamarackcc.com				
Telluride Ski & GC,	Telluride	18	[R]	970-728-2606
tellurideskiandgolfclub.com				
The Black Bear GC,	Parker	18	[V]	303-840-3100
canongatecolorado.com				
The Bridges G&CC,	Montrose	18	[S]	970-252-8899
montrosebridges.com				
The Broadlands GC,	Broomfield	18	[P]	303-466-8285
thebroadlandsgc.com				
The Broadmoor,	Colorado Springs	54	[R]	719-577-5790
broadmoor.com				
The CC at Castle Pines,	Castle Rock	18	[V]	303-660-6807
ccatcastlepines.com				
The Club At Crested Butte,	Crested Butte	18	[R]	970-349-8603
theclubatcrestedbutte.com				
The Club At Flying Horse,	Colorado Springs	18	[V]	719-487-2620
flyinghorseclub.com				
The Divide Ranch & Club,	Ridgway	18	[S]	970-626-5284
eqresorts.com				
The GC At Bear Dance,	Larkspur	18	[P]	303-681-4653
beardancegolf.com				
The GC At Ravenna,	Littleton	18	[V]	720-956-1600
ravennagolf.com				
The GC At Redlands Mesa,	Grand Junction	18	[S]	970-263-9270
redlandsmesa.com				
The Homestead GC,	Lakewood	18	[M]	720-963-5181
lakewoodgolf.org				
The Links At Highlands Ranch,	Highlands Ranch	18	[P]	303-470-9292
highlandsranchgolf.com				
The Meadows GC,	Littleton	18	[M]	303-409-2250
foothillsgolf.org				
The Olde Course At Loveland,	Loveland	18	[M]	970-667-5256
oldecourse.com				
The Ranch CC,	Westminster	18	[V]	303-466-2111
theranchcc.com				
The Ridge At Castle Pines North,	Castle Rock	18	[P]	303-688-4301
theridgecpn.com				
The River Course At Keystone,	Dillon	18	[R]	970-496-1444
golfkeystone.com				
The Roaring Fork Club,	Basalt	18	[V]	970-927-9100
roaringforkclub.com				
The Signature GC,	Colorado Springs	18	[P]	719-382-3649
signaturegolfclub.com				
The Snowmass Club,	Snowmass Village	18	[R]	970-923-5700
snowmassclub.com				
Thorncreek GC,	Thornton	18	[M]	303-450-7055
thorncreekgc.com				

[S] = SEMI-PRIVATE   [V] = PRIVATE   [U] = UNIVERSITY   [N] = UNIVERSITY-PRIVATE

COLORADO

Golf Yellow Pages, 18th Edition

Tiara Rado GC, *Grand Junction* ....18 [M] 970-254-3830
golfgrandjunction.net
Trinidad Muni GC, *Trinidad* ....9 [M] 719-846-4015
trinidadgc.com
Twin Peaks GC, *Longmont*.........................18 [M] 303-651-8401
golflongmont.com
Ute Creek GC, *Longmont* ....18 [M] 303-774-4342
golflongmont.com
Vail GC, *Vail* ....18 [R] 970-479-2260
vailgolfclub.net
Valley CC, *Aurora* .... 18 [V] 303-690-6377
valleycountryclub.org
Valley Hi GC, *Colorado Springs*..................18 [M] 719-385-6911
valleyhigolfcourse.com
Vineyard GC, *Colorado Springs* ....9 [P] 719-226-2466
Walking Stick GC, *Pueblo* ....18 [M] 719-553-1181
pueblocitygolf.com
Walsenburg GC, *Walsenburg*........................9 [M] 719-738-2730
Washington County GC, *Akron*.....................9 [M] 970-345-2309
Wellshire GC, *Denver* ....18 [M] 303-757-1352
cityofdenvergolf.com
West Woods GC, *Arvada* ....27 [M] 720-898-7370
westwoodsgolf.com
Willis Case GC, *Denver* ....18 [M] 720-865-0700
cityofdenvergolf.com
Wray CC, *Wray* ....9 [M] 970-332-5934
Yampa Valley GC, *Craig*............................18 [P] 970-824-3673
yampavalleygolf.com

CONNECTICUT

Airways GC & CC, *West Suffield* ....18 [P] 860-668-4973
airwaysgolf.com
Alling Memorial GC, *New Haven* ....18 [M] 203-946-8014
allingmemorialgolfclub.com
Aspetuck Valley CC, *Weston* .... 18 [V] 203-226-9989
aspetuckvalley.com
Banner Resort & CC, *Moodus* ....18 [R] 860-873-9075
bannercountryclub.com
Birch Plain GC, *Groton*.............................18 [P] 860-445-9918
birchplaingolf.com
Birchwood CC, *Westport* .... 9 [V] 203-221-3282
birchwoodcc.org
Black Hall Club, *Old Lyme*......................... 18 [V] 860-434-2038
blackhallclub.com
Blackledge CC, *Hebron*.............................36 [P] 860-228-0250
blackledgecc.com
Blue Fox Run GC, *Avon*.............................27 [P] 860-678-1699
bluefoxent.com
Brooklawn CC, *Fairfield*............................ 18 [V] 203-334-9033
brooklawncc.com
Brooklyn CC, *Brooklyn*...............................9 [P] 860-779-9333
brooklyngolfcourse.com
Brownson CC, *Shelton*............................. 18 [V] 203-929-0282
brownsoncc.com
Buena Vista GC, *West Hartford* ....9 [M] 860-521-7359
Bulls Bridge GC, *South Kent* ....18 [V] 860-927-7135
bullsbridgegolfclub.com
Burning Tree CC, *Greenwich* .... 18 [V] 203-869-9004
burningtreecc.org
Canaan GC, *Canaan*..................................9 [P] 860-824-7683
Candlewood Lake Club, *Brookfield*................ 9 [R] 860-354-4004
candlewoodlakeclub.org

Candlewood Valley CC, *New Milford*...............18 [P] 860-354-9359
candlewoodvalleygolf.com
CC of Darien, *Darien*............................... 18 [V] 203-655-9726
ccdarien.org
CC of Fairfield, *Fairfield*............................ 18 [V] 203-255-3951
ccfairfield.com
CC of Farmington, *Farmington* .... 18 [V] 860-677-1754
farmingtoncountryclub.com
CC of New Canaan, *New Canaan* .... 18 [V] 203-966-3033
ccnc.org
CC of Waterbury, *Waterbury* .... 18 [V] 203-756-6644
ccwaterbury.com
CC of Woodbridge, *Woodbridge* .... 18 [V] 203-387-2278
thecountryclubofwoodbridge.com
Cedar Knob GC, *Somers*............................18 [P] 860-749-3550
cedarknobgolfcourse.com
Cedar Ridge GC, *East Lyme* ....18 [P] 860-691-4568
cedarridgegolf.com
Chanticlair GC, *Colchester* ....9 [P] 860-537-3223
chanticlair.com
Chippanee GC, *Bristol* .... 18 [V] 860-585-7931
chippanee.com
Clinton CC, *Clinton* .... 18 [V] 860-669-6074
clintoncc.org
Connecticut Golf Land, *Vernon* ....9 [P] 860-643-2654
ctgolfland.com
Connecticut National GC, *Putnam*.................18 [P] 860-928-7748
ctnationalgolf.com
Copper Hill GC, *East Granby* ....9 [P] 860-653-6191
copperhillgolf.com
Crestbrook Park GC, *Watertown*..................18 [M] 860-945-5249
watertownct.org
E Gaynor Brennan Muni GC, *Stamford*...........18 [M] 203-356-0046
brennangolf.com
East Mountain GC, *Waterbury*.....................18 [M] 203-753-1425
waterburyct.org
Eastwood CC, *Torrington* ....9 [P] 860-489-2630
playeastwood.com
Ellington Golf Ctr, *Ellington*.........................9 [P] 860-872-9574
Ellington Ridge CC, *Ellington* .... 18 [V] 860-872-9060
ellingtonridge.org
Elmridge GC, *Pawcatuck* ....27 [P] 860-599-2248
elmridgegolf.com
Fairchild Wheeler GC, *Fairfield* ....36 [M] 203-373-5911
fairchildwheelergolf.com
Fairview CC, *Greenwich* .... 18 [V] 203-531-4283
fairviewcountryclub.org
Fairview Farm GC, *Harwinton* ....18 [P] 860-689-1000
fairviewfarmgolfcourse.com
Farmingbury Hills GC, *Wolcott* ....9 [P] 203-879-8038
Farmington Woods CC, *Avon* .... 18 [V] 860-673-0062
farmingtonwoods.com
Fenwick GC, *Old Saybrook* ....9 [M] 860-388-3499
Fox Hopyard GC, *East Haddam* ....18 [S] 800-943-1903
golfthefox.com
Gainfield Farms GC, *Southbury* ....9 [P] 203-262-1100
gainfieldfarmsgolf.com
GC of Avon, *Avon* ....27 [V] 860-673-4577
golfclubofavon.com
Gillette Ridge, *Bloomfield*..........................18 [P] 860-726-1430
gilletteridgegolf.com
Glastonbury Hills CC, *South Glastonbury*........... 18 [V] 860-657-9499
glastonburyhills.com

[A] = MILITARY   [M] = MUNICIPAL   [P] = PUBLIC   [R] = RESORT

Golf Yellow Pages, 18th Edition — CONNECTICUT

Goodwin GC, *Hartford* .... 27 [M] 860-956-3601
  goodwin.americangolf.com
Goose Run GC at Naval Submarine Base, *Groton* .. 9 [A] 860-694-3763
Grassmere CC, *Enfield* .... 9 [P] 860-749-7740
  grassmerecountryclub.com
Grassy Hill CC, *Orange* .... 18 [P] 203-795-3100
  grassyhillcountryclub.com
Great River GC, *Milford* .... 18 [P] 203-876-8051
  greatrivergolfclub.com
Green Woods CC, *Winsted* .... 9 [V] 860-379-8302
  greenwoodscc.net
Greenwich CC, *Greenwich* .... 18 [V] 203-869-1000
  greenwichcountryclub.org
Griffith E Harris GC, *Greenwich* .... 18 [M] 203-531-7261
  greenwichct.org
Guilford Lakes GC, *Guilford* .... 9 [V] 203-453-8214
  guilfordlakesgc.com
H Smith Richardson GC, *Fairfield* .... 18 [M] 203-255-7356
  hsrgolf.com
Harrisville GC, *Woodstock* .... 9 [P] 860-928-6098
  harrisvillegolfcourse.com
Hartford GC, *West Hartford* .... 27 [V] 860-233-5432
  hartfordgolfclub.org
Hawks Landing CC, *Southington* .... 18 [P] 860-793-6000
  hawkslandingcc.com
Heritage Village CC, *Southbury* .... 27 [V] 203-264-8081
  heritagevillagecc.com
Highfield Club, *Middlebury* .... 9 [V] 203-758-9101
Highland GC, *Shelton* .... 9 [V] 203-924-9754
  highlandgolfclub.com
Highland Greens GC, *Prospect* .... 9 [P] 203-758-4022
  highlandgreens.com
Hillside Links, *Deep River* .... 9 [P] 860-526-8893
Homewood Acres, *Woodbridge* .... 18 [V] 203-397-2114
Hop Brook GC, *Naugatuck* .... 9 [M] 203-729-8013
  naugatuck-ct.gov
Hop Meadow CC, *Simsbury* .... 18 [V] 860-651-0686
  hopmeadowcc.net
Hotchkiss School GC, *Lakeville* .... 9 [U] 860-435-4400
  hotchkiss.org
Hunter Memorial GC, *Meriden* .... 18 [M] 203-634-3366
  huntergolfshop.com
Indian Hill CC, *Newington* .... 18 [V] 203-666-5447
  ihccgolf.com
Indian Springs GC, *Middlefield* .... 9 [P] 203-349-8109
  indiansprings-golf.com
Innis Arden GC, *Old Greenwich* .... 18 [V] 203-637-6900
  innisardengolfclub.com
Keney GC, *Hartford* .... 18 [M] 860-525-3656
  keney.americangolf.com
Lake of Isles GC & Resort - South,
  North Stonington .... 18 [V] 860-312-3636
  lakeofisles.com
Lake of Isles GC & Resort-No, *North Stonington* ... 18 [R] 860-312-3636
  lakeofisles.com
Lake Waramaug CC, *New Preston* .... 9 [V] 860-868-2255
  lakewaramaugcc.com
Laurel View CC, *Hamden* .... 18 [P] 203-281-0670
  laurelviewcc.com
Litchfield CC, *Litchfield* .... 9 [V] 860-567-8383
  litchfieldcc.net
Long Hill CC, *East Hartford* .... 18 [V] 860-528-5082
  longhillcc.com

Longshore Club Park GC, *Westport* .... 18 [S] 203-222-7535
  longshoregolf.com
Lyman Orchards GC, *Middlefield* .... 36 [S] 860-349-1793
  lymangolf.com
Madison CC, *Madison* .... 18 [V] 203-245-2336
  madisoncountryclub.org
Manchester CC, *Manchester* .... 18 [S] 860-646-0226
  mancc.com
Milbrook Club, *Greenwich* .... 9 [V] 203-869-4540
  milbrookclub.com
Mill River CC, *Stratford* .... 18 [V] 203-375-9001
  millrivercc.com
Miner Hills Family Golf LLC, *Middletown* .... 9 [P] 860-635-0051
  minerhillsgolf.com
Minnechaug GC, *Glastonbury* .... 9 [P] 860-643-9914
  minnechauggolf.com
New Haven CC, *Hamden* .... 18 [V] 203-248-4531
  newhavencc.com
New London CC, *Waterford* .... 18 [V] 860-443-6864
  newlondoncountryclub.org
Newtown CC, *Newtown* .... 9 [V] 203-426-9371
  newtowncountryclub.com
Norfolk CC, *Norfolk* .... 9 [V] 860-542-5282
  norfolkcountryclub.com
Norwich GC, *Norwich* .... 18 [M] 860-889-6973
  norwichgolf.com
Oak Hills Park GC, *Norwalk* .... 18 [M] 203-838-1015
  oakhillsgc.com
Oak Lane G&CC, *Woodbridge* .... 18 [V] 203-389-5055
  oaklanecc.org
Old Lyme CC, *Old Lyme* .... 9 [V] 860-434-2144
  oldlymecountryclub.com
Orange Hills CC, *Orange* .... 18 [P] 203-795-4161
  orangehillscountryclub.com
Oronoque CC, *Stratford* .... 18 [V] 203-377-6307
  oronoquecc.com
Pequabuck GC, *Pequabuck* .... 18 [S] 203-583-7307
  pequabuckgolf.com
Pequot GC, *Stonington* .... 18 [P] 203-535-1898
  pequotgolf.com
Pine Orchard Y&CC, *Branford* .... 9 [V] 203-488-0481
  poycc.com
Pine Valley GC, *Southington* .... 18 [P] 860-628-0879
  pinevalleygolfct.com
Pomperaug GC, *Southbury* .... 9 [P] 203-264-9484
  heritagesouthbury.com
Portland GC, *Portland* .... 18 [P] 860-342-6107
  portlandgolfcourse.com
Portland GC West, *Portland* .... 18 [P] 860-342-4043
  portlandgolfwest.com
Quarry Ridge GC, *Portland* .... 18 [P] 860-342-6113
  quarryridge.com
Quarry View, *East Canaan* .... 9 [P] 860-824-4252
Quinnatisset CC, *Thompson* .... 18 [V] 860-928-7516
  quinnatissetcc.org
Race Brook CC, *Orange* .... 27 [V] 203-397-9806
  racebrook.org
Raceway GC, *Thompson* .... 18 [S] 860-923-9591
  racewaygolf.com
Redding CC, *West Redding* .... 18 [V] 203-938-9832
  reddingcc.org
Richter Park GC, *Danbury* .... 18 [M] 203-792-2550
  richterpark.com

[S] = SEMI-PRIVATE   [V] = PRIVATE   [U] = UNIVERSITY   [N] = UNIVERSITY-PRIVATE

CONNECTICUT
Golf Yellow Pages, 18th Edition

Ridgefield GC, *Ridgefield* .... 18 [M] 203-748-7008
  ridgefieldgc.com
Ridgewood CC, *Danbury* .... 18 [V] 203-748-8757
  ridgewoodcc.com
River Ridge GC, *Jewett City* .... 18 [P] 860-376-3268
  riverridgegolf.com
Rock Ridge CC, *Newtown* .... 9 [V] 203-426-2658
  rockridgecountryclub.com
Rockledge GC, *West Hartford* .... 18 [M] 860-521-3156
  golfrockledge.com
Rockrimmon CC, *Stamford* .... 18 [V] 203-322-3408
  rockrimmoncc.org
Rolling Greens GC, *Rocky Hill* .... 9 [P] 860-257-9775
Rolling Hills CC, *Wilton* .... 18 [V] 203-762-4636
  rhcconline.com
Rolling Meadows CC, *Ellington* .... 18 [P] 860-870-5328
  rollingmeadowscountryclub.com
Sharon CC, *Sharon* .... 9 [V] 860-364-5964
  sharonclub.com
Shennecossett GC, *Groton* .... 18 [M] 860-448-1867
  shennygolf.com
Shorehaven GC, *Norwalk* .... 18 [V] 203-838-8717
  shorehavengc.org
Short Beach GC, *Stratford* .... 9 [M] 203-381-2070
  townofstratford.com
Shuttle Meadow CC, *Kensington* .... 18 [V] 860-229-6100
  shuttlemeadowcc.com
Silver Spring CC, *Ridgefield* .... 18 [V] 860-438-0100
  silverspringcc.org
Silvermine GC, *Norwalk* .... 27 [V] 203-846-2552
  silverminegolf.com
Simsbury Farms GC, *West Simsbury* ..... 18 [M] 860-658-6246
  simsburyfarms.com
Skungamaug River GC, *Coventry* .... 18 [P] 860-742-9348
  skungamauggolf.com
Sleeping Giant GC, *Hamden* .... 9 [P] 203-281-9456
South Pine Creek GC, *Fairfield* .... 9 [M] 203-256-3173
Southington CC, *Southington* .... 18 [P] 860-628-7032
  southingtoncountryclub.com
Stanley GC, *New Britain* .... 27 [M] 860-827-8570
  stanleygolf.com
Sterling Farms GC, *Stamford* .... 18 [M] 203-461-9090
  sterlingfarmsgc.com
Stonington CC, *Stonington* .... 18 [V] 860-535-4035
  stoningtoncountryclub.com
Stonybrook GC, *Litchfield* .... 9 [P] 860-567-9977
Suffield CC, *Suffield* .... 9 [V] 860-668-7260
  suffieldcc.com
Sunset Hill GC, *Brookfield* .... 9 [P] 203-740-7800
Tallwood CC, *Hebron* .... 18 [P] 860-646-1151
  ctgolfer.com/tallwoodcc
Tamarack CC, *Greenwich* .... 18 [V] 203-531-7300
  tamarackcountryclub.com
Tashua Knolls GC, *Trumbull* .... 27 [M] 203-452-5186
  tashuaknolls.com
The Club At River Oaks, *Sherman* .... 18 [V] 860-354-3330
  clubriveroaks.com
The Connecticut GC, *Easton* .... 18 [V] 203-261-2544
  ctgolfclub.com
The Course At Yale, *New Haven* .... 18 [N] 203-392-2376
  thecourseatyale.com
The Farms CC, *Wallingford* .... 18 [V] 203-269-9000
  farmscc.com

The GC At Oxford Greens, *Oxford* .... 18 [P] 203-888-1600
  oxfordgreens.com
The Orchards, *Milford* .... 9 [M] 203-877-8200
The Patterson Club, *Fairfield* .... 18 [V] 203-259-5244
  thepattersonclub.com
The Round Hill Club, *Greenwich* .... 18 [V] 203-661-1648
The Stanwich Club, *Greenwich* .... 18 [V] 203-869-2072
  stanwich.com
The Tradition GC At Wallingford, *Wallingford* ...... 18 [P] 203-269-6023
  wallingfordtradition.com
The Tradition GC At Windsor, *Windsor* ..... 18 [P] 860-688-2575
  traditionalclubs.com
The Univ Club of Connecticut, *North Windham* ...18 [P] 860-456-1971
  uclubct.com
Timberlin GC, *Berlin* .... 18 [M] 860-828-7054
  timberlingolf.com
Topstone GC, *South Windsor* .... 18 [P] 860-648-4653
  topstonegc.com
Torrington CC, *Goshen* .... 18 [V] 860-491-2440
  torringtoncountryclub.com
Tower Ridge CC, *Simsbury* .... 18 [S] 860-658-9767
  towerridgecc.com
TPC River Highlands, *Cromwell* .... 18 [V] 860-635-2211
  tpcriverhighlands.com
Tumble Brook CC, *Bloomfield* .... 27 [V] 860-242-4600
  tumblebrookcc.com
Tunxis Plantation GC, *Farmington* .... 45 [P] 860-677-1367
  tunxisgolf.com
Twin Hills CC, *Coventry* .... 18 [P] 860-742-9705
  twinhillscountryclub.com
Twin Lakes GC, *North Branford* .... 9 [P] 203-481-3776
Vineyard Valley GC, *Pomfret Center* ...... 9 [P] 860-974-2100
  vineyardvalleygolfclub.com
Wallingford CC, *Wallingford* .... 18 [V] 203-284-9189
  wallingfordcc.com
Wampanoag CC, *West Hartford* .... 18 [V] 860-236-1691
  wampanoagcc.com
Washington GC, *Washington* .... 9 [V] 860-868-0166
  washingtonclub.net
Watertown GC, *Watertown* .... 18 [V] 203-274-4387
  watertowngolfclub.org
Wee Burn CC, *Darien* .... 18 [V] 203-655-2929
  weeburn.com
Western Hills GC, *Waterbury* .... 18 [M] 203-755-6828
  waterburyct.com
Westwoods GC, *Farmington* .... 18 [M] 203-675-2548
  farmington-ct.org
Wethersfield CC, *Wethersfield* .... 18 [V] 860-529-1772
  wethersfieldcc.com
Whitney Farms GC, *Monroe* .... 18 [P] 203-268-0707
  whitneyfarmsgc.com
Willow Brook GC, *South Windsor* .... 18 [P] 860-648-2061
  willowbrookgc.com
Wintonbury Hills GC, *Bloomfield* .... 18 [M] 860-242-1401
  wintonburyhillsgolf.com
Woodhaven GC, *Bethany* .... 9 [P] 203-393-3230
Woodstock GC & DR, *Woodstock* .... 9 [P] 860-928-4130
Woodway CC, *Darien* .... 18 [V] 203-322-2360
  woodway.org

DELAWARE

Back Creek GC, *Middletown* .... 18 [P] 302-378-6499
  backcreekgc.com

32   [A] = MILITARY   [M] = MUNICIPAL   [P] = PUBLIC   [R] = RESORT

Golf Yellow Pages, 18th Edition — FLORIDA

Bayside Resort GC, *Selbyville* .... 18 [V]   302-436-3400
golfbayside.com
Baywood Greens, *Long Neck* .... 18 [P]   302-947-9800
baywoodgreens.com
Bear Trap Dunes GC, *Ocean View* .... 27 [S]   302-537-5600
beartrapdunes.com
Bethany Bay GC, *Ocean View* .... 9 [P]   302-539-3833
bethany-bay.com
Bidermann GC, *Wilmington* .... 18 [V]   302-655-3336
vicmead.com
Brandywine CC, *Wilmington* .... 18 [V]   302-478-4604
brandywinecountryclub.net
Cavaliers CC, *Newark* .... 18 [V]   302-738-4573
cavaliersgolf.com
Cripple Creek G&CC, *Dagsboro* .... 18 [V]   302-539-1446
cripplecreekgolf.com
Deerfield G&TC, *Newark* .... 18 [P]   302-368-6640
deerfieldgolfclub.com
Delcastle GC, *Wilmington* .... 18 [P]   302-998-9505
delcastlegc.com
Dover Par 3 & DR, *Dover* .... 18 [P]   302-674-8275
Du Pont CC, *Wilmington* .... 54 [V]   302-654-4435
dupontcountryclub.com
Eagle Creek GC, *Dover AFB* .... 18 [A]   302-677-2988
doverafbservices.com
Ed Oliver GC, *Wilmington* .... 18 [M]   302-571-9041
edolivergolfclub.com
Fieldstone GC, *Wilmington* .... 18 [V]   302-658-2600
fieldstonegolf.com
Frog Hollow GC, *Middletown* .... 18 [P]   302-376-6500
froghollowgolfclub.com
Garrisons Lake GC, *Smyrna* .... 18 [P]   302-659-1206
garrisonslakegolf.com
Golf Acad of Delaware, *Middletown* .... 9 [P]   302-378-3000
Heritage Inn & GC, *Rehoboth Beach* .... 9 [R]   302-644-3860
rehobothheritage.com
Heritage Shores GC, *Bridgeville* .... 18 [S]   302-337-7767
heritageshoresgolf.com
Hoopers Landing GC, *Seaford* .... 18 [V]   302-629-2890
seafordde.com
Jonathans Landing, *Magnolia* .... 27 [P]   302-697-8204
jonathanslandinggolf.com
Kings Creek CC, *Rehoboth Beach* .... 18 [V]   302-227-8953
kingscreekcountryclub.com
Maple Dale CC, *Dover* .... 18 [V]   302-674-2877
mapledaleclub.com
Marsh Island GC, *Lewes* .... 18 [P]   302-945-4653
Midway Par 3 & DR, *Lewes* .... 18 [P]   302-645-7955
Newark CC, *Newark* .... 18 [V]   302-368-7008
newarkcc.com
Odessa National GC, *Townsend* .... 18 [S]   302-464-1007
odessanationalgolfclub.com
Old Landing GC, *Rehoboth Beach* .... 18 [P]   302-227-3131
Pike Creek GC, *Wilmington* .... 18 [S]   302-737-1877
pikecreekgolf.com
Rehoboth Beach CC, *Rehoboth Beach* .... 18 [V]   302-227-3616
rehobothbeachcc.com
Rock Manor GC, *Wilmington* .... 18 [S]   302-295-1400
rockmanorgolf.com
Salt Pond GC, *Bethany Beach* .... 18 [P]   302-539-7525
saltpondgolf.com
Shamrock Farms Par 3, *Milton* .... 18 [P]   302-684-1808

Shawnee CC, *Milford* .... 18 [V]   302-422-7010
shawneegolf.net
Sussex Pines GC, *Georgetown* .... 18 [V]   302-856-3363
sussexpinescountryclub.com
The Peninsula G&CC, *Millsboro* .... 18 [V]   302-945-4768
peninsula-delaware.com
The Rookery GC, *Milton* .... 18 [P]   302-684-3000
rookerygolf.com
Vinces Sports Ctr Par 3 GC, *Newark* .... 9 [P]   302-738-4859
vincessports.com
White Clay Creek CC, *Wilmington* .... 18 [V]   302-994-6700
whiteclaycreek.com
Wild Quail G&CC, *Camden Wyoming* .... 18 [V]   302-697-4653
wildquail.net
Wilmington CC, *Wilmington* .... 36 [V]   302-655-6022
wilmingtoncc.com

DISTRICT OF COLUMBIA

East Potomac GC, *Washington* .... 36 [P]   202-554-7660
golfdc.com
Langston GC, *Washington* .... 18 [P]   202-397-8638
golfdc.com
Rock Creek Park GC, *Washington* .... 18 [P]   202-882-7332
golfdc.com
US Soldiers & Airmens Home GC, *Washington* ... 9 [A]   202-730-3050
afrh.gov

FLORIDA

A C Read GC, *Pensacola* .... 45 [A]   850-452-2454
Abacoa GC, *Jupiter* .... 18 [P]   561-622-0036
abacoagolfclub.com
Abbey Course At St Leo Univ, *St Leo* .... 18 [P]   352-588-2016
saintleo.edu
Aberdeen G&CC, *Boynton Beach* .... 18 [V]   561-737-8662
aberdeencountryclub.com
Adara GC, *Crestview* .... 18 [S]   850-689-1111
adaragolf.com
Addison Reserve, *Delray Beach* .... 27 [V]   561-637-9555
addisonreserve.cc
Adios GC, *Coconut Creek* .... 18 [V]   954-574-1455
adiosgolfclub.org
Airco GC, *Clearwater* .... 18 [M]   727-573-4653
pinellascounty.org/park/golf.htm
Alaqua CC, *Longwood* .... 18 [V]   407-333-2582
alaquacc.com
Alden Pines GC, *Bokeelia* .... 18 [S]   239-283-3766
Amelia Island Plantation, *Amelia Island* ..... 36 [R]   904-261-6161
aipfl.com
Amelia Island Plantation - Long Point,
Amelia Island .... 18 [R]   904-261-6161
aipfl.com
Amelia National G&CC, *Fernandina Beach* ..... 18 [V]   904-652-0660
amelianationalgolf.com
Amelia River GC, *Amelia Island* .... 18 [R]   904-491-8500
golfameliariver.com
Anglers Green GC, *Mulberry* .... 9 [V]   863-425-4332
Apollo Beach GC, *Apollo Beach* .... 18 [P]   813-645-6212
apollobeachgolf.com
Aquarina Beach & CC, *Melbourne Beach* .... 18 [P]   321-728-0600
Arcadia GC, *Arcadia* .... 18 [M]   863-494-4223
arcadiamunicipalgolfcourse.webs.com
Arcadia Village CC, *Arcadia* .... 9 [V]   800-538-2590
arcadiavillage.com

[S] = SEMI-PRIVATE   [V] = PRIVATE   [U] = UNIVERSITY   [N] = UNIVERSITY-PRIVATE

FLORIDA

Golf Yellow Pages, 18th Edition

Arlington Ridge GC, *Leesburg* .... 18 [P] 352-728-4660
myarlingtonridge.com
Arrowhead GC At Heritage Greens, *Naples* .... 18 [P] 239-596-1000
arrowheadgolfnaples.com
Atlantis CC, *Lake Worth* .... 18 [S] 561-965-7700
atlantiscountryclub.com
Atlantis GC, *Lake Worth* .... 27 [V] 561-966-7626
atlantisgolf.org
Audubon CC, *Naples* .... 18 [V] 239-566-9800
auduboncountryclub.org
Avila G&CC, *Tampa* .... 18 [V] 813-961-1754
avilagolf.com
Babe Zaharias GC, *Tampa* .... 18 [M] 813-631-4374
babezahariasgc.com
BallenIsles CC, *Palm Beach Gardens* .... 54 [V] 561-622-0220
ballenisles.com
Banyan GC, *West Palm Beach* .... 18 [V] 561-793-0177
banyangolfclub.com
Bardmoor G&TC, *Largo* .... 18 [P] 727-392-1234
bardmoorgolf.com
Barefoot Bay GC, *Barefoot Bay* .... 18 [P] 772-664-3174
bbrd.org
Bartow GC, *Bartow* .... 18 [M] 863-533-9183
bartow.govoffice.com
Baseline GC, *Ocala* .... 18 [P] 352-245-4414
Bay Colony GC, *Naples* .... 18 [V] 239-592-9530
baycolonygolfclub.com
Bay Dunes, *Panama City* .... 18 [P] 850-872-1704
baydunes.com
Bay Hill C&Lodge, *Orlando* .... 27 [R] 407-876-2429
bayhill.com
Bay Palms G Complex, *MacDill AFB* .... 36 [A] 813-840-6904
macdillservices.com
Bay Point Marriott Golf Resort & Spa, *Panama City* 36 [R] 850-235-6950
baypointgolf.com
Bay Tree GC, *Tavares* .... 18 [S] 352-343-7227
Bayou GC, *Largo* .... 18 [V] 727-399-1000
bayouclubgolf.com
Baypoint GC, *Seminole* .... 18 [S] 727-595-2095
Baytree National Golf Links, *Melbourne* .... 18 [S] 321-259-9050
baytreenational.com
Beachview GC, *Sanibel* .... 18 [R] 239-472-2626
beachviewgolfclub.com
Beacon Woods GC, *Bayonet Point* .... 18 [V] 727-868-9528
beaconwoodsgolf.com
Bear Lakes CC, *West Palm Beach* .... 36 [V] 561-478-0001
bearlakes.org
Bears Paw CC, *Naples* .... 18 [V] 239-262-1836
bearspawcc.com
Bella Collina GC, *Montverde* .... 18 [V] 407-469-4961
bellacollina.com
Belleair CC, *Belleair* .... 36 [V] 727-461-7171
belleaircc.com
Belleview Biltmore GC, *Belleair* .... 18 [R] 727-581-5498
belleviewbiltmore.com
Bent Creek GC, *Jacksonville* .... 18 [M] 904-779-0800
golfbentcreek.com
Bent Pine GC, *Vero Beach* .... 18 [V] 772-567-6838
bentpinegolf.com
Bent Tree CC, *Sarasota* .... 18 [V] 941-371-8200
benttreecc.net
Bentley Village GC, *Naples* .... 18 [V] 239-513-1125
viliving.com
Betmar Acres GC, *Zephyrhills* .... 27 [V] 813-782-0043

Big Cypress G&CC, *Lakeland* .... 36 [S] 863-859-6871
cypresslakesfla.com
Biltmore GC, *Coral Gables* .... 18 [R] 305-460-5364
biltmorehotel.com
Binks Forest GC, *West Palm Beach* .... 18 [P] 561-333-5731
binksforestgc.com
Bird Bay Exec GC, *Venice* .... 18 [S] 941-485-9333
Black Bear GC, *Eustis* .... 18 [P] 352-357-4732
blackbeargolfclub.com
Black Diamond Ranch, *Lecanto* .... 45 [V] 352-746-3446
blackdiamondranch.com
Blackstone GC, *Mossy Head* .... 18 [P] 850-520-4670
blackstonemossyhead.com
Bloomingdale Golfers Club, *Valrico* .... 18 [S] 813-685-4105
bloomingdalegolf.com
Blue Cypress GC, *Jacksonville* .... 9 [P] 904-762-1971
bluecypressgolf.net
Blue Cypress Golf & RV Resort, *Okeechobee* .... 9 [R] 863-467-5774
bluecypressrental.com
Blue Heron G&CC, *Okeechobee* .... 18 [S] 863-467-4677
Blue Heron Pines GC, *Punta Gorda* .... 18 [P] 941-637-6191
Bluewater Bay Resort, *Niceville* .... 36 [R] 850-897-3241
Bluffs GC, *Zolfo Springs* .... 18 [P] 863-735-2363
Bobby Jones GC, *Sarasota* .... 45 [M] 941-955-8041
bobbyjonesgolfclub.com
Bobcat Run, *Sebring* .... 9 [P] 863-655-0202
springlakegolf.com
Bobcat Trail GC, *North Port* .... 18 [S] 941-429-0500
bobcattrailgc.com
Boca Delray G&CC, *Delray Beach* .... 18 [V] 561-495-1616
bocadelray.net
Boca Dunes G&CC, *Boca Raton* .... 27 [S] 561-451-1600
bocadunes.com
Boca Greens CC, *Boca Raton* .... 18 [V] 561-852-8800
boca-greens.com
Boca Grove G&TC, *Boca Raton* .... 18 [V] 561-488-2582
bocagrove.org
Boca Lago CC, *Boca Raton* .... 36 [V] 561-482-5000
bocalago.com
Boca Pointe CC, *Boca Raton* .... 18 [V] 561-864-8500
bocapointecc.com
Boca Raton Muni GC, *Boca Raton* .... 27 [M] 561-483-5014
bocacitygolf.com
Boca Raton Resort & Club, *Boca Raton* .... 36 [R] 561-447-3099
bocaresort.com
Boca Rio GC, *Boca Raton* .... 18 [V] 561-482-3300
Boca Royale G&CC, *Englewood* .... 18 [S] 941-474-7475
bocaroyale.com
Boca West Club, *Boca Raton* .... 72 [V] 561-488-6924
bocawestcc.org
Boca Woods CC, *Boca Raton* .... 36 [V] 561-487-2800
bocaratongolfandcountryclub.com
Bocaire CC, *Boca Raton* .... 18 [V] 561-998-1602
bocairecc.com
Boggy Creek GC, *Orlando* .... 9 [P] 407-857-0280
Bonaventure CC, *Fort Lauderdale* .... 36 [V] 954-389-2100
golfbonaventure.com
Bonifay GC, *Lady Lake* .... 18 [P] 352-753-1776
golfthevillages.com
Bonita Bay East, *Naples* .... 36 [V] 239-353-5100
bonitabayclub.net
Bonita Bay West, *Bonita Springs* .... 54 [V] 239-498-2626
bonitabayclub.net

[A] = MILITARY   [M] = MUNICIPAL   [P] = PUBLIC   [R] = RESORT

FLORIDA

Golf Yellow Pages, 18th Edition

Bonita Fairways, *Bonita Springs* .... 18 [P]   239-947-9100
  bonitafairwaysgolf.com
Bonita Springs G&CC, *Bonita Springs* .... 18 [P]   239-992-2800
  bonitaspringsgolfclub.com
Bradenton CC, *Bradenton* .... 18 [V]   941-792-4159
  bradentoncc.org
Bramble Ridge GC, *Lakeland* .... 27 [P]   863-667-1988
  brgolf.com
Breakers Ocean GC, *Palm Beach* .... 18 [R]   561-655-6611
  thebreakers.com
Breakers Rees Jones Course, *West Palm Beach* .... 18 [R]   561-653-6320
  thebreakers.com
Breckenridge G&TC, *Estero* .... 18 [V]   239-992-5959
  breckenridgehomeowners.com
Brentwood Farms GC, *Lecanto* .... 9 [P]   352-527-2600
Briar Bay GC, *Miami* .... 9 [M]   305-235-6667
  briarbaygolf.com
Broken Sound Club - Club Course, *Boca Raton* ... 36 [V]   561-241-6860
  brokensoundclub.org
Broken Sound Club - Old Course, *Boca Raton* ..... 36 [V]   561-994-8505
  brokensoundclub.org
Brooker Creek GC, *Palm Harbor* .... 18 [S]   727-784-7606
  brookercreekgc.com
Brookridge CC, *Brooksville* .... 18 [V]   352-596-3028
  springhillonline.com
Brooksville CC At Majestic Oaks, *Brooksville* .... 18 [P]   352-796-8236
  brooksvillecc.com
Buckhorn Springs G&CC, *Valrico* .... 18 [V]   813-689-7766
  hamptongolfclubs.com
Buffalo Creek GC, *Palmetto* .... 18 [M]   941-776-2611
  co.manatee.fl.us
Burnt Store Golf & Activity Club, *Punta Gorda* ..... 27 [R]   941-637-1577
  bsgac.org
Caloosa G&CC, *Sun City Center* .... 18 [V]   813-634-2870
  caloosagolf.com
Caloosa Greens Exec GC, *Sun City Center* .... 18 [V]   813-633-3958
Calusa CC, *Miami* .... 18 [S]   305-386-5533
  calusacountryclub.com
Calusa Lakes GC, *Nokomis* .... 18 [S]   941-484-8995
  golfinvenice.com
Calusa Pines GC, *Naples* .... 18 [V]   239-348-2220
Camp Creek GC, *Panama City Beach* .... 18 [S]   850-231-7600
  campcreekgolfclub.com
Candler Hills G&CC, *Ocala* .... 18 [S]   352-861-9712
  candlerhillsgolfclub.com
Cane Garden GC, *Lady Lake* .... 27 [V]   352-751-7029
  golfthevillages.com
Cape Coral Exec Course, *Cape Coral* .... 9 [P]   239-574-4454
Capitol City CC, *Tallahassee* .... 18 [V]   850-224-1815
  capitalcitycc.com
Capri Isle GC, *Venice* .... 18 [P]   941-485-3371
  golfinvenice.com
Captiva Island GC, *Captiva Island* .... 9 [R]   239-472-5111
  southseasresort.com
Card Sound GC, *Key Largo* .... 18 [V]   305-367-2555
  cardsoundgolfclub.com
Carefree RV GC, *Winter Haven* .... 9 [P]   863-324-7970
  carefreecountryclub.org
Carriage Hills GC, *Pensacola* .... 18 [P]   850-497-6266
Casselberry GC, *Casselberry* .... 18 [P]   407-699-9310
  casselberrygc.com
Caverns GC, *Marianna* .... 9 [S]   850-482-4257

CC At Mirasol, *Palm Beach Gardens* .... 36 [V]   561-775-9800
  mirasolclub.com
CC At Silver Springs Shores, *Ocala* .... 18 [S]   352-687-2828
CC of Coral Springs, *Coral Springs* .... 18 [V]   954-753-2930
  ccofcs.com
CC of Florida, *Village of Golf* .... 18 [V]   561-734-1341
  ccfgolf.com
CC of Miami, *Hialeah* .... 36 [M]   305-829-8456
  golfmiamicc.com
CC of Mount Dora, *Mt Dora* .... 18 [S]   352-735-2263
  ccofmtdora.com
CC of Naples, *Naples* .... 18 [V]   239-261-1267
  ccnaples.net
CC of Ocala, *Ocala* .... 18 [V]   352-237-6644
  thecountryclubofocala.com
CC of Orange Park, *Orange Park* .... 18 [V]   904-276-7664
  ccofop.com
CC of Orlando, *Orlando* .... 18 [V]   407-425-2319
  countrycluboforlando.com
Cecil Field GC, *Jacksonville* .... 18 [P]   904-778-5245
  capstonegolf.net
Cedar Hammock G&CC, *Naples* .... 18 [S]   239-793-1134
  cedarhammockgolf.com
Celebration GC, *Kissimmee* .... 18 [P]   407-566-4653
  celebrationgolf.com
Champion GC, *Cantonment* .... 9 [S]   850-968-9325
Champions Club at Julington Creek, *Jacksonville* 18 [P]   904-287-4653
  championsclubgolf.com
Champions Club At Summerfield, *Stuart* .... 18 [P]   772-283-1500
  thechampionsgolfclub.com
ChampionsGate Golf Resort, *Davenport* .... 36 [R]   407-787-4653
  championsgategolf.com
Cheeca Lodge Resort, *Islamorada* .... 9 [R]   305-664-4651
  cheeca.com
Cheval G&CC, *Lutz* .... 18 [V]   813-949-4231
  chevalgolfandcountryclub.com
Chi Chi Rodriguez GC, *Clearwater* .... 18 [M]   727-726-8829
  chichi.org
Chiefland G&CC, *Chiefland* .... 18 [P]   352-493-2375
Cimarrone G&CC, *Jacksonville* .... 18 [S]   904-287-2000
  cimarronegolf.com
Citrus Hills GC, *Hernando* .... 36 [S]   352-746-4425
  citrushills.com
Citrus Springs CC, *Dunnellon* .... 18 [S]   352-489-5045
  citrusspringsgolf.com
Clearwater CC, *Clearwater* .... 18 [M]   727-443-5078
  clearwatercountryclub.com
Clearwater Exec GC, *Clearwater* .... 18 [M]   727-447-5272
  myclearwater.com/gov/depts/parksrec/athletics/golf.asp
Clerbrook Resort, *Clermont* .... 18 [R]   352-394-6165
  clerbrook.com
Cleveland Heights GC, *Lakeland* .... 27 [M]   863-682-3277
  lakelandgov.net
Clewiston GC, *Clewiston* .... 18 [M]   863-983-1448
  clewiston-fl.gov
Club Med Sandpiper, *Port St Lucie* .... 24 [R]   772-337-6638
Cocoa Beach CC, *Cocoa Beach* .... 27 [M]   321-868-3351
  golfcocoabeach.com
Colliers Reserve CC, *Naples* .... 18 [V]   239-597-7020
  colliersreserve.com
Colonial CC, *Fort Myers* .... 18 [S]   239-768-9421
  colonialgolfclub.com
Colony West CC, *Tamarac* .... 36 [P]   954-726-8430
  golfcolonywest.com

[S] = SEMI-PRIVATE   [V] = PRIVATE   [U] = UNIVERSITY   [N] = UNIVERSITY-PRIVATE

FLORIDA

Golf Yellow Pages, 18th Edition

Continental CC, *Wildwood* .... 18 [S] 352-748-3293
continentalcountryclub.com
Cooper Colony CC, *Cooper City* .... 18 [S] 954-434-2181
Copperhead GC, *Lehigh Acres* ....18 [P] 239-369-8200
copperheadgc.com
Copperleaf GC, *Bonita Springs* .... 18 [V] 239-390-2030
copperleafgc.com
Coral Creek Club, *Placida* .... 18 [V] 941-697-9100
coralcreekclub.com
Coral Oaks GC, *Cape Coral* ....18 [M] 239-573-3100
coraloaksgolf.com
Coral Ridge CC, *Fort Lauderdale* .... 18 [V] 954-449-4406
coralridgecc.com
Costa Greens GC, *Miami* ....18 [P] 305-592-9210
costagreensgolfclub.com
Countryside CC, *Clearwater* .... 27 [V] 727-796-1135
countrysideclub.com
Countryside Exec GC, *Clearwater* ....9 [P] 727-796-1555
Countryside G&CC, *Naples* .... 18 [V] 239-455-0001
countrysidegcc.net
Countryway GC, *Tampa* ....18 [P] 813-854-1182
countrywaygolfclub.com
Cove Cay CC, *Clearwater* .... 18 [S] 727-535-1406
covecaycountryclub.com
Crandon Golf At Key Biscayne, *Key Biscayne*.......18 [M] 305-361-9129
crandongolfclub.com
Crane Creek Reserve GC, *Melbourne*..................18 [M] 321-674-5716
melbourneflorida.org
Crane Lakes G&CC, *Port Orange*................18 [P] 386-767-4653
cranelakes.com
Creek Course At Hammock Dunes, *Palm Coast* ... 18 [V] 386-447-7116
hammockdunes.com
Crescent Oaks CC, *Tarpon Springs* .... 18 [V] 727-942-6182
crescentoaksgolf.com
Cross Creek CC, *Fort Myers* .... 18 [S] 239-768-1922
crosscreekfl.com
Cross Creek CC, *Arcadia* ....9 [P] 863-494-7300
Cross Creek GC & DR, *Tallahassee* ....9 [P] 850-656-4653
Crown Colony G&CC, *Fort Myers*..................... 18 [V] 239-590-9860
crowncolonygcc.com
Crystal Lake CC, *Pompano Beach*......................... 18 [S] 954-943-2902
crystallakecountryclub.com
Crystal Lake Club, *Avon Park* .... 18 [V] 863-385-7727
crystallakeclub.com
Cypress Creek CC, *Boynton Beach* .... 18 [S] 561-732-4202
cypresscreekcountryclub.com
Cypress Greens, *Lake Alfred* ....9 [P] 863-956-4179
americanlandlease.com/cypressgreens
Cypress Lake CC, *Fort Myers* .... 18 [V] 239-481-3222
cypresslakecc.com
Cypress Lakes, *West Palm Beach* .... 18 [V] 561-640-1044
Cypress Lakes GC, *Cantonment* ....18 [S] 850-937-3820
cypresslakesgolfclub.net
Cypress Point RV GC, *Osteen*........................ 9 [R] 407-323-0760
Cypress Run GC, *Tarpon Springs* .... 18 [V] 727-938-3774
cypressrun.com
Cypress Woods G&CC, *Naples* ....18 [P] 239-592-7860
cypresswoodsgolf.com
Cypresswood G&CC, *Winter Haven* ....18 [P] 863-324-6174
cypresswoodcc.com
Davie G&CC, *Davie*..18 [P] 954-797-4653
golfdavie.com

Daytona Beach GC, *Daytona Beach* ....36 [M] 386-671-3500
ci.daytona-beach.fl.us
DeBary G&CC, *Debary*..........................18 [P] 386-668-1705
debarycc.com
Deep Creek GC, *Punta Gorda* ....18 [P] 941-625-6911
deepcreekgc.com
Deer Creek CC, *Deerfield Beach* ....18 [P] 954-421-5550
deercreekflorida.com
Deer Creek RV Golf Resort, *Davenport*..................18 [R] 863-424-2839
deercreekrv.com
Deer Island CC, *Deer Island* ....18 [S] 352-343-7550
deerislandgolf.com
Deercreek CC, *Jacksonville* .... 18 [V] 904-363-1507
deercreekclub.com
Deerfield CC, *Deerfield Beach*.......................18 [P] 954-427-4400
dccfl.com
Deerfield Lakes GC, *Callahan* ....18 [P] 904-879-1210
Deering Bay Y&CC, *Coral Gables*...................... 18 [V] 305-254-2111
dbycc.com
DeFuniak Springs CC, *Defuniak Springs*...............18 [P] 850-892-3812
defuniakspringsgolf.com
Del Tura CC, *Fort Myers* ....27 [S] 239-731-7814
delturagolfclub.com
Delaire CC, *Delray Beach* .... 27 [V] 561-499-0770
delaire.org
Deland CC, *Deland*...................................... 18 [V] 386-734-9675
delandcountryclub.com
Delray Beach GC, *Delray Beach* ....18 [M] 561-243-7380
delraybeachgolfclub.com
Delray Dunes G&CC, *Boynton Beach*.............. 18 [V] 561-737-4749
delraydunes.org
Diamond Hill G&CC, *Dover*.......................18 [S] 813-689-7219
Diamondback GC, *Haines City* ....18 [S] 863-421-0437
diamondbackgc.net
Dogwood Lakes GC, *Bonifay* ....18 [P] 850-547-4653
dogwoodlakesgolfclub.com
Don Shulas GC, *Miami Lakes* ....36 [R] 305-821-1150
donshulahotel.com
Doral Golf Resort, *Miami* ....72 [R] 305-592-2000
doralresort.com
Dubsdread GC, *Orlando* ....18 [M] 407-246-2551
historicaldubsdread.com
Duffys Golf Ctr, *Port Charlotte* ....18 [P] 941-697-3900
Duran GC, *Viera* ....27 [P] 321-504-7776
durangolf.com
Eagle Creek G&CC, *Naples*................... 18 [V] 239-774-2202
eaglecreekgcc.com
Eagle Creek GC, *Orlando* ....18 [R] 407-273-4653
eaglecreekgolf.info/
Eagle Dunes GC, *Sorrento* ....18 [P] 352-357-0123
eagledunes.com
Eagle Harbor GC, *Orange Park* ....18 [S] 904-269-9300
hamptongolfclubs.com/eharbor.html
Eagle Lakes GC, *Naples* ....18 [S] 239-732-0034
eaglelakesgolfclub.com
Eagle Landing GC, *Orange Park*.................18 [S] 904-291-5600
eaglelandingonline.com
Eagle Marsh GC, *Jensen Beach* ....18 [S] 772-692-3322
eaglemarsh.com
Eagle Ridge At Spruce Creek CC, *Summerfield*.....27 [R] 352-307-1668
playeagleridgegolf.com
Eagle Ridge G&TC, *Fort Myers* ....18 [P] 239-768-1888
playeagleridge.com

[A] = MILITARY [M] = MUNICIPAL [P] = PUBLIC [R] = RESORT

Golf Yellow Pages, 18th Edition — FLORIDA

Eaglewood Home Owners Assoc, *Hobe Sound* ... 18 [V] 772-546-3656
  eaglewoodhoa.net
East Bay GC, *Largo* .... 27 [S] 727-581-3333
  eastbaygolfclub.com
East Lake Woodlands CC, *Oldsmar* .... 36 [V] 727-784-7270
  eastlakewoodlandscc.com
Eastpointe CC, *Palm Beach Gardens* .... 18 [V] 561-626-6863
  eastpointe-cc.com
Eastpointe Golf & Racquet CC, *Palm Beach Gardens* 18 [V] 561-627-5502
  eastpointegolfandracquetclub.com
Eastwood GC, *Fort Myers* .... 18 [M] 239-321-7487
  cityftmyers.com
EastWood GC, *Orlando* .... 18 [P] 407-281-4653
  eastwoodgolf.com
Eco GC, *Hollywood* ....9 [M] 954-922-8755
  hollywoodbeachgolf.com
Edgewater Beach Resort, *Panama City Beach* ...... 9 [R] 850-235-4044
  edgewaterbeachresort.com
Eglin GC, *Niceville* .... 36 [A] 850-882-2949
  eglinservices.com
El Diablo G&CC, *Citrus Springs* .... 18 [P] 352-465-0986
  eldiablogolf.com
El Rio GC, *Fort Myers* .... 18 [S] 239-995-2204
Emerald Bay GC, *Destin* .... 18 [S] 850-837-5197
  emeraldbaygolfclub.com
Emerald Dunes GC, *West Palm Beach* .... 18 [V] 561-687-1700
  edgclub.com
Emerald Greens Golf Resort & CC, *Tampa* ....27 [R] 813-961-1369
  emeraldgreensgcc.com
Errol Estates CC, *Apopka* ....27 [S] 407-886-3676
  errolestatecc.com
Estero CC, *Estero* .... 18 [V] 239-267-7003
  esterocc.com
Everglades Club, *Palm Beach* .... 18 [V] 561-820-2662
Fairway Village GC, *Largo* .... 9 [V] 727-531-8134
Fairways CC, *Orlando* .... 18 [P] 407-282-7535
  golffairwayscc.com
Fairways GC, *West Palm Beach* .... 18 [P] 561-686-0948
Fairwinds GC, *Fort Pierce* .... 18 [M] 772-462-2722
  stlucieco.gov/fairwinds
Falcon Watch GC, *Sun City Center* .... 27 [V] 813-634-3038
  falconwatch.org
Falcons Fire GC, *Kissimmee* .... 18 [R] 407-239-5445
  falconsfire.com
Falling Waters GC, *Chipley* ....9 [P] 850-638-7398
Falls CC, *Lake Worth* .... 18 [V] 561-964-5700
  fallscountryclub.org
Feather Sound CC, *Clearwater* .... 18 [V] 727-572-6677
  feathersoundcc.com
Fernandina Beach GC, *Fernandina Beach* ....27 [M] 904-277-7370
  fernandinabeachgolfclub.com
Fiddlesticks CC, *Fort Myers* .... 36 [V] 239-768-1114
  fiddlestickscc.com
Fisher Island Club, *Miami Beach* ....9 [V] 305-535-6016
  fisherislandclub.com
Fishermans Cove Golf & Marina, *Tavares* ....9 [P] 352-343-1233
  lakeharrisresort.com
Flamingo Lakes CC, *Pembroke Pines* .... 18 [P] 954-435-6110
Floridian Yacht & GC, *Palm City* .... 18 [R] 772-781-1000
Forest Glen G&CC, *Naples* .... 18 [V] 239-348-1332
  forestglengcc.com
Forest Hills GC, *Holiday* ....9 [P] 727-934-7517

Forest Lake GC, *Ocoee* .... 18 [P] 407-654-4653
  forestlakegolf.com
Forest Oaks GC, *Lake Worth* .... 18 [R] 561-967-6810
Fort Lauderdale CC, *Plantation* .... 36 [V] 954-587-4700
  fortlauderdalecc.com
Fort Myers Beach GC, *Fort Myers Beach* .... 18 [P] 239-463-2064
  fmbgolfclub.com
Fort Myers CC, *Fort Myers* .... 18 [M] 239-321-7488
  cityftmyers.com
Fort Walton Beach GC, *Fort Walton Beach* .... 36 [M] 850-833-9664
  fwb.org
Fountain Lakes Community GC, *Estero* .... 9 [V] 239-495-3555
Fountains CC, *Lake Worth* .... 54 [V] 561-642-2719
  fountainscc.com
Four Lakes GC, *Winter Haven* .... 18 [V] 863-291-0930
Fox Hollow GC, *Trinity* .... 18 [P] 727-376-6333
  golfthefox.com
Foxfire CC, *Naples* .... 27 [V] 239-643-2402
  foxfirecc.com
Foxwood CC, *Crestview* .... 18 [S] 850-682-2012
  foxwoodcc.com
Freedom Fairways, *Sun City Center* .... 18 [P] 813-633-4653
Frenchmans Creek CC, *Palm Beach Gardens* ..... 36 [V] 561-622-8300
  frenchmanscreek.com
Frenchmans Reserve, *Palm Beach Gardens* .... 18 [V] 561-630-0333
  frenchmansreserve.com
Gainesville G&CC, *Gainesville* .... 18 [V] 352-372-1458
  gainesvillegolf.cc
Gasparilla Inn GC, *Boca Grande* .... 18 [R] 941-964-2201
  the-gasparilla-inn.com
Gateway G&CC, *Fort Myers* .... 18 [V] 239-561-1014
  gatewaygolf.com
Gator Creek GC, *Sarasota* .... 18 [V] 941-924-1111
Gator Lakes GC, *Hurlburt Field* .... 18 [A] 850-581-0007
  myhurlburt.com/gatorlakes
Gator Trace G&CC, *Fort Pierce* .... 18 [S] 772-464-0407
  gatortracecountryclub.com
GC At North Hampton, *Fernandina Beach* .... 18 [S] 904-548-0000
  hamptongolfclubs.com
GC At South Hampton, *St Augustine* .... 18 [S] 904-287-7529
  hamptongolfclubs.com
GC of Amelia Island, *Amelia Island* .... 18 [R] 904-277-0012
  golfclubofamelia.com
GC of the Everglades, *Naples* .... 18 [V] 239-354-4727
Glen Abbey GC, *Debary* .... 18 [S] 386-668-4209
Glen Eagle G&CC, *Naples* .... 18 [V] 239-354-3167
  gleneaglecountryclub.com
Glen Kernan G&CC, *Jacksonville* .... 18 [V] 904-646-1116
  glenkernanrealty.com
Glen Lakes CC, *Brooksville* .... 18 [V] 352-597-1118
  glenlakes.com
Gleneagles CC, *Delray Beach* .... 36 [V] 561-496-1333
  gleneagles.cc
Glenview Champions CC, *The Villages* .... 27 [P] 352-753-3245
  golfthevillages.com
Golden Eagle GC, *Tallahassee* .... 18 [V] 850-893-7700
  goldeneaglecc.org
Golden Gate CC, *Naples* .... 18 [R] 239-455-9498
  naplesgolfresort.com
Golden Hills G&TurfC, *Ocala* .... 18 [P] 352-629-7980
  goldenhillscc.com
Golden Lakes GC, *Plant City* .... 9 [V] 813-752-6010

[S] = SEMI-PRIVATE   [V] = PRIVATE   [U] = UNIVERSITY   [N] = UNIVERSITY-PRIVATE

FLORIDA

Golf Yellow Pages, 18th Edition

Golden Ocala Golf & Equestrian Club, *Ocala* .... 18 [V] 352-629-6229
goldenocala.com
Golf Hammock CC, *Sebring* .... 18 [S] 863-382-2151
golfhammockcc.net
Golfview G&RC, *Fort Myers* .... 9 [S] 239-489-2264
golfview-grc.com
Granada GC, *Coral Gables* .... 9 [M] 305-460-5367
Grand Cypress Resort, *Orlando* .... 45 [R] 407-239-4700
grandcypress.com
Grand Harbor CC, *Vero Beach* .... 36 [V] 772-778-9200
grandharbor.com
Grand Haven GC, *Palm Coast* .... 18 [R] 386-445-2327
hamptongolfclubs.com
Grand Lacuna G&CC, *Lake Worth* .... 18 [S] 561-433-3006
grandlacuna.com
Grand Lake RV & Golf Resort, *Citra* .... 9 [R] 352-591-3474
grandlakeresort.com
Grand Palms Hotel & Golf Resort, *Pembroke Pines* 27 [R] 954-437-3334
grandpalmsresort.com
Grand Reserve GC, *Bunnell* .... 18 [S] 386-313-2966
grandreserveandgolfclub.com
Grande Oaks GC, *Davie* .... 18 [V] 954-916-2900
grandeoaks.com
Grande Pines GC, *Orlando* .... 18 [R] 407-239-6108
grandepinesgolfclub.com
Grasslands G&CC, *Lakeland* .... 18 [V] 863-680-1616
oakbridge.com
Green Valley CC, *Clermont* .... 18 [S] 352-394-2133
gvcountryclub.com
Grenelefe G&T Resort, *Haines City* .... 36 [R] 863-422-7511
thelefe.com
Grey Oaks CC, *Naples* .... 54 [V] 239-262-5550
greyoakscc.com
Greynolds Park GC, *North Miami Beach* ..... 9 [M] 305-949-1741
golfmiamidade.com
Gulf Gate GC, *Sarasota* .... 27 [P] 941-921-5515
Gulf Harbors GC, *New Port Richey* .... 18 [P] 727-849-7675
Gulf Harbour Y&CC, *Fort Myers* .... 18 [V] 239-433-3015
gulfharbour.com
Gulf Stream GC, *Delray Beach* .... 18 [V] 561-276-4421
Hacienda Hills G&CC, *The Villages* .... 27 [P] 352-753-5155
golfthevillages.com
Haile Plantation G&CC, *Gainesville* .... 18 [V] 352-335-0055
haileplantationgolf.com
Halifax Plantation GC, *Ormond Beach* .... 18 [P] 386-676-9600
halifaxplantation.com
Hamlet CC, *Delray Beach* .... 18 [V] 561-498-7600
thehamletcc.com
Hammock Bay, *Naples* .... 18 [V] 239-394-4811
hammockbaygcc.com
Hammock Creek GC, *Palm City* .... 18 [P] 772-220-2599
hammockcreekgolfclub.com
Hammock Dunes Club, *Palm Coast* .... 18 [V] 386-446-6222
hammockdunes.com
Hamptons GC, *Auburndale* .... 18 [P] 863-666-8442
Harbor Hills GC, *Lady Lake* .... 18 [S] 352-753-7000
harborhills.com
Harbour Ridge Y&CC, *Palm City* .... 36 [V] 772-336-8900
hrycc.com
Harbour Village G&YC, *Ponce Inlet* .... 9 [R] 386-760-3434
Harder Hall CC, *Sebring* .... 18 [R] 863-382-0500
Harder Hall Exec GC, *Sebring* .... 9 [P] 863-382-0744

Harmony Golf Preserve, *Harmony* .... 18 [P] 407-891-8525
harmonygolfpreserve.com
Haulover Beach GC, *Bal Harbour* .... 9 [M] 305-940-6719
miamigov.com
Havana CC, *Lady Lake* .... 27 [V] 352-750-8085
golfthevillages.com
Havana G&CC, *Havana* .... 9 [V] 850-539-6767
Hawks Landing GC, *Orlando* .... 18 [R] 407-238-8660
golfhawkslanding.com
Hawks Nest GC, *Vero Beach* .... 18 [V] 772-569-9402
hawksnestgolf.com
Heather G&CC, *Weeki Wachee* .... 9 [S] 352-596-2019
hgcc.20m.com
Heather Hills GC, *Bradenton* .... 18 [P] 941-755-8888
Heathrow CC, *Heathrow* .... 18 [V] 407-333-1469
heathrowcc.com
Heritage Bay GC, *Naples* .... 27 [P] 239-353-2561
golfheritagebay.com
Heritage Harbor G&CC, *Lutz* .... 18 [P] 813-949-4886
heritageharborgolf.com
Heritage Isles G&CC, *Tampa* .... 18 [P] 813-907-7447
heritageislesgolf.com
Heritage Oaks G&CC, *Sarasota* .... 18 [V] 941-926-7600
heritageoaksgcc.com
Heritage Palms G&CC, *Fort Myers* .... 27 [P] 239-278-9090
hpgcc.com
Heritage Pines CC, *Hudson* .... 18 [V] 727-861-1645
heritagepines.net
Heritage Plantation G&CC, *Laurel Hill* .... 18 [S] 850-652-2555
heritageplantationfla.com
Heritage Ridge GC, *Hobe Sound* .... 18 [S] 772-546-2800
heritageridgegolf.com
Heritage Springs CC, *New Port Richey* ...... 18 [V] 727-372-5281
heritagespringscommunity.com
Hernando Oaks G&CC, *Brooksville* .... 18 [P] 352-799-9908
hernandooaksgolf.com
Heron Bay GC, *Coral Springs* .... 18 [S] 954-796-2000
heronbaygolfclub.net
Heron Creek G&CC, *North Port* .... 27 [S] 941-423-6955
heron-creek.com
Herons Glen G&CC, *Fort Myers* .... 18 [P] 239-731-4520
heronsglenrecdist.com
Hibiscus GC, *Naples* .... 18 [V] 239-774-0088
hibiscusgolf.com
Hidden Hills CC, *Jacksonville* .... 18 [V] 904-641-8121
hiddenhillscc.com
Hidden Lakes GC, *New Smyrna Beach* ..... 18 [P] 386-427-4138
hiddenlakesgolfclub.com
Hideaway Beach GC, *Marco Island* .... 9 [V] 239-394-5555
hideawaybeachclub.org
Hideaway CC, *Fort Myers* .... 18 [V] 239-275-5581
Hideout GC, *Naples* .... 18 [V] 239-352-4444
hideoutgolfclub.com
High Point CC, *Naples* .... 9 [S] 239-261-4442
High Point GC, *Brooksville* .... 18 [V] 352-596-0833
retireflorida.com
High Ridge CC, *Lantana* .... 18 [V] 561-586-3333
highridgecc.com
Highland Fairways GC, *Lakeland* .... 18 [V] 863-858-0947
highlandfairways.net
Highland Lakes Exec GC, *Palm Harbor* ...... 27 [V] 727-784-1402
highlandlakeshoa.org
Highland Woods G&CC, *Bonita Springs* ..... 18 [V] 239-498-0553
hwgcc.com

[A] = MILITARY   [M] = MUNICIPAL   [P] = PUBLIC   [R] = RESORT

Golf Yellow Pages, 18th Edition   FLORIDA

Highlands Reserve GC, *Davenport* .... 18 [P] 863-420-1724
   highlandsreserve-golf.com
Highlands Ridge GC North, *Avon Park* .... 18 [P] 863-453-9991
   highlandsridge.com
Highlands Ridge GC South, *Avon Park* .... 18 [S] 863-471-2299
   highlandsridge.com
Hilaman Park GC, *Tallahassee* .... 18 [M] 850-891-2560
   hilamangolfcourse.com
Hillcrest G&CC, *Hollywood* .... 27 [P] 954-987-5000
   hillcrestgcc.com
Hillsboro Pines Golf, *Deerfield Beach* .... 18 [S] 954-421-1188
   hillsboropinesgolfcourse.com
Hobe Sound GC, *Hobe Sound* .... 18 [V] 772-546-4600
   hobesoundgolfclub.com
Hole in the Wall GC, *Naples* .... 18 [V] 239-261-0756
   holeinthewallgolf.org
Holiday GC, *Panama City Beach* .... 27 [P] 850-234-1800
   holidaygolfclub.com
Hollybrook G&TC, *Pembroke Pines* .... 36 [V] 954-431-4545
   hollybrook.com
Hollywood Beach G&CC, *Hollywood* .... 18 [R] 954-927-1751
   hollywoodbeachgolf.com
Hombre GC, *Panama City Beach* .... 27 [S] 850-234-3673
   hombregolfclub.com
Hunters Creek GC, *Orlando* .... 18 [P] 407-240-6003
   golfhunterscreek.com
Hunters Green CC, *Tampa* .... 18 [V] 813-973-1000
   huntersgreencc.com
Hunters Ridge CC, *Bonita Springs* .... 18 [V] 239-947-6467
   huntersridge.net
Hunters Run POA, *Boynton Beach* .... 54 [V] 561-737-2582
   huntersrun.net
Huntington GC, *Ocala* .... 18 [P] 352-347-3333
Huntington Hills G&CC, *Lakeland* .... 18 [S] 863-859-3689
Hyde Park GC, *Jacksonville* .... 18 [P] 904-786-5410
   hydeparkgolfclub.com
Ibis G&CC, *West Palm Beach* .... 54 [V] 561-625-8500
   ibisgolf.com
IMG Academies G&CC, *Bradenton* .... 18 [V] 941-758-1466
   imggcc.com
Imperial GC, *Naples* .... 36 [V] 239-597-7186
   imperialgolfclub.org
Imperial Lakes CC, *Mulberry* .... 18 [P] 863-425-1154
   imperiallakes.cc
Imperial Lakewoods GC, *Palmetto* .... 18 [P] 941-747-4653
   ilwgc.com
Indian Bayou G&CC, *Destin* .... 27 [S] 850-837-6191
   indianbayougolf.com
Indian Creek CC, *Indian Creek Village* .... 18 [V] 305-866-1263
   indiancreekcountryclub.org
Indian Hills GC, *Fort Pierce* .... 18 [M] 772-461-9620
   cityoffortpierce.com
Indian Lake Estates CC, *Lake Wales* .... 27 [S] 863-692-1514
   indianlakeestates.net
Indian Pines GC, *Fort Pierce* .... 18 [P] 772-464-7018
Indian River Club, *Vero Beach* .... 18 [V] 772-569-5066
   indianriverclub.com
Indian River Colony Club, *Melbourne* .... 18 [V] 321-255-6058
   indianrivercolonyclub.com
Indian Spring CC, *Boynton Beach* .... 36 [V] 561-737-5544
   indianspringcc.com
Indian Springs GC, *Marianna* .... 18 [S] 850-482-8787
   indianspringsgolfcourse.net

Indianwood G&CC, *Indiantown* .... 18 [P] 772-597-3794
   indianwoodgolfclub.com
Indigo Lakes GC, *Daytona Beach* .... 18 [S] 386-254-3607
   indigolakesgolf.com
Innisbrook Resort & GC, *Palm Harbor* .... 72 [R] 727-942-2000
   innisbrookgolfresort.com
Interlachen CC, *Winter Park* .... 18 [V] 407-657-5220
   interlachenccfl.com
Intl Links Miami Melreese GC, *Miami* .... 18 [M] 305-633-4583
   internationallinksgolfclub.com
Inverness G&CC, *Inverness* .... 18 [V] 352-637-2526
   golfinverness.com
Inverrary CC, *Lauderhill* .... 54 [S] 954-733-7550
   inverrarygolf.com
Ironhorse G&CC, *West Palm Beach* .... 18 [V] 561-624-5550
   ironhorsecountryclub.com
Ironwood GC, *Gainesville* .... 18 [M] 352-334-3120
   ironwoodgolfcourse.com
Isla Del Sol Y&CC, *St Petersburg* .... 18 [R] 727-864-2417
   isladelsolycc.com
Island CC, *Marco Island* .... 18 [V] 239-394-3151
   island-countryclub.org
Island Dunes CC, *Jensen Beach* .... 9 [V] 772-229-2739
Isleworth CC, *Windermere* .... 18 [V] 407-876-5944
   isleworth.com
Jacaranda GC, *Plantation* .... 36 [R] 954-472-5836
   golfjacaranda.com
Jacaranda West CC, *Venice* .... 18 [V] 941-493-2664
   jacwestcc.com
Jacksonville Beach GC, *Jacksonville Beach* .... 18 [M] 904-247-6184
   jacksonvillebeachgolfclub.com
Jacksonville G&CC, *Jacksonville* .... 18 [V] 904-223-5555
   jaxgcc.com
Jake Gaither GC, *Tallahassee* .... 9 [M] 850-891-3942
   talgov.com/parks
Jefferson CC, *Monticello* .... 9 [P] 850-997-5484
Jo Daddys Lighted GC, *Palm Bay* .... 9 [P] 321-723-1956
Johns Island Club, *Vero Beach* .... 36 [V] 772-231-1700
   johnsislandclub.org
Johns Island Club - West, *Vero Beach* .... 18 [V] 772-231-1700
   johnsislandclub.org
Jonathans Landing At Old Trail, *Jupiter* .... 36 [V] 561-744-8200
   jonathanslanding.com
Jonathans Landing GC, *Jupiter* .... 18 [V] 561-744-4231
   jonathanslanding.com
Juliette Falls Golf & Spa Club, *Dunnellon* .... 18 [S] 352-522-0309
   juliettefalls.com
Jupiter CC, *Jupiter* .... 18 [V] 561-746-3950
   jupitercountryclub.com
Jupiter Dunes GC, *Jupiter* .... 9 [P] 561-746-6654
   jupiterdunesgolf.com
Jupiter Hills Club, *Tequesta* .... 36 [V] 561-746-5228
   jupiterhillsclub.org
Jupiter Island Club, *Hobe Sound* .... 18 [R] 772-546-2301
   thejic.com
Kelly Greens G&CC, *Fort Myers* .... 18 [V] 239-466-9552
   kellygreens.com
Kelly Plantation GC, *Destin* .... 18 [P] 850-650-7600
   kellyplantationgolf.com
Kensington G&CC, *Naples* .... 18 [V] 239-649-0071
   kensingtoncc.com
Key Colony Beach Par 3, *Key Colony Beach* .... 9 [P] 305-289-1533
   kcbpar3.com

[S] = SEMI-PRIVATE   [V] = PRIVATE   [U] = UNIVERSITY   [N] = UNIVERSITY-PRIVATE

FLORIDA

Key Royale Club, *Holmes Beach* .... 9 [V] 941-778-3055
 keyroyaleclub.com
Key West GC, *Key West* .... 18 [R] 305-294-5232
 keywestgolf.com
Keys Gate GC, *Homestead* .... 18 [P] 305-230-0362
 keysgategolf.com
Keystone Heights G&CC, *Keystone Heights* .... 18 [S] 352-473-4540
Killearn CC & Inn, *Tallahassee* .... 27 [R] 850-893-2186
 killearncc.com
Killian Greens GC, *Miami* .... 18 [P] 305-271-0917
 killiangreensgolfclub.com
King & Bear GC World Golf Village, *St Augustine* .18 [R] 904-940-6088
 golfwgv.com
Kings Gate GC, *Port Charlotte* .... 18 [S] 941-625-0680
 kingsgatehomes.com
Kings Island GC, *Punta Gorda* .... 18 [S] 941-629-7800
Kings Point Exec GC, *Sun City Center* .... 18 [V] 813-634-6261
 suncitycenter.wcicommunities.com
Kings Point Golf, *Delray Beach* .... 18 [P] 561-499-7840
 kingspointdelray.com
Kings Ridge GC, *Clermont* .... 36 [P] 352-242-4653
 kingsridgegc.com
Kingsway CC, *Lake Suzy* .... 18 [V] 941-625-8898
 kingswaycountryclub.com
Kissimmee Bay CC, *Kissimmee* .... 18 [S] 407-348-4653
 playgolfinkissimmee.com
Kissimmee GC, *Kissimmee* .... 18 [P] 407-847-2816
 kissgolfclub.com
KOA Campground & Golf Resort, *Okeechobee* .... 9 [R] 863-763-0231
 okeechobeekoa.com
La Cita CC, *Titusville* .... 18 [V] 321-267-2955
 lacitacc.com
La Gorce CC, *Miami Beach* .... 18 [V] 305-867-8204
 lagorcecc.com
Lago Mar CC, *Plantation* .... 18 [V] 954-472-7047
 lagomarcc.com
Lake Ashton GC, *Winter Haven* .... 36 [V] 863-326-1032
 lakeashton.com
Lake Bess GC, *Winter Haven* .... 9 [P] 863-326-9171
Lake Diamond G&CC, *Ocala* .... 18 [P] 352-687-1000
 lakediamond.com
Lake Fairways CC, *Fort Myers* .... 18 [S] 239-731-5220
Lake Henry GC, *Winter Haven* .... 18 [V] 863-299-2683
Lake Jovita G&CC, *Dade City* .... 36 [S] 352-588-2233
 lakejovita.com
Lake June West G&AC, *Lake Placid* .... 9 [S] 863-465-2888
Lake Nona GC, *Orlando* .... 18 [V] 407-857-6216
 lakenona.com
Lake Orlando GC, *Orlando* .... 18 [P] 407-298-1230
 golflakeorlando.com
Lake Region Yacht CC, *Winter Haven* .... 18 [V] 863-324-4579
 lakeregionycc.com
Lake Venice GC, *Venice* .... 27 [S] 941-488-3948
 lakevenicegolf.com
Lake Wales CC, *Lake Wales* .... 18 [V] 863-676-6519
 lakewalescc.com
Lake Worth Muni GC, *Lake Worth* .... 18 [M] 561-582-9713
 lakeworth.org
Lakes at Leesburg, *Leesburg* .... 9 [V] 352-326-3130
Lakes of Lady Lake GC, *Lady Lake* .... 18 [P] 352-750-4414
LakeSide GC, *Inverness* .... 18 [P] 352-726-1461
 lakesideccgolf.com

Lakeview GC, *Delray Beach* .... 18 [M] 561-498-3229
 lakeviewgcdelray.com
Lakewood CC, *Naples* .... 18 [V] 239-775-0765
Lakewood Ranch G&CC, *Bradenton* .... 54 [V] 941-907-4710
 lakewoodranchgolf.com
Lansbrook GC, *Palm Harbor* .... 18 [S] 727-784-7333
 lansbrook-golf.com
LaPlaya GC, *Naples* .... 18 [V] 239-254-5001
 laplayaresort.com
Largo GC, *Largo* .... 18 [M] 727-518-3024
 largogolf.com
Lauderhill GC, *Fort Lauderdale* .... 9 [M] 954-730-2990
Laurel Oak CC, *Sarasota* .... 36 [V] 941-378-3600
 laureloak.com
Legacy GC, *Bradenton* .... 18 [P] 941-907-7920
 legacygolfclub.com
Legends G&CC, *Fort Myers* .... 18 [V] 239-561-7757
 legendscc.com
Leisureville Community Assoc, *Pompano Beach*... 9 [V] 954-946-0350
Leisureville Community GC, *Boynton Beach* .... 18 [V] 561-732-0593
Lekarica Hills GC Rest & Country Inn, *Lake Wales* 18 [R] 863-679-9478
 lekarica.com
Lely Resort G&CC, *Naples* .... 36 [R] 239-793-2600
 lely-resort.net
Lemon Bay GC, *Englewood* .... 18 [V] 941-697-4190
 lemonbaygolfclub.com
Lexington CC, *Fort Myers* .... 18 [V] 239-437-3380
 lexingtoncountryclub.com
Lexington Oaks GC, *Wesley Chapel* .... 18 [P] 813-907-7270
 lexoaks.com
Lily Lake Golf & RV Resort, *Frostproof* .... 9 [R] 863-635-1344
 lilylake.com
Links At Greenfield Plantation, *Bradenton* .... 18 [P] 941-747-9432
 linksatgreenfieldplantation.com
Little Cypress G&CC, *Wauchula* .... 9 [P] 863-735-1333
Live Oak G&CC, *Crescent City* .... 18 [S] 386-467-2512
 liveoakgolf.com
Live Oak GC & RV Park, *Arcadia* .... 9 [R] 863-993-4014
Loblolly, *Hobe Sound* .... 18 [V] 772-546-8705
 loblollyinfo.com
Lone Palm GC, *Lakeland* .... 18 [V] 863-499-5481
Lone Pine GC, *West Palm Beach* .... 18 [P] 561-842-0480
Long Marsh GC, *Rotonda West* .... 27 [P] 941-698-0918
 rotondagolf.com
Longboat Key Club, *Longboat Key* .... 45 [R] 941-387-1632
 longboatkeyclub.com
Lost Key GC, *Pensacola* .... 18 [P] 850-492-1300
 lostkey.com
Lost Lake GC, *Hobe Sound* .... 18 [S] 772-220-6666
 lostlakegolfclub.com
Lost Tree Club, *North Palm Beach* .... 18 [V] 561-626-1400
 losttreeclub.com
LPGA International, *Daytona Beach* .... 36 [V] 386-274-5742
 lpgainternational.com
Lutz Exec Golf Ctr, *Lutz* .... 9 [P] 813-949-6687
 lutzgolf.com
Lynx At Vista GC, *Vero Beach* .... 27 [S] 772-562-1221
 LynxatVista.com
Madison CC, *Madison* .... 9 [V] 850-973-6701
 madisoncountryclub-fl.com
Magnolia Plantation GC, *Lake Mary* .... 18 [P] 407-771-4343
 magnoliaplantationgolfclub.com

[A] = MILITARY   [M] = MUNICIPAL   [P] = PUBLIC   [R] = RESORT

FLORIDA

Magnolia Plantation Gc, *Lake Mary* .... 18 [S] 407-833-0818
magnoliaplantationgolfclub.com
Magnolia Point G&CC, *Green Cove Springs* .... 27 [P] 904-269-9315
magnoliapointgolfclub.com
Magnolia Valley GC, *New Port Richey* .... 27 [S] 727-847-2342
magnoliavalleygolfclub.com
Mainlands GC, *Pinellas Park* .... 18 [P] 727-577-4847
mainlandsgolf.com
Majestic GC, *Lehigh Acres* .... 18 [S] 239-369-8216
majesticgolfclub.com
Majors GC At Bayside Lakes, *Palm Bay* .... 18 [P] 321-952-8617
majorsgolfclub.com
Mallards Landing GC, *Melbourne* .... 18 [M] 321-255-4606
melbourneflorida.org
Mallory Hill CC, *Lady Lake* .... 27 [V] 352-753-3730
golfthevillages.com
Manatee County GC, *Bradenton* .... 18 [M] 941-792-6773
co.manatee.fl.us/golf.html
Manatee Cove GC, *Patrick AFB* .... 18 [A] 321-494-7856
patrick.af.mil
Mangrove Bay GC, *St Petersburg* .... 27 [M] 727-893-7800
stpete.org
Maple Leaf G&CC, *Port Charlotte* .... 18 [S] 941-629-1666
mapleleafgcc.net
Marcus Pointe GC, *Pensacola* .... 18 [P] 850-484-9770
marcus-pointe.com
Margate Exec GC, *Margate* .... 9 [P] 954-971-0807
oriolegolfclub.com
Marina Lakes GC, *Delray Beach* .... 18 [S] 561-499-2424
marinalakesgolfcourse.webs.com
Mariner Sands CC, *Stuart* .... 36 [V] 772-221-7304
marinersands.com
Marion Oaks CC, *Ocala* .... 18 [P] 352-347-1271
marionoakscountryclub.com
Mark Bostick GC At Univ of Florida, *Gainesville* .. 18 [N] 352-375-4866
ufgolfcourse.com
Marriotts Grande Vista GC, *Orlando* .... 9 [R] 407-238-7677
gofaldo.com
Marsh Creek GC, *St Augustine* .... 18 [V] 904-461-1145
marshcreek.com
Marsh Landing CC, *Ponte Vedra Beach* .... 18 [V] 904-285-6459
marshlandingcc.com
Martin County G&CC, *Stuart* .... 36 [M] 772-287-3747
martincountygolfandcountryclub.com
Martin Downs CC, *Palm City* .... 36 [V] 772-286-6818
martindownscc.com
Mayacoo Lakes CC, *West Palm Beach* .... 18 [V] 561-793-1700
mayacoolakescc.com
Mayfair CC, *Sanford* .... 18 [S] 407-322-2531
mayfairlinks.com
McArthur GC, *Hobe Sound* .... 18 [V] 772-545-3838
mcarthurgolf.com
Meadow Oaks G&CC, *Hudson* .... 18 [S] 727-856-2878
meadowoakscountryclub.com
Meadowbrook GC, *Gainesville* .... 18 [S] 352-332-0577
playmeadowbrook.com
Meadowood G&TC, *Fort Pierce* .... 18 [V] 772-466-4000
meadowoodgolfandtennis.com
Medalist GC, *Hobe Sound* .... 18 [V] 772-545-9500
medalistgolfclub.org
MetroWest GC, *Orlando* .... 18 [S] 407-299-8800
metrowestgolf.com
Miami Beach GC, *Miami Beach* .... 18 [S] 305-532-3350
miamibeachgolfclub.com

Miami Shores CC, *Miami Shores* .... 18 [S] 305-795-2366
miamishoresgolf.com
Miami Springs G&CC, *Miami Springs* .... 18 [M] 305-805-5180
miamispringsgolfcourse.com
Miccosukee G&CC, *Miami* .... 27 [P] 305-382-3931
miccosukeegolf.com
Miles Grant CC, *Stuart* .... 18 [V] 772-286-2220
milesgrant.net
Mill Cove GC, *Jacksonville* .... 18 [P] 904-642-6140
millcovegolfcourse.com
Miona Lake GC, *Wildwood* .... 18 [S] 352-748-4200
brassboys.com
Miromar Lakes GC, *Miromar Lakes* .... 18 [S] 239-482-7644
miromarlakes.com
Mirror Lakes GC, *Lehigh Acres* .... 18 [R] 239-369-1322
Mission Inn Golf Resort, *Howey In The Hills* .... 36 [R] 352-324-3101
missioninnresort.com
Mission Valley CC, *Nokomis* .... 18 [V] 941-488-7747
missionvalleycc.com
Misty Creek GC, *Sarasota* .... 18 [V] 941-922-2188
mistycreek.net
Mizner CC, *Delray Beach* .... 18 [V] 561-638-5600
miznercc.info
Monarch CC, *Palm City* .... 18 [V] 772-286-3715
monarchclub.com
Monterey Y&CC, *Stuart* .... 9 [V] 772-283-7600
montereyyachtandcountryclub.com
Moorings GC, *Vero Beach* .... 18 [V] 772-231-5990
themooringsclub.com
Mount Dora GC, *Mt Dora* .... 18 [P] 352-383-3954
mountdoragolf.com
Mountain Lake GC, *Lake Wales* .... 18 [V] 863-676-3494
mountainlakecc.com
Myakka Pines GC, *Englewood* .... 27 [P] 941-474-3296
myakkapinesgolfclub.com
Myerlee CC, *Fort Myers* .... 18 [V] 239-481-1440
myerleecc.com
Mystic Dunes Resort & GC, *Kissimmee* .... 18 [R] 407-787-5678
mysticdunesgolf.com
Nancy Lopez Legacy G&CC, *Lady Lake* .... 27 [P] 352-753-1450
golfthevillages.com
Naples Beach Hotel & GC, *Naples* .... 18 [R] 239-261-2222
naplesbeachhotel.com
Naples Grande GC, *Naples* .... 18 [R] 239-659-3700
naplesgrandegolf.com
Naples Heritage G&CC, *Naples* .... 18 [V] 239-417-9990
nhgcc.com
Naples Lakes CC, *Naples* .... 18 [V] 239-732-1011
napleslakesfl.com
Naples National GC, *Naples* .... 18 [V] 239-775-8911
naplesnationalgolfclub.com
NAS Jacksonville GC, *Jacksonville* .... 27 [A] 904-542-3249
Nature Walk GC, *Lynn Haven* .... 18 [P] 850-265-2582
naturewalkgolfcourse.com
New Smyrna Beach GC, *New Smyrna Beach* ..... 18 [M] 386-424-2191
cityofnsb.com
Normandy Shores GC, *Miami Beach* .... 18 [M] 305-868-6502
normandyshoresgolfclub.com
North Lakes GC, *Sun City Center* .... 18 [V] 813-634-1024
wcicommunities.com
North Palm Beach CC, *North Palm Beach* .... 18 [M] 561-691-3433
village-npb.org
North Shore GC, *Orlando* .... 18 [P] 407-277-9277
golfatnorthshore.com

[S] = SEMI-PRIVATE   [V] = PRIVATE   [U] = UNIVERSITY   [N] = UNIVERSITY-PRIVATE

FLORIDA — Golf Yellow Pages, 18th Edition

Northdale G&TC, *Tampa* .... 18 [S] 813-962-0428
  northdalegolf.com
Oak Ford GC, *Sarasota* .... 27 [P] 941-371-3680
  oakfordgolfclub.com
Oak Harbor CC, *Vero Beach* .... 9 [V] 772-562-3808
  oakharborcc.com
Oak Hills CC, *Spring Hill* .... 18 [P] 352-683-6830
  teetalk.net
Oak Run CC, *Ocala* .... 9 [P] 352-854-0126
Oakwood GC, *Lake Wales* .... 18 [P] 863-676-8558
  golfoakwood.com
Ocala GC, *Ocala* .... 18 [M] 352-401-6917
  ocalagolfcourses.com
Ocala Palms G&CC, *Ocala* .... 18 [P] 352-732-4653
  ocalapalmsgolf.com
Ocean Breeze G&CC, *Boca Raton* .... 27 [V] 561-994-0400
  oceanbreezegolf.com
Ocean Club-Hutchinson Island Beach, *Stuart* ...... 18 [R] 772-225-6819
Ocean Course at Hammock Beach Resort,
  Palm Coast .... 18 [R] 386-447-4612
  hammockbeach.com
Ocean Reef Club, *Key Largo* .... 36 [P] 305-367-2611
  oceanreef.com
Ocean Village GC, *Fort Pierce* .... 9 [V] 772-467-0102
  oceanvillage.com
Oceans GC, *Daytona Beach* .... 9 [S] 386-788-2998
  members.aol.com/oceansgolfclub/index.html
Oceanside CC, *Ormond Beach* .... 18 [V] 386-672-1991
  occ1907.com
Okeechobee G&CC, *Okeechobee* .... 18 [P] 863-763-6228
  okeechobeegolf.com
Okeeheelee GC, *West Palm Beach* .... 27 [M] 561-964-4653
  pbcgolf.com
Old Corkscrew GC, *Estero* .... 18 [S] 239-949-4700
  oldcorkscrew.com
Old Marsh GC, *Palm Beach Gardens* .... 18 [V] 561-626-7400
  oldmarshgolf.com
Old Memorial GC, *Tampa* .... 18 [V] 813-926-8888
  oldmemorialgolfclub.com
Old Palm GC, *Palm Beach Gardens* .... 18 [V] 561-472-5120
  oldpalmgc.com
Olde Florida GC, *Naples* .... 18 [V] 239-353-7667
Olde Hickory G&CC, *Fort Myers* .... 18 [V] 239-768-2400
  oldehickory.cc
On Top Of The World GC, *Clearwater* .... 27 [V] 727-726-7773
On Top of the World GC, *Ocala* .... 36 [V] 352-854-8430
  ontopoftheworld.com
Orange Blossom Hills G&CC, *The Villages* .... 18 [S] 352-753-5200
  golfthevillages.com
Orange County National GCtr&Lodge,
  Winter Garden .... 45 [R] 407-656-2626
  ocngolf.com
Orange Tree GC, *Orlando* .... 18 [V] 407-351-2521
  orangetreegolfclub.com
Orangebrook G&CC, *Hollywood* .... 36 [M] 954-967-4653
  orangebrook.com
Orchid Island G&BC, *Vero Beach* .... 18 [V] 772-388-9393
  orchidislandgolfandbeachclub.com
Oriole G&TC, *Margate* .... 18 [S] 954-972-8140
  oriolegolfclub.com
Osceola Muni GC, *Pensacola* .... 18 [P] 850-453-7599
  osceolagolf.com
Osprey Point GC, *Boca Raton* .... 27 [P] 561-482-2868
  pbcgolf.com

Oyster Creek GC, *Englewood* .... 18 [P] 941-475-0334
  oystercreekgolfclub.com
Pablo Creek Club, *Jacksonville* .... 18 [V] 904-992-6900
Palatka GC, *Palatka* .... 18 [M] 386-329-0141
  palatkagolfclub.com
Palisades CC, *Clermont* .... 18 [S] 352-394-0085
  palisadesgolfproperties.com
Palm Aire CC & Resort, *Pompano Beach* .... 72 [R] 954-975-6225
  palmairegolf.com
Palm Aire CC of Sarasota, *Sarasota* .... 36 [V] 941-355-9733
  palmaire.net
Palm Beach CC, *Palm Beach* .... 18 [V] 561-844-3501
  palmbeachcountryclub.org
Palm Beach Gardens GC, *Palm Beach Gardens* .... 18 [M] 561-626-7888
  gardensgolf.com
Palm Beach National G&CC, *Lake Worth* .... 18 [S] 561-965-3381
  palmbeachnational.com
Palm Beach Par 3 GC, *Palm Beach* .... 18 [M] 561-547-0598
  golfontheocean.com
Palm Beach Polo & CC, *West Palm Beach* .... 36 [V] 561-798-7405
  palmbeachpolo.com
Palm Cove G&YC, *Palm City* .... 18 [P] 772-287-5605
  palmcovegolf.com
Palm Gardens GC, *Melbourne* .... 9 [P] 321-723-3182
  palmgardensgolfcourse.com
Palm Harbor GC, *Palm Coast* .... 18 [S] 386-986-4653
  palmharborgolfclub.com
Palm Hill GC, *Largo* .... 9 [V] 727-581-1710
  palmhillcountryclub.net
Palm Valley GC, *Ponte Vedra Beach* .... 9 [P] 904-824-9279
  palmvalleygolfing.com
Palm View Hills GC, *Palmetto* .... 18 [P] 941-722-2392
Palma Ceia G&CC, *Tampa* .... 18 [V] 813-253-3061
  pcgc.org
Palmer Legends CC, *The Villages* .... 27 [P] 352-753-5300
  golfthevillages.com
Palmetto GC, *Miami* .... 18 [M] 305-235-1069
  golfpalmetto.com
Palmetto Pine CC, *Cape Coral* .... 18 [V] 239-574-2141
  palmettopine.com
Palmetto Pines GC, *Parrish* .... 36 [P] 941-776-1375
  palmettopinesgolfcourse.com
Palmira G&CC, *Bonita Springs* .... 27 [V] 239-949-4466
  golfclubatpalmira.org
Panama CC, *Lynn Haven* .... 18 [V] 850-265-2911
  panamacountryclub.com
Panther Creek GC, *Jacksonville* .... 18 [P] 904-783-2600
  panthercreekgolf.com
Panther Run GC, *Ave Maria* .... 18 [S] 239-304-2835
  pantherrungolfclub.com
Park Ridge GC, *Lake Worth* .... 18 [M] 561-966-7044
  pbcgolf.com
Parkland GC, *Parkland* .... 18 [V] 954-753-7737
  theclubatparklandgcc.com
Pasadena Y&CC, *Gulfport* .... 18 [V] 727-381-8337
  pyccgolf.com
Pebble Creek GC, *Tampa* .... 18 [S] 813-973-3870
  pebblecreekclub.com
Pelican Marsh GC, *Naples* .... 18 [V] 239-597-1858
  pelicanmarshgc.com
Pelican Point GC, *Tyndall AFB* .... 18 [A] 850-286-2565
Pelican Pointe G&CC, *Venice* .... 27 [P] 941-496-4653
  pelicanpointeclub.com

[A] = MILITARY   [M] = MUNICIPAL   [P] = PUBLIC   [R] = RESORT

FLORIDA

Golf Yellow Pages, 18th Edition

Pelican Preserve GC, *Fort Myers* .... 27 [S]   239-985-1707
  pelicanpreservelifestyles.com
Pelican Sound G&RiverC, *Estero* .... 27 [V]   239-948-4333
  pelicansoundgrc.com
Pelicans Nest GC, *Bonita Springs* .... 36 [V]   239-947-4600
  nestgolf.com
Pembroke Lakes GC, *Pembroke Pines* .... 18 [M]   954-431-4144
  pcmgolf.com
Pennbrooke Fairways, *Leesburg* .... 27 [P]   352-728-3200
  pennbrooke.org
Penney Retirement Community, *Penney Farms* ... 9 [V]   904-284-8200
  pennyretirementcommunity.org
Pensacola CC, *Pensacola* .... 18 [V]   850-455-1488
  pensacolacountryclub.com
Perdido Bay GC, *Pensacola* .... 18 [R]   850-492-1223
  perdidobaygolf.com
Peridia G&CC, *Bradenton* .... 18 [S]   941-758-2582
  peridiagcc.net
Perry G&CC, *Perry* .... 9 [S]   850-584-3590
PGA GC in PGA Village, *Port St Lucie* .... 54 [R]   772-467-1300
  pgavillage.com
PGA National Estates GC, *West Palm Beach* .... 18 [R]   561-625-6833
  pgaresorts.com
PGA National GC, *Palm Beach Gardens* .... 72 [R]   561-627-1800
  pgaresort.com
Pine Island Ridge CC, *Fort Lauderdale* .... 18 [V]   954-472-1080
Pine Lakes CC, *Fort Myers* .... 18 [S]   239-731-5822
Pine Lakes GC, *Stuart* .... 18 [P]   772-692-0346
Pine Oaks GC, *Ocala* .... 18 [M]   352-401-6941
Pine Ridge Community G&CC, *Beverly Hills* .... 27 [S]   352-746-5177
Pine Tree GC, *Boynton Beach* .... 18 [S]   561-732-6404
  pinetreegolfclub.net
Pinebrook Ironwood GC, *Bradenton* .... 18 [S]   941-792-3288
  pinebrookironwood.com
Pinecrest GC, *Largo* .... 18 [P]   727-584-6497
Pinecrest on Lotela, *Avon Park* .... 18 [P]   863-453-7555
  golfpinecrestgc.com
Pinemoor East GC, *Rotonda West* .... 9 [P]   941-697-9492
Pinemoor West GC, *Rotonda West* .... 18 [P]   941-697-7006
Pipers Landing CC, *Palm City* .... 18 [V]   772-283-1155
  piperslanding.com
Placid Lakes CC, *Lake Placid* .... 18 [S]   863-465-1626
  placidlakescc.com
Plantation Bay, *Ormond Beach* .... 27 [V]   386-437-4776
  plantationbaygolf.com
Plantation Bay - Prestwick Course, *Ormond Beach* 18 [V] 386-437-6664
  plantationbaygolf.com
Plantation G&CC, *Venice* .... 36 [V]   941-493-2000
  plantationgcc.com
Plantation Golf Resort & Spa, *Crystal River* .... 27 [R]   352-795-4211
  plantationgolfandspa.com
Plantation Oaks of Ormond Beach, *Ormond Beach* 9 [S] 800-873-6125
  plantationoaksoformondbeach.com
Plantation Palms GC, *Land O Lakes* .... 18 [P]   813-996-7122
  plantationpalms.net
Plantation Preserve GC, *Plantation* .... 18 [M]   954-585-5020
  plantationpreserve.org
Poinciana GC, *Lake Worth* .... 18 [P]   561-439-4721
  golfpoinciana.com
Point O Woods GC, *Inverness* .... 9 [S]   352-726-3113
  pointowoodsgolfclub.com
Polo Club of Boca Raton, *Boca Raton* .... 36 [V]   561-995-1150
  poloclub.net

Polo Park East, *Davenport* .... 9 [P]   863-424-0093
  poloparkeast.com
Polo Park GC, *Davenport* .... 9 [P]   863-424-3341
  polopark.home.att.net
Polo Trace GC, *Delray Beach* .... 18 [P]   561-495-5300
  polotracegolf.com
Pompano Beach GC, *Pompano Beach* .... 36 [M]   954-781-0426
  mypompanobeach.org/parksrec/golf
Ponte Vedra G&CC At Sawgrass, *Ponte Vedra Beach* 18 [P] 904-285-0204
  pontevedragolfandcc.com
Ponte Vedra Inn & Club, *Ponte Vedra Beach* .... 36 [R]   904-285-6911
  pvresorts.com
Port Charlotte GC, *Port Charlotte* .... 18 [S]   941-625-4109
  portcharlottegc.com
Providence GC, *Davenport* .... 18 [P]   863-420-2652
  providence-golf.com
Punta Gorda CC, *Punta Gorda* .... 18 [S]   941-639-1494
Quail Creek GC, *Naples* .... 36 [V]   239-597-2831
  quailcreekcc.com
Quail Heights CC, *Lake City* .... 27 [S]   386-752-3339
  quailheightscc.com
Quail Ridge CC, *Boynton Beach* .... 36 [V]   561-737-5100
  quailridgecc.com
Quail Ridge Golf CC, *Brooksville* .... 18 [S]   813-996-2630
  quailridgegolfcountryclub.com
Quail Run GC In Naples, *Naples* .... 18 [V]   239-261-3930
  naplesquailrun.com
Quail Valley GC, *Vero Beach* .... 18 [V]   772-299-0093
  quailvalleygolfclub.com
Quail Village GC, *Naples* .... 18 [V]   239-598-9922
  quailcreekvillage.org
Quail West G&CC, *Naples* .... 36 [V]   239-593-4100
  quailwest.com
Quarry GC, *Brooksville* .... 9 [M]   352-544-5485
  thefirstteebrooksville.org
Queens Harbour Y&CC, *Jacksonville* .... 18 [S]   904-221-1012
  clubcorp.com
Rainbow Springs G&CC, *Dunnellon* .... 27 [S]   352-489-3566
  myrainbowspringsflorida.com/golf.html
Rainbows End GC, *Dunnellon* .... 9 [P]   352-489-4566
Raptor Bay GC, *Bonita Springs* .... 18 [R]   239-390-4610
  raptorbaygolfclub.com
Red Reef Exec GC, *Boca Raton* .... 9 [M]   561-391-5014
  bocacitygolf.com
Red Tail GC, *Sorrento* .... 18 [V]   352-383-2700
  redtailclub.com
Redland G&CC, *Homestead* .... 18 [S]   305-247-8503
  redlandgolf.com
RedStick GC, *Vero Beach* .... 18 [V]   772-388-3200
  redstickgolfclub.com
Regatta Bay G&CC, *Destin* .... 18 [R]   850-337-8080
  regattabay.com
Remington GC, *Kissimmee* .... 18 [P]   407-344-4004
  remington-gc.com
Reservation GC, *Mulberry* .... 18 [S]   863-425-3818
Reunion Resort & Club, *Reunion* .... 54 [R]   407-396-3195
  reunionresort.com
Ridgewood Lakes G&CC, *Davenport* .... 18 [S]   863-424-8688
  ridgewoodlakesgolf.com
Rio Pinar G&CC, *Orlando* .... 18 [V]   407-277-5121
  riopinar.com
Riomar CC, *Vero Beach* .... 18 [V]   772-231-6888
Ritz Carlton GC & Spa, *Jupiter* .... 18 [R]   561-514-6021
  ritzcarltonclubjupiter.com

[S] = SEMI-PRIVATE   [V] = PRIVATE   [U] = UNIVERSITY   [N] = UNIVERSITY-PRIVATE

43

FLORIDA
Golf Yellow Pages, 18th Edition

Ritz Carlton GC, Grande Lakes Orlando, *Orlando* .18 [R] 407-393-4900
grandelakes.com
Ritz Carlton Members GC, *Bradenton* ....18 [R] 941-309-2900
rcmcsarasota.com
Rivard G&CC, *Brooksville* ....18 [S] 352-796-1410
River Bend GC, *Ormond Beach* ....18 [P] 386-673-6000
playriverbendgolf.com
River Greens GC, *Avon Park* ....18 [P] 863-453-5210
rgreens.com
River Hall CC, *Alva* .... 18 [V] 239-313-4653
riverhall.cc
River Hills CC, *Valrico* .... 18 [V] 813-653-1554
riverhillscountryclub.com
River Isles GC, *Bradenton* .... 9 [V] 941-720-2712
riverislesfl.com
River Ridge GC, *New Port Richey* .... 18 [S] 727-847-4762
myriverridgegolf.com
River Run Golf Links, *Bradenton* ....18 [M] 941-708-8459
riverrungolflinks.com
River Strand G&CC At Heritage Harbour, *Bradenton*27 [P] 941-708-3517
riverstrandgolf.com
River Wilderness G&CC, *Parrish* .... 18 [V] 941-776-2602
riverwildernesscc.com
Riverbend G&CC, *North Fort Myers* ....18 [P] 239-543-2200
Riverbend GC, *Tequesta* .... 18 [V] 561-746-5108
riverbendfl.com
Riverwood GC, *Port Charlotte* .... 18 [S] 941-764-6661
riverwoodgc.com
Riviera CC, *Coral Gables* .... 18 [V] 305-661-5331
rivieracc.org
Riviera CC, *Ormond Beach* ....18 [P] 386-677-2464
rivcc.com
Riviera GC, *Naples* ....18 [P] 239-774-1081
rivieragolf.com
Rock Springs Ridge GC, *Apopka* ....18 [P] 407-814-7474
rockspringsridgegc.com
Rockledge CC, *Rockledge* .... 18 [V] 321-636-3160
rockledgecc.com
Rocky Bayou CC, *Niceville* .... 18 [V] 850-678-3271
rockybayoucc.com
Rocky Point GC, *Tampa* ....18 [M] 813-673-4316
rockypointgc.com
Rogers Park GC, *Tampa* ....18 [M] 813-356-1670
rogersparkgc.com
Rolling Green GC, *Sarasota* .... 18 [S] 941-355-7621
rollinggreengc.com
Rolling Greens Exec Golf Community, *Ocala*........18 [P] 352-624-0511
rollinggreensocala.com
Rolling Hills GC, *Longwood* ....18 [P] 407-831-1312
rollinghillsgolfclub.com
Rosedale G&TC, *Bradenton* .... 18 [S] 941-756-0004
rosedalegcc.com
Rotonda G&CC - The Hills, *Rotonda West* ....18 [P] 941-697-2414
rotondagolf.com
Rotonda G&CC - The Links, *Rotonda West* ....18 [P] 941-697-2414
rotondagolf.com
Rotonda G&CC - The Palms, *Rotonda West* ....18 [P] 941-697-2414
rotondagolf.com
Royal Oak GC, *Titusville* ....18 [R] 321-269-4500
royaloakgolfresort.com
Royal Oaks GC, *Ocala* .... 18 [P] 352-861-1818
Royal Palm CC, *Naples* .... 18 [V] 239-775-1150
royalpalmcc.com
Royal Palm Y&CC, *Boca Raton* .... 18 [V] 561-395-2202
rpycc.org
Royal Poinciana GC, *Naples* .... 36 [V] 239-261-2558
rpgolfclub.com
Royal St Augustine G&CC, *St Augustine*...............18 [P] 904-824-4653
royalstaugustine.com
Royal St Cloud Golf Links, *St Cloud* ....27 [P] 407-891-7010
royalstcloudgolflinks.com
Royal Tee GC, *Cape Coral* ....27 [S] 239-283-5522
royaltee.net
Royal Wood G&CC, *Naples* .... 18 [V] 239-774-2213
royalwoodgcc.com
Sabal Springs Golf & Racquet, *North Fort Myers*.. 18 [S] 239-731-0101
Sabal Trace G&CC, *North Port* .... 18 [P] 941-426-4883
Saddlebrook Resort, *Wesley Chapel* ....36 [R] 813-973-1111
saddlebrookresort.com
Sailfish Point GC, *Stuart* .... 18 [V] 772-225-1500
sailfishpoint.com
Sam Exec GC, *Sharpes* ....18 [P] 321-632-2890
San Carlos GC, *Fort Myers* .... 18 [S] 239-267-3131
sancarlosgolfclub.com
San Jose CC, *Jacksonville* .... 18 [V] 904-733-1511
sjccjax.com
Sanctuary Ridge Golf, *Clermont* ....18 [S] 352-243-0411
sanctuaryridgegc.com
Sandestin G&B Resort, *Destin* ....72 [R] 850-267-8155
playsandestingolf.com
Sandpiper Cove GC, *Destin* .... 9 [V] 850-837-9121
sandpipercove.com
Sandpiper GC, *Sun City Center* .... 27 [V] 813-634-3377
wcicommunities.com
Sandpiper GC, *Lakeland* .... 18 [S] 863-859-5461
Sandridge GC, *Vero Beach* ....36 [M] 772-770-5003
sandridgegc.com
Santa Lucia River Club, *Port St Lucie* .... 18 [V] 772-398-0888
santaluciariverclub.net
Santa Rosa G&BC, *Santa Rosa Beach* .... 18 [S] 850-267-2229
santarosaclub.com
Sara Bay CC, *Sarasota* .... 18 [V] 941-355-6544
sarabaycc.org
Sarabande Golf Estates & Marina,
  Howey In The Hills .... 18 [P] 352-324-2511
sarabandegolf.com
Sarasota GC, *Sarasota* .... 18 [S] 941-371-2431
sarasotagc.com
Sarasota National GC, *Venice* .... 18 [P] 941-496-8676
sarasotanationalgolf.com
Saufley GC, *Netpmsa-Pensacola* .... 9 [A] 850-452-1097
Savanna GC, *Port St Lucie* .... 18 [S] 772-879-1316
Savannahs GC, *Merritt Island* .... 18 [M] 321-455-1375
golfspacecoast.com
Sawgrass CC, *Ponte Vedra Beach* .... 27 [V] 904-273-3720
sawgrasscountryclub.com
Scenic Hills CC, *Pensacola* .... 18 [S] 850-476-0611
scenichills.com
Scepter GC, *Sun City Center* .... 18 [V] 813-634-4593
falconwatch.org
Schalamar Creek G&CC, *Lakeland* .... 18 [S] 863-666-1623
schalamar.com
Scotland Yards GC, *Dade City* .... 18 [S] 352-567-7600
scotlandyards.com
Sea Pines GC, *Hudson* .... 18 [S] 727-863-1214
seapinesgolfclub.com

44   [A] = MILITARY   [M] = MUNICIPAL   [P] = PUBLIC   [R] = RESORT

FLORIDA

Golf Yellow Pages, 18th Edition

Name	Holes	Type	Phone
Seascape Resort, *Destin*	18	[R]	850-654-7888
seascape-resort.com			
Sebastian Muni GC, *Sebastian*	18	[M]	772-589-6801
sebastiangolfcourse.org			
Sebring GC, *Sebring*	18	[M]	863-314-5919
mysebring.com			
Sebring Lakeside Golf Resort, *Sebring*	9	[R]	863-385-7113
2sebring.com			
Selva Marina CC, *Atlantic Beach*	18	[V]	904-246-3144
selvamarina.com			
Seminole GC, *Tallahassee*	18	[U]	850-644-2582
seminolegolfcourse.com			
Seminole GC, *Juno Beach*	18	[V]	561-626-0280
Seminole Lake CC, *Seminole*	18	[V]	727-391-6255
seminolelake.net			
Seminole Lakes CC, *Punta Gorda*	18	[S]	941-639-5440
seminolelakes.net			
Serenoa GC, *Sarasota*	18	[P]	941-925-2755
serenoagc.com			
Seven Bridges at Springtree GC, *Sunrise*	18	[M]	954-572-2270
sunrisefl.gov/2golf.html			
Seven Hills Golfers Club, *Spring Hill*	18	[S]	352-688-8888
sevenhillsgolfersclub.com			
Seven Lakes G&TC, *Fort Myers*	18	[V]	239-481-6560
Seven Rivers G&CC, *Crystal River*	18	[V]	352-795-2100
7riversgolf.com			
Seven Springs G&CC, *New Port Richey*	36	[S]	727-376-0035
ssgcc.com			
Shadow Wood CC, *Bonita Springs*	54	[P]	239-992-6616
shadowwoodcc.com			
Shadow Wood Preserve, *Fort Myers*	18	[V]	239-590-6911
shadowwoodpreserve.com			
Shady Brook Golf & RV, *Sumterville*	18	[P]	352-568-1808
Shalimar Pointe G&CC, *Shalimar*	18	[S]	850-651-1416
shalimarpointe.com			
Sharks Tooth GC, *Panama City Beach*	18	[V]	850-249-3041
sharkstoothgolfclub.com			
Shell Point GC, *Fort Myers*	18	[P]	239-433-9790
shellpointgolf.com			
Sherbrooke G&CC, *Lake Worth*	18	[V]	561-964-6011
Sherman Hills GC, *Brooksville*	18	[P]	352-544-0990
shermanhills.org			
Sherwood GC, *Titusville*	18	[R]	321-269-4653
golfsherwood.com			
Sherwood Park GC, *Delray Beach*	18	[P]	561-499-3559
Shingle Creek GC, *Orlando*	18	[R]	407-996-9933
shinglecreekgolf.com			
Signal Hill GC, *Panama City*	18	[P]	850-234-5051
signalhillgolfcourse.com			
Silver Dollar G&TrapC, *Odessa*	27	[P]	813-920-3884
silverdollargolf.com			
Silver Lakes Resort & GC, *Naples*	9	[R]	239-417-3446
silverlakesrvandgolfresort.net			
Silverado GC, *Zephyrhills*	27	[S]	813-788-1225
golfsilverado.com			
Silverthorn GC, *Spring Hill*	18	[P]	352-799-2600
silverthornclub.net			
Six Lakes CC, *Fort Myers*	18	[V]	239-995-5434
sixlakescountryclub.com			
Skyview At Terra Vista G&CC, *Hernando*	18	[P]	352-746-3664
citrushills.com			
Skyview G&CC, *Lakeland*	18	[P]	863-665-4008
Slammer & Squire GC World Golf Village, *St Augustine*	18	[R]	904-940-6100
slammerandsquire.com			
Sombrero CC, *Marathon*	18	[V]	305-743-2551
sombrerocc.com			
Sorrento Par 3, *Nokomis*	9	[P]	941-966-4884
Southern Dunes G&CC, *Haines City*	18	[S]	863-421-4653
southerndunes.com			
Southern Hills Plantation Club, *Brooksville*	18	[V]	352-277-5000
southernhillsplantation.com			
Southern Woods GC, *Homosassa*	18	[V]	352-382-1200
southernwoodsgc.com			
Southport Springs GC, *Zephyrhills*	18	[P]	813-780-7637
southportsprings.com			
Southridge GC, *Deland*	18	[P]	386-736-0560
Southwinds GC, *Boca Raton*	18	[M]	561-483-1305
southwindsgolfcourse.com			
Southwood GC, *Tallahassee*	18	[P]	850-942-4653
southwoodgolf.com			
Spanish Lakes CC, *Fort Pierce*	9	[V]	772-466-0777
Spanish Lakes Fairways, *Fort Pierce*	18	[V]	772-489-0943
Spanish Lakes Golf Village, *Port St Lucie*	9	[V]	772-335-4510
Spanish Lakes I, *Port St Lucie*	9	[V]	772-878-3416
Spanish Wells G&CC, *Bonita Springs*	27	[V]	239-992-5522
spanishwellscountryclub.com			
Spessard Holland GC, *Melbourne Beach*	18	[M]	321-952-4529
golfspacecoast.com			
Spring Hill G&CC, *Spring Hill*	18	[P]	352-683-2261
springhillgolfclub.com			
Spring Lake Golf Resort, *Sebring*	36	[R]	863-655-0900
springlakegolf.com			
Spring Run GC, *Bonita Springs*	18	[P]	239-949-0707
springrun.com			
Spruce Creek CC, *Port Orange*	18	[S]	386-756-6114
sprucecreekgolf.com			
St Andrews CC of Boca Raton, *Boca Raton*	36	[V]	561-487-1110
standrewscc.com			
St Andrews Links, *Dunedin*	18	[P]	727-733-6728
saintandrewslinks.com			
St Andrews South GC, *Punta Gorda*	18	[V]	941-639-3971
standrewssouth.com			
St Augustine Shores GC, *St Augustine*	18	[S]	904-794-0303
capstonegolf.net			
St James Bay, *Carrabelle*	18	[S]	850-697-9606
stjamesbay.com			
St James GC, *Port St Lucie*	18	[P]	772-336-4653
stjamesgolfclub.net			
St Johns G&CC, *St Augustine*	18	[P]	904-940-3215
stjohnsgolf.com			
St Johns GC, *Elkton*	27	[M]	904-209-0350
sjgc.com			
St Josephs Bay CC, *Port St Joe*	18	[S]	850-227-1751
stjoebaygolf.com			
St Petersburg CC, *St Petersburg*	18	[P]	727-867-2111
stpetecc.com			
Starke G&CC, *Starke*	9	[P]	904-964-5441
Stone Creek GC, *Ocala*	18	[S]	352-854-1272
delwebb.com/stonecreek			
Stonebridge CC, *Naples*	18	[V]	239-592-5252
stonebridgecountryclub.com			
Stonebridge G&CC, *Boca Raton*	18	[P]	561-488-0808
stonebridgefl.com			

[S] = SEMI-PRIVATE [V] = PRIVATE [U] = UNIVERSITY [N] = UNIVERSITY-PRIVATE

FLORIDA — Golf Yellow Pages, 18th Edition

Stonebrook GC, *Pace*..................................18 [P] 850-994-7171
  stonebrook-golf.com
Stonecrest GC, *Summerfield*......................18 [P] 352-245-0565
  stonecrestgolfclub.com
Stonegate GC, *Kissimmee*........................36 [R] 863-427-7150
  solivita.com
Stoneybrook East GC, *Orlando*...................18 [P] 407-384-6888
  golfstoneybrookeast.com
Stoneybrook G&CC, *Sarasota*.................... 18 [V] 941-966-1800
  stoneybrook.net
Stoneybrook GC, *Estero*............................18 [P] 239-948-3933
  stoneybrookgolffm.com
Stoneybrook GC At Heritage Harbour, *Bradenton* 18 [P] 941-746-2696
  stoneybrookgolfbradenton.com
Stoneybrook West, *Winter Garden*..............18 [P] 407-877-8533
  golfstoneybrookwest.com
Sugar Cane GC, *Belle Glade*.......................18 [P] 561-996-6605
  sugarcanegolfclub.com
Sugar Mill CC, *New Smyrna Beach*.............. 27 [V] 386-426-5210
  sugarmillcc.com
Sugarloaf Mountain Golf & Town Club, *Clermont* 18 [S] 407-544-1104
  hamptongolfclubs.com/smountain.html
Sugarmill Woods CC, *Homosassa*................ 27 [V] 352-382-2663
  sugarmillwoodscc.com
Summerfield Crossing GC, *Riverview*............18 [P] 813-671-3411
  summerfieldgc.com
SummerGlen CC, *Ocala*............................18 [P] 352-307-1766
  summerglen.com
Summertree GC, *New Port Richey*.................9 [P] 727-856-0471
Sun Air GC, *Haines City*............................18 [S] 863-439-4958
  sunairgolfclub.net
Sun n Lake G&CC, *Sebring*........................36 [S] 863-385-4830
  sunlakegolfclub.com
Suncoast Golf Ctr, *Sarasota*........................9 [P] 941-351-2666
  suncoastgolfcenter.com
Sunny Hills G&CC, *Sunny Hills*....................27 [P] 850-773-3619
  sunnyhillsgolfandcountryclub.com
Sunnybreeze GC, *Arcadia*..........................27 [S] 863-494-2521
  sunnybreezegolf.com
Sunrise CC, *Sunrise*................................18 [S] 954-742-4333
  sunrisefl.gov/2golf.html
Sunrise GC, *Sarasota*...............................18 [S] 941-924-1402
  sunrisegolf.com
Sunrise Lakes Phase III, *Sunrise*..................9 [V] 954-741-8352
  sunriselakesfl.com
Sunrise Lakes Phase IV GC, *Sunrise*..............9 [R] 954-748-4567
Sunset GC, *Hollywood*..............................9 [P] 954-923-2008
Suntree GC, *Melbourne*...........................36 [P] 321-242-6235
  suntree.com
Suwannee CC, *Live Oak*............................9 [S] 386-362-1147
Suwannee River Valley GC, *Jasper*...............9 [P] 386-792-1990
Sweetwater CC, *Apopka*...........................18 [P] 407-889-4666
  sweetwatergolfandcountryclub.com
Sweetwater G&TC, *Haines City*..................18 [P] 863-956-5530
  golflink.com
Swiss Fairways, *Clermont*........................18 [S] 352-429-9065
Talis Park GC, *Naples*..............................18 [V] 239-514-1051
  talispark.com
Tampa Bay G&CC, *San Antonio*..................27 [P] 352-588-5454
  tbgolfclub.com
Tampa Palms G&CC, *Tampa*.....................18 [P] 813-972-1444
  tampa-palmscc.com

Tanglewood GC, *Milton*...........................18 [S] 850-623-6176
  tanglewood-golf.com
Tara G&CC, *Bradenton*.............................18 [V] 941-756-7775
  taragcc.com
Tarpon Springs GC, *Tarpon Springs*..............18 [M] 727-937-6906
  ci.tarpon-springs.fl.us/golfcourse.htm
Tatum Ridge Golf Links, *Sarasota*................18 [P] 941-378-4211
  tatumridgegolflinks.com
Temple Terrace G&CC, *Temple Terrace*..........18 [V] 813-988-1791
  templeterracegolf.com
Tequesta CC, *Tequesta*............................18 [V] 561-746-4501
  tequestacountryclub.net
Terra Ceia G&CC, *Palmetto*.......................18 [P] 941-729-7663
  terraceiabay.com
Terrace Hill GC, *Tampa*..............................9 [P] 813-985-4653
  terracehillgolfclub.com
Terraverde CC, *Fort Myers*...........................9 [P] 239-433-7733
The Bears Club, *Jupiter*............................18 [V] 561-626-2327
  thebearsclub.com
The Boca CC, *Boca Raton*..........................18 [V] 561-447-3865
  bocaresort.com
The Carolina Club, *Margate*.......................18 [S] 954-753-4000
  carolinagolfclub.com
The CC At Deer Run, *Casselberry*................18 [S] 407-699-9710
  deerruncc.com
The CC At Lake City, *Lake City*...................18 [S] 386-752-2266
  playsouthernoaks.com
The CC of Sebring, *Sebring*.......................18 [S] 863-382-3500
  countryclubofsebring.net
The Classics CC, *Naples*...........................18 [V] 239-732-1200
  theclassics.americangolf.com
The Claw At USF, *Tampa*..........................18 [U] 813-632-6893
  theclawatusfgolf.com
The Club at Admirals Cove - East Course, *Jupiter* 18 [V] 561-745-2630
  admiralscove.net
The Club At Admirals Cove Golf Village, *Jupiter*.. 27 [V] 561-745-2603
  admiralscove.net
The Club At Eaglebrooke, *Lakeland*..............18 [S] 863-701-0101
  eaglebrooke.com
The Club at Emerald Hills, *Hollywood*...........18 [S] 954-961-4000
  theclubatemeraldhills.com
The Club At Grandezza, *Estero*...................18 [V] 239-948-2900
  grandezzacc.com
The Club At Hidden Creek, *Navarre*..............18 [P] 850-939-4604
  hiddengolf.com
The Club At Mediterra, *Naples*...................36 [V] 239-254-3034
  mediterra-naples.com
The Club At Olde Cypress, *Naples*...............18 [V] 239-596-6857
  oldecypress.com
The Club at Pelican Bay, *Naples*..................27 [V] 239-597-2105
  theclubpelicanbay.com
The Club At Pelican Bay, North Course,
  Daytona Beach...................................18 [P] 386-756-0040
  pelicanbaycc.com
The Club At Pelican Bay, South Course,
  Daytona Beach...................................18 [S] 386-788-4653
  pelicanbaycc.com
The Club At Pointe West, *Vero Beach*...........18 [P] 772-770-4653
  pointewestflorida.com
The Club At Renaissance, *Fort Myers*............18 [V] 239-561-6335
  theclubatrenaissance.com
The Club At Strand, *Naples*.......................27 [V] 239-592-9944
  thestrandcc.com

FLORIDA

Course	Location	Holes	Type	Phone
The Club At TwinEagles,	Naples	36	[V]	239-352-2121
twineagles.com				
The Club at Winston Trails,	Lake Worth	18	[P]	561-439-3700
winstontrailsgolfclub.com				
The Club Renaissance,	Sun City Center	18	[P]	813-642-9091
clubrenaissancescc.com				
The Colony G&CC,	Bonita Springs	18	[V]	239-390-4710
thecolonygolfcc.com				
The Concession GC,	Bradenton	18	[V]	941-322-1465
theconcession.com				
The Conservatory At Hammock Beach,	Palm Coast	18	[R]	386-246-5435
hammockbeach.com				
The Deerwood CC,	Jacksonville	18	[V]	904-642-5917
deerwoodclub.com				
The Deltona Club,	Deltona	18	[S]	386-789-4911
thedeltonaclub.com				
The Dunedin CC,	Dunedin	18	[S]	727-733-7836
dunedincc.com				
The Dunes G&TC,	Sanibel	18	[S]	239-472-2535
dunesgolfsanibel.com				
The Dunes GC,	Weeki Wachee	18	[P]	352-596-7888
dunesgolfclub.com				
The Dye Preserve,	Jupiter	18	[V]	561-575-7891
thedyepreserve.com				
The Eagles GC,	Odessa	36	[S]	813-920-6681
eaglesgolf.com				
The Evergreen Club,	Palm City	18	[V]	772-286-2113
theevergreenclub.com				
The First Tee of Jacksonville,	Jacksonville	9	[P]	904-924-0401
thefirstteejacksonville.org				
The Florida Club,	Stuart	18	[P]	772-287-3680
floridaclubgolf.com				
The Forest CC,	Fort Myers	36	[V]	239-481-5700
theforestcc.com				
The Founders GC,	Sarasota	18	[V]	941-379-3701
thefoundersclub.com				
The Fox Club,	Palm City	18	[S]	772-597-4222
foxclubfl.com				
The GC At Bridgewater,	Lakeland	18	[P]	863-682-3000
golfbridgewater.com				
The GC At Cypress Head,	Port Orange	18	[M]	386-756-5449
cypressheadgolf.com				
The GC At Fiddlers Creek,	Naples	18	[V]	239-732-3030
fiddlerscreek.com				
The GC At Fleming Island,	Orange Park	18	[P]	904-269-1440
flemingislandgolf.com				
The GC At Magnolia Landing,	North Fort Myers	18	[V]	239-652-0102
magnolialandingclub.com				
The GC At Summerbrooke,	Tallahassee	18	[P]	850-894-4653
summerbrookegolf.com				
The GC of Cypress Creek,	Ruskin	27	[P]	813-634-8888
cypresscreekgolfclub.com				
The GC of Jupiter,	Jupiter	18	[P]	561-747-6262
golfclubofjupiter.com				
The GC of Quincy,	Quincy	18	[S]	850-627-8386
The Glades GC,	Naples	36	[P]	239-774-1443
gladescountryclub.com				
The Glades Resort,	Moore Haven	9	[R]	863-983-8464
thegladesresort.com				
The Golden Bear Club At Keenes Pointe,				
Windermere		18	[V]	407-876-5775
thegoldenbearclub.com				
The Golf Garden of Destin,	Destin	9	[P]	850-837-7422
The Golf Lodge At the Quarry,	Naples	18	[V]	239-304-0172
thequarrynaples.com				
The Grand Club Cypress Course,	Palm Coast	18	[R]	386-437-5807
hamptongolfclubs.com				
The Grand Club Matanzas Course,	Palm Coast	18	[R]	386-446-6330
hamptongolfclubs.com				
The Grand Club Pine Course,	Palm Coast	18	[R]	386-445-0852
hamptongolfclubs.com				
The Great Outdoors G&CC,	Titusville	18	[R]	321-269-5524
tgogolf.com				
The Groves G&CC,	Land O Lakes	18	[P]	813-996-0161
thegrovesgolfandcountryclub.com				
The Habitat GC,	Malabar	18	[M]	321-952-6312
golfspacecoast.com				
The Jim McLean Signature Course,	Miami	18	[P]	305-477-1906
doralresort.com				
The Kissimmee Oaks GC,	Kissimmee	18	[P]	407-933-4055
kissimmeeoaksgolf.com				
The Landings Yacht, G&TC,	Fort Myers	18	[V]	239-482-0242
landingsygtc.com				
The Legacy Club At Alaqua Lakes,	Longwood	18	[V]	407-444-9995
alaqualakesgolfclub.com				
The Legacy G&TC,	Port St Lucie	27	[V]	772-466-7888
legacygolfandtennis.com				
The Legends at Orange Lake,	Kissimmee	18	[R]	407-239-0000
golforangelake.com				
The Legends G&CC,	Clermont	18	[P]	352-243-1118
legendsgolforlando.com/golf/proto/legendsgolfclub/index.htm				
The Legends Walk at Orange Lake,	Kissimmee	9	[R]	407-239-0000
golforangelake.com				
The Links at 434,	Altamonte Springs	9	[P]	407-774-4653
The Links At Boynton Beach,	Boynton Beach	27	[M]	561-742-6502
boynton-beach.org				
The Links At Madison Green,	Royal Palm Beach	18	[P]	561-784-5225
madisongreengolf.com				
The Links GC,	Hudson	18	[P]	727-868-1091
The Links of Lake Bernadette,	Zephyrhills	18	[S]	813-788-7888
linksoflakebernadette.com				
The Links of Naples,	Naples	18	[P]	239-417-1313
thelinksofnaples.com				
The Links of Spruce Creek,	Summerfield	18	[P]	352-347-6172
The Little Club,	Delray Beach	18	[V]	561-278-5830
The Little Club,	Tequesta	9	[V]	561-746-1869
The Loxahatchee Club,	Jupiter	18	[V]	561-744-6168
theloxahatcheeclub.org				
The Meadows At Countrywood,	Plant City	18	[V]	813-752-4636
The Meadows CC,	Sarasota	54	[V]	941-378-5153
meadowscc.org				
The Monarch At Royal Highlands,	Leesburg	18	[P]	352-314-9000
monarchgolfclub.com				
The Moorings CC,	Naples	18	[V]	239-261-1033
mooringscc.com				
The Moors Golf & Lodging,	Milton	18	[P]	850-995-4653
moors.com				
The Oaks Club,	Osprey	36	[V]	941-966-2161
theoaksclub.com				
The Old Collier GC,	Naples	18	[V]	239-597-9898
theoldcolliergc.com				
The Palencia Club,	St Augustine	18	[V]	904-599-9030
vivapalencia.com				
The PGA CC,	Port St Lucie	18	[V]	772-340-1911
pgavillage.com				

[S] = SEMI-PRIVATE [V] = PRIVATE [U] = UNIVERSITY [N] = UNIVERSITY-PRIVATE

FLORIDA — Golf Yellow Pages, 18th Edition

The Plantation at Ponte Vedra, *Ponte Vedra Beach* 18 [V] 904-543-2960
theplantationpv.com
The Plantation G&CC, *Fort Myers* .... 18 [V] 239-561-8650
plantationgolfcc.com
The Plantation GC, *Leesburg* .... 36 [P] 352-365-0526
plantationatleesburggolf.com
The Preserve GC At Tara, *Bradenton* .... 18 [P] 941-756-2944
golfthepreserve.com
The President CC, *West Palm Beach* .... 36 [V] 561-686-4700
presidentcc.com
The Ravines C&Lodge, *Middleburg* .... 18 [V] 904-282-0028
theravinesclubandlodge.com
The Reserve at Orange Lake, *Kissimmee* ...... 27 [R] 407-239-0000
golforangelake.com
The River Club, *Bradenton* .... 18 [S] 941-751-4211
riverclubgc.com
The Riverside GC, *Ruskin* .... 18 [P] 813-645-2000
allriversideclub.com
The Rookery At Marco, *Naples* .... 18 [R] 239-389-6600
therookeryatmarco.com
The Saints At Port St Lucie GC, *Port St Lucie* ...... 18 [M] 772-398-2901
cityofpsl.com/golf
The Sanctuary GC, *Sanibel* .... 18 [V] 239-472-6223
sanctuarygc.net
The Spruce Creek Preserve GC, *Dunnellon* .... 18 [S] 352-861-3131
playthepreserve.com
The St Andrews Club, *Delray Beach* .... 18 [V] 561-272-5050
standrewsclub.org
The Tesoro Club, *Port St Lucie* .... 36 [V] 772-345-4030
golfandwater.com
The Tides GC, *Seminole* .... 18 [V] 727-392-5345
tidesgc.com
The Venice G&CC, *Venice* .... 18 [V] 941-493-3400
venicegolfandcc.com
The Villages Exec Golf Trail-26 Par 3, *Lady Lake* 234 [V] 352-753-3396
golfthevillages.com
The Vinoy Club, *St Petersburg* .... 18 [R] 727-896-8000
vinoyclub.com
The Wanderers Club, *Wellington* .... 18 [S] 561-795-3510
wanderersclubwellington.com
The Westin Diplomat Golf & Spa, *Hallandale Beach* 18 [R] 954-883-4444
diplomatgolfresortandspa.com
Tiburon GC, *Naples* .... 36 [R] 239-594-2040
tiburongcnaples.com
Tierra Del Sol G&CC, *The Villages* .... 18 [S] 352-750-4600
golfthevillages.com
Tiger Point G&CC, *Gulf Breeze* .... 27 [S] 850-932-1333
tigerpointclub.com
Timacuan G&CC, *Lake Mary* .... 18 [S] 407-321-0010
golftimacuan.com
Timber Creek GC, *Bradenton* .... 9 [P] 941-794-8381
Timber Greens CC, *New Port Richey* .... 18 [P] 727-372-0789
timbergreens.net
Timber Pines GC, *Spring Hill* .... 63 [V] 352-666-2311
timberpines.com
Timuquana CC, *Jacksonville* .... 18 [V] 904-388-2664
timuquana.net
Tomoka Oaks G&CC, *Ormond Beach* .... 18 [P] 386-677-5931
tomokaoaks.com
Torrey Oaks GC, *Bowling Green* .... 18 [S] 863-767-0302
TPC Eagle Trace, *Coral Springs* .... 18 [V] 954-753-7222
tpceagletrace.com
TPC of Tampa Bay, *Lutz* .... 18 [P] 813-949-0090
tpctampabay.com

TPC Prestancia, *Sarasota* .... 36 [V] 941-922-8800
tpcprestancia.com
TPC Sawgrass, *Ponte Vedra Beach* .... 36 [R] 904-273-3230
tpcsawgrass.com
TPC Treviso Bay, *Naples* .... 18 [V] 239-643-1414
tpctrevisobay.com
Travelers Rest Resort Golf, *Dade City* .... 9 [R] 352-588-2013
travelersrestresort.com
Treasure Bay G&TC, *Treasure Island* .... 9 [M] 727-360-6062
treasurebaygolfandtennis.com
Triple S Golf Ranch, *Dade City* .... 18 [R] 352-567-6622
Trump Intl GC -West Palm Beach, *West Palm Beach* 27 [V] 561-682-0700
trumpinternationalpalmbeaches.com
Turkey Creek G&CC, *Alachua* .... 18 [S] 386-462-4655
plantationoaksgolf.com
Turnberry Isle Resort & Club, *Aventura* .... 36 [R] 305-932-6200
turnberryisle.com
Turnbull Bay GC, *New Smyrna Beach* .... 18 [P] 386-427-8727
turnbullbay.com
Turtle Creek Club, *Tequesta* .... 18 [V] 561-746-8884
turtlecreekclub.com
Turtle Creek GC, *Rockledge* .... 18 [P] 321-632-2520
turtlecreekgolfclub.com
Tuscawilla CC, *Winter Springs* .... 18 [V] 407-366-1851
tuscawillacc.com
Twin Brooks GC, *St Petersburg* .... 18 [M] 727-893-7445
stpete.org
Twin Isles CC, *Punta Gorda* .... 18 [V] 941-637-1612
twinislescc.org
Twin Lakes Reserve & GC, *Umatilla* .... 9 [P] 352-669-2222
Twin Rivers GC, *Oviedo* .... 18 [P] 407-366-1211
twinriversgolfclub.com
Twisted Oaks GC, *Beverly Hills* .... 18 [S] 352-746-6257
Univ Park CC, *University Park* .... 27 [S] 941-359-9999
universitypark-fl.com
Valencia G&CC, *Naples* .... 18 [P] 239-352-0777
valenciagolfandcountryclub.com
Vanderbilt CC, *Naples* .... 18 [V] 239-348-2663
vanderbiltcountryclub.com
Vasari CC, *Bonita Springs* .... 18 [V] 239-596-0645
vasaricountryclub.com
Venetian Bay GC, *New Smyrna Beach* .... 18 [V] 386-424-5775
venetianbaygolf.com
Venetian G&RiverC, *North Venice* .... 18 [V] 941-483-4811
venetiangolfandriverclub.com
Venice East GC, *Venice* .... 18 [P] 941-493-0005
Ventura CC, *Orlando* .... 18 [S] 407-277-2640
venturacountryclub.org
Verandah GC, *Fort Myers* .... 36 [V] 239-694-4229
verandah.com
Vero Beach CC, *Vero Beach* .... 18 [V] 772-567-3320
verobeachcountryclub.com
Via Mizner G&CC, *Boca Raton* .... 18 [V] 561-392-7991
viamiznergcc.com
Victoria Hills GC, *DeLand* .... 18 [P] 386-738-6000
victoriahillsgolf.com
Viera East GC, *Viera* .... 18 [M] 321-639-6500
vieragolf.com
Villa Del Ray GC, *Delray Beach* .... 18 [P] 561-498-1444
villadelraygc.com
Village GC, *Royal Palm Beach* .... 18 [P] 561-793-1400
thevillagegolfclub.com
Village Green GC of Sarasota, *Sarasota* .... 18 [S] 941-922-9500
villagegreengolfclub.com

[A] = MILITARY   [M] = MUNICIPAL   [P] = PUBLIC   [R] = RESORT

Golf Yellow Pages, 18th Edition — GEORGIA

Villages of Country Creek GC, *Estero* .... 18 [S] 239-947-3840
  villagesatcountrycreek.org
Vineyards CC, *Naples* .... 36 [V] 239-353-0505
  vineyardscountryclub.net
Vista Plantation GC, *Vero Beach* .... 18 [S] 772-569-2223
  myvistagolf.com
Walden Lake G&CC, *Plant City* .... 36 [P] 813-754-8575
  waldenlakegolf.com
Waldorf Astoria GC, *Orlando* .... 18 [R] 407-597-3782
  waldorfastoriagolfclub.com
Walkabout G&CC, *Mims* .... 18 [R] 321-385-2099
  walkaboutgolf.com
Walt Disney World GC, *Lake Buena Vista* .... 45 [R] 407-938-4653
  golf.disneyworld.com
Walt Disney World-Lake Buena Vista,
  Lake Buena Vista .... 18 [R] 407-938-4653
  golf.disneyworld.com
Walt Disney World-Osprey Ridge, *Lake Buena Vista* 18 [R] 407-938-4653
  golf.disneyworld.com
Water Oak CC Estates, *Lady Lake* .... 18 [P] 352-753-3905
  wateroakgolf.net
Waterford GC, *Venice* .... 27 [S] 941-484-6621
  golfinvenice.com
Waterlefe G&RiverC, *Bradenton* .... 18 [S] 941-744-0393
  waterlefegolfandriverclub.com
Wedgefield GC, *Orlando* .... 18 [S] 407-568-2116
  wedgefieldgolf.com
Wedgewood GC, *Grand Island* .... 9 [S] 352-589-0072
Wedgewood GC, *Lakeland* .... 18 [S] 863-858-4451
Wekiva GC, *Longwood* .... 18 [S] 407-862-5113
  wekivagc.com
Wentworth GC, *Tarpon Springs* .... 18 [V] 727-942-4760
  wentworthgolfclub.org
West Bay Beach & GC, *Estero* .... 18 [V] 239-948-3482
  westbayclub.com
West End GC, *Newberry* .... 18 [P] 352-332-2721
  westendgolf.com
West Orange CC, *Winter Garden* .... 18 [V] 407-656-1914
  woclub.com
West Palm Beach GC, *West Palm Beach* .... 18 [M] 561-582-2019
  wpalmbeachgc.com
Westchase GC, *Tampa* .... 18 [P] 813-854-2331
  westchasegc.com
Westchester G&CC, *Boynton Beach* .... 45 [P] 561-734-6300
  westchesterccc.com
Westgate River Ranch Resort, *River Ranch* .... 9 [R] 863-692-0727
  westgateriverranch.com
Westminster GC, *Lehigh Acres* .... 18 [S] 239-368-1110
  westminster-golf.com
Weston Hills CC, *Weston* .... 36 [V] 954-384-4653
  westonhillsgolfclub.com
Westview CC, *Miami* .... 18 [V] 305-685-2411
  westviewcc.com
Whiskey Creek CC, *Fort Myers* .... 18 [V] 239-481-3021
  whiskeycreekcc.com
White Oak Plantation, *Yulee* .... 18 [P] 904-225-3218
Whiting Field Navy GC, *Milton* .... 18 [A] 850-623-7348
Wildcat Run G&CC, *Estero* .... 18 [V] 239-495-3031
  wildcatrunec.com
Wilderness CC, *Naples* .... 18 [V] 239-261-5505
  wildernessccc.com
Wildwood GC, *Crawfordville* .... 18 [S] 850-926-4653
  wildwoodforgolf.com

Williston Highlands G&CC, *Williston* .... 18 [S] 352-528-2520
  willistongolf.com
Willoughby GC, *Stuart* .... 18 [V] 772-220-6000
  willoughbygolfclub.com
Willow Brook GC, *Winter Haven* .... 18 [M] 863-291-5899
  mywinterhaven.com
Willow Lakes RV & Golf Resort, *Titusville* .... 9 [R] 321-264-4653
  willowlakes.com
Windermere CC, *Windermere* .... 18 [V] 407-876-4410
  windermeregolf.com
Windsor CC, *Vero Beach* .... 18 [V] 772-388-8440
  windsorflorida.com
Windsor Parke GC, *Jacksonville* .... 18 [P] 904-223-4653
  windsorparke.com
Windstar on Naples Bay, *Naples* .... 18 [V] 239-775-3500
  windstarclub.com
Windswept Dunes GC, *Freeport* .... 18 [P] 850-835-1847
  windsweptdunes.com
Windy Harbor GC, *Mayport* .... 18 [A] 904-270-5380
Winter Park CC, *Winter Park* .... 9 [M] 407-599-3339
  winterparkcountryclub.com
Winter Pines GC, *Winter Park* .... 18 [P] 407-671-3172
  winterpines.com
Woodfield CC, *Boca Raton* .... 18 [V] 561-994-1000
  woodfield.org
Woodlands CC, *Tamarac* .... 36 [V] 954-731-2500
  woodlandscountryclub.net
Woodlands GC & Dr Rg, *Parrish* .... 9 [P] 941-729-8999
  golfthewoodlands.com
Woodmont CC, *Tamarac* .... 36 [S] 954-722-4300
  woodmontcountryclub.net
World Woods GC, *Brooksville* .... 45 [R] 352-796-5500
  worldwoods.com
Worthington CC, *Bonita Springs* .... 18 [V] 239-495-1750
  worthingtoncc.net
Wycliffe G&CC, *Wellington* .... 36 [V] 561-641-2000
  wycliffecc.com
Wyndemere CC, *Naples* .... 27 [V] 239-263-1700
  wyndemere.com
Wynmoor GC, *Coconut Creek* .... 18 [V] 954-978-2677
Yacht & Country Club, *Stuart* .... 18 [V] 772-283-1966
  yachtandcountryclub.com
YMCA Par 3 Home of the First Tee-Lakeland,
  Lakeland .... 9 [P] 863-577-0236
  thefirstteelakeland.org
Zellwood Station CC, *Zellwood* .... 18 [S] 407-886-3303
  zellwoodgolf.com
Zephyrhills Muni GC, *Zephyrhills* .... 18 [M] 813-782-0714

GEORGIA

Achasta GC, *Dahlonega* .... 18 [P] 888-988-6222
  achasta.com
Alfred Tup Holmes GC, *Atlanta* .... 18 [M] 404-753-6158
  alfredtup.americangolf.com
Alpharetta Ath Club East, *Alpharetta* .... 18 [V] 770-475-2300
  alpharettaac.com
Alpharetta Ath Club West, *Alpharetta* .... 18 [V] 770-410-9360
  alpharettaac.com
American Legion GC, *Lagrange* .... 9 [P] 706-884-4379
Ansley GC, *Atlanta* .... 9 [V] 404-897-7717
  ansleygolfclub.org
Ansley GC At Settindown Creek, *Roswell* .... 18 [V] 770-640-4620
  ansleygolfclub.org

[S] = SEMI-PRIVATE   [V] = PRIVATE   [U] = UNIVERSITY   [N] = UNIVERSITY-PRIVATE

GEORGIA
Golf Yellow Pages, 18th Edition

Apple Mountain GC, *Clarkesville*	18 [P]	706-754-2255	
applemountaingolfga.com			
Applewood GC, *Keysville*	18 [P]	706-554-0028	
Appling CC, *Baxley*	9 [S]	912-367-3582	
Arrowhead CC, *Jasper*	9 [V]	706-692-5634	
arrowheadgolf.org			
Arrowhead Pointe At Lake Richard B Russell,			
Elberton	18 [M]	706-283-6000	
golfgeorgia.org			
Athens CC, *Athens*	27 [V]	706-354-7111	
athenscountryclub.com			
Atlanta Ath Club, *Johns Creek*	36 [V]	770-448-2166	
atlantaathleticclub.org			
Atlanta CC, *Marietta*	18 [V]	770-953-2100	
atlantacountryclub.org			
Atlanta National GC, *Alpharetta*	18 [V]	770-442-8801	
atlantanationalgolfclub.com			
Augusta CC, *Augusta*	18 [V]	706-736-5322	
augcc.com			
Augusta Muni GC, *Augusta*	18 [M]	706-731-9344	
Augusta National GC, *Augusta*	27 [V]	706-667-6000	
masters.org			
Bacon Park GC, *Savannah*	27 [M]	912-354-2625	
baconparkgolf.com			
Bainbridge CC, *Bainbridge*	18 [S]	229-246-1986	
bainbridgecountryclub.com			
Barrens GC, *Doerun*	18 [P]	229-782-7172	
Bartram Trail GC, *Evans*	18 [P]	706-210-4681	
bartramtrailgolfclub.org			
Battlefield GC, *Ringgold*	18 [V]	706-866-1363	
battlefieldgolf.com			
Bear Creek GC, *Monroe*	18 [P]	770-207-5511	
bearcreekmonroe.com			
Bears Best Atlanta GC, *Suwanee*	18 [P]	678-714-2582	
bearsbest.com			
Beaver Kreek GC, *Douglas*	18 [S]	912-384-8230	
Beaver Lake G&CC, *Gay*	18 [P]	706-538-6994	
Beckart Employees Athletic Assoc, *Lindale*	9 [S]	706-234-8010	
Belle Meade CC, *Thomson*	18 [S]	706-595-1553	
bellemeadecountryclub.com			
Bent Tree GC, *Jasper*	18 [V]	770-893-2626	
bent-tree.com			
Bentwater GC, *Acworth*	18 [S]	770-529-9554	
bentwatergolfclub.com			
Berkeley Hills CC, *Duluth*	18 [V]	770-448-4661	
berkeleyhillscc.org			
Big Canoe GC, *Jasper*	27 [R]	706-268-3323	
bigcanoe.com			
Black Creek GC, *Ellabell*	18 [S]	912-858-4653	
blackcreekgolfclub.com			
Blueberry Plantation G&CC, *Alma*	18 [P]	912-632-2772	
blueberryplantation.com			
Bobby Jones GC, *Atlanta*	18 [M]	404-355-1009	
bobbyjones.americangolf.com			
Bowden GC, *Macon*	18 [P]	478-742-1610	
cityofmacon.net			
Bowdon GC, *Bowdon*	18 [P]	770-258-3477	
Braelinn GC, *Peachtree City*	18 [V]	770-631-3100	
canongategolf.com			
Brasstown Valley Resort & Spa, *Young Harris*	18 [R]	706-379-4613	
brasstownvalley.com			
Brazells Creek At Gordonia Alatamaha, *Reidsville*	18 [M]	912-557-7745	
golfgeorgia.org			
Briar Creek CC, *Sylvania*	9 [V]	912-863-4161	
Brickyard At Riverside GC, *Macon*	18 [V]	478-477-6765	
brickyardgolf.com			
Brickyard Plantation GC, *Americus*	27 [S]	229-874-1234	
brickyardgolfclub.com			
Bridgemill Ath Club, *Canton*	18 [P]	770-345-5500	
hmsgolf.com			
Bridgewood GC, *Macon*	9 [P]	478-788-5812	
Brookfield CC, *Roswell*	18 [V]	770-993-1990	
brookfieldcountryclub.com			
Brookstone G&CC, *Acworth*	18 [V]	770-425-8500	
brookstonecc.com			
Browns Mill GC, *Atlanta*	18 [M]	404-366-3573	
brownsmill.americangolf.com			
Brunswick CC, *Brunswick*	18 [V]	912-264-4377	
brunswickcountryclub.com			
Bull Creek GC, *Midland*	36 [M]	706-561-1614	
columbusga.org/bullcreek/index.htm			
Butternut Creek GC, *Blairsville*	18 [M]	706-439-6097	
butternutcreekgolf.com			
Cabin Creek GC, *Griffin*	18 [V]	770-227-9794	
Cairo CC, *Cairo*	18 [V]	229-377-4506	
cairocountryclub.net			
Calhoun Elks GC, *Calhoun*	18 [S]	706-629-4091	
Callahan Golf Links, *Waleska*	18 [P]	770-720-1900	
callahangolflinks.com			
Callaway Gardens Golf Resort, *Pine Mountain*	36 [R]	706-663-2281	
callawaygardens.com			
Callier Springs CC, *Rome*	9 [V]	706-234-1691	
Candler Park GC, *Atlanta*	9 [M]	404-371-1260	
candlerpark.americangolf.com			
Canongate At Eagle Watch GC, *Woodstock*	18 [V]	770-591-1000	
canongategolf.com			
Canongate At Georgia National GC, *McDonough*	18 [V]	770-914-9994	
canongategolf.com			
Canongate At Healy Point CC, *Macon*	18 [V]	478-743-1495	
canongategolf.com			
Canongate At Heron Bay, *Locust Grove*	18 [V]	770-320-8500	
canongategolf.com			
Canongate At Olde Atlanta GC, *Suwanee*	18 [V]	770-497-0097	
canongategolf.com			
Canongate At Planterra Ridge, *Peachtree City*	18 [V]	770-487-8141	
canongategolf.com			
Canongate at River Forest, *Forsyth*	18 [V]	478-974-0974	
canongategolf.com			
Canongate GC, *Sharpsburg*	36 [V]	770-463-3949	
canongategolf.com			
Canongate Golf At Sun City Peachtree, *Griffin*	18 [V]	678-242-1933	
canongategolf.com			
Canongate On White Oak GC, *Newnan*	36 [V]	770-251-6700	
canongategolf.com			
Canton GC, *Canton*	9 [V]	770-479-2772	
Canyon Ridge GC, *Rising Fawn*	18 [V]	706-398-0882	
golfcanyonridge.com			
Capitol City Club Brookhaven, *Atlanta*	18 [V]	404-233-2121	
capitalcityclub.org			
Capitol City Club Crabapple, *Woodstock*	18 [V]	770-667-6931	
capitalcityclub.org			
Cartersville CC, *Cartersville*	18 [V]	706-382-4882	
cartersvillecountryclub.com			
Cateechee GC, *Hartwell*	18 [P]	706-856-4653	
cateechee.com			

[A] = MILITARY [M] = MUNICIPAL [P] = PUBLIC [R] = RESORT

Golf Yellow Pages, 18th Edition — GEORGIA

CC of Columbus, *Columbus* .... 18 [V] 706-322-6869
  ccofcolumbus.com
CC of Gwinnett, *Snellville* .... 18 [S] 770-978-7755
  countryclubofgwinnett.com
CC of Roswell, *Roswell* .... 18 [V] 770-475-7800
  ccroswell.com
CC of the South, *Johns Creek* .... 18 [V] 770-475-6779
  thecountryclubofthesouth.com
Cedar Creek G&CC, *Buena Vista* .... 9 [S] 229-649-3381
Cedar Lake GC, *Loganville* .... 18 [P] 770-466-4043
  cedarlakegolf.com
Cedar Valley GC, *Cedartown* .... 18 [S] 770-748-9671
Cedars GC, *Zebulon* .... 18 [S] 770-567-8808
Celebrity GC International, *Tucker* .... 27 [P] 770-493-4653
  celebritygolfclub.com
Champions Retreat GC, *Evans* .... 27 [V] 706-854-6960
  championsretreat.net
Chapel Hills G&CC, *Douglasville* .... 18 [V] 770-949-0030
  canongategolf.com
Charlie Yates GC, *Atlanta* .... 18 [P] 404-373-4655
  charlieyatesgolfcourse.com
Chateau Elan GC, *Braselton* .... 45 [P] 800-233-9463
  chateauelan.com
Chattahoochee GC, *Gainesville* .... 18 [M] 770-532-0066
  gainesville.org
Cherokee G&CC, *Cedartown* .... 18 [V] 770-748-2800
Cherokee Golf Ctr, *Woodstock* .... 9 [P] 770-924-2062
Cherokee Rose CC, *Hinesville* .... 18 [S] 912-876-5503
Cherokee Run GC, *Conyers* .... 18 [P] 770-785-7904
  cherokeerun.com
Cherokee Town & CC, *Atlanta* .... 36 [V] 770-993-4401
  cherokeetcc.org
Chestatee GC, *Dawsonville* .... 18 [P] 706-216-7336
  chestateegolf.net
Chicopee Woods GC, *Gainesville* .... 27 [P] 770-534-7322
  chicopeewoodsgolfcourse.com
Circlestone CC, *Adel* .... 18 [S] 229-896-3893
  ccscrosby.com/CircleStone
City Club Marietta, *Marietta* .... 18 [R] 770-528-4653
  cityclubmarietta.com
Coastal Pines GC, *Brunswick* .... 18 [P] 912-261-0503
  coastalpinesgolf.com
Cobblestone GC, *Acworth* .... 18 [M] 770-917-5151
  cobblestonegolf.com
College Park Muni GC, *College Park* .... 9 [P] 404-761-0731
  collegeparkgolfcourse.com
Collins Hill GC, *Lawrenceville* .... 18 [S] 770-822-5400
  collinshillgolf.com
Community GC, *Douglas* .... 9 [U] 912-384-7353
Coosa CC, *Rome* .... 18 [V] 706-234-2200
  coosacountryclub.org
Cordele Crisp Municipal GC, *Cordele* .... 9 [M] 229-276-2797
Cottonfields GC, *McDonough* .... 18 [S] 770-914-1442
  cottonfieldsgolf.com
Country Land GC, *Cumming* .... 18 [R] 770-887-0006
  countrylandgolf.com
Country Oaks GC, *Thomasville* .... 18 [M] 229-225-4333
  countryoaksgolfcourse.org
Coweta Club, *Newnan* .... 18 [S] 770-683-4727
  cowetaclub.com
Creekside G&CC, *Hiram* .... 18 [P] 770-445-7655
  creeksidegolf.com
Crooked Creek GC, *Baxley* .... 9 [P] 912-367-6300
Crooked Oak GC, *Colquitt* .... 18 [M] 229-758-9200
  golfcrookedoak.com
Cross Creek GC, *Atlanta* .... 18 [P] 404-352-5612
  crosscreek-atlanta.com
Crosswinds GC, *Savannah* .... 27 [P] 912-966-1909
  crosswindsgolfclub.com
Crystal Falls GC, *Dawsonville* .... 18 [R] 770-894-4972
  crystalfallsgc.com
Crystal Lake G&CC, *Hampton* .... 18 [P] 770-471-3233
  crystallakecc.com
Currahee Club, *Toccoa* .... 18 [R] 706-827-1800
  curraheeclub.com
Cuscowilla on Lake Oconee, *Eatonton* .... 18 [S] 706-484-0050
  cuscowilla.com
Dalton G&CC, *Dalton* .... 18 [V] 706-259-8547
  daltongcc.org
Dawson CC, *Dawson* .... 9 [V] 229-995-2255
Deer Trail CC, *Barnesville* .... 18 [V] 770-358-0349
Deer Trail CC, *Commerce* .... 9 [S] 706-335-3987
Dodge County GC, *Eastman* .... 9 [P] 478-374-3616
Dogwood GC, *Austell* .... 18 [S] 770-941-2202
  dogwoodgolf.org
Donalsonville CC, *Donalsonville* .... 18 [S] 229-524-2955
  donalsonvillecountryclub.com
Double Oaks GC, *Commerce* .... 18 [P] 706-335-8100
  doubleoaksgolfclub.net
Doublegate CC, *Albany* .... 18 [V] 229-436-6501
  doublegatecc.com
Douglas G&CC, *Douglas* .... 18 [V] 912-383-4653
  douglasgolf.net
Druid Hills GC, *Atlanta* .... 18 [V] 404-377-1768
  dhgc.org
Dublin CC, *Dublin* .... 18 [V] 478-272-1549
  dublincountryclub.com
Dunwoody CC, *Atlanta* .... 18 [V] 770-394-4492
  dunwoodycc.org
Durham Lakes CC, *Fairburn* .... 18 [P] 770-306-7200
  durhamlakes.com
Eagle Creek GC, *Statesboro* .... 18 [P] 912-839-3933
Eagles Brooke G&CC, *Locust Grove* .... 18 [V] 770-954-1999
  eaglesbrooke.com
Eagles Landing CC, *Stockbridge* .... 27 [V] 770-389-2000
  eagleslandingcc.com
East Lake GC, *Atlanta* .... 18 [V] 404-373-5722
  eastlakegolfclub.com
Echelon GC, *Alpharetta* .... 18 [V] 770-888-4653
  echelonliving.com
Elberton CC, *Elberton* .... 18 [V] 706-283-5921
Fairfield Plantation G&CC, *Villa Rica* ..... 18 [R] 770-836-1112
  fairfieldplantationgolf.com
Fargo GC, *Fargo* .... 9 [M] 912-637-5106
Fayetteville GC, *Fayetteville* .... 18 [P] 770-460-1098
  fayettevillegc.com
Fields Ferry GC, *Calhoun* .... 18 [M] 706-625-5666
  fieldsferry.net
Fieldstone CC, *Conyers* .... 18 [S] 770-483-4372
Flat Creek CC, *Peachtree City* .... 27 [V] 770-487-8140
  canongategolf.com
Flint River Muni GC, *Albany* .... 18 [M] 229-430-5267
Forest Heights CC, *Statesboro* .... 18 [V] 912-764-3084
  forestheightscc.com
Forest Hills GC, *Augusta* .... 18 [U] 706-733-0001
  theforesthillsgolfcourse.com

[S] = SEMI-PRIVATE [V] = PRIVATE [U] = UNIVERSITY [N] = UNIVERSITY-PRIVATE

GEORGIA
Golf Yellow Pages, 18th Edition

Forest Lakes GC, *Tifton*..........................9 [U] 229-382-7626
 abac.edu
Forsyth GC, *Forsyth*..............................18 [P] 478-994-5328
Four Seasons GC, *Wrens*.....................18 [S] 706-547-4131
Fox Creek GC, *Smyrna*........................18 [M] 770-435-1000
 legacyfoxcreek.com
Fox Run CC, *Macon*.............................18 [S] 478-757-8358
 foxruncountryclub.com
Francis Lake GC, *Lake Park*................18 [P] 229-559-7961
 francislake.com
Frederica GC, *St Simons Island*...........18 [V] 912-634-6900
 fredericamembers.com
GC at Osprey Cove, *St Marys*.............18 [V] 912-882-5575
 hamptongolfclubs.com
GC of South Georgia, *Tifton*...............18 [P] 229-386-4653
 golfclubofsouthgeorgia.com
Georgia Vets Memorial-Blackshear Resort, *Cordele* 18 [R] 229-276-2377
 lakeblackshearresort.com
Glen Arven CC, *Thomasville*................18 [V] 229-226-1780
 glenarven.com
Glynco GC, *Brunswick*............................9 [P] 912-264-9521
Godwin Creek GC, *Columbus*................9 [P] 706-324-0583
 thefirstteecolumbusgeorgia.org
Golden Leaf G&CC, *Cairo*....................18 [P] 229-872-3907
Golf Junction, *Auburn*............................9 [P] 770-586-5276
Gordon Lakes GC, *Fort Gordon*..........27 [A] 706-791-2433
 fortgordon.com
Goshen Plantation GC, *Augusta*........18 [S] 706-793-1168
 goshenplantation.com
Grand Island GC, *Albany*....................18 [M] 229-878-0071
 grandislandclub.com
Great Waters at Reynolds Plantation, *Eatonton*...18 [R] 706-485-0235
 reynoldsplantation.com
Green Acres G&RecC, *Dexter*..............18 [S] 478-875-3110
 greenacresgolfclub.com
Green Island CC, *Columbus*.................18 [V] 706-324-3706
 greenislandcc.org
Green Meadows GC, *Augusta*............18 [V] 706-798-1533
Green Valley Greens GC, *Cartersville*....9 [P] 770-382-8510
Greene County CC, *Union Point*.........18 [V] 706-486-4513
Greystone GC, *Douglasville*.................18 [P] 706-489-9608
 greystonegolfga.com
Griffin Bell Golf & Conf Center, *Americus*............18 [P] 229-924-2914
 gsw.edu/golf
Griffin CC, *Griffin*.................................18 [V] 770-228-4744
Griffin GC, *Griffin*...............................18 [M] 770-229-6615
 cityofgriffin.com
Hamilton Mill GC, *Dacula*....................18 [V] 770-945-4653
 canongategolf.com
Hammers Glen G&CC, *Homer*............18 [P] 706-677-3333
 hammersglen.com
Hampton Club-The King&Prince GC,
 St Simons Island................................18 [R] 912-634-0255
 hamptonclub.com
Hampton Golf Village, *Cumming*........18 [P] 770-205-7070
 hamptongolfvillage.net
Harbor Club, *Greensboro*.....................18 [R] 706-453-4414
 harborclub.com
Hartwell GC, *Hartwell*..........................18 [S] 706-376-8161
 hartwellgolf.com
Hawks Point GC, *Vidalia*......................18 [S] 912-537-9256
 hawkspointgolfclub.com

Hawks Ridge GC, *Ball Ground*..............27 [V] 770-205-6886
 hawksridge.com
Henderson GC, *Savannah*....................18 [M] 912-920-4653
 hendersongolfclub.com
Hickory Hills GC, *Jackson*.....................27 [S] 770-775-2433
Hickory Ridge GC, *Meansville*..............18 [P] 706-648-2955
 hickoryridgecourse.com
High Point GC, *Chickamauga*.................9 [P] 706-931-2487
Highland CC, *Lagrange*.........................18 [V] 706-882-3026
 highlandcountryclub.net
Highland GC, *Conyers*...........................18 [S] 770-483-4235
 highlandgolf.com
Highland Walk At Victoria Bryant, *Royston*........18 [M] 706-245-6770
 georgiagolf.com
Hinson Hills Golf Ctr, *Douglas*..............18 [P] 912-384-8984
Hogansville GC, *Hogansville*..................9 [P] 706-637-4538
Holiday Hills CC, *Gordon*.....................18 [V] 478-628-5150
Honey Creek CC, *Conyers*....................18 [S] 770-483-6343
 honeycreekgolf.com
Horseshoe Bend CC, *Roswell*...............18 [V] 770-992-1818
 horseshoebendcc.com
Houston Lake CC, *Perry*......................18 [P] 478-218-5252
 houstonlake.com
Houston Springs Resort & GC, *Perry*.....9 [R] 478-988-8200
 houstonsprings.com
Hunter GC, *Savannah*.........................18 [A] 912-315-9115
 stewartmwr.com
Hunter Pope CC, *Monticello*................18 [P] 706-468-6222
Idle Hour G&CC, *Macon*......................18 [V] 478-477-2092
 ihcgolf.com
Indian Creek GC, *Covington*................18 [P] 770-385-0064
 indiancreekgolfclub.net
Indian Hills CC, *Marietta*.....................27 [V] 770-971-7663
 indianhillscc.com
Indian Trace GC, *Chatsworth*..............18 [P] 706-695-7353
Innsbruck Resort & GC, *Helen*.............18 [R] 706-878-2100
 innsbruckgolfclub.com
Ironwood GC, *Cordele*.........................18 [S] 229-535-3014
Jekyll Island Golf Resort, *Jekyll Island*.................63 [R] 912-635-2368
 golf.jekyllisland.com
Jennings Mill CC, *Bogart*.....................18 [V] 706-548-1852
 jenningsmillclub.com
John A White GC, *Atlanta*.....................9 [M] 404-756-1868
 thefirstteeatlanta.org
Johnson County CC, *Wrightsville*..........9 [V] 478-864-3301
Jones Creek GC, *Evans*........................18 [P] 706-860-4228
 jonescreekgolfclub.com
Kinderlou Forest GC, *Valdosta*.............18 [S] 229-219-2300
 kinderlou.com
Kingwood GC & Resort, *Clayton*..........18 [R] 706-212-4100
 kingwoodresort.com
Kraftsmans Club, *Rome*........................9 [P] 706-235-9377
La Vida CC, *Savannah*...........................9 [V] 912-925-2440
Lafayette GC, *La Fayette*....................18 [M] 706-639-1580
 cityoflafayettega.org
Lake Jonesco GC, *Gray*........................18 [M] 478-986-3206
Lake Spivey GC, *Jonesboro*.................27 [S] 770-477-9836
 lakespivey.net
Lakeview G&CC, *Blackshear*................18 [P] 912-449-4411
Landings Club - Deer Creek, *Savannah*............18 [V] 912-598-2535
 landingsclub.com
Landings Club - Marshwood/Magnolia, *Savannah* 36 [V] 912-598-2535
 landingsclub.com

52   [A] = MILITARY   [M] = MUNICIPAL   [P] = PUBLIC   [R] = RESORT

Golf Yellow Pages, 18th Edition — GEORGIA

Landings Club - Oakridge, *Savannah* .... 18 [V] 912-598-2535
landingsclub.com
Landings Club - Palmetto/Plantation, *Savannah* 36 [V] 912-598-2535
landingsclub.com
Landings GC, *Warner Robins* .... 27 [S] 478-923-5222
landingsgolfclub.com
Lane Creek GC, *Bishop* .... 18 [P] 706-769-6699
lanecreekgolfclub.com
Lanier GC, *Cumming* .... 18 [P] 770-887-6114
laniergolfclub.com
Laurel Island Links, *Kingsland* .... 18 [P] 912-729-7277
laurelislandlinks.com
Laurel Springs GC, *Suwanee* .... 18 [V] 770-884-0064
laurelspringsclub.com
Legacy Links At Windy Hill, *Smyrna* .... 18 [M] 770-434-6331
legacyfoxcreek.com
Legacy on Lanier GC, *Buford* .... 18 [V] 678-318-7861
lakelanierislands.com
Little Fishing Creek GC, *Milledgeville* .... 18 [M] 478-445-0796
Little Mountain GC, *Ellenwood* .... 18 [P] 770-981-7921
Little Ocmulgee At Wallace Adams Course,
  Mc Rae .... 18 [M] 229-868-6651
littleocmulgee.com
Long Shadow GC, *Madison* .... 18 [P] 706-431-6638
madisonlakes.net
Lookout Mountain GC, *Lookout Mountain* .... 18 [V] 706-820-0719
lookoutmountaingolfclub.com
Lost Plantation GC, *Rincon* .... 18 [S] 912-826-2092
lostplantationgolf.com
Magnolia CC, *Millen* .... 9 [P] 478-982-5717
Manor G&CC, *Alpharetta* .... 18 [V] 678-366-3975
themanorgolfandcountryclub.com
Maple Ridge GC, *Columbus* .... 18 [V] 706-569-0966
golfmapleridge.com
Marietta CC, *Kennesaw* .... 27 [V] 770-426-1808
mariettacountryclub.org
Mary Calder GC, *Savannah* .... 9 [S] 912-238-7100
McKenzie Memorial GC, *Montezuma* .... 9 [P] 478-472-6126
Meadow Lakes GC, *Cedartown* .... 18 [S] 770-748-4942
meadowlakescedartown.com
Meadow Links At George T Bagby, *Fort Gaines* ...18 [M] 229-768-3714
golfgeorgia.org
Milledgeville CC, *Milledgeville* .... 18 [V] 478-452-3220
mccga.com
Mirror Lake GC, *Villa Rica* .... 36 [V] 770-459-5599
canongategolf.com
Monroe G&CC, *Monroe* .... 18 [V] 770-267-8424
monroegcc.com
Moody Quiet Pines GC, *Valdosta* .... 9 [A] 229-257-3297
Morgan Dairy GC, *Griffin* .... 18 [P] 770-358-2221
morgandairygolfclub.com
Mossy Creek GC, *Cleveland* .... 18 [P] 706-865-2277
Mystery Valley GC, *Lithonia* .... 18 [M] 770-469-6913
mysteryvalley.com
Newnan CC, *Newnan* .... 18 [V] 706-253-9856
newnancc.org
Nob North GC, *Cohutta* .... 18 [M] 706-694-8505
North Fulton GC, *Atlanta* .... 18 [P] 404-255-0723
northfulton.americangolf.com
Northwood CC, *Lawrenceville* .... 18 [V] 770-923-2991
northwoodcc.com
Oak Grove Island G&CC, *Brunswick* .... 18 [P] 912-280-9525
oakgroveislandgolf.com

Oak Haven GC, *Macon* .... 18 [P] 478-474-8080
oakhavengolfclub.com
Oak Mountain Champ GC, *Carrollton* .... 18 [P] 770-834-7065
oakmountaingolf.com
Oakview G&CC, *Macon* .... 18 [S] 478-785-1833
oakviewgolfcc.com
Ocean Forest GC, *Sea Island* .... 18 [V] 912-638-5835
Ocilla CC, *Ocilla* .... 9 [V] 229-468-7512
Ogeechee Valley CC, *Louisville* .... 9 [V] 478-625-3502
Okefenokee CC, *Blackshear* .... 18 [V] 912-283-7235
Old Union GC, *Braselton* .... 18 [P] 706-745-4653
olduniongolf.com
Orchard Hills GC, *Newnan* .... 27 [P] 770-251-5683
orchardhills.com
Overlook Golf Links, *Lagrange* .... 18 [P] 706-845-7425
overlookgolflinks.com
Oxbow Creek GC, *Columbus* .... 9 [M] 706-689-9977
columbusga.org
Peachtree CC, *Atlanta* .... 18 [V] 404-233-4428
Peachtree Golf Ctr, *Duluth* .... 18 [P] 770-497-9265
peachgolf.com
Pebblebrook GC, *Woodbury* .... 9 [S] 706-846-3809
Perry CC, *Perry* .... 18 [P] 478-987-1033
perrycountryclub.com
Piedmont Driving Club GC, *Atlanta* .... 18 [V] 404-346-4174
drivingclub.com
Pine Forest CC, *Jesup* .... 18 [S] 912-427-6505
Pine Hills G&CC, *Cordele* .... 18 [P] 229-273-1238
playpinehills.com
Pine Hills GC, *Winder* .... 18 [P] 770-867-3150
Pine Islands GC, *Tifton* .... 9 [P] 229-387-7600
Pine Needles CC, *Fort Valley* .... 9 [P] 478-825-3816
pnccgolf.com
Pine Oaks GC, *Robins AFB* .... 18 [A] 478-926-4103
robins.af.mil
Pinecrest CC, *Pelham* .... 9 [V] 229-294-8525
canongategolf.com
Pineknoll GC, *Sylvester* .... 9 [P] 229-776-3455
Pines GC, *Williamson* .... 18 [P] 770-229-4107
midgagolf.com
Pines GC, *Edison* .... 9 [P] 229-835-3056
Pinetree CC, *Kennesaw* .... 18 [V] 770-422-5902
pinetreecc.org
Plantation Course at Reynolds Plantation,
  Greensboro .... 18 [R] 706-467-1142
reynoldsplantation.com
Pointe South GC, *Hephzibah* .... 18 [S] 706-592-2222
pointesouthgolfclub.com
Polo G&CC, *Cumming* .... 18 [V] 770-887-4049
pologolfandcountryclub.com
Prospect Valley GC, *Rockmart* .... 9 [P] 770-684-5961
Quitman CC, *Quitman* .... 18 [P] 229-560-4141
Rabbit Run GC, *Adairsville* .... 9 [P] 706-236-6006
rabbitrungolf.com
Rabun County GC, *Clayton* .... 9 [M] 706-782-5500
Raintree GC, *Thomaston* .... 18 [P] 706-647-7358
midgagolf.com
Randolph CC, *Cuthbert* .... 9 [V] 229-732-2351
Red Oak GC, *Cusseta* .... 18 [P] 706-989-3312
Retreat GC At St Simons Island, *St Simons Island* 18 [V] 912-638-3611
Reunion GC, *Hoschton* .... 18 [P] 770-967-8300
reuniongolfclub.com
Reynolds GC, *Reynolds* .... 9 [S] 478-847-4556

[S] = SEMI-PRIVATE   [V] = PRIVATE   [U] = UNIVERSITY   [N] = UNIVERSITY-PRIVATE

GEORGIA — Golf Yellow Pages, 18th Edition

River Pines Golf, *Alpharetta* .... 27 [P] 770-442-5960
  riverpinesgolf.com
River Pointe GC, *Albany* .... 18 [S] 229-883-4885
  riverpointegolfcourse.com
Rivermont G&CC, *Alpharetta* .... 18 [V] 770-993-1779
  rivermontcountryclub.com
Riverview Park GC, *Dublin* .... 18 [M] 478-275-4064
  dublinriverview.com
Rocky Branch GC, *Lincolnton* .... 18 [P] 706-359-4303
Rocky Creek GC, *Vidalia* .... 18 [P] 912-538-1110
  rockycreekgolfclub.com
Rogers Gardens GC, *Moultrie* .... 9 [P] 229-891-2433
Roosevelt Memorial GC, *Warm Springs* .... 9 [M] 706-655-5230
Royal Lakes G&CC, *Flowery Branch* .... 18 [S] 770-535-8800
  royallakesgolfcc.com
Rum Creek, *Stockbridge* .... 9 [P] 770-507-3538
Sapelo Hammock GC, *Townsend* .... 18 [P] 912-832-4653
  sapelohammockgolfclub.com
Savannah Quarters CC, *Pooler* .... 18 [V] 912-450-2280
  savannahquarterscc.com
Sea Island GC, *St Simons Island* .... 36 [R] 912-638-5118
  seaisland.com
Sea Palms G&T Resort, *St Simons Island* ...... 27 [R] 912-638-9041
  seapalms.com
Sky Valley Resort & CC, *Sky Valley* .... 18 [R] 706-746-5302
  skyvalley.com
Smoke Rise G&CC, *Stone Mountain* .... 18 [V] 770-908-2582
  smokerisecc.com
South Wind GC, *Fairburn* .... 18 [S] 770-774-3336
  southwindgolfcourse.com⊠
Southbridge GC, *Savannah* .... 18 [S] 912-651-5455
  southbridgegolfclub.com
Southern Hills GC, *Hawkinsville* .... 18 [P] 478-783-0600
  southernhillsgolf.com
Southern Links GC, *Statesboro* .... 18 [P] 912-839-3191
  playsouthernlinks.com
Southland CC, *Stone Mountain* .... 18 [S] 770-469-2717
  southlandcountryclub.com
Spring Hill CC, *Tifton* .... 18 [V] 229-382-3144
Spring Lakes GC, *Chatsworth* .... 18 [S] 706-695-9300
  springlakesgolfclub.com
St Andrews G&CC, *Winston* .... 18 [S] 770-489-2200
  standrewsga.com
St Ives CC, *Duluth* .... 18 [V] 770-497-9432
  stivescountryclub.org
St Marlo CC, *Duluth* .... 18 [P] 770-495-7725
  stmarlo.com
Steel Canyon GC, *Atlanta* .... 18 [P] 770-390-0424
  steelcanyongolfclub.com
Sterling Links GC, *Richmond Hill* .... 18 [P] 912-727-4653
  sterlinglinksgolf.com
Stone Creek GC, *Valdosta* .... 18 [S] 229-247-2527
  gagolf.com
Stone Mountain GC, *Stone Mountain* .... 36 [R] 770-465-3278
  stonemountaingolf.com
Stonebridge G&CC, *Albany* .... 18 [V] 229-889-8270
  stonebridgegcc.com
Stonebridge GC, *Rome* .... 18 [M] 706-236-5046
  romestonebridge.com
Sugar Creek GC, *Atlanta* .... 18 [P] 404-241-7671
  sugarcreekga.com
Sugar Hill GC, *Sugar Hill* .... 18 [P] 770-271-0519
  sugarhillgolfclub.com

Summergrove GC, *Newnan* .... 18 [V] 770-251-1800
  canongategolf.com
Summit Chase CC, *Snellville* .... 18 [V] 770-979-9000
  summitchasecc.com
Sunrise GC, *Colbert* .... 18 [P] 706-788-2720
  sunrisegolfclub.com
Sunset CC, *Moultrie* .... 18 [V] 229-890-5555
Sunset Hills CC, *Carrollton* .... 18 [V] 770-832-2441
  sunsethillscc.com
Swainsboro G&CC, *Swainsboro* .... 18 [P] 478-237-6116
Tally Mountain GC, *Tallapoosa* .... 18 [M] 770-574-3122
Taylors Creek GC, *Fort Stewart* .... 18 [M] 912-767-2370
  stewart.army.mil/dcaf
The Chimneys GC, *Winder* .... 18 [P] 770-307-4900
  chimneysgc.com
The Club At Savannah Harbor, *Savannah* ... 18 [R] 912-201-2240
  theclubatsavannahharbor.com
The Creek At Hard Labor, *Rutledge* .... 18 [M] 706-557-3006
  georgiagolf.com
The Creek Club at Reynolds Plantation, *Greensboro* 18 [V] 706-467-1680
  reynoldsplantation.com
The Fairways of Canton GC, *Canton* .... 18 [V] 770-704-6531
  fairwaysofcanton.net
The Farm GC, *Rocky Face* .... 18 [V] 706-673-4546
  thefarmgolfclub.org
The First Tee of Albany, *Albany* .... 9 [P] 229-888-0800
  thefirstteealbany.org
The First Tee of Augusta, *Augusta* .... 9 [P] 706-364-4653
  thefirstteeaugusta.org
The First Tee of Troup County, *Lagrange* ..... 9 [P] 706-883-1655
  thefirstteetroupco.org
The Ford Plantation, *Richmond Hill* .... 18 [V] 912-756-2742
  fordplantation.com
The Fort Benning GC, *Fort Benning* .... 27 [A] 706-687-1940
  benningmwr.com
The Frog GC, *Villa Rica* .... 18 [R] 770-459-4400
  golfthefrog.com
The GC at Bradshaw Farm, *Woodstock* .... 27 [S] 770-592-2222
  bradshawfarmgc.com
The GC At Sanctuary Cove, *Waverly* .... 18 [P] 912-466-0080
  sanctuarycovegolf.com
The GC of Georgia, *Alpharetta* .... 36 [V] 770-664-8644
  golfclubofgeorgia.com
The General At Barnsley Gardens, *Adairsville* ... 18 [R] 770-773-2555
  barnsleyresort.com
The Georgia Club, *Statham* .... 27 [R] 770-725-8100
  thegeorgiaclub.com
The Georgia Trail At Sugarloaf, *Duluth* .... 9 [P] 770-497-4653
  gatrail.com
The Golfers Club At Fort McPherson,
  Fort McPherson .... 18 [A] 404-464-2178
The Governors Towne Club, *Acworth* .... 18 [V] 770-966-5353
  governorstowneclub.com
The Highlands GC at Lake Arrowhead Resort,
  Waleska .... 18 [R] 770-721-7900
  lakearrowheadclub.net
The Hooch GC, *Duluth* .... 18 [P] 770-476-2525
  thehoochgolfclub.com
The International City GC, *Warner Robins* .. 18 [M] 478-322-0276
  warner-robins.org
The Lakes At Laura S Walker, *Waycross* ...... 18 [M] 912-285-6154
  golfgeorgia.org
The Landing at Reynolds Plantation, *Greensboro* 18 [R] 706-467-1670
  reynoldslanding.com

[A] = MILITARY   [M] = MUNICIPAL   [P] = PUBLIC   [R] = RESORT

Golf Yellow Pages, 18th Edition — HAWAII

The Legends at Chateau Elan, *Braselton* .... 18 [V] 770-932-8653
  chateauelan.net
The Links GC, *Jonesboro*..27 [P] 770-461-5100
  golfatthelinks.com
The Lion GC, *Bremen*...............................18 [P] 770-537-1400
  theliongolfclub.com
The National at Reynolds Plantation, *Greensboro* 27 [R] 706-467-1142
  reynoldsplantation.com
The Oaks Course, *Covington* ....18 [P] 770-786-3801
  golfoaks.com
The Oconee at Reynolds Plantation, *Greensboro* .18 [R] 706-467-1142
  reynoldsplantation.com
The Orchard G&CC, *Clarkesville* .... 18 [V] 706-754-3156
  theorchardclub.com
The Pines GC, *Bainbridge* ....18 [M] 229-246-8545
The Pines GC, *Toccoa*..9 [P] 706-886-1915
  thepinesoftoccoa.com
The Plantation GC, *Cartersville*........................... 18 [S] 770-382-3999
  plantationgolfclub.net
The Providence Club, *Monroe* ....18 [P] 770-207-4332
  theprovidenceclubgolf.com
The River Club, *Suwanee* .... 18 [V] 770-271-2582
  theriverclub-ga.com
The Savannah GC, *Savannah* .... 18 [V] 912-236-4305
  thesavannahgolfclub.com
The Standard Club, *Duluth*................................ 18 [V] 770-497-1920
  standardclub.org
Thomson CC, *Thomson* ....9 [S] 706-595-2727
Town & CC, *Blakely* .... 9 [V] 229-723-4737
Town Creek CC, *Hawkinsville*................................9 [P] 478-783-0128
Towne Lake Hills GC, *Woodstock* ....18 [P] 770-592-9969
  townelakehillsgc.com
TPC Sugarloaf, *Duluth*... 27 [V] 770-418-1113
  tpcsugarloaf.com
Traditions of Braselton GC, *Jefferson*................. 18 [S] 706-363-9963
  canongategolf.com
Trenton GC, *Trenton* .... 18 [S] 706-657-3616
  trentongolfclub.com
Trident Lakes GC, *Kings Bay* ....18 [A] 912-573-8475
Trion GC, *Trion* ....9 [P] 706-734-2712
Trophy Club of Apalachee, *Dacula*..................... 18 [S] 770-822-9220
  trophyclubapalachee.com
Trophy Club of Atlanta, *Alpharetta*..................... 18 [S] 770-343-9700
  tcatlanta.americangolf.com
Tunnel Hill GC, *Tunnel Hill*....................................9 [P] 706-673-4131
Turtle Cove GC, *Monticello* .... 9 [V] 706-468-0341
  turtlecovepoa.com
Twin City CC, *Tennille* ....18 [P] 478-552-7894
  twincitycc.com
Twin Oaks GC, *Albany* .... 9 [A] 229-639-5211
Twisted Pine GC, *Hazlehurst* ....9 [M] 912-375-6697
Uchee Trail CC, *Cochran* ....18 [P] 478-934-7891
Uncle Remus GC, *Eatonton* ....9 [M] 706-485-6850
Univ of Georgia GC, *Athens*............................... 18 [U] 706-369-5739
  golfcourse.uga.edu
Valdosta CC, *Valdosta* .... 27 [V] 229-241-2000
  valdostacc.com
Valley Pines GC, *Cairo* ....9 [P] 229-377-2000
Wanee Lake GC, *Ashburn* ....9 [P] 229-567-2727
  waneelake.com
Warrenton GC, *Warrenton* .... 18 [A] 706-465-3032
Washington Wilkes CC, *Washington*................... 9 [V] 706-678-2046
Waterfall CC, *Clayton* .... 18 [V] 706-212-4000
  waterfallcountryclub.com
Waterford CC, *Bonaire* ....18 [S] 478-328-7533
  thewaterfordgolfclub.com
Waterford Landing GC, *Richmond Hill*................18 [P] 912-727-4848
  waterfordlandinggolf.com
Waynesboro CC, *Waynesboro*............................ 18 [V] 706-554-2262
Wendell Coffee Golf Ctr, *Tyrone*..........................9 [P] 770-969-4469
  coffeegolfcenter.com
West Lake CC, *Augusta* .... 18 [V] 706-863-4640
  westlakecountryclub.com
West Pines GC, *Douglasville*...............................18 [S] 678-391-1600
  westpinesgc.com
White Columns CC, *Alpharetta* .... 18 [V] 770-343-9025
  whitecolumnscountryclub.com
White Path GC, *Ellijay* ....18 [P] 706-276-3080
  whitepathgolfclub.net
Whitewater Creek, *Fayetteville* .... 18 [V] 770-461-6545
  canongategolf.com
Willow Lake GC, *Metter* ....18 [P] 912-685-2724
  willowlakegolfclub.com
Wilmington Island Club, *Savannah*...................18 [R] 912-897-1612
  wilmingtonislandclub.com
Windermere GC, *Cumming* .... 18 [V] 678-513-1000
  canongategolf.com
Windstone GC, *Ringgold*.................................... 18 [V] 423-894-1231
  windstone.com
Windy Hills GC, *Covington*....................................9 [P] 770-786-2820
Wolf Creek GC, *Americus*....................................18 [S] 229-928-4040
Wolf Creek GC, *Atlanta* ....18 [P] 404-344-1334
  wolfcreekgc.com
Woodlands Hills GC, *Midland*............................. 18 [P] 706-563-5511
Woodmont G&CC, *Canton*................................. 18 [P] 770-345-9260
  woodmontgolfclub.com
Woods GC, *Cochran*.. 27 [P] 478-934-0731

HAWAII

Ala Wai GC, *Honolulu* ....18 [M] 808-733-7384
  honolulu.gov/des/golf
Barbers Point GC, *Pearl Harbor* ....18 [A] 808-682-1911
Bay View Golf Park, *Kaneohe* .... 18 [S] 808-247-0451
  bayviewgolfparkhi.com
Big Island CC, *Kailua Kona* ....18 [P] 808-325-5044
Cavendish GC, *Lanai City*......................................9 [P] 808-565-7300
Club At Hokulia, *Kailua Kona* .... 18 [V] 808-930-4101
  hokulia.com
Coral Creek GC, *Ewa Beach* ....18 [P] 808-441-4653
  coralcreekgolfhawaii.com
Discovery Harbor G&CC, *Naalehu* ....18 [P] 808-929-7353
Ewa Beach GC, *Ewa Beach* .... 18 [S] 808-689-6565
  ewabeachgc.com
Ewa Villages GC, *Ewa Beach*...............................18 [M] 808-681-0220
  co.honolulu.hi.us/golf
Hamakua CC, *Honokaa* ....9 [S] 808-775-7244
Hapuna GC, *Kamuela* ....18 [R] 808-880-3000
  princegolfhawaii.com
Hawaii CC, *Wahiawa*..18 [P] 808-622-1744
  hawaiicc.com
Hawaii Kai GC, *Honolulu* .... 36 [S] 808-395-2358
  hawaiikaigolf.com
Hawaii Prince GC, *Ewa Beach* ....27 [R] 808-944-4567
  princegolfhawaii.com
Hilo Muni GC, *Hilo* ....18 [M] 808-959-7711

[S] = SEMI-PRIVATE   [V] = PRIVATE   [U] = UNIVERSITY   [N] = UNIVERSITY-PRIVATE

HAWAII

Course	Holes	Type	Phone
Hoakalei CC At Ocean Pointe, *Ewa Beach*	18	[V]	808-388-4049
hoakaleicountryclub.com			
Honolulu CC, *Honolulu*	18	[V]	808-441-9400
honolulucountryclub.com			
Hualalai GC - Hualalai Course, *Kailua*	18	[V]	808-325-8480
hualalairesort.com			
Hualalai GC - Keolu Course, *Kailua*	18	[V]	808-325-8480
hualalairesort.com			
Ironwood Hills GC, *Kualapuu Molokai*	9	[P]	808-567-6000
Kaanapali Golf Resort, *Lahaina*	36	[R]	808-661-3691
kaanapali-golf.com			
Kahili GC, *Wailuku*	18	[R]	808-242-4653
kahiligolf.com			
Kahuku GC, *Kahuku*	9	[M]	808-293-5842
honolulu.gov/des/golf/kahuku.htm			
Kaneohe Klipper Marine GC, *Kaneohe Bay*	18	[A]	808-254-2107
mccshawaii.com/golf.htm			
Kapalua GC - Bay, *Lahaina*	18	[R]	808-669-8877
golfatkapalua.com			
Kapalua GC - Plantation, *Lahaina*	18	[R]	808-669-8877
golfatkapalua.com			
Kapolei GC, *Kapolei*	18	[P]	808-674-2227
kapoleigolfcourse.com			
Kauai Lagoons GC, *Lihue*	18	[R]	808-241-6000
bad link			
Kealohi GC, *Hickam AFB*	9	[A]	808-448-2318
hickamservices.com			
Kiahuna GC, *Koloa*	18	[R]	808-742-9595
kiahunagolf.com			
King Kamehameha GC, *Wailuku*	18	[R]	808-249-0033
kamehamehagolf.com			
Ko Olina GC, *Kapolei*	18	[R]	808-676-5300
koolinagolf.com			
Kona CC, *Kailua Kona*	36	[R]	808-322-2595
konagolf.com			
Koolau GC, *Kaneohe*	18	[P]	808-236-4653
koolaugolfclub.com			
Kukio Makai Beach GC, *Kailua Kona*	28	[V]	808-325-4000
kukio.com			
Kukuiolono GC, *Kalaheo*	9	[P]	808-332-9151
kukuiolono.com			
Leilehua GC, *Schofield Barracks*	18	[A]	808-655-4653
mwrarmyhawaii.com			
Luana Hills CC, *Kailua*	18	[P]	808-262-2139
luanahills.com			
Makaha Resort GC, *Waianae*	18	[R]	808-695-9544
makaharesort.com			
Makaha Valley CC, *Waianae*	18	[P]	808-695-9578
makahavalleycc.com			
Makai GC At Princeville, *Princeville*	27	[R]	808-826-5070
makaigolf.com			
Makalei Hawaii CC, *Kailua Kona*	18	[S]	808-325-6625
makalei.com			
Makena GC, *Kihei*	18	[R]	808-891-4000
makenagolf.com			
Mamala Bay GC, *Hickam AFB*	18	[A]	808-449-2300
hickamservices.com			
Maui CC, *Paia*	9	[V]	808-877-0516
mauicountryclub.org			
Maui Elleair GC, *Kihei*	18	[S]	808-874-0777
elleairmauigolfclub.com			
Mauna Kea Resort, *Kamuela*	18	[R]	808-882-5404
maunakeabeachhotel.com			
Mauna Lani Resort GC, *Kamuela*	36	[R]	808-885-6655
maunalani.com			
Mid Pacific CC, *Kailua*	18	[V]	808-262-8161
mpcchi.org			
Mililani GC, *Mililani*	18	[S]	808-623-2222
mililanigolfclub.com			
Moanalua GC, *Honolulu*	9	[V]	808-839-2311
Nanea GC, *Kailua Kona*	18	[V]	808-930-1300
Naniloa Volcanoes Resort, *Hilo*	9	[R]	808-935-3000
hottours.us			
Navy Marine GC, *Honolulu*	18	[A]	808-471-0142
Oahu CC, *Honolulu*	18	[V]	808-595-3256
oahucountryclub.com			
Olomana Golf Links, *Waimanalo*	18	[P]	808-259-7926
olomanagolflinks.com			
Pali Muni GC, *Kaneohe*	18	[M]	808-266-7612
honolulu.gov/des/golf			
Pearl CC, *Aiea*	18	[P]	808-487-3802
pearlcc.com			
Poipu Bay Resort GC, *Koloa*	18	[R]	808-742-8711
poipubaygolf.com			
Prince GC at Princeville, *Princeville*	18	[R]	808-826-5001
princeville.com			
Puakea GC, *Lihue*	18	[P]	808-245-8756
puakeagolf.com			
Pukalani CC, *Makawao*	18	[P]	808-572-1314
pukalanigolf.com			
Royal Kunia CC, *Waipahu*	18	[R]	808-688-9222
royalkuniacc.com			
Sea Mountain GC, *Pahala*	18	[R]	808-928-6222
Ted Makalena GC, *Waipahu*	18	[M]	808-675-6052
honolulu.gov/des/golf			
The Challenge at Manele, *Lanai*	18	[R]	808-565-2222
golfonlanai.com			
The Dunes At Maui Lani GC, *Kahului*	18	[P]	808-873-7911
dunesatmauilani.com			
The Experience at Koele, *Lanai*	18	[R]	808-565-4653
golfonlanai.com			
The Turtle Bay Resort & GC, *Kahuku*	36	[R]	808-293-8574
turtlebayresort.com			
Volcano G&CC, *Volcanoes Natl Pk*	18	[S]	808-967-7331
volcanogolfshop.com			
Waialae CC, *Honolulu*	18	[V]	808-734-2151
waialaecc.com			
Waiehu Muni GC, *Wailuku*	18	[M]	808-270-7400
co.maui.hi.us			
Waikele GC, *Waipahu*	18	[S]	808-676-9000
golfwaikele.com			
Waikoloa Beach Resort GC, *Waikoloa*	36	[R]	808-886-7888
waikoloabeachresort.com			
Waikoloa Village GC, *Waikoloa*	18	[R]	808-883-9621
waikoloa.org			
Wailea GC - Gold/Emerald, *Kihei*	36	[R]	808-875-5143
waileagolf.com			
Wailea GC - Old Blue, *Kihei*	18	[R]	808-875-5155
waileagolf.com			
Wailua Muni GC, *Lihue*	18	[M]	808-241-6666
kauai.gov/golf			
Waimea CC, *Kamuela*	18	[P]	808-885-8053
waimeagolf.com			
Walter J Nagorski GC, *Schofield Barracks*	9	[A]	808-438-9587
mwrarmyhawaii.com			
West Loch Muni GC, *Ewa Beach*	18	[M]	808-675-6076
honolulu.gov/des/golf			

[A] = MILITARY   [M] = MUNICIPAL   [P] = PUBLIC   [R] = RESORT

IDAHO

Course	Location	Holes	Type	Phone
93 Golf Ranch	Jerome	18	[S]	208-324-9693
American Falls GC	American Falls	9	[M]	208-226-5827
Aspen Acres GC	Ashton	18	[R]	208-652-3524
aspenacresrvpark.com				
Avondale G&TC	Hayden Lake	18	[S]	208-772-5963
avondalegolfcourse.com				
BanBury GC	Eagle	18	[P]	208-939-3600
banburygolf.com				
Bear Lake West G&CC	Fish Haven	9	[S]	208-945-2744
bearlakewest.com				
Bigwood GC	Ketchum	9	[P]	208-726-4024
thunderspring.com				
Blackfoot Muni GC	Blackfoot	18	[M]	208-785-9960
blackfootgc.com				
Blue Lakes CC	Twin Falls	18	[V]	208-733-2337
bluelakescc.com				
Boise Ranch GC	Boise	18	[P]	208-362-6501
boiseranchgc.com				
Broadmore CC	Nampa	9	[V]	208-466-0561
broadmorecc.com				
Bryden Canyon GC	Lewiston	18	[M]	208-746-0863
brydencanyongolf.net				
Burley GC	Burley	18	[M]	208-878-9807
burleyidaho.org				
Candleridge GC	Twin Falls	9	[P]	208-733-6577
Canyon Springs GC	Twin Falls	18	[P]	208-734-7609
canyonspringsgolf.com				
Caribou Highlands GC & RV Park	Grace	9	[R]	208-425-3233
caribouhighlandsgolf.com				
Carmela Vineyards GC	Glenns Ferry	9	[P]	208-366-7531
carmelavineyards.com				
Cascade GC	Cascade	9	[P]	208-382-4835
Cedar Park GC	Rigby	9	[P]	208-745-0103
cedarparkgolf.com				
Centennial GC	Nampa	18	[P]	208-468-5889
centennialgolf.net				
Challis GC	Challis	9	[M]	208-879-5440
challisgolfcourse.com				
Circling Raven GC	Worley	18	[R]	208-686-0248
circlingraven.com				
Clear Lake CC	Buhl	18	[S]	208-543-4849
clearlakecc.org				
Coeur DAlene GC	Coeur D Alene	18	[P]	208-765-0218
Coeur DAlene Resort GC	Coeur D Alene	18	[R]	208-765-5595
cdaresort.com				
Cottonwood Links GC & RV Park	Leslie	18	[R]	208-588-3394
Council Mountain GC	Council	9	[P]	208-253-6908
Crane Creek CC	Boise	18	[V]	208-344-6529
cranecreekcountryclub.com				
Dempsey Ridge GC	Lava Hot Springs	9	[P]	208-776-5048
dempseyridgegolfcourse.com				
Desert Canyon GC	Mountain Home	18	[M]	208-587-3293
mountain-home.us				
Eagle Hills GC	Eagle	18	[P]	208-939-0402
eaglehillsgolfcourse.com				
Elkhorn GC	Sun Valley	18	[V]	208-622-3309
elkhorngolfclub.com				
Fairview GC	Caldwell	9	[M]	208-455-3090
cityofcaldwell.com				
Falcon Crest GC	Kuna	36	[P]	208-362-8897
falconcrestgolf.com				
Foxtail GC & DR	Meridian	18	[P]	208-887-4653
Fremont County GC	St Anthony	9	[M]	208-624-7074
co.fremont.id.us				
Galena Ridge at Silver Mountain Resort	Kellogg	9	[R]	208-783-1522
silvermt.com				
Gem County Emmett GC	Emmett	9	[M]	208-365-2675
emmettidaho.com				
Gooding CC	Gooding	9	[M]	208-934-9977
goodingcc.com				
Gozzer Ranch Golf & Lake Club	Harrison	18	[V]	208-665-6655
gozzerranchclub.com				
Grangeville CC	Grangeville	9	[S]	208-983-1299
grangevilleidaho.com				
Hayden Lake CC	Hayden Lake	18	[V]	208-772-0555
haydenlakecc.com				
Hazard Creek GC	Aberdeen	9	[M]	208-397-5308
Headwaters Club At Teton Springs	Victor	27	[R]	208-787-3600
tetonsprings.com				
Heise Hills GC	Ririe	9	[P]	208-538-7327
heiseexpeditions.com				
Highland GC	Pocatello	18	[M]	208-237-9922
Hillcrest CC	Boise	18	[V]	208-343-1769
hillcrest.cc				
Hunters Point GC	Nampa	18	[P]	208-465-1903
hunterspointgolfclub.com				
Huntsman Springs GC	Driggs	18	[V]	877-354-9660
huntsmansprings.com				
Idaho Falls CC	Idaho Falls	18	[V]	208-523-5762
ifcountryclub.com				
Indian Lakes GC	Boise	9	[P]	208-362-5771
indianlakesgolf.com				
Island Park Village Resort GC	Island Park	9	[R]	208-558-7550
islandparkvillageresort.com				
Jefferson Hills GC	Rigby	18	[P]	208-745-6492
jeffersonhillsgolfcourse.com				
Jerome CC	Jerome	18	[P]	208-324-5281
jeromecountryclub.com				
Jug Mountain Ranch GC	McCall	18	[S]	208-634-5072
jugmountainranch.com				
Juniper Hills CC	Pocatello	18	[V]	208-233-0269
jhcc.us				
Kaylers Bend Golf	Peck	9	[P]	208-486-6841
kaylersbend.com				
Lakeview GC	Meridian	18	[M]	208-888-4080
golflakeviewgc.com				
Lewiston G&CC	Lewiston	18	[V]	208-746-2801
lewistongolfcountryclub.com				
McCall Muni GC	McCall	27	[M]	208-634-7200
mccallgolfclub.com				
Meadow Creek GC	New Meadows	18	[R]	208-347-2164
meadowcreekgolfcourse.net				
Meadow Lake Village & GC	Meridian	9	[V]	888-978-5050
meadowlakevillage.com				
Mirror Lake GC	Bonners Ferry	9	[M]	208-267-5314
kvpress.com				
Montpelier GC	Montpelier	9	[M]	208-847-1981
Moscow Elks GC	Moscow	18	[V]	208-882-3015
elks249.com				
Oregon Trail CC	Soda Springs	9	[P]	208-547-2204
oregontrailcountryclub.com				
Orofino G&CC	Orofino	9	[P]	208-476-3117
Osprey Meadows GC At Tamarack Resort	Donnelly	18	[R]	208-325-4653
tamarackidaho.com				
Pierce Park Greens	Boise	9	[P]	208-853-3302
pierceparkgreens.com				

[S] = SEMI-PRIVATE   [V] = PRIVATE   [U] = UNIVERSITY   [N] = UNIVERSITY-PRIVATE

IDAHO

Course	City	Holes	Type	Phone
Pinecrest GC,	Idaho Falls	18	[M]	208-612-8485
idahofallsidaho.gov				
Plantation CC,	Boise	18	[V]	208-853-4793
plantationcc.com				
Pleasant Valley GC,	Kimberly	9	[P]	208-423-5800
Ponderosa GC,	Burley	9	[P]	208-679-5730
Ponderosa Springs GC,	Coeur D Alene	9	[P]	208-664-1101
Prairie Falls GC,	Post Falls	18	[P]	208-457-0210
prairiefallsgolf.com				
Preston G&CC,	Preston	18	[S]	208-852-2408
Priest Lake G&TC,	Priest Lake	18	[P]	208-443-2525
priestlakegolfcourse.com				
Purple Sage GC,	Caldwell	18	[M]	208-459-2223
purplesagegolfcourse.com				
Quail Hollow GC,	Boise	18	[S]	208-344-7807
quailhollowgolfclub.com				
Ranch Club GC,	Priest River	9	[P]	208-448-1731
ranchclubgolfcourse.com				
Rexburg GC,	Rexburg	9	[M]	208-359-3037
tetonlakesgc.com				
Ridgecrest GC,	Nampa	27	[M]	208-468-5888
ridgecrestgolf.com				
Rimrock GC,	Athol	9	[P]	208-762-5054
River Bend GC,	Wilder	18	[P]	208-482-7169
River Birch GC,	Star	18	[P]	208-286-0801
riverbirchgolfcourse.com				
River Park GC & RV Pk,	Mackay	9	[R]	208-588-2296
Riverside GC,	Pocatello	18	[M]	208-232-9515
Rolling Hills GC,	Weiser	9	[P]	208-549-0456
Rupert CC,	Rupert	18	[V]	208-436-9168
Sage Lakes Muni GC,	Idaho Falls	18	[M]	208-612-8535
idahofallsidaho.gov				
Salmon Valley GC,	Salmon	9	[P]	208-756-4734
Sand Creek GC,	Idaho Falls	18	[M]	208-612-8115
idahofallsidaho.gov				
Sandpoint Elks GC,	Sandpoint	9	[P]	208-263-4321
sandpointelksgolfcourse.com				
Scotch Pines GC,	Payette	18	[M]	208-642-1829
scotchpinesgolf.com				
Shadow Valley GC,	Boise	18	[P]	208-939-6699
shadowvalley.com				
Shoshone G&TC,	Osburn	9	[P]	208-784-0161
shoshonegolf.com				
Silver Sage GC,	Mountain Home AFB	18	[A]	208-828-6559
mhafbfun.com				
Soldier Mt Ranch & Resort,	Fairfield	18	[R]	208-764-2506
soldiermountainranch.com				
SpurWing CC,	Meridian	18	[V]	208-887-1177
spurwing.com				
St Maries GC,	St Maries	9	[M]	208-245-3842
Stoneridge GC,	Blanchard	18	[R]	208-437-4682
stoneridgeidaho.com				
Sun Valley Resort,	Sun Valley	27	[R]	208-622-4111
sunvalley.com				
Terrace Lakes Golf Resort,	Garden Valley	18	[R]	208-462-3250
terracelakes.com				
Teton Lakes GC,	Rexburg	27	[P]	208-359-3036
tetonlakesgc.com				
Teton Reserve,	Victor	18	[P]	208-787-4224
tetonreserve.com				
The Club At Black Rock,	Coeur D Alene	18	[V]	208-676-8999
blackrockidaho.com				
The Highlands GC,	Post Falls	18	[P]	208-773-3673
thehighlandsgc.com				
The Idaho Club,	Sandpoint	18	[R]	208-265-2345
theidahoclub.com				
The Links GC,	Post Falls	18	[P]	208-777-7611
golfthelinks.net				
The Pinehurst GC,	Pinehurst	9	[P]	208-682-2013
golfpinehurstidaho.com				
The Valley Club,	Hailey	27	[V]	208-788-5400
thevalleyclub.org				
Timberline GC,	Ashton	9	[P]	208-652-3219
timberlinegolfresort.com				
TimberStone GC,	Caldwell	18	[P]	208-639-6900
playtimberstone.com				
Twin Falls GC,	Twin Falls	18	[M]	208-733-3326
tfid.org				
Twin Lakes Village GC,	Rathdrum	18	[R]	208-687-1312
golftwinlakes.com				
Univ of Idaho GC,	Moscow	18	[U]	208-885-6171
uidaho.edu/golf				
Warm Springs GC,	Boise	18	[M]	208-343-5661
cityofboise.org				
Whitetail GC,	McCall	18	[R]	208-634-2244
whitetailclub.com				

ILLINOIS

Course	City	Holes	Type	Phone
Acorns Golf Links,	Waterloo	18	[P]	618-939-7800
acornsgolflinks.com				
Addison Links & Tees,	Addison	9	[M]	630-458-2660
addisonparkdistrict.org				
Aldeen GC,	Rockford	18	[M]	815-282-4653
aldeengolfclub.com				
Alpine Hills GC,	Rockford	9	[P]	815-398-8066
golfalpinehills.com				
American Legion Post GC,	Edwardsville	9	[P]	618-656-9774
Anderson Field GC,	Streator	9	[M]	815-672-3702
ci.streator.il.us				
Anetsberger GC,	Northbrook	9	[M]	847-291-2971
Angus Links GC,	Windsor	18	[P]	217-459-2805
anguslinks.com				
Annbriar GC,	Waterloo	18	[P]	618-939-4653
annbriar.com				
Antioch GC,	Antioch	18	[S]	847-395-3004
antiochgolfclub.com				
Apple Canyon Lake GC,	Apple River	9	[P]	815-492-2477
applecanyonlake.org				
Apple Orchard GC,	Bartlett	9	[M]	630-540-4807
bartletparkdistrict.com				
Arlington Greens GC,	Granite City	18	[M]	618-931-5232
arlingtongreens.com				
Arlington Lakes GC,	Arlington Heights	18	[M]	847-577-3030
ahpd.org/algc				
Arrowhead CC,	Edelstein	18	[V]	309-274-4675
arrowheadcc.net				
Arrowhead GC,	Wheaton	27	[M]	630-653-5800
arrowheadgolfclub.com				
Arrowhead Heights GC,	Camp Point	18	[P]	217-593-6619
arrowheadheights.com				
Aspen Ridge GC,	Bourbonnais	18	[P]	815-939-1742
aspenridgegolf.com				
Atwood Homestead GC,	Rockford	18	[M]	815-623-2411
wcfpd.org				

[A] = MILITARY [M] = MUNICIPAL [P] = PUBLIC [R] = RESORT

Golf Yellow Pages, 18th Edition — ILLINOIS

Aurora CC, *Aurora* .... 18 [V] 630-892-3785
  auroracc.com
Baker Park GC, *Kewanee* .... 18 [M] 309-852-4653
Balmoral Woods GC, *Crete* .... 18 [P] 708-672-7448
  balmoralwoods.com
Barrington Hills CC, *Barrington* .... 18 [V] 847-381-4200
  barringtonhillscc.com
Bartlett Hills GC, *Bartlett* .... 18 [M] 630-837-2741
  bartletthills.com
Barwood GC, *Rockton* .... 9 [P] 815-624-2280
Beaver Creek GC, *Capron* .... 9 [P] 815-569-2427
  golfthebeaver.com
Bel Mar CC, *Belvidere* .... 18 [V] 815-544-6268
  belmarcc.com
Belk Park GC, *Wood River* .... 18 [M] 618-251-3115
  belkpark.com
Bent Oak GC, *Breese* .... 9 [P] 618-526-8181
  bentoakgolf.org
Bent Tree GC, *Charleston* .... 18 [P] 217-348-1611
  benttreegolfcourse.com
Benton CC, *Benton* .... 9 [P] 618-439-0921
Bergen GC, *Springfield* .... 9 [M] 217-753-6211
  springfieldparks.org
Beverly CC, *Chicago* .... 18 [V] 708-636-8700
  beverlycc.org
Big Run GC, *Lockport* .... 18 [P] 815-838-1057
  bigrungolf.com
Billy Caldwell GC, *Chicago* .... 9 [M] 773-792-1930
  forestpreservegolf.com
Biltmore CC, *Barrington* .... 18 [V] 847-381-6884
  biltmore-cc.com
Bittersweet GC, *Gurnee* .... 18 [P] 847-855-9031
  bittersweetgolf.com
Black Sheep GC, *Sugar Grove* .... 27 [V] 630-879-2000
  blacksheepgolfclub.com
Blackberry Oaks GC, *Bristol* .... 18 [P] 630-553-7170
  blackberryoaks.com
Blackhawk Run GC, *Stockton* .... 18 [P] 815-947-3011
  blackhawkrun.com
Blackstone GC, *Marengo* .... 18 [P] 815-923-1800
  blackstonegc.com
Bliss Creek GC, *Sugar Grove* .... 18 [P] 630-466-4177
  blisscreekgolf.com
Bloomingdale GC, *Bloomingdale* .... 18 [S] 630-529-6232
  bloomingdalegc.com
Bloomington CC, *Bloomington* .... 18 [V] 309-829-6166
  bloomcc.com
Blue Grass Creek GC, *Minier* .... 9 [P] 309-392-2094
Blue Needles GC, *Fairmount* .... 18 [P] 217-427-5536
  blueneedles.com
Bob O Link GC, *Highland Park* .... 18 [V] 847-432-0917
Bolingbrook GC, *Bolingbrook* .... 18 [S] 630-771-9400
  bolingbrookgolfclub.com
Bonnie Brook GC, *Waukegan* .... 18 [M] 847-360-4730
  waukeganparks.org
Bonnie Dundee GC, *Carpentersville* .... 18 [M] 847-426-5511
  bonniedundeegc.com
Boone Creek GC, *McHenry* .... 27 [P] 815-455-6900
  boonecreekgolfacademy.com
Boughton Ridge GC, *Bolingbrook* .... 9 [M] 630-739-4100
  bolingbrookparks.org
Boulder Ridge GC, *Lake In The Hills* .... 27 [V] 847-854-3030
  boulderridge.com

Bow Lake GC, *Barry* .... 9 [P] 217-335-7043
Bowes Creek CC, *Elgin* .... 18 [M] 847-214-5880
  bowescreekcountryclub.com
Brae Loch CC, *Grayslake* .... 18 [M] 847-968-3444
  lcfpd.org
Briarwood CC, *Deerfield* .... 18 [V] 847-945-2660
  briarwoodcountryclub.com
Broken Arrow GC, *Lockport* .... 36 [P] 815-836-8858
  golfbrokenarrow.com
Brookhill GC, *Rantoul* .... 18 [M] 217-893-1200
  golfbrookhillgc.com
Brookhills GC, *Springfield* .... 9 [P] 217-787-8576
  brookhillsgolfclub.com
Brushcreek GC, *Orangeville* .... 9 [P] 815-789-4042
Bryn Mawr CC, *Lincolnwood* .... 18 [V] 847-676-2660
  brynmawrcountryclub.com
Bucks Barn Golf Resort, *Thomson* .... 18 [R] 815-259-8278
  bucksbarngolf.com
Buena Vista GC, *Dekalb* .... 9 [M] 815-758-4812
  dekalbparkdistrict.com
Buffalo Grove GC, *Buffalo Grove* .... 18 [M] 847-459-5520
  buffalogrovegolf.com
Bull Valley GC, *Woodstock* .... 18 [V] 815-337-4411
  bullvalleygolfclub.com
Bunker Links GC, *Galesburg* .... 18 [M] 309-344-1818
  ci.galesburg.il.us/parks/bunkerlinks.htm
Bunn GC, *Springfield* .... 18 [M] 217-522-2633
  springfieldparks.org
Burnham Woods GC, *Burnham* .... 18 [M] 708-862-9043
  forestpreservegolf.com
Butler National GC, *Oak Brook* .... 18 [V] 630-990-3333
  butlernational.org
Butterfield CC, *Oak Brook* .... 27 [V] 630-323-1307
  butterfieldcc.org
Byron Hills GC, *Port Byron* .... 18 [S] 309-523-2664
  byronhills.com
Calumet CC, *Homewood* .... 18 [V] 708-799-2230
  calumetcc.com
Cantigny G&TC, *Wheaton* .... 36 [P] 630-668-3323
  cantignygolf.com
Canyata GC, *Marshall* .... 18 [V] 217-826-9500
  canyata.com
Cardinal Creek GC, *Scott AFB* .... 18 [A] 618-744-1400
Cardinal Creek GC, *Beecher* .... 27 [P] 708-946-2800
  cardinalcreekgolf.com
Cardinal GC, *Effingham* .... 18 [P] 217-868-2860
Carlinville CC, *Carlinville* .... 9 [V] 217-854-9316
Carlyle Lake GC, *Carlyle* .... 9 [P] 618-594-2758
Carmi CC, *Carmi* .... 9 [S] 618-384-5011
Carriage Greens CC, *Darien* .... 18 [P] 630-985-3730
  carriagegreens.com
Carthage GC, *Carthage* .... 9 [P] 217-357-3625
Cary CC, *Cary* .... 18 [S] 847-639-3161
  carycountryclub.com
Casey CC, *Casey* .... 9 [P] 217-932-2030
CC of Decatur, *Decatur* .... 18 [V] 217-429-7823
  ccofdecatur.com
CC of Peoria, *Peoria Heights* .... 18 [V] 309-685-1212
  ccofpeoria.org
Cedar Crest CC, *Quincy* .... 9 [P] 217-223-1210
Cedarbrooke Par 3 Golf, *Sumner* .... 9 [P] 618-936-9393
Cedardell GC, *Plano* .... 9 [S] 630-552-3242

[S] = SEMI-PRIVATE   [V] = PRIVATE   [U] = UNIVERSITY   [N] = UNIVERSITY-PRIVATE

ILLINOIS — Golf Yellow Pages, 18th Edition

Course	Holes	Type	Phone
Chalet Hills GC, *Cary*	18	[P]	847-639-0666
chaletgolf.com			
Champaign CC, *Champaign*	18	[V]	217-356-1391
champaigncountryclub.com			
Champion Exec GC At Hillcrest Resort, *Orion*	9	[R]	309-526-8700
hillcrest-resort.com			
Chapel Hill CC, *McHenry*	18	[P]	815-385-3337
chapelhillgolf.com			
Charleston CC, *Charleston*	18	[V]	217-345-9711
Chester CC, *Chester*	9	[P]	618-826-3168
Chicago GC, *Wheaton*	18	[V]	630-665-2988
Chicago Heights Park District-East, *Chicago Heights*	9	[M]	708-754-3673
Chicago Heights Park District-West, *Chicago Heights*	9	[M]	708-754-1400
Chicago Highlands Club, *Westchester*	18	[V]	708-947-2190
chicagohighlands.com			
Chick Evans GC, *Morton Grove*	18	[M]	847-965-5353
forestpreservegolf.com			
Cinder Ridge Golf Links, *Wilmington*	18	[P]	815-476-4000
cinderridge.com			
Clinton CC, *Clinton*	9	[V]	217-935-2918
clintoncountryclub.org			
Clinton Hill CC, *Swansea*	18	[S]	618-277-3700
clintonhillgolf.com			
Cloverleaf GC, *Alton*	18	[P]	618-462-3022
Cog Hill G&CC, *Lemont*	72	[P]	630-257-5872
coghillgolf.com			
Colonial GC, *Sandoval*	18	[P]	618-247-3307
sandovalcolonialgolf.com			
Columbia GC, *Columbia*	18	[P]	618-286-9653
columbiagolfclub.net			
Columbus Park GC, *Chicago*	9	[M]	312-746-5573
cpdgolf.com			
Conway Farms GC, *Lake Forest*	18	[V]	847-234-7160
conwayfarms.com			
Country Hills GC, *Greenview*	18	[P]	217-632-7242
countryhillsgc.com			
Country Lakes GC, *Naperville*	18	[P]	630-420-1060
countrylakesgolfclub.com			
Country View GC, *Geneseo*	9	[P]	309-441-5272
Countryside GC, *Mundelein*	36	[M]	847-968-3466
lcfpd.org			
Coyote Creek GC, *Bartonville*	18	[P]	309-633-0911
golfcoyotecreek.com			
Coyote Run GC, *Flossmoor*	27	[M]	708-957-8700
coyoterungolf.com			
Crab Orchard GC, *Carterville*	18	[S]	618-985-2321
craborchardgolfclub.com			
Craig Woods GC, *Woodstock*	9	[P]	815-338-3111
crystalwoodsgc.com			
Crane Creek GC, *Kilbourne*	18	[P]	309-538-9141
golfcranecreek.com			
Cranes Landing GC, *Lincolnshire*	18	[R]	847-634-5935
craneslandinggolf.com			
Cress Creek CC, *Naperville*	18	[V]	630-355-7300
cresscreekcc.com			
Crestwicke CC, *Bloomington*	18	[V]	309-829-8092
crestwicke.com			
Crooked Creek Golf Links, *Mt Vernon*	18	[S]	618-735-2445
Crooked Knee GC, *Henry*	18	[P]	309-364-3012
Cross Creek GC, *Morrison*	9	[P]	815-772-7966
Crystal Highlands, *Lake in the Hills*	9	[P]	847-659-1766
Crystal Lake CC, *Crystal Lake*	18	[V]	815-459-1068
clcountryclub.com			
Crystal Tree G&CC, *Orland Park*	18	[V]	708-403-3010
crystaltreecc.org			
Crystal Woods GC, *Woodstock*	18	[P]	815-338-3111
crystalwoodsgc.com			
Danville CC, *Danville*	18	[V]	217-442-6027
golfdanvillecc.com			
Dayton Ridge GC, *Ottawa*	9	[P]	815-434-0145
drgolf.com			
Deer Creek GC, *University Park*	18	[P]	708-672-6667
deercreekgolfcourse.com			
Deer Park CC, *Oglesby*	18	[V]	815-667-4239
deerparkcountryclub.com			
Deer Run GC, *Hamilton*	18	[S]	217-847-3623
playdeerrun.com			
Deer Run Mary Heath Mem GC, *Robinson*	9	[M]	618-544-2350
cityofrobinson.com			
Deer Trail GC At Lake Shelbyville, *Shelbyville*	9	[S]	217-774-3030
Deer Valley GC, *Deer Grove*	27	[P]	815-438-4653
dvforegolf.com			
Deer Valley GC, *Big Rock*	9	[M]	630-556-3333
Deerfield GC, *Deerfield*	18	[M]	847-945-8333
deerfieldgolf.org			
Deerpath GC, *Lake Forest*	18	[M]	847-615-4290
cityoflakeforest.com			
Detweiller Park GC, *Peoria*	9	[M]	309-692-7518
peoriaparks.org			
Downers Grove GC, *Downers Grove*	9	[M]	630-963-1306
dgparks.org			
Dwight CC, *Dwight*	18	[S]	815-584-1399
dwightcountryclub.com			
Eagle Brook CC, *Geneva*	18	[V]	630-208-4653
eaglebrookclub.com			
Eagle Creek Resort GC, *Findlay*	18	[R]	217-756-3458
eaglecreekresort.com			
Eagle Ridge Inn & Resort, *Galena*	63	[R]	815-777-2444
eagleridge.com			
Eaglewood Conf Resort & Spa, *Itasca*	18	[R]	630-773-3510
eaglewoodresort.com			
Earlville CC, *Earlville*	9	[S]	815-246-9329
East Fork Par 3 GC, *Olney*	9	[P]	618-395-3505
Edgebrook CC, *Sandwich*	18	[S]	815-786-3058
sandwichgolf.com			
Edgebrook GC, *Chicago*	18	[M]	773-763-8320
forestpreservegolf.com			
Edgewood GC, *Auburn*	18	[P]	217-438-3221
golfedgewood.com			
Edgewood GC, *Polo*	9	[P]	815-946-3636
clubedgewood.com			
Edgewood Park GC, *Mc Nabb*	18	[P]	815-882-2317
Edgewood Valley CC, *La Grange*	18	[V]	708-246-2800
edgewoodvalleycc.com			
Effingham CC, *Effingham*	18	[V]	217-347-0424
effinghamcc.com			
Egyptian CC, *Mounds*	9	[P]	618-745-6412
El Paso CC, *El Paso*	18	[S]	309-527-5225
elpasogolfclub.com			
Elgin CC, *Elgin*	18	[V]	847-741-2707
elgincc.com			
Elliot GC, *Rockford*	18	[M]	815-332-5130
rockfordparks.org			

[A] = MILITARY   [M] = MUNICIPAL   [P] = PUBLIC   [R] = RESORT

ILLINOIS

Elmwood GC, *Belleville* .... 9 [P] 618-538-5826
  golfatelmwood.com
Emerald Hill G&LearnCtr, *Sterling* .... 18 [M] 815-622-6204
  sterlingparkdistrict.org
Evanston GC, *Skokie* .... 18 [V] 847-676-0300
  evanstongolfclub.org
Evergreen G&CC, *Evergreen Park* .... 18 [P] 773-238-6680
Exmoor CC, *Highland Park* .... 18 [V] 847-432-3600
  exmoorcountryclub.org
Fairfield CC, *Fairfield* .... 18 [S] 618-847-7222
  fairfieldcountryclub.com
Fairfield GC, *Columbia* .... 18 [P] 618-281-7773
  fairfieldgolfclub.com
Fairlakes GC, *Secor* .... 18 [P] 309-744-2222
  fairlakesgc.com
Fairway Hills GC, *Virginia* .... 9 [P] 217-452-3488
Far Oaks GC, *Caseyville* .... 27 [P] 618-628-2900
  faroaksgolfclub.com
Flagg Creek GC, *Countryside* .... 9 [M] 708-246-3336
  flaggcreekgolfcourse.org
Flora G&CC, *Flora* .... 9 [P] 618-662-2500
Flossmoor CC, *Flossmoor* .... 18 [V] 708-798-4700
  flossmoorcc.org
Flying M Ranch GC, *Centralia* .... 9 [P] 618-532-8602
Fon du Lac GC, *East Peoria* .... 9 [M] 309-699-4222
  fondulacpark.com
Forest Hills CC, *Rockford* .... 18 [V] 815-877-5733
  foresthillscountryclub.com
Fore-Way GC, *Effingham* .... 9 [P] 217-868-5418
  forewaygolfcourse.com
Foss Park GC, *North Chicago* .... 18 [M] 847-689-7490
  fosspark-district.org
Fountain Hills GC, *Alsip* .... 9 [P] 708-388-4653
  alsipparks.org
Four Willows GC, *Mason City* .... 9 [P] 217-482-3349
Fox Bend GC, *Oswego* .... 18 [P] 630-554-3939
  foxbendgolfcourse.com
Fox Creek GC, *Edwardsville* .... 18 [P] 618-692-9400
  golffoxcreek.com
Fox Lake CC, *Fox Lake* .... 18 [P] 847-587-6411
  foxlakecc.net
Fox Run Golf Links, *Elk Grove Village* .... 18 [P] 847-228-3544
  foxrungolflinks.com
Fox Valley G&CC, *North Aurora* .... 18 [M] 630-879-1030
  aurora-il.org
Foxford Hills GC, *Cary* .... 18 [M] 847-639-0400
  foxfordhillsgolfclub.com
Frank Govern Memorial GC, *Evanston* .... 18 [M] 847-475-9173
  frankgoverngolf.org
Franklin County GC, *West Frankfort* .... 18 [P] 618-937-3020
Freeport CC, *Freeport* .... 18 [V] 815-232-2012
  freeportcountryclub.com
Fresh Meadow GC, *Hillside* .... 18 [P] 708-449-3434
  freshmeadowgc.com
Fulton GC, *Fulton* .... 9 [V] 815-589-2440
Galena GC, *Galena* .... 18 [P] 815-777-3599
  galenagolf.webs.com
Gateway National Golf Links, *Madison* .... 18 [P] 314-421-4653
  gatewaynational.com
Geneseo CC, *Geneseo* .... 9 [V] 309-944-3666
  geneseocountryclub.com
Geneva GC, *Geneva* .... 9 [V] 630-232-2055

George Dunne National GC, *Oak Forest* ...... 18 [M] 708-429-6886
  forestpreservegolf.com
Gibson Woods GC, *Monmouth* .... 18 [M] 309-734-9968
  gibsonwoods.com
Gillespie CC, *Gillespie* .... 9 [P] 217-839-2703
Glen Flora CC, *Waukegan* .... 18 [V] 847-244-6304
  glenfloracc.com
Glen Oak CC, *Glen Ellyn* .... 18 [V] 630-469-5600
  glenoakcountryclub.org
Glen View Club, *Golf* .... 18 [V] 847-729-3611
  glenviewclub.com
Glencoe GC, *Glencoe* .... 18 [S] 847-835-0250
  glencoegolfclub.com
Glendale Lakes GC, *Glendale Heights* .... 18 [M] 630-260-0018
  glendalelakes.com
Gleneagles CC, *Lemont* .... 36 [P] 630-257-5466
  golfgleneagles.com
Glenview National 9 GC, *Glenview* .... 9 [M] 847-657-1637
  golfglenview.com
Glenview Park GC, *Glenview* .... 18 [M] 847-724-0250
  golfglenview.com
Glenwoodie GC, *Glenwood* .... 18 [M] 708-758-1212
  glenwoodiegolf.com
Gold Hills GC, *Colchester* .... 18 [P] 309-837-2930
  gold-hills.com
Golf Ctr, *Des Plaines* .... 9 [M] 847-803-4653
  thegolfcenter.org
Golf Vista Estates GC, *Monee* .... 9 [P] 708-534-8204
Golfmohr GC, *East Moline* .... 18 [P] 309-496-2434
  golfmohr.com
Governors Run, *Carlyle* .... 36 [P] 618-594-4585
  governorsrun.com
Grand Marais GC, *East St Louis* .... 18 [M] 618-398-9999
  grandmaraisgolf.com
Grayslake GC, *Grayslake* .... 9 [M] 847-223-7529
  glpd.com
Graystone Golf Links, *Tinley Park* .... 9 [P] 708-720-6600
Great River Road GC, *Nauvoo* .... 18 [P] 217-453-2417
  golfnauvoo.com
Green Acres CC, *Northbrook* .... 18 [V] 847-291-2200
  greenacrescountryclub.com
Green Garden CC, *Frankfort* .... 36 [P] 815-469-3350
  greengardencc.com
Green Hills GC, *Mt Vernon* .... 18 [S] 618-244-3961
  greenhillsgolfclub.net
Green Meadows, *Westmont* .... 9 [M] 630-810-5330
  dupagegolf.com
Green River CC, *Walnut* .... 9 [S] 815-379-2227
Greenshire GC, *Beach Park* .... 9 [M] 847-360-4777
  waukeganparks.org
Greenview GC, *Centralia* .... 18 [S] 618-532-7395
Greenville CC, *Greenville* .... 9 [V] 618-664-1536
Harborside International Golf Ctr, *Chicago* ... 36 [P] 312-782-7837
  harborsideinternational.com
Harrison Park GC, *Danville* .... 18 [S] 217-431-2266
  cityofdanville.org
Harry Mussatto GC At Western Illinois Univ,
  Macomb .... 18 [U] 309-298-3676
  golf.wiu.edu
Hawthorn Ridge GC, *Aledo* .... 18 [P] 309-582-5641
Hawthorn Woods CC, *Hawthorn Woods* .... 18 [V] 847-847-3259
  hwccgolf.com
Hazy Hills GC, *Hudson* .... 9 [P] 309-726-9200

[S] = SEMI-PRIVATE [V] = PRIVATE [U] = UNIVERSITY [N] = UNIVERSITY-PRIVATE

ILLINOIS
Golf Yellow Pages, 18th Edition

Heather Ridge GC, *Gurnee* ....9 [P]   847-367-6010
 heatherridgegolf.com
Hend Co Hills CC, *Biggsville* ....18 [P]   309-627-2779
Heritage Bluffs Public GC, *Channahon* ....18 [M]   815-467-7888
 heritagebluffs.com
Hickory Hills CC, *Hickory Hills* ....27 [P]   708-598-6460
 hickoryhillscntryclub.com
Hickory Knoll GC, *Lake Villa* ....9 [P]   847-356-8640
Hickory Point GC, *Forsyth* ....18 [M]   217-421-7444
 decatur-parks.org
Hickory Ridge Public Golf Ctr, *Carbondale* ....18 [P]   618-529-4386
 cpkd.org
Hidden Lakes GC, *Sheffield* ....18 [P]   815-454-2660
 hiddenlakecountryclub.com
High Point GC, *Essex* ....9 [P]   815-365-4000
 golfhighpoint.com
Highland CC, *Highland* ....9 [V]   618-654-4653
 hccgolf.net
Highland Park CC, *Highland Park* ....18 [M]   847-433-9015
 highlandparkcc.com
Highland Park GC, *Bloomington* ....18 [M]   309-434-2200
 highlandparkgc.com
Highland Springs GC, *Rock Island* ....18 [M]   309-732-7265
 rigov.org
Highland Woods GC, *Hoffman Estates* ....18 [M]   847-359-5850
 forestpreservegolf.com
Hillcrest CC, *Long Grove* ....18 [V]   847-540-5100
 hillcrestcc.org
Hillcrest Golf Ctr, *Washington* ....18 [P]   309-444-9033
Hilldale GC, *Hoffman Estates* ....18 [P]   847-310-1100
 hilldalegolf.com
Hillsboro CC, *Hillsboro* ....9 [V]   217-532-2045
Hinsdale GC, *Clarendon Hills* ....18 [V]   630-986-5339
 hinsdalegolfclub.org
Howard D Kellogg GC, *Peoria* ....27 [M]   309-691-0293
 peoriaparks.org
Hubbard Trail G&CC, *Hoopeston* ....9 [S]   217-748-6759
Hughes Creek GC, *Elburn* ....18 [P]   630-365-9200
 hughescreek.com
Hunter CC, *Richmond* ....18 [P]   815-678-7940
Hunters Ridge GC, *Princeton* ....18 [P]   815-875-1151
 huntersridgegc.com
Idlewild CC, *Flossmoor* ....18 [V]   708-798-0514
 idlewildcc.net
Illini CC, *Springfield* ....18 [V]   217-546-2830
 illinicc.net
Indian Bluff GC, *Milan* ....18 [M]   309-799-3868
 indianbluffgolfcourse.com
Indian Boundary GC, *Chicago* ....18 [M]   773-625-9630
 forestpreservegolf.com
Indian Creek G&CC, *Fairbury* ....9 [S]   815-692-2655
Indian Hill Club, *Winnetka* ....18 [V]   847-251-1711
 indianhillclub.org
Indian Hills GC, *Mt Vernon* ....18 [S]   618-244-9697
Indian Hills CC, *Tiskilwa* ....9 [P]   815-646-4856
Indian Lakes Resort, *Bloomingdale* ....27 [R]   630-529-4466
 golfindianlakes.com
Indian Mounds GC, *Fairmont City* ....18 [P]   618-271-4000
 indianmoundsgolfcourse.com
Indian Oaks CC, *Shabbona* ....9 [P]   815-824-2202
 indianoakscountryclub.com
Indian Springs GC, *Saybrook* ....9 [S]   309-475-4111
 golfatindiansprings.com

Indian Springs GC, *Fillmore* ....18 [P]   217-538-2392
 indianspringsgolf.net
Ingersoll GC & Learning Links, *Rockford* ....18 [M]   815-987-8834
 rockfordparkdistrict.org
Inverness GC, *Palatine* ....18 [V]   847-359-0244
 invernessgolfclub.org
Inwood GC, *Joliet* ....18 [M]   815-741-7265
 inwoodgc.com
Ironhorse GC, *Tuscola* ....18 [P]   217-253-6644
 ironhorsegc.com
Ironwood GC, *Normal* ....18 [M]   309-454-9620
 normal.org
Itasca CC, *Itasca* ....18 [V]   630-773-1800
 itascacountryclub.com
Jackson CC, *Murphysboro* ....18 [P]   618-684-2387
Jackson Park GC, *Chicago* ....18 [M]   773-667-0524
 cpdgolf.com
Jacksonville CC, *Jacksonville* ....18 [V]   217-245-7717
 jacksonvillecc.com
Joe Louis "The Champ" GC, *Riverdale* ....18 [M]   708-849-1731
 forestpreservegolf.com
Joliet CC, *Joliet* ....18 [V]   815-727-3677
 jolietcountryclub.com
Kankakee CC, *Kankakee* ....18 [V]   815-933-6615
 kankakeecountryclub.com
Kankakee Elks GC, *St Anne* ....18 [S]   815-937-9547
 elksgolf627.com
Kaskaskia CC, *Arcola* ....9 [V]   217-268-3001
 kaskaskiacountryclub.com
Kaufman Park GC, *Eureka* ....9 [P]   309-467-2523
Kemper Lakes GC, *Kildeer* ....18 [P]   847-320-3450
 kemperlakesgolf.com
Ken Loch Golf Links, *Lombard* ....9 [P]   630-620-9665
Kewanee Dunes, *Kewanee* ....18 [P]   309-852-4508
 kewaneedunes.com
Kishwaukee CC, *Dekalb* ....18 [V]   815-758-6849
 kishwaukeecc.org
Klein Creek GC, *Winfield* ....18 [P]   630-690-0101
 kleincreek.com
Knights of Columbus Par 3 GC, *Quincy* ....9 [P]   217-222-4105
 quincykofc.org
Knollwood Club, *Lake Forest* ....18 [V]   847-234-1600
 knollwoodclub.org
Kokopelli GC, *Marion* ....18 [P]   618-997-5656
 kokopelligolf.com
La Grange CC, *La Grange* ....18 [V]   708-352-0066
 lagrangecc.org
Lacoma GC, *East Dubuque* ....45 [S]   815-747-3874
 lacomagolf.com
Lacon CC, *Lacon* ....9 [S]   309-246-7650
Lake Barrington Shores GC, *Barrington* ....18 [V]   847-382-4240
 lbsgolf.com
Lake Bluff GC, *Lake Bluff* ....18 [M]   847-234-6771
 lakebluffgolfclub.com
Lake Bracken CC, *Galesburg* ....18 [V]   309-343-5915
 lakebracken.com
Lake Calhoun GC, *La Fayette* ....9 [V]   309-995-3343
Lake Carroll GC, *Lanark* ....18 [V]   815-493-2808
 lakecarrollassociation.com
Lake Erie CC, *Erie* ....9 [P]   309-659-2250
Lake of Egypt CC, *Marion* ....9 [R]   618-995-2661
 loecc.com

62   [A] = MILITARY   [M] = MUNICIPAL   [P] = PUBLIC   [R] = RESORT

ILLINOIS

Course	Holes	Phone
Lake of the Woods GC, *Mahomet*	27 [M]	217-586-2183
golfthelake.com		
Lake Park GC, *Des Plaines*	18 [M]	847-391-5730
desplainesparks.org		
Lake Shore CC, *Glencoe*	18 [V]	847-835-3000
lakeshorecc.com		
Lake Shore GC, *Taylorville*	18 [M]	217-824-5521
lakeshoregolfcourse.com		
Lake View GC, *Sterling*	18 [S]	815-626-2886
Lake Zurich GC, *Lake Zurich*	9 [V]	847-438-2431
Lakemoor GC, *Lakemoor*	18 [P]	815-759-0011
countrylakesgolfclubnaperville.com		
Lakeside CC, *Bloomington*	9 [V]	309-828-4711
lakesideblm.com		
Lakeview CC, *Loda*	9 [V]	217-386-2335
Lakewood Golf Assoc, *Bath*	9 [S]	309-546-2274
Lamoine Valley GC, *La Harpe*	9 [M]	217-659-3918
Lansing CC, *Lansing*	18 [V]	708-474-1590
lanscc.com		
Laurel Greens GC, *Knoxville*	36 [P]	309-289-4146
Lawrence County CC, *Lawrenceville*	9 [V]	618-943-2011
Ledges GC, *Roscoe*	18 [M]	815-389-0979
wcfpd.org		
Leisure Village GC, *Fox Lake*	9 [V]	847-587-6795
Lena GC, *Lena*	27 [P]	815-369-5513
lenagolfclub.com		
Leo Donovan GC, *Peoria*	18 [M]	309-691-8361
peoriaparks.org/golf		
LeRoy CC, *Le Roy*	9 [P]	309-962-3421
leroycountryclub.org		
Libertyville GC, *Libertyville*	9 [M]	847-362-5733
libertyville.com		
Lick Creek GC, *Pekin*	18 [M]	309-346-0077
pekin.net/pekinparkdistrict		
Lincoln Elks CC, *Lincoln*	18 [S]	217-732-4010
Lincoln Greens GC, *Springfield*	18 [M]	217-786-4111
springfieldparks.org		
Lincoln Oaks GC, *Crete*	18 [P]	708-672-9401
lincolnoaksgolfcourse.com		
Lincoln Trail GC, *Taylorville*	9 [P]	217-824-5161
Lincolnshire CC, *Crete*	18 [V]	708-672-5090
lincolnshirecountryclub.com		
Lincolnshire Fields CC, *Champaign*	18 [V]	217-352-1911
lincolnshirefieldscc.com		
Links at Jacksonville, *Jacksonville*	27 [M]	217-479-4663
jacksonvilleil.com		
Litchfield CC, *Litchfield*	9 [V]	217-324-4115
cityoflitchfieldil.com		
Lockhaven CC, *Godfrey*	18 [V]	618-466-2441
lockhavencountryclub.com		
Lockport G&RecC, *Lockport*	9 [V]	815-838-8692
Locust Hills GC, *Lebanon*	18 [P]	618-537-4590
locusthillsgolf.com		
Lone Oak GC, *Carrollton*	9 [P]	217-942-6166
Long Bridge GC, *Springfield*	9 [P]	217-744-8311
longbridgegc.com		
Longwood CC, *Crete*	18 [S]	708-758-1811
Lost Nation GC, *Dixon*	18 [P]	815-652-4212
lostnationgolf.com		
Macktown GC, *Rockton*	18 [M]	815-624-7410
wcfpd.org		
Macomb CC, *Macomb*	18 [S]	309-837-2132
mccgolf.org		
Madison Park GC, *Peoria*	18 [M]	309-673-7161
peoriaparks.org		
Makray Memorial GC, *Barrington*	18 [P]	847-381-6500
makraygolf.com		
Manteno GC, *Manteno*	18 [M]	815-468-8827
mantenogolf.com		
Maple Bluff GC, *Geneseo*	18 [P]	309-944-5418
golfmaplebluffgeneseo.com		
Maple Lane CC, *Elmwood*	9 [V]	309-742-8212
maplelanecountryclub.com		
Maple Meadows GC, *Wood Dale*	27 [M]	630-616-8424
dupagegolf.com		
Marengo Ridge GC, *Marengo*	18 [P]	815-923-2332
marengoridgegolfclub.com		
Marquette Park GC, *Chicago*	9 [M]	312-747-2761
cpdgolf.com		
Marshall GC, *Marshall*	9 [P]	217-826-2404
Mascoutah CC, *Mascoutah*	9 [P]	618-566-4884
Mattoon G&CC, *Mattoon*	18 [V]	217-234-7735
mgcc.com		
Mauh Nah Tee See CC, *Rockford*	18 [V]	815-399-0682
mntscc.org		
McHenry CC, *McHenry*	18 [V]	815-385-3435
mchenrycc.net		
McLeansboro GC, *McLeansboro*	9 [S]	618-643-2400
Meadow View GC, *Mattoon*	18 [P]	217-258-7888
meadowviewgolf.com		
Meadow Woods GC, *Centralia*	9 [P]	618-532-8142
Meadowlark GC, *Hinsdale*	9 [M]	708-562-2977
forestpreservegolf.com		
Medinah CC, *Medinah*	54 [V]	630-438-6825
medinahcc.org		
Mendota GC, *Mendota*	18 [S]	815-538-7241
Metropolis CC, *Metropolis*	18 [V]	618-524-4414
metropoliscountryclub.net		
Mid Iron Club, *Lemont*	9 [P]	630-257-3340
Midland Hills GC, *Makanda*	9 [P]	618-529-3698
midlandhillsgolf.com		
Midlane Champ Golf Resort, *Wadsworth*	18 [R]	847-360-0550
midlaneresort.com		
Midlothian CC, *Midlothian*	18 [V]	708-388-0596
midlothiancc.org		
Mill Creek GC, *Geneva*	27 [P]	630-208-7272
millcreekgolfcourse.com		
Miller Golf Complex, *Dixon*	9 [M]	815-284-1033
Minne Monesse GC, *Grant Park*	18 [S]	815-465-6653
minnemonesse.com		
Mission Hills CC, *Northbrook*	18 [V]	847-498-3200
missionhillsclub.com		
Mistwood GC, *Romeoville*	18 [P]	815-254-3333
mistwoodgolf.net		
Monmouth CC, *Monmouth*	9 [V]	309-734-7909
monmouthcountryclub.com		
Monticello CC, *Monticello*	9 [V]	217-762-2831
Morris CC, *Morris*	18 [V]	815-942-3628
morriscountryclub.com		
Mount Hawley CC, *Peoria*	18 [V]	309-691-6731
mthawleycc.com		
Moweaqua GC, *Moweaqua*	18 [M]	217-768-3411
Mt Carmel Muni GC, *Mt Carmel*	18 [M]	618-262-5771
mtcarmelgolfcourse.com		
Mt Prospect GC, *Mt Prospect*	18 [S]	847-259-4200
mppd.org		

[S] = SEMI-PRIVATE [V] = PRIVATE [U] = UNIVERSITY [N] = UNIVERSITY-PRIVATE

ILLINOIS
Golf Yellow Pages, 18th Edition

Naperbrook GC, *Plainfield*..................................18 [M] 630-378-4215
  naperbrookgolfcourse.org
Naperville CC, *Naperville* .... 18 [V] 630-355-0747
  napervillecc.org
Nashville GC, *Nashville* ....9 [M] 618-327-3821
Nettle Creek CC, *Morris* ....18 [M] 815-941-4300
  nettlecreek.com
Newburg Village GC, *Cherry Valley*......................9 [P] 815-332-9002
  newburgvillage.net
Newman GC, *Peoria*...18 [M] 309-674-1663
  peoriaparks.org
Nickol Knoll GC, *Arlington Heights* ....9 [M] 847-590-6050
  ahpd.org/nkgc
North County CC, *Red Bud* ....9 [P] 618-282-6590
North Greens GC, *Atlanta* ....9 [P] 217-648-5500
  northgreensgc.com
North Shore CC, *Glenview* .... 18 [V] 847-724-9240
  north-shorecc.org
Northmoor CC, *Highland Park*........................... 27 [V] 847-926-5200
  northmoor.org
Northridge Hills GC, *Jacksonville*..........................9 [P] 217-243-4241
  northridgehills.com
Norton Knolls GC, *Oakland* ....9 [P] 217-346-3102
Oak Brook CC, *Edwardsville*................................27 [P] 618-656-5600
Oak Brook GC, *Oak Brook* ....18 [M] 630-990-3032
  oak-brook.org
Oak Club of Genoa, *Genoa* ....18 [P] 815-784-5678
  oakclubgolf.com
Oak Glen GC, *Robinson* ....18 [P] 618-592-3030
Oak Grove GC, *Harvard* ....18 [P] 815-648-2550
  oakgrovegolfcourse.com
Oak Hills CC, *Palos Heights* ....9 [S] 708-448-5544
  oakhills.com
Oak Leaf CC, *Girard* ....9 [S] 217-627-3015
  oakleafcountryclub.com
Oak Meadows GC, *Addison* ....18 [M] 630-595-0071
  dupagegolf.com
Oak Park CC, *River Grove* .... 18 [V] 708-456-7600
  opcc.ws
Oak Run GC, *Dahinda*..18 [P] 309-879-2582
Oak Springs GC, *St Anne* ....18 [P] 815-937-1648
  oakspringsgolfclub.com
Oak Terrace Resort, *Pana* ....18 [R] 217-539-4477
  oakterraceresort.com
Oak View CC, *Aledo* .... 9 [V] 309-582-7916
Oakville CC, *Mt Carroll*...9 [S] 815-684-5295
  oakvillegolfing.com
Oakwood CC, *Coal Valley* .... 18 [V] 309-799-3153
  oakwoodgolf.org
Odyssey CC, *Tinley Park*.....................................18 [P] 708-429-7402
  odysseycountryclub.com
Old Elm Club, *Highland Park* .... 18 [V] 847-432-6272
  oldelmclub.com
Old Oak CC, *Homer Glen* ....18 [P] 708-301-3344
  oldoakcc.com
Old Orchard CC, *Mt Prospect*..............................18 [M] 847-255-2025
  oldorchardcc.com
Old Orchard CC, *Pittsfield* .... 9 [V] 217-285-9041
Old Top Farm GC, *Crystal Lake* ....9 [P] 815-479-9361
Old Wayne GC, *West Chicago*............................. 27 [V] 630-231-1350
Olympia Fields CC, *Olympia Fields*...................... 36 [V] 708-748-0495
  ofcc.info
Onwentsia Club, *Lake Forest* .... 18 [V] 847-234-0120

Orchard Valley GC, *Aurora* ....18 [M] 630-907-0500
  orchardvalleygolf.com
Oregon CC, *Oregon* .... 9 [V] 815-732-7405
  oregonil.com
Palatine Hills GC, *Palatine*...................................18 [M] 847-359-4020
  palatinehills.org
Palisades GC, *Savanna*..9 [P] 815-273-2141
  palisadesgolfcourse.com
Palos CC, *Orland Park*...9 [P] 708-448-6064
  paloscountryclub.com
Palos Hills Muni GC, *Palos Hills* ....9 [M] 708-599-0202
  paloshillsweb.org
Pana CC, *Pana* .... 9 [V] 217-562-2641
Panther Creek CC, *Springfield*............................. 18 [V] 217-546-4432
  panthercreekcc.com
Park Hills GC, *Freeport* ....36 [M] 815-235-3611
  golfparkhills.com
Park Ridge CC, *Park Ridge* .... 18 [V] 847-823-0410
  parkridgecc.org
Parkview GC, *Pekin*...18 [M] 309-346-8494
  pekinparkdistrict.org
Pasfield GC, *Springfield*..9 [M] 217-753-6226
  springfieldparks.org
Pekin CC, *Pekin* .... 18 [V] 309-346-6888
  pekincc.com
Peoria Golf Learning Ctr, *Peoria* ....9 [M] 309-690-7162
Pheasant Run Resort & Spa, *St Charles* ....18 [R] 630-584-4914
  pheasantrun.com/golf
Phillips Park GC, *Aurora* ....18 [M] 630-499-0670
  phillipsparkaurora.com
Pine Hills GC, *Ottawa* ....9 [S] 815-434-3985
  ottawapinehillsgolfclub.com
Pine Lakes GC, *Washington*................................18 [P] 309-745-9344
  pinelakesgc.com
Pine Lakes GC, *Herrin*..18 [S] 618-942-6816
Pine Meadow GC, *Mundelein*..............................18 [P] 847-566-4653
  pinemeadowgc.com
Pinecrest G&CC, *Huntley*....................................18 [M] 847-669-3111
  pinecrestgc.com
Pinnacle CC, *Milan*... 18 [V] 309-787-5446
  pinnaclecountryclub.com
Piper Glen GC, *Springfield*...................................18 [P] 217-483-6537
  piperglen.com
Pistakee CC, *McHenry* ....9 [P] 815-385-9854
Plum Creek GC, *Winchester*.................................9 [P] 217-742-9018
Plum Tree National GC, *Harvard*..........................18 [P] 815-943-7474
  plumtreegolf.com
Pontiac Elks CC, *Pontiac* ....18 [S] 815-842-1249
  pontiacelks.com
Poplar Creek CC, *Hoffman Estates* ....18 [M] 847-884-0219
  poplarcreekcc.com
Pottawatomie GC, *St Charles* ....9 [P] 630-584-8356
  st-charlesparks.com
Prairie Bluff GC, *Lockport* ....18 [M] 815-836-4653
  lockportpark.org
Prairie Isle GC, *Prairie Grove* ....18 [P] 815-356-0202
  prairieisle.com
Prairie Lake GC, *Marseilles* ....9 [P] 815-795-5107
Prairie Landing GC, *West Chicago*.......................18 [P] 630-208-7600
  prairielanding.com
Prairie Pines GC, *Dekalb*......................................9 [P] 815-758-5249
Prairie Ridge Golf, *Morrison*................................18 [P] 815-772-8989
  prairieridgegolfcourse.com

[A] = MILITARY   [M] = MUNICIPAL   [P] = PUBLIC   [R] = RESORT

Golf Yellow Pages, 18th Edition — ILLINOIS

Prairie Vista GC, *Bloomington* ....18 [M] 309-434-2217
  prairievistagc.com
PrairieView GC, *Byron*.........................18 [M] 815-234-4653
  prairieviewgolf.com
Prestwick CC, *Frankfort*....................... 18 [V] 815-469-2136
  prestwickcc.com
Prophet Hills CC, *Prophetstown*................9 [S] 815-537-5226
Pyramid Oaks GC, *Percy*........................9 [P] 618-497-8484
Quail Creek CC, *Robinson* ....18 [R] 618-544-8674
  quailcreekclub.com
Quail Meadows GC, *Washington*.............18 [M] 309-694-3139
  quailmeadowsgolf.com
Quincy CC, *Quincy*............................. 18 [V] 217-222-1052
  quincycountryclub.org
Railside GC, *Gibson City* ....18 [P] 217-784-5000
  railside.com
Ramsey Lake GC, *Ramsey* ....9 [P] 618-423-2261
Randall Oaks GC, *West Dundee* ....18 [M] 847-428-5661
  randalloaksgc.com
Ravinia Green CC, *Riverwoods*.............. 18 [V] 847-945-6200
  raviniagreen.com
Ravisloe CC, *Homewood* ....18 [P] 708-798-5600
  ravisloecountryclub.com
Red Barn GC, *Rockton* ....9 [P] 815-624-8037
  redbarngolfcourse.com
Red Dog Run GC, *East Moline*.................9 [P] 309-496-9355
Red Hawk CC, *Tamaroa*......................18 [S] 618-357-8712
  redhawkgc.net
Red Tail Run GC, *Decatur*....................18 [M] 217-422-2211
  redtailrun.org
RedTail GC, *Village of Lakewood*...........18 [M] 815-477-0055
  redtailgolf.com
Rend Lake GC, *Whittington* ....27 [M] 618-629-2353
  rendlake.org
Renwood GC, *Round Lake Beach* ....18 [M] 847-231-4711
  renwoodgolf.com
Rich Harvest Farms, *Sugar Grove* .... 18 [V] 630-466-7610
  richharvestfarms.com
Richland CC, *Olney*...........................18 [S] 618-395-1661
  rccgolf.net
Ridge CC, *Chicago*............................ 18 [V] 773-238-9400
  ridgecc.org
Ridgemoor CC, *Chicago*...................... 18 [V] 708-867-8400
  ridgemoorcc.com
River Bend GC, *Lisle*...........................9 [M] 630-968-1920
  riverbendgolfclub.org
River Forest CC, *Elmhurst* .... 18 [V] 630-279-5444
  riverforestcc.org
River Heights GC, *Dekalb* ....18 [M] 815-758-1550
  riverheightsgc.com
River Lakes GC, *Columbia*...................18 [P] 618-281-5400
  riverlakesgolfcourse.com
River Oaks GC, *Calumet City* ....18 [M] 708-868-4090
  forestpreservegolf.com
Riverside GC, *North Riverside*.............. 18 [V] 708-447-8152
  rgc.org
Rob Roy GC, *Prospect Heights*.................9 [M] 847-253-4544
  rtpd.org
Robert Black GC, *Chicago*......................9 [M] 312-742-7931
  cpdgolf.com
Robert P Wadlow Muni GC, *Alton* ....9 [M] 618-465-9861
  alton-il.com
Rochelle CC, *Rochelle*........................ 18 [V] 815-562-6666

Rock Island Arsenal GC, *Rock Island* .... 18 [V] 309-793-1604
  riagolfclub.com
Rock River CC, *Rock Falls* ....18 [P] 815-625-2322
  rrgap.com
Rock Springs GC, *Alton* ....9 [M] 618-465-9898
Rockford CC, *Rockford*...................... 18 [V] 815-962-0948
  rockfordcountryclub.com
Rogala Public Links, *Mattoon* ....9 [P] 217-235-5518
Roland Barkau Memorial GC, *Okawville*...18 [M] 618-243-6610
  rbmgolfcourse.com
Rolling Green CC, *Arlington Heights*.......... 18 [V] 847-253-0400
  rollinggreen.org
Rolling Greens GC, *Mt Sterling* ....9 [P] 217-773-3085
Rolling Hills GC, *Godfrey* ....27 [P] 618-466-8363
  rollinghillsgc.com
Rolling Knoll CC, *Elgin* ....18 [P] 847-888-2888
  rollingknollscc.com
Royal Fox CC, *St Charles* .... 18 [V] 630-584-4000
  royalfoxcc.com
Royal Hawk CC, *St Charles* .... 18 [V] 630-443-3500
  royalfoxcc.com
Royal Melbourne, *Long Grove* .... 18 [V] 847-913-8380
  royalmelbourne.net
Ruffled Feathers GC, *Lemont*................18 [S] 630-257-1000
  ruffledfeathersgc.com
Ruth Lake CC, *Hinsdale* .... 18 [V] 630-986-2060
  ruthlakecc.org
Salem CC, *Salem* .... 18 [V] 618-548-2975
  salemcc.net
Saline County G&CC, *Eldorado* ....18 [P] 618-273-9002
Salt Creek GC, *Wood Dale*...................18 [M] 630-773-0184
  saltcreekgolfclub.com
Sanctuary GC, *New Lenox* ....18 [M] 815-462-4653
  golfsanctuary.com
Sandy Hollow GC, *Rockford*.................18 [M] 815-987-8836
  rockfordparks.org
Saukie Muni GC, *Rock Island* ....18 [M] 309-732-2277
  rigov.org
Savannah Oaks GC of Candlewick Lake, *Poplar Grove* .9 [P] 815-765-0111
  candlewick-lake.org
Schaumburg GC, *Schaumburg* ....27 [M] 847-885-9000
  schaumburggolf.com
Scovill GC, *Decatur*...........................18 [M] 217-429-6243
  decatur-parks.org
Scripps Park GC, *Rushville*...................18 [M] 217-322-4444
Senicas Oak Ridge GC, *La Salle* ....18 [P] 815-223-7273
  senicasoakridge.net
Settlers Hill GC, *Batavia*......................18 [M] 630-232-1636
  settlershill.com
Seven Bridges GC, *Woodridge* ....18 [M] 630-964-7777
  sevenbridges.com
Shady Oaks CC, *Amboy* ....18 [P] 815-849-5424
  shadyoakscc.com
Shagbark G&CC, *Onarga* ....9 [P] 815-268-7308
Shambolee GC, *Petersburg* ....18 [S] 217-632-2140
  shamboleegolfclub.com
Shamrock GC, *St Anne* ....18 [P] 815-937-9355
Shaw Creek GC, *Bushnell* ....9 [P] 309-772-3422
  golfbushnell.com
Shawnee Hills CC, *Harrisburg*................9 [P] 618-253-7294
Shepherds Crook GC, *Zion* ....18 [M] 847-872-2080
  shepherdscrook.org
Shewami CC, *Sheldon* .... 18 [V] 815-429-3769

[S] = SEMI-PRIVATE   [V] = PRIVATE   [U] = UNIVERSITY   [N] = UNIVERSITY-PRIVATE

ILLINOIS — Golf Yellow Pages, 18th Edition

Shiloh Park GC, *Zion* ....9 [M] 847-746-5500
  zionparkdistrict.com
Shoal Creek GC, *Raymond* ....9 [M] 217-229-4545
Shoreacres, *Lake Bluff*............................... 18 [V] 847-234-1472
  shoreacres1916.com
Short Hills CC, *East Moline* .... 18 [V] 309-755-0618
  shorthillscc.com
Silver Lake CC, *Orland Park* ....45 [P] 708-349-6940
  silverlakecc.com
Silver Oaks GC, *Braidwood* .... 9 [V] 815-458-2068
Silver Ridge GC, *Oregon* ....18 [P] 815-734-4440
  silverridgegolfcourse.com
Sinnissippi Park GC, *Rockford*.................9 [M] 815-987-8838
  rockfordparks.org
Skokie CC, *Glencoe*..................................... 18 [V] 847-835-5835
  skokiecc.com
Snag Creek GC, *Washburn* ....18 [P] 309-248-7300
Soangetaha CC, *Galesburg*...................... 18 [V] 309-342-5410
  soangetaha.com
South Bluff CC, *Peru* ....9 [P] 815-223-0603
  southbluffgolf.com
South Shore Cultural Ctr GC, *Chicago* ....9 [P] 773-256-0986
  cpdgolf.com
South Shore GC, *Momence*......................18 [P] 815-472-4407
  ssgcm.com
South Side CC, *Decatur* .... 18 [V] 217-428-4851
  southsidecountryclub.com
Sparta CC, *Sparta* .... 9 [V] 618-443-4911
Spencer T Olin Community GC, *Alton* ....27 [P] 618-465-3111
  spencertolingolf.com
Sportsmans CC, *Northbrook*....................27 [M] 847-291-2351
  sportsmansgolf.com
Spring Creek GC, *Spring Valley*...............18 [P] 815-894-2137
Spring Lake CC, *Quincy* .... 18 [V] 217-222-5021
  springlakecountryclub.com
Springbrook GC, *Naperville*.....................18 [P] 630-848-5060
  springbrookgolfcourse.org
Square Links GC&DR, *Frankfort*...................9 [P] 815-469-1600
  fspd.org
St Andrews G&CC, *West Chicago* ....36 [P] 630-231-3100
  standrewsgc.com
St Charles GC, *St Charles* .... 18 [V] 630-377-9340
  stcharlescountryclub.com
St Clair CC, *Belleville* .... 18 [V] 618-398-3402
  stclaircc.com
St Elmo GC, *St Elmo* ....9 [S] 618-829-3390
Stagecoach GC, *Lena*...................................9 [P] 815-369-2222
  stagecoachgolfcourse.com
Star Dust GC, *Johnston City* ....9 [P] 618-983-8822
Staunton CC, *Staunton*............................... 9 [V] 618-635-2430
Steeple Chase GC, *Mundelein*.................18 [P] 847-949-8900
  mundeleinparks.org/steeplechasegc
Stone Creek GC, *Makanda*.......................18 [P] 618-457-5455
  stonecreekgolf.com
Stone Creek GC, *Urbana*...........................18 [P] 217-367-3000
  stonecreekgolfclub.com
Stonebridge CC, *Aurora* .... 18 [V] 630-820-1007
  stonebridge-cc.org
Stonebridge GC, *Maryville*.......................18 [P] 618-346-8800
  golfatstonebridge.com
Stonehenge GC, *Barrington* .... 18 [V] 847-381-8600
Stones Throw GC, *Newton* ....18 [P] 618-783-3790
  stonesthrowgolfcourse.com

Stonewall Orchard GC, *Grayslake*...........18 [P] 847-740-4890
  stonewallorchard.com
Stonewolf GC, *Fairview Heights* ....18 [P] 618-624-4653
  stonewolfgolf.com
Stony Creek GC, *Oak Lawn* ....18 [M] 708-857-2433
  golfstonycreek.com
Storybrook CC, *Hanover* ....18 [P] 815-591-2210
  storybrook.com
Streamwood Oaks GC, *Streamwood* ....9 [M] 630-483-1881
  streamwood.org
Streator CC, *Streator* .... 9 [V] 815-673-5553
Sugar Creek GC, *Villa Park*......................9 [M] 630-834-3325
  sugarcreekgolfcourse.org
Sugar River Greens, *Rockton* ....9 [P] 815-629-2227
Sullivan CC, *Sullivan* .... 9 [V] 217-728-4406
Summertime Nine GC, *Kell* ....9 [P] 618-822-6242
Sun N Fun Swim & GC, *Decatur* ....9 [P] 217-877-6622
Sunset GC, *Mt Morris* ....9 [P] 815-734-4839
Sunset Hills CC, *Edwardsville*................. 18 [V] 618-656-9380
  sunsethillscountryclub.com
Sunset Hills GC, *Pekin*..............................27 [P] 309-347-7553
  sunsethillsgolfclub.com
Sunset Ridge CC, *Northfield* .... 22 [V] 847-446-5222
  sunsetridgecc.com
Sunset Valley GC, *Highland Park* ....18 [M] 847-432-7140
  sunsetvalleygolfcourse.org
Swan Creek GC, *Avon*..................................9 [P] 309-465-3127
  swancreekgolfclub.com
Swan Hills GC, *Belvidere* ....18 [P] 815-547-3232
Sycamore GC, *Sycamore*...........................18 [P] 815-895-3884
  sycamoreparkdistrict.com
Sycamore Hills GC, *Paris* ....18 [S] 217-465-4031
  sycamorehillsgc.com
Sydney R Marovitz GC, *Chicago*..............9 [M] 312-742-7930
  cpdgolf.com
Tall Oaks CC, *Toluca*.................................. 9 [V] 815-452-9392
Tamarack CC, *O Fallon*..............................18 [P] 618-632-6666
Tamarack GC, *Naperville*...........................18 [P] 630-904-4000
  tamarackgc.com
Tanna Farms GC, *Geneva*........................18 [P] 630-232-4300
  tannafarms.com
Terrace Hill GC, *Algonquin* .... 18 [V] 847-658-4653
  terracehillgc.com
Terry Park GC, *Palmyra* ....9 [M] 217-436-2531
The Arboretum Club, *Buffalo Grove*.....18 [M] 847-913-1112
  arboretumgolf.com
The Bourne, *Marseilles* ....18 [P] 815-496-2301
The Bridges GC, *Columbia* ....18 [P] 618-281-3900
  columbiagolfclub.net
The Den at Fox Creek, *Bloomington* ....18 [M] 309-434-2300
  thedengc.com
The Gambit GC, *Vienna*............................18 [P] 618-658-6022
  gambitgolf.com
The GC of Illinois, *Algonquin* ....18 [P] 847-658-4400
  golfclubofil.com
The Glen Club, *Glenview* ....18 [S] 847-724-7272
  theglenclub.com
The Highlands of Elgin, *Elgin* ....18 [M] 847-931-5950
  highlandsofelgin.com
The Ivanhoe Club, *Mundelein*................. 27 [V] 847-970-3800
  ivanhoeclub.com
The Legacy GC, *Granite City*...................18 [P] 618-931-4653
  thelegacygolfcourse.com

66 [A] = MILITARY   [M] = MUNICIPAL   [P] = PUBLIC   [R] = RESORT

ILLINOIS

Course	Location	Holes	Type	Phone
The Legends of Bensenville,	Bensenville	9	[M]	630-594-1100
bensenville.il.us				
The Legends of Champaign,	Champaign	9	[P]	217-863-2145
legendsofchampaign.com				
The Links at Carillon,	Plainfield	27	[P]	815-886-2132
carillongolf.com				
The Links At Ireland Grove,	Bloomington	9	[P]	309-661-8040
thelinksatirelandgrove.com				
The Meadows GC of Blue Island,	Blue Island	18	[M]	708-385-1994
meadowsgc.com				
The Merit Club,	Libertyville	18	[V]	847-918-8800
meritclub.org				
The Oaks GC,	Springfield	18	[P]	217-528-6600
theoaksgolfcourse.com				
The Orchards GC,	Belleville	18	[P]	618-233-8921
orchardsgolfclub.com				
The Prairies,	Cahokia	18	[M]	618-332-6944
The Rail GC,	Springfield	18	[P]	217-525-0365
railgolf.com				
The Ridge GC,	Waterloo	18	[S]	618-939-4646
The Tam O Shanter GC,	Niles	9	[M]	847-965-2344
niles-parks.org				
The Windmills GC,	Rio	9	[P]	309-972-5321
windmillsgc.com				
The Woodlands GC,	Alton	18	[P]	618-462-1456
playthewoodlands.com				
ThunderHawk GC,	Zion	18	[M]	847-968-4295
lcfpd.org				
Timber Creek Golf,	Dixon	18	[P]	815-288-5110
timbercreekdixon.com				
Timber Lake CC,	Peoria	9	[V]	309-674-2171
timberlakeclub.com				
Timber Lakes GC,	Staunton	18	[P]	618-635-4653
timberlakesgc.com				
Timber Pointe GC,	Poplar Grove	18	[P]	815-544-1935
golfthepointe.com				
Timber Trails CC,	La Grange	18	[P]	708-246-0275
timbertrailscc.com				
Timberlake GC,	Sullivan	9	[P]	217-797-6496
TPC Deere Run,	Silvis	18	[S]	309-796-6000
tpc.com/deererun				
Traditions At Chevy Chase,	Wheeling	18	[M]	847-465-2300
chevychasecountryclub.com				
Tri City CC,	Villa Grove	9	[V]	217-832-9782
Tri County CC,	Augusta	9	[P]	309-458-3226
Triple Lakes GC,	Millstadt	18	[P]	618-476-9985
TTI GC,	Cave in Rock	9	[P]	618-289-4587
Tuckaway GC,	Crete	18	[P]	708-946-2259
tuckawaygc.com				
Turnberry CC,	Crystal Lake	18	[V]	815-459-3356
turnberrycc.com				
Turtle Run GC,	Danville	18	[P]	217-442-8876
turtlerungolfclub.com				
Twin Creeks GC,	Manville	9	[S]	815-672-4220
Twin Lakes GC,	Palatine	9	[P]	847-934-6050
saltcreekpd.com				
Twin Lakes GC,	Westmont	9	[M]	630-852-7167
Twin Oaks G&CC,	Blandinsville	9	[P]	309-652-9519
Twin Oaks GC,	Greenville	9	[P]	618-749-5611
twinoaksgolf.net				
Twin Orchard CC,	Long Grove	36	[V]	847-634-3800
twinorchardcc.org				
Union County CC,	Anna	18	[S]	618-833-7912
Univ GC&CCtr,	University Park	18	[S]	708-747-0306
universitygolfclub.com				
Univ of Illinois GC,	Savoy	36	[U]	217-359-5613
uofigolf.com				
Urbana G&CC,	Urbana	18	[V]	217-344-8673
urbanacountryclub.com				
Valley Green GC,	North Aurora	18	[P]	630-897-3000
valleygreengc.com				
Valley Lo Club,	Glenview	18	[V]	847-729-5557
valleylo.org				
Valley View Club,	Cambridge	18	[V]	309-937-3938
Vandalia G&CC,	Vandalia	9	[S]	618-283-1365
Vernon Hills GC,	Vernon Hills	9	[P]	847-680-9310
vernonhillsgolf.com				
Villa Olivia CC,	Bartlett	18	[P]	630-289-1000
villaolivia.com				
Village Green CC,	Mundelein	18	[P]	847-566-7373
villagegreencc.com				
Village Greens of Woodridge GC,	Woodridge	18	[M]	630-985-3610
villagegreensgolf.com				
Village Links of Glen Ellyn,	Glen Ellyn	27	[M]	630-469-8194
villagelinksgolf.com				
Walnut Greens GC,	Schaumburg	9	[M]	847-490-7878
walnutgreensgolf.com				
Waterloo CC,	Waterloo	9	[V]	618-939-9810
waterloocountryclub.com				
Waters Edge GC,	Marengo	9	[P]	815-568-5983
Waters Edge GC,	Worth	18	[M]	708-671-1032
watersedgegolf.com				
WeaverRidge GC,	Peoria	18	[P]	309-691-3344
weaverridge.com				
Weber Park GC,	Skokie	9	[M]	847-674-1500
skokieparkdistrict.org				
Wedgewood GC,	Plainfield	18	[M]	815-741-7270
wedgewoodgc.com				
Wee Ma Tuk Hills CC,	Cuba	18	[V]	309-789-6208
wmtcc.com				
Weibring GC At Illinois State Univ,	Normal	18	[U]	309-438-8065
isugolf.com				
West Haven GC,	Belleville	9	[P]	618-233-9536
Western Acres GC,	Lombard	9	[M]	630-469-6768
westernacres.com				
Westlake CC,	Jerseyville	9	[V]	618-498-2011
westlakecc.net				
Westlake Village,	Winnebago	18	[P]	815-335-7177
golfwestlake.com				
Westmoreland CC,	Wilmette	18	[V]	847-251-4600
westmorelandcc.org				
Westview GC,	Quincy	27	[M]	217-223-7499
westviewgolf.com				
Whisper Creek GC,	Huntley	18	[P]	847-515-7680
whispercreekgolf.com				
White Deer Run GC,	Vernon Hills	18	[P]	847-680-6100
whitedeergolf.com				
White Eagle GC,	Naperville	27	[V]	630-983-6806
whiteaglegc.com				
White Mountain Golf Park,	Tinley Park	9	[P]	708-478-4653
whitemountaingolfpark.com				
White Oak GC,	Marissa	9	[R]	618-295-2889
White Pines GC,	Bensenville	36	[M]	630-766-0304
whitepinesgolf.com				
Whitetail Ridge GC,	Yorkville	18	[S]	630-882-8988
whitetailridgegolf.us				

[S] = SEMI-PRIVATE   [V] = PRIVATE   [U] = UNIVERSITY   [N] = UNIVERSITY-PRIVATE

ILLINOIS

Golf Yellow Pages, 18th Edition

Willow Crest GC, *Oak Brook* .... 18 [R] 630-850-5515
  willowcrestgolf.com
Willow Glen GC, *Great Lakes* .... 18 [A] 847-688-4593
  mwrgl.com
Willow Pond GC, *Rantoul* .... 18 [P] 217-893-9000
Willow Run GC, *Mokena* .... 9 [P] 815-485-2119
  willowrungolf.net
Willowhill GC, *Northbrook* .... 9 [P] 847-480-7888
  willowhillgolfcourse.com
Wilmette GC, *Wilmette* .... 18 [M] 847-256-9646
  golfwilmette.com
Wing Park GC, *Elgin* .... 9 [M] 847-931-5952
Winnetka GC, *Winnetka* .... 27 [M] 847-501-2050
  winnetkagolfclub.com
Wolf Creek GC, *Danville* .... 9 [P] 217-446-9226
Wolf Creek GC, *Pontiac* .... 18 [P] 815-842-9008
  golfatwolfcreek.com
Wolf Run GC, *Aurora* .... 18 [P] 630-906-1402
  wolfrungolfcourse.net
Wolves Crossing GC, *Jerseyville* .... 18 [P] 618-498-3178
  wolvescrossing.com
Woodbine Bend GC, *Stockton* .... 18 [P] 815-858-3939
  woodbinebend.com
Woodbine GC, *Homer Glen* .... 18 [P] 708-301-1252
  woodbinegolf.com
Woodlawn CC, *Farmer City* .... 9 [P] 309-928-3215
  woodlawnccgolf.com
Woodruff GC, *Joliet* .... 18 [M] 815-741-7272
  woodruffgc.com
Woodstock CC, *Woodstock* .... 9 [V] 815-338-5355
  woodstockcountryclub.com
Wyaton Hills GC, *Princeton* .... 9 [P] 815-872-2641
Wynstone GC, *North Barrington* .... 18 [V] 847-304-2810
  wynstone.org
Yorktown G Complex, *Belleville* .... 18 [P] 618-233-2000
  yorktowngolf.net
Zigfield Troy Par3, *Woodridge* .... 9 [P] 630-985-9860
  zigfieldtroygolf.com

INDIANA

A J Thatcher GC, *Indianapolis* .... 9 [M] 317-244-0713
  indy.gov/eGov/City/DPR/Golf
Albany GC, *Albany* .... 18 [P] 765-789-4366
Alvin C Ruxer Park Muni GC, *Jasper* .... 9 [P] 812-482-5554
American Legion GC, *Kokomo* .... 18 [P] 765-453-9864
Anderson CC, *Anderson* .... 18 [V] 765-643-4252
  andersonclub.com
Angel Hill GC, *Rossville* .... 18 [P] 765-379-3533
  angelhillgolfcourse.com
Antler Pointe GC, *Rushville* .... 18 [S] 765-932-3072
  antlerpointe.com
Arbor Trace GC, *Marion* .... 18 [P] 765-662-8236
  arbortracegc.com
Arlington Park Assoc, *Fort Wayne* .... 9 [P] 260-485-2774
Arrowhead GC, *Greenfield* .... 18 [P] 317-326-2226
  arrowheadgc.com
Autumn Ridge GC, *Fort Wayne* .... 18 [P] 260-637-8727
  autumnridgegc.com
Balmoral GC, *Fishers* .... 9 [V] 317-849-4409
  balmoralgolfclub.com
Bass Lake GC, *Knox* .... 18 [P] 574-772-2432
Battle Ground GC, *Battle Ground* .... 18 [P] 765-567-2178
  golfbattleground.com

Bear Chase GC, *Shelbyville* .... 18 [P] 317-392-9010
  bearchasegc.com
Bear Slide GC, *Cicero* .... 18 [P] 317-984-3837
  bearslide.com
Beechwood GC, *La Porte* .... 18 [M] 219-362-2651
Belterra GC, *Florence* .... 18 [R] 812-427-7783
  belterracasino.com
Bent Oak GC, *Elkhart* .... 18 [V] 574-295-1602
  bentoakgc.com
Benton County CC, *Fowler* .... 18 [S] 765-884-1864
Bicknell CC, *Bicknell* .... 18 [S] 812-735-4518
  bicknellcountryclub.com
Big Pine GC, *Attica* .... 18 [S] 765-762-2027
Birch Tree GC, *New Carlisle* .... 9 [P] 574-654-7311
Birck Boilermaker G Complex, *West Lafayette* .... 36 [U] 765-494-3139
  purduegolf.com
Black Squirrel GC, *Goshen* .... 18 [P] 574-533-1828
  blacksquirrelgolfclub.com
Blackford CC, *Hartford City* .... 18 [P] 765-348-0700
Blackthorn GC, *South Bend* .... 18 [M] 574-232-4653
  blackthorngolf.com
Bledsoes Lakeview GC, *Angola* .... 9 [P] 260-833-2240
Bloomington CC, *Bloomington* .... 18 [V] 812-332-3025
  bloomingtoncc.com
Bluewater GC, *Montpelier* .... 9 [P] 765-728-2800
Bluff Creek GC, *Greenwood* .... 18 [P] 317-422-4736
  bluffcreekgolf.com
Boltenwood GC Range & Acad, *Linton* .... 18 [P] 812-847-4480
Boonville GC, *Boonville* .... 18 [V] 812-897-1370
  boonvillecountryclub.com
Bowlers CC, *South Bend* .... 9 [V] 574-237-9150
  bowlcc.org
Brendonwood GC, *Indianapolis* .... 9 [V] 317-547-8717
  brendonwood.org
Briar Leaf GC, *La Porte* .... 18 [P] 219-326-1992
  briarleaf.com
Briar Ridge CC, *Schererville* .... 27 [V] 219-322-3660
  briarridgecc.com
Brickyard Crossing GC, *Indianapolis* .... 18 [R] 317-492-6570
  brickyardcrossing.com
Bridgewater GC, *Auburn* .... 36 [P] 260-925-8184
  bridgewatergolf.com
Broadmoor CC, *Indianapolis* .... 18 [V] 317-251-9444
  broadmoorcc.com
Brockway GC, *Lapel* .... 9 [P] 765-534-4194
Brook Hill GC, *Brookville* .... 18 [P] 765-647-4522
  brookhillgc.com
Brookshire GC, *Carmel* .... 18 [S] 317-846-7431
  brookshiregolf.com
Brookwood GC, *Fort Wayne* .... 27 [P] 260-747-3136
  brookwoodgc.com
Buffer Park GC, *Indianapolis* .... 9 [P] 317-241-5046
  bufferpark.com
Burke Memorial GC at Notre Dame, *Notre Dame* .. 9 [U] 574-631-6425
  nd.edu
Cambridge GC, *Evansville* .... 18 [P] 812-868-4653
  villageofcambridge.com
Canterbury Green CC, *Fort Wayne* .... 18 [P] 260-486-7888
  canterburygreengolf.com
Cardinal Hills GC, *Selma* .... 18 [P] 765-288-2731
  cardinalhills.com
Carroll County CC, *Delphi* .... 9 [S] 765-564-2155

[A] = MILITARY   [M] = MUNICIPAL   [P] = PUBLIC   [R] = RESORT

Golf Yellow Pages, 18th Edition — INDIANA

Cascades GC, *Bloomington* .... 27 [M] 812-349-3764
  bloomington.in.gov
Cattails GC, *Elwood* .... 18 [P] 765-552-2027
  cattailselwood.com
CC of Indianapolis, *Indianapolis* .... 18 [V] 317-291-3798
  ccindianapolis.com
CC of Old Vincennes, *Vincennes* .... 18 [S] 812-882-9800
  countryclubofoldvincennes.com
CC of Terre Haute, *Terre Haute* .... 18 [V] 812-299-1558
  ccth.org
Cedar Creek GC, *Leo* .... 18 [P] 260-627-5623
  cedarcreekgc.com
Cedar Creek Golf Ctr, *Cedar Lake* .... 12 [P] 219-365-2902
  lakecountyparks.com
Cedar Lake GC, *Howe* .... 18 [P] 260-562-3923
  cedarlakegolfcourse.com
Cedar Valley GC, *Mitchell* .... 18 [P] 812-849-2255
Centennial Park GC, *Munster* .... 9 [M] 219-836-6931
  munster.org
Champions Pointe GC, *Henryville* .... 18 [P] 812-294-1800
  championspointe.com
Chariot Run GC, *Laconia* .... 18 [R] 812-969-6205
  harrahs.com/golf
Cherry Hill GC, *Fort Wayne* .... 18 [P] 260-485-8727
  cherryhillgc.com
Cherry Valley GC, *New Albany* .... 9 [P] 812-945-2777
  cherryvalleygolf.com
Chesapeake Run GC, *North Judson* .... 18 [P] 574-896-2424
  chesapeakerungolf.com
Chestnut Hills GC, *Fort Wayne* .... 18 [P] 260-625-4146
  chestnuthillsgolf.com
Chippendale GC, *Kokomo* .... 27 [P] 765-453-7079
  chippendalegolf.com
Christiana Creek CC, *Elkhart* .... 18 [V] 574-264-3025
  christianacreek.com
Christmas Lake GC, *Santa Claus* .... 18 [P] 812-544-2271
  christmaslake.com
Clear Creek GC, *Huntington* .... 18 [P] 260-344-1665
  clearcreekgc.com
Clearcrest Pines G&BanqCtr, *Evansville* .... 18 [P] 812-867-3311
  members.evansville.net/ccpines
Clermont GC, *Brownsburg* .... 18 [P] 317-852-8284
Clifty Creek GC, *Hope* .... 9 [P] 812-372-6031
Clover Meadow GC, *Cloverdale* .... 18 [P] 765-795-6001
  clovermeadowsgolf.com
Cobblestone GC, *Kendallville* .... 18 [P] 260-349-1550
  cobblestonegc.com
Coffin GC, *Indianapolis* .... 18 [M] 317-327-7845
  coffingolf.com
Cold Springs GC, *Hamilton* .... 18 [R] 260-488-2920
  cold-springs-resort.com
Colonial Oaks GC, *Fort Wayne* .... 18 [P] 260-489-5121
  colonialoaksgc.com
Cool Lake GC, *Lebanon* .... 18 [P] 765-325-9271
  coollakegolf.com
Country Mark Co Op, *Mt Vernon* .... 9 [V] 812-838-8109
Country Meadows Golf Resort, *Fremont* .... 18 [R] 260-495-4525
  countrymeadowsgolfresort.com
Country Oaks GC, *Montgomery* .... 18 [P] 812-486-3300
  countryoaksgolf.com
Country View GC, *Guilford* .... 18 [P] 812-576-5000
Covered Bridge GC, *Sellersburg* .... 18 [P] 812-246-8880
  coveredbridge.com

Coyote Creek GC, *Fort Wayne* .... 18 [V] 260-483-3148
  coyotecreekonline.com
Coyote Crossing GC, *West Lafayette* .... 18 [P] 765-497-1061
  coyotecrossinggolf.com
Crawfordsville CC, *Crawfordsville* .... 18 [V] 765-362-2353
  crawfordsvillecountryclub.com
Crawfordsville Muni GC, *Crawfordsville* .... 18 [M] 765-364-5171
  crawfordsvilleparkandrec.com
Creekside GC & Training Ctr, *Valparaiso* .... 9 [M] 219-477-5579
  creeksidegolfcourse.com
Cressmoor CC, *Hobart* .... 18 [P] 219-942-9300
Crestview GC, *Muncie* .... 27 [P] 765-289-6952
Cricket Ridge CC, *Batesville* .... 9 [P] 812-934-6348
  cricketridge.com
Crooked Lake GC, *Columbia City* .... 9 [P] 260-691-2157
Crooked Stick GC, *Carmel* .... 18 [V] 317-844-9938
  crookedstick.org
Cross Creek GC, *Decatur* .... 18 [P] 260-724-4316
  golfatcrosscreek.com
Culver GC, *Culver* .... 9 [N] 574-842-8218
  culver.org
Curtis Creek CC, *Rensselaer* .... 18 [V] 219-866-7729
  curtiscreekcountryclub.com
Cypress Run GC, *Franklin* .... 9 [P] 317-738-2555
  cypressrungc.com
Dakota Landing GC, *Indianapolis* .... 9 [P] 317-862-8255
  dakotalanding.com
Dearborn CC, *Aurora* .... 18 [V] 812-926-0487
  dearborncc.net
Deer Creek GC, *Clayton* .... 18 [P] 317-539-2013
  deercreekgolfclub.com
Deer Track GC, *Frankfort* .... 18 [P] 765-296-2595
Deer Track GC, *Auburn* .... 18 [S] 260-627-2121
  deertrackgolf.com
Deer Valley GC, *Franklin* .... 9 [P] 317-738-4441
Delaware CC, *Muncie* .... 18 [V] 765-282-3301
  delawarecc.com
Dogwood Glen GC, *Warren* .... 9 [P] 260-375-4750
  dogwoodglengc.com
Donald Ross GC, *Fort Wayne* .... 18 [P] 260-745-7093
Douglass GC, *Indianapolis* .... 9 [P] 317-924-0018
  indy.gov/eGov/City/DPR/Golf
Duck Creek GC, *Hobart* .... 18 [P] 219-759-5870
  duckcreekgolfcourse.com
Dyes Walk CC, *Greenwood* .... 18 [V] 317-535-9666
  dyeswalkcc.com
Dykeman Park GC, *Logansport* .... 18 [M] 574-753-0222
  dykemanpark.com
Eagle Creek GC, *Indianapolis* .... 36 [M] 317-297-3366
  eaglecreekgolfclub.com
Eagle Glen GC, *Columbia City* .... 18 [P] 260-248-4653
  linksofeagleglen.com
Eagle Pines GC, *Mooresville* .... 18 [S] 317-831-4774
  eaglepines.com
Eagle Valley GC, *Evansville* .... 18 [P] 812-867-7888
  eaglevalleygolfcourse.net
Eagle View GC, *Loogootee* .... 18 [A] 812-854-0100
  crane.navy.mil
Eberhart Park GC, *Mishawaka* .... 18 [M] 574-255-5508
  mishawakacity.com
Edgewood GC, *Anderson* .... 18 [S] 765-643-6336
Edwood Glen CC, *West Lafayette* .... 18 [S] 765-463-1100
  edwoodglencc.com

[S] = SEMI-PRIVATE   [V] = PRIVATE   [U] = UNIVERSITY   [N] = UNIVERSITY-PRIVATE

INDIANA　　　　　　　　　　　　Golf Yellow Pages, 18th Edition

Name	Holes	Type	Phone
Eel River GC, *Churubusco*	18	[P]	260-693-3464
eelrivergc.com			
Elbel Park GC, *South Bend*	18	[M]	574-271-9180
sbparks.org			
Elcona CC, *Bristol*	18	[V]	574-295-6373
elconacc.com			
Elks CC, *Richmond*	18	[V]	765-966-0952
elks649.org			
Elks CC, *Sullivan*	18	[S]	812-268-6874
Erskine Park GC, *South Bend*	18	[M]	574-291-3216
sbpark.org			
Etna Acres GC, *Andrews*	18	[P]	260-468-2906
etnaacres.com			
Evansville CC, *Evansville*	18	[V]	812-425-2243
evansvillecountryclub.org			
Fair Way GC, *Lebanon*	9	[S]	765-482-4906
Fall Creek GC, *Pendleton*	18	[S]	765-778-8071
fallcreekgc.com			
Fendrich GC, *Evansville*	18	[M]	812-435-6070
fendrichgolfcourse.org			
Fords Crossing GC, *North Vernon*	9	[P]	812-346-4653
fordscrossinggc.com			
Fore Seasons G Complex, *Terre Haute*	18	[P]	812-234-9212
foreseasonsgolfcomplex.com			
Forest Hills CC, *Richmond*	18	[V]	765-962-7414
fhcclub.com			
Forest Park GC, *Noblesville*	9	[P]	317-773-2881
forestparkgolf.com			
Forest Park GC, *Valparaiso*	18	[M]	219-476-1876
forestparkgolfcourse.com			
Forest Park GC, *Brazil*	18	[M]	812-442-5681
ugolfbrazil.com			
Fort Wayne CC, *Fort Wayne*	18	[V]	260-432-4573
ftwaynecc.org			
Foster Park GC, *Fort Wayne*	18	[P]	260-427-6735
fortwayneparks.org			
Fox Prairie GC, *Noblesville*	27	[M]	317-776-6357
foxprairie.com			
Foxcliff GC, *Martinsville*	18	[V]	765-342-0409
foxcliffgc.com			
Frankfort Golf & Community Club, *Frankfort*	18	[P]	765-659-1324
frankfortcc.com			
Frazanda GC, *Huntington*	9	[P]	260-468-2579
French Lick Springs Resort, *French Lick*	54	[R]	812-936-9300
frenchlick.com			
Friendswood GC, *Camby*	9	[P]	317-856-5372
friendswoodgolfcourse.com			
Garrett CC, *Garrett*	18	[P]	260-357-5165
garrettcc.com			
GC of Indiana, *Lebanon*	18	[S]	317-769-6388
golfindiana.com			
GC of the Limberlost, *Geneva*	18	[P]	260-368-7388
golfclubofthelimberlost.com			
Geneva Hills GC, *Clinton*	18	[P]	765-832-8384
genevahills.org			
Glendarin Hills GC, *Angola*	18	[P]	260-624-3550
glendarinhills.com			
Grand Oak GC, *West Harrison*	18	[P]	812-637-3943
grandoakgolfclub.net			
Grandview GC, *Anderson*	18	[M]	765-648-6880
Grassy Creek GC, *Indianapolis*	9	[P]	317-894-5855
Gray Eagle GC & Acad, *Fishers*	18	[P]	317-845-2900
grayeaglegolf.com			
Green Acres GC, *Kokomo*	18	[P]	765-883-7355
Green Valley GC, *Bluffton*	9	[P]	260-824-4510
Greenbelt GC, *Columbus*	9	[M]	812-376-2684
columbus.in.gov			
Greensburg CC, *Greensburg*	18	[S]	812-663-2229
greensburgcountryclub.com			
Grey Goose GC, *Decatur*	18	[P]	260-724-4512
greygoosegolfclub.com			
Griffith Golf Ctr, *Griffith*	18	[P]	219-923-3223
Hamlet GC, *Hamlet*	18	[P]	574-867-4000
hamletgolf.com			
Harbour Trees GC, *Noblesville*	18	[V]	317-877-3611
harbourtrees.com			
Harrison Hills CC, *Attica*	18	[P]	765-762-1135
harrisonhills.com			
Harrison Lake CC, *Columbus*	18	[V]	812-342-6012
harrisonlakecc.com			
Hartley Hills CC, *Hagerstown*	9	[S]	765-489-4373
hartleyhillsgolf.com			
Hawks Tail of Greenfield, *Greenfield*	18	[S]	317-462-2706
hawkstail.com			
Hazelden CC, *Brook*	18	[P]	219-275-5551
hazeldencountryclub.com			
Heartland Crossing Golf Links, *Camby*	18	[P]	317-630-1785
heartlandcrossinggolf.com			
Heartland Resort, *Greenfield*	9	[R]	317-326-3181
heartlandresort.com			
Helfrich Hills GC, *Evansville*	18	[M]	812-435-6075
helfrichmensgolfclub.com			
Heron Creek GC, *La Grange*	18	[P]	260-463-2906
heroncreekgc.com			
Hickory Bend GC, *Zionsville*	9	[P]	317-769-2363
Hickory Hills GC, *Brownstown*	9	[V]	812-358-4529
Hickory Hills GC, *Farmland*	18	[P]	765-468-6321
hickoryhillsgolf.us			
Hickory Stick GC, *Greenwood*	18	[P]	317-422-8300
hickorystickgolf.com			
Hidden Creek GC, *Sellersburg*	27	[P]	812-246-2556
hiddencreekgolfclub.com			
Hidden Hills GC, *Springville*	18	[P]	812-863-2500
hiddenhillsgolf.com			
Hidden Valley GC, *Lawrenceburg*	18	[V]	812-537-5033
hiddenvalleylakegolfclub.com			
Hidden Valley GC, *Angola*	18	[P]	260-665-6064
Highland G&CC, *Indianapolis*	18	[V]	317-253-3030
highlandgc.com			
Highland Hills GC, *Roann*	18	[P]	260-982-2679
Highland Lake GC, *Richmond*	18	[M]	765-983-7287
richmondindiana.gov			
Hillcrest CC, *Indianapolis*	18	[V]	317-251-8653
hillcrestcindy.com			
Hillcrest G&CC, *Batesville*	18	[P]	812-934-4350
hillcrest-gcc.com			
Hillview CC, *Franklin*	18	[V]	317-736-5556
hillviewcountryclub.net			
Hollow Acres Golf Ctr, *Monticello*	9	[P]	574-965-2182
hollowacres.com			
Honeywell Public GC, *Wabash*	18	[P]	260-563-8663
honeywellgolf.com			
Hoosier Heights CC, *Tell City*	9	[V]	812-547-2196
Hoosier Hills GC, *Cory*	9	[P]	812-864-2304
Hoosier Links GC, *Milan*	18	[S]	812-654-2440
hoosierlinksgolf.com			

[A] = MILITARY　　[M] = MUNICIPAL　　[P] = PUBLIC　　[R] = RESORT

Golf Yellow Pages, 18th Edition — INDIANA

Horseshoe Bend GC, *Lewisville* .... 18 [P] 765-345-5242
   horseshoebendgolf.com
Howell Park GC, *Evansville* .... 9 [M] 812-422-8495
Hulman Links GC, *Terre Haute* .... 18 [M] 812-877-2096
   hulmanlinks.com
Huntingburg CC, *Huntingburg* .... 9 [S] 812-683-3376
   huntingburgcc.com
Idle Creek GC, *Terre Haute* .... 18 [P] 812-299-4653
   idlecreek.com
Indian Hills GC, *Leesburg* .... 9 [P] 574-453-3912
Indian Lake GC, *Indianapolis* .... 9 [V] 317-823-6552
   indianlakecc.com
Indian Lakes GC, *Sunman* .... 9 [R] 812-623-4653
Indian Oaks GC, *Peru* .... 9 [S] 765-473-7312
   indianoaksgolf.net
Indian Ridge GC, *Hobart* .... 18 [P] 219-942-6850
   indianridgehobart.com
Indian Springs GC, *Trafalgar* .... 9 [P] 317-878-5926
   indianspringsgolf.com
Indiana National GC at Swan Lake, *Plymouth* .... 36 [R] 574-936-9798
   swanlakeresort.com
Indiana Univ GC, *Bloomington* .... 27 [U] 812-855-7543
   iuhoosiers.cstv.com/facilities/ind-facilities-golf.html
Innsbrook CC, *Merrillville* .... 18 [V] 219-980-9143
   innsbrookcc.com
Ironwood GC, *Fishers* .... 27 [P] 317-842-0551
   ironwoodgc.com
J Rock Ridge Golf Community, *Orleans* ...... 18 [P] 812-849-1200
Jasper CC, *Jasper* .... 9 [P] 812-482-1994
   jaspercountryclub.com
Jasper Muni GC, *Jasper* .... 18 [M] 812-482-4600
Jeffersonville Elks GC, *Jeffersonville* .... 18 [V] 812-283-9022
   jeffelksclub.com
Juday Creek GC, *Granger* .... 18 [P] 574-277-4653
   judaycreek.com
Kendallville GC, *Kendallville* .... 9 [S] 260-347-3440
   kendallvillegc.com
Ki Ann GC, *Hartford City* .... 18 [P] 765-348-4876
Killbuck GC, *Anderson* .... 18 [P] 765-643-1877
   killbuckgolf.com
Knollwood CC, *Granger* .... 36 [V] 574-277-2620
   knollwoodclub.com
Kokomo CC, *Kokomo* .... 18 [V] 765-457-2290
   kokomocountryclub.com
La Fontaine GC, *Huntington* .... 18 [P] 260-356-5820
   lafontainegc.com
Lafayette CC, *Lafayette* .... 9 [V] 765-474-3461
   lafayettecountryclub.net
Lafayette Elks CC, *West Lafayette* .... 18 [P] 765-463-2332
   elksgolf.com
Lafayette GC, *Lafayette* .... 18 [M] 765-807-1130
   lafayetteparks.org
Lake Dalecarlia Fairways GC, *Lowell* .... 9 [V] 219-696-0771
   lakedalecarlia.org
Lake Hills G&CC, *St Joseph* .... 27 [S] 219-365-8661
Lake James GC, *Angola* .... 18 [P] 260-833-3967
   golflakejames.com
Lake View GC, *Marion* .... 9 [P] 765-998-7671
Lakes of the Four Seasons CC, *Crown Point* ..... 18 [P] 219-988-2201
   lofs.org
Lakeside GC, *Fort Wayne* .... 27 [P] 260-422-8714
   lakesidegolfandbowling.com
Lakeview GC, *Eaton* .... 18 [P] 765-396-9010

Lakeview GC, *Loogootee* .... 9 [M] 812-295-5678
   golflakeview.com
Lakewood CC, *Rockport* .... 9 [V] 812-649-9258
Leaning Tree GC, *Peru* .... 9 [P] 765-689-9705
Legacy Hills GC, *La Porte* .... 18 [P] 219-324-4777
   legacyhillsgolf.com
Legends of Indiana GC, *Franklin* .... 27 [P] 317-736-8186
   legendsofindiana.com
Liberty CC, *Liberty* .... 18 [S] 765-458-5664
   libertycountryclub.com
Limberlost GC, *Rome City* .... 18 [P] 260-854-4878
Little Big Horn GC, *Pierceton* .... 18 [P] 574-267-5431
   littlebighorngc.com
Little Mountain GC, *Walton* .... 9 [P] 574-626-2831
Logans Run Family GC, *Logansport* .... 18 [P] 574-753-6700
Logansport GC, *Logansport* .... 18 [P] 574-722-1110
   logansportgolf.com
Long Beach CC, *Long Beach* .... 18 [V] 219-872-8547
   longbeachcc.org
Lost Marsh GC, *Hammond* .... 27 [M] 219-932-4046
   lostmarshgolf.com
Lu Gene Links, *Lake Village* .... 9 [P] 219-992-3337
Mac Arthur GC, *East Chicago* .... 9 [M] 219-391-8362
Magic Hills GC, *Columbia City* .... 9 [S] 260-691-2788
Maple Creek GC, *Indianapolis* .... 18 [V] 317-894-3837
   maplecreekgc.com
Maplecrest CC, *Goshen* .... 18 [V] 574-533-1925
   maplecrestcountryclub.org
Maplewood GC, *Muncie* .... 18 [P] 765-284-8007
Marion Elks GC, *Marion* .... 18 [V] 765-662-3481
   elks195.tripod.com
Marks Par 3 GC, *Terre Haute* .... 18 [P] 812-877-1467
   markspar3.com
Martinsville GC, *Martinsville* .... 18 [P] 765-342-4336
   martinsvillegolf.com
Matthews Park GC, *Clinton* .... 9 [M] 765-832-9016
Maxinkuckee CC, *Culver* .... 9 [V] 574-842-2391
Maxwelton GC, *Syracuse* .... 18 [P] 574-457-3504
   maxweltongolf.com
McCormick Creek Muni GC, *Nappanee* .... 18 [M] 574-773-2725
   mccormickcreekgc.com
McDonald GC, *Evansville* .... 9 [M] 812-475-2578
   mcdonaldgolfcourse.com
McMillen Park GC, *Fort Wayne* .... 27 [M] 260-427-6710
   mcmillengolfcourse.com
Meadowbrook GC, *Anderson* .... 18 [P] 765-644-9754
   meadowbrookgolfcourse.com
Memorial Park GC, *New Castle* .... 18 [P] 765-529-9856
Meridian Hills CC, *Indianapolis* .... 18 [V] 317-255-3369
   meridianhillscc.org
Meshingomesia CC, *Marion* .... 18 [V] 765-662-6881
   mccmarion.com
Michigan City GC, *Michigan City* .... 36 [M] 219-873-1516
   michigancitygolfcourse.com
Mink Lake GC, *Valparaiso* .... 9 [P] 219-462-2585
Mohawk Hills GC, *Carmel* .... 9 [P] 317-844-3112
Morning Star GC, *Indianapolis* .... 18 [P] 317-899-4653
   morningstargc.com
Morris Park CC, *South Bend* .... 18 [V] 574-282-3727
   morrisparkcc.com
Moss Creek GC, *Winamac* .... 18 [P] 574-595-3112
   golfmosscreek.com

[S] = SEMI-PRIVATE   [V] = PRIVATE   [U] = UNIVERSITY   [N] = UNIVERSITY-PRIVATE

INDIANA — Golf Yellow Pages, 18th Edition

Muncie Elks CC, *Muncie* .... 18 [V] 765-759-7770
  muncieelks.com
Mystic Hills GC, *Culver* .... 18 [P] 574-842-2687
  mystichills.com
New Albany CC, *New Albany* .... 9 [V] 812-945-9091
  newalbanycc.com
New Salisbury GC, *New Salisbury* .... 9 [P] 812-347-2396
  golfnewsalisbury.com
Noble Hawk Golf Links, *Kendallville* .... 18 [P] 260-349-0900
  noblehawk.com
North Branch GC, *Greensburg* .... 27 [P] 812-663-6062
  northbranchgc.com
Norwood GC, *Huntington* .... 18 [P] 260-356-5929
  norwoodgc.com
Oak Grove CC, *Oxford* .... 18 [P] 765-385-2713
  oakgrovecc.com
Oak Knoll GC, *Crown Point* .... 18 [P] 219-663-3349
Oak Knoll GC, *Columbus* .... 18 [P] 812-342-2000
  oakknollgc.com
Oak Meadow GC, *Evansville* .... 18 [V] 812-867-1900
  oakmeadowgolfclub.com
Oak Ridge GC, *Brazil* .... 18 [P] 812-446-4653
Oakland City GC, *Oakland City* .... 9 [P] 812-749-3923
Oaktree GC, *Plainfield* .... 18 [S] 317-839-6205
  oaktreegc.com
Old Capitol GC, *Corydon* .... 18 [P] 812-738-2277
  oldcapitalgolf.com
Old English GC, *English* .... 18 [P] 812-338-3748
  oldenglishgolf.com
Old Hickory GC, *Greencastle* .... 18 [P] 765-653-2019
Old Oakland GC, *Indianapolis* .... 27 [V] 317-823-4791
  oldoaklandgc.com
Old Orchard GC, *Elkhart* .... 18 [P] 574-293-1121
  golfoldorchard.com
Orchard Golf Ctr, *Greenwood* .... 18 [P] 317-883-3840
Orchard Ridge CC, *Fort Wayne* .... 18 [V] 260-747-3117
  orchardridgecc.com
Otis Park GC, *Bedford* .... 18 [M] 812-279-9092
  otisparkgolf.com
Otte Golf Ctr, *Greenwood* .... 18 [P] 317-881-4620
  ottegolf.com
Otter Creek GC, *Columbus* .... 27 [P] 812-579-5227
  ottercreekgolf.com
Palmira G&CC, *St John* .... 18 [S] 219-365-4331
  palmiragolf.com
Paoli CC, *Paoli* .... 9 [S] 812-723-2110
Parke County GC, *Rockville* .... 9 [P] 765-569-3556
Parmore GC & DR, *New Paris* .... 9 [P] 574-831-4434
Pebble Brook GC, *Noblesville* .... 36 [P] 317-896-5596
  pebblebrookgolfclub.com
Persimmon Ridge GC, *Mitchell* .... 18 [P] 812-849-5188
Peru Muni GC, *Peru* .... 18 [M] 765-473-6806
  perugolfcourse.com
Pheasant Valley CC, *Crown Point* .... 18 [P] 219-663-5000
Phil Harris GC, *Linton* .... 18 [M] 812-847-4790
Pine Hills GC, *Holton* .... 9 [P] 812-689-3533
  pinehillsholton.com
Pine Valley CC, *Fort Wayne* .... 18 [V] 260-637-6414
  pinevalleycc.com
Pine View GC, *Monticello* .... 27 [R] 574-583-3339
  pineviewgolf.net
Pine Woods GC, *Spencer* .... 9 [P] 812-829-9028
  pinewoodsgc.com

Pittsboro GC, *Pittsboro* .... 9 [P] 317-892-3335
Players Club At Woodland Trails, *Yorktown* ..... 18 [P] 765-759-8536
  theplayersclubgolf.com
Pleasant Run GC, *Indianapolis* .... 18 [M] 317-357-0829
  pleasantrungolf.com
Plum Creek GC, *Carmel* .... 18 [P] 317-573-9900
  plumcreekgolfclub.com
Plymouth CC, *Plymouth* .... 18 [V] 574-936-9008
  plymouthcountryclub.com
Plymouth Rock GC, *Plymouth* .... 18 [P] 574-936-4405
Pond A River GC, *Woodburn* .... 18 [P] 260-632-5481
Pond View GC, *Star City* .... 18 [P] 574-595-7431
  pondviewgolf.net
Portland GC, *Portland* .... 18 [S] 260-726-4646
  portlandgc.com
Pottawattomie CC, *Michigan City* .... 18 [V] 219-872-0624
  pottawattomie.com
Prairie View GC, *Carmel* .... 18 [P] 317-816-3100
  prairieviewgc.com
Prestwick CC, *Avon* .... 18 [V] 317-745-6448
  prestwickcountryclub.net
Prides Creek GC, *Petersburg* .... 9 [P] 812-354-3059
  pridescreekgolf.com
Princeton CC, *Princeton* .... 9 [S] 812-385-5669
Purgatory GC, *Noblesville* .... 18 [S] 317-776-4653
  purgatorygolf.com
Quail Creek GC, *Pittsboro* .... 18 [P] 317-892-2582
  quailcreekgc.com
Quail Crossing GC, *Boonville* .... 18 [P] 812-897-1247
  quailcrossing.com
Raber GC, *Bristol* .... 27 [P] 574-848-4020
Raccoon Run GC, *Warsaw* .... 18 [P] 574-269-2902
  raccoonrungolf.com
Racoon Lake GC, *Rockville* .... 9 [P] 765-344-1134
  raccoonlakegolfcourse.com
Rea Park GC, *Terre Haute* .... 18 [M] 812-232-0709
  reapark.com
Rices Golf Ctr, *Kokomo* .... 18 [P] 765-453-3650
River Glen CC, *Fishers* .... 18 [P] 317-849-8274
  riverglencc.com
River Pointe CC, *Hobart* .... 27 [V] 219-947-1711
  riverpointecountryclub.com
Riverbend GC, *Fort Wayne* .... 18 [P] 260-485-2732
Rivercrest GC, *Covington* .... 18 [P] 765-793-7888
Riverside GC, *Indianapolis* .... 18 [M] 317-327-7300
  riversidegolfindy.com
Riverside Golf Acad, *Indianapolis* .... 9 [M] 317-327-7303
  riversidegolfacademy.com
Robbinhurst GC & DR, *Valparaiso* .... 18 [P] 219-762-9711
  robbinhurst.com
Robin Hood GC, *South Bend* .... 9 [P] 574-291-2450
Rochester Elks GC, *Rochester* .... 9 [S] 574-223-4427
Rock Hollow GC, *Peru* .... 18 [P] 765-473-6100
  rockhollowgolf.com
Rocky Ford Par 3 GC, *Columbus* .... 18 [P] 812-376-2687
Rocky Ridge GC, *Crawfordsville* .... 18 [P] 765-794-4444
  rockyridgegolf.com
Rolling Hills CC, *Newburgh* .... 18 [V] 812-925-3301
Rolling Meadows GC, *Gosport* .... 18 [P] 812-829-0717
  golfus.com/rollingmeadows
Round Barn GC at Mill Creek, *Rochester* ..... 18 [M] 574-223-5717
  rtcol.com/millcreek

[A] = MILITARY   [M] = MUNICIPAL   [P] = PUBLIC   [R] = RESORT

Golf Yellow Pages, 18th Edition — INDIANA

Royal Hylands GC, *Knightstown* ....18 [P] 765-345-2123
royalhylands.com
Rozella Ford GC, *Warsaw* ....18 [P] 574-269-9582
rozellaford.com
Saddlebrook GC, *Indianapolis*......................18 [P] 317-290-0539
saddlebrookgolf.com
Sagamore GC, *Noblesville* ....18 [V] 317-776-2000
thesagamoreclub.com
Salt Creek Golf Retreat, *Nashville*.................18 [R] 812-988-7888
saltcreekgolf.com
Sand Creek CC, *Chesterton* ....27 [P] 219-395-5210
sandcreek.com
Sandy Pines GC, *Demotte*.............................18 [P] 219-987-3611
sandypinesgc.com
Sarah Shank GC, *Indianapolis* ....18 [M] 317-784-0631
sarahshankgolf.com
Scherwood Golf Concessions, *Schererville*..........27 [P] 219-865-2554
scherwood.com
Seymour CC, *Seymour*......................................9 [P] 812-522-3495
seymourcc.com
Shadowood GC, *Seymour* ....18 [P] 812-522-8164
shadowoodgolf.com
Shady Hills GC, *Marion* ....18 [S] 765-668-8256
shadyhillsgolf.com
Shekinah on Brandywine, *Greenfield*................9 [P] 317-462-7813
Shoaff Park GC, *Fort Wayne* ....18 [M] 260-427-6745
shoaffgolfcourse.com
Shortees Golf, *Indianapolis*...........................18 [P] 317-582-1850
shorteesgolf.net
Sims Oak Hills GC, *Middlebury*....................18 [M] 574-825-5767
Smock GC, *Indianapolis* ....18 [M] 317-888-0036
smockgolf.com
South Bend CC, *South Bend* ....18 [V] 574-289-2277
southbendcc.com
South Gleason Park GC, *Gary*.......................18 [M] 219-980-1089
South Grove GC, *Indianapolis*......................18 [M] 317-327-7351
southgrovegolf.com
South Shore CC, *Cedar Lake*........................18 [P] 219-374-6070
golfsscc.com
South Shore GC, *Syracuse* ....18 [P] 574-457-2832
golftheshore.com
Southern Dunes GC, *Indianapolis*.................27 [P] 317-865-1800
southerndunesgolfcourse.com
Speed Employees CC, *Speed* ....9 [P] 812-246-9570
Sprig OMint GC, *Bremen* ....18 [P] 574-546-2640
sprigomint.com
Spring Hills GC, *Hanover*..............................18 [P] 812-866-4727
springhillsgc.com
Spring Meadow Farm GC, *Middlebury*..........18 [P] 574-825-3422
springmeadowgolf.com
St Annes GC, *North Vernon* ....18 [P] 812-346-0066
Stone Crest Golf Community, *Bedford*..........27 [P] 812-276-4653
stonecrestgolf.com
Stone Eagle GC, *Aurora*..................................9 [P] 812-926-3595
Stonehenge GC, *Winona Lake* ....18 [V] 574-269-6111
stonehengegolfclub.com
Stony Creek GC, *Noblesville*........................27 [P] 317-773-1820
stonycreekgolfclub.com
Studebaker GC, *South Bend* ....9 [M] 574-287-6634
sbpark.org
Sugar Ridge GC, *Lawrenceburg*....................18 [P] 812-537-9300
sugarridgegc.com

Sullivan County Park & Lake GC, *Sullivan*............9 [R] 812-268-5537
sullivancountyparkandlake.com
Sultans Run GC, *Jasper* ....18 [P] 812-482-1009
sultansrun.com
Summertree GC, *Crown Point* ....18 [P] 219-663-0800
Sunrise GC, *Madison*....................................18 [M] 812-265-8334
madisonparks.com
Sunrise Golf, *Indianapolis*..............................9 [P] 317-574-0427
Sycamore GC, *North Manchester* ....18 [P] 260-982-2279
sycamoregc.com
Sycamore GC, *Columbus* ....18 [S] 812-579-9173
sycamoregolfclub.com
Sycamore Hills GC, *Fort Wayne* ....18 [V] 260-625-4397
sycamorehillsgolfclub.com
Tameka Woods GC, *Trafalgar* ....18 [P] 317-878-4331
tamekawoods.com
Taylors Par 3, *Bloomington* ....9 [P] 812-330-8611
taylorspar3.com
Tee Time G Complex, *Evansville*.....................9 [P] 812-473-2010
teetimegolfcomplex.com
The Brassie GC, *Chesterton*..........................18 [P] 219-921-1192
thebrassie.com
The Bridgewater Club, *Carmel* ....27 [V] 317-867-4653
thebridgewaterclub.com
The Course at Aberdeen, *Valparaiso*.............18 [P] 219-462-5050
golfataberdeen.com
The Cozy Acres G Complex, *Madison* ....9 [P] 812-273-3137
cozyacresgolf.com
The Eagle Pointe Golf Resort, *Bloomington*.........18 [R] 812-824-4040
eaglepointe.com
The Fort GC, *Indianapolis*.............................18 [R] 317-543-9597
thefortgolfcourse.com
The Hawthorns G&CC, *Fishers* ....18 [V] 317-845-9100
hawthornscountryclub.com
The Landing At Fort Harrison, *Terre Haute*...18 [P] 812-460-4000
thelandingatfortharrison.com
The Links at Rising Star Casino Resort, *Rising Sun*18 [R] 812-438-5149
risingstarcasino.com
The Links GC, *New Palestine*........................18 [P] 317-861-4466
linksindy.com
The Ravines GC, *West Lafayette* ....18 [P] 765-497-7888
ravinesgolf.com
The Trophy Club, *Lebanon* ....18 [P] 765-482-7272
thetrophyclubgolf.com
Thunderbolt Pass GC, *Evansville*...................27 [P] 812-426-2166
thunderboltpass.com
Timber Ridge GC, *Millersburg* ....18 [P] 574-642-3252
trgolfclub.com
Timber Ridge GC, *Bluffton* ....18 [S] 260-824-2728
timberridgegc.com
Timbergate GC, *Edinburgh*..........................18 [M] 812-526-3523
timbergate.com
Tippecanoe CC, *Monticello* ....18 [S] 574-583-9977
tippecanoecc.com
Tippecanoe Lake CC, *Leesburg* ....18 [V] 574-453-3641
tippylakecc.com
Tipton Muni GC, *Tipton*...............................18 [M] 765-675-6027
Tomahawk Hills GC, *Jamestown* ....9 [P] 765-676-6022
tomahawkhillsgc.com
Tri County GC, *Middletown*........................18 [P] 765-533-4107
Tri Ponds GC, *Tipton*......................................9 [P] 765-963-2547
Tri way GC, *Plymouth*..................................18 [P] 574-936-9517
triwaygolf.com

[S] = SEMI-PRIVATE   [V] = PRIVATE   [U] = UNIVERSITY   [N] = UNIVERSITY-PRIVATE

INDIANA

Golf Yellow Pages, 18th Edition

Turkey Creek GC, *Merrillville* .... 18 [M] 219-980-5170
Turkey Run GC, *Waveland* .... 18 [P] 765-435-2048
   turkeyrungolf.com
Twilight GC, *Jeffersonville* .... 9 [P] 812-288-8871
   twilightgolfcourse.com
Twin Bridges GC, *Danville* .... 18 [P] 317-745-9098
   twinbridgesgolfclub.com
Twin Lakes GC, *Carmel* .... 18 [V] 317-872-6206
   twinlakesclub.com
Ulen CC, *Lebanon* .... 18 [V] 765-482-3480
   ulencc.com
Valle Vista CC, *Greenwood* .... 18 [P] 317-888-5313
   vallevista.com
Valley Hills GC, *Rolling Prairie* .... 9 [P] 219-778-2823
Valley View GC, *Floyds Knobs* .... 18 [S] 812-923-7291
   valleyviewgolfclub.org
Valley View GC, *Middletown* .... 18 [S] 765-354-2698
   valleyviewgc.com
Valparaiso CC, *Valparaiso* .... 18 [V] 219-464-1600
   valparaisocountryclub.com
Victoria National GC, *Newburgh* .... 18 [V] 812-858-8230
   victorianational.com
Vincennes GC, *Vincennes* .... 18 [P] 812-895-1020
   vincennesgolfclub.com
Vineyard GC, *Rising Sun* .... 18 [P] 812-594-2627
Walnut Creek & Club Run GC, *Marion* ...... 36 [P] 765-998-7651
   walnutcreekgolf.com
Walnut Ridge GC, *Greenwood* .... 18 [P] 317-881-1710
   haguegolf.com
Warren GC At Notre Dame, *Notre Dame* .... 18 [U] 574-631-4653
   warrengolfcourse.com
Washington CC, *Washington* .... 9 [P] 812-254-2060
Wawasee GC, *Syracuse* .... 9 [P] 574-457-0224
   wawaseegolfclub.com
Wesselman Par 3 GC, *Evansville* .... 18 [M] 812-475-2579
West Chase GC, *Brownsburg* .... 18 [P] 317-892-7888
   westchasegolf.com
Western Hills CC, *Mt Vernon* .... 9 [V] 812-838-5631
Western Hills CC, *Salem* .... 9 [P] 812-883-5138
Westwood GC, *Scottsburg* .... 9 [P] 812-752-3233
   westwoodgolf.org
Westwood GC, *New Castle* .... 18 [P] 765-529-1300
   westwoodgc.com
Whispering Creek GC, *New Haven* .... 18 [P] 260-749-5025
   whisperingcreekgc.com
Whispering Hills GC, *Indianapolis* .... 9 [M] 317-862-9000
   indy.gov/eGov/City/DPR/Golf
Whispering Pines GC, *Walkerton* .... 18 [P] 574-656-3295
White Hawk GC, *Crown Point* .... 36 [P] 219-661-1300
   whitehawkcountryclub.com
White Lick GC, *Brownsburg* .... 9 [P] 317-852-2931
Wicker Memorial Park GC, *Highland* .... 18 [M] 219-838-9809
   wickermemorialpark.com
Wildcat Creek GC, *Kokomo* .... 18 [P] 765-455-3673
   wildcatcreek.com
William Sahm GC, *Castleton* .... 18 [M] 317-842-3848
   sahmgolf.com
Willow Ridge GC, *Fort Wayne* .... 18 [P] 260-637-3243
Willowbrook CC, *Connersville* .... 18 [P] 765-825-2315
   willowbrookconnersville.com
Winchester GC, *Winchester* .... 27 [P] 765-584-5151
   winchestergc.com

Winding Branch GC, *Cambridge City* .... 18 [P] 765-478-5638
   windingbranch.com
Winding Ridge GC, *Indianapolis* .... 18 [P] 317-826-3020
   windingridgegolf.com
Winding River GC, *Indianapolis* .... 18 [M] 317-856-7257
   windingrivergc.com
Windy Hill CC, *Greencastle* .... 9 [V] 765-653-5470
Wolf Run GC, *Zionsville* .... 18 [V] 317-769-5260
   wolfrungc.com
Wood Wind GC, *Westfield* .... 18 [S] 317-896-2474
   woodwindgolf.com
Wooded View GC, *Clarksville* .... 18 [M] 812-283-9274
   clarksvilleparks.com
Woodland CC, *Carmel* .... 18 [V] 317-846-5044
   woodlandcc.com
Woodmar CC, *Hammond* .... 18 [V] 219-845-0300
Woodstock Club, *Indianapolis* .... 9 [V] 317-923-9912
   woodstockclub.com
Wyaloosing Creek GC, *Greensburg* .... 18 [P] 812-591-4100
Youche CC, *Crown Point* .... 18 [V] 219-663-1418
   youchecc.org
Yule GC, *Alexandria* .... 18 [P] 765-724-3229
   yulegc.com
Zionsville GC, *Zionsville* .... 9 [M] 317-873-4218
   zionsvillegolf.com
Zollner GC, *Angola* .... 18 [U] 260-665-4269
   zollnergc.com

IOWA

3 30 G&CC, *Lowden* .... 9 [P] 563-941-7695
A H Blank Muni Course, *Des Moines* .... 18 [M] 515-248-6300
   blankgolfcourse.com
Ackley CC, *Ackley* .... 9 [P] 641-847-3475
Acorn Park GC, *St Ansgar* .... 9 [M] 641-713-4450
Airport National G Complex, *Cedar Rapids* .. 27 [P] 319-848-4500
   airportnationalpublicgolf.com
Akron GC, *Akron* .... 9 [P] 712-568-3146
Albia CC, *Albia* .... 9 [V] 641-932-5002
Algona CC, *Algona* .... 9 [V] 515-295-7308
   algonacountryclub.com
All Golf Ctr, *Waterloo* .... 9 [P] 319-236-1010
   g3golf.com
All Veterans GC, *Clear Lake* .... 9 [P] 641-357-4457
   allvetsgolf.com
Alta G&CC, *Alta* .... 9 [P] 712-200-2442
Amana Colonies GC, *Amana* .... 18 [P] 319-622-6222
   amanagolfcourse.com
American Legion CC, *Shenandoah* .... 18 [S] 712-246-3308
American Legion GC, *Marshalltown* .... 18 [P] 641-752-1834
American Legion GC, *Villisca* .... 9 [P] 712-826-2702
Ames G&CC, *Ames* .... 18 [V] 515-232-8334
   amesgolfcc.com
Ankeny G&CC, *Ankeny* .... 9 [V] 515-964-3647
   ankenygolf.com
Anthon GC, *Anthon* .... 9 [P] 712-373-5774
   anthoniowa.com
Aplington Rec Complex, *Aplington* .... 9 [P] 319-347-6059
   aplingtonia.com
Appanoose CC, *Centerville* .... 9 [V] 641-856-2222
Arrowhead GC, *Clear Lake* .... 9 [P] 641-357-7519
Atlantic CC, *Atlantic* .... 18 [P] 712-243-3656
   theagcc.com
Audubon G&CC, *Audubon* .... 9 [S] 712-563-2348

[A] = MILITARY   [M] = MUNICIPAL   [P] = PUBLIC   [R] = RESORT

Golf Yellow Pages, 18th Edition — IOWA

Aurelia GC, *Aurelia* .... 9 [S] 712-434-5498
Avoca GC, *Avoca* .... 9 [M] 712-343-6979
  avocagolf.tripod.com
Backbone G&CC, *Strawberry Point* .... 9 [S] 563-933-4545
Ballard G&CC, *Huxley* .... 9 [V] 515-597-2266
  ballardgolf.com
Bear Creek GC, *Forest City* .... 18 [P] 641-585-1353
  bearcreekfc.com
Beaver Creek GC, *Grimes* .... 27 [P] 515-986-3221
  beavercreek-golf.com
Beaver Hills GC, *Cedar Falls* .... 18 [V] 319-266-1975
  beaverhills.com
Beaver Meadow G&CC, *Parkersburg* .... 9 [P] 319-346-1870
Bedford GC, *Bedford* .... 9 [P] 712-523-3373
Belle Plaine CC, *Belle Plaine* .... 9 [S] 319-444-3113
  belleplainecc.com
Bellevue GC, *Bellevue* .... 9 [S] 563-872-4262
Belmond CC, *Belmond* .... 9 [P] 641-444-4183
Bent Tree GC, *Council Bluffs* .... 18 [P] 712-566-9441
  benttreegolfcb.com
Big Rock CC, *Fayette* .... 18 [S] 563-425-3687
  bigrockcc.com
Bloomfield CC, *Bloomfield* .... 9 [V] 641-664-2089
  bloomfieldcountryclub.com
Blue Top Ridge At Riverside, *Riverside* ....18 [R] 319-648-1234
  riversidecasinoandresort.com
Bos Landen GC, *Pella* .... 18 [P] 641-628-4625
  boslanden.com
Breda GC, *Breda* .... 9 [P] 712-673-4653
Briarwood Club of Ankeny, *Ankeny* ...... 18 [P] 515-964-4653
  briarwoodclubofankeny.com
Briggs Woods GC, *Webster City* .... 18 [M] 515-832-9572
  briggswoods.com
Britt CC, *Britt* .... 9 [P] 641-843-3249
Brooklyn Victor CC, *Brooklyn* .... 9 [V] 641-522-7608
Brooks National GC, *Okoboji* .... 27 [R] 712-332-5011
  brooksgolfclub.com
Brookside GC, *Kingsley* .... 9 [P] 712-378-2595
Brown Deer GC, *Coralville* .... 18 [P] 319-248-9300
  browndeergolf.com
Buffalo Creek Club, *Winthrop* .... 9 [S] 319-935-3697
Bunker Hill GC, *Dubuque* .... 18 [M] 563-589-4261
  cityofdubuque.org
Burlington GC, *Burlington* .... 18 [V] 319-752-3720
  bgciowa.com
Canyon Creek GC, *Clinton* .... 9 [P] 563-243-3534
CARD GC, *Clarksville* .... 9 [P] 319-278-4787
Carroll CC, *Carroll* .... 18 [V] 712-792-1255
  carrollcountryclub.com
Carroll Muni GC, *Carroll* .... 18 [M] 712-792-9190
  cityofcarroll.com
Cedar Creek GC, *Ottumwa* .... 18 [M] 641-683-0646
  cedarcreekgolfcourse.com
Cedar Pointe GC, *Boone* .... 18 [P] 515-432-6002
  cedarpointegolfcourse.com
Cedar Rapids CC, *Cedar Rapids* .... 18 [V] 319-362-4878
  thecrcc.org
Cedar Ridge GC, *Charles City* .... 18 [P] 641-228-6465
Cedar Valley GC, *Tipton* .... 18 [P] 563-886-0218
  site.cedarvalleygolfcourse.com
Cedarcrest G&CC, *Columbus Junction* ... 9 [P] 319-728-8461
  cedarcrestcc.com

Centennial Oaks GC, *Waverly* .... 18 [V] 319-483-1765
  centennialoaks.com
Cherokee G&CC, *Cherokee* .... 9 [P] 712-225-4687
Clarinda CC, *Clarinda* .... 18 [P] 712-542-5417
  clarindacountryclub.com
Clarmond CC, *Clarion* .... 9 [V] 515-532-2911
Clinton CC, *Clinton* .... 18 [V] 563-242-4961
  clintoncc.net
Coldwater Golf Links, *Ames* .... 18 [P] 515-233-4664
  coldwatergolf.com
Colfax CC, *Colfax* .... 9 [S] 515-674-3776
Collison Par3 GC, *Marshalltown* .... 18 [P] 641-753-0055
Coon Rapids GC, *Coon Rapids* .... 9 [P] 712-999-2880
  coonrapidsgolfcourse.com
Copper Creek GC, *Pleasant Hill* .... 18 [P] 515-263-1600
  coppergolf.com
Correctionville GC, *Correctionville* .... 9 [P] 712-372-4916
  correctionville.govoffice2.com
Corydon GC, *Corydon* .... 9 [M] 641-872-1826
  cityofcorydoniowa.com
Council Bluffs CC, *Council Bluffs* .... 18 [V] 712-366-1639
  councilbluffscountryclub.com
Country Greens GC, *Armstrong* .... 9 [P] 712-868-3048
Country Hills Community Golf, *West Union* .....9 [P] 563-422-3482
Country View GC, *Decorah* .... 18 [P] 563-382-2315
Countryside GC, *Norwalk* .... 18 [P] 515-981-0266
  countrysideiowa.com
Cresco CC, *Cresco* .... 9 [V] 563-547-2374
Crestmoor GC, *Creston* .... 9 [V] 641-782-2771
Crestwood Hills GC, *Anita* .... 18 [P] 712-762-3803
  anitagolf.com
Crow Valley GC, *Davenport* .... 18 [V] 563-359-0531
  crowvalleygolfclub.com
Davenport CC, *Pleasant Valley* .... 18 [V] 563-332-5022
  davenportcc.com
Deer Creek GC, *Humboldt* .... 9 [P] 515-546-6312
Deer Run GC, *Hinton* .... 9 [P] 712-947-4653
  hintoniowa.com
Deer Run GC & DR, *Indianola* .... 18 [P] 515-961-5445
Deerwood GC, *New London* .... 9 [P] 319-367-5216
Derby Grange Golf & Rec, *Dubuque* ..... 9 [P] 563-556-4653
  derbygrangegolf.com
Des Moines G&CC, *West Des Moines* .... 36 [V] 515-440-7500
  dmgcc.org
Diamond Trail GC, *Lynnville* .... 9 [P] 641-527-2600
  diamondtrailgolf.com
Dodge Riverside GC, *Council Bluffs* ... 18 [M] 712-328-4660
  cbparksandrec.org/golf.asp
Don Williams GC, *Ogden* .... 9 [M] 515-353-9225
Donald K Gardner Memorial GC, *Marion* ..... 18 [V] 319-286-5586
  playcedarrapidsgolf.com
Dougusta Par 3 GC, *Webster City* .... 9 [P] 515-297-0135
  dougusta.com
Dows GC, *Dows* .... 9 [P] 515-852-4751
Dubuque G&CC, *Dubuque* .... 18 [V] 563-583-9150
  dubuquegolf.org
Duck Creek GC, *Davenport* .... 18 [M] 563-326-7824
  cityofdavenportiowa.com
Dunlap GC, *Dunlap* .... 9 [S] 712-643-5945
Dyersville G&CC, *Dyersville* .... 9 [V] 563-875-8497
  dgcc.ghinclub.com
Dysart Rec GC, *Dysart* .... 9 [S] 319-476-3274
  dysartgolfclub.com

[S] = SEMI-PRIVATE   [V] = PRIVATE   [U] = UNIVERSITY   [N] = UNIVERSITY-PRIVATE

IOWA — Golf Yellow Pages, 18th Edition

Course	Location	Holes	Type	Phone
Eagle Grove GC	Eagle Grove	9	[S]	515-448-4166
Echo Valley CC	Norwalk	27	[V]	515-285-0101
echovalleycc.com				
Edgewater GC	Oelwein	9	[P]	319-283-3258
golfedgewater.com				
Edmundson GC	Oskaloosa	18	[M]	641-673-5120
Elkader GC	Elkader	9	[S]	563-245-2230
Elks Fairview GC	Keokuk	9	[V]	319-524-1074
Elks Lodge 590	Iowa City	9	[V]	319-351-3700
elks590.org				
Ellis Park GC	Cedar Rapids	18	[M]	319-286-5589
playcedarrapidsgolf.com				
Elmcrest CC	Cedar Rapids	18	[V]	319-363-7980
elmcrestcountryclub.com				
Elmwood CC	Marshalltown	18	[V]	641-753-8111
Emeis GC	Davenport	18	[M]	563-326-7825
Emerald Hills GC	Arnolds Park	18	[P]	712-332-7100
golfemeraldhills.com				
Essex GC	Essex	9	[P]	712-379-3805
Fairfield G&CC	Fairfield	9	[V]	641-472-4212
Fairview CC	Malvern	9	[P]	712-624-8557
Fawn Creek GC	Anamosa	9	[S]	319-462-4115
fawncreekcc.com				
Fillmore Fairways GC	Cascade	9	[M]	563-852-3377
fillmorefairways.com				
Finkbine GC	Iowa City	18	[U]	319-335-9556
finkbine.com				
Five By Eighty CC	Menlo	9	[P]	641-524-2345
5by80golf.com				
Five Island Golf & Community Ctr	Emmetsburg	9	[P]	712-852-3422
emmetsburg.com				
Flint Hills Muni GC	Burlington	18	[M]	319-752-2018
flinthillsgolf.com				
Floyd Park GC	Sioux City	18	[M]	712-274-1059
greenvalleyfloyd.org				
Fonda GC	Fonda	9	[P]	712-288-6419
Fort Dodge CC	Fort Dodge	18	[V]	515-955-8551
fortdodgecountryclub.com				
Fox Ridge GC	Dike	18	[P]	319-989-2213
golffoxridge.com				
Fox Run G&CC	West Branch	9	[S]	319-643-2100
Fox Run GC	Council Bluffs	27	[P]	712-366-4653
foxrungc.com				
Fremont County GC	Sidney	9	[M]	712-374-2347
co.fremont.ia.us				
Garner G&CC	Garner	9	[P]	641-923-2819
Gates Park GC	Waterloo	18	[M]	319-291-4485
waterlooleisureservices.org/golf				
Gateway Rec	Monroe	9	[P]	641-259-3246
gatewayrecreation.com				
Geneva G&CC	Muscatine	18	[V]	563-262-8894
genevacc.com				
Glen Oaks CC	West Des Moines	18	[V]	515-221-9000
glenoakscc.com				
Glenwood CC	Glenwood	9	[P]	712-527-9798
Glynns Creek GC	Long Grove	18	[M]	563-328-3484
glynnscreek.com				
Grand View GC	Des Moines	18	[M]	515-248-6301
dmgov.org				
Green Acres GC	Donnellson	9	[S]	319-835-5011
greenacresclub.com				
Green Valley GC	Sioux City	18	[M]	712-252-2025
greenvalleyfloyd.org				
Green Valley GC	Waukon	9	[P]	563-568-4866
Greenbrier GC	Exira	9	[S]	712-268-2209
Greenfield CC	Greenfield	9	[V]	641-743-2113
Grinnell G&CC	Grinnell	9	[V]	641-236-3590
Griswold G&CC	Griswold	9	[S]	712-778-4104
showcase.netins.net/web/nvra				
Guthrie Ctr GC	Guthrie Center	9	[P]	641-332-3558
Guttenberg GC	Guttenburg	9	[P]	563-252-1423
guttenberggolfcourse.com				
Hampton CC	Hampton	9	[V]	641-456-3256
hamptoncountryclub.com				
Happy Hollow CC	Corning	9	[P]	641-322-4333
Harlan G&CC	Harlan	9	[V]	712-755-5951
harlangolf.com				
Hart Ridge GC	Manchester	9	[P]	563-927-5494
Harvest Point GC	Oskaloosa	9	[P]	641-673-3100
Hawarden GC	Hawarden	9	[M]	712-551-4444
Hi Point GC	Iowa City	18	[P]	319-351-9434
Hickory Grove GC	Oelwein	9	[S]	319-283-2674
golfedgewater.com				
Hidden Acres CC	Sioux City	9	[P]	712-239-9942
Hidden Hills GC	Bettendorf	18	[P]	563-332-5616
Highland CC	Iowa Falls	9	[P]	641-648-4021
Highland Park GC	Mason City	18	[M]	641-423-9693
masoncity.net				
Hillcrest CC	Mt Vernon	9	[P]	319-895-8193
hillcrestcountryclubmv.com				
Hillcrest CC	Adel	9	[V]	515-993-3630
hccadel.com				
Hillcrest GC	Graettinger	9	[P]	712-859-3766
Hillside Golf	Wesley	9	[P]	515-679-4262
Holstein CC	Holstein	9	[P]	712-368-2530
Homewood GC	Ames	9	[M]	515-239-5363
city.ames.ia.us/parkrecweb				
Honey Creek GC	Boone	18	[P]	515-432-6162
golfhoneycreek.com				
Hubbard G&RecC	Hubbard	9	[P]	641-864-2647
Humboldt CC	Humboldt	9	[P]	515-332-3364
Hunters Ridge GC	Marion	18	[P]	319-377-3500
hrgolfcourse.com				
Hyperion Field Club	Johnston	18	[V]	515-276-1596
hyperionfc.com				
Ida Grove CC	Ida Grove	9	[P]	712-364-2320
Indian Creek CC	Nevada	9	[V]	515-382-9070
indiancreekcc.com				
Indian Hills G&CC	Wapello	18	[P]	319-868-7747
ihgcc.com				
Indian Hills GC	Spirit Lake	9	[P]	712-336-4768
Indianola G&CC	Indianola	18	[V]	515-961-3303
indianolacountryclub.com				
Irv Warren Memorial GC	Waterloo	18	[M]	319-234-9271
Jackson Heights GC	Jackson Junction	9	[P]	563-776-9181
jacksonheightsgolf.com				
Jester Park GC	Granger	27	[M]	515-999-2903
jesterparkgolf.com				
Jesup GC	Jesup	9	[P]	319-827-1152
jesupgolf.com				
Jewell G&CC	Jewell	9	[S]	515-827-5631
Jones Park GC	Cedar Rapids	18	[M]	319-286-5581
playcedarrapidsgolf.com				
Kalona GC	Kalona	9	[S]	319-656-3844
kalonagolfclub.com				

[A] = MILITARY   [M] = MUNICIPAL   [P] = PUBLIC   [R] = RESORT

Golf Yellow Pages, 18th Edition — IOWA

Keokuk CC, *Keokuk* .... 9 [V] 319-524-2002
  keokukcountryclub.com
Knoll Ridge CC, *North English* .... 9 [P] 319-664-3700
La Porte City GC, *La Porte City* .... 9 [P] 319-342-2249
Lagos Acres GC, *Keota* .... 9 [P] 641-636-3411
Lake City CC, *Lake City* .... 9 [S] 712-464-3344
  lakecitycountryclub.com
Lake Creek CC, *Storm Lake* .... 18 [P] 712-732-1548
  lakecreekgolf.com
Lake MacBride GC, *Solon* .... 9 [P] 319-624-2500
  lakemacbride.com
Lake Panorama National GC, *Panora* .... 18 [P] 641-755-2024
  lakepanoramanational.com
Lakeshore G&CC, *Afton* .... 9 [P] 641-347-5221
Lakeside GC, *Jefferson* .... 9 [S] 515-738-2403
Lakeside Muni GC, *Fort Dodge* .... 18 [M] 515-576-6741
Lakeview CC, *Winterset* .... 9 [S] 515-462-9962
Lakeview G&CC, *Chariton* .... 9 [V] 641-774-5964
Lamoni GC, *Lamoni* .... 9 [P] 641-784-6022
Landsmeer GC, *Orange City* .... 18 [M] 712-737-3429
  landsmeergolfclub.com
Latimer GC, *Latimer* .... 9 [P] 641-579-6090
Laurens G&CC, *Laurens* .... 9 [V] 712-841-2287
  laurens-ia.com
Legend Trail GC, *Parkersburg* .... 9 [P] 319-346-1499
  legendtraildevelopment.com
Lenox Muni GC, *Lenox* .... 9 [M] 641-333-2990
Leon G&CC, *Leon* .... 9 [P] 641-446-4529
Lincoln Valley GC, *State Center* .... 18 [S] 641-483-2054
  lincolnvalleygolf.com
Linn Grove CC, *Rockwell* .... 9 [P] 641-822-4990
Little Bear Rec Club, *Wyoming* .... 9 [S] 563-488-2559
  littlebeargolfcourse.com
Little Sioux G&CC, *Sioux Rapids* .... 9 [S] 712-283-2162
Logan Missouri Valley CC, *Logan* .... 9 [S] 712-644-3050
Lone Pine G&CC, *Colesburg* .... 9 [P] 563-856-3445
Lost Island GC, *Ruthven* .... 9 [P] 712-837-4800
Majestic Hills GC At Denison, *Denison* .... 18 [P] 712-263-5194
  majestichillsgolf.com
Manchester GC, *Manchester* .... 18 [P] 563-927-4155
  manchestergolfcourse.net
Manhattan GC, *Centerville* .... 9 [S] 641-856-8165
  themanhattangolfclub.com
Manning Manilla G&CC, *Manning* .... 9 [P] 712-653-3515
Manson G&CC, *Manson* .... 9 [P] 712-469-3996
  golfmanson.com
Maple Heights G&CC, *Elma* .... 9 [P] 641-393-2120
  golfelma.com
Maple Hills GC, *Tripoli* .... 9 [V] 319-882-4229
Maquoketa GC, *Maquoketa* .... 9 [V] 563-652-4515
  maquoketacountryclub.com
Marcus Community GC, *Marcus* .... 9 [P] 712-376-4492
Marengo G&CC, *Marengo* .... 9 [S] 319-642-3508
Mason City CC, *Mason City* .... 18 [V] 641-424-2173
  masoncitycountryclub.com
Meadow Acres GC, *Larchwood* .... 9 [P] 712-477-2576
Meadow Hills GC, *Iowa Falls* .... 9 [P] 641-648-4421
Meadowbrook CC, *Sumner* .... 9 [V] 563-578-8123
Meadowbrook G&CC, *Hartley* .... 9 [P] 712-728-2060
Meadowbrook GC, *Wellsburg* .... 9 [P] 641-869-3766
Meadowridge Golf DR, *Cedar Rapids* .... 9 [P] 319-396-2234
  meadowridgegolf.com
Meadowview GC, *Central City* .... 9 [P] 319-438-1063

Montezuma CC, *Montezuma* .... 9 [V] 641-623-5714
Monticello GC, *Monticello* .... 9 [P] 319-465-5225
Mount Ayr CC, *Mt Ayr* .... 9 [P] 641-464-2430
Mt Pleasant G&CC, *Mt Pleasant* .... 9 [V] 319-986-6157
Muscatine Muni GC, *Muscatine* .... 18 [M] 563-263-4735
  ci.muscatine.ia.us
Nashua Town & CC, *Nashua* .... 9 [V] 641-435-4466
New Hampton G&CC, *New Hampton* .... 9 [P] 641-394-4340
Newell Golf Park, *Newell* .... 9 [M] 712-272-4424
  newelliowa.com
Newton CC, *Newton* .... 9 [V] 641-792-6619
  newtoncc.com
Nishna Hills GC, *Atlantic* .... 18 [V] 712-243-9931
Nora Springs West Hills G&CC, *Nora Springs* .... 9 [P] 641-749-5522
North Kossuth GC, *Bancroft* .... 9 [P] 515-885-2352
Northwood CC, *Northwood* .... 9 [P] 641-324-1662
Oak Hills GC, *Clear Lake* .... 9 [P] 641-357-2216
Oak Leaf CC, *Reinbeck* .... 9 [P] 319-345-2079
Oak Park Golf & Rec, *Dayton* .... 9 [P] 515-547-2712
  daytonia.govoffice2.com
Oak Ridge Rec Associaton, *Goldfield* .... 9 [P] 515-825-3611
Oakland Acres GC, *Grinnell* .... 18 [P] 641-236-7111
Oakland CC, *Oakland* .... 9 [P] 712-482-6614
Oaks GC, *Ames* .... 9 [P] 515-232-9862
  oaksgolfcourse.com
Oakwood GC, *Conrad* .... 9 [S] 641-366-2211
Okoboji View GC, *Spirit Lake* .... 18 [P] 712-337-3372
  okobojiview.net
Olathea GC, *Le Claire* .... 9 [P] 563-289-4653
Olde Indian Creek CC, *Marion* .... 9 [V] 319-377-4489
  indiancreekcountryclub.net
Onawa CC, *Onawa* .... 9 [V] 712-433-1712
Oneota G&CC, *Decorah* .... 18 [S] 563-382-4407
Osceola CC, *Osceola* .... 9 [V] 641-342-3717
Oskaloosa Golf, *Oskaloosa* .... 18 [P] 641-676-4653
  oskaloosagolf.com
Otter Creek GC, *Ankeny* .... 18 [M] 515-965-6464
  ankenyiowa.gov
Otter Valley CC, *George* .... 9 [P] 712-475-3861
  golfovcc.com
Ottumwa CC, *Ottumwa* .... 18 [V] 641-684-4471
  ottumwacountryclub.com
Palmer Hills GC, *Bettendorf* .... 18 [M] 563-332-8296
  palmerhillsgolf.com
Paullina GC, *Paullina* .... 9 [S] 712-448-3477
Pebble Creek GC, *Le Claire* .... 9 [P] 563-332-5072
  pebblecreekgolf.org
Pella G&CC, *Pela* .... 9 [V] 641-628-4564
Perry G&CC, *Perry* .... 9 [P] 515-465-3852
  perryiagolf.com
Pheasant Ridge Muni GC, *Cedar Falls* .... 27 [M] 319-266-8266
  golfcedarfalls.com
Pierson GC, *Pierson* .... 9 [P] 712-375-5011
Pine Creek GC, *Mason City* .... 9 [P] 641-423-6831
Pine Knolls CC, *Knoxville* .... 9 [P] 641-842-3730
  pineknollscountryclub.com
Pine Lake GC, *Eldora* .... 9 [S] 641-858-3031
  plccgolf.net
Pine Valley GC, *Creston* .... 9 [P] 641-782-4917
Pioneer Town & CC, *Manly* .... 9 [S] 641-454-2414
Pleasant Valley GC, *Iowa City* .... 18 [P] 319-337-2622
  pleasantvalleyic.com
Pleasant Valley CC, *Thornton* .... 9 [P] 641-998-2117

[S] = SEMI-PRIVATE   [V] = PRIVATE   [U] = UNIVERSITY   [N] = UNIVERSITY-PRIVATE

IOWA

Golf Yellow Pages, 18th Edition

Pleasant Valley Sports Club, *Clermont*....................9 [P] 563-423-7396
Pleasantville G&CC, *Pleasantville*..........................9 [V] 515-848-5716
  pleasantvillecc.com
Plum Creek GC, *Fredericksburg*..............................9 [P] 563-237-6401
Plum River GC, *Preston*...9 [P] 563-689-4653
Pocahontas GC, *Pocahontas*...................................9 [P] 712-335-4375
Ponderosa Public GC, *West Des Moines*..................9 [P] 515-225-1766
Prairie Creek, *Maquoketa*......................................9 [P] 563-652-1833
Prairie Knolls CC, *New Sharon*...............................9 [S] 641-637-4200
Prairie Rose GC, *Brunsville*...................................9 [P] 712-533-6774
Prairie View GC, *Nevada*.......................................9 [P] 515-382-4653
Prairie View Golf & Grill, *Gowrie*...........................9 [P] 515-352-3320
Primghar G&CC, *Primghar*.....................................9 [P] 712-957-6781
  primghar.com
Quail Creek GC, *North Liberty*...............................9 [P] 319-626-2281
Quail Run GC, *Neola*..9 [P] 712-485-2266
  quailrunia.com
Quimby GC, *Quimby*..9 [P] 712-445-2236
Raccoon Valley GC, *Jefferson*................................9 [P] 515-386-4178
Radcliffe Friendly Fairways, *Radcliffe*....................9 [P] 515-899-7969
Raleigh Hill CC, *Ionia*..9 [P] 641-394-3256
Red Carpet GC, *Waterloo*....................................18 [P] 319-235-1242
  redcarpetgolf.com
Red Hawk GC, *Davenport*......................................9 [M] 563-386-0348
  cityofdavenportiowa.com
Red Oak CC, *Red Oak*..18 [S] 712-623-4281
  redoakcc.com
Remsen GC, *Remsen*...9 [P] 712-786-2266
Rice Lake G&CC, *Lake Mills*................................18 [S] 641-592-8022
  ricelakegolfandcountryclub.com
Riceville GC, *Riceville*..9 [P] 641-985-2447
  riceville.govoffice2.com
Ridgestone GC, *Sheffield*....................................18 [P] 641-892-8040
  ridgestonegolfclub.com
River Bend GC, *Story City*.....................................9 [M] 515-733-2611
River Ridge GC, *Independence*..............................9 [P] 319-334-6576
River Road GC, *Algona*..9 [P] 515-295-7351
River Valley GC, *Adel*..18 [P] 515-993-4029
  rivervalleygolf.com
River View Club, *Keosauqua*.................................9 [S] 319-293-3200
  keosauqua.com/riverviewclub
Riverview GC, *Estherville*......................................9 [P] 712-362-3911
Rock River G&CC, *Rock Rapids*............................9 [P] 712-472-3168
  countryclub.rockrapids.org
Rock Valley GC, *Rock Valley*.................................9 [S] 712-476-2427
Rolfe GC, *Rolfe*...9 [P] 712-848-3662
Rolling Acres GC, *Center Point*.............................9 [P] 319-849-2996
Rolling Hills CC, *Hull*..9 [P] 712-439-2310
Rolling Hills GC, *Norwalk*...................................18 [P] 515-981-1500
Rolling Knolls GC, *Dyersville*................................9 [P] 563-875-7466
Rosman Glendale Shelby County GC, *Harlan*........9 [P] 712-627-4224
Round Grove G&CC, *Greene*.................................9 [P] 641-816-5621
Rustic Ridge GC, *Eldridge*....................................9 [P] 563-285-8119
  golfrusticridge.com
Sac CC, *Sac City*..9 [S] 712-662-7342
  saccountryclub.com
Saddleback Ridge GC, *Solon*..............................18 [P] 319-624-1477
  saddlebackridgegolf.com
Sanborn G&CC, *Sanborn*.......................................9 [M] 712-930-5600
Schleswig CC, *Schleswig*.......................................9 [P] 712-676-3343
  schleswigia.com
Shadow Valley GC, *Woodbine*..............................9 [P] 712-647-3442
Shady Oaks GC, *Ackworth*..................................18 [P] 515-961-0262

Sheaffer Memorial GC, *Fort Madison*..................18 [P] 319-528-6214
Sheldon G&CC, *Sheldon*.......................................9 [S] 712-324-4275
  sheldongolf.com
Shoreline GC, *Carter Lake*..................................18 [P] 712-347-5173
  golfshoreline.com
Sibley G&CC, *Sibley*..9 [P] 712-754-2729
Sigourney G&CC, *Sigourney*.................................9 [V] 641-622-3400
Silver Lake CC, *Lake Park*.....................................9 [P] 712-832-3213
  slccgolf.com
Silver Spring GC, *Ossian*.......................................9 [P] 563-532-8904
Silvercrest G&CC, *Decorah*...................................9 [S] 563-382-5296
  silvercrestgolf.com
Sioux City CC, *Sioux City*...................................18 [V] 712-277-4612
  sccountryclub.com
Sioux G&CC, *Alton*..9 [S] 712-756-4513
  altoniowa.org/Siouxgolf.htm
Sleepy Hollow Sports Park, *Des Moines*..............9 [P] 515-262-4100
  sleepyhollowsportspark.com
Slippery Elm GC, *Klemme*.....................................9 [P] 641-587-2670
Sloan Community Recr Assn GC, *Sloan*................9 [P] 712-428-9993
South Hardin Rec Area, *Union*..............................9 [P] 641-486-2335
South Hills GC, *Waterloo*...................................18 [M] 319-291-4268
  golfsouthhills.com
South Winn G&CC, *Calmar*...................................9 [S] 563-562-3191
Spencer G&CC, *Spencer*.....................................18 [P] 712-262-2028
  spencergolfcc.com
Spencer Muni GC, *Spencer*................................18 [M] 712-580-7281
  spencermunigolf.com
Spirit Hollow GC, *Burlington*..............................18 [P] 319-752-0004
  spirithollowgolfcourse.com
Spring Hills CC, *Mallard*.......................................9 [P] 712-425-3582
Spring Lake CC, *Wall Lake*....................................9 [S] 712-664-2204
Spring Lake GC, *Fort Madison*..............................9 [P] 319-372-9937
Spring Valley GC, *Livermore*...............................18 [P] 515-379-1259
  springvalleygc.com
Springbrook CC, *de Witt*.....................................18 [V] 563-659-3187
St Andrews GC, *Cedar Rapids*.............................18 [P] 319-393-9915
  standrewsiowa.com
Stone Creek GC, *Williamsburg*..............................9 [S] 319-668-2225
  stonecreekiowa.com
Sugar Creek GC, *Waukee*......................................9 [M] 515-987-5247
  waukee.org
Sun Valley GC, *Sioux City*...................................18 [P] 712-258-9770
Sun Valley Lake GC, *Ellston*..................................9 [P] 641-772-4380
Sunkissed Meadows GC, *Fort Dodge*....................9 [M] 515-576-4313
Sunny Brae G&CC, *Osage*.....................................9 [S] 641-732-3435
Sunnyside GC, *Waterloo*.....................................18 [V] 319-234-1125
  sunnysidecountryclub.com
Sunrise GC, *Bettendorf*...9 [P] 563-332-6386
Sunrise Pointe GC, *Storm Lake*............................9 [M] 712-732-8025
  stormlake.org
Tama Toledo CC, *Tama*..9 [P] 641-484-2027
  golf.tamatoledo.org
Tara Hills CC, *Van Horne*......................................9 [P] 319-228-8771
  tarahills.com
Terrace Hills GC, *Altoona*...................................18 [P] 515-967-2932
  golfthills.com
The Barn Gruis Rec Area GC, *Buffalo Center*........9 [M] 641-926-5393
The Harvester, *Rhodes*..18 [P] 641-227-4653
  harvestergolf.com
The Hill GC, *Grand Junction*..................................9 [P] 515-738-2633
The Inn At Okoboji GC, *Okoboji*............................9 [R] 712-332-2113
  theinnatokoboji.com

[A] = MILITARY [M] = MUNICIPAL [P] = PUBLIC [R] = RESORT

Golf Yellow Pages, 18th Edition — KANSAS

The Legacy GC, *Norwalk* ....18 [P] 515-287-7885
  thelegacygolfclub.com
The Meadows CC, *Moville* ....9 [S] 712-873-3184
  meadowscountryclub.com/index.html
The Meadows GC, *Dubuque* ....18 [M] 563-583-7385
  meadowsgolf.com
The Preserve At Lake Rathbun, *Moravia* ....18 [R] 641-724-1400
  honeycreekresort.com
The Ridge GC, *Sioux Center* ....18 [S] 712-722-4866
  siouxcenterridge.com
The Rockford Public GC, *Rockford* ....9 [S] 641-756-3314
Three Elms Golf, *Independence* ....9 [P] 319-334-4235
Thunder Hills CC, *Peosta* ....18 [V] 563-556-3363
  thunderhillscc.com
Timberline GC, *Peosta* ....18 [P] 563-876-3210
  timberlinegolf.com
Tipton CC, *Tipton* ....9 [P] 563-886-2848
Toad Valley Public GC, *Pleasant Hill* ....18 [P] 515-967-9575
  toadvalley.com
Tournament Club of Iowa, *Polk City* ....18 [P] 515-984-9440
  tcofiowa.com
Town & Country GC, *Grundy Center* ....9 [P] 319-824-3712
  tcgolfclub.com
Traer G&CC, *Traer* ....9 [P] 319-478-2700
  traer.com
Treynor Rec Area, *Treynor* ....9 [P] 712-487-3302
  TRAclubhouse.com
Tri City GC, *Luana* ....9 [P] 563-539-4435
Twin Anchors GC, *Colo* ....9 [P] 641-377-2245
Twin Lakes GC, *Rockwell City* ....9 [P] 712-297-8712
  twinlakesgolfclub.org
Twin Lakes GC, *Winfield* ....9 [P] 319-257-6253
Twin Pines GC, *Cedar Rapids* ....18 [M] 319-286-5583
  playcedarrapidsgolf.com
Urbandale G&CC, *Urbandale* ....9 [V] 515-276-5496
  urbandalegolf.com
Valley Oaks GC, *Clinton* ....27 [S] 563-242-7221
  valleyoaksgolf.com
Veenker Memorial GC, *Ames* ....18 [U] 515-294-6727
  veenkergolf.com
Vinton CC, *Vinton* ....9 [P] 319-472-4052
Wahkonsa CC, *Durant* ....9 [S] 563-785-6328
  wahkonsa.com
Wakonda Club, *Des Moines* ....18 [V] 515-285-4962
  wakondaclub.com
Walton Club, *Fairfield* ....9 [V] 641-472-4909
  thewaltonclub.com
Wapsi Oaks CC, *Calamus* ....9 [S] 563-246-2216
  wapsioaks.com
Wapsie Ridge GC, *Fairbank* ....9 [P] 319-638-4653
  wapsieridgecountrygolf.com
Wapsipinicon GC, *Anamosa* ....9 [R] 319-462-3930
Washington G&CC, *Washington* ....9 [P] 319-653-2080
Waukon G&CC, *Waukon* ....9 [P] 563-568-9939
Waveland GC, *Des Moines* ....18 [M] 515-271-8725
  wavelandgolfcourse.org
Waverly Muni GC, *Waverly* ....18 [M] 319-352-1530
  golfwaverly.com
Webster City Links, *Webster City* ....9 [P] 515-832-1533
Wellman GC, *Wellman* ....9 [P] 319-646-9717
West Bend G&CC, *West Bend* ....9 [P] 515-887-6217
West Liberty GC, *West Liberty* ....9 [P] 319-627-2085
  westlibertycountryclub.homestead.com

West Links Estates GC, *Alta* ....9 [P] 712-200-2137
Westwood GC, *Newton* ....18 [M] 641-792-3087
  westwoodgolfcourse.com
Westwood Park GC, *Council Bluffs* ....9 [M] 712-322-9913
  cbparksandrec.org/golf.asp
Whispering Creek GC, *Sioux City* ....18 [P] 712-276-3678
  whisperingcreekgolfclub.com
Whispering Pines GC, *Muscatine* ....9 [P] 563-288-4324
Whittemore GC, *Whittemore* ....9 [P] 515-884-2775
Wildcat GC, *Shellsburg* ....18 [P] 319-436-4653
Wildwood Muni GC, *Charles City* ....9 [P] 641-257-6322
  charlescity.govoffice.com
Willow Creek GC, *West Des Moines* ....36 [P] 515-285-4558
  willowgolf.com
Willow Creek GC, *Le Mars* ....27 [M] 712-546-6849
Willow Ridge GC, *Fort Dodge* ....9 [S] 515-576-5711
  willowridgegolf.com
Willow Run CC, *Denver* ....9 [S] 319-984-5762
  willowruncc.com
Willow Vale GC, *Mapleton* ....9 [P] 712-881-1002
Woodland Hills Golf, *Des Moines* ....27 [P] 515-289-1326
  golfwoodlandhills.com
Woodlyn Hills GC, *Milford* ....18 [P] 712-338-9898
  woodlynhillsgolf.com
Woods Edge GC, *Edgewood* ....9 [P] 563-928-6668
Woodward Golf & Rec, *Woodward* ....9 [V] 515-438-2198

KANSAS

Abilene CC, *Abilene* ....9 [V] 785-263-3811
Allen County CC, *Iola* ....9 [P] 620-365-2682
Alvamar CC, *Lawrence* ....18 [V] 785-842-2929
  alvamar.com
Alvamar Orchards, *Lawrence* ....9 [P] 785-843-7456
Alvamar Public GC, *Lawrence* ....18 [S] 785-842-1907
  alvamar.com
American Legion GC, *El Dorado* ....9 [P] 316-321-1295
Anthony CC, *Anthony* ....9 [P] 620-842-5965
Arkansas City CC, *Arkansas City* ....18 [V] 620-442-5560
  members.cox.net/arkcitycc
Arthur B Sim Park GC, *Wichita* ....18 [M] 316-337-9100
  golfwichita.com
Ashland CC, *Ashland* ....9 [V] 620-635-2281
Atwood CC, *Atwood* ....9 [V] 785-626-9542
Auburn Hills GC, *Wichita* ....18 [M] 316-219-9700
  golfwichita.com
Augusta CC, *Augusta* ....9 [P] 316-775-7281
  augustaccgolf.com
Baldwin GC, *Baldwin City* ....9 [M] 785-594-3435
Baxter CC, *Baxter Springs* ....9 [S] 620-856-3538
Belleville CC, *Belleville* ....9 [P] 785-527-2745
Bellevue GC, *Atchison* ....18 [V] 913-367-3022
Beloit CC, *Beloit* ....9 [V] 785-738-5381
  beloitcountryclub.com
Bentwood GC, *Ulysses* ....9 [M] 620-356-3097
Big Creek GC, *Wakeeney* ....9 [P] 785-743-2420
Bird City GC, *Bird City* ....9 [P] 785-734-2708
Braeburn GC at Wichita State Univ, *Wichita* ....18 [U] 316-978-4653
  braeburngolfcourse.com
Brookridge G&CC - Regulation, *Overland Park* ....18 [V] 913-648-1600
  brookridgecc.net
Brookridge G&CC - West 9, *Overland Park* ....9 [V] 913-648-1600
  brookridgecc.net

[S] = SEMI-PRIVATE   [V] = PRIVATE   [U] = UNIVERSITY   [N] = UNIVERSITY-PRIVATE

KANSAS — Golf Yellow Pages, 18th Edition

Buffalo Dunes GC, *Garden City* ....18 [M] 620-276-1210
  buffalodunes.net
Burning Tree GC, *De Soto* ....9 [P] 913-301-9631
  burningtreegolfclub.com
Caney CC, *Caney* ....9 [P] 620-879-2055
Cannonball GC, *Greensburg* .... 9 [V] 620-723-3056
Carey Park GC, *Hutchinson* ....18 [M] 620-694-2698
  hutchgov.com
Cedar Brook GC, *Iola* ....18 [P] 620-365-2176
Cedar Hills GC, *Washington*....................................9 [P] 785-325-2424
  washingtonks.net
Cedar Links G&CC, *Plainville* ....9 [P] 785-434-4766
Cedar Pines GC, *Andover*..9 [P] 316-733-8070
  andoverks.com
Chanute CC, *Chanute* .... 9 [V] 620-431-9560
Chase GC, *Chase* ....9 [P] 620-938-2911
Cherry Oaks GC, *Cheney*..18 [M] 316-540-0133
  cheneyks.com
Cimarron GC, *Cimarron* ....9 [M] 620-855-7003
  cimarronkansas.net/cgc.htm
Cimarron Valley GC, *Satanta* ....9 [P] 620-649-2202
City Of Willowbrook GC, *Hutchinson* .... 9 [V] 620-662-5701
Claflin GC, *Great Bend*... 9 [V] 620-587-3460
Clay Ctr CC, *Clay Center* .... 9 [V] 785-632-3551
Clearwater GC, *Clearwater*.......................................9 [P] 620-584-2799
  clearwatergolfclub.com
Coffeyville CC, *Coffeyville*..................................... 18 [V] 620-251-5236
  coffeyvillecountryclub.com
Colbert Hills GC, *Manhattan* .... 27 [U] 785-776-6475
  colberthills.com
Coldwater CC, *Coldwater*... 9 [V] 620-582-2733
Columbus CC, *Columbus* ....9 [S] 620-674-3383
Concordia American Legion GC, *Concordia*...........9 [P] 785-243-3305
  concordiaamericanlegionpost76.org
Cool Springs GC, *Onaga* ....9 [P] 785-889-7128
Cottonwood Falls CC, *Cottonwood Falls*................9 [S] 620-273-8583
Cottonwood Hills GC, *Hutchinson*........................18 [R] 620-802-9150
  cottonwoodhills.net
Council Grove CC, *Council Grove* ....9 [P] 620-767-5516
Countryside GC, *Pittsburg* ....9 [P] 620-232-3654
  countrysidegc.com
Crestview CC, *Wichita* .... 36 [V] 316-733-1344
  crestviewcountryclub.com
Crestwood CC, *Pittsburg* .... 18 [V] 620-231-6530
  countryclubatcrestwood.com
Crooked Creek CC, *Montezuma*.............................9 [M] 620-846-2264
Custer Hill GC, *Fort Riley* ....18 [A] 785-784-6000
  rileymwr.com
Cypress Ridge GC, *Topeka* ....18 [M] 785-273-0811
  cypressridgegc.com
Deer Creek GC, *Overland Park* .... 18 [S] 913-681-3100
  deercreekgc.com
Deer Trace GC, *Linn Valley* .... 18 [V] 913-757-4597
  lvlpoa.com
Dodge City CC, *Dodge City*................................... 18 [P] 620-225-4242
  dccountryclub.com
Downs GC, *Downs* ....9 [P] 785-454-3805
Dubs Dread GC, *Kansas City* ....18 [P] 913-721-1333
  dubsdreadgolfclub.com
Eagle Bend GC, *Lawrence*......................................18 [M] 785-748-0600
  lprd.org
Echo Hills GC, *Wichita* ....18 [M] 316-838-0143
  echohills.com

Elks CC, *Salina* .... 18 [V] 785-827-8585
Ellis CC, *Ellis*..9 [S] 785-726-4711
  elliscountryclub.com
Ellsworth GC, *Ellsworth* ....9 [M] 785-472-4236
  ellsworthks.net/golf
Emporia CC, *Emporia* .... 9 [V] 620-342-0349
  emporiacc.org
Emporia Muni GC, *Emporia*...................................18 [M] 620-342-7666
  emporia.ws
Eureka CC, *Eureka* .... 9 [V] 620-583-5642
Falcon Lakes GC, *Basehor*......................................18 [P] 913-724-4653
  falconlakesgolf.com
Falcon Ridge GC, *Lenexa* ....18 [P] 913-393-4653
  falconridgegolf.com
Falcon Valley GC, *Lenexa* ....9 [P] 913-780-5976
  falconvalleygolf.com
Firekeeper GC, *Mayetta* ....18 [P] 785-966-2100
  firekeepergolf.com
Flint Hills National GC, *Andover*......................... 18 [V] 316-733-7272
  flinthillsnational.com
Forbes Public GC, *Topeka* ....9 [M] 785-862-0114
  co.shawnee.ks.us
Forewinds Muni GC, *Hugoton* ....9 [P] 620-544-8269
Fort Hays Muni GC, *Hays*.......................................18 [M] 785-625-9949
  haysusa.com
Fort Scott CC, *Fort Scott* ....18 [P] 620-223-5060
Four Oaks GC, *Pittsburg* ....18 [M] 620-231-8070
  pittks.org
Fox Ridge GC, *Newton* ....9 [P] 316-283-4666
  foxridgegc.com
Fredonia GC, *Fredonia* ....9 [P] 620-378-3270
Gardner GC, *Gardner* ....18 [M] 913-856-8858
  gardnergolf.com
Garnett CC, *Garnett* ....9 [S] 785-448-6191
Geneseo GC, *Geneseo* .... 9 [V] 620-824-6217
Girard Muni GC, *Girard*.. 9 [V] 620-724-8855
Glasco GC, *Glasco*...9 [P] 785-568-2448
Golden Locket GC, *Garden City* ....9 [P] 620-275-1953
GreatLife Golf & Fitness - Berkshire, *Topeka*....... 18 [V] 785-267-7888
  greatlifegolf.com
GreatLife Golf & Fitness - Chisholm Trail, *Abilene* 18 [P] 785-263-3313
  greatlifegolf.com
GreatLife Golf & Fitness - Lake Perry, *Ozawkie*... 18 [V] 785-484-2339
  greatlifegolf.com
GreatLife Golf & Fitness - Prairie View, *Topeka*... 18 [V] 785-478-9733
  greatlifegolf.com
GreatLife Golf & Fitness - Western Hills, *Topeka*..18 [P] 785-478-4000
  greatlifegolf.com
GreatLife Golf-Junction City, *Junction City* .... 9 [V] 785-238-1161
  greatlifegolf.com
Greeley County GC, *Tribune* ....9 [P] 620-376-4845
Green Valley GC, *Pratt*...9 [P] 620-672-3990
Grinnel Cowpaddy GC, *Grinnel*...............................9 [P] 785-824-3909
Grove Park GC, *Ellinwood* .... 9 [V] 620-564-3123
  groveparkgolf.com
Haddam Community GC, *Haddam*..........................9 [P] 785-778-2524
Hallbrook CC, *Leawood*... 18 [V] 913-345-1011
  hallbrookcc.org
Haven GC, *Haven* ....9 [P] 620-465-3618
Herington CC, *Herington*.. 9 [V] 785-258-2052
Heritage Park GC, *Olathe* ....18 [M] 913-829-4653
  jcprd.com

[A] = MILITARY [M] = MUNICIPAL [P] = PUBLIC [R] = RESORT

KANSAS

Hesston Golf Park, *Hesston* .... 18 [M] 620-327-2331
  hesstongolf.com
Hiawatha CC, *Hiawatha*.................................... 9 [V] 785-742-3361
Hickory Hollow GC, *Ottawa* ....9 [P] 785-566-3733
Hidden Lakes GC, *Derby*................................18 [P] 316-788-2855
  hiddenlakesgolfcourse.com
Hidden Springs GC, *Overbrook*....................9 [P] 785-665-7372
Hillcrest GC, *Coffeyville* ....18 [M] 620-252-6190
  coffeyville.com
Hillsboro Muni GC, *Hillsboro* ....9 [M] 620-947-3067
Holton CC, *Holton* ....9 [P] 785-364-3558
  holtonks.net
Horton Lakeview CC, *Horton*........................9 [P] 785-486-3829
Hoxie GC, *Hoxie* ....9 [P] 785-675-3241
Independence CC, *Independence* .... 18 [V] 620-331-1274
  independence-cc.com
Indian Hills CC, *Shawnee Mission*............... 18 [V] 913-362-6204
  ihcckc.com
Indian Hills GC, *Chapman* ....9 [M] 785-922-6203
  cityofchapman.org
Indian Plains GC, *New Strawn*.....................9 [P] 620-364-5606
Ironhorse GC, *Leawood*..............................18 [M] 913-685-4653
  ironhorsegolf.com
Katy GC, *Parsons*..9 [M] 620-421-4532
Kingman Country GC, *Kingman* .... 9 [V] 620-532-2373
  kingmanks.com
Kinsley Golf & The Fairways, *Kinsley* ....9 [S] 620-659-2538
L W Clapp Memorial GC, *Wichita*................18 [M] 316-688-9341
  golfwichita.com
La Crosse CC, *La Crosse*...............................9 [S] 785-222-2517
Lake Barton GC, *Great Bend*...................... 18 [S] 620-653-4255
Lake of the Forest GC, *Bonner Springs*.................. 9 [V] 913-441-3252
  lakeforestclubhouse.com
Lake Quivira CC, *Lake Quivira* .... 18 [V] 913-631-7577
  lakequivira.org
Lake Shawnee GC, *Topeka* ....18 [M] 785-267-2295
  lakeshawneegolf.com
Lakeside GC, *Yates Center* ....9 [P] 620-496-6910
Lakeside GC, *Cawker City* ....9 [M] 785-781-4713
Lakin Municipal GC, *Lakin*............................9 [M] 620-355-6945
  lakinkansas.org/serv/golf.html
Lamont Hill Resort GC, *Vassar* .... 9 [R] 785-828-3131
Lane County CC, *Dighton* .... 9 [V] 620-397-2549
Larned CC, *Larned*.......................................9 [M] 620-285-3935
Lawrence CC, *Lawrence*.............................. 18 [V] 785-843-2938
  lawrencecountryclub.com
Leavenworth CC, *Lansing*........................... 18 [V] 913-727-6600
  leavenworthcountryclub.com
Leawood South CC, *Leawood*..................... 18 [V] 913-469-4172
  leawoodsocc.com
Leonardville GC, *Leonardville*......................9 [P] 785-293-5647
Leoti CC, *Leoti* ....9 [S] 620-375-2263
Liberal CC, *Liberal* .... 9 [V] 620-624-3992
Lincoln GC, *Lincoln* ....9 [P] 785-524-4624
Lindsborg GC, *Lindsborg* ....9 [P] 785-227-2244
Logan GC, *Logan*..9 [M] 785-689-4816
Luray GC (Pasture), *Luray*............................9 [S] 785-698-2320
  pasturegolf.com/courses/luray.htm
Lyons Town & CC, *Lyons* .... 9 [V] 620-257-2962
MacDonald GC, *Wichita* ....18 [M] 316-688-9341
  golfwichita.com
Madison GC, *Madison* .... 9 [V] 620-437-2120

Manhattan CC, *Manhattan*......................... 18 [V] 785-539-6221
  themanhattancountryclub.com
Mankato CC, *Mankato* .... 9 [V] 785-378-3140
Mariah Hills GC, *Dodge City*........................18 [M] 620-225-8182
  mariahhillsgolf.com
Marion CC, *Marion*...................................... 9 [V] 620-382-2281
Marysville CC, *Marysville*............................ 9 [V] 785-562-2296
Mc Pherson CC, *McPherson*........................ 9 [V] 620-241-3541
  mcphersonks.org
McCracken CC, *Mc Cracken* ....9 [P] 785-394-1101
  mccrackencountryclub.com
Meade CC, *Meade*..9 [P] 620-873-7400
  meadecountyecodevo.com/golf.htm
Meadow Lake GC, *Colby*..............................9 [P] 785-460-6443
Meadowbrook G&CC, *Prairie Village* .... 18 [V] 913-642-3161
  meadowbrookcc.org
Medicine Lodge GC, *Medicine Lodge* ....9 [S] 620-886-9852
Metcalf Ridge GC, *Louisburg* .... 18 [V] 913-837-5476
  metcalfridge.com
Milburn G&CC, *Overland Park* .... 18 [V] 913-432-1224
  milburn.org
Miltonvale GC, *Miltonvale*...........................9 [P] 785-427-2285
Minneapolis GC, *Minneapolis* ....9 [M] 785-392-3546
Mission Hills CC, *Mission Hills* .... 18 [V] 913-722-1085
  missionhillscc.com
Ness County CC, *Ness City*.......................... 9 [V] 785-798-2609
Newton Public GC, *Newton*.........................9 [P] 316-283-4168
  golfnewton.com
Nicklaus GC At LionsGate, *Overland Park*.... 18 [V] 913-402-1000
  nicklausgolflg.com
North Topeka Golf Ctr, *Topeka* ....9 [P] 785-357-0026
Oak Country GC, *de Soto* ....18 [P] 913-583-3503
  oakcountrygolfcourse.com
Oakley CC, *Oakley*....................................... 9 [V] 620-672-3081
  discoveroakley.com
Osage City CC, *Osage City*...........................9 [P] 785-528-3329
Osage Hills GC, *Saint Paul* .... 9 [V] 316-449-2713
Osawatomie GC, *Osawatomie*...................18 [M] 913-755-4769
  osawatomieks.org
Osborne CC, *Osborne* ....9 [P] 785-346-5933
Oswego GC, *Oswego* ....9 [S] 620-795-4767
Ottawa CC, *Ottawa* .... 9 [V] 785-242-6527
Painted Hills GC, *Kansas City*......................18 [P] 913-334-1111
  paintedhillsgolfcourse.com
Paola CC, *Paola* .... 9 [V] 913-294-2910
  paolacountryclub.com
Park Hills CC, *Pratt* .... 18 [V] 620-672-7541
Parsons GC, *Parsons*....................................9 [P] 620-421-5290
  parsonsgolfclub1.com
Peabody GC, *Peabody*..................................9 [P] 785-349-2307
Phillipsburg GC, *Phillipsburg*.......................9 [P] 785-543-5545
Pine Bay GC, *Wichita* ....9 [P] 316-524-7300
Pine Edge GC, *Newton* ....9 [P] 620-367-2664
  pineedgegolf.com
Pineview CC, *Atchison* .... 9 [V] 913-367-2832
Plains GC, *Plains* ....9 [M] 620-563-7611
Point Rock GC, *Elkhart*.................................9 [M] 620-697-9801
Prairie Dog Rec Assoc, *Norton* .... 9 [V] 785-877-3643
Prairie Dunes CC, *Hutchinson* .... 18 [V] 620-662-7301
  prairiedunes.com
Prairie Highlands GC, *Olathe*......................18 [P] 913-856-7235
  prairiehighlands.com
Prairie Ridge GC, *Erie* ....9 [P] 620-244-3454

[S] = SEMI-PRIVATE   [V] = PRIVATE   [U] = UNIVERSITY   [N] = UNIVERSITY-PRIVATE

KANSAS
Golf Yellow Pages, 18th Edition

Prairie Trail GC, *Hill City*..................9 [M] 785-421-2437
Prairie Trails G&CC, *El Dorado*..............18 [P] 316-321-4114
  prairietrails.com
Quail Ridge GC, *Winfield*....................18 [M] 620-221-5645
  golfquailridgeonline.com
Quinter GC, *Quinter*..........................9 [V] 785-754-2108
Reflection Ridge GC, *Wichita*................18 [V] 316-721-4653
River Bend GC, *Salina*........................9 [P] 785-452-9333
Riverside Rec Assoc, *St Francis*..............9 [S] 785-332-3401
Rock Creek CC, *Burlington*....................9 [V] 620-364-2145
Rolling Acres GC, *McPherson*..................9 [P] 620-241-0630
  rollingacres-mcpherson.com
Rolling Hills CC, *Wichita*...................18 [V] 316-722-1181
  rollinghillswichita.com
Rolling Meadows GC, *Milford*.................18 [M] 785-238-4303
  jcrollingmeadows.com
Russell GC, *Russell*..........................9 [M] 785-483-2852
  russellcity.org
Sabetha GC, *Sabetha*..........................9 [V] 785-284-2023
  sabethagolfclub.com
Safari Public GC, *Chanute*....................9 [P] 620-431-5200
Salina CC, *Salina*...........................18 [V] 785-827-6131
  salinacountryclub.com
Salina Muni GC, *Salina*......................18 [M] 785-826-7450
Sand Creek Station GC, *Newton*...............18 [M] 316-284-6161
  sandcreekgolfclub.com
Scott City CC, *Scott City*....................9 [P] 620-872-7109
Sedan CC, *Sedan*..............................9 [P] 316-725-5555
Seidel GC, *Pratt*.............................9 [P] 620-672-7468
Shadow Glen GC, *Olathe*......................18 [V] 913-764-4536
  shadowglen.org
Shady Bend GC, *Osborne*.......................9 [M] 785-346-2024
Sharon Springs GC, *Sharon Springs*............9 [V] 785-852-4220
Shawnee CC, *Topeka*..........................18 [V] 785-233-5544
  shawneecountryclub.org
Shawnee G&CC, *Shawnee*.......................27 [S] 913-422-8357
  shawneegolfcc.com
Sierra Hills GC, *Wichita*....................18 [P] 316-733-9333
  sierrahillsgolfclub.com
Smileys G Complex, *Lenexa*...................18 [P] 913-782-1323
  smileysgolf.com
Smith Ctr Muni GC, *Smith Center*..............9 [M] 785-282-6806
Smoky Hill CC, *Hays*.........................18 [V] 785-625-8297
  smokyhillcc.com
Southwind CC, *Garden City*...................18 [V] 620-275-2117
  southwindcc.com
Spring Creek GC, *Seneca*.....................18 [M] 785-336-3568
  springcreek-seneca.com
Springhill Golf & Recr Assoc, *Arkansas City*..9 [M] 620-441-4330
  springhillgolf.net
St Andrews GC, *Overland Park*................18 [M] 913-897-3804
  standrewsopgolf.com
St Marys Public GC, *St Marys*.................9 [P] 785-437-6454
Stafford County CC, *St John*..................9 [P] 620-549-6597
Stagg Hill GC, *Manhattan*....................18 [P] 785-539-1041
  stagghillgolfclub.com
Stanton County Prairie Pines, *Johnson*........9 [M] 620-492-6818
Sterling CC, *Sterling*........................9 [P] 620-278-9956
  sterlingcountryclub.com
Sugar Hills GC, *Goodland*....................18 [P] 785-899-2785
  sugarhillsgolf.com

Sugar Valley Lakes GC, *Mound City*............9 [V] 913-795-2120
  sugarvalleyhiddenvalleylakes.com
Sunflower Hills GC, *Bonner Springs*..........18 [M] 913-573-8570
  wycokck.org
Sunny Meadows GC, *Moran*......................9 [P] 620-237-4653
Suppesville GC, *Milton*.......................9 [P] 620-478-2772
  suppesville.com
Sycamore Ridge GC, *Spring Hill*..............18 [P] 913-592-5292
  sycamoreridgegolf.com
Sycamore Valley GC, *Independence*............18 [P] 620-331-2828
Sykes/Lady Overland Park GC, *Overland Park*..27 [P] 913-897-3809
  opkansas.org
Tallgrass CC, *Wichita*.......................18 [V] 316-684-5663
  tallgrasscc.com
Tamarisk GC, *Syracuse*........................9 [M] 620-384-7832
Terradyne Resort Hotel GC, *Andover*..........18 [R] 316-733-5851
  terradynecountryclub.com
Tex Consolver GC, *Wichita*...................18 [M] 316-337-9494
  golfwichita.com
The Club At StoneRidge, *Great Bend*..........18 [P] 620-792-4306
  theclubatstoneridge.com
The Derby G&CC, *Derby*.......................18 [P] 316-788-3070
  derbygolfcc.com
The GC of Kansas, *Lenexa*....................18 [P] 913-888-4894
  gcofkansas.com
The Highlands Golf & Supper Club, *Hutchinson*..18 [V] 620-663-5301
The Kansas City CC, *Mission Hills*...........18 [V] 913-236-2122
  kccc.com
The Links at Pretty Prairie, *Pretty Prairie*..9 [P] 620-459-4653
  prettyprairiegolf.com
The Oaks GC, *Leavenworth*.....................9 [S] 913-651-5845
  oaks-golf.com
Tomahawk Hills GC, *Shawnee*..................18 [M] 913-631-8000
  jcprd.com
Topeka CC, *Topeka*...........................18 [V] 785-354-8563
  topekacountryclub.com
Trails West GC, *Fort Leavenworth*............18 [A] 913-651-7176
  fortleavenworthmwr.com/golf.htm
Turkey Creek GC, *McPherson*..................18 [P] 620-241-8530
  turkeycreekgolfcourse.com
Twin Lakes GC, *McConnell AFB*................18 [A] 316-759-4038
Village Greens GC, *Meriden*..................18 [P] 785-876-2255
  villagegreenskansas.com
Wamego CC, *Wamego*...........................18 [S] 785-456-2649
  wamegogolf.com
Waterville Community Golf Assoc, *Blue Rapids*..9 [P] 785-363-2479
Wedgewood GC, *Halstead*.......................9 [M] 316-835-2991
Wellington GC, *Wellington*...................18 [M] 620-326-7904
  wellingtongolfclub.com
Wichita CC, *Wichita*.........................18 [V] 316-634-0412
  wichitacountryclub.org
Wildcat Creek Golf & Fitness, *Manhattan*......9 [P] 785-539-7529
  wildcatgolfandfitness.com
Willow Tree GC, *Liberal*.....................18 [M] 620-626-0175
Willowbend GC, *Wichita*......................18 [V] 316-636-4653
  willowbendgolfclub.com
Winfield CC, *Winfield*.......................18 [V] 620-221-1570
  winfieldcountryclub.com
Wolf Creek Golf Links, *Olathe*...............18 [V] 913-592-4020
  wolfcreekks.com
Yucca Ridge GC, *Liberal*......................9 [P] 620-624-4653
  yuccaridge.com

[A] = MILITARY   [M] = MUNICIPAL   [P] = PUBLIC   [R] = RESORT

Golf Yellow Pages, 18th Edition

KENTUCKY

KENTUCKY

A J Jolly GC, *Alexandria*..................................18 [M] 859-635-2106
  ajjollygolf.com
Andover G&CC, *Lexington* .... 18 [V] 859-263-4335
  golfandover.com
Arlington Assoc, *Richmond*........................ 18 [N] 859-622-4976
  arlington.eku.edu/golf
Arrowhead GC, *Cadiz* ....18 [P] 270-522-8001
  arrowheadgolf.com
Audubon CC, *Louisville*............................. 18 [V] 502-637-5625
  auduboncc.org
Avon GC, *Lexington* ....9 [M] 859-299-8356
  lexingtonky.gov/golf
Ballard County CC, *La Center* .... 18 [V] 270-665-5557
Bardstown CC, *Bardstown*..........................36 [P] 502-348-6600
  bardstowncountryclub.com
Bardstown CC At Woodlawn Springs, *Bardstown* 18 [P] 502-348-2200
  bardstowncountryclub.com
Barren River St Park GC, *Lucas* ....18 [M] 270-646-4653
  parks.ky.gov/golftrail
Battlefield G&CC, *Richmond* ....18 [P] 859-624-8005
  battlefieldgolfclub.net
Beattyville CC, *Beattyville*...........................9 [S] 606-464-8320
Beechfork GC, *Clay City*..............................9 [P] 606-663-9479
Bellarmine Univ GC, *Louisville* .... 9 [U] 502-452-8378
  bellarmine.edu
Bellefonte CC, *Ashland* .... 18 [V] 606-329-1966
  bellefontecc.com
Ben Hawes St Park GC, *Owensboro* ....27 [M] 270-687-7137
  parks.ky.gov/golftrail
Benton G&CC, *Benton* ....18 [P] 270-527-9673
Berea CC, *Berea* ....9 [S] 859-986-7141
Big Hickory GC, *Manchester* ....9 [S] 606-598-8053
Big Spring CC, *Louisville*........................... 18 [V] 502-459-2622
  bigspringcc.com
Birmingham Pointe GC, *Benton* ....18 [P] 270-354-5050
  birminghampointe.com
Blackfish G&HuntC, *Winchester*...................9 [P] 859-744-0900
  mahanmanor.com
Bluegrass Army Depot GC, *Richmond* .... 9 [A] 859-779-6405
Bobby Nichols GC, *Louisville* ....9 [M] 502-937-9051
  louisvilleky.gov/metroparks/golf
Boone Links GC, *Florence* ....27 [M] 859-371-7550
  boonecountygolf.com
Boots Randolph GC at Lake Barkley St Park, *Cadiz* 18 [R] 270-924-9076
  parks.ky.gov/golftrail
Bowling Green CC, *Bowling Green*................. 18 [V] 270-842-4581
  bgcc1913.com
Breckenridge G&CC, *Morganfield*........................18 [S] 270-389-3186
Breckinridge County Comm Ctr, *Hardinsburg* ....9 [P] 270-756-2841
Bright Leaf GC, *Harrodsburg* ....36 [P] 859-734-5481
  brightleafgolfresort.com
Calvert City G&CC, *Calvert City* .... 18 [S] 270-395-5831
  calvertcitycountryclub.com
Campbellsville CC, *Campbellsville* .... 18 [V] 270-465-3620
  campbellsvillecc.com
Canewood GC, *Georgetown*........................18 [P] 502-868-0245
  canewoodgolf.com
Cardinal Club, *Simpsonville*....................... 18 [V] 502-722-2225
  cardinalclub.cc
Cardinal Hills GC, *Bedford* ....18 [P] 502-255-7770
Carnico GC, *Carlisle* ....9 [P] 859-289-5400

Carrington Greens GC, *Salt Lick*................18 [P] 606-768-2100
Carter Caves St Park GC, *Olive Hill*................9 [M] 606-286-4411
  cartercaves.com
Cassell Creek GC, *Winchester*...................18 [P] 859-744-9959
Cave Land Par 3, *Cave City* ....9 [P] 270-773-2377
Cave Valley GC at Park Mammoth Resort, *Park City* 18 [R] 270-749-4101
  parkmammothresort.us
Caveland CC, *Horse Cave* ....9 [P] 270-786-1950
  cavelandcountryclub.com
CC of Paducah, *Paducah* .... 18 [V] 270-554-5330
  ccofpaducah.com
Cedar Fil GC, *Bardstown*............................18 [P] 502-348-8981
Cedar Rapids CC, *Mt Vernon*.......................9 [P] 606-256-4112
Central City CC, *Central City*.................... 18 [V] 270-754-4312
Champion Trace GC, *Nicholasville* .... 18 [V] 859-223-7275
  championtrace.com
Charlie Vettiner GC, *Jeffersontown*..............18 [M] 502-267-9958
  charlievettiner.com
Cherokee GC, *Louisville* ....9 [M] 502-458-9450
  louisvilleky.gov/metroparks/golf
Cherry Blossom G&CC, *Georgetown* ....18 [P] 502-570-9849
  cherryblossomgolf.com
Cherry Grove GC, *Trenton* ....18 [P] 270-466-3610
Clear Creek GC, *Shelbyville*........................9 [S] 502-633-0375
Coal Ridge GC, *Georgetown*.......................18 [P] 502-863-0754
Connemara GC, *Nicholasville* ....18 [P] 859-885-4331
  connemaralinks.com
Crescent Hill GC, *Louisville* ....9 [M] 502-896-9193
  louisvilleky.gov/metroparks/golf
Crooked Creek GC, *London* .... 18 [V] 606-877-1993
  crookedcreekgcky.com
CrossWinds GC, *Bowling Green*................18 [M] 270-393-3559
  bgky.org/golf
Cynthiana CC, *Cynthiana*........................... 9 [V] 859-234-5364
  cynthianacc.com
Dale Hollow Lake GC, *Burkesville* ....18 [R] 270-433-7888
  parks.ky.gov/golftrail
Danville CC, *Danville*................................. 18 [V] 859-236-2838
  danvillecountryclub.net
Deer Lakes GC, *Salem* ....18 [P] 270-988-4653
  deerlakesgolfcourse.com
Devou Park GC, *Covington*........................18 [M] 859-431-8030
  devouparkgolf.com
Diamond Caverns GC, *Park City* ....18 [R] 270-749-9466
Diamond Links GC, *Catlettsburg*................18 [P] 606-928-5335
Different Strokes English Springs GC, *Louisville*.....9 [P] 502-245-0229
  dsgolfcenters.com
Different Strokes New Cut, *Fairdale* ....9 [P] 502-363-2004
  dsgolfcenters.com
Dix River CC, *Stanford*.............................. 18 [V] 606-365-2620
Doe Valley CC, *Brandenburg*......................18 [S] 270-422-3397
  doevalleyky.com
Dogwood Hills, *Cunningham* ....9 [P] 270-642-2244
Drake Creek GC, *Ledbetter*........................18 [P] 270-898-4653
  drakecreek.com
Duckers Lake GC, *Frankfort* ....18 [P] 502-695-4653
  duckerslakegolfresort.com
Dunmor Lakeside GC, *Dunmor*..................18 [P] 270-657-8260
  dunmorlakesidegolf.com
Eagle Creek CC, *Dry Ridge* .... 18 [V] 859-428-1772
  eaglecreekky.com
Eagle Creek GC, *La Grange* ....18 [M] 502-222-7927
  eaglecreekgolfky.com

[S] = SEMI-PRIVATE   [V] = PRIVATE   [U] = UNIVERSITY   [N] = UNIVERSITY-PRIVATE

KENTUCKY Golf Yellow Pages, 18th Edition

Eagle Ridge GC At Yatesville Lake St Park, *Louisa*18 [M] 606-673-4300
parks.ky.gov/golftrail
Eagle Trace GC, *Morehead* ....18 [P] 606-783-9073
moreheadstate.edu/eagletrace
Eagles Nest CC, *Somerset* .... 18 [V] 606-679-7754
eaglesnestcc.com
Elizabethtown CC, *Elizabethtown* .... 18 [V] 270-737-7707
etowncc.com
Elizabethtown Muni Par 3, *Elizabethtown* ....9 [M] 270-765-4030
Elk Fork CC, *Elkton* .... 9 [V] 270-265-5340
elkforkcc.com
Elkwood GC, *Sturgis* ....9 [M] 270-333-2299
Estill County GC, *Ravenna* .... 9 [S] 606-723-5166
Fairway GC, *Wheatley* ....18 [P] 502-463-2338
fairwaygolfcourse.com
Flagg Springs GC, *California* ....18 [P] 859-635-2170
flaggsprings.com
Fleming County Golf Assoc, *Flemingsburg* ....9 [P] 606-849-8161
Fort Mitchell CC, *Fort Mitchell* .... 9 [V] 859-331-4580
fortmitchellcc.com
Fox Hollow GC, *Glasgow* ....18 [P] 270-678-7277
foxhollowgolf.com
Frankfort CC, *Frankfort* .... 18 [V] 502-695-1403
frankfortcountryclub.com
Franklin CC, *Franklin* .... 18 [V] 270-586-6580
Gay Brewer Jr GC at Picadome, *Lexington* .... 18 [S] 859-288-2990
lexingtonky.gov/golf
GC of The Bluegrass, *Nicholasville* ....18 [P] 859-223-4516
General Burnside Island GC, *Burnside* ....18 [M] 606-561-4192
parks.ky.gov/golftrail
General Butler St Park GC, *Carrollton* ....9 [M] 502-732-4384
parks.ky.gov/golftrail
Gibson Bay GC, *Richmond* ....27 [M] 859-623-0225
gibsonbay.com
Glasgow CC, *Glasgow* .... 18 [V] 270-651-8955
glasgowcountryclub.com
Glenmary Golf CC, *Louisville* ....18 [P] 502-239-3500
glenmarycountryclub.com
GlenOaks GC, *Prospect* .... 18 [V] 502-339-0215
glenoakscountryclub.com
Green County CC, *Greensburg* ....9 [S] 270-932-7031
greencountygolf.com
Green Meadow CC, *Pikeville* .... 9 [V] 606-432-0712
Greenbrier G&CC, *Lexington* .... 18 [V] 859-299-2811
greenbriergcc.com
Greenville CC, *Greenville* .... 9 [V] 270-338-3233
greenvillekycc.com
Griffin Gate Golf Resort, *Lexington* ....18 [R] 859-288-6193
griffingategolf.com
Harlan CC, *Harlan* .... 9 [V] 606-573-2510
Harmony Landing CC, *Goshen* .... 18 [V] 502-228-8316
harmonylandingcc.com
Hazard CC, *Hazard* .... 9 [V] 606-436-5320
Henderson CC, *Henderson* .... 18 [V] 270-827-3444
hendersoncountryclub.org
Henderson Muni GC, *Henderson* ....9 [M] 270-831-1263
Henry County CC, *New Castle* ....18 [P] 502-845-2375
hcccky.com
Heritage Hill GC, *Shepherdsville* ....18 [P] 502-531-0660
hhgolfclub.com
Hickman CC, *Hickman* ....9 [P] 270-236-9128
Hickory Hills CC, *Liberty* ....9 [P] 606-787-7368

Hickory Sticks GC, *California* .... 18 [P] 859-635-4653
hickorysticks.com
Hidden Cove GC at Grayson Lake St Park, *Olive Hill*18 [M] 606-474-2553
parks.ky.gov/golftrail
Hidden Hills G&CC, *Tompkinsville* .... 18 [S] 270-487-8172
geocities.com/hiddenhillsgolf
Hidden Valley GC, *Morgantown* ....18 [P] 270-526-4643
Highland CC, *Fort Thomas* .... 18 [V] 859-441-0221
hcc-ky.com
Highpoint GC, *Nicholasville* ....18 [P] 859-887-4614
highpointgolfclubky.com
Hillcrest CC, *Brandenburg* .... 9 [S] 270-422-4455
Hillcrest Muni GC, *Owensboro* .... 9 [M] 270-687-8717
owensboroparks.org
Hopkinsville G&CC, *Hopkinsville* .... 18 [V] 270-886-2498
hgcc.cc
Houston Oaks GC, *Paris* ....18 [P] 859-987-5600
Hunting Creek CC, *Prospect* .... 18 [V] 502-228-8129
huntingcreekcc.com
Hurstbourne CC, *Louisville* .... 27 [V] 502-425-0097
hurstbournecc.com
Idle Hour CC, *Lexington* .... 18 [V] 859-266-7901
idlehour.cc
Indian Hills CC, *Bowling Green* .... 18 [V] 270-843-8256
indianhills-bgky.com
Indian Springs G&CC, *Barbourville* .... 9 [S] 606-546-5607
Indian Springs GC, *Louisville* .... 18 [S] 502-426-7111
isgolfclub.com
Iroquois Park GC, *Louisville* ....18 [M] 502-363-9520
louisvilleky.gov/metroparks/golf
John J Audubon St Park GC, *Henderson* ....9 [M] 270-826-5546
parks.ky.gov
Juniper Hill GC, *Frankfort* ....18 [M] 502-875-8559
frankfort.ky.gov
Kearney Hill Links, *Lexington* ....18 [M] 859-253-1981
lexingtonky.gov/golf/golf
Keene Run GC, *Nicholasville* .... 18 [V] 859-224-4653
keenerun.com
Kenlake Par 3 State Resort Park GC, *Hardin* .... 9 [R] 270-474-2213
parks.ky.gov/golftrail
Kenny Perrys Country Creek GC, *Franklin* ....18 [P] 270-586-9373
kpcountrycreek.com
Kenton County GC, *Independence* ....54 [M] 859-371-3200
kentoncounty.org
Kenton Station GC, *Maysville* ....9 [S] 606-759-7154
Kentucky Dam Village State Resort Pk, *Gilbertsville*18 [R]270-362-4276
parks.ky.gov/golftrail
Kentucky Hills GC, *Summer Shade* ....9 [P] 270-428-4444
Kincaid Lake St Park GC, *Falmouth* ....9 [M] 859-654-8555
parks.ky.gov
Knob View GC, *Lebanon Junction* ....9 [P] 502-833-2253
Lake Forest CC, *Louisville* .... 18 [V] 502-245-6184
lakeforestgolf.com
Lakeshore CC, *Madisonville* ....18 [P] 270-821-2069
Lakeside GC, *Lexington* ....18 [M] 859-263-5315
lexingtonky.gov/golf
Lakeview Springs GC, *Frankfort* ....9 [M] 502-695-5870
Lakewood CC, *Russell Springs* .... 18 [S] 270-343-3921
Larue County CC, *Hodgenville* .... 18 [S] 270-358-9727
Lassing Pointe GC, *Union* ....18 [M] 859-384-2266
boonecountygolf.com
Laurel Oaks GC, *Maysville* ....18 [P] 606-759-5011

84 [A] = MILITARY [M] = MUNICIPAL [P] = PUBLIC [R] = RESORT

KENTUCKY

Lebanon CC, *Lebanon* .... 9 [V] 270-692-3541
   lebanoncountryclub.net
Legacy GC, *Leitchfield* .... 18 [P] 270-242-3348
Lexington CC, *Lexington* .... 18 [V] 859-299-4388
   lexingtoncc.com
Lincoln Homestead St Park GC, *Springfield* .... 18 [M] 859-336-7461
   parks.ky.gov/golftrail
Lincoln Trail CC, *Vine Grove* .... 18 [S] 270-877-2181
   lincolntrailcc.com
Lindsey GC, *Fort Knox* .... 18 [A] 502-624-4218
   knox.army.mil
Links At Lily Creek Resort, *Jamestown* .... 18 [R] 270-343-4653
   linksatlilycreek.com
Links At Novadell GC, *Hopkinsville* .... 18 [P] 270-886-1101
   novadell.com
London CC, *London* .... 18 [V] 606-864-2282
   londoncountryclub.com
Lone Oak CC, *Nicholasville* .... 18 [V] 859-887-2212
   loneoakcountryclub.com
Long Run GC, *Louisville* .... 18 [M] 502-245-9015
   louisvilleky.gov/metroparks/golf
Longview GC, *Georgetown* .... 18 [S] 502-863-2165
   duckerslakegolfresort.com
Louisville CC, *Louisville* .... 18 [V] 502-895-8477
   loucc.net
Madison CC, *Richmond* .... 9 [V] 859-623-6468
Madisonville City Park GC, *Madisonville* .... 9 [M] 270-824-2156
Madisonville G&CC, *Madisonville* .... 18 [V] 270-821-3700
   mgccgolf.com
Maplehurst GC, *Shepherdsville* .... 18 [P] 502-957-3370
Marion CC, *Marion* .... 9 [P] 270-965-1604
Mayfield Graves CC, *Mayfield* .... 18 [V] 270-247-1862
   mayfieldgravescountryclub.com
Maysville CC, *Maysville* .... 18 [V] 606-564-6351
   maysvillecountryclub.com
Meadowbrook GC, *Lexington* .... 18 [M] 859-272-3115
   lexingtonky.gov/golf
Meadowood GC, *Burlington* .... 9 [P] 859-586-0422
   meadowoodgolf.com
Meadows GC, *Clay City* .... 9 [P] 606-663-4000
Members of Farnsley Golf, *Louisville* .... 9 [M] 502-640-1260
Middlesboro CC, *Middlesboro* .... 9 [V] 606-248-3831
   middlesborocc.com
Midland Trail GC, *Louisville* .... 18 [V] 502-245-0223
   midlandtrailgc.com
Midtown GC, *Paducah* .... 9 [M] 270-444-9124
Miller Memorial GC, *Murray* .... 18 [U] 270-809-2238
   murraystate.edu/millergolf
Mineral Mound GC, *Eddyville* .... 18 [M] 270-388-3673
   parks.ky.gov/golftrail
Monticello CC, *Monticello* .... 9 [V] 606-348-7321
Mountain Public Links, *Meta* .... 18 [P] 606-437-0339
   mountainpublinks.com
Mountain View GC, *Albany* .... 18 [P] 606-387-0910
Mt Sterling G&CC, *Mt Sterling* .... 18 [V] 859-498-3142
   mountsterlingcc.com
Murray CC, *Murray* .... 18 [V] 270-753-9430
   murraycountryclub.com
My Old Kentucky Home St Park GC, *Bardstown* .. 18 [M] 502-349-6542
   parks.ky.gov/golftrail
Nevel Meade GC, *Prospect* .... 18 [P] 502-228-9522
   nevelmeade.com
Oak Hill Rec Assoc, *Clinton* .... 9 [P] 270-653-6001

Oaks CC, *Murray* .... 18 [V] 270-753-6454
   theoaks.cc
Old Bridge GC, *Danville* .... 18 [P] 859-236-6051
   oldbridgeinc.com
Old Silo GC, *Mt Sterling* .... 18 [P] 859-498-4697
   oldsilo.com
Oldham County CC, *La Grange* .... 18 [S] 502-222-9133
   oldhamcountycc.com
Owensboro CC, *Owensboro* .... 18 [V] 270-683-3387
   owensborocountryclub.com
Owl Creek CC, *Anchorage* .... 9 [V] 502-245-4156
   owlcreekcc.com
Oxmoor CC, *Louisville* .... 18 [V] 502-491-7061
   oxmoorcc.com
Paintsville CC, *Paintsville* .... 18 [S] 606-789-4234
Panther Creek GC, *Utica* .... 18 [P] 270-785-4565
   panthercreekgolfclub.com
Paul Hunt Thompson GC, *Allen* .... 9 [P] 606-874-2837
Paul R Walker GC, *Bowling Green* .... 9 [M] 270-393-3821
   bgky.org
Paxton Park GC, *Paducah* .... 18 [M] 502-444-9514
   paxtonpark.com
Pendleton CC, *Butler* .... 18 [V] 859-472-2150
   pendletonky.com
Peninsula Golf Resort, *Lancaster* .... 18 [R] 859-548-5055
   peninsulagolf.com
Pennsylvania Run GC, *Louisville* .... 18 [P] 502-957-5940
Pennyrile Forest St Resort Park GC,
   Dawson Springs .... 18 [P] 270-797-7888
   parks.ky.gov/golftrail
Perry Park Golf Resort, *Perry Park* .... 27 [R] 502-484-5776
   perryparkgolfresort.com
Persimmon Ridge GC, *Louisville* .... 18 [V] 502-241-0819
   persimmonridge.com
Pine Valley Golf Resort, *Elizabethtown* .... 18 [P] 502-737-8300
   pinevalleygolfandresort.com
Planters Row Golf Links, *Nicholasville* .... 18 [P] 859-885-1254
   plantersrowgolflinks.com
Players Club of Henderson, *Henderson* .... 18 [P] 270-827-9999
   playersclubofhenderson.com
Pleasant Valley CC, *West Liberty* .... 9 [P] 606-743-3329
Polo Fields G&CC, *Louisville* .... 18 [V] 502-244-6688
   polofieldscc.com
Princeton G&CC, *Princeton* .... 18 [P] 270-365-6110
Quail Chase GC, *Louisville* .... 27 [P] 502-239-2110
   quailchase.com
Raven Rock GC, *Jenkins* .... 18 [P] 606-832-2955
River Bend GC, *Argillite* .... 18 [P] 606-473-6773
River Road CC, *Louisville* .... 9 [P] 502-893-2536
Rolling Hills CC, *Paducah* .... 18 [V] 270-554-3025
   rhccgolf.com
Rolling Hills GC, *Russellville* .... 18 [P] 270-726-8700
Rolling Meadows GC, *Catlettsburg* .... 9 [P] 606-739-4140
Rosewood G&CC, *Lebanon* .... 18 [P] 270-692-0506
   rosewoodgolfcourse.com
Rough Creek GC, *Livermore* .... 9 [P] 270-278-4653
Rough River Dam State Resort Park GC,
   Falls of Rough .... 9 [R] 270-257-2311
   parks.ky.gov/golftrail
Royal Cypress GC, *Sacramento* .... 18 [P] 270-736-5515
Royal Oaks GC, *Hartford* .... 9 [V] 270-256-2588
Russellville CC, *Russellville* .... 9 [V] 270-726-7460
Ryland Lakes CC, *Covington* .... 9 [V] 859-356-9444

[S] = SEMI-PRIVATE   [V] = PRIVATE   [U] = UNIVERSITY   [N] = UNIVERSITY-PRIVATE

KENTUCKY

Golf Yellow Pages, 18th Edition

Name	Holes	Type	Phone
Sag Hollow GC, *Booneville*	9	[P]	606-593-4653
saghollow.com			
Sandy Creek GC, *Ashland*	18	[P]	606-928-6321
sandycreekgc.com			
Scottsville CC, *Scottsville*	9	[S]	270-237-3662
Seneca GC, *Louisville*	18	[M]	502-458-9298
louisvilleky.gov/metroparks/golf			
Seventy-Six Falls CC, *Albany*	9	[P]	606-387-5908
Shady Brook GC, *Paris*	9	[P]	859-987-1544
Shady Hollow GC, *Cub Run*	18	[P]	270-286-6165
shadyhollowgolf.net			
Shawnee GC, *Louisville*	18	[M]	502-776-9389
shawneegolfcourse.com			
Shelbyville CC, *Shelbyville*	18	[V]	502-633-0542
shelbyvillecc.com			
Sheltowee Trail CC & GC, *Morehead*	9	[P]	606-784-2582
Silos CC, *Kevil*	18	[S]	270-488-2182
siloscc.com			
Sleepy Hollow GC, *Cumberland*	9	[P]	606-589-2502
Sleepy Hollow GC, *Prospect*	9	[P]	502-241-4475
Somerset CC, *Somerset*	18	[V]	606-678-4623
South Highland CC, *Mayfield*	18	[P]	270-247-2918
southhighlandcc.com			
South Park CC, *Fairdale*	18	[V]	502-969-5757
southparkcountryclub.com			
Southwind GC, *Winchester*	18	[S]	859-744-0375
Spring Valley GC, *Lexington*	18	[V]	859-254-9646
Standard CC, *Louisville*	18	[V]	502-425-2857
standardcc.net			
Stearns GC, *Stearns*	9	[S]	606-376-2666
StoneCrest GC, *Prestonsburg*	18	[P]	606-886-1006
Stoner Creek CC, *Paris*	9	[V]	859-987-0025
stonercreekcountryclub.com			
Sugar Bay GC, *Warsaw*	18	[S]	859-567-2601
Sugar Camp GC, *Jackson*	9	[P]	606-693-4727
sugarcampgolfclub.com			
Sullivans Par Three, *Murray*	18	[P]	270-753-1152
sullivansgolf.com			
Summit Hills CC, *Crestview Hills*	18	[V]	859-344-7949
summithillscc.com			
Sun Valley CC, *Valley Station*	18	[M]	502-937-9228
louisvilleky.gov/metroparks/golf			
Sundowner GC, *Ashland*	9	[P]	606-329-9093
Sweet Hollow GC, *Corbin*	9	[S]	606-523-1241
sweethollowresort.com			
Sweetbrier GC, *Danville*	9	[V]	859-936-1404
bad link			
Tanglewood GC, *Taylorsville*	18	[S]	502-477-2468
golftanglewood.com			
Tates Creek GC, *Lexington*	18	[M]	859-272-3428
lexingtonky.gov/golf			
The Brook GC, *Versailles*	18	[V]	859-873-8404
mcqueenfamilygolf.com			
The Bull At Boones Trace, *Richmond*	18	[P]	859-623-4653
thebullgolf.com			
The Club At Olde Stone, *Alvaton*	18	[V]	270-393-4654
olde-stone.com			
The Crossings, *Brooks*	18	[P]	502-957-6523
playthecrossings.com			
The Falls Resort &GC, *Falls of Rough*	18	[R]	270-879-3462
thefallsresortandgolfclub.com			
The GC At Riverview, *Bowling Green*	9	[M]	270-393-3877
bgky.org/golf			
The Golf Course, *Williamsburg*	9	[S]	606-549-4215
The Lakes GC, *South Shore*	9	[S]	606-932-4266
The Marvel GC, *Benton*	18	[P]	270-354-9050
marvelgolf.com			
The Oaks GC, *Flatwoods*	18	[P]	606-833-5565
The Pines At Lindsey Wilson College, *Columbia*	18	[P]	270-384-3613
lindsey.edu			
The Summit CC, *Owensboro*	18	[S]	270-281-4653
summitky.com			
The Trace at Bays Fork GC, *Alvaton*	18	[P]	270-796-6677
baysfork.com			
Traditions GC, *Hebron*	18	[V]	859-586-5079
traditionsgolfclub.com			
Tri County CC, *Corbin*	9	[V]	606-528-2166
Triple Crown CC, *Union*	18	[V]	859-384-5362
triplecrowngolfclub.com			
Twin Oaks Golf & Plantation Club, *Covington*	18	[P]	859-581-2410
golfattwinoaks.com			
Univ Club of Kentucky, *Lexington*	36	[V]	859-977-1235
uckygolf.com			
Valhalla GC, *Louisville*	18	[V]	502-245-4475
valhallagolfclub.com			
Waits Boro Hill GC, *Somerset*	18	[P]	606-679-3113
Wasioto Winds, *Pineville*	18	[R]	606-337-1066
kystateparks.com			
Weissinger Hills GC, *Shelbyville*	18	[M]	502-633-7332
weissingerhills.com			
Western Hills GC, *Hopkinsville*	18	[P]	270-885-6023
westernhillsgolf.com			
Wild Turkey Trace GC, *Lawrenceburg*	18	[P]	502-839-4029
wildturkeytrace.com			
Wildwood CC, *Louisville*	18	[V]	502-499-1001
wildwoodcc.com			
Winchester CC, *Winchester*	18	[V]	859-744-4884
winchester-cc.com			
Windridge CC, *Owensboro*	18	[V]	270-685-3639
Windward Heights CC, *Hawesville*	9	[V]	270-927-6603
Woodford Hills CC, *Versailles*	18	[V]	859-873-8122
woodfordhillscountryclub.com			
Woodhaven CC, *Louisville*	27	[V]	502-491-9100
woodhavencountryclub.org			
Woodson Bend Resort, *Bronston*	18	[R]	606-561-5316
woodsonbendresort.com			
World of Sports GC, *Florence*	18	[M]	859-371-8255
landrumgolf.com			

LOUISIANA

Name	Holes	Type	Phone
Abbeville CC, *Abbeville*	18	[P]	337-893-5203
Abita Springs G&CC, *Abita Springs*	18	[P]	985-893-2463
abitagolf.com			
Acadian Hills CC, *Lafayette*	18	[V]	337-232-4010
acadianhills.com			
Advance CC, *Hodge*	9	[V]	318-259-7247
Alexandria G&CC, *Woodworth*	18	[V]	318-442-2806
alexandriagolfandcountryclub.com			
Audubon Park GC, *New Orleans*	18	[S]	504-212-5290
auduboninstitute.org			
Aviation Oaks GC, *New Orleans*	18	[A]	504-678-3453
Baton Rouge CC, *Baton Rouge*	18	[V]	225-925-5466
batonrougecc.org			
Bay Hills Rec Park, *Bunkie*	9	[S]	318-346-6245
bayhillscc.com			

[A] = MILITARY   [M] = MUNICIPAL   [P] = PUBLIC   [R] = RESORT

Golf Yellow Pages, 18th Edition — LOUISIANA

Name	Holes	Type	Phone
Bayou Barriere GC, *Belle Chasse*	27	[P]	504-394-9500
bayoubarriere.com			
Bayou Bend CC, *Crowley*	18	[P]	337-783-3214
Bayou Bend Golf, *Bastrop*	9	[P]	318-283-2279
Bayou CC, *Thibodaux*	9	[P]	985-447-9987
Bayou De Siard CC, *Monroe*	18	[V]	318-322-2127
bayoudesiardcc.com			
Bayou Oaks CC, *Sulphur*	18	[P]	337-583-7129
Bayou Side GC, *Napoleonville*	9	[S]	985-369-7676
Beau Chene CC, *Mandeville*	36	[V]	985-845-3572
beauchenecc.com			
Beauregard CC, *Deridder*	18	[V]	337-463-4444
Beaver Creek GC, *Zachary*	18	[M]	225-658-6338
brec.org			
Belle Terre CC, *La Place*	18	[S]	985-652-5000
belleterregolf.com			
Black Bear GC, *Delhi*	18	[P]	318-878-2162
blackbear-golf.com			
Blue Wing GC, *Kentwood*	9	[S]	985-229-4122
Boeuf River CC, *Rayville*	9	[P]	318-728-7800
Bogalusa CC, *Bogalusa*	9	[V]	985-735-6546
Bringhurst GC, *Alexandria*	9	[P]	318-448-9021
Broken Pines CC, *Franklin*	9	[P]	337-828-2572
Cajun Pine GC, *Branch*	9	[S]	337-334-9904
Caldwell CC, *Grayson*	9	[V]	318-649-5035
Carter Plantation, *Springfield*	18	[P]	225-294-9855
carterplantation.com			
CC of Louisiana, *Baton Rouge*	18	[V]	225-755-4655
ccofla.com			
Champion Links, *Shreveport*	9	[P]	318-865-7888
Chateau G&CC, *Kenner*	18	[V]	504-467-1351
chateaugc.com			
Chennault Park GC, *Monroe*	18	[M]	318-329-2454
monroe-westmonroe.org			
City Park GC, *Baton Rouge*	9	[M]	225-387-9523
brec.org			
Colonial Acres GC, *Houma*	9	[P]	985-868-5051
Colonial CC, *Harahan*	18	[V]	504-737-0601
colonialcountryclubno.com			
Contraband Bayou GC At LAuberge Du Lac, *Lake Charles*	18	[R]	337-395-7220
ldlcasino.com			
Copper Mill GC, *Zachary*	18	[P]	225-658-0656
coppermillgolf.com			
Coushatta CC, *Coushatta*	9	[V]	318-932-5924
Covington CC, *Covington*	18	[S]	985-892-1900
covingtoncountryclub.com			
Crooked Hollow GC, *Greenwood*	18	[P]	318-938-5060
Cypress Bend Golf Resort & CCtr, *Many*	18	[R]	318-256-0346
cypressbend.com			
Cypress Lakes CC at Ormond, *Destrehan*	18	[P]	985-764-6868
cypresslakescc.com			
Delhi CC, *Delhi*	9	[P]	318-878-3619
Denham Springs CC, *Denham Springs*	9	[P]	225-665-6437
Dumas GC, *Baton Rouge*	18	[M]	225-775-9166
brec.org			
East Ridge GC, *Shreveport*	18	[V]	318-868-6571
eastridgecc.com			
Eastland CC, *Haughton*	9	[P]	318-949-0161
Ellendale CC, *Houma*	18	[V]	985-876-4394
ellendalecountryclub.net			
Emerald Hills Golf Resort, *Florien*	18	[R]	318-586-4661
emeraldhillsresort.com			
English Turn G&CC, *New Orleans*	18	[V]	504-391-8018
englishturn.com			
Eunice CC, *Eunice*	9	[P]	337-457-3273
False River G&CC, *Ventress*	9	[V]	225-638-6309
Farm DAllie GC, *Carencro*	18	[P]	337-886-2227
golfcarencro.com			
Fashion G&CC, *Hahnville*	9	[S]	985-783-6486
Fennwood Hills CC, *Zachary*	9	[P]	225-654-8586
Fox Run GC, *Barksdale AFB*	18	[A]	318-456-2263
barksdaleservices.com			
Franklinton CC, *Franklinton*	18	[P]	985-839-4195
Frasch Park GC, *Sulphur*	18	[M]	337-527-2515
sulphurparks.com			
Frenchmans Bend CC, *Monroe*	18	[P]	318-387-2363
frenchmansbend.com			
Gemstone Plantation CC, *Franklinton*	18	[P]	985-795-8900
Gray Plantation GC, *Lake Charles*	18	[S]	337-562-1663
graywoodllc.com			
Greystone G&CC, *Denham Springs*	18	[S]	225-667-6744
greystonecountryclub.com			
Grove GC, *Minden*	18	[P]	318-377-9800
grovegolfretreat.com			
Hammond Golf Ctr, *Hammond*	9	[P]	985-542-7908
hammondgolfcenter.com			
Haynesville CC, *Haynesville*	9	[M]	318-624-0022
Homer CC, *Homer*	9	[M]	318-927-9502
Howell Park GC, *Baton Rouge*	18	[M]	225-357-9292
brec.org			
Huntington Park GC, *Shreveport*	18	[M]	318-673-7765
myspar.org			
Indian Hills CC, *Opelousas*	18	[P]	337-948-9688
Jay & Lionel Hebert Muni GC, *Lafayette*	18	[M]	337-291-5557
Jennings GC, *Jennings*	18	[P]	337-824-1274
Jerry Tim Brooks GC, *Shreveport*	9	[P]	318-673-7782
myspar.org			
Joseph M Bartholomew, Sr GC, *New Orleans*	18	[M]	504-288-0928
Koasati Pines At Coushatta, *Kinder*	18	[R]	337-738-4777
koasatipines.com			
La Salle GC, *Jena*	9	[V]	318-992-4283
lasallegolf.com			
Lake Bruin G&CC, *St Joseph*	9	[V]	318-766-4303
Lake Charles CC, *Lake Charles*	18	[V]	337-477-0047
lakecharlescc.net			
Lake DArbonne CC, *Farmerville*	9	[V]	318-368-2474
Lake Providence CC, *Lake Providence*	9	[V]	318-559-2650
Lakewood GC, *New Orleans*	18	[P]	504-373-5926
lakewoodgolf.com			
LaTour GC, *Mathews*	18	[R]	985-532-7111
latourgolfclub.com			
Le Triomphe G&CC, *Broussard*	18	[V]	337-856-9005
letriomphe.com			
Leesville Muni GC, *Leesville*	9	[M]	337-239-2526
Les Vieux Chenes GC, *Youngsville*	18	[M]	337-837-1159
lesvieuxchenesgolfcourse.com			
Links on the Bayou, *Alexandria*	18	[P]	318-473-1331
linksonthebayou.com			
Louisiana State Univ GC, *Baton Rouge*	18	[U]	225-578-3394
golf.lsu.edu			
Louisiana Tech Univ GC, *Ruston*	9	[N]	318-247-8331
LSU at Alexandria GC, *Alexandria*	9	[U]	318-473-6507
Magnolia Creek GC, *Ethel*	9	[P]	225-658-2270
Mallard Cove GC, *Lake Charles*	18	[M]	337-491-1204
cityoflakecharles.com			

[S] = SEMI-PRIVATE   [V] = PRIVATE   [U] = UNIVERSITY   [N] = UNIVERSITY-PRIVATE

LOUISIANA

Course	Location	Holes	Type	Phone
Mansfield G&CC	Mansfield	9	[V]	318-872-2959
Meadow Lake G&CC	Bernice	9	[S]	318-285-7425
Meadow Lake GC	Keithville	18	[S]	318-925-9547
golfmeadowlake.com				
Metairie CC	Metairie	18	[V]	504-218-4615
metairiecc.info				
Money Hill GC & CC	Abita Springs	18	[V]	985-892-8250
moneyhill.com				
Monterey CC	Vivian	9	[V]	318-375-3043
Morehouse CC	Bastrop	18	[V]	318-281-0466
morehousecountryclub.com				
Natchitoches CC	Natchitoches	9	[P]	318-352-5538
natchitochescountryclub.com				
New Orleans CC	New Orleans	18	[V]	504-482-7594
Northwestern Hills GC	Natchitoches	18	[U]	318-357-6300
Northwood Hills CC	Shreveport	18	[S]	318-929-2380
Oak Harbor GC	Slidell	18	[P]	985-646-0110
oakharborgolf.com				
Oak Knoll CC	Hammond	18	[V]	985-542-5756
oakknollcountryclub.com				
Oak Lake GC	Clinton	9	[P]	225-683-3037
Oakbourne CC	Lafayette	18	[V]	337-235-2324
oakbournecc.com				
Oakland Plantation CC	Plain Dealing	9	[V]	318-326-5555
OakWing GC	Alexandria	18	[P]	318-561-0260
oakwinggolf.com				
Olde Oaks GC	Haughton	27	[P]	318-742-0333
oldeoaksgolf.com				
Palmetto CC	Benton	18	[V]	318-965-2400
palmettocountryclub.com				
Panola Woods CC	Ferriday	9	[V]	318-757-2301
Pelican Point GC	Gonzales	36	[P]	225-746-9900
golfthepoint.com				
Pine Hills CC	Minden	9	[P]	318-377-3024
Pine Ridge CC	Winnfield	9	[V]	318-628-7739
Pine Shadows GC	Lake Charles	18	[P]	337-433-8681
Pinewood CC	Slidell	18	[V]	985-643-6893
pinewoodcc.net				
Querbes Park GC	Shreveport	18	[M]	318-673-7773
myspar.org				
Rapides G&CC	Alexandria	18	[V]	318-442-8746
Riverlands G&CC	La Place	18	[V]	985-652-6316
Royal GC	Slidell	18	[P]	985-643-3000
Ruston G&CC	Ruston	9	[V]	318-255-1307
Sandy Hills GC	Dubach	9	[P]	318-777-8714
Santa Maria GC	Baton Rouge	18	[M]	225-752-9667
brec.org				
Shenandoah CC	Baton Rouge	18	[V]	225-753-3358
Shreveport CC	Shreveport	18	[V]	318-631-1200
shreveportcc.com				
Southern Oaks GC	Houma	9	[P]	985-851-6804
sogolfclub.com				
Southern Pines - Pine Hills GC	Calhoun	18	[V]	318-644-5370
sopinesgolf.com				
Southern Pines GC - Calvert Crossing	Calhoun	18	[V]	318-397-0064
sopinesgolf.com				
Southern Trace GC	Shreveport	18	[V]	318-798-8301
southern-trace.com				
Spanish Trail GC	Cade	18	[S]	337-364-2263
Spring Bayou CC	Marksville	9	[S]	318-253-9264
Springhill GC	Cullen	9	[V]	318-994-3134
Springview GC	Roseland	18	[V]	985-748-9760
springviewcountryclub.com				
Squire Creek CC	Choudrant	18	[S]	318-768-7000
squirecreek.com				
Squirrel Run GC	New Iberia	27	[P]	337-367-7820
squirrel-run.com				
St Mary G&CC	Berwick	9	[V]	985-384-8500
Stonebridge GC of New Orleans	Gretna	27	[P]	504-394-1300
stonebridgegolfofno.com				
Sugar Oaks G&CC	New Iberia	18	[S]	337-364-7611
sugaroakscc.com				
Sugarland G&CC	Raceland	18	[V]	985-537-6436
Tallulah G&CC	Tallulah	9	[V]	318-574-4173
Tamahka Trails GC	Marksville	18	[R]	318-240-6300
paragoncasinoresort.com				
Tchefuncta CC	Covington	18	[V]	985-892-1949
The Atchafalaya At Idlewild GC	Patterson	18	[M]	985-395-4653
atchafalayagolf.com				
The Bluffs CC	St Francisville	18	[R]	225-634-5757
thebluffs.com				
The First Tee At Clark Park GC	Baton Rouge	9	[M]	225-774-5946
thefirstteeebrp.org				
The GC At StoneBridge	Bossier City	18	[P]	318-747-2004
gcstonebridge.com				
The GC At Timber Trails	Pineville	9	[P]	318-640-4030
tgcatt.com				
The Island CC	Plaquemine	18	[S]	225-685-0808
theislandgolf.com				
The Links At Muny	Monroe	9	[M]	318-387-2396
monroe-westmonroe.org				
The National GC of Louisiana	Westlake	18	[M]	337-433-2255
nationalgcla.com				
The North Course At City Park	New Orleans	18	[M]	504-483-9410
cityparkgolf.com				
The Oaks at Sherwood	Baton Rouge	18	[V]	225-272-1141
theoaksatsherwood.com				
The Prison View GC	Angola	9	[P]	225-655-2978
prisonviewgolf.com				
Tidelands G&CC	Galliano	9	[S]	985-632-3915
Timberlane GC	Gretna	18	[V]	504-361-3612
timberlanecc.com				
TPC Louisiana	Avondale	18	[P]	504-436-8721
tpc.com				
Trails End GC	Arcadia	18	[M]	318-263-7420
Trenton Street GC	West Monroe	9	[P]	318-361-9345
Twin Oaks CC	Winnsboro	9	[V]	318-435-6426
Univ Club of Baton Rouge	Baton Rouge	18	[V]	225-819-0800
universityclubbr.com				
Ville Platte G&CC	Ville Platte	9	[V]	337-363-4116
Warrior Hills GC	Fort Polk	18	[A]	337-531-4661
Webb Park GC	Baton Rouge	18	[M]	225-383-4919
brec.org				
West Side GC	Brusly	18	[S]	225-749-8832
Westwood Exec GC	Shreveport	18	[P]	318-636-3162
Wetlands GC	Lafayette	18	[M]	337-291-7151
lafayettela.gov				
Willowdale CC	Luling	18	[S]	985-785-2478
willowdalecc.com				

MAINE

Course	Location	Holes	Type	Phone
Abenakee Club	Biddeford Pool	9	[V]	207-283-3811
Allen Mountain CC	Denmark	9	[P]	207-452-2282
Apple Valley GC	Lewiston	9	[P]	207-784-9773
Aroostook Valley CC	Fort Fairfield	18	[P]	506-273-9184
avcc.ca				

[A] = MILITARY   [M] = MUNICIPAL   [P] = PUBLIC   [R] = RESORT

MAINE

Golf Yellow Pages, 18th Edition

Course	Location	Holes	Type	Phone
Augusta CC,	Manchester	18	[V]	207-623-9624
augustacountryclub.org				
Bangor Muni GC,	Bangor	27	[M]	207-941-0232
bangorgc.com				
Bar Harbor GC,	Trenton	18	[P]	207-667-7505
Barren View GC,	Jonesboro	9	[P]	207-434-6531
barrenview.com				
Bath CC,	Bath	18	[P]	207-442-8411
skipworkplaygolf.com				
Belgrade Lakes GC,	Belgrade Lakes	18	[P]	207-495-4653
belgradelakesgolf.com				
Bethel Inn & CC,	Bethel	18	[R]	207-824-6276
bethelinn.com				
Biddeford Saco CC,	Saco	18	[S]	207-282-5883
bscc.ghinclub.com				
Blink Bonnie Golf Links,	Sorrento	9	[P]	207-422-3930
Blue Hill CC,	Blue Hill	9	[V]	207-374-2271
Boothbay CC,	Boothbay	18	[V]	207-633-6085
boothbaycountryclub.com				
Bridgton Highlands CC,	Bridgton	18	[P]	207-647-3491
bridgtonhighlands.com				
Brunswick GC,	Brunswick	18	[P]	207-725-8224
brunswickgolfclub.com				
Bucksport G&CC,	Bucksport	9	[P]	207-469-7612
bucksportgolfclub.com				
Cape Arundel GC,	Kennebunkport	18	[S]	207-967-3494
capearundelgolfclub.com				
Cape Neddick CC,	Cape Neddick	18	[P]	207-361-2011
capeneddickgolf.com				
Capital City GC,	Augusta	18	[P]	207-623-0504
Caribou GC,	Caribou	9	[P]	207-493-3933
caribougolf.com				
Castine GC,	Castine	9	[S]	207-326-8844
castinegolfclub.com				
Causeway Club,	Southwest Harbor	9	[P]	207-244-3780
thecausewayclub.org				
Cedar Springs GC,	Albion	9	[P]	207-437-2073
cedarspringsgc.com				
Cobbossee Colony GC,	Monmouth	9	[P]	207-268-4182
golfcobbossee.com				
Country Fareways Par 3,	Bowdoin	9	[P]	207-666-5603
countryfareways.com				
Country View GC,	Brooks	9	[P]	207-722-3161
Deep Brook GC,	Saco	9	[P]	207-283-3500
deepbrookgolfcourse.com				
Dexter Muni GC,	Dexter	9	[M]	207-924-6477
dextermaine.org/golf				
Dunegrass GC,	Old Orchard Beach	27	[P]	207-934-4513
dunegrass.com				
Dutch Elm GC,	Arundel	18	[P]	207-282-9850
dutchelmgolf.com				
Evergreen GC,	Rangeley	9	[P]	207-864-9055
evergreengolfrangeley.net				
Fairlawn G&CC,	Poland	18	[P]	207-998-4277
fairlawngolf.com				
Falmouth CC,	Falmouth	18	[V]	207-878-2384
falmouthcc.org				
Fort Kent GC,	Fort Kent	9	[P]	207-834-3149
Fox Ridge GC,	Auburn	18	[P]	207-777-4653
foxridgegolfclub.com				
Foxcroft GC,	Dover Foxcroft	9	[P]	207-564-8887
Freeport CC,	Freeport	9	[P]	207-865-0711
harrisgolfonline.com				
Frye Island GC,	Frye Island	9	[P]	207-655-3551
fryeisland.com				
Goose River GC,	Rockport	9	[P]	207-236-8488
gooserivergolf.com				
Gorham CC,	Gorham	18	[P]	207-839-3490
gorhamcountryclub.com				
Great Chebeague GC,	Chebeague Island	9	[P]	207-846-9478
Great Cove GC,	Roque Bluffs	9	[P]	207-434-7200
greatcovegolf.com				
Green Valley GC,	West Enfield	9	[P]	207-732-3006
barnesbrookgolfandski.com				
Grindstone Neck GC,	Winter Harbor	9	[P]	207-963-7760
grindstonegolf.com				
Hampden CC,	Hampden	9	[P]	207-862-4653
hampdencountryclub.net				
Hermon Meadow GC,	Hermon	18	[P]	207-848-3741
hermonmeadow.com				
Hidden Meadows GC,	Old Town	9	[P]	207-827-4779
oldtowngolf.com				
Highland Green GC,	Topsham	9	[S]	207-725-8066
highlandgreenmaine.com				
Hillcrest GC,	Millinocket	9	[S]	207-723-8410
Houlton Community GC,	Houlton	9	[P]	207-532-2662
houltongolf.com				
Island CC,	Sunset	9	[P]	207-348-2379
islandcountryclub.net				
Island Green Golf Ctr,	Holden	9	[P]	207-989-9909
J W Parks GC,	Pittsfield	9	[S]	207-487-5545
jwparksgolf.com				
JaTo Highlands GC,	Lincoln	18	[P]	207-794-2433
jatohighlands.com				
Katahdin CC,	Milo	9	[P]	207-943-8734
Kebo Valley GC,	Bar Harbor	18	[P]	207-288-3000
kebovalleyclub.com				
Kenduskeag Valley GC,	Kenduskeag	9	[P]	207-884-7330
kenduskeaggolf.com				
Lake Kezar CC,	Lovell	18	[P]	207-925-2462
lakekezargolf.com				
Lakeview GC,	Burnham	9	[P]	207-948-5414
Lakewood GC,	Madison	18	[P]	207-474-5955
lakewoodgolfmaine.com				
Limestone CC,	Limestone	9	[P]	207-328-7277
limestonecountryclub.com				
Long Lake CC,	St David	9	[P]	207-895-6957
Loons Cove GC.	Skowhegan	9	[P]	207-474-9550
Lucerne In Maine GC,	Dedham	9	[P]	207-843-6282
lucernegolf.com				
Maple Lane GC,	Livermore	9	[R]	207-897-3770
maplelaneinn.com/golf				
Mars Hill CC,	Mars Hill	18	[P]	207-425-4802
golfmhcc.com				
Martindale CC,	Auburn	18	[V]	207-782-1107
martindalecc.com				
Megunticook GC,	Rockport	9	[V]	207-236-2666
megunticookgolf.com				
Mere Creek GC,	Brunswick Nas	9	[A]	207-721-9995
Merriland Farm Par 3 GC,	Wells	9	[P]	207-646-0508
merrilandfarm.com				
Mingo Springs GC,	Rangeley	18	[P]	207-864-5021
mingosprings.com				
Moose River GC,	Jackman	9	[M]	207-668-9050
mooserivergolfcourse.com				

[S] = SEMI-PRIVATE   [V] = PRIVATE   [U] = UNIVERSITY   [N] = UNIVERSITY-PRIVATE

MAINE

Mt Kineo GC, *Augusta*..........................9 [R] 207-534-9012
mooseheadlakegolf.com
Naples G&CC, *Naples*......................18 [P] 207-693-6424
naplesgolfcourse.com
Natanis GC, *Vassalboro*..................36 [P] 207-622-3561
natanisgc.com
Newport CC, *Newport*.......................9 [P] 207-368-5600
Nonesuch River GC, *Scarborough*....18 [P] 207-883-0007
nonesuchgolf.com
North Haven GC, *North Haven*..........9 [S] 207-867-2054
Northeast Harbor GC, *Northeast Harbor*....18 [S] 207-276-5335
nehgc.com
Northport GC, *Northport*..................9 [P] 207-338-2270
Norway CC, *Norway*.........................9 [S] 207-743-9840
norwaycountryclub.com
Oakdale CC, *Mexico*.........................9 [S] 207-364-3951
oakdalecc.com
Old Marsh CC, *Wells*.......................18 [S] 207-251-4653
oldmarshcountryclub.com
Palmyra GC, *Palmyra*......................18 [R] 207-938-4947
palmyra-me.com
Paris Hill CC, *Paris*............................9 [P] 207-743-2371
Penobscot Valley CC, *Orono*............18 [V] 207-866-2423
penobscotvalleycc.com
Pine Hill GC, *Orrington*....................9 [P] 207-989-3824
Pine Ridge GC, *Waterville*................9 [M] 207-873-0474
Piscataquis CC, *Guilford*..................9 [P] 207-876-3203
piscataquisgolfcourse.com
Point Sebago Golf Beach Resort, *Casco*......18 [P] 207-655-3821
pointsebago.com
Portage Hills CC, *Portage*..................9 [P] 207-435-8221
Portland CC, *Falmouth*....................18 [V] 207-781-3053
portlandcountryclub.org
Presque Isle CC, *Presque Isle*............18 [S] 207-764-0430
picountryclub.com
Prospect Hill GC, *Auburn*.................18 [P] 207-782-9220
Prouts Neck CC, *Scarborough*..........18 [V] 207-883-9851
Province Lake Golf, *Parsonsfield*......18 [S] 207-793-4040
provincelakegolf.com
Purpoodock Club, *Cape Elizabeth*.....18 [V] 207-799-2273
purpoodock.com
Rivermeadow GC, *Westbrook*............9 [P] 207-854-1625
rivermeadowgolf.com
Riverside Muni GC, *Portland*...........27 [M] 207-797-3524
portlandmaine.gov
Rockland GC, *Rockland*...................18 [P] 207-594-9322
rocklandgolf.com
Rocky Knoll CC, *Orrington*..............18 [P] 207-989-0109
rockyknollcc.com
Roys All Steak Hamburgers & Golf Ctr, *Auburn*....9 [P] 207-782-2801
roysgolf.com
Sable Oaks GC, *South Portland*........18 [P] 207-775-6257
sableoaks.com
Salmon Falls GC, *Hollis*.....................9 [P] 207-929-5233
salmonfalls-resort.com
Samoset Resort GC, *Rockport*...........18 [P] 207-593-1511
samoset.com/golf.html
Sandy River Golf, *Farmington Falls*...9 [P] 207-778-2492
Sanford CC, *Sanford*.......................18 [S] 207-324-5462
sanfordcountryclub.com
Sawmill Woods GC, *Clifton*...............9 [P] 207-843-7481
sawmillwoodsgolf.com

Searsport Pines GC, *Searsport*..........9 [P] 207-548-2854
searsportpines.com
Sheepscot Links, *Whitefield*..............9 [P] 207-549-7060
sheepscotlinks.com
Shore Acres GC, *Sebasco Estates*......9 [R] 207-389-9060
sebasco.com
South Portland Muni GC, *South Portland*....9 [M] 207-775-0005
Spring Meadows GC, *Gray*...............18 [P] 207-657-2586
springmeadowsgolf.com
Springbrook GC, *Leeds*....................18 [P] 207-946-5900
springbrookgolfclub.com
Squaw Mountain Village GC, *Greenville Junction*...9 [P] 207-695-3609
St Croix CC, *Calais*............................9 [S] 207-454-8875
stcroixcc.com
Streamside GC, *Winterport*..............9 [P] 207-223-9009
Sugarloaf GC, *Carrabassett Valley*....18 [R] 207-237-2000
sugarloaf.com
Summit Springs Golf, *Poland Spring*...18 [P] 207-998-4515
Sunday River GC, *Newry*.................18 [R] 207-824-4653
harrisgolfonline.com
Sunset Ridge Golf Links, *Westbrook*...27 [S] 207-854-9463
golfmaine.com
Tarratine GC, *Islesboro*......................9 [V] 207-734-2248
The Ledges GC, *York*........................18 [P] 207-351-3000
ledgesgolf.com
The Links At Outlook, *South Berwick*...18 [P] 207-384-4653
outlookgolf.com
The Links Poland Spring, *Poland*......18 [R] 207-998-6002
polandspringresort.com
The Meadows GC, *Litchfield*.............18 [P] 207-268-3000
themeadowsgolfclub.com
The Woodlands Club, *Falmouth*......18 [R] 207-781-3104
thewoodlands.org
Toddy Brook GC, *North Yarmouth*....18 [P] 207-829-5100
toddybrookgolf.com
Turner Highlands, *Turner*................18 [P] 207-224-7060
turnerhighlands.com
Twin Falls GC, *Westbrook*..................9 [P] 207-854-5397
Va Jo Wa GC, *Island Falls*................18 [P] 207-463-2128
vajowa.com
Val Halla GC, *Cumberland*..............18 [M] 207-829-2225
valhallagolf.com
Waterville CC, *Oakland*...................18 [P] 207-465-9861
watervillecountryclub.com
Wawenock CC, *Walpole*.....................9 [P] 207-563-3938
wawenockgolfclub.com
Webhannet GC, *Kennebunk*............18 [S] 207-967-2061
webhannetgolfclub.com
Western View GC, *Augusta*................9 [P] 207-622-5309
White Birches GC, *Ellsworth*.............9 [P] 207-667-3621
acadiabirchesmotel.com
White Tail GC, *Charleston*..................9 [P] 207-285-7730
golfwhitetailinmaine.com
Willowdale GC, *Scarborough*...........18 [P] 207-883-9351
willowdalegolf.com
Wilson Lake CC, *Wilton*.....................9 [P] 207-645-2016
harrisgolfonline.com
York G&TC, *York*..............................18 [V] 207-363-2683
ygtclub.com
York Par 3 GC, *York*...........................9 [P] 207-363-7070
yorkpar3.com

[A] = MILITARY   [M] = MUNICIPAL   [P] = PUBLIC   [R] = RESORT

MARYLAND

Andrews AFB GC, *Andrews AFB*..........................54 [A] 301-736-4595
 aafbgc.com
Annapolis GC, *Annapolis*...................................9 [S] 410-263-6771
 annapolisgolfclub.net
Argyle CC, *Silver Spring*................................. 18 [V] 301-598-6949
 argylecc.net
Assateague Greens Golf Ctr, *Ocean City*.................9 [P] 410-213-7526
Atlantic Golf At Queenstown Harbor, *Queenstown*36 [S] 410-827-6611
 qhgolf.com
Baltimore CC, *Lutherville* .... 36 [V] 410-889-4400
 bcc1898.com
Bay Hills GC, *Arnold* .... 18 [V] 410-974-0669
 bayhillsgolf.com
Beaver Creek CC, *Hagerstown* .... 18 [S] 301-733-5152
 beavercreekcc.com
Bethesda CC, *Bethesda* .... 18 [V] 301-365-1703
 bethesdacountryclub.org
Bittersweet GC, *Elkton*..................................... 18 [S] 410-398-8848
 bittersweetgc.us
Black Horse G&LearnCtr, *White Hall*....................9 [P] 410-557-0100
Black Rock GC, *Hagerstown* ....18 [M] 240-313-2816
 blackrockgolfcourse.com
Blue Heron GC, *Stevensville*............................18 [M] 410-643-5721
 parksnrec.org
Blue Mash GC, *Gaithersburg* ....18 [P] 301-670-1966
 bluemash.com
Bonnie View CC, *Baltimore*............................... 18 [S] 410-486-1100
Bowie G&CC, *Bowie* .... 18 [S] 301-262-8141
 bowiegolf.com
Bren-Mar Park GC, *Bel Air*..................................9 [P] 410-836-8855
Breton Bay CC, *Leonardtown*............................ 18 [S] 301-475-2300
 bretonbaygolf.com
Bretton Woods Rec Ctr, *Germantown*.................. 18 [V] 301-948-5405
 bwrc.org
Bulle Rock, *Havre de Grace*...............................18 [P] 410-939-8887
 bullerock.com
Burning Tree Club, *Bethesda* .... 18 [V] 301-365-2588
Caroline CC, *Denton* .... 18 [V] 410-479-1425
 carolinecountryclub.com
Carroll Park GC, *Baltimore*..................................9 [M] 410-685-8344
 bmgcgolf.com
Cattail Creek CC, *Glenwood* .... 18 [V] 410-442-1787
 cattailcreekcc.com
Caves Valley GC, *Owings Mills* .... 18 [V] 410-356-1313
 cavesvalley.net
CC at Woodmore, *Mitchellville*........................... 18 [V] 301-249-6100
 ccwoodmore.com
CC of Maryland, *Towson* .... 18 [V] 410-823-3869
 ccofmd.com
Cedar Point GC, *Patuxent River*..........................18 [A] 301-342-3597
Chartwell G&CC, *Severna Park* .... 18 [V] 410-987-4480
 chartwellgcc.com
Chesapeake Bay GC At North East, *North East*.....18 [P] 410-287-0200
 chesapeakegolf.com
Chesapeake Bay GC At Rising Sun, *Rising Sun*.....18 [P] 410-658-4343
 chesapeakegolf.com
Chesapeake Hills GC, *Lusby*............................... 18 [S] 410-326-4653
 chesapeakehills.com
Chester River Y&CC, *Chestertown* .... 18 [V] 410-778-1372
 crycc.org
Chestnut Ridge CC, *Lutherville*.......................... 18 [V] 410-252-8779
 chestnutridge.net

Chevy Chase Club, *Chevy Chase*........................ 18 [V] 301-652-4100
 chevychaseclub.org
Clearview At Horns Point, *Cambridge* .... 18 [S] 410-221-0521
 clearviewathornspoint.com
Clifton Park GC, *Baltimore*................................18 [M] 410-243-3500
 bmgcgolf.com
Clustered Spires GC, *Frederick* ....18 [M] 301-624-1295
 cityoffrederick.com
Columbia CC, *Chevy Chase* .... 18 [V] 301-951-5050
 columbiacc.org
Compass Pointe GC, *Pasadena*...........................36 [P] 410-255-7764
 compasspointegolf.com
Congressional CC, *Bethesda*.............................. 36 [V] 301-469-2032
 ccclub.org
Crofton CC, *Crofton* .... 18 [V] 410-721-3111
 croftonclub.com
Cross Creek GC, *Beltsville* ....18 [P] 301-595-8901
 crosscreekgolfclub.net
Cumberland CC, *Cumberland* .... 18 [V] 301-724-0440
 cumberlandcountryclub.net
Deer Run GC, *Berlin* ....18 [P] 410-629-0060
 golfdeerrun.com
Diamond Ridge GC, *Windsor Mill* .... 36 [M] 410-887-1349
 baltimoregolfing.com
Eagles Landing GC, *Berlin* ....18 [M] 410-213-7277
 eagleslandinggolf.com
Eisenhower GC, *Crownsville*.............................. 18 [P] 410-571-0973
 eisenhowergolf.com
Elkridge Hunt Club, *Baltimore*........................... 18 [V] 410-377-9201
 elkridgeclub.com
Elks GC, *Salisbury* .... 9 [V] 410-749-2695
Enterprise GC, *Mitchellville* .... 18 [M] 301-249-2040
 pgparks.com
Evening Breeze GC, *Deer Park* ....9 [P] 301-533-4448
 deepcreektimes.com/eveningbreeze.html
Exton GC, *Aberdeen Proving Gnd*....................... 9 [A] 410-436-2213
 apgmwr.com
Fairway Hills GC, *Columbia* ....18 [P] 410-730-1112
 fairwayhillsgolfclub.com
Falls Road GC, *Potomac*....................................18 [M] 301-299-5156
 montgomerycountygolf.com
Fore Sisters GC, *Rawlings*................................. 18 [P] 301-729-4000
Forest Park GC, *Baltimore* ....18 [M] 410-448-4653
 bmgcgolf.com
Fort Meade GC, *Fort Meade* ....27 [A] 301-677-4333
 ftmeadegolf.com
Fountain Head CC, *Hagerstown*.......................... 18 [V] 301-733-5940
 fhcc1924.com
Four Streams GC, *Beallsville*.............................. 18 [V] 301-349-2900
 fourstreams.com
Fox Hollow GC, *Lutherville Timonium*.................18 [M] 410-887-7735
 baltimoregolfing.com
Frederick GC, *Frederick*.................................... 18 [S] 301-846-0694
Furnace Bay GC, *Perryville* ....18 [P] 410-642-6816
 furnacebaygolf.com
GC At South River, *Edgewater* .... 18 [V] 410-798-5865
 golfclubsr.com
Geneva Farm GC, *Street* .... 18 [P] 410-452-8800
 genevafarmgolf.com
Gibson Island Club, *Gibson Island* .... 9 [V] 410-255-1040
 gibsonisland.com
Glade Valley GC, *Walkersville* ....18 [P] 301-898-5555
 gladevalleygolf.com

[S] = SEMI-PRIVATE   [V] = PRIVATE   [U] = UNIVERSITY   [N] = UNIVERSITY-PRIVATE

MAINE

Golf Yellow Pages, 18th Edition

Glenn Dale GC, *Glenn Dale* .... 18 [S] 301-262-1166
  glenndalegolfclub.com
GlenRiddle Man OWar Course, *Berlin* .... 18 [P] 410-213-2325
  glenriddlegolf.com
GlenRiddle War Admiral Course, *Berlin* .... 18 [V] 410-213-2325
  glenriddlegolf.com
Great Hope GC, *Westover* .... 18 [M] 410-651-5900
  greathopegolf.com
Great Oak Landing Marina, *Chestertown* .... 9 [R] 410-778-5007
  mearsgreatoaklanding.com
Green Hill Y&CC, *Quantico* .... 18 [V] 410-749-1605
  greenhillgolf.org
Green Spring Valley Hunt Club, *Owings Mills* ...... 18 [V] 410-363-0462
  gsvhc.org
Greystone GC, *White Hall* .... 18 [M] 410-887-1945
  baltimoregolfing.com
Gunpowder GC, *Laurel* .... 18 [P] 301-725-4532
  gunpowdergolf.com
Hagerstown Greens At Hamilton Run, *Hagerstown* 9 [M] 301-733-8630
  hagerstownmd.org
Hampshire Greens GC, *Silver Spring* .... 18 [S] 301-476-7999
  montgomerycountygolf.com
Harbourtowne Golf Resort, *St Michaels* .... 18 [R] 410-745-5183
  harbourtowne.com
Hawthorne CC, *La Plata* .... 9 [V] 301-934-2433
  hawthornecc.com
Hayfields CC, *Hunt Valley* .... 18 [V] 410-527-4653
  hayfieldscc.com
Henson Creek GC, *Fort Washington* .... 9 [M] 301-567-4646
  pgparks.com
Heritage Harbour GC, *Annapolis* .... 9 [V] 410-224-3580
Hillendale CC, *Phoenix* .... 18 [V] 410-592-3027
  hillendalecc.com
Hobbits Glen GC, *Columbia* .... 18 [S] 410-730-5980
  hobbitsglengolfclub.com
Hog Neck GC, *Easton* .... 27 [M] 410-822-6079
  hogneck.com
Hollow Creek GC At Glenbrook, *Middletown* .... 18 [P] 301-371-9166
  hollowcreekgolfclub.com
Holly Hills CC, *Ijamsville* .... 18 [V] 301-694-7210
  hollyhillsgolf.com
Hope Valley GC, *Mt Airy* .... 18 [P] 301-865-0026
  hopevalleygolf.com
Horse Bridge GC, *Salisbury* .... 18 [P] 410-543-4446
Hunt Valley GC, *Phoenix* .... 27 [V] 410-527-3304
  huntvalleygc.com
Hunters Oak GC, *Queenstown* .... 27 [R] 410-827-3499
  theriverplantation.com
Kenwood G&CC, *Bethesda* .... 18 [V] 301-320-3605
  kenwoodcc.net
Lake Arbor GC, *Mitchellville* .... 18 [S] 410-336-7771
  lakearborgc.com
Lake Presidential GC, *Upper Marlboro* .... 18 [S] 301-627-8577
  lakepresidential.com
Lakewood CC, *Rockville* .... 18 [V] 301-762-5430
  lakewoodcc.org
Laytonsville GC, *Laytonsville* .... 18 [M] 301-948-5288
  montgomerycountygolf.com
Leisure World GC, *Silver Spring* .... 18 [V] 301-598-1570
  lwmc.com
Liberty Road Golf Ctr, *Frederick* .... 9 [P] 301-898-3035
Linkwood Family Golf Park Llc, *Linkwood* .... 18 [P] 410-221-8700
Little Bennett GC, *Clarksburg* .... 18 [P] 410-253-1515
  montgomerycountygolf.com

Lodestone GC, *McHenry* .... 18 [V] 301-387-4653
  lodestonegolf.com
Manor CC, *Rockville* .... 27 [V] 301-929-1131
  manorcc.org
Maple Run GC LLC, *Thurmont* .... 18 [P] 301-271-7870
  maplerungolf.com
Maplehurst CC, *Frostburg* .... 18 [P] 301-689-6602
  maplehurstcc.com
Marlborough CC, *Upper Marlboro* .... 18 [S] 301-952-1300
  marlboroughgolfclub.com
Marlton GC, *Upper Marlboro* .... 18 [P] 301-856-7566
  marltongolf.com
Maryland G&CC, *Bel Air* .... 18 [V] 410-838-5022
  marylandgcc.org
Maryland National GC, *Middletown* .... 18 [P] 301-371-0000
  marylandnational.com
McDaniel College GC, *Westminster* .... 9 [U] 410-848-7667
  mcdaniel.edu
Mellomar Golf Park, *Owings* .... 18 [P] 410-286-8212
  mellomar.com
Mitchells Golf Ctr, *Reisterstown* .... 9 [P] 410-833-7721
  mitchellsgolf.com
Montgomery CC, *Laytonsville* .... 18 [V] 240-912-9529
  montgomerycc.com
Montgomery Village GC, *Montgomery Village* ..... 18 [V] 301-948-6204
  montgomeryvillagegolf.com
Mount Pleasant GC, *Baltimore* .... 18 [M] 410-254-5100
  bmgcgolf.com
Mountain Branch GC, *Joppa* .... 18 [P] 410-836-9600
  mountainbranch.com
Musket Ridge GC, *Myersville* .... 18 [P] 301-293-9930
  musketridge.com
Nassawango CC, *Snow Hill* .... 18 [S] 410-632-3114
  nassawango.com
National GC At Tantallon, *Fort Washington* .... 18 [V] 301-292-0003
  nationalgolfclubusa.com
Needwood GC, *Derwood* .... 27 [M] 301-948-1075
  montgomerycountygolf.com
Night Hawk Golf Ctr, *Gambrills* .... 9 [P] 410-721-9349
  nighthawkgolfcenter.com
Norbeck CC, *Rockville* .... 18 [V] 301-774-7706
  norbeckcc.com
Northwest GC, *Silver Spring* .... 27 [M] 301-598-6100
  montgomerycountygolf.com
Nutters Crossing GC, *Salisbury* .... 18 [S] 410-860-4653
  nutterscrossing.com
Oak Creek GC, *Upper Marlboro* .... 18 [V] 301-390-1595
  oakcreekclub.com
Oakland GC, *Oakland* .... 18 [P] 301-334-3883
  golfatoakland.com
Oakmont Green GC, *Hampstead* .... 18 [P] 410-374-1500
  oakmontgreen.com
Ocean City GC, *Berlin* .... 36 [R] 410-641-1779
  oceancitygolfclub.com
Ocean Pines G&CC, *Berlin* .... 18 [S] 410-641-6057
  oceanpines.org
Ocean Resorts WWCC GC, *Berlin* .... 18 [R] 410-641-5643
  oceanresortsgolfclub.com
Old South CC, *Lothian* .... 18 [V] 410-741-1793
  oldsouthcountryclub.org
P B Dye GC, *Ijamsville* .... 18 [P] 301-607-4653
  pbdyegolf.com
Paint Branch G Complex, *College Park* .... 9 [M] 301-935-0330
  pgparks.com

92 [A] = MILITARY [M] = MUNICIPAL [P] = PUBLIC [R] = RESORT

MASSACHUSETTS

Patuxent Greens CC, *Laurel* .... 18 [S] 301-776-5533
  patuxentgolf.com
Pine Ridge GC, *Lutherville* .... 18 [M] 410-252-1408
  classic5golf.com
Pine Shore GC, *Berlin* .... 27 [R] 410-641-5100
  pineshoregolf.com
Piney Branch G&CC, *Hampstead* .... 18 [V] 410-239-7114
  pineybranchgolf.com
Poolesville GC, *Poolesville* .... 18 [M] 301-428-8143
  montgomerycountygolf.com
Potomac Ridge, *Waldorf* .... 27 [S] 301-372-1305
  golfpotomacridge.com
Prospect Bay CC, *Grasonville* .... 18 [V] 410-827-6924
  prospectbay.com
Rattlewood GC, *Mt Airy* .... 18 [M] 301-607-9000
  montgomerycountygolf.com
Redgate Muni GC, *Rockville* .... 18 [M] 240-314-8730
  redgategolf.com
Renditions, *Davidsonville* .... 18 [P] 410-798-9798
  renditionsgolf.com
River Downs GC, *Finksburg* .... 18 [S] 410-526-2000
  riverdownsgolf.com
River Marsh GC, *Cambridge* .... 18 [R] 410-901-6397
  chesapeakebay.hyatt.com
River Run GC, *Berlin* .... 18 [P] 410-641-7200
  riverrungolf.com
Rocky Gap Lodge & Golf Resort, *Flintstone* .... 18 [R] 301-784-8400
  rockygapresort.com/maryland-golf-resorts.cfm
Rocky Point GC, *Essex* .... 18 [M] 410-391-2906
  baltimoregolfing.com
Rolling Road GC, *Catonsville* .... 18 [V] 410-747-6070
  rollingroadgc.com
Ruggles GC, *Aberdeen Proving Gnd* .... 18 [A] 410-278-4794
  apgmwr.com
Rum Pointe Seaside Golf Links, *Berlin* .... 18 [P] 410-629-1414
  rumpointe.com
Severna Park Golf Ctr, *Arnold* .... 9 [P] 410-647-8618
  severnaparkgolf.com
Sherwood Forest Club, *Sherwood Forest* .... 9 [V] 410-841-6491
Sligo Creek GC, *Silver Spring* .... 9 [M] 301-585-6006
  montgomerycountygolf.com
Sparrows Point CC, *Baltimore* .... 27 [V] 410-477-3636
  sparrowspointcc.org
Swan Point Y&CC, *Issue* .... 18 [S] 301-259-0047
  swanpointgolf.com
Talbot CC, *Easton* .... 18 [V] 410-822-4757
  talbotcc.com
The Bay Club, *Berlin* .... 36 [S] 410-641-4081
  thebayclub.com
The Beach Club Golf Links, *Berlin* .... 27 [S] 410-641-4653
  beachclubgolflinks.com
The Club At Patriots Glen, *Elkton* .... 18 [P] 410-392-9552
  patriotsglen.com
The Cove Creek Club, *Stevensville* .... 9 [V] 410-643-4868
  covecreekclub.com
The Easton Club, *Easton* .... 18 [P] 410-820-9017
  eastonclub.com
The Links At Challedon, *Mt Airy* .... 18 [P] 410-552-0320
  thelinksatchalledon.com
The Links At Lighthouse Sound, *Bishopville* .... 18 [R] 410-352-5767
  lighthousesound.com
The Suburban Club of Baltimore County, *Pikesville* 18 [V] 410-484-4051
  suburban.org

The Timbers at Troy, *Elkridge* .... 18 [M] 410-313-4653
  timbersgolf.com
The Wetlands GC, *Aberdeen* .... 18 [P] 410-273-7488
  golfwetlands.com
Thousand Acres Lake Side GC, *Swanton* .... 9 [S] 301-387-0387
  thousandacresgolf.com
Towson G&CC, *Phoenix* .... 18 [V] 410-252-5960
  tgcc.net
TPC Potomac At Avenel Farm, *Potomac* .... 18 [V] 301-469-3700
  tpcpotomac.com
Trotters Glen, *Olney* .... 18 [P] 301-570-4951
  trottersglen.com
Turf Valley Resort, *Ellicott City* .... 36 [R] 410-465-1504
  turfvalley.com
Twin Shields GC, *Dunkirk* .... 18 [S] 410-257-7800
  twinshields.com
Univ of Maryland GC, *College Park* .... 18 [U] 301-314-4653
  golf.umd.edu
US Naval Acad GC, *Annapolis* .... 18 [A] 410-293-9747
  usna.edu/usnaathletics/golfclub.htm
VFW CC, *Frederick* .... 9 [V] 301-663-9768
  vfwpost3285.org
Wakefield Valley GC, *Westminster* .... 27 [S] 410-876-6662
  wakefieldvalley.com
Walden GC, *Crofton* .... 18 [V] 410-721-8268
  waldengc.com
Waterfront Greens GC, *Swanton* .... 9 [S] 301-387-8851
  waterfrontgreens.net
Waverly Woods GC, *Marriottsville* .... 18 [P] 410-313-9182
  waverlywoods.com
West Winds GC, *New Market* .... 18 [S] 301-831-6191
  westwindsgc.com
Westminster National GC, *Westminster* .... 18 [S] 410-876-4653
  westminsternationalgc.com
Whiskey Creek GC, *Ijamsville* .... 18 [P] 301-694-2900
  whiskeycreekgolf.com
White Plains GC, *White Plains* .... 18 [M] 301-645-1300
  charlescounty.org
Wicomico Shores GC, *Mechanicsville* .... 18 [M] 301-884-4601
  co.saint-marys.md.us
Willow Springs GC, *West Friendship* .... 18 [P] 410-442-7700
  willowspringsgolfcourse.com
Winter Quarters GC, *Pocomoke City* .... 9 [M] 410-957-1171
Winters Run GC, *Bel Air* .... 18 [V] 410-879-1200
  wintersrun.com
Wisp Resort GC, *Mc Henry* .... 18 [R] 301-387-4911
  wispresort.com
Wood Creek Golf Links, *Delmar* .... 18 [P] 410-896-3000
  wcgolflinks.com
Woodholme CC, *Pikesville* .... 18 [V] 410-486-3700
  woodholme.org
Woodmont CC, *Rockville* .... 36 [V] 301-424-8496
  woodmontcc.com
Worthington Manor GC, *Frederick* .... 18 [P] 301-874-5500
  worthingtonmanor.com
Yinglings Golf Ctr, *Hagerstown* .... 18 [P] 301-790-2494
  yinglingsgolfcenter.com

MASSACHUSETTS

Acoaxet Club, *Westport* .... 9 [V] 508-636-4782
  acoaxet.com
Acushnet River Valley GC, *Acushnet* .... 18 [M] 508-998-7777
  golfacushnet.com

[S] = SEMI-PRIVATE   [V] = PRIVATE   [U] = UNIVERSITY   [N] = UNIVERSITY-PRIVATE

MASSACHUSETTS — Golf Yellow Pages, 18th Edition

Agawam Muni GC, *Feeding Hills* .... 18 [M] 413-786-2194
  agawamgc.com
Allendale CC, *North Dartmouth* .... 18 [V] 508-992-8682
  allendalecountryclub.com
Amesbury G&CC, *Amesbury* .... 9 [S] 978-388-5153
  amesburygolf.com
Amherst GC, *Amherst* .... 9 [U] 413-256-6894
  amherstgolfclub.org
Andover CC, *Andover* .... 18 [V] 978-475-2024
  andovercountryclub.com
Ashfield Community GC, *Ashfield* .... 9 [P] 413-628-4413
Atlantic CC, *Plymouth* .... 18 [P] 508-759-6644
  atlanticcountryclub.com
Atlantic Golf Ctr, *South Attleboro* .... 9 [P] 508-761-5484
  atlanticgolfcenter.com
Ballymeade CC, *North Falmouth* .... 18 [S] 508-540-4005
  ballymeade.com
Bass Ridge GC, *Hinsdale* .... 18 [P] 413-655-2605
Bass River GC, *Amesbury* .... 18 [M] 508-398-9079
  golfyarmouthcapecod.com
Bass Rocks GC, *Gloucester* .... 18 [V] 978-283-1866
  bassrocksgolfclub.org
Bay Path GC, *East Brookfield* .... 9 [P] 508-867-8161
Bay Pointe GC, *Buzzards Bay* .... 18 [P] 508-759-8802
  baypointecc.net
Bayberry Hills GC, *West Yarmouth* .... 27 [M] 508-394-5597
  golfyarmouthcapecod.com
Bear Hill GC, *Stoneham* .... 9 [V] 781-245-1529
  bearhillgolfclub.com
Beaver Brook GC, *Haydenville* .... 9 [V] 413-268-7229
Bedrock GC, *Rutland* .... 9 [P] 508-886-0202
  bedrockgc.com
Bellevue GC, *Melrose* .... 9 [V] 781-665-9733
  bellevuegolfclub.com
Belmont CC, *Belmont* .... 18 [V] 617-484-5360
  belmontcc.org
Berkshire Hills CC, *Pittsfield* .... 18 [V] 413-442-1451
  berkshirehillscc.com
Berlin CC, *Berlin* .... 9 [P] 978-838-2733
Beverly G&TC, *Beverly* .... 18 [S] 978-922-9072
  beverlygolfandtennis.net
Black Rock CC, *Hingham* .... 18 [V] 781-749-1919
  blackrockcc.com
Black Swan CC, *Georgetown* .... 18 [V] 978-352-7926
  blackswancountryclub.com
Blackstone National GC, *Sutton* .... 18 [P] 508-865-2111
  bngc.net
Blissful Meadows GC, *Uxbridge* .... 18 [S] 508-278-6110
  blissfulmeadows.com
Blue Hill CC, *Canton* .... 27 [V] 781-828-2000
  bluehillcc.com
Blue Rock GC, *South Yarmouth* .... 18 [R] 508-398-9295
  bluerockgolfcourse.com
Boston GC, *Hingham* .... 18 [V] 781-741-5123
  bostongolfclub.org
Bradford CC, *Bradford* .... 18 [P] 978-372-8587
  bradfordcc.com
Brae Burn CC, *West Newton* .... 27 [V] 617-244-4411
  braeburngolf.com
Braintree Muni GC, *Braintree* .... 18 [M] 781-843-6513
  braintreegolf.com
Brockton CC, *Brockton* .... 9 [V] 508-588-8439
  brocktoncountryclub.us

Brookmeadow CC, *Canton* .... 18 [P] 781-828-4444
  brookmeadowgolf.com
Bungay Brook GC, *Bellingham* .... 9 [P] 508-883-1600
  bungaybrook.com
Butter Brook Crossing GC, *Westford* .... 18 [P] 978-692-6560
  butterbrookgc.com
Butternut Farm GC, *Stow* .... 18 [P] 978-897-3400
  butternutfarm.com
Candlewood GC, *Ipswich* .... 9 [P] 978-356-5377
Cape Ann CC, *Essex* .... 9 [P] 978-768-7544
  capeanngolf.com
Cape Cod CC, *Village of Hatchville* .... 18 [P] 508-563-9842
  capecodcountryclub.com
Cape Cod National GC, *Brewster* .... 18 [V] 508-240-6800
  capecodnational.net
Carriage Pines GC, *Rowley* .... 9 [P] 978-948-2731
  rowleygolf.com
CC of Billerica, *Billerica* .... 18 [P] 978-667-9121
  countryclubofbillerica.com
CC of Greenfield, *Greenfield* .... 18 [V] 413-773-7530
  countryclubofgreenfield.net
CC of Halifax, *Halifax* .... 18 [V] 781-293-9063
  halifaxcc.com
CC of New Bedford, *North Dartmouth* .... 18 [V] 508-992-9339
  ccnbgolfclub.com
CC of Pittsfield, *Pittsfield* .... 18 [V] 413-447-8500
  ccpittsfield.org
CC of Wilbraham, *Wilbraham* .... 18 [V] 413-596-8887
  countryclubofwilbraham.com
Cedar Glen GC, *Saugus* .... 9 [P] 781-233-3609
Cedar Hill GC, *Stoughton* .... 9 [M] 781-344-8913
  cedarhill-stoughton.com
Charles River CC, *Newton* .... 18 [V] 617-527-8300
  charlesrivercc.org
Charter Oak CC, *Hudson* .... 18 [V] 978-562-0800
  charteroakcc.com
Chatham Seaside Links, *Chatham* .... 9 [M] 508-945-4774
Chelmsford CC, *Chelmsford* .... 9 [S] 978-256-1818
  sterlinggolf.com
Chemawa GC, *North Attleboro* .... 18 [P] 508-399-7330
  chemawagolf.com
Chequessett Y&CC, *Wellfleet* .... 9 [P] 508-349-3704
  cycc.net
Cherry Hill GC, *Amherst* .... 9 [M] 413-256-4071
  cherryhillgolf.org
Chicopee CC, *Chicopee* .... 18 [M] 413-594-9295
  chicopeema.gov
Cityview Golfland, *North Dartmouth* .... 18 [P] 508-995-8266
Clearview GC, *Millbury* .... 9 [P] 508-754-5654
Cohasse CC, *Southbridge* .... 9 [V] 508-764-6290
  cohasse.com
Cohasset GC, *Cohasset* .... 18 [V] 781-383-9890
  cohassetgc.org
Cold Springs CC, *Belchertown* .... 18 [P] 413-323-4888
  coldspringcc.com
Coldbrook Golf & RV Resort, *Barre* .... 9 [R] 978-355-2090
  coldbrookcountry.com
Concord CC, *Concord* .... 18 [V] 978-371-1089
  concordcc.org
Cotuit Highground CC, *Cotuit* .... 9 [P] 508-428-9863
  cotuithighground.com
Cranberry Valley GC, *Harwich* .... 18 [M] 508-430-5234
  cranberrygolfcourse.com

[A] = MILITARY   [M] = MUNICIPAL   [P] = PUBLIC   [R] = RESORT

MASSACHUSETTS

Cranwell Resort, Spa & GC, *Lenox* ....18 [R] 413-637-1364
   cranwell.com
Crestview CC, *Agawam*................................ 18 [V] 413-786-0917
   crestviewcc.org
Crestwood CC, *Rehoboth*............................. 18 [V] 508-336-8582
   crestwoodcc.com
Crumpin Fox Club, *Bernardston*..................18 [S] 413-648-9101
   golfthefox.com
Crystal Springs GC, *Haverhill*.......................18 [S] 978-374-9621
Cummaquid GC, *Yarmouth Port*..................18 [S] 508-362-2022
   cummaquidgc.com
Cyprian Keyes GC, *Boylston*.........................27 [P] 508-869-9900
   cypriankeyes.com
D W Field GC, *Brockton*................................18 [M] 508-580-7855
   2doggolf.com
Dedham Country & Polo Club, *Dedham* .... 18 [V] 781-326-3181
   dedhamclub.org
Dennis Highlands GC, *Dennis*......................18 [M] 508-385-1554
   dennisgolf.com
Dennis Pines GC, *East Dennis* ....18 [M] 508-385-8347
   dennisgolf.com
Donnybrook CC, *Lanesboro* ....9 [P] 413-499-7888
Dudley Hill GC Nichols College, *Dudley* ....9 [S] 508-943-4538
   dudleyhill.org
Dunroamin CC, *Gilbertville*..........................9 [S] 413-477-0004
Duxbury Yacht Club, *Duxbury* .... 18 [V] 781-934-2578
East Mountain CC, *Westfield* ....18 [P] 413-568-1539
   eastmountaincc.com
Easton CC, *South Easton*.............................18 [S] 508-238-2500
   eastoncountryclub.com
Eastward Ho! CC, *Chatham* ....18 [R] 508-945-0620
   eastwardho.net
Edgartown GC, *Edgartown* .... 9 [V] 508-627-5343
Edge Hill GC, *Ashfield* ....9 [P] 413-625-6018
   edgehillgolfcourse.com
Edgewood GC, *Southwick* .... 18 [S] 413-569-6826
   edgewood4golf.com
Edgewood GC, *Uxbridge* ....9 [S] 508-278-6027
   edgewoodgolfcourse.com
Egremont CC, *Great Barrington*...................18 [P] 413-528-4222
   egremontcountryclub.com
Ellinwood CC, *Athol* ....18 [P] 978-249-7460
   ellinwoodcc.com
Elmcrest CC, *East Longmeadow*.................. 18 [V] 413-525-8444
   elmcrest.cc
Essex CC, *Manchester*................................. 18 [V] 978-526-7691
   essexcc.org
Evergreen GC, *Newburyport*........................9 [P] 978-463-8600
   evergreenvalleygolf.com
Falcon GC, *Otis Ang Base*............................. 9 [A] 508-968-6453
Fall River CC, *Fall River*................................ 18 [V] 508-678-9374
   fallrivercc.com
Falmouth CC, *East Falmouth*.......................27 [M] 508-548-3211
   falmouthcountryclub.com
Far Corner GC, *Boxford*................................27 [P] 978-352-9838
   farcornergolf.com
Farm Neck GC, *Oak Bluffs*............................ 18 [S] 508-693-3057
Ferncroft CC, *Middleton* ....27 [R] 978-739-4032
   ferncroftcc.com
Firefly GC, *Seekonk* ....18 [P] 508-336-6622
Fore Kicks GC, *Norfolk*..................................9 [P] 508-384-4533
   forekicks.com

Forest Park CC, *Adams*.................................9 [P] 413-743-3311
   forestparkadams.com
Foxborough CC, *Foxboro* .... 18 [S] 508-543-4661
   foxboroughcc.com
Framingham CC, *Framingham* .... 18 [V] 508-872-9790
   framinghamcc.com
Franconia GC, *Springfield*...........................18 [M] 413-734-9334
   veteransgolfcourse.com
Franklin CC, *Franklin*................................... 18 [V] 508-528-9852
   franklincc.com
Fresh Pond GC, *Cambridge*..........................9 [M] 617-349-6282
   freshpondgolf.com
Furnace Brook GC, *Quincy* ....9 [S] 617-472-8466
   furnacebrookgolfclub.com
Gannon GC, *Lynn*..18 [M] 781-592-8238
   gannongolfclub.com
Gardner Muni GC, *Gardner*.........................18 [M] 978-632-9703
Garrison Golf Ctr, *Haverhill*..........................9 [P] 978-374-9380
   garrisongolf.com
GC of Cape Cod, *North Falmouth* .... 18 [S] 508-457-7200
   tgccc.com
General Electric Athletic Assn, *Pittsfield*...........9 [S] 413-443-5746
George Wright GC, *Hyde Park*.....................18 [M] 617-364-2300
   cityofbostongolf.com
Glen Ellen CC, *Millis* ....18 [P] 508-376-2978
   glenellencc.com
Golf City, *West Bridgewater* ....18 [P] 508-588-5020
Granite Links GC At Quarry Hills, *Quincy* ....27 [S] 617-689-1900
   granitelinksgolfclub.com
Green Harbor GC, *Marshfield* ....18 [P] 781-834-7303
   greenharborgolfclub.com
Green Hill GC, *Worcester* ....18 [M] 508-799-1359
   greenhillgc.com
Greenock CC, *Lee* ....9 [S] 413-243-3323
   greenockcc.com
Groton CC, *Groton* ....9 [M] 978-448-2564
   grotoncountryclub.com
Hampden CC, *Hampden*.............................. 18 [S] 413-566-8010
   hampdencountryclub.com
Harmon Golf & Fitness Club, *Rockland*................ 9 [V] 781-871-7775
   harmongolf.com
Harwich Port GC, *Harwich Port*....................9 [P] 508-432-0250
Hatherly CC, *North Scituate*........................ 18 [V] 781-545-9814
   hatherlycc.com
Haverhill G&CC, *Haverhill*........................... 18 [V] 978-374-8522
   haverhillcc.com
Hawthorne CC, *North Dartmouth*................9 [P] 508-996-1766
   hawthornecountryclub.com
Heather Hill GC, *Plainville* ....27 [P] 508-695-0309
Hemlock Ridge GC, *Fiskdale*.........................9 [S] 508-347-9935
   hemlockridgegolfcourse.com
Heritage CC, *Charlton* .... 18 [S] 508-248-3591
   heritagecountryclub.com
Hickory Hill GC, *Methuen* ....18 [P] 978-686-0822
Hickory Ridge CC, *Amherst* .... 18 [S] 413-253-9320
   hickoryridgecc.com
Hidden Hollow CC, *Rehoboth* ....9 [P] 508-252-9392
Highfields G&CC, *Grafton*............................18 [P] 508-839-1945
   highfieldsgolfcc.com
Highland CC, *Attleboro* .... 9 [V] 508-222-0569
   highlandcountryclubattleboro.com
Highland Links GC, *North Truro*...................9 [P] 508-487-9201
   truro-ma.gov

[S] = SEMI-PRIVATE   [V] = PRIVATE   [U] = UNIVERSITY   [N] = UNIVERSITY-PRIVATE

MASSACHUSETTS — Golf Yellow Pages, 18th Edition

Hillcrest CC, *Leicester* .... 9 [S] 508-892-0963
Hillside CC, *Rehoboth* .... 9 [S] 508-252-9761
 hillsidecountryclub.com
Hillview GC, *North Reading* .... 18 [M] 978-664-4435
 hillviewgc.com
Holden Hills CC, *Holden* ....18 [P] 508-829-3129
 holdenhillsgolf.com
Holly Ridge GC, *Sandwich* ....18 [P] 508-428-5577
 hollyridgegolf.com
Holyoke CC, *Holyoke* .... 9 [S] 413-534-1933
 holyokecountryclub.com
Hopedale CC, *Hopedale* .... 9 [S] 508-473-9876
 hopedalecc.com
Hopkinton CC, *Hopkinton* .... 18 [V] 508-435-4630
 hopkintoncc.com
Hyannis GC, *Hyannis* ....18 [M] 508-362-2606
 hyannisgc.com
Hyannisport Club, *Hyannisport* .... 18 [V] 508-775-2978
 hyannisportclub.com
Indian Meadows GC, *Westborough* ....9 [P] 508-836-5460
 indianmeadowsgolf.com
Indian Pond CC, *Kingston* .... 18 [V] 781-585-0555
 indianpondcountryclub.com
Indian Ridge CC, *Andover* .... 18 [V] 978-475-5233
 indianridgecountryclub.us
International GC, *Bolton* .... 36 [V] 978-779-6911
 theinternational.com
Ipswich CC, *Ipswich* .... 18 [V] 978-356-3999
 ipswichclub.com
John F Parker GC, *Taunton* ....9 [P] 508-822-1797
 johnparker.com
Juniper Hill GC, *Northborough* .... 36 [U] 508-393-2444
 juniperhillgc.com
Kelley Greens GC, *Nahant* ....9 [M] 781-581-0840
 kelleygreens.com
Kernwood CC, *Salem* .... 18 [V] 978-745-1210
 kernwoodcc.org
Kettle Brook GC, *Paxton* ....18 [P] 508-799-4653
 kettlebrookgolfclub.com
King Rail Reserve GC, *Lynnfield* ....9 [M] 781-334-2877
 town.lynnfield.ma.us
Lakeview GC, *Wenham* ....9 [P] 978-468-9584
 lakeviewgc.com
Lakeville CC, *Lakeville* ....18 [P] 508-947-6630
 lakevillecountryclub.com
LeBaron Hills CC, *Lakeville* .... 18 [V] 508-923-5710
 lebaronhills.com
Ledgemont CC, *Seekonk* .... 18 [V] 508-761-3300
 ledgemontcc.com
Ledges Muni GC, *South Hadley* ....18 [M] 413-532-2307
 ledgesgc.com
Leicester CC, *Leicester* ....18 [P] 508-892-1390
 leicestercc.com
Leo J Martin Memorial GC, *Weston* ....18 [M] 781-891-1119
 state.ma.us/mdc
Lexington GC, *Lexington* .... 9 [V] 781-862-9614
 lex-golf.com
Little Harbor CC, *Wareham* ....18 [P] 508-295-2617
 littleharborcountryclub.com
Locust Valley CC, *Attleboro* ....9 [P] 508-222-1500
 longmeadowgolfclub.com
Long Meadow GC, *Lowell* ....9 [P] 978-452-8561
 longmeadowgolfclub.com
Longhis Exec Golf, *Southwick* ....9 [P] 413-569-0093

Longmeadow CC, *Longmeadow* .... 18 [V] 413-567-3381
 longmeadowcc.net
Lost Brook GC, *Norwood* ....18 [P] 781-769-2550
 lostbrookgolfclub.com
Ludlow CC, *Ludlow* .... 18 [V] 413-583-3434
 ludlowcountryclub.com
Maplegate CC, *Bellingham* ....18 [P] 508-966-4040
 maplegate.com
Maplewood GC, *Lunenburg* ....9 [P] 978-582-6694
Marion CC, *Marion* ....9 [P] 508-748-0199
Marlborough CC, *Marlborough* .... 18 [S] 508-481-5340
 marlboroughcountryclub.com
Marshfield CC, *Marshfield* .... 18 [V] 781-837-9353
 marshfieldcc.com
Maynard CC, *Maynard* .... 9 [V] 978-897-9885
 maynardcc.com
Meadow Brook GC, *Reading* .... 9 [V] 781-944-9703
 meadowbrookgolfclub.org
Meadow Creek GC, *Dracut* .... 18 [S] 978-459-5129
 meadowcreekgolfclub.com
Meadows GC, *Greenfield* ....9 [P] 413-773-9047
Merrimack GC, *Methuen* .... 18 [S] 978-685-9717
 merrimackvalleygolfclub.net
MGA Links At Mamantapett, *Norton* ....18 [P] 508-222-0555
 mamantapett.com
Miacomet GC, *Nantucket* .... 18 [S] 508-325-0333
 miacometgolf.com
Middlebrook CC, *Rehoboth* ....9 [P] 508-252-9395
Middleton GC, *Middleton* ....18 [P] 978-774-4075
 middletongolf.com
Milford CC Condominiums, *Milford* .... 9 [V] 508-478-1250
Mill Valley Golf Links, *Belchertown* ....18 [P] 413-323-4079
 millvalleygolflinks.com
Millwood Farms GC, *Framingham* ....18 [P] 508-877-1221
Milton Hoosic Club, *Canton* .... 9 [V] 781-828-9717
 miltonhoosicclub.com
Mink Meadows GC, *Vineyard Haven* ....9 [S] 508-693-0600
 minkmeadowsgc.com
Monoosnock CC, *Leominster* ....9 [S] 978-537-1872
 monoosnock.com
Mount Hood GC, *Melrose* ....18 [M] 781-665-6656
 mounthoodgolfclub.com
Mt Pleasant CC, *Boylston* .... 18 [V] 508-869-2000
 mountpleasantcc.org
Mt Pleasant GC, *Lowell* .... 9 [V] 978-453-2949
 mpgc.net
Myopia Hunt Club, *South Hamilton* .... 18 [V] 978-468-1402
 myopiahuntclub.org
Nabnasset Lake CC, *Westford* .... 9 [V] 978-692-2560
 nabnassetlakecc.com
Nantucket GC, *Nantucket* .... 18 [V] 508-257-8500
 nantucketgolfclub.com
Nashawtuc CC, *Concord* .... 18 [V] 978-369-6420
 nashawtuc.com
Needham GC, *Needham* .... 9 [V] 781-444-9692
 needhamgolfclub.com
Nehoiden GC, *Wellesley* .... 9 [N] 781-283-3398
 ngcwc.org
New England CC, *Bellingham* ....18 [P] 508-883-2300
 newenglandcountryclub.com
New Meadows GC, *Topsfield* ....9 [P] 978-887-9307
 newmeadowsgolf.com

96 [A] = MILITARY [M] = MUNICIPAL [P] = PUBLIC [R] = RESORT

MASSACHUSETTS

Newton Commonwealth GC, *Newton* .... 18 [P]   617-630-1971
  sterlinggolf.com
Nonquitt GC, *South Dartmouth* .... 9 [V]   508-997-2023
Norfolk GC, *Westwood* .... 9 [V]   781-326-9793
  norfolkgc.com
North Adams CC, *Clarksburg* .... 9 [S]   413-664-7149
  northadamscountryclub.com
North Andover CC, *North Andover* .... 9 [V]   978-683-1914
  northandovercountryclub.com
North Hill CC, *Duxbury* .... 9 [M]   781-934-3249
  johnsongolfmanagement.com
Northampton CC, *Leeds* .... 9 [V]   413-586-1898
  hampgolf.com
Northfield GC, *Northfield* .... 9 [P]   413-498-2432
Northfields GC, *Haverhill* .... 9 [V]   978-469-0464
Norton CC, *Norton* .... 18 [S]   508-285-2400
  nortoncountryclub.com
Norwood CC, *Norwood* .... 18 [P]   781-769-5880
  sterlinggolf.com
Oak Hill CC, *Fitchburg* .... 18 [V]   978-342-0237
  oakhillcc.org
Oak Ridge GC, *Feeding Hills* .... 18 [S]   413-789-7307
  oakridgegc.com
Oak Ridge GC, *Gill* .... 9 [P]   413-863-9693
  oakridgegolfclub.net
Oakley CC, *Watertown* .... 18 [V]   617-484-7748
  oakleycountryclub.org
Ocean Edge Resort & GC, *Brewster* .... 18 [R]   774-323-6200
  oceanedge.com
Old Sandwich GC, *Plymouth* .... 18 [V]   508-209-2200
  osgolfclub.com
Olde Barnstable Fairgrounds GC, *Marstons Mills* 18 [M]   508-420-1141
  obfgolf.com
Olde Salem Greens GC, *Salem* .... 9 [M]   978-744-2149
Olde Scotland Links, *Bridgewater* .... 18 [M]   508-279-3344
  oldescotlandlinks.com
Ould Newbury GC, *Newbury* .... 9 [S]   978-465-9888
  ouldnewbury.com
Oyster Harbors Club, *Osterville* .... 18 [V]   508-428-6666
  oysterharborsclub.org
Pakachoag GC, *Auburn* .... 9 [M]   508-755-3291
  johnsongolfmanagement.com
Patriot GC, *Bedford* .... 9 [A]   781-687-2396
  patriotgc.com
Paul Harney GC, *East Falmouth* .... 18 [P]   508-563-3454
  paulharneygolf.com
Pembroke CC, *Pembroke* .... 18 [S]   781-829-2273
  pembrokegolf.com
Petersham CC, *Petersham* .... 9 [P]   978-724-3388
  petershamcc.com
Pine Brook CC, *Weston* .... 18 [V]   781-893-4820
  pbccma.com
Pine Grove GC, *Florence* .... 18 [P]   413-584-4570
Pine Knoll GC, *East Longmeadow* .... 18 [P]   413-525-4444
Pine Meadows GC, *Lexington* .... 9 [M]   781-862-5516
  pinemeadowsgolfclub.com
Pine Oaks GC, *South Easton* .... 9 [S]   508-238-2320
  pineoaks.com
Pine Ridge CC, *North Oxford* .... 18 [S]   508-892-9188
  pineridgegolf.net
Pine Valley GC, *Rehoboth* .... 9 [P]   508-336-9815
Pinecrest GC, *Holliston* .... 18 [P]   508-429-9871
  pinecrestgolfclub.org

Pinehills GC, *Plymouth* .... 36 [R]   508-209-3000
  pinehillsgolf.com
Pleasant Valley CC, *Sutton* .... 18 [V]   508-865-5244
  pleasantvalleycc.com
Plymouth CC, *Plymouth* .... 18 [V]   508-746-0476
  plyccma.com
Pocasset GC, *Pocasset* .... 18 [V]   508-563-7171
  pocassetgolfclub.com
Ponkapoag GC, *Canton* .... 36 [M]   781-401-3191
  ponkapoaggolf.com
Pontoosuc Lake CC, *Pittsfield* .... 18 [P]   413-445-4217
Poquoy Brook GC, *Lakeville* .... 18 [P]   508-947-5261
  poquoybrook.com
Presidents GC, *North Quincy* .... 18 [M]   617-328-3444
  presidentsgc.com
Quaboag CC, *Monson* .... 9 [S]   413-267-5294
  quaboagcountryclub.com
Quail Hollow GC, *Oakham* .... 18 [P]   508-882-5516
  quailhollowgolf.net
Quail Ridge CC, *Acton* .... 18 [P]   978-264-0399
  quailridgecc.org
Quashnet Valley CC, *Mashpee* .... 18 [P]   508-477-4412
  quashnetvalley.com
Red Tail GC, *Devens* .... 18 [P]   978-772-3273
  redtailgolf.net
Reedy Meadow GC, *Lynnfield* .... 9 [M]   781-334-9877
  town.lynnfield.ma.us
Rehoboth CC, *Rehoboth* .... 18 [P]   508-252-6259
  rehobothcc.com
Renaissance GC, *Haverhill* .... 18 [V]   978-556-0900
  renaissancegolfclub.com
Reservation GC, *Mattapoisett* .... 9 [V]   508-758-3792
Ridder Farm GC, *East Bridgewater* .... 18 [P]   781-447-9003
  ridderfarm.com
River Bend CC, *West Bridgewater* .... 18 [P]   508-580-3673
  riverbendcc.com
Robert T Lynch Muni GC, *Chestnut Hill* .... 18 [M]   617-730-2078
  brooklinegolf.com
Rochester GC, *Rochester* .... 18 [P]   508-763-5155
Rockland GC, *Rockland* .... 18 [P]   781-878-5836
  rocklandgolfcourse.com
Rockport GC, *Rockport* .... 9 [S]   978-546-3340
  rockportgolfclub.net
Rolling Green GC, *Andover* .... 9 [P]   978-475-4066
Round Hill Community GC, *South Dartmouth* ... 9 [V]   508-992-4800
Royal Crest CC, *Walpole* .... 9 [V]   508-850-0003
Royal Oaks CC, *Southbridge* .... 18 [P]   508-764-4653
Sagamore Spring GC, *Lynnfield* .... 18 [P]   781-334-3151
  sagamoregolf.com
Salem CC, *Peabody* .... 18 [V]   978-538-5400
  salemcountryclub.org
Sandwich Hollows GC, *East Sandwich* .... 18 [S]   508-888-3384
  sandwichhollows.com
Sandy Burr CC, *Wayland* .... 18 [P]   508-358-7211
  sandyburr.com
Sankaty Head GC, *Siasconset* .... 18 [V]   508-257-6655
  sankatyheadgc.com
Sassamon Trace, *Natick* .... 9 [M]   508-655-1330
  sassamontrace.com
Scituate CC, *Scituate* .... 9 [V]   781-545-9768
  scituatecc.com
Scottish Meadow GC, *Warren* .... 9 [P]   413-436-5108
  scottishmeadowgolfclub.com

[S] = SEMI-PRIVATE   [V] = PRIVATE   [U] = UNIVERSITY   [N] = UNIVERSITY-PRIVATE

MASSACHUSETTS — Golf Yellow Pages, 18th Edition

Segregansett CC, *Taunton* .... 18 [V]   508-824-9144
  segregansett.com
Shaker Farms CC, *Westfield* .... 18 [P]   413-562-2770
  shakerfarmscc.com
Shaker Hills GC, *Harvard* .... 18 [P]   978-772-2227
  shakerhills.com
Sharon CC, *Sharon* .... 9 [V]   781-784-3878
  sharoncountryclub.com
Shining Rock GC, *Northbridge* .... 18 [S]   508-234-0400
  shiningrock.com
Siasconset GC, *Siasconset* .... 9 [P]   508-257-6596
Skyline CC, *Lanesboro* .... 18 [S]   413-445-5584
  skyline-cc.com
South Shore CC, *Hingham* .... 18 [M]   781-749-1747
  southshorecc.com
Southampton CC, *Southampton* .... 18 [P]   413-527-9815
Southers Marsh GC, *Plymouth* .... 18 [P]   508-830-3535
  southersmarsh.com
Southwick CC, *Southwick* .... 18 [P]   413-569-0136
  southwickcountryclub.com
Spring Valley CC, *Sharon* .... 18 [V]   781-784-5991
  springvalleycountryclub.com
Springfield CC, *West Springfield* .... 18 [P]   413-787-1560
  springfieldcc.org
Squirrel Run G&CC, *Plymouth* .... 18 [P]   508-746-5001
  squirrelrungolf.com
St Anne CC, *Feeding Hills* .... 18 [P]   413-786-2088
  stannecc.com
St Marks GC, *Southborough* .... 9 [U]   508-460-0946
  newenglandgolfcorp.com
Sterling National, *Sterling* .... 18 [V]   978-422-0275
  sterlingcc.com
Stockbridge GC, *Stockbridge* .... 18 [V]   413-298-3423
  stockbridgegc.com
Stone E Lea GC, *Attleboro* .... 18 [P]   508-222-9735
Stone Meadow Golf, *Lexington* .... 9 [P]   781-863-0445
  stonemeadowgolf.com
Stoneham Oaks GC, *Stoneham* .... 9 [M]   781-438-7888
Stonybrook GC, *Southborough* .... 9 [P]   508-485-3151
  stonybrook.com
Stow Acres CC, *Stow* .... 36 [P]   978-568-8690
  stowacres.com
Stowaway GC, *Stow* .... 9 [P]   978-897-4532
Strawberry Valley GC, *Abington* .... 9 [M]   781-878-2845
  johnsongolfmanagement.com
Sun Valley GC, *Rehoboth* .... 18 [P]   508-336-8686
Swansea CC, *Swansea* .... 27 [S]   508-379-9886
  swanseacountryclub.com
Swanson Meadows GC, *North Billerica* .... 9 [P]   978-670-7777
  swansonmeadows.com
Taconic GC, *Williamstown* .... 18 [U]   413-458-3997
  taconicgolf.net
Tatnuck CC, *Worcester* .... 9 [V]   508-757-0231
  tatnuckcc.com
Tedesco CC, *Marblehead* .... 18 [V]   781-631-2803
  tedescocc.org
Tekoa CC, *Westfield* .... 18 [S]   413-568-1064
  tekoacc.com
Templewood GC, *Templeton* .... 18 [P]   978-939-5031
  templewoodgolfcourse.com
Tewksbury CC, *Tewksbury* .... 9 [P]   978-640-0033
  tewksburycc.com

The Back Nine Club, *Lakeville* .... 18 [P]   508-947-9991
  thebacknineclub.com
The Bay Club At Mattapoisett, *Mattapoisett* .... 18 [V]   508-207-9200
  bayclubmatt.com
The Blandford Club, *Blandford* .... 9 [V]   413-848-2443
  theblandfordclubgolf.com
The Brookside Club, *Bourne* .... 18 [P]   508-743-4653
  thebrooksideclub.com
The Captains GC, *Brewster* .... 36 [M]   508-896-1716
  captainsgolfcourse.com
The CC At New Seabury, *Mashpee* .... 36 [R]   508-539-8322
  newseabury.com
The CC Brookline, *Chestnut Hill* .... 27 [V]   617-566-0240
  tcclub.org
The Club at Yarmouthport, *Yarmouth Port* ...... 18 [V]   508-362-8870
The Crosswinds GC, *Plymouth* .... 27 [P]   508-830-1199
  golfcrosswinds.com
The GC At Southport, *Mashpee* .... 9 [V]   508-477-7911
  southportoncapecod.com
The Kittansett Club, *Marion* .... 18 [V]   508-748-0192
  kittansett.org
The Meadow At Peabody, *Peabody* .... 18 [M]   978-532-9390
  peabodymeadowgolf.com
The Orchards GC, *South Hadley* .... 18 [N]   413-535-2582
  orchardsgolf.com
The Ranch GC, *Southwick* .... 18 [S]   413-569-9333
  theranchgolfclub.com
The Ridge Club, *Sandwich* .... 18 [V]   508-428-6800
  ridgeclubcapecod.com
The Woods of Westminster, *Westminster* .... 18 [S]   978-874-0278
  woodsofwestminster.com
Thomas Memorial G&CC, *Turners Falls* .... 9 [S]   413-863-8003
  tmgcc.net
Thomson CC, *North Reading* .... 18 [V]   978-664-2016
  thomsoncc.com
Thorny Lea GC, *Brockton* .... 18 [V]   508-586-2171
  thornyleagc.com
Touisset CC, *Swansea* .... 9 [P]   508-679-9577
  touissetcc.com
Townsend Ridge CC, *Townsend* .... 18 [P]   978-597-8400
  townsendridge.com
TPC of Boston At Great Woods, *Norton* .... 18 [V]   508-285-3200
  thetpcofboston.com
Trull Brook GC, *Tewksbury* .... 18 [P]   978-851-6731
  trullbrook.com
Turner Hill G&RC, *Ipswich* .... 18 [V]   978-356-7070
  turnerhill.com
Twin Brooks GC, *Hyannis* .... 18 [R]   508-775-7775
  twinbrooksgolf.net
Twin Hills CC, *Longmeadow* .... 18 [P]   413-567-0181
  twinhillscc.com
Twin Springs GC, *Bolton* .... 9 [P]   978-779-5020
  twinspringsgolf.com
Tyngsboro CC, *Tyngsboro* .... 9 [P]   978-649-7334
Unicorn Golf GC, *Stoneham* .... 9 [M]   781-438-9732
  ci.stoneham.ma.us
Vesper CC, *Tyngsboro* .... 18 [V]   978-459-3070
  vespercc.com
Veterans Memorial GC, *Springfield* .... 18 [M]   413-787-6449
  veteransgolfcourse.com
Village Links GC, *Plymouth* .... 18 [P]   508-830-4653
Vineyard GC, *Edgartown* .... 18 [V]   508-627-8930
  vineyardgolf.com

[A] = MILITARY   [M] = MUNICIPAL   [P] = PUBLIC   [R] = RESORT

Golf Yellow Pages, 18th Edition — MICHIGAN

Wachusett CC, *West Boylston* .... 18 [S] 508-835-2264
   wachusettcc.com
Wahconah CC, *Dalton* .... 18 [S] 413-684-1333
   wahconahcountryclub.com
Walpole CC, *Walpole* .... 18 [V] 508-668-7184
   walpolecc.com
Wampanoag GC, *Swansea* .... 9 [P] 508-379-9832
   wapanoagolf.com
Wampatuck CC of Canton, *Canton* .... 9 [V] 781-828-3771
   wampatuck.com
Waubeeka Golf Links, *Williamstown* .... 18 [P] 413-458-8355
   waubeeka.com
Waverly Oaks GC, *Plymouth* .... 27 [P] 508-224-6700
   waverlyoaksgolfclub.com
Wayland CC, *Wayland* .... 18 [P] 508-358-4775
   wayland-country-club.com
Wedgewood Pines CC, *Stow* .... 18 [V] 978-897-1790
   wedgewoodpines.com
Wellesley CC, *Wellesley Hills* .... 18 [V] 781-235-8497
   wellesleycc.com
Wenham CC, *Wenham* .... 18 [S] 978-468-4714
   wenhamcountryclub.com
Wentworth Hills GC, *Plainville* .... 18 [P] 508-699-9406
   wentworthhillsgolf.com
Westborough CC, *Westborough* .... 9 [M] 508-366-9947
   westborocountryclub.com
Westminster CC, *Westminster* .... 18 [S] 978-874-5938
   westminstercountryclub.com
Weston GC, *Weston* .... 18 [V] 781-894-2503
   westongolfclub.com
Westover Muni GC, *Granby* .... 18 [M] 413-547-8610
   ludlow.ma.us/golf/index.htm
Whaling City GC At New Bedford, *New Bedford* .. 18 [P] 508-996-9393
   johnsongolfmanagement.com
White Cliffs CC, *Plymouth* .... 18 [V] 508-888-2110
   whitecliffscc.com
White Pines GC, *Brockton* .... 9 [P] 508-586-3260
Whitinsville GC, *Whitinsville* .... 9 [V] 508-234-6210
   whitinsvillegolfcourse.com
Wianno GC, *Osterville* .... 18 [V] 508-428-9840
   wiannogolf.net
Widows Walk GC, *Scituate* .... 18 [M] 781-544-0032
   widowswalkgolf.com
William Devine GC At Franklin Park, *Dorchester* . 18 [M] 617-265-4084
   cityofbostongolf.com
Willowbend GC, *Mashpee* .... 27 [V] 508-539-5000
   willowbendcountryclub.com
Willowdale GC, *Mansfield* .... 9 [P] 508-339-3197
Winchendon GC, *Winchendon* .... 18 [U] 978-297-9897
   winchgolf.com
Winchester CC, *Winchester* .... 18 [V] 781-729-4085
   winchestercc.org
Winthrop GC, *Winthrop* .... 9 [V] 617-799-1455
   winthropgolf.com
Woburn CC, *Woburn* .... 9 [M] 781-933-9880
Wollaston GC, *Milton* .... 18 [V] 617-698-0909
   wollastongc.org
Woodbriar GC, *Falmouth* .... 9 [P] 508-495-5500
Woodland GC, *Auburndale* .... 18 [V] 617-527-9675
   woodlandgolfclub.com
Woods Hole GC, *Falmouth* .... 18 [V] 508-548-2932
   woodsholegolfclub.com
Worcester CC, *Worcester* .... 18 [V] 508-853-5087
   worcestercc.org

Worthington GC, *Worthington* .... 9 [V] 413-238-4464
   worthingtongolfclub.net
Wyantenuck CC, *Great Barrington* .... 18 [V] 413-528-3229
   wyantenuck.org
Wyckoff CC, *Holyoke* .... 18 [V] 413-536-3602
   wyckoffcountryclub.com

MICHIGAN

A Ga Ming Golf Resort, *Kewadin* .... 36 [R] 231-264-5081
   a-ga-ming.com
Alpena GC, *Alpena* .... 18 [P] 989-354-5052
   alpenagolfclub.com
Alpine GC, *Comstock Park* .... 18 [P] 616-784-1064
   alpinegolfmichigan.com
Alwyn Downs GC, *Marshall* .... 18 [P] 269-781-3905
Angels Crossing GC, *Vicksburg* .... 18 [S] 269-649-2700
   golfangelscrossing.com
Ann Arbor CC, *Ann Arbor* .... 18 [V] 734-426-4693
   annarborcc.com
Ann Arbor Golf & Outing Club, *Ann Arbor* .... 9 [V] 734-663-4044
   aagoc.org
Antrim Dells GC, *Ellsworth* .... 18 [P] 231-599-2679
   antrimdellsgolf.com
Apple Valley GC, *West Branch* .... 18 [P] 989-345-2971
   applevalleygolf.com
Arbor Hills GC, *Jackson* .... 18 [P] 517-750-2290
   arborhillsgolf.com
Arcadia Bluffs GC, *Arcadia* .... 18 [P] 231-889-3001
   arcadiabluffs.com
Arcadia Hills GC, *Attica* .... 9 [P] 810-724-6967
Arrowhead GC, *Lowell* .... 18 [P] 616-897-7264
   arrowheadontheweb.com
Arrowhead GC, *Caro* .... 18 [P] 989-673-2017
   1arrowhead.net
Atlas Valley CC, *Grand Blanc* .... 18 [V] 810-636-7977
   atlasvalleycountryclub.com
Back Nine of Barton City, *Barton City* .... 9 [P] 989-736-9556
Bald Mountain GC, *Lake Orion* .... 27 [P] 248-373-1110
   baldmountaingolf.com
Barton Hills CC, *Ann Arbor* .... 18 [V] 734-662-4955
   bhcconline.com
Battle Creek CC, *Battle Creek* .... 18 [V] 269-962-6121
   battlecreekcc.com
Bay City CC, *Bay City* .... 18 [V] 989-684-2611
   baycitycountryclub.com
Bay County GC, *Essexville* .... 18 [M] 989-892-2161
   baycounty-mi.gov/GolfCourse
Bay Harbor GC, *Bay Harbor* .... 27 [R] 231-439-4028
   bayharborgolf.com
Bay Meadows GC, *Traverse City* .... 18 [P] 231-946-7927
   baymeadowstc.com
Bay Pointe GC, *West Bloomfield* .... 18 [P] 248-360-0600
   oakmanagement.com
Bay Valley GC, *Bay City* .... 18 [R] 989-686-5400
   bayvalley.com
Beacon Hill GC, *Commerce Township* .... 18 [P] 248-684-2200
   beaconhillgc.com
Bear Lake County Highlands GC, *Bear Lake* .... 18 [P] 231-864-3817
   golfbearlake.com
Bear River Links GC, *Walloon Lake* .... 9 [P] 231-535-2400
Beaver Island GC, *Beaver Island* .... 9 [P] 231-448-2301
   beaverislandgolf.com

[S] = SEMI-PRIVATE   [V] = PRIVATE   [U] = UNIVERSITY   [N] = UNIVERSITY-PRIVATE

MICHIGAN — Golf Yellow Pages, 18th Edition

Bedford Hills GC, *Temperance* ....27 [P] 734-854-4653
  bedfordhillsgolf.com
Bedford Valley GC, *Battle Creek* ....18 [R] 269-965-3385
  gulllakeview.com
Beech Hollow GC, *Freeland* ....18 [P] 989-695-5427
  beechhollowgolf.com
Beech Woods GC, *Southfield* ....9 [M] 248-796-4655
  cityofsouthfield.com
Beeches GC, *South Haven* ....18 [P] 269-637-2600
  beechesgolfclub.com
Beechwood Greens GC, *Mt Morris* ....9 [P] 810-686-4200
Bella Vista GC, *Coldwater* ....18 [P] 517-238-8686
  bellavistagolf.org
Belle Isle GC, *Detroit* ....9 [M] 313-852-4086
  ci.detroit.mi.us
Belle River G&CC, *Riley* ....18 [P] 810-392-2121
  bellerivergolf.com
Bello Woods GC, *Macomb* ....27 [P] 586-949-1200
Belvedere GC, *Charlevoix* ....18 [S] 231-547-2512
  belvederegolfclub.com
Bennington GC, *Owosso* ....9 [P] 989-725-9194
Benona Shores GC, *Shelby* ....18 [P] 231-861-2098
  westmichigan.com
Bent Pine GC, *Whitehall* ....18 [P] 231-766-2045
  bentpinegolfclub.com
Berrien Hills GC, *Benton Harbor* ....18 [S] 269-925-9002
  berrienhills.com
Binder Park GC, *Battle Creek* ....27 [M] 269-979-8250
  binderparkgolf.com
Birch Pointe GC, *St Helen* ....9 [P] 989-389-7009
Birch Valley GC, *Sears* ....18 [P] 231-734-9112
Birchwood Farms G&CC, *Harbor Springs* ....27 [V] 231-526-6245
  birchwoodcc.com
Birchwood GC, *Howard City* ....18 [P] 231-762-4424
Bird Creek GC, *Port Austin* ....18 [P] 989-738-4653
  birdcreekgolf.com
Birmingham CC, *Birmingham* ....18 [V] 248-220-5144
  bhamcc.com
Black Bear GC, *Vanderbilt* ....18 [P] 989-983-4441
  golfblackbear.net
Black Forest At Wilderness Valley, *Gaylord* ....36 [P] 231-585-7090
  blackforestgolf.com
Black Lake GC, *Onaway* ....27 [P] 989-733-4653
  blacklakegolf.com
Black River CC, *Port Huron* ....18 [S] 810-982-5251
  blackrivergolfclub.com
Blackheath GC, *Oakland Township* ....18 [P] 248-601-8000
  blackheathgolf.com
Bloomfield Hills CC, *Bloomfield Hills* ....18 [V] 248-644-6262
  bloomfieldhillscc.org
Blossom Trails GC, *Benton Harbor* ....27 [S] 269-925-4951
  blossomtrailsgolfclub.com
Blythefield CC, *Belmont* ....18 [V] 616-361-2661
  blythefieldcc.org
Bonnie View GC, *Eaton Rapids* ....9 [P] 517-663-4363
  bonnieviewgolf.com
Boulder Creek GC, *Bessemer* ....9 [P] 906-932-9066
  bouldercreekgolfmi.com
Boulder Creek GC, *Belmont* ....18 [P] 616-363-1330
  bouldercreekgolfclub.com
Boulder Lakes GC, *Chesterfield* ....18 [P] 586-949-0633
  boulderlakesgolf.com

Boulder Pointe GC&CCtr, *Oxford* ....27 [P] 248-969-1500
  boulderpointe.net
Boyne Highlands GC, *Harbor Springs* ....81 [R] 231-526-3029
  boyne.com
Boyne Mountain Resort, *Boyne Falls* ....36 [R] 231-549-6028
  boyne.com
Brae Burn GC, *Plymouth* ....18 [P] 734-453-1900
  braeburngc.com
Braeside GC, *Rockford* ....18 [P] 616-866-1402
  braesidegolf.com
Bramblewood GC, *Holly* ....18 [P] 248-634-3481
  bramblewoodgolfcourse.com
Branson Bay GC, *Mason* ....18 [P] 517-663-4144
  bransonbay.com
Brentwood G&CC, *White Lake* ....18 [P] 248-684-2662
  brentwoodgc.com
Briar Hill GC, *Fremont* ....18 [P] 231-924-2070
  briarhillgolf.com
Briar Ridge GC, *Montrose* ....18 [P] 810-639-4653
Briarwood GC, *Caledonia* ....27 [P] 616-698-8720
  briarwoodlinks.com
Bridgeport CC, *Bridgeport* ....9 [P] 989-777-1750
  bridgeportgolfgrille.com
Brigadoon GC, *Grant* ....27 [P] 231-834-8200
  brigadoongolf.com
Broadmoor CC, *Caledonia* ....18 [P] 616-891-8000
  golfbroadmoor.com
Bronson GC, *Bronson* ....18 [S] 517-369-6745
  bronsongolfclub.com
Brookshire Inn & GC, *Williamston* ....18 [R] 517-655-4694
  brookshiregolfclub.com
Brookside GC, *Saline* ....18 [P] 734-429-4276
  brooksidesaline.com
Brookside GC, *Gowen* ....18 [P] 616-984-2381
  brooksidegolf.com
Brookwood GC, *Rochester Hills* ....9 [V] 248-651-4820
  mybrookwood.com
Brookwood GC, *Buchanan* ....18 [P] 269-695-7818
  golfbrookwood.com
Bruce Hills GC, *Romeo* ....18 [P] 586-752-7244
  golfbrucehills.com
Bucks Run GC, *Mt Pleasant* ....18 [P] 989-773-6830
  bucksrun.com
Bunker Hill GC, *Cadillac* ....9 [P] 231-775-3330
  netonecom.net/~bunker
Burning Oak CC, *Roscommon* ....18 [P] 989-821-9800
  burningoakcc.com
Burning Tree G&CC, *Macomb* ....18 [V] 586-468-1486
  burningtreegolf.com
Burr Oak GC, *Parma* ....18 [P] 517-531-4741
Bushwood GC, *Northville* ....9 [P] 734-420-3200
  bushwoodgc.com
Byron Hills GC, *Byron Center* ....27 [P] 616-878-1522
Caberfae Peaks Resort, *Cadillac* ....9 [R] 231-862-3000
  caberfaepeaks.com
Cadillac CC, *Cadillac* ....18 [S] 231-775-9442
  golfcadillac.com/countryclub
Calderone Farms GC, *Grass Lake* ....18 [P] 517-522-6661
  calderonegolfclub.com
Calumet GC, *Calumet* ....9 [P] 906-337-3911
  calumetgolfclub.com
Canadian Lakes CC, *Stanwood* ....36 [V] 231-972-8979
  clpoc.org

[A] = MILITARY   [M] = MUNICIPAL   [P] = PUBLIC   [R] = RESORT

Golf Yellow Pages, 18th Edition — MICHIGAN

Candlestone Golf & Resort, *Belding* .... 18 [R] 616-794-1580
  candlestone.com
Carleton Glen GC, *Carleton* .... 18 [P] 734-654-6201
Caro GC, *Caro* .... 9 [P] 989-673-7797
Carrington GC, *Monroe* .... 18 [S] 734-241-0707
  carringtongolf.net
Cascade GC - Championship, *Jackson* .... 18 [M] 517-788-4323
  cascadesgolfcourse.com
Cascade GC - Executive 9, *Jackson* .... 9 [M] 517-768-5846
  cascadesgolfcourse.com
Cascade Hills CC, *Grand Rapids* .... 27 [V] 616-949-0740
  cascadehillscc.com
Caseville GC, *Caseville* .... 9 [P] 989-856-2613
Castle Creek GC, *Lum* .... 27 [P] 810-724-0851
  castlecreekgolfclub.com
Cattails GC, *South Lyon* .... 18 [P] 248-486-8777
  cattailsgolfclub.com
CC of Detroit, *Grosse Pointe Farms* .... 27 [V] 313-881-8000
  ccofd.com
CC of Jackson, *Jackson* .... 27 [V] 517-782-5347
  countryclubofjackson.com
CC of Lansing, *Lansing* .... 18 [V] 517-318-5219
  cclansing.org
Cedar Chase GC, *Cedar Springs* .... 18 [P] 616-696-2308
  cedarchasegolfclub.com
Cedar Creek GC, *Battle Creek* .... 18 [P] 269-965-6423
  cedargolfclub.com
Cedar Farms GC, *Battle Creek* .... 18 [P] 269-979-7277
  cedargolfclub.com
Cedar Glen GC, *New Baltimore* .... 18 [S] 586-725-8156
  cedarglengolfclub.com
Cedar Valley GC, *Comins* .... 18 [P] 989-848-2792
Centennial Acres, *Sunfield* .... 27 [P] 517-566-8055
  centennialacres.com
Centennial CC, *Grand Rapids* .... 18 [V] 616-954-0444
  centennialcc.com
Centerview GC, *Adrian* .... 18 [P] 517-263-8081
Century Oaks GC, *Elkton* .... 9 [P] 989-375-4419
Champion Hill GC, *Beulah* .... 18 [P] 231-882-9200
  championhill.com
Chandler Park GC, *Detroit* .... 18 [M] 313-331-7755
  chandlerpark.americangolf.com
Chardell GC, *Bath* .... 9 [P] 517-641-4123
Charlevoix G&CC, *Charlevoix* .... 18 [V] 231-547-9796
  chxcountryclub.com
Charlevoix GC, *Charlevoix* .... 9 [M] 231-547-3268
  cityofcharlevoix.org
Charlotte CC, *Charlotte* .... 9 [V] 517-543-4018
Chase Hammond GC, *Muskegon* .... 18 [P] 231-766-3035
  chasehammondgolfclub.com
Cheboygan G&CC, *Cheboygan* .... 18 [S] 231-627-4264
  cheboygangolf.com
Chemung Hills GC, *Howell* .... 18 [P] 517-546-7706
  chemunghillsgolfclub.com
Cherry Creek GC, *Shelby Township* .... 18 [P] 586-254-7700
  cherrycreekgolf.com
Cherrywood GC, *Ottawa Lake* .... 9 [S] 734-856-6669
  cherrywoodgolfclub.com
Cheshire Hills GC, *Allegan* .... 27 [P] 269-673-2882
  cheshirehills.com
Chestnut Hills GC, *Bear Lake* .... 18 [P] 231-864-2458
Chestnut Valley GC, *Harbor Springs* .... 18 [P] 231-526-9100
  chestnutvalleygolf.com

Chikaming CC, *Lakeside* .... 18 [V] 269-469-5484
  chikamingcc.org
Chippewa Hills CC, *Durand* .... 9 [P] 989-743-3277
Chisholm Hills GC, *Lansing* .... 18 [S] 517-694-0169
  chisholmhillsgolfclub.com
Clark Lake GC, *Brooklyn* .... 27 [P] 517-592-6259
  clarklakegolfcourse.com
Clearbrook GC, *Saugatuck* .... 18 [P] 269-857-2000
  clearbrookgolfclub.com
Clio GC, *Clio* .... 18 [V] 810-687-0340
  cliocountryclub.com
College Fields GC, *Okemos* .... 18 [P] 517-332-8100
  collegefields.net
Concord Hills GC, *Concord* .... 18 [P] 517-524-8337
Copper Creek GC, *Farmington Hills* .... 9 [P] 248-489-1777
  coppercreekgolf.net
Copper Hills G&CC, *Oxford* .... 27 [P] 248-969-9808
  copperhills.com
Copper Ridge GC, *Davison* .... 18 [P] 810-658-7775
  copperridgegolfclub.com
Corunna Hills GC, *Corunna* .... 9 [P] 989-743-4693
Country Meadows GC, *Escanaba* .... 9 [P] 906-786-1565
Country Town GC, *Springport* .... 9 [P] 517-857-4653
County Line GC, *Reese* .... 9 [P] 989-868-4991
  countylinegolfcourse.com
Coyote GC, *New Hudson* .... 18 [P] 248-486-1228
  coyotegolfclub.com
Coyote Preserve GC, *Fenton* .... 18 [P] 810-714-3206
  coyotepreserve.com
Cracklewood GC, *Macomb* .... 18 [P] 586-781-0808
  cracklewood.com
Crestview GC, *Kalamazoo* .... 18 [P] 269-349-1111
  crestviewgolfcourse.com
Crestview GC, *Zeeland* .... 18 [P] 616-875-8101
  crestviewgolf.com
Crooked Creek GC, *Saginaw* .... 18 [P] 989-781-0050
  thecreekandthevalley.com
Crooked Tree GC, *Petoskey* .... 18 [P] 231-439-4030
  boyne.com
Crown GC, *Traverse City* .... 18 [P] 231-946-2975
  golfthecrown.com
Crystal Downs CC, *Frankfort* .... 18 [V] 231-352-7979
Crystal GC, *Crystal* .... 18 [R] 989-235-6616
Crystal Lake GC, *Beulah* .... 18 [P] 231-882-4061
  clgolfclub.com
Crystal Mountain GC, *Thompsonville* .... 36 [R] 231-378-2911
  crystalmountain.com
Crystal View Muni GC, *Crystal Falls* .... 9 [M] 906-875-3029
  crystalfalls.org
Currie Muni GC, *Midland* .... 27 [M] 989-839-9600
  curriegolf.com
Custer Greens, *Battle Creek* .... 9 [P] 269-968-7398
Davison GC, *Davison* .... 18 [V] 810-653-5301
  davisoncc.com
De Mor Hills GC, *Morenci* .... 18 [P] 517-458-6679
  demorhills.com
Dearborn CC, *Dearborn* .... 18 [V] 313-561-4433
  dearborncountryclub.net
Dearborn Hills GC, *Dearborn* .... 18 [M] 313-563-4653
  dearbornhills.com
Deer Run GC, *Lowell* .... 18 [P] 616-897-8481
  deerrungolfclub.net
Deer Run GC, *Horton* .... 9 [P] 517-688-3350

[S] = SEMI-PRIVATE   [V] = PRIVATE   [U] = UNIVERSITY   [N] = UNIVERSITY-PRIVATE

MICHIGAN — Golf Yellow Pages, 18th Edition

Course	Location	Holes	Type	Phone
Deer View GC	Imlay City	9	[P]	810-395-7495
Deme Acres GC	Petersburg	18	[P]	734-279-1151
demeacres.com				
Detroit GC	Detroit	36	[V]	313-345-1818
detroitgolfclub.org				
Devils Knob GC	Harrison	9	[P]	989-539-9742
Devils Lake GC	Manitou Beach	18	[P]	517-547-3653
Devils Ridge GC	Oxford	18	[P]	248-969-0100
devilsridgegolfclub.com				
Diamond Lake GC	Cassopolis	9	[P]	269-445-3143
Diamond Springs GC	Hamilton	18	[P]	269-751-4545
diamondspringsgolf.com				
Double R Ranch Resort	Belding	9	[R]	616-794-0520
doublerranch.com				
Dowagiac Elks GC	Dowagiac	9	[S]	269-782-3889
Downing Farms GC	Northville	18	[P]	248-486-0990
downingfarmsgolf.com				
Drummond Island GC	Drummond Island	9	[M]	906-493-5406
drummondisland.com				
Duck Lake CC	Albion	18	[V]	517-629-9015
ducklakecc.com				
Dundee GC	Dundee	9	[P]	734-529-2321
Dunham Hills G&CC	Hartland	18	[P]	248-887-9170
dunhamhills.com				
Dunmaglas GC	Charlevoix	18	[P]	231-547-4653
dunmaglas.com				
Dutch Hollow GC	Durand	18	[P]	989-288-3960
E M S Links	Sandusky	9	[P]	810-648-2256
Eagle Creek GC	Allegan	9	[S]	269-673-8261
eaglecreekallegan.com				
Eagle Crest GC	Ypsilanti	18	[P]	734-487-2441
eaglecrestresort.com				
Eagle Eye GC	East Lansing	18	[P]	517-641-4570
hawkhollow.com				
Eagle Glen GC	Farwell	18	[P]	989-588-4424
golfeagleglen.biz				
Eagle Island GC	Muskegon	9	[P]	231-773-7171
Eagle Mountain GC	Iron Mountain	9	[P]	906-774-0003
Eagle Ridge GC	Glennie	18	[P]	989-735-3500
eagleridgemi.com				
Eagle View GC	Mason	18	[P]	517-676-5366
Earhart GC	Ann Arbor	9	[P]	734-994-5314
Eastern Hills GC	Kalamazoo	27	[M]	269-385-8175
kalamazoogolf.org				
Edgewood CC	Commerce Township	18	[V]	248-363-7111
edgewoodcountryclub.org				
Edgewood Greens GC	Prescott	9	[P]	989-873-5427
Egypt Valley CC	Ada	36	[V]	616-676-2626
egyptvalley.com				
Eldorado GC	Cadillac	18	[P]	231-779-9977
golfeldorado.com				
Eldorado GC	Mason	27	[S]	517-676-2854
eldorado27.com				
Elk Rapids GC	Elk Rapids	9	[P]	231-264-8891
golfelkrapids.com				
Elk Ridge GC	Atlanta	18	[P]	989-785-2275
elkridgegolf.com				
Ella Sharp Park GC	Jackson	18	[P]	517-788-4066
ellasharppark.com				
Elmbrook GC	Traverse City	18	[P]	231-946-9180
elmbrookgolf.com				
Emerald at Maple Creek GC	St Johns	18	[P]	989-224-6287
emeraldgolfcourse.com				
Emerald Vale GC	Manton	18	[S]	231-824-3631
emeraldvale.com				
English Hills CC	Grand Rapids	18	[P]	616-784-3420
englishhills.net				
Epworth Heights GC	Ludington	9	[R]	231-843-8011
Escanaba CC	Escanaba	18	[P]	906-786-4430
escanabacc.com				
Evergreen GC	Grand Haven	18	[P]	616-296-1200
evergreenexecgolfclub.com				
Evergreen Hills GC	Southfield	9	[M]	248-796-4666
cityofsouthfield.com				
Fairview Hills GC	Mio	9	[P]	989-848-5810
Fairway Farms GC	Muskegon	9	[V]	231-780-0196
Falcon GC	East Lansing	9	[P]	517-371-3484
hawkhollow.com				
Falcon Head GC	Big Rapids	18	[P]	231-796-2613
falconheadgc.com				
Family Golf	North Muskegon	9	[P]	231-766-2217
Farmington Hills GC	Farmington Hills	18	[M]	248-476-5910
ci.farmington-hills.mi.us				
Faulkwood Shores GC	Howell	18	[P]	517-546-4180
faulkwoodshoresgolf.com				
Fawn Crest GC	Wellston	9	[P]	231-848-4174
fawncrestgolf.com				
Fellows Creek GC	Canton	27	[M]	734-728-1300
fellowscreekgolf.com				
Fellowship Greens GC	Grand Rapids	18	[P]	616-942-1330
Fenton Farms GC	Fenton	18	[P]	810-629-1212
fentonfarms.com				
Fern Hill CC	Clinton Township	18	[P]	586-286-4700
fernhillcc.com				
Fields GC	Ithaca	18	[P]	989-875-4612
thefieldsgolfcourse.com				
Fieldstone GC of Auburn Hill	Auburn Hills	18	[M]	248-370-9354
fieldstonegolfclub.com				
Firefly Golf Links	Clare	18	[S]	989-386-3510
fireflygolflinks.com				
Flint Elks GC	Grand Blanc	18	[V]	810-743-0730
elks.org/Lodges/LodgeFacilities.cfm?LodgeNumber=222				
Flint GC	Flint	18	[V]	810-743-6750
flintgolfclub.com				
Flushing Valley G&CC	Flushing	18	[V]	810-487-0471
flushingvalleycc.com				
Fore Lakes GC	Kimball	18	[P]	810-982-3673
forelakes.com				
Forest Akers GC MSU	Lansing	36	[U]	517-355-1635
golf.msu.edu				
Forest Dunes GC	Roscommon	18	[R]	989-275-0700
forestdunesgolf.com				
Forest Lake CC	Bloomfield Hills	18	[V]	248-332-7070
flcc.us				
Forest View Golf Ctr	Midland	9	[P]	989-837-6704
forestviewgolf.com				
Fountains Golf & Banquet	Clarkston	18	[P]	248-625-3731
golfthefountains.com				
Four Lakes CC	Edwardsburg	18	[P]	269-699-5701
Four Winds GC	East Lansing	9	[P]	517-339-1500
Fox Creek GC	Livonia	18	[M]	248-471-3400
golflivonia.com				
Fox Hills G&BanqCtr	Plymouth	63	[P]	734-453-7272
foxhills.com				
Fox Run CC	Grayling	18	[P]	989-348-4343
foxruncc.com				

102 [A] = MILITARY [M] = MUNICIPAL [P] = PUBLIC [R] = RESORT

MICHIGAN

Course	Holes	Type	Phone
Frankfort GC, *Frankfort*	9	[P]	231-352-4101
Franklin Hills CC, *Franklin*	18	[V]	248-851-6632
franklinhills.com			
Fruitport CC, *Muskegon*	18	[P]	231-798-3355
fruitportbanquetcenter.com			
Garden GC, *Garden*	18	[R]	906-644-2693
gardengolfcourse.com			
Garland Resort, *Lewiston*	72	[R]	989-786-2211
garlandusa.com			
Garver Lake GC, *Edwardsburg*	9	[P]	269-663-6463
Gateway GC, *Romulus*	18	[P]	734-721-4100
gatewaygolfclub.org			
Gausss Green Valley GC, *Jackson*	18	[P]	517-764-0270
Gaylord CC, *Gaylord*	18	[S]	231-546-3376
gaylordcountryclub.org			
GC At Apple Mountain, *Freeland*	18	[R]	989-781-0170
applemountain.com			
Genesee Hills GC, *Grand Blanc*	18	[V]	810-344-9844
geneseehills.com			
Genesee Valley Meadows, *Swartz Creek*	18	[P]	810-732-1401
Gentzs Homestead GC, *Marquette*	9	[P]	906-249-1002
gentzhomestead.com			
George Young GC, *Gaastra*	18	[P]	906-265-3401
georgeyoung.com			
Georgetown CC, *Ann Arbor*	9	[S]	734-971-5500
georgetowncc.org			
Germania Town & CC, *Saginaw*	18	[V]	989-799-5522
germaniatcc.com			
Giant Oak GC, *Temperance*	27	[P]	734-847-6733
giantoakgolfclub.com			
Gladstone GC, *Gladstone*	18	[P]	906-428-9646
gladstonegolf.com			
Gladwin Heights GC, *Gladwin*	18	[P]	989-426-9941
Glen Oaks GC, *Farmington*	18	[M]	248-851-8356
destinationoakland.com			
Glenbrier GC, *Perry*	18	[P]	517-625-3800
glenbrier.com			
Gleneagle GC, *Hudsonville*	18	[P]	616-457-8800
gegolfclub.com			
Glenhurst GC, *Redford*	18	[M]	313-592-8758
redfordtwp.com			
Glenkerry GC, *Greenville*	18	[P]	616-225-4653
glenkerrygolf.com			
Glenlore GC, *Commerce Township*	18	[P]	248-363-7997
Glenn Shores GC, *South Haven*	9	[P]	269-227-3226
glennshores.com			
Gogebic CC, *Ironwood*	18	[S]	906-932-2515
Golden Hawk GC, Rest & Banquet Ctr, *Casco*	18	[P]	586-727-4681
goldenhawkgolfclub.com			
Golden Sands GC, *Mears*	9	[P]	231-873-4909
goldensandsgolfcourse.com			
Goodrich CC, *Goodrich*	18	[S]	810-636-2493
goodrichcountryclub.com			
Gowanie GC, *Harrison Township*	18	[V]	586-468-1374
Gracewil GC, *Grand Rapids*	36	[P]	616-784-2455
gracewil.com			
Grand Beach Muni GC, *New Buffalo*	9	[S]	269-469-4888
Grand Haven GC, *Grand Haven*	18	[P]	616-842-4040
grandhavengolfclub.com			
Grand Ledge GC, *Grand Ledge*	18	[P]	517-627-2495
grandledgecountryclub.com			
Grand Prairie GC, *Kalamazoo*	9	[M]	269-388-4447
grandprairiegc.com			
Grand Rapids CC, *Grand Rapids*	27	[P]	616-949-2820
grandrapidsgolf.net			
Grand Rapids Sparta Moose GC, *Sparta*	9	[V]	616-887-9126
moose50.org			
Grand Traverse Resort & Spa, *Acme*	54	[R]	231-534-6000
grandtraverseresort.com			
Grand View GC, *Kalkaska*	18	[S]	231-258-3244
grandviewgolf.com			
Grand View GC, *New Era*	18	[P]	231-861-6616
grandviewgc.com			
Grande GC, *Jackson*	18	[P]	517-768-9494
grandegolfclub.com			
Grayling CC, *Grayling*	18	[S]	989-348-5618
graylingcountryclub.net			
Great Oaks CC, *Rochester*	18	[V]	248-651-6566
greatoakscc.com			
Green Acres GC, *Bridgeport*	18	[P]	989-777-3510
greenacresgc.com			
Green Briar GC, *Lupton*	18	[P]	989-473-4900
greenbriargolf.net			
Green Hills GC, *Pinconning*	18	[P]	989-697-3011
Green Meadows GC, *Monroe*	18	[P]	734-242-5566
greenmeadowsgolf.com			
Green Oaks GC, *Ypsilanti*	18	[M]	734-485-0881
ytown.org			
Green Trees GC, *Gaylord*	18	[P]	989-732-6006
Green Valley GC, *Sturgis*	18	[P]	269-651-6331
Greenbriar GC & RV Park, *Brooklyn*	18	[R]	517-592-6943
greenbriargolfclub.com			
Greenbrier GC, *Mayville*	18	[P]	989-843-6575
Greenbush GC, *Greenbush*	9	[R]	989-724-6356
greenbushgc.com			
Greenville CC, *Greenville*	9	[V]	616-754-5451
Greystone GC, *Washington*	18	[P]	586-752-7030
golfgreystone.com			
Groesbeck Muni GC, *Lansing*	18	[M]	517-483-4333
lansingmi.gov/parks/golf			
Grosse Ile G&CC, *Grosse Ile*	18	[V]	734-676-1169
gigcc.com			
Gull Lake CC, *Richland*	18	[V]	269-629-9311
gulllakecc.com			
Gull Lake View GC & Resort, *Augusta*	36	[R]	269-731-4149
gulllakeview.com			
Gun Ridge GC, *Hastings*	9	[P]	269-948-8366
gunridgegolf.com			
Hadley Acres G&CC, *Hadley*	18	[P]	810-797-4820
Hampshire GC, *Dowagiac*	36	[S]	269-782-7476
Hampton G&RecC, *Rochester Hills*	9	[P]	248-852-3250
golfthehampton.com			
Hankerd Hills GC, *Pleasant Lake*	27	[P]	517-769-2507
hankerdhills.com			
Harbor Beach GC, *Harbor Beach*	9	[R]	989-479-3423
Harbor Point GC, *Harbor Springs*	18	[S]	231-526-2951
harborpointgolfclub.com			
Harbour Club GC, *Belleville*	9	[P]	734-699-8844
golfharbourclub.com			
Hartland Glen GC, *Hartland*	36	[P]	248-887-3777
hartlandglen.com			
Hastings CC, *Hastings*	18	[P]	269-945-2756
hastingscc.org			
Hawk Hollow GC, *Bath*	27	[P]	517-641-4295
hawkhollow.com			

[S] = SEMI-PRIVATE [V] = PRIVATE [U] = UNIVERSITY [N] = UNIVERSITY-PRIVATE

MICHIGAN

Golf Yellow Pages, 18th Edition

Hawk Meadows At Dama Farms, *Howell*............18 [P] 517-546-4635
  hawkmeadows.com
Hawks Eye GC, *Bellaire*...........................18 [R] 231-533-4295
  golfhawkseye.com
HawksHead Links, *South Haven*...................18 [P] 269-639-2121
  hawksheadlinks.com
Heather Highlands GC, *Holly*....................27 [P] 248-634-6800
  heatherhighlands.com
Heather Hills GC, *Romeo*........................18 [P] 810-798-3971
  heatherhills.net
Hemlock GC, *Ludington*..........................18 [R] 231-845-1300
  hemlockgolfclub.com
Heritage Glen GC, *Paw Paw*......................18 [S] 269-657-2552
  heritageglengolf.com
Hessel Ridge GC, *Hessel*........................18 [P] 906-484-2107
  hesselridge.com
Hiawatha Sportsmans GC, *Engadine*...............9 [V] 906-477-6683
  hiawathaclub.com
Hickory Creek GC, *Ypsilanti*....................18 [P] 734-454-1850
  hickorycreekgolf.com
Hickory Hill GC, *Wixom*.........................9 [P] 248-624-4733
Hickory Hills GC, *Jackson*......................36 [P] 517-750-3636
  hickoryhillsclub.com
Hickory Hollow GC, *Macomb*......................18 [P] 586-949-9033
Hickory Knoll GC, *Whitehall*....................36 [P] 231-894-5535
Hickory Ridge, *Galesburg*.......................27 [P] 269-382-6212
  golfhickoryridge.com
Hickory Sticks GC, *Ann Arbor*...................18 [P] 734-913-8140
  hickorysticks.org
Hidden Harbour GC, *Caseville*...................9 [P] 989-856-3991
Hidden Oaks GC, *St Louis*.......................18 [P] 989-681-3404
  hiddenoaksgolf.com
Hidden River Golf & Casting, *Brutus*............18 [P] 231-529-4653
  hiddenriver.com
Hidden Valley GC, *Shelbyville*..................18 [S] 269-672-7866
  hiddenvalleygc.com
Highland GC, *Escanaba*..........................18 [S] 906-466-7457
  highlandgolfclub.net
Highland Hills GC, *Highland*....................18 [P] 248-887-4481
  highlandhillsgolfclub.com
Highland Hills GC, *Dewitt*......................18 [P] 517-669-9873
Hills Heart of the Lakes GC, *Brooklyn*..........18 [P] 517-592-2110
  hillsgolfcourse.com
Hillsdale G&CC, *Hillsdale*......................9 [V] 517-437-2201
Hilltop GC, *Plymouth*...........................18 [S] 734-453-9800
  hilltopgolfclub.com
Holiday Greens GC, *Mt Pleasant*.................18 [R] 989-772-2905
Holiday Meadows GC, *Durand*.....................9 [R] 810-621-5454
  holidayshoresrv.com
Holland CC, *Holland*............................18 [V] 616-396-1255
  hollandcc.org
Holland Lake GC, *Sheridan*......................9 [P] 989-291-5757
Holly Meadows GC, *Capac*........................18 [P] 810-395-4653
  hollymeadows.com
Huckleberry Creek GC, *Pewamo*...................18 [P] 989-593-3305
Hudson Mills Metropark GC, *Dexter*..............18 [M] 734-426-0466
  metroparks.com
Hunters Ridge GC, *Howell*.......................18 [P] 517-545-4653
  golfhuntersridge.com
Huntmore GC, *Brighton*..........................18 [P] 810-225-4498
  huntmoregolfclub.com
Huron Breeze GC, *Au Gres*.......................18 [P] 989-876-6868
  huronbreeze.com

Huron Hills GC, *Ann Arbor*......................18 [M] 734-971-6840
  a2gov.org
Huron Meadows Metropark GC, *Brighton*...........18 [M] 810-231-4084
  metroparks.com
Huron Shores GC, *Port Sanilac*..................18 [S] 810-622-9961
  huronshoresgolfclub.com
Idyl Wyld CC, *Livonia*..........................18 [M] 734-464-6325
  golflivonia.com
IMA Brookwood GC, *Burton*.......................18 [S] 810-742-4930
  brookwoodgolfclub.com
Independence Green GC, *Farmington Hills*........18 [P] 248-477-7092
Indian Hills GC, *Stephenson*....................9 [P] 906-753-4781
  nuttall.net/ihills
Indian Hills GC, *Okemos*........................9 [P] 517-349-1010
  ihcustomgolf.com
Indian Lake G&CC, *Manistique*...................18 [S] 906-341-5600
  indianlakegolfclub.net
Indian Lake Hills GC, *Eau Claire*...............27 [R] 269-782-2540
  indianlakehills.com
Indian River GC, *Indian River*..................18 [S] 231-238-7011
  indianrivergolfclub.com
Indian Run GC, *Scotts*..........................18 [P] 269-327-1327
  irgolfclub.com
Indian Springs Metropark GC, *White Lake*........18 [M] 248-625-7870
  metroparks.com
Indian Trails GC, *Grand Rapids*.................18 [M] 616-245-2021
  grand-rapids.mi.us
Indianhead Mountain Resort, *Wakefield*..........9 [R] 906-229-5181
  indianheadmtn.com
Indianwood G&CC, *Lake Orion*....................36 [V] 248-693-8049
  indianwoodgolfandcountryclub.com
Inkster Valley GC, *Inkster*.....................18 [M] 734-722-8020
  waynecountyparks.org
Interlochen G&CC, *Interlochen*..................18 [S] 231-275-7311
  interlochengolf.com
Inverness CC, *Chelsea*..........................9 [V] 734-475-8746
  inverness-mi.com
Irish Hills GC, *Onsted*.........................9 [P] 517-467-2997
  tcapts.com/IHG.htm
Irish Oaks GC, *Gladstone*.......................18 [P] 906-428-2616
  lakebluffretirement.com
Iron River CC, *Iron River*......................9 [S] 906-265-3161
Ironwood GC, *Byron Center*......................18 [P] 616-538-4000
  golfironwoodgc.com
Ironwood GC, *Howell*............................18 [P] 517-546-3211
  golfironwood.com
Ironwood Links GC, *Mason*.......................18 [P] 517-676-3116
  ironwoodlinksgolfcourse.com
Island Hills GC, *Centreville*...................18 [P] 269-467-7261
  islandhillsgolf.com
Iyopawa Island GC, *Coldwater*...................9 [P] 517-238-2216
  iyopawaisland.com
Jenkins GC, *Litchfield*.........................9 [P] 517-542-3121
Jeptha Lake GC, *Bloomingdale*...................9 [P] 269-427-7502
  jepthalakegolf.com
Kalamazoo CC, *Kalamazoo*........................27 [V] 269-344-0752
  kalamazoocountryclub.com
Katke GC Ferris State U, *Big Rapids*............18 [U] 231-591-3765
  ferris.edu/katke
Kearsley Lake GC, *Flint*........................18 [M] 810-736-0930
  cityofflint.com
Kensington Metropark GC, *Milford*...............18 [M] 248-685-9332
  metroparks.com

104   [A] = MILITARY   [M] = MUNICIPAL   [P] = PUBLIC   [R] = RESORT

Golf Yellow Pages, 18th Edition — MICHIGAN

Kent CC, *Grand Rapids* .... 18 [V] 616-363-6811
  kentcountryclub.com
Keweenaw Mountain Lodge, *Copper Harbor*........9 [M] 906-289-4403
  atthelodge.com
Kimberley Oaks GC, *St Charles* .... 18 [S] 989-865-8261
  kimberleyoaks.com
King Par GC, *Flushing*.........................9 [P] 810-732-2470
  kingpar.com
Klinger Lake CC, *Sturgis* .... 18 [V] 269-651-4653
  klingerlakecc.com
Knoll View GC, *Au Gres*..................... 18 [S] 989-876-4653
  golfknollview.com
Knollwood CC, *West Bloomfield* .... 18 [V] 248-855-1800
  knollwoodcountryclub.net
L Anse GC, *Lanse*..............................9 [S] 906-524-6600
L E Kaufman GC, *Wyoming* ....18 [M] 616-538-5050
  accesskent.com/parks
Lac Vieux Desert GC, *Watersmeet*...........18 [P] 906-358-0303
  lvdcasino.com
Lake Cora Hills GC, *Paw Paw* .... 18 [P] 269-657-4074
  lakecorahillsgolfclub.com
Lake Doster GC, *Plainwell* .... 18 [S] 269-685-5308
  lakedostergolf.com
Lake Erie Metropark GC, *Brownstown* ....18 [M] 734-379-5020
  metroparks.com
Lake Forest GC, *Ann Arbor* ....18 [P] 734-994-8580
  lakeforestgc.com
Lake LeAnn GC, *Jerome*.........................9 [P] 517-688-3445
Lake Michigan Hills GC, *Benton Harbor*.......18 [P] 269-849-2722
  lakemichiganhills.com
Lake Monterey GC, *Dorr*.....................18 [P] 616-896-8118
Lake O The Hills GC, *Haslett*...................9 [P] 517-339-9445
Lakeland Hills GC, *Jackson* ....18 [P] 517-764-5292
Lakelands G&CC, *Brighton* .... 18 [V] 810-231-3010
  lakelandsgolf.com
Lakes of Taylor GC, *Taylor* ....18 [M] 734-287-2100
  taylorgolf.com
Lakes of the North Deer Run GC, *Mancelona* ....18 [S] 231-585-6000
  lakesofthenorth.com
Lakeside GC, *Gladwin* ....9 [P] 989-426-1664
Lakeside Links, *Ludington*....................27 [P] 231-843-3660
  lakesidelinks.com
Lakeview Hills CC & Resort, *Lexington*.................36 [R] 810-359-8901
  lakeviewhills.com
Lakewood Shores Resort, *Oscoda* ....72 [R] 989-739-2075
  lakewoodshores.com
Lapeer CC, *Lapeer* .... 18 [S] 810-664-2442
  lapeercountryclub.com
Lawton GC, *Lawton* ....9 [P] 269-624-2051
Leaning Tree GC, *Wales*......................18 [P] 810-367-3528
  leaningtreegolf.com
Ledge Meadows GC, *Grand Ledge*.............18 [P] 517-627-7492
  ledgemeadowsgolfcourse.com
Leland CC, *Leland* .... 18 [V] 231-256-9721
Lenawee CC, *Adrian*......................... 18 [V] 517-265-8227
  lenaweecc.com
Les Cheneaux GC, *Cedarville* ....9 [P] 906-484-3606
  lescheneauxgolfclub.com
Leslie Park GC, *Ann Arbor* ....18 [M] 734-794-6245
  a2gov.org
Lincoln CC, *Grand Rapids* ....18 [P] 616-453-6348
Lincoln GC, *Muskegon* .... 18 [S] 231-766-2226
  lincolngolfcourse.com

Lincoln Hills GC, *Birmingham* ....9 [M] 248-647-4468
  ci.birmingham.mi.us
Lincoln Hills GC, *Ludington*................... 18 [S] 231-843-4666
  golflincolnhillsludington.com
Links At Lake Erie, *Monroe*...................18 [P] 734-384-1177
  linksatlakeerie.com
Links of Novi, *Novi*..........................27 [P] 248-380-9595
  linksofnovi.com
Little Bear GC, *Wallace* ....9 [P] 906-788-4162
Little Traverse Bay GC & Rest, *Harbor Springs*......18 [P] 231-526-6200
  ltbaygolf.com
Loch Lomond GC, *Flint* ....9 [P] 810-742-1434
LochenHeath, *Williamsburg* .... 18 [S] 231-938-9800
  lochenheath.com
Lochmoor Club, *Grosse Pointe Woods*................. 18 [V] 313-884-0563
  lochmoorclub.com
Lost Dunes GC, *Bridgman* .... 18 [V] 269-465-9300
  lostdunes.com
Lost Lake Woods Club, *Lincoln* .... 18 [V] 989-736-8412
Lower Huron par 3, *Belleville* ....18 [M] 734-697-9181
  metroparks.com
Lynx GC, *Otsego*............................18 [P] 269-694-5969
  lynxgolfcourse.com
Lyon Oaks GC, *Wixom* ....18 [P] 248-437-1488
  destinationoakland.com
Macatawa Legends G&CC, *Holland* .... 18 [V] 616-738-7000
  macatawalegends.com
Macon GC & Proshop, *Clinton*...................9 [P] 517-423-4259
Majestic at Lake Walden, *Hartland* ....27 [P] 810-632-5235
  majesticgolf.com
Mallard GC, *East Jordan* ....9 [P] 231-536-3636
  mallardgolf.com
Manistee G&CC, *Manistee*.................... 18 [V] 231-723-2509
  manisteegolfandcc.com
Manistee National Golf & Resort, *Manistee*........36 [R] 231-398-0123
  manisteenational.com
Manitou Passage GC, *Cedar* ....18 [R] 231-228-6000
  manitoupassagegolfclub.com
Maple Grove GC, *Lambertville*....................27 [P] 734-854-6777
Maple Hill GC, *Grandville* ....18 [P] 616-538-0290
  maplehillgc.com
Maple Hill GC, *Hemlock*..................... 18 [V] 989-642-8680
  maplehillgolfclub.com
Maple Hills GC, *Augusta* ....9 [P] 269-731-4430
Maple Lane GC, *Sterling Heights* ....54 [P] 586-795-4000
  maplelanegolf.com
Maple Leaf GC, *Linwood* ....27 [P] 989-697-3531
  golfmapleleaf.com
Maple Ridge GC, *Brutus* ....36 [R] 231-529-6574
  mapleridgegc.com
Maple Springs Golf Range, *Metamora*...........9 [P] 810-664-0484
Marlette GC, *Marlette*.........................9 [P] 989-635-3009
  marlettegolf.com
Marquette GC, *Marquette*....................36 [S] 906-225-0721
  marquettegolfclub.com
Marquette Trails GC, *Baldwin* ....18 [P] 231-898-2450
  marquettetrailsgc.com
Marsh Ridge GC, *Gaylord* ....18 [P] 989-732-5552
  marshridge.com
Marshall CC, *Marshall* .... 18 [V] 269-781-5310
  marshallcountryclub.com
Marysville GC, *Marysville*...................18 [M] 810-364-4653
  cityofmarysvillemi.com/golf

[S] = SEMI-PRIVATE   [V] = PRIVATE   [U] = UNIVERSITY   [N] = UNIVERSITY-PRIVATE

MICHIGAN — Golf Yellow Pages, 18th Edition

Course	Location	Holes	Type	Phone
Marywood GC,	Battle Creek	18	[S]	269-968-1168
marywoodgolf.com				
McGuires Resort & GC,	Cadillac	27	[R]	231-775-9947
mcguiresresort.com				
Meadow Lane Golf Crse,	Grand Rapids	18	[P]	616-698-8034
Meadowbrook CC,	Northville	18	[V]	248-349-3606
meadowbrookcountryclub.com				
Meadows Family Golf Ctr,	Baroda	9	[P]	269-422-2828
Meadows GC at GVSU,	Allendale	18	[U]	616-331-1000
gvsu.edu/meadows				
Meceola CC,	Big Rapids	18	[P]	231-796-9004
meceolacc.com				
Meridian Sun GC,	Haslett	18	[P]	517-339-8281
meridiansungc.com				
Metamora G&CC,	Metamora	18	[V]	248-969-2120
metamoragolfclub.com				
Metropolitan Beach GC,	Mt Clemens	18	[M]	586-463-4581
metroparks.com				
Michaywe Pines Course,	Gaylord	18	[P]	989-939-8911
michaywe.com				
Michigan Meadows GC,	Casco	18	[P]	586-727-7029
Middle Channel G&CC,	Harsens Island	18	[P]	810-748-9922
Midland CC,	Midland	18	[V]	989-832-3074
midlandcc.net				
Milham Park,	Kalamazoo	18	[P]	269-344-7639
kalamazoogolf.org				
Mill Race GC,	Jonesville	9	[P]	517-849-9439
Mines GC,	Grand Rapids	18	[P]	616-791-7544
minesgolfcourse.com				
Missaukee GC,	Lake City	18	[S]	231-825-2901
missaukeegolfclub.com				
Mistwood GC,	Lake Ann	27	[P]	231-275-5500
mistwoodgolf.com				
Monroe G&CC,	Monroe	18	[V]	734-241-6531
mgcc.net				
Moose Ridge GC,	South Lyon	18	[P]	248-446-9030
mooseridgegolf.com				
Morrison Lake CC,	Saranac	18	[P]	616-642-9528
Moss Ridge GC,	Ravenna	18	[P]	231-853-5665
mossridge.com				
Mott Park GC,	Flint	9	[M]	810-766-7077
cityofflint.com				
Mountain Flowers GC,	Glen Arbor	9	[R]	231-334-5000
thehomesteadresort.com				
Mt Pleasant CC,	Mt Pleasant	18	[V]	989-772-1591
Mulberry Fore GC,	Nashville	18	[P]	517-852-0760
mulberryfore.com				
Mulberry Hills GC,	Oxford	18	[P]	248-628-2808
mulberryhills.com				
Mullenhurst GC,	Delton	18	[S]	269-623-8383
Mullette Lake G&CC,	Mullette Lake	9	[S]	231-627-5971
Mulligans Irish Links,	Cass City	9	[P]	989-872-8002
Munoscong GC,	Pickford	18	[P]	906-647-9812
Muskegon CC,	Muskegon	18	[P]	231-755-1481
muskegoncc.com				
Mystic Creek GC,	Milford	27	[P]	248-684-3333
mysticcreekgc.com				
Nahma Club,	Rapid River	9	[P]	906-644-2648
New Hawthorne Valley GC,	Westland	9	[P]	734-422-1970
hawthornevalley.com				
Newberry CC,	Newberry	18	[S]	906-293-8422
golfnewberry.com				
NMU GC - Chocolay,	Marquette	18	[U]	906-227-3111
chocolaydownsgolfcourse.com				
Normandy Oaks GC,	Royal Oak	9	[M]	248-554-0027
ci.royal-oak.mi.us				
North Forty GC,	Marcellus	18	[P]	269-919-9003
northfortygolf.com				
North Kent GC,	Rockford	18	[P]	616-866-2659
northkentgolf.com				
North Shore GC,	Menominee	18	[P]	906-863-3026
North Star GC,	Ithaca	18	[P]	989-875-3841
Northport Point GC,	Northport	9	[V]	231-386-5871
Northville Hills GC,	Northville	18	[P]	734-667-4653
northvillehillsgolfclub.com				
Northwood GC,	Fremont	18	[S]	231-924-3380
Oak Crest GC,	Norway	18	[M]	906-563-5891
oakcrestgolf.com				
Oak Lane GC,	Webberville	18	[P]	517-521-3900
oaklanegolf.com				
Oak Pointe CC,	Brighton	36	[V]	810-227-9194
oak-pointe.com				
Oak Pointe/Champ Course,	Brighton	18	[V]	810-227-1381
oak-pointe.com				
Oak Ridge GC,	New Haven	36	[P]	586-749-5151
oakridgegolf.com				
Oak Ridge GC,	Muskegon	18	[S]	231-798-3660
Oakhurst G&CC,	Clarkston	18	[V]	248-391-3300
oakhurstgolf.com				
Oakland Hills CC,	Bloomfield Hills	36	[V]	248-644-2500
oakland-hills.com				
Oakland Hills GC,	Battle Creek	18	[P]	269-965-0809
oaklandhillsgolfclub.com				
Oakland Hills GC,	Portage	9	[P]	269-327-1493
Oakland Univ,	Rochester	36	[N]	248-370-4150
ougolf.com				
Oceana GC,	Shelby	18	[P]	231-861-4211
oceanagolfclub.com				
Old Channel Trail GC,	Montague	27	[P]	231-894-5076
golfoct.com				
Old Town Golf & Sportland,	Monroe	9	[P]	734-242-2525
Olde Mill GC,	Schoolcraft	18	[S]	269-679-5625
oldemillgolfclub.com				
Olivet GC,	Olivet	9	[P]	269-749-9051
Ontonagon GC,	Ontonagon	9	[S]	906-884-4130
Orchard Hills CC,	Buchanan	18	[V]	269-695-5722
orchardhillscc.org				
Orchard Hills GC,	Shelbyville	27	[S]	269-672-7096
orchardhillsgc.com				
Orchard Lake CC,	Orchard Lake	18	[V]	248-682-2500
orchardlakecountryclub.com				
Otsego Club & Resort,	Gaylord	36	[R]	989-732-5181
otsegoclub.com				
Overbrook GC,	Middleton	9	[P]	989-236-5357
golfoverbrook.com				
Owosso CC,	Owosso	18	[V]	989-723-2592
owossocc.com				
Oxford Hills GC,	Oxford	18	[P]	248-628-2518
oxfordhillsgolf.com				
Paint Creek CC,	Lake Orion	18	[V]	248-693-9292
paintcreekgolf.com				
Palmer Park GC,	Detroit	18	[M]	313-883-2525
palmerpark.americangolf.com				
Park Shore GC,	Cassopolis	18	[P]	269-445-2834
parkshoregolfclub.com				

[A] = MILITARY [M] = MUNICIPAL [P] = PUBLIC [R] = RESORT

Golf Yellow Pages, 18th Edition — MICHIGAN

Course	Holes	Type	Phone
Patsy Lou Williamsons Sugarbush G&CC, *Davison*	18	[P]	810-653-3326
sugarbushgolfclub.com			
Paw Paw Lake GC, *Watervliet*	18	[P]	269-463-3831
pawpawlakegolfcourse.com			
Pebblewood CC, *Bridgman*	18	[P]	269-465-5611
Perttus Big Spruce GC, *Bruce Crossing*	9	[P]	906-827-3727
Petoskey Bay View CC, *Petoskey*	18	[R]	231-347-3394
pbvcc.com			
Pheasant GC, *Zeeland*	9	[P]	616-875-4653
Pheasant Run GC, *Canton*	27	[M]	734-397-6460
canton-mi.org			
Pictured Rocks G&CC, *Munising*	18	[S]	906-387-3970
picturedrocksgolfcourse.com			
Pierce Lake GC, *Chelsea*	18	[M]	734-475-5858
ewashtenaw.org			
Pierce Park GC, *Flint*	18	[M]	810-766-7297
cityofflint.com			
Pigeon Creek GC, *West Olive*	18	[P]	616-875-4300
golfpigeoncreek.com			
Pilgrims Run GC, *Pierson*	18	[P]	888-533-7742 x4
pilgrimsrun.com			
Pine Creek GC, *Belleville*	18	[P]	734-483-5010
Pine Grove CC, *Iron Mountain*	18	[V]	906-774-3493
pinegrovecc.org			
Pine Hills GC, *Laingsburg*	18	[P]	517-651-9700
golfpinehills.com			
Pine Hollow GC, *Jackson*	18	[P]	517-764-4200
pinehollowgc.com			
Pine Knob GC, *Clarkston*	27	[P]	248-625-4430
pineknobmansion.com			
Pine Lake CC, *Orchard Lake*	18	[V]	248-682-1300
pinelakecc.com			
Pine River CC, *Alma*	18	[V]	989-463-4610
Pine River GC, *Standish*	18	[P]	989-846-6819
Pine Shores GC, *St Clair*	9	[M]	810-329-4294
Pine Trace GC, *Rochester*	18	[P]	248-852-7100
pinetrace.com			
Pine Valley GC, *Ray*	27	[P]	586-752-5300
pinevalleygolfcc.com			
Pine View GC, *Three Rivers*	36	[P]	269-279-5131
pineviewgolf.com			
Pine View GC, *Ypsilanti*	27	[P]	734-481-0500
pineviewgc.com			
Pine View Highlands GC, *Houghton Lake*	18	[P]	989-366-7726
pineviewhighlands.com			
Pinecroft Golf Plantation, *Beulah*	18	[P]	231-882-9100
pinecroftgolf.com			
Pipestone Creek GC, *Eau Claire*	18	[P]	269-944-1611
Pleasant Hills GC, *Mt Pleasant*	18	[P]	989-772-0487
pleasanthillsgolfcourse.com			
Pleasant View GC, *Saginaw*	9	[P]	989-791-4768
Plum Brook GC, *Sterling Heights*	18	[P]	586-264-9411
plumbrookgolf.com			
Plum Hollow CC, *Southfield*	18	[V]	248-357-5353
plumhollowcc.com			
Plym Park GC, *Niles*	9	[M]	269-684-7331
ci.niles.mi.us			
Pohlcat GC, *Mt Pleasant*	18	[R]	989-773-4221
pohlcat.net			
Point O Woods CC, *Benton Harbor*	18	[V]	269-944-5851
pointowoods.com			
Pointe Aux Barques GC, *Port Austin*	9	[V]	989-738-7585
Polo Fields G&CC, *Ann Arbor*	18	[V]	734-998-1555
polofieldsccmi.com			
Pontiac CC, *Waterford*	18	[S]	248-682-6333
pontiaccountryclub.com			
Pontiac Muni GC, *Pontiac*	18	[M]	248-758-3966
pontiac.mi.us			
Port Huron Elks GC, *Port Huron*	18	[V]	810-984-1204
porthuronelkslodge.com			
Port Huron GC, *Fort Gratiot*	18	[V]	810-385-3881
phgc.net			
Portage Lake GC Mich Tech, *Houghton*	18	[U]	906-487-2641
golf.mtu.edu			
Portland CC, *Portland*	18	[P]	517-647-4521
portlandcountryclub.us			
Prairie Creek GC, *Dewitt*	18	[P]	517-669-1958
golfprairiecreek.com			
Prairiewood GC, *Otsego*	18	[P]	269-694-6633
prairiewoodgolf.com			
Prestwick Village GC, *Highland*	18	[V]	248-887-4334
pvgcc.com			
Quail Ridge GC, *Ada*	18	[P]	616-676-2000
quailridgegc.com			
Quincy GC, *Quincy*	9	[P]	517-639-4491
Rackham GC, *Huntington Woods*	18	[M]	248-543-4040
rackham.americangolf.com			
Radrick Farms GC, *Ann Arbor*	18	[N]	734-998-7040
umich.edu/~radrick			
Railside GC, *Byron Center*	18	[V]	616-878-0202
railsidegolf.com			
Raisin River CC, *Monroe*	36	[P]	734-289-3700
raisinrivergolf.com			
Raisin Valley GC, *Tecumseh*	18	[P]	517-423-2050
raisinvalleygolfclub.com			
Rammler GC, *Sterling Heights*	27	[P]	586-264-4101
rammlergolf.com			
Ramshorn on the Lakes, *Fremont*	18	[P]	231-924-2640
Rattle Run GC, *St Clair*	18	[P]	810-329-2070
rattlerun.com			
Ravenna Creeks GC, *Ravenna*	18	[P]	231-853-6736
Ravines GC, *Saugatuck*	18	[P]	269-857-1616
ravinesgolfclub.com			
Red Arrow GC, *Kalamazoo*	9	[M]	269-345-8329
kalamazoogolf.org			
Red Fox Run GC, *Gwinn*	18	[P]	906-346-7010
redfoxrun.com			
Red Hawk GC, *East Tawas*	18	[S]	989-362-0800
redhawkgolf.net			
Red Oaks GC, *Madison Heights*	9	[M]	248-541-5030
destinationoakland.com			
Red Run GC, *Royal Oak*	18	[V]	248-548-7500
redrungolfclub.com			
Reddeman Farms GC, *Chelsea*	18	[P]	734-475-3020
reddemanfarms.com			
Richmond Forest, *Lenox*	18	[P]	586-727-4742
richmondforestgolf.com			
Ridgeview GC, *Kalamazoo*	18	[P]	269-375-8821
ridgeviewgolf.com			
Ridgeview GC, *Belding*	9	[P]	616-794-1860
ridgeviewgc.biz			
Rippling Rapids GC, *Cheboygan*	18	[S]	231-625-2770
River Bank GC, *South Lyon*	18	[P]	248-486-6251
riverbankgolfclub.com			
River Bend GC, *Hastings*	27	[P]	269-945-3238
golfhastings.com			

[S] = SEMI-PRIVATE [V] = PRIVATE [U] = UNIVERSITY [N] = UNIVERSITY-PRIVATE

MICHIGAN

Golf Yellow Pages, 18th Edition

Course	Holes	Type	Phone
River Forest GC, *Flint*	9	[P]	810-732-9240
Rivers Edge GC, *Alpena*	18	[P]	989-354-4312
riversedgealpena.com			
Riverside CC, *Battle Creek*	18	[V]	269-962-3921
bcriversidecountryclub.com			
Riverside CC, *Menominee*	18	[P]	906-863-2590
Riverview Highlands GC, *Riverview*	27	[M]	734-479-2266
riverviewhighlands.com			
Riverwood Golf Resort, *Mt Pleasant*	27	[R]	989-772-5726
riverwoodresort.com			
Rogell GC, *Detroit*	18	[P]	313-255-4653
golfnewrogell.com			
Rogers City CC, *Rogers City*	18	[P]	989-734-4909
Rogue River GC, *Sparta*	18	[P]	616-887-7182
theroguegolfclub.com			
Rolling Hills GC, *Hudsonville*	18	[P]	616-669-9768
Rolling Hills GC, *Cass City*	9	[P]	989-872-3569
Rolling Hills GC, *Lapeer*	18	[P]	810-664-2281
Rolling Hills Golf Estate, *Ionia*	9	[P]	616-527-3480
golfionia.com			
Rolling Meadows GC, *Whitmore Lake*	18	[P]	734-662-5144
golfrmcc.com			
Romeo G&CC, *Romeo*	36	[P]	586-752-9673
Rouge Park GC, *Detroit*	18	[M]	313-837-5900
rougepark.americangolf.com			
Royal Oak GC, *Royal Oak*	9	[M]	248-554-0019
ci.royal-oak.mi.us/golf/index.html			
Royal Scot, *Lansing*	27	[P]	517-321-6220
royalscot.net			
Rush Lake Hills GC, *Pinckney*	18	[S]	734-878-9790
rushlakehills.com			
Rustic Glen GC, *Saline*	18	[P]	734-429-7679
rusticglen.com			
Saginaw CC, *Saginaw*	18	[V]	989-793-3461
saginawcountryclub.com			
Salem Hills GC, *Northville*	18	[P]	248-437-2152
salemhillsgolfclub.com			
Salt River CC, *Chesterfield*	18	[P]	586-725-0311
golfsaltriver.com			
Sanctuary Lake, *Troy*	18	[M]	248-619-7671
troymi.gov			
Sand Creek GC & DR, *Marne*	9	[P]	616-677-3379
sandcreekgolf.com			
Sand Wedge GC, *Ottawa Lake*	18	[P]	734-854-4909
Sandy Creek GC, *Monroe*	18	[P]	734-242-7200
sandycreekgolf.com			
Sandy Pebbles GC, *Ahmeek*	9	[P]	906-337-3516
Sandy Ridge GC, *Midland*	18	[P]	989-631-6010
golfsandyridge.com			
Saskatoon GC, *Alto*	36	[P]	616-891-9229
saskatoongolf.com			
Sauganash CC, *Three Rivers*	18	[P]	269-278-7825
sauganashgc.com			
Sault Sainte Marie CC, *Sault Sainte Marie*	18	[S]	906-632-7812
saultgolfing.com			
Scenic G&CC, *Pigeon*	18	[S]	989-453-3350
scenicgolfandcountryclub.com			
Scott Lake CC, *Comstock Park*	27	[P]	616-784-1355
scottlake.com			
Seifert Golf Plus, *Grand Blanc*	9	[P]	810-655-8070
seifertgolfplus.com			
Selfridge GC, *Harrison TWP*	18	[A]	583-269-4659
selfridgemwr.com/recreation/golf.htm			
Shadow Ridge GC, *Ionia*	9	[P]	616-527-1180
shadowridgegc.com			
Shaffers Evergreen GC, *Hudson*	9	[P]	517-448-8174
Shallow Creek GC, *Fort Gratiot*	9	[P]	810-385-3542
Shamrock Hills GC, *Gobles*	18	[P]	269-628-2070
shamrockhillsgolfclub.com			
Shanty Creek, *Bellaire*	36	[R]	231-533-7002
shantycreek.com			
Shanty Creek - Cedar River, *Bellaire*	18	[R]	231-533-6076
shantycreek.com			
Shanty Creek - Schuss Mountain, *Bellaire*	18	[R]	231-533-6076
shantycreek.com			
Shenandoah CC, *West Bloomfield*	18	[P]	248-683-6363
shenandoahcc.net			
Shepherds Hollow GC, *Clarkston*	27	[P]	248-922-0300
shepherdshollow.com			
Sherwood On The Hill, *Gagetown*	9	[R]	989-665-9971
SideWinder GC, *Mio*	18	[P]	989-826-8020
sidewindergolf.com			
Signal Point Club, *Niles*	18	[V]	269-683-7073
signalpointgolf.com			
Silver Lake CC, *Rockford*	18	[V]	616-874-7100
Silver Lake GC, *Brooklyn*	9	[P]	517-592-8036
Singing Bridge GC, *Tawas City*	18	[P]	989-362-0022
singingbridgegolfcourse.com			
Snow Snake Ski & Golf, *Harrison*	18	[R]	989-539-6583
snowsnake.net			
Somerset GC, *Troy*	9	[V]	248-643-8737
South Haven GC, *South Haven*	18	[S]	269-637-3896
Southgate Muni GC, *Southgate*	18	[M]	734-258-3004
southgate-mi.org/golf			
Southmoor CC, *Burton*	18	[P]	810-743-4080
Spring Brook Golf & Grill, *Battle Creek*	9	[P]	269-441-7529
springbrookgolf.net			
Spring Lake CC, *Spring Lake*	18	[V]	616-842-4200
springlakecc.com			
Spring Meadows CC, *Linden*	18	[V]	810-735-7836
springmeadowscountryclub.com			
Spring Valley GC, *Kawkawlin*	9	[P]	989-686-0330
Spring Valley GC, *Hersey*	18	[P]	231-832-5041
Springbrook GC, *Walloon Lake*	18	[P]	231-535-5155
springbrookgolf.com			
Springdale GC, *Birmingham*	9	[M]	248-530-1660
ci.birmingham.mi.us			
Springfield Oaks GC, *Davisburg*	18	[M]	248-625-2540
destinationoakland.com			
Springport Hills GC, *Harrisville*	18	[P]	989-724-5611
loggerstrace.com			
Spruce Ridge GC, *Dowagiac*	18	[R]	269-782-5827
St Clair River CC, *St Clair*	18	[V]	810-329-7300
scrcc.net			
St Clair Shores CC, *St Clair Shores*	18	[M]	586-294-2000
scsgolf.com			
St Ignace G&CC, *St Ignace*	9	[P]	906-643-8071
St Ives GC, *Stanwood*	18	[P]	231-972-4837
tullymoregolf.com			
St Joe Valley GC, *Sturgis*	18	[P]	269-467-6275
rivercountry.com			
States GC, *Vicksburg*	18	[P]	269-649-1931
Stonebridge GC, *Ann Arbor*	18	[P]	734-429-8383
stonebridgegolfclub.net			
Stonegate GC, *Twin Lake*	18	[P]	231-744-7200
stonegategolfclub.com			

[A] = MILITARY   [M] = MUNICIPAL   [P] = PUBLIC   [R] = RESORT

Golf Yellow Pages, 18th Edition — MICHIGAN

Course	Info	Phone
Stonehedge GC, *Augusta*	36 [R]	269-731-2300
gulllakeview.com		
StoneWater CC, *Caledonia*	18 [P]	616-656-9898
stonewatercc.com		
Stoney Creek GC, *Lake City*	18 [P]	231-839-7777
Stoney Links, *Onaway*	18 [P]	989-733-2683
stoneylinksgolfcourse.com		
Stony Creek Metropark GC, *Shelby Township*	18 [M]	586-781-9166
metroparks.com		
Stony Point GC, *Manistique*	9 [S]	906-341-3419
Stonycroft Hills GC, *Bloomfield Hills*	9 [P]	248-647-1294
stonycroft.com		
Sugar Loaf The Old Course, *Cedar*	18 [R]	231-228-2040
sugarloaftheoldcourse.com		
Sugar Springs CC, *Gladwin*	18 [S]	989-426-4391
sugarsprings.net		
Sultana Par 3, *Brownstown*	18 [P]	734-285-7480
Summer Breeze Par 3, *Fremont*	9 [P]	231-924-9759
Summergreen Golf Links, *Hudsonville*	9 [P]	616-669-0950
summergreengolflinks.com		
Sunnybrook CC, *Grandville*	18 [V]	616-457-1102
sunnybrookcc.com		
Sunnybrook GC, *Sterling Heights*	27 [P]	586-977-9759
sunnybrookgolfandbowl.com		
Swan Valley GC, *Saginaw*	18 [P]	989-781-4945
thecreekandthevalley.com		
Swartz Creek GC, *Flint*	27 [M]	810-766-7043
cityofflint.com		
Sweetgrass GC, *Harris*	18 [R]	906-723-2251
sweetgrassgolfclub.com		
Sycamore Hills GC, *Macomb*	27 [P]	586-598-9500
sycamorehills.com		
Sylvan Glen GC, *Troy*	18 [M]	248-619-7600
troymi.gov		
Tam OShanter CC, *West Bloomfield*	18 [V]	248-855-1900
Tanglewood GC, *South Lyon*	27 [P]	248-486-3355
tanglewoodthelion.com		
Tanglewood Marsh, *Sault Sainte Marie*	18 [P]	906-635-7651
tanglewoodmarsh.com		
Tawas Creek GC, *Tawas City*	18 [R]	989-362-6262
golftawascreek.com		
Taylor Meadows GC, *Taylor*	18 [M]	734-287-2100
taylorgolf.com		
Tecumseh CC, *Tecumseh*	18 [V]	517-423-3930
tecumsehcountryclub.com		
Tee J's GC, *Macomb*	18 [P]	586-598-5010
Terra Verde GC, *Nunica*	18 [P]	616-837-8249
terraverdegc.com		
Terrace Bluff GC, *Gladstone*	18 [P]	906-428-2343
terracebay.com		
The Bayou GC, *Freeland*	9 [P]	989-781-8181
bayougolfclub.net		
The Briar North At Mesick, *Mesick*	18 [P]	231-885-1220
golfmesick.com		
The Briar South At Cadillac, *Cadillac*	18 [P]	231-885-1220
golfmesick.com		
The Captains Club At Woodfield, *Grand Blanc*	18 [P]	810-695-4653
captainsclubatwoodfield.com		
The Centennial Farm GC, *Bellaire*	18 [P]	231-533-6886
thefarmgolfclub.com		
The Chief GC, *Bellaire*	18 [R]	231-533-9000
golfthechief.com		
The Colonial GC, *Hart*	27 [P]	231-873-8333
colonialgolfhart.com		
The Dream, *West Branch*	18 [R]	989-345-6300
teedream.com		
The Dunes Club, *New Buffalo*	9 [V]	269-469-5539
The Dunes GC, *Empire*	18 [P]	231-326-5390
dunesgolf.com		
The Falls At Barber Creek, *Kent City*	9 [P]	616-675-7345
thefallsatbarbercreek.com		
The Fortress, *Frankenmuth*	18 [P]	989-652-0460
zehnders.com		
The GC at Harbor Shores, *Benton Harbor*	18 [R]	269-927-4653
harborshoreslife.com		
The GC At Thornapple Pointe, *Grand Rapids*	18 [P]	616-554-4747
thornapplepointe.com		
The GC of Coldwater, *Coldwater*	18 [S]	517-279-2100
golfclubofcoldwater.com		
The Glacier Club, *Washington*	18 [S]	586-786-0800
glaciersgolf.com		
The Heathers Club, *Bloomfield Hills*	9 [V]	248-334-4494
heathersclub.com		
The Heathlands, *Onekama*	18 [P]	231-889-5644
heathlands.com		
The Highlands GC, *Grand Rapids*	18 [S]	616-453-1504
grhighlands.com		
The Inn At St Johns GC, *Plymouth*	27 [R]	734-453-1047
stjohnsgolfconference.com		
The Jackal GC At Mt Brighton, *Brighton*	18 [P]	810-229-9581
jackalgolfclub.com		
The Jewel GC, *Mackinac Island*	18 [P]	906-847-3331
grandhotel.com		
The Jewel of Grand Blanc, *Grand Blanc*	36 [P]	810-694-5960
jewelgolf.com		
The Kingsley Club, *Kingsley*	18 [V]	231-263-3000
kingsleyclub.com		
The Lakes GC, *Gaylord*	18 [P]	989-732-4454
mountainlakegolf.com		
The Leelanau Club At Bahle Farms, *Suttons Bay*	18 [P]	231-271-2020
leelanauclub.com		
The Legacy GC, *Ottawa Lake*	18 [P]	734-854-1101
legacybyarthurhills.com		
The Links At Edmore, *Edmore*	9 [P]	989-427-3241
The Links At Rolling Meadows, *Holland*	9 [P]	616-395-5926
rollingmeadows.net		
The Links at Whitmore Lake, *Whitmore Lake*	18 [P]	734-449-4653
linksatwhitmorelake.com		
The Links of Bowen Lake, *Gowen*	18 [P]	616-984-9916
linksatbowenlake.com		
The Loon GC, *Gaylord*	18 [P]	989-732-4454
theloongolfclub.com		
The Mackinaw Club, *Carp Lake*	18 [P]	231-537-4955
mackinawclub.com		
The Maples Club, *Novi*	9 [P]	248-960-3033
maplesclub.com		
The Medalist GC, *Marshall*	18 [S]	269-789-4653
themedalist.com		
The Moors GC, *Portage*	18 [V]	269-323-8873
moorsgolf.com		
The Myth Golf & Banquets, *Oakland*	27 [P]	248-693-7170
golfthemyth.com		
The Natural, *Gaylord*	18 [R]	989-732-1785
golfthenatural.com		
The Nightmare, *West Branch*	18 [P]	989-345-1500
golfnightmare.com		

[S] = SEMI-PRIVATE   [V] = PRIVATE   [U] = UNIVERSITY   [N] = UNIVERSITY-PRIVATE

MICHIGAN — Golf Yellow Pages, 18th Edition

The Oaks At Kincheloe, *Kincheloe* ...... 18 [M] 906-495-5706
  kinross.net
The Orchards GC, *Washington* .... 18 [P] 586-786-7200
  orchards.com
The Pines GC, *Wyoming* .... 18 [P] 616-538-8380
  pinesgolfcourse.com
The Pines GC at Lake Isabella, *Lake Isabella* .... 18 [R] 989-644-2300
  thepinesgolfcourse.com
The Players Club GC, *Lansing* .... 9 [P] 517-627-8687
The Polo Fields G&CC-Washtenaw, *Ypsilanti* ...... 18 [V] 734-434-2150
  polofieldsccmi.com
The Prairies, *Kalamazoo* .... 18 [P] 269-343-3906
  prairiesgolf.com
The Quest at Houghton Lake, *Houghton Lake* ...... 18 [P] 989-422-4516
  questgolfcourse.com
The Ridge GC, *Breckenridge* .... 9 [P] 989-842-1510
The Rock At Drummond Island, *Drummond Island* 18 [R] 906-493-1006
  drummondisland.com
The Rose GC, *Leroy* .... 18 [P] 231-768-5060
  golftherose.com
The Sawmill GC, *Saginaw* .... 18 [S] 989-793-2692
  thesawmill.com
The Tamaracks, *Harrison* .... 18 [P] 989-539-5441
  tamaracksgolf.com
The Tamaracks West, *Harrison* .... 9 [P] 989-539-5441
The Timbers GC, *Vassar* .... 18 [P] 989-871-4884
  timbersgolfclub.com
The Woodlands, *Wayne* .... 18 [P] 734-729-3812
  thewoodlandsgc.com
The Wyndgate G&CC, *Rochester* .... 18 [V] 248-652-4283
  thewyndgate.com
Thornapple Creek GC, *Kalamazoo* .... 18 [P] 269-344-0040
  thornapplecreek.com
Thorne Brothers at Lilac GC, *Newport* .... 18 [P] 734-586-7555
  lilacgolf.com
Thorne Hills GC, *Carleton* .... 18 [P] 734-587-2332
  thornehills.com
Thoroughbred GC, *Rothbury* .... 18 [R] 231-894-3939
  doublejj.com
Thousand Oaks GC, *Grand Rapids* .... 18 [P] 616-447-7750
  thousandoaksgolf.com
Thunder Bay Golf Resort, *Hillman* .... 18 [R] 989-742-4875
  thunderbaygolf.com
Timber Ridge GC, *East Lansing* .... 18 [P] 517-339-8000
  golftimberridge.com
Timber Trace GC, *Pinckney* .... 18 [P] 734-878-1800
  timbertracegolfclub.com
Timber Wolf GC, *Kalkaska* .... 18 [P] 231-258-5685
  timberwolfgolfclub.com
TimberStone At Pine Mountain, *Iron Mountain* ..18 [R] 906-776-0111
  timberstonegolf.com
Timberwood GC, *Ray* .... 18 [P] 586-784-6000
  timberwoodgc.com
Tomac Woods GC, *Albion* .... 18 [S] 517-629-8241
  tomacwoods.com
TPC Michigan, *Dearborn* .... 18 [P] 313-436-3100
  tpcmichigan.com
Traverse City G&CC, *Traverse City* .... 18 [V] 231-947-3553
  tcgcc.com
Travis Pointe CC, *Ann Arbor* .... 18 [V] 734-662-5703
  travispointe.com
Treetops Resort, *Gaylord* .... 63 [R] 989-732-6711
  treetops.com

Treetops Resort - Jones Masterpiece, *Gaylord* ..... 18 [R] 989-732-6711
  treetops.com
True North GC, *Harbor Springs* .... 18 [V] 231-526-3300
  truenorthgolf.com
Tullymore GC, *Stanwood* .... 18 [S] 231-972-4837
  tullymoregolf.com
Turtle Creek GC, *Burlington* .... 27 [P] 517-765-2232
Tustin Trails GC, *Tustin* .... 9 [P] 231-829-5455
Twin Beach CC, *West Bloomfield* .... 9 [V] 248-363-3335
  twinbeachcc.com
Twin Birch GC, *Kalkaska* .... 18 [P] 231-258-9691
  twinbirchgolf.com
Twin Bridges GC, *Merrill* .... 18 [P] 989-643-7475
Twin Brook GC, *Charlotte* .... 18 [P] 517-543-0570
  twinbrookgolfclub.com
Twin Brooks GC, *Chesaning* .... 18 [P] 989-845-6403
  twinbrooksgolfcourse.com
Twin Knolls GC, *Grass Lake* .... 9 [P] 517-522-8944
Twin Lakes GC, *Oakland* .... 27 [P] 248-650-4960
  twinlakesgc.com
Twin Oaks GC, *St Johns* .... 9 [P] 989-224-7342
Twin Oaks GC, *Freeland* .... 27 [P] 989-695-9746
Tyler Creek Golf, *Alto* .... 18 [P] 616-868-6751
  tylercreekgolf.com
Tyrone Hills GC, *Fenton* .... 18 [P] 810-629-5011
  tyronehillsgolf.com
Ubly Heights GC, *Ubly* .... 18 [P] 989-658-2374
  ublyheights.com
Union Lake GC, *Commerce Township* .... 9 [P] 248-363-4666
  unionlakegolfcourse.com
Univ Park GC, *Muskegon* .... 9 [U] 231-773-0023
  muskegon.cc.mi.us
Valley View Farm GC, *Saginaw* .... 18 [S] 989-781-1248
  valleyviewfarmgolf.com
Vassar G&CC, *Vassar* .... 18 [P] 989-823-7221
  vassargolf.com
Verona Hills GC, *Bad Axe* .... 18 [S] 989-269-8132
  veronahillsgolf.com
Vienna Greens GC, *Clio* .... 18 [P] 810-686-1443
Village Green GC, *Newaygo* .... 18 [P] 231-652-6513
Wabeek CC, *Bloomfield Hills* .... 18 [V] 248-855-0700
  wabeekcc.org
Wallinwood Springs, *Jenison* .... 18 [S] 616-457-9920
  wallinwoodspringsgolf.com
Walloon Lake CC, *Petoskey* .... 18 [V] 231-535-2992
  walloonlakecc.com
Walnut Creek CC, *South Lyon* .... 27 [V] 248-437-7470
  walnutcreekcc.net
Walnut Hills CC, *East Lansing* .... 18 [V] 517-332-8647
  walnuthillsgolf.com
Warfield Greens GC, *Fraser* .... 9 [P] 586-293-9887
Warren Valley GC, *Dearborn Heights* .... 36 [M] 313-561-1040
  co.wayne.mi.us
Warwick Hills G&CC, *Grand Blanc* .... 18 [V] 810-694-4103
  warwickhills.org
Washakie Golf & RV Resort, *North Branch* ...... 18 [R] 810-688-3235
  washakiegolfrv.com
Waterloo GC, *Grass Lake* .... 18 [P] 517-522-8527
  waterloogolfcourse.com
Watermark CC, *Grand Rapids* .... 18 [V] 616-949-6411
  watermarkcc.com
Waters Edge CC, *Grosse Ile* .... 9 [S] 734-675-0777
  grosseile.com

Wawashkamo CC, *Mackinac Island* .... 9 [R] 906-847-3871
  wawashkamo.com
Wawonowin CC, *Champion* .... 18 [S] 906-485-5660
  wawonowin.com
Wequetonsing GC, *Harbor Springs* .... 18 [V] 231-526-5351
Wesburn GC, *South Rockwood* .... 18 [P] 734-379-3555
  wesburngolf.com
West Branch CC, *West Branch* .... 18 [S] 989-345-2501
  westbranchcc.com
West Ottawa GC, *Holland* .... 27 [P] 616-399-1678
  westottawagolfclub.com
West Shore G&CC, *Grosse Ile* .... 18 [V] 734-676-0330
  golfwestshore.com
West Shore GC, *Douglas* .... 18 [R] 269-857-2500
  westshoregolfclub.com
Westbrooke GC, *Novi* .... 18 [P] 248-349-2723
Western G&CC, *Redford* .... 18 [V] 313-531-2323
  westerngcc.net
Western Greens GC, *Marne* .... 18 [P] 616-677-3677
  westerngreensgolf.com
Westland Muni GC, *Westland* .... 9 [M] 734-721-6660
Westwind GC, *Muskegon* .... 18 [P] 231-773-8814
Westwynd GC, *Rochester Hills* .... 18 [P] 248-608-7820
  westwyndgrille.com
Wheatfield Valley GC, *Williamston* .... 18 [P] 517-655-6999
  wheatfieldvalley.com
Whiffletree Hill GC, *Concord* .... 18 [P] 517-524-6655
Whispering Pines GC, *Pinckney* .... 18 [P] 734-878-0009
  whisperingpinesgc.com
Whispering Willows GC, *Livonia* .... 18 [M] 248-476-4493
  golflivonia.com
White Birch Hills GC, *Bay City* .... 18 [P] 989-662-6523
White Deer CC, *Prudenville* .... 18 [P] 989-366-5812
  golfwhitedeer.com
White Lake GC, *Whitehall* .... 18 [V] 231-893-4232
White Lake Oaks GC, *Waterford* .... 18 [M] 248-698-2700
  destinationoakland.com
White Oaks GC, *Hillsdale* .... 18 [P] 517-437-3434
White Oaks GC, *Goodells* .... 9 [P] 810-325-9292
  whiteoaksgolfcourse.com
White Pine Natl Golf Resort, *Spruce* .... 18 [R] 989-736-3279
  whitepinenational.com
Whitefish Lake GC, *Pierson* .... 18 [P] 616-636-5260
  whitefishgolfandgrill.com
Whiteford Valley GC, *Ottawa Lake* .... 72 [P] 734-856-4545
  whitefordgolf.com
Whittaker Woods GC, *New Buffalo* .... 18 [P] 269-469-3400
  golfwhittaker.com
Wicker Hills CC, *Hale* .... 18 [P] 989-728-9971
  wickerhillsgolf.com
Wild Bluff GC, *Brimley* .... 18 [R] 906-248-5860
  wildbluff.com
Wilderness GC, *Carp Lake* .... 9 [P] 231-537-4973
  golfwilderness.com
Wilderness Hills GC, *Plainwell* .... 18 [P] 269-664-4653
  wildernesshills.com
Wildwood Lakes, *Wolverine* .... 9 [P] 231-525-8949
  wildwoodlakesgolf.com
Willow Brook Public GC, *Byron* .... 18 [P] 810-266-4660
  hawkmeadows.com
Willow Creek, *Walkerville* .... 9 [P] 231-873-8489
Willow Creek GC, *Stockbridge* .... 9 [P] 517-851-7856

Willow Metropark GC, *New Boston* .... 18 [M] 734-697-9181
  metroparks.com
Willow Ridge GC, *Fort Gratiot* .... 9 [P] 810-982-7010
Willow Springs G&CC, *Vassar* .... 18 [P] 989-871-9703
  golfthewillow.com
Willow Tree GC, *Melvin* .... 9 [P] 810-387-4001
Willow Wood GC, *Portland* .... 18 [P] 517-647-1984
  willowwoodgc.com
Winding Brook GC, *Shepherd* .... 18 [P] 989-828-6618
  windingbrookgolfclub.com
Winding Creek GC, *Holland* .... 27 [P] 616-396-4516
  windingcreekgolfclub.com
Windmill Farms Par-3, *Mancelona* .... 9 [P] 231-587-5258
Wolcott Mill Metropark GC, *Ray* .... 18 [M] 586-749-3415
  metroparks.com
Wolf Creek GC, *Adrian* .... 18 [P] 517-265-3944
Woodland Hills GC, *Sandusky* .... 18 [P] 810-648-2400
  woodlandhillsontheweb.com
Woodlawn GC, *Adrian* .... 18 [P] 517-263-3288
Woodside Meadows GC, *Romulus* .... 18 [P] 734-782-5136
Wuskowhan Players Club, *West Olive* .... 18 [V] 616-738-6000
  wuskowhan.com
Wyandotte Hills GC, *Toivola* .... 9 [R] 906-288-3720
  wyandottehills.com
Wyandotte Shores GC, *Wyandotte* .... 9 [M] 734-324-7270
  wyandotte.net
Yankee Springs GC, *Wayland* .... 27 [P] 269-795-3356
  playyankeegolf.com
Yarrow Golf & Conf Ctr, *Augusta* .... 18 [P] 269-731-2090
  yarrowgolf.com
Ye Nyne Olde Holles GC, *East Jordan* .... 9 [P] 231-582-7609
  yenyne.com
Ye Olde CC, *Roscommon* .... 9 [P] 989-275-5582
  yeoldecountryclub.com

MINNESOTA

Adrian CC, *Adrian* .... 9 [S] 507-483-2722
Afton Alps GC, *Hastings* .... 18 [P] 651-436-1320
  aftonalps.com
Albany GC, *Albany* .... 18 [M] 320-845-2505
  albanygc.com
Albion Ridges GC, *Annandale* .... 27 [P] 320-963-5500
  albionridges.com
Alexandria GC, *Alexandria* .... 18 [S] 320-763-3605
  alexandriagolfclub.com
Angushire GC, *St Cloud* .... 18 [P] 320-251-9619
  angushiregolf.com
Apple Valley GC, *St Paul* .... 9 [P] 952-432-4647
Appleton GC, *Appleton* .... 9 [S] 320-289-2511
Applewood Hills GC, *Stillwater* .... 18 [P] 651-439-7276
  applewoodhillsgolf.com
Arbor Pointe GC, *Inver Grove Heights* .... 9 [P] 651-451-9678
  arborpointegolf.com
Atikwa GC at Arrowwood Resort, *Alexandria* .... 18 [R] 320-762-1124
  arrowwoodresort.com
Austin CC, *Austin* .... 18 [V] 507-437-7631
  austincountryclub.net
Babbitt GC, *Babbitt* .... 9 [P] 218-827-2603
Baker National GC, *Medina* .... 27 [M] 763-694-7670
  bakernational.com
Balmoral GC, *Battle Lake* .... 18 [P] 218-367-2055
  golfbalmoral.com

[S] = SEMI-PRIVATE   [V] = PRIVATE   [U] = UNIVERSITY   [N] = UNIVERSITY-PRIVATE

MINNESOTA — Golf Yellow Pages, 18th Edition

Bearpath G&CC, *Eden Prairie*..................... 18 [V] 952-975-0123
bearpathgolf.com
Bears Den GC, *Park Rapids*........................ 9 [R] 218-732-8489
timberlaneresort.com
Begin Oaks Golf, *Plymouth* .... 9 [P] 763-559-7574
beginoaksgolf.com
Bellwood Oaks GC, *Hastings* .... 18 [P] 651-437-4141
bellwoodoaksgolf.com
Bemidji Town & CC, *Bemidji* .... 18 [P] 218-751-4535
bemidjigolf.com
Benson GC, *Benson*.................................... 18 [M] 320-842-7901
bensongolfclub.com
Bent Creek GC, *Eden Prairie*..................... 18 [V] 952-937-9347
bentcreekgolfclub.com
Bentwood GC, *Climax* .... 9 [P] 218-857-3545
Big Lake GC, *Cloquet* .... 9 [P] 218-879-4221
Birch Bay GC, *Nisswa* .... 9 [R] 218-963-4488
birchbaygolfresort.com
Birch Creek GC, *Sturgeon Lake* .... 9 [P] 218-658-4555
Birchwood GC, *Pelican Rapids* .... 9 [P] 218-863-6486
Birnamwood GC, *Burnsville* .... 9 [P] 952-641-1370
burnsville.org
Black Bear G Complex, *Backus* .... 18 [P] 218-587-8800
pinerivercountryclub.com
Black Bear GC, *Carlton* .... 18 [P] 218-722-8633
golfatthebear.com
Blackberry Ridge GC, *Sartell* .... 18 [P] 320-257-4653
blackberryridgegolf.com
Blackduck GC, *Blackduck* .... 9 [M] 218-835-7757
blackduckmn.com
Blooming Prairie CC, *Blooming Prairie* ...... 9 [P] 507-583-2887
Blueberry Hills CC, *Deer River*................... 9 [P] 218-246-8010
blueberryhillsgolf.com
Blueberry Pines GC, *Menahga* .... 18 [P] 218-564-4653
blueberrypinesgolf.com
Bluff Creek GC, *Chaska*............................ 18 [P] 952-445-5685
golfbluffcreekmn.com
Boulder Pointe GC, *Elko*........................... 18 [P] 952-461-4900
boulderpointegolf.com
Boulder Ridge GC, *St Cloud* .... 9 [P] 320-259-7944
Bracketts Crossing CC, *Lakeville* .... 18 [V] 952-435-7600
brackettscrossingcc.com
Braemar Executive Course and DR, *Edina*....9 [M] 952-903-5760
braemargolf.com
Braemar GC, *Edina*................................... 36 [M] 952-903-5750
braemargolf.com
Breezy Point Resort, *Breezy Point* .... 36 [R] 218-562-7811
breezypointresort.com
Brightwood Hills GC, *New Brighton* .... 9 [P] 651-638-2150
newbrightonmn.gov
Brockway GC, *Rosemount*......................... 9 [S] 651-423-5222
Brookland Exec Nine Hole GC, *Brooklyn Park*...9 [P] 763-561-3850
Brookside Resort GC, *Park Rapids* .... 9 [R] 218-732-4093
brookside-resort.com
Brooktree GC, *Owatonna* .... 18 [M] 507-444-2467
ci.owatonna.mn.us
Brookview GC, *Golden Valley* .... 18 [M] 763-512-2300
brookviewgolf.com
Buffalo Heights GC, *Buffalo* .... 9 [P] 763-682-2854
buffaloheights.com
Bulrush GC, *Rush City*.............................. 18 [P] 320-358-1050
bulrushgc.com

Bunker Hills GC, *Coon Rapids* .... 36 [M] 763-755-4141
bunkerhillsgolf.com
Burl Oaks GC, *Mound*............................... 18 [V] 952-472-4909
burloaksgolfclub.com
Canby GC, *Canby*....................................... 9 [S] 507-223-5607
Cannon GC, *Cannon Falls* .... 18 [P] 507-263-3126
cannongolfclub.com
Carefree GC, *Big Lake* .... 18 [R] 763-263-6050
carefreecc.com
Carriage Hills CC, *Eagan*......................... 18 [P] 651-452-7211
Castle Highlands GC, *Bemidji*.................. 18 [S] 218-586-2681
golfcastles.com
Castlewood GC, *Forest Lake*..................... 9 [P] 651-464-6233
castlewoodgolf.com
Cedar Creek GC, *Albertville*..................... 18 [P] 763-497-8245
cedarcreekmn.com
Cedar River CC, *Adams*........................... 18 [P] 507-582-3595
cedarrivercountryclub.com
Cedar Valley GC, *Winona*........................ 27 [P] 507-457-3129
cedarvalleymn.com
Centerbrook GC, *Brooklyn Center*............. 9 [M] 763-561-3239
cityofbrooklyncenter.org
Chaska Town Course, *Chaska* .... 18 [M] 952-443-3748
chaskatowncourse.com
Chisago Lakes GC, *Lindstrom* .... 18 [P] 651-257-1484
chisagolakesgolf.com
Chomonix GC, *Lino Lakes* .... 18 [M] 651-482-8484
chomonix.com
Chosen Valley GC, *Chatfield* .... 9 [S] 507-867-4305
Cimarron Park GC, *Lake Elmo*................... 9 [P] 651-436-6188
City View GC, *Cold Spring* .... 9 [P] 320-685-7000
Clarks Grove GC, *Clarks Grove*.................. 9 [P] 507-256-7737
Cleary Lake GC, *Prior Lake*....................... 9 [M] 763-694-7777
threeriversparkdistrict.org
Cloquet CC, *Cloquet* .... 18 [V] 218-879-7997
cloquetcc.com
Coffee Mill G&CC, *Wabasha* .... 18 [S] 651-565-4332
coffeemillgolf.com
Cokato Town & CC, *Cokato* .... 9 [P] 320-286-2007
Columbia GC, *Minneapolis*...................... 18 [M] 612-789-2627
minneapolisparks.org
Como GC, *St Paul* .... 18 [M] 651-488-9679
golfstpaul.org
Cottonwood CC, *Cottonwood* .... 9 [S] 507-423-6335
Country View GC, *Maplewood*................. 18 [P] 651-484-9809
Countryside GC, *Minneota* .... 9 [P] 507-872-6335
Countryside GC, *Shafer* .... 9 [P] 651-257-6387
CreeksBend GC, *New Prague* .... 18 [P] 952-758-7200
creeksbendgolfcourse.com
Crosswoods GC, *Crosslake*..................... 27 [P] 218-692-4653
crosslakegolf.com
Crow River GC, *Hutchinson* .... 18 [P] 320-587-3070
crowrivercc.com
Crystal Lake GC, *Lakeville*...................... 18 [P] 952-432-6566
crystallakegolfcourse.com
Cuyuna CC, *Deerwood*............................. 18 [S] 218-534-3489
cuyunacountryclub.com
Dacotah Ridge GC, *Morton* .... 18 [R] 507-697-8050
dacotahridge.com
Dahlgreen GC, *Chaska* .... 18 [S] 952-448-7463
dahlgreen.com
Dawson GC, *Dawson*................................. 9 [P] 320-769-2280

[A] = MILITARY   [M] = MUNICIPAL   [P] = PUBLIC   [R] = RESORT

Golf Yellow Pages, 18th Edition — MINNESOTA

Daytona GC, *Dayton* .... 18 [P] 763-427-6110
  daytonagolfclub.com
Deacons Lodge GC, *Pequot Lakes* .... 18 [P] 218-562-6262
  deaconslodge.com
Deer Run GC, *Victoria* .... 18 [P] 952-443-2351
  deerrungolf.com
Dellwood Hills GC, *Dellwood* .... 18 [V] 651-426-4733
  dellwoodhillsgc.org
Detroit CC, *Detroit Lakes* .... 36 [R] 218-847-5790
  detroitcountryclub.com
Dodge CC, *Dodge Center* .... 18 [P] 507-374-2374
  dodgecountryclub.com
Double Eagle GC, *Eagle Bend* .... 9 [P] 218-738-5155
Driftwood Family Resort & GC, *Pine River* ...... 9 [R] 218-568-4221
  driftwoodresort.com
Dwan GC, *Bloomington* .... 18 [M] 952-563-8702
  ci.bloomington.mn.us
Eagle Creek GC, *Willmar* .... 18 [S] 320-235-1166
  willmargolf.com
Eagle Lake Golf Ctr, *Plymouth* .... 9 [M] 763-694-7695
  eaglelakegolf.com
Eagle Ridge GC, *Coleraine* .... 18 [M] 218-245-2217
  golfeagleridge.com
Eagle Trace Golfers Club, *Clearwater* .... 18 [P] 320-558-4653
  eagletracegolf.com
Eagle Valley GC, *Woodbury* .... 18 [M] 651-714-3750
  eaglevalleygc.com
Eagle View GC, *Park Rapids* .... 18 [P] 218-732-7102
Eagles Landing GC, *Fort Ripley* .... 18 [P] 320-632-5721
  eagleslanding-golf.com
East Bay 9 GC, *Balaton* .... 9 [M] 507-734-4711
  swmngolf.com
East Mill Nine GC, *Alexandria* .... 9 [M] 320-886-5500
  eastmillnine.com
Eastwood GC, *Rochester* .... 18 [M] 507-281-6173
  rochestermngolf.com
Edina CC, *Edina* .... 18 [V] 952-927-5775
  edinacountryclub.org
Edinburgh USA, *Brooklyn Park* .... 18 [M] 763-315-8550
  edinburghusa.org
Elk River GC, *Elk River* .... 18 [S] 763-441-4111
  elkrivergc.com
Elm Creek GC, *Minneapolis* .... 18 [P] 763-478-6716
  elmcreekgc.com
Ely GC, *Ely* .... 9 [S] 218-365-5932
  elymngolfclub.com
Emerald Greens GC, *Hastings* .... 36 [P] 651-480-8558
  emeraldgreensgolf.com
Emerald Valley GC, *Lakefield* .... 9 [S] 507-662-5755
Emily Greens GC, *Emily* .... 18 [P] 218-763-2169
  emilygreens.com
Enger Park GC, *Duluth* .... 27 [M] 218-723-3451
  golfinduluth.com
Eshquaguma CC, *Gilbert* .... 9 [V] 218-865-4706
  eshquaguma.com
Eveleth Muni GC, *Eveleth* .... 9 [M] 218-744-7558
  minnesotagolf.com
Fair Havens GC, *Menahga* .... 18 [P] 218-732-0519
  fairgolf.com
Fairway Shores Exec GC, *Zimmerman* .... 9 [P] 763-856-3334
Fairways At Howards Barn, *Fifty Lakes* .... 9 [P] 218-763-2038
Falcon Ridge GC, *Stacy* .... 27 [P] 651-462-5797
  falconridgegolf.net

Falls CC, *International Falls* .... 18 [S] 218-283-4491
  fallscc.com
Faribault G&CC, *Faribault* .... 18 [P] 507-334-3810
  faribaultgolf.com
Farmers GC, *Sanborn* .... 9 [P] 507-648-3629
  rrcnet.org/~golfclub
Ferndale GC, *Rushford* .... 9 [P] 507-864-7626
  ferndalegolfcourse.com
Fiddlestix GC, *Isle* .... 18 [P] 320-676-3636
  golffiddlestix.com
Forest Hills GC, *Forest Lake* .... 18 [V] 651-464-3097
  foresthillsgc.com
Forest Hills Golf Resort, *Detroit Lakes* .... 18 [R] 218-439-6400
  foresthillsgolfrv.com
Fort Ridgley GC, *Fairfax* .... 9 [M] 507-426-7840
  dnr.state.mn.us
Fort Snelling GC, *St Paul* .... 9 [M] 612-726-6222
  minneapolisparks.org
Fosston GC, *Fosston* .... 9 [S] 218-435-6535
Fountain Valley GC, *Farmington* .... 18 [P] 651-463-2121
Fox Hollow GC, *St Michael* .... 27 [S] 763-428-4468
  foxhollowgolf.net
Fox Lake GC, *Sherburn* .... 9 [P] 507-764-8381
Frazee GC, *Frazee* .... 9 [P] 218-334-3831
French Lake GC, *Dayton* .... 9 [P] 763-428-4544
  frenchlakegolf.com
Gem Lake Hills GC, *White Bear Lake* .... 18 [P] 651-429-8715
  gemlakehillsgolf.com
Geneva GC, *Alexandria* .... 27 [P] 320-762-7089
  genevagolfclub.com
Glen Lake Golf & Practice Ctr, *Minnetonka* ... 9 [M] 763-694-7824
  glenlakegolf.com
Glencoe CC, *Glencoe* .... 18 [S] 320-864-3023
  glencoecountryclub.net
Golden Eagle GC, *Fifty Lakes* .... 18 [P] 218-763-4653
  golfgoldeneagle.com
Golden Valley G&CC, *Golden Valley* .... 18 [V] 763-732-4140
  gvccclub.com
Golf at the Legacy, *Faribault* .... 18 [P] 507-332-7177
  legacygolf.net
Golf on the Edge, *Bigfork* .... 9 [P] 218-743-3626
  golfontheedge.com
Goodrich GC, *Maplewood* .... 18 [M] 651-748-2525
  ramseycountygolf.com
Gopher Hills GC, *Cannon Falls* .... 27 [P] 507-263-2507
  gopherhills.com
Graceville GC, *Graceville* .... 9 [S] 320-748-7557
Grand National GC, *Hinckley* .... 18 [P] 320-384-7427
  grandnationalgolf.com
Grandview GC, *Duluth* .... 9 [P] 218-628-3727
Grandy Nine GC, *Stanchfield* .... 9 [P] 763-689-1417
Granite Park GC, *Granite Falls* .... 9 [S] 320-564-4755
Green Lea GC, *Albert Lea* .... 18 [P] 507-373-1061
  greenlea.com
Green Valley GC, *Lake Park* .... 9 [P] 218-532-7447
  greenvalleygolf.net
Greenhaven CC, *Anoka* .... 18 [M] 763-576-2970
  greenhavengolfcourse.com
Greenwood GC, *Bemidji* .... 18 [P] 218-751-3875
  greenwoodgolfcourse.com
Greenwood Golf Links, *Wyoming* .... 18 [P] 651-462-4653
Greystone GC, *Sauk Centre* .... 18 [P] 320-351-4653
  greystonegc.net

[S] = SEMI-PRIVATE   [V] = PRIVATE   [U] = UNIVERSITY   [N] = UNIVERSITY-PRIVATE

MINNESOTA
Golf Yellow Pages, 18th Edition

Gross National GC, *Minneapolis* .... 18 [M] 612-789-2542
  minneapolisparks.org
Gunflint Hills GC, *Grand Marais* .... 9 [M] 218-387-9988
  grandmarais.com
Hadley Creek GC, *Rochester* .... 9 [M] 507-328-2533
  rochestermngolf.com
Halla Green Exec GC, *Chanhassen* .... 9 [P] 952-252-2525
  hallagreens.com
Hardwoods GC At Mille Lacs, *Garrison* .... 18 [R] 320-692-4325
  millelacsgolf.com
Harmony GC, *Harmony* .... 9 [S] 507-886-5622
  harmonygolfclub.com
Hastings CC, *Hastings* .... 18 [V] 651-437-4612
  hastingscountryclub.org
Havana Hills GC, *Owatonna* .... 9 [P] 507-451-2577
Hawk Creek CC, *Raymond* .... 9 [P] 320-967-4653
  hawkcreekcc.com
Hawley G&CC, *Hawley* .... 18 [M] 218-483-4808
  hawleygolf.com
Hayden Hills GC, *Dayton* .... 18 [P] 763-421-0060
  haydenhillsgolf.com
Hazeltine National GC, *Chaska* .... 18 [V] 952-566-5400
  hngc.com
Headwaters CC, *Park Rapids* .... 18 [P] 218-732-4832
  headwatersgolf.com
Heart of the Valley GC, *Ada* .... 9 [P] 218-784-4746
Heritage Links GC, *Lakeville* .... 18 [P] 952-440-4653
  heritagelinks.com
Hiawatha GC, *Minneapolis* .... 18 [M] 612-724-7715
  minneapolisparks.org
Hibbing Muni GC, *Hibbing* .... 9 [P] 218-362-5950
Hidden Creek GC, *Owatonna* .... 18 [P] 507-444-9229
  hiddencreekmn.com
Hidden Greens GC, *Hastings* .... 18 [P] 651-437-3085
  hiddengreensgolf.com
Hidden Haven GC, *Cedar* .... 18 [P] 763-434-6867
  hiddenhavengolfclub.com
Higbees GC, *Onamia* .... 9 [P] 320-495-3333
  higbeesgolfcourse.com
Highland National GC, *St Paul* .... 18 [P] 651-695-3774
  golfstpaul.org
Highland Park 9 Hole GC, *St Paul* .... 9 [M] 651-695-3708
  golfstpaul.org
Hillcrest GC of St Paul, *St Paul* .... 18 [V] 651-771-1515
  hillcreststpaul.com
Holiday Park GC, *Hayward* .... 9 [R] 507-373-3886
Hollydale GC, *Plymouth* .... 18 [P] 763-559-9847
  hollydalegolf.com
Hoyt Lakes GC, *Hoyt Lakes* .... 9 [M] 218-225-2841
  hoytlakes.com
Hyland Greens GC, *Bloomington* .... 18 [M] 952-563-8868
  ci.bloomington.mn.us
Indian Hills GC, *Stillwater* .... 18 [V] 651-770-2366
  minnesotagolfatindianhills.com
Interlachen CC, *Edina* .... 18 [V] 952-929-1661
  interlachencc.org
Interlaken GC, *Fairmont* .... 18 [V] 507-238-1693
  interlakengolfclub.com
Inver Wood GC, *Inver Grove Heights* .... 27 [M] 651-457-3667
  inverwood.org
Irish Hills GC, *Pine River* .... 18 [P] 218-587-2296
  pineyridge.com
Ironman GC, *Detroit Lakes* .... 9 [P] 218-847-5592
  ironmangolf.com

Island Lake Golf & Training Ctr, *Shoreview* .... 9 [P] 651-787-0483
  islandlakegolf.com
Island Pine CC, *Atwater* .... 18 [P] 320-974-8600
  islandpinegolf.com
Island View GC, *Waconia* .... 18 [S] 952-442-6116
  islandviewgolfclub.com
Izatys G&YC, *Onamia* .... 36 [R] 320-532-3101
  izatys.com
Jackson GC, *Jackson* .... 9 [S] 507-847-2660
Karlstad GC, *Karlstad* .... 9 [M] 218-436-4653
  karlstadgolfclub.com
Kate Haven GC, *Circle Pines* .... 9 [P] 763-786-2945
  katehaven.com
Keller GC, *Maplewood* .... 18 [M] 651-766-4170
  ramseycountygolf.com
Kenyon CC, *Kenyon* .... 9 [S] 507-789-6307
Kimball GC, *Kimball* .... 18 [P] 320-398-2285
  kimballgolf.com
Koronis Hills GC, *Paynesville* .... 18 [S] 320-243-4111
  koronishillsgolf.com
Lafayette CC, *Minnetonka Beach* .... 9 [V] 952-471-8493
  lafayetteclub.com
Lake City GC, *Lake City* .... 18 [S] 651-345-3221
  lakecitygolf.com
Lake Hendricks GC, *Hendricks* .... 9 [S] 507-275-3852
Lake Miltona GC, *Alexandria* .... 18 [S] 320-852-7078
  lakemiltonagolfclub.com
Lake Pepin GC, *Lake City* .... 18 [P] 651-345-5768
  lakepepingolf.com
Lakeview Golf of Orono, *Mound* .... 18 [P] 952-472-3459
  lakeviewgolfoforono.com
Lakeview National GC, *Two Harbors* .... 18 [M] 218-834-2664
  lakeviewnational.com
Lancaster Riverside GC, *Lancaster* .... 9 [P] 218-762-4653
  wiktel.net/lancasterriverside
Lanesboro GC, *Lanesboro* .... 9 [S] 507-467-3742
Le Sueur CC, *Le Sueur* .... 18 [V] 507-665-6292
  lesueurcountryclub.com
Legacy Course At Craguns, *Brainerd* .... 45 [R] 218-825-2800
  legacygolfcourses.com
Legends Club, *Prior Lake* .... 18 [R] 952-226-4777
  legendsgc.com
Lester Park GC, *Duluth* .... 27 [M] 218-525-1400
  golfinduluth.com
Lewiston CC, *Lewiston* .... 18 [P] 507-523-2060
Lida Greens GC, *Pelican Rapids* .... 9 [P] 218-863-1531
  lidagreensgolf.biz
Litchfield GC, *Litchfield* .... 18 [M] 320-693-6059
  litchfieldgolfclub.com
Little Crow CC, *Spicer* .... 27 [P] 320-354-2296
  littlecrowgolf.com
Little Falls GC, *Little Falls* .... 18 [M] 320-616-5520
  littlefallsgolf.com
Loggers Trail GC, *Stillwater* .... 18 [P] 651-439-7862
  sawmillgc.com
Long Prairie CC, *Long Prairie* .... 18 [S] 320-732-3312
  longprairiecountryclub.com
Longbow GC, *Walker* .... 18 [R] 218-547-4121
  longbowgolfclub.com
Loon Lake GC, *Jackson* .... 9 [P] 507-847-4036
Lost Spur GC, *Eagan* .... 9 [P] 651-454-5681
  wpgolf.com/lostspur

[A] = MILITARY [M] = MUNICIPAL [P] = PUBLIC [R] = RESORT

MINNESOTA

Golf Yellow Pages, 18th Edition

Luverne CC, *Luverne* .... 9 [S] 507-283-4383
luvernecountryclub.com
Ma Cal Grove CC, *Caledonia* .... 9 [S] 507-725-2733
macalgrove.com
Maddens on Gull Lake - Classic, *Brainerd* .... 18 [R] 218-829-2811
maddens.com
Maddens on Gull Lake - Pine Beach West, *Brainerd* 18 [R] 218-829-2811
maddens.com
Maddens on Gull Lake-Pine Beach E-Social 9,
  Brainerd .... 63 [R] 218-829-2811
maddens.com
Madelia GC, *Madelia* .... 9 [M] 507-642-3608
madeliamn.com
Madison CC, *Madison* .... 9 [V] 320-598-7587
Mahnomen CC, *Mahnomen* .... 9 [P] 218-935-5188
Majestic Oaks GC, *Ham Lake* .... 45 [P] 763-755-2140
majesticoaksgolfclub.com
Manitou Ridge GC, *White Bear Lake* .... 18 [M] 651-777-2987
manitouridge.com
Mankato GC, *Mankato* .... 18 [V] 507-387-5636
mankatogolfclub.com
Maple Hills GC, *Frazee* .... 9 [P] 218-847-9532
maplehillsgolfclub.com
Maple Ridge GC, *Bemidji* .... 9 [P] 218-751-8401
mapleridgebemidji.com
Maple Valley G&CC, *Rochester* .... 18 [P] 507-285-9100
maplevalleygolf.com
MarHaven Greens GC, *Belgrade* .... 9 [V] 320-254-8416
marhavengreens.com
Marshall GC, *Marshall* .... 18 [V] 507-537-1622
marshallgolfclub.com
Mayflower CC, *Fairfax* .... 9 [P] 507-426-9964
Meadow Greens GC, *Austin* .... 18 [P] 507-433-4878
meadowgreensgc.com
Meadow Lakes GC, *Rochester* .... 18 [P] 507-285-1190
meadowlakesgolfclub.com
Meadow Links GC, *Hutchinson* .... 9 [P] 320-234-9533
Meadowbrook CC, *Mabel* .... 9 [P] 507-493-5708
Meadowbrook GC, *Hopkins* .... 18 [M] 952-929-2077
minneapolisparks.org
Meadowlark CC, *Melrose* .... 9 [P] 320-256-4989
meadowlarkcountryclub.com
Meadowwood GC, *Minnetonka* .... 9 [P] 612-470-4000
Medina G&CC, *Hamel* .... 27 [V] 763-478-6020
medinagolfcc.com
Mendakota CC, *Mendota Heights* .... 18 [V] 651-454-4200
mendakotacc.com
Mendota Heights Par 3, *Mendota Heights* .... 9 [M] 651-454-9822
mendota-heights.com
Mesaba CC, *Hibbing* .... 18 [P] 218-262-2851
mesabacc.com
Midland Hills CC, *St Paul* .... 18 [V] 651-631-0440
midlandhillscc.org
Milaca GC, *Milaca* .... 18 [P] 320-983-2110
stonesthrowgolf.com
Minakwa CC, *Crookston* .... 9 [P] 218-281-1773
Minn Iowa GC, *Elmore* .... 9 [P] 507-943-3149
Minneapolis GC, *Minneapolis* .... 18 [V] 952-544-0021
minneapolisgolfclub.com
Minneopa GC, *Mankato* .... 9 [P] 507-625-5777
minneopagolf.com
Minnesota National GC, *McGregor* .... 27 [S] 218-426-3117
minnesotanationalgolfcourse.com

Minnesota Valley CC, *Bloomington* .... 18 [V] 952-884-1744
mvccgolf.com
Minnetonka CC, *Excelsior* .... 18 [V] 952-474-5222
minnetonkacc.com
Minnewaska GC, *Glenwood* .... 18 [P] 320-634-3680
minnewaskagolfclub.com
Mississippi Dunes Golf Links, *Cottage Grove* .... 18 [P] 651-768-7611
mississippidunes.com
Mississippi National Golf Links, *Red Wing* .... 36 [P] 651-388-1874
wpgolf.com/mississippi
Montgomery National GC, *Montgomery* .... 18 [P] 507-364-5602
montgomerynationalgolf.com
Monticello CC, *Monticello* .... 18 [P] 763-295-4653
montigolf.com
Moorhead CC, *Moorhead* .... 18 [V] 218-236-0200
moorheadcountryclub.com
Moorhead Village Green GC, *Moorhead* .... 18 [P] 218-299-7888
moorheadgolf.com
Moose Lake GC, *Sturgeon Lake* .... 9 [S] 218-485-4886
Mount Frontenac GC, *Frontenac* .... 18 [P] 651-388-5826
mountfrontenac.com
Mountain Lake GC, *Mountain Lake* .... 9 [S] 507-427-3869
mtlakegolfcourse.com
New Hope Village GC, *New Hope* .... 9 [M] 763-531-5178
ci.new-hope.mn.us
New Prague GC, *New Prague* .... 18 [P] 952-758-5326
newpraguegolf.com
New Ulm CC, *New Ulm* .... 18 [S] 507-354-8896
Nordic Trails GC, *Alexandria* .... 9 [P] 320-762-5420
North Branch GC, *North Branch* .... 9 [M] 651-674-9989
nbgolfcourse.com
North Links GC, *North Mankato* .... 18 [P] 507-947-3355
northlinksgolf.com
North Oaks GC, *North Oaks* .... 18 [V] 651-484-1635
northoaksgolfclub.com
Northern Hills GC, *Rochester* .... 18 [M] 507-281-6170
rochestermngolf.com
Northfield GC, *Northfield* .... 18 [S] 507-645-4026
northfieldgolfclub.com
Northland CC, *Duluth* .... 18 [V] 218-525-1941
northlandcountryclub.com
Oak Glen GC, *Stillwater* .... 27 [P] 651-439-6981
oakglengolf.com
Oak Harbor G&TC, *Baudette* .... 18 [S] 218-634-9939
oakharborgolfcourse.com
Oak Hill GC, *Rice* .... 18 [P] 320-259-8969
oakhillgolfclub.com
Oak Knolls GC, *Red Lake Falls* .... 9 [M] 218-253-4423
Oak Lake GC, *Erskine* .... 9 [S] 218-687-4653
Oak Marsh GC, *Oakdale* .... 18 [P] 651-730-8886
wpgolf.com/oakmarsh
Oak Ridge CC, *Hopkins* .... 18 [V] 952-935-7721
oakridgecountryclub.net
Oakcrest GC, *Roseau* .... 18 [P] 218-463-3016
oakcrestgolfcourse.com
Oakdale CC, *Buffalo Lake* .... 18 [P] 320-833-5518
oakdalegolfclub.com
Oaks CC, *Hayfield* .... 18 [P] 507-477-3233
oaksinhayfield.com
Oaks Summit GC, *Rochester* .... 18 [P] 507-252-1808
oaksummitgolf.com
Oakview GC, *Greenbush* .... 9 [M] 218-782-2380
greenbushmn.govoffice2.com

[S] = SEMI-PRIVATE   [V] = PRIVATE   [U] = UNIVERSITY   [N] = UNIVERSITY-PRIVATE

115

MINNESOTA

Golf Yellow Pages, 18th Edition

Oakview GC, *Alden* ....9 [P] 507-863-2288
 oakviewgc.com
Oakwood GC, *Henning* ....9 [P] 218-583-2127
Old Barn Resort Course, *Preston* ....18 [R] 507-467-2512
 barnresort.com
Olivia GC, *Olivia* ....9 [P] 320-523-2313
Olympic Hills CC, *Eden Prairie* .... 18 [V] 952-941-6265
 olympichills.com
Oneka Ridge GC, *White Bear Lake* ....18 [P] 651-429-2390
 onekaridgegc.com
Orono GC, *Wayzata* ....9 [M] 952-473-9904
Ortonville Muni GC, *Ortonville* ....18 [M] 320-839-3606
 ortonvillegolfcourse.com
Osakis CC, *Osakis* ....9 [S] 320-859-2140
 osakiscountryclub.com
Owatonna CC, *Owatonna* .... 18 [V] 507-451-1363
 owatonnacc.com
Parkview GC, *Eagan* ....18 [P] 651-994-8000
 parkviewgolfclub.com
Pebble Creek GC, *Becker* ....27 [M] 763-263-4653
 pebblecreekgolf.com
Pebble Lake GC, *Fergus Falls* ....18 [M] 218-736-7404
 playpebblelake.com
Perham Lakeside CC, *Perham* ....27 [M] 218-346-6070
 perhamlakeside.com
Pezhekee National GC, *Glenwood* ....18 [P] 320-634-4502
 petersresort.com
Phalen Park GC, *St Paul* ....18 [M] 651-778-0413
 golfstpaul.org
Pheasant Acres GC, *Rogers* ....18 [P] 763-428-8244
 pheasantacresgolf.com
Pheasant Links, *Emmons* .... 9 [V] 507-297-5800
 pheasantlinks.com
Pierz Muni GC, *Pierz* ....9 [M] 320-468-2662
 pierzmn.org
Pike Lake GC, *Duluth* ....9 [S] 218-729-8160
 pinelakegolf.com
Pine City CC, *Pine City* ....9 [P] 320-629-3848
Pine Creek GC, *La Crescent* ....9 [M] 507-895-2410
 lacrescent.govoffice.com
Pine Hill GC, *Carlton* ....9 [P] 218-384-3727
Pine Island GC, *Pine Island* ....18 [P] 507-356-8252
 pigc.net
Pine Meadows at Brainerd GC, *Baxter* .... 18 [S] 218-829-5733
 brainerdgolf.com
Pine Ridge GC, *Evansville* ....9 [P] 320-834-4028
 pineridgegolfcourse.net
Pine Ridge GC, *Motley* ....18 [P] 218-575-3300
 brainerd.net/~prgolfcl
Pine Ridge GC - Sartell, *Sartell* ....18 [P] 320-259-0551
 sartellmn.com
Pine River CC, *Pine River* ....18 [P] 218-587-4774
 pinerivercountryclub.com
Pinewood GC, *Elk River* ....9 [M] 763-441-3451
 ci.elk-river.mn.us
Pioneer Creek GC, *Maple Plain* ....18 [P] 952-955-3982
 pioneercreek.com
Piper Hills GC, *Plainview* ....9 [P] 507-534-2613
Pipestone CC, *Pipestone* ....9 [S] 507-825-2592
 pipestonecc.com
Pokegama GC, *Grand Rapids* ....18 [P] 218-326-3444
 pokegamagolf.com

Pomme De Terre CC, *Morris* .... 18 [S] 320-589-1009
 pdtgolfclub.com
Ponderosa GC, *Glyndon* ....9 [U] 218-498-2201
Prairie Ridge GC, *Janesville* ....9 [M] 507-234-5505
Prairie View Community GC, *Brooten* ....9 [P] 320-346-2677
Prairie View Golf Links, *Worthington* .... 18 [M] 507-372-8670
 ci.worthington.mn.us
Preston G&CC, *Preston* ....9 [P] 507-765-4485
 prestongolf.net
Prestwick GC At Wedgewood, *Woodbury* ....18 [S] 651-731-4779
 prestwick.com
Princeton GC, *Princeton* ....18 [S] 763-389-5109
 princetongc.com
Proctor GC, *Proctor* ....9 [M] 218-624-2255
 ci.proctor.mn.us
Purple Hawk CC, *Cambridge* ....18 [S] 763-689-3800
 purplehawk.com
Quadna Mtn Resort GC, *Hill City* .... 9 [R] 218-697-2880
 quadna-resort.com
Red Oak GC, *Mound* ....9 [P] 952-472-3999
 lakeviewgolfoforono.com/redoakpage.htm
Red Rock GC, *Hoffman* ....9 [P] 320-986-2342
Red Wing GC, *Red Wing* .... 18 [S] 651-388-9524
 redwinggolfclub.com
Redwood Falls GC, *Redwood Falls* ....18 [P] 507-627-8901
 redwoodfallsgolf.com
Retreat GC, *Floodwood* ....9 [P] 218-476-3131
 retreatgolfclub.com
Rich Spring GC, *Cold Spring* ....18 [P] 320-685-8810
 richspringgolf.com
Rich Valley GC, *Rosemount* ....27 [P] 651-437-4653
 rich-valley-golf-course.com
Ridges At Sand Creek, *Jordan* ....18 [P] 952-492-2644
 ridgesatsandcreek.com
Ridgeview CC, *Duluth* .... 18 [V] 218-728-5128
 ridgeviewcountryclub.com
Ridgewood GC, *Longville* ....27 [P] 218-363-2444
 ridgewoodgolf.com
River Hills GC, *Detroit Lakes* ....9 [P] 218-847-1223
 riverhillsdl.com
River Oaks GC, *Cottage Grove* ....18 [M] 651-438-2121
 riveroaksmunigolf.com
River Oaks GC, *Cold Spring* ....18 [P] 320-685-4138
 River Oaks GC, *Austin* ....18 [P] 507-433-9098
Rivers Edge Golf, *Watertown* ....9 [P] 952-955-3343
 bontheriver.com
Riverside Town & CC, *Winnebago* .... 9 [V] 507-526-2764
Riverview GC, *New Richland* ....9 [P] 507-465-3516
Riverview Greens GC, *Stewartville* ....18 [P] 507-533-9393
 riverviewgreens.com
Riverwood National, *Monticello* ....18 [P] 763-271-5000
 riverwoodnational.com
Rochester G&CC, *Rochester* .... 18 [V] 507-282-3170
 rgcc.org
Rodina GC, *Alexandria* ....9 [P] 320-554-3385
Rolling Hills GC, *Pelican Rapids* ....9 [P] 218-532-2214
Rolling Hills GC, *Westbrook* ....9 [P] 507-274-5166
Root River CC, *Spring Valley* ....9 [P] 507-346-2501
 rootrivercountryclub.com
Rose Lake GC, *Fairmont* ....18 [P] 507-235-5274
 roselakegolfclub.com
Roseville Cedarholm GC, *Roseville* ....9 [M] 651-633-8337
 cityofroseville.com

116 [A] = MILITARY [M] = MUNICIPAL [P] = PUBLIC [R] = RESORT

MINNESOTA

Rum River Hills GC, *Ramsey* ....18 [P] 763-753-3339
  rumriverhills.com
Rush Creek GC, *Maple Grove* ....18 [P] 763-494-8844
  rushcreek.com
Ruttgers Bay Lake Lodge, *Deerwood*..................27 [R] 218-678-4647
  ruttgers.com
Ruttgers Sugar Lake Lodge, *Cohasset* ....18 [R] 218-327-1462
  sugarlakelodge.com
Sanbrook GC, *Isanti* ....27 [P] 763-444-9904
  sanbrook.com
Sandhill River GC, *Fertile* ....9 [P] 218-945-3535
  sandhillrivergolf.com
Sandstone Area CC, *Sandstone* ....9 [M] 320-245-0471
Sandtrap GC, *Cass Lake*..................9 [P] 218-335-6531
Sauk Centre CC, *Sauk Centre*..................9 [P] 320-352-3860
Savannah Oaks GC, *Lynd*..................9 [P] 507-865-1135
  golfsavannahoaks.com
Sawmill GC, *Stillwater* ....18 [S] 651-439-7862
  sawmillgc.com
ShadowBrooke GC, *Lester Prairie* ....18 [P] 320-395-4250
  shadowbrooke.com
Shamrock GC, *Hamel* ....18 [P] 763-478-9977
  shamrockgolfcourse.com
Shoreland G&TC, *St Peter*..................18 [S] 507-931-3470
  shorelandcc.com
Silver Bay CC, *Silver Bay*..................9 [S] 218-226-3111
  silverbaygolf.com
Silver Springs GC, *Monticello* ....36 [P] 763-295-2951
  silverspringsgolf.com
Slayton CC, *Slayton*..................9 [S] 507-836-8154
Sleepy Eye GC, *Sleepy Eye* ....9 [S] 507-794-5249
Soldiers Memorial Field GC, *Rochester*..................18 [M] 507-281-6176
  rochestermngolf.com
Somerby GC, *Byron* ....18 [V] 507-775-3700
  somerby.com
Somerset CC, *Mendota Heights* ....18 [V] 651-457-1224
Southbrook GC, *Annandale*..................18 [S] 320-274-2341
  southbrookgolf.com
Southern Hills GC, *Farmington*..................18 [P] 651-463-4653
  southernhillsgolfcourse.com
Southview CC, *St Paul*..................18 [V] 651-451-1169
  southviewcc.com
Spring Brook CC, *Mora*..................18 [S] 320-679-2317
  springbrookgc.com
Spring Hill GC, *Wayzata*..................18 [V] 952-473-1500
  springhillgc.com
Springfield GC, *Springfield*..................9 [P] 507-723-5888
St Charles GC, *St Charles* ....18 [S] 507-932-5444
  stcharlesgolfclub.com
St Cloud CC, *St Cloud*..................18 [V] 320-253-1331
  stcloudcountryclub.com
St James CC, *St James*..................18 [P] 507-375-7484
  stjamesgc.com
Stalker Lake GC, *Dalton* ....9 [P] 218-589-8591
  stalkerlake.com
Stephen Riverside GC, *Stephen*..................9 [P] 218-478-2735
Stillwater CC, *Stillwater* ....18 [V] 651-439-7979
  sccgolf.com
Stone Bridge GC, *Otsego* ....9 [P] 763-441-0900
  stonebridgegolfcourse.com
Stone Creek GC, *Foley*..................9 [P] 320-968-6017
Stonebrooke GC, *Shakopee*..................27 [P] 952-496-3171
  stonebrooke.com

Stonebrooke GC, *Shakopee*..................27 [P] 952-496-3171
  stonebrooke.com
StoneRidge GC, *Stillwater*..................18 [P] 651-436-4653
  stoneridgegc.com
Stoney Creek GC, *Renville* ....9 [P] 320-329-8400
  stoneycreekonline.com
Straight River GC, *Faribault* ....18 [P] 507-334-5108
  straightrivergc.com
Sundance Golf & Bowl, *Maple Grove*..................18 [P] 763-420-4700
  sundancegolfbowl.com
Superior National at Lutsen, *Lutsen*..................27 [R] 218-663-7195
  superiornational.com
Swan Lake CC, *Pengilly* ....9 [S] 218-885-3543
Tanners Brook GC, *Forest Lake*..................18 [P] 651-464-2300
  tannersbrook.com
Tartan Park GC, *Lake Elmo* ....27 [S] 651-733-3480
Terrace View GC, *Mankato* ....18 [P] 507-625-7665
Territory GC, *St Cloud*..................18 [P] 320-258-4653
  territorygc.com
The Bridges GC, *Minneapolis* ....9 [M] 763-785-9063
  bridgesgolf.com
The Bridges GC, *Winona* ....18 [S] 507-452-3535
  winonagolf.com
The Chaska Par 30 GC, *Chaska*..................9 [M] 952-448-7454
  chaskapar30.com
The Crossings at Montevideo, *Montevideo*..................18 [P] 320-269-6828
  montegolf.com
The Fred Richards GC, *Edina*..................9 [M] 612-915-6606
  braemargolf.com
The Garden Course At Grandview Lodge, *Nisswa*..................9 [R] 218-963-8745
  grandviewlodge.com
The Greens At Howard Lake, *Howard Lake*..................9 [P] 320-543-3330
The Jewel GC, *Lake City*..................18 [S] 651-345-5999
  jewelgolfclub.com
The Legend at Giants Ridge, *Biwabik*..................18 [R] 218-865-3001
  giantsridge.com
The Links At Northfork, *Ramsey*..................18 [P] 763-241-0506
  golfthelinks.com
The Links of Byron, *Byron* ....9 [P] 507-775-2004
The Lynx National GC, *Sauk Centre*..................18 [P] 320-352-0243
  lynxnationalgolf.com
The Meadows, *Moorhead* ....18 [M] 218-299-7888
  moorheadgolf.com
The Meadows At Mystic Lake, *Prior Lake*..................18 [P] 952-233-5533
  mysticlakegolf.com
The Minikahda Club, *Minneapolis* ....18 [V] 612-926-1601
  minikahdaclub.org
The Pines At Grand View Lodge, *Nisswa*..................27 [R] 218-963-2234
  grandviewlodge.com
The Ponds At Battle Creek GC, *Maplewood*..................9 [P] 651-501-6321
  ramseycountygolf.com
The Ponds, *St Francis* ....27 [P] 763-753-1100
  thepondsgolf.com
The Preserve At Grand View Lodge, *Pequot Lakes*..................18 [R] 218-568-4944
  grandviewlodge.com
The Quarry at Giants Ridge, *Biwabik*..................18 [R] 218-865-3001
  giantsridge.com
The Refuge GC, *Cedar* ....18 [P] 763-753-8383
  refugegolfclub.com
The Summit GC, *Cannon Falls* ....27 [P] 507-263-4648
  summitgolfclub.com
The Veterans GC, *St Cloud* ....9 [M] 320-255-7273
  stcloudmac.com

MINNESOTA

Golf Yellow Pages, 18th Edition

The Vintage at Staples, *Staples* .... 18 [P] 218-894-9907
  vintagegolfclub.com
The Wilderness At Fortune Bay, *Tower* .... 18 [R] 218-753-8917
  thewildernessgolf.com
The Wilds GC, *Prior Lake* .... 18 [P] 952-445-3500
  golfthewilds.com
Theodore Wirth GC, *Golden Valley* .... 27 [M] 763-522-4584
  minneapolisparks.org
Thief River Falls GC, *Thief River Falls* .... 18 [S] 218-681-2955
  thiefrivergolfclub.com
Thompson Oaks GC, *St Paul* .... 9 [M] 651-457-6042
  ci.west-saint-paul.mn.us
Three Brothers Vermilion River Greens, *Buyck* ..... 9 [P] 218-993-2246
Thumper Pond GC, *Ottertail* .... 18 [P] 218-367-2000
  thumperpond.com
Tianna CC, *Walker* .... 18 [S] 218-547-1712
  tianna.com
Timber Creek GC, *Watertown* .... 18 [P] 952-955-3600
  timbercreekgolf.com
Tipsinah Mounds GC, *Elbow Lake* .... 18 [P] 218-685-4271
  tmoundsgolf.com
Town & CC of St Paul, *St Paul* .... 18 [V] 651-659-2549
  tcc-club.com
Town & Country GC, *Fulda* .... 9 [P] 507-425-3328
TPC Twin Cities, *Blaine* .... 18 [V] 763-795-0816
  tpctwincities.com
Tracy CC, *Tracy* .... 9 [P] 507-629-4666
Travelers CC, *Clear Lake* .... 9 [R] 320-743-3133
  travelerscconmiss.com
Twenty Nine Pines GC, *Mahtonen* .... 9 [P] 218-389-3136
  29pinesgolfcourse.com
Twin Pines CC, *Bagley* .... 9 [M] 218-694-2454
Two Rivers GC, *Hallock* .... 9 [S] 218-843-2155
Tyler Community GC, *Tyler* .... 18 [P] 507-247-3242
  tylergolfclub.com
Univ of Minnesota Les Bolstad GC, *St Paul* .... 18 [U] 612-627-4000
  uofmgolf.com
Valley GC, *Willmar* .... 9 [P] 320-235-6790
Valley Golf Assn GC, *East Grand Forks* .... 18 [P] 218-773-1207
  valleygolfegf.com
Valley High GC, *Houston* .... 18 [P] 507-894-4444
Valley View GC, *Belle Plaine* .... 18 [P] 952-873-4653
  vvgolf.com
Valleywood GC, *Apple Valley* .... 18 [M] 952-953-2323
  cityofapplevalley.org
Vermilion Fairways, *Cook* .... 9 [S] 218-666-2679
Victory Links GC, *Blaine* .... 18 [P] 763-717-3240
  nscsports.org
Viking Meadows GC, *Cedar* .... 27 [P] 763-434-4205
  vikingmeadows.com
Vintage GC, *Monticello* .... 18 [P] 763-271-5000
  riverwoodnational.com
Virginia GC, *Virginia* .... 18 [M] 218-748-7530
Wapicada GC, *Sauk Rapids* .... 18 [S] 320-251-7804
  wapicada.com
Warren Riverside GC, *Warren* .... 9 [P] 218-745-4028
Warroad Estates GC, *Warroad* .... 18 [P] 218-386-2025
  warroadestates.com
Waseca Lakeside Club, *Waseca* .... 18 [S] 507-835-2574
  wasecagolf.com
Wayzata CC, *Wayzata* .... 18 [V] 952-475-9769
  wayzatacc.com

Wedgewood Cove GC, *Albert Lea* .... 18 [P] 507-373-2007
  wedgewoodcove.com
Wedgewood GC, *Walker* .... 9 [P] 218-547-2666
Wells GC, *Wells* .... 9 [P] 507-553-3313
Wendigo GC, *Grand Rapids* .... 18 [P] 218-327-2211
  wendigogolfclub.com
Westfield GC, *Winona* .... 9 [P] 507-452-6901
  westfieldgolfclub.com
Wheaton CC, *Wheaton* .... 9 [P] 320-563-4079
Whispering Pines GC, *Annandale* .... 18 [P] 320-274-8721
  whisperingpinesgolf.com
White Bear Yacht Club, *White Bear Lake* .... 18 [V] 651-429-5002
  wbyc.com
White Tail Run GC, *Wadena* .... 18 [M] 218-631-7718
  whitetailrungolfcourse.com
Whitefish GC, *Pequot Lakes* .... 18 [P] 218-543-4900
  whitefishgolf.com
Wild Marsh GC, *Buffalo* .... 18 [P] 763-682-4476
  wildmarsh.com
Wilderness Trail Golf & Village, *Longville* .... 9 [P] 218-363-2552
Wildflower At Fair Hills Resort, *Detroit Lakes* ...... 27 [R] 888-752-9945
  wildflowergolfcourse.com
Wildwedge Golf & Mini Golf, *Pequot Lakes* .... 9 [R] 218-568-6995
  wildwedge.com
Willinger GC, *Northfield* .... 18 [P] 952-652-2500
  willingersgc.com
Willow Creek GC, *Barnesville* .... 9 [M] 218-493-4486
Willow Creek GC, *Rochester* .... 27 [S] 507-285-0305
  wpgolf.com
Windom CC, *Windom* .... 9 [P] 507-831-3489
  windomcountryclub.com
Windsong Farms GC, *Maple Plain* .... 18 [V] 763-479-3535
  wsfarm.com
Winthrop GC, *Winthrop* .... 9 [S] 507-647-5828
Wolfridge GC, *Angora* .... 9 [P] 218-666-0218
  wolfridgegolf.com
Woodhill CC, *Wayzata* .... 18 [S] 952-473-5024
  woodhillcc.com
Woodland Creek GC, *Andover* .... 9 [P] 763-323-0517
Worthington CC, *Worthington* .... 18 [S] 507-376-4281
Zumbro Falls GC, *Zumbro Falls* .... 9 [P] 507-753-3131
  zfgolfclub.com
Zumbro Valley GC, *Mantorville* .... 9 [S] 507-635-2821
  zvrc.com
Zumbrota GC, *Zumbrota* .... 18 [S] 507-732-5817
  zumbrotagolfclub.com

MISSISSIPPI

Aberdeen G&CC, *Aberdeen* .... 9 [V] 662-369-6251
Ackerman CC, *Ackerman* .... 9 [V] 662-285-6025
Amory GC, *Amory* .... 9 [P] 662-256-9454
Annandale GC, *Madison* .... 18 [V] 601-856-0886
Back Acres CC, *Senatobia* .... 18 [V] 662-562-9838
Bay Breeze GC, *Biloxi* .... 18 [A] 228-377-3832
  keeslerservices.us
Bay Pointe Golf & Resort, *Brandon* .... 18 [R] 601-829-1862
  baypointegolfresort.com
Bay Springs CC, *Louin* .... 9 [P] 601-764-2621
Bayou Bend CC, *Sumner* .... 9 [V] 662-458-0430
Bayou Vista GC, *Gulfport* .... 18 [P] 228-868-9953
Bear Creek GC, *Laurel* .... 18 [P] 601-425-5670
Beau Pre CC, *Natchez* .... 18 [P] 601-442-5493
  beauprecc.com

[A] = MILITARY   [M] = MUNICIPAL   [P] = PUBLIC   [R] = RESORT

MISSISSIPPI

Bel Air GC, *Tupelo* .... 9 [M] 662-841-6446
Benton CC, *Benton* .... 9 [V] 662-673-9881
Big Oaks GC, *Saltillo* .... 18 [P] 662-844-8002
  bigoaksgolfclub.com
Booneville G&CC, *Booneville* .... 9 [S] 662-728-6812
Briarwood CC, *Meridian* .... 18 [V] 601-681-6185
  briarwoodcc.org
Brookhaven CC, *Brookhaven* .... 18 [V] 601-833-6841
Brookwood Byram CC, *Jackson* .... 18 [P] 601-372-5981
  brookwoodbyramcc.com
Canebrake CC, *Hattiesburg* .... 18 [V] 601-271-2010
  canebrakegolf.com
Castlewoods GC, *Brandon* .... 27 [V] 601-992-1942
  castlewoodscountryclub.com
CC of Canton, *Canton* .... 18 [V] 601-859-6359
  countryclubofcanton.com
CC of Jackson, *Jackson* .... 27 [V] 601-956-1415
  ccjackson.com
Cherokee Valley GC, *Olive Branch* .... 18 [P] 662-893-4444
  olivebranchgolf.com
Clarksdale CC, *Clarksdale* .... 18 [V] 662-624-8962
Clear Creek GC, *Vicksburg* .... 18 [M] 601-638-9395
  clearcreekgolfcourse.net
Cleveland CC, *Cleveland* .... 18 [V] 662-843-3456
Coahoma CC, *Clarksdale* .... 9 [S] 662-624-9484
Colonial CC Deerfield, *Canton* .... 18 [V] 601-856-6966
  colonialcc.org
Colonial CC Jackson Course, *Jackson* ... 18 [V] 601-956-4655
  colonialcc.org
Columbia CC, *Columbia* .... 9 [P] 601-736-0383
Columbus CC, *Columbus* .... 18 [V] 662-328-5584
County Line CC, *Union* .... 18 [S] 601-416-9553
Dancing Rabbit GC, *Philadelphia* .... 36 [R] 601-663-0011
  dancingrabbitgolf.com
Decatur GC, *Decatur* .... 9 [V] 601-635-2077
Deer Creek Town & Racquet Club, *Leland* .... 9 [V] 662-686-4611
Delta St College GC, *Cleveland* .... 9 [U] 662-846-4585
Diamondhead GC, *Diamondhead* .... 36 [P] 228-255-3910
  diamondheadms.org
Dixie Golf Assoc, *Laurel* .... 18 [V] 601-649-3384
Dogwood Hills GC, *Biloxi* .... 18 [P] 228-392-9805
  dogwoodhills.com
Drew CC, *Drew* .... 9 [V] 662-745-6127
Duncan Park GC, *Natchez* .... 18 [M] 601-442-5955
  natchezcitypark.com
Eagle Ridge GC, *Raymond* .... 18 [U] 601-857-5993
  hindscc.edu
Elm Lake GC, *Columbus* .... 18 [S] 662-329-8964
  elmlakegolfcourse.com
Eupora CC, *Eupora* .... 9 [V] 662-258-9796
  euporacountryclub.org
Fallen Oak GC, *Saucier* .... 18 [R] 228-386-7015
  fallenoak.com
Fernwood CC, *McComb* .... 18 [V] 601-249-2833
  fernwoodcc.com
Forest CC, *Forest* .... 18 [V] 601-469-9137
Fulton CC, *Fulton* .... 9 [S] 662-862-9711
Great Southern GC, *Gulfport* .... 18 [P] 228-896-3536
Green Oaks GC, *Columbus* .... 18 [V] 662-328-3879
  greenoaksgolfclub.com
Greenville G&CC, *Greenville* .... 18 [V] 662-332-7210
  greenvillegolfandcountryclub.com
Greenville Muni GC, *Greenville* .... 18 [M] 662-332-4079

Greenwood CC, *Greenwood* .... 18 [V] 662-453-3414
Grenada CC, *Grenada* .... 18 [V] 662-226-8839
  grenadacc.net
Grove Park GC, *Jackson* .... 9 [M] 601-960-2074
Gulf Hills GC, *Ocean Springs* .... 18 [R] 228-872-9663
  gulfhillsgolf.com
Hattiesburg CC, *Hattiesburg* .... 18 [V] 601-264-5078
  hattiesburgcountryclub.com
Hernando Hills CC, *Hernando* .... 18 [V] 662-429-0317
  hernandohillscc.com
Highlands Plantation, *Starkville* .... 18 [S] 662-323-7271
  highlandsplantation.com
Hillandale CC, *Corinth* .... 18 [P] 662-286-8020
Holmes County CC, *Lexington* .... 9 [V] 662-834-4029
Houston CC, *Houston* .... 9 [V] 662-448-5885
Humphreys County CC, *Silver City* .... 9 [V] 662-247-3141
Indianola CC, *Indianola* .... 9 [V] 662-887-3832
Iuka CC, *Iuka* .... 9 [P] 662-423-3475
Kirkwood National GC, *Holly Springs* .. 18 [S] 662-252-4888
  kirkwoodgolf.com
Lake Caroline GC, *Madison* .... 18 [V] 601-853-4023
  randywatkinsgolf.com
Lakeview GC, *Meridian* .... 18 [M] 601-693-3301
Laurel CC, *Laurel* .... 18 [V] 601-649-7132
  laurelcountryclub.org
Le Fleurs Bluff GC, *Jackson* .... 9 [M] 601-362-5485
Leake CC, *Carthage* .... 9 [V] 601-267-9496
Leflore County CC, *Itta Bena* .... 9 [P] 662-453-2971
Links of Whispering Woods, *Olive Branch* .... 18 [R] 662-893-2874
  whisperingwoods.com
Live Oaks GC, *Jackson* .... 18 [S] 601-982-1231
  liveoaksgc.com
Louisville CC, *Louisville* .... 18 [V] 662-773-3303
Lucedale CC, *Lucedale* .... 9 [S] 601-947-2798
Mallard Pointe GC, *Sardis* .... 27 [M] 662-487-2400
  mallardpointegc.com
Middlefork GC, *Meadville* .... 18 [V] 601-384-5730
Millbrook CC, *Picayune* .... 18 [S] 601-798-8711
  millbrookcountryclub.com
Mississippi National GC, *Gautier* .... 18 [S] 228-497-2372
  mississippinational.com
Mississippi State Univ GC, *Starkville* ... 18 [U] 601-325-3028
  golfcourse.msstate.edu
Mosswood CC, *Port Gibson* .... 9 [V] 601-437-4111
Natchez Trace GC, *Saltillo* .... 18 [S] 662-869-2166
Newton CC, *Newton* .... 9 [V] 601-683-3521
North Creek GC, *Southaven* .... 18 [P] 662-280-4653
  northcreekgolf.com
Northwood CC, *Meridian* .... 18 [V] 601-483-5551
  northwoodcountryclub.org
Oaks CC, *New Albany* .... 9 [P] 662-534-3239
Okatoma GC, *Collins* .... 18 [S] 601-765-1841
  okatomagolfclub.com
Okolona CC, *Okolona* .... 9 [V] 662-447-2033
Old Waverly GC, *West Point* .... 18 [R] 662-494-6463
  oldwaverly.com
Ole Miss GC, *Oxford* .... 18 [U] 662-234-4816
  olemiss.edu/depts/golf
Olive Branch CC, *Olive Branch* .... 18 [V] 662-895-1555
  olivebranchcountryclub.com
Panola CC, *Batesville* .... 18 [V] 662-563-9935
Pascagoula CC, *Pascagoula* .... 9 [P] 228-762-1466

[S] = SEMI-PRIVATE   [V] = PRIVATE   [U] = UNIVERSITY   [N] = UNIVERSITY-PRIVATE

MISSISSIPPI

Golf Yellow Pages, 18th Edition

Pass Christian Isles GC, *Pass Christian* .... 18 [V]   228-452-4851
  pci-golf.com
Patrick Farms GC, *Jackson* .... 18 [S]   601-664-0304
  randywatkinsgolf.com
Pearl Muni GC, *Pearl* .... 18 [M]   601-932-3562
Pearl River GC, *Poplarville* .... 18 [P]   601-795-1011
Philadelphia CC, *Philadelphia* .... 18 [P]   601-656-8512
Pine Bayou GC, *Gulfport* .... 18 [A]   228-871-2494
Pine Belt National GC, *Moselle* .... 18 [R]   601-584-6531
  pinebeltgolf.com
Pine Burr CC, *Wiggins* .... 18 [S]   601-928-4911
Pine Creek GC, *Purvis* .... 18 [P]   601-794-6427
Pine Hill G&CC, *Ripley* .... 9 [V]   662-837-7863
Pine Hills CC, *Calhoun City* .... 9 [P]   662-983-8662
Pine Hills CC, *Gloster* .... 9 [V]   601-225-7741
Ponta Creek GC, *Meridian* .... 18 [A]   601-679-2526
Pontotoc CC, *Pontotoc* .... 18 [P]   662-489-1962
  pontotoccc.com
Prentiss CC, *Prentiss* .... 9 [V]   601-792-5062
Quail Hollow GC, *McComb* .... 27 [M]   601-684-2903
  quailhollowgc.com
Quitman CC, *Quitman* .... 18 [V]   601-776-2582
Redbud Springs G&CC, *Kosciusko* .... 9 [V]   662-289-5446
Reunion G&CC, *Madison* .... 18 [V]   601-605-8784
  reuniongolfandcc.com
River Bend Links, *Tunica Resorts* .... 18 [R]   662-363-1005
  riverbendlinks.com
River Birch GC, *Amory* .... 18 [P]   662-256-5976
Rolling Hills CC, *Crystal Springs* .... 9 [V]   601-892-1621
Rolling Hills GC, *Richton* .... 18 [P]   601-788-6999
Shadow Ridge GC, *Hattiesburg* .... 18 [P]   601-296-0286
  shadowridgegolf.com
Sharkey CC, *Rolling Fork* .... 9 [V]   662-873-2222
Shelby CC, *Shelby* .... 9 [V]   662-398-7777
Shell Landing GC, *Gautier* .... 18 [P]   228-497-5683
  shelllanding.com
Shiloh Ridge Ath Club, *Corinth* .... 18 [P]   662-286-8000
  shilohridge.net
Simpson County CC, *Mendenhall* .... 9 [P]   601-849-3567
Sonny Guy Muni GC, *Jackson* .... 18 [M]   601-960-1905
Southaven Golf Ctr, *Southaven* .... 9 [M]   662-393-0370
St Andrews GC, *Ocean Springs* .... 18 [S]   228-875-7730
Starkville CC, *Starkville* .... 18 [V]   662-323-1733
  starkvillecc.org
Sunkist CC, *Biloxi* .... 18 [S]   228-388-3961
  sunkistcc.com
Tallahatchie CC, *Charleston* .... 9 [V]   662-647-9498
The Bridges GC At Hollywood Casino, *Bay St Louis* 18 [P] 228-463-4047
  hollywoodcasinobsl.com
The CC of Oxford, *Oxford* .... 18 [V]   662-234-2866
  countryclubofoxford.com
The Dogwoods GC At Hugh White St Park,
  Grenada .... 18 [M]   601-226-4123
  thedogwoodsgolf.com
The Grand Bear, *Saucier* .... 18 [R]   228-539-7806
  harrahs.com/golf
The Kings Arrow Ranch, *Lumberton* .... 18 [P]   601-796-3423
The Links At Cottonwoods, *Tunica Resorts* .... 18 [R]   662-357-6079
  harrahsgolf.com
The Links At Oxford G&CC, *Oxford* .... 9 [S]   662-234-4875
The Links At Starkville, *Starkville* .... 9 [P]   662-323-1280
  lindseymanagement.com
The Links of Madison County G&CC, *Canton* .... 9 [P]   601-859-0585
  lindseymanagement.com
The Meadows GC, *Tupelo* .... 9 [P]   662-840-1985
The Oaks GC, *Pass Christian* .... 18 [P]   228-452-0909
  theoaksgolfclub.com
The Plantation GC, *Olive Branch* .... 18 [P]   662-895-3530
  olivebranchgolf.com
The Preserve GC, *Vancleave* .... 18 [R]   228-386-2500
  preservegc.com
The Refuge, *Flowood* .... 18 [M]   601-664-1414
  playthefuge.com
The River Resort, *Rosedale* .... 9 [R]   662-759-3774
Timberton GC, *Hattiesburg* .... 18 [S]   601-584-4653
  timbertongolf.com
Tunica National G&TC, *Tunica Resorts* .... 18 [M]   662-357-0777
  tunicanational.com
Tupelo CC, *Belden* .... 18 [V]   662-840-3277
  tupcc.com
Twin Pines CC, *Petal* .... 9 [S]   601-544-8318
Tylertown CC, *Tylertown* .... 9 [V]   601-876-2510
USM Van Hook GC, *Hattiesburg* .... 18 [U]   601-264-1872
Vicksburg CC, *Vicksburg* .... 18 [V]   601-636-8692
  vicksburgcc.com
Waynesboro CC, *Waynesboro* .... 9 [R]   601-735-6494
Wedgewood Golfers Club, *Olive Branch* .... 18 [S]   662-895-7490
  wwncgolf.com
West Point CC, *West Point* .... 9 [V]   662-494-3535
Whisper Lake CC, *Madison* .... 18 [V]   601-853-0202
  randywatkinsgolf.com
Whispering Pines Columbus AFB, *Columbus AFB* . 9 [A]   662-434-7932
Whispering Pines GC, *Corinth* .... 9 [P]   662-286-6151
Whispering Pines Jackson Co GC, *Hurley* .... 18 [M]   228-588-6111
  co.jackson.ms.us/ds/golfcourse.html
Wilson Lakes CC, *Marks* .... 18 [V]   662-326-2241
Windance CC, *Gulfport* .... 18 [R]   228-832-4871
  windancecc.com
Winona CC, *Winona* .... 9 [V]   662-283-4211
Wolf Hollow GC, *Wesson* .... 18 [U]   601-643-8379
  colin.edu/wolfhollow
Yalobusha CC, *Water Valley* .... 9 [V]   662-473-2401
Yazoo CC, *Yazoo City* .... 9 [V]   662-746-4441
Yoda Creek GC, *Bruce* .... 9 [S]   662-983-9632
  yodacreek.com
Zach Brooks GC, *Macon* .... 9 [P]   662-726-5610

MISSOURI

Aberdeen GC, *Eureka* .... 18 [P]   636-938-5465
  aberdeengolf.com
Adams Pointe GC, *Blue Springs* .... 18 [M]   816-220-3673
  adamspointegolfclub.com
Albany CC, *Albany* .... 9 [V]   660-726-7493
  albanymo.net
Algonquin GC, *St Louis* .... 18 [V]   314-962-3700
  algonquingolfclub.com
American Legion GC, *Hannibal* .... 9 [P]   573-221-5831
Arcadia Valley CC, *Ironton* .... 9 [S]   573-546-9508
Arthur Hills GC, *Mexico* .... 18 [M]   573-581-1330
Ava CC, *Ava* .... 9 [S]   417-683-5750
Ballwin GC, *Ballwin* .... 9 [M]   636-227-1750
  ballwin.mo.us
Bayview GC, *Linn Creek* .... 9 [P]   573-346-6617
Bear Creek GC, *Wentzville* .... 18 [P]   636-332-5018
  bearcreekgolf.com

[A] = MILITARY   [M] = MUNICIPAL   [P] = PUBLIC   [R] = RESORT

MISSOURI

Golf Yellow Pages, 18th Edition

Bear Creek Valley GC, *Osage Beach* ....18 [P] 573-302-1000
  bearcreekvalley.com
Bellerive CC, *St Louis*............................. 18 [V] 314-434-4405
  bellerivecc.org
Bent Creek GC, *Jackson*........................18 [S] 573-243-6060
  bentcreekgc.com
Bent Oak GC, *Oak Grove*.......................18 [P] 816-690-3028
  bentoakgolfclub.com
Berry Hill GC, *Bridgeton*.........................9 [M] 314-731-7979
  bridgetonmo.com
Bethany CC, *Bethany*..............................9 [P] 660-425-3745
Bill & Payne Stewart GC, *Springfield*..........27 [M] 417-833-9962
  parkboard.org
Birch Creek GC, *Union*...........................18 [P] 636-584-7200
  birchcreekgc.com
Blackberry Trails GC, *Archie*.....................9 [P] 816-430-5737
  blackberrytrails.net
Blue Hills CC, *Kansas City* ....18 [V] 816-942-1683
  bluehillscc.com
Bogey Club, *St Louis*............................18 [V] 314-993-0161
Bogey Hills G&CC, *St Charles*................18 [V] 636-946-1511
  bogeyhillscc.com
Bolivar GC, *Bolivar*...............................9 [P] 417-326-6600
Boone Valley GC, *Augusta*....................18 [V] 636-928-5200
  boonevalley.org
Boot Heel GC, *Sikeston*.......................18 [P] 573-472-6111
  bootheelgolf.com
Branson Creek GC, *Hollister*..................18 [R] 417-339-4653
  bransoncreekgolf.com
Briarbrook GC, *Carl Junction* ....18 [V] 417-649-6777
Brookfield CC, *Brookfield* ....9 [S] 660-258-7802
  brookfieldclub.com
Bryce Oaks GC, *Monett*........................18 [P] 417-235-7307
Butler CC, *Butler* ....9 [V] 660-679-3637
California CC, *California* ....9 [S] 573-796-2089
Cameron Veteran's Memorial GC, *Cameron* ....18 [P] 816-632-2626
  camerongolfclub.com
Cape Girardeau CC, *Cape Girardeau* ....18 [V] 573-335-7224
  cggolfclub.com
Cape Jaycee Muni GC, *Cape Girardeau*........18 [M] 573-334-2031
  cityofcapegirardeau.org
Cardinal Hill GC, *Liberty*.......................18 [U] 816-781-6522
  cardinalhillgolf.com
Carrollton CC, *Carrollton*.......................9 [V] 660-542-9888
Carthage Muni GC, *Carthage* ....18 [M] 417-237-7030
  carthagegolfcourse.com
Caruthersville Golf Assn, *Caruthersville*.........9 [P] 573-333-1443
  caruthersvillecity.com
Cassville GC, *Cassville* ....18 [S] 417-847-2399
  cassvillegolfclub.com
CC at the Legends, *Eureka*...................27 [V] 636-938-5548
  thelegendsgolf.com
CC of Blue Springs, *Blue Springs*............18 [V] 816-229-8103
  ccofbluesprings.com
CC of Missouri, *Columbia* ....18 [V] 573-442-1310
  ccmo.net
CC of St Albans, *St Albans* ....36 [V] 636-458-3062
  ccstalbans.com
CC of Sugar Creek, *High Ridge*..............18 [P] 636-677-4070
  sugarcreekstl.com
Cedar Oak Lodge GC, *Stockton* ....9 [R] 417-276-3193
  cedaroaklodge.com
Center Creek Recal Club, *Sarcoxie*............9 [S] 417-548-7755

Centralia CC, *Centralia* ....9 [V] 573-682-2914
Charleston CC, *Charleston* ....9 [V] 573-683-4433
Chillicothe CC, *Chillicothe*....................9 [V] 660-646-2922
  chillicothecountryclub.com
Clinton CC, *Clinton*...........................18 [S] 660-885-2521
  clinton-country-club.com
Columbia CC, *Columbia*......................18 [V] 573-449-4115
  columbiacc.net
Cottonwood GC, *de Soto* ....9 [S] 636-586-8803
Country Creek GC, *Pleasant Hill*...........36 [P] 816-540-5225
  countrycreekgolf.com
Country Lake GC, *Warrenton*..............18 [P] 636-456-1165
  countrylakegc.com
Crescent Farms GC, *Crescent*................ 18 [V] 636-938-6200
  CrescentFarms.com
Creve Coeur GC, *Creve Coeur*................9 [M] 314-432-4263
  creve-coeur.org
Crowleys Ridge Rec Ctr, *Bloomfield*..........9 [P] 573-568-4698
Crown Pointe GC, *Farmington*.............18 [P] 573-756-6660
  crownpointegolfclub.com
Crystal Springs Quarry GC, *Maryland Heights*......18 [P] 314-344-4448
  crystalspringsquarry.com
Cuba Lakes CC, *Cuba* ....9 [S] 573-885-2234
Dalhousie GC, *Cape Girardeau*.............18 [V] 573-332-0818
  dalhousiegolfclub.com
Daviess County CC, *Gallatin* ....9 [S] 660-663-2922
Deer Creek GC, *House Springs* ....18 [P] 636-671-0447
  deercreekstlouis.com
Deer Lake GC, *Springfield*...................18 [P] 417-865-8888
  deerlakegolf.com
Deer Run GC, *Van Buren*......................9 [P] 573-323-8475
Dogwood Hills GC, *Osage Beach* ....18 [R] 573-348-3153
  dogwoodhillsresort.com
Don Gardner Par 3 GC, *Branson*.............9 [M] 417-337-8510
  cityofbranson.org
Dream Valley GC, *Buffalo* ....18 [P] 417-345-4653
Drumm Farm GC, *Independence*..........27 [P] 816-350-9900
  drummfarmgolfclub.com
Duncan Hills GC, *Savannah*.................18 [M] 816-324-7575
Eagle Creek GC, *Joplin*.......................18 [V] 417-623-5050
  downstreamcasino.com
Eagle Crest CC, *Republic*.....................18 [P] 417-732-8500
Eagle Knoll GC, *Hartsburg*...................18 [P] 573-761-4653
  eagleknoll.com
Eagle Springs GC, *St Louis*..................27 [P] 314-355-7277
  eaglesprings.com
Eagles Bluff GC, *Clarksville* ....9 [P] 573-242-3309
  clarksvillemo.us/eaglebluffgolf.html
Eagles Landing GC, *Belton* ....18 [M] 816-318-0004
  eagleslandinggolfcourse.com
Edina CC, *Edina*..................................9 [V] 660-397-9992
Eldon CC, *Eldon*................................18 [S] 573-392-4172
  eldoncountryclub.com
Elk River GC, *Noel*...............................9 [S] 417-475-3208
  freewebs.com/elkrivergolfcourse
Elm Hills GC, *Sedalia*...........................9 [P] 660-826-6171
Elmwood GC, *Washington* ....9 [P] 636-239-6841
  elmwoodgolfcourse.net
Emerald Greens GC, *St Louis* ....18 [P] 314-355-2777
  emeraldgreensgc.com
Excelsior Springs GC, *Excelsior Springs* ....18 [M] 816-630-3731
  ci.excelsior-springs.mo.us

[S] = SEMI-PRIVATE   [V] = PRIVATE   [U] = UNIVERSITY   [N] = UNIVERSITY-PRIVATE

MISSOURI
Golf Yellow Pages, 18th Edition

Fairview GC, *St Joseph* ....18 [M]   816-271-5351
  fairviewgolf.net
Family Golf & Learning Center, *St Louis*.................9 [P]   636-861-2500
Family Golf Park, *Blue Springs* ....9 [P]   816-228-1550
  familygolfpark.com
Fayette GC, *Fayette* .... 9 [V]   660-248-5106
Fisher Creek CC, *Kimberling City*............................9 [P]   417-739-4370
  fishercreekcountryclub.com
Forest Hills CC, *Chesterfield*............................... 27 [V]   636-227-1528
  foresthillscc.net
Forest Park GC, *St Louis*.....................................27 [P]   314-367-1337
  forestparkgc.com
Four Seasons CC, *Chesterfield*............................ 9 [V]   314-469-5986
Fourche Valley GC, *Potosi*......................................9 [P]   573-438-7888
  fourchevalley.org
Fox Run GC, *Eureka* .... 18 [V]   636-938-4653
  foxrungolfclub.com
Frank E Peters GC, *Nevada* ....18 [M]   417-448-2750
Franklin County CC, *Washington*........................ 18 [V]   636-239-6678
  fcccgolf.com
Fred Arbanas GC At Longview Lakes, *Kansas City* 27 [M]   816-763-3500
  jacksongov.org
Fremont Hills CC, *Nixa* .... 18 [V]   417-725-1506
  fremonthillsgolf.com
Fulton CC, *Fulton* .... 9 [V]   573-642-3005
  fultoncountryclub.com
GC At Deer Chase, *Linn Creek* ....18 [P]   573-346-6117
  deerchasegolf.com
GC of Creekmoor, *Raymore* ....18 [P]   816-331-2621
  creekmoor.com
GC of Wentzville, *Wentzville* ....18 [P]   636-332-0500
  gcofwentzville.com
Gene Pray Memorial GC, *El Dorado Springs* ....9 [M]   417-876-9968
  eldomo.org
Glen Echo CC, *St Louis* .... 18 [V]   314-383-1500
  gecc.org
Grand Summit G&CC, *Grandview*......................18 [P]   816-331-3978
  grandsummitgolfcc.com
GreatLife Golf & Fitness - Maple Creek, *Kansas City* 9 [P]   816-459-8400
  greatlifegolf.com
GreatLife Golf & Fitness - River Oaks, *Grandview* 18 [P]   816-966-8111
  greatlifegolf.com
Green Hills GC, *Chillicothe*..................................18 [M]   660-646-6669
  greenhillsgolfcourse.com
Greenbriar Hills CC, *Kirkwood* .... 18 [V]   314-822-3011
  greenbriarcc.com
Greene Hills CC, *Willard* .... 18 [V]   417-742-3086
Gustin GC, *Columbia*... 18 [U]   573-882-6016
  missouri.edu/~gustin
Hail Ridge GC, *Boonville* ....18 [S]   660-882-2223
  hailridgegolf.com
Hannibal CC, *Hannibal*... 9 [V]   573-221-0629
  hannibalcountryclub.com
Harrisonville GC, *Harrisonville*..............................9 [M]   816-380-3845
Hawk Ridge GC, *Lake St Louis*.............................18 [P]   636-561-2828
Heart of America Golf Acad, *Kansas City* ....18 [M]   816-513-8940
  kcmo.org
Heritage Hills GC, *Moberly* .... 18 [V]   660-269-8659
  heritagehillsgolfcourse.com
Hghlands G&TC, *St Louis*......................................9 [P]   314-531-7773
  highlandsgolfandtennis.com
Hickory Hills CC, *Springfield*............................... 18 [V]   417-869-3878
  hichoryhillscountryclub.com

Hidden Pines CC, *Warrensburg*........................... 18 [V]   660-747-8817
  hiddenpinescc.com
Hidden Trails CC, *Dexter*......................................18 [S]   573-624-3638
  hiddentrailscc.com
Hidden Valley CC, *Eureka* .... 18 [V]   636-938-5373
  hiddenvalleyski.com
Hidden Valley GC, *Lawson* ....18 [P]   816-580-3444
Hidden Valley Golf Links, *Clever* ....18 [P]   417-743-2860
Higginsville CC, *Higginsville*..................................9 [S]   660-584-3600
Highland Springs CC, *Springfield* .... 18 [V]   417-886-0408
  highlandsprings.com
Hillcrest CC, *Kansas City* .... 18 [V]   816-523-8601
  hillcrestkc.com
Hodge Park GC, *Kansas City* ....18 [M]   816-781-4152
  hodgeparkgolf.com
Holiday Hills Resort & Golf, *Branson* ....18 [R]   417-334-4838
  holidayhills.com
Honey Creek GC, *Aurora*.....................................18 [P].   417-678-3353
  honeycreekgolfclub.com
Hoots Hollow At Country Creek, *Pleasant Hill* .....18 [P]   816-380-4920
  countrycreekgolf.com
Horton Smith GC, *Springfield*..............................18 [M]   417-891-1639
  parkboard.org
House Springs GC, *House Springs*........................9 [P]   636-671-0560
  housespringsgolf.com
Hub G&SwimC, *Bethany*......................................9 [P]   660-425-3022
Incline Village GC, *Foristell* ....18 [P]   636-463-7274
  inclinevillagegc.com
Indian Foothills GC, *Marshall*...............................18 [M]   660-831-0929
Indian Rock GC, *Laurie*..18 [P]   573-372-3023
  indianrockgolfclub.com
Innsbrook Resort GC, *Innsbrook*.........................18 [R]   636-928-3366
  innsbrook-resort.com
Island Green GC, *Republic* ....18 [S]   417-732-7622
  islandgreengolfclub.com
Jackson Park GC, *Palmyra* ....9 [P]   573-769-3000
  showmepalmyra.com
Jefferson City CC, *Jefferson City*........................ 18 [V]   573-893-3400
  jeffersoncitycountryclub.com
Joachim GC, *Herculaneum* ....9 [S]   636-479-4101
John Knox Village GC, *Lees Summit*..................... 9 [V]   816-524-8400
  johnknoxvillage.org
Kennett CC, *Kennett*..18 [S]   573-888-9945
  kennettcountryclub.com
Keth Memorial GC, *Warrensburg*........................ 18 [U]   660-543-4182
  kethmemorialgolf.com
Kimbeland CC, *Jackson*....................................... 18 [V]   573-243-5926
  kimbeland.com
Kings River GC, *Shell Knob* ....18 [P]   417-858-6330
  kingsrivergolf.com
Kirksville CC, *Kirksville* .... 18 [V]   660-665-5335
  kirksvillecountryclub.com
L A Nickell Muni GC, *Columbia* ....18 [M]   573-445-4213
  gocolumbiamo.com
La Plata GC, *La Plata*...18 [M]   660-332-4584
  laplatagolfcourse.com
Lake Forest G&CC, *Lake St Louis* .... 18 [V]   636-561-2221
  lakeforestgolf.org
Lake of the Woods, *Columbia*..............................18 [M]   573-474-7011
  gocolumbiamo.com/dept/park
Lake St Louis Par 3, *Lake St Louis* .... 9 [V]   636-625-8276
  lslca.com

[A] = MILITARY [M] = MUNICIPAL [P] = PUBLIC [R] = RESORT

MISSOURI

Club	City	Holes	Type	Phone
Lake Thunderhead at Wildflower	Unionville	9	[V]	660-947-3267
thunderheadlake.com				
Lake Valley CC	Camdenton	18	[S]	573-346-7218
lakevalleygolf.com				
Lake View GC	Hamilton	9	[P]	816-583-7914
Lakesite Club Incorporated	Maysville	9	[V]	816-449-2570
Lakewood Oaks GC	Lees Summit	18	[V]	816-373-6886
logc.org				
Lamar CC	Lamar	9	[S]	417-682-3977
golflamar.com				
Lancaster CC	Lancaster	9	[P]	660-457-2277
Landings At Spirit GC	Chesterfield	18	[P]	636-728-1927
landingsatspirit.com				
Lead Belt GC	Bonne Terre	9	[P]	573-358-3573
Lebanon Community G&CC	Lebanon	18	[S]	417-532-2901
Ledgestone CC	Reeds Spring	18	[R]	417-335-8187
ledgestonegolf.com				
Liberty Hills CC	Liberty	18	[V]	816-781-6833
libertyhillscountryclub.com				
Loch Lloyd CC	Village of Loch Lloyd	18	[V]	816-322-2117
lochlloyd.com				
Lockwood GC	Lockwood	9	[P]	417-232-4777
lockwoodgolf.com				
Log Cabin Club	St Louis	18	[V]	314-993-0154
Loutre Shore CC	Hermann	9	[P]	573-486-5815
loutreshoregolf.com				
Lowe CC	Clinton	9	[V]	660-885-8151
Macon CC	Macon	9	[P]	660-385-2614
Malden CC	Malden	9	[S]	573-276-9991
Malden Recal Park GC	Malden	9	[M]	573-276-3879
Marceline CC	Marceline	9	[P]	660-376-3174
marcelinegolf.com				
Mari Mac G Complex	Kearney	18	[P]	816-628-4800
Mark Twain CC	Paris	9	[V]	660-327-4411
Marshfield CC	Marshfield	18	[P]	417-859-4470
Maryville CC	Maryville	9	[V]	660-582-5122
Meadow Lake Acres CC	New Bloomfield	18	[P]	573-491-3417
mlacc.org				
Meadow Lake GC	Clinton	18	[S]	660-885-5124
meadowlakecc.com				
Meadowbrook CC	Ballwin	18	[V]	636-227-5365
meabrk.org				
Meramec Lakes GC	St Clair	18	[P]	636-629-0900
merameclakes.com				
Mexico CC	Mexico	9	[V]	573-581-5374
mexicocountryclub.com				
Mid Rivers Golf Links	St Peters	18	[P]	636-939-3663
midriversgolf.com				
Millwood G&RC	Ozark	18	[P]	417-889-2889
millwoodgolf.com				
Miner GC at Missouri S&T	Rolla	9	[U]	573-341-4217
mst.edu				
Minor Park GC	Kansas City	18	[M]	816-942-4033
minorparkgolfcourse.com				
Missouri Bluffs GC	St Charles	18	[P]	636-939-6494
mobluffs.com				
Moila Shrine CC	St Joseph	18	[V]	816-232-9681
moila.org/golf.htm				
Monetts Windmill Ridge GC	Monett	18	[M]	417-235-6076
cityofmonett.com				
Montgomery County GC	Montgomery City	9	[V]	573-564-3010
Mosswood Meadows GC	Monroe City	9	[P]	573-735-2088
Mound City CC	Mound City	9	[P]	660-442-5780
Mountain View GC	Mountain View	18	[M]	417-934-6959
Mozingo Lake GC	Maryville	18	[M]	660-562-3864
mozingolf.com				
Mt Vernon Muni GC	Mt Vernon	9	[P]	417-466-7831
Murder Rock CC	Hollister	18	[P]	417-332-3259
murderrock.com				
National GC of Kansas City	Kansas City	18	[V]	816-741-0634
thenationalgolfclub.com				
Nehai Property Owners CC	Keytesville	9	[V]	660-222-3453
Neosho Muni GC	Neosho	27	[M]	417-451-1543
neoshomo.com				
Nevada CC	Nevada	9	[V]	417-667-7182
New Madrid CC	New Madrid	9	[V]	573-748-5022
newmadridcountryclub.com				
New Melle Lakes GC	Wentzville	18	[P]	636-398-4653
newmellegolf.com				
Normandie GC	St Louis	18	[P]	314-862-4884
normandiegolf.com				
Norwood Hills CC	St Louis	36	[V]	314-521-4802
norwoodhills.com				
Norwoods GC	Hannibal	18	[P]	573-248-1998
norwoodsgolfclub.com				
Oak Hills CC	Dixon	9	[S]	573-759-2323
Oak Hills Golf Ctr	Jefferson City	18	[M]	573-634-6532
jeffcitymo.org				
Oak Meadow CC	Rolla	18	[V]	573-341-2363
golfomcc.com				
Oakmont Community GC	Ridgedale	9	[S]	417-334-1572
Oakwood CC	Kansas City	18	[V]	816-761-5501
oakwoodcountryclub.org				
Oakwood CC	Houston	9	[P]	417-967-3968
theoakwoodgolfclub.com				
Old Hickory GC	St Charles	18	[V]	636-477-8960
oldhickorygc.com				
Old Warson CC	St Louis	18	[V]	314-961-0005
oldwarson.com				
Osage CC	Linn	9	[S]	573-897-3631
Osage National GC	Lake Ozark	27	[R]	573-365-1950
osagenational.com				
Owensville GC	Owensville	9	[M]	573-437-8877
owensvillemissouri.com				
Ozark Ridge GC	Poplar Bluff	18	[M]	573-686-8634
Paradise Pointe G Complex	Smithville	36	[M]	816-532-4100
paradisepointegolf.com				
Paradise Valley CC	High Ridge	18	[P]	636-225-5157
paradisevalleygolf.com				
Payne Stewart GC	Branson	18	[P]	417-337-2963
paynestewartgolfclub.com				
Perche Creek GC	Columbia	18	[P]	573-445-7546
Perryville CC	Perryville	9	[P]	573-547-8036
pccgolf.net				
Persimmon Woods GC	St Charles	18	[V]	636-926-8841
pwgolf.com				
Pevely Farms GC	Crescent	18	[P]	636-938-7000
pevelyfarms.com				
Pheasant Run GC	O Fallon	18	[P]	636-379-0099
golf-headquarters.com				
Piedmont Canyon Club	Piedmont	9	[S]	573-223-7908
Pike County CC	Louisiana	9	[V]	573-754-7944
pikecountycountryclub.com				
Pineridge GC	Belle	9	[P]	573-859-6056
Piney Valley GC	Fort Leonard Wood	18	[A]	573-329-4770
wood.army.mil				

[S] = SEMI-PRIVATE   [V] = PRIVATE   [U] = UNIVERSITY   [N] = UNIVERSITY-PRIVATE

MISSOURI — Golf Yellow Pages, 18th Edition

Plattsburg CC, *Plattsburg*	18 [S]	816-539-3328	
plattsburgcc.com			
Pleasant Hills G&CC, *Pleasant Hill*	9 [P]	816-987-2188	
Pointe Royale Village CC, *Branson*	18 [R]	417-334-4477	
pointeroyale.com			
Pomme Creek GC, *Arnold*	18 [M]	636-296-4653	
arnoldmo.org/parks/parks.htm			
Quail Creek GC, *St Louis*	18 [P]	314-487-1988	
quailcreekgolfclub.com			
Railwood GC, *Holts Summit*	18 [P]	573-896-4653	
railwoodgolf.com			
Raintree CC, *Hillsboro*	18 [S]	636-797-3774	
raintreemo.com			
Randel Hinkle Muni GC, *Mountain Grove*	18 [M]	417-926-5700	
Rangeline GC, *Joplin*	9 [P]	417-624-1160	
Red Field GC, *Eugene*	18 [P]	573-498-0110	
redfieldgolf.com			
Richland GC & CC, *Richland*	9 [S]	573-765-4825	
River View GC, *Canton*	9 [S]	573-288-3083	
Rivercut GC, *Springfield*	18 [M]	417-891-1645	
rivercut.com			
Riverside CC, *Trenton*	9 [V]	660-359-6004	
Riverside GC, *Fenton*	27 [P]	636-343-6333	
Rock Port G&CC, *Rock Port*	9 [S]	660-744-2590	
Rockwood GC, *Independence*	18 [P]	816-252-2000	
rockwoodgolfclub.com			
Rolling Hills CC, *Versailles*	18 [P]	573-378-5109	
playrollinghills.com			
Roy L Beck Muni GC, *Eminence*	9 [M]	573-226-3018	
eminencecanoescottagescamp.com			
Royal Meadows GC, *Kansas City*	18 [P]	816-353-1323	
royalmeadowsgc.com			
Ruth Park Muni GC, *St Louis*	9 [M]	314-727-4800	
ruthparkgolf.com			
Sainte Genevieve GC, *Sainte Genevieve*	18 [S]	573-883-2949	
Salisbury Muni GC, *Salisbury*	9 [M]	660-388-5721	
salisburymo.org			
Schifferdecker GC, *Joplin*	18 [M]	417-624-3533	
joplinparks.org/brochure.html			
Sedalia CC, *Sedalia*	18 [V]	660-826-2230	
Shadow Lake G&CC, *Wheatland*	18 [S]	417-282-6544	
Shamrock Hills GC, *Lees Summit*	18 [P]	816-537-6556	
shamrockhills.com			
Shawnee Bend GC, *Warsaw*	9 [M]	660-438-6115	
welcometowarsaw.com			
Shelbina Lakeside GC, *Shelbina*	9 [M]	573-588-4755	
Sherwood CC, *St Louis*	9 [V]	314-846-8850	
Shiloh Springs GC, *Platte City*	18 [M]	816-270-2582	
shilohspringsgolf.com			
Shirkey GC, *Richmond*	18 [S]	816-470-2582	
shirkeygolfcourse.com			
Shoal Creek GC, *Kansas City*	18 [M]	816-407-7242	
shoalcreekgolf.com			
Sikeston CC, *Sikeston*	18 [S]	573-472-4225	
sikestoncc.com			
Silo Ridge G&CC, *Bolivar*	18 [V]	417-326-7456	
siloridgecc.com			
Southern Oaks CC, *Fredericktown*	9 [P]	573-783-6044	
Spring Creek GC, *Salem*	9 [V]	573-729-3080	
Springfield G&CC, *Springfield*	18 [P]	417-833-6821	
springfieldgolfcc.com			
St Ann GC, *St Ann*	9 [P]	314-423-6400	
St Francois CC, *Farmington*	18 [V]	573-756-7574	
sfccgolf.com			
St James GC, *St James*	9 [P]	573-265-8688	
St Joseph CC, *St Joseph*	18 [V]	816-233-6373	
stjoecc.com			
St Louis CC, *St Louis*	18 [V]	314-994-0017	
stlouiscountryclub.org			
St Peters GC, *St Peters*	18 [M]	636-397-2227	
stpgolf.com			
St. Charles GC, Inc., *Saint Charles*	27 [P]	636-946-6190	
Staley Farms GC, *Kansas City*	18 [V]	816-734-3839	
staleyfarms.com			
Stanberry GC, *Stanberry*	9 [M]	660-783-2261	
Stockton CC, *Stockton*	9 [S]	417-276-5417	
Stone Canyon GC, *Blue Springs*	18 [P]	816-228-3333	
stonecanyongolfclub.com			
Stone Hedge GC, *Marshall*	9 [V]	660-886-4653	
Sullivan CC, *Sullivan*	18 [S]	573-468-5803	
sullivancountryclub.com			
Sullivan County CC, *Milan*	9 [S]	660-265-4150	
Sun Valley GC, *Elsberry*	18 [P]	573-898-2613	
sunvalleygc.com			
Sunset CC, *St Louis*	18 [V]	314-843-7119	
sunsetcountryclub.org			
Sunset Lakes GC & DR, *St Louis*	18 [P]	314-843-3000	
sunsetlakesgolf.net			
Swope Memorial GC, *Kansas City*	18 [M]	816-513-8910	
swopememorialgolfcourse.com			
Sycamore Creek GC, *Osage Beach*	18 [P]	573-348-9593	
sycamorecreekgolfclub.com			
Sycamore Hills GC, *Doniphan*	9 [V]	573-996-2900	
Tan Tar A GC, *Osage Beach*	27 [R]	573-348-8521	
tan-tar-a.com			
Tanglewood GC, *Fulton*	18 [P]	573-642-7277	
tanglewoodgolfcourse.com			
Tapawingo National GC, *St Louis*	27 [P]	636-349-3100	
tapawingogolf.com			
Tarkio GC, *Tarkio*	9 [P]	660-736-4776	
tarkiogolfclub.com			
Teetering Rocks Links, *Kansas City*	18 [R]	816-356-1111	
teeteringrocks.com			
Terre Du Lac G&CC, *Bonne Terre*	27 [P]	573-562-7091	
terredulac.com			
Thayer CC, *Thayer*	9 [S]	417-264-7854	
The Club At Old Hawthorne, *Columbia*	18 [V]	573-442-5280	
oldhawthorne.com			
The Club At Old Kinderhook, *Camdenton*	18 [S]	573-346-4444	
oldkinderhook.com			
The Club At Porto Cima, *Sunrise Beach*	18 [V]	573-964-3100	
portocima.com			
The Deuce-National GC of Kansas City, *Kansas City*	18 [V]	816-505-0650	
thedeucegolf.org			
The Falls GC, *O Fallon*	18 [P]	636-240-4653	
fallsgolf.com			
The GC of Florissant, *Florissant*	18 [M]	314-741-7444	
golfclubofflorissant.com			
The GC of St Joseph, *St Joseph*	9 [P]	816-253-9310	
thegolfclubofsaintjoseph.com			
The Links At Columbia, *Columbia*	9 [V]	573-474-4459	
lindseymanagement.com			
The Links At Dardenne, *O Fallon*	18 [P]	636-978-7173	
linksatdardenne.com			

[A] = MILITARY   [M] = MUNICIPAL   [P] = PUBLIC   [R] = RESORT

The Lodge of Four Seasons - Cove, *Lake Ozark*.....18 [R] 573-365-3000
4seasonsresort.com
The Lodge of Four Seasons - Ridge, *Lake Ozark*...18 [R] 573-365-3000
4seasonsresort.com
Theodosia CC, *Theodosia*...9 [S] 417-273-4877
theodosiacc.50megs.com
Thousand Hills Golf Resort, *Branson* ....18 [R] 417-336-5874
thousandhills.com
Three Pines GC, *Ewing* ....9 [P] 573-494-3435
Tiffany Greens GC, *Kansas City* ....18 [R] 816-880-9600
tiffanygreensgolf.com
Timber Creek Resort, *De Soto* .... 9 [V] 636-586-7448
silverleafresorts.com/resorts/timber-creek-resort
Timber Lake GC, *Moberly*...................................18 [P] 660-263-8542
timberlakegolf.com
Timber Ridge GC, *Memphis*............................9 [P] 660-883-5341
Tipton CC, *Tipton* ....9 [S] 660-433-2321
Top of the Rock GC, *Ridgedale*............................ 9 [R] 417-339-5312
bigcedar.com
Tour 3 GC, *St Peters* ....18 [P] 636-477-9779
tour3golf.com
Tower Tee Golf, *St Louis*.....................................9 [P] 314-481-5818
towertee.com
Tri-City CC, *Emma* ....9 [S] 660-463-7841
Turkey Creek Golf Ctr, *Jefferson City* ....9 [P] 573-636-7833
turkeycreekgolfcenter.com
Twin Hills G&CC, *Joplin* .... 18 [V] 417-624-1611
twinhillsgolf.net
Twin Lakes Public GC, *Kahoka* ....9 [P] 660-727-3120
Twin Oaks GC, *Springfield*................................. 18 [V] 417-881-1800
twinoakscountryclub.com
Twin Pines CC, *Harrisonville* ....9 [V] 816-380-5818
twinpinesgolfclub.com
Union Hills GC, *Pevely* .... 18 [V] 636-475-4474
unionhillsgolfcourse.org
Unionville CC, *Unionville*................................... 9 [V] 660-947-3100
Unity CC, *Unity Village* .... 9 [N] 816-969-2069
unityworldhq.org
Vandalia CC, *Vandalia*...................................9 [P] 573-594-6666
Viburnam G&CC, *Viburnum*.............................9 [P] 573-244-5688
Warrenton GC, *Warrenton*...............................18 [P] 636-456-8726
warrentongolfcourse.com
Wedgewood CC, *Mountain Grove*.......................9 [V] 417-926-5374
West Branson Bluffs Resort, *Galena*.................. 9 [R] 417-538-2291
West Plains CC, *West Plains* ....18 [P] 417-257-2726
West Plains Muni GC, *West Plains* ....18 [M] 417-256-9824
westplains.net
Westborough CC, *Kirkwood* .... 18 [V] 314-968-5180
westboroughcc.com
Westwood CC, *St Louis*.................................... 27 [V] 314-432-2312
westwood-cc.com
Westwood Hills CC, *Poplar Bluff*......................... 18 [V] 573-785-8211
Whiteman AFB Royal Oaks GC, *Whiteman AFB* ...18 [A] 660-687-5572
Whitmoor CC, *St Charles* .... 36 [V] 636-926-2266
whitmoorgolf.com
Willow Springs Muni GC, *Willow Springs* ....9 [M] 417-469-1214
willowspringsmo.com
Windmill GC, *Clark*..9 [P] 573-641-5737
Windsor CC, *Windsor* .... 9 [V] 660-647-2175
Winghaven CC, *O Fallon* .... 18 [V] 636-561-9464
winghavencc.com
Winterstone GC, *Independence*..........................18 [P] 816-257-5755
winterstonegolf.com

Wolf Hollow GC, *Labadie* .... 18 [P] 636-390-8100
wolfhollowgolf.com
Woods Fort CC, *Troy*... 18 [S] 636-528-0040
woodsfortcc.com

MONTANA

Airport GC, *Wolf Point*... 9 [V] 406-653-2161
Anaconda CC, *Anaconda*....................................9 [P] 406-797-3220
Anaconda Hills GC, *Black Eagle* ....18 [M] 406-761-8459
greatfallsmt.net/people_offices/golf
Arrowhead Meadows Golf Assoc,
White Sulphur Springs...............................9 [M] 406-547-3993
Beaver Creek GC, *Havre*......................................9 [P] 406-265-4201
Beaverhead CC, *Dillon* .... 9 [S] 406-683-9933
beaverheadgolf.com
Big Mountain GC, *Kalispell*..................................18 [P] 406-751-1950
bigmountainclub.com
Big Sky of Montana GC, *Big Sky* ....18 [R] 406-995-4706
bigskyresort.com
Bill Roberts Muni GC, *Helena* ....18 [M] 406-442-2191
billrobertsgolf.com
Bridger Creek GC, *Bozeman* ....18 [P] 406-586-2333
bridgercreek.com
Buffalo Hill GC, *Kalispell* ....27 [M] 406-756-4547
golfbuffalohill.com
Butte CC, *Butte* .... 18 [V] 406-494-3383
Cabinet View CC, *Libby* ....9 [P] 406-293-7332
cabinetviewcountryclub.com
Canyon River GC, *Missoula*.................................18 [P] 406-721-0222
canyonrivergolfclub.com
Cedar Creek GC, *Superior* ....9 [P] 406-822-4443
Chinook G&CC, *Chinook* ....9 [P] 406-357-2112
chinookmontana.com
Choteau CC, *Choteau* ....9 [P] 406-466-2020
Circle Inn Golf Links, *Billings*................................ 9 [R] 406-248-4201
Cottonwood CC, *Glendive*...................................9 [S] 406-377-8797
cottonwoodcc.com
Cottonwood Hills GC, *Bozeman*..........................27 [P] 406-587-1118
cottonwoodhills.com
Crystal Lakes GC, *Fortine* .... 18 [V] 406-882-4432
Cut Bank G&CC, *Cut Bank*...................................9 [P] 406-873-2574
Deer Park GC, *Deer Lodge*...................................9 [M] 406-846-1625
deerlodgegolf.com
Double Arrow Lodge, *Seeley Lake* ....18 [R] 406-677-3247
doublearrowresort.com
Eagle Bend GC, *Bigfork* ....27 [S] 406-837-7310
golfmt.com
Eagle Falls GC, *Great Falls* ....18 [M] 406-761-1078
greatfallsmt.net/people_offices/golf
EagleRock GC, *Billings* ....18 [P] 406-655-4445
eaglerockgolfcourse.com
Emerald Greens GC, *Great Falls* ....18 [P] 406-453-4844
Exchange City GC, *Billings*.................................. 18 [M] 406-652-2553
Fairmont Hot Springs Resort, *Anaconda* ....18 [R] 406-797-3241
fairmontmontana.com
Forsyth CC, *Forsyth* ....9 [P] 406-356-7710
Fort Custer GC, *Hardin* ....9 [P] 406-665-2597
Fox Ridge GC, *Helena* ....18 [P] 406-227-8304
foxridgegolfcourse.com
Frontier Road House, *Kalispell* ....9 [P] 406-755-0111
frontierroadhouse.com
Glacier Park GC, *East Glacier Park* .... 9 [R] 406-226-5642
glacierparkinc.com

[S] = SEMI-PRIVATE [V] = PRIVATE [U] = UNIVERSITY [N] = UNIVERSITY-PRIVATE

MONTANA

Golf Yellow Pages, 18th Edition

Glacier View GC, *West Glacier* .... 18 [P] 406-888-5471
  glacierviewgolf.com
Green Meadow CC, *Helena* .... 18 [V] 406-442-1420
  gmcchelena.com
Hamilton GC, *Hamilton* .... 18 [P] 406-363-4251
Harlem GC, *Harlem* .... 9 [P] 406-353-2213
Harvest Hills GC, *Fairfield* .... 9 [P] 406-467-2052
Headwaters GC, *Three Forks* .... 9 [P] 406-285-3700
  golfthreeforks.com
Heaven on Earth Par 3 Ranch & GC, *Ulm* .... 9 [R] 406-866-3316
  deepcreekoutfitters.com
Highland View GC, *Butte* .... 18 [M] 406-494-7900
Hilands GC, *Billings* .... 9 [V] 406-259-0419
  hilandsgolfclub.com
Indian Springs Ranch, *Eureka* .... 18 [P] 406-889-5056
  indianspringsmontana.com
Iron Horse GC, *Whitefish* .... 18 [V] 406-863-3100
  ironhorsegolfclub.com
Jawbone Creek GC, *Harlowton* .... 9 [M] 406-632-4206
  jawbonecreekcc.com
Judith Shadows GC, *Lewistown* .... 18 [P] 406-538-6062
  judithshadows.com
Lake Hills GC, *Billings* .... 18 [P] 406-252-9244
  lakehillsgolfclub.com
Lakeview CC, *Baker* .... 9 [S] 406-778-3166
Larchmont GC, *Missoula* .... 18 [M] 406-721-4416
Laurel GC, *Laurel* .... 18 [V] 406-628-4504
  laurelgolfclub.com
Linda Vista GC, *Missoula* .... 9 [P] 406-251-3655
Livingston G&CC, *Livingston* .... 9 [S] 406-222-1100
Madison Meadows GC, *Ennis* .... 9 [M] 406-682-7468
  madisonmeadowsgolfcourse.com
Marian Hills GC, *Malta* .... 9 [P] 406-654-5527
Marias Valley G&CC, *Shelby* .... 18 [P] 406-434-5940
  mvgcc.com
Meadow Creek GC, *Fortine* .... 9 [P] 406-882-4474
Meadow Lake Golf Resort, *Columbia Falls* .... 18 [R] 406-892-2111
  meadowlake.com
Meadow Lark CC, *Great Falls* .... 18 [V] 406-453-6531
  meadowlarkcc.net
Miles City Town & CC, *Miles City* .... 9 [S] 406-234-1600
  milescitytcc.com
Mission Mountain CC, *Ronan* .... 18 [V] 406-676-4653
  golfmissionmountain.com
Missoula CC, *Missoula* .... 18 [V] 406-251-2751
  missoulacountryclub.com
Norwegian Wood GC, *Helena* .... 9 [P] 406-475-3229
  norwegianwoodgolf.com
Old Baldy GC, *Townsend* .... 9 [M] 406-266-3337
Overland GC, *Big Timber* .... 9 [M] 406-932-4297
Peter Yegen, Jr GC, *Billings* .... 18 [P] 406-656-8099
  yegengolfclub.com
Pine Meadows GC, *Lewistown* .... 9 [S] 406-538-7075
Pine Ridge GC, *Roundup* .... 9 [P] 406-323-2880
Plains GC, *Plains* .... 9 [M] 406-826-5626
Plentywood CC, *Plentywood* .... 9 [M] 406-765-2532
Polson Bay GC, *Polson* .... 27 [R] 406-883-8230
  polsonbaygolf.com
Pondera GC, *Conrad* .... 9 [P] 406-278-3402
Ponderosa Butte Public GC, *Colstrip* .... 9 [P] 406-748-2700
Prairie Farms GC, *Havre* .... 9 [P] 406-265-4790
  prairiefarmsgolf.com

Pryor Creek GC, *Huntley* .... 36 [V] 406-348-3900
  pryorcreekgolf.com
Red Lodge GC, *Red Lodge* .... 18 [R] 406-446-3344
  redlodgemountain.com
Reserve At Moonlight Basin GC, *Big Sky* .... 18 [V] 888-893-7698
  moonlightbasin.com
Rising Sun GC at Mountain Sky, *Emigrant* ..... 9 [R] 406-333-4911
  mtnsky.com
Rivers Bend GC, *Thompson Falls* .... 9 [M] 406-827-3438
Riverside CC, *Bozeman* .... 18 [V] 406-586-2251
  riverside-country-club.com
Rock Creek Cattle Company, *Deer Lodge* ...... 18 [V] 406-846-3474
  rockcreekcattlecompany.com
Rolling Hills GC, *Broadus* .... 9 [M] 406-436-9984
Scobey G&CC, *Scobey* .... 9 [P] 406-487-5322
Sidney CC, *Sidney* .... 18 [P] 406-433-1894
  sidneycountryclub.com
Signal Point GC, *Fort Benton* .... 9 [P] 406-622-3666
  fortbenton.com/signalpoint
Silver Fox GC, *Pablo* .... 9 [U] 406-275-4734
  silverfoxgolf.com
Sleepy Hollow GC, *Dillon* .... 9 [P] 406-683-6118
Stillwater Golf & Rec, *Columbus* .... 9 [P] 406-322-4298
Stock Farm Club, *Hamilton* .... 18 [V] 406-375-1886
  stockfarm.com
Sunnyside GC, *Glasgow* .... 9 [V] 406-228-9519
The Black Bull Run GC, *Bozeman* .... 18 [V] 406-556-5011
  blackbullbozeman.com
The Briarwood GC, *Billings* .... 18 [V] 406-248-2702
  thebriarwoodgc.com
The Club At Spanish Peaks, *Big Sky* .... 18 [R] 406-993-5801
  spanish-peaks.com
The Highlands GC, *Missoula* .... 9 [P] 406-728-7360
The King Ranch GC, *Frenchtown* .... 18 [P] 406-626-4000
The Old Works GC, *Anaconda* .... 21 [P] 406-563-5989
  oldworks.org
The Ranch Club, *Missoula* .... 18 [P] 406-532-1000
  ranchclub.com
Trestle Creek GC, *St Regis* .... 9 [P] 406-649-2680
  trestlecreek-golf.com
Univ of Montana GC, *Missoula* .... 9 [U] 406-728-8629
  umt.edu/golf
Valley View GC, *Bozeman* .... 18 [V] 406-586-2145
  vvgcbozeman.com
Village Greens GC, *Kalispell* .... 18 [P] 406-752-4666
  villagegreensmontana.com
Whitefish Lake GC, *Whitefish* .... 36 [P] 406-862-5960
  golfwhitefish.com
Whitetail GC, *Stevensville* .... 9 [S] 406-777-3636
Wilderness Club, *Eureka* .... 18 [V] 406-889-6501
  thewildernessclub.com
Yellowstone CC, *Billings* .... 18 [V] 406-656-1706
  yellowstonecc.com
Yellowstone GC, *Big Sky* .... 18 [V] 406-539-4110
  theyellowstoneclub.com

NEBRASKA

Ainsworth Muni GC, *Ainsworth* .... 9 [M] 402-387-1658
Albion CC, *Albion* .... 9 [V] 402-395-2900
  albioncountryclub.com
Alma GC, *Alma* .... 9 [M] 308-928-2341
  almacity.com
Antelope CC, *Neligh* .... 9 [S] 402-887-5211

[A] = MILITARY   [M] = MUNICIPAL   [P] = PUBLIC   [R] = RESORT

NEBRASKA

Golf Yellow Pages, 18th Edition

Arapahoe Muni GC&CC, *Arapahoe* ....9 [M] 308-962-9555
  arapahoe-ne.com
ArborLinks GC, *Nebraska City* .... 18 [V] 402-873-4334
  arborlinks.com
Arnold GC, *Arnold*.. 9 [V] 308-848-3372
Arrowhead Meadows Golf & Rec, *Curtis*................9 [P] 308-367-4123
Ashland CC, *Ashland*..18 [S] 402-944-3388
  ashlandgolfclub.com
Atkinson Stuart CC, *Atkinson* ....9 [S] 402-925-5330
Auburn CC, *Auburn*...9 [S] 402-274-4500
Augusta Wind GC, *Stapleton*...............................9 [P] 308-636-2907
Awarii Dunes GC, *Axtell* .... 18 [V] 308-743-1111
  awariidunes.com
Bassett CC, *Bassett* ....9 [P] 402-684-3449
Bay Hills GC, *Plattsmouth* ....18 [P] 402-298-8191
  bayhillsgolfclub.com
Bayside GC, *Brule* ....18 [P] 308-287-4653
  baysidegolf.com
Beatrice CC, *Beatrice*...................................... 18 [V] 402-223-2710
  beatricecc.com
Benkelman GC, *Benkelman*..................................9 [V] 308-423-4653
Benson Park GC, *Omaha* ....18 [M] 402-444-4626
  ci.omaha.ne.us/parks
Blue Hill GC, *Blue Hill*..9 [P] 402-756-2418
  bluehillne.com/directory.htm
Broken Bow CC, *Broken Bow* ....9 [S] 308-872-6444
  brokenbowcountryclub.com
Buffalo Ridge GC, *Kearney* ....9 [P] 308-236-5879
  buffaloridgegc.com
Calamus GC, *Burwell* ....9 [P] 308-346-5559
  calamusgolf.com
Callaway GC, *Callaway* ....9 [P] 308-836-2806
Cardinal CC, *Oxford* ....9 [P] 308-824-3511
Cedar View CC, *Laurel* ....9 [P] 402-256-3184
Centura Hills CC, *Cairo* ....18 [P] 402-485-4650
  centurahills.com
Champions Run, *Omaha*................................... 18 [V] 402-498-8989
  championsomaha.com
Chappell GC, *Chappell* ....9 [M] 308-874-2729
Chimney Rock GC, *Bayard*..................................9 [M] 308-586-1606
  bayardne.net
Club 91 GC, *Leigh*...9 [P] 402-487-2636
College Heights CC, *Crete* ....9 [S] 402-826-4653
Cottonwood Greens GC, *Spalding* ....9 [P] 308-497-2151
Country Drive GC, *Ashland* ....9 [P] 402-944-2333
Country Shadows GC, *Columbus* ....9 [P] 402-563-4040
Courthouse & Jail Rock GC, *Bridgeport*.................9 [M] 308-262-9925
Covington Links GC, *South Sioux City* ....18 [P] 402-494-9841
Cozad CC, *Cozad*... 18 [V] 308-784-2585
Creighton Community GC, *Creighton* ....9 [P] 402-358-3565
Crofton Lakeview CC, *Crofton* ....9 [M] 402-388-4552
Crooked Creek CC, *Clay Center* ....9 [P] 402-762-3807
  clay-center.net/crookedcreek
Crooked Creek GC, *Lincoln*...............................18 [P] 402-489-7899
  crookedcreekgolfclub.com
Cross Creek Golf Links, *Cambridge*.....................18 [S] 402-697-4768
  crosscreekgolflinks.com
Dannebrog GC, *Dannebrog* ....9 [P] 402-226-2359
David City GC, *David City* ....9 [P] 402-367-4292
Dismal River Club LLC, *Mullen*...........................18 [R] 308-546-2900
  dismalriver.com
Eagle Hills GC, *Papillion* ....18 [M] 402-592-7788
  eaglehills.org

Eagle Run G Complex, *Omaha* ....18 [P] 402-498-9900
  eaglerungolf.com
Eldorado Hills GC, *Norfolk*................................18 [S] 402-371-1453
  1golf.com/ne/eldorado.htm
Elk Creek CC, *Nelson*...9 [P] 402-225-4401
Elkhorn Acres GC, *Stanton* ....9 [M] 402-439-2191
  elkhornacresgolf.com
Elkhorn Ridge GC, *Elkhorn* ....9 [P] 402-289-4332
  elkhornridge.net
Elkhorn Valley GC, *Hooper* ....9 [P] 402-654-3512
Elks GC, *Columbus* .... 18 [V] 402-564-4930
Elks Country GC, *Kearney* ....9 [P] 308-238-0760
Elmwood Park GC, *Omaha* ....18 [M] 402-444-4683
  ci.omaha.ne.us/parks
Enders Lake GC, *Enders* .... 9 [R] 308-394-5491
Evergreen Hill GC, *Battle Creek*............................9 [P] 402-675-5004
Fair Play Golf, *Norfolk* ....18 [P] 402-371-9877
  fairplaygolfcourse.com
Fairbury CC, *Fairbury* ....9 [V] 402-729-2080
Fairview GC, *Pawnee City* ....9 [V] 402-852-2188
Falls City CC, *Falls City* ....9 [V] 402-245-3624
  fallscitycountryclub.com
Field Club of Omaha, *Omaha*............................. 18 [V] 402-345-6347
  fcomaha.com
Firethorn GC, *Lincoln* .... 27 [V] 402-483-6099
  firethorngolfclub.com
Fonner View GC, *Grand Island* ....9 [P] 308-382-0202
Fontenelle GC, *Omaha* ....9 [M] 402-444-5019
  ci.omaha.ne.us/parks
Fontenelle Hills CC, *Bellevue* ....18 [S] 402-292-2500
  fontenellehillsgolf.com
Four Winds GC, *Kimball* ....18 [M] 308-235-4241
  ci.kimball.ne.us
Fox Hollow CC, *Sutton*.......................................9 [P] 402-773-5365
Franklin CC, *Franklin*.. 9 [V] 308-425-3614
Fremont GC, *Fremont*...................................... 18 [V] 402-721-6642
  fremontgolfclub.org
Friend CC GC & Rest, *Friend*................................9 [V] 402-947-6501
  friendcountryclub.com
Galaway Creek GC, *Henderson* ....9 [M] 402-723-4828
  cityofhenderson.org/golf.html
Gordon CC, *Gordon* ....9 [S] 308-282-1146
Grandpas Woods GC, *Murdock* ....9 [P] 402-994-2100
Grant GC, *Grant* ....9 [P] 308-352-2716
Happy Hollow Club, *Omaha* .... 18 [V] 402-391-0239
  happyhollowclub.com
Hartington GC, *Hartington* ....9 [M] 402-254-7312
  ci.hartington.ne.us
Hastings Elks Lodge & GC, *Hastings* ....18 [S] 402-462-6616
  hastingselksgolf.com
Hay Springs GC, *Hay Springs* ....9 [M] 308-638-7275
Hebron CC, *Hebron* ....9 [P] 402-768-6350
Hemingford Muni GC, *Hemingford* ....9 [M] 308-487-3639
Heritage Hills GC, *Mc Cook* ....18 [P] 308-345-5032
  mccookgolf.com
Hi Line GC, *Bertrand* ....9 [P] 308-991-7132
  hilinegolf.com
Hidden Acres GC, *Beatrice* ....18 [S] 402-228-2146
Hidden Hills CC, *Geneva* ....9 [S] 402-759-3084
Hidden Valley G&CC, *Lincoln* ....18 [P] 402-483-2532
  hiddenvalleylincoln.com
Highland Oaks, *Ponca* .... 9 [R] 402-755-4222

[S] = SEMI-PRIVATE   [V] = PRIVATE   [U] = UNIVERSITY   [N] = UNIVERSITY-PRIVATE

127

NEBRASKA
Golf Yellow Pages, 18th Edition

Highlands GC, *Lincoln* .... 18 [M] 402-441-6081
   highlandsgolfcourse.net
Hillcrest CC, *Lincoln* .... 18 [V] 402-489-8181
   hillcrestcountryclub.com
Hillside GC, *Sidney* .... 18 [M] 308-254-2311
   cityofsidney.org
Hilltop CC, *Wahoo* .... 9 [V] 402-443-3338
   wahoogolf.com
HiMark GC, *Lincoln* .... 27 [P] 402-488-7888
   himarkgolf.com
Holdrege CC, *Holdrege* .... 18 [V] 308-995-5744
   holdregecc.com
Holmes GC, *Lincoln* .... 18 [M] 402-441-8960
   ci.lincoln.ne.us
Imperial CC, *Imperial* .... 9 [P] 308-882-4697
Indian Creek GC, *Elkhorn* .... 27 [P] 402-289-0900
   golfatindiancreek.com
Indian Meadows GC, *North Platte* .... 9 [S] 308-532-6955
Indian Trails GC, *Beemer* .... 18 [S] 402-528-3404
   indiantrailsclub.com
Indianhead GC, *Grand Island* .... 18 [P] 402-381-4653
   indianheadgolf.com
Iron Eagle Muni GC, *North Platte* .... 18 [M] 402-535-6730
   ci.north-platte.ne.us
Iron Horse GC, *Ashland* .... 18 [P] 402-944-9800
   golfironhorse.com
Ironwood G&CC of Omaha, *Omaha* .... 18 [V] 402-333-3606
   ironwoodgolfclub.com
Jackrabbit Run GC, *Grand Island* .... 18 [M] 308-385-5340
   jackrabbitgolf.com
Jim Ager Memorial GC, *Lincoln* .... 9 [M] 402-441-8963
   agergolf.com
Johnny Goodman GC, *Omaha* .... 18 [M] 402-444-4656
   ci.omaha.ne.us/parks
Kearney CC, *Kearney* .... 18 [V] 308-237-2553
   kearneycountryclub.com
Kellys CC, *Norfolk* .... 9 [P] 402-371-9959
Kemp CC, *Fullerton* .... 9 [P] 308-536-2119
Kirkmans Lakeview GC, *Humboldt* .... 9 [P] 402-862-2828
Knolls GC, *Lincoln* .... 18 [V] 402-423-1776
La Vista Falls Muni GC, *La Vista* .... 9 [M] 402-339-9147
Lake Maloney GC, *North Platte* .... 18 [S] 402-532-9998
   lakemaloneygc.tripod.com
Lake Ridge CC, *Plattsmouth* .... 9 [S] 402-235-4653
   lake-ridgegolf.com
Lakeside CC, *Elwood* .... 18 [S] 308-785-2818
Lakeview GC, *Ralston* .... 9 [P] 402-339-2522
Legend Butte GC, *Crawford* .... 9 [P] 308-665-2431
Lochland CC, *Hastings* .... 18 [V] 402-462-8783
   lochlandcc.com
Logan Valley GC, *Wakefield* .... 9 [S] 402-287-2343
Loup City GC, *Loup City* .... 9 [S] 402-745-9982
Mahoney GC, *Lincoln* .... 18 [M] 402-441-8969
   ci.lincoln.ne.us
Meadowlark Hills GC, *Kearney* .... 18 [M] 402-233-3265
   meadowlarkhillsgolf.com
Milts Golf Ctr, *Omaha* .... 9 [P] 402-731-2001
Minden CC, *Minden* .... 9 [S] 402-832-1965
Miracle Hill G&T Ctr, *Omaha* .... 18 [P] 402-498-0220
   miraclehillgolf.com
Monument Shadows GC, *Gering* .... 18 [M] 402-635-3881
   gering.org
Mullen GC, *Mullen* .... 9 [P] 402-546-2455

Newman Grove GC, *Newman Grove* .... 9 [P] 402-447-6111
Niobrara Valley GC, *Niobrara* .... 9 [M] 402-857-3412
Norfolk CC, *Norfolk* .... 18 [V] 402-379-1188
North Bend GC, *North Bend* .... 18 [P] 402-652-3666
North Platte CC, *North Platte* .... 18 [V] 308-532-7550
Northridge GC, *Tekamah* .... 9 [P] 402-374-2661
Oak Hills CC, *Omaha* .... 18 [V] 402-895-4383
   oakhillscountryclub.org
Oakland GC, *Oakland* .... 18 [S] 402-685-5339
Omaha CC, *Omaha* .... 18 [V] 402-571-7470
   omahacc.org
ONeill CC, *O'Neill* .... 9 [P] 402-336-1676
   oneillcountryclub.com
Ord GC, *Ord* .... 9 [M] 308-728-3970
   ordgolfclub.com
Oshkosh CC, *Oshkosh* .... 9 [P] 308-772-3881
Overton GC, *Overton* .... 9 [P] 308-324-7764
Pacific Springs GC, *Omaha* .... 18 [P] 402-330-4300
   pacificsprings.com
Papio Greens Golf Ctr, *Papillion* .... 18 [P] 402-331-4621
   papiogreens.com
Pawnee Hills GC, *Fullerton* .... 9 [P] 308-536-2274
Pelican Beach GC, *Hyannis* .... 9 [P] 210-410-1889
Pierce Community GC, *Pierce* .... 9 [P] 402-329-4790
   ptcnet.net/golfcourse.htm
Pine Lake G&TC, *Lincoln* .... 9 [P] 402-488-7105
Pioneers GC, *Lincoln* .... 18 [M] 402-441-8966
   pioneersgolf.com
Plainview CC, *Plainview* .... 9 [S] 402-582-3445
Platteview CC, *Bellevue* .... 18 [V] 402-291-5927
   platteviewcc.com
Plattsmouth CC, *Plattsmouth* .... 9 [S] 402-298-8033
Players Club At Deer Creek, *Omaha* .... 27 [V] 402-963-9950
   playersclubomaha.com
Poco Creek GC (Aurora CC), *Aurora* .... 9 [P] 402-694-3662
Prairie Hills GC, *Pleasanton* .... 18 [P] 308-388-5115
   prairiehillsgolf.com
Quail Run GC, *Columbus* .... 18 [M] 402-564-1313
   quailrungolf.com
Quarry Oaks GC, *Ashland* .... 18 [P] 402-944-6000
   quarryoaks.com
Randolph Community GC, *Randolph* .... 9 [M] 402-337-1405
   ci.randolph.ne.us
Ravenna GC, *Ravenna* .... 9 [S] 308-452-3150
   ci.ravenna.ne.us
Red Cloud Muni GC, *Red Cloud* .... 9 [M] 402-746-2567
Ridgeview CC, *Chadron* .... 9 [P] 308-432-4468
River Wilds GC, *Blair* .... 18 [S] 402-426-2941
   riverwilds.com
Riverside CC, *Grand Island* .... 18 [V] 308-382-2648
   riversidegolfclub.org
Riverside GC, *Central City* .... 9 [P] 308-940-3070
Riverview G&CC, *Scottsbluff* .... 18 [P] 308-635-1555
Rolling Greens GC, *Morrill* .... 9 [M] 308-247-2817
Rolling Hills CC, *Wausa* .... 9 [P] 402-586-2507
Ryan Hill CC, *Osceola* .... 9 [P] 402-747-6661
Sand Hills GC, *Mullen* .... 18 [S] 308-546-2237
Sand Ridge GC, *Rushville* .... 9 [P] 308-327-2966
Sandy Meadows GC, *Waco* .... 9 [P] 402-728-5358
Sargent Comstock GC, *Sargent* .... 9 [V] 308-527-4200
Scenic Knolls GC, *Mitchell* .... 9 [M] 308-623-2468
Schuyler GC, *Schuyler* .... 9 [V] 402-352-2900

Scottsbluff CC, *Scottsbluff* .... 18 [V] 308-635-1844
scottsbluffcountryclub.com
Seward CC, *Seward* .... 9 [S] 402-643-6650
sewardgolf.com
Shadow Ridge CC, *Omaha* .... 18 [V] 402-333-0500
shadowridgecountryclub.com
Skyview GC, *Alliance* ....18 [M] 308-762-1446
cityofalliance.net
South Ridge GC, *South Sioux City* .... 9 [S] 402-494-4323
southridgedome.com
Southern Hills GC, *Hastings* .... 18 [S] 402-463-8006
Spring Lake Park GC, *Omaha* ....9 [M] 402-444-4630
ci.omaha.ne.us/parks
Springview GC, *Springview* ....9 [P] 402-497-3108
St Paul CC, *St Paul* ....9 [P] 308-754-4203
Steepleview GC, *Humphrey* ....9 [P] 402-923-1914
steepleviewgolf.com
Steve Hogan GC, *Omaha*.....................................9 [M] 402-444-5396
ci.omaha.ne.us/parks
Stone Creek GC, *Omaha* ....27 [P] 402-965-9000
golfstonecreek.com
Summerland GC, *Ewing* ....9 [P] 402-626-7555
golfsummerland.com
Sunset Valley CC, *Omaha* .... 9 [V] 402-393-3770
sunsetvalleygolf.org
Superior CC, *Superior* ....9 [P] 402-879-3146
Syracuse GC, *Syracuse* ....9 [S] 402-269-2924
syracusene.com
Tara Hills GC, *Papillion* .... 18 [M] 402-592-7550
tarahills.org
Taylor Creek GC, *Madison* ....9 [S] 402-454-3925
Tecumseh CC, *Tecumseh* ....9 [V] 402-335-2337
The CC of Lincoln, *Lincoln* .... 18 [V] 402-423-2271
ccl.cc
The GC At Table Creek, *Nebraska City* ....18 [P] 402-873-7750
tablecreek.com
The Knolls GC, *Omaha* .... 18 [M] 402-493-1740
knollsgolf.com
The Links At Lincoln G&CC, *Lincoln* ....9 [P] 402-476-1012
The Oregon Trail GC, *Sutherland*..........................9 [S] 308-386-4653
The Pines CC, *Valley* .... 18 [S] 402-359-4311
pinescountryclub.com
The Prairie Club, *Valentine* ....45 [R] 970-390-5273
theprairieclub.com
Thedford GC, *Thedford* ....9 [P] 308-645-2634
Thornridge GC, *Milford* ....9 [P] 402-761-3606
Tiburon GC, *Omaha* ....27 [S] 402-895-2688
tiburongolf.com
Tregaron GC, *Bellevue* .... 18 [P] 402-292-9300
tregarongolf.com
Twin Creeks GC, *Pender* ....9 [P] 402-385-2376
Valentine GC, *Valentine* ....9 [P] 402-376-6004
heartcity.com
Valley View CC, *Central City* ....9 [S] 308-946-2730
Valley View GC, *Fremont* .... 18 [P] 402-721-7772
Valley View GC, *Gibbon* ....9 [P] 308-468-5884
Van Berg Muni GC, *Columbus* ....9 [P] 402-564-0561
quailrungolf.com
Warren Swigart Muni GC, *Omaha* ....9 [M] 402-444-4623
ci.omaha.ne.us/parks
Wayne CC, *Wayne* .... 18 [S] 402-375-1152
waynecountryclub.org
Wellington Greens GC, *Lincoln* .... 9 [V] 402-483-4504

West Nine at Firethorne, *Lincoln* ....9 [P] 402-486-4653
west9golf.com
Westwind GC, *Ogallala* .... 18 [S] 308-284-4358
westwindgolf.com
Westwood Heights GC, *Omaha* ....9 [M] 402-444-4658
ci.omaha.ne.us/parks
White Tail Run GC, *Fremont* ....9 [P] 402-727-4403
Wild Horse GC At Gothenburg, *Gothenburg*.........18 [P] 308-537-7700
playwildhorse.com
Wilderness Ridge GC, *Lincoln* ....27 [S] 402-434-5106
wildernessridgegolf.com
Wildwood GC, *Nebraska City* ....9 [M] 402-873-3661
Willow Lakes Warrior Nine, *Bellevue* ....27 [A] 402-292-1680
Wood River CC, *Wood River* ....9 [S] 402-583-2225
Woodland Hills GC, *Eagle* .... 18 [P] 402-475-4653
woodlandhillsgolf.com
Wymore CC, *Wymore* ....9 [S] 402-645-9904
Yankee Hill CC, *Lincoln* .... 18 [V] 402-421-8300
yankeehillcc.com
York CC, *York* .... 18 [S] 402-362-3720
yorkcountryclub.net

NEVADA

Aliante GC, *North Las Vegas* .... 18 [P] 702-399-4888
aliantegolf.com
Angel Park GC, *Las Vegas* ....45 [R] 702-254-4653
angelpark.com
Anthem CC, *Henderson* .... 18 [V] 702-614-5050
anthemcc.com
ArrowCreek CC, *Reno* .... 36 [V] 775-850-4471
arrowcreekcc.com
Arroyo GC at Red Rock, *Las Vegas* ....18 [P] 702-258-2300
thearroyogolfclub.com
Badlands GC, *Las Vegas* ....27 [P] 702-242-4653
badlandsgc.com
Bali Hai GC, *Las Vegas* .... 18 [R] 702-450-8000
balihaigolfclub.com
Bears Best Las Vegas GC, *Las Vegas* ....18 [P] 702-804-8500
bearsbestlasvegas.com
Black Mountain G&CC, *Henderson* ....27 [S] 702-565-7933
golfblackmountain.com
Boulder City Muni GC, *Boulder City* ....18 [M] 702-293-9236
golfbouldercity.com
Boulder Creek GC, *Boulder City* ....27 [M] 702-294-6534
bouldercreekgc.com
Burning Sands GC, *Empire* ....9 [P] 775-557-2341
Callaway Golf Ctr, *Las Vegas* ....9 [P] 702-896-4100
cgclv.com
Canyon Gate CC, *Las Vegas* .... 18 [V] 702-363-0481
canyon-gate.com
Carson Valley GC, *Gardnerville* .... 18 [P] 775-265-3181
carsonvalleygolf.com
CasaBlanca Resort & Casino, *Mesquite* ....18 [R] 702-346-7529
casablancaresort.com
Cascata, *Boulder City* .... 18 [R] 702-294-2000
golfcascata.com
Chimney Rock GC, *Wells* ....9 [M] 775-752-3928
Conestoga GC, *Mesquite* ....18 [P] 702-346-4292
conestogagolf.com
Coyote Willows GC, *Mesquite* ....9 [S] 702-345-3222
coyotewillowsgolf.com
Craig Ranch GC, *North Las Vegas* ....18 [M] 702-642-9700

NEVADA — Golf Yellow Pages, 18th Edition

Crystal Peak GC, *Verdi* ....9 [P] 775-345-1551
verdi.us
Dayton Valley GC At Legado, *Dayton* ....18 [S] 775-246-7888
daytonvalley.com
Desert Pines GC, *Las Vegas* ....18 [R] 702-388-4400
desertpinesgolfclub.com
Desert Rose GC, *Las Vegas* ....18 [M] 702-431-4653
desertrosegc.com
Desert Willow GC, *Henderson* ....18 [P] 702-263-4653
desertwillowlasvegas.com
Dragon Ridge CC, *Henderson* ....18 [V] 702-614-4444
dragonridgegolf.com
Durango Hills GC, *Las Vegas* ....18 [P] 702-229-4653
durangohillsgolf.com
Eagle Crest GC, *Las Vegas* ....18 [P] 702-240-1320
golfsummerlin.com
Eagle Valley GC, *Carson City* ....36 [M] 775-887-2380
eaglevalleygolf.com
Edgewood Tahoe GC, *Stateline* ....18 [R] 775-588-3566
edgewoodtahoe.com
Empire Ranch GC, *Carson City* ....27 [P] 775-885-2100
empireranchgolf.com
Falcon Ridge GC, *Mesquite* ....18 [P] 702-346-6363
golffalcon.com
Genoa Lakes GC & Resort - Lakes Course, *Genoa* .18 [R] 775-782-4653
genoalakes.com
Genoa Lakes GC & Resort - Resort Course, *Genoa* 18 [R] 775-782-4653
genoalakes.com
Glenbrook GC, *Glenbrook* ....9 [R] 775-749-5201
Hidden Valley CC, *Reno* ....18 [V] 775-857-4735
hvccreno.com
Highland Falls GC, *Las Vegas* ....18 [P] 702-254-7010
golfsummerlin.com
Incline Village Champ GC, *Incline Village* ....18 [R] 775-832-1146
golfincline.com
Incline Village GC - Mountain, *Incline Village* ....18 [R] 775-832-1150
golfincline.com
Jackpot GC, *Jackpot* ....18 [M] 775-755-2260
LakeRidge GC, *Reno* ....18 [P] 775-825-2200
lakeridgegolf.com
Lakeview Executive GC, *Pahrump* ....18 [S] 775-727-4040
lakeviewgolfpahrump.com
Las Vegas CC, *Las Vegas* ....18 [V] 702-734-1132
lasvegascc.com
Las Vegas GC, *Las Vegas* ....18 [M] 702-646-3003
lasvegasgc.com
Las Vegas National GC, *Las Vegas* ....18 [R] 702-734-1796
lasvegasnational.com
Las Vegas Paiute Golf Resort, *Las Vegas* ....54 [R] 702-658-1400
lvpaiutegolf.com
Los Prados GC, *Las Vegas* ....18 [S] 702-645-5696
losprados-golf.com
Mojave Resort GC, *Laughlin* ....18 [R] 702-535-4653
mojaveresortgolfclub.com
Montreux G&CC, *Reno* ....18 [V] 775-849-9496
montreuxgolf.com
Mountain Falls GC, *Pahrump* ....18 [P] 775-537-6553
mountainfallsgolfclub.com
Mountain View GC, *Battle Mountain* ....9 [M] 775-635-2380
mvgolfclub.com
North Las Vegas Par 3, *North Las Vegas* ....9 [M] 775-633-1833
cityofnorthlasvegas.com
Painted Desert GC, *Las Vegas* ....18 [P] 702-645-2570
painteddesertgc.com

Palm Valley GC, *Las Vegas* ....18 [S] 702-363-4373
golfsummerlin.com
Palms GC, *Mesquite* ....18 [R] 702-346-5234
casablancaresort.com
PGA Village At Coyote Springs, *Coyote Springs* ....18 [P] 702-422-1400
coyotesprings.com
Red Rock CC - Mountain Course - Private,
Las Vegas ....18 [V] 702-304-5614
redrockcountryclub.com
Reflection Bay GC, *Henderson* ....18 [R] 702-740-4653
lakelasvegas.com
Resort At Red Hawk - Hills, *Sparks* ....18 [R] 775-626-6000
resortatredhawk.com
Resort At Red Hawk - Lakes, *Sparks* ....18 [R] 775-626-6000
resortatredhawk.com
Revere GC, *Henderson* ....36 [P] 702-259-4653
reveregolf.com
Rhodes Ranch GC, *Las Vegas* ....18 [R] 702-740-4114
rhodesranchgolf.com
Rio Secco GC, *Henderson* ....18 [R] 702-889-2400
harrahs.com/golf
Rosewood Lakes GC, *Reno* ....18 [M] 775-857-2892
rosewoodlakes.com
Round Mountain GC, *Round Mountain* ....9 [P] 775-377-2880
rmgcgolf.com
Royal Links GC, *Las Vegas* ....18 [R] 702-450-8123
waltersgolf.com
Ruby View GC, *Elko* ....18 [M] 775-777-7277
ci.elko.nv.us
Shadow Creek GC, *North Las Vegas* ....18 [R] 702-399-7111
shadowcreek.com
Siena GC, *Las Vegas* ....18 [R] 702-341-9200
sienagolfclub.com
Sierra Sage GC, *Reno* ....18 [M] 775-972-1564
sierrasagegolf.org
Silver Oak GC, *Carson City* ....18 [P] 775-841-7000
silveroakgolf.com
Silverstone GC, *Las Vegas* ....27 [P] 702-562-3770
silverstonegolf.com
Somersett CC, *Reno* ....18 [V] 775-787-1800
somersett.com
Somersett CC Canyon Nine, *Reno* ....9 [V] 775-787-4500
somersett.com
South Shore At Lake Las Vegas, *Henderson* ......18 [R] 702-558-0022
lakelasvegas.com
Southern Highlands GC, *Las Vegas* ....18 [V] 702-263-1000
southernhighlands.com
Spanish Trail G&CC, *Las Vegas* ....27 [V] 702-364-0357
spanishtrailcc.com
Spring Creek GC, *Spring Creek* ....18 [P] 775-753-6331
Sun Ridge GC, *Carson City* ....18 [P] 775-267-4448
sunridgegolfclub.com
Sunrise Vista GC, *Nellis AFB* ....36 [A] 702-652-2602
nellis.af.mil
The Club At Clear Creek, *Carson City* ....18 [V] 775-782-5888
clearcreektahoe.com
The GC At Fallon, *Fallon* ....9 [P] 775-423-4616
The GC of Fernley, *Fernley* ....18 [P] 775-835-6933
fernleygolfclub.com
The Legacy GC, *Henderson* ....18 [P] 702-897-2200
thelegacygc.com
The Links At Kiley Ranch, *Sparks* ....9 [P] 775-354-2100
The Oasis GC, *Mesquite* ....36 [R] 702-346-7820
theoasisgolfclub.com

[A] = MILITARY [M] = MUNICIPAL [P] = PUBLIC [R] = RESORT

NEW HAMPSHIRE

The Wynn GC, *Las Vegas* .... 18 [R] 702-770-7100
 wynnlasvegas.com
Thunder Canyon, *Washoe Valley* .... 18 [V] 775-882-0882
 thundercanyon.com
Toana Vista GC, *Wendover* ....18 [R] 775-664-4300
TPC Las Vegas, *Las Vegas* ....18 [R] 702-256-2000
 tpclasvegas.com
TPC Summerlin, *Las Vegas* .... 18 [V] 702-256-0222
 tpcsummerlin.com
Tuscany GC, *Henderson* ....18 [P] 702-951-1500
 tuscanygolfclub.com
Walker Lake GC, *Hawthorne* .... 9 [A] 775-945-1111
 golfhawthorne.com
Washoe County GC, *Reno*......................18 [M] 775-828-6640
 washoegolf.org
Whispering Pines GC, *Glenbrook*............. 9 [V] 775-588-7300
White Pine County GC, *Ely* ....18 [M] 775-289-4095
 elygolfing.com
Wildcreek GC, *Sparks* ....27 [P] 775-673-3100
 playreno.com
WildHorse GC, *Henderson* ....18 [M] 702-434-9000
 golfwildhorse.com
Winnemucca GC, *Winnemucca*................9 [M] 775-623-9920
 winnemuccacity.org
Wolf Creek At Paradise Canyon, *Mesquite* ....18 [R] 866-252-4653
 golfwolfcreek.com
Wolf Run GC, *Reno*..............................18 [P] 775-851-3301
 wolfrungolfclub.com

NEW HAMPSHIRE

Abenaqui CC, *Rye Beach* .... 18 [V] 603-964-5335
 abenaquicc.com
Amherst CC, *Amherst*..........................18 [P] 603-673-9908
 amherstcountryclub.com
Androscoggin Valley CC, *Gorham* .... 18 [S] 603-466-9468
 avccgolf.com
Angus Lea GC, *Hillsborough* ....9 [P] 603-464-5404
 anguslea.com
Apple Hill GC, *East Kingston* ....27 [P] 603-642-4414
 applehillgolf.com
Applewood Golf Links, *Windham* ....9 [S] 603-890-1015
Atkinson CC & Resort, *Atkinson*............27 [R] 603-362-8700
 atkinsonresort.com
Baker Hill GC, *Newbury*....................... 18 [V] 603-763-8900
 bakerhill.org
Bald Peak Colony Club, *Moultonborough* .... 18 [V] 603-544-9923
 baldpeak.org
Balsams Panorama GC, *Colebrook*.........27 [R] 603-255-4961
 thebalsams.com
Beaver Meadow GC, *Concord* ....18 [M] 603-228-8954
 beavermeadowgolfcourse.com
Bethlehem CC, *Bethlehem* ....18 [M] 603-869-5745
 bethlehemccnhgolf.com
Bill Flynns Windham CC, *Windham*....................18 [P] 603-434-2093
 windhamcc.us
Blackmount CC, *North Haverhill* ....9 [P] 603-787-6564
Bolduc Park GC, *Gilford* ....9 [P] 603-524-1370
 bolducpark.com
Bramber Valley GC, *Greenland* ....9 [P] 603-436-4288
 brambervalleygolf.com
Breakfast Hill GC, *Greenland* ....18 [P] 603-436-5001
 breakfasthill.com

Bretwood GC, *Keene* ....36 [P] 603-352-7626
 bretwoodgolf.com
Brookstone Park G Complex, *Derry* ....9 [P] 603-894-7336
 brookstone-park.com
Buckmeadow GC, *Amherst* ....9 [P] 603-673-7077
Campbells Scottish Highlands GC, *Salem*............18 [P] 603-894-4653
 scottishhighlandsgolf.com
Candia Woods Golf Links, *Candia* ....18 [P] 603-483-2307
 candiawoods.com
Canterbury Woods CC, *Canterbury* .... 18 [S] 603-783-9400
 canterburywoodscc.com
Carter GC, *Lebanon*..............................9 [P] 603-448-4483
 cartercc.com
CC Of New Hampshire, *North Sutton* ....18 [R] 603-927-4246
 playgolfne.com
Claremont CC, *Claremont*......................9 [S] 603-542-9550
 claremontcountryclubnh.com
Cochecho CC, *Dover* .... 18 [V] 603-742-8580
 cochechocc.com
Colebrook CC, *Colebrook* .... 9 [R] 603-237-5566
 colebrookcountryclub.com
Concord CC, *Concord* .... 18 [V] 603-228-8936
 concordcountryclub.org
Countryside GC, *Dunbarton* ....9 [P] 603-774-5031
 golfcountryside.net
Crotched Mountain GC, *Francestown* ....18 [M] 603-588-2000
 crotchedmountaingolf.com
Den Brae GC, *Sanbornton* ....9 [P] 603-934-9818
 denbrae.com
Derryfield CC, *Manchester* ....18 [M] 603-669-0235
 derryfieldgolf.com
Dublin Lake Club, *Dublin* .... 9 [V] 603-563-8559
Duston CC, *Hopkinton*..........................9 [P] 603-746-4234
 dustoncc.com
Eagle Mountain Resort GC, *Jackson* ...... 9 [R] 603-383-9090
 eaglemt.com
Eastman Golf Links, *Grantham* ....18 [S] 603-863-4500
 eastmangolflinks.com
Exeter CC, *Exeter* ....9 [S] 603-772-4752
 exetercountryclub.com
Farmington CC, *Farmington* ....9 [S] 603-755-2412
 farmingtoncountryclubnh.com
Granite Fields GC, *Kingston*..................18 [P] 603-642-9977
 granitefields.com
Granliden On Sunapee GC, *Sunapee* ...... 9 [V] 603-763-5606
 granliden.com
Green Meadow GC, *Hudson* ....36 [P] 603-882-9565
 greenmeadowgolfclub.com
Hales Location GC, *Hales Location* .... 9 [R] 603-356-2140
 haleslocationgolf.com
Hanover CC at Dartmouth College, *Hanover* .... 18 [U] 603-646-2000
 dartmouth.edu/~hccweb
Hickory Pond Inn & GC, *Durham* .... 9 [R] 603-659-2227
 hickorypondinn.com
Hidden Creek GC, *Litchfield* ....9 [P] 603-262-9272
 hiddencreekgolfnh.com
Hidden Valley RV & Golf Park, *Derry* ....27 [R] 603-887-3767
 hiddenvalleyrv.com
Highland Links GC, *Holderness*...............9 [P] 603-536-3452
Hoodkroft CC, *Derry*..............................9 [S] 603-434-0651
 hoodkroftcc.com
Hooper GC, *Walpole*.............................9 [P] 603-756-4080
 hoopergolfclub.com

[S] = SEMI-PRIVATE [V] = PRIVATE [U] = UNIVERSITY [N] = UNIVERSITY-PRIVATE

NEW HAMPSHIRE — Golf Yellow Pages, 18th Edition

Course	Location	Holes	Type	Phone
Indian Mound GC	Center Ossipee	18	[P]	603-539-7733
	indianmoundgc.com			
Intervale CC	Manchester	9	[S]	603-647-6811
	intervalecc.com			
Jack O Lantern Resort	Woodstock	18	[R]	603-745-3636
	jackolanternresort.com			
Jade Trace Golf At Mystic Meadows	Laconia	9	[P]	603-528-3057
	jadetrace.com			
Keene CC	Keene	18	[V]	603-352-9722
	keenecc.com			
Kingston Fairways	Kingston	18	[P]	603-642-7722
	kingstonfairwaysgolf.com			
Kingswood GC	Wolfeboro	18	[S]	603-569-3569
	kingswoodgolfclub.com			
Kona Par 3 Club	Center Harbor	9	[R]	603-253-4900
Laconia CC	Laconia	18	[V]	603-524-1274
	laconiacountryclub.com			
Lake Sunapee CC	New London	18	[R]	603-526-6440
	lakesunapeecc.com			
Lakeview GC	Belmont	9	[S]	603-524-2220
Linderhof CC	Glen	9	[V]	603-383-9074
Lisbon Village CC	Lisbon	9	[R]	603-838-6004
	lisbonvillagecountryclub.com			
Lochmere G&CC	Tilton	18	[S]	603-528-4653
	lochmeregolf.com			
Londonderry CC	Londonderry	18	[P]	603-432-9789
	londonderrycountryclub.com			
Loudon CC	Loudon	18	[P]	603-783-3372
	loudoncc.com			
Manchester CC	Bedford	18	[V]	603-623-8270
	manchestercountryclub.com			
Maplewood CC & Hotel	Bethlehem	18	[P]	603-869-3335
	maplewoodgolfresort.com			
Mojalaki GC	Franklin	9	[S]	603-934-3033
	mojalaki.com			
Monadnock CC	Peterborough	9	[S]	603-924-7769
	monadnockcc.com			
Montcalm GC	Enfield	18	[V]	603-448-5665
	montcalmgolfclub.com			
Mount Washington Hotel & Resort	Bretton Woods	27	[R]	603-278-4653
	mtwashington.com			
Mountain View Grand GC	Whitefield	9	[P]	603-837-2100
	mountainviewgrand.com			
Nashua CC	Nashua	18	[V]	603-888-9858
	nashuacountryclub.com			
Newport GC	Newport	18	[S]	603-863-7787
	newport-golf.com			
Nippo Lake GC	Barrington	18	[S]	603-664-7616
	nippolake.com			
North Conway CC	North Conway	18	[P]	603-356-5244
	northconwaycountryclub.com			
Oak Brook Golf	Weare	9	[P]	603-529-4653
	oakbrookgolf.com			
Oak Hill GC	Meredith	9	[P]	603-279-4438
	oakhillgc.com			
Owls Nest GC	Campton	18	[P]	603-726-3076
	owlsnestgolf.com			
Passaconaway CC	Litchfield	18	[P]	603-424-4653
	passaconawaycc.com			
Pease GC	Portsmouth	27	[P]	603-433-1331
	peasegolf.com			
Pheasant Ridge CC	Gilford	18	[P]	603-524-7808
	playgolfne.com			
Pine Grove Springs CC	Spofford	9	[P]	603-399-4886
	pgscc.com			
Pine Valley Golf Links	Pelham	9	[P]	603-635-8305
Plausawa Valley CC	Pembroke	18	[P]	603-928-7473
	plausawavalleycc.com			
Ponemah Green Family Golf Ctr	Amherst	9	[P]	603-672-4732
	amherstcountryclub.com			
Portsmouth CC	Greenland	18	[S]	603-436-9719
	portsmouthcc.net			
Profile GC	Franconia	9	[V]	603-823-7083
Ragged Mountain GC	Danbury	18	[R]	603-768-3600
	ragged-mt.com			
Ridgewood CC	Moultonborough	18	[P]	603-476-5930
	ridgewoodcc.net			
Rochester CC	Rochester	18	[V]	603-332-9892
	rochestercc.com			
Rockingham CC	Newmarket	9	[P]	603-659-9956
	rockinghamgolf.com			
Sagamore Hampton GC	North Hampton	18	[P]	603-964-5341
	sagamorehampton.com			
Shattuck GC	Jaffrey	18	[S]	603-532-4300
	sterlinggolf.com			
Sky Meadow CC	Nashua	18	[V]	603-888-3000
	skymeadow.com			
Souhegan Woods GC	Amherst	18	[P]	603-673-0200
	playgolfne.com			
Steele Hill Resort GC	Sanbornton	9	[R]	603-524-0500
	steelehillresorts.com			
Stonebridge CC	Goffstown	18	[P]	603-497-8633
	golfstonebridgecc.com			
Sunningdale GC	Somersworth	9	[R]	603-742-8056
	sunningdalegolfshop.com			
Sunset Hill GC	Sugar Hill	9	[R]	603-823-7244
	sunsethillgolf.com			
The GC of New England	Stratham	18	[V]	603-772-4900
	golfclubofnewengland.com			
The Lake Winnipesaukee GC	New Durham	18	[V]	603-569-3055
	lwgcnh.com			
The Oaks Golf Links	Somersworth	18	[P]	603-692-6257
	theoaksgolflinks.com			
The Overlook CC	Hollis	18	[P]	603-465-2909
	overlookgolfclub.com			
Twin Lake Village GC	New London	9	[R]	603-526-2034
Waterville Valley GC	Waterville Valley	9	[R]	603-236-4805
	waterville.com/info/summer			
Waukewan GC	Center Harbor	18	[P]	603-279-6661
	waukewan.com			
Waumbek CC	Jefferson	18	[S]	603-586-7777
	playgolfne.com			
Wentworth By The Sea	Rye	18	[V]	603-433-5010
	wentworthbytheseacc.com			
Wentworth GC	Jackson	18	[P]	603-383-9641
	wentworthgolf.com			
Whip Poor Will GC	Hudson	9	[P]	603-889-9706
	playgolfne.com			
White Mountain CC	Ashland	18	[R]	603-536-2227
	playgolfne.com			
Woodbound Inn GC	Rindge	9	[P]	603-532-8341
	woodbound.com			

NEW JERSEY

Course	Location	Holes	Type	Phone
Alpine CC	Demarest	18	[V]	201-768-2121
	alpinecc.org			

[A] = MILITARY   [M] = MUNICIPAL   [P] = PUBLIC   [R] = RESORT

Golf Yellow Pages, 18th Edition — NEW JERSEY

Apple Mountain G&CC, *Belvidere* .... 18 [S] 908-453-3023
  applemountaingolf.com
Apple Ridge CC, *Mahwah* .... 18 [V] 201-327-8000
  appleridgecountryclub.com
Arcola CC, *Paramus* .... 18 [V] 201-843-3990
  arcolacc.org
Ash Brook GC, *Scotch Plains* .... 27 [M] 908-756-0414
  ashbrookgolfcourse.com
Atlantic City CC, *Northfield* .... 18 [S] 609-641-7575
  accountryclub.com
Avalon GC, *Cape May Court House* .... 18 [S] 609-465-4653
  avalongolfclub.com
B L England GC, *Marmora* .... 9 [P] 609-390-0472
Ballamor GC, *Egg Harbor Township* .... 18 [P] 609-601-6220
  ballamor.com
Ballyowen GC, *Hamburg* .... 18 [R] 973-827-5996
  crystalgolfresort.com
Baltusrol GC, *Springfield* .... 36 [V] 973-376-1900
  baltusrol.org
Bamm Hollow CC, *Lincroft* .... 27 [V] 732-741-4131
  bammhollowcountryclub.com
Basking Ridge CC, *Basking Ridge* .... 18 [V] 908-766-8200
  baskingridgecc.com
Battleground CC, *Manalapan* .... 18 [V] 732-462-7575
  battlegroundcc.com
Bayonne GC, *Bayonne* .... 18 [V] 201-823-4800
  bayonnegolfclub.com
Beacon Hill CC, *Atlantic Highlands* .... 18 [V] 732-291-3344
  beaconhillcc.org
Bear Brook GC, *Newton* .... 18 [P] 973-383-2327
  bearbrookgolf.com
Beaver Brook CC, *Annandale* .... 18 [S] 908-735-4200
  beaverbrookcc.com
Beckett CC, *Woolwich Township* .... 27 [P] 856-467-4700
  beckettgc.com
Bedens Brook Club, *Skillman* .... 18 [V] 609-466-3063
  bedensbrook.com
Bel Aire GC, *Wall* .... 27 [M] 732-449-6024
  monmouthcountyparks.com
Bella Vista CC, *Marlboro* .... 18 [V] 732-308-4600
  bellavistacc.com
Berkshire Valley GC, *Oak Ridge* .... 18 [M] 973-208-0018
  morrisparks.net
Bey Lea GC, *Toms River* .... 18 [M] 732-349-0566
  usegolf.com
Black Bear GC, *Franklin* .... 18 [P] 973-209-2521
  crystalgolfresort.com
Black Oak GC, *Long Valley* .... 18 [P] 908-876-9887
  blackoakgolfclub.com
Blair Acad GC, *Blairstown* .... 9 [U] 908-362-6121
  blair.edu
Blue Heron Pines GC, *Cologne* .... 36 [P] 609-965-1800
  blueheronpines.com
Bowling Green GC, *Oak Ridge* .... 18 [S] 973-697-8688
  bowlinggreengolf.com
Brooklake CC, *Florham Park* .... 18 [V] 973-377-2235
  brooklakecc.com
Buena Vista CC, *Buena* .... 18 [P] 856-697-3733
  allforeclub.com
Bunker Hill GC, *Princeton* .... 18 [P] 908-359-6535
  distinctgolf.com
Burlington CC, *Mt Holly* .... 18 [V] 609-267-1887
  burlingtonccnj.com

Canoe Brook CC, *Summit* .... 36 [V] 908-277-0100
  canoebrook.com
Cape May National GC, *Erma* .... 18 [P] 609-898-1005
  cmngc.com
Cape May Par 3 & DR, *Rio Grande* .... 18 [P] 609-889-2600
  capemaypar3.com
Cedar Creek GC, *Bayville* .... 18 [M] 732-269-4460
  twp.berkeley.nj.us
Cedar Hill G&CC, *Livingston* .... 18 [V] 973-992-4700
  cedarhillcc.com
Centerton CC, *Elmer* .... 18 [P] 856-358-2220
  centertoncc.com
Charleston Springs GC, *Millstone Township* .... 36 [M] 732-409-7227
  monmouthcountyparks.com
Cherry Valley CC, *Skillman* .... 18 [V] 609-466-4244
  cherryvalleycc.com
Clearbrook GC, *Monroe Twp* .... 9 [P] 609-655-3443
  clearbrookgc.com
Coakley Russo Memorial GC, *Lyons* .... 9 [M] 908-204-3003
Cohanzick CC, *Fairton* .... 18 [S] 856-455-2127
  allforeclub.com/ccc
Colonia CC, *Colonia* .... 18 [V] 732-381-9500
  coloniacc.net
Colonial Terrace GC, *Ocean* .... 9 [M] 732-775-3636
  oceanhsd.org/golfcourse.html
Colts Neck GC, *Colts Neck* .... 18 [S] 732-303-9330
  coltsneckgolfclub.com
Concordia GC, *Cranbury* .... 18 [V] 609-655-5631
  concordiagolf.com
Copper Hill CC, *Ringoes* .... 18 [V] 908-782-4455
  copper-hill.com
Cranbury GC, *West Windsor* .... 18 [S] 609-799-0341
  cranburygolf.com
Cream Ridge GC, *Cream Ridge* .... 18 [P] 609-259-2849
  creamridgegolfclub.com
Crestmont CC, *West Orange* .... 18 [V] 973-731-2060
  crestmontcountryclub.com
Cruz Golf CC, *Farmingdale* .... 18 [P] 732-938-3378
Crystal Springs GC, *Hamburg* .... 27 [P] 973-827-1587
  crystalgolfresort.com
Culver Lake GC, *Branchville* .... 9 [P] 973-948-5610
  culverlakegolf.com
Darlington GC & DR, *Mahwah* .... 18 [M] 201-327-8770
  bergengolf.org
Deal G&CC, *Deal* .... 18 [V] 732-531-1190
  dealcountryclub.com
Deer Run GC, *Lincoln Park* .... 9 [V] 973-694-0758
Deerwood CC, *Westampton* .... 18 [V] 609-265-1800
  deerwoodcc.com
Due Process Stable, *Colts Neck* .... 18 [V] 732-542-0317
Eagle Oaks GC, *Farmingdale* .... 18 [V] 732-938-9696
  eagleoaks.com
Eagle Ridge GC, *Lakewood* .... 27 [P] 732-901-4900
  eagleridgegolf.com
East Orange GC, *Short Hills* .... 18 [S] 973-379-6775
Eastlyn GC, *Vineland* .... 18 [P] 856-691-5558
Echo Lake CC, *Westfield* .... 18 [V] 908-232-4288
  echolakecc.com
Edgewood CC, *Rivervale* .... 27 [V] 201-666-1200
  edgewoodnj.com
Emerson GC, *Emerson* .... 18 [P] 201-261-1100
  emersongolfcourse.com

[S] = SEMI-PRIVATE   [V] = PRIVATE   [U] = UNIVERSITY   [N] = UNIVERSITY-PRIVATE

NEW JERSEY

Golf Yellow Pages, 18th Edition

Essex County CC, *West Orange* .... 18 [V] 973-731-1400
essexcountycc.com
Essex Fells CC, *Essex Fells* .... 18 [V] 973-226-3800
essexfellscc.com
Fairmount CC, *Chatham* .... 18 [V] 973-377-8901
fairmountcc.com
Fairway Golf Ctr, *Piscataway* .... 9 [P] 732-819-0111
fairwaygolfcenter.com
Fairway Mews GC, *Spring Lake Heights* .... 18 [V] 732-449-8883
fairwaymews.org
Fairway Valley GC, *Washington* .... 9 [P] 908-689-1530
fairwayvalleygolfclub.com
Falcon Creek GC, *Mc Guire AFB* .... 18 [A] 609-754-2169
Farmstead G&CC, *Lafayette* .... 27 [P] 973-383-1666
farmsteadgolf.com
Fiddlers Elbow CC, *Bedminster* .... 54 [V] 908-439-2513
fiddlerselbowcc.com
Flanders Valley GC, *Flanders* .... 36 [M] 973-584-5382
morrisparks.net
Forest Hill Field Club, *Bloomfield* .... 18 [V] 973-743-9611
foresthillfc.com
Forsgate CC, *Monroe Township* .... 36 [M] 732-521-0070
forsgatecc.com
Fountain Green GC, *Fort Dix* .... 18 [A] 609-562-5443
Four Seasons Spa & CC, *Lakewood* .... 9 [V] 732-477-2730
Fox Hollow GC, *Branchburg* .... 18 [V] 908-526-0010
foxhollowgc.com
Francis A Byrne GC, *West Orange* .... 18 [P] 973-736-2306
Freeway GC, *Sicklerville* .... 18 [P] 856-227-1115
freewaygolfclub.com
Frog Rock CC, *Hammonton* .... 18 [P] 609-561-5504
frogrockgolf.com
Galloping Hill GC, *Kenilworth* .... 27 [M] 908-686-1556
gallopinghillgolfcourse.com
Galloway National GC, *Absecon* .... 18 [V] 609-748-1000
gallowaynationalgolf.com
Gambler Ridge GC, *Cream Ridge* .... 18 [P] 609-758-3588
gamblerridge.com
Glen Ridge CC, *Glen Ridge* .... 18 [V] 973-744-7803
glenridgecc.com
Glenwild Greens, *Bloomingdale* .... 9 [P] 973-283-0888
glenwildgreens.com
Glenwood GC, *Old Bridge* .... 18 [V] 732-607-2582
njgolfclub.com
Golden Pheasant CC, *Lumberton* .... 18 [R] 609-267-4276
goldenpheasantgc.com
Great Gorge CC, *McAfee* .... 27 [P] 973-827-7603
crystalgolfresort.com
Greate Bay GC, *Somers Point* .... 18 [R] 609-927-5071
greatebay.com
Green Brook CC, *Caldwell* .... 18 [V] 973-228-1800
greenbrookcc.org
Green Knoll GC, *Bridgewater* .... 18 [M] 908-722-1301
somersetcountyparks.org
Green Tree GC, *Egg Harbor Township* .... 18 [M] 609-625-9131
greentree.aclink.org
Greenacres CC, *Lawrenceville* .... 18 [V] 609-896-0259
greenacres-cc.com
Greenbriar At Ocean Aire G&CC, *Waretown* .... 18 [V] 609-693-8885
Greenbriar At Whittingham GC, *Monroe Twp* .... 9 [P] 609-860-6521
gbcainc.net
Greenbriar Woodlands, *Toms River* .... 9 [V] 732-286-6889
greenbriarwoodlandsnj.com

Hackensack GC, *Oradell* .... 18 [V] 201-261-5505
hgc.org
Hamilton Farm GC, *Gladstone* .... 36 [P] 908-901-4000
hamiltonfarmgolfclub.com
Hamilton Trails GC, *Mays Landing* .... 9 [P] 609-641-6824
hamiltontrails.com
Hanover GC, *Wrightstown* .... 18 [P] 609-758-8301
hanovergc.com
Harbor Pines GC, *Egg Harbor Township* .... 18 [P] 609-927-0006
harborpines.com
Harkers Hollow CC, *Phillipsburg* .... 18 [V] 908-859-0977
harkershollow.com
Hawk Pointe GC, *Washington* .... 18 [R] 908-689-1870
hawkpointegolf.com
Haworth CC, *Haworth* .... 18 [V] 201-384-7300
haworthcountryclub.com
Hendricks Field GC, *Belleville* .... 18 [M] 973-751-0178
Heritage Links GC, *Ocean View* .... 9 [P] 609-390-4500
linfieldnational.com/heritage
Heron Glen GC, *Ringoes* .... 18 [M] 908-806-6804
heronglen.com
Hidden Acres GC, *Hainesville* .... 9 [P] 973-948-9804
Hidden Creek GC, *Egg Harbor Township* .... 18 [V] 609-909-2990
hiddencreekclub.com
High Bridge Hills GC, *High Bridge* .... 18 [M] 908-638-5055
highbridgehills.com
High Mountain GC, *Franklin Lakes* .... 18 [S] 201-891-4653
highmountaingolf.com
High Point GC, *Montague* .... 18 [S] 973-293-3282
highpointgc.com
Hillsborough CC, *Hillsborough Twp* .... 18 [S] 908-369-3322
hillsboroughgolf.com
Hole in One Golf Ctr, *Millstone Township* .... 9 [P] 732-792-2818
Hollywood GC, *Deal* .... 18 [V] 732-531-8950
hollywoodgolfclub.org
Hominy Hill GC, *Colts Neck* .... 18 [M] 732-462-9222
monmouthcountyparks.com
Hopewell Valley CC, *Hopewell* .... 18 [V] 609-466-9070
hvgc.com
Howell Park GC, *Farmingdale* .... 18 [M] 732-938-4771
monmouthcountyparks.com
Hyatt Hills GC, *Clark* .... 9 [P] 908-669-9100
hyatthills.com
Indian Spring CC, *Marlton* .... 18 [M] 856-983-0222
indianspringgolf.com
Jumping Brook CC, *Neptune* .... 18 [V] 732-922-6140
jumpingbrookcc.com
Knickerbocker CC, *Tenafly* .... 18 [V] 201-568-1460
knickerbocker.cc
Knob Hill GC, *Manalapan* .... 18 [P] 732-792-7722
knobhillgc.com
Knoll East CC, *Lake Hiawatha* .... 18 [M] 973-263-7115
knollgolfclub.com
Knoll West CC, *Lake Hiawatha* .... 18 [M] 973-263-7110
knollgolfclub.com
Kresson GC, *Voorhees* .... 18 [P] 856-435-3355
Laguna Oaks GC, *Cape May Court House* .... 10 [P] 609-465-4560
Lake Lackawanna GC, *Stanhope* .... 9 [P] 973-448-1313
lakelackawannagolfcourse.com
Lake Mohawk GC, *Sparta* .... 18 [V] 973-729-9200
lakemohawkgolfclub.com
Lakewood CC, *Lakewood* .... 18 [P] 732-364-8899
thelakewoodcountryclub.com

134 [A] = MILITARY [M] = MUNICIPAL [P] = PUBLIC [R] = RESORT

NEW JERSEY

Golf Yellow Pages, 18th Edition

Latona CC, *Buena* .... 9 [P] 856-692-8149
  latonagolfcourse.com
Laurel Creek CC, *Mt Laurel* .... 18 [V] 856-273-7663
  laurelcreek.org
Lawrenceville School GC, *Lawrenceville* ...... 9 [N] 609-896-1481
Leisure Village East, *Lakewood* .... 9 [V] 732-477-7902
Leisure Village GC, *Lakewood* .... 9 [V] 732-364-1820
Leisure Village West Assoc, *Manchester* ...... 18 [V] 732-657-8997
  lvwa.net
Liberty National, *Jersey City* .... 18 [V] 201-333-4105
  libertynationalgc.com
Links GC, *Marlton* .... 18 [V] 856-983-2000
  thelinksgc.com
Linwood CC, *Linwood* .... 18 [V] 609-927-6134
  linwoodcountryclub.com
Lions Head CC, *Brick* .... 9 [V] 732-477-7277
Little Mill CC, *Marlton* .... 27 [V] 856-767-0559
  littlemill.com
Madison GC, *Madison* .... 9 [V] 973-377-5264
  mgc.cc
Manasquan River GC, *Brielle* .... 18 [V] 732-528-9678
  mrgc.com
Maplewood CC, *Maplewood* .... 18 [V] 973-762-2100
Mattawang GC, *Belle Mead* .... 18 [S] 908-281-0778
  mattawang-golf.com
Mays Landing G&CC, *Mays Landing* .... 18 [P] 609-641-4411
  mayslandinggolf.com
McCulloughs Emerald Golf Links,
  Egg Harbor Township .... 18 [P] 609-926-3900
  mcculloughsgolf.com
Meadows At Middlesex, *Plainsboro* .... 18 [S] 609-799-4000
  mciauth.com
Meadows GC, *Lincoln Park* .... 18 [P] 973-696-7212
  meadowsgolfclub.com
Medford Lakes CC, *Medford Lakes* .... 18 [V] 609-654-5108
  medfordlakescountryclub.com
Medford Village CC, *Medford* .... 18 [V] 609-654-8211
  medfordvillage.com
Mendham G&TC, *Mendham* .... 18 [V] 973-543-6524
  mendhamgolfandtennis.com
Mercer Oaks GC, *Princeton Junction* .... 36 [M] 609-936-1383
  golfmercercounty.com
Merchantville CC, *Cherry Hill* .... 9 [V] 856-662-7835
  merchantvillecc.com
Metedeconk National GC, *Jackson* .... 27 [V] 732-928-0111
  metedeconk.org
Metuchen G&CC, *Edison* .... 18 [V] 732-548-4980
  metuchengolf.com
Millburn Township Par 3 GC, *Short Hills* ..... 9 [M] 973-379-4156
  twp.millburn.nj.us
Minebrook GC, *Hackettstown* .... 18 [P] 908-979-0366
  minebrookgc.com
Minerals GC, *Vernon* .... 9 [R] 973-827-3710
  crystalgolfresort.com
Miry Run CC, *Robbinsville* .... 18 [P] 609-259-1010
  miryruncc.com
Montammy GC, *Alpine* .... 18 [P] 201-768-9016
  montammy.com
Montclair GC, *West Orange* .... 36 [V] 973-239-1800
  montclairgolfclub.org
Moorestown Field Club, *Moorestown* .... 9 [V] 856-235-2326
  moorestownfc.com
Morris County CC, *Morristown* .... 18 [V] 973-539-7200
  morriscgc.com

Mountain Ridge CC, *West Caldwell* .... 18 [R] 973-575-0734
  mountainridgecc.org
Mountain View GC, *West Trenton* .... 18 [M] 609-882-4093
  golfmercercounty.com
Mt Tabor CC, *Mt Tabor* .... 9 [V] 973-627-5995
  mounttaborcc.com
Navesink CC, *Middletown* .... 18 [V] 732-842-3111
  navesinkcc.com
Neshanic Valley GC, *Neshanic Station* .... 36 [M] 908-369-8200
  neshanicvalleygolf.com
New Jersey National GC, *Basking Ridge* .... 18 [V] 908-781-9400
  newjerseynational.com
Newton CC, *Newton* .... 18 [V] 973-383-9394
  newtoncountryclub.org
North Jersey CC, *Wayne* .... 18 [V] 973-595-5150
  northjerseycc.com
Oak Hill GC, *Milford* .... 18 [V] 908-995-2285
  oakhillgolf.com
Ocean Acres CC, *Manahawkin* .... 18 [P] 609-597-9393
  allforeclub.com
Ocean City Muni GC, *Ocean City* .... 9 [V] 609-399-1315
  ocnj.us
Ocean County GC At Atlantis,
  Little Egg Harbor Twp .... 18 [M] 609-296-2444
  oceancountygov.com/county/parks
Ocean County GC At Forge Pond, *Brick* .... 18 [M] 732-920-8899
  co.ocean.nj.us
Old Orchard CC, *Eatontown* .... 18 [S] 732-542-7666
Old Tappan GC, *Old Tappan* .... 9 [V] 201-767-1199
  oldtappan.net
Olde York CC, *Chesterfield* .... 18 [V] 609-298-0212
  oldeyork.com
Orchard Hills GC, *Paramus* .... 9 [M] 201-447-3788
  bergengolf.org
Overpeck GC, *Teaneck* .... 18 [M] 201-837-3020
  bergengolf.org
Packanack GC, *Wayne* .... 9 [V] 973-694-9754
Panther Valley G&CC, *Allamuchy* .... 18 [V] 908-852-6120
  panthervalleygolfcc.com
Paramus GC, *Paramus* .... 18 [M] 201-447-6079
  paramusborough.org
Passaic County GC, *Wayne* .... 36 [M] 973-881-4921
Peace Pipe CC, *Denville* .... 9 [V] 973-625-5041
  peacepipecc.com
Pebble Creek GC, *Colts Neck* .... 18 [P] 732-303-9090
  pebblecreekgolfclub.com
Peddie School GC, *Hightstown* .... 18 [N] 609-490-7542
  peddie.org
Pennsauken CC, *Pennsauken* .... 18 [M] 856-662-4961
  pennsaukengolf.com
Picatinny Arsenal GC, *Picatinny Arsenal* ..... 18 [A] 973-989-2466
  pica.army.mil
Pinch Brook GC, *Florham Park* .... 18 [M] 973-377-2039
  morrisparks.net
Pine Barrens GC, *Jackson* .... 18 [V] 732-408-1154
  pinebarrensgolf.com
Pine Brook GC, *Englishtown* .... 18 [M] 732-536-7272
  monmouthcountyparks.com
Pine Ridge GC, *Lakehurst* .... 9 [A] 732-323-7483
  lakehurst.navy.mil
Pine Valley GC, *Clementon* .... 27 [V] 856-783-3000
Pinelands GC, *Hammonton* .... 18 [P] 609-561-8900
  allforeclub.com

[S] = SEMI-PRIVATE   [V] = PRIVATE   [U] = UNIVERSITY   [N] = UNIVERSITY-PRIVATE

NEW JERSEY
Golf Yellow Pages, 18th Edition

Pines At Clermont, *Cape May Court House*............9 [P] 609-624-0100
  pinesatclermont.com
Pitman GC, *Sewell* ....18 [M] 856-589-6688
  co.gloucester.nj.us/golf
Plainfield CC, *Edison* .... 27 [V] 908-757-1800
  plainfieldcc.com
Pomona G&CC, *Pomona*.................................9 [P] 609-965-3232
Preakness Hills CC, *Wayne* ....18 [V] 973-694-2910
  preaknesshills.org
Princeton CC, *Princeton*....................................18 [M] 609-452-9382
  golfmercercounty.com
Quail Brook GC, *Somerset* ....18 [M] 732-560-9528
  somersetcountyparks.org
Raintree GC, *Freehold* .... 9 [V] 732-431-3526
Ramblewood CC, *Mt Laurel*.............................27 [P] 856-235-2118
  ramblewoodcc.com
Ramsey G&CC, *Ramsey*................................... 18 [V] 201-327-3877
  ramseycountryclub.com
Rancocas GC, *Willingboro* ....18 [P] 609-877-5534
  rancocas.americangolf.com
Raritan Landing GC, *Piscataway* ....18 [M] 732-885-9600
  mciauth.com
Raritan Valley CC, *Bridgewater*..........................18 [V] 908-722-2000
  rvcc1911.org
Regency At Monroe G&CC, *Monroe Township*.......9 [P] 732-605-9057
  regencyatmonroe.com
Renaissance GC, *Manchester TWP*...................18 [V] 732-657-8900
River Vale CC, *Westwood*..................................18 [S] 201-391-2300
  rivervalecc.com
RiverWinds G&TC, *West Deptford* ....18 [P] 856-848-1033
  riverwindsgolfandtennis.com
Rock Spring Club, *West Orange* ....18 [V] 973-731-6466
  rockspringclub.com
Rockaway River CC, *Denville* ....18 [V] 973-627-4461
  rockawayrivercc.com
Rockleigh GC, *Rockleigh* ....27 [M] 201-768-6353
  bergengolf.org
Rolling Greens GC, *Newton* ....18 [P] 973-383-3082
  rollinggreensgolf.com
Ron Jaworskis Valleybrook GC, *Blackwood*...........18 [S] 856-227-3171
  valleybrookgolf.com
Roselle GC, *Roselle*.. 9 [V] 908-245-7175
Rossmoor GC, *Monroe Township* .... 18 [V] 609-655-3182
  rossmoor-nj2.com/rossmoor_golf
Roxiticus GC, *Mendham*....................................18 [V] 973-543-4017
  roxiticus.com
Royce Brook GC, *Hillsborough* .... 36 [V] 908-904-4786
  roycebrook.com
Rumson CC, *Rumson*...18 [V] 732-842-3333
  rumsoncc.org
Running Deer GC, *Elmer* ....18 [P] 856-358-2000
  runningdeergolfclub.com
Rutgers Univ GC, *Piscataway* ....18 [U] 732-445-2637
  golfcourse.rutgers.edu
Sakima CC, *Carneys Point*.................................. 9 [V] 856-299-0201
Salem CC, *Salem*.. 9 [V] 856-935-1603
Sand Barrens GC, *Cape May Court House*...........27 [P] 609-465-3555
  sandbarrensgolf.com
Scotch Hills CC, *Scotch Plains* ....9 [M] 908-232-9748
  scotchplainsnj.com
Scotland Run GC, *Williamstown*........................18 [P] 856-863-3737
  scotlandrun.com

Sea Oaks GC, *Tuckerton*.....................................18 [P] 609-296-2656
  seaoakscc.com
Seaview Golf Resort, *Absecon*...........................36 [R] 609-748-7680
  seaviewgolf.com
Shackamaxon G&CC, *Scotch Plains*.....................18 [V] 908-233-1300
  shackamaxoncc.com
Shadow Lake Village, *Red Bank* ....9 [V] 732-842-9580
  shadowlakevillage.com
Shark River GC, *Neptune*...................................18 [M] 732-922-4141
  monmouthcountyparks.com
Shore Gate GC, *Ocean View*..............................18 [R] 609-624-8337
  shoregategolfclub.com
Sky View GC, *Sparta* ....18 [R] 973-726-4653
  skyviewgolf.com
Somerset Hills CC, *Bernardsville*........................ 18 [V] 908-766-0044
  somersetcc.org
Spooky Brook GC, *Somerset* ....18 [M] 732-873-2242
  somersetcountyparks.org
Spring Brook CC, *Morristown* ....18 [V] 973-539-6660
  springbrookcc.net
Spring Lake GC, *Spring Lake*..............................18 [V] 732-449-7185
  springlakegolfclub.org
Spring Meadow GC, *Farmingdale*......................18 [M] 732-449-0806
Springdale GC, *Princeton* ....18 [V] 908-924-3198
  princeton.edu/~golf/sgc.html
Springfield Golf Ctr, *Mt Holly* ....18 [P] 609-267-8440
  springfieldgc.com
Stanton Ridge G&CC, *Whitehouse Station* .... 18 [V] 908-534-1234
  stantonridgecc.com
Stone Harbor GC, *Cape May Court House*............18 [V] 609-465-9270
  stoneharborgolf.com
Stony Brook GC, *Hopewell*.................................18 [P] 609-466-2215
Suburban GC, *Union* ....18 [V] 908-686-0444
  suburbangolfclub.com
Summit Muni GC, *Summit*.................................9 [M] 908-277-6828
  ci.summit.nj.us
Sun Eagles GC At Fort Monmouth, *Fort Monmouth*18 [A] 732-532-4307
  bad link
Sunset Valley GC, *Pompton Plains* ....18 [M] 973-835-1515
  morrisparks.net
Tamarack GC, *East Brunswick*............................36 [M] 732-821-8881
  mciauth.com
Tara Greens Golf Ctr, *Somerset* ....9 [P] 732-247-8284
  taragreensgolf.com
Tavistock CC, *Haddonfield* .... 18 [V] 856-429-1827
  tavistockcc.org
The Architects GC, *Phillipsburg* ....18 [P] 908-213-3080
  thearchitectsclub.com
The Fernwood Club, *Roseland*............................9 [P] 973-226-8800
  fernwoodclub.com
The Links At Brigantine Beach, *Brigantine*..........18 [R] 609-266-1388
  brigantinegolf.com
The Ridge at Back Brook, *Ringoes*.....................18 [V] 609-466-0242
  theridgegc.com
The Ridgewood CC, *Paramus* .... 27 [V] 201-599-3900
  rcc1890.com
The Riverton CC, *Riverton* ....18 [V] 856-829-1919
  therivertoncountryclub.com
Toms River CC, *Toms River*.................................9 [V] 732-349-8867
  trcc.net
Town & Country Golf Links, *Woodstown* ....18 [P] 856-769-8333
  tcgolflinks.com
TPC Jasna Polana, *Princeton* .... 18 [V] 609-688-2000
  tpcatjasnapolana.com

[A] = MILITARY   [M] = MUNICIPAL   [P] = PUBLIC   [R] = RESORT

Golf Yellow Pages, 18th Edition

NEW MEXICO

Trenton CC, *West Trenton* .... 18 [V]   609-883-3800
   trentoncc.com
Trump National GC Philadelphia, *Pine Hill* .... 18 [V]   856-435-3100
   trumpnationalphiladelphia.com
Trump National GC, Bedminster, *Bedminster* ...... 36 [V]   908-470-4400
   trumpnationalbedminster.com
Trump National GC, Colts Neck, *Colts Neck* .... 27 [V]   732-625-9244
   trumpcoltsneck.com
Twin Brook Golf Ctr, *Tinton Falls* .... 9 [P]   732-922-1600
   twinbrookgolfcenter.com
Twin Brooks CC, *Watchung* .... 18 [V]   908-561-8558
   twinbrooks.com
Twin Willows Par 3 GC, *Lincoln Park* .... 9 [P]   973-692-0179
   par3golfnj.com
Twisted Dune GC, *Egg Harbor Township* .... 18 [P]   609-653-8019
   twisteddune.com
Upper Montclair CC, *Clifton* .... 27 [V]   973-779-7505
   uppermontclaircountryclub.com
Valley Brook GC, *Riverdale* .... 18 [M]   201-664-5886
   bergengolf.org
Victors Par 3 GC, *Mays Landing* .... 18 [P]   609-625-4931
Vineyard Golf At Renault, *Egg Harbor City* .... 18 [R]   609-965-2111
   renaultwinery.com
Walkill CC, *Franklin* .... 9 [V]   973-827-9620
Warrenbrook GC, *Warren* .... 18 [M]   908-754-8402
   somersetcountyparks.org
Washington Twnsp Muni Course, *Turnersville* ...... 9 [M]   856-227-1435
Wedgwood CC, *Turnersville* .... 18 [P]   856-227-5522
   wedgwoodcc.com
Weequahic Park GC, *Newark* .... 18 [M]   973-923-1838
Westlake G&CC, *Jackson* .... 18 [V]   732-833-7274
   westlakegolfandcountryclub.com
Westwood GC, *Woodbury* .... 18 [S]   856-845-2000
   westwoodgolfclub.com
White Beeches G&CC, *Haworth* .... 18 [V]   201-385-3100
   wbgcc.com
White Oaks CC, *Newfield* .... 18 [P]   856-697-8900
   whiteoaksgolf.com
Wild Oaks GC, *Salem* .... 27 [S]   856-935-0705
   wildoaksgolfcourse.com
Wild Turkey GC, *Hamburg* .... 18 [P]   973-827-1587
   crystalgolfresort.com
Wildwood G&CC, *Cape May Court House* .... 18 [V]   609-465-7824
   wildwoodgolf.com
Willowbrook CC, *Moorestown* .... 18 [S]   856-461-0131
   willowbrookcountryclub.com
Woodbury CC, *Woodbury* .... 9 [V]   856-848-5000
   woodburycountryclub.org
Woodcrest CC, *Cherry Hill* .... 18 [V]   856-428-1243
   woodcrestcc.com
Woodlake CC, *Lakewood* .... 18 [V]   732-370-1002
   woodlakecountryclub.com

NEW MEXICO

Albuquerque CC, *Albuquerque* .... 18 [V]   505-243-7156
   albuquerquecountryclub.com
Alto Lakes G&CC, *Alto* .... 18 [V]   575-336-4231
   altolakesgolf.com
Angel Fire Resort CC, *Angel Fire* .... 18 [R]   575-377-3055
   angelfireresort.com
Anthony CC, *Anthony* .... 9 [V]   575-882-2723
Apache Mesa GC, *Holloman AFB* .... 9 [A]   575-572-3574

Arroyo Del Oso GC, *Albuquerque* .... 27 [M]   505-884-7505
   cabq.gov/golf
Artesia CC, *Artesia* .... 18 [V]   575-746-6732
Black Mesa GC, *Espanola* .... 18 [R]   505-747-8946
   blackmesagolfclub.com
Chamisa Hills CC, *Rio Rancho* .... 27 [V]   505-896-5017
   chamisahillsgolfandcountryclub.com
Champ GC At Univ of New Mexico, *Albuquerque* 18 [U]   505-277-4546
   unmgolf.com
Chaparral CC, *Clovis* .... 27 [S]   575-762-4775
   chaparralcountryclub.com
Civitan GC, *Farmington* .... 9 [M]   505-599-1184
   fmtn.org/civitan
Clayton GC, *Clayton* .... 9 [P]   575-374-9643
Clovis Muni GC, *Clovis* .... 27 [M]   575-769-7871
   cityofclovis.org
Coyote del Malpais GC, *Grants* .... 18 [M]   505-285-5544
   coyotedelmalpaisgolfcourse.com
Cree Meadows CC, *Ruidoso* .... 18 [P]   575-257-2733
   playcreemeadows.com
Desert Greens GC, *Albuquerque* .... 18 [R]   505-898-7001
   desertgreensgolf.com
Desert Lakes GC, *Alamogordo* .... 18 [M]   575-437-0290
   desertlakesgolf.com
Dos Lagos GC, *Anthony* .... 18 [P]   575-882-2830
   doslagos.com
Eunice Muni GC, *Eunice* .... 9 [M]   575-394-2881
   cityofeunice.org
Four Hills CC, *Albuquerque* .... 18 [V]   505-299-9555
   fourhillscc.com
Fox Run GC, *Gallup* .... 18 [M]   505-863-9224
Gene Torres GC, *Las Vegas* .... 9 [U]   505-425-7711
   nmhu.edu
Hidden Valley GC, *Aztec* .... 18 [P]   505-334-3248
Hobbs CC, *Hobbs* .... 18 [V]   575-393-5212
   hobbscountryclub.com
Inn of the Mountain Gods Resort, *Mescalero* ...... 18 [R]   505-464-7777
   innofthemountaingods.com
Innsbrook Village CC, *Ruidoso* .... 9 [P]   505-258-3589
   innsbrookcondos.com
Isleta Eagle GC, *Albuquerque* .... 27 [P]   505-848-1900
   isletaeagle.com
Jal CC, *Jal* .... 9 [S]   575-395-2330
Kokopelli Club, *Alto* .... 18 [V]   575-336-1818
   kokopelliclub.com
Ladera GC, *Albuquerque* .... 27 [M]   505-836-4396
   cabq.gov/golf
Lake Carlsbad GC, *Carlsbad* .... 27 [M]   575-885-5444
   lakecarlsbadgolfcourse.com
Las Cruces CC (1), *Las Cruces* .... 18 [V]   575-526-8731
   lccc-golf.com
Los Alamos County GC, *Los Alamos* .... 18 [M]   505-662-8139
   losalamosgolf.org
Los Altos GC, *Albuquerque* .... 27 [M]   505-298-1897
   cabq.gov/golf
Lovington CC, *Lovington* .... 18 [V]   575-396-6619
Marty Sanchez Links De Santa Fe, *Santa Fe* ...... 27 [M]   505-955-4400
   linksdesantafe.com
New Mexico Military Institute GC, *Roswell* .... 18 [U]   575-622-6033
   nmmi.edu
New Mexico St Univ GC, *Las Cruces* .... 18 [U]   575-646-3219
   nmsugolf.com

[S] = SEMI-PRIVATE   [V] = PRIVATE   [U] = UNIVERSITY   [N] = UNIVERSITY-PRIVATE

NEW MEXICO

New Mexico Tech GC, *Socorro* .... 18 [U] 575-835-5335
 nmt.edu
Ocotillo Park GC, *Hobbs* .... 18 [M] 505-397-9297
 ocotillogolfcourse.com
Outlaw Club At Lincoln Hill, *Alto* .... 18 [V] 575-336-1111
 outlawgolfclub.com
Paa Ko Ridge GC, *Sandia Park* .... 27 [P] 505-281-6000
 paakoridge.com
Pendaries Village Community Assoc, *Rociada* ..... 18 [R] 505-425-9890
 pendaries.net
Picacho Hills CC, *Las Cruces* .... 18 [V] 575-523-8641
 picachohillscc.com
Pinon Hills GC, *Farmington* .... 18 [M] 505-326-6066
 fmtn.org/pinonhills
Ponderosa Pines GC, *Cloudcroft* .... 9 [P] 575-682-2995
Portales CC, *Portales* .... 9 [V] 575-356-8943
Pueblo De Cochiti GC, *Cochiti Lake* .... 18 [P] 505-465-2239
 golfcochititoday.com
Puerto Del Sol GC, *Albuquerque* .... 9 [M] 505-265-5636
 cabq.gov/golf
Quail Run GC, *Santa Fe* .... 9 [V] 505-986-2255
 quailrunsantafe.com
Raton CC & GC, *Raton* .... 9 [S] 575-445-8113
 ratongolf.com
Rio Mimbres CC, *Deming* .... 18 [S] 575-546-9481
Riverside CC, *Carlsbad* .... 18 [S] 575-885-4253
 riversidenm.com
Riverview GC, *Kirtland* .... 18 [U] 505-598-0140
Roswell CC, *Roswell* .... 9 [V] 575-622-2050
 roswellcountryclub.com
San Juan CC, *Farmington* .... 18 [V] 505-327-4451
 sanjuancountryclub.org
Sandia GC, *Albuquerque* .... 18 [R] 505-798-3990
 sandiagolf.com
Santa Ana GC, *Santa Ana Pueblo* .... 27 [P] 505-867-9464
 mynewmexicogolf.com
Santa Fe CC, *Santa Fe* .... 18 [S] 505-471-2626
 santafecountryclub.com
Santa Rosa GC, *Santa Rosa* .... 9 [M] 575-472-4653
Santa Teresa CC, *Santa Teresa* .... 36 [V] 575-589-3466
Sierra Del Rio GC, *Elephant Butte* .... 18 [R] 575-744-4653
 sierradelrio.com
Silver City GC, *Silver City* .... 18 [M] 575-538-5041
 silvercity.org/golf.shtml
Sonoma Ranch GC, *Las Cruces* .... 18 [P] 575-521-1818
 sonomaranchgolf.com
Spring River GC, *Roswell* .... 18 [M] 575-622-9506
 roswell-nm.gov/golf.htm
Tanoan CC, *Albuquerque* .... 27 [V] 505-822-0422
 tanoancountryclub.com
Taos CC, *Rancho de Taos* .... 18 [S] 575-758-7300
 taoscc.americangolf.com
The Club At Las Campanas, *Santa Fe* .... 36 [V] 575-995-3535
 lascampanas.com
The GC At Rainmakers, *Alto* .... 18 [V] 575-336-4653
 rainmakersusa.com
The Links at Sierra Blanca, *Ruidoso* .... 18 [R] 575-258-5330
 thelinksatsierrablanca.com
The Lodge GC, *Cloudcroft* .... 9 [R] 575-682-2098
 thelodgeresort.com
Tierra Del Sol GC, *Belen* .... 18 [S] 505-864-1000
Tijeras Arroyo GC, *Kirtland AFB* .... 18 [A] 505-846-1169
 kirtland.af.mil

Timberon GC, *Timberon* .... 9 [P] 575-987-2260
 timberon.info/GolfCourse/Index.html
Towa GC, *Santa Fe* .... 27 [R] 505-455-9000
 buffalothunderresort.com
Truth Or Consequence City GC,
 Truth or Consequences................................... 9 [M] 575-894-2603
Tucumcari Muni GC, *Tucumcari* .... 9 [M] 575-461-1849
Twelve Shores GC, *Tucumcari* .... 9 [S] 575-403-7177
 12shores.com
Twin Warriors GC, *Bernalillo* .... 18 [R] 575-771-6155
 twinwarriorsgolf.com
Univ of New Mexico North Course, *Albuquerque* .. 9 [U] 505-277-4146
 unm.edu/~bdae/golf/golf.htm
Valle Del Sol GC, *Carrizozo* .... 9 [P] 575-648-2770
Valle Escondido GC, *Taos* .... 9 [S] 575-758-3475
 eveha.com
Whispering Winds GC, *Cannon AFB* .... 18 [A] 575-784-2800
White Sands GC, *White Sands MR* .... 9 [A] 575-678-1759
 wsmrmwr.com
Zuni Mountain GC, *Milan* .... 9 [M] 505-287-9239

NEW YORK

1000 Acres Ranch Resort, *Stony Creek* .... 9 [R] 518-696-5246
 1000acres.com
Adams CC, *Adams* .... 18 [P] 315-232-4842
 adamscountryclub.com
Adirondack G&CC, *Peru* .... 18 [P] 518-643-8403
 adirondackgolfclub.com
Afton GC, *Afton* .... 18 [P] 607-639-2454
 aftongolf.com
Airway Meadows GC, *Gansevoort* .... 18 [P] 518-792-4144
 airwaymeadowsgolf.com
Alapaha Golf Links, *Kingston* .... 9 [P] 845-331-2334
Albany CC, *Voorheesville* .... 18 [V] 518-765-2854
 albanycc.cc
Alder Creek GC, *Alder Creek* .... 9 [P] 315-831-5222
 golfadirondacks.com
Alexandria Bay Muni GC, *Alexandria Bay* .... 9 [M] 315-482-3474
Allegany Hills GC, *Cuba* .... 18 [P] 585-437-2163
Amherst Audubon GC, *Buffalo* .... 27 [M] 716-631-7139
 amherst.ny.us
Amsterdam Muni GC, *Amsterdam* .... 18 [M] 518-842-4265
 amsterdammuni.com
Anglebrook GC, *Lincolndale* .... 18 [V] 914-245-5588
 anglebrookgc.com
Apalachin GC, *Apalachin* .... 18 [P] 607-625-2682
 apalachingolfcourse.net
Apple Creek CC, *De Ruyter* .... 9 [P] 315-852-6466
 applecreekcc.com
Apple Greens GC, *Highland* .... 27 [P] 845-883-5500
 applegreens.com
Archie's Par 3 GC, *Java Center* .... 11 [P] 585-457-9505
 archiesgolfclub.com
Ardsley CC, *Ardsley-On-Hudson* .... 18 [V] 914-591-8403
 ardsleycc.org
Arrowhead GC, *East Syracuse* .... 27 [S] 315-656-7563
Arrowhead GC, *Spencerport* .... 18 [P] 585-352-5500
 arrowhead-golfclub.com
Arrowhead GC, *Akron* .... 18 [P] 716-542-4653
 arrowheadgolfclub.net
Atlantic GC, *Bridgehampton* .... 18 [V] 631-537-1818
 atlanticgolf.org
Attica GC, *Attica* .... 9 [V] 585-591-0133

138 [A] = MILITARY [M] = MUNICIPAL [P] = PUBLIC [R] = RESORT

NEW YORK

Golf Yellow Pages, 18th Edition

Ausable Club, *Keene Valley* .... 9 [R] 518-576-4411
ausableclub.org
AuSable Valley GC, *Au Sable Forks* .... 9 [P] 518-647-8666
avgolfcourse.com
Baiting Hollow Club, *Calverton* .... 18 [V] 631-369-4455
baitinghollowclub.com
Ballston Spa CC, *Ballston Spa* .... 18 [S] 518-885-7935
ballstonspacc.com
Barker Brook GC, *Oriskany Falls* .... 18 [P] 315-821-6438
Bartlett CC, *Olean* .... 18 [V] 716-372-5175
bartlettcountryclub.com
Batavia CC, *Batavia* .... 18 [S] 585-343-7600
bataviacc.com
Bath CC, *Bath* .... 18 [S] 607-776-5043
Battenkill CC, *Greenwich* .... 9 [P] 518-692-9179
battenkillcc.com
Battle Island St Park GC, *Fulton* .... 18 [M] 315-592-3361
nysparks.state.ny.us
Bay Breeze Golf Links, *Chaumont* .... 9 [P] 315-649-4653
Bay Meadows GC, *Queensbury* .... 9 [P] 518-792-1650
Bay Park GC, *East Rockaway* .... 9 [M] 516-571-7242
nassaucountyny.gov
Bear Creek Lodge GC, *Forestport* .... 9 [V] 315-392-4574
Beaver Creek GC, *Rome* .... 9 [P] 315-337-0920
Beaver Island St Park GC, *Grand Island* .... 18 [M] 716-773-7143
Beaver Meadows GC, *Phoenix* .... 18 [P] 315-695-5187
beavermeadowsgolf.com
Bedford Creek GC, *Sackets Harbor* .... 9 [P] 315-646-3400
Bedford G&TC, *Bedford* .... 18 [V] 914-234-3325
Beekman CC, *Hopewell Junction* .... 27 [S] 845-226-7700
beekmangolf.com
Belden Hill GC, *Harpursville* .... 18 [P] 607-693-3257
beldenhillgolf.com
Bellevue CC, *Syracuse* .... 18 [V] 315-475-1984
bellevuecountryclub.com
Bellport CC, *Bellport* .... 18 [M] 631-286-7206
bellportvillage.org
Bemus Point Golf, *Bemus Point* .... 9 [P] 716-386-2893
Bend Of The River GC, *Hadley* .... 9 [P] 518-696-3415
bendoftheriver.com
Bergen Point GC, *West Babylon* .... 18 [M] 631-661-8282
co.suffolk.ny.us
Bethany Hills GC, *East Bethany* .... 18 [P] 585-591-2763
Bethpage St Park GC, *Farmingdale* .... 90 [M] 516-249-0701
nysparks.com/golf
Big Oak Public GC, *Geneva* .... 27 [P] 315-789-9419
bigoakgc.com
Binghamton CC, *Endwell* .... 18 [V] 607-797-2339
binghamtoncountryclub.com
Birch Run CC, *Allegany* .... 9 [P] 716-373-3113
Birdies, Eagles & Ducks GC, *Clinton* .... 9 [P] 315-853-4661
Blackhead Mountain Lodge & CC, *Roundtop* .... 18 [R] 518-622-3157
blackheadmtn.com
Blind Brook Club, *Purchase* .... 18 [V] 914-939-1450
blindbrookclub.org
Blue Heron Hills CC, *Macedon* .... 18 [V] 315-986-5888
blueheronhillscc.com
Blue Hill GC, *Pearl River* .... 27 [S] 845-735-2094
orangetown.com
Blue Ridge GC, *Medford* .... 9 [V] 631-698-8394
Blue Stone GC, *Oxford* .... 18 [P] 607-843-8352
Bluff Point Golf Resort, *Plattsburgh* .... 18 [R] 518-563-3420
bluffpoint.com

Bob O Link GC, *Orchard Park* .... 18 [P] 716-662-4311
bobolinkgolf.com
Bonavista State GC, *Ovid* .... 9 [M] 607-869-5482
nysparks.state.ny.us
Bonnie Briar CC, *Larchmont* .... 18 [V] 914-834-1627
bonniebriar.org
Brae Burn CC, *Purchase* .... 18 [V] 914-761-8300
braeburncc.org
Brae Burn GC, *Dansville* .... 9 [P] 585-335-8840
60redjacketstreet.com
Braemar CC, *Spencerport* .... 18 [P] 585-352-5360
Brantingham GC, *Brantingham* .... 18 [P] 315-348-8861
Breezewood Golf Links, *Falconer* .... 18 [P] 716-287-2138
Breezy Point Exec Course, *Breezy Point* .... 9 [S] 718-474-1623
Brentwood CC, *Brentwood* .... 18 [M] 631-436-6060
brentwoodcc.com
Bretton Woods CC, *Coram* .... 9 [V] 631-698-4861
brettonwoodshoa.org
Briar Creek GC, *Duanesburg* .... 18 [P] 518-355-6145
briarcreekgolf.com
Brierwood CC, *Hamburg* .... 18 [V] 716-648-7034
brierwoodcc.com
Bright Meadows GC - Bright / White(Rothland),
  Akron .... 18 [P] 716-542-4653
brightmeadowsgolf.com
Brighton Park GC, *Tonawanda* .... 18 [M] 716-504-3663
tonawanda.ny.us
Bristol Harbour GC, *Canandaigua* .... 18 [R] 585-396-2460
bristolharbour.com
Broadacres GC, *Orangeburg* .... 9 [M] 845-359-8218
orangetown.com
Brockport CC, *Brockport* .... 18 [S] 585-638-6486
brockportcc.com
Brook Lea CC, *Rochester* .... 18 [V] 585-247-4577
brookleacc.com
Brookfield CC, *Clarence* .... 18 [V] 716-632-2500
brookfieldcc.com
Brookhaven GC, *Porter Corners* .... 18 [S] 518-893-7458
brookhavengolfclub.com
Brooklawn GC, *Mattydale* .... 18 [P] 315-463-1831
Brookville GC, *Glen Head* .... 18 [V] 516-671-5440
brookvillecc.com
Brunswick Greens, *Troy* .... 9 [P] 518-279-3848
brunswickgreens.com
Brynwood G&CC, *Armonk* .... 18 [V] 914-273-9300
brynwoodclub.com
Buffalo Tournament Club, *Lancaster* .... 18 [P] 716-681-4653
btcgolf.com
Burden Lake CC, *Averill Park* .... 18 [P] 518-674-1770
blccgolf.com
Burnet GC, *Syracuse* .... 9 [M] 315-487-6285
syracuse.ny.us
Butternut Creek GC, *Jamesville* .... 9 [P] 315-251-1100
hickoryhillgolfcenter.com/?page=78662
Buttonwood GC, *Spencerport* .... 18 [P] 585-352-4720
buttonwoodgolfcourse.com
Byrncliff Resort & CCtr, *Varysburg* .... 18 [R] 585-535-7300
byrncliff.com
C Way GC, *Clayton* .... 18 [R] 315-686-4562
cwayresort.com
Caledonia CC, *Caledonia* .... 18 [V] 585-538-9956
caledoniacc.com
Calverton Links, *Calverton* .... 18 [P] 631-369-5200
calvertonlinks.com

[S] = SEMI-PRIVATE   [V] = PRIVATE   [U] = UNIVERSITY   [N] = UNIVERSITY-PRIVATE

NEW YORK

Golf Yellow Pages, 18th Edition

Camillus CC, *Camillus*..........................18 [P] 315-672-3770
  camilluscountryclub.com
Camroden GC, *Rome*...............................9 [P] 315-865-5771
Canajoharie CC, *Canajoharie*................18 [S] 518-673-8183
  canajohariecountryclub.com
Canandaigua CC, *Canandaigua*................9 [V] 585-394-4370
  canadaiguacountryclub.com
Canasawacta G&CC, *Norwich*.................18 [P] 607-336-2685
  canasawactacc.com
Cantiague Park GC, *Hicksville*..................9 [M] 516-571-7061
  nassaucountyny.gov
Capitol Hills At Albany, *Albany*..............18 [M] 518-438-2208
  caphills.com
Cardinal Creek GC, *Brockport*................18 [S] 585-637-4302
Cardinal Hills GC, *Randolph*..................18 [P] 716-358-5409
Carlowden CC, *Carthage*.......................18 [P] 315-493-0624
  carlowden.com
Casolwood GC, *Canastota*.....................18 [P] 315-697-9164
  casolwoodgc.com
Casperkill GC, *Poughkeepsie*..................18 [S] 845-463-0900
  casperkillgolf.com
Cassadaga CC, *Cassadaga*......................9 [P] 716-595-3003
  cassadagacountryclub.com
Catatonk GC, *Candor*...........................18 [S] 607-659-4600
  catatonkgolfclub.com
Catskill GC, *Catskill*............................18 [S] 518-943-0302
  catskillgolfclub.com
Cazenovia CC, *Cazenovia*.......................18 [V] 315-655-8880
  caz-cc.com
Cazenovia GC, *Cazenovia*........................9 [V] 315-655-8575
  cazgolf.com
Cazenovia GC, *Buffalo*............................9 [M] 716-823-1517
  bfloparks.org
CC of Buffalo, *Williamsville*.................18 [V] 716-632-1100
  ccofbuffalo.org
CC of Ithaca, *Ithaca*............................18 [V] 607-257-1808
  countryclubofithaca.com
CC of Mendon, *Mendon*.........................18 [V] 585-624-5015
  ccmendon.org
CC of Rochester, *Rochester*...................18 [V] 585-381-1800
  ccrochester.org
CC of Troy, *Troy*.................................18 [V] 518-274-4207
  countrycluboftroy.com
Cedar Beach GC, *Babylon*......................18 [M] 631-321-4562
Cedar Brook Club, *Glen Head*................18 [V] 516-759-8447
Cedar Lake Club, *Clayville*....................18 [V] 315-839-5838
  cedarlakeclub.com
Cedar River GC, *Indian Lake*....................9 [P] 518-648-5906
  cedarrivergolf.com
Cedar View GC, *Rooseveltown*...............18 [P] 315-764-9104
Cedars GC, *Cutchogue*............................9 [P] 631-734-6363
Cedars GC, *Lowville*.............................18 [P] 315-376-6267
Cedarview GC, *Lansing*...........................9 [P] 315-364-7598
Centennial GC of NY, *Carmel*................27 [P] 845-225-5700
  centennialgolf.com
CenterPointe CC, *Canandaigua*.............18 [S] 585-394-0346
Century CC, *Purchase*..........................18 [V] 914-761-0400
  centurycc.org
Champion Hills Club, *Victor*....................9 [V] 585-924-8383
  championhillscountryclub.com
Chautauqua GC, *Chautauqua*................36 [P] 716-357-6211
  ciweb.org
Chautauqua Point GC, *Dewittville*............9 [P] 716-753-7271

Chemung GC, *Waverly*.........................18 [P] 607-565-2323
Chenango Commons GC, *Chenango Bridge*...9 [P] 607-648-2380
Chenango Valley St Park GC, *Chenango Forks*.....18 [M] 607-648-9804
  nysparks.state.ny.us
Cherry Creek Golf Links, *Riverhead*........18 [P] 631-369-6500
  cherrycreeklinks.com
Cherry Valley Club, *Garden City*............18 [V] 516-741-1980
  cherryvalleyclub.com
Chestnut Hill CC, *Darien Center*.............18 [P] 585-547-9699
  chestnuthillcc.com
Chili CC, *Scottsville*.............................18 [P] 585-889-9325
  chilicountryclub.com
Christmas Windham House, *Windham*....27 [R] 518-734-6990
  windhamhouse.com
Christopher Morley Park GC, *Roslyn*........9 [M] 516-571-8120
  nassaucountyny.gov
Churchville Park GC, *Churchville*............27 [M] 585-293-0680
  golftheparks.com
Clayton CC, *Clayton*..............................9 [P] 315-686-4242
  claytoncountryclub.com
Clearview Park GC, *Bayside*...................18 [M] 718-229-2570
  nycteetimes.com
Clifton Fine Muni GC, *Star Lake*..............9 [P] 315-848-3570
Clifton Knolls Exec GC, *Clifton Park*.........9 [P] 518-373-1435
Clifton Springs CC, *Clifton Springs*.........18 [V] 315-462-9885
  cliftonspringscountryclub.com
Cobble Hill GC, *Elizabethtown*.................9 [M] 518-873-6555
  elizabethtown-ny.com
Cobblestone Creek CC, *Victor*................18 [V] 585-924-6460
  cobblestonecreekcc.com
Cobleskill G&CC, *Cobleskill*...................18 [S] 518-234-4045
  cobygolf.com
Cold Spring CC, *Cold Spring Harbor*........18 [V] 631-692-6550
  coldspringcc.com
Cold Springs GC, *Mannsville*....................9 [P] 315-465-6515
College Hill GC, *Poughkeepsie*..................9 [M] 845-486-9112
Colonial Acres GC, *Glenmont*....................9 [P] 518-439-2089
  townofbethlehem.org
Colonial CC, *Tannersville*.........................9 [P] 518-589-9807
Colonial Ridge GC, *Laurens*....................18 [P] 607-263-5291
  ceejaygolf.com
Colonial Springs GC, *Farmingdale*............27 [V] 631-643-0051
  colonialspringsgolf.com
Colonie G&CC, *Voorheesville*..................18 [V] 518-765-4103
  coloniegcc.com
Columbia G&CC, *Claverack*....................18 [V] 518-851-9894
  columbiagolf.org
Concord Crest GC, *East Concord*.............18 [P] 716-592-7636
  concordcrest.com
Concord Resort & GC, *Kiamesha Lake*......36 [R] 845-794-4000
  concordresort.com
Conesus GC, *Conesus*............................18 [S] 585-346-2100
  conesusgolf.com
Conklin Players Club, *Conklin*.................18 [P] 607-775-3042
  conklinplayers.com
Copake CC, *Craryville*...........................18 [P] 518-325-4338
  copakecountryclub.com
Corning CC, *Corning*.............................18 [V] 607-936-3392
  corningcountryclub.com
Cortland CC, *Cortland*..........................18 [V] 607-753-8811
  cortlandcc.com
Country Meadows Golf, *Fort Ann*............12 [P] 518-792-5927
  countrymeadowsgolf.net

[A] = MILITARY   [M] = MUNICIPAL   [P] = PUBLIC   [R] = RESORT

Golf Yellow Pages, 18th Edition

NEW YORK

Crab Meadow GC, *Northport* .... 18 [M] 631-757-8800
crabmeadow.com
Crag Burn GC, *East Aurora* .... 18 [V] 716-655-0000
cragburn.com
Cragie Brae GC, *Scottsville* .... 18 [P] 585-889-1440
cragiebrae.com
Craig Wood GC, *Lake Placid* .... 18 [M] 518-523-9811
craigwoodgolfclub.com
Cranebrook GC, *Auburn* .... 9 [P] 315-252-7887
Crestwood GC, *Marcy* .... 18 [P] 315-797-6068
Cronins Golf Resort, *Warrensburg* .... 18 [R] 518-623-9530
croninsgolfresort.com
Crooked Pines GC, *Macedon* .... 18 [S] 315-986-4455
crookedpinesgc.com
Crystal Springs GC, *Vernon* .... 9 [P] 315-829-3210
Dande Farms CC, *Akron* .... 18 [P] 716-542-2027
Davis Countryside Meadows, *Pavilion* .... 18 [P] 585-584-8390
dcmeadows.com
Deepdale GC, *Manhasset* .... 18 [V] 516-365-9111
deepdalegolfclub.com
Deerfield CC, *Brockport* .... 27 [S] 585-392-8080
deerfieldcc.com
Deerwood GC, *North Tonawanda* .... 27 [M] 716-695-8529
northtonawanda.org
Delaware Park GC, *Buffalo* .... 18 [M] 716-835-2533
bfloparks.org
Dellwood GC, *New City* .... 18 [V] 845-634-2386
dellwoodcc.com
Delphi Falls GC, *Delphi Falls* .... 18 [P] 315-662-3611
Delta Knolls Golf Ctr, *Rome* .... 9 [P] 315-339-1280
Diamond Hawk GC, *Cheektowaga* .... 18 [P] 716-651-0700
diamondhawkgolf.com
Dimmock Hill GC, *Binghamton* .... 18 [P] 607-729-5511
dimmockhill.com
Dinsmore St Park GC, *Staatsburg* .... 18 [M] 845-889-4071
nysparks.state.ny.us
Dix Hills CC, *Dix Hills* .... 9 [P] 631-271-4788
Dix Hills Park GC, *Dix Hills* .... 9 [M] 631-499-8005
crabmeadow.com
DJs Golf Ctr, *Waverly* .... 9 [P] 607-565-2618
Dogwood Knolls GC, *Hopewell Junction* .... 9 [P] 845-226-7317
Domenicos GC, *Whitesboro* .... 18 [P] 315-736-9812
Doral Arrowwood GC, *Rye Brook* .... 9 [R] 914-323-4478
doralarrowwood.com
Dotys GC, *Ilion* .... 9 [P] 315-894-2860
Douglaston Park GC, *Little Neck* .... 18 [P] 718-224-6566
golfnyc.com
Drumlins GC, *Syracuse* .... 36 [N] 315-446-4580
drumlins.com
Dryden Lake GC, *Dryden* .... 9 [P] 607-844-8300
Dunwoodie GC, *Yonkers* .... 18 [P] 914-231-3490
westchestergov.com
Durand Eastman Park GC, *Rochester* ... 18 [M] 585-266-0110
golftheparks.com
Dutch Hollow CC, *Owasco* .... 18 [P] 315-784-5052
dutchhollow.com
Dutchaven GC, *Buskirk* .... 9 [P] 518-753-7533
Dutcher GC, *Pawling* .... 9 [P] 845-855-9845
Dutchess G&CC, *Poughkeepsie* .... 18 [V] 845-452-5403
dutchessgolf.com
Dyker Beach GC, *Brooklyn* .... 18 [P] 718-836-9722
nycteetimes.com
E Donald Conroy GC, *Babylon* .... 9 [P] 631-669-2340

Eagle Crest GC, *Clifton Park* .... 27 [P] 518-877-7082
eaglecrestgolf.com
Eagle Vale GC, *Fairport* .... 18 [P] 585-377-5200
eaglevale.com
East Aurora CC, *East Aurora* .... 18 [V] 716-652-6800
eastauroracc.com
East Hampton GC, *East Hampton* .... 18 [V] 631-267-2100
ehgc.com
Eddy Farm Golf, *Sparrowbush* .... 18 [R] 845-858-4300
eddyfarm.com
Eden Valley GC, *Eden* .... 18 [P] 716-337-2190
Edgewood Club of Tivoli, *Tivoli* .... 9 [V] 845-757-3184
Eisenhower Park GC, *East Meadow* ...... 54 [M] 516-222-2620
nassaucountyny.gov
Elkdale CC, *Salamanca* .... 18 [P] 716-945-5553
elkdalecc.com
Elm Tree GC, *Cortland* .... 18 [P] 607-753-1341
elmtreegolfcourse.com
Elma Meadows GC, *Elma* .... 18 [M] 716-652-5475
erie.gov
Elmira CC, *Elmira* .... 18 [V] 607-734-6251
elmiracountryclub.com
Elmwood CC, *White Plains* .... 18 [V] 914-592-6600
elmwoodcc.org
Ely Park Muni GC, *Binghamton* .... 18 [M] 607-772-7231
Emerald Crest GC, *Fulton* .... 18 [P] 315-593-1016
Emerald Green, *Gouverneur* .... 9 [S] 315-287-4497
En Joie GC, *Endicott* .... 18 [M] 607-785-1661
enjoiegolf.com
Endwell Greens GC, *Endwell* .... 18 [P] 607-785-4653
endwellgreensgolf.com
Engineers CC, *Roslyn* .... 18 [V] 516-621-5350
engineerscc.com
Erie Falcon Golf & Rec, *Newark* .... 9 [P] 315-331-2370
eriefalcon.com
Evergreen CC, *Castleton On Hudson* ... 36 [P] 518-477-7921
evergreencountryclub.com
Evergreen GC, *Buffalo* .... 9 [P] 716-688-6204
Evergreen Hills GC & DR, *Oswego* .... 9 [P] 315-342-7888
evergreenhillsgolf.com
Exec South Family Golf Ctr, *Henrietta* ... 9 [S] 585-334-1300
henriettafoundation.org
Fairways of Half Moon, *Mechanicville* .... 27 [P] 518-664-1578
fairwaysofhalfmoon.com
Falkirk Estate & CC, *Central Valley* .... 18 [S] 845-928-6924
falkirkestate.com
Fallsview GC At Honors Haven, *Ellenville* .... 9 [R] 845-210-3106
honorshaven.com
FarView GC, *Avon* .... 18 [P] 585-226-8210
farviewgc.com
Fenway GC, *Scarsdale* .... 18 [V] 914-723-1095
fenwaygolf.com
Fillmore GC, *Locke* .... 18 [P] 315-497-3145
Fishers Island Club, *Fishers Island* .... 18 [V] 631-788-7223
fishersislandclub.com
Fishkill GC & DR, *Fishkill* .... 9 [P] 845-896-5220
fishkillgolf.com
Flushing Meadows Pitch & Putt, *Flushing* .... 18 [M] 718-271-8182
golfnyc.com
Ford Hill CC, *Whitney Point* .... 36 [P] 607-692-8938
Forest Park GC, *Woodhaven* .... 18 [M] 718-296-0999
golfnyc.com
Forestburgh CC, *Forestburgh* .... 18 [S] 845-791-5070

[S] = SEMI-PRIVATE   [V] = PRIVATE   [U] = UNIVERSITY   [N] = UNIVERSITY-PRIVATE

NEW YORK
Golf Yellow Pages, 18th Edition

Foster Ponds GC, *Durhamville* ....9 [P] 315-363-9879
Fox Hill G&CC, *Massena* ....9 [P] 315-764-8633
  foxhillgolfonline.com
Fox Run GC, *Rock Stream* ....9 [P] 607-535-4413
Fox Run GC, *Johnstown* ....18 [P] 518-762-3717
  foxrungolfclub.net
Fox Valley Club, *Lancaster* ....18 [V] 716-683-6241
  palmergolf.com
Foxfire at Village Green, *Baldwinsville* ....18 [P] 315-638-2930
  foxfire247.com
Frear Park Muni GC, *Troy* ....18 [M] 518-270-4553
  troyny.gov
French Woods G&CC, *Hancock* ....18 [P] 607-637-1800
Frenchs Hollow Fairways, *Altamont* ....9 [P] 518-861-8837
Fresh Meadow CC, *Lake Success* ....18 [V] 516-482-7300
  freshmeadow.org
Friars Head, *Riverhead* ....18 [V] 631-722-5200
  friarshead.org
Galway GC, *Galway* ....9 [P] 518-882-6395
  galwaygolfclub.com
Garden City CC, *Garden City* ....18 [V] 516-747-2929
  gardencitycc.org
Garden City GC, *Garden City* ....18 [V] 516-746-8360
  gardencitycc.org
Gardiners Bay CC, *Shelter Island Hts* ....18 [V] 631-749-1033
  gardinersbay.org
Garrison GC, *Garrison* ....18 [S] 845-424-3604
  thegarrison.com
Genegantslet GC, *Greene* ....18 [P] 607-656-8191
  genygolf.com
Genesee Valley GC, *Rochester* ....36 [M] 585-424-2920
  golftheparks.com
Geneva CC, *Geneva* ....9 [V] 315-789-8786
  gccgenevany.com
Gilbert Greens CC, *Heuvelton* ....18 [P] 315-344-2222
Glen Cove GC, *Glen Cove* ....18 [S] 516-671-0033
  glencove-li.com
Glen Head CC, *Glen Head* ....18 [V] 516-676-4050
  glenheadcountryclub.org
Glen Oak GC, *East Amherst* ....18 [P] 716-688-5454
  glenoak.com
Glen Oaks Club, *Old Westbury* ....27 [V] 516-626-2900
  glenoaksclub.org
GlenArbor GC, *Bedford Hills* ....18 [V] 914-241-0700
  glenarborclub.com
Glens Falls CC, *Queensbury* ....18 [V] 518-793-0021
  glensfallscountryclub.com
Glenwood GC & DR, *West Monroe* ....18 [P] 315-676-3114
Golden Oaks GC, *Windsor* ....18 [P] 607-655-3217
Gothic Hill GC, *Lockport* ....9 [P] 716-438-5477
  gothichillgolf.com
Gouverneur CC, *Gouverneur* ....9 [S] 315-287-2130
Gowanda CC, *Collins* ....18 [P] 716-337-2100
  gowandacc.com
Grandview Farms GC, *Berkshire* ....18 [P] 607-657-2619
Grandview GC, *Angola* ....9 [P] 716-549-4930
  grandviewgolfcourse.com
Great Rock GC, *Wading River* ....18 [P] 631-929-1200
  greatrockgolfclub.com
Green Acres GC, *Kingston* ....9 [P] 845-331-2283
  greenacresgolf.com
Green Lakes GC, *Fayettville* ....18 [P] 315-637-4653
  nysparks.state.ny.us

Green Mansions GC, *Chestertown* ....9 [P] 518-494-7222
  greenmansionsgolf.com
Green Ridge GC, *Johnson* ....18 [P] 845-355-1317
  greenridgegolfclub.com
Greenview CC, *West Monroe* ....36 [P] 315-668-2244
  greenviewcountryclub.com
Greenwood GC, *Clarence Center* ....9 [P] 716-741-3395
Greystone GC, *Walworth* ....18 [P] 315-524-0022
  234golf.com
Griffins Greens, *Oswego* ....18 [P] 315-343-2996
Grossinger CC, *Liberty* ....27 [R] 845-292-9000
  grossingergolf.net
Grover Cleveland GC, *Amherst* ....18 [M] 716-836-7398
  erie.gov
Gull Haven GC, *Central Islip* ....9 [M] 631-436-6059
Hales Mills CC, *Johnstown* ....18 [P] 518-736-4622
Hamburg Town GC, *Hamburg* ....18 [M] 716-648-4410
  townofhamburgny.com
Hamilton College Tompkins GC, *Clinton* ....9 [N] 315-859-4011
  hamilton.edu
Hamilton Lake Conf Ctr, *Lake Pleasant* ....9 [V] 518-548-6171
Hamlet G&CC, *Commack* ....18 [V] 631-864-9048
  hamletgolfandcountryclub.com
Hamlet Wind Watch GC, *Hauppauge* ....18 [R] 631-232-9850
  hamletwindwatch.com
Hampshire CC, *Mamaroneck* ....18 [V] 914-698-4610
  hampshirecountryclub.org
Hampton Hills G&CC, *Riverhead* ....18 [V] 631-727-6862
Hanah Country Resort GC, *Margaretville* ....18 [R] 845-586-4849
  hanahcountryclub.com
Hancock GC, *Hancock* ....9 [S] 607-637-2480
  hancockgolfcourse.com
Harbor Links GC, *Port Washington* ....27 [M] 516-767-4816
  harborlinks.com
Harbour Pointe CC, *Waterport* ....18 [P] 585-682-3922
Hardwood Hills GC, *Masonville* ....18 [P] 607-467-1031
Harlem Valley GC, *Wingdale* ....9 [P] 845-832-9957
  harlemvalleygolfclub.com
Harmony GC, *Port Kent* ....9 [P] 518-834-9785
  harmonygolfclubandcommunity.com
Harris Hill Golf Ctr, *Bowmansville* ....9 [P] 716-684-4653
  harrishillgolf.com
Harvest Hill Golf Center, *Orchard Park* ....18 [S] 716-662-1980
  harvesthillgc.com
Hay Harbor Club, *Fishers Island* ....9 [V] 631-788-7514
Heartland Golf Park, *Edgewood* ....9 [P] 631-667-7400
  heartlandgolfpark.com
Heatherwood GC, *Centereach* ....18 [P] 631-473-9000
  pinehillsgolfproshop.com/Heatherwood.html
Hempstead GC, *Hempstead* ....18 [V] 516-486-7800
  hempsteadgolfandcc.com
Hiawatha Trails Exec Course, *Guilderland* ......18 [P] 518-456-9512
Hickory Hill GC, *Baldwinsville* ....18 [P] 315-652-9822
  hickoryhillgolfcenter.com
Hickory Hill GC, *Warwick* ....18 [M] 845-988-9501
  orangecountygov.com
Hickory Ridge G&CC, *Holley* ....18 [P] 585-638-4653
  hickoryridgegolfandcountryclub.com
Hickory Ridge GC, *Cato* ....9 [P] 315-626-2291
  golfathickoryridge.com
Hidden Acres Exec Golf, *Warsaw* ....18 [P] 585-237-2190
Hidden Valley GC, *Whitesboro* ....18 [P] 315-736-9953
  golfhiddenvalley.com

[A] = MILITARY   [M] = MUNICIPAL   [P] = PUBLIC   [R] = RESORT

Golf Yellow Pages, 18th Edition — NEW YORK

Course	Holes	Type	Phone
High Peaks GC, *Newcomb*	9	[M]	518-582-2300
newcombny.com			
Highland Greens GC, *Brushton*	18	[P]	518-529-0563
highlandgreensgolf.com			
Highland Meadows G&CC, *Watertown*	18	[P]	315-785-0108
golf342.com			
Highland Park GC, *Auburn*	18	[S]	315-253-3381
highlandparkgolfclub.com			
Highlands CC, *Garrison*	9	[S]	845-424-3727
highlandscountryclub.net			
Hiland Park CC, *Queensbury*	18	[P]	518-761-4653
hilandparkcc.com			
Hill N Dale CC, *Tully*	9	[P]	315-696-5338
Hillcrest GC, *Duanesburg*	9	[P]	518-355-9817
Hillendale GC, *Ithaca*	18	[S]	607-273-2363
hillendale.com			
Hillview GC, *Fredonia*	18	[P]	716-679-4571
Holbrook CC GC, *Holbrook*	18	[M]	631-467-3417
holbrookccgolf.com			
Holiday Valley Resort, *Ellicottville*	18	[R]	716-699-2345
holidayvalley.com			
Holland Heights GC, *Herkimer*	9	[P]	315-866-8716
Holland Hills CC, *Holland*	18	[S]	716-537-2345
Holland Meadows GC, *Gloversville*	18	[P]	518-883-3318
hollandmeadowsgolfcourse.com			
Hollow Brook GC, *Cortlandt Manor*	18	[V]	914-734-1500
golfhollowbrook.com			
Hollow Hills CC, *Dix Hills*	9	[P]	631-242-0010
Hollybrook CC, *Spencer*	18	[P]	607-589-4431
hollybrookcc.com			
Homowack Lodge GC, *Spring Glen*	9	[R]	845-647-6800
Hoosick Falls CC, *Hoosick Falls*	9	[P]	518-686-1967
hoosickgolf.com			
Hornell GC, *Hornell*	9	[S]	607-324-1735
hornellgolfclub.com			
Hudson Hills GC, *Ossining*	18	[M]	914-864-3000
hudsonhillsgolf.com			
Hudson National GC, *Croton On Hudson*	18	[V]	914-271-7600
hudsonnational.org			
Hudson Valley Resort, *Kerhonkson*	18	[R]	845-626-8888
hudsonvalleyresort.com			
Huletts GC, *Huletts Landing*	9	[R]	518-499-1234
hulettsonlakegeorge.com			
Huntington CC, *Huntington*	18	[V]	631-427-0876
huntingtoncc.org			
Huntington Crescent Club, *Huntington*	18	[V]	631-427-3400
huntingtoncrescentclub.com			
Hyde Park Muni GC, *Niagara Falls*	36	[P]	716-297-2067
niagarafallsusa.org/GolfCourse.cfm			
Indian Head GC, *Cayuga*	9	[P]	315-253-6812
Indian Hills CC, *Northport*	18	[P]	631-757-7718
indianhillscc.net			
Indian Island GC, *Riverhead*	18	[M]	631-727-7776
indianislandcountryclub.com			
Indian River Golf Links, *Philadelphia*	9	[P]	315-681-7355
indianrivergolflinks.com			
Inlet GC, *Inlet*	18	[P]	315-357-3503
inletgolfclub.com			
Inwood CC, *Inwood*	18	[V]	516-239-2800
inwoodcc.org			
Irondequoit CC, *Rochester*	18	[P]	585-586-0156
irondequoitcc.org			
Ironwood G&CC, *Baldwinsville*	9	[P]	315-635-9826
golf-ironwood.com			
Ironwood GC, *Cowlesville*	18	[P]	585-805-0350
playironwood.com			
Ischua Valley CC, *Franklinville*	9	[P]	716-676-3630
Island Glen CC, *Bethel*	9	[P]	845-583-1010
Island Hills GC, *Sayville*	18	[V]	631-589-2200
islandhillsgolfclub.com			
Island Valley GC, *Fairport*	9	[P]	585-586-1300
islandvalley.com			
Islands End G&CC, *Greenport*	18	[P]	631-477-0777
islandsendgolf.com			
Ives Hill CC, *Watertown*	18	[P]	315-775-4653
iveshillcountryclub.com			
James Baird GC, *Pleasant Valley*	18	[M]	845-473-6200
nysparks.state.ny.us			
Jones Beach St Park GC, *Wantagh*	18	[M]	516-785-1600
nysparks.state.ny.us			
Kanon Valley CC, *Oneida*	18	[V]	315-363-8283
kanonvalley.com			
King Ferry GC, *King Ferry*	9	[P]	315-364-7343
kingferrygolfclub.com			
Kingsboro GC, *Gloversville*	9	[P]	518-773-4600
kingsborogolf.net			
Kingswood GC, *Hudson Falls*	18	[P]	518-747-8888
kingswoodgolf.com			
Kis N Greens GC, *Alden*	18	[P]	716-937-4741
kis-n-greens.com			
Kissena Park GC, *Flushing*	18	[M]	718-939-4594
golfnyc.com			
Knickerbocker CC, *Cincinnatus*	18	[P]	607-863-3800
Knollwood CC, *Elmsford*	18	[V]	914-592-6182
kccclub.org			
Kutshers CC & Hotel, *Monticello*	18	[R]	845-794-6000
kutshers.com			
L A GC, *Clayton*	9	[P]	315-686-3748
La Tourette GC, *Staten Island*	18	[P]	718-351-1889
nycteetimes.com			
Lafayette Hills G&CC, *Jamesville*	18	[P]	315-469-3296
lafayettehillsgcc.com			
Lake Isle GC, *Eastchester*	18	[M]	914-961-3453
eastchester.org			
Lake Mohonk GC, *New Paltz*	9	[R]	845-256-2154
mohonk.com			
Lake Placid Resort GC, *Lake Placid*	45	[R]	518-523-2556
lakeplacidcp.com			
Lake Pleasant GC, *Lake Pleasant*	9	[P]	518-548-7071
Lake Shore CC, *Rochester*	27	[P]	585-663-9100
lakeshore-cc.com			
Lake Shore Y&CC, *Cicero*	18	[V]	315-699-2798
lakeshoreycc.com			
Lake View GC, *Highland Lake*	9	[P]	845-557-6406
Lakeside CC, *Penn Yan*	18	[S]	315-536-7252
lccgolfny.com			
Lakeside GC, *Ripley*	9	[P]	716-736-7637
Lakeview G&CC, *Owasco*	18	[P]	315-253-3152
Lakewinds GC, *Rushville*	9	[P]	585-554-6735
lakewindsgolf.com			
Lancaster CC, *Lancaster*	18	[V]	716-683-1854
lccny.com			
Langbrook Meadows G&CC, *Brier Hill*	18	[P]	315-375-6372
langbrookmeadows.com			

[S] = SEMI-PRIVATE   [V] = PRIVATE   [U] = UNIVERSITY   [N] = UNIVERSITY-PRIVATE

NEW YORK
Golf Yellow Pages, 18th Edition

Latta Lea GC, *Rochester* .... 9 [P] 585-663-9440
   lattalea.com
Laurel Links CC, *Laurel* .... 18 [V] 631-298-4300
   laurellinkscc.com
Lawrence Y&CC, *Lawrence* .... 18 [M] 516-239-8263
   lycc.cc
Le Roy CC, *Le Roy* .... 18 [P] 585-768-7330
   leroycc.com
Leatherstocking GC, *Cooperstown* .... 18 [R] 607-547-5275
   otesaga.com
Leewood GC, *Eastchester* .... 18 [V] 914-793-5821
   leewoodgolfclub.com
Leisure Village GC, *Ridge* .... 9 [V] 631-744-0334
Lido Beach GC, *Lido Beach* .... 18 [P] 516-889-8181
   lidogolf.com
Lima G&CC, *Lima* .... 36 [S] 585-624-1490
   limagolf.com
Links At Sunset Ridge, *Marcellus* .... 18 [S] 315-673-2255
   linksatsunsetridge.com
Little Falls Muni GC, *Little Falls* .... 9 [M] 315-823-4442
Liverpool G&CC, *Liverpool* .... 18 [P] 315-457-7170
   lgpcc.com
Livingston CC, *Geneseo* .... 18 [S] 585-243-4430
   livingstoncc.com
Lochmor Muni GC, *Loch Sheldrake* .... 18 [M] 845-434-1257
   tarrybrae.com
Lockport Town & CC, *Lockport* .... 18 [V] 716-433-4581
   lockportcountryclub.com
Locust Hill CC, *Pittsford* .... 18 [V] 585-427-7010
   locusthill.org
Long Island National GC, *Riverhead* .... 18 [P] 631-727-4653
   longislandnationalgc.com
Lyndon GC, *Fayetteville* .... 18 [P] 315-446-1885
Madrid GC, *Madrid* .... 9 [P] 315-322-0502
Mahopac GC, *Mahopac* .... 18 [V] 845-628-9335
   mahopacgolfclub.com
Maidstone Club, *East Hampton* .... 27 [V] 631-324-5530
   maidstoneclub.com
Majestic Hills GC, *Naples* .... 9 [P] 585-554-3609
   majestichillsgolfny.com
Malone GC, *Malone* .... 36 [P] 518-483-2926
   malonegolfclub.com
Manhattan Woods GC, *West Nyack* .... 18 [V] 845-627-2222
   manhattanwoodsgc.com
Maple Crest GC, *Frankfort* .... 9 [P] 315-894-3970
Maple Hill GC, *Marathon* .... 18 [P] 607-849-3285
   golfmaplehill.com
Maple Moor GC, *White Plains* .... 18 [P] 914-995-9200
   westchestergov.com
Maplehurst CC, *Lakewood* .... 18 [P] 716-763-1225
   maplehurstccgolf.com
Marine Park GC, *Brooklyn* .... 18 [M] 718-252-4625
   golfmarinepark.com
Mark Twain GC, *Elmira Heights* .... 18 [M] 607-737-5770
   marktwaingolf.com
Massena CC, *Massena* .... 18 [P] 315-769-2293
   massenacountryclub.com
Mc Cann Memorial GC, *Poughkeepsie* .... 18 [P] 845-454-1968
   mccanngolfcourse.com
McConnellsville GC, *McConnellsville* .... 18 [P] 315-245-1157
   mcconnellsvillegolfclub.com
McGregor Links GC, *Gansevoort* .... 18 [P] 518-584-6664
   mcgregorlinks.com

Meadow Brook Club, *Jericho* .... 18 [V] 516-822-3354
Meadow Links GC, *Richfield Springs* .... 18 [P] 315-858-1646
   meadowlinks.com
Meadowbrook GC, *Weedsport* .... 9 [P] 315-834-9358
Meadowbrook GC, *Winthrop* .... 9 [P] 315-389-4562
Meadowgreens GC, *Ghent* .... 9 [P] 518-828-0663
Mechanicville GC, *Mechanicville* .... 9 [P] 518-664-3866
Merrick GC, *Merrick* .... 9 [M] 516-868-4650
Metropolis CC, *White Plains* .... 18 [V] 914-949-4840
   metropoliscc.org
Middle Bay CC, *Oceanside* .... 18 [V] 516-766-1880
   middlebaycc.com
Middle Island CC, *Middle Island* .... 27 [P] 631-924-3000
   middleislandcc.com
Midvale CC, *Penfield* .... 18 [V] 585-586-1030
   midvalecountryclub.com
Mill Creek GC, *Churchville* .... 27 [P] 585-889-4110
   millcreekgolf.com
Mill Creek GC, *Newburgh* .... 9 [P] 845-236-3160
Mill Pond GC, *Medford* .... 27 [P] 631-732-8249
   golfatmillpond.com
Mill River Club, *Oyster Bay* .... 18 [V] 516-922-3556
Mill Road Acres GC, *Latham* .... 18 [P] 518-785-4653
   millroadacres.com
Millbrook G&TC, *Millbrook* .... 9 [V] 845-677-3810
   millbrookgt.com
Millstone GC, *Weedsport* .... 18 [P] 315-689-3600
   golfmillstone.com
Minisceongo GC, *Pomona* .... 18 [V] 845-362-8200
   minisceongogolfclub.com
Mohansic GC, *Yorktown Heights* .... 18 [M] 914-862-5283
   westchestergov.com
Mohawk GC, *Schenectady* .... 27 [V] 518-374-9124
   mohawkgolfclub.com
Mohawk Glen GC, *Rome* .... 9 [P] 315-334-4652
   callmohawkvalleyhome.org
Mohawk River GC, *Rexford* .... 18 [P] 518-399-2345
   mohawkrivercc.com
Mohawk Valley CC, *Little Falls* .... 9 [S] 315-823-0330
   mohawkvalleycountryclub.com
Monroe CC, *Monroe* .... 9 [S] 845-783-9045
   monroecountryclubny.com
Monroe GC, *Pittsford* .... 18 [V] 585-586-3608
   monroegolfclub.com
Montauk Downs St Park GC, *Montauk* ...... 18 [M] 631-668-1100
   nysparks.com/golf
Moon Brook CC, *Jamestown* .... 18 [V] 716-484-1720
   moonbrookcc.com
Morefar GC, *Brewster* .... 18 [V] 845-279-5086
Moriah CC, *Port Henry* .... 9 [P] 518-546-9979
Mosholu GC, *Bronx* .... 9 [M] 718-655-9164
   thefirstteemetny.org
Mount Kisco CC, *Mt Kisco* .... 18 [V] 914-666-2116
   mountkiscocc.org
Mountain Top GC, *Sherburne* .... 9 [P] 607-674-4005
Muttontown Club, *East Norwich* .... 18 [V] 516-922-7500
   muttontownclub.com
Nassau CC, *Glen Cove* .... 18 [V] 516-676-0554
   nassaucc.com
National Golf Links of America, *Southampton* ... 18 [V] 631-283-0410
New Paltz GC, *New Paltz* .... 9 [P] 845-255-8282
   newpaltzgolf.com

[A] = MILITARY   [M] = MUNICIPAL   [P] = PUBLIC   [R] = RESORT

NEW YORK

New York CC, *Spring Valley*..................18 [P] 845-362-5800
  nycountryclub.com
New York Hospital GC, *White Plains*.............9 [V] 914-997-5819
Newark Valley GC, *Newark Valley*...............18 [P] 607-642-3376
  newarkvalleygolfclub.com
Newfane Pro Am Par 3 GC, *Newfane*..............9 [P] 716-778-8302
Newman Muni GC, *Ithaca*.........................9 [M] 607-273-6262
Niagara County GC, *Lockport*...................18 [M] 716-439-7954
  niagaracounty.com
Niagara Falls CC, *Lewiston*....................18 [V] 716-285-1331
  niagarafallscc.com
Niagara Frontier CC, *Youngstown*...............18 [V] 716-745-3667
  niagarafrontiercc.com
Niagara Orleans CC, *Middleport*................18 [P] 716-735-9000
  noccgolf.com
Niagara's Golf Wonderland, *Niagara Falls*........9 [P] 716-731-5155
Nick Stoner GC, *Caroga Lake*...................18 [M] 518-835-4220
Nissequogue GC, *St James*......................18 [V] 631-584-2453
  nissequoguegolf.com
Normanside CC, *Delmar*.........................18 [V] 518-475-9445
  normanside.com
North Country GC, *Champlain*...................18 [P] 518-297-5814
  northcountrygolfclub.com
North Fork CC, *Cutchogue*......................18 [V] 631-734-7139
North Hempstead CC, *Port Washington*...........18 [V] 516-365-7500
  nhccli.com
North Hills CC, *Manhasset*.....................18 [V] 516-627-9100
  northhillscc.com
North Shore CC, *Glen Head*.....................18 [V] 516-676-0500
  nsccli.com
North Shore GC, *Cleveland*......................9 [P] 315-675-8101
North Woodmere GC, *Valley Stream*...............9 [M] 516-571-7814
  nassaucountyny.gov
Northern Pines GC, *Cicero*.....................18 [P] 315-699-2939
Northport GC At the VA, *Northport*..............9 [M] 631-261-8000
Noyac GC, *Sag Harbor*..........................18 [V] 631-725-1800
  noyacgolfclub.com
Oak Hill CC, *Rochester*........................36 [V] 585-586-1660
  oakhillcc.com
Oak Run GC, *Lockport*..........................18 [P] 716-434-8851
  oakrungolf.com
Oakwood GC, *Buffalo*............................9 [M] 716-689-1421
  amherst.ny.us
Old Hickory GC, *Livonia*.......................18 [S] 585-346-2450
  theoldhickorygolfclub.com
Old Oak GC, *Kirkville*.........................18 [P] 315-656-3522
Old Oaks CC, *Purchase*.........................18 [V] 914-683-6000
  oldoakscc.org
Old Westbury G&CC, *Old Westbury*...............27 [V] 516-626-1810
  owgolf.com
Olde Kinderhook GC, *Valatie*...................18 [V] 518-766-6542
Olde Vine GC, *Riverhead*.......................18 [V] 631-369-7151
  oldevinegolfclub.com
Oneida Community GC, *Oneida*...................18 [S] 315-361-6111
  oneidagolf.com
Oneonta CC, *Oneonta*...........................18 [V] 607-432-8950
  oneontacountryclub.org
Onondaga G&CC, *Fayetteville*...................18 [V] 315-446-1630
  ogccgolf.com
Onteora GC, *Tannersville*.......................9 [V] 518-589-5310
Orange County GC, *Middletown*..................18 [V] 845-341-1899
  orangecountygolfclub.com

Orchard Creek GC, *Altamont*....................18 [P] 518-861-5000
  orchardcreek.com
Orchard Park CC, *Orchard Park*.................18 [V] 716-662-4471
  orchardparkcc.com
Orchard Vali GC, *La Fayette*...................18 [P] 315-677-3303
  orchardvali.com
Oriskany Hills GC, *Oriskany*....................9 [P] 315-339-4653
Osiris CC, *Walden*.............................18 [V] 845-778-5795
  osiriscc.com
Oswego CC, *Oswego*.............................18 [V] 315-343-1941
  oswegocountryclub.com
Otsego GC, *Springfield Center*..................9 [P] 607-547-9290
  otsegogolf.com
Otterkill G&CC, *Campbell Hall*.................18 [V] 845-427-2020
  otterkillcountryclub.com
Ouleout GC, *Franklin*..........................18 [P] 607-829-2100
  ouleoutgolf.com
Owasco CC, *Auburn*..............................9 [V] 315-253-3971
  owascocountryclub.com
Oyster Bay GC, *Woodbury*.......................18 [M] 516-677-5980
  oysterbaytown.com
Ozzies Corner GC, *Hamlin*......................18 [P] 585-964-5440
Pap Pap Par 3 GC, *Albion*.......................9 [P] 585-589-4004
Park CC, *Williamsville*........................18 [V] 716-632-2286
  parkclub.org
Parkview Fairways, *Victor*.....................18 [P] 585-657-7539
  parkviewgc.com
Partridge Run G&CC, *Canton*....................18 [M] 315-386-4444
  partridgerun.com
Patriot Hills GC, *Stony Point*.................18 [M] 845-947-7085
  patriothillsgolfclub.com
Pearl Lakes GC & DR, *Skaneateles*...............9 [P] 315-685-6799
Peekn Peak GC, *Findley Lake*...................36 [R] 716-355-4141
  pknpk.com
Pehquenakonck CC, *North Salem*..................9 [S] 914-669-6776
Pelham CC, *Pelham*.............................18 [V] 914-738-2730
  pelhamcc.com
Pelham Split Rock GC, *Bronx*...................36 [M] 718-885-1258
  pelhamsplitrock.americangolf.com
Penfield CC, *Penfield*.........................18 [V] 585-377-7050
  penfieldcc.org
Peninsula GC, *Massapequa*.......................9 [P] 516-798-9776
Perinton G&CC, *Fairport*.......................18 [P] 585-223-7651
  bad link
Pheasant Hill CC, *Owego*.......................18 [P] 607-687-0722
  pheasanthillcc.com
Pheasant Hollow GC, *Castleton On Hudson*........9 [P] 518-479-4653
  evergreencountryclub.com
Phillip J Rotella Memorial GC, *Thiells*........18 [M] 845-354-1616
  rotellagolfcourse.com
Pine Brook GC, *Gloversville*....................9 [V] 518-725-1621
  pinebrookgolfclub.org
Pine Grove CC, *Camillus*.......................18 [P] 315-672-8107
  pinegrovecountryclub.com
Pine Hills CC, *Manorville*.....................18 [P] 631-878-4343
  pinehillsgolfproshop.com
Pine Hills GC, *Frankfort*......................18 [P] 315-733-5030
Pine Hollow CC, *East Norwich*..................18 [V] 516-922-0300
  pinehollowcc.com
Pine Meadows Greens, *Clarence*..................9 [P] 716-741-3970
Pine Ridge GC, *Coram*..........................18 [P] 631-331-7930
  pineridgegc.com

[S] = SEMI-PRIVATE   [V] = PRIVATE   [U] = UNIVERSITY   [N] = UNIVERSITY-PRIVATE

NEW YORK

Golf Yellow Pages, 18th Edition

Pinehaven CC, *Guilderland* .... 18 [V] 518-456-7111
  pinehavencc.com
Pinehurst GC, *Westfield* .... 9 [P] 716-326-4424
  pinehurst.jimdo.com
Pinewood CC, *Spencerport* .... 9 [S] 585-352-5314
Pinnacle St Park GC, *Addison* .... 9 [M] 607-359-2767
  nysparks.state.ny.us
Pioneer Hills GC, *Ballston Spa* .... 18 [P] 518-885-7000
  pioneerhillsgolf.com
Piping Rock Club, *Locust Valley* .... 18 [V] 516-676-2332
  pipingrockclub.org
Plandome CC, *Manhasset* .... 18 [V] 516-627-1273
  plandomecc.com
Pleasant Knolls GC, *Verona* .... 9 [R] 315-829-5192
  turning-stone.com
Pleasantville CC, *Pleasantville* .... 9 [V] 914-769-2809
  pleasantvillecountryclub.com
Pole Valley Players Club, *Hartford* .... 18 [P] 518-632-9632
  polevalley.com
Poolsbrook GC, *Kirkville* .... 18 [P] 315-687-3096
Popes Grove GC, *Syracuse* .... 9 [P] 315-487-9075
Port Bay GC, *Wolcott* .... 18 [P] 315-594-8295
  portbaygolf.com
Port Jefferson CC At Harbor Hills, *Port Jefferson*. 18 [V] 631-285-1814
Port Jervis CC, *Port Jervis* .... 18 [V] 845-856-5391
  portjerviscountryclub.com
Potsdam Town & CC, *Potsdam* .... 18 [P] 315-265-2141
  potsdamgolf.com
Pound Ridge GC, *Pound Ridge* .... 18 [S] 914-764-5771
  poundridgegolf.com
Poxabogue Golf Ctr, *Wainscott* .... 9 [P] 631-537-0025
  poxaboguegolf.com
Putnam National Golf, *Mahopac* .... 18 [M] 845-628-4200
  putnamnational.com
Quaker Hill CC, *Pawling* .... 9 [V] 845-855-1040
  quakerhill.cc
Quaker Ridge GC, *Scarsdale* .... 18 [V] 914-723-3701
  quakerridgegc.org
Queensbury CC, *Lake George* .... 18 [S] 518-793-3711
  lakegeorgegolf.com/queensbury
Quiet Times GC, *Attica* .... 18 [P] 585-591-1747
Quogue Field Club, *Quogue* .... 9 [V] 631-653-9885
Radisson Greens GC, *Baldwinsville* .... 18 [P] 315-638-0092
  radissongreens.com
Rainbow GC, *Greenville* .... 18 [R] 518-966-5343
  rainbowgolfclub.com
Ravenwood GC, *Victor* .... 18 [P] 585-924-5100
  ravenwoodgolf.com
Raymondville G&CC, *Massena* .... 9 [P] 315-769-2759
Red Hook GC, *Red Hook* .... 18 [S] 845-758-8652
  redhookgolfclub.com
Red Pines GC, *Edmeston* .... 9 [P] 607-965-6714
Reservoir Creek GC, *Naples* .... 18 [P] 585-374-6828
  rcgolf.com
Ricci Meadows GC, *Albion* .... 18 [P] 585-682-3280
Richmond County GC, *Staten Island* ..... 18 [V] 718-351-0600
  richmondcountycc.org
Ridgemont CC, *Rochester* .... 18 [V] 585-225-1370
  rccgolf.com
Ridgeway CC, *White Plains* .... 18 [V] 914-946-0681
  ridgewaycc.com
Rip Van Winkle CC, *Palenville* .... 9 [P] 518-678-9779
  rvwcc.com

River Oaks GC, *Grand Island* .... 18 [V] 716-773-3337
  riveroaksinc.com
River Run II Golf Links, *Kirkwood* .... 9 [P] 607-775-9280
  riverrunii.com/index.shtml
Riverbend GC, *New Berlin* .... 18 [P] 607-847-8481
Riverside CC, *Central Square* .... 18 [P] 315-676-7714
Riverton GC, *West Henrietta* .... 9 [P] 585-334-6196
  rivertongolfclub.com
Robert Moses St Park GC, *Babylon* .... 18 [M] 631-669-0449
  nysparks.state.ny.us
Robert Trent Jones GC At Cornell Univ, *Ithaca* .... 18 [N] 607-254-6531
  cornell.edu
Rock Hill G&CC, *Manorville* .... 18 [P] 631-878-2250
  rockhillgolf.com
Rockaway Hunting Club, *Lawrence* ...... 18 [V] 516-569-0600
  rhcny.com
Rockland CC, *Sparkill* .... 18 [V] 845-359-9702
  rocklandcountryclub.org
Rockland Lake GC, *Congers* .... 36 [M] 845-268-6250
  nysparks.state.ny.us
Rockville Links Club, *Rockville Centre* .. 18 [V] 516-766-9200
  rockvillelinks.com
Rogues Roost G&CC, *Bridgeport* .... 36 [P] 315-633-9406
  roguesroost.com
Rolling Acres GC, *Pike* .... 18 [R] 585-567-8557
Rolling Hills CC, *Fort Johnson* .... 18 [P] 518-829-7423
  golfrollinghills.com
Rolling Hills GC, *Chaffee* .... 9 [P] 716-496-5016
  rollinghillspar3.com
Rolling Oaks CC, *Rocky Point* .... 18 [P] 631-744-3200
  golfrollingoaks.com
Rome CC, *Rome* .... 18 [P] 315-336-6464
  romecountryclub.com
Rondout CC, *Accord* .... 18 [S] 845-626-2513
  rondoutgolfclub.com
Rose Brook GC, *Silver* .... 18 [P] 716-934-2825
  rosebrookgolfcourse.com
Rothland GC, *Akron* .... 27 [P] 716-542-4325
  rothlandgolf.com
Rustic G&CC, *Dexter* .... 9 [P] 315-639-6800
  rusticgolf.com
Rye GC, *Rye* .... 18 [V] 914-835-3200
  ryegolfclub.com
Sacandaga GC, *Northville* .... 9 [P] 518-863-4887
  officialsacgolf.com
Sadaquada GC, *Whitesboro* .... 9 [V] 315-736-3231
  sadaquada.cc
Sag Harbor GC, *Sag Harbor* .... 9 [M] 631-725-2503
  nysparks.state.ny.us
Sagamore Resort & GC, *Bolton Landing* .... 18 [R] 518-644-9400
  thesagamore.com
Salem GC, *North Salem* .... 18 [V] 914-669-5551
  salemgolfclub.org
Salmon Creek CC, *Spencerport* .... 18 [S] 585-352-4300
  salmoncreekcountryclub.com
Sands Point GC, *Sands Point* .... 18 [V] 516-883-3077
  sandspointgc.com
Sandy Pond GC, *Riverhead* .... 9 [P] 631-727-0909
Saranac Inn G&CC, *Saranac Lake* .... 18 [R] 518-891-1402
  saranacinn.com
Saranac Lake GC, *Ray Brook* .... 9 [P] 518-891-2675
Saratoga Golf & Polo Club, *Saratoga Springs* .... 9 [V] 518-584-8121
  saratogagolfpoloclub.org

146   [A] = MILITARY   [M] = MUNICIPAL   [P] = PUBLIC   [R] = RESORT

Golf Yellow Pages, 18th Edition — NEW YORK

Saratoga Lake GC, *Saratoga Springs*.................18 [P] 518-581-6611
  saratogalakegolf.com
Saratoga National GC, *Saratoga Springs*.............18 [P] 518-583-4653
  golfsaratoga.com
Saratoga Spa St Park GC, *Saratoga Springs* ....27 [M] 518-584-2006
  saratogaspagolf.com
Sauquoit Knolls GC, *Sauquoit* ....9 [P] 315-737-8959
Saxon Woods GC, *Scarsdale* ....18 [M] 914-231-3461
  westchestergov.com
Scarsdale GC, *Hartsdale*................................ 18 [V] 914-723-2840
  scarsdalegolfclub.org
Scenic Farms GC, *Pine Island*............................9 [P] 845-258-4455
  scenicfarmsgolf.com
Schenectady Muni GC, *Schenectady*................18 [M] 518-382-5155
  schenectadygolf.com
Schroon Lake Muni GC, *Schroon Lake*................9 [M] 518-532-9359
Schuyler Meadows Club, *Loudonville*................. 18 [V] 518-785-8191
  schuylermeadows.com
Scotts Corner GC, *Montgomery* ....9 [P] 845-457-9141
Scotts GC, *Deposit*.......................................18 [R] 607-467-3094
  scottsfamilyresort.com
Seawane Club, *Hewlett*................................. 18 [V] 516-374-1110
  seawane.com
Sebonack GC, *Southampton*........................... 18 [V] 631-287-4444
  sebonack.com
Seneca Falls CC, *Seneca Falls*..........................18 [P] 315-568-5202
  senecafallscountryclub.com
Seneca GC & DR, *Baldwinsville*..........................9 [P] 315-635-7571
Seneca Hickory Stick GC, *Lewiston* ....18 [P] 716-754-2424
  senecahickorystick.com
Seneca Lake CC, *Geneva*............................... 18 [S] 315-789-4681
Seven Oaks GC, *Hamilton*.............................. 18 [U] 315-824-1432
  sevenoaksgolf.com
Shadow Lake G&RC, *Penfield*..........................27 [P] 585-385-2010
  234golf.com
Shadow Pines GC, *Penfield* ....18 [P] 585-385-8550
  234golf.com
Shady Brook GC, *Beaver Dams* ....9 [P] 607-936-6608
  shadybrookgolfcourse.com
Shaker Ridge CC, *Loudonville*.......................... 18 [V] 518-869-5101
  shakerridge.com
Shallow Creek GC, *Shrub Oak*...........................9 [P] 914-962-0302
Shamrock G&CC, *Oriskany* .... 18 [S] 315-336-9858
Shawangunk CC, *Ellenville*................................9 [P] 845-647-6090
Shawnee CC, *Sanborn*.....................................9 [P] 716-731-5177
Shelridge CC, *Medina* .... 18 [V] 585-798-0391
  shelridgecc.com
Shelter Island CC, *Shelter Island Hts* ....9 [M] 631-749-0416
Shephard Hills GC, *Roxbury* ....9 [P] 607-326-7121
  shephardhills.com
Sheridan Park GC, *Tonawanda*........................18 [M] 716-875-1811
  tonawanda.ny.us
Shinnecock Hills GC, *Southampton* .... 18 [V] 631-283-1310
Shorewood CC, *Dunkirk* .... 18 [V] 716-366-5197
Sidney G&CC, *Sidney*......................................9 [V] 607-563-8381
Silver Creek GC, *Waterloo*..............................18 [P] 315-539-5076
  silvercreekgc.com
Silver Lake CC, *Perry*.....................................18 [P] 585-237-6308
  golf-silverlake.com
Silver Lake GC, *Staten Island*..........................18 [M] 718-447-5640
  silverlakegolf.com
Siwanoy CC, *Bronxville*................................. 18 [V] 914-337-8858
  siwanoycc.com

Six S GC, *Belfast*...36 [P] 585-365-2201
  sixsgolf.com
Skaneateles CC, *Skaneateles* .... 18 [V] 315-685-7131
  skaneatelescc.com
Skenadoa Club Of Clinton, *Clinton* .... 18 [V] 315-853-6612
  skenandoa.com
Skene Valley CC, *Whitehall*..............................18 [P] 518-499-1685
Skyridge GC, *Chittenango* ....9 [P] 315-687-6900
  skyridgegolf.com
Sleepy Hollow CC, *Scarborough* ....27 [V] 914-941-3062
  sleepyhollowcc.org
Sleepy Hollow GC, *Rome*................................18 [P] 315-336-4110
  sleepyhollow-golf.com
Smithtown Landing CC, *Smithtown*..................27 [M] 631-979-6534
  michaelhebron.com/schoolpages/smithtownlanding.html
Soaring Eagles GC Mark Twain St Park,
  Horseheads..18 [M] 607-739-0551
  nysparks.com/golf
Sodus Bay Heights GC, *Sodus Point* .... 18 [S] 315-483-6777
  sodusbayheights.com
Somers Pointe GC, *Somers* ....27 [V] 914-276-1000
  somerspointe.com
Sonyea GC, *Sonyea* ....9 [P] 585-658-4545
  sonyeagolf.com
South Fork CC, *Amagansett* .... 18 [V] 631-267-3575
  southforkcc.net
South Hills CC, *Jamestown*..............................18 [V] 716-487-1471
  southillscc.com
South Hills Par 3, *Jamestown* ....9 [S] 716-484-7987
South Park GC, *Buffalo* ....9 [M] 716-825-9504
  bfloparks.org
South Shore CC, *Hamburg*.............................. 18 [S] 716-649-6674
  southshoregolfcourse.com
South Shore GC, *Staten Island*........................18 [M] 718-984-0101
  nycteetimes.com
Southampton GC, *Southampton* .... 18 [V] 631-283-0623
  southamptongolfclub.com
Southern Dutchess CC, *Beacon* ....9 [V] 845-831-0762
  southerndutchesscc.com
Southern Meadows GC, *Rush*............................9 [P] 585-533-2440
  southernmeadows.com
Southward Ho CC, *Bay Shore*.......................... 18 [V] 631-665-1710
  southwardho.com
Spook Rock GC, *Suffern*.................................18 [M] 845-357-6466
  ramapo.org
Sprain Lake GC, *Yonkers*................................18 [M] 914-779-9827
  westchestergov.com
Spring Lake GC, *Middle Island*.........................27 [P] 631-924-5115
  springlakegolfclub.com
Springbrook Greens State GC, *Sterling* ....18 [M] 315-947-6115
  nysparks.com/golf
Springville CC, *Springville* .... 18 [V] 716-592-2122
  springvillecc.com
Spruce Ridge CC, *Arcade* ....9 [P] 585-492-4122
  spruceridgecc.com
St Andrews GC, *Hastings On Hudson* .... 18 [V] 914-478-3500
  saintandrewsgolfclub.com
St Bonaventure Univ GC, *St Bonaventure* ....9 [U] 716-372-7692
St Georges G&CC, *East Setauket* .... 18 [V] 631-751-0585
  stgeorgesgolf.com
St John Fisher GC, *Rochester* ....9 [U] 585-385-8458
  home.sjfc.edu/golfcourse
St Lawrence St Park GC, *Ogdensburg* ....9 [M] 315-393-2286
  nysparks.state.ny.us

[S] = SEMI-PRIVATE [V] = PRIVATE [U] = UNIVERSITY [N] = UNIVERSITY-PRIVATE

NEW YORK

Golf Yellow Pages, 18th Edition

St Lawrence Univ G&CC, *Canton*.......................... 18 [U]   315-386-4600
    stlawu.edu/sports/slgc/page1.htm
Stadium GC, *Schenectady* ....18 [P]   518-374-9104
    stadiumgolfclub.com
Stafford CC, *Stafford* .... 18 [V]   585-343-9281
    staffordcc.com
Stamford GC, *Stamford*...18 [P]   607-652-7398
    stamfordgolfclub.com
Stone Dock GC, *High Falls* ....9 [P]   845-687-7107
    stonedockgolfclub.com
Stonebridge G&CC, *New Hartford* ....18 [P]   315-733-5663
    stonebridgecc1.com
Stonebridge Golf Links & CC, *Smithtown*........... 18 [S]   631-724-7500
    stonebridgeglcc.com
Stonegate CC At Summit Lakes, *West Winfield*....18 [P]   315-855-4389
    stonegategc.com
Stonehedges CC, *Groton* ....18 [P]   607-898-3754
    stonehedgesgolfcourse.com
Stony Ford GC, *Montgomery* ....18 [M]   845-457-4949
    orangecountygov.com
Storm King GC, *Cornwall*...................................... 9 [V]   845-534-3844
    stormkinggolf.com
Streamside GC & CC, *Pulaski* ....9 [P]   315-298-6887
    streamsidecg.com
Sugar Hill GC, *Westfield* ....9 [P]   716-326-4653
    freewebs.com/newcaddyshackrestaurant
Sullivan County G&CC, *Liberty* ....9 [S]   845-292-9584
Sundown G&CC, *Bainbridge* ....9 [P]   607-895-6888
Sunken Meadow St Park GC, *Kings Park*............27 [M]   631-269-5451
    nysparks.com/golf
Sunningdale CC, *Scarsdale*.................................. 18 [V]   914-723-3200
    sunningdale.org
Sunny Hill GC, *Greenville*......................................18 [R]   518-634-7698
    sunnyhill.com
Sunnycrest Park GC, *Syracuse*..............................9 [M]   315-463-9358
    syracuse.ny.us
Sunnyside Par 3 GC, *Glens Falls*...........................9 [P]   518-792-0148
    sunnysidepar3.com
Sunset Valley Golf, *Lakewood* ....18 [P]   716-664-7508
SUNY Delhi College GC, *Delhi*.............................. 18 [U]   607-746-4650
    delhi.edu/golfcourse
Swan Lake G&CC, *Swan Lake* ....18 [P]   845-292-0323
    golfswanlake.com
Swan Lake GC, *Manorville* .... 18 [P]   631-369-1818
    swanlakegolf.com
Sweetland Pines GC, *Stafford*................................9 [P]   585-343-7059
Tallgrass At Shoreham, *Shoreham* ....18 [P]   631-209-9359
    golfattallgrass.com
Tam OShanter GC, *Glen Head* ....18 [V]   516-626-1980
    tamoshanterclub.com
Tamarack GC, *Oswego*...18 [P]   315-342-6614
    tamarackgolf.homestead.com
Tan Tara GC, *North Tonawanda* ....18 [V]   716-694-6954
    tantaragc.com
Tanner Valley GC, *Syracuse*...................................27 [P]   315-492-8113
Taranwould GC, *Newark* ....18 [P]   315-331-9128
    taranwould.com
Tarry Brae Muni GC, *South Fallsburg* ....18 [M]   845-434-2620
    tarrybrae.com
Tecumseh GC, *Syracuse*..9 [P]   315-445-0963
    tecumsehclub.com
Tee Bird GC - Tee-Bird North, *Fort Edward*...........18 [P]   518-792-7727
    teebirdgolf.com

Tee Bird GC - Tee-Bird South, *Moreau* ....9 [P]   518-747-0280
    teebirdgolf.com
Tennanah Lake G&TC, *Roscoe*..............................18 [R]   607-498-5502
    tennanah.com
Terry Hills GC, *Batavia* ....27 [P]   585-343-0860
    terryhills.com
Teugega CC, *Rome*... 18 [V]   315-337-7151
    teugega.com
The Apawamis Club, *Rye*....................................... 18 [V]   914-967-2100
    apawamis.org
The Barracks GC, *Plattsburgh*...............................18 [P]   518-566-7150
The Bolivar GC, *Bolivar* ....18 [P]   585-928-1266
The Bridge, *Bridgehampton*................................. 18 [V]   631-537-8902
The Bridgehampton Club, *Bridgehampton*.......... 9 [V]   631-537-9875
    bridgehamptonclub.org
The Brookwoods CC, *Ontario*...............................18 [P]   315-524-8495
    brookwoodcc.com
The Cavalry Club, *Manlius*.................................... 18 [V]   315-682-9510
    cavalryclub.org
The Club At Caughdenoy Creek, *Central Square*...18 [P]   315-676-4653
    caughdenoycreek.com
The Club At Shepard Hills, *Waverly* ....18 [P]   607-565-8522
    shepardhills.com
The Creek Club, *Locust Valley* .... 18 [V]   516-671-1001
The Edison Club, *Rexford*......................................27 [V]   518-399-2992
    edisonclub.com
The Elms GC, *Sandy Creek* ....18 [P]   315-387-5297
    theelmsgolfclub.com
The GC at Mansion Ridge, *Monroe* ....18 [S]   845-782-7888
    mansionridgegc.com
The GC of Newport, *Newport* ....18 [P]   315-845-8333
    golfclubofnewport.com
The GC of Purchase, *Purchase* .... 18 [V]   914-328-5047
The Greens at Beaumont, *Brewerton* ....18 [P]   315-699-5338
    greensatbeaumont.com
The Greens At Half Hollow, *Melville* .... 18 [V]   631-271-4514
    greensgolfshop.com
The Lazy Swan G&CC, *Saugerties* ....9 [S]   845-247-0075
    thelazyswan.com
The Links at Erie Village, *East Syracuse*................18 [P]   315-656-4653
    golferielinks.com
The Links at Hiawatha, *Apalachin*........................18 [P]   607-687-6952
    hiawathalinks.com
The Links At Ivy Ridge, *Akron* ....18 [P]   716-542-6342
    thelinksativyridge.com
The Links At Shirley, *Shirley*..................................27 [P]   631-395-7272
    linksatshirley.com
The Links At Union Vale, *Lagrangeville*................18 [S]   845-223-1000
    thelinksatunionvale.com
The Meadows Golf Ctr, *Margaretville* ....9 [P]   845-586-4104
    meadowsgolfcenter.com
The Pines GC, *Pulaski*..18 [P]   315-298-8100
The Pompey Club, *Pompey* .... 18 [V]   315-677-3559
    pompeyclub.com
The Powelton Club of Newburgh, *Newburgh* ..... 18 [P]   845-561-7409
    powelton.com
The Sedgewood GC, *Carmel* ....9 [V]   845-225-5227
    thesedgewoodclub.com
The Sycamore GC, *Ravena*....................................18 [P]   518-756-9555
    evergreencountryclub.com
The Tuxedo Club, *Tuxedo Park* .... 18 [V]   845-351-4543
    thetuxedoclub.com

148 [A] = MILITARY   [M] = MUNICIPAL   [P] = PUBLIC   [R] = RESORT

NEW YORK

Golf Yellow Pages, 18th Edition

The Village Club at Lake Success, *Great Neck*.......18 [P] 516-482-4012
villageoflakesuccess.com
The Witch GC at Fire Fox RV Park, *Lisle*...............18 [R] 607-692-4093
firefoxresorts.com
The Woods At Cherry Creek, *Riverhead*...............18 [P] 631-506-0777
thewoodsatcherrycreek.com
Thendara GC, *Thendara*..18 [P] 315-369-3136
thendaragolfclub.com
Thomas Carvel CC, *Pine Plains*............................18 [P] 518-398-7101
carvelcountryclub.com
Thousand Island CC Lake Course, *Wellesley Island* 18 [R] 315-482-9454
ticountryclub.com
Thousand Islands CC Old Course, *Wellesley Island* 18 [R] 315-482-9454
ticountryclub.com
Three Ponds Farm, *Water Mill*........................... 18 [V] 631-537-0664
Thunderhart GC, *Freehold*.................................18 [R] 518-634-7816
thunderhartgolf.com
Ticonderoga CC, *Ticonderoga*...........................18 [P] 518-585-2801
ticonderogacountryclub.com
Timber Banks GC & Marina, *Baldwinsville*............9 [S] 315-635-8800
timberbanks.com
Timber Creek GC, *Ashville* ....9 [P] 716-782-4550
Timber Point GC, *Great River*.............................27 [M] 631-581-2401
timberpointgolfcourse.com
Tioga CC, *Nichols* ....18 [P] 607-699-3881
tiogacc.com
Top Of The World Golf Resort, *Lake George*.........18 [R] 518-668-3000
topoftheworldgolfresort.com
Towers CC, *Floral Park* .... 18 [V] 718-279-1848
Town Of Colonie GC, *Albany*.............................36 [M] 518-374-4852
colonie.org
Town of Wallkill GC, *Middletown*.......................18 [M] 845-361-1022
townofwallkill.com/golfclub
Traditions At the Glen, *Johnson City*..................18 [S] 607-797-2381
traditionsresort.com
Transit Valley CC, *East Amherst* .... 18 [V] 716-688-5500
transitvalley.com
Tri County CC, *Forestville*...................................18 [S] 716-965-9723
tricountycountryclub.com
Triple Creek GC, *Nunda* ....18 [P] 585-468-2116
triplecreekgolfclub.com
Trumansburg GC, *Trumansburg* ....18 [P] 607-387-8844
trumansburggolf.com
Trump National GC, Westchester, *Briarcliff Manor* 18 [V] 914-944-0900
trumpnationalwestchester.com
Trump National-Hudson Valley ,
Hopewell Junction.. 18 [V] 845-223-1600
trumpnationalhudsonvalley.com
Tsuga Links GC, *New Berlin* ....9 [P] 607-965-2380
tsugalinks.com
Tupper Lake CC, *Tupper Lake*.............................18 [P] 518-359-3701
tupperlakegolf.com
Turin Highlands GC, *Turin* .... 18 [S] 315-348-4327
turinhighlands.com
Turkey Run GC, *Arcade* ....9 [P] 716-492-2888
Turning Stone Resort, *Verona* ....45 [R] 315-361-8518
turning-stone.org
Turtle Creek GC At Garden Cathay, *Wallkill*...........9 [R] 845-564-3220
gardencathayresort.com
Tuscarora GC, *Marcellus* .... 18 [V] 315-673-2679
tuscarorolfclub.com
Twaalfskill Club, *Kingston* ....9 [V] 845-331-6266
twaalfskillgolf.org

Twin Brooks GC, *Waddington*.............................18 [P] 315-388-4480
Twin Hickory GC, *Hornell* .... 18 [S] 607-324-1441
twinhickorygc.com
Twin Hills GC, *Spencerport* ....18 [P] 585-352-4800
twinhillsgolfcourse.com
Twin Ponds G&CC, *New York Mills* ....18 [P] 315-736-0550
twinpondsgolf.net
Twin Village GC, *Roscoe* ....9 [P] 607-498-5829
roscoegolf.com
Undermountain GC, *Copake*................................9 [P] 518-329-4444
undermountaingolf.com
Vails Grove GC, *Brewster*......................................9 [S] 845-669-5721
Valley View GC, *Whitehall* ....9 [P] 518-499-2634
valleyviewgolf.com
Valley View GC, *Utica*...18 [M] 315-732-8755
cityofutica.com
Valor GC, *Canandaigua* ....9 [A] 585-394-0040
Van Cortlandt Park GC, *Bronx*............................18 [M] 718-543-4595
vancortlandtgc.com
Van Patten GC, *Clifton Park* ....27 [P] 518-877-5400
vanpattengolf.com
Van Schaick Island CC, *Cohoes*............................9 [V] 518-237-6127
vsiccgolf.com
Vassar GC, *Poughkeepsie*.....................................9 [P] 845-473-9838
vassargolfcourse.com
Vesper Hills GC, *Tully* ....18 [P] 315-696-8328
vesperhillsgolf.com
Vestal Hills CC, *Binghamton* .... 18 [V] 607-723-7658
vestalhillscc.com
Victor Hills CC, *Victor* ....63 [P] 585-924-3480
victorhills.com
Villa Roma Resort, *Callicoon* ....18 [R] 845-887-4880
villaroma.com
Village Club of Sands Point, *Sands Point* .... 18 [V] 516-944-7840
villageclub.org
Wa Noa GC, *East Syracuse* ....18 [P] 315-656-8213
Waccabuc CC, *Waccabuc* .... 18 [V] 914-763-3144
waccabuccc.com
Wakely Lodge GC, *Indian Lake* ....9 [R] 518-648-5011
wakelylodgegc.com
Walden Oaks CC, *Cortland*................................. 18 [S] 607-753-9452
waldenoakscc.com
Walker Valley GC, *Pine Bush*................................9 [P] 845-744-2714
Wanakah CC, *Hamburg*..................................... 18 [V] 716-627-3472
wanakahcc.com
Warwick Valley CC, *Warwick* ....9 [V] 845-987-9923
warwickvalleycc.org
Water Way Hills GC, *Cuba*..................................18 [P] 716-372-9144
waterwayhills.com
Watertown GC, *Watertown*.................................18 [P] 315-782-4040
watertowngolfclubinc.com
Watkins Glen GC, *Watkins Glen* ....9 [P] 607-535-2340
Wayne Hills CC, *Lyons* ....18 [P] 315-946-6944
waynehillscc.com
Webster GC, *Webster*...36 [P] 585-265-1920
webstergolf.com
Wedgewood GC, *Fort Edward* ....9 [P] 518-747-0003
wedgewoodfe.com
Wellesley Island St Park GC, *Wellesley Island* ....9 [M] 315-482-5244
nysparks.state.ny.us
Wells College GC, *Aurora* ....9 [S] 315-364-8024
Wellsville GC, *Wellsville*..................................... 18 [V] 585-593-6337
wellsvillecountryclub.com

[S] = SEMI-PRIVATE   [V] = PRIVATE   [U] = UNIVERSITY   [N] = UNIVERSITY-PRIVATE

NEW YORK

Golf Yellow Pages, 18th Edition

West Hill CC, *Camillus* ....18 [P] 315-672-8677
westhillgolfcourse.com
West Point GC, *West Point* ....18 [A] 845-938-2435
westpointmwr.com
West Sayville GC, *West Sayville*..................18 [M] 631-567-1704
co.suffolk.ny.us
Westchester CC, *Rye* ....45 [V] 914-967-6000
wccclub.org
Westchester Hills GC, *White Plains*..................18 [V] 914-948-5020
westchesterhills.org
Western Turnpike GC, *Guilderland*..................27 [S] 518-456-0786
westernturnpike.com
Westhampton CC, *Westhampton Beach*..................18 [V] 631-288-1110
westhamptoncc.org
Westmoreland GC, *Westmoreland*..................9 [P] 315-853-8914
Westport CC, *Westport* ....18 [R] 518-962-4470
westportcountryclub.com
Westvale GC, *Camillus* ....18 [P] 315-487-0130
westvalegolfcourse.com
Westwood CC, *Williamsville*..................18 [V] 716-632-3040
westwoodcc.net
Wheatley Hills GC, *East Williston* ....18 [V] 516-747-7358
wheatleyhills.com
Whippoorwill Club, *Armonk* ....18 [V] 914-273-3059
whippoorwillclub.org
Whispering Pines Exec GC, *Schenectady* ....18 [P] 518-355-2724
White Birch GC, *Lyndonville* ....9 [P] 585-765-2630
White Pines GC, *Black River* ....9 [P] 315-773-3744
Whiteface Club & Resort, *Lake Placid*..................18 [R] 518-523-2551
whitefaceclubresort.com
Wild Wood CC, *Rush* ....18 [P] 585-334-5860
golfwildwood.com
Willow Creek G&CC, *Mt Sinai* ....27 [P] 631-928-3680
hamletwillowcreek.com
Willow Ridge CC, *Harrison* ....18 [V] 914-967-6161
willowridgecc.org
Willow Run GC, *Mayville*..................9 [P] 716-789-3162
Willowbrook GC, *Watertown* ....27 [P] 315-782-8192
willowbrookgolfclubwatertown.com
Willowbrook GC, *Cortland*..................18 [P] 607-756-7382
willowbrookgolfclubcortland.com
Willowbrook GC, *Lockport* ....27 [P] 716-434-0111
willowbrook.biz
Willowcreek GC, *Big Flats* ....27 [P] 607-562-8898
willowcreekgolfclub.com
Willsboro GC, *Willsboro* ....9 [P] 518-963-8989
willsborony.com
Wiltwyck GC, *Kingston*..................18 [V] 845-331-7878
wiltwyck.org
Windham CC, *Windham* ....18 [P] 518-734-9910
windhamcountryclub.com
Winding Brook CC, *Valatie*..................18 [P] 518-758-9117
windingbrookcountryclub.com
Winding Creek Exec Course, *Victor*..................9 [P] 585-924-0280
Winding Hills GC, *Montgomery*..................18 [P] 845-457-3187
windinghillsgolfcourse.com
Windy Hills GC, *Greenwich*..................18 [P] 518-695-4902
Winged Foot GC, *Mamaroneck*..................36 [V] 914-698-8400
wfgc.org
Winged Pheasant GC, *Shortsville*..................27 [P] 585-289-8846
wingedpheasant.com
Wolferts Roost CC, *Albany* ....18 [V] 518-462-2115
wolfertsroost.com
Woodcliff Hotel & Spa, *Fairport* ....9 [R] 585-248-4880
woodcliffhotelspa.com
Woodcrest GC, *Cazenovia*..................18 [P] 315-687-3086
woodcrestgolfclub.com
Woodcrest GC, *Mayville*..................18 [P] 716-789-4653
woodcrestgolf.com
Woodgate Pines GC, *Boonville* ....18 [P] 315-942-5442
Woodhaven GC, *West Oneonta* ....9 [P] 607-267-4367
Woodlynn Hills GC, *Nunda*..................18 [P] 585-468-5010
woodlynnhills.com
Woodmere Club, *Woodmere* ....18 [V] 516-295-2500
woodmereclub.com
Woodside Acres CC, *Syosset* ....18 [V] 516-802-2900
wsagolf.com
Woodstock GC, *Woodstock*..................9 [V] 845-679-2914
woodstockgolf.com
Wykagyl CC, *New Rochelle* ....18 [V] 914-636-8700
wykagylcc.org
Yahnundasis GC, *New Hartford* ....18 [V] 315-732-3950
yahnundasis.com

NORTH CAROLINA

401 Par Golf, *Raleigh* ....9 [P] 919-772-5261
401pargolf.com
Alamance CC, *Burlington* ....18 [V] 336-584-1326
alamancecc.net
Anderson Creek GC, *Spring Lake* ....18 [P] 910-814-2115
andersoncreekgolf.com
Angels Trace Golf Links, *Sunset Beach*..................36 [P] 910-579-2277
golfangelstrace.com
Apple Creek Exec GC, *Dallas*..................18 [P] 704-922-4440
applecreekgolf.com
Arrowhead GC, *Mebane*..................18 [P] 919-563-5255
Asheboro CC, *Asheboro*..................18 [S] 336-625-6810
asheborocc.com
Asheboro Muni GC, *Asheboro* ....9 [M] 336-625-4158
Asheville Muni GC, *Asheville*..................18 [M] 828-298-1867
ashevilleparks.org
Ayden G&CC, *Ayden*..................18 [S] 252-746-3389
aydengolf.com
Badin Inn Golf Resort & Club, *Badin* ....18 [R] 704-422-3683
badininn.com
Bald Head Island Club, *Southport* ....18 [R] 910-457-7300
bhigolf.com
Ballantyne CC, *Charlotte*..................18 [V] 704-341-3113
ballantyneclub.com
Balsam Mountain Preserve GC, *Sylva*..................18 [V] 828-631-1009
balsammountainpreserve.com
Bayonet At Puppy Creek GC, *Raeford*..................18 [P] 910-904-1500
bayonetgolf.com
Bayview GC, *Bath*..................9 [P] 252-923-8191
Baywood GC, *Fayetteville*..................18 [P] 910-483-4330
dsgolfcenters.com
Beacon Ridge G&CC, *West End*..................18 [R] 910-673-2950
beaconridgegolfcc.com
Bear Lake GC, *Tuckasegee*..................9 [V] 828-293-5005
bearlakereserve.com
Bear Trail GC, *Jacksonville*..................18 [S] 910-346-8160
beartrailgolf.com
Beau Rivage Golf & Resort, *Wilmington*..................18 [R] 910-392-9021
beaurivagegolf.com
Beaver Creek GC, *Dobson*..................9 [P] 336-374-5670
Beechwood CC, *Ahoskie*..................18 [S] 252-332-2905

[A] = MILITARY   [M] = MUNICIPAL   [P] = PUBLIC   [R] = RESORT

Golf Yellow Pages, 18th Edition — NORTH CAROLINA

Course	Info	Phone
Belvedere CC, *Hampstead*	18 [R]	910-270-2703
belvederecc.com		
Bentwinds G&CC, *Fuquay Varina*	18 [V]	919-552-5656
bentwinds.org		
Benvenue CC, *Rocky Mount*	18 [V]	252-443-3926
benvenuecc.com		
Bermuda Run CC - Champ, *Advance*	18 [V]	336-998-8154
bermudaruncc.com		
Bermuda Run CC - West, *Advance*	18 [V]	336-998-8154
bermudaruncc.com		
Biltmore Forest CC, *Asheville*	18 [V]	828-274-1261
biltmoreforestcc.com		
Birchwood CC, *Nashville*	18 [V]	252-459-3910
birchwoodcountryclub.com		
Birkdale GC, *Huntersville*	18 [P]	704-895-8038
birkdale.com		
Black Mountain GC, *Black Mountain*	18 [M]	828-669-2710
townofblackmountain.org		
Blair Park GC, *High Point*	18 [M]	336-883-3497
blairparkgc.com		
Blowing Rock GC, *Blowing Rock*	18 [V]	828-295-7311
blowingrockcountryclub.com		
Bluff Golf Links, *Pinebluff*	18 [R]	910-281-0275
thebluffgolflinks.com		
Boone GC, *Boone*	18 [P]	828-264-8760
boonegolfclub.com		
Bradford Creek GC, *Greenville*	18 [M]	252-329-4653
greenvillenc.gov		
Brandywine Bay GC, *Morehead City*	18 [P]	252-247-2541
brandywinegolf.com		
Brevofield Golf Links, *Wake Forest*	18 [S]	919-562-1900
wakeforestgolf.com		
Brick Landing Plantation Yacht&GC, *Ocean Isle Beach*	18 [R]	910-754-5545
bricklandinggc.com		
Brier Creek CC, *Raleigh*	18 [V]	919-206-4600
briercreekcc.com		
Brierwood GC, *Shallotte*	18 [P]	910-754-4660
brierwood.com		
Brights Creek GC, *Mill Spring*	18 [V]	828-894-5032
brightscreek.com		
Broadmoor Golf Links, *Fletcher*	18 [P]	828-687-1500
broadmoorlinks.com		
Brook Valley CC, *Greenville*	18 [V]	252-756-5500
brookvalleycountryclub.com		
Brookwood GC, *Whitsett*	18 [P]	336-449-5544
Brunswick Plantation & Golf Resort, *Calabash*	27 [R]	910-845-6935
brunswickplantation.com		
Brushy Mountain GC, *Taylorsville*	18 [P]	828-632-4804
brushymountaingolf.com		
Bryan Park GC, *Browns Summit*	36 [M]	336-375-2200
bryanpark.com		
Bull Creek G&CC, *Louisburg*	18 [P]	919-496-7888
bullcreekgolf.com		
Bur Mil Park GC, *Greensboro*	9 [M]	336-373-3800
burmilpark.org		
Burlingame CC at Sapphire Lakes, *Sapphire*	18 [V]	828-966-9202
burlingamecc.com		
Cabarrus CC, *Concord*	18 [V]	704-786-8154
cabarruscc.org		
Cape Fear CC, *Wilmington*	18 [V]	910-762-4652
capefearcountryclub.net		
Cape Fear National At Brunswick Forest, *Leland*	18 [P]	910-371-2434
capefearnational.com		
Cardinal CC, *Selma*	18 [P]	919-284-3647
Cardinal G&CC, *Greensboro*	18 [V]	336-668-2749
cardinalcc.com		
Carmel CC, *Charlotte*	36 [V]	704-945-3300
carmelcountryclub.org		
Carolina CC, *Raleigh*	18 [V]	919-787-2134
carolinacc.net		
Carolina Club, *Grandy*	18 [S]	252-453-3588
thecarolinaclub.com		
Carolina Colours GC, *New Bern*	18 [V]	877-356-2304
carolinacolours.com		
Carolina GC, *Charlotte*	18 [V]	704-392-6363
carolinagolfclub.org		
Carolina Lakes CC, *Sanford*	18 [P]	919-499-5421
carolina-lakes.com		
Carolina Meadows, *Chapel Hill*	9 [P]	800-458-6756
carolinameadows.org		
Carolina National GC, *Bolivia*	27 [S]	910-755-5200
carolinanationalgolf.com		
Carolina Pines CC, *New Bern*	18 [P]	252-444-1000
carolinapinesgolf.com		
Carolina Sands At White Lake, *Elizabethtown*	18 [P]	910-862-8796
carolinasandsgolf.com		
Carolina Shores GC, *Calabash*	18 [R]	910-579-2181
Carolina Trace CC, *Sanford*	36 [V]	919-499-5121
carolinatracecc.com		
Cashie G&CC, *Windsor*	9 [P]	252-794-4942
Castle Bay G&CC, *Hampstead*	18 [S]	910-270-1978
castlebaycc.com		
Caswell Pines GC, *Blanch*	18 [P]	336-694-2255
caswellpines.com		
Catawba CC, *Newton*	18 [V]	828-294-3737
catawbacc.org		
Catawba Springs Golf-Lake Hickory CC, *Hickory*	27 [V]	828-256-2171
lakehickorycc.com		
CC of Asheville, *Asheville*	18 [V]	828-258-9762
countryclubofasheville.net		
CC of Johnston County, *Smithfield*	18 [V]	919-934-4544
ccjohnstoncounty.com		
CC of Landfall - Dye, *Wilmington*	18 [V]	910-256-9050
countrycluboflandfall.com		
CC of Landfall - Nick, *Wilmington*	27 [V]	910-256-9050
countrycluboflandfall.com		
CC of North Carolina, *Pinehurst*	36 [V]	910-692-6565
ccofnc.com		
CC of Salisbury, *Salisbury*	18 [V]	704-636-7070
ccofsalisbury.com		
CC of Whispering Pines, *Whispering Pines*	36 [R]	910-949-3000
whisperingpinesnc.com		
Cedar Grove GC, *Hillsborough*	18 [P]	919-732-8397
cedargrovegolfcourse.com		
Cedar Lake GC, *Jonesville*	9 [P]	336-835-5041
Cedar Rock CC, *Lenoir*	18 [P]	828-758-4421
cedarrockcountryclub.com		
Cedarbrook CC, *State Road*	18 [V]	336-835-2320
cedarbrookcountryclub.com		
Cedarcrest GC, *Mc Leansville*	18 [P]	336-697-8251
Cedarwood CC, *Charlotte*	18 [V]	704-542-0206
cedarwoodcc.com		
Challenger 3 GC, *Shelby*	18 [P]	704-482-5061
challenger3.com		
Champion Hills Club, *Hendersonville*	18 [V]	828-693-3600
championhills.com		

[S] = SEMI-PRIVATE   [V] = PRIVATE   [U] = UNIVERSITY   [N] = UNIVERSITY-PRIVATE

NORTH CAROLINA

Chapel Hill CC, *Chapel Hill* .... 18 [V]   919-932-2857
  chapelhillcc.org
Chapel Ridge GC, *Pittsboro* .... 18 [S]   919-545-2242
  chapelridgegolfclub.com
Charles T Myers GC, *Charlotte* .... 18 [M]   704-536-1692
  charlottepublicgolf.com
Charlotte CC, *Charlotte* .... 18 [V]   704-334-0836
  charlottecountryclub.org
Charlotte Golf Links, *Charlotte* .... 18 [P]   704-846-7990
  charlottegolflinks.com
Charlotte National GC, *Indian Trail* .... 18 [S]   704-882-8282
Chatuge Shores GC, *Hayesville* .... 18 [M]   828-389-8940
  chatugeshoresgolf.com
Cherokee Hills CC, *Murphy* .... 18 [P]   828-837-5853
  wellswest.com
Cherryville G&CC, *Cherryville* .... 9 [S]   704-435-6597
Chicora GC, *Dunn* .... 18 [P]   910-897-7366
  chicoracountryclub.com
Chockoyote CC, *Weldon* .... 18 [V]   252-536-3166
Chowan G&CC, *Edenton* .... 18 [P]   252-482-3606
  chowangolfandcountryclub.com
Cleghorn Plantation GC, *Rutherfordton* ...... 18 [R]   828-286-9117
  cleghornplantation.com
Cleveland CC, *Shelby* .... 18 [V]   704-487-4643
  clevelandcountryclub.us
Cliffwood GC, *Lumberton* .... 18 [P]   910-738-9400
Club At Irish Creek, *Kannapolis* .... 18 [V]   704-932-2525
  playatirishcreek.com
Coharie CC, *Clinton* .... 18 [V]   910-592-2951
  cohariecc.com
Colonial CC, *Thomasville* .... 18 [V]   336-472-7501
  colonialcountryclubnc.com
Connestee Falls GC, *Brevard* .... 18 [S]   828-885-2005
  connesteefalls.com
Corbin Hills GC, *Salisbury* .... 18 [P]   704-636-0672
Country Hills GC, *Gibsonville* .... 18 [P]   336-375-8649
  countryhillsgolfnc.com
Countryside GC, *Elkin* .... 9 [P]   336-957-2629
Cowans Ford CC, *Stanley* .... 18 [V]   704-827-3219
  cowansford.com
Cramer Mountain CC, *Cramerton* .... 18 [V]   704-824-2772
  cramermountain.com
Crestview GC, *Ennice* .... 18 [P]   336-657-3471
Croasdaile CC, *Durham* .... 18 [V]   919-383-2517
  croasdailecountryclub.com
Crooked Creek GC, *Hendersonville* .... 18 [P]   828-692-2011
Crooked Creek GC, *Fuquay Varina* .... 18 [S]   919-557-7529
  playcrookedcreek.com
Crooked Tree GC, *Browns Summit* .... 18 [P]   336-656-3211
  crookedtreegolfcourse.com
Cross Creek CC, *Mt Airy* .... 18 [V]   336-789-5131
  crosscreekcc.com
Crow Creek GC, *Calabash* .... 18 [P]   910-287-3081
  crowcreek.com
Crowders Mountain Golf, *Kings Mountain* .. 18 [P]   704-739-7681
  golfholes.com/nc/crowders-mountain.htm
Crowne Plaza T&G Resort, *Asheville* .... 9 [R]   828-254-3211
  ashevillecp.com
Cullasaja Club, *Highlands* .... 18 [V]   828-526-3531
  cullasaja-club.com
Cummings Cove G&CC, *Hendersonville* ..... 18 [S]   828-891-9412
  cummingscove.com

Golf Yellow Pages, 18th Edition

Cutter Creek GC, *Snow Hill* .... 18 [S]   252-747-4653
  cuttercreekgolfclub.com
Cypress Creek Golf Links, *Laurinburg* .... 18 [P]   910-277-0311
Cypress Lakes GC, *Hope Mills* .... 18 [P]   910-483-0359
  cypresslakesnc.com
Cypress Landing GC, *Chocowinity* .... 18 [S]   252-946-7788
  cypresslandinggolf.com
Dan Valley GC, *Stoneville* .... 18 [P]   336-548-6808
Dawn Acres GC, *Stokesdale* .... 18 [P]   336-643-5397
Deep Springs CC, *Stoneville* .... 18 [V]   336-427-0950
  deepspringscc.com
Deer Brook GC, *Shelby* .... 18 [S]   704-482-4653
  deerbrookgolfclub.com
Deercroft G&CC, *Wagram* .... 18 [S]   910-369-3107
  deercroft.com
Devils Ridge GC, *Holly Springs* .... 18 [V]   919-557-6101
  devilsridgecc.com
Diamond Creek, *Banner Elk* .... 18 [V]   828-898-1800
  diamondcreekgc.com
Dogwood Valley GC, *Forest City* .... 9 [P]   828-657-6214
Dormie Club, *West End* .... 18 [V]   910-947-3240
  dormieclub.com
Dr Charles Sifford GC at Revolution Park, *Charlotte* 9 [M]   704-333-3949
  charlottepublicgolf.com
Duck Haven GC, *Wilmington* .... 18 [P]   910-791-7983
Duck Woods CC, *Kitty Hawk* .... 18 [S]   252-261-2609
  duckwoodscc.com
Duke Univ GC, *Durham* .... 18 [U]   919-681-2288
  golf.duke.edu
Eagle Chase GC, *Marshville* .... 18 [S]   704-385-9000
  eaglechasegolf.com
Eagle Point GC, *Wilmington* .... 27 [V]   910-686-4653
  eaglepointgc.com
Eagle Ridge GC, *Raleigh* .... 18 [P]   919-661-6300
  playateagleridge.com
Echo Farms G&CC, *Wilmington* .... 18 [S]   910-791-9318
  echofarmsnc.com
Emerald GC, *New Bern* .... 18 [P]   252-633-4440
  emeraldgc.com
Emerald Lake GC, *Matthews* .... 18 [S]   704-882-7888
  emeraldlakegolfclub.com
Etowah Valley GC, *Etowah* .... 27 [R]   828-891-7141
  etowahvalley.com
Fairfield GC, *High Point* .... 9 [P]   336-431-2913
Fairfield Harbour GC, *New Bern* .... 36 [R]   252-514-0050
  hoatown.com
Fairmont GC, *Fairmont* .... 18 [P]   910-628-9931
  fairmontgolfcourse.com
Falling Creek CC, *Kinston* .... 18 [P]   252-522-1828
  fallingcreekgolf.com
Falls Village GC, *Durham* .... 18 [S]   919-596-4653
  fallsvillagegolf.com
Farmstead Golf Links, *Calabash* .... 18 [P]   866-749-7277
  farmsteadgolflinks.com
Farmville G&CC, *Farmville* .... 18 [S]   252-753-3660
Firethorne CC, *Marvin* .... 18 [V]   704-843-3111
  firethornecountryclub.com
Fletchers Landing At Swingin Things, *Jacksonville* 9 [P]   910-347-7711
Fords Colony CC At Rocky Mount, *Rocky Mount* ...18 [P]   252-557-1600
  rockymountgolfclub.com
Forest City Muni GC, *Forest City* .... 9 [M]   828-248-5222
  townofforestcity.com/golf.html

[A] = MILITARY   [M] = MUNICIPAL   [P] = PUBLIC   [R] = RESORT

NORTH CAROLINA

Forest Creek GC, *Pinehurst* .... 36 [V] 910-693-1996
  forestcreekgolfclub.com
Forest Oaks CC, *Greensboro* .... 18 [V] 336-674-2241
  forestoakscc.com
Forsyth CC, *Winston Salem* .... 18 [V] 336-768-7559
Fort Bragg Ryder GC, *Fort Bragg* .... 18 [A] 910-907-4653
  fortbraggmwr.com/ryder.php
Fort Bragg Stryker GC, *Fort Bragg* .... 18 [A] 910-396-3980
  fortbraggmwr.com/stryker.php
Founders Club At St James Plantation, *Southport* 18 [R] 910-253-3011
  theclubsatstjames.com
Fox Den CC, *Statesville* .... 18 [P] 704-872-9990
  foxdencc.com
Foxfire G&CC, *Foxfire Village* .... 36 [R] 910-295-5555
  visitfoxfire.com
Foxwood GC, *Salisbury* .... 18 [P] 704-637-2528
Franklin GC, *Franklin* .... 9 [R] 828-524-2288
  franklingolfcourse.com
Garner CC, *Raleigh* .... 9 [V] 919-772-2587
Gaston CC, *Gastonia* .... 18 [V] 704-867-9561
  gastoncc.com
Gastonia Muni GC, *Gastonia* .... 18 [M] 704-866-6945
  cityofgastonia.com
Gates Four G&CC, *Fayetteville* .... 18 [V] 910-425-2176
  gatesfour.com
GC at Ballantyne Resort, *Charlotte* .... 18 [R] 704-248-4383
  golfballantyne.com
Gillespie Park GC, *Greensboro* .... 9 [M] 336-373-5850
Glen Cannon CC, *Brevard* .... 18 [S] 828-884-9160
  glencannoncc.com
Glen Oaks GC, *Maiden* .... 18 [P] 828-428-2451
  glenoaksgolf.com
Goldsboro Muni GC, *Goldsboro* .... 18 [S] 919-735-0411
  gmgcgolf.com
Golf Village, *Pineville* .... 9 [P] 704-889-5086
Goose Creek G&CC, *Grandy* .... 18 [S] 252-453-4008
  obxgolfgoosecreek.com
Governors Club, *Chapel Hill* .... 27 [V] 919-933-7500
  governorsclub.cc
Granada Farms CC, *Granite Falls* .... 18 [S] 828-396-2313
Grandfather G&CC, *Linville* .... 36 [R] 828-898-4388
  grandfatherclub.org
Grandover Resort, *Greensboro* .... 36 [R] 336-294-1800
  grandover.com
Grassy Creek G&CC, *Spruce Pine* .... 18 [P] 828-765-7436
  grassycreek.com
Green Acres Camping Resort, *Williamston* . 9 [R] 252-792-3939
Green Acres GC, *Randleman* .... 9 [P] 336-498-2247
Green Hill CC, *Louisburg* .... 9 [V] 919-496-3236
Green Hills GC, *Leland* .... 18 [P] 910-253-8333
Green Meadows GC, *Mt Holly* .... 18 [P] 704-827-9264
  greenmeadowsgolfsite.com
Green Oaks GC, *Concord* .... 18 [P] 704-786-4412
Greensboro CC - Farm Course, *Greensboro* .. 18 [V] 336-272-4364
  greensborocc.org
Greensboro CC - Irving Park Course, *Greensboro* 18 [V] 336-272-4364
  greensborocc.org
Greensboro National GC, *Summerfield* ..... 18 [P] 336-342-1113
  greensboronatl.com
Greensbridge GC, *Garland* .... 18 [S] 910-529-1662
  greensbridge.com
Greenville CC, *Greenville* .... 18 [V] 252-756-0504
  greenvillecountryclub.com

Hampton Heights GC, *Hickory* .... 18 [P] 828-328-5010
  hamptonheightsgc.com
Happy Valley GC, *Wilson* .... 18 [P] 252-237-6611
Hardys Custom Golf Ctr, *Mount Airy* .... 9 [P] 336-789-7888
  hardrockgolf.net
Headwaters GC, *Cashiers* .... 9 [V] 828-743-6047
Hedingham G&AC, *Raleigh* .... 18 [P] 919-250-3030
  fredsmithcompany.com
Hemlock GC, *Walnut Cove* .... 18 [P] 336-591-7934
Henderson CC, *Henderson* .... 18 [V] 252-438-3095
Hendersonville CC, *Hendersonville* .... 18 [V] 828-692-2261
  hendersonvillecc.com
Henry River GC, *Hickory* .... 18 [P] 828-294-2638
  henryrivergolf.com
Heritage GC, *Wake Forest* .... 18 [S] 919-453-2020
  playheritagegolf.com
Hickory Meadows GC, *Whitakers* .... 18 [P] 252-437-0591
  hickorymeadows.com
High Hampton Inn & CC, *Cashiers* .... 18 [R] 828-743-2450
  highhamptoninn.com
High Meadows G&CC, *Roaring Gap* .... 18 [V] 336-363-2445
  highmeadowscountryclub.com
High Point CC - Emerywood Course, *High Point* ... 9 [P] 336-869-2416
High Point CC - Willow Creek Course, *High Point* 18 [V] 336-869-2416
High Vista CC, *Mills River* .... 18 [P] 828-891-1986
  highvistagolf.com
Highland CC, *Fayetteville* .... 18 [V] 910-485-8141
  hcconline.net
Highland Creek GC, *Charlotte* .... 18 [P] 704-875-9000
  highlandcreekgolfclub.com
Highland Lake GC, *Flat Rock* .... 9 [P] 828-692-0143
Highlands GC, *Highlands* .... 18 [V] 828-526-2181
  highlandscountryclub.com
Highlands Falls CC, *Highlands* .... 18 [P] 828-526-4118
  clubhfcc.com
Hillandale GC, *Durham* .... 18 [P] 919-286-4211
  hillandalegolf.com
Hilma CC, *Tarboro* .... 9 [V] 252-823-4443
  hilmacountryclub.com
Holly Ridge GC, *Harbinger* .... 18 [S] 252-491-2893
  hollyridgeobx.com
Holly Ridge Golf Links, *Archdale* .... 18 [P] 336-861-4653
  hollyridgegolflinks.com
Hope Mills G&CC, *Hope Mills* .... 18 [P] 910-425-7171
Hope Valley CC, *Durham* .... 18 [V] 919-489-6676
  hvcc.org
Hound Ears Club, *Boone* .... 18 [R] 828-963-4321
  houndears.com
Hyland GC, *Southern Pines* .... 18 [P] 910-692-3752
  hylandgolfclub.com
Indian Trails GC, *Grifton* .... 18 [P] 252-524-5485
Indian Valley GC, *Burlington* .... 18 [M] 336-584-7871
  burlingtonnc.gov
Inland Greens, *Wilmington* .... 9 [P] 910-452-9900
  inlandgreens.com
Iron Play GC, *Summerfield* .... 18 [P] 336-644-7991
  ironplay.com
Iron Tree GC, *Waynesville* .... 9 [P] 828-627-1933
Ironwood G&CC, *Greenville* .... 18 [V] 252-752-6659
  ironwoodgolf.com
Jacksonville CC, *Jacksonville* .... 18 [V] 910-346-9255
  jacksonvillecountryclub.net

[S] = SEMI-PRIVATE   [V] = PRIVATE   [U] = UNIVERSITY   [N] = UNIVERSITY-PRIVATE

NORTH CAROLINA
Golf Yellow Pages, 18th Edition

Jamestown Park GC, *Jamestown* .... 18 [M] 336-454-4912
  jamestownparkgolf.com
Jefferson Landing Club, *Jefferson* .... 18 [R] 336-982-7767
  jeffersonlandingclub.com
Keith Hills CC, *Buies Creek* .... 36 [U] 910-893-5051
  campbell.edu/keithhills
Kenmure CC, *Flat Rock* .... 18 [V] 828-697-1200
  kenmure.com
Kerr Lake CC, *Henderson* .... 18 [S] 252-492-1895
  kerrlakecc.com
Key Vista CC, *Pink Hill* .... 9 [P] 252-568-4880
Kilmarlic GC, *Powells Point* .... 18 [S] 252-491-4220
  kilmarlic.com
Kings Grant G&CC, *Fayetteville* .... 18 [S] 910-630-1111
  kingsgrantlife.com
Kings Mountain CC, *Kings Mountain* .... 18 [P] 704-739-5871
Kinston CC, *Kinston* .... 18 [V] 252-523-5730
  kinstoncc.com
Knights Play Golf Ctr, *Apex* .... 27 [P] 919-303-4653
  knightsplay.com
Knobbs Creek Par 3 GC, *Elizabeth City* .... 9 [M] 252-337-6618
  cityofec.com
Knollwood Fairways & DR, *Southern Pines* .... 9 [R] 910-692-3572
  knollwood-midland.com
Lake Gaston GC, *Macon* .... 9 [P] 252-257-1777
Lake Hickory Town Course, *Hickory* .... 9 [V] 828-327-8716
  lakehickorycc.com
Lake Junaluska GC, *Waynesville* .... 18 [R] 828-456-5777
  lakejunaluska.com
Lake Louise GC, *Mocksville* .... 18 [P] 336-998-8746
  lakelouisegolfclubnc.com
Lake Toxaway CC, *Lake Toxaway* .... 18 [V] 828-966-4661
  laketoxawaycountryclub.com
Lake Winds GC, *Rougemont* .... 18 [S] 919-471-4653
  lakewindsgolfcourse.com
Lakeshore GC, *Durham* .... 18 [P] 919-596-2401
  lakeshoregc.com
Lakewood CC, *Salemburg* .... 18 [P] 910-525-4424
  lakewoodcc.us
Lakewood GC, *Statesville* .... 18 [S] 704-873-6441
  lakewoodgolfclub.net
Lakewood Golf Links, *Belmont* .... 18 [P] 704-825-2852
Land Harbor GC, *Linville* .... 18 [V] 828-733-8325
  linvillelandharbor.com
Land O Lakes GC, *Whiteville* .... 18 [P] 910-642-5757
  landolakesgolfclub.com
Lane Tree GC, *Goldsboro* .... 18 [S] 919-734-1245
  lanetree.com
Larkhaven GC, *Charlotte* .... 18 [P] 704-545-4653
  larkhavengolf.com
Laurel Ridge CC, *Waynesville* .... 18 [V] 828-456-3200
  laurelridgegolf.com
Legacy Golf Links, *Aberdeen* .... 18 [P] 910-944-8825
  legacygolfnc.com
Lennon Hills GC, *Bolivia* .... 9 [V] 910-754-4200
  lennonhills.com
Lenoir GC, *Lenoir* .... 18 [P] 828-754-5093
  lenoirgolfclub.com
Lexington GC, *Lexington* .... 18 [M] 336-248-3950
  lexingtongolfclub.com
Lincoln CC, *Lincolnton* .... 18 [P] 704-735-1382
  lincolncountryclub.net
Linville Falls Mountain Club & Preserve, *Marion* 18 [V] 828-756-4653
  linvillefallsmountainclub.com

Linville GC, *Linville* .... 18 [R] 828-733-4363
  eseeola.com
Linville Ridge CC, *Linville* .... 18 [V] 828-898-9741
  linvilleridge.com
Little River Golf & Resort, *Carthage* .... 18 [R] 910-949-5013
  littleriver.com
Loch Haven GC, *Rockingham* .... 18 [P] 910-895-3295
Lochmere GC, *Cary* .... 18 [S] 919-851-0611
  lochmere.com
Lockwood Folly CC, *Supply* .... 18 [P] 910-842-5666
  lockwoodfolly.com
Longleaf G&CC, *Southern Pines* .... 18 [R] 910-692-6100
  longleafgolf.com
Lonnie Poole GC At NC State Univ, *Raleigh* .... 18 [U] 919-833-3338
  lonniepoolegolfcourse.com
Lynrock GC, *Eden* .... 18 [S] 336-623-6110
Maccripine CC, *Pinetops* .... 18 [V] 252-827-5537
  maccripine.com
MacGregor Downs CC, *Cary* .... 18 [V] 919-467-1895
  macgregordowns.org
Maggie Valley Club, *Maggie Valley* .... 18 [R] 828-926-6013
  maggievalleyclub.com
Magnolia Greens Golf Plantation, *Leland* .... 27 [P] 910-383-0999
  magnoliagreens.com
Majestic Pines G&CC, *Kenansville* .... 18 [P] 910-296-0919
Mallard Head CC, *Mooresville* .... 18 [P] 704-664-7031
  mallardheadcc.com/mhcc
Maple Leaf GC, *Kernersville* .... 18 [P] 336-769-9122
Marion Lake Club, *Nebo* .... 18 [P] 828-652-6232
  marionlakeclub.com
Masonboro CC, *Wilmington* .... 18 [V] 910-397-9162
  masonborocountryclub.com
Matthew Creek Par 3, *Elizabeth City* .... 9 [P] 252-330-2229
McCanless GC, *Salisbury* .... 18 [P] 704-637-1235
  themacgc.com
Meadow Greens CC, *Eden* .... 18 [P] 336-623-6381
  meadowgreens.com
Meadowbrook GC, *Rutherfordton* .... 18 [P] 828-863-2690
  meadowbrookgolfclub.com
Meadowlands GC, *Winston Salem* .... 18 [P] 336-769-1011
  meadowlandsgolfclub.com
Meadowlands GC, *Calabash* .... 18 [R] 910-287-7529
  meadowlandsgolf.com
Members Club At St James Plantation, *Southport* 27 [S] 910-253-9500
  theclubsatstjames.com
Methodist Univ GC, *Fayetteville* .... 18 [N] 910-630-7144
  methodist.edu/pgm
Mid Pines Inn & GC, *Southern Pines* .... 18 [R] 910-692-9362
  pineneedles-midpines.com
Mid South Club, *Southern Pines* .... 18 [V] 910-695-3193
  talamore.com
Midland CC, *Pinehurst* .... 9 [S] 910-295-3241
  pinehurstarearealty.com
Mill Creek CC, *Franklin* .... 18 [S] 828-524-6458
  millcreekcountryclub.com
Mill Creek GC, *Mebane* .... 18 [S] 919-563-4653
  millcreekgc.com
Mill Run GC, *Moyock* .... 18 [S] 252-435-6455
  millrungolfclub.us
Mimosa Hills GC, *Morganton* .... 18 [V] 828-437-2967
  mimosahills.org
Minnesott G&CC, *Arapahoe* .... 18 [S] 252-249-0813
  minnesottgolf.com

NORTH CAROLINA

Monroe CC, *Monroe* .... 18 [M] 704-282-4661
  monroenc.org
Monroeton GC, *Reidsville* .... 18 [P] 336-342-1043
Mooresville GC, *Mooresville* .... 18 [M] 704-663-2539
  ci.mooresville.nc.us
Morehead City CC, *Morehead City* .... 18 [V] 252-726-4917
  moreheadcitycc.com
Mount Airy CC, *Mt Airy* .... 9 [V] 336-786-2577
Mountain Air CC, *Burnsville* .... 18 [V] 828-682-4600
  mountainaircc.com
Mountain Aire GC, *West Jefferson* .... 18 [P] 336-877-4716
  mountainaire.com
Mountain Glen GC, *Newland* .... 18 [P] 828-733-5804
  mountainglengolfclub.com
Mountaintop Golf & Lake Club, *Cashiers* ... 18 [V] 828-743-4758
  mountaintopgolfclub.com
Mt Brook GC, *Albemarle* .... 18 [P] 704-983-4653
Mt Mitchell GC, *Burnsville* .... 18 [R] 828-675-5454
  mountmitchellgolfresort.com
Myers Park CC, *Charlotte* .... 18 [V] 704-376-0745
  myersparkcc.com
Myrick Hills CC, *Littleton* .... 18 [V] 252-586-4066
Nags Head Golf Links, *Nags Head* .... 18 [R] 252-441-8073
  nagsheadgolflinks.com
Natures Walk At Chinquapin, *Glenville* .... 9 [V] 828-743-5878
  chinquapinnc.com
New Bern G&CC, *New Bern* .... 18 [V] 252-637-4061
  nbgcc.com
New River CC, *Sparta* .... 18 [P] 336-372-4869
  newrivercountryclub.com
North Carolina State Univ Club, *Raleigh* ...... 9 [N] 919-828-0308
  ncsuclub.com
North Ridge CC, *Raleigh* .... 36 [V] 919-847-0796
  northridgecountryclub.org
North River Club, *Beaufort* .... 18 [R] 252-728-5525
  northrivergolfclub.com
North Shore CC, *Sneads Ferry* .... 18 [P] 910-327-2410
  northshorecountryclub.com
Northgreen CC, *Rocky Mount* .... 18 [S] 252-446-7224
  northgreengolf.com
Northstone CC, *Huntersville* .... 18 [V] 704-948-4286
  northstoneclub.com
Northwoods GC, *Asheville* .... 9 [P] 828-253-1659
Oak Hills GC, *Charlotte* .... 18 [P] 704-394-2834
  oakhillsinc.com
Oak Hollow GC, *High Point* .... 18 [M] 336-883-3260
  oakhollowgc.com
Oak Island GC, *Oak Island* .... 18 [P] 910-278-5275
  oakislandgc.com
Oak Valley GC, *Advance* .... 18 [S] 336-940-2000
  oakvalleygolfclub.com
Oakwoods CC, *Wilkesboro* .... 18 [V] 336-838-3011
  oakwoodscc.com
Occoneechee GC, *Hillsborough* .... 18 [P] 919-732-3435
  occoneechee.com
Ocean Rdg Plantation-Leopards Chase ,
  Ocean Isle Bch .... 18 [S] 800-233-1801
  big-cats.com
Ocean Ridge Plantation, *Ocean Isle Beach* ... 36 [S] 910-287-1703
  big-cats.com
Old Chatham GC, *Durham* .... 18 [V] 919-361-1400
  oldchathamgolf.com
Old Edwards Club, *Cashiers* .... 18 [P] 828-526-8044
  oldedwardsinn.com

Old Fort GC, *Winnabow* .... 18 [P] 910-371-9940
Old Fort GC, *Old Fort* .... 9 [P] 828-668-4256
Old North State Club, *New London* .... 18 [V] 336-461-2610
  oldnorthstateclub.com
Old Town Club, *Winston Salem* .... 18 [V] 336-722-1584
  oldtownclub.org
Olde Beau GC, *Roaring Gap* .... 18 [R] 336-363-3333
  oldebeau.com
Olde Homeplace GC, *Winston Salem* .... 18 [P] 336-769-1076
  oldehomeplacegolfclub.com
Olde Liberty G&CC, *Youngsville* .... 18 [S] 919-554-4690
  oldelibertygolf.com
Olde Point G&CC, *Hampstead* .... 18 [S] 910-270-2403
  oldepointgolf.com
Olde Sycamore Golf Plantation, *Charlotte* ... 18 [S] 704-573-1000
  oldesycamoregolf.com
Orchard Hills GC, *Granite Falls* .... 18 [S] 828-728-3560
Orchard Trace GC, *Hendersonville* .... 18 [P] 828-685-1006
Oyster Bay Golf Links, *Sunset Beach* .... 18 [P] 910-579-3528
  legendsgolf.com
Par Three- Bistro, *Winston-Salem* .... 9 [P] 336-924-5850
Paradise Point GC, *Camp Lejeune* .... 36 [A] 910-451-5445
  mccslejeune.com/golf
Paradise Valley GC, *Charlotte* .... 18 [P] 704-548-1808
  charlottepublicgolf.com
Paschal GC, *Wake Forest* .... 9 [P] 919-556-5861
Peachtree Hills CC, *Spring Hope* .... 9 [P] 252-478-5745
Pearl Golf Links, *Calabash* .... 36 [P] 910-579-8132
  thepearlgolf.com
Pebble Creek GC, *Indian Trail* .... 18 [P] 704-821-7276
  pebblecreekgolfpar3.com
Pennrose Park CC, *Reidsville* .... 9 [V] 336-349-5163
  pennrosepark.com
Pilot Knob Park CC, *Pilot Mountain* .... 18 [P] 336-368-2828
  pilotknobparkgolf.org
Pine Brook CC, *Winston Salem* .... 18 [V] 336-767-0034
  pinebrookcc.com
Pine Burr Golf, *Lillington* .... 18 [P] 910-893-5788
Pine Grove GC, *Shelby* .... 18 [P] 704-487-0455
  pinegrovegolfclub.com
Pine Hollow GC, *Clayton* .... 18 [P] 919-553-4554
  pinehollowgolf.com
Pine Island CC, *Charlotte* .... 18 [V] 704-394-1011
  pineislandcc.com
Pine Knolls GC, *Kernersville* .... 18 [P] 336-993-5478
  pineknolls.com
Pine Lake CC, *Charlotte* .... 18 [V] 704-545-5213
  pinelakecountryclub.com
Pine Mountain GC, *Connelly Springs* .... 18 [P] 828-433-4950
  realtyassociates.com
Pine Needles Lodge & GC, *Southern Pines* ... 18 [R] 910-692-7111
  pineneedles-midpines.com
Pine Ridge Classic GC, *Mt Airy* .... 18 [P] 336-320-2233
Pine Valley GC, *Wilmington* .... 18 [V] 910-791-3971
  pvccnc.com
Pinecrest CC, *Lumberton* .... 18 [P] 910-738-6541
Pinehurst Resort & CC, *Pinehurst* .... 90 [R] 910-235-8507
  pinehurst.com
Pinehurst Resort & CC #8, *Pinehurst* .... 18 [R] 910-235-8760
  pinehurst.com
Pinehurst Resort & CC No 6, *Village of Pinehurst* . 18 [R] 910-235-8507
  pinehurst.com

[S] = SEMI-PRIVATE   [V] = PRIVATE   [U] = UNIVERSITY   [N] = UNIVERSITY-PRIVATE

NORTH CAROLINA
Golf Yellow Pages, 18th Edition

Pinehurst Resort & CC No 7, *Village of Pinehurst* .18 [R] 910-235-8507
  pinehurst.com
Pinewild CC of Pinehurst, *Pinehurst* .... 48 [S] 910-295-5145
  pinewildcc.com
Pinewood CC, *Asheboro* .... 18 [V] 336-629-4266
  pinewoodclub.com
Piney Point GC, *Norwood* .... 18 [P] 704-474-3985
  pineypointgolfclub.com
Plantation GC, *Reidsville* .... 18 [P] 336-342-6191
  plantationgolfclub.org
Players Club At St James Plantation, *Southport* .. 18 [S] 910-457-0049
  theclubsatstjames.com
Pleasant Ridge GC, *Greensboro* .... 18 [P] 336-668-7107
Plymouth CC, *Plymouth* .... 9 [V] 252-793-3034
Ponderosa GC, *Stoneville* .... 9 [P] 336-573-9025
Ponderosa GC, *Cameron* .... 18 [P] 919-499-4013
Porters Neck CC, *Wilmington* .... 18 [S] 910-686-1177
  portersneckcountryclub.com
Prestonwood CC, *Cary* .... 54 [V] 919-467-9601
  prestonwoodcc.com
Providence CC, *Charlotte* .... 18 [V] 704-846-8475
  providencecc.com
Pudding Ridge GC, *Mocksville* .... 18 [P] 336-940-4653
  puddingridge.com
Quail Hollow Club, *Charlotte* .... 18 [V] 704-552-1726
  quailhollowclub.com
Quail Ridge GC, *Sanford* .... 18 [P] 919-776-6623
  quailridgegolfcourse.com
Quaker Creek GC, *Mebane* .... 18 [P] 336-578-5789
  quakercreekgolf.com
Quaker Meadows GC, *Morganton* .... 27 [P] 828-437-2677
  qmgolf.com
Quaker Neck GC, *Trenton* .... 18 [P] 252-224-5736
Quarry Hills GC, *Graham* .... 18 [P] 336-578-2602
  quarryhillsgolfclub.com
Rain Tree Par 3, *Jonesville* .... 9 [P] 336-835-4153
Raintree CC, *Charlotte* .... 36 [V] 704-541-8880
  raintreecountryclub.com
Raleigh CC, *Raleigh* .... 18 [V] 919-231-6055
  raleighcc.com
Raleigh Golf Assoc, *Raleigh* .... 27 [P] 919-772-9987
  rgagolf.net
Red Bird Golf Links, *Sapphire* .... 9 [P] 828-743-1991
Red Bridge G&CC, *Locust* .... 18 [S] 704-781-5231
  redbridgegolfclub.com
Red Fox CC, *Tryon* .... 18 [P] 828-894-8251
  redfoxcc.com
Reedy Creek GC, *Four Oaks* .... 18 [P] 919-934-7502
  reedycreekgolf.com
Reems Creek GC, *Weaverville* .... 18 [P] 828-645-4393
  reemscreekgolf.com
Renaissance Park GC, *Charlotte* .... 18 [M] 704-357-3373
  charlottepublicgolf.com
Reserve Club At St James Plantation, *Southport* 18 [V] 910-253-5100
  theclubsatstjames.com
Reynolds Park GC, *Winston Salem* .... 18 [M] 336-650-7660
  reynoldspark.americangolf.com
Richmond Pines CC, *Rockingham* .... 18 [P] 910-997-2300
  richmondpines.com
Riegelwood CC, *Riegelwood* .... 9 [P] 910-655-3333
River Bend G&CC, *New Bern* .... 18 [P] 252-638-2819
  golfriverbendcc.com

River Bend YMCA GC, *Shelby* .... 18 [P] 704-482-4286
  clevecoymca.org
River Crest GC, *Hickory* .... 18 [P] 828-495-0017
  rivercrestgolfclub.net
River G&CC, *Louisburg* .... 18 [S] 252-478-3832
  rivergolf.net
River Landing, *Wallace* .... 36 [V] 910-285-6693
  riverlanding.com
River Landing At Sandy Ridge, *Colfax* .... 9 [P] 336-668-1171
  riverlandingsr.org
River Mont GC, *Siloam* .... 18 [P] 336-374-2384
River Oaks GC at lake Norman, *Statesville* .... 18 [S] 704-883-8724
  golfriveroaks.com
River Ridge GC, *Raleigh* .... 18 [P] 919-661-8374
  golfriverridge.com
River Run CC, *Davidson* .... 18 [V] 704-896-7355
  riverruncc.com
River View GC, *Pine Hall* .... 9 [P] 336-548-6908
Rivers Edge GC, *Shallotte* .... 18 [S] 910-755-3434
  river18.com
Riverside CC, *Robbins* .... 18 [P] 910-464-3686
Riverside CC, *Maxton* .... 18 [P] 910-521-8433
Riverwood G&AC, *Clayton* .... 27 [S] 919-550-1919
  rwgac.com
Roanoke CC, *Williamston* .... 18 [V] 252-792-2502
  roanokecountryclub.net
Roaring Gap Club, *Roaring Gap* .... 18 [V] 336-363-5042
  roaringgapclub.com
Robersonville CC, *Robersonville* .... 9 [V] 252-795-4212
Rock Barn Golf & Spa, *Conover* .... 36 [S] 828-459-9279
  rockbarn.com
Rock Creek CC, *North Wilkesboro* .... 18 [P] 336-696-2146
Rock Creek CC, *Jacksonville* .... 18 [P] 910-324-5151
  golfatrockcreek.com
Rockfish CC, *Wallace* .... 18 [P] 910-285-2744
Rocky River GC At Concord, *Concord* .... 18 [M] 704-455-1200
  rockyrivergolf.com
Rolling Hills CC, *Monroe* .... 18 [V] 704-283-8201
  rollinghillscountryclub.org
Rolling Hills GC, *Salisbury* .... 18 [P] 704-633-8125
Roxboro CC, *Roxboro* .... 18 [P] 336-599-2332
  roxborocountryclub.com
Royster Memorial GC, *Shelby* .... 9 [M] 704-484-6823
  cityofshelby.com
Rumbling Bald-Lake Lure-Apple Valley, *Lake Lure* 18 [R] 828-625-3043
  rumblingbald.com
Rumbling Bald-Lake Lure-Bald Mountain,
  Lake Lure .... 18 [R] 828-625-3043
  rumblingbald.com
Rutherfordton GC, *Rutherfordton* .... 9 [P] 828-287-3406
Salem Glen GC, *Clemmons* .... 18 [P] 336-712-1010
  salemglen.com
Sandpiper Bay G&CC, *Sunset Beach* .... 27 [P] 910-579-9120
  sandpipergolf.com
Sandy Creek GC, *Staley* .... 18 [P] 336-622-1802
Sandy Ridge CC, *Dunn* .... 18 [P] 910-892-6424
Sanford Muni GC, *Sanford* .... 18 [M] 919-775-8320
  sanfordnc.net
Sapona CC, *Lexington* .... 18 [V] 336-956-6245
  saponacc.com
Sapphire National GC, *Sapphire* .... 18 [R] 828-743-1174
  sapphirenational.com

[A] = MILITARY   [M] = MUNICIPAL   [P] = PUBLIC   [R] = RESORT

NORTH CAROLINA

Course	Location	Holes	Type	Phone
Scotch Hall Preserve,	Merry Hill	18	[S]	252-482-5300
scotchhallpreserve.com				
Scotch Meadows CC,	Laurinburg	18	[V]	910-276-0169
scotchmeadowscc.tripod.com				
Scotfield CC,	Enfield	18	[V]	252-826-3218
scotfieldcountryclub.com				
Sea Scape Golf Links,	Kitty Hawk	18	[P]	252-261-2158
seascapegolf.com				
Sea Trail Golf Links - Jones/Byrd,	Sunset Beach	36	[R]	910-287-1122
seatrail.com				
Sea Trail Golf Links - Maples,	Sunset Beach	18	[R]	910-287-1122
seatrail.com				
Sedgefield CC,	Greensboro	18	[V]	336-299-5324
sedgefieldcc.org				
Sequoyah National GC,	Whittier	18	[R]	828-497-3000
sequoyahnational.com				
Seven Falls Golf & River Club,	Hendersonville	9	[V]	828-233-1070
sevenfallsnc.com				
Seven Lakes CC,	Seven Lakes	18	[V]	910-673-1092
sevenlakescountryclub.com				
Shamrock GC,	Burlington	18	[P]	336-227-8566
Sherwood Forest GC,	Brevard	18	[P]	828-884-7825
Shillelagh GC,	Burlington	18	[P]	336-449-4882
Siler City CC,	Siler City	18	[V]	919-742-3721
silercitycountryclub.com				
Silo Run GC,	Boonville	18	[P]	336-367-3133
silorungolf.com				
Silver Creek GC,	Swansboro	18	[P]	252-393-8058
golfemeraldisle.com				
Silver Creek Plantation CC,	Morganton	18	[P]	828-584-6911
silvercreekplantation.com				
Skybrook GC,	Huntersville	18	[P]	704-948-6611
skybrookgolf.com				
Sleepy Creek GC,	Dudley	18	[P]	919-734-6661
Smoky Mountain CC,	Whittier	18	[P]	828-497-7622
carolinamountaingolf.com				
Somerset GC,	North Wilkesboro	9	[P]	336-667-9595
Sound of Freedom Cherry Point GC,	Cherry Point	18	[A]	252-466-3044
mccscherrypoint.com				
Sourwood Forest GC,	Snow Camp	18	[P]	336-376-8166
sourwoodgolf.com				
South Granville CC,	Creedmoor	18	[V]	919-528-0003
sgcconline.com				
South Harbour Golf Links,	Southport	18	[R]	910-454-0905
oakislandnc.com				
Southern Pines CC,	Southern Pines	18	[S]	910-692-6551
southernpinesgc.com				
Southern Tee GC,	Fletcher	18	[P]	828-687-7273
Southern Wayne GC,	Mt Olive	18	[P]	919-658-4269
Southwick GC,	Graham	18	[P]	336-227-2582
southwickgolf.com				
Springdale CC,	Canton	18	[P]	828-235-8451
springdalegolf.com				
St Augustines College GC & Rec-Meadowbrook,				
Garner		9	[U]	919-516-5010
Star Hill GC,	Cape Carteret	27	[P]	252-393-8111
starhillgolf.com				
Starmount Forest GC,	Greensboro	18	[V]	336-299-0427
starmountforest.com				
Statesville CC,	Statesville	18	[V]	704-873-8376
statesvillecountryclub.com				
Stone Mountain GC,	Traphill	18	[R]	336-957-4422
stonemountainclub.com				
Stonebridge GC,	Monroe	18	[P]	704-283-8998
stonebridgegolfclub.com				
Stonewall GC,	Germanton	18	[P]	336-591-4653
Stoney Creek GC,	Whitsett	18	[P]	336-449-5688
stoneycreekgolf.com				
Sugar Mountain GC,	Sugar Mountain	18	[M]	828-898-6464
seesugar.com				
Sunset Hills GC,	Charlotte	18	[M]	704-399-0980
charlottepublicgolf.com				
Taberna CC,	New Bern	18	[V]	252-514-2854
tabernacc.com				
Talamore GC,	Southern Pines	18	[P]	910-692-5884
talamoregolfresort.com				
Tanglewood GC,	Clemmons	54	[R]	336-778-6320
tanglewoodpark.org				
The Beech Mountain Club,	Beech Mountain	18	[V]	828-387-2372
beechmtnclub.org				
The Buccaneer Club,	Burgaw	18	[S]	910-259-2809
The Carolina Club,	Whispering Pines	18	[S]	910-949-2811
thecarolina.com				
The CC of Sapphire Valley,	Sapphire Valley	18	[V]	828-743-2462
ccsapphirevalley.org				
The CC of the Crystal Coast,	Pine Knoll Shores	18	[P]	252-726-1034
cccrystalcoast.com				
The Challenge GC,	Graham	18	[S]	336-578-5070
thechallenge.com				
The Cliffs At Walnut Cove,	Arden	18	[V]	828-687-7965
cliffscommunities.com				
The Club At Longview,	Waxhaw	18	[V]	704-443-2520
theclubatlongview.com				
The Coves At Round Mountain,	Lenoir	18	[P]	828-754-1992
thecovesnc.com				
The Crescent GC,	Salisbury	18	[S]	704-647-0025
crescentgolfclub.com				
The Crossings at Grove Park,	Durham	18	[P]	919-598-8686
crossingsgolf.com				
The Currituck Club,	Corolla	18	[R]	252-453-9400
thecurrituckgolfclub.com				
The Divide GC,	Matthews	18	[P]	704-882-8088
thedividegolfclub.com				
The Elk River Club,	Banner Elk	18	[V]	828-898-9773
elkriverclub.com				
The Grove Park Inn Resort & Spa,	Asheville	18	[R]	828-252-2711
groveparkinn.com				
The Hasentree Club,	Wake Forest	18	[V]	919-569-0256
hasentreeclub.com				
The Lakes CC,	Southport	18	[S]	910-845-2625
thelakescountryclub.com				
The Links At Cotton Valley GC,	Tarboro	18	[P]	252-824-0818
thelinksatcottonvalley.com				
The Links At Plantation Harbor,	Havelock	18	[S]	252-444-4653
The Long Creek Club,	Bethania	18	[P]	336-924-5226
longcreekgolf.com				
The National GC,	Pinehurst	18	[S]	910-295-4300
nationalgolfclub.com				
The Neuse GC,	Clayton	18	[P]	919-550-0550
neusegolf.com				
The Palisades CC,	Charlotte	18	[V]	704-504-0099
thepalisadescc.com				
The Peninsula Club,	Cornelius	18	[V]	704-896-7080
thepeninsulaclub.com				
The Pines At Elizabeth City,	Elizabeth City	18	[S]	252-335-0278
thepinesatelizabethcity.com				

[S] = SEMI-PRIVATE   [V] = PRIVATE   [U] = UNIVERSITY   [N] = UNIVERSITY-PRIVATE

NORTH CAROLINA

Golf Yellow Pages, 18th Edition

The Pit Golf Links, *Aberdeen* .... 18 [P] 910-944-1600
  pitgolf.com
The Point Lake & GC, *Mooresville* .... 18 [V] 704-663-4653
  the-pointclub.com
The Pointe GC, *Powells Point* .... 18 [P] 252-491-8388
  thepointegolfclub.com
The Preserve At Jordan Lake GC, *Chapel Hill* .... 18 [S] 919-542-5501
  thepreservegolf.com
The Ridges CC, *Hayesville* .... 18 [P] 828-389-4111
  hamptongolfclubs.com
The Sound Golf Links, *Hertford* .... 18 [R] 252-426-5555
  soundgolflinks.com
The Tillery Tradition CC, *Mt Gilead* .... 18 [P] 910-439-5578
  tillerytradition.com
The Tradition GC, *Charlotte* .... 18 [M] 704-503-7529
  thetraditiongolfclub.com
The UNC Finley GC, *Chapel Hill* .... 18 [U] 919-962-2349
  uncfinley.com
The Waynesville Inn Golf Resort & Spa,
  Waynesville .... 27 [R] 828-452-4617
  thewaynesvilleinn.com
Third Creek GC, *Statesville* .... 9 [P] 704-873-1098
Thistle GC, *Sunset Beach* .... 27 [P] 910-575-8700
  thistlegolf.com
Thorndale CC, *Oxford* .... 9 [V] 919-693-7404
Three Eagles GC, *Seymour Johnson AFB* .... 18 [A] 919-722-0395
  sjafbservices.com/tegc/golf.htm
Tigers Eye Golf Links, *Ocean Isle Beach* ..... 18 [R] 910-287-7227
  big-cats.com
TimberLake GC, *Clinton* .... 18 [P] 910-596-2211
  timberlakegolfclub.com
Tobacco Road GC, *Sanford* .... 18 [P] 919-775-1940
  tobaccoroadgolf.com
Topsail Greens GC, *Hampstead* .... 18 [P] 910-270-2883
  topsailgreens.com
Tot Hill Farm GC, *Asheboro* .... 18 [P] 336-857-4455
  tothillfarm.com
Town of Lake Lure Muni GC, *Lake Lure* .... 9 [M] 828-625-4472
  townoflakelure.com
TPC Piper Glen, *Charlotte* .... 18 [V] 704-846-1515
  tpcpiperglen.com
TPC Wakefield Plantation, *Raleigh* .... 27 [V] 919-488-5200
  tpcwakefieldplantation.com
Treyburn CC, *Durham* .... 18 [V] 919-620-0055
  treyburncc.com
Trillium Links, *Cashiers* .... 18 [V] 828-743-4251
  trilliumnc.com
Tryon CC, *Tryon* .... 9 [V] 828-859-9561
  tryoncountryclub.com
Tuscarora Greens, *Winton* .... 18 [P] 252-358-4671
  tuscaroragreens.com
Twelve Oaks GC, *Holly Springs* .... 18 [S] 919-557-6850
  12oaksnc.com
Twin Cedars GC, *Mocksville* .... 18 [P] 336-751-5824
Twin Lakes GC, *Chapel Hill* .... 9 [P] 919-933-1024
  golf-twinlakes.com
Twin Oaks GC, *Statesville* .... 18 [P] 704-872-3979
Twin Valley CC, *Wadesboro* .... 18 [V] 704-694-2336
Umstead Pines Golf & Swim At Willowhaven,
  Durham .... 18 [P] 919-383-1022
  willowhavencc.com
Upland Trace GC, *Raeford* .... 18 [P] 910-875-3524
  uplandtracegolfcourse.com
Uwharrie G&CC, *Asheboro* .... 18 [P] 336-857-2651

Valley Pine CC, *Lasker* .... 18 [S] 252-539-4124
Verdict Ridge G&CC, *Denver* .... 18 [P] 704-489-1206
  verdictridge.com
Wade Hampton GC, *Cashiers* .... 18 [V] 828-743-5465
  wadehamptongc.com
Walnut Creek GC, *Goldsboro* .... 18 [V] 919-778-2363
  walnutcreekcountryclub.org
Walnut Wood GC, *Julian* .... 18 [P] 336-697-8140
Warrenton GC, *Warrenton* .... 9 [P] 252-257-1909
Warrior GC, *China Grove* .... 18 [P] 704-856-0871
  warriorgolf.com
Washington Y&CC, *Washington* .... 18 [V] 252-946-3245
  wyccnc.com
Wedgewood GC, *Wilson* .... 18 [M] 252-237-4761
  wilsonnc.org
Wendell CC, *Wendell* .... 18 [P] 919-365-7337
  wendellcc.com
Westport GC, *Denver* .... 18 [S] 704-489-8088
  westportgc.com
Whispering Woods, *Whispering Pines* .... 18 [S] 910-949-4653
  whisperingwoodsgolf.com
White Oak Par 3, *Alexis* .... 18 [P] 704-263-9990
White Pines CC, *Mt Airy* .... 9 [P] 336-786-6616
Whiteville CC, *Whiteville* .... 9 [V] 910-642-3623
Wil Mar GC, *Raleigh* .... 18 [S] 919-266-1800
  wil-margolfclub.com
Wildcat Cliffs CC, *Highlands* .... 18 [V] 828-526-2164
  wildcatcliffscountryclub.com
Wildwood Green GC, *Raleigh* .... 18 [P] 919-846-8376
  wildwoodgreen.com
Willow Creek GC, *Boone* .... 9 [R] 828-963-6865
  willowvalley-resort.com
Willow Lakes GC, *Pope AFB* .... 18 [A] 910-394-4653
  43dservices.com
Willow Springs CC, *Wilson* .... 18 [P] 252-291-5171
  willowspringscc.com
Wilmington Muni GC, *Wilmington* .... 18 [M] 910-791-0558
  wilmingtonmuni.com
Wilshire GC, *Winston Salem* .... 18 [P] 336-788-7016
Wilson CC, *Wilson* .... 18 [V] 252-291-1144
  wilsoncc.org
Winding Creek GC, *Thomasville* .... 18 [M] 336-475-5580
  ci.thomasville.nc.us
Winston Lake GC, *Winston Salem* .... 18 [M] 336-727-2703
  cityofws.org/recreation
Wolf Creek GC, *Reidsville* .... 18 [P] 336-349-7660
Wolf Laurel CC, *Mars Hill* .... 18 [R] 828-680-9772
  wolflaurelcountryclub.com
Woodbridge Golf Links, *Kings Mountain* .... 18 [S] 704-482-0353
Woodlake CC, *Vass* .... 36 [S] 910-245-4031
  woodlakecc.com
Yadkin CC, *Yadkinville* .... 18 [P] 336-679-8590
Zebulon CC, *Zebulon* .... 18 [P] 919-269-8311

NORTH DAKOTA

Apple Creek CC, *Bismarck* .... 18 [V] 701-223-5955
  applecreekcountryclub.com
Apple Grove CC, *Minot* .... 9 [P] 701-852-5460
Ashley CC, *Ashley* .... 9 [P] 701-288-9566
Beaver Valley GC, *Wishek* .... 9 [P] 701-452-2128
Berthold GC, *Berthold* .... 9 [P] 701-453-3158
Birchwood GC, *Bottineau* .... 9 [P] 701-263-4186
  birchwoodgolf.com

[A] = MILITARY   [M] = MUNICIPAL   [P] = PUBLIC   [R] = RESORT

NORTH DAKOTA

Golf Yellow Pages, 18th Edition

Bjornson Park GC, *Valley City* ....9 [M] 701-845-5452
   vcparks.com
Black Sand GC, *Beulah* ....9 [M] 701-873-2929
   lewisandclarkgolftrail.com
Bois De Sioux GC, *Wahpeton* ....18 [P] 701-642-3673
Bottineau CC, *Bottineau* ....9 [P] 701-228-3857
   golfbcc.com
Bowbells CC, *Bowbells* ....9 [P] 701-377-2601
Bully Pulpit GC, *Medora* ....18 [P] 701-623-4653
   medora.com
Cando GC, *Cando* ....9 [P] 701-968-3813
   candond.com
Cavalier CC, *Cavalier* ....9 [P] 701-265-4506
Columbus GC, *Columbus* ....9 [M] 701-939-4005
Cooperstown CC, *Cooperstown* ....9 [M] 701-797-2599
Cottonwood GC, *Casselton* ....9 [P] 701-347-9882
Cottonwood GC, *Steele* ....9 [M] 701-475-2416
Crosby CC, *Crosby* ....9 [M] 701-965-6157
Crossroads GC, *Glen Ullin* ....9 [S] 701-348-3645
Crossroads Golf & Rec Parkway, *Carrington* ....18 [R] 701-652-2601
   crossroadsgolf.com
Dakota Winds GC, *Hankinson* ....36 [R] 701-634-3000
   dakotamagic.com
Devils Lake Town & CC, *Devils Lake* ....18 [S] 701-662-2408
   golfdevilslake.com
Dr Blatherwick GC, *Parshall* ....9 [P] 701-862-3752
Drake GC, *Drake* ....9 [P] 701-465-3049
Drayton GC, *Drayton* ....9 [M] 701-454-6547
Eagle Ridge GC, *Williston* ....18 [P] 701-572-6500
   golfateagleridge.com
Edgeley Splicken CC, *Edgeley* ....9 [S] 701-493-2884
Edgewater CC, *New Town* ....9 [P] 701-627-9407
Edgewood Muni GC, *Fargo* ....18 [M] 701-232-2824
   fargogolf.net
El Zagal GC, *Fargo* ....9 [M] 701-232-8156
   fargogolf.net
Ellendale CC, *Ellendale* ....9 [P] 701-349-4292
   ellendalend.com
Enderlin GC, *Enderlin* ....9 [P] 701-437-2369
Fair Oaks GC, *Grafton* ....9 [P] 701-352-3956
Fairmont GC, *Fairmount* ....9 [V] 701-474-5789
Fargo CC, *Fargo* ....27 [V] 701-237-6746
   fargocc.com
Fessenden GC, *Fessenden* ....9 [P] 701-547-3598
Forman GC, *Forman* ....9 [M] 701-724-3411
Gackle GC, *Gackle* ....9 [P] 701-485-3542
Garden Gate GC, *Dunseith* ....9 [M] 701-244-5211
   rolettecounty.com
Garrison GC, *Garrison* ....9 [M] 701-337-5420
Gateway Cities GC, *Portal* ....9 [P] 701-926-3145
Goose River GC, *Hillsboro* ....9 [P] 701-636-5556
   gooserivergolfclub.com
Grand Forks CC, *Grand Forks* ....18 [V] 701-772-3912
   gfcountryclub.com
Harvey CC, *Harvey* ....9 [S] 701-324-2069
Hawktree GC, *Bismarck* ....18 [P] 701-355-0995
   hawktree.com
Hazen GC, *Hazen* ....9 [P] 701-748-2011
Heart River Muni GC, *Dickinson* ....18 [M] 701-456-2050
   dickinsonparks.org
Hettinger GC, *Hettinger* ....9 [P] 701-567-2339
Hillcrest CC, *Park River* ....9 [P] 701-284-6733

Hillcrest Muni Golf, *Jamestown* ....18 [M] 701-252-4320
   jamestownparksandrec.com
Hope GC, *Hope* ....9 [P] 701-945-2572
Jack Hoeven Wee Links GC, *Minot* ....9 [P] 701-857-1570
   weelinks.org
Jamestown CC, *Jamestown* ....18 [P] 701-252-8448
   jamestowncountryclub.com
Kenmare CC, *Kenmare* ....9 [P] 701-385-4384
Kings Walk, *Grand Forks* ....18 [M] 701-787-5464
   kingswalk.org
Kulm CC, *Kulm* ....9 [S] 701-269-3456
   kulmcc.com
La Moure CC, *Lamoure* ....9 [M] 701-883-4238
Lakeview GC, *Milnor* ....9 [M] 701-427-5280
Lakota Rock Creek GC, *Lakota* ....9 [M] 701-247-2580
   lakota-nd.com
Langdon CC, *Langdon* ....9 [P] 701-256-5938
Lansford GC, *Lansford* ....9 [P] 701-784-5585
Larimore GC, *Larimore* ....9 [P] 701-343-2201
Leeds GC, *Leeds* ....9 [P] 701-466-2858
Leonard CC, *Leonard* ....9 [P] 701-645-2582
   leonardcc.com
Lidgerwood GC, *Lidgerwood* ....9 [S] 701-538-4312
Lincoln Park Muni GC, *Grand Forks* ....9 [M] 701-746-2788
   gfparks.org
Linton CC, *Linton* ....9 [P] 701-254-9093
Lisbon Bissell GC, *Lisbon* ....9 [P] 701-683-4510
Louse Creek GC, *Flasher* ....9 [P] 701-597-3914
Mandan Muni GC, *Mandan* ....9 [M] 701-667-3272
   mandanparks.com
Manvel Rivers Edge GC, *Manvel* ....9 [P] 701-696-8268
Maple River GC, *Mapleton* ....18 [P] 701-282-5415
   maplerivergolfclub.com
Mayville GC, *Mayville* ....9 [M] 701-788-3659
McVille CC, *McVille* ....9 [M] 701-322-5625
   mcville.com
Medicine Hole GC, *Killdeer* ....9 [P] 701-764-4653
   medicineholegolfcourse.com
Memorial Park CC, *Lamoure* ....9 [S] 701-883-4296
   memorialparkcc.com
Michigan Duffers GC, *Michigan* ....9 [P] 701-259-2488
   michigannd.com
Minot CC, *Minot* ....18 [P] 701-839-6169
   minotcountryclub.com
Mohall CC, *Mohall* ....9 [P] 701-756-6948
Mott GC, *Mott* ....9 [M] 701-824-2825
Napoleon CC, *Napoleon* ....9 [P] 701-754-2903
New England GC, *New England* ....9 [M] 701-579-4887
New Rockford GC, *New Rockford* ....9 [M] 701-947-2385
New Salem GC, *New Salem* ....9 [M] 701-843-7828
Northwood GC, *Northwood* ....9 [M] 701-587-5373
Oakes GC, *Oakes* ....9 [M] 701-742-2405
Osgood GC, *Fargo* ....9 [M] 701-356-3070
   fargogolf.net
Oxbow G&CC, *Oxbow* ....18 [V] 701-588-4666
   oxbowcc.com
Painted Woods GC, *Washburn* ....9 [M] 701-462-8480
Pebble Creek Muni GC, *Bismarck* ....9 [M] 701-223-3600
   bisparks.org
Pembina GC, *Pembina* ....9 [P] 701-825-6619
Pheasant Country GC, *South Heart* ....18 [M] 701-677-4653
   pheasantcountrygolf.com

[S] = SEMI-PRIVATE   [V] = PRIVATE   [U] = UNIVERSITY   [N] = UNIVERSITY-PRIVATE

NORTH DAKOTA

Plainsview GC, *Grand Forks*........................9 [A] 701-747-4279
gf-services.com
Prairie West GC, *Mandan*........................18 [M] 701-667-3222
mandanparks.com
Prairiewood Muni GC, *Fargo*....................9 [M] 701-232-1445
fargogolf.net
Ray Richards GC, *Grand Forks*................9 [U] 701-777-4340
rrgc.und.edu
Riverdale GC, *Riverdale*............................9 [M] 701-654-7607
Riverwood GC, *Bismarck*........................18 [M] 701-222-6462
bisparks.org
Rolette CC, *Rolette*....................................9 [M] 701-246-3644
rolettecounty.com
Rolla CC, *Rolla*..9 [M] 701-477-6202
rolettecounty.com
Rose Creek GC, *Fargo*............................18 [M] 701-235-5100
fargogolf.net
Roughrider GC, *Minot AFB*....................9 [A] 701-723-3164
5thservices.com
Rugby GC, *Rugby*....................................9 [P] 701-776-6917
Scranton GC, *Scranton*............................9 [P] 701-275-6332
Sherwood GC, *Sherwood*......................9 [P] 701-459-2261
Souris Valley GC, *Minot*........................18 [M] 701-838-4112
Square Butte Creek GC, *Center*..............9 [P] 701-794-3623
Stanley CC, *Stanley*..................................9 [P] 701-628-2135
Starcity GC, *Velva*....................................9 [P] 701-338-2363
velva.net/golfclub
Sweetwater GC, *Bowman*......................9 [P] 701-523-5800
The Links of North Dakota, *Ray*............18 [P] 701-568-2600
thelinksofnorthdakota.com
The Springs GC, *Gwinner*......................9 [M] 701-678-3910
gwinnernd.com
Tioga G&CC, *Tioga*..................................9 [P] 701-664-3822
Tom OLeary GC, *Bismarck*....................18 [M] 701-222-6531
bisparks.org
Valley City Town & CC, *Valley City*........9 [P] 701-845-4626
Walhalla CC, *Walhalla*............................9 [P] 701-549-2357
Watford City GC, *Watford City*..............9 [M] 701-842-2074
Westhope CC, *Westhope*......................9 [P] 701-245-6553
Westridge GC, *Underwood*..................9 [P] 701-442-5555
Wildwood GC, *Burlington*....................18 [P] 701-725-4653
Williston Muni GC, *Williston*..................9 [P] 701-577-1321
willistonparks.com

OHIO

Acacia CC, *Beachwood*..........................18 [V] 440-442-2686
acaciacountryclub.com
Adams County CC, *West Union*..............9 [P] 937-544-8021
Airport GC, *Columbus*............................18 [M] 614-645-3127
columbuscitygolfcourses.com
Airport Greens GC, *Wickliffe*..................18 [P] 440-944-6164
Alliance CC, *Alliance*..............................18 [V] 330-821-2828
alliancecountryclub.com
Andover GC, *Andover*..............................9 [P] 440-293-7155
Apple Valley GC, *Howard*......................18 [P] 740-397-7664
applevalleygolfcourse.com
Aqua Marine GC, *Avon Lake*..................9 [R] 440-933-7607
Arrowhead GC, *Minster*........................18 [P] 419-628-3111
arrowhead-golf.com
Arrowhead Lakes GC, *Galena*................9 [P] 740-965-5422
arrowheadlakesgolf.com
Arrowhead Pines GC, *Lowell*................18 [P] 740-984-4165
Aston Oaks GC, *North Bend*..................18 [P] 513-467-0070
astonoaksgolfclub.com
Astorhurst CC, *Walton Hills*..................18 [P] 440-439-3636
golfastorhurst.com
Athens CC, *Athens*....................................9 [V] 740-592-1655
Atwood Lake Resort GC, *Sherrodsville*....27 [R] 330-735-2211
atwoodlakeresort.com
Auburn Springs CC, *Chagrin Falls*..........18 [P] 440-543-4448
auburnspringsgolf.com
Auglaize CC, *Defiance*............................18 [P] 419-393-2211
auglaizegolf.com
Auman Timbers GC, *Dover*....................18 [P] 330-602-6865
Aurora G&CC, *Aurora*............................18 [V] 330-562-2672
auroragc.com
Avalon G&CC - Avalon Lakes, *Warren*....18 [S] 330-856-8898
avalonlakes.com
Avalon G&CC - Squaw Creek, *Vienna*....18 [P] 330-856-8850
avalonlakes.com
Avon Dale GC, *Avon*..............................18 [P] 440-934-4398
avondale-gc.com
Avon Fields GC, *Cincinnati*....................18 [M] 513-281-0322
bad link
Avon Oaks CC, *Avon*..............................18 [V] 440-892-0660
avonoakscc.com
Barberton Brookside CC, *Barberton*......18 [P] 330-825-4539
barbertonbrookside.com
Barrington GC, *Aurora*............................18 [V] 330-995-0667
barringtongolf.org
Bay Point GC, *Marblehead*......................9 [P] 419-798-4434
baypointmarina.com
Bayview Retirees GC, *Toledo*..................9 [M] 419-726-8081
Beaver Creek Meadows GC, *Lisbon*......18 [P] 330-385-3020
Beaver Creek Par 3 GC, *Lisbon*..............9 [P] 330-385-5315
Beavercreek GC, *Beavercreek*..............18 [M] 937-320-0742
beavercreekgolfclub.com
Bec Wood Hills GC, *Rayland*................18 [S] 740-769-2698
Beckett Ridge GC, *West Chester*..........18 [P] 513-874-2840
beckettridgegolf.com
Bedford Trails GC, *Lowellville*................18 [P] 330-536-2234
bedfordtrails.com
Beech Creek GC, *Cincinnati*....................9 [P] 513-522-8700
Beechmont CC, *Cleveland*....................18 [V] 216-831-9100
beechmontcc.com
Beechwood GC, *Arcanum*....................27 [P] 937-678-4422
beechwoodgc.com
Bel Wood CC, *Morrow*..........................18 [V] 513-899-3361
belwoodcc.com
Belmont CC, *Perrysburg*........................18 [V] 419-666-1472
thebelmontcountryclub.com
Belmont Hills CC, *St Clairsville*..............18 [V] 740-695-2263
belmonthillscc.net
Bent Tree GC, *Sunbury*..........................18 [P] 740-965-5140
benttreegc.com
Berkshire Hills GC, *Chesterland*............18 [P] 440-729-9516
berkshirehills.com
Big Beaver Creek GC, *Piketon*................18 [P] 740-289-3643
Big Bend GC, *Uhrichsville*........................9 [P] 740-922-1766
Big Dawgs GC, *Minerva*........................18 [P] 330-868-3294
Big Met GC, *Fairview Park*....................18 [M] 440-331-1070
clemetparks.com
Big Walnut GC, *Sunbury*..........................9 [P] 740-524-8642
bigwalnutgolf.com

[A] = MILITARY [M] = MUNICIPAL [P] = PUBLIC [R] = RESORT

Golf Yellow Pages, 18th Edition — OHIO

Birch Run GC, *North Baltimore* ....18 [P] 419-257-3641
  birchrungolf.com
Black Brook GC, *Mentor* ....18 [M] 440-951-0010
  cityofmentor.com
Black Diamond GC, *Millersburg* ....18 [P] 330-674-6110
  blackdiamondgolfcourse.com
Blackhawk GC, *Galena* ....18 [P] 740-965-1042
  golfblackhawk.com
Blacklick Woods Metro GC, *Reynoldsburg* ....36 [M] 614-861-3193
  metroparks.net
Blackmoor GC, *Richmond* ....18 [P] 740-765-5502
  theblackmoor.com
Blue Ash GC, *Cincinnati* ....18 [M] 513-686-1280
  blueash.com
Blue Heron GC, *Medina* ....27 [P] 330-722-0227
  golfblueheron.com
Blues Creek GC, *Marysville* ....18 [P] 937-644-9686
Bluffton GC, *Bluffton* ....18 [P] 419-358-6230
  blufftongolfclub.com
Bob O Link GC, *Avon* ....36 [P] 440-934-6217
  bobolinkgolfcourse.com
Bobs Countryside GC, *Carey* ....9 [P] 419-396-6956
  bobscountrysidegolf.com
Boulder Creek GC, *Streetsboro* ....18 [P] 330-626-2828
  bouldercreekohio.com
Bowling Green CC, *Bowling Green* ....9 [P] 419-352-5546
Brandywine CC, *Peninsula* ....27 [P] 330-467-7066
  golfbrandywine.com
Brandywine CC, *Maumee* ....27 [V] 419-866-3444
  brandywinecc.com
Brass Ring GC, *Logan* ....18 [S] 740-385-3806
  brassringgolfclub.com
Breakaway Racquet & Health Club, *Celina* ....9 [P] 419-586-6688
Brentwood GC, *Grafton* ....18 [P] 440-322-9254
  golfbrentwood.com
Briardale Greens GC, *Euclid* ....18 [M] 216-289-8574
  briardalegreens.com
Briarwood GC At Wiltshire, *Broadview Heights* ..27 [P] 440-237-5271
  briarwoodgolf.net
Bridgeview GC The First Tee of Columbus, *Columbus* 9 [U] 614-471-1565
  bridgeviewgc.com
Bristolwood GC, *North Bloomfield* ....9 [P] 330-889-3771
Broadview, *Pataskala* ....9 [P] 740-927-8900
Bronzewood GC, *Kinsman* ....18 [P] 330-876-5300
  bronzwoodgolfclub.com
Brookledge GC, *Cuyahoga Falls* ....18 [M] 330-971-8416
  cityofcf.com/brookledge
Brookside CC, *Canton* ....18 [V] 330-477-6505
  brooksidecc.com
Brookside G&CC, *Columbus* ....18 [V] 614-889-2581
  brooksidegcc.com
Brookside GC, *Ashland* ....18 [M] 419-289-7933
  ashlandbrooksidegolfcourse.com
Browns Run CC, *Middletown* ....18 [V] 513-423-6291
  brownsruncc.com
Brunswick Hills GC, *Brunswick* ....18 [P] 330-225-7370
Buck Run GC, *Salem* ....9 [P] 330-537-4218
Buckeye Hills GC, *Greenfield* ....18 [P] 937-981-4136
  buckeyehillsgolf.com
Buckridge GC, *Marysville* ....18 [P] 937-642-6516
  buckridgegc.com
Bunker Hill GC, *Medina* ....18 [P] 330-722-4174
  bunkerhillgolfclub.com

Burning Tree GC, *Newark* ....18 [P] 740-522-3464
Buttermilk Falls GC, *Georgetown* ....9 [P] 937-378-3786
Cadiz CC, *Cadiz* ....18 [V] 740-942-3610
  cadizcc.com
California GC, *Cincinnati* ....18 [M] 513-231-6513
  cincygolf.org
Cambridge CC, *Byesville* ....18 [V] 740-439-2744
  cambridgecountryclub.net
Candywood GC, *Vienna* ....18 [P] 330-399-4217
  candywoodgolfclub.com
Canterbury GC, *Cleveland* ....18 [V] 216-561-1914
  canterburygc.org
Cardinal Glen GC, *Buchtel* ....18 [P] 740-753-3216
Carlisle GC, *Grafton* ....27 [P] 440-458-8011
Carroll Meadows GC, *Carrollton* ....18 [P] 330-627-2663
  carrollmeadows.com
Cassel Hills GC, *Vandalia* ....18 [M] 937-890-1300
  casselhills.com
Castle Shannon GC, *Hopedale* ....18 [P] 740-937-2373
  castleshannongolf.com
Catawba Island Club, *Port Clinton* ....18 [V] 419-797-4424
  cicclub.com
CC At Muirfield Village, *Dublin* ....18 [V] 614-764-7705
  tccmv.com
CC of Ashland, *Ashland* ....18 [V] 419-289-2917
  ccashland.com
CC of the North, *Xenia* ....18 [V] 937-374-5000
  countryclubofthenorth.com
Cedar Hills GC, *East Liverpool* ....9 [P] 330-386-6094
Cedar Trace GC, *Batavia* ....18 [P] 513-625-4400
  cedartracegolfclub.com
Chagrin Valley CC, *Chagrin Falls* ....18 [V] 440-248-4314
  cvcclub.com
Champions of Columbus GC, *Columbus* ....18 [M] 614-645-7111
  columbuscitygolfcourses.com
Chapel Hill GC, *Mt Vernon* ....18 [P] 740-393-3999
  chapelhillgolfcourse.com
Chapel Hills Golf, *Ashtabula* ....18 [P] 440-997-3791
  chapelhillsgolf.com
Chardon Lakes GC, *Chardon* ....18 [P] 440-285-4653
  chardonlakes.com
Chenoweth GC, *Akron* ....18 [P] 330-644-0058
  chenowethgolf.com
Cherokee Hills GC, *Bellefontaine* ....18 [P] 937-599-3221
  cherokeehillsgolfclub.com
Cherokee Hills GC, *Valley City* ....18 [P] 330-225-6122
  cherokeehillsgolf.com
Cherry Ridge GC, *Elyria* ....9 [P] 440-324-3713
Chillicothe Golf Ctr, *Chillicothe* ....18 [P] 740-772-2683
  runningfoxgc.com
Chillicothe Jaycees GC, *Chillicothe* ....18 [P] 740-775-7659
  jcgolfcourse.com
Chippewa GC, *Doylestown* ....18 [P] 330-658-6126
  chippewagolfclub.com
Chippewa GC, *Curtice* ....18 [P] 419-836-8111
  chippewagolfonline.com
Cincinnati CC, *Cincinnati* ....18 [V] 513-533-5265
  cincinnaticountryclub.com
Circling Hills GC, *Harrison* ....18 [P] 513-367-5858
  circlinghills.com
Clair Mar GC, *Powhatan Point* ....9 [P] 740-795-5856
Clear Creek At The Practice Ctr, *Franklin* ....18 [P] 937-743-5588
  tpcgolf.com

[S] = SEMI-PRIVATE [V] = PRIVATE [U] = UNIVERSITY [N] = UNIVERSITY-PRIVATE

OHIO

Clearview GC, *East Canton* .... 18 [P] 330-488-0404
  clearview-gc.com
Cliffside GC, *Gallipolis* .... 18 [P] 740-446-4653
  cliffsidegolf.com
Cliffside GC, *Tipp City* .... 27 [P] 937-667-6686
Clinton Heights GC, *Tiffin* .... 18 [P] 419-447-8863
Clover Valley GC, *Johnstown* .... 18 [P] 740-966-5533
  clovervalleygolfclub.com
Clovernook CC, *Cincinnati* .... 18 [V] 513-521-0335
  clovernookcc.com
Club Walden, *Aurora* .... 18 [V] 330-562-7145
  yourwalden.com
Coldstream CC, *Cincinnati* .... 18 [V] 513-624-2783
  coldstreamcc.com
Collins Park GC, *Toledo* .... 9 [M] 419-693-1991
  collinsparkgc.com
Colonial Golfers Club, *Harrod* .... 18 [P] 419-649-3350
  colonialgolfersclub.com
Colonial Pines GC, *Bethel* .... 18 [S] 513-876-4653
  colonialpinesgolf.com
Columbia Hills CC, *Columbia Station* ... 18 [P] 440-236-8277
  columbiahills.org
Columbus CC, *Columbus* .... 27 [P] 614-861-0800
  columbuscc.com
Community Golf Ctr, *Dayton* .... 36 [M] 937-293-2341
  cityofdayton.org
Congress Lake Club, *Hartville* .... 18 [V] 330-877-9318
  congresslakeclub.com
Cooks Creek GC, *Ashville* .... 18 [P] 740-983-3636
  cookscreek.com
Coolridge GC, *Mansfield* .... 9 [P] 419-522-1452
  coolridgegc.com
Copeland Hills GC, *Columbiana* .... 18 [P] 330-482-3221
  copelandhillsgolf.com
Copley Greens GC, *Copley* .... 9 [P] 330-864-3111
Coshocton Town & CC, *Coshocton* .... 9 [V] 740-622-4504
  coshoctoncountryclub.com
Cottonwood Creek Executive GC, *Sylvania* .... 9 [P] 419-829-2891
  sdgcohiogolf.com
Country Acres GC, *Ottawa* .... 18 [P] 419-532-3434
  countryacresgolfclub.com
Country View GC, *Thornville* .... 9 [P] 740-246-8439
Countryside GC, *New Paris* .... 9 [P] 937-437-1122
  csgolfclub.com
Cranberry Hills GC, *New Washington* ... 9 [P] 419-492-2192
Cranberry Hills GC, *Warren* .... 9 [P] 330-847-2884
Creek Side GC, *Chandlersville* .... 9 [P] 740-674-6885
Creekwood GC, *Columbia Station* .... 18 [P] 440-748-3188
  creekwoodgolfcourse.com
Crooked Creek GC, *Belmont* .... 18 [P] 740-782-1695
Crooked Tree GC, *Mason* .... 18 [P] 513-398-3933
  crookedtree.com
Cross Winds GC, *Perrysburg* .... 9 [P] 419-872-4653
Crown Hill GC, *Williamsport* .... 18 [P] 740-986-4653
  crownhillgolf.com
Crystal Springs GC, *Hopewell* .... 18 [S] 740-787-1114
  crystalspringsgolfclub.com
Cumberland Trail GC, *Pataskala* .... 18 [P] 740-964-9331
  cumberlandtrailgc.com
Darby Creek GC, *Marysville* .... 18 [P] 937-349-7491
  darbycreekgolf.com
Darby Dan Farm, *Galloway* .... 9 [V] 614-374-6377
  forehope.org

Golf Yellow Pages, 18th Edition

Dayton CC, *Dayton* .... 18 [V] 937-294-2735
  daytoncountryclub.com
Deer Creek GC, *Hubbard* .... 18 [P] 330-534-1395
  deercreekgolfhubbardoh.com
Deer Creek St Park GC, *Mt Sterling* ...... 18 [M] 740-869-3088
  ohiostateparks.org
Deer Lake GC, *Geneva* .... 18 [P] 440-466-8450
Deer Ridge GC, *Bellville* .... 18 [P] 419-886-7090
  deerridgegc.com
Deer Run GC, *Cincinnati* .... 18 [V] 513-941-8000
  deerruncountryclub.com
Deer Track GC, *Goshen* .... 18 [P] 513-625-2500
  deertrackgolfcourse.com
Deerfield GC, *Rockford* .... 9 [P] 419-363-9400
Deerpass GC, *Seville* .... 18 [P] 330-769-9955
Delaware GC, *Delaware* .... 18 [V] 740-362-2582
  delawaregolf.com
Delhi Hills Par 3, *Cincinnati* .... 9 [P] 513-941-9827
Delphos CC, *Delphos* .... 18 [P] 419-453-3812
  delphoscountryclub.com
Detwiler Park GC, *Toledo* .... 18 [M] 419-726-9353
  detwilergc.com
Diamond Back GC, *Canfield* .... 18 [P] 330-533-3053
Dogwood Hills GC, *Chillicothe* .... 18 [P] 740-663-2700
Donnybrook GC, *Hubbard* .... 9 [P] 330-534-1872
Dorlon GC, *Columbia Station* .... 18 [P] 440-236-8234
  dorlon.com
Double Eagle Club, *Galena* .... 18 [V] 740-548-7799
  doubleeagleclub.net
Double Eagle Golf Ctr, *Waynesville* .... 9 [P] 513-897-2721
  doubleeaglegolfcenter.com
Doughton GC, *Hubbard* .... 18 [P] 330-568-7005
Dragon Ranch GC, *Elyria* .... 18 [P] 440-986-5881
  dragonranchgolf.com
Duck Creek GC, *Warren* .... 18 [P] 330-872-3825
Dunham GC, *Cincinnati* .... 9 [M] 513-251-1157
  cincygolf.org
Dyer CC, *Toronto* .... 9 [V] 740-537-1681
Eagle Creek GC, *Norwalk* .... 18 [P] 419-668-8535
  eaglecreekgolf.com
Eagle Crest GC, *Sullivan* .... 9 [P] 419-736-3472
Eagle Eye GC, *Columbus* .... 9 [A] 614-692-2075
  dsccmwr.com
Eagle Pass GC, *East Rochester* .... 9 [P] 330-223-1773
Eagle Sticks GC, *Zanesville* .... 18 [P] 740-454-4900
  eaglesticks.com
Eagles Landing GC, *Oregon* .... 18 [S] 419-697-4653
  eagleslandinggolfclub.net
Eagles Nest GC, *Loveland* .... 18 [P] 513-722-1241
East Liverpool CC, *East Liverpool* .... 9 [V] 330-385-0624
  eastliverpoolcc.com
East Palestine CC, *Negley* .... 9 [P] 330-426-9761
Eaton CC, *Eaton* .... 9 [P] 937-456-6922
  eatoncc.com
Echo Hills GC, *Piqua* .... 18 [M] 937-778-2086
  piquaoh.org
Echo Valley GC, *Wellington* .... 18 [P] 440-647-2065
Edgewater GC, *Minerva* .... 18 [P] 330-862-2630
Edgewood GC, *Canton* .... 9 [P] 330-499-2353
  golfatedgewood.com
Elks CC, *Mc Dermott* .... 18 [S] 740-259-6241
  elkscountryclub.com
Elks GC of Hillsboro, *Hillsboro* .... 9 [S] 937-393-3047

162 [A] = MILITARY [M] = MUNICIPAL [P] = PUBLIC [R] = RESORT

Elks Run GC, *Batavia*..........................18 [P]   513-735-6600
elksrun.com
Ellsworth Meadows GC, *Hudson*..........18 [M]   330-656-2103
ellsworthmeadows.com
Elm GC, *Athens*.......................................9 [P]   740-594-0130
Elms CC, *North Lawrence*...................27 [P]   330-833-2668
elmscc.com
Elyria CC, *Elyria*....................................18 [V]   440-323-8225
theelyriacountryclub.com
Emerald Valley CC, *Lorain*...................9 [P]   440-282-5663
Emerald Woods GC, *Columbia Station*..........45 [P]   440-236-8940
emeraldwoodsgc.com
Erie Islands Resort, *Port Clinton*..........9 [R]   419-734-9117
erieislandsresort.com
Erie Shores GC, *Madison*.....................18 [M]   440-428-3164
lakemetroparks.com
Fair Greens CC, *Jackson*.......................9 [V]   740-286-4242
Fairfield GC South Trace, *Fairfield*.......18 [M]   513-858-7750
fairfield-city.org
Fairfield Greens North Trace, *Fairfield*..........9 [M]   513-939-3741
fairfield-city.org
Fairlawn CC, *Akron*..............................18 [V]   330-836-5541
fairlawncountryclub.org
Fairway River Links GC, *Rayland*.......18 [P]   740-859-9304
fairwayriverlinks.bizland.com
Fairways Riverside GC, *Sardis*...........27 [P]   740-483-1536
riverside.bizland.com
Fallen Timbers Fairways, *Waterville*....18 [P]   419-878-4653
fallentimbersfairways.com
Fernbank G&TC, *Cincinnati*..................9 [P]   513-941-9960
Findlay CC, *Findlay*..............................18 [V]   419-422-9263
findlaycc.com
Fire Ridge GC, *Millersburg*..................18 [P]   330-674-3921
fireridgegolf.com
Firestone CC, *Akron*............................54 [V]   330-644-8441
firestonecountryclub.com
Five Waters GC, *Midvale*....................18 [P]   740-922-2182
Flying B GC, *Salem*..............................18 [P]   330-337-8138
Forest E Everhart Memorial GC, *Chillicothe*..........9 [P]   740-773-1141
Forest Hills CC, *Middletown*.................9 [V]   513-423-4797
foresthillsclub4me.com
Forest Hills GC, *Springfield*..................9 [P]   937-322-1385
foresthillspar3.com
Forest Hills GC, *Chesapeake*................9 [P]   740-867-4445
Forest Hills GC, *Mansfield*...................18 [P]   419-589-3331
Forest Hills GC, *Glouster*......................9 [P]   740-767-4623
Forest Hills GC, *Heath*..........................9 [P]   740-283-4653
Forest Hills Golf Ctr, *Elyria*..................18 [M]   440-323-2632
golftheforest.com
Forrest Creason GC, *Bowling Green*..........18 [U]   419-372-2674
bgsu.edu/offices/sa/recsports/golf
Fostoria CC, *Fostoria*..........................18 [P]   419-435-4248
fostoriacc.com
Four Bridges CC, *Middletown*..............18 [V]   513-759-4620
fourbridges.com
Fowlers Mill GC, *Chesterland*..............27 [P]   440-729-7569
fowlersmillgc.com
Fox Creek G&RC, *Lorain*.....................18 [P]   440-282-9106
foxcreeksports.com
Fox Den GC, *Stow*...............................18 [M]   330-673-3443
foxdengolf.com
Fox Meadow CC, *Medina*....................18 [P]   330-723-5536
foxmeadowcc.com

Foxfire GC, *Lockbourne*.......................36 [P]   614-224-3694
foxfiregolfclub.com
Foxs Den GC, *Celina*............................18 [P]   419-586-3102
foxsdengolf.com
Franklin GC, *Franklin*............................9 [S]   937-746-2319
Franklin Valley GC, *Jackson*.................18 [P]   740-286-4903
Fremont CC, *Fremont*...........................18 [V]   419-332-2646
fremontcountryclub.com
Friendly Meadows GC, *Hamersville*....18 [P]   937-379-1050
friendlymeadowsgolf.com
Fullers Fairways, *Zanesville*.................18 [P]   740-452-9830
Gahanna Muni GC, *Gahanna*.................9 [M]   614-342-4270
gahanna.gov
Galion CC, *Galion*.................................18 [V]   419-468-2640
galioncc.com
GC of Dublin, *Dublin*............................18 [S]   614-792-3825
golfclubofdublin.net
Geauga Hidden Valley CC, *Thompson*...........9 [P]   440-298-3912
General Electric Employees Activity, *Cincinnati*..18 [V]   513-346-2720
geeaa.org
Geneva On The Lake Muni GC,
   Geneva-on-the-Lake.........................18 [M]   440-466-8797
gotlgolf.com
Glen Ross GC, *Delaware*......................18 [P]   740-657-3752
glenrossgc.com
Gleneagles GC, *Twinsburg*...................18 [M]   330-425-3334
gleneaglesgc.com
Glenmoor CC, *Canton*...........................18 [V]   330-966-3600
glenmoorcc.com
Glenview GC, *Cincinnati*.......................27 [M]   513-771-1747
cincygolf.org
Golden Tee At Tri-County, *Springdale*...........9 [P]   513-771-6001
goldenteetri-county.com
Golf Ctr at Kings Island, *Mason*...........36 [R]   513-398-5200
thegolfcenter.com
Grandview GC, *Middlefield*..................18 [P]   440-834-1824
grandviewcountryclub.com
Grantwood GC, *Solon*...........................18 [M]   440-248-4646
grantwoodgolf.com
Granville CC, *Granville*........................18 [P]   740-587-0843
granvillegolf.com
Great Trail GC, *Minerva*.......................27 [P]   330-868-6770
greattrailgolf.com
Green Acres GC, *Marion*......................18 [P]   740-387-6114
greenacresgolf.com
Green Crest GC, *Middletown*...............18 [P]   513-777-2090
greencrestgolf.com
Green Hills GC, *Cincinnati*.....................9 [M]   513-589-3585
Green Hills GC, *Clyde*..........................27 [P]   419-547-7947
greenhillsgolf.com
Green Hills GC, *Kent*..............................9 [P]   330-678-2601
Green Ridge GC, *Wickliffe*....................9 [P]   440-943-0007
cityofwickliffe.com/html/greenridgegolf.htm
Green Valley GC, *New Philadelphia*....18 [P]   330-364-2812
greenvalleygolfclub.com
Green Valley GC, *Zanesville*.................18 [P]   740-452-7105
greenvalleygc.com
Greene CC, *Fairborn*............................18 [V]   937-767-5621
greenecc.com
Greentree GC, *Lebanon*..........................9 [P]   513-727-1009
greentreegc.com
Greenville GC, *Greenville*....................18 [P]   937-548-3563
greenvillegolfcourse.com

[S] = SEMI-PRIVATE   [V] = PRIVATE   [U] = UNIVERSITY   [N] = UNIVERSITY-PRIVATE

OHIO
Golf Yellow Pages, 18th Edition

Grey Hawk GC, *Lagrange* .... 18 [S] 440-355-4844
  greyhawkgolf.com
Hamilton Elks GC, *Hamilton* .... 27 [V] 513-887-4384
Hara Greens, *Dayton* .... 18 [P] 937-278-4272
Harbor Hills CC, *Hebron* .... 9 [P] 740-928-3596
Harmon GC, *Lebanon* .... 9 [P] 513-934-3433
  harmongolfclub.com
Hartwell GC, *Cincinnati* .... 9 [P] 513-821-9855
Hawks Nest At Ohio State ATI, *Creston* .... 18 [U] 330-435-4611
  hawksnest.osu.edu
Hawthorne Hills CC, *Lima* .... 27 [P] 419-221-1891
  hawthornegolf.com
Hawthorne Valley CC, *Solon* .... 18 [V] 440-439-7417
  hawthornevalleycc.com
Heather Downs CC, *Toledo* .... 18 [S] 419-385-0248
  heatherdowns.com
Heatherwoode GC, *Springboro* .... 18 [M] 937-748-3222
  golfheatherwoode.com
Hemlock Springs GC, *Geneva* .... 18 [P] 440-466-4044
  hemlocksprings.com
Henry Stambaugh GC, *Youngstown* .... 9 [M] 330-743-5370
Heritage GC, *Hilliard* .... 18 [V] 614-684-7102
  heritagegc.com
Hiawatha Running Water GC, *Mt Vernon* .... 18 [P] 740-393-2886
  hiawathagolf.com
Hickory Flat Greens, *West Lafayette* .... 18 [P] 740-545-7796
Hickory Grove GC, *Jefferson* .... 18 [P] 440-576-3776
  hickorygrovegc.com
Hickory Grove GC, *Harpster* .... 18 [P] 740-496-2631
  hickorygrovegolfclub.com
Hickory Grove GC, *London* .... 9 [P] 740-852-9280
Hickory Hills GC, *Grove City* .... 18 [V] 614-878-1057
  hickoryhills.com
Hickory Hills GC, *Hicksville* .... 9 [P] 419-542-6400
Hickory Hollow GC, *Salem* .... 9 [V] 330-222-1064
Hickory Nut GC, *Columbia Station* .... 18 [P] 440-236-8008
  hickorynutgolfcourse.com
Hickory Sticks GC, *Van Wert* .... 27 [P] 419-238-0441
  hickorysticksohio.com
Hickory Woods GC, *Loveland* .... 18 [P] 513-575-3900
  hickorywoods.com
Hidden Creek GC, *Lima* .... 18 [P] 419-643-8562
  hiddencreekgolfclub.net
Hidden Hills GC, *Woodville* .... 18 [P] 419-849-3693
Hidden Hills GC, *Howard* .... 9 [P] 740-599-6628
Hidden Holes GC, *Fredericktown* .... 9 [P] 740-694-0631
Hidden Lake GC, *Tipp City* .... 18 [P] 937-667-8880
Hidden Oaks GC, *Vienna* .... 9 [P] 330-856-6872
Hidden Valley GC, *Delaware* .... 9 [M] 740-363-1739
Hide A Way Hills Club, *Sugar Grove* .... 9 [V] 614-837-3866
High Acres, *Huron* .... 9 [P] 419-588-2503
High Lands GC, *Pataskala* .... 18 [V] 740-927-3966
  highlandsgc.com
Highgrove GC, *Diamond* .... 18 [P] 330-538-2305
  highgrovegolf.com
Highland Meadows GC, *Sylvania* .... 18 [V] 419-882-4040
  hmgolfclub.org
Highland Park GC, *Highland Hills* .... 36 [M] 216-348-7273
  city.cleveland.oh.us
Hillcrest CC, *Montpelier* .... 18 [P] 419-485-3368
Hillcrest GC, *Johnstown* .... 9 [P] 740-967-7921
  hillcrestgc.com
Hillcrest GC, *Findlay* .... 18 [S] 419-423-7511

Hilliard Lakes CC, *Westlake* .... 18 [P] 440-871-9578
  hilliardlakesgc.com
Hilltop GC, *Manchester* .... 18 [P] 937-549-2904
Hilltop GC, *Coshocton* .... 18 [M] 740-622-8083
Hillview GC, *Cleves* .... 18 [P] 513-574-6670
  hillviewgolfcourse.com
Hinckley Hills GC, *Hinckley* .... 18 [P] 330-278-4861
  hinckleyhillsgolf.com
Holly Hills GC, *Waynesville* .... 18 [P] 513-897-4921
  golfhollyhills.com
Homestead GC, *Tipp City* .... 18 [P] 937-698-4876
Homestead Springs GC, *Groveport* .... 18 [P] 614-836-5872
  homesteadsprings.com
Horseshoe Bend GC, *Jacobsburg* .... 18 [P] 740-686-2351
  horseshoebendgolfcourse.com
Hueston Woods St Park GC, *Oxford* .... 18 [M] 513-523-8081
  home.earthlink.net/~hwgolf
Hyde A Way GC, *Beloit* .... 9 [P] 330-584-2200
Hyde Park G&CC, *Cincinnati* .... 18 [V] 513-871-3111
  hydeparkcc.com
Indian Hills GC, *Granville* .... 9 [P] 740-587-0706
Indian Hollow Lake GC, *Grafton* .... 18 [P] 440-355-5344
Indian Ridge GC, *Oxford* .... 18 [P] 513-524-4653
  golfindianridge.com
Indian Springs GC - Reserve / Woods,
  Mechanicsburg .... 18 [P] 937-834-2111
  golfindiansprings.com
Inverness Club, *Toledo* .... 18 [V] 419-578-9000
  invernessclub.com
Irish Hills GC, *Mt Vernon* .... 18 [P] 740-397-6252
Ironton CC, *Ironton* .... 9 [P] 740-532-2511
  ironcc.com
Ironwood GC, *Hinckley* .... 18 [P] 330-278-7171
  ironwoodgolfcoursehinckleyohio.com
Ironwood GC, *Wauseon* .... 18 [P] 419-335-0587
Ivy Hills CC, *Cincinnati* .... 18 [V] 513-561-6177
  ivyhillscountryclub.com
J Edward Good Park GC, *Akron* .... 18 [M] 330-864-0020
  ci.akron.oh.us
Jamaica Run GC, *Germantown* .... 18 [P] 937-866-4333
  jamaicarun.com
Jaycee GC, *Zanesville* .... 18 [P] 740-452-1860
  zanesvillejcgolfcourse.com
Jefferson G&CC, *Blacklick* .... 18 [V] 614-759-7500
  jeffersoncountryclub.com
Johnny Cake Ridge GC, *Willoughby* .... 9 [P] 440-946-3154
Kennsington GC, *Canfield* .... 18 [P] 330-533-8733
  kennsingtongolf.com
Kent State Univ GC, *Kent* .... 18 [U] 330-672-2500
  kent.edu
Kenwood CC, *Cincinnati* .... 36 [V] 513-561-7397
  kenwoodcc.com
Kettenring CC, *Defiance* .... 18 [V] 419-784-5571
Keys GC, *Huron* .... 9 [P] 419-433-5585
  keysgolfcourse.com
Kings Mill GC, *Waldo* .... 18 [P] 740-726-2626
  kingsmillgolf.com
Kinsale Golf & Fitness Club, *Powell* .... 18 [P] 740-881-6500
  golfkinsale.com
Kittyhawk Golf Ctr, *Dayton* .... 54 [M] 937-237-5424
  kittyhawkgolfcenter.com
Knoll Run GC, *Lowellville* .... 18 [P] 330-755-2499
  knollrun.com

164   [A] = MILITARY   [M] = MUNICIPAL   [P] = PUBLIC   [R] = RESORT

OHIO

Course	Location	Holes	Type	Phone
Knollbrook GC	Lodi	9	[P]	330-948-1482
Kyber Run GC	Johnstown	18	[P]	740-967-1404
kyberrungolf.com				
L C Boles Memorial GC	Wooster	9	[U]	330-263-2316
Lake Forest CC	Hudson	18	[V]	330-656-3804
lakeforestcc.org				
Lake Front GC	Columbiana	9	[P]	330-482-3466
Lakeland GC	St Paris	18	[P]	937-663-4707
lakelandgolfclub.com				
Lakeland GC	Fostoria	18	[P]	419-894-6440
Lakeside GC	Lake Milton	18	[P]	330-547-2797
Lakeside GC	Beverly	18	[R]	740-984-4265
lakesidegolfcourse.net				
Lakeview GC	Hartville	9	[P]	330-877-2390
Lakewood CC	Westlake	18	[V]	440-871-5338
lakewoodcountryclub.com				
Lakewood GC	Georgetown	18	[P]	937-378-4200
thelakewoodgolfcourse.com				
Lancaster CC	Lancaster	18	[V]	740-654-3535
lancastercc.org				
Larch Tree GC	Trotwood	18	[P]	937-854-1951
Legend Lake GC	Chardon	18	[V]	440-285-3110
legendlakegolfclub.com				
Legendary Run GC	Cincinnati	18	[S]	513-753-1717
legendaryrungolf.com				
Leisure Time Rec Ctr	Stow	18	[P]	330-688-4162
leisuretimerecreation.com				
Liberty Hills GC	Bellefontaine	18	[P]	937-592-4653
playlibertyhills.com				
Licking Springs Trout & GC	Newark	18	[P]	740-366-7328
lickingsprings.com				
Lincoln Hills GC	Upper Sandusky	9	[P]	419-294-3037
golflincolnhills.com				
Lindale GC	Amelia	18	[P]	513-797-7300
lindalegolfclub.com				
Little Apple GC	Bellville	18	[P]	419-886-4400
littleapplegolfcourse.com				
Little Bear GC	Lewis Center	11	[P]	740-548-8532
littlebearvillage.com				
Little Met GC	Cleveland	9	[M]	216-941-9672
clemetparks.com				
Little Miami Golf Ctr	Cincinnati	18	[M]	513-561-5650
greatparks.org				
Little Mountain CC	Painesville	18	[P]	440-358-7888
littlemountaincc.com				
Little Scioto Golf	Wheelersburg	9	[P]	740-776-9976
Little Turtle GC	Westerville	18	[V]	614-882-5940
littleturtlegc.com				
Locust Hills GC	Springfield	36	[P]	937-265-5152
locusthillsgc.com				
London CC	London	9	[V]	740-852-1762
Longaberger GC	Nashport	18	[P]	740-763-1100
longabergergolfclub.com				
Losantiville CC	Cincinnati	18	[V]	513-366-4080
losantivillecc.com				
Lost Creek CC	Lima	18	[P]	419-229-2026
thelostcreekcountryclub.com				
Lost Nation Muni GC	Willoughby	18	[M]	440-953-4280
willoughbyohio.com				
Loudon Meadows GC	Fostoria	18	[P]	419-435-8500
loudonmeadows.com				
Loyal Oak GC	Norton	27	[P]	330-825-2904
Lyons Den GC	Canal Fulton	18	[P]	330-854-9910
lyonsdengolf.com				
Madden Golf Ctr	Dayton	18	[M]	937-268-0111
daytonrecreationandyou.com				
Madison CC	Madison	18	[V]	440-428-2641
madisoncountryclub.com				
Mahoning CC	Girard	18	[P]	330-545-2517
mahoningcountryclub.com				
Majestic Springs GC	Wilmington	18	[P]	937-383-1474
majesticsprings.com				
Maketewah CC	Cincinnati	18	[V]	513-242-9200
maketewah.com				
Mallard Creek GC	Columbia Station	27	[P]	440-748-8231
golfmallardcreek.com				
Manakiki GC	Willoughby	18	[M]	440-942-2500
clemetparks.com				
Maple Ridge GC	Austinburg	18	[P]	440-969-1368
mapleridgegolfcourse.com				
Maplecrest GC	Kent	18	[P]	330-673-2722
maplecrestgolf.com				
Marietta CC	Marietta	18	[V]	740-373-6889
mariettacc.org				
Marion CC	Marion	18	[V]	740-387-0974
marioncountryclub.com				
Marks GC	Circleville	18	[P]	740-420-0420
marksgolf.com				
Marysville GC	Marysville	18	[P]	937-642-1816
marysvillegolfclub.com				
Mastick Woods GC	Cleveland	9	[M]	216-267-5626
clemetparks.com				
Maumee Bay Resort	Oregon	18	[R]	419-836-9009
maumeebayresort.com				
Mayfair CC	Uniontown	18	[P]	330-699-2209
mayfaircountryclub.com				
Meadow Links & Golf Acad	Cincinnati	9	[M]	513-825-3701
greatparks.org				
Meadowbrook CC	Clayton	18	[V]	937-836-6353
daytonmeadowbrook.com				
Meadowlake Golf & Swim	Canton	18	[P]	330-492-2010
meadowlakegs.com				
Meadowood GC	Westlake	27	[M]	440-835-6442
cityofwestlake.org				
Meander GC	North Jackson	9	[P]	330-538-3933
Medina CC	Medina	27	[V]	330-725-6621
medinacc.com				
Mentel Memorial GC At Bolton Field	Galloway	18	[M]	614-645-3050
columbuscitygolfcourses.com				
Mercer County Elks GC	Celina	18	[S]	419-925-4215
Metro Parks Par 3 GC	Youngstown	18	[M]	330-740-7114
Miami Shores GC	Troy	18	[M]	937-335-4457
troyohio.gov				
Miami Valley GC	Dayton	18	[V]	937-278-7381
miamivalleygolfclub.com				
Miami View GC	Miamitown	18	[P]	513-353-2384
miamiview.net				
Miami Whitewater Forest GC	Harrison	18	[M]	513-367-4627
greatparks.org				
Mill Creek GC	Ostrander	18	[P]	740-666-7711
millcreekgolfclub.com				
Mill Creek Park GC	Boardman	36	[M]	330-740-7122
millcreekmetroparks.com				
Mills Creek GC	Sandusky	9	[M]	419-627-5803
ci.sandusky.oh.us/recreation/millscreek.htm				
Millstone Hills GC	New London	18	[P]	419-929-6477

[S] = SEMI-PRIVATE   [V] = PRIVATE   [U] = UNIVERSITY   [N] = UNIVERSITY-PRIVATE

OHIO — Golf Yellow Pages, 18th Edition

Minerva Lake GC, *Columbus* .... 18 [P]   614-882-9988
  minervalakegolf.com
Mitchell Hills Club, *Springfield* .... 9 [V]   937-399-0711
  mitchellhills.com
Mohawk GC, *Tiffin* .... 18 [V]   419-447-5951
  mohawkgolf.com
Mohican Hills GC, *Jeromesville* .... 18 [P]   419-368-3303
  bestcourses.com
Moose CC, *Sidney* .... 9 [P]   937-492-7222
Moraine CC, *Dayton* .... 18 [V]   937-293-6391
  morainecountryclub.com
Morgan County Fairgrounds GC, *McConnelsville* ..... 9 [P]   740-962-3245
Moss Creek GC, *Clayton* .... 18 [S]   937-837-4653
  mosscreekgolfclub.com
Mound GC, *Miamisburg* .... 9 [M]   937-866-2211
  moundgolf.com
Moundbuilders CC, *Newark* .... 18 [V]   740-344-4500
  moundbuilderscc.com
Mt Vernon CC, *Mt Vernon* .... 18 [V]   740-392-4216
  mtvcountryclub.com
Mud Run GC, *Akron* .... 9 [M]   330-375-2728
  cityofakrongolf.com/mudrun/
Muirfield Village GC, *Dublin* .... 18 [V]   614-889-6740
  thememorialtournament.com
Mulligan Springs, *Mogadore* .... 9 [P]   330-628-5139
Napoleon Muni GC, *Napoleon* .... 9 [M]   419-592-5526
  napoleonohio.com
National Golf Links, *South Charleston* ... 18 [P]   937-568-9660
  nationalgolflinks.org
National Road GC, *West Jefferson* .... 18 [P]   614-879-7880
Nature Trails GC, *Kansas* .... 18 [P]   419-986-5229
  naturetrailsgolf.com
NCR CC, *Kettering* .... 36 [V]   937-643-6940
  ncrcountryclub.com
Neumann GC, *Cincinnati* .... 27 [M]   513-574-1320
  cincygolf.org
New Albany CC, *New Albany* .... 27 [V]   614-939-8520
  nacc.com
New Albany Links GC, *New Albany* .... 18 [P]   614-855-8532
  newalbanylinks.com
New Winchester GC, *Bucyrus* .... 9 [P]   419-985-5190
  newwinchestergolfcourse.com
North Olmsted GC, *North Olmsted* .... 9 [P]   440-777-0220
  noga.org
Northmoor GC, *Celina* .... 18 [P]   419-394-4896
Northstar GC, *Sunbury* .... 18 [R]   740-524-4653
  thenorthstargolfclub.com
Northwood GC, *Warren* .... 9 [P]   330-847-7608
Northwood Hills CC, *Springfield* .... 18 [S]   937-399-2304
  northwoodhillscc.com
Norwalk Sycamore Hills GC, *Norwalk* ..... 9 [P]   419-668-8460
Norwich Valley GC, *Norwich* .... 9 [S]   614-872-3644
Oak Grove GC, *Atwater* .... 18 [P]   440-823-8823
  ohio-oakgrovegolfcourse.com
Oak Knolls GC, *Kent* .... 18 [P]   330-673-6713
  kent.edu
Oak Mallett GC, *Findlay* .... 9 [P]   419-422-7035
Oak Shadows GC, *New Philadelphia* ...... 18 [P]   330-343-2425
  oakshadowsgolf.com
Oakhaven GC, *Delaware* .... 18 [P]   740-548-5636
  oakhaven.com
Oakhurst CC, *Grove City* .... 18 [V]   614-878-6443
  oakhurstgc.com

Oaks GC, *Lima* .... 18 [P]   419-999-2586
  oaksgolfclub.com
Oaktree GC, *Mansfield* .... 18 [P]   419-747-4653
  oaktreeclub.com
Oakwood CC, *Canton* .... 9 [V]   330-499-7211
Oakwood Club, *Cleveland* .... 18 [V]   216-291-0679
  oakwoodclub.org
Oasis GC&CCtr, *Loveland* .... 18 [V]   513-583-8383
  oasisgolfclub.com
OBannon Creek GC, *Loveland* .... 18 [V]   513-683-5657
  obannoncreek.com
Oberlin GC, *Oberlin* .... 18 [V]   440-774-3923
  oberlingc.com
Ohio Prestwick CC, *Uniontown* .... 18 [V]   330-492-4180
  ohioprestwick.com
Ohio State Univ GC, *Columbus* .... 36 [N]   614-459-4653
  ohiostategolfclub.com
Ohio Univ GC, *Athens* .... 9 [U]   740-593-9405
  ohiou.edu/recreation
Old Avalon GC, *Warren* .... 18 [M]   330-856-4329
Old Pine GC, *Richfield* .... 9 [P]   330-659-4900
  oldpinegolfcourse.com
Old Pines GC, *Wauseon* .... 9 [P]   419-337-3116
Olde Dutch Mill GC, *Lake Milton* .... 18 [P]   330-654-4100
  oldedutchmill.com
Orchard Hills CC, *Bryan* .... 18 [V]   419-636-6984
Ottawa Park GC, *Toledo* .... 18 [M]   419-472-2059
  ottawaparkgc.com
Oxbow G&CC, *Belpre* .... 18 [P]   740-423-6771
  oxbow-golf.com
Oxford CC, *Oxford* .... 9 [P]   513-524-0801
  theoxfordcountryclub.com
Painesville CC, *Painesville* .... 18 [P]   440-354-3469
  painesvillecountryclub.com
Paradise Hills GC, *Ashland* .... 18 [P]   419-289-8531
Paradise Hills GC, *Rayland* .... 18 [S]   740-859-5028
Paradise Lake Golf & Banquet, *Mogadore* .. 18 [P]   330-628-1313
  paradiselakecc.com
Pebble Creek GC, *Cincinnati* .... 18 [P]   513-385-4442
  pebblecreekgc.com
Pebble Creek GC, *Lexington* .... 18 [P]   419-884-3434
  golfatpebble.com
Penn Terra GC, *Lewisburg* .... 18 [P]   937-962-4515
  pennterragc.com
Pepper Pike Club, *Pepper Pike* .... 18 [V]   216-831-9466
Pepperidge Tree GC, *Madison* .... 9 [P]   440-428-1398
Perry CC, *New Lexington* .... 9 [P]   740-342-1781
Pheasant Run GC, *Lagrange* .... 18 [P]   440-355-5035
Pickaway CC, *Circleville* .... 18 [V]   740-474-4786
Pike Run GC, *Ottawa* .... 18 [S]   419-538-7000
  pikerungolf.com
Pine Brook GC, *Grafton* .... 18 [P]   440-748-2939
  pinebrookgc.com
Pine Hill GC, *Carroll* .... 18 [P]   614-837-3911
  pinehillgolfclub.com
Pine Hills GC, *Hinckley* .... 18 [P]   330-225-4477
  golfpinehills.net
Pine Hills GC, *Pomeroy* .... 9 [P]   740-992-6312
Pine Lakes GC, *Mt Gilead* .... 18 [P]   419-946-1856
  pinelakesgolfohio.com
Pine Lakes GC, *Hubbard* .... 18 [P]   330-534-9026
  golfpinelakes.com
Pine Meadows Golf, *Salem* .... 9 [P]   330-581-8888

[A] = MILITARY   [M] = MUNICIPAL   [P] = PUBLIC   [R] = RESORT

Golf Yellow Pages, 18th Edition — OHIO

Course	Holes	Type	Phone
Pine Ridge CC, *Wickliffe* — lakemetroparks.com	18	[M]	440-943-0293
Pine Valley GC, *Wadsworth*	18	[P]	330-335-3375
Pinnacle GC, *Grove City* — pinnaclegc.com	18	[V]	614-539-0722
Pioneer Family Golf Center, *Marietta* — pioneer-golf.com	9	[P]	740-376-9009
Pipestone GC, *Miamisburg* — pipestonegolf.com	18	[M]	937-866-4653
Piqua CC, *Piqua* — pcc1896.com	18	[V]	937-778-9005
Pleasant Hill GC, *Perrysville* — pleasanthillgolf.com	18	[P]	419-938-5311
Pleasant Hill GC, *Middletown*	18	[P]	513-539-7220
Pleasant Hill GC, *Chardon* — pleasanthillgolfchardon.com	27	[P]	440-285-2428
Pleasant Valley CC, *Medina* — neohiogolf.com	18	[P]	330-725-5770
Pleasant Valley GC, *Lancaster*	27	[P]	740-654-3293
Pleasant Valley GC, *Payne*	9	[P]	419-263-2037
Pleasant View GC, *Paris* — pleasantviewgolfclub.com	18	[P]	330-862-2034
Plum Brook CC, *Sandusky* — plumbrookcc.com	18	[V]	419-625-5394
Port Clinton GC, *Port Clinton*	9	[P]	419-635-9993
Portage CC, *Akron* — portagecc.org	18	[V]	330-836-4994
Potters Park GC, *Hamilton* — cityofhamilton.org	18	[M]	513-868-5983
Powderhorn GC, *Madison* — powderhorngolf.com	18	[P]	440-428-5951
Prairie Trace GC, *Wright Patterson AFB* — 88thservices.com/golfcourses.htm	27	[A]	937-879-5311
Prairie View GC, *Waynesfield* — prairieviewgolf.com	18	[P]	419-568-7888
Prestwick G&CC, *Cortland*	9	[P]	330-637-7901
Punderson Resort GC, *Newbury* — pundersonmanorstateparklodge.com	18	[R]	440-564-5465
Quail Hollow Resort & CC, *Painesville* — quailhollowcc.com	36	[R]	440-639-3800
Raccoon Hill GC, *Kent* — raccoonhillgolfclub.com	18	[P]	330-673-2111
Raccoon International GC, *Granville* — raccooninternational.com	18	[P]	740-587-0921
Raintree CC, *Uniontown* — raintreegc.com	18	[P]	330-699-3232
Rattlesnake Ridge GC, *Sunbury* — rrgolfclub.com	18	[V]	614-410-1399
Ravenswood GC, *Ravenna* — ravenswoodgolfcourse.com	18	[P]	330-296-4103
Rawiga CC, *Seville* — rawigacc.com	18	[V]	330-336-2220
Raymond C Firestone GC, *Akron* — clubcorpgolf.com	9	[P]	330-724-4444
Raymond Memorial GC, *Columbus* — columbuscitygolfcourses.com	18	[M]	614-645-3276
Red Hawk Run GC, *Findlay* — redhawkrun.com	18	[P]	419-894-4653
Red Oaks GC, *Bloomingdale*	18	[S]	740-944-1400
Red Tail GC, *Avon* — redtailgolfclub.com	18	[S]	440-937-6286
Reeves GC, *Cincinnati* — cincygolf.org	27	[M]	513-321-2740
Reid Memorial Park GC, *Springfield* — ci.springfield.oh.us	36	[M]	937-324-7725
Reserve Run GC, *Poland* — reserverungolf.com	18	[P]	330-758-1017
Riceland GC, *Orrville*	18	[P]	330-683-1876
Ridge Top GC, *Medina* — ridgetopgolfcourse.net	18	[P]	330-725-5500
Ridgewood GC, *Parma* — ridgewoodgolfclub.com	18	[M]	440-888-1057
River Cliff, *Fremont* — greenhillsgolf.com	9	[P]	419-334-2452
River Greens GC, *West Lafayette* — rivergreens.com	27	[P]	740-545-7817
River Oaks GC, *Bucyrus* — riveroaksgcbucyrus.com	18	[P]	419-562-0381
Riverby Hills GC, *Bowling Green* — riverbyhills.com	18	[P]	419-878-5941
Riverside Greens GC, *Stryker* — riversidegreens.net	18	[P]	419-682-2053
Riverview GC, *Newton Falls*	18	[P]	330-898-5674
Riverwood GC Pine Valley Sports, *Akron*	18	[P]	330-928-2669
Riviera GC, *Dublin* — rivieragolfclub.net	18	[V]	614-889-2395
Robins Nest Par 3 & DR, *Cleves* — robinsnestgolf.com	9	[P]	513-367-6280
Robins Ridge GC, *Senecaville*	18	[P]	740-685-6029
Rocky Lakes GC, *Springfield* — rockylakes.com	18	[P]	937-322-3211
Rollandia Golf Ctr, *Dayton* — gorollandia.com	18	[P]	937-434-4911
Rolling Acres GC, *Nova* — rollingacresgolfclub.com	18	[P]	419-652-3160
Rolling Green GC, *Huntsburg* — rollinggreenghuntsburg.com	18	[P]	440-636-5171
Rolling Green GC, *Massillon*	18	[P]	330-854-3800
Rolling Meadows GC, *Marysville* — rollingmeadowsgolfclub.com	18	[P]	614-873-4567
Rosemont CC, *Fairlawn* — rosemontcountryclub.com	18	[V]	330-666-8109
Roses Run CC, *Stow* — rosesrun.com	18	[S]	330-688-4653
Round Lake GC, *Lakeville* — roundlakegolfcourse.com	9	[P]	419-827-2097
Royal American Links, *Galena* — royalamericanlinks.com	18	[P]	740-965-1215
Royal Crest GC, *Columbia Station*	18	[P]	440-236-5644
Royal Oak CC, *Cincinnati* — royaloakcountryclub.com	18	[V]	513-752-6500
Royal Oaks GC, *Grafton* — royaloaksgolfclub.net	18	[P]	440-926-2959
Running Fox GC, *Chillicothe* — runningfoxgc.com	45	[P]	740-775-9955
Rushcreek GC, *Thornville*	9	[P]	740-743-1036
Rustic Hills CC, *Medina* — rustichills.com	9	[V]	330-725-4281
Sable Creek GC, *Hartville* — sablecreekgolf.com	27	[P]	330-877-9606
Safari GC, *Powell* — safarigc.com	18	[P]	614-645-3444
Salem GC, *Salem* — thesalemgolfclub.com	18	[V]	330-332-0111
Salem Hills G&CC, *Salem* — salemhillsgolf.com	18	[P]	330-337-8033

[S] = SEMI-PRIVATE [V] = PRIVATE [U] = UNIVERSITY [N] = UNIVERSITY-PRIVATE

OHIO

Golf Yellow Pages, 18th Edition

Salt Fork St Park GC, *Lore City* .... 18 [M] 740-432-7185
Sand Ridge GC, *Chardon* .... 18 [V] 440-285-8088
  mayfieldsandridge.com
Saunders GC, *Put In Bay* .... 9 [R] 419-285-3917
Sawmill Creek GC & Resort, *Huron* .... 18 [R] 419-433-3789
  golfsawmillcreek.com
Scioto CC, *Columbus* .... 18 [V] 614-486-1039
  sciotocc.com
Scioto Reserve G&AC, *Powell* .... 18 [V] 740-881-9082
  sciotoreserve.com
Sebastian Hills GC, *Xenia* .... 18 [P] 937-372-2468
  sebastianhills.com
Sebring CC, *North Benton* .... 9 [V] 330-584-9231
Seneca GC, *Broadview Heights* .... 36 [M] 216-348-7274
Seneca Hills GC, *Tiffin* .... 18 [P] 419-447-9446
  senecahillsgolf.com
Seven Hills CC, *Hartville* .... 18 [P] 330-877-9303
  sevenhillscc.com
Shady Acres GC, *Mc Comb* .... 9 [P] 419-293-9656
  shadyacresgolf.com
Shady Grove Par 3 GC, *Findlay* .... 18 [P] 419-422-7494
Shady Hollow CC, *Massillon* .... 18 [V] 330-832-1804
  shadyhollowcc.com
Shaker Heights CC, *Cleveland* .... 18 [V] 216-991-3660
  shakerheightscc.org
Shaker Run GC, *Lebanon* .... 27 [P] 513-727-0007
  shakerrungolfclub.com
Shale Creek GC, *Medina* .... 18 [P] 330-723-8774
  shalecreekgolfclubggp.com
Shamrock GC, *Powell* .... 18 [P] 614-792-6630
  shamrockgc.com
Sharon Woods GC, *Cincinnati* .... 18 [M] 513-769-4325
  greatparks.org
Shawnee CC, *Lima* .... 18 [V] 419-227-7177
  shawneecountryclub.com
Shawnee Hills GC, *Bedford* .... 27 [M] 440-232-7184
  clemetparks.com
Shawnee Lookout GC, *North Bend* .... 18 [M] 513-941-0120
  greatparks.org
Shawnee St Park Lodge GC, *Friendship* .... 18 [M] 740-858-6681
  shawneestateparklodge.com
Shelby CC, *Shelby* .... 18 [V] 419-347-1824
Shelby DR & Par 3, *Shelby* .... 9 [P] 419-347-7883
Shelby Oaks GC, *Sidney* .... 27 [P] 937-492-2883
  shelbyoaks.com
Signature of Solon CC, *Solon* .... 18 [V] 440-248-4573
  signatureofsoloncc.com
Silver Lake CC, *Silver Lake* .... 18 [V] 330-688-6016
  silverlakeclub.com
Skyland GC, *Hinckley* .... 18 [P] 330-225-5698
  skylandgolfcourse.com
Skyland Pines GC, *Canton* .... 18 [P] 330-454-5131
  skylandpines.net
Sleepy Hollow CC, *Alliance* .... 18 [P] 330-821-8865
  sleepyhollowcountryclub.com
Sleepy Hollow GC, *Brecksville* .... 18 [P] 440-526-4285
  clemetparks.com
Sleepy Hollow GC, *Clyde* .... 18 [P] 419-547-0770
  sleepyhollowclyde.com
Snow Hill CC, *New Vienna* .... 18 [V] 937-987-2491
  snowhillcountryclub.com
Snyder Park GC, *Springfield* .... 18 [M] 937-324-7383
  ntprd.org

South Toledo GC, *Toledo* .... 18 [P] 419-385-4678
  southtoledogolf.com
Southington GC, *Southington* .... 27 [P] 330-898-2852
Split Rock GC, *Orient* .... 18 [P] 614-877-9755
  splitrockgolf.com
Spring Hills GC, *East Springfield* .... 18 [P] 740-543-3270
Spring Hills GC, *Clinton* .... 18 [P] 330-825-2439
Spring Valley G&AC, *Elyria* .... 18 [P] 440-365-1411
  springvalleygolfohio.com
Spring Valley GC, *East Sparta* .... 18 [P] 330-484-1886
Springbrook GC, *Lima* .... 18 [P] 419-225-8037
  springbrookgolfinlima.com
Springfield CC, *Springfield* .... 18 [V] 937-399-0351
  springfieldccoh.org
Springvale GC, *North Olmsted* .... 18 [M] 440-777-0678
Spruce Tree GC, *Wooster* .... 9 [P] 330-345-8010
Spuyten Duyval GC, *Sylvania* .... 27 [P] 419-829-2891
  sdgcohiogolf.com
St Albans GC, *Alexandria* .... 18 [P] 740-924-8885
  stalbansgolfclub.com
St Bernard GC, *Richfield* .... 18 [V] 330-659-3451
  stbernardgolf.com
St Denis GC & Party Ctr, *Chardon* .... 18 [P] 440-285-2183
  stdenispc.com
St Mikes GC, *Defiance* .... 18 [P] 419-497-4675
Steubenville CC, *Steubenville* .... 18 [V] 740-264-2821
  steubenvillecc.com
Stillwater Ridge GC, *West Milton* .... 9 [P] 937-698-5806
Stillwater Valley GC, *Versailles* .... 18 [P] 937-526-3041
  stillwatervalleygolfclub.com
Stone Crossing GC, *Upper Sandusky* .... 9 [P] 419-294-4425
Stone Oak CC, *Holland* .... 18 [V] 419-867-8400
  stoneoakcountryclub.org
Stone Ridge GC, *Bowling Green* .... 18 [S] 419-353-2582
  stoneridgegolfclub.org
Stonelick Hills GC, *Batavia* .... 18 [P] 513-735-4653
  stonelickhills.com
StoneWater GC, *Highland Heights* .... 18 [V] 440-461-4653
  stonewatergolf.com
Suburban GC, *Bryan* .... 18 [P] 419-636-9988
Suffield Springs GC, *Mogadore* .... 9 [P] 330-628-1500
Sugar Bush GC, *Garrettsville* .... 18 [P] 330-527-4202
  sugarbushgolf.com
Sugar Creek GC, *Elmore* .... 18 [P] 419-862-2551
  sugarcreekelmore.com
Sugar Isle Golf CC, *New Carlisle* .... 18 [P] 937-845-8699
  sugarislegolf.com
Sugar Valley CC, *Bellbrook* .... 18 [V] 937-372-9400
  sugarvalleycc.com
Sunbury GC, *Sunbury* .... 9 [P] 740-965-5441
  sunburygolfcourse.com
Sunnyhill Golf & Rec, *Kent* .... 27 [P] 330-673-1785
  sunnyhillgolfcourse.com
Sweetbriar GC, *Avon Lake* .... 36 [P] 440-933-9001
  sweetbriargolfclub.com
Switzerland of Ohio CC, *Beallsville* .... 9 [P] 740-926-9985
Sycamore Creek CC, *Springboro* .... 18 [V] 937-748-0791
  sycamorecreekcc.com
Sycamore Hills GC, *Fremont* .... 27 [P] 419-332-5716
  sycamorehillsgolf.com
Sycamore Springs GC, *Arlington* .... 18 [P] 419-365-5109
  sycamorespringsgolf.com
Sycamore Valley GC, *Akron* .... 9 [P] 330-928-3329

[A] = MILITARY   [M] = MUNICIPAL   [P] = PUBLIC   [R] = RESORT

Name	Holes	Type	Phone
Sylvania CC, *Sylvania*	18	[V]	419-882-3197
sylvaniacc.org			
Table Rock GC, *Centerburg*	18	[P]	740-625-6859
tablerock.com			
Tam OShanter GC, *Canton*	36	[P]	330-477-5111
tamoshantergolf.com			
Tamarac GC, *Lima*	27	[P]	419-331-2951
tamaracgolfclub.com			
Tamaron CC, *Toledo*	18	[P]	419-474-5067
tamaroncc.com			
Tamer Win G&CC, *Cortland*	18	[P]	330-637-2881
tamerwin.com			
Tanglewood GC, *Perrysburg*	18	[P]	419-833-1725
Tanglewood National GC, *Chagrin Falls*	18	[V]	440-543-3752
tanglewoodnational.com			
Tannenhauf GC, *Alliance*	18	[P]	330-823-4402
tannenhaufgolf.com			
Tartan Fields GC, *Dublin*	18	[V]	614-792-0727
tartanfields.com			
Taylor Glen GC, *Bethel*	18	[P]	513-734-6400
taylorglengolfclub.com			
Terrace Park CC, *Milford*	18	[V]	513-831-2464
terraceparkcc.com			
The 797 Elks GC, *Wilmington*	18	[P]	937-382-2666
the797elksgolfclub.com			
The Camargo Club, *Cincinnati*	18	[V]	513-561-7213
camargoclub.com			
The CC of Hudson, *Hudson*	18	[V]	330-650-1188
cchudson.org			
The Chillicothe CC, *Chillicothe*	9	[V]	740-774-2467
The Country Club, *Pepper Pike*	18	[V]	216-831-9252
thecountryclub.com			
The Estate Club, *Lancaster*	18	[P]	740-654-4444
The Fairways at Arrowhead, *North Canton*	18	[P]	330-433-1880
fairwaysnc.com			
The First Tee of Canton, *Canton*	9	[P]	330-452-5331
thefirstteecanton.org			
The GC At Rocky Fork, *Hillsboro*	18	[P]	937-393-9004
The GC At Yankee Trace, *Centerville*	27	[M]	937-438-4533
yankeetrace.org			
The Golf Club, *New Albany*	18	[V]	614-855-7326
The Harbor GC, *Ashtabula*	18	[S]	440-964-5824
harborgolfclubashtabula.com			
The Heritage Club, *Mason*	18	[V]	513-459-7711
heritageclub.com			
The Islander G&CC, *Port Clinton*	18	[P]	419-734-2524
catawbaislander.com			
The Kirtland CC, *Willoughby*	18	[V]	440-951-8422
kirtlandcc.org			
The Lake Club, *Poland*	18	[V]	330-549-2629
thelakeclubohio.com			
The Lakes G&CC, *Westerville*	18	[V]	614-899-3080
lakesclub.com			
The Landings At Rickenbacker GC, *Groveport*	18	[A]	614-491-5000
thelandingsgolf.com			
The Legends of Massillon, *Massillon*	27	[M]	330-830-4653
thelegends.com			
The Links at Echo Springs, *Johnstown*	18	[P]	740-587-1890
thelinksatechosprings.com			
The Links At Firestone Farms, *Columbiana*	18	[P]	330-482-7888
linksatfirestonefarms.com			
The Links At Groveport, *Groveport*	18	[A]	614-836-5874
linksatgroveport.com			
The Links at the Renaissance, *Olmsted Falls*	9	[P]	440-235-0501
therenaissance.org			
The Mayfield Sandridge Club, *South Euclid*	18	[V]	216-382-3958
mayfieldsandridge.com			
The Medallion Club, *Westerville*	27	[V]	614-794-6988
medallionclub.com			
The Mill Course, *Cincinnati*	18	[M]	513-825-3770
greatparks.org			
The Oak Harbor Club, *Oak Harbor*	18	[P]	419-898-1493
oakharborgolfclub.com			
The Phoenix Golf Links, *Grove City*	18	[P]	614-539-3636
phoenixgl.com			
The Pines GC, *Orrville*	18	[P]	330-684-1010
thepinesgolf.com			
The Quarry GC, *Canton*	18	[P]	330-488-3178
quarrygolfclubgp.com			
The Ridge Club, *Cincinnati*	18	[V]	513-731-6800
The Sanctuary, *North Canton*	18	[P]	330-499-7721
thesanctuarygolfclub.com			
The Sharon GC, *Sharon Center*	18	[V]	330-239-2383
The Vineyard GC, *Cincinnati*	18	[M]	513-474-3007
greatparks.org			
Thorn Apple CC, *Galloway*	18	[P]	614-878-7703
thornapplegolf.com			
Thunder Hill GC, *Madison*	36	[P]	440-298-3474
thunderhillgolf.com			
Thunderbird Hills GC, *Huron*	36	[P]	419-433-4552
thunderbirdhills.com			
Timberview GC, *Marysville*	18	[P]	937-644-4653
timberviewgolfclub.com			
Tippecanoe CC, *Canfield*	18	[V]	330-758-2380
Toledo CC, *Toledo*	18	[V]	419-385-0862
toledocountryclub.com			
Tomahawk Hollow GC, *Gambier*	18	[P]	740-427-2081
TPC Rivers Bend, *Maineville*	18	[V]	513-677-0550
tpcriversbend.com			
Tree Links GC, *Bellefontaine*	18	[P]	937-592-7888
treelinks.com			
Troy CC, *Troy*	18	[V]	937-335-5691
troycc.com			
Trumbull CC, *Warren*	18	[V]	330-372-5127
trumbullcountryclub.net			
Turkana Farms GC, *East Liverpool*	18	[P]	330-382-1187
Turkeyfoot Lake Golf Links, *Akron*	27	[P]	330-644-5971
turkeyfootgolf.com			
Turnberry GC, *Pickerington*	18	[M]	614-645-2582
columbuscitygolfcourses.com			
Twin Base GC, *Wright Patterson AFB*	18	[A]	937-253-6181
88thservices.com/golfcourses.htm			
Twin Lakes CC, *Kent*	9	[V]	330-673-3515
twinlakescountryclub.com			
Twin Lakes GC, *Mansfield*	18	[P]	419-529-3777
Twin Lakes GC, *Bellevue*	9	[P]	419-483-2842
twinlakesbellevue.com			
Twin Oaks GC, *Dublin*	9	[P]	614-873-8511
Twin Run Muni GC, *Hamilton*	18	[M]	513-868-5833
twinrun.com			
Twin Springs GC, *Lisbon*	9	[P]	330-222-2335
Union CC, *Dover*	18	[V]	330-343-2334
Union City CC, *Union City*	9	[P]	937-968-6518
Upper Lansdowne Golf Links, *Ashville*	18	[P]	740-983-2989
upperlansdownegolf.com			

[S] = SEMI-PRIVATE [V] = PRIVATE [U] = UNIVERSITY [N] = UNIVERSITY-PRIVATE

OHIO

Golf Yellow Pages, 18th Edition

Urbana CC, *Urbana* .... 18 [V] 937-653-1689
 urbanacc.net
Valleaire GC, *Hinckley* ....18 [P] 440-237-9191
 valleairegolf.com
Valley GC, *Columbiana* ....9 [P] 330-482-9464
Valley View Club, *Lancaster*................................18 [P] 740-687-1112
 golfvalleyview.com
Valley View GC, *Crestline*....................................18 [P] 419-468-1226
Valley View GC, *Akron*..27 [P] 330-928-9034
Valley Vista GC, *Bainbridge*................................18 [P] 740-634-2221
 valleyvistagolf.com
Valleywood GC, *Swanton*..................................18 [P] 419-826-3991
 valleywoodgc.com
Vermilion CC, *Vermilion* ....9 [P] 440-967-3492
 vermilioncountryclub.com
Veterans Memorial Park GC, *Kenton*..................18 [M] 419-674-4573
 vmpgc.com
Vienna Short Holes GC, *Vienna* ....9 [P] 330-394-2626
Village Green GC, *North Kingsville*......................18 [M] 440-224-0931
Village View GC, *Croton*....................................18 [P] 740-893-4653
Vista Verde GC, *Hamilton* ....18 [P] 513-868-6948
 vistaverdegolf.com
Vista View GC, *Nashport* ....18 [P] 740-453-4758
 vistaviewgolf.com
Walden Ponds GC, *Hamilton* ....18 [P] 513-785-2999
 waldenponds.com
Walnut Grove CC, *Dayton* .... 18 [V] 937-253-6451
 walnutgrovecc.net
Walnut Hill GC, *Columbus* ....9 [M] 614-645-3100
 columbuscitygolfcourses.com
Walnut Run GC, *Cortland* ....27 [P] 330-638-4653
 walnutrun.com
Wapakoneta CC, *Wapakoneta*..............................9 [V] 419-657-2020
Washington CC, *Washington Ct House*.................9 [P] 740-335-3490
Washington Golf Learning Ctr, *Newburgh Heights* 9 [M] 216-641-1864
 clemetparks.com
Waverly GC, *Waverly*..9 [P] 740-947-7422
Wayside GC, *Findlay* ....9 [P] 419-423-5089
Weatherwax GC, *Middletown* ....36 [M] 513-425-7886
 playweatherwax.com
Wedgewood G&CC, *Powell* .... 18 [V] 614-793-9600
 wedgewoodgolfcc.com
Westbrook CC, *Mansfield* .... 18 [V] 419-747-2556
 westbrookcc.org
Westchester GC, *Canal Winchester* ....18 [P] 614-834-4653
 westchestergolfcourse.com
Western Hills CC, *Cincinnati* .... 18 [V] 513-922-0019
 westernhillscountryclub.com
Westfield Group CC, *Westfield Center* .... 36 [V] 330-887-0391
 westfieldgrp.com
Westgate Golf Ctr, *Newton Falls* ....9 [P] 330-872-7984
 tesslergolf.net
Wests Mogadore CC, *Mogadore* ....18 [P] 330-628-2611
Westville Lake GC, *Beloit* ....9 [P] 330-537-4042
Westwood, *Rocky River* .... 18 [P] 440-331-2120
 westwoodcountryclub.org
Wetherington G&CC, *West Chester* ....18 [V] 513-755-2278
 wetheringtoncc.com
Weymouth CC, *Medina* .... 18 [V] 330-725-6497
 weymouthcc.com
WGC GC, *Xenia*..18 [P] 937-372-1202
 wgcgolfcourse.com

Whetstone GC, *Caledonia* ....18 [P] 740-389-4343
 whetstonegolf.com
Whiskey Run GC, *Quaker City*.............................18 [R] 740-679-2422
 whiskeyrun.8m.com
Whispering Pines GC, *Columbiana*.......................9 [P] 330-482-3733
 whisperingpinesvillage.com
White Oak GC, *Sardinia*.....................................18 [P] 937-444-2888
 whiteoakgolf.com
White Pines GC, *Swanton* ....18 [P] 419-875-5535
 whitepinesgc.com
White Springs GC, *Greenville*................................9 [P] 937-548-6546
Wicked Woods GC, *Newbury* ....18 [P] 440-564-7960
Wildfire GC, *New Concord* ....18 [P] 740-826-7606
 wildfiregolfclub.com
Wildwood CC, *Fairfield* ....9 [P] 513-874-3754
Wildwood GC, *Middletown* .... 18 [V] 513-422-7138
 wildwoodgc.com
Wilkshire GC, *Bolivar* ....18 [P] 330-874-2525
Willandale GC, *Sugarcreek* ....27 [P] 330-852-4395
 willandalegolf.com
Willard GC, *Willard* ....9 [P] 419-935-0252
Willow Bend GC, *Van Wert* ....9 [V] 419-238-1041
 willow-bend.com
Willow Creek GC, *Vermilion* ....18 [P] 440-967-4101
 golfwillow.com
Willow Ponds GC, *Tipp City* ....9 [P] 937-667-0100
Willow Run GC, *Pataskala*..................................18 [P] 740-927-1932
 golfwillowrun.com
Wilson Road GC, *Columbus*..................................9 [M] 614-645-3221
 columbuscitygolfcourses.com
Winding Hollow GC, *New Albany*.......................18 [P] 614-855-8600
 windinghollow.com
Windmill Lakes GC, *Ravenna* ....18 [P] 330-297-0440
 golfwindmilllakes.com
Windwood Hollow GC, *Edon*..............................18 [P] 419-272-3310
 windwoodhollow.com
Windy Acres GC, *New Bloomington*...................18 [P] 740-499-3438
Windy Hill GC & Campground, *Conneaut* ....18 [R] 440-594-5251
 windyhillgolf.com
Windy Hills GC, *Rockbridge* ....9 [P] 740-385-7886
Windy Knoll GC, *Springfield*...............................18 [P] 937-399-0001
 windyknollgolfclub.com
Woodland GC, *Cincinnati* ....9 [M] 513-451-4408
 cincygolf.org
Woodland GC, *Cable* ....18 [P] 937-653-8875
 golfwoodland.com
Woody Ridge GC, *Shelby*...................................18 [P] 419-347-1588
Wooldridge Woods G&SwimC, *Mansfield*........... 18 [S] 419-756-1026
Wooster CC, *Wooster* .... 18 [V] 330-263-1988
 woostercountryclub.com
Worthington Hills CC, *Columbus* .... 18 [V] 614-885-9128
 worthingtonhills.com
Wosusickett GC, *Sandusky* ....18 [P] 419-359-1141
 greenhillsgolf.com
Wyandot GC, *Centerburg*..................................18 [P] 740-625-5370
 wyandotgolf.com
Wyoming GC, *Cincinnati* ....9 [P] 513-821-8226
Yankee Run GC, *Brookfield* ....18 [P] 330-448-8096
 yankeerun.com
York GC, *Columbus*... 18 [V] 614-885-5459
 yorkgolfclubonline.com
Youngstown CC, *Youngstown*............................ 18 [V] 330-759-1040
 youngstowncountryclub.com

170 [A] = MILITARY [M] = MUNICIPAL [P] = PUBLIC [R] = RESORT

Golf Yellow Pages, 18th Edition

OKLAHOMA

Zanesville CC, *Zanesville* .... 18 [V] 740-452-1563
zanesvillecc.com
Zoar Village GC, *Dover*.......................................18 [P] 330-874-4653
zoargolf.com

OKLAHOMA

Adams Muni GC, *Bartlesville*...........................18 [M] 918-331-3900
cityofbartlesville.org
Alva G&CC, *Alva*..9 [P] 580-327-2296
Antlers Springs GC, *Antlers* ....9 [P] 580-298-9900
Arrowhead St Park GC, *Canadian* ....18 [M] 918-339-2769
touroklahoma.com/golf_courses.asp
Atoka Trails GC, *Atoka* ....9 [P] 580-889-7171
Bailey Ranch GC, *Owasso*.................................18 [M] 918-274-4653
baileyranchgolf.com
Battle Creek GC, *Broken Arrow*.........................18 [M] 918-355-4850
battlecreekgolf.net
Beaver GC, *Beaver* ....9 [P] 580-625-3633
Belmar GC, *Norman*.. 18 [V] 405-364-0111
ilovethiscourse.com
Blackmer Muni GC, *Hooker*................................9 [M] 580-652-2856
Blackwell Muni GC, *Blackwell* ....9 [M] 580-363-1228
Boiling Springs GC, *Woodward*.......................18 [P] 580-256-1206
boilingspringsgolfcourse.com
Brent Bruehl Mem GC, *Purcell*........................18 [P] 405-527-5114
Brier Creek GC, *Stigler*......................................9 [P] 918-967-8225
Bristow Community G&CC, *Bristow*................9 [P] 918-367-5156
Broadmoore GC, *Moore* ....18 [P] 405-794-1529
Broken Arrow G&AC, *Broken Arrow* .... 18 [V] 918-355-0602
lindseymanagement.com
Brookside GC, *Oklahoma City*...........................9 [P] 405-632-9666
Buffalo Hills GC, *Pawhuska* ....9 [P] 918-287-1695
buffalohillsgolf.com
Buncombe Creek GC, *Kingston*........................9 [P] 580-564-1260
buncombecreekgolf.com
Cedar Creek GC At Beavers Bend St Park,
  Broken Bow ....18 [M] 580-494-6456
touroklahoma.com/golf_courses.asp
Cedar Crest GC, *Skiatook* ....9 [P] 918-396-0200
Cedar Lakes GC, *Fort Sill* ....18 [A] 580-442-3875
Cedar Ridge CC, *Broken Arrow*....................... 18 [V] 918-252-2505
cedarridgecountryclub.com
Cedar Valley Exec Par 3, *Guthrie*........................ 9 [R] 405-282-4478
cedarvalleygolfclub.com
Cedar Valley GC, *Guthrie* ....36 [P] 405-282-4800
cedarvalleygolfclub.com
Chandler GC, *Chandler* ....9 [M] 405-258-3068
Cherokee Grove GC, *Grove*................................9 [P] 918-786-9852
Cherokee Hills GC, *Catoosa* ....18 [R] 918-384-7600
cherokeecasino.com
Cherokee Trails GC, *Tahlequah*.........................9 [P] 918-458-4294
cherokeecasino.com
Cherry Springs GC, *Tahlequah*.......................18 [P] 918-456-5100
cherryspringsgolfclub.com
Cheyenne GC, *Cheyenne* ....9 [P] 580-497-2460
Chickasaw Pointe GC, *Kingston*......................18 [P] 580-564-2581
pointe-vista.com
Choctaw CC, *Poteau*... 9 [V] 918-647-3488
choctawcountryclub.com
Choctaw Creek GC, *Choctaw* ....18 [P] 405-769-7166
choctawcreekgolf.com
Cimarron County GC, *Boise City*......................9 [M] 580-544-2589

Cimarron National GC, *Guthrie*........................36 [P] 405-282-7888
cimarronnational.com
Cimarron Trails GC, *Perkins* ....18 [P] 405-547-5701
cimarrontrails.com
Clary Fields GC, *Sapulpa* ....18 [P] 918-248-4080
claryfields.com
Cobblestone Creek GC, *Muskogee* ....18 [P] 918-682-4845
cobblestonecreekgolf.com
Cobblestone Creek GC, *Norman* ....9 [P] 405-872-2582
cobblestonecreekgolfclub.com
Coffee Creek GC, *Edmond* ....18 [P] 405-340-4653
coffeecreekgolfclub.com
Comanche GC, *Comanche* ....9 [P] 580-439-8879
Cordell G&CC, *Cordell* ....9 [P] 580-832-2232
Cotton Creek GC, *Mounds* ....18 [P] 918-827-3673
Cottonwood Creek At Chickasha, *Chickasha*......... 9 [V] 405-224-1250
Crimson Creek GC, *El Reno* ....18 [M] 405-422-4653
crimsoncreekgolf.com
Cushing CC, *Cushing* ....18 [P] 918-225-6734
cushingcountryclub.com
Deer Valley GC, *Kansas* ....9 [P] 918-597-3636
Dietrich Memorial GC, *Anadarko* ....9 [P] 405-247-2274
dietrichmemorialgolf.com
Doby Springs GC, *Buffalo*..................................9 [P] 580-735-2654
dobyspringsgolf.com
Dornick Hills G&CC, *Ardmore*........................ 18 [V] 580-223-2957
dornickhills.com
Dr Gil Morgan Muni GC, *Wewoka*....................9 [M] 405-257-3292
wewoka.com/recreation.htm
Drumright GC, *Drumright* ....9 [P] 918-352-9424
Duncan G&CC, *Duncan*....................................18 [S] 580-255-7706
Durant CC, *Durant*..18 [P] 580-924-0622
durantgolf.com
Eagle Crest GC, *Muskogee* ....18 [P] 918-682-0866
Earlywine GC, *Oklahoma City*..........................36 [M] 405-691-1727
okcgolf.com
Eccentric Duffer GC & Range, *Ada* .... 9 [R] 405-332-4950
eccentricduffer.com
Elk City G&CC, *Elk City* ....18 [P] 580-225-5454
Elks CC, *Shawnee*... 18 [V] 405-275-1060
Emerald Falls GC, *Broken Arrow* ....18 [P] 918-806-6563
emeraldfalls.com
Fairfax GC, *Edmond* ....18 [P] 405-359-8333
fairfaxgolfclubofedmond.com
Fairview Lakeside CC, *Longdale* ....9 [P] 580-227-3225
Falconhead Resort & CC, *Burneyville*..............18 [R] 580-276-9284
falconheadgolf.com
Firelake GC, *Shawnee* ....18 [M] 405-275-4471
potawatomi.org
Forest Ridge GC, *Broken Arrow*.......................18 [P] 918-357-2443
forestridge.com
Fort Cobb St Park GC, *Fort Cobb* ....18 [M] 405-643-2398
touroklahoma.com/golf_courses.asp
Fort Sill GC, *Fort Sill* ....18 [A] 580-442-5441
army.mil
Fountainhead GC At Eufalla St Park, *Checotah*....18 [P] 918-689-3209
fountainheadgolf.com
Frederick G&CC, *Frederick* .... 9 [V] 580-335-2911
Gaillardia CC, *Oklahoma City*......................... 18 [V] 405-302-2810
gaillardia.com
GC At Surrey Hills, *Yukon* ....18 [P] 405-373-2770
surreyhillsok.com
Generation GC, *Marlow* ....18 [P] 580-658-3021

[S] = SEMI-PRIVATE   [V] = PRIVATE   [U] = UNIVERSITY   [N] = UNIVERSITY-PRIVATE

OKLAHOMA

Golf Yellow Pages, 18th Edition

Golden Oaks Village Green Golf, *Enid* .... 9 [P] 580-249-2600
  goldenoaks.com
Gordon GC, *Claremore* .... 9 [P] 918-283-3333
Grand Cherokee St Park GC, *Langley* .... 9 [M] 918-435-8727
  touroklahoma.com/golf_courses.asp
Guthrie G&CC, *Guthrie* .... 9 [V] 405-282-1315
  guthriegolfandcountryclub.wetpaint.com
Henryetta G&CC, *Henryetta* .... 9 [P] 918-652-8664
Heritage Hills GC, *Claremore* .... 18 [P] 918-341-0055
  heritagehillsgc.com
Hickory Ridge GC, *Hendrix* .... 9 [S] 580-283-3051
  golf-hickoryridge.com
Hillcrest CC, *Bartlesville* .... 18 [V] 918-333-0687
  hillcrestok.com
Hilltop GC, *Porter* .... 9 [P] 918-483-9551
Hobart Muni GC, *Hobart* .... 9 [P] 580-726-3534
Hollis G&CC, *Hollis* .... 9 [P] 580-688-3673
Hugo GC, *Hugo* .... 9 [P] 580-326-6549
Hummingbird GC, *Cache* .... 9 [P] 580-429-4400
Idabel CC, *Idabel* .... 18 [P] 580-286-7545
  idabelcountryclub.com
Indian Springs CC, *Broken Arrow* .... 36 [V] 918-455-9515
  indianspringscc.com
James E Stewart GC, *Oklahoma City* .... 9 [M] 405-424-4353
  okcgolf.com
Jimmy Austin GC, *Seminole* .... 18 [M] 405-382-3365
Jimmy Austin GC Univ Oklahoma, *Norman* .... 18 [U] 405-325-6716
  ougolfclub.com
John Conrad GC, *Midwest City* .... 18 [M] 405-732-2209
  midwestcityok.org/golfcourse.html
Kah Wah C CC, *Fairfax* .... 9 [P] 918-642-5351
Karsten Creek GC, *Stillwater* .... 18 [P] 405-743-1658
  karstencreek.net
Keystone GC, *Cleveland* .... 9 [P] 918-358-2277
  keystonegolfcourse.com
KickingBird GC, *Edmond* .... 18 [M] 405-341-5350
  kickingbirdgolf.com
Kingfisher GC, *Kingfisher* .... 18 [M] 405-375-3941
  kingfisher.ok.gov
LaFortune Park GC, *Tulsa* .... 27 [M] 918-496-6200
  parks.tulsacounty.org
Lake Hefner GC, *Oklahoma City* .... 36 [M] 405-843-1565
  okcgolf.com
Lake Murray St Park GC, *Ardmore* .... 18 [M] 580-223-6613
  touroklahoma.com/golf_courses.asp
Lakeside GC, *Stillwater* .... 18 [M] 405-372-3399
Lakeside GC, *Walters* .... 18 [M] 580-875-3829
Lakeside GC, *Moore* .... 9 [P] 405-794-0252
Lakeview GC, *Ardmore* .... 18 [M] 580-223-4260
  ardmorecity.com
Lakeview GC, *Shidler* .... 9 [P] 918-793-2721
Lakewood GC, *Ada* .... 9 [P] 580-332-5151
Laverne G&CC, *Laverne* .... 9 [P] 580-921-5228
Lawton CC, *Lawton* .... 18 [V] 580-353-2073
Lawton Muni GC, *Lawton* .... 18 [M] 580-353-4493
Lew Wentz GC, *Ponca City* .... 18 [M] 580-767-0433
  wentzgolf.com
Lincoln Park GC, *Oklahoma City* .... 36 [M] 405-424-1421
  okcgolf.com
Lindsay Muni GC, *Lindsay* .... 9 [M] 405-756-3611
Links on Memorial Golf & Athletic Club, *Bixby* ... 9 [P] 918-369-6035
Litl Links GC, *Broken Arrow* .... 18 [P] 918-481-3673
  litlinks.com

Mangum GC, *Mangum* .... 9 [M] 580-782-3676
McAlester CC, *McAlester* .... 18 [V] 918-423-3599
  mcalesterproshop.com
Meadowbrook CC, *Tulsa* .... 18 [V] 918-252-4121
  meadowbrook.americangolf.com
Meadowlake GC, *Enid* .... 18 [M] 580-234-3080
  enid.org
Miami G&CC, *Miami* .... 18 [P] 918-542-2512
Midwest City Muni GC, *Midwest City* .... 9 [M] 405-732-9999
Mohawk Park GC, *Tulsa* .... 36 [M] 918-425-6871
  tulsagolf.org
Moore G&AC, *Moore* .... 18 [V] 405-790-0264
  lindseymanagement.com
Muskogee CC, *Muskogee* .... 18 [V] 918-682-3721
  muskogeecountryclub.com
Nashoba Valley GC & Cabins, *Nashoba* .... 9 [P] 918-755-4519
New Kirk CC, *Newkirk* .... 9 [M] 580-362-2240
Northern Hills GC, *Enid* .... 9 [U] 580-234-5131
Nowata CC, *Nowata* .... 9 [P] 918-273-0928
Oak Hills CC, *Ada* .... 18 [V] 580-332-3762
  oakhillsada.com
Oak Tree CC, *Edmond* .... 36 [V] 405-844-4653
  oaktreecc.net
Oak Tree National, *Edmond* .... 18 [V] 405-348-2004
  oaktreenational.com
Oaks CC, *Tulsa* .... 18 [V] 918-446-5518
  oakscountryclub.com
Oakwood CC, *Enid* .... 18 [V] 580-234-5811
  occofenid.org
Oil Field Rec Assoc, *Healdton* .... 9 [P] 580-229-2520
Okeene GC, *Okeene* .... 9 [M] 580-822-3435
Okemah GC, *Okemah* .... 9 [M] 918-623-9516
Oklahoma City G&CC, *Oklahoma City* .... 18 [V] 405-848-5611
  okcgcc.com
Okmulgee GC, *Okmulgee* .... 18 [P] 918-756-8000
Osage Creek GC, *Adair* .... 18 [P] 918-785-4166
Owasso G&AC, *Owasso* .... 18 [V] 918-274-4884
  lindseymanagement.com
Page Belcher GC, *Tulsa* .... 36 [M] 918-446-1529
  tulsagolf.org
Panhandle State Univ GC, *Goodwell* .... 9 [U] 580-349-2611
  opsu.edu
Patricia Island GC, *Grove* .... 18 [R] 918-786-3338
  patriciaisland.com
Pauls Valley GC, *Pauls Valley* .... 9 [M] 405-238-7462
Pawnee Muni GC, *Pawnee* .... 9 [M] 918-762-3785
Pebble Creek GC, *Mustang* .... 9 [P] 405-376-8892
Pecan Valley GC, *Fort Gibson* .... 9 [P] 918-478-9774
Peoria Ridge GC, *Miami* .... 18 [P] 918-542-7676
  peoriaridge.com
Perry G&CC, *Perry* .... 9 [V] 580-336-2326
Persimmon Hills GC, *Meeker* .... 9 [P] 405-279-3424
Pheasant Run, *Enid* .... 18 [P] 580-233-2355
  pheasantrunenid.com
Ponca City CC, *Ponca City* .... 18 [V] 580-762-4413
  poncacitycountryclub.net
Prague GC, *Prague* .... 9 [P] 405-567-2857
Prairie West GC At Weatherford, *Weatherford* .... 18 [P] 580-772-3832
Pryor Creek GC, *Pryor* .... 18 [M] 918-825-3056
  pryorcreekgolf.org
Quail Creek G&CC, *Oklahoma City* .... 18 [V] 405-751-0811
  quailcreekgcc.com
Quail Run GC, *Muldrow* .... 9 [P] 918-427-5315

[A] = MILITARY   [M] = MUNICIPAL   [P] = PUBLIC   [R] = RESORT

Quartz Mountain GC, *Lone Wolf* .... 18 [P] 580-563-2520
  quartzmountainresort.com
River Bend GC, *Chickasha* .... 27 [P] 405-222-1995
  riverbendok.com
River Oaks GC, *Edmond* .... 18 [V] 405-771-5800
  riveroaksgolf.com
Riverside GC, *Clinton* .... 18 [M] 405-323-5958
  clintonokla.org
Rock Creek GC, *Hugo* .... 9 [P] 580-326-6130
  rockcreekhugo.com
Rolling Meadows GC, *Covington* .... 9 [P] 580-863-2207
Roman Nose Resort Park GC, *Watonga* .... 18 [R] 580-623-7989
  touroklahoma.com/golf_courses.asp
Rose Creek GC, *Edmond* .... 18 [P] 405-330-8220
  rosecreekok.com
Sapulpa Muni GC, *Sapulpa* .... 18 [M] 918-224-0237
Sayre GC, *Sayre* .... 9 [M] 580-928-9046
Scissortail GC, *Claremore* .... 18 [P] 918-266-5000
  scissortailgolfclub.com
Seiling GC, *Seiling* .... 9 [P] 580-922-3565
Sequoyah St Park GC, *Hulbert* .... 18 [M] 918-772-2297
  touroklahoma.com/golf_courses.asp
Shadow Creek CC, *Sallisaw* .... 18 [P] 918-775-6997
Shangri La CC, *Monkey Island* .... 36 [R] 918-257-4204
  shangrilaok.com
Shattuck GC, *Shattuck* .... 9 [P] 580-938-2445
Shawnee CC, *Shawnee* .... 18 [V] 405-273-2764
  shawneecc.com
Silverado GC, *Durant* .... 18 [P] 580-924-1899
  silveradogolf.com
Silverhorn GC, *Oklahoma City* .... 18 [P] 405-752-1181
  silverhorn.americangolf.com
South Lakes GC, *Jenks* .... 18 [M] 918-746-3760
  southlakesgolf.com
Southern Hills CC, *Tulsa* .... 27 [V] 918-494-0001
  southernhillscc.org
Stillwater CC, *Stillwater* .... 18 [V] 405-372-8987
  thestillwatercountryclub.com
Stroud Muni GC, *Stroud* .... 9 [M] 918-968-2105
Sugar Creek Canyon GC, *Hinton* .... 18 [M] 405-542-3974
  sugarcreekcanyon.com
Sulphur Hills GC, *Sulphur* .... 9 [P] 580-622-5057
Sunset Hills GC, *Guymon* .... 18 [M] 580-338-7404
Sycamore Springs GC, *Wilburton* .... 9 [P] 918-465-3161
Tahlequah City GC, *Tahlequah* .... 9 [M] 918-456-3761
  cityoftahlequah.com
The Canyons At Blackjack Ridge, *Sand Springs* ... 18 [M] 918-246-2606
  sandspringsok.org
The Coves at Bird Island, *Afton* .... 18 [V] 918-782-3220
  thecoves.com
The GC at Indian Ridge, *Blanchard* .... 18 [P] 405-485-8608
The GC of Oklahoma, *Broken Arrow* .... 18 [V] 918-486-6575
  golfcluboklahoma.com
The Greens, *Burns Flat* .... 9 [P] 580-562-4204
The Greens CC, *Oklahoma City* .... 18 [P] 405-751-6266
  thegreenscc.com
The Greens of Altus, *Altus* .... 9 [P] 580-480-0209
The Links At Mustang Creek, *Yukon* .... 9 [P] 405-577-5858
  lindseymanagement.com
The Links at Norman G&CC, *Norman* .... 18 [V] 405-329-6549
  linksatnormangolf.com
The Links At Oklahoma City, *Oklahoma City* ..... 9 [P] 405-936-9214

The Links At Stillwater, *Stillwater* .... 18 [P] 405-780-7167
  lindseymanagement.com
The Patriot At Stone Canyon, *Owasso* .... 18 [V] 918-272-1260
  patriotgolfclub.com
The Territory G&CC, *Duncan* .... 18 [V] 580-475-0075
  territorygolf.com
The Trails GC, *Norman* .... 18 [V] 405-360-1920
  trailsgolf.com
The Woods GC, *Coweta* .... 18 [P] 918-486-3117
Thundercreek GC, *McAlester* .... 18 [P] 918-423-5799
Tinker GC, *Tinker AFB* .... 18 [A] 405-734-2909
Tishomingo G&RecC, *Tishomingo* .... 9 [P] 580-371-2604
Trosper Park GC, *Oklahoma City* .... 18 [M] 405-677-8874
  okcgolf.com
Tulsa CC, *Tulsa* .... 18 [V] 918-585-8719
  tulsacountryclub.com
Turkey Creek GC, *Hennessey* .... 18 [P] 405-853-2100
Twin Hills G&CC, *Oklahoma City* .... 18 [V] 405-427-3947
  twin-hills.com
Twin Oaks GC, *Duncan* .... 18 [V] 580-252-4714
  twinoaksgolfclub.com
Watonga GC, *Watonga* .... 9 [M] 580-623-4674
Westbury CC, *Yukon* .... 18 [P] 405-324-0707
Westwood Park GC, *Norman* .... 18 [M] 405-292-9700
  westwoodparkgolf.com
Wetumka GC, *Wetumka* .... 9 [M] 405-452-3273
White Hawk GC, *Bixby* .... 18 [P] 918-366-4653
  whitehawk.americangolf.com
White Sands GC, *Valliant* .... 9 [P] 580-933-7355
  whitesandsgolfclubok.com
Wildhorse GC, *Velma* .... 9 [P] 580-444-3338
Willow Creek CC, *Oklahoma City* .... 18 [V] 405-685-7751
  willowcreekcc.org
Windy Trails Altus Air Force GC, *Altus AFB* .... 18 [A] 580-481-7207
  altusservices.com
WinStar GC, *Thackerville* .... 18 [R] 580-276-1240
  winstargolfcourse.com
Winter Creek GC, *Blanchard* .... 18 [P] 405-224-3338
  wintercreekgolf.com
Wolf Ridge GC, *Wister* .... 18 [P] 918-647-2582
  wolfridgegolfclub.com
Woodward Muni GC, *Woodward* .... 9 [P] 580-256-9028

OREGON

Agate Beach GC, *Newport* .... 9 [P] 541-265-7331
  agatebeachgolf.net
Alderbrook GC, *Tillamook* .... 18 [P] 503-842-6413
  tillamoo.com/alderbrookgolf.html
Alpine Meadows GC, *Enterprise* .... 9 [P] 541-426-3246
  alpinemeadowsgolfcourse.com
Applegate River Golf, *Grants Pass* .... 9 [P] 541-955-0480
Arrowhead GC, *Molalla* .... 18 [V] 503-829-8080
  golfarrowhead.com
Aspen Lakes GC, *Sisters* .... 18 [P] 541-549-4653
  aspenlakes.com
Astoria G&CC, *Warrenton* .... 18 [V] 503-861-2545
  astoriagolf.com
Auburn Ctr GC, *Salem* .... 9 [P] 503-363-4404
Awbrey Glen GC, *Bend* .... 18 [V] 541-385-6011
  awbreyglen.com
Bandon Crossings GC, *Bandon* .... 18 [P] 541-347-3232
  bandoncrossings.com

OREGON

Golf Yellow Pages, 18th Edition

Bandon Dunes Golf Resort, *Bandon* ....72 [R] 541-347-4380
  bandondunesgolf.com
Bay Breeze GC, *Tillamook* ....9 [P] 503-842-1166
Bayou GC, *McMinnville* ....18 [P] 503-472-4651
  bayougolfcourse.com
Bear Creek GC, *Medford* ....9 [P] 541-773-1822
  golfbearcreek.com
Bear Valley Meadows GC, *Seneca* ....9 [M] 541-542-2161
  pasturegolf.com/bear.htm
Bend G&CC, *Bend* ....18 [V] 541-382-2878
  bendgolfclub.com
Big River GC, *Umatilla* ....18 [P] 541-922-3006
  golfbigriver.com
Black Butte Ranch GC - Big Meadow, *Sisters* ....18 [R] 541-595-1500
  blackbutteranch.com
Black Butte Ranch GC - Glaze Meadow, *Sisters* ...18 [R] 541-595-1500
  blackbutteranch.com
Brasada Canyons GC at Brasada Ranch,
  Powell Butte..18 [R] 541-526-6380
  brasada.com
Broadmoor GC, *Portland* ....18 [P] 503-281-1337
  broadmoor-1931.com
Broken Top Club, *Bend* ....18 [V] 541-383-7683
  brokentop.com
Buffalo Peak GC, *Union* ....18 [M] 541-562-5527
  buffalopeakgolf.com
Cedar Bend GC, *Gold Beach* ....9 [P] 541-247-6911
  cedarbendgolf.com
Cedar Links GC, *Medford* ....9 [P] 541-773-4373
  cedarlinks.com
Centennial GC, *Medford* ....18 [P] 541-773-4653
  centennialgolfclub.com
Charbonneau GC, *Wilsonville* ....27 [P] 503-694-1246
  charbonneaugolf.com
Chehalem Glenn GC, *Newberg* ....18 [R] 503-538-5800
  chehalemglenn.com
China Creek GC, *Arlington* ....9 [M] 541-454-2000
  honkernet.net/visitarlington/golf_course.htm
Chinook Winds Golf Resort, *Lincoln City* ....18 [R] 541-994-8442
  chinookwindscasino.com
Christmas Valley GC, *Christmas Valley* ....9 [M] 541-576-2216
  cvgolfcourse.org
Circle Bar GC, *Oakridge* ....9 [P] 541-782-3541
Claremont GC, *Portland* ....9 [P] 503-690-4589
  claremontgolfclub.com
Colonial Valley Links, *Grants Pass* ....9 [P] 541-479-5568
Columbia Edgewater CC, *Portland* ....27 [V] 503-285-3676
  cecc.com
Colwood National GC, *Portland* ....18 [P] 503-254-5515
  colwoodgolfclub.com
Condon GC, *Condon* ....9 [M] 541-384-4266
  cityofcondon.com
Coquille Valley Elk GC, *Coquille* ....9 [V] 541-572-5367
Corvallis CC, *Corvallis* ....18 [P] 541-752-3471
  corvalliscc.info
Cottonwood Lakes Golf Ctr, *Salem* ....9 [P] 503-364-3673
Country View GC, *Ontario* ....9 [P] 541-881-1171
Creekside GC, *Salem* ....18 [P] 503-363-4653
  golfcreekside.com
Crestview GC, *Waldport* ....9 [P] 541-563-3020
  crestviewgolfclub.com
Crooked River Ranch GC, *Crooked River Ranch* .....18 [R] 541-923-6343
  crookedriverranch.com

Cross Creek GC, *Dallas* ....18 [P] 503-623-6666
  crosscreekgc.com
Crosswater Club At Sunriver, *Sunriver* ....18 [R] 541-593-1145
  crosswater.com
Dallas GC, *Dallas* ....9 [P] 503-623-6832
Desert Peaks GC, *Madras* ....9 [M] 541-475-6368
  ci.madras.or.us
Diamond Woods GC, *Monroe* ....18 [P] 541-998-9707
  diamondwoods.com
Dutcher Creek GC, *Grants Pass* ....18 [P] 541-474-2188
  dutchercreekgolf.com
Eagle Creek GC, *Eagle Creek* ....18 [P] 503-630-4676
Eagle Crest Golf Resort, *Redmond* ....54 [R] 541-923-4653
  eagle-crest.com
Eagle Landing Family Golf Ctr, *Happy Valley* ......27 [P] 503-698-7888
  eaglelandingsite.com
Eagle Point GC, *Eagle Point* ....18 [P] 541-826-8225
  eaglepointgolf.com
Eastmoreland GC, *Portland* ....18 [M] 503-775-2900
  eastmorelandgolfcourse.com
Echo Hills Muni GC, *Echo* ....9 [M] 541-376-8244
  echo-oregon.com
Elkhorn Valley GC, *Lyons* ....18 [P] 503-897-3368
  elkhorngolf.com
Emerald Valley GC, *Creswell* ....18 [R] 541-895-2174
  emeraldvalleygolf.com
Eugene CC, *Eugene* ....18 [V] 541-344-5124
  eugenecountryclub.com
Eugene Eagles #275 FOE, *Eugene* ....9 [P] 541-688-9471
Evergreen GC, *Mt Angel* ....9 [P] 503-845-9911
  evergreenoregon.com
Fiddlers Green GC, *Eugene* ....18 [P] 541-689-8464
  fiddlersgreen.com
Forest Hills CC, *Cornelius* ....18 [P] 503-357-3347
  golfforesthills.com
Forest Hills CC, *Reedsport* ....9 [P] 541-271-2626
  golfreedsport.com
Frontier GC, *Canby* ....9 [P] 503-266-4435
  pasturegolf.com/courses/frontier.htm
Gearhart Golf Links, *Gearhart* ....18 [P] 503-738-3538
  gearhartgolflinks.com
Glendoveer GC, *Portland* ....36 [P] 503-253-7507
  golfglendoveer.com
Golf City Par 3, *Corvallis* ....9 [P] 541-753-6213
Grants Pass GC, *Grants Pass* ....18 [P] 541-476-0849
  grantspassgolfclub.com
Greenlea GC, *Boring* ....9 [P] 503-663-3934
  greenleagolfcourse.com
Gresham GC, *Gresham* ....18 [P] 503-665-3352
  greshamgolf.com
Harbor Links GC, *Klamath Falls* ....18 [P] 541-882-0609
  harborlinksgolf.net
Hawk Creek GC, *Neskowin* ....9 [P] 503-392-4120
  hawkcreekgolfcourse.com
Heron Lakes GC, *Portland* ....36 [M] 503-289-1818
  heronlakesgolf.com
Hidden Valley GC, *Cottage Grove* ....9 [P] 541-942-3046
  playhiddenvalleygolf.com
Highlands GC, *Gearhart* ....9 [P] 503-738-5248
  highlandsgolfgearhart.com
Hood River GC, *Hood River* ....18 [P] 541-386-3009
  hoodrivergolf.com
Illahe Hills CC, *Salem* ....18 [V] 503-364-0117
  illahehills.com

[A] = MILITARY   [M] = MUNICIPAL   [P] = PUBLIC   [R] = RESORT

OREGON

Illinois Valley GC, *Cave Junction* .... 9 [P] 541-592-3151
Indian Creek GC, *Hood River* .... 18 [P] 541-386-7770
　indiancreekgolf.com
John Day GC, *John Day* .... 9 [P] 541-575-0170
Juniper GC, *Redmond* .... 18 [P] 541-548-3121
　junipergolfcourse.com
Kah Nee Ta GC, *Warm Springs* .... 18 [R] 541-553-1112
　kahneeta.com
Kentuck GC, *North Bend* .... 18 [P] 541-756-4464
　kentuckgolfcourse.com
Killarney West GC, *Hillsboro* .... 9 [P] 503-648-7634
King City GC, *Portland* .... 9 [P] 503-639-7986
La Grande CC, *La Grande* .... 9 [V] 541-963-4241
　lagrandecountryclub.com
Lake Oswego Public GC, *Lake Oswego* .... 18 [M] 503-636-8228
　lakeoswegogolf.org
Lakeridge GC, *Lakeview* .... 9 [P] 541-947-3855
Langdon Farms GC, *Aurora* .... 18 [R] 503-678-4653
　langdonfarms.com
Laurel Hill GC, *Central Point* .... 9 [P] 541-855-7965
Laurelwood GC, *Eugene* .... 9 [M] 541-484-4653
　golflaurelwood.com
Lewis & Clark Public GC, *Astoria* .... 9 [P] 503-338-3386
　lewisandclarkatthecrossing.com
Lost Tracks GC, *Bend* .... 18 [P] 541-385-1818
　losttracks.com
Mallard Creek Golf & RV Resort, *Lebanon* ...... 18 [R] 541-259-4653
　mallardcreekgc.com
Manzanita GC, *Manzanita* .... 9 [P] 503-368-5744
　doormat.com
Marysville GC, *Corvallis* .... 9 [P] 541-753-3421
McKay Creek GC, *Hillsboro* .... 9 [P] 503-693-7612
　mckaycreekgolf.com
McKenzie River GC, *Springfield* .... 9 [P] 541-896-3454
McMenamins Pub Course, *Troutdale* .... 32 [P] 503-669-8610
　mcmenamins.com
McNary GC, *Keizer* .... 18 [P] 503-393-4653
　mcnarygolfclub.org
Meadow Lakes GC, *Prineville* .... 18 [M] 541-447-7113
　meadowlakesgc.com
Meadowlawn GC, *Salem* .... 9 [P] 503-363-7391
　meadowlawngolf.net
Meriwether National GC, *Hillsboro* .... 36 [P] 503-648-4143
　meriwethergolfclub.com
Michelbook CC, *McMinnville* .... 18 [V] 503-472-2129
　michelbook.com
Middlefield GC, *Cottage Grove* .... 18 [M] 541-942-8730
　middlefieldgolf.com
Milton Freewater GC, *Milton Freewater* .... 18 [M] 541-938-7284
　mfcity.com
Mountain View GC, *Boring* .... 18 [P] 541-663-4869
Myrtle Creek GC, *Myrtle Creek* .... 18 [P] 541-863-4653
　myrtlecreekgolf.com
Neskowin Marsh GC, *Neskowin* .... 9 [P] 503-392-3377
Oak Knoll GC, *Independence* .... 18 [P] 503-378-0344
　oakknollgolfcourse.com
Oak Knoll GC, *Ashland* .... 9 [M] 541-482-4311
　oakknollgolf.org
Oakway GC, *Eugene* .... 18 [P] 541-484-1927
　oakwaygolf.com
Ocean Dunes Golf Links, *Florence* .... 18 [P] 541-997-3232
　oceandunesgolf.com

OGA GC, *Woodburn* .... 18 [P] 503-981-6105
　ogagolfcourse.com
Olalla Valley GC, *Toledo* .... 9 [P] 541-336-2121
Old Bandon Golf Links, *Bandon* .... 9 [P] 541-329-1927
　oldbandongolflinks.com
Ontario GC, *Ontario* .... 18 [P] 541-889-9022
　oregongolf.com/ontario
Oregon City GC, *Oregon City* .... 18 [P] 503-518-2846
　ocgolfclub.com
Orion Greens GC, *Bend* .... 9 [P] 541-388-3999
Oswego Lake CC, *Lake Oswego* .... 18 [V] 503-635-3659
　oswegolakecountryclub.com
Pendleton CC, *Pendleton* .... 18 [V] 541-443-4653
　pendletoncc.com
Persimmon CC, *Gresham* .... 18 [V] 503-667-7500
　persimmoncc.americangolf.com
Pineway GC, *Lebanon* .... 9 [P] 541-258-8815
Pleasant Valley GC, *Clackamas* .... 18 [V] 503-658-3101
　pleasantvalleygolfclub.com
Portland GC, *Portland* .... 18 [P] 503-292-2778
　portlandgolfclub.com
Portland Meadows GC, *Portland* .... 9 [P] 503-289-3405
Prineville G&CC, *Prineville* .... 9 [V] 541-447-7266
　golfprineville.com
Pumpkin Ridge GC - Ghost Creek, *North Plains* .. 36 [V] 503-647-9977
　pumpkinridge.com
Pumpkin Ridge GC - Witch Hollow, *North Plains* 36 [V] 503-647-9977
　pumpkinridge.com
Quail Point GC, *Medford* .... 9 [P] 541-857-7000
　quailpointgolf.com
Quail Ridge GC, *Baker City* .... 18 [M] 541-523-2358
　bakercity.com
Quail Run GC, *La Pine* .... 18 [P] 541-536-1303
　golfquailrun.com
Quail Valley GC, *Banks* .... 18 [P] 503-324-4444
　quailvalleygolf.com
Ranch Hills GC, *Mulino* .... 9 [P] 503-829-5666
Reames G&CC, *Klamath Falls* .... 18 [V] 541-884-7446
　reamescc.com
Red Mountain GC, *Grants Pass* .... 9 [P] 541-479-2297
　redmountaingolf.com
RedTail Golf Ctr, *Beaverton* .... 18 [M] 503-646-5166
　golfredtail.com
RiverRidge G Complex, *Eugene* .... 36 [P] 541-345-9160
　riverridgeor.com
Rivers Edge Golf Resort, *Bend* .... 18 [R] 541-389-2828
　riverhouse.com
Riverside G&CC, *Portland* .... 18 [V] 503-282-7265
　riversidegcc.com
Rock Creek CC, *Portland* .... 18 [V] 503-645-1115
　rockcreekcountryclub.com
Rogue Valley CC, *Medford* .... 27 [V] 541-772-5965
　rvcc.com
Rose City GC, *Portland* .... 18 [M] 503-253-4744
　rosecitygc.com
Roseburg CC, *Roseburg* .... 18 [V] 541-672-4041
　roseburgcountryclub.com
Round Lake Resort, *Klamath Falls* .... 9 [R] 541-884-2520
　roundlakerv.com
Running Y Ranch Resort, *Klamath Falls* .... 18 [R] 541-850-5580
　runningy.com
Sah Hah Lee GC, *Clackamas* .... 18 [P] 503-655-9249
　sah-hah-lee.com

[S] = SEMI-PRIVATE   [V] = PRIVATE   [U] = UNIVERSITY   [N] = UNIVERSITY-PRIVATE

OREGON

Salem GC, *Salem* .... 18 [P] 503-363-6652
salemgolfclub.com
Salemtowne GC, *Salem* .... 9 [V] 503-362-2215
Salishan Spa & Golf Resort, *Gleneden Beach* .... 18 [R] 541-764-3632
salishan.com
Salmon Run, *Brookings* .... 18 [R] 541-469-4888
salmonrun.net
Sandelie 18 Hole GC, *West Linn* .... 18 [P] 503-655-1461
sandeliegolfcourse.com
Sandelie West 9 GC, *Wilsonville* .... 9 [P] 503-655-1461
sandeliegolfcourse.com
Sandpines Golf Links, *Florence* .... 18 [P] 541-997-1940
sandpines.com
Santiam GC, *Aumsville* .... 18 [P] 503-769-3485
santiamgolfclub.com
Seaside GC, *Seaside* .... 9 [P] 503-738-5261
Senior Estates G&CC, *Woodburn* .... 18 [V] 503-981-0189
seniorestatesgolf.com
Shadow Hills CC, *Junction City* .... 18 [V] 541-998-8441
shadowhillscc.org
Shield Crest GC, *Klamath Falls* .... 18 [P] 541-884-5305
shieldcrestgc.com
South Fork GC, *Dayville* .... 9 [P] 541-987-2488
Spring Hill CC, *Albany* .... 18 [V] 541-926-6059
springhillcc.com
Springfield CC, *Springfield* .... 18 [V] 541-747-2517
springfieldcountryclub.com
Springwater GC, *Estacada* .... 9 [P] 503-630-4586
St Helens GC, *Warren* .... 9 [P] 503-397-0358
Stewart Meadows GC, *Medford* .... 9 [P] 541-770-6554
stewartmeadows.com
Stewart Park Muni GC, *Roseburg* .... 9 [M] 541-672-4592
ci.roseburg.or.us
Stone Creek GC, *Oregon City* .... 18 [P] 503-518-4653
stonecreekgolfclub.net
Stone Ridge GC, *Eagle Point* .... 18 [P] 541-830-4653
oregongolf.com/stoneridge
Summerfield G&CC, *Tigard* .... 9 [P] 503-620-1200
summerfield55.org
Sunriver Lodge & Resort - Meadows, *Sunriver* .... 18 [R] 541-593-4402
sunriver-resort.com
Sunriver Lodge & Resort - Woodlands, *Sunriver* .. 18 [R] 541-593-4402
sunriver-resort.com
Sunset Bay GC, *Coos Bay* .... 9 [P] 541-888-9301
sunsetbaygolf.com
Sunset Grove GC, *Forest Grove* .... 9 [P] 503-357-6044
Tetherow GC, *Bend* .... 18 [P] 541-388-2582
tetherow.com
The Childrens Course, *Gladstone* .... 9 [P] 503-722-1530
thefirstteechildrenscourse.org
The Club At Pronghorn, *Bend* .... 36 [R] 541-693-5365
pronghornclub.com
The Dalles CC, *The Dalles* .... 9 [V] 541-296-5252
The GC of Oregon, *Albany* .... 18 [P] 541-928-8338
The Greens at Redmond, *Redmond* .... 18 [P] 541-923-0694
thegreensatredmond.com
The Old Back Nine At Mountain High, *Bend* ...... 9 [P] 541-382-1111
oldbacknine.com
The Oregon GC, *West Linn* .... 18 [V] 503-650-6900
oregongc.americangolf.com
The Reserve Vineyards & GC, *Aloha* .... 36 [S] 503-649-8191
reservegolf.com

The Resort at the Mountain, *Welches* .... 27 [R] 503-622-3101
theresort.com
Tokatee GC, *Blue River* .... 18 [P] 541-822-3220
tokatee.com
Trysting Tree GC, *Corvallis* .... 18 [U] 541-752-3332
trystingtree.com
Tualatin CC, *Tualatin* .... 18 [V] 503-692-4620
tualatincountryclub.com
Umpqua Golf Resort, *Sutherlin* .... 18 [R] 541-459-4422
umpquagolfresort.com
V A Medical Ctr GC, *Roseburg* .... 9 [V] 541-580-5679
Valley GC, *Hines* .... 9 [M] 541-573-6251
Vernonia GC, *Vernonia* .... 18 [P] 503-429-6811
Veterans Memorial GC, *White City* ..... 9 [V] 541-830-7406
veteransgolf.org
Watson Ranch Golf, *Coos Bay* .... 18 [S] 541-267-7257
watsonranchgolf.com
Waverley CC, *Portland* .... 18 [V] 503-654-6521
waverley.cc
Widgi Creek GC, *Bend* .... 18 [P] 541-382-4449
widgi.com
Wildhorse Resort GC, *Pendleton* .... 18 [R] 541-276-5588
wildhorseresort.com
Wildwood GC, *Portland* .... 18 [P] 503-621-3402
golfingwildwood.com
Willamette Valley CC, *Canby* .... 18 [V] 503-266-2102
willamettevalleycc.com
Willow Creek CC, *Heppner* .... 9 [P] 541-676-5437
Wilsons Willow Run GC, *Boardman* .... 9 [P] 541-481-4381

PENNSYLVANIA

3 Lakes GC, *Pittsburgh* .... 18 [S] 412-793-7111
3lakesgolf.com
Abington CC, *Jenkintown* .... 9 [V] 215-885-0734
abingtonclub.com
Allegheny CC, *Sewickley* .... 18 [V] 412-741-7500
alleghenycountryclub.com
Allentown Muni Benner Fairways GC, *Allentown* 18 [M] 610-395-5108
allentowngolf.com
Alverthorpe Park GC, *Jenkintown* .... 9 [M] 215-884-6538
abington.org
American Legion CC, *Mt Union* .... 18 [S] 814-542-4343
Apollo Elks CC, *Apollo* .... 18 [V] 724-478-2939
apolloelks.org
Applebrook GC, *Malvern* .... 18 [V] 610-647-7667
applebrookgolfclub.com
Applecross CC, *Downingtown* .... 18 [V] 215-641-1300
talamorepa.com
Appledale GC, *Ebensburg* .... 9 [P] 814-472-6080
Applewood GC, *Pittston* .... 9 [P] 570-388-2500
applewoodgolf.com
Armitage GC, *Mechanicsburg* .... 18 [M] 717-737-5344
armitagegolfclub.com
Arnolds GC, *Mlfflinville* .... 18 [P] 570-752-7022
Aronimink GC, *Newtown Square* .... 18 [V] 610-356-8000
aronimink.org
Arrowhead GC, *Douglassville* .... 27 [P] 610-582-4258
arrowheadgolf.net
Aubreys Dubbs Dred GC, *Butler* .... 18 [P] 724-287-4832
aubreysdubbsdred.com
Avalon G&CC - Buhl Park, *Sharon* .... 18 [P] 724-981-6705
avalonlakes.com

176   [A] = MILITARY   [M] = MUNICIPAL   [P] = PUBLIC   [R] = RESORT

PENNSYLVANIA

Bala GC, *Philadelphia* .... 18 [V]   215-877-0661
balagolfclub.com
Bavarian Hills GC, *St Marys* .... 18 [M]   814-834-3602
bavarianhillsgolf.net
Beaver Bend Par 3, *Hummelstown* .... 18 [P]   717-566-5858
beaverbendpar3.com
Beaver Valley GC, *Patterson Heights* .... 18 [P]   724-846-2212
beavervalleygc.com
Bedford Elks CC, *Bedford* .... 9 [P]   814-623-9314
Bedford Springs GC, *Bedford* .... 18 [R]   814-624-5637
bedfordspringsresort.com
Beechwood CC, *Fairview* .... 18 [P]   814-833-0527
beechwoodgolf.net
Beechwood GC, *Falls Creek* .... 18 [P]   814-371-7611
Bella Vista GC, *Gilbertsville* .... 18 [P]   610-705-1855
bellavistagc.com
Belles Spring GC, *Mill Hall* .... 18 [M]   570-726-4222
bellessprings.com
Bellewood GC, *Pottstown* .... 18 [R]   610-718-9100
bellewoodgolf.com
Bensalem Twnsp CC, *Bensalem* .... 18 [M]   215-639-5556
bensalemtownshipcountryclub.com
Bent Creek CC, *Lititz* .... 18 [V]   717-560-7700
bentcreekcc.com
Berkleigh CC, *Kutztown* .... 18 [S]   610-683-8268
berkleighcountryclub.com
Berkshire CC, *Reading* .... 18 [V]   610-376-2536
berkshirecc.net
Berwick GC, *Berwick* .... 18 [V]   570-752-2506
berwickgc.com
Bethlehem GC, *Bethlehem* .... 27 [M]   610-691-9393
bethlehem-pa.gov/parks/golf/index.htm
Birdsfoot GC, *Freeport* .... 18 [P]   724-295-3656
birdsfoot.com
Black Hawk GC, *Beaver Falls* .... 36 [P]   724-843-5512
blackhawkgolfcourse.com
Blackwood GC, *Douglassville* .... 18 [P]   610-385-6200
blackwoodgolf.com
Blue Bell CC, *Blue Bell* .... 18 [V]   215-616-8101
bluebellcc.com
Blue Knob Rec Area GC, *Claysburg* .... 9 [R]   814-239-5111
blueknob.com
Blue Mountain GC, *Fredericksburg* .... 18 [P]   717-865-4401
bluemountaingc.com
Blue Ridge CC, *Harrisburg* .... 18 [V]   717-545-8311
blueridgecc.org
Blue Ridge CC, *Palmerton* .... 18 [V]   610-826-2504
blueridgecountryclub.net
Blue Ridge Trail GC, *Mountain Top* .... 27 [S]   570-868-4653
blueridgetrail.com
Blueberry Hill GC, *Russell* .... 18 [P]   814-757-8690
blueberryhillgc.com
Bon Air CC, *Glen Rock* .... 18 [V]   717-235-2091
bonaircc.com
Borland Golf Ctr, *New Wilmington* .... 18 [P]   724-946-2371
borlandgolfcenter.com
Bostonia CC, *Distant* .... 9 [P]   814-275-2553
Brackenridge Heights CC, *Natrona Heights* ... 9 [P]   724-226-1146
bhccgolf.com
Briarwood GC, *York* .... 36 [P]   717-792-9776
briarwoodgolfclubs.com
Broad Run Golfers Club, *West Chester* ...... 18 [P]   610-738-4510
broadrungc.com

Brookside CC, *Pottstown* .... 18 [V]   610-323-9755
brooksidepottstown.com
Brookside CC, *Macungie* .... 18 [V]   610-966-4041
brooksidecountryclub.org
Buck Hill GC, *Buck Hill Falls* .... 27 [V]   570-595-7730
buckhillfalls.com
Bucknell GC, *Lewisburg* .... 18 [U]   570-523-8193
departments.bucknell.edu/golfclub
Buffalo GC, *Sarver* .... 18 [P]   724-353-2440
buffalogolfpa.com
Buhl Farm GC, *Hermitage* .... 9 [P]   724-962-1943
buhlfarmpark.com
Burgis Back Nine, *Altoona* .... 9 [P]   814-201-2105
Butler CC, *Butler* .... 18 [V]   724-586-6030
butlercc.org
Butlers GC, *Elizabeth* .... 36 [P]   412-751-9121
butlersgolf.com
Butter Valley Golf Port, *Barto* .... 18 [P]   610-845-2491
buttervalley.com
Cabin Greens GC, *Freeport* .... 9 [P]   724-295-3744
cabingreens.com
Cable Hollow GC, *Russell* .... 18 [P]   814-757-4765
cablehollow.com
Caesars Pocono Palace Resort, *Marshalls Creek* .... 9 [R]   570-588-6692
caesarspoconoresorts.com
Caledonia GC, *Fayetteville* .... 18 [M]   717-352-7271
Cambrian Hills CC, *Barnesboro* .... 9 [P]   814-247-8521
Carlisle Barracks GC, *Carlisle* .... 18 [A]   717-243-3262
Carlisle CC, *Carlisle* .... 18 [P]   717-243-6866
carlislecountryclub.org
Carmichaels GC, *Carmichaels* .... 18 [P]   724-966-7500
carmichaelsgolf.com
Carroll Valley Resort GC, *Fairfield* .... 18 [R]   717-642-8211
carrollvalley.com
Carter Heights GC, *Corry* .... 9 [P]   814-739-2083
carterheights.com
Castle Hills GC, *New Castle* .... 18 [P]   724-652-8122
CC of Scranton, *Clarks Summit* .... 27 [V]   570-586-2311
ccscranton.com
CC of the Poconos, *Marshalls Creek* .... 18 [P]   570-223-8099
poconosbestgolf.com
CC of York, *York* .... 18 [V]   717-843-9303
ccyork.org
Cedar Ridge GC, *Gettysburg* .... 18 [P]   717-359-4480
Cedarbrook CC, *Blue Bell* .... 18 [P]   215-643-3560
cedarbrookcc.org
Cedarbrook GC, *Belle Vernon* .... 36 [P]   724-929-8300
cedarbrookgolfcourse.com
Center Square GC, *Norristown* .... 18 [P]   610-584-5700
centersquaregolfclub.com
Centre Hills CC, *State College* .... 27 [V]   814-238-0111
centrehillscc.com
Chambersburg CC, *Chambersburg* .... 18 [V]   717-263-8296
chambersburgcountryclub.org
Champion Lakes GC, *Bolivar* .... 18 [P]   724-238-5440
pagolf.com
Chapel Hill GC, *Reading* .... 18 [P]   610-775-8815
chapelhillgolf.net
Chartiers CC, *Pittsburgh* .... 18 [V]   412-921-5360
chartierscc.com
Cherokee GC, *Danville* .... 18 [P]   570-275-2005
cherokeegolfcourse.com

[S] = SEMI-PRIVATE   [V] = PRIVATE   [U] = UNIVERSITY   [N] = UNIVERSITY-PRIVATE

PENNSYLVANIA
Golf Yellow Pages, 18th Edition

Cherry Creek GC, *Greensburg* ....18 [P] 724-925-8665
  cherrycreekgolfclub.com
Cherry Valley GC, *Stroudsburg*................18 [P] 570-421-1350
  cherryvalleygolfcourse.com
Cherry Wood GC, *Apollo*........................18 [P] 724-727-2546
Cherrywood GC, *Penn Run*.....................9 [P] 724-349-6909
Chester Valley GC, *Malvern* .... 18 [V] 610-647-4007
  chestervalleygc.org
Chestnut Ridge GC, *Blairsville*..............36 [R] 724-459-7180
  chestnutridgeresort.com
Chetremon GC, *Cherry Tree* ....9 [P] 814-743-6205
Chippewa GC, *Bentleyville* ....18 [P] 724-239-4841
  golfchippewa.com
Chisel Creek GC, *Landenberg*................18 [P] 610-255-3961
  chiselcreekgolf.com
Churchill Valley CC, *Pittsburgh* .... 18 [V] 412-243-7600
  cvccgolf.com
Clarion Oaks GC, *Clarion*..................... 18 [S] 814-226-8888
  clarionoaks.com
Clayton Park GC, *Glen Mills* ....9 [M] 610-459-4510
Clearfield Curwensville CC, *Clearfield*......... 9 [V] 814-765-8232
Cliff Park Inn & GC, *Milford* .... 9 [R] 570-296-6491
  cliffparkinn.com
Clinton CC, *Mill Hall* .... 18 [V] 570-748-6061
  clintoncountryclub.com
Clover Hill GC, *Pittsburgh*.....................9 [M] 412-364-2447
  franklinparkborough.us/cloverhill
Cloverleaf GC, *Delmont* ....27 [P] 724-468-4173
Club At Nevillewood, *Presto*...................18 [P] 412-276-4653
  theclubatnevillewood.com
Coatesville CC, *Coatesville* .... 18 [V] 610-384-0442
  coatesvillecountryclub.com
Cobbs Creek GC, *Philadelphia* ....36 [M] 215-877-8707
  golfphilly.org
Colonial G&TC, *Harrisburg*................... 18 [S] 717-657-3212
  colonialgolftennis.com
Commonwealth National GC, *Horsham* .... 18 [V] 215-672-3356
  commonwealthgolfclub.com
Concord CC, *West Chester*................... 18 [V] 610-459-2200
  concordclub.org
Conestoga CC, *Lancaster* .... 18 [V] 717-394-8411
  conestogacc.com
Conewango Valley CC, *Warren* .... 18 [V] 814-723-3421
  conewangovalleycc.com
Conleys Resort Inn, *Butler* ....18 [R] 724-586-7711
  conleyresort.com
Connoquenessing CC, *Ellwood City* .... 18 [V] 724-752-2294
  ccc.wpga.org
Conocodell GC, *Fayetteville* ....9 [P] 717-352-3222
Cool Creek GC, *Wrightsville* ....18 [P] 717-252-3691
  coolcreekgolf.com
Corey Creek GC, *Mansfield* ....18 [P] 570-662-3520
  coreycreekgolf.com
Corry CC, *Corry*....................................... 9 [V] 814-665-9282
  corrycountryclub.com
Coudersport GC, *Coudersport* ....18 [P] 814-274-9122
  coudersportgolf.com
Country Meadows GC, *Venango*...........18 [P] 814-398-2881
  countrymeadows.com
Crab Apple Ridge GC, *Waterford* ....18 [P] 814-796-3106
  crabappleridge.com
Cranberry Highlands GC, *Cranberry Township*....18 [M] 724-776-7372
  cranberryhighlands.com

Cricket Hill GC, *Hawley* ....18 [P] 570-226-4366
  cricketgolf.com
Cross Creek Resort, *Titusville*................27 [R] 814-827-9611
  crosscreekresort.com
Crossgates GC, *Millersville*....................18 [P] 717-872-4500
  crossgatesgolf.com
Culbertson Hills Golf Resort, *Edinboro* .... 18 [R] 814-734-3114
  culbertsonhills.com
Cumberland GC, *Carlisle* ....18 [P] 717-249-5538
  golf.81fun.com
Dauphin Highlands GC, *Harrisburg* ....18 [M] 717-986-1984
  golfdauphinhighlands.com
Deep Valley GC, *Harmony* ....18 [P] 724-452-8021
  hartmannsresort.com
Deer Point GC, *Newburg* ....9 [P] 717-423-5915
Deer Trails CC, *Industry* .... 9 [V] 724-643-4710
  deertrailscountryclub.com
Deer Valley GC, *Hummelstown*.............18 [P] 717-583-4653
  deervalleygc.com
Del Mar GC, *Wampum* ....18 [P] 724-758-9499
  delmargolf.com
Diamond Run GC, *Sewickley* .... 18 [V] 412-741-3002
  diamond-run.com
Dick Kidds Par 3 GC, *Selinsgrove*...........9 [P] 570-743-1425
Dogwood Hills GC, *Claysville*................18 [P] 724-663-5870
  dogwoodhillsgolfcourse.com
Donegal Highlands GC, *Donegal* ....18 [P] 724-423-7888
  donegalhighlandsgolf.com
Double Eagle Golf At Snipes Farm, *Morrisville*.....18 [P] 215-295-1337
  golfatdoubleeagle.com
Down River GC, *Everett* ....18 [P] 814-652-5193
Downing GC, *Harborcreek*....................18 [M] 814-899-5827
  ci.erie.pa.us/golf
Downingtown CC, *Downingtown*..........18 [P] 610-269-2000
  golfdowningtown.com
Doylestown CC, *Doylestown*............... 18 [V] 215-348-2112
  doylestowncountryclub.com
DuBois CC, *Du Bois*...............................18 [P] 814-371-3581
  duboiscountryclub.com
Duck Hollow GC, *Uniontown*................18 [P] 724-439-3150
  duckhollowgolfclub.com
Eagle Rock Golf & Ski Resort, *Hazleton* ....18 [R] 570-384-6616
  eaglerockresort.com
Eagles Crossing GC, *Carlisle*.................18 [P] 717-960-0500
  eaglescrossing.com
Eagles Mere CC, *Eagles Mere*................18 [R] 570-525-3460
  eaglesmerecc.com
Eagles Ridge GC, *Curwensville* ....18 [P] 814-236-3669
  eaglesridgegolfclub.com
Ebensburg CC, *Ebensburg* ....18 [P] 814-472-6550
  ebensburgcc.com
Edgewood CC, *Pittsburgh*..................... 18 [V] 412-823-2220
  eccgolf.com
Edgewood In The Pines GC, *Drums*......18 [P] 570-788-1101
  edgewoodpinesgc.com
Edgmont CC, *Edgmont*......................... 18 [V] 610-353-1800
  edgmont.com
Eighty-Four GC, *Eighty Four*..................18 [P] 724-746-1510
Elk Valley Golf & Rec, *Girard*.................18 [P] 814-474-2356
  elkvalleygolfcourse.com
Elkview CC, *Carbondale*....................... 18 [V] 570-222-4555
Elmhurst CC, *Moscow* .... 18 [V] 570-842-7011
  elmhurstcc.com

[A] = MILITARY   [M] = MUNICIPAL   [P] = PUBLIC   [R] = RESORT

PENNSYLVANIA

Emanon CC, *Falls* .... 18 [P] 570-388-6112
Emporium CC, *Emporium* .... 18 [P] 814-486-7715
   emporiumcc.com
Erie GC, *Erie* .... 18 [M] 814-866-0641
   eriegolflinks.com
Evergreen GC, *Analomink* .... 9 [P] 570-421-7721
Evergreen Golf, *Manheim* .... 18 [P] 717-898-7852
   evergreengolfinc.com
Exeter GC, *Reading* .... 9 [P] 610-779-1211
Fairview GC, *Lebanon* .... 18 [P] 717-273-3411
   distinctgolf.com
Fairways G&CC, *Warrington* .... 18 [P] 215-343-9979
   fairwaysgolfclub.com
Fernwood Hotel & Resort, *Bushkill* .... 18 [R] 570-588-9500
   fernwoodhotel.com
Flatbush GC, *Littlestown* .... 18 [P] 717-359-7125
   flatbushgolfcourse.com
Flourtown CC, *Flourtown* .... 9 [V] 215-233-1550
   flourtowncc.com
Flying Hills GC, *Reading* .... 18 [P] 610-775-4063
   flyinghills.com
Forest Lake Club, *Hawley* .... 9 [V] 570-685-7171
Fort Cherry GC, *Mc Donald* .... 18 [P] 724-926-4181
   fortcherrygolfclub.com
Four Seasons GC, *Landisville* .... 18 [M] 717-898-0104
   4seasonsgolfcourse.com
Four Seasons GC, *Exeter* .... 18 [P] 570-655-8869
   troongolf.com
Fox Chapel GC, *Pittsburgh* .... 18 [V] 412-963-7885
   foxchapelgolfclub.org
Fox Hill CC, *Exeter* .... 18 [V] 570-654-9242
   foxhillcc.net
Fox Hollow GC, *Quakertown* .... 18 [P] 215-538-1920
   golfatfoxhollow.com
Fox Run GC, *Beaver Falls* .... 18 [P] 724-847-3568
   foxrungolfcourse.net
Fox Run GC, *Waterford* .... 9 [P] 814-796-6400
   foxrungolfcourse.com
Foxburg CC, *Foxburg* .... 9 [P] 724-659-3196
   foxburggolf.com
Foxchase GC, *Stevens* .... 18 [P] 717-336-3673
   foxchasegolf.com
Foxwood Acres GC, *Eighty Four* .... 9 [P] 724-945-5400
Franklin D Roosevelt GC, *Philadelphia* .... 18 [M] 215-462-8997
   golfphilly.org
Franklin Park GC, *Pittsburgh* .... 9 [P] 412-364-7688
Freeport Mills GC, *Lebanon* .... 9 [P] 717-865-3005
Freestone GC, *Port Matilda* .... 18 [P] 814-692-4249
   freestonegolf.com
French Creek GC, *Elverson* .... 18 [V] 610-913-6330
   frenchcreekgolf.com
Frosty Valley CC, *Danville* .... 18 [V] 570-275-4700
   frostyvalleycc.com
Frosty Valley Golf Links, *Pittsburgh* ...... 9 [P] 724-941-5003
   frostyvalleygolf.com
Galen Hall GC, *Wernersville* .... 18 [R] 610-678-9535
   galenhallgc.com
GC at Felicita, *Harrisburg* .... 18 [R] 717-599-5028
   felicitaresort.com
Gilbertsville GC, *Gilbertsville* .... 27 [P] 610-323-3222
   golfgilbertsvillegc.com
Glen Brook GC, *Stroudsburg* .... 18 [M] 570-421-3680
   glenbrookgolfclub.com

Glen Oak CC, *Clarks Summit* .... 18 [V] 570-587-4024
   glenoakcc.com
Glengarry Golf Links, *Latrobe* .... 18 [P] 724-423-4653
   golfglengarry.com
Glenhardie CC, *Wayne* .... 9 [V] 610-687-3180
   glenhardiecc.com
Glenmaura National GC, *Moosic* .... 18 [V] 570-341-9552
   gngc.net
Golden Oaks GC, *Fleetwood* .... 18 [S] 610-944-6000
   goldenoaksgolfclub.com
Gospel Hill CC, *Erie* .... 18 [P] 814-899-5700
   gospelhillgolf.com
Grand View GC, *Braddock* .... 18 [P] 412-351-5390
   pittsburghgolf.com
Grandview GC, *York* .... 18 [P] 717-764-2674
   golfgrandview.com
Grassy Lane GC, *Darlington* .... 9 [P] 724-336-5006
Great Bear G&CC, *East Stroudsburg* ... 18 [V] 570-223-4653
   greatbeargolf.com
Great Cove G&RecC, *Mc Connellsburg* .... 18 [P] 717-485-4157
   greatcovegolfclub.com
Green Acres GC, *Titusville* .... 9 [P] 814-827-3589
Green Acres GC, *Bernville* .... 18 [P] 610-488-6698
Green Hills GC, *Birdsboro* .... 9 [P] 610-856-8633
   golfgreenhills.com
Green Meadows GC, *North East* .... 18 [P] 814-725-5009
   greenmeadowsgolfcourse.com
Green Meadows GC, *Volant* .... 18 [P] 724-530-7330
Green Oaks CC, *Verona* .... 18 [V] 412-793-2200
   greenoakscc.com
Green Pond GC, *Bethlehem* .... 18 [P] 610-253-2505
   greenpondcc.com
Green Valley CC, *Lafayette Hill* .... 18 [V] 610-828-3000
   greenvalleycc.org
Green Valley GC, *Pittsburgh* .... 9 [P] 412-364-9980
Greencastle Greens GC, *Greencastle* . 18 [P] 717-597-1188
   greencastlegreensgolfclub.com
Greene County GC, *Waynesburg* .... 9 [P] 724-883-4880
Greensburg CC, *Greensburg* .... 18 [V] 724-837-1810
   greensburgcc.com
Groff Farm GC, *Mt Joy* .... 18 [P] 717-653-2048
   groffsfarmgolfclub.com
Grove City CC, *Grove City* .... 18 [V] 724-748-3493
   grovecitycc.com
Gulph Mills GC, *King of Prussia* .... 18 [V] 610-828-9370
   gulphmillsgc.com
Hailwood GC, *Meadville* .... 9 [P] 814-333-2505
Hannastown GC, *Greensburg* .... 18 [V] 724-836-8643
   hannastowngc.com
Hanover CC, *Abbottstown* .... 18 [V] 717-259-0411
   hanovercc.com
Harbor Ridge GC, *Erie* .... 9 [P] 814-898-4653
   harborridgegolf.com
Harmony Ridge GC, *Ambridge* .... 9 [P] 724-266-8445
   harmonyridgegolf.com
Harrisburg CC, *Harrisburg* .... 18 [V] 717-599-5162
   ccharrisburg.com
Hartefeld National GC, *Avondale* .... 18 [V] 610-268-8800
   hartefeld.com
Hartstown GC, *Hartstown* .... 9 [P] 724-932-3017
Hawk Valley GC, *Denver* .... 18 [P] 717-445-5445
Hawthorne Valley GC, *Midland* .... 18 [P] 724-643-9091

[S] = SEMI-PRIVATE   [V] = PRIVATE   [U] = UNIVERSITY   [N] = UNIVERSITY-PRIVATE

PENNSYLVANIA — Golf Yellow Pages, 18th Edition

Heidelberg CC, *Bernville* .... 18 [V] 610-488-6021
 heidelbergcc.com
Hemlock View GC, *Punxsutawney* .... 9 [P] 814-938-9294
Heritage Creek GC, *Jamison* .... 9 [S] 215-674-8283
Heritage Hills Golf Resort, *York* .... 18 [R] 717-755-4653
 hhgr.com
Hershey CC, *Hershey* .... 36 [R] 717-533-2464
 hersheygolfcollection.com
Hershey Links, *Hummelstown* .... 18 [P] 717-533-0890
 hersheylinks.com
Hersheys Mill GC, *West Chester* .... 18 [V] 610-692-6592
 hersheysmillgolfclub.com
Hi Level GC, *Kossuth* .... 23 [P] 814-797-1813
Hickory Heights GC, *Spring Grove* .... 18 [P] 717-225-4247
 golfhickoryheights.com
Hickory Heights GC, *Bridgeville* .... 18 [S] 412-257-0300
 hickoryheightsgc.com
Hickory Valley GC, *Gilbertsville* .... 36 [P] 610-754-9862
 hickoryvalley.com
Hidden Valley GC, *Hidden Valley* .... 18 [R] 814-443-8000
 hiddenvalleyresort.com
Hidden Valley GC, *Pine Grove* .... 18 [P] 570-739-4455
 distinctgolf.com
Highland CC, *Pittsburgh* .... 18 [V] 412-761-3556
 highlandcc.net
Hiland GC, *Butler* .... 18 [P] 724-287-8814
Hill Crest CC, *Lower Burrell* .... 18 [V] 724-339-8840
 hillcrestcountryclub.net
Hollenback GC, *Wilkes Barre* .... 9 [M] 570-821-1169
Homestead GC, *Carbondale* .... 18 [P] 570-282-5197
Honesdale GC, *Honesdale* .... 9 [V] 570-253-5616
 hgclub.net
Honey Run GC, *York* .... 18 [P] 717-792-9771
 honeyrungolf.com
Honeybrook GC, *Honey Brook* .... 18 [P] 610-273-0207
 honeybrookgolf.com
Horsham Valley GC, *Ambler* .... 18 [P] 215-646-4707
 horshamvalleygolf.com
Hunter Station GC, *Forest City* .... 18 [P] 814-755-4558
 hunterstation.com
Huntingdon CC, *Huntingdon* .... 18 [S] 814-627-0631
 huntingdoncc.com
Huntingdon Valley CC, *Huntingdon Valley* .... 27 [V] 215-657-1610
 hvccpa.org
Huntsville GC, *Dallas* .... 18 [V] 570-674-3673
 golf-huntsville.com
Immergrun GC, *Loretto* .... 9 [U] 814-471-9650
 immergrungolfclub.com
Indian Creek GC, *Emmaus* .... 18 [P] 610-965-8486
 indiancreek.com
Indian Hills CC, *Paxinos* .... 18 [P] 570-644-1972
 indianhillscountryclub.com
Indian Lake GC, *Central City* .... 18 [V] 814-754-5601
 indianlakegolfclub.com
Indian Mountain GC, *Kunkletown* .... 9 [P] 610-681-4534
Indian Run GC, *Mc Clure* .... 18 [P] 570-658-2080
 indianrungolf.com
Indian Run GC, *Avella* .... 18 [S] 814-587-0330
 golfindianrun.com
Indian Valley CC, *Telford* .... 18 [V] 215-723-9886
 indianvalleycc.com
Indiana CC, *Indiana* .... 18 [V] 724-465-5222
 indiana-countryclub.com

Ingleside GC, *Thorndale* .... 18 [M] 610-384-9128
 calntownship.org
Inniscrone GC, *Avondale* .... 18 [S] 610-268-8200
 inniscronegolfcourse.com
Irem CC, *Dallas* .... 18 [V] 570-675-4653
 iremgolf.com
Iron Lakes GC, *Allentown* .... 18 [P] 610-395-3369
 ironlakescountryclub.com
Iron Masters CC, *Roaring Spring* .... 18 [S] 814-224-5217
 wpga.org
Iron Valley GC, *Lebanon* .... 18 [S] 717-279-7409
 ironvalley.com
Iron Wood GC, *Conneaut Lake* .... 9 [R] 814-382-8438
Ironwood GC, *Mc Veytown* .... 18 [P] 717-899-0900
Irwin CC, *Irwin* .... 18 [P] 724-863-6016
 irwincountryclub.com
Island Green CC, *Philadelphia* .... 18 [P] 215-677-3500
 islandgreencc.com
Island Green GC, *Cochranton* .... 9 [P] 814-425-7704
Jack Frost National GC, *Blakeslee* .... 18 [R] 866-268-5503
 jackfrostnational.com
Jackson Valley GC, *Warren* .... 18 [P] 814-489-7803
JC Melrose CC, *Cheltenham* .... 18 [V] 215-379-5300
 jcmelrosecc.com
Jeffersonville GC, *Norristown* .... 18 [M] 610-539-0422
 westnorritontwp.org
Jericho National GC, *New Hope* .... 18 [V] 215-862-8800
 jerichonational.biz
John F Byrne GC, *Philadelphia* .... 18 [M] 215-632-8668
 golfphilly.org
Johnstown Muni GC, *Johnstown* .... 9 [M] 814-288-3011
Joseph Martin GC, *Erie* .... 9 [M] 814-864-1821
 ci.erie.pa.us/golf
Juniata GC, *Philadelphia* .... 18 [M] 215-743-4060
 fairmountpark.org
Kahkwa Club, *Erie* .... 18 [V] 814-838-1901
 kahkwa.com
Kane CC, *Kane* .... 18 [P] 814-837-9491
 kanecountryclub.com
Kennett Square G&CC, *Kennett Square* ...... 18 [V] 610-444-2640
 ksgcc.com
Kimberton GC, *Phoenixville* .... 18 [P] 610-933-8836
 kimbertongolfclub.com
King Valley GC, *Imler* .... 18 [P] 814-239-0199
Kings Mountain GC, *Rockwood* .... 9 [R] 814-926-2021
Kiski Prep School GC, *Saltsburg* .... 9 [N] 724-639-3586
 kiski.org
Kistlers Golf, *Jeannette* .... 18 [P] 724-527-9815
Kittanning CC, *Kittanning* .... 9 [V] 724-543-2014
 kittanningcountryclub.com
Knoebels Three Ponds GC, *Elysburg* .... 18 [P] 570-672-9064
 knoebels.com
Krendale Public GC, *Butler* .... 27 [P] 724-482-4065
 krendalegolfcourse.com
Lake Arthur CC, *Butler* .... 18 [P] 724-865-2765
 lakearthur.com
Lake Lorain GC, *Poyntelle* .... 9 [P] 570-448-2232
Lake Naomi Timber Trails GC, *Pocono Pines* ... 9 [P] 570-646-9060
 lakenaomiclub.com
Lake Pleasant GC, *Erie* .... 9 [P] 814-825-5642
 lakepleasantgolfcourse.com
Lake Shore CC, *Erie* .... 18 [V] 814-833-7822
 lakeshorecountryclub.com

180   [A] = MILITARY   [M] = MUNICIPAL   [P] = PUBLIC   [R] = RESORT

PENNSYLVANIA

Lake View CC, *North East* .... 18 [V]   814-725-9561
lakeviewcc.com
Lakeland GC, *Fleetville* .... 9 [P]   570-945-9983
Lakeview North GC, *Butler* .... 18 [P]   724-586-7097
Lancaster CC, *Lancaster* .... 33 [V]   717-393-4064
lancastercc.com
Lancaster Host Golf Resort, *Lancaster* .... 18 [R]   717-397-7756
lancasterhost.com
Latrobe CC, *Latrobe* .... 18 [V]   724-539-8588
latrobecountryclub.com
Latrobe Elks GC, *Latrobe* .... 18 [V]   724-539-8511
latrobe-elks.org
Laurel Mill GC, *Ridgeway* .... 9 [P]   814-772-1015
Laurel Run GC, *Sigel* .... 18 [P]   814-752-2872
laurelrungolf.com
Laurel Valley GC, *Ligonier* .... 18 [V]   724-238-2422
Lawrence Park GC, *Erie* .... 18 [V]   814-899-9601
lawrenceparkgc.com
Lebanon CC, *Lebanon* .... 18 [V]   717-272-1893
lebcc.com
Lebanon Valley GC, *Myerstown* .... 18 [P]   717-866-4481
lebanonvalleygc.com
Lederach GC, *Harleysville* .... 18 [M]   215-513-3034
lederachgolfclub.com
Ledgerock GC, *Mohnton* .... 18 [V]   610-777-9705
ledgerockgolf.com
Lehigh CC, *Allentown* .... 18 [V]   610-437-1451
lehighcc.com
Lehman GC, *Dallas* .... 9 [P]   570-675-1686
lehmangolfclub.com
Lenape Heights GC, *Ford City* .... 18 [P]   724-763-2201
lenapeheights.com
Lewistown CC, *Lewistown* .... 18 [P]   717-248-9822
lewistowncountryclub.com
Liberty Forge GC, *Mechanicsburg* ..... 18 [R]   717-795-9880
libertyforge.net
Liberty Valley CC, *Danville* .... 18 [P]   570-275-4647
libertyvalleygolf.com
Ligonier CC, *Ligonier* .... 18 [V]   724-238-5438
ligoniercountryclub.com
Limekiln GC, *Ambler* .... 27 [P]   215-643-0643
limegolf.com
Limerick GC, *Limerick* .... 18 [P]   610-495-6945
limerickgolfclub.com
Lincoln Hills CC, *North Huntingdon* .... 18 [P]   724-863-4650
Linden Hall GC, *Dawson* .... 18 [R]   724-529-2366
lindenhallpa.com
Lindenwood GC, *Canonsburg* .... 27 [P]   724-745-9889
lindenwoodgolf.com
Linfield National GC, *Linfield* .... 18 [P]   610-495-8455
linfieldnational.com
Links At Gettysburg, *Gettysburg* .... 18 [S]   717-359-8000
thelinksatgettysburg.com
Little Creek GC, *Spring Grove* .... 18 [P]   717-225-1702
Llanerch CC, *Havertown* .... 18 [V]   610-446-2232
llanerchcc.org
Loch Nairn GC, *Avondale* .... 18 [P]   610-268-2234
lochnairn.com
Locust Valley GC, *Coopersburg* .... 18 [P]   610-282-4711
Lone Pine GC, *Washington* .... 18 [V]   724-222-4700
lonepinecc.com
Longue Vue GC, *Verona* .... 18 [V]   412-793-2375
longuevueclub.net

Lookaway GC, *Buckingham* .... 18 [V]   215-794-0531
lookawaygc.com
Lords Valley CC, *Hawley* .... 18 [V]   570-775-6013
lordsvalleycountryclub.org
Lost Creek GC, *Oakland Mills* .... 18 [P]   717-463-2450
lostcreekgolfpa.com
Lu Lu CC, *Glenside* .... 18 [V]   215-576-7030
lulucc.com
Lucky Hills GC, *Franklin* .... 9 [P]   814-432-3900
Lykens Valley GC, *Millersburg* .... 18 [R]   717-692-3664
lykensvalley.com
Macoby Run GC, *Green Lane* .... 18 [P]   215-541-0161
macobyrun.com
Mahoning Valley CC, *Lehighton* .... 18 [P]   570-386-2588
mahoningvalleycc.com
Mainland GC, *Mainland* .... 18 [P]   215-256-9548
mainlandgolf.com
Majestic Ridge GC, *Chambersburg* .... 18 [P]   717-267-3444
majesticridgegolfclub.com
Makefield Highlands GC, *Yardley* ...... 18 [M]   215-321-7000
makefieldhighlands.com
Manada GC, *Grantville* .... 18 [P]   717-469-2400
golfatmanadagc.com
Mannitto GC, *New Alexandria* .... 18 [P]   724-668-8150
mannittogolfclub.com
Manor GC, *Sinking Spring* .... 18 [P]   610-678-9597
themanorgolfclub.com
Manor Valley GC, *Export* .... 18 [P]   724-744-4242
manorvalleygolf.com
Manufacturers G&CC, *Fort Washington* ...... 18 [V]   215-886-3200
mg-cc.org
Maple Crest GC, *Monroeville* .... 9 [P]   412-372-7770
Maple Crest GC, *Portage* .... 9 [P]   814-736-3098
maplecrestgolfcourse.com
Maple Hills Public GC, *Springville* .... 9 [P]   570-965-2324
maplehillsgolf.net
Marada GC, *Clinton* .... 9 [P]   724-899-2600
maradagolfcourse.com
Marjon GC, *Moscow* .... 9 [P]   570-842-7922
Mars Bethel GC, *Mars* .... 9 [P]   724-625-2759
Mayapple Golf Links, *Carlisle* .... 18 [P]   717-258-4088
McCall G&CC, *Upper Darby* .... 18 [V]   610-734-7934
mccallgolf.com
Meadia Heights GC, *Lancaster* .... 18 [V]   717-393-9761
meadiaheightsgolf.com
Meadow Brook GC, *Phoenixville* .... 9 [P]   610-933-2929
meadowbrookgc.com
Meadow Brook GC, *Gettysburg* .... 18 [P]   717-334-0569
Meadow Lane GC, *Indiana* .... 18 [P]   724-465-5604
meadowlanegolf.com
Meadowbrook GC, *Huntingdon Valley* .... 18 [S]   215-947-8477
Meadowink GC, *Murrysville* .... 18 [P]   724-327-8243
meadowinkgolf.com
Meadowlands CC, *Blue Bell* .... 18 [V]   215-646-2300
meadowlandscc.com
Melody Lakes GC, *Quakertown* .... 9 [S]   215-538-1191
Memorial Links GC, *Waymart* .... 9 [P]   570-448-9200
Mercer Public GC, *Mercer* .... 18 [P]   724-662-9951
Merion GC, *Ardmore* .... 36 [V]   610-642-5600
meriongolfclub.com
Mermaid Swim & GC, *Blue Bell* .... 9 [P]   610-275-9191
mermaidlake.com

[S] = SEMI-PRIVATE   [V] = PRIVATE   [U] = UNIVERSITY   [N] = UNIVERSITY-PRIVATE

PENNSYLVANIA
Golf Yellow Pages, 18th Edition

Middlecreek GC, *Rockwood*..........................9 [P] 814-926-3524
   middlecreekgolf.com
Middletown CC, *Langhorne* ....18 [M] 215-757-6953
   middletowncc.com
Midlantic GC, *Dover*....................................9 [P] 717-292-9727
Mill Race Golf & Camping Resort, *Benton* ....18 [R] 570-925-2040
   millracegolf.com
Millcreek G&LearnCtr, *Erie*........................9 [M] 814-835-5168
   eriegolflinks.com
Moccasin Run GC, *Atglen* ....18 [P] 610-593-2600
   moccasinrun.com
Mohawk Trails GC, *New Castle*.................18 [P] 724-667-8570
   mohawktrails.com
Monongahela Valley CC, *Monongahela*.................9 [V] 724-258-7660
Monroe Valley GC, *Jonestown* ....18 [P] 717-865-2375
   monroevalleygolfpa.com
Monterey CC, *Blue Ridge Summit* ....9 [P] 717-794-2809
   montereycountryclub.net
Montour Heights CC, *Coraopolis*.................. 18 [V] 412-262-4653
   montourheightscc.com
Moon GC, *Moon Township* ....18 [M] 412-262-2992
   moongolfclub.com
Morgan Hills, *Hunlock Creek* ....9 [P] 570-256-3444
Moselem Springs GC, *Fleetwood*......................18 [V] 610-944-7616
   moselemgolf.com
Mound Grove GC, *Waterford* ....18 [P] 814-796-2767
   moundgrovegc.com
Mount Airy GC, *Mt Pocono* ....18 [R] 570-839-8816
   mountairygolfclub.com
Mount Chestnut DR & 9 Hole Exec Course, *Butler*..9 [P] 724-285-1010
Mount Odin Park GC, *Greensburg* ....18 [M] 724-834-2640
   city.greensburg.pa.us
Mount Pocono GC, *Mt Pocono*....................9 [P] 570-839-6061
   poconomanor.com
Mount Summit GC, *Farmington* .... 9 [R] 724-438-8986
   summitinnresort.com
Mountain Laurel GC, *White Haven* ....18 [P] 570-443-7424
   mountainlaurelgolf.com
Mountain Manor GC, *Marshalls Creek* ....27 [P] 570-223-1290
   mountainmanor.com
Mountain Valley GC, *Barnesville* ....27 [P] 570-467-2242
   mtvalleygolf.com
Mountain View GC, *Fairfield* ....18 [R] 717-642-5848
   mtviewgc.com
Mt Hope GC, *Guys Mills*............................18 [P] 814-789-2475
   mthopegolfcourse.com
Mt Lebanon GC, *Pittsburgh*........................9 [M] 412-561-9761
   mtlebanon.org
Murrysville GC, *Murrysville* ....18 [P] 724-327-0726
   murrysvillegolfclub.com
Nemacolin CC, *Beallsville* .... 18 [V] 724-632-5443
   nemacolin.org
Nemacolin Woodlands Resort & Spa, *Farmington*36 [R] 724-329-8555
   nemacolin.com
Neshaminy Valley GC, *Jamison* ....18 [P] 215-343-6930
New Castle CC, *New Castle* .... 18 [V] 724-654-1431
   newcastlecc.com
Newberry Estate CC, *Dallas*....................... 9 [V] 570-675-5236
   newberryestate.us
Newfoundland GC, *South Sterling* ....9 [S] 570-676-9013
Nine Flags GC, *Olyphant* ....9 [P] 570-254-9933
Nittany CC, *Mingoville* .... 9 [V] 814-383-2611
   nittanycountryclub.com

North Fork G&TC, *Johnstown* ....18 [S] 814-288-2822
   freewebs.com/northforkcc
North Hills CC, *Glenside* .... 18 [V] 215-576-9875
   northhillscc.org
North Hills GC, *Corry* ....18 [M] 814-664-4477
   northhillsgolf.com
North Park Dr Range & Par 3, *Pittsburgh*..........9 [P] 412-367-2406
North Park GC, *Allison Park* ....18 [M] 724-935-1967
   county.allegheny.pa.us/parks
Northampton CC, *Easton* ....18 [V] 610-258-6125
   northamptoncountryclub.org
Northampton Valley GC, *Richboro*..............18 [P] 215-355-2234
   nvgc.com
Northwinds GC, *Central City* ....18 [R] 814-754-4653
   northwindsgolf.com
Norvelt GC, *Mt Pleasant*............................27 [P] 724-423-5400
   norveltgolfclub.com
Oak Lake GC, *New Kensington* ....18 [P] 724-727-2400
Oak Tree GC, *West Middlesex* ....18 [P] 724-528-9984
   oaktree-cc.com
Oakbrook GC, *Stoystown* ....18 [P] 814-629-5892
Oakland Beach GC, *Conneaut Lake*............18 [P] 814-382-5665
   oaklandbeach.com
Oakmont CC - Main Course, *Oakmont* ...... 18 [V] 412-828-4653
   oakmont-countryclub.org
Oakview GC, *Slippery Rock*........................18 [S] 724-794-1173
   oakviewgolfclub.com
Old Town Run Par 3 GC, *Hollidaysburg* ....9 [P] 814-693-8955
Old York Road CC, *Spring House* .... 18 [V] 215-643-2182
   oyrcc.com
Olde Hickory GC, *Lancaster* ....9 [P] 717-569-9107
   boydwilson.com/oldehickorygolf.asp
Olde Homestead GC, *New Tripoli*...............27 [P] 610-298-4653
   oldehomesteadgolfclub.com
Olde Masters GC, *Newtown Square* ....9 [P] 610-356-7606
Olde Stonewall GC, *Ellwood City* ....18 [P] 724-752-4653
   oldestonewall.com
Orchard Pond GC, *Erie*...............................9 [P] 814-864-3621
Out Door CC, *York* .... 18 [V] 717-764-1188
   odcc.com
Over Lake GC, *Girard* ....18 [P] 814-774-3361
Overbrook GC, *Bryn Mawr* .... 18 [V] 610-687-6135
   overbrookgolf.com
Overlook GC, *Lancaster* ....18 [M] 717-569-9551
   overlookgolfcourse.com
Owens Brockway GC, *Brockport*..................9 [P] 814-268-4325
   owensbrockwaygolfcourse.com
Oxford Valley GC, *Fairless Hills*....................9 [M] 215-945-8644
Panorama GC, *Forest City* ....18 [P] 570-222-3525
   panoramagc.com
Par Line GC, *Elizabethtown* ....18 [P] 717-367-7794
   parlinegolfcourse.com
Park GC, *Conneaut Lake* ....18 [P] 814-382-9974
Park Hills CC, *Altoona* .... 18 [V] 814-944-2631
   parkhillscc.com
Parkview GC, *Hershey*................................18 [P] 717-534-3450
   hersheypa.com
Paupack Hills G&CC, *Greentown* .... 18 [V] 570-857-0251
   paupackhills.com
Paxon Hollow CC, *Media* ....18 [M] 610-353-0220
   paxonhollowgolf.com
Penn National GC & Inn, *Fayetteville*..................36 [R] 717-352-2400
   penngolf.com

PENNSYLVANIA

Penn Oaks GC, *West Chester*.................... 18 [V] 610-399-0501
 pennoaksgolfclub.com
Penn State GC, *State College* .... 36 [U] 814-863-4653
 pennstategolfcourses.com
Pennhills Club, *Bradford* .... 18 [V] 814-368-3464
 pennhillsclub.com
Pennsylvania Delaware Conf Ctr, *Carlisle*...........9 [P] 717-243-7381
 penndel.org
Perry GC, *Shoemakersville*.........................18 [P] 610-562-3510
Pheasant Ridge GC, *Gibsonia*.....................18 [P] 724-443-1908
 pheasantridgegc.com
Philadelphia CC, *Gladwyne*........................ 27 [V] 610-525-6000
 philadelphiacc.net
Philadelphia Cricket Club At Flourtown, *Flourtown*18 [V]215-247-6001
 philacricket.com
Philadelphia Cricket Club-Militia Hill,
 Plymouth Mtg .... 18 [V] 215-247-6001
 philacricket.com
Philipsburg Elks Lodge & CC, *Philipsburg* ....9 [P] 814-342-1114
 philipsburgcc.com
Philmont CC, *Huntingdon Valley* .... 36 [V] 215-947-0541
 philmontcc.org
Phoenixville CC, *Phoenixville* .... 9 [V] 610-935-9320
 phoenixvillecc.com
Pickering Valley GC, *Phoenixville*.................18 [P] 610-933-2223
 golfpickeringvalley.com
Pike Run CC, *Jones Mills* .... 9 [V] 724-593-2444
 pikeruncc.com
Pilgrims Oak GC, *Peach Bottom*........................18 [P] 717-548-3011
 pilgrimsoak.com
Pine Acres CC, *Bradford*................................18 [P] 814-362-2005
 pineacrescc.com
Pine Crest GC, *Lansdale*..............................18 [P] 215-855-6112
 pinecrestcountryclub.com
Pine Grove GC, *Grove City*............................18 [P] 724-458-8394
 pinegrovegolf.com
Pine Hill GC, *Greenville*................................18 [P] 724-588-8053
Pine Hills GC, *Taylor*....................................27 [P] 570-562-0138
 pinehillscc.net
Pine Marsh GC, *Morris* .... 9 [V] 570-353-2721
Pine Meadows G Complex, *Lebanon*...................18 [P] 717-865-4995
 pinemeadowsgolf.com
Pinecrest CC, *Brookville*................................ 18 [S] 814-849-4666
 pinecrestcc.com
Pinecroft GC, *Gillett* ....18 [P] 570-596-4653
Piney Apple GC, *Biglerville*............................18 [P] 717-677-9264
 pineyapplegolf.com
Piney Run GC, *Garrett*......................................9 [P] 814-634-8660
 somersetcounty.com/pineyrun
Pittsburgh Field Club, *Pittsburgh*...................... 18 [V] 412-963-7700
 fieldclub.org
Pittsburgh National GC, *Gibsonia*...................... 18 [S] 724-265-4800
 pittsburghnationalgolfclub.com
Pittsburgh North GC, *Bakerstown*......................27 [P] 724-443-3800
 pghnorthgolf.com
Pleasant Acres GC, *Jamestown*.........................18 [P] 724-932-5907
Pleasant Hill GC, *Fleetwood*............................18 [P] 610-926-2741
Pleasant Valley CC, *Connellsville*................... 18 [P] 724-628-0101
 pleasantvalleycountryclub.com
Pleasant Valley GC, *Vintondale*........................18 [P] 814-446-6244
Pleasant Valley GC Of York Co, *Stewartstown*.......18 [P] 717-993-2184
 playpleasantvalley.com
Pleasure GC, *Edinboro*.......................................9 [P] 814-734-4093

Plymouth CC, *Plymouth Meeting* .... 18 [V] 610-272-4050
 plymouthcc.com
Pocono Farms CC, *Tobyhanna* .... 18 [V] 570-894-8441
 poconofarms.com
Pocono Manor GC, *Pocono Manor* ....36 [R] 570-839-7111
 poconomanor.com
Ponderosa GC, *Hookstown* ....18 [P] 724-947-4745
 ponderosagolfcourse.com
Punxsutawney CC, *Punxsutawney* .... 18 [V] 814-938-9760
 punxsutawneycountryclub.com
Quail Valley GC, *Littlestown* .... 18 [S] 717-359-8453
 quailvalleygc.com
Quartette GC, *Philadelphia* ....9 [P] 215-676-3939
 pqcc.org
Quicksilver GC, *Midway* ....18 [P] 724-796-1594
 quicksilvergolf.com
Radley Run CC, *West Chester*............................. 18 [V] 610-793-1662
 radleyruncountryclub.com
Radnor Valley CC, *Villanova* .... 18 [V] 610-688-0153
 radnorvalleycc.com
Range End CC, *Dillsburg*....................................18 [P] 717-432-4213
 rangeendgolfclub.com
Ravens Claw GC, *Pottstown* ....18 [P] 610-495-4710
 ravensclawgolfclub.com
Reading CC, *Reading* ....18 [M] 610-779-1626
 exetertownship.com
Red Maples GC, *Waymart*....................................9 [P] 570-937-4543
Regents Glen CC, *York*.......................................18 [R] 717-505-4653
 regentsglen.com
Rich Maiden GC, *Fleetwood* ....18 [P] 610-926-1606
 richmaiden.com
Rich Valley Golf, *Mechanicsburg*........................18 [P] 717-691-8805
 richvalleygolf.net
Richland Green Golf Ctr, *Johnstown*....................9 [P] 814-266-1684
Ridgeview GC, *Ligonier*..9 [P] 724-238-7655
Rittswood GC, *Valencia*......................................18 [P] 724-586-2721
 rittswoodgolf.com
River Forest CC, *Freeport*..................................18 [R] 724-295-2217
 golfriverforest.com
River Ridge GC, *Franklin* ....9 [P] 814-676-3712
River Valley GC, *Westfield* ....18 [P] 814-367-2202
 rivervalleygolf.net
Rivers Edge GC, *Industry*....................................9 [P] 724-643-4110
Riverside GC, *Cambridge Springs*........................18 [P] 814-398-4537
 riversidegolfclub.com
Riverview CC, *Easton* ....18 [P] 610-559-9700
 riverviewcountryclub.com
Riverview GC, *New Cumberland*...........................9 [A] 717-770-5199
Riverview GC, *Elizabeth*.....................................18 [P] 412-384-7596
 riverviewpa.com
Robershaw Acres GC, *Youngwood*.......................9 [P] 724-834-9730
Rock Creek GC, *Nicholson*...................................18 [P] 570-222-2500
Rocky Spring GC, *Chambersburg*.........................9 [P] 717-264-7742
 rockyspringgc.com
Rohannas GC, *Waynesburg*...............................18 [P] 724-627-6423
Rolling Acres GC, *Beaver Falls* ....27 [P] 724-843-6736
 rollingacresgolf.com
Rolling Acres GC, *York*.......................................18 [P] 717-755-1406
Rolling Fields GC, *Murraysville*............................18 [P] 724-335-7522
Rolling Green GC, *Eighty Four* ....18 [P] 724-222-9671
 rollinggreengolf.net
Rolling Green GC, *Springfield*............................ 18 [V] 610-328-5535
 rggc.org

[S] = SEMI-PRIVATE   [V] = PRIVATE   [U] = UNIVERSITY   [N] = UNIVERSITY-PRIVATE

PENNSYLVANIA

Rolling Hills CC, *McMurray* .... 18 [V] 724-941-5520
   rollinghillscountryclub.us
Rolling Hills GC, *Pulaski* .... 18 [P] 724-964-8201
Rolling Meadows GC, *Ashland* .... 18 [P] 570-875-1204
Rolling Pines GC, *Berwick* .... 18 [R] 570-752-1000
Rolling Rock Club, *Ligonier* .... 18 [V] 724-238-9501
Rolling Turf GC, *Schwenksville* .... 9 [P] 610-287-7297
   rollingturf.4t.com
Rose Ridge GC, *Allison Park* .... 18 [P] 724-443-5020
   roseridgegolf.com
Royal Manchester Golf Links, *Mt Wolf*...18 [S] 717-268-0490
   royalmanchestergolflinks.com
Royal Oaks GC, *Lebanon* .... 18 [P] 717-274-2212
   royaloaksgolfpa.com
Sand Springs CC, *Drums* .... 18 [P] 570-788-5845
   sandspringsgolf.com
Sandy Run CC, *Oreland* .... 18 [V] 215-836-5055
   sandyruncc.com
Saucon Valley CC, *Bethlehem* .... 54 [P] 610-758-7177
   sauconvalleycc.org
Sawmill GC, *Easton* .... 18 [P] 610-759-8200
   sawmillgolfcourse.com
Saxon GC, *Sarver* .... 27 [P] 724-353-2130
Scallys Golf Ctr, *Coraopolis* .... 18 [P] 412-264-9940
   scallysgolfcenter.com
Scenic Heights GC, *Erie* .... 18 [P] 814-739-9700
   scenicheightsgolfcourse.com
Scenic Valley GC, *Finleyville* .... 18 [P] 412-833-1988
   scenicvalleygolf.com
Schuylkill CC, *Orwigsburg* .... 18 [V] 570-366-0733
   schuylkillcc.com
Scotch Valley CC, *Hollidaysburg*............ 18 [V] 814-695-1478
   scotchvalleycc.com
Scottish Glen GC, *Clifford* .... 9 [P] 570-222-3676
   fernhallinn.com
Scottish Heights GC, *Brockport* .... 18 [S] 814-265-4653
   scottishheights.com
Scranton Canoe Club, *Lake Winola* .... 9 [V] 570-378-9982
   scrantoncanoeclub.com
Scranton GC, *Mt Cobb* .... 18 [P] 570-689-2686
Serene Valley GC, *Butler* .... 18 [P] 724-285-1236
Seven Oaks GC, *Beaver* .... 18 [P] 724-495-2770
   sevenoakscc.com
Seven Springs CC, *Elizabeth* .... 18 [P] 412-384-7730
   golf7springs.com
Seven Springs Mountain Resort, *Champion*........18 [R] 814-352-7777
   7springs.com
Sewickley Heights GC, *Sewickley* .... 18 [P] 412-741-6450
   shgc.org
Shade Mountain GC, *Middleburg* .... 18 [P] 570-837-2155
   shademountaingolf.com
Shadowbrook Inn & Resort GC, *Tunkhannock*.....18 [P] 570-836-5417
   shadowbrookresort.com
Shamrock Public GC, *Slippery Rock* .... 9 [P] 724-794-3030
Shannopin CC, *Pittsburgh* .... 18 [P] 412-761-6377
   shannopincc.com
Shawnee Inn & Golf Resort, *Shawnee On Delaware*27 [R]570-424-4000
   shawneeinn.com
Shenango Lake GC, *Transfer* .... 18 [P] 724-962-9875
   shenangolakegolfclub.com
Shepherd Hills GC, *Wescosville* .... 18 [P] 610-391-0444
Silver Creek GC, *Hellertown* .... 27 [V] 610-838-6664
   silvercreekcountryclub.com

Silver Spring GC, *Mechanicsburg* ....18 [P] 717-766-0462
   silverspringgolfcourse.com
Sinking Valley CC, *Altoona* .... 18 [P] 814-684-0662
   sinkingvalleycc.com
Skippack GC At Evansburg St Park, *Skippack*......18 [M] 610-584-4226
   skippackgolfclub.com
Skyline GC, *Greenfield Township* .... 18 [P] 570-282-5993
   skylinegolfcourse.com
Skytop Lodge GC, *Skytop* .... 18 [R] 570-595-8910
   skytop.com
Sleepy Hollow GC, *Greenfield Twp*.......... 18 [P] 570-254-4653
   sleepyhollowgolf.com
Sliding Rock GC, *Boswell* .... 9 [P] 814-629-6561
Smethport CC, *Smethport* .... 9 [S] 814-887-5641
Somerset CC, *Somerset* .... 18 [P] 814-445-5179
   thegolfclubofsomerset.com
South Hills CC, *Pittsburgh* .... 18 [V] 412-884-5111
   southhillscc.org
South Hills GC, *Hanover* .... 27 [P] 717-637-7500
   southhillsgc.com
South Mountain GC, *South Mountain* ...... 9 [P] 717-749-3286
South Park GC, *South Park* .... 27 [M] 412-835-3545
   county.allegheny.pa.us/parks
South Woods GC, *McKean* .... 9 [P] 814-476-7907
Southmoore GC, *Bath*......................... 18 [P] 610-837-7200
   southmooregolf.com
Southpointe GC, *Canonsburg* .... 18 [V] 724-746-2950
   southpointegolfclub.com
Speers Public GC, *Franklin* .... 9 [P] 814-676-3890
Split Rock Resort & CC, *Lake Harmony* ...27 [R] 570-722-9111
   splitrockresort.com
Sportsmans GC, *Harrisburg*.................. 18 [P] 717-545-0023
   sportsmansgolfcourse.com
Spring Creek Frontier GC, *Spring Creek*.... 9 [P] 814-664-2821
Spring Creek GC, *Hershey*..................... 9 [P] 717-533-2847
   hersheygolfcollection.com
Spring Ford GC, *Royersford* .... 18 [V] 610-948-0580
   springfordcc.com
Spring Hollow GC, *Spring City* .... 18 [P] 610-948-5566
   springhollowgolf.com
Spring Mill GC, *Ivyland* .... 18 [V] 215-675-6000
   springmillcountryclub.com
Spring Valley GC, *Mercer* .... 18 [P] 724-662-1999
   springvalleygolfcourse.net
Springdale GC, *Uniontown* .... 18 [P] 724-439-4400
   springdalegolfclub.net
Springfield CC, *Springfield* .... 18 [M] 610-543-9860
   springfieldgolf.com
Springside Par 3 GC, *Reinholds* .... 18 [P] 717-336-6098
Springwood GC, *York* .... 18 [S] 717-747-9663
   hhgr.com
Squires GC, *Ambler* .... 18 [V] 215-643-7244
   squiresgolf.com
St Clair CC, *Pittsburgh* .... 27 [V] 412-833-5550
   stclaircc.org
St Davids CC, *Wayne* .... 18 [V] 610-688-9708
   stdavidsgc.com
St Jude GC, *Chicora* .... 18 [V] 724-445-3784
   stjudegolfclub.com
St Marys CC, *St Marys* .... 9 [V] 814-834-7888
   thesmcc.com
Standing Stone GC, *Huntingdon* .... 18 [S] 814-643-4800

PENNSYLVANIA

State College Elks CC, *Boalsburg* .... 18 [V] 814-466-6451
elks1600.com
Stone Hedge GC, *Factoryville* ....18 [P] 570-836-5108
stone-hedge.com
Stone Meadows GC, *White Haven* ....18 [P] 570-472-5465
stonemeadowsgolf.com
Stonecrest GC, *Wampum* ....18 [P] 724-535-8971
stonecrestgc.com
Stonewall Links, *Elverson* .... 36 [V] 610-286-3090
stonewalllinks.com
Stop & Sock, *New Brighton* ....18 [P] 724-843-7043
stopandsock.com
Stoughton Acres GC, *Butler*........................18 [P] 724-285-3633
stoughtonacres.com
Strawberry Ridge GC, *Harmony* ....18 [P] 724-452-4022
strawberryridgegolfcourse.com
Sugarloaf GC, *Sugarloaf*..............................18 [P] 570-384-4097
sugarloafgolfclub.com
Summit CC, *Cresson* ....18 [P] 814-886-9985
Summit Hills GC, *Clarks Summit* ....18 [P] 570-586-4427
Suncrest GC, *Butler*....................................18 [P] 724-586-5508
suncrestgolf.com
Sunnehanna CC, *Johnstown*....................... 18 [V] 814-255-4121
sunnehannacountryclub.com
Sunny Hill GC, *Sunbury*.................................9 [P] 570-286-5980
Sunnybrook GC, *Plymouth Meeting*.............. 18 [P] 610-828-9631
sunnybrook.org
Sunset GC, *Middletown*..............................18 [M] 717-944-5415
sunsetgc.com
Susquehanna Valley CC, *Hummels Wharf*...... 18 [V] 570-743-7052
svccgolf.com
Sweet Water GC, *Pennsburg*..........................9 [P] 215-541-3111
golfsweetwater.com
Sylvan Heights Muni GC, *New Castle*.............18 [M] 724-658-8021
newcastlepa.org
Sylvan Hills GC, *Hollidaysburg* ....9 [P] 814-695-4769
Talamore CC, *Ambler* .... 18 [V] 215-646-8900
talamorepa.com
Tall Pines Players Club, *Friendsville* ....18 [P] 570-553-4653
Tam OShanter GC, *Hermitage* ....18 [P] 724-981-3552
tamoshanterpa.com
Tamiment GC, *Tamiment*............................18 [P] 570-588-6652
tamiment.com
Tanglewood GC, *Pulaski* ....18 [P] 724-964-8702
tanglewoodgc.com
Tanglewood Manor GC, *Quarryville* ....18 [P] 717-786-2500
twgolf.com
Terra Greens GC, *East Stroudsburg*................9 [M] 570-421-0120
terragreens.com
The ACE Club, *Lafayette Hill*........................ 18 [V] 610-940-4785
theaceclubonline.com
The Bob OConnor GC At Schenley Park, *Pittsburgh*18 [P] 412-622-6959
thebobgc.com/
The Bridges GC, *Abbottstown* ....18 [P] 717-624-9551
bridgesgc.com
The Bucks Club, *Jamison*............................18 [P] 215-343-0350
golfbucks.com
The CC of Meadville, *Meadville* .... 18 [V] 814-724-7453
meadvillecc.com
The Center Valley Club, *Center Valley*............18 [P] 610-791-5580
centervalleyclubgolf.com
The Club At Blackthorne, *Jeannette* ....9 [P] 724-325-2052
theclubatblackthorne.com

The Club At Morgan Hill, *Easton* ....18 [P] 610-923-8480
theclubatmorganhill.com
The Club at Shadow Lakes, *Aliquippa* .... 18 [V] 724-375-5511
clubatshadowlakes.com
The Club At Shannondell, *Audubon* ....18 [M] 610-666-7600
theclubatshannondell.com
The GC At Glen Mills, *Glen Mills*...................18 [P] 610-558-2142
glenmillsgolf.com
The GC of Washington, *Washington*............... 9 [P] 724-222-9664
golfclubofwashington.com
The Greens of Greenville, *Greenville*..............18 [P] 724-588-6020
greensofgreenville.com
The Hideaway Hills GC, *Kresgeville*................18 [P] 610-681-6000
hideawaygolf.com
The Hideout Golf, *Lake Ariel*......................... 9 [V] 570-698-5682
hideoutassoc.com
The Indian Springs G&CC, *Indiana* ....18 [S] 724-465-5131
indianspringsvfw.com
The Links At Spring Church, *Apollo* ....18 [P] 724-478-5478
playthelinks.com
The Madison Club, *Madison*........................18 [P] 724-446-4000
themadisonclub.com
The Montrose Club, *Montrose* .... 9 [V] 570-278-3460
themontroseclub.com
The Phoenix at Buffalo Valley, *Freepost*..........18 [P] 724-295-4001
thephoenixbv.com
The RiverCrest GC & Preserve, *Phoenixville* ....18 [P] 610-933-4700
rivercrestgolfclub.com
The Springhaven Club, *Wallingford*............... 18 [V] 610-872-8461
springhavengolf.com
Thornhurst CC, *Thornhurst*...........................9 [P] 570-472-9079
thornhurst.org
Timber Ridge GC, *Mt Pleasant* ....18 [P] 724-547-1909
timberridgegolfclub.org
Timberlink GC, *Ligonier* ....18 [P] 724-238-7314
Toftrees Resort & Four Star GC, *State College*.......18 [R] 814-238-7600
toftrees.com
Torresdale Frankford CC, *Philadelphia* .... 18 [V] 215-824-2155
tfccgolf.com
Totteridge GC, *Greensburg* .... 18 [V] 724-837-6700
totteridge.com
Towanda CC, *Towanda* ....18 [S] 570-265-6939
towandacountryclub.com
Treasure Lake, *Du Bois* ....36 [R] 814-375-1808
treasurelakepoa.com
Tree Top GC, *Manheim* ....18 [P] 717-665-6262
treetopgolf.com
Treesdale G&CC, *Gibsonia* .... 27 [V] 724-625-4653
treesdalegolf.com
Tumblebrook GC, *Coopersburg*......................9 [P] 610-282-0377
Turtle Creek GC, *Limerick* ....27 [P] 610-489-5133
turtlecreekgolf.com
Tussey Mountain GC, *Boalsburg* ....9 [P] 814-466-6266
tusseymountain.com
Twin Lakes P 3 GC, *Kittanning*.......................9 [P] 724-543-2609
Twin Oaks GC, *Dallas* ....9 [P] 570-333-4360
Twin Ponds GC, *Gilbertsville*........................18 [P] 610-369-1901
twinpondsgolf.com
Twin Woods GC, *Hatfield*..............................9 [P] 215-822-9263
twinwoodsgolfcourse.com
Twining Valley GC, *Dresher* ....18 [S] 215-659-9917
twiningvalley.com
Two T'S Par-3 9-Hole GC, *Easton* ....9 [P] 610-923-7225
twotsgolf.com

[S] = SEMI-PRIVATE [V] = PRIVATE [U] = UNIVERSITY [N] = UNIVERSITY-PRIVATE

PENNSYLVANIA
Golf Yellow Pages, 18th Edition

Tyoga CC, *Wellsboro* .... 18 [P] 570-724-1653
  tyogacc.com
Union City CC, *Union City* .... 18 [P] 814-438-2810
Uniontown CC, *Uniontown* .... 18 [V] 724-438-7831
Valley Brook CC, *McMurray* .... 27 [V] 412-563-3500
  valleybrookcc.com
Valley CC, *Sugarloaf* .... 18 [V] 570-788-1194
  vcc1909.com
Valley Green G&CC, *Greensburg* .... 18 [P] 724-837-6366
  valleygreengolfclub.com
Valley Green GC, *Etters* .... 18 [P] 717-938-4200
  valleygreengolfcourse.com
Valley View GC, *Harrisville* .... 9 [P] 724-735-2158
Valley View GC, *Wattsburg* .... 9 [S] 814-825-4906
Vandergrift GC, *Vandergrift* .... 9 [P] 724-567-7413
Venango Trail GC, *Mars* .... 18 [P] 724-776-4400
Venango Valley Inn & GC, *Venango* .... 18 [R] 814-398-4330
  venangovalley.com
VFW GC, *Hermitage* .... 18 [P] 724-346-6903
  hickoryvfw-normandy.com
Village Green GC, *Hickory* .... 18 [P] 724-356-2282
  golfvillagegreen.com
Village Greens GC, *Sinking Spring* .... 18 [P] 610-678-3988
Villas Crossing GC, *Tamaqua* .... 18 [P] 570-386-4515
  villascrossing.com
Walnut Acres GC, *Hamburg* .... 9 [P] 610-562-8282
  walnutacresgolf.com
Walnut Creek GC, *Jamestown* .... 9 [P] 724-932-5219
Walnut Lane GC, *Philadelphia* .... 18 [M] 215-482-3470
  golfphilly.com
Wanango GC, *Reno* .... 18 [V] 814-677-5130
  wanango.com
Warminsters Five Ponds GC, *Warminster* .... 18 [M] 215-956-9727
  5pondsgc.com
Water Gap CC, *Delaware Water Gap* .... 18 [P] 570-476-0300
  watergapcountryclub.com
Waynesboro CC, *Waynesboro* .... 18 [V] 717-762-2603
  waynesborocc.com
Waynesboro Muni GC, *Waynesboro* .... 9 [M] 717-762-3734
  waynesboropa.com
Waynesborough CC, *Paoli* .... 18 [V] 610-296-2122
  waynesborough-cc.com
Wedgewood GC, *Coopersburg* .... 27 [P] 610-797-4551
  distinctgolf.com
Wemberly Hills GC, *Scott Township* .... 9 [P] 570-563-1902
West Chester G&CC, *West Chester* .... 9 [V] 610-692-2161
  westchestercc.net
West Hills Par 3 GC, *Moon Twp.* .... 9 [S] 412-262-9331
West Shore CC, *Camp Hill* .... 18 [P] 717-737-5164
  westshorecc.com
West View GC, *Akron* .... 18 [P] 717-859-2333
Westmoreland CC, *Export* .... 27 [V] 724-733-7747
  westmorelandcc.com
Westover GC, *Norristown* .... 18 [P] 610-539-4500
  westovercountryclub.com
Westwood GC, *West Mifflin* .... 18 [P] 412-462-9555
  westwoodlinks.com
Whispering Pines GC, *Meadville* .... 18 [P] 814-333-2827
  golfwhisperingpines.com
Whispering Woods GC, *McKean* .... 18 [S] 814-838-9942
  whisperingwoodsgc.com
White Birch GC, *Barnesville* .... 27 [P] 570-467-2525
  whitebirchgolfcourse.com

White Deer GC, *Montgomery* .... 45 [M] 570-547-2186
  wdgc.net
White Manor CC, *Malvern* .... 18 [V] 610-647-1070
  whitemanorcc.com
White Oak GC, *Dayton* .... 9 [P] 814-257-0113
  whiteoakfarmsinc.com
Whitemarsh Valley CC, *Lafayette Hill* .... 18 [V] 215-233-3901
  whitemarshvalleycc.com
Whitetail GC, *Bath* .... 18 [P] 610-837-9626
  whitetailgolfclub.com
Whitetail Golf Resort, *Mercersburg* .... 18 [R] 717-328-4169
  golfatwhitetail.com
Whitetail Run GC, *Franklin* .... 9 [P] 814-676-0633
Whitford CC, *Exton* .... 18 [V] 610-269-2151
  whitfordgolf.com
Wild Pines GC, *Pocono Pines* .... 18 [V] 570-646-4444
  wildpines.com
Wildwood GC, *Allison Park* .... 18 [V] 412-486-4300
  wildwoodgolfclub.org
Wilkes Barre GC, *Wilkes Barre* .... 18 [M] 570-472-3590
  wilkes-barregolfclub.com
Williamsport CC, *Williamsport* .... 18 [V] 570-323-3709
  wcc1909.com
Willow Brook GC, *Catasauqua* .... 18 [P] 610-264-9904
  golfwillowbrook.com
Willow Hills GC, *Grove City* .... 9 [P] 724-748-3375
  willowhillsgolf.com
Willow Hollow GC, *Leesport* .... 18 [P] 610-373-1505
  distinctgolf.com
Willow Valley GC, *Lancaster* .... 9 [R] 717-464-4448
  willowvalley.com
Willowbrook CC, *Apollo* .... 18 [V] 724-727-3442
  willowbrookcc.org
Willowbrook GC, *Belle Vernon* .... 9 [P] 724-872-7272
Windber CC, *Salix* .... 18 [V] 814-266-4536
  windbercountryclub.com
Windsor Heights GC, *Bloomsburg* .... 18 [P] 570-784-5673
  windsorheightsgc.com
Windy Hill GC, *Plum* .... 9 [P] 412-793-7771
Wolf Hollow Golf Ctr, *Bloomsburg* .... 9 [P] 570-784-5994
Woodbridge GC, *Kutztown* .... 18 [P] 610-683-5355
  playwoodbridge.com
Woodland Hills CC, *Hellertown* .... 18 [P] 610-838-7192
  woodlandhillscountryclub.com
Woodlawn GC, *Tarentum* .... 9 [P] 724-224-4730
Woodloch Springs GC, *Hawley* .... 18 [R] 570-685-8102
  woodloch.com
Woods Golf Ctr, *Norristown* .... 18 [P] 610-279-0678
  woodysgolfcenter.com
Woodstone CC, *Danielsville* .... 18 [V] 610-760-2777
  woodstonegolf.com
Worcester GC, *Collegeville* .... 9 [P] 610-222-0200
  tendollargolf.com
Wyncote GC, *Oxford* .... 18 [S] 610-932-8900
  wyncote.com
Wynding Brook GC, *Milton* .... 18 [P] 570-742-7455
  wyndingbrookgolf.com
Wyndon Links, *Scottdale* .... 9 [P] 724-887-8858
Wyoming Valley CC, *Wilkes Barre* .... 18 [V] 570-825-9489
  wyomingvalleycountryclub.com
Yardley G&CC, *Yardley* .... 18 [V] 215-493-3260
  yardleycc.com

[A] = MILITARY [M] = MUNICIPAL [P] = PUBLIC [R] = RESORT

Youghiogheny CC, *McKeesport*............................ 18 [V]   412-751-2943
youghcc.com

RHODE ISLAND

Agawam Hunt, *Rumford*...................................... 18 [V]   401-434-3254
agawamhunt.org
Alpine CC, *Cranston* .... 18 [V]   401-944-9760
alpinecountryclubri.com
Beaver River GC, *West Kingston* ....18 [P]   401-539-2100
beaverrivergolf.com
Bristol GC, *Bristol*... 9 [P]   401-253-9844
Button Hole Short Course & Teaching Ctr,
Providence ....9 [P]   401-421-1664
buttonhole.org
Carnegie Abbey Club, *Portsmouth* .... 18 [V]   401-682-6000
carnegieabbeyclub.com
Country View GC, *Harrisville* ....18 [P]   401-568-7157
countryviewgolf.net
Coventry Pines CC, *Coventry*..................................9 [P]   401-397-9482
Cranston CC, *Cranston*.. 18 [P]   401-826-1683
cranstoncc.com
Crystal Lake GC, *Harrisville* ....18 [P]   401-567-4500
crystallakegolfclub.com
East Greenwich Golf & Country, *East Greenwich*....9 [P]   401-884-5656
rigolf.com/eg
Exeter CC, *Exeter*... 18 [P]   401-295-8212
exetercc.us
Fairlawn GC, *Lincoln* .... 9 [P]   401-334-3937
fairlawngolfcourse.com
Fenner Hill GC, *Hope Valley* ....18 [P]   401-539-8000
fennerhill.com
Foster CC, *Foster* ....18 [P]   401-397-5990
fostercountryclub.com
Foxwoods G&CC, *Richmond* ....18 [P]   401-539-4653
foxwoodsgolf.com
Glocester CC, *Harmony* .... 9 [V]   401-949-3330
Goddard Memorial St Park GC, *East Greenwich* ....9 [M]   401-884-9834
riparks.com
Green Valley CC, *Portsmouth*...............................18 [P]   401-849-2162
greenvalleyccofri.com
Jamestown GC, *Jamestown* ....9 [P]   401-423-9930
jamestowngolf.com
Kirkbrae CC, *Lincoln* .... 18 [V]   401-333-1303
kirkbrae.com
Laurel Lane CC, *West Kingston* ....18 [P]   401-783-3844
laurellanecountryclub.com
Lincoln CC, *Lincoln*... 9 [V]   401-334-2200
lincolncountryclub.com
Lindhbrook GC, *Hope Valley* ....18 [P]   401-539-8700
Louisquisset GC, *North Providence* .... 9 [V]   401-353-1620
LouisquissetGolfClub.com
Meadow Brook GC, *Wyoming*.............................18 [P]   401-539-8491
meadowbrookgolfri.com
Melody Hill GC, *Harmony*....................................18 [P]   401-949-9851
Metacomet CC, *East Providence* .... 18 [P]   401-434-9588
metacometcc.org
Midville CC, *West Warwick*....................................9 [P]   401-821-0324
midvillegolfclub.com
Misquamicut Club, *Westerly* .... 18 [V]   401-348-8121
themisquamicutclub.com
Montap GC, *Portsmouth*......................................18 [S]   401-683-0955
montaupcc.com

SOUTH CAROLINA

Mulligans Island Golf & Entertainment Ctr, *Cranston*9 [P]401-464-8855
mulligansisland.com
Newport CC, *Newport*.. 18 [V]   401-846-0461
newportcountryclub.us
Newport National GC, *Middletown* ....18 [P]   401-848-9690
newportnational.com
North Kingstown GC, *North Kingstown*.............18 [M]   401-294-4051
nkgc.com
Pawtucket CC, *Pawtucket* .... 18 [V]   401-726-6320
pawtucketcountryclub.com
Pinecrest GC, *Carolina*..9 [P]   401-364-8600
pinecrestri.com
Point Judith CC, *Narragansett* .... 18 [V]   401-792-9770
pointjudithcountryclub.com
Potowomut GC, *East Greenwich* .... 18 [V]   401-884-9773
potowomut.com
Quidnessett CC, *North Kingstown* .... 18 [V]   401-885-5613
quidnessett.com
Rhode Island CC, *Barrington* .... 18 [V]   401-245-7370
ricc.org
Richmond CC, *Richmond*.....................................18 [P]   401-364-9200
richmondcountryclub.net
Rolling Greens GC, *North Kingstown* ....9 [P]   401-294-9859
rollinggreensri.com
Rose Hill GC, *Wakefield* ....9 [P]   401-788-1088
rosehillri.com
Sakonnet GC, *Little Compton* .... 18 [V]   401-635-4821
sakonnetgc.com
Seaview CC, *Warwick*..9 [P]   401-681-4133
Shelter Harbor GC, *Charlestown* .... 27 [V]   401-322-0600
shgcri.com
Triggs Memorial GC, *Providence*..........................18 [P]   401-521-8460
triggs.us
Valley CC, *Warwick* .... 18 [V]   401-821-1115
valleycountryclub.net
Wannamoisett CC, *Rumford*................................ 18 [V]   401-434-1200
wannamoisett.com
Wanumetonomy G&CC, *Middletown* .... 18 [V]   401-847-3420
wanumetonomy.com
Warwick CC, *Warwick*.. 18 [V]   401-737-9878
warwickcc.com
Washington Village GC, *Coventry* ....9 [P]   401-823-0010
Weekapaug GC, *Westerly*....................................... 9 [V]   401-322-7870
weekapauggolfclub.com
West Warwick CC, *West Warwick* ....9 [V]   401-641-9546
westwarwickcc.com
Windmill Hill GC, *Warren* ....9 [P]   401-245-1463
windmillgolfri.com
Winnapaug G&CC, *Westerly*................................18 [P]   401-596-1237
winnapaugcountryclub.com
Wood River Golf, *Hope Valley*..............................18 [P]   401-364-0700
woodrivergolf.com
Woodland Greens GC, *North Kingstown*................9 [P]   401-294-2872
Yawgoo Valley GC, *Exeter*.......................................9 [P]   401-294-3802
yawgoo.com

SOUTH CAROLINA

Aberdeen CC, *Longs*... 27 [S]   843-399-2660
mbn.com
Anderson CC, *Anderson* .... 18 [S]   864-225-8291
golfaag.com
Arcadian Shores GC, *Myrtle Beach* ....18 [R]   843-449-5217
kingstonplantation.com/golf

[S] = SEMI-PRIVATE   [V] = PRIVATE   [U] = UNIVERSITY   [N] = UNIVERSITY-PRIVATE

SOUTH CAROLINA

Arrowhead CC, *Myrtle Beach*..........................27 [P] 843-236-3243
 arrowheadcc.com
Arthur Hills GC-Palmetto Dunes, *Hilton Head Is* ..18 [R] 843-785-1136
 palmettodunes.com
Azalea Sands GC, *North Myrtle Beach* ....18 [P] 843-272-6191
 azaleasandsgc.com
Barefoot Resort & GC, *North Myrtle Beach* ....54 [R] 843-390-3200
 barefootgolf.com
Barefoot Resort Dye, *North Myrtle Beach*............18 [R] 843-399-7238
 barefootgolf.com
Beachwood GC, *North Myrtle Beach*....................18 [P] 843-272-6168
 beachwoodgolf.com
Bear Creek GC, *Hilton Head Island* .... 18 [V] 843-681-2667
 bearcreekgolfclub.org
Beaver Creek GC, *Darlington* ....18 [P] 843-393-5441
Beech Creek GC, *Sumter*......................................18 [P] 803-499-4653
 beechcreekgolfclub.com
Belfair GC, *Bluffton* .... 36 [V] 843-757-0715
 belfair1811.com
Berkeley CC, *Moncks Corner* .... 18 [P] 843-761-4880
Berkeley Hall GC, *Bluffton*................................... 36 [V] 843-815-2444
 berkeleyhallclub.com
Bermuda Run GC, *Jefferson* ....18 [P] 803-475-2884
Bethune CC, *Bethune*...9 [P] 843-334-7179
Bishopville CC, *Bishopville* ....18 [P] 803-428-3675
 bishopvillecountryclub.com
Black Bear GC, *Longs* ....18 [P] 843-249-1478
 classicgolfgroup.com
Blackmoor GC, *Murrells Inlet*..............................18 [P] 843-650-5555
 blackmoor.com
Blue Ridge Golf Ctr, *Walhalla*.................................9 [P] 864-882-7949
 blueridgepar3.com
Bonnie Brae GC, *Greenville* ....18 [P] 864-277-4178
Boscobel GC, *Pendleton* ....18 [P] 864-646-3991
 golfaag.com
Brays Island Plantation, *Sheldon* .... 18 [V] 843-846-3100
 braysisland.com
Brookstone Meadows GC, *Anderson* ....18 [P] 864-964-9966
 golfaag.com
Bulls Bay GC, *Awendaw* .... 18 [V] 843-881-2223
 bullsbaygolf.com
Burning Ridge GC, *Conway* ....36 [R] 843-347-0538
 classicgolfgroup.com
Caledonia Golf & Fish Club, *Pawleys Island* ....18 [P] 843-237-3675
 fishclub.com
Calhoun CC, *St Matthews*....................................18 [P] 803-823-2465
 calhouncountryclub.com
Callawassie Island Club, *Okatie*.......................... 27 [V] 843-987-2161
 mycallawassieisland.com
Camden CC, *Camden*.. 18 [V] 803-432-3322
 camdencountryclub.com
Cane Patch Par 3 GC & DR, *Myrtle Beach* ....27 [P] 843-315-0301
 myrtlebeachtrips.com
Carolina Crossing GC, *York* ....18 [P] 803-684-5878
 carolinacrossinggc.com
Carolina Golf, *Greenville*....................................... 9 [V] 864-244-6702
 carolinagolfbw.com
Carolina Lakes GC, *Indian Land* ....18 [P] 843-547-9668
 carolinalakesgc.com
Carolina Lakes GC, *Shaw AFB* ....18 [A] 803-895-1399
Carolina Springs GC, *Fountain Inn*......................27 [P] 864-862-3551
CC of Charleston, *Charleston* .... 18 [V] 843-795-2312
 countryclubofcharleston.com

CC of Hilton Head, *Hilton Head Island*.................18 [R] 843-681-4653
 hiltonheadclub.com
CC of Lexington, *Lexington* .... 18 [V] 803-359-8838
 ccoflexington.com
CC of South Carolina, *Florence*........................... 18 [V] 843-669-1838
 countryclubsc.com
CC of Spartanburg, *Spartanburg* .... 18 [V] 864-582-1646
 sbrg.org
Cedar Springs GC, *Greenwood*.............................9 [P] 864-374-3396
Charleston Muni GC, *Charleston*........................18 [M] 843-795-6517
 charlestoncity.info
Charleston Natl GC, *Mt Pleasant* ....18 [P] 843-884-7799
 charlestonnationalgolf.com
Charwood CC, *West Columbia* ....27 [P] 803-755-2000
 charwood.com
Chechessee Creek Club, *Okatie*.......................... 18 [V] 843-987-7070
 chechesseecreekclub.com
Cheraw CC, *Cheraw*..18 [P] 843-537-3412
 cherawgolf.com
Cheraw St Park GC, *Cheraw*................................18 [M] 800-868-9630
 southcarolinaparks.com
Cherokee National G&CC, *Gaffney*..................... 18 [V] 864-489-9417
 cherokeenational.net
Cherokee Plantation, *Yemassee* ....18 [R] 843-844-8000
 cherokeeplantation.com
Cherry Hill CC, *Andrews* .... 9 [V] 843-264-5422
Chesnee CC, *Chesnee* .... 9 [V] 864-461-9687
Chester GC, *Chester*.. 18 [S] 803-581-5733
 playchester.com
Clio CC, *Clio*..9 [P] 843-586-9361
Club At Rawls Creek, *Columbia* ....18 [P] 803-781-0114
 golfrawlscreek.com
Cobbs Glen CC, *Anderson* ....18 [P] 864-226-7688
 cobbsglen.com
Cokesbury Hills GC, *Hodges*..................................9 [P] 864-374-7820
Colleton River Plantation Club, *Bluffton*............ 45 [V] 843-836-4400
 colletonriverclub.com
Columbia CC, *Blythewood* .... 27 [V] 803-754-8100
 columbiacountryclub.com
Conway CC, *Conway*..9 [P] 843-365-3621
Coopers Creek GC, *Leesville* ....18 [S] 803-894-3666
Coosaw Creek CC, *North Charleston* ....18 [S] 843-767-9000
 coosawcreek.com
Crescent Pointe GC, *Bluffton* ....18 [S] 843-706-2600
 crescentpointegolf.com
Crestwood CC, *Denmark* ....9 [S] 803-793-0108
Cross Creek Plantation, *Seneca* .... 18 [V] 864-882-8337
 crosscreekplantation.com
Crosswinds GC, *Greenville* ....18 [P] 864-233-6336
 crosswinds-golf.com
Crowfield G&CC, *Goose Creek* .... 18 [M] 843-764-4618
 crowfieldgolf.com
Crown Park GC, *Longs* ....27 [P] 843-756-3200
 crownparkmb.com
Crystal Lake GC, *Sumter*.....................................18 [M] 803-775-1902
Cypress Bay GC, *Little River* ....18 [R] 843-249-1025
Cypress Point Par 3, *Moncks Corner* ....18 [P] 843-761-5599
Daniel Island Club, *Charleston* .... 36 [V] 843-971-3555
 danielislandclub.com
Darlington CC, *Darlington*.................................. 18 [V] 843-393-2196
 darlingtoncountryclub.com
Dataw Island Club, *St Helena Island* .... 36 [V] 843-838-8250
 dataw.org

188 [A] = MILITARY   [M] = MUNICIPAL   [P] = PUBLIC   [R] = RESORT

SOUTH CAROLINA

Daufuskie Island Resort-Bloody Point,
Hilton Head Is .... 18 [V] 843-785-5029
daufuskieresort.com
Daufuskie Island Resort-Melrose Club,
Hilton Head Is .... 18 [V] 843-785-5029
DeBordieu Club, *Georgetown* .... 18 [V] 843-527-6000
debordieuclub.com
Dogwood Hills CC, *Walterboro* .... 9 [V] 843-538-8316
dogwoodhillscountryclub.com
Dolphin Head GC, *Hilton Head Island* ... 18 [V] 843-681-5550
dolphinheadgc.com
Donaldson Ctr GC, *Greenville* .... 9 [P] 864-277-8414
Dunes West GC, *Mt Pleasant* .... 18 [P] 843-856-9000
duneswestgolfclub.com
Dusty Hills CC, *Marion* .... 18 [P] 843-423-2721
Eagle Landing GC, *Hanahan* .... 18 [P] 843-797-1667
Eagle Nest GC, *Little River* .... 18 [P] 843-249-1449
eaglenestgolf.com
Eagles Pointe GC, *Bluffton* .... 18 [S] 843-757-5900
eaglespointegolf.com
Edgewater GC, *Lancaster* .... 18 [P] 803-283-9800
edgewatergc.com
Fairdale CC, *Fairfax* .... 9 [P] 803-584-7117
Fairfield CC, *Winnsboro* .... 9 [V] 803-635-2111
Falcons Lair GC, *Walhalla* .... 18 [S] 864-638-0000
golfaag.com
Florence CC, *Florence* .... 18 [V] 843-669-3554
florencecc.com
Forest Lake Club, *Columbia* .... 18 [V] 803-738-0500
forestlakeclub.com
Fort Jackson GC, *Fort Jackson* .... 36 [A] 803-787-4344
jackson.army.mil
Fort Mill GC, *Fort Mill* .... 18 [P] 803-547-2044
playfortmill.com
Fox Creek GC, *Lydia* .... 18 [P] 843-332-0613
Fox Run CC, *Simpsonville* .... 18 [V] 864-967-9505
Foxboro GC, *Summerton* .... 18 [P] 803-478-7000
foxborogolfsc.com
Foxwood Hills GC, *Westminster* .... 9 [P] 864-647-9503
fwhgolf.com
Furman Univ GC, *Greenville* .... 18 [U] 864-294-9090
furmangolfclub.com
Gaffney CC, *Gaffney* .... 9 [V] 864-489-4607
GC At Wescott Plantation, *Summerville* .... 27 [M] 843-871-2135
wescottgolf.com
George Fazio GC-Palmetto Dunes, *Hilton Head Is* 18 [R] 843-785-1136
palmettodunes.com
Gifford Golf, *Beaufort* .... 9 [P] 843-521-9555
giffordsgolf.com
Glen Dornoch Waterway Golf Links, *Little River* ... 18 [P] 843-249-2541
glendornoch.com
Golden Hills G&CC, *Lexington* .... 18 [P] 803-957-3355
goldenhillsgolf.com
Golf Ctr, *Columbia* .... 9 [P] 803-736-9193
Goodale St Park GC, *Camden* .... 9 [M] 843-432-2772
southcarolinaparks.com
Governors Run GC, *Lamar* .... 18 [P] 843-326-5513
Grande Dunes GC, *Myrtle Beach* .... 18 [R] 843-449-7070
grandedunes.com
Green Hill GC, *Lugoff* .... 9 [P] 803-438-1917
Green River CC, *Chesterfield* .... 18 [P] 843-623-2533
Green Valley GC, *Greenville* .... 18 [V] 864-246-3941
greenvalley.lc

Greenville CC, *Greenville* .... 36 [V] 864-233-6227
gccsc.com
Greenwood CC, *Greenwood* .... 27 [V] 864-942-8861
greenwoodcountryclub.com
Greer G&CC, *Greer* .... 18 [V] 864-877-9279
Haig Point Club, *Hilton Head Island* .... 27 [V] 843-341-8100
haigpoint.com
Hampton Hall Club, *Bluffton* .... 18 [V] 843-815-8720
hamptonhallsc.com
Hampton Pointe CC, *Hardeeville* .... 18 [V] 866-375-8655
hamptonpointesc.com
Harbour Town Golf Links, *Hilton Head Island* ... 18 [R] 843-363-8385
seapines.com
Harbour View Par 3 & DR, *Little River* ... 18 [P] 843-249-9117
harbourviewgolf.com
Hartsville CC, *Hartsville* .... 18 [V] 843-332-1441
hartsvillecountryclub.com
Heather Glen Golf Links, *Little River* ... 27 [V] 843-249-9000
heatherglen.com
Hejaz Shrine Rec Club, *Mauldin* .... 18 [V] 864-277-4491
hejazgolfclub.com
Heritage Club, *Pawleys Island* .... 18 [P] 843-237-3424
legendsgolf.com
Heron Point GC, *Myrtle Beach* .... 18 [P] 843-650-6664
heronpointgolfclub.com
Hickory Knob St Park GC, *McCormick* ... 18 [M] 864-391-2450
discoversouthcarolina.com
Hidden Valley CC, *Gaston* .... 18 [P] 803-794-8087
hvgolf.com
Hideaway Golf, *Hemingway* .... 9 [P] 843-558-3647
High Meadows CC, *Abbeville* .... 9 [P] 864-446-2043
Hillcrest GC, *Orangeburg* .... 18 [M] 803-533-6030
orangeburg.sc.us/hillcrest
Hilton Head National GC, *Bluffton* ..... 27 [P] 843-842-5900
golfhiltonheadnational.com
Holly Hill CC, *Holly Hills* .... 9 [V] 803-496-3460
Holly Tree CC, *Simpsonville* .... 18 [V] 864-967-9510
hollytreecountryclub.net
Houndslake CC, *Aiken* .... 27 [V] 803-648-3333
houndslakecc.com
Hunters Creek G&CC, *Greenwood* ...... 27 [S] 864-223-9286
hunterscreekcc.com
Indian River GC, *West Columbia* .... 18 [P] 803-955-0080
indianrivergolfclub.net
Indian Trail GC, *Batesburg* .... 18 [P] 803-532-9010
indiantrail.peachhost.com
Indian Wells GC, *Murrells Inlet* .... 18 [P] 843-651-1505
classicgolfgroup.com
Indigo Creek GC, *Murrells Inlet* .... 18 [R] 843-650-1809
indigocreekgolfclub.com
International Club of Myrtle Beach, *Murrells Inlet* 18 [P] 843-651-9995
internationalclubmb.com
Island Green GC, *Myrtle Beach* .... 18 [P] 843-650-2186
islandgreengc.com
Island West GC, *Bluffton* .... 18 [P] 843-689-6660
islandwestgolf.net
Jim & Lilie GC, *Jackson* .... 9 [P] 803-471-9446
Keowee Key G&CC, *Salem* .... 18 [V] 864-944-2222
keowee-key.com
Kershaw CC & GC, *Kershaw* .... 18 [M] 803-475-2104
Kiawah Island Club - Cassique, *Johns Island* ... 18 [V] 843-768-5752
kiawahislandclub.com

[S] = SEMI-PRIVATE [V] = PRIVATE [U] = UNIVERSITY [N] = UNIVERSITY-PRIVATE

SOUTH CAROLINA
Golf Yellow Pages, 18th Edition

Kiawah Island Club - River Course, *Johns Island*..18 [R] 843-768-5715
  kiawahislandclub.com
Kiawah Island Resort - Cougar Point,
  Kiawah Island....................................18 [R] 843-768-2121
  kiawahresort.com
Kiawah Island Resort - Oak Point, *Kiawah Island* 18 [R] 843-768-2121
  kiawahresort.com
Kiawah Island Resort - Ocean, *Kiawah Island* .....18 [R] 843-768-2121
  kiawahresort.com
Kiawah Island Resort - Osprey Point,
  Kiawah Island....................................18 [R] 843-768-2121
  kiawahresort.com
Kiawah Island Resort - Turtle Point, *Kiawah Island* 18 [R] 843-768-2121
  kiawahresort.com
Kountryside GC, *Cope* ....18 [P] 803-536-5888
Ladys Island CC, *Beaufort* ....36 [R] 843-524-3635
  ladysislandcc.com
Lake City CC, *Lake City*................................18 [V] 843-374-3415
Lake Marion GC, *Santee*................................18 [R] 843-854-2554
  santeecoopergolf.com
Lake Murray Golf Ctr, *Chapin* ....9 [P] 803-345-0199
  lakemurraygolf.com
Lakeside CC, *Laurens* ....18 [V] 864-682-3614
Lakeview GC, *Piedmont* ....18 [P] 843-277-2680
  lakeviewgolfclub.net
Lan Yair CC, *Spartanburg*.............................18 [V] 864-579-0360
Lancaster GC, *Lancaster*..............................18 [S] 803-416-4500
  leroysprings.com
Legend Oaks Plantation GC, *Summerville* ....18 [P] 843-821-4077
  legendoaksgolf.com
Links OTryon, *Campobello*...........................18 [P] 864-468-4961
  linksotryon.com
LinRick GC, *Columbia* ....18 [M] 803-754-6331
  richlandcountyrecreation.com
Litchfield CC, *Pawleys Island* ....18 [S] 843-237-3411
  litchcc.com
Long Bay Club, *Longs*..................................18 [P] 843-399-2222
  mbn.com
Long Cove Club, *Hilton Head Island* ....18 [V] 843-686-1020
  longcoveclub.org
Man OWar Golf Links, *Myrtle Beach* ....18 [P] 843-236-8000
  manowargolfcourse.com
Marlboro CC, *Bennettsville*..........................18 [P] 843-479-7741
  marlborocc.com
May River GC At Palmetto Bluff, *Bluffton* ....18 [R] 843-706-6580
  palmettobluffresort.com
Mc Cormick CC, *Mc Cormick*..........................9 [P] 864-391-3657
Mid Carolina CC, *Prosperity* ....18 [P] 803-364-3193
  midcarolinaclub.com
Midland Valley CC, *Graniteville* ....18 [S] 843-663-7332
  playmidlandvalley.com
Midway Par 3, *Myrtle Beach* ....27 [P] 843-913-5335
  myrtlebeachfamilygolf.com
Miler CC, *Summerville*..................................18 [P] 843-873-2210
  ra2.biz/s/miler
Monticello GC At Savannah Lakes, *Mc Cormick*... 18 [V] 864-391-4175
  savannahlakesvillage.net
Moss Creek CC, *Hilton Head Island* ....36 [R] 843-837-2231
  mosscreek-hiltonhead.com
Mount Vintage Plantation & GC, *North Augusta*.. 27 [S] 803-279-5422
  mountvintage.com
Mountainview Par 3 Golf, *Gramling*.................9 [P] 864-472-0652
Musgrove Mill GC, *Clinton* ....18 [V] 864-833-6921
  musgrovemill.com

Myrtle Beach National GC, *Myrtle Beach*............54 [R] 843-448-2308
  mbn.com
Myrtlewood GC, *Myrtle Beach* ....36 [S] 843-913-4516
  myrtlewoodgolf.com
New Ellenton GC, *New Ellenton*......................9 [P] 803-652-7867
Newberry CC, *Newberry*...............................18 [P] 803-276-2385
  ccofnewberry.com
North Augusta G&CC, *North Augusta* .... 18 [V] 803-279-0704
  northaugustagolf.com
Northern Pines, *Loris*......................................9 [S] 843-756-4141
Northwoods GC, *Columbia*............................18 [P] 803-786-9242
  northwoodsgolfsc.com
Oak Hills GC, *Columbia*................................18 [P] 803-735-9830
  oakhillsgolf.com
Oak Ridge CC, *Spartanburg*..........................18 [P] 864-582-7579
Oakdale CC, *Florence*..................................18 [P] 843-662-0368
Oaks G&CC, *Goose Creek*..............................9 [P] 843-553-4141
  golftheoaks.net
Ocean Creek GC, *Fripp Island*........................18 [R] 843-838-1576
  frippislandresort.com
Ocean Point Golf Links, *St Helena* ....18 [R] 843-838-1521
  frippislandresort.com
Oconee CC, *Seneca*......................................18 [V] 864-882-8037
Old Carolina GC, *Bluffton* ....9 [P] 843-785-6363
  oldcarolinagolf.com
Old South Golf Links, *Bluffton*.......................18 [R] 843-785-5353
  oldsouthgolf.com
Old Tabby Links on Spring Island, *Okatie* ....18 [V] 843-987-2013
  springisland-sc.com
Oldfield GC, *Okatie* ....18 [R] 843-379-5051
  oldfield1732.com
Orangeburg CC, *Orangeburg* ....18 [V] 803-534-6069
  orangeburgcc.com
Oyster Reef GC, *Hilton Head Island*...................18 [P] 843-681-7717
  oysterreefgolfclub.com
Palmetto GC, *Aiken* ....18 [V] 803-649-2951
  palmettogolfclub.net
Palmetto Greens G&CC, *Longs* ....18 [S] 843-399-4653
Palmetto Hall, *Hilton Head Island* ....36 [R] 843-342-2582
  palmettohallgolf.com
Par 3 West, *Greenwood*..................................9 [P] 864-223-4482
Patriots Point Links-Charleston Harbor,
  Mt Pleasant ....18 [R] 843-881-0042
  patriotspointlinks.com
Pawleys Plantation G&CC, *Pawleys Island*...........18 [R] 843-237-6200
  pawleysplantation.com
Pawpaw CC, *Bamberg*..................................18 [S] 803-245-4171
  pawpawcc.com
Pebble Creek GC, *Taylors*.............................36 [P] 864-244-8937
  pebblecreek-club.com
Penny Branch Club, *Furman*..........................18 [P] 803-625-0222
  pennybranchclub.com
Persimmon Hill GC, *Saluda*...........................18 [P] 803-275-2561
  persimmonhill-golf.com
Pickens GC, *Pickens*....................................18 [P] 864-878-6083
  golfaag.com
Pine Forest CC, *Summerville*.........................18 [S] 843-851-1193
  pineforestcountryclub.com
Pine Lake GC, *Anderson*...............................18 [P] 864-296-9960
Pine Lakes CC, *Myrtle Beach*..........................18 [P] 843-315-7700
  pinelakes.com
Pine Ridge CC, *Edgefield* ....18 [P] 803-637-3570
  pineridgeplantation.com

190 [A] = MILITARY [M] = MUNICIPAL [P] = PUBLIC [R] = RESORT

SOUTH CAROLINA

Course	Location	Holes	Type	Phone
Pinecrest GC,	Bluffton	18	[V]	843-757-8960
canongategolf.com				
Pineland CC,	Nichols	18	[P]	843-526-2175
Pinetuck GC,	Rock Hill	18	[P]	843-327-1141
pinetuck.com				
Pintail Creek GC,	Hardeeville	18	[P]	843-784-2426
Players Course At Wyboo Plantation,	Manning	18	[P]	843-478-2500
Ponderosa CC,	Batesburg-Leesville	18	[V]	803-532-3472
ponderosacountryclub.com				
Port Royal Golf Club,	Hilton Head Island	54	[R]	843-681-1760
portroyalgolfclub.com				
Possum Trot GC,	North Myrtle Beach	18	[P]	843-272-5341
possumtrot.com				
Prestwick GC,	Myrtle Beach	18	[P]	843-293-4100
prestwickcountryclub.com				
Quail Creek GC Costal Carolina Univ,	Conway	18	[U]	843-347-0549
coastal.edu				
Redbank Plantation GC,	Goose Creek	18	[A]	843-764-7802
Regent Park GC,	Fort Mill	18	[P]	803-547-1300
regentparkgolfclub.com				
Republic GC,	Great Falls	9	[P]	803-482-3300
River Chase GC,	Union	18	[P]	864-427-3055
River Club,	Pawleys Island	18	[R]	843-237-8755
mbn.com				
River Falls Plantation,	Duncan	18	[S]	843-433-9192
riverfallsgolf.com				
River Hills CC,	Lake Wylie	18	[V]	803-831-2249
riverhillscc.org				
River Hills G&CC,	Little River	18	[S]	843-399-2100
riverhillsgolf.com				
River Oaks Golf Plantation,	Myrtle Beach	27	[R]	843-236-2222
riveroaksgolfplantation.com				
Riverside Golf Ctr,	Columbia	9	[P]	803-750-1015
riversidegolfcolombia.com				
RiverTowne CC,	Mt Pleasant	18	[P]	843-849-2400
rivertownecountryclub.com				
Robert Trent Jones GC-Palmetto Dunes,				
Hilton Head Is		18	[R]	843-785-1136
palmettodunes.com				
Rock Hill CC,	Rock Hill	18	[V]	803-327-7790
rockhillcountryclub.net				
Rolling Green GC,	Easley	27	[P]	864-859-7716
Rolling S GC,	Waterloo	18	[P]	864-677-4566
rollingsgolfclub.us				
Rose Hill GC,	Bluffton	18	[S]	843-757-9030
golfrosehill.com				
Royal Oaks GC,	Manning	18	[P]	843-478-7272
royaloaksgolfcourse.com				
Sage Valley GC,	Graniteville	18	[V]	803-663-0900
sagevalleygolf.com				
Saluda Valley CC,	Williamston	18	[P]	864-847-7102
saludavalleycc.com				
Sandy Point CC,	Hartsville	18	[P]	843-335-8950
Santee Cooper CC,	Santee	18	[P]	843-854-2467
santeecoopergolf.com				
Santee National GC,	Santee	18	[P]	843-854-3531
santeenational.com				
Sea Pines CC,	Hilton Head Island	18	[P]	843-671-4417
seapinescountryclub.com				
Sea Pines Resort,	Hilton Head Island	36	[R]	843-842-8484
seapines.com				
Secession GC,	Beaufort	18	[P]	843-522-4600
secessiongolf.com				
Sedgewood CC,	Hopkins	18	[P]	803-776-2177
pasturegolf.com				
Sergeant Jasper CC,	Ridgeland	9	[P]	843-726-8977
Shadowmoss Plantation GC,	Charleston	18	[P]	843-556-8251
shadowmossgolf.com				
Shaftesbury Glen Golf & Fish Club,	Conway	18	[R]	866-587-1457
shaftesburyglen.com				
Shannon Greens GC,	Manning	18	[P]	803-435-8752
shannongreens.com				
Shipyard GC,	Hilton Head Island	27	[R]	843-681-1503
shipyardgolfclub.com				
Smithfields CC,	Easley	18	[V]	864-859-9545
smithfields.cc				
Snee Farm CC,	Mt Pleasant	18	[P]	843-884-2600
sneefarmcc.com				
South Edisto GC,	Ridge Spring	18	[P]	803-649-3366
southedistogolf.com				
Southern Oaks GC,	Easley	18	[P]	864-859-6698
southernoaks.com				
Spanish Wells Club,	Hilton Head Island	9	[R]	843-681-2819
spanishwellsclub.com				
Spring Lake CC,	York	18	[P]	803-684-4898
Spring Valley CC,	Columbia	18	[V]	803-788-3084
springvalleycc.com				
Springfield GC,	Fort Mill	18	[P]	803-548-3318
playspringfield.com				
St George CC,	St George	9	[P]	843-563-2816
St Stephens GC,	St Stephen	9	[P]	843-567-4653
Stone Creek Cove GC,	Anderson	9	[P]	864-261-0888
stonecreekcove.org				
Stoney Point GC,	Greenwood	18	[P]	864-942-0900
Sugar Foot GC,	Honea Path	9	[P]	864-369-1751
Summersett GC,	Greenville	18	[P]	864-834-4781
summersett.net				
Sun City Hilton Head - Argent Lakes,	Hardeeville	18	[P]	843-645-0507
Sun City Hilton Head - Hidden Cypress,	Bluffton	18	[P]	843-705-4999
Sun City Hilton Head - Okatie Creek,	Bluffton	18	[S]	843-705-4653
Sunset CC,	Sumter	18	[V]	803-773-7220
sunsetcountryclubsc.com				
Surf G&BC,	North Myrtle Beach	18	[V]	843-249-1021
surfgolf.com				
Swamp Fox GC,	Greeleyville	18	[P]	843-382-3436
Sweetwater CC,	Barnwell	18	[P]	803-259-5004
sweetwatercountryclub.org				
Tara GC At Savannah Lakes,	Mc Cormick	18	[V]	864-391-4115
savannahlakesvillage.net				
Tega Cay GC,	Tega Cay	27	[P]	803-548-2918
tegacaygolfclub.com				
The Aiken GC,	Aiken	18	[S]	803-649-6029
aikengolfclub.com				
The Caddy Shak,	Lexington	12	[P]	803-356-4653
mycaddyshak.com				
The Carolina CC,	Spartanburg	18	[V]	864-573-7540
thecarolinacountryclub.com				
The Cliffs At Glassy G&CC,	Landrum	18	[P]	864-895-8104
cliffscommunities.com				
The Cliffs At Keowee Falls,	Salem	18	[P]	864-944-2010
cliffscommunities.com				
The Cliffs At Keowee Springs,	Six Mile	18	[V]	864-868-0422
cliffscommunities.com				
The Cliffs At Keowee Vineyards GC,	Sunset	18	[V]	864-868-4444
cliffscommunities.com				

[S] = SEMI-PRIVATE   [V] = PRIVATE   [U] = UNIVERSITY   [N] = UNIVERSITY-PRIVATE

SOUTH CAROLINA

Golf Yellow Pages, 18th Edition

The Cliffs Valley GC, *Travelers Rest*...................... 18 [V] 864-836-4653
  cliffscommunities.com
The Clubs At Cherokee Valley, *Travelers Rest*........ 18 [S] 864-895-6758
  cherokeevalleygolfclub.com
The Creek GC, *Spartanburg*................................. 18 [S] 864-583-7084
  thecreekgolfclub.com
The Crossing GC, *Florence* .... 18 [P] 843-665-8040
  crossingsgolfclub.com
The Dunes G&BC, *Myrtle Beach*........................... 18 [R] 843-449-5914
  thedunesclub.net
The Exec GC, *Bluffton*..9 [P] 843-686-6400
The Founders Club At Pawleys Island,
  Pawleys Island ....18 [P] 843-237-2299
  classicgolfgroup.com
The GC At Briars Creek, *Johns Island*................... 18 [V] 843-768-3050
  briarscreek.com
The GC At Cedar Creek, *Aiken* ....18 [P] 803-648-4206
  cedarcreek.net
The GC at Indigo Run, *Hilton Head Island* .... 18 [V] 843-689-5666
  thegolfclub-indigorun.com
The GC At Star Fort, *Ninety Six* .... 18 [V] 864-543-2757
  starfortgolf.com
The GC of South Carolina At Crickentree,
  Blythewood .... 18 [S] 803-754-8600
  golfclubsc.com
The Golden Bear GC At Indigo Run,
  Hilton Head Island... 18 [S] 843-689-2200
  goldenbear-indigorun.com
The Legends At Parris Island, *Parris Island* .... 18 [A] 843-228-2240
  mccssc.com
The Legends G Complex, *Myrtle Beach* .... 54 [R] 843-236-9318
  legendsgolf.com
The Links At Lakewood, *Sumter* ....18 [P] 803-481-5700
  southernlinks.net
The Links at Stono Ferry, *Hollywood* ....18 [R] 843-763-1817
  stonoferrygolf.com
The Links of Summerville, *Summerville*.................9 [P] 843-832-0809
The Members Club At Grande Dunes, *Myrtle Beach* 18 [R] 843-913-1343
  grandedunes.com
The Members Club At WildeWood, *Columbia* ..... 18 [V] 803-788-8000
  wildewoodwoodcreek.com
The Members Club At Woodcreek Farms, *Elgin* .. 18 [V] 803-699-2411
  wildewoodwoodcreek.com
The Patriot GC At Grand Harbor, *Ninety Six* .... 18 [V] 864-543-2000
  grandharbor.net
The Plantation Course At Edisto, *Edisto Island*.....18 [P] 843-869-1111
  theplantationcourseatedisto.com
The Reserve At Lake Keowee, *Sunset*................. 18 [V] 864-869-2106
  reserveatlakekeowee.com
The Reserve Club At Woodside Plantation, *Aiken* 27 [V] 803-648-2442
  thereserveclubatwoodside.com
The Reserve GC At Pawleys Island, *Pawleys Island* 18 [V] 843-235-0755
  thereservegolfclub.net
The River GC, *North Augusta*............................. 18 [S] 803-202-0110
  rivergolfclub.com
The Rock At Jocassee, *Pickens*............................18 [P] 864-878-2030
  golftherock.com
The Sanctuary GC At Cat Island, *Beaufort* .... 18 [S] 843-524-0300
  sanctuarygolfcatisland.com
The Seabrook Island Club, *Johns Island*............... 36 [V] 843-768-2529
  discoverseabrook.com
The Traces GC, *Florence* ....27 [P] 843-662-7775
  thetracesgolfclub.com

The Tradition GC, *Pawleys Island*.........................18 [P] 843-237-5041
  traditiongolfclub.com
The Trail At Chickasaw Pointe, *Westminster* ....18 [P] 864-972-9623
  chickasawpoint.org
The Univ Club At Cobblestone Park, *Blythewood* 27 [V] 803-714-2620
  cobblestonesc.com
The Valley At Eastport, *Little River* ....18 [P] 843-427-4424
  valleyateastport.com
The Walker GC At Clemson Univ, *Clemson* .... 18 [U] 864-656-0236
  walkergolfcourse.com
The Wellman Club, *Johnsonville*...........................18 [P] 843-386-2521
  southernlinks.net
The Windermere Club, *Blythewood*.................... 18 [V] 803-786-7888
  thewindermereclub.com
The Witch Golf Links, *Conway* ....18 [P] 843-448-1300
  witchgolf.com
The Wizard GC, *Myrtle Beach* ....18 [P] 843-236-9393
  wizardgolfcourse.com
The Woodlands CC, *Columbia* .... 18 [V] 803-788-7771
  woodlandscc.com
Thornblade Club, *Greer*...................................... 18 [V] 843-234-5100
  thornbladeclub.com
Three Pines CC, *Woodruff*................................... 18 [V] 864-476-3614
Tidewater GC & Plantation, *North Myrtle Beach*.. 18 [P] 843-249-3829
  tidewater-golf.com
Timberlake CC, *Chapin*..18 [P] 803-345-9909
  timberlakecountryclub.com
TPC Myrtle Beach, *Murrells Inlet* ....18 [P] 843-357-3399
  tpc-mb.com
Tradition National GC, *Hardeeville* .... 18 [V] 843-208-5353
  traditionhh.com
True Blue Plantation, *Pawleys Island* ....18 [R] 843-237-7270
  truebluegolf.com
Tupelo Bay G Complex, *Murrells Inlet*..................27 [P] 843-215-7888
  tupelobay.com
Twin Lakes CC, *Hamer*..18 [P] 843-774-3740
Twin Oaks Par 3 Golf & DR, *Inman* ....18 [P] 864-877-2269
Verdae Greens GC, *Greenville* ....18 [R] 864-676-1500
  verdaegreens.com
Village Greens CC, *Gramling*................................18 [P] 864-472-2411
  villagegreensgolfclub.com
Wachesaw Plantation Club, *Murrells Inlet*........... 18 [V] 843-357-1500
  wachesaw.com
Wachesaw Plantation East GC, *Murrells Inlet* ......18 [R] 843-357-5252
  wachesaweast.com
Ware Shoals GC, *Ware Shoals*................................9 [P] 864-456-2623
Waterford GC, *Rock Hill*.......................................18 [P] 803-324-0300
  charlottegolf.com
Waterway Hills GC, *Myrtle Beach* ....27 [P] 843-449-6488
Wedgefield Plantation GC, *Georgetown*...............18 [P] 843-546-8587
  wedgefield.com
Wexford GC, *Hilton Head Island* .... 18 [V] 843-686-8812
  wexfordplantation.com
Whispering Pines, *Myrtle Beach* ....18 [M] 843-918-2305
  wpinesgolf.com
White Pines GC, *Camden* ....18 [P] 803-432-7442
White Plains CC, *Pageland* ....18 [P] 843-672-7200
Whitmire GC, *Whitmire* ....9 [P] 803-694-2141
Wicked Stick Golf Links, *Myrtle Beach*.................18 [P] 843-215-2500
  wickedstick.com
Wild Dunes Resort, *Isle of Palms* ....36 [R] 843-886-2180
  wilddunes.com

[A] = MILITARY   [M] = MUNICIPAL   [P] = PUBLIC   [R] = RESORT

Golf Yellow Pages, 18th Edition

SOUTH DAKOTA

Wild Wing Plantation, *Conway* ....27 [R]   800-736-9404
  wildwing.com
Willbrook Plantation, *Pawleys Island*.................18 [P]   843-237-4900
  mbn.com
Williston CC, *Williston*......................................9 [P]   803-266-7616
Willow Creek GC, *Greer* ....18 [P]   864-848-4999
  willow-creekgolf.com
Winthrop Univ GC, *Rock Hill* .... 9 [N]   803-323-2112
  winthrop.edu
Winyah Bay GC, *Georgetown*.......................18 [P]   843-527-7765
  winyahbaygolfclub.com
Woodfin Ridge GC, *Inman* ....18 [P]   864-578-0023
  woodfinridge.com
Woodhaven GC, *Pendleton*............................9 [P]   864-646-9511
  golfaag.com
Woodland Valley CC, *Loris*..........................18 [P]   843-756-3264
  woodlandvalleycc.com
Woodside Plantation CC, *Aiken*..................... 45 [V]   803-649-3383
  woodside-plantation.com
World Tour Golf Links, *Myrtle Beach*............27 [R]   877-377-7773
  worldtourmb.com
Wrenwoods At Charleston AFB, *Charleston AFB*..18 [A]   843-963-1833
  jbcharleston.com
Wyboo GC, *Manning*....................................18 [R]   803-478-7899
  wyboogolfclub.com
Yeamans Hall Club, *Charleston*..................... 18 [P]   843-747-8855
  yeamanshallclub.com

SOUTH DAKOTA

Alcester GC, *Alcester* .... 9 [V]   605-934-1839
  alcestergolfclub.org
Arrowhead CC, *Rapid City* .... 18 [V]   605-342-6477
  arrowheadccrc.com
Bakker Crossing GC, *Sioux Falls*....................18 [P]   605-368-9700
  bakkercrossing.com
Belle Fourche CC, *Belle Fourche*....................9 [P]   605-892-3472
Bison CC, *Bison* ....9 [M]   605-244-5669
Bon Homme CC, *Tyndall* ....9 [P]   605-589-3186
Boulder Canyon CC, *Sturgis*...........................9 [P]   605-347-5108
  bouldercanyoncountryclub.com
Bowdle GC, *Bowdle* ....9 [P]   605-285-6500
Brandon Muni GC, *Brandon* ....18 [M]   605-582-7100
  brandongc.com
Britton CC, *Britton* ....9 [P]   605-448-2512
Broadland Creek National GC, *Huron*........18 [M]   605-353-8525
  huronsd.com
Brookings CC, *Brookings* .... 18 [V]   605-693-4315
  brookingscc.com
Buffalo GC, *Buffalo* ....9 [P]   605-375-3313
Burke CC, *Burke*...9 [P]   605-775-9190
Castlewood GC, *Castlewood*.........................9 [P]   605-793-2510
Cattail Crossing GC, *Watertown* ....27 [M]   605-882-6262
  watertownsd.us
Central Valley GC, *Hartford* ....18 [S]   605-528-6122
  golfcentralvalley.com
Chamberlain CC, *Chamberlain* ....9 [M]   605-734-4451
Clark GC, *Clark* ....9 [P]   605-532-5871
Clearlake GC, *Clear Lake*..............................9 [P]   605-874-2641
  golf.gotoclearlake.com
Colman Area Rec GC, *Colman* ....9 [S]   605-534-3121
Dakota Dunes GC, *Dakota Dunes* ....18 [P]   605-232-3080
  dakotadunescountryclub.com

Dells Rocky Run GC, *Dell Rapids*..................18 [P]   605-428-3498
  rockyrungolf.com
Dunes GC, *Fort Pierre*..................................18 [P]   605-223-2525
  golfdunes.com
Edgebrook GC, *Brookings*...........................18 [M]   605-692-6995
Edgemont GC, *Edgemont* ....9 [P]   605-662-5100
Elk Point CC, *Elk Point* ....9 [S]   605-356-2874
Elkhorn Ridge GC, *Spearfish* ....9 [M]   605-722-4653
  golfelkhorn.com
Elmwood Park GC, *Sioux Falls* ....27 [M]   605-367-7092
  dakotagolf.com
Eureka Muni GC, *Eureka*..............................9 [M]   605-284-5266
Fish Lake CC, *Plankinton*..............................9 [P]   605-942-7269
Fisher Grove GC, *Redfield* ....9 [M]   605-472-1336
Flandreau Park GC, *Flandreau* ....9 [P]   605-997-3031
Fountain Springs GC, *Rapid City*..................9 [P]   605-342-4653
Fox Run Muni GC, *Yankton* ....18 [M]   605-668-5205
  cityofyankton.org
Gary Gate City GC, *Gary*..............................9 [P]   605-272-5651
  garysd.com
GC At Red Rock, *Rapid City*......................18 [P]   605-718-4710
  golfclubatredrock.com
Gettysburg CC, *Gettysburg*...........................9 [P]   605-765-2656
  gettysburgsd.net
Glenridge GC, *Irene*.................................... 9 [V]   605-263-3546
Gregory GC, *Gregory*...................................9 [M]   605-835-8134
Hart Ranch GC, *Rapid City*........................18 [P]   605-341-5703
  hartranch.com
Hiawatha GC, *Canton*..................................9 [P]   605-987-2474
Hidden Valley GC, *Brandon*.......................18 [P]   605-582-2424
  golfthevalley.com
Highmore GC, *Highmore*..............................9 [P]   605-852-2099
Hillcrest G&CC, *Yankton* ....18 [P]   605-665-4621
  hillcrest.4t.com
Hillsview GC, *Pierre*....................................18 [M]   605-773-6191
  hillsviewgolfcourse.com
Howard GC, *Howard* ....9 [P]   605-772-4669
Huron CC, *Huron* .... 9 [V]   605-352-3354
Kadoka GC, *Kadoka*.....................................9 [M]   605-837-2229
Kimball GC, *Kimball*....................................9 [P]   605-778-6361
Kingsbury County CC, *de Smet*.....................9 [P]   605-854-3134
Kuehn Park GC, *Sioux Falls* ....9 [M]   605-362-2811
  dakotagolf.com
Lake Platte GC, *Platte* ....9 [P]   605-337-3300
Lake Region GC, *Arlington* ....18 [P]   605-983-5437
  lakeregionalgolfcourse.com
Lake Waggoner GC, *Philip*.............................9 [P]   605-859-2211
Lakes GC, *Wentworth* ....9 [P]   605-483-3535
  golfatthelakes.com
Lakeside CC, *Faulkton*...................................9 [P]   605-598-6558
Lakeview GC, *Corsica* ....9 [P]   605-946-5609
Lakeview Muni GC, *Mitchell* ....18 [M]   605-995-8460
  cityofmitchell.org
Lead CC, *Lead* ....9 [P]   605-584-1852
  leadcountryclub.com
Lee Park GC, *Aberdeen* ....18 [M]   605-626-7092
  aberdeen.sd.us
Lemmon GC, *Lemmon* ....9 [M]   605-374-3176
  lemmonsd.com
Lenkota GC, *Lennox*......................................9 [P]   605-647-5335
  lenkota.com
Leola CC, *Leola* .... 9 [V]   605-439-3299
Little Moreau GC, *Timber Lake*.................. 9 [V]   605-865-3643

[S] = SEMI-PRIVATE   [V] = PRIVATE   [U] = UNIVERSITY   [N] = UNIVERSITY-PRIVATE

SOUTH DAKOTA
Golf Yellow Pages, 18th Edition

Course	City	Holes	Type	Phone
Madison G&CC,	Madison	18	[P]	605-256-3991
Markota Acres GC,	Martin	9	[M]	605-685-6525
McCook CC,	Salem	9	[P]	605-425-2073
Meadow Creek GC,	Volga	9	[P]	605-627-5444
golfvolga.com				
Meadowbrook GC,	Rapid City	18	[P]	605-394-4191
golfatmeadowbrook.com				
Medicine Creek GC,	Presho	9	[P]	605-895-2659
Memorial Park GC,	Huron	9	[M]	605-353-8527
huronsd.com				
Miller CC,	Miller	9	[V]	605-853-2652
turtlecreek.net/mgc.htm				
Minnehaha CC,	Sioux Falls	18	[V]	605-336-1419
minnehahacc.com				
Mobridge CC,	Mobridge	9	[P]	605-845-2307
Moccasin Creek GC,	Aberdeen	18	[V]	605-226-0989
moccasincreekcc.com				
Murdo GC,	Murdo	9	[M]	605-669-2300
Newell GC,	Newell	9	[M]	605-456-2195
North Shore GC,	Faith	9	[P]	605-967-2191
Northern Links GC,	Sioux Falls	9	[P]	605-334-6679
Olive Grove GC,	Groton	9	[S]	605-397-4653
Par Mar Valley CC,	Parker	9	[V]	605-297-4819
Parkston CC,	Parkston	9	[V]	605-928-3092
Pine Hills GC,	Milbank	18	[P]	605-432-4124
pinehillsgolfcourse.org				
Pony Hills CC,	Woonsocket	9	[V]	605-796-4694
Prairie Dunes GC,	Goodwin	9	[P]	605-795-2321
Prairie Green GC,	Sioux Falls	18	[M]	605-367-6056
dakotagolf.com				
Prairie Ridge GC,	Box Eller	9	[A]	605-923-4999
ellsworthservices.com				
Prairie Winds GC,	Watertown	18	[V]	605-886-3554
pwgolfclub.com				
Randall Hills GC,	Pickstown	9	[P]	605-487-7884
Rapid City Elks GC,	Rapid City	18	[S]	605-393-0522
rcelks.org				
Rapid City Exec GC,	Rapid City	9	[M]	605-394-4124
golfatmeadowbrook.com				
River Ridge GC,	Garretson	9	[P]	605-594-6234
Rocky Knolls GC,	Custer	9	[P]	605-673-4481
Rolling Hills GC,	Aberdeen	9	[P]	605-226-4487
Roscoe Legion GC,	Roscoe	9	[P]	605-287-4508
Scotland Dawson Creek GC,	Scotland	9	[P]	605-583-4244
scotlandsd.org				
Six Mile Creek GC,	White	9	[P]	605-629-2121
Southern Hills GC,	Hot Springs	18	[M]	605-745-6400
southernhillsmunicipalgolfcourse.com				
Spearfish Canyon CC,	Spearfish	18	[V]	605-717-4653
spearfishcanyoncountryclub.com				
Split Rock CC,	Ipswich	9	[P]	605-426-6961
splitrockccgolf.com				
Spring Creek CC,	Harrisburg	18	[P]	605-743-2000
springcreekcountryclub.com				
Springfield GC,	Springfield	9	[P]	605-369-5525
Sutton Bay Golf,	Agar	18	[P]	605-264-5530
suttonbay.com				
The Bluffs GC,	Vermillion	18	[P]	605-677-7058
thebluffsgc.com				
The Bridges At Beresford,	Beresford	9	[M]	605-763-2202
beresfordbridges.com				
The Trails Golf Resort,	Pierre	9	[R]	605-224-9340
oahetrails.com				
Tomahawk Lake CC,	Deadwood	9	[P]	605-578-2080
Tri Del GC,	Delmont	9	[P]	605-779-6081
Two Rivers GC,	Dakota Dunes	18	[P]	605-232-3241
Valley View CC,	Sisseton	9	[P]	605-698-3742
Valley View GC,	Freeman	9	[P]	605-925-4929
Wall Community GC,	Wall	9	[P]	605-279-4653
Webster GC,	Webster	9	[M]	605-345-3971
Wessington Springs CC,	Wessington Springs	9	[V]	605-539-1944
Westward Ho GC,	Sioux Falls	27	[V]	605-336-3766
westwardhocountryclub.com				
Wild Oak GC,	Mitchell	18	[P]	605-996-2084
wildoakgolfclub.com				
Willow Creek GC,	Fort Pierre	9	[P]	605-223-3154
Willow Run GC,	Sioux Falls	18	[P]	605-335-5900
willowrungolfcourse.com				
Winner CC,	Winner	9	[P]	605-842-0686
YMCA LaCroix Links GC,	Rapid City	9	[M]	605-718-9953
rcymca.org				

TENNESSEE

Course	City	Holes	Type	Phone
4 Seasons Golf,	Crossville	18	[P]	931-484-0995
fourseasonsgolfcourse.com				
Andrew Johnson GC,	Greeneville	18	[P]	423-636-1476
andrewjohnson.com				
Arnold GC,	Arnold AFB	9	[A]	931-455-5870
arnoldgolf.com				
Baileyton GC,	Greeneville	18	[P]	423-234-5131
Baneberry Golf & Resort Club,	Baneberry	18	[R]	865-674-2500
baneberrygolf.com				
Bays Mountain GC,	Seymour	18	[P]	865-577-8172
Bear Trace At Cumberland Mountain,	Crossville	18	[P]	931-707-1640
beartrace.com				
Bear Trace At Harrison Bay,	Harrison	18	[M]	423-326-0885
tngolftrail.net				
Beaver Brook G&CC,	Knoxville	18	[V]	865-689-4479
beaverbrook.net				
Belle Acres GC,	Cookeville	9	[P]	931-526-8834
belleacresgolf.com				
Belle Meade CC,	Nashville	18	[V]	615-298-5744
bellemeadecc.org				
Bent Creek GC,	Gatlinburg	18	[R]	865-436-3947
bentcreekgolfcourse.com				
Beverly Park Par 3,	Knoxville	9	[V]	865-689-6445
knoxareajuniorgolf.org				
Big Hollow Par 3,	Blountville	9	[P]	423-323-6615
Black Creek Club,	Chattanooga	18	[V]	423-822-2582
blackcreekclub.com				
Blackberry Ridge GC,	Shelbyville	18	[S]	931-437-2343
blackberryridgegc.com				
Blackthorn Club at the Ridges,	Jonesborough	18	[V]	423-913-3164
blackthornclub.com				
Bluegrass Y&CC,	Hendersonville	18	[V]	615-824-6566
bluegrasscountryclub.com				
Bogey's Golf & Family Ent Ctr,	Cordova	9	[P]	901-757-2649
bogeys.com				
Brainerd GC,	Chattanooga	18	[M]	423-855-2692
chattanooga.gov				
Brentwood CC,	Brentwood	18	[V]	615-373-9922
bcctn.org				
Brown Acres GC,	Chattanooga	18	[M]	423-855-2680
chattanooga.gov				
Brownsville CC,	Brownsville	18	[V]	731-772-0892
Buffalo River GC,	Lobelville	9	[S]	931-589-3340

[A] = MILITARY [M] = MUNICIPAL [P] = PUBLIC [R] = RESORT

TENNESSEE

Golf Yellow Pages, 18th Edition

Buffalo Valley GC, *Unicoi* .... 18 [M] 423-743-5021
  johnsoncitygolf.org
Camelot GC, *Rogersville* .... 18 [P] 423-272-7570
Carroll Lake GC, *McKenzie* .... 18 [P] 731-352-2998
Cattails at MeadowView GC, *Kingsport* .... 18 [R] 423-578-6622
  cattailsgolf.com
CC of Bristol, *Bristol* .... 18 [V] 423-652-1700
  countryclubofbristol.com
Cedar Crest GC, *Murfreesboro* .... 18 [P] 615-849-7837
  cedarcrestgolfclub.net
Cedar Hills GC, *Lenoir City* .... 18 [P] 865-986-6521
Cedars GC, *Bristol* .... 18 [P] 423-989-0064
  cedarsgolfcourse.com
Centennial GC, *Oak Ridge* .... 18 [M] 865-483-2291
  centennialgc.com
Champions Run GC, *Rockvale* .... 18 [P] 615-274-2301
  championsrungolf.com
Chatata Valley GC, *Cleveland* .... 18 [S] 423-339-9784
  chatatavalleygolf.com
Chattanooga G&CC, *Chattanooga* .... 18 [V] 423-266-1049
  chattanoogagcc.org
Cherokee CC, *Knoxville* .... 18 [V] 865-584-4637
  cherokeecountryclub.com
Chickasaw CC, *Memphis* .... 18 [V] 901-323-6216
  chickasawcc.com
Chickasaw GC, *Henderson* .... 18 [M] 731-989-4700
  chickasawgc.com
Clarksville G&CC, *Clarksville* .... 18 [V] 931-647-4300
  clarksvillecountryclub.com
Claxbranch GC, *Loretto* .... 18 [P] 931-853-4653
  claxbranch.com
Cleveland CC, *Cleveland* .... 18 [V] 423-336-3566
  clevelandcountryclub.org
Cliff View GC, *Kingston Springs* .... 9 [P] 615-952-9077
  cliffviewgolf.net
Clinchview G&CC, *Bean Station* .... 18 [P] 865-993-2892
Cole Park GC, *Fort Campbell* .... 18 [A] 931-431-4087
Colonial GC, *Cordova* .... 36 [V] 901-388-6150
  colonialcountryclub.org
Concord GC, *Chattanooga* .... 18 [P] 423-894-4536
Concord Park Par 3, *Knoxville* .... 9 [P] 865-966-9103
  knoxareajuniorgolf.org
Cookeville CC, *Cookeville* .... 18 [P] 931-526-5526
  cookville-golf-club.com
Copper Basin GC, *Copperhill* .... 9 [S] 423-496-3579
Cordova CC, *Cordova* .... 18 [V] 901-758-8188
  cordovacc.com
Council Fire GC, *Chattanooga* .... 18 [V] 423-499-6300
  councilfire.net
Country Hills GC, *Hendersonville* .... 18 [M] 615-824-1100
  chillsgc.com
Covington CC, *Covington* .... 18 [V] 901-476-8676
Creeks Bend GC, *Hixson* .... 18 [V] 423-842-5911
Creekside Plantation, *Seymour* .... 9 [P] 865-577-4653
  creeksideplantation.com
Crocket G&CC, *Alamo* .... 9 [V] 731-696-5619
Crocketts Ridge GC, *Kingsport* .... 18 [P] 423-279-1500
  crockettridgegolfcourse.com
Cumberland Bend GC, *Gainesboro* .... 9 [P] 931-268-0259
Dandridge G&CC, *Dandridge* .... 27 [P] 865-397-2655
  dandridgegolf.com
Dayton G&CC, *Evensville* .... 18 [P] 423-775-2313
  daytongolfclub.com

Dead Horse Lake GC, *Knoxville* .... 18 [P] 865-693-5270
  deadhorselake.com
Deer Creek GC, *Crossville* .... 18 [S] 931-456-0178
  deercreekgolfer.com
Diamond Oaks GC, *Trenton* .... 18 [P] 731-855-3677
Dickson CC, *Dickson* .... 18 [V] 615-446-2879
  dicksoncountryclub.com
Dixie Oaks GC, *Summertown* .... 18 [P] 931-964-4991
  dixieoaksgolfclub.com
Doe Valley Golf Ctr, *South Fulton* .... 18 [P] 731-479-9309
Dogwood Hills CC, *Portland* .... 9 [V] 615-325-4648
Dorchester CC, *Crossville* .... 18 [S] 931-484-3709
  fairfieldglade.cc
Druid Hills GC, *Crossville* .... 18 [S] 931-484-3711
  fairfieldglade.cc
Dyersburg CC At The Farms, *Dyersburg* ...... 18 [P] 731-286-2155
Dyersburg Muni GC, *Dyersburg* .... 18 [M] 731-286-7620
Eagle Bluff GC, *Chattanooga* .... 18 [S] 423-326-0202
  eaglebluffgolf.com
Eastland Green GC, *Clarksville* .... 27 [P] 931-358-9051
Egwani Farms GC, *Rockford* .... 18 [P] 865-970-7132
  egwanifarmsgolf.com
Elizabethton Muni GC, *Elizabethton* .... 18 [M] 423-542-8051
  elizabethtongolf.com
Elks Lodge Par 3 GC, *Erwin* .... 9 [V] 423-743-8559
Emory G&CC, *Harriman* .... 9 [M] 865-882-9977
Fair Oaks GC, *Oakland* .... 18 [P] 901-466-1445
Fairways on Spencer Creek, *Franklin* .... 9 [V] 615-794-8223
Falcon Ridge GC, *Cedar Grove* .... 18 [P] 731-968-1212
  golffalconridge.com
Fall Creek St Park GC, *Pikeville* .... 18 [M] 423-881-5706
  tngolftrail.net
Fayetteville CC, *Fayetteville* .... 9 [V] 931-433-2962
Five Oaks G&CC, *Lebanon* .... 18 [V] 615-444-2784
  five-oaks.com
Forest Hill GC, *Drummonds* .... 18 [P] 901-835-3918
  foresthillgolfcourse.com
Forrest Crossing GC, *Franklin* .... 18 [P] 615-794-9400
  forrestcrossing.americangolf.com
Fox Chase GC, *Counce* .... 9 [P] 731-689-4500
Fox Den GC, *Knoxville* .... 18 [V] 865-966-5533
  foxdencountryclub.com
Franklin County CC, *Winchester* .... 9 [V] 931-967-1827
Fulton CC, *South Fulton* .... 18 [V] 731-479-3016
Futures GC, *Puryear* .... 18 [P] 731-247-3264
Gallatin CC, *Gallatin* .... 9 [V] 615-452-6988
  gallatincountryclub.com
Gatlinburg GC, *Pigeon Forge* .... 18 [M] 865-453-3912
  golf.gatlinburg-tn.com
Gaylord Springs At Gaylord Opryland, *Nashville*..18 [R] 615-458-1730
  gaylordsprings.com
GC of Tennessee, *Kingston Springs* .... 18 [V] 615-952-2020
  thegolfcluboftn.com
Germantown CC, *Germantown* .... 18 [V] 901-754-6453
  germantowncountryclub.com
Gettysvue Polo, G&CC, *Knoxville* .... 18 [V] 865-522-4653
  gettysvuecc.com
Glen Eagle GC, *Millington* .... 18 [A] 901-874-5168
GrandView GC, *Spencer* .... 18 [P] 423-881-5686
  grandviewgolfresort.com
Graymere CC, *Columbia* .... 18 [V] 931-388-4422
  graymerecc.com

[S] = SEMI-PRIVATE   [V] = PRIVATE   [U] = UNIVERSITY   [N] = UNIVERSITY-PRIVATE

TENNESSEE

Golf Yellow Pages, 18th Edition

Graysburg Hills GC, *Chuckey* .... 27 [P] 423-234-8061
 graysburghillsgolf.com
Green Hills Golf, *Riddleton* .... 9 [S] 615-735-2895
Green Meadow CC, *Alcoa* .... 18 [V] 865-982-8783
 greenmeadowcc.com
Greystone GC, *Dickson* .... 18 [P] 615-446-0044
 greystonegc.com
Hardeman County G&CC, *Bolivar* .... 9 [V] 731-658-2731
Harpeth Hills GC, *Nashville* .... 18 [M] 615-862-8493
 nashvillefairways.com
Harpeth Valley Golf Ctr, *Nashville* .... 9 [P] 615-646-8858
 harpethvalleygolf.com
Hazelburn GC, *Cornersville* .... 9 [P] 931-293-4653
Heatherhurst GC, *Crossville* .... 36 [S] 931-484-3799
 fairfieldglade.cc
Henry Horton St Park GC, *Chapel Hill* .... 18 [M] 931-364-2319
 tngolftrail.net
Hermitage GC, *Old Hickory* .... 36 [P] 615-847-4001
 hermitagegolf.com
Hidden Falls At Mt Airy Golf, *Dunlap* ...... 18 [S] 423-949-2582
Hidden Valley G&CC, *Livingston* .... 9 [S] 931-823-1313
Highland Green Golf Links, *Jackson* .... 9 [P] 731-664-4653
Highland Rim GC, *Joelton* .... 18 [P] 615-746-0400
 ttggolf.com
Hillcrest CC, *Pulaski* .... 9 [V] 931-363-5630
Hillwood CC, *Nashville* .... 18 [P] 615-352-5600
 hillwoodcc.org
Hohenwald GC, *Hohenwald* .... 9 [M] 931-796-5421
Holston Hills CC, *Knoxville* .... 18 [V] 865-525-0626
 holstonhills.com
Humboldt G&CC, *Humboldt* .... 18 [V] 731-784-4127
Hunters Point GC, *Lebanon* .... 18 [P] 615-444-7521
 hunterspointgolf.com
Indian Hills GC, *Murfreesboro* .... 18 [P] 615-895-3642
 indianhillsgc.com
Irene G&CC, *Memphis* .... 18 [V] 901-752-1521
 lindseymanagement.com
Ironwood GC, *Cookeville* .... 18 [P] 931-528-2331
Jackson CC, *Jackson* .... 18 [V] 731-668-0688
 jacksoncclub.com
Jackson National GC, *Jackson* .... 18 [P] 731-424-3146
 hiddenvalleygac.com
Johnson City CC, *Johnson City* .... 18 [V] 423-928-5161
 jccountryclub.com
Jones Creek GC, *Jackson* .... 18 [M] 731-425-8620
 jonescreekgolf.net
Kings Creek GC, *Spring Hill* .... 18 [P] 931-486-1253
 kingscreekgolf.com
Kinser Park GC, *Greeneville* .... 9 [P] 423-639-6406
 kinserpark.org/golf.htm
Knoxville GC, *Knoxville* .... 18 [P] 865-691-7143
 golfknox.com
La Follette CC, *La Follette* .... 9 [P] 423-562-9130
Lake Haven G&CC, *Decatur* .... 9 [S] 423-334-3654
Lake Tansi Village GC, *Crossville* .... 18 [R] 931-788-3301
 laketansipoa.com
Lakeside GC, *Kingston* .... 9 [P] 865-376-5497
Lakewood G&CC, *Tullahoma* .... 18 [V] 931-455-8606
 lakewoodgcc.com
Lambert Acres GC, *Maryville* .... 27 [P] 865-982-9838
 lambertacresgc.com
Landmark GC At Avalon, *Lenoir City* ..... 18 [S] 865-986-4653
 avalongolf.com

Laurel Valley GC, *Townsend* .... 18 [R] 865-448-6690
 golflaurelvalley.com
Lawrenceburg G&CC, *Lawrenceburg* ...... 18 [V] 931-762-2500
Lebanon G&CC, *Lebanon* .... 9 [V] 615-444-5010
Lewisburg Rec Ctr, *Lewisburg* .... 9 [M] 931-359-2482
Link Hills CC, *Greeneville* .... 18 [V] 423-639-2961
 linkhills.org
Long Hollow GC, *Gallatin* .... 18 [M] 615-451-3120
Lost Creek GC, *New Market* .... 18 [S] 865-475-9661
 lostcreekgolfclub.com
Lupton City GC, *Chattanooga* .... 9 [V] 423-280-3754
Macon County GC, *Lafayette* .... 9 [S] 615-666-8799
Madisonville GC, *Madisonville* .... 9 [P] 423-442-6423
Magic Valley GC, *Camden* .... 9 [V] 731-584-9964
MAM Park GC, *Memphis* .... 9 [P] 901-606-7332
 mamsports.org
Mason Rudolph GC, *Clarksville* .... 9 [M] 931-645-7479
 cityofclarksville.com
Mc Donald Hills GC, *Rogersville* .... 18 [P] 423-272-1477
McCabe GC, *Nashville* .... 27 [M] 615-862-8491
 nashvillefairways.com
McMinnville CC, *Mc Minnville* .... 18 [V] 931-668-4143
Memphis CC, *Memphis* .... 18 [V] 901-452-2131
Memphis National GC, *Collierville* .... 45 [P] 901-853-8058
 palmergolf.com
Milan G&CC, *Milan* .... 18 [V] 731-686-0616
Millstone GC, *Morristown* .... 18 [P] 423-586-4000
 millstonegolfclub.net
Mirimichi GC, *Millington* .... 27 [P] 901-259-3800
 mirimichi.com
Moccasin Bend GC, *Chattanooga* .... 18 [P] 423-267-3585
 moccasinbendgc.com
Mont Lake GC, *Soddy Daisy* .... 18 [P] 423-332-3111
 montlakegolf.com
Montgomery Bell St Park, *Burns* .... 18 [M] 615-797-2578
 tngolftrail.net
Morristown G&CC, *Morristown* .... 9 [P] 423-586-9953
Mountain Ridge GC, *Monterey* .... 18 [P] 931-839-3313
 mountainridgegolfclub.com
Mt Pleasant CC, *Mt Pleasant* .... 9 [V] 931-379-3130
Nashboro GC, *Nashville* .... 18 [P] 615-367-2311
 nashborogolf.com
Nashville G&AC, *Brentwood* .... 18 [V] 615-370-3346
 ngac.net
Nolichucky View GC, *Greeneville* .... 18 [P] 423-638-7888
 nolichuckyview.com
Oak Hills GC, *Greenbrier* .... 18 [S] 615-643-4505
 oakhillsgolfcourse.com
Oak Ridge CC, *Oak Ridge* .... 18 [V] 865-483-1031
 oakridgecountryclub.org
Oak View Links, *Newbern* .... 9 [P] 731-627-0047
 westtngolf.com
Old Fort GC, *Murfreesboro* .... 18 [M] 615-896-2448
 murfreesborotn.gov
Old Hickory CC, *Old Hickory* .... 18 [V] 615-847-5056
 oldhickorycountryclub.net
Old Natchez CC, *Franklin* .... 18 [V] 615-373-3200
 oldnatchezcc.com
Old Stone Fort St Park GC, *Manchester* ... 9 [M] 931-723-5075
 tngolftrail.net
Oneida Muni GC, *Oneida* .... 9 [M] 423-569-9506
Orgill Park GC, *Millington* .... 18 [M] 901-872-3610
 orgillpark.com

[A] = MILITARY [M] = MUNICIPAL [P] = PUBLIC [R] = RESORT

TENNESSEE

Paris CC, *Paris* .... 9 [V] 731-642-0591
Paris Landing St Park GC, *Buchanan* .... 18 [M] 731-641-4459
   tngolftrail.net
Patriot Hills GC, *Jefferson City* .... 18 [P] 865-475-4466
   patriothillsgolf.com
Pebble Brook GC, *Greenbrier* .... 18 [S] 615-382-3045
Percy Warner GC, *Nashville* .... 9 [M] 615-352-9958
   nashvillefairways.com
Persimmon Hills GC, *Sharon* .... 18 [S] 731-456-2323
Pickwick Landing St Park GC, *Pickwick Dam* .... 18 [M] 731-689-3149
   tngolftrail.net
Pine Creek GC, *Mt Juliet* .... 18 [P] 615-449-7272
   pinecreekgolf.net
Pine Lakes GC, *Rockford* .... 18 [P] 865-970-9018
   pinelakesgolfcourse.com
Pine Oaks GC, *Johnson City* .... 18 [M] 423-434-6250
   johnsoncitygolf.org
Pinetree CC, *Lexington* .... 9 [V] 731-968-7081
Poplar Meadows CC, *Union City* .... 9 [V] 731-885-3650
Quail Ridge GC, *Bartlett* .... 18 [P] 901-386-6951
   thequailgolf.com
Rarity Bay CC, *Vonore* .... 18 [S] 423-884-3030
   raritybay.com/baygolf.htm
Rarity Pointe GC, *Lenoir City* .... 18 [V] 865-988-0370
   raritypointe.com
Ravenwood CC, *Hermitage* .... 18 [V] 615-889-6394
   ravenwoodcountryclub.net
Red Tail Mountain Club, *Mountain City* .... 18 [S] 423-727-7931
   redtailmountain.com
Renegade National Golf Resort, *Crab Orchard* .... 18 [R] 931-484-5285
   renegadenational.com
Richland CC, *Nashville* .... 18 [V] 615-370-0030
   richlandcc.com
Ridgefields CC, *Kingsport* .... 18 [V] 423-392-8373
   ridgefieldscc.org
Ridgeway CC, *Memphis* .... 18 [V] 901-853-0929
   ridgewaycountryclub.com
Ridgewood GC, *Athens* .... 18 [P] 423-263-5672
River Islands GC, *Kodak* .... 18 [P] 865-933-0100
   riverislandsgolf.com
River Run GC, *Crossville* .... 18 [R] 931-456-4060
Riverbend CC, *Shelbyville* .... 18 [V] 931-684-4894
   rbcountryclub.com
Riverside Golf Ctr, *Old Hickory* .... 27 [P] 615-847-5074
   riversidegolfcourse.net
Riverview GC, *Loudon* .... 18 [P] 865-986-6972
Riverwatch GC, *Sparta* .... 18 [P] 931-761-8124
   riverwatchgolfclub.com
Rock Springs GC, *Athens* .... 18 [P] 423-453-5455
   rockspringsgolf.com
Rockwood G&CC, *Rockwood* .... 9 [M] 865-354-2121
Rolling Hills CC, *Ripley* .... 9 [S] 731-635-2957
Ross Creek Landing, *Clifton* .... 18 [R] 931-676-3174
   rosscreeklandinggolfclub.com
Royal Oaks GC, *Maryville* .... 18 [S] 865-984-4260
Ruggles Ferry GC, *Strawberry Plains* .... 18 [P] 865-932-4450
Saddle Creek GC, *Lewisburg* .... 18 [P] 931-270-7280
   saddlecreekgc.com
Scenic View GC, *Winchester* .... 9 [P] 931-967-5224
Sculley GC, *Jackson* .... 9 [P] 731-424-4500
Selmer G&CC, *Selmer* .... 9 [V] 731-645-9915
Sequatchie Valley G&CC, *South Pittsburg* .... 9 [S] 423-837-6532
Sewanee G&TC, *Sewanee* .... 9 [U] 931-598-1104

Shelby GC, *Nashville* .... 18 [M] 615-862-8474
   nashvillefairways.com
Shiloh Falls GC, *Counce* .... 18 [R] 731-689-5050
   shilohfallsgolf.com
Shiloh GC, *Adamsville* .... 18 [S] 731-632-0678
   golfshiloh.com
Signal Mountain G&CC, *Signal Mountain* .... 18 [V] 423-886-2241
   smgcc.org
Silver Lake GC, *Church Hill* .... 9 [V] 423-357-9940
Skyview GC, *Centerville* .... 9 [V] 931-729-2444
Smithville GC, *Smithville* .... 9 [M] 615-597-6648
Smoky Mountain CC, *Newport* .... 18 [V] 423-623-7321
Smoky Mountain Par 3 GC, *Sevierville* .... 18 [P] 865-774-7749
   par3golfcourse.com
Smyrna Muni GC, *Smyrna* .... 27 [M] 615-459-2666
   townofsmyrna.org/golf
Somerville CC, *Somerville* .... 9 [V] 901-465-8111
Southern Hills G&CC, *Cookeville* .... 18 [P] 931-432-5149
   southernhillsgolf.net
Southwest Point GC, *Kingston* .... 18 [P] 865-376-5282
Sparta G&CC, *Sparta* .... 9 [S] 931-738-5836
Spring Creek Ranch, *Collierville* .... 18 [V] 901-853-5660
   springcreekranch.org
Springbrook G&CC, *Niota* .... 18 [V] 423-568-2161
   springbrookgcc.com
Springfield CC, *Springfield* .... 9 [P] 615-384-7346
Steele Creek GC, *Bristol* .... 9 [M] 423-764-6411
   bristoltn.org
Stonebridge GC, *Lakeland* .... 18 [P] 901-382-1886
   stonebridgegolf.com
Stonehenge GC, *Crossville* .... 18 [R] 931-484-3731
   stonehengegolf.com
Stones River CC, *Murfreesboro* .... 18 [V] 615-893-1353
   stonesrivercc.com
Stoneybrook GC, *Columbia* .... 18 [P] 931-388-5143
   stoneybrook.us
Swan Lake GC, *Clarksville* .... 18 [M] 931-648-0479
   cityofclarksville.com
Sycamore Valley GC, *Ashland City* .... 18 [P] 615-246-1410
T O Fuller St Park GC, *Memphis* .... 18 [M] 901-543-7771
   tngolftrail.net
Tanasi GC, *Loudon* .... 18 [V] 865-458-4707
   tvpoa.org
Ted Rhodes GC, *Nashville* .... 18 [M] 615-862-8463
   nashvillefairways.com
Temple Hills Club, *Franklin* .... 27 [P] 615-646-4785
   templehillsgolf.com
Tennessee Golf Trail At Warriors Path, *Kingsport* 18 [M] 423-323-4990
   tngolftrail.net
Tennessee Hills GC, *Pikeville* .... 9 [P] 423-447-2304
Tennessee National GC, *Loudon* .... 18 [V] 865-657-2001
   tennesseenational.com
Tennessee River GC, *Decaturville* .... 18 [R] 731-852-2582
   tennesseerivergolfclub.com
The Bear Trace At Tims Ford, *Winchester* .... 18 [M] 931-968-0995
   beartrace.com
The Champions Club At Hampton Creek, *Ooltewah* 18 [V] 423-238-6812
The Club At Fairvue Plantation, *Gallatin* .... 36 [V] 615-451-0919
   fairvueplantation.com
The Country Club, *Morristown* .... 18 [V] 423-581-2763
   the-countryclub.com
The Crossings GC, *Jonesborough* .... 18 [V] 423-348-8855
   thecrossingsgolfclub.net

[S] = SEMI-PRIVATE   [V] = PRIVATE   [U] = UNIVERSITY   [N] = UNIVERSITY-PRIVATE

TENNESSEE

Golf Yellow Pages, 18th Edition

The Golf Club, *Maryville*................................... 18 [P] 865-856-4400
The Governors Club, *Brentwood*.......................... 18 [V] 615-776-2323
   thegovernorsclub.com
The Greens at Deerfield, *La Follette*.................... 18 [R] 423-566-0040
   greensatdeerfield.com
The Grove, *College Grove*................................. 18 [V] 615-368-3032
   groveliving.com
The Honors Course, *Ooltewah* .... 18 [V] 423-238-4272
   honorscourse.net
The Legacy, *Springfield*....................................18 [M] 615-384-4653
   golfthelegacy.com
The Links At Audubon, *Memphis* ....18 [M] 901-683-6941
   thelinksataudubon.com
The Links At Davey Crockett, *Memphis*...............18 [M] 901-358-3375
   cityofmemphis.org
The Links At Fox Meadows, *Memphis*..................18 [M] 901-362-0232
   foxmeadowsgolf.com
The Links At Galloway, *Memphis* ....18 [M] 901-685-7805
   thelinksatgalloway.com
The Links at Kahite GC, *Vonore* .... 18 [V] 865-408-2639
   tvpoa.org
The Links at Overton Park, *Memphis*...................9 [M] 901-725-9905
   cityofmemphis.org
The Links at Pine Hill, *Memphis* ....18 [M] 901-775-9434
   cityofmemphis.org
The Links at Riverside, *Memphis*........................9 [M] 901-576-4296
   cityofmemphis.org
The Links At Whitehaven, *Memphis*.....................9 [S] 901-396-1608
   cityofmemphis.org
The Little Course, *Franklin* ....9 [P] 615-790-0222
   golfhousetennessee.com
The Pines, *Dyer*... 18 [S] 731-692-3690
The Quarry, *Chattanooga*..................................9 [P] 423-875-8888
The Reserve At Collins River, *Mc Minnville*............9 [P] 931-668-7749
   collinsriver.com
The Sevierville GC, *Sevierville* ....18 [M] 865-429-4223
   seviervilletn.org
The Tennessean GC, *Springville*..........................18 [P] 731-642-7271
   tennesseangolfclub.com
The Wee Course At Williams Creek, *Knoxville* ......18 [P] 865-546-5828
   weecourseatwilliamscreek.com
Three Ridges GC, *Knoxville*...............................18 [M] 865-687-4797
   knoxcounty.org
Toqua GC, *Loudon*.. 18 [V] 865-458-6546
   tvpoa.org
TPC Southwind, *Memphis*................................. 18 [V] 901-748-0330
   tpcsouthwind.com
Tri Cities GC, *Blountville* .... 27 [S] 423-323-4178
   tricitiesgc.com
Twelve Stones Crossing GC, *Goodlettsville*............18 [P] 615-851-4653
   twelvestonesgolfclub.com
Twin Creeks GC, *Chuckey*..................................18 [M] 423-257-5192
Two Rivers GC, *Nashville* ....18 [M] 615-889-2675
   nashvillefairways.com
Valleybrook G&CC, *Hixson*................................ 18 [V] 423-842-4646
   valleybrookcountryclub.com
Vanderbilt Legends Club, *Franklin* .... 36 [V] 615-791-8100
   legendsclub.com
Veterans Administration Hospital GC, *Murfreesboro*9 [M]615-893-2543
VinnyLinks GC, *Nashville*...................................9 [M] 615-880-1720
   nashvillefairways.com
Waterville GC, *Cleveland* .... 18 [S] 423-559-3348
Waverly CC, *Waverly* ....9 [V] 931-296-4644

Waynesboro Muni GC, *Waynesboro* ....9 [M] 931-722-3948
   cityofwaynesboro.org
Westhaven GC, *Franklin*................................... 18 [V] 615-599-4420
   golfwesthaven.com
White Oaks GC, *Athens* ....18 [P] 423-745-3349
White Pine GC, *White Pine*.................................9 [M] 865-674-9986
White Plains GC, *Cookeville*...............................18 [P] 931-537-6397
   whiteplainsgolf.net
Whittle Springs GC, *Knoxville* ....18 [M] 865-525-1022
   golfwhittlesprings.com
Willow Creek GC, *Knoxville* ....18 [S] 865-675-0100
   willowcreekgolf.com
Willow Ridge GC, *Mc Ewen* ....18 [P] 931-582-9966
Willowbrook GC, *Manchester*.............................18 [S] 931-728-8989
   golfwillowbrook.net
Windtree GC, *Mt Juliet*......................................18 [P] 615-754-4653
   windtreegolf.com
Windyke CC, *Memphis* .... 54 [V] 901-754-1888
   windyke.com
Wingfoot GC, *Union City* .... 18 [V] 731-885-9922
   wingfootgolfcourse.com
Woodlake GC, *Tazewell* ....18 [S] 423-626-6010
   woodlakegolf.com
Woodland Hills G&CC, *Pinson* .... 18 [V] 731-988-5311
   woodlandhills.samsbiz.com
WynRidge Greens, *Troy*.....................................18 [P] 731-536-4653
   wynridgegolfclub.homestead.com

TEXAS

A 1 Golf Ctr, *Rockwall*..9 [P] 972-771-3996
Abernathy GC, *Abernathy* ....9 [S] 806-328-5286
Alamo CC, *Alamo*... 9 [V] 956-787-0910
   myalamocountryclub.com/index.php
Alamo GC, *San Antonio*....................................18 [P] 210-696-4000
   alamogolfclub.net
Albany GC, *Albany* ....9 [M] 325-762-2844
Alice CC, *Alice* .... 9 [V] 361-664-3723
Alice Muni GC, *Alice*...18 [M] 361-664-7033
   cityofalice.org
All Golf, *Kingwood*..9 [P] 281-359-3995
Alpine GC, *Longview*..18 [P] 903-753-4515
Alpine GC, *Alpine*..9 [S] 432-837-2752
Alsatian GC, *Castroville* ....18 [P] 830-931-3100
   alsatiangolfcourse.com
Alvin G&CC, *Alvin* ....9 [S] 281-331-4541
   alvingolf.com
Amarillo CC, *Amarillo* .... 18 [V] 806-355-5021
   amarillocountryclub.memberstatements.com
Andrews County GC, *Andrews*............................18 [M] 432-524-1462
Anson Muni GC, *Anson*......................................9 [M] 325-823-2822
April Sound GC, *Montgomery* .... 27 [V] 936-588-1101
   april-sound.com
Archer City CC, *Archer City*.................................9 [S] 940-574-4322
Arrowhead GC, *Tyler*..18 [P] 903-509-3555
   tylergolf.net
Ascarate Muni GC, *El Paso*.................................27 [M] 915-772-7381
   cityofelpaso.org
Aspermont City GC, *Aspermont*...........................9 [S] 940-989-2288
Atascocita CC at Kingwood, *Humble* .... 27 [V] 281-852-8111
   theclubsofkingwood.com
Athens CC, *Athens* .... 18 [V] 903-677-3844
   athenscctx.org

[A] = MILITARY   [M] = MUNICIPAL   [P] = PUBLIC   [R] = RESORT

TEXAS

Augusta Pines GC, *Spring* .... 18 [P] 281-290-1910
augustapinesgolf.com
Austin Bayou GC & RV Park, *Danbury*............ 9 [R] 979-922-1234
garrettsrvpark-golf.com
Austin CC, *Austin* .... 18 [V] 512-328-0090
austincountryclub.com
Austin GC, *Spicewood* .... 18 [V] 512-264-9787
Avery Ranch GC, *Austin* .... 18 [P] 512-248-2442
averyranchgolf.com
Babe Zaharias GC, *Port Arthur* .... 18 [M] 409-722-8286
aquilagolf.com
Balcones CC, *Austin* .... 36 [V] 512-258-1621
balconescountryclub.com
Ballinger CC, *Ballinger* .... 9 [P] 325-365-3214
ballingercc.com
Battle Lake GC, *Mart* .... 18 [P] 254-876-2837
battlelakegolf.com
Bay Cel GC, *Bay City* .... 9 [V] 979-241-4075
Bay City CC, *Bay City* .... 9 [V] 979-245-3990
Bay Forest GC, *La Porte* .... 18 [M] 281-471-4653
bayforestgolf.com
Bay Oaks CC, *Houston* .... 18 [V] 281-488-9753
bayoakscountryclub.com
Bayou Din GC, *Beaumont* .... 27 [P] 409-796-1327
aquilagolf.com
Bayou GC, *Texas City* .... 18 [M] 409-643-5850
texas-city-tx.org
Beacon Lakes GC, *Dickinson* .... 18 [P] 281-337-1459
beaconlakesgolf.com
Bear Creek, *Houston* .... 54 [P] 281-859-8188
bearcreekgolfworld.com
Bear Creek GC, *Dallas* .... 36 [R] 972-456-3200
bearcreek-golf.com
Beaumont CC, *Beaumont* .... 18 [V] 409-898-7011
beaumontcountryclub.com
Beaver Brook CC, *Daingerfield* .... 9 [S] 903-645-2976
Beeville CC, *Beeville* .... 9 [V] 361-358-1216
Belle Oaks GC, *Beaumont* .... 18 [S] 409-796-1312
Bellville G&RecC, *Bellville* .... 9 [P] 979-865-9058
Benbrook Lighted 3 Par, *Benbrook* .... 9 [P] 817-249-0770
Bent Tree CC, *Dallas* .... 18 [V] 972-931-7326
benttreecc.org
Bentwater Y&CC, *Montgomery* .... 54 [V] 936-597-6224
bentwaterclub.com
Bentwood CC, *San Angelo* .... 18 [V] 325-944-8575
bentwoodcc.com
Bergstrom GC, *Austin* .... 18 [M] 512-530-4653
Berry Creek CC, *Georgetown* .... 18 [V] 512-930-4615
berrycreekcc.com
Big Cedar GC, *Teague* .... 18 [P] 254-739-5500
Big Lake GC, *Big Lake* .... 9 [P] 325-884-2633
Big Spring CC, *Big Spring* .... 18 [V] 432-267-5354
bigspringcountryclub.com
Birdees Golf Ctr & DR, *New Braunfels* .... 9 [P] 830-620-4653
birdeesgolfcenter.com
Birmingham Forest GC, *Rusk* .... 9 [P] 903-683-9518
birminghamgolfclub.net
Black Jacks Crossing GC, *Terlingua* .... 18 [R] 432-424-5080
blackjackscrossing.com
Blackhawk GC, *Pflugerville* .... 18 [P] 512-251-9000
blackhawkgolf.com
BlackHorse GC, *Cypress* .... 36 [S] 281-304-1747
blackhorsegolfclub.com

Blaketree National GC, *Montgomery* .... 18 [P] 936-449-4907
blaketreegolf.com
Blossom Golf Ctr, *San Antonio* .... 9 [P] 210-494-0002
blossomgolfcenter.com
Blue Lake GC, *Horseshoe Bay* .... 9 [P] 830-598-5524
bluelakegolf.com
Bluebonnet CC, *Navasota* .... 18 [P] 936-894-2207
bluebonnetcountry.com
Bluebonnet CC, *Hico* .... 9 [P] 254-796-4122
Bluebonnet Hill GC, *Austin* .... 18 [P] 512-272-4228
bluebonnethillgolf.com
Booker CC, *Booker* .... 9 [M] 806-658-9663
Boot Ranch GC, *Fredericksburg* .... 18 [V] 830-990-7888
bootranch.com
Borger CC, *Borger* .... 18 [P] 806-273-2231
borgercountryclub.com
Bosque Valley GC, *Meridian* .... 9 [V] 254-435-2692
Bowie CC, *Bowie* .... 18 [P] 940-872-5401
bowiegolfclub.com
Brackenridge Park GC, *San Antonio* .... 18 [M] 210-226-5612
brackenridgegolfsa.com
Brady Muni GC, *Brady* .... 9 [M] 325-597-6010
bradytx.com
BraeBurn CC, *Houston* .... 18 [V] 713-774-8788
braeburncc.com
Breckenridge CC, *Breckenridge* .... 9 [S] 254-559-3466
Brenham CC, *Brenham* .... 18 [S] 979-836-1733
brenhamcc.com
Brentwood CC, *Beaumont* .... 18 [P] 409-840-9440
brentwoodccbeaumont.com
Briarcrest CC, *Bryan* .... 18 [V] 979-776-1490
briarcrestcc.org
Bridgeport CC, *Bridgeport* .... 9 [S] 940-683-9438
Bridlewood GC, *Flower Mound* .... 18 [P] 972-355-4800
bridlewoodgolf.com
Brock Park GC, *Houston* .... 18 [M] 281-458-1350
houstontx.gov/municipalgolf
Brook Hollow CC, *Dallas* .... 18 [V] 214-637-1900
brookhollowgc.org
Brookhaven CC, *Dallas* .... 54 [V] 972-241-2761
brookhavenclub.com
Brownfield GC, *Brownfield* .... 9 [S] 806-637-3656
Brownsville Golf Ctr, *Brownsville* .... 18 [M] 956-541-2582
Brownwood CC, *Brownwood* .... 18 [V] 325-646-1086
brownwoodcountryclub.com
Bryan Muni GC, *Bryan* .... 18 [M] 979-823-0126
bryangolf.com
Buckhorn CC, *Comfort* .... 18 [P] 830-995-5351
buckhorngolfcourse.com
Buffalo Creek GC, *Rockwall* .... 18 [P] 972-771-4003
buffalocreek.americangolf.com
Butler Park Pitch & Putt GC, *Austin* .... 9 [P] 512-477-4430
butlerparkpitchandputt.com
Butterfield Trail GC, *El Paso* .... 18 [M] 915-772-1038
butterfieldtrailgolf.com
Calvert CC, *Calvert* .... 9 [V] 979-364-2892
Cameron CC, *Cameron* .... 9 [V] 254-697-2371
Canadian CC, *Canadian* .... 9 [M] 806-323-5512
Canongate At Lake Windcrest GC, *Magnolia* ....18 [P] 281-259-2279
canongatetexas.com
Canongate At Magnolia Creek GC, *League City*... 27 [P] 281-557-0555
canongatetexas.com

TEXAS
Golf Yellow Pages, 18th Edition

Canongate At the Woodlands, *The Woodlands*....36 [R] 281-364-6329
  canongatetexas.com
Canongate of South Shore, *League City* ....27 [R] 281-334-0525
  canongatetexas.com
Canyon CC, *Canyon* ....9 [S] 806-499-3397
  canyontxcountryclub.com
Canyon Creek CC, *Richardson* .... 18 [V] 972-231-1466
  canyoncreekclub.com
Canyon Lake GC, *Canyon Lake* .... 18 [S] 830-899-3301
  canyonlakegolfclub.com
Canyon Springs GC, *San Antonio*..........................18 [P] 210-497-1770
  canyonspringsgc.com
Canyon West GC, *Weatherford* .... 18 [S] 817-596-4653
  canyonwestgolf.com
Cape Royale GC, *Coldspring*................................18 [P] 936-653-2388
  caperoyalegolfclub.com
Caprock GC, *Post*...9 [P] 806-495-3029
Carrizo Springs Muni GC, *Carrizo Springs*...............9 [M] 830-876-2596
Carthage CC, *Carthage*.. 9 [V] 903-693-9062
Casa Blanca GC, *Laredo*.....................................18 [M] 956-726-2019
  golfcasablanca.com
Cascades GC, *Tyler*... 18 [V] 903-525-0016
  cascadesoftexas.com
CC of Dimmitt, *Dimmitt*......................................9 [P] 806-647-4502
Cedar Creek CC, *Kemp*...................................... 18 [V] 903-498-6761
  cedarcreekcountryclub.com
Cedar Creek GC, *San Antonio*.............................18 [M] 210-695-5050
  cedarcreekgolfsa.com
Cedar Crest GC, *Dallas*......................................18 [M] 214-670-7615
  cedarcrestgolf.com
Center CC, *Center*..9 [P] 936-598-5513
Chambers County GC, *Anahuac*..........................18 [P] 409-267-8235
  chamberscountygolf.com
Champions GC, *Houston* .... 36 [V] 281-444-6449
  championsgolfclub.com
Chaparral Ridge GC, *Lubbock*...............................9 [P] 806-771-8970
Chapparral Rec Assoc GC, *Dickinson*.................... 9 [V] 281-337-2411
Chase Oaks GC, *Plano* ....27 [M] 214-509-4653
  chaseoaks.com
Chemcel Club GC, *Bishop* .... 9 [V] 361-584-6107
Chemlake GC, *Pasadena* .... 9 [V] 281-474-6402
Cherokee Country Golf Assn, *Longview*.................9 [P] 903-643-3571
Chester W Ditto GC, *Arlington*...........................18 [M] 817-275-5941
  arlingtongolf.com
Cimarron Hills G&CC, *Georgetown*...................... 18 [V] 512-763-8700
  cimarronhills.com
Clarendon CC, *Howardwick* .... 18 [S] 806-874-2166
Clarksville CC, *Clarksville*....................................9 [P] 903-427-3450
Clay County CC, *Henrietta* .... 9 [V] 940-538-4339
Clear Creek GC, *Houston*...................................18 [P] 713-738-8000
  clearcreekgolfclub.com
Clear Lake GC, *Houston*.....................................18 [P] 281-488-0252
  clearlakegolfclub.com
Cleburne Golf Ranch, *Cleburne* ....9 [P] 817-774-1999
  golf-ranch.com
Cleburne Muni GC, *Cleburne* ....18 [M] 817-641-4501
  gocleburne.com
Club at Carlton Woods - Fazio, *The Woodlands*.. 18 [V] 281-863-5820
  carltonwoods.com
Club at Carlton Woods - Nicklaus, *The Woodlands*18 [V] 281-863-5820
  carltonwoods.com
Club Course At Abilene CC, *Abilene* .... 18 [V] 325-692-1855
  abilenecountryclub.com

Coleman CC, *Coleman*..9 [S] 325-625-2922
  colemancountryclub.com
Colonial CC, *Fort Worth*..................................... 18 [V] 817-927-4221
  colonialfw.com
Colony Creek CC, *Victoria* ....18 [P] 361-576-0018
  colonycreek.net
ColoVista CC & Resort, *Bastrop*..........................18 [R] 512-303-4045
  colovista.com
Columbia Lakes Resort, *West Columbia*...............18 [R] 979-345-7888
  columbia-lakes.com
Columbus GC, *Columbus*....................................9 [P] 979-732-5575
  columbustexas.net
Comanche Creek GC, *Mason* ....9 [P] 325-347-5798
Comanche Trail GC, *Big Spring* ....18 [M] 432-264-2366
Comanche Trail GC, *Amarillo*..............................36 [M] 806-378-4281
  comanchetrail.com
Concho Springs GC, *Eden* ....9 [M] 325-869-8180
  edentexas.com
Conroe CC, *Conroe*.. 9 [V] 936-756-5222
Copperas Hollow CC, *Caldwell*.............................9 [S] 979-567-4422
  copperashollow.com
Coronado CC, *El Paso*....................................... 18 [V] 915-584-1171
  coronadocountryclub.com
Corpus Christi CC, *Corpus Christi*....................... 18 [V] 361-991-7870
  cccountryclub.com
Corsicana CC, *Corsicana*.................................... 18 [V] 903-874-2441
  corsicanacountryclub.com
Cottonwood Creek GC, *Waco*.............................18 [M] 254-745-6009
  waco-texas.com
Cottonwood Valley, *Irving*..................................18 [R] 972-717-2502
  thesportsclubfourseasons.com
Cottonwood XXI GC, *Harlingen* ....9 [P] 956-428-7758
  cottonwood21.com
Country Campus GC, *Huntsville*...........................9 [P] 936-291-0008
Country Oaks GC, *Athens* ....18 [P] 903-489-3325
Country Place GC, *Pearland* .... 18 [V] 713-436-1533
  countryplacegolfclub.com
Country View GC, *Lancaster* ....18 [P] 972-227-0995
  countryviewgolfcourse.com
Cowan Creek GC, *Georgetown*........................... 18 [S] 512-864-1111
  sctxca.org
Cowboys GC, *Grapevine* ....18 [R] 817-481-7277
  cowboysgolfclub.com
Coyote Ridge GC, *Carrollton* ....18 [P] 972-395-0786
  coyoteridgegolf.com
Crane CC, *Crane* ....9 [P] 432-558-2651
Creek Bend GC, *Blanket* ....9 [P] 325-748-4404
Creekview GC, *Crandall*....................................18 [M] 972-472-8400
  creekviewgolf.com
Crenshaw Cliffside At Barton Creek, *Austin*.........18 [R] 512-329-4610
  bartoncreek.com
Crooked Creek GC (Pasture), *Electra* ....9 [M] 940-495-3832
Cross Timbers GC, *Azle*....................................18 [M] 817-444-4940
  crosstimbersgc.com
Crow Hollow GC, *Trinity*.....................................9 [P] 936-594-2583
Crown Colony CC, *Lufkin*................................... 18 [V] 936-637-8800
  crown-colony.com
Cuero Park Muni GC, *Cuero*................................9 [M] 361-275-3233
Cypress GC, *Cypress*..9 [P] 281-373-0727
Cypress Lakes GC, *Cypress* ....18 [P] 281-304-8515
  cypresslakesgc.com
Cypresswood GC, *Spring* ....54 [P] 281-821-6300
  cypresswood.com

200   [A] = MILITARY   [M] = MUNICIPAL   [P] = PUBLIC   [R] = RESORT

Golf Yellow Pages, 18th Edition — TEXAS

Course	City	Holes	Type	Phone
Dalhart CC	Dalhart	18	[V]	806-244-5597
Dallas Ath Club	Dallas	36	[V]	972-279-6517
dallasathleticclub.org				
Dallas CC	Dallas	18	[V]	214-521-2151
thedallascc.org				
Dallas National GC	Dallas	18	[V]	214-331-4195
dallasnationalgolfclub.com				
Decatur G&CC	Decatur	9	[P]	940-627-3789
DeCordova Bend CC	Granbury	27	[V]	817-326-2381
dcbeweb.com				
Delaware Springs GC	Burnet	18	[M]	512-756-8471
delawaresprings.com				
Delta CC	Cooper	9	[S]	903-395-4712
Denison CC	Denison	18	[V]	903-465-4488
denisoncc.com				
Denton CC	Argyle	18	[V]	940-387-1717
dentoncc.org				
Desert Pines GC	Fort Stockton	18	[M]	432-336-2050
ci.fort-stockton.tx.us				
Devine GC	Devine	18	[P]	830-665-9943
Diamond Back GC	Abilene	18	[P]	325-690-9190
diamondbackgolfclub.biz				
Diamond Oaks G&CC	Fort Worth	18	[V]	817-834-6261
diamondoaksclub.com				
Dogwood Hills CC	Woodville	9	[P]	409-283-8725
Eagle Lake GC & Rec Ctr	Eagle Lake	9	[P]	979-234-5981
meldahl.com				
Eagle Pass GC	Eagle Pass	9	[M]	830-773-9761
Eagle Pointe GC	Mont Belvieu	18	[M]	281-385-6666
eaglepointeonline.com				
Eagle Rock GC	Ennis	18	[P]	972-878-4653
eaglerockgolfclub.com				
Eastern Hills CC	Garland	18	[V]	972-840-3484
easternhillscc.com				
Ebony Hills Public GC	Edinburg	9	[M]	956-292-2144
Echo Creek CC	Murchison	18	[S]	903-852-7094
Edna CC	Edna	9	[P]	361-782-3010
El Campo CC	El Campo	9	[V]	979-543-6592
El Paso CC	El Paso	18	[V]	915-584-1511
elpasocountryclub.com				
Eldorado CC	McKinney	18	[V]	972-529-2770
eldoradocc.com				
Eldorado GC	Eldorado	9	[M]	325-853-2036
Elk Hollow GC	Paris	9	[P]	903-785-6585
Elkhart GC	Elkhart	18	[S]	903-764-2461
Elkins Lake Rec Assoc	Huntsville	27	[P]	936-295-4312
elkinslake.net				
Elm Grove GC	Lubbock	18	[P]	806-799-7801
elmgrovegolfclub.com				
Embassy Hills GC	Big Sandy	9	[P]	903-636-9890
embassyhills.com				
Emerald Bay Club	Bullard	18	[P]	903-825-3444
emeraldbayclub.org				
Emerald Springs Golf & Conf Ctr	Horizon City	18	[P]	915-852-9110
emeraldspringsgolf.com				
Ennis CC	Ennis	18	[P]	972-875-3641
enniscc.com				
Escondido Golf & Lake Club	Horseshoe Bay	18	[P]	830-598-5301
escondidotexas.com				
Evergreen Point GC	Baytown	18	[P]	281-837-9000
evergreenpointgolf.com				
Fair Oaks Ranch G&CC	Fair Oaks	36	[P]	210-582-6500
fairoaksclub.com				
Fairway Course At Abilene CC	Abilene	18	[V]	325-692-1855
abilenecountryclub.com				
Falconhead GC	Austin	18	[P]	512-402-1558
falconheadaustin.com				
Falfurrias Golfers	Falfurrias	9	[M]	361-325-5348
Falls Creek GC	Midlothian	18	[V]	972-989-8939
Farwell CC	Farwell	9	[P]	806-481-9210
Fazio Canyons at Barton Creek	Austin	18	[R]	512-301-6569
bartoncreek.com				
Fazio Foothills At Barton Creek	Austin	18	[R]	512-329-4519
bartoncreek.com				
Feather Bay GC	Brownwood	18	[R]	325-784-4653
Firewheel Golf Park	Garland	27	[M]	972-205-2795
golffirewheel.com				
Firewheel Golf Park	Garland	36	[M]	972-205-2795
golffirewheel.com				
Flatonia GC	Flatonia	9	[P]	361-865-2922
flatoniagolf.com				
Flintrock Falls	Austin	36	[V]	512-263-6090
flintrockfalls.com				
Floydada CC	Floydada	9	[P]	806-983-2769
Flying L Guest Ranch	Bandera	18	[R]	830-796-8466
flyingl.com				
Forest Creek GC	Round Rock	18	[P]	512-388-2874
forestcreek.com				
Fort Bend CC	Richmond	18	[V]	281-342-8368
fortbendcc.com				
Fort Brown Memorial GC	Brownsville	18	[P]	956-541-0394
fortbrowngolf.com				
Fort Clark Springs GC	Brackettville	18	[P]	830-563-9204
ftclarksprings.com				
Fort Sam Houston GC	San Antonio	36	[A]	210-222-9386
Four Seasons Resort & Club (TPC Las Colinas)	Irving	18	[R]	972-717-2500
thesportsclubfourseasons.com				
Fox Creek GC	Hempstead	18	[P]	979-826-2131
foxcreekgolf.com				
Freeport GC	Freeport	18	[M]	979-233-8311
Friona CC	Friona	9	[V]	806-250-3125
Frisch Auf Valley CC	La Grange	9	[P]	979-968-6113
Fun City Golf Ctr	Grand Prairie	9	[P]	972-262-0022
funcitygolf.com				
Gabe Lozano Sr Golf Ctr	Corpus Christi	27	[M]	361-826-8016
cctexas.com				
Gaines County GC	Seminole	18	[M]	432-758-3808
Gainesville Muni GC	Gainesville	18	[M]	940-668-4560
gainesville.tx.us				
Galveston CC	Galveston	18	[V]	409-737-9800
galvestoncountryclub.com				
Ganado G&CC	Ganado	9	[P]	361-771-2424
Garden Valley Golf Resort	Lindale	27	[R]	903-882-6108
gardenvalleytx.com				
Gatesville CC	Gatesville	18	[S]	254-865-6917
Gateway Hills GC at Lackland	Lackland AFB	18	[A]	210-671-3466
lacklandservices.com				
Gateway Valley GC Lackland	Kelly AFB	18	[A]	210-925-7610
GC at Cinco Ranch	Katy	18	[P]	281-395-4653
golfclubatcincoranch.com				
GC of Seguin	Seguin	18	[P]	830-379-6313
thegolfclubofseguin.com				
Gentle Creek GC	Prosper	18	[V]	972-346-2550
gentlecreek.com				

[S] = SEMI-PRIVATE   [V] = PRIVATE   [U] = UNIVERSITY   [N] = UNIVERSITY-PRIVATE

TEXAS Golf Yellow Pages, 18th Edition

Georgetown CC, *Georgetown* .... 18 [V] 512-930-4577
  georgetowncountryclub.net
Giddings CC & Muni GC, *Giddings* ....9 [M] 979-542-3777
  giddings.net
Gilmer CC, *Gilmer* .... 9 [V] 903-734-4125
  gilmercountryclub.net
Gleannloch Pines GC, *Spring* ....27 [P] 281-225-1200
  playgleannlochpines.com
Glen Garden G&CC, *Fort Worth* .... 18 [V] 817-535-7582
  glengarden.com
Glenbrook GC, *Houston* ....18 [M] 713-649-8089
  glenbrookgolfcourse.com
Gleneagles CC, *Plano* .... 36 [V] 972-867-8888
  gleneaglesclub.com
Goldthwaite Muni GC, *Goldthwaite* ......9 [M] 325-938-5652
  golfgoldthwaitetx.com
Golf Utopia Riveroaks, *Utopia* ....9 [P] 830-966-5577
  golfutopiaoftexas.com
Golfcrest CC, *Pearland* .... 18 [V] 281-485-4593
  golfcrestcountryclub.com
Goliad County GC, *Goliad* ....9 [P] 361-645-8322
  goliadgolf.com
Goose Creek CC, *Baytown* .... 18 [V] 281-424-5565
Graham CC, *Graham* ....9 [P] 940-549-7721
Granbury CC, *Granbury* ....9 [P] 817-573-9912
Grand Lake GC, *Montgomery* .... 18 [V] 936-447-4653
  grandlakegolfclub.com
Grand Oaks GC, *Grand Prairie* ....18 [P] 972-264-2974
  grandoaksgolfclub.com
Grapevine GC, *Grapevine* ....27 [M] 817-410-3377
  grapevinetexas.gov
Grayson College GC, *Denison* .... 18 [U] 903-786-9719
  grayson.edu/update/golfcourse.asp
Great Hills CC, *Austin* .... 18 [V] 512-345-0505
  greathillscc.org
Great Southwest GC, *Grand Prairie*..................... 18 [V] 972-647-0116
  greatsouthwestgc.com
Greatwood GC, *Sugar Land* ....18 [P] 281-343-9999
  greatwoodgolf.com
Green Caye GC, *Dickinson* ....9 [P] 281-337-2021
  thelinksatgreencaye.com
Green Tree CC, *Midland* .... 27 [V] 432-694-7726
  greentreecc.com
Greenbrier GC, *Moody* ....18 [P] 254-853-2927
  greenbriergolfclub.com
Grey Rock GC, *Austin* ....18 [P] 512-288-4297
  greyrockgolfclub.com
Gulf Winds GC, *Corpus Christi* ....18 [A] 361-961-3250
Gus Wortham Park GC, *Houston* ....18 [M] 713-928-4260
  houstontx.gov/municipalgolf
Hackberry Creek CC, *Irving* .... 18 [V] 972-869-2631
  hackberrycreekcc.com
Hackberry GC, *Houston* ....9 [P] 281-575-7791
Hallettsville GC, *Hallettsville* ....9 [P] 361-798-9908
Hamlin GC, *Hamlin* ....9 [P] 325-576-3581
Hancock GC, *Austin* ....9 [P] 512-453-0270
  ci.austin.tx.us/parks/hancockgc.htm
Hancock Park GC, *Lampasas* ....18 [P] 512-556-3202
  ci.lampasas.tx.us/golf
Hank Haney Golf Ranch at Vista Ridge, *Lewisville* .9 [P] 972-315-5300
  hankhaneygolf.com
Hansford GC, *Spearman* ....9 [P] 806-659-2233

Harbor Lakes GC, *Granbury* ....18 [P] 817-578-8600
  harborlakesgc.com
Harlingen CC, *Harlingen* .... 18 [V] 956-412-4100
  harlingencc.com
Hartlines Golf Ctr, *Greenville* ....9 [P] 903-455-7888
Harvey Penick Golf Campus, *Austin* ....9 [P] 512-926-1100
  harveypenickgc.com
Haskell County CC, *Haskell* ....9 [P] 940-864-3400
Hatch Bend CC, *Port Lavaca* ....9 [P] 361-552-3037
Hawks Creek GC, *Fort Worth* ....18 [P] 817-738-8402
  hawkscreek.com
Hearne Muni GC, *Hearne* ....9 [M] 979-279-3112
Hearthstone CC, *Houston* .... 27 [V] 281-463-2204
  hearthstoneclub.com
Henderson CC, *Henderson* .... 9 [V] 903-657-4719
Henry Homberg GC, *Beaumont* ....18 [M] 409-842-3220
  cityofbeaumont.com
Heritage Ranch G&CC, *Fairview* ....18 [P] 972-886-4700
  heritageranchgolf.com
Hermann Park GC, *Houston* ....18 [P] 713-526-0077
  hermannparkgc.com
Heron Lakes GC, *Houston* ....18 [P] 281-807-0207
  heronlakesgc.com
Hidden Creek GC, *Burleson* ....18 [M] 817-447-4444
  hiddencreekgolfcourse.com
Hidden Falls GC, *Meadowlakes* ....18 [S] 830-693-3300
  hiddenfallsgolfclub.com
Hidden Hills Muni GC, *Pampa* ....18 [M] 806-669-5866
  cityofpampa.org
Hidden Oaks, *Granbury* ....18 [P] 817-279-1078
  hiddenoaksgolf.net
Hidden Springs GC, *Harper* ....18 [P] 830-990-4122
  golf.double-b-ranch.com
Hide A Way Lake GC, *Hideaway* .... 27 [V] 903-882-8511
  hideawaytexas.net
High Meadow Ranch GC, *Magnolia* ....18 [P] 281-356-7700
  highmeadowranchgolf.com
Highland Lakes CC, *Lago Vista* ....18 [R] 512-617-4950
  lagovistagc.com
Highland Lakes GC, *Burnet* ....9 [S] 512-793-2859
  highlandlakesgolfclub.com
Hillcrest CC, *Lubbock* .... 18 [V] 806-765-5208
  hillcrestcc.com
Hillcrest CC, *Vernon* .... 9 [V] 940-552-5406
  hillcrestcc.com
Hillcrest GC, *Alvin* ....9 [P] 281-331-3505
  hillcrestnightgolf.com
Hills of Cove Muni GC, *Copperas Cove* ....18 [M] 254-547-2606
  ci.copperas-cove.tx.us
Hillsboro CC, *Hillsboro* ....9 [P] 254-582-8211
Hilltop CC, *Troup* ....9 [S] 903-842-3516
Hilltop Lakes Resort GC, *Hilltop Lakes* ....18 [R] 936-855-2100
  hilltoplakes.com
Hogan Park GC, *Midland* ....36 [M] 432-685-7360
  hoganparkgolf.com
Holiday Hills CC, *Mineral Wells* ....18 [P] 940-325-8403
  hhccmw.com
Holly Lake Ranch GC, *Holly Lake Ranch* ....18 [P] 903-769-2397
Hollytree CC, *Tyler* .... 18 [V] 903-581-7723
  hollytreeclub.com
Hondo GC, *Hondo* ....9 [M] 830-741-4653
  cityofhondo.com

202 [A] = MILITARY [M] = MUNICIPAL [P] = PUBLIC [R] = RESORT

TEXAS

Name	Holes	Type	Phone
Honors GC Dallas, *Carrollton*	18	[V]	972-416-2131
thehonorsgolfclubdallas.com			
Horseshoe Bay Resort & CCtr, *Horseshoe Bay*	36	[R]	830-598-2561
hsbresort.com			
Horseshoe Bay Resort-Slick Rock, *Horseshoe Bay*	18	[R]	830-598-2561
hsbresort.com			
Horseshoe Bend CC, *Weatherford*	9	[P]	817-594-6454
Houston CC, *Houston*	18	[V]	713-465-8381
houstoncc.com			
Houston National GC, *Houston*	27	[S]	281-304-1400
houstonnationalgolf.com			
Houston Oaks G&CC, *Hockley*	27	[S]	713-888-0000
houstonoaks.com			
Houstonian G&CC, *Richmond*	18	[R]	281-494-4244
houstoniangolf.com			
Humble Oil Patch Golf Ctr, *Humble*	9	[P]	281-548-7273
Hurricane Creek CC, *Anna*	18	[V]	972-924-3247
hurricanecreekcc.com			
Hyatt Hill Country GC, *San Antonio*	27	[R]	210-520-4040
hyatthillcountrygolf.com			
Idylwild GC, *Sour Lake*	18	[S]	409-753-2521
Independence GC, *Gonzales*	9	[M]	830-672-1324
cityofgonzales.org			
Indian Creek GC, *Carrollton*	36	[M]	972-466-9850
indiancreekgolfclub.com			
Indian Hills CC, *Atlanta*	9	[S]	903-796-4146
Indian Oaks GC, *Nocona*	18	[M]	940-825-4213
Indian Oaks GC, *Kemp*	27	[P]	903-498-3564
indianoaksgolfcourse.com			
Indian Shores Rec Assoc, *Crosby*	9	[S]	281-324-2592
Iraan GC, *Iraan*	9	[P]	432-639-8892
Iron Horse GC, *North Richland Hills*	18	[M]	817-485-6666
ironhorsetx.com			
Iron Oaks GC, *Beaumont*	18	[P]	409-866-9191
Island Oaks GC, *Idalou*	9	[P]	806-892-2839
Jacksboro GC, *Jacksboro*	9	[P]	940-567-3726
James Connally Muni GC, *Waco*	18	[M]	254-799-6561
Jasper CC, *Jasper*	9	[V]	409-384-4342
Jersey Meadow GC, *Houston*	18	[M]	713-896-0900
jerseymeadow.com			
Jim McLean Golf Center At Texas, *Fort Worth*	9	[P]	817-303-4370
texas.jimmclean.com			
Jimmy Clay Roy Kizer Muni GC, *Austin*	36	[M]	512-444-0999
ci.austin.tx.us/parks/jimmyclay.htm			
John C Beasley Muni Golf, *Beeville*	9	[M]	361-362-7618
John Pitman Muni GC, *Hereford*	18	[M]	806-363-7139
Junction GC, *Junction*	9	[P]	325-446-2968
Karnes County CC, *Kenedy*	9	[P]	830-583-3200
Keeton Park GC, *Dallas*	18	[M]	214-670-8784
keetonpark.com			
Kent County GC, *Jayton*	9	[M]	806-237-4970
co.kent.tx.us			
Kings Creek GC, *Kemp*	18	[S]	903-498-8888
kingscreekgolfclub.com			
Kingwood GC, *Kingwood*	72	[V]	281-358-2171
theclubsofkingwood.com			
Kingwood Cove GC, *Kingwood*	18	[P]	281-358-1155
kingwoodcove.com			
Kirbywood GC, *Cleveland*	9	[P]	281-593-3303
kirbywoodgolf.com			
Knox City GC, *Knox City*	9	[P]	940-658-3911
L B Houston GC, *Dallas*	18	[M]	214-670-6522
golflbhouston.com			
L E Ramey GC, *Kingsville*	18	[M]	361-592-1101
lerameygolf.com			
La Cantera GC Palmer Course, *San Antonio*	18	[R]	210-558-2365
lacanteragolfclub.com			
La Paloma GC, *Amarillo*	18	[S]	806-342-3051
lapalomagolf.com			
La Torretta Del Lago Resort, *Montgomery*	18	[R]	936-448-4400
latorrettalakeresort.com			
Lady Bird Johnson GC, *Fredericksburg*	18	[M]	830-997-4010
golffredericksburg.com			
LaFloresta GC, *Mercedes*	9	[R]	956-565-6314
Lago Vista GC, *Lago Vista*	18	[R]	512-267-1170
lagovistagc.com			
Lake Arlington GC, *Arlington*	18	[M]	817-451-6101
arlingtongolf.com			
Lake Cisco CC, *Cisco*	9	[S]	254-442-2725
Lake Creek GC, *Munday*	9	[M]	940-422-4331
mundaytexas.com			
Lake Fork GC, *Emory*	18	[P]	903-473-3112
lakeforkgolfcourse.com			
Lake Kiowa GC, *Lake Kiowa*	18	[V]	940-668-7394
lakekiowatx.com			
Lake Park Exec GC, *Lewisville*	9	[P]	972-436-3113
lakeparkgc.com			
Lake Park GC - Regulation, *Lewisville*	18	[P]	972-219-5661
lakeparkgc.com			
Lake Ridge CC, *Lubbock*	18	[V]	806-794-4445
lakeridgecc.com			
Lake Sweetwater Muni GC, *Sweetwater*	18	[M]	325-235-8816
lakesweetwater.com			
Lake Whitney RV & Golf, *Whitney*	18	[R]	254-694-2313
Lakecliff GC, *Spicewood*	18	[V]	888-798-0695
lakecliff.net			
Lakeside CC, *Eastland*	18	[P]	254-629-2892
Lakeside CC, *Houston*	18	[V]	281-497-2222
lakesidecc.com			
Lakeside Village GC, *Rockwall*	9	[P]	972-771-0131
Lakeway GC Yaupon Course, *Austin*	18	[R]	512-261-7172
clubcorp.com			
Lakewood CC, *Dallas*	18	[V]	214-821-7690
lakewoodcc.com			
Lamesa CC, *Lamesa*	9	[P]	806-872-3059
Lamesa Muni GC, *Lamesa*	9	[M]	806-872-8100
ci.lamesa.tx.us			
Landa Park GC, *New Braunfels*	18	[M]	830-221-4340
tx-newbraunfels.civicplus.com			
Lantana GC, *Lantana*	18	[P]	940-728-4653
lantanatx.com			
Laredo CC, *Laredo*	18	[V]	956-727-2900
laredocc.com			
Las Colinas CC, *Irving*	18	[V]	972-541-1141
lascolinascc.com			
Leaning Pines GC, *Laughlin AFB*	9	[A]	830-298-5451
Legacy Hills GC, *Georgetown*	18	[P]	512-864-1222
sctxca.org			
Legacy Ridge GC, *Bonham*	18	[P]	903-640-4800
legacyridge.com			
Legendary Oaks GC, *Hempstead*	18	[P]	979-826-4001
legendaryoaksgolf.com			
Legends CC, *Stephenville*	18	[P]	254-968-2200
Leon Valley GC, *Belton*	18	[M]	254-939-5271
beltongolf.com			
Levelland CC, *Levelland*	9	[V]	806-894-3288

[S] = SEMI-PRIVATE   [V] = PRIVATE   [U] = UNIVERSITY   [N] = UNIVERSITY-PRIVATE

TEXAS

Golf Yellow Pages, 18th Edition

Links At Lands End, *Yantis* .... 18 [P] 903-383-3290
  golflakefork.com
Lions Muni GC, *Austin* .... 18 [M] 512-477-6963
  lionsgolfcourse.com
Littlefield GC, *Littlefield* .... 9 [P] 806-385-3309
Live Oak At The Clubs of Lakeway, *Austin* .... 18 [R] 512-261-7173
  clubcorp.com
Live Oak CC, *Rockport* .... 9 [V] 361-729-7311
Livingston GC, *Livingston* .... 9 [P] 936-327-4777
Llano Grande GC, *Mercedes* .... 18 [P] 956-565-3351
  llanograndresort.com
Llano River GC, *Llano* .... 18 [P] 325-247-5100
  llanorivergolfcourse.com
Lochinvar CC, *Houston* .... 18 [V] 281-821-0220
Lockhart St Park GC, *Lockhart* .... 9 [M] 512-398-3479
  tpwd.state.tx.us
Lone Cedar CC, *Eastland* .... 18 [S] 254-647-3613
  lonecedarcountryclub.com
Lone Oak GC, *Lone Oak* .... 9 [V] 903-634-5059
  thevillagesatloneoak.com
Lone Star GC, *El Paso* .... 18 [M] 915-591-4927
  lonestargolfclub.net
Long Island GC, *Port Isabel* .... 18 [R] 956-943-7520
  longislandvillage.com
Longview CC, *Longview* .... 18 [P] 903-759-9251
Longwood GC, *Cypress* .... 27 [S] 281-373-4100
  longwoodgc.com
Lorenzo CC, *Lorenzo* .... 9 [P] 806-634-5787
Los Ebanos GC, *Zapata* .... 9 [P] 956-765-8336
Los Lagos GC, *Edinburg* .... 18 [M] 956-316-0444
  loslagosgolfclub.com
Los Rios CC, *Plano* .... 18 [P] 972-422-8068
  losrioscountryclub.com
Lost Creek CC, *Austin* .... 18 [V] 512-892-2032
  lostcreekclub.com
Lost Creek GC, *Aledo* .... 18 [P] 817-244-4513
  lostcreekgolf.com
Lost Pines GC, *Bastrop* .... 18 [R] 512-321-2327
  tpwd.state.tx.us
Lost Valley Resort Ranch, *Bandera* .... 18 [P] 830-460-7958
Lubbock CC, *Lubbock* .... 18 [V] 806-763-1871
  lubbockcc.org
Lufkin CC, *Lufkin* .... 18 [P] 936-632-2848
  lufkincountryclub.com
Luling GC, *Luling* .... 9 [M] 830-875-5114
Magnolia Ridge CC, *Liberty* .... 9 [P] 936-336-3551
Mansfield National GC, *Mansfield* .... 18 [P] 817-477-3366
  mansfield-national.com
Marfa Muni GC, *Marfa* .... 9 [M] 432-729-4043
Marlin CC, *Marlin* .... 9 [V] 254-803-6101
Marshall Lakeside CC, *Marshall* .... 9 [V] 903-938-4211
Martin Valley Ranch GC, *Mission* .... 27 [R] 956-585-6330
  martinvalley.com
Maverick GC, *Floresville* .... 18 [P] 830-216-2800
  maverickgolfclub.com
Max Starcke Park GC, *Seguin* .... 18 [P] 830-401-2490
  ci.seguin.tx.us/general/golf.htm
Maxwell GC, *Abilene* .... 18 [P] 325-692-2737
  golfmaxwell.com
McAllen CC, *McAllen* .... 18 [V] 956-631-1103
  mcallencountryclub.com
McCamey CC, *McCamey* .... 9 [P] 432-652-8904

McLean CC, *McLean* .... 9 [P] 806-779-2688
Meadow Creek in the Valley, *Mission* .... 18 [R] 956-581-6267
  meadowcreekinthevalley.net
Meadowbrook CC, *Kilgore* .... 9 [V] 903-984-3387
  mbcckilgore.com
Meadowbrook Farms GC, *Katy* .... 18 [P] 281-693-4653
  meadowbrookfarmsgolfclub.com
Meadowbrook GC, *Fort Worth* .... 18 [M] 817-457-4616
  fortworthgolf.org
Meadowbrook GC, *Lubbock* .... 36 [M] 806-765-6679
  golfmeadowbrook.com
Meadowbrook Park GC, *Arlington* .... 9 [M] 817-275-0221
  arlingtongolf.com
Melrose GC, *Houston* .... 9 [M] 281-931-4666
  houstontx.gov/municipalgolf
Memorial Park GC, *Houston* .... 18 [M] 713-862-4033
  houstontx.gov/municipalgolf
Memphis CC, *Memphis* .... 9 [P] 806-259-2169
Menard GC, *Menard* .... 9 [M] 325-396-3319
Mesquite GC, *Mesquite* .... 18 [M] 972-270-7457
  mesquitegc.com
Mesquite Grove GC, *Dyess AFB* .... 18 [A] 325-696-5067
Mid Valley GC, *Mercedes* .... 18 [P] 956-565-3211
Midland CC, *Midland* .... 18 [V] 432-683-3621
  midlandcc.com
Mill Creek GC, *Salado* .... 27 [R] 254-947-5698
  millcreek-golf.com
Mineola CC, *Mineola* .... 9 [V] 903-569-2472
Mira Vista CC, *Fort Worth* .... 18 [V] 817-294-6600
  miravistacountryclub.com
Miramont CC, *Bryan* .... 18 [R] 979-774-7474
  miramont.cc
Mission Del Lago Muni GC, *San Antonio* .... 18 [M] 210-627-2522
  missiondellagogolfsa.com
Mitchell Resort & RV Park Par 3, *Perrin* ...... 9 [R] 940-798-4615
  mitchellparkandresort.com
Monte Cristo G&CC, *Edinburg* .... 18 [P] 956-381-0964
  montecristogcc.com
Moody Gardens GC, *Galveston* .... 18 [M] 409-683-4653
  moodygardensgolf.com
Morris Williams GC, *Austin* .... 18 [M] 512-926-1298
  ci.austin.tx.us/parks/morriswilliams.htm
Morton CC, *Morton* .... 9 [P] 806-266-5941
Mount Pleasant CC, *Mt Pleasant* .... 18 [P] 903-572-0751
  golfmtpleasant.com
Mountain Creek GC, *Robert Lee* .... 9 [P] 325-453-2317
Mountain Valley CC, *Joshua* .... 18 [V] 817-295-7126
  mountainvalleycc.com
Mountain View GC, *Van Horn* .... 9 [M] 432-283-2628
Muleshoe CC, *Muleshoe* .... 9 [P] 806-272-4250
Mulligans, *Houston* .... 9 [P] 281-890-6026
  mulligansgolf.com
Mustang Creek GC, *Taylor* .... 9 [P] 512-365-1332
  mustangcreektaylor.com
Navasota Municipal GC, *Navasota* .... 9 [P] 936-825-7284
Neches Pines GC, *Diboll* .... 18 [M] 936-829-5086
Newgulf GC, *Boling* .... 9 [S] 979-657-4639
  newgulfgolfclub.com
Newport GC&CCtr, *Crosby* .... 18 [P] 281-328-3576
  newport-tx.com
Nocona Hills GC, *Nocona* .... 18 [P] 940-825-3444
North Texas Golf Ctr, *Dallas* .... 9 [P] 972-247-4653
  northtexasgolf.com

[A] = MILITARY   [M] = MUNICIPAL   [P] = PUBLIC   [R] = RESORT

Golf Yellow Pages, 18th Edition — TEXAS

Course	Holes	Phone
Northcliffe CC, *Cibolo*	18 [P]	830-606-7351
northcliffegc.com		
Northern Challenge GC, *Sherman*	18 [P]	903-891-8700
northernchallenge.com		
Northern Hills GC, *San Antonio*	18 [P]	210-655-8026
northernhillsgolfclub.com		
Northgate CC, *Houston*	27 [V]	281-440-1223
northgatecountryclub.com		
Northridge CC, *Texarkana*	18 [V]	903-792-9331
northridgecountryclub.net		
Northshore CC, *Portland*	18 [V]	361-643-2798
northshore.cc		
Northwest Golf DR, *Dallas*	9 [P]	214-348-3693
Nueva Vista GC, *Midland*	18 [P]	432-520-0500
nuevavistagolf.com		
Nutcracker GC, *Granbury*	18 [V]	817-279-0936
Oak Creek CC, *Greenville*	9 [V]	903-455-3971
Oak Grove CC, *Franklin*	9 [V]	979-828-2301
Oak Grove GC, *New Boston*	18 [P]	903-223-8402
oakgrovegolf.com		
Oak Grove GC, *Terrell*	9 [P]	972-563-8553
Oak Hills CC, *San Antonio*	18 [P]	210-349-5151
oakhillscc.com		
Oak Hollow GC, *McKinney*	18 [M]	972-542-4523
oakhollowgolf.com		
Oak Lawn Muni GC, *Marshall*	9 [M]	903-935-7555
Oak Valley DR & Par 3, *Helotes*	9 [P]	210-695-2606
Oakhurst GC, *Porter*	18 [P]	281-354-4653
oakhurstgolfclub.com		
Oakmont GC, *Corinth*	18 [V]	940-321-5599
oakmontclub.com		
Oakridge CC, *Madisonville*	9 [P]	936-348-6264
Oakridge CC, *Garland*	18 [V]	972-530-8008
oakridgecctexas.com		
Oaks Trail GC, *Corsicana*	9 [P]	903-872-1801
Occidental Chemical GC, *Deer Park*	9 [V]	281-476-2101
Odessa CC, *Odessa*	36 [V]	432-272-4500
odessacc.com		
Old Brickyard GC, *Ferris*	18 [P]	972-842-8700
oldbrickyardgolf.com		
Oldham County CC, *Vega*	9 [P]	806-267-2595
Olmos Basin Muni GC, *San Antonio*	18 [M]	210-826-4041
olmosbasingolfsa.com		
Olney CC, *Olney*	9 [M]	940-564-2424
Olton Rec Ctr GC, *Olton*	9 [P]	806-285-2595
Olympia Hills Golf & Conf Ctr, *Universal City*	18 [P]	210-945-4653
olympiahillsgolf.com		
Onion Creek Club, *Austin*	27 [V]	512-282-2162
onioncreekclub.com		
Oso Beach Muni GC, *Corpus Christi*	18 [M]	361-826-8010
cctexas.com		
Overton Muni GC, *Overton*	9 [M]	903-834-6414
Ozona CC, *Ozona*	9 [V]	325-392-2520
P A R CC, *Comanche*	18 [S]	254-879-2296
parcountryclub.net		
Packsaddle CC, *Kingsland*	18 [P]	325-388-6660
packsaddlegolf.com		
Padre Isles CC, *Corpus Christi*	18 [V]	361-949-8056
padreislescc.com		
Paducah CC, *Paducah*	9 [S]	806-492-2245
Painted Dunes Desert GC, *El Paso*	27 [M]	915-821-2122
painteddunes.com		
Palacios GC, *Palacios*	9 [P]	361-972-5947
Palm View GC, *McAllen*	18 [M]	956-681-3444
mcallen.net		
Palmer Lakeside At Barton Creek, *Spicewood*	18 [R]	830-693-3528
bartoncreek.com		
Palo Duro Creek GC, *Canyon*	18 [S]	806-655-1106
pdcgc.com		
Pamcel GC, *Pampa*	9 [V]	806-663-4342
Pampa CC, *Pampa*	18 [V]	806-665-8431
pampacountryclub.com		
Panhandle CC, *Panhandle*	9 [P]	806-537-3300
Paris G&CC, *Paris*	18 [V]	903-785-6512
parisgcc.com		
Pasadena Muni GC, *Houston*	18 [M]	281-481-0834
Patterson Ranch GC, *Snyder*	9 [V]	325-573-0853
Peach Tree GC, *Bullard*	36 [P]	903-894-7079
easttexasgolf.com		
Pebble Creek CC, *College Station*	18 [S]	979-690-0996
pebblecreek.org		
Pecan Grove Plantation CC, *Richmond*	27 [V]	281-342-9940
pecangrovecc.com		
Pecan Hollow GC, *Plano*	18 [M]	972-941-7600
pecanhollowgc.com		
Pecan Lakes GC, *Navasota*	18 [P]	936-870-3889
pecanlakesgolfclub.com		
Pecan Plantation CC, *Granbury*	18 [V]	817-573-2645
ppoaweb.com		
Pecan Ridge GC, *Scurry*	18 [P]	972-486-4653
pecanridgegolfclub.com		
Pecan Trails GC, *Midlothian*	18 [P]	972-723-1376
pecantrailsgolf.com		
Pecan Valley GC, *San Antonio*	18 [P]	210-333-9018
pecanvalleygc.com		
Pecan Valley Muni GC, *Fort Worth*	36 [M]	817-249-1845
fortworthgolf.com		
Pedernales GC, *Spicewood*	9 [P]	512-264-1489
pedernalesgolfclub.com		
Perry CC, *Hamilton*	9 [P]	254-386-3383
Perryton Muni GC, *Perryton*	18 [M]	806-435-5381
perrytongolfclub.com		
Pharaohs GC, *Corpus Christi*	18 [S]	361-991-2477
Pheasant Trails GC, *Dumas*	18 [M]	806-935-7375
pheasanttrailsgolfcourse.com		
Phillips CC, *Borger*	18 [M]	806-274-6812
phillipscountryclub.com		
Pine Crest GC, *Houston*	18 [P]	713-462-4914
Pine Dunes Resort, *Frankston*	18 [R]	903-876-4336
pinedunes.com		
Pine Forest CC, *Houston*	27 [V]	281-463-1234
pfcc.com		
Pine Forest GC, *Bastrop*	18 [P]	512-321-1181
pineforestgolfclub.com		
Pine Ridge GC, *Paris*	18 [P]	903-785-8076
Pine Springs GC, *Tyler*	18 [P]	903-526-4653
pinespringsgolfcourse.com		
Pinecrest GC, *Longview*	18 [P]	903-758-8000
pinecrestcc.org		
Piney Woods CC, *Nacogdoches*	18 [V]	936-569-9821
pineywoodscountryclub.com		
Pinnacle CC, *Mabank*	18 [R]	903-451-9797
pinnaclegolfclub.com		
Plainview CC, *Plainview*	18 [M]	806-296-6148
Plantation GC, *Frisco*	18 [R]	972-335-4653
plantationgolf.net		

[S] = SEMI-PRIVATE   [V] = PRIVATE   [U] = UNIVERSITY   [N] = UNIVERSITY-PRIVATE

TEXAS
Golf Yellow Pages, 18th Edition

Pleasanton CC, *Pleasanton* .... 18 [P]   830-281-3486
   pleasantoncountryclub.com
Plum Creek GC, *Kyle* .... 18 [P]   512-262-5555
   plumcreekgolf.com
Point Venture GC, *Point Venture* .... 9 [P]   512-267-2768
   prismnet.com/~jerrym/golf.htm
Prairie Lakes GC, *Grand Prairie* .... 27 [M]   972-263-0661
   prairielakesgolf.com
Prairie Oaks Ranch, *Bowie* .... 9 [R]   214-673-7552
   poranch.net
Preston Trail GC, *Dallas* .... 18 [V]   972-380-0469
Preston West Par 3 GC, *Amarillo* .... 18 [P]   806-353-7003
Prestonwood CC - Creek, *Dallas* .... 18 [V]   972-239-7111
   prestonwoodcc.org
Prestonwood CC - Hills, *Plano* .... 18 [V]   972-239-7111
   prestonwoodcc.org
Prestwick GC, *Midlothian* .... 18 [P]   972-723-2232
Princedale GC, *Pittsburg* .... 9 [P]   903-856-3737
Quail Creek CC, *San Marcos* .... 18 [P]   512-353-1665
   quailcreek-cc.com
Quail Valley GC, *Missouri City* .... 36 [S]   281-403-5910
   golfquailvalley.com
Quanah CC, *Quanah* .... 9 [V]   940-663-2069
Quicksand At Woodcreek GC, *Wimberley* ... 18 [R]   512-847-9700
Quicksand GC, *San Angelo* .... 18 [P]   325-482-8337
   quicksandsanangelo.com
Ranchland Hills GC, *Midland* .... 18 [P]   432-683-2041
   ranchlandhillsgolf.com
Rancho Viejo Resort & CC, *Rancho Viejo* .... 36 [R]   956-350-4000
   playrancho.com
Randolph Oaks GC, *Randolph* .... 18 [A]   210-652-4570
Rankin GC, *Rankin* .... 9 [M]   432-693-2401
Ratliff Ranch Golf Links, *Odessa* .... 18 [P]   432-550-8181
   ratliffranchgolfodessa.com
Raven Nest GC, *Huntsville* .... 18 [P]   936-438-8588
   ravennestgolf.com
Raveneaux CC, *Spring* .... 36 [V]   281-370-6370
   raveneaux.com
Rayburn CC, *Brookeland* .... 27 [R]   409-698-2271
   rayburnresort.com
Raymondville GC, *Raymondville* .... 9 [M]   956-689-3594
Red Oak Valley GC, *Red Oak* .... 18 [P]   972-617-3249
Red Wolf Golf Resort, *Huffman* .... 18 [P]   281-324-1841
   redwolfgolf.com
Redstone GC, *Humble* .... 36 [P]   281-454-6590
   redstonegolfclub.com
Reese Golf Ctr, *Lubbock* .... 18 [P]   806-885-1247
Reeves County GC, *Pecos* .... 9 [M]   432-447-2858
Refugio County CC, *Refugio* .... 9 [P]   361-526-5554
Reindeer Hill GC (Pasture), *Pritchett* .... 9 [P]   903-734-3006
   pasturegolf.com/courses/reindeerhill.htm
Ridgeview Ranch GC, *Plano* .... 18 [P]   972-390-1039
   ridgeviewgc.com
Ridgewood CC, *Waco* .... 18 [V]   254-772-2050
   ridgewoodwaco.com
Ridglea CC - North Family, *Fort Worth* .... 18 [V]   817-732-8111
   ridgleacountryclub.com
Ridglea CC - South Championship, *Fort Worth*... 18 [V]   817-732-8111
   ridgleacountryclub.com
Rio Colorado GC, *Bay City* .... 18 [P]   979-244-2955
   riocoloradogolfcourse.com
River Bend GC, *Brownsville* .... 18 [R]   956-548-0192
   riverbendresort.us

River Creek Park GC, *Burkburnett* .... 18 [M]   940-855-3361
   rivercreekpark.com
River Crest CC, *Fort Worth* .... 18 [V]   817-738-9221
   rivercrest-cc.org
River Crossing Club, *Spring Branch* .... 18 [V]   830-904-4653
   rivercrossingclub.com
River Hills CC, *Corpus Christi* .... 18 [V]   361-387-3563
River Oaks CC, *Houston* .... 18 [V]   713-529-4321
   riveroakscc.net
River Place CC, *Austin* .... 18 [V]   512-346-1114
   riverplaceclub.com
River Plantation CC, *Conroe* .... 27 [V]   936-271-1083
   riverplantationcc.com
River Pointe GC, *Richmond* .... 18 [P]   281-343-9995
   riverpointegolf.com
River Ridge GC, *Sealy* .... 27 [P]   979-885-3333
   riverridgegolfclub.com
River Terrace GC, *Houston* .... 18 [P]   281-452-2183
Riverbend CC, *Sugar Land* .... 18 [V]   281-491-2500
   riverbendcountryclub.org
Riverchase GC, *Coppell* .... 18 [P]   972-462-8281
   palmergolf.com
Riverhill CC, *Kerrville* .... 18 [V]   830-792-1143
   riverhillcc.com
Riverside GC, *Grand Prairie* .... 18 [P]   817-640-7800
   riverside-golfclub.com
Riverside GC, *San Antonio* .... 27 [M]   210-533-8371
   riversidegolfsa.com
Riverside GC, *Victoria* .... 27 [V]   361-573-4521
Riverside GC, *Austin* .... 18 [P]   512-386-7077
   riverside-gc.com
Riverside Hills GC, *San Angelo* .... 18 [P]   325-653-6130
Roaring Springs Ranch GC, *Roaring Springs* ... 9 [V]   806-348-7267
Rock Creek GC, *Gordonville* .... 9 [R]   903-523-5105
   rockcreekontexoma.com
Rockdale CC, *Rockdale* .... 9 [V]   512-446-4013
Rockport CC Members Assoc, *Rockport* ..... 18 [V]   361-729-8324
   rockportcountryclub.net
Rocksprings CC, *Rocksprings* .... 9 [V]   830-683-4224
Rockwood Muni GC, *Fort Worth* .... 27 [M]   817-624-1771
   fortworthgolf.org
Rockwood Par-3 GC & DR, *Fort Worth* .... 9 [P]   817-624-8311
Rolling Hills CC, *Arlington* .... 18 [V]   817-261-6221
   rollinghills.cc
Rolling Hills GC, *Rusk* .... 9 [P]   903-683-8442
   rollinghillsgolf.com
Rolling Oaks GC, *Rising Star* .... 18 [P]   254-643-4563
Ross Rogers Muni GC, *Amarillo* .... 36 [M]   806-378-3086
   amarilloparks.org
Rotan GC, *Rotan* .... 9 [M]   325-735-2251
Royal Oaks CC, *Dallas* .... 18 [V]   214-691-0339
   roccdallas.com
Royal Oaks CC Houston, *Houston* .... 18 [V]   281-899-3200
   royaloakscc.com
Rusty Rail GC, *Jefferson* .... 9 [P]   903-665-7245
   rustyrailgolfclub.com
Salt Fork River Estates G Complex, *Seymour* ... 9 [M]   940-889-2833
Sammons Golf Links, *Temple* .... 18 [M]   254-771-2030
   golfsammons.com
San Angelo CC, *San Angelo* .... 18 [V]   325-651-7395
   sanangelocountryclub.net
San Antonio CC, *San Antonio* .... 18 [V]   210-824-8861
   sanantoniocc.com

[A] = MILITARY   [M] = MUNICIPAL   [P] = PUBLIC   [R] = RESORT

Golf Yellow Pages, 18th Edition — TEXAS

San Felipe CC, *del Rio*..9 [S] 830-775-3953
sanfelipecc.com
San Jacinto College GC, *Pasadena*..................... 9 [U] 281-476-1880
sanjac.edu
San Pedro GC & DR, *San Antonio*......................9 [M] 210-349-5113
alamocitygolftrail.com
San Saba River GC, *San Saba* ....18 [M] 325-372-3212
Sand Hills G&CC, *Campbell*................................ 9 [U] 903-886-4455
Sante Fe Park GC, *San Angelo* ....9 [P] 325-657-4485
Scott Schriener Muni GC, *Kerrville*....................18 [M] 830-257-4982
kerrville.org
Scurry County GC, *Snyder* ....9 [P] 325-573-7101
Shadow Glen GC, *Manor*...................................18 [P] 512-278-1304
shadowglengolf.com
Shadow Hawk GC, *Richmond*............................ 18 [V] 281-340-7205
shadowhawkgolfclub.com
Shadow Hills GC, *Lubbock*.................................18 [P] 806-793-9700
shadowhillsgolf.com
Shadow Lakes GC, *Mt Pleasant* ....9 [P] 903-572-1288
shadowlakescorp.com
Shady Oaks CC, *Fort Worth* .... 27 [V] 817-732-1271
shadyoaksclub.com
Shady Oaks GC, *Baird*.. 18 [S] 325-854-1757
Shady Valley GC, *Arlington*................................ 18 [V] 817-275-8771
shadyvalley.com
Shamrock CC, *Shamrock* ....9 [P] 806-256-3622
Sharpstown Park GC, *Houston* ....18 [M] 713-988-2099
houstontx.gov/municipalgolf
Shary Muni GC, *Mission*.....................................27 [M] 956-580-8770
Sherrill Park GC, *Richardson*..............................36 [P] 972-234-1416
sherrillparkgolf.com
Sienna Plantation GC, *Missouri City* .... 18 [S] 281-778-4653
siennagolf.com
Silsbee CC, *Silsbee* .... 9 [V] 409-385-4372
Silverhorn GC, *San Antonio*...............................18 [P] 210-545-5300
silverhorngolfclub.com
Singing Winds GC, *Bronte*...................................9 [P] 325-473-2156
Sinton Muni GC, *Sinton*.....................................18 [M] 361-364-9013
Sky Creek Ranch GC, *Keller*...............................18 [P] 817-498-1414
skycreekranch.com
Slaton Muni GC, *Slaton*.......................................9 [M] 806-828-3269
Sonora GC, *Sonora*...9 [M] 325-387-3680
South Padre Island GC (Private) , *Port Isabel*..... 9 [V] 956-943-5678
spigolf.com
South Padre Island GC (Public), *Port Isabel* ....18 [V] 956-943-5678
spigolf.com
Southern Hills GC, *Gladewater*..........................18 [P] 903-984-5335
southernhillsclub.com
Southern Oaks GC, *Burleson* ....18 [S] 817-426-2400
Southwyck GC, *Pearland*....................................18 [P] 713-436-9999
southwyckgc.com
Spanish Oaks GC, *Bee Cave*............................... 18 [V] 512-421-8530
spanishoaks.com
Spirit Lake GC, *Tioga*... 9 [R] 940-437-5000
spiritofthewestresort.net
Split Rail Links & GC, *Aledo*..............................18 [P] 817-441-4653
Spring Creek CC, *Crockett* ....9 [V] 936-544-7848
Spring Valley GC, *Spring* ....9 [P] 281-351-8628
springvalleygolfclub.com
Spur GC, *Spur* ....9 [M] 806-271-3671
Squaw Creek GC, *Willow Park* ....18 [P] 817-441-8185
lmra.org

Squaw Valley GC, *Glen Rose* ....36 [M] 254-897-7956
squawvalleygc.com
Stamford G&CC, *Stamford*................................. 9 [P] 325-773-5001
Star Harbor GC, *Malakoff*...................................9 [M] 903-489-0091
Starr Hollow GC, *Tolar*.. 9 [V] 254-834-3464
Stephen F Austin CC, *San Felipe*........................18 [P] 979-885-2811
sfaustingc.com
Stevens Park GC, *Dallas* ....18 [M] 214-670-7506
stevensparkgolf.com
Stewart Peninsula GC, *The Colony*......................9 [P] 972-625-8700
stewartpeninsulagolf.com
Stone Creek GC, *Sherman* ....18 [P] 903-870-7980
stonecreekcc.com
Stone Gate GC, *Lubbock* ....18 [P] 806-748-1448
playstonegategolf.com
Stone River GC, *Royse City*................................18 [P] 972-636-2254
stonerivergolf.com
Stonebriar CC, *Frisco*.. 36 [V] 972-625-8916
stonebriar.com
Stonebridge Ranch CC - Dye Course, *McKinney* .. 18 [V] 972-529-5992
stonebridgeranch.com
Stonebridge Ranch CC - Hills Course, *McKinney* . 27 [V] 972-540-2000
stonebridgeranch.com
Stonetree GC, *Killeen* ....18 [M] 254-699-6034
golfkilleen.com
StoneyRidge GC, *Childress* ....18 [M] 940-937-2481
childresstexas.net
Stratford CC, *Stratford*.. 9 [V] 806-396-2259
Sugar Creek GC, *Sugar Land* ....27 [V] 281-494-9131
sugarcreekcctexas.com
Sugar Hill GC, *Houston*......................................18 [P] 281-561-5252
Sugar Tree G&CC, *Lipan*.................................... 18 [S] 817-341-1111
sugartreegolf.com
Sulphur Springs CC, *Sulphur Springs* ....18 [P] 903-885-4861
Sundance GC, *New Braunfels*............................18 [P] 830-629-3817
sundancegolf.com
Sundown Muni GC, *Sundown* ....9 [M] 806-229-6186
sundowntx.com
Sunset CC, *Odessa* ....27 [P] 432-366-1061
Sunset Golf Ctr, *Grand Prairie*.............................9 [P] 214-331-8057
sunsetgolfdallas.com
Sunset Grove CC, *Orange* .... 18 [V] 409-883-9454
sunsetgrovecc.com
Sunshine CC Estates, *Harlingen*.......................... 9 [V] 956-425-1420
Sweetwater CC, *Sugar Land* .... 36 [V] 281-980-4653
swcclub.com
Sweetwater CC, *Sweetwater*.............................18 [P] 325-235-8093
Sycamore Creek GC, *Fort Worth* ....9 [M] 817-535-7241
fortworthgolf.org
T Bar CC, *Tahoka* .... 9 [V] 806-998-5305
Tangle Oaks GC, *Hawley* ....18 [P] 325-537-9023
Tangle Ridge GC, *Grand Prairie* ....18 [M] 972-299-6637
tangleridge.com
Tanglewood Resort, *Pottsboro*...........................18 [R] 903-786-4140
tanglewoodresort.com
Tapatio Springs CC & Resort, *Boerne*................27 [R] 830-537-4611
tapatio.com
Tascosa CC, *Amarillo*... 18 [V] 806-374-2351
Tawakoni GC, *West Tawakoni*...........................18 [P] 903-447-2981
Tejas GC, *Stephenville* .... 9 [V] 254-965-3904
Temple College GC, *Temple* .... 9 [U] 254-773-0888
templejc.edu

[S] = SEMI-PRIVATE [V] = PRIVATE [U] = UNIVERSITY [N] = UNIVERSITY-PRIVATE

TEXAS — Golf Yellow Pages, 18th Edition

Tenison Park, *Dallas* .... 36 [S] 214-670-1402
  tenisonpark.com
Teravista GC, *Round Rock* .... 18 [P] 512-651-9850
  teravistagolf.com
Texaco CC, *Houston* .... 18 [M] 713-453-7501
  texacogolfclub.com
Texarkana Golf Ranch, *Texarkana* .... 18 [P] 903-334-7401
  hankhaneygolf.com
Texas A&M Univ GC, *College Station* .... 18 [U] 979-845-1723
  recsports.tamu.edu/programs/golf
Texas National GC, *Willis* .... 18 [P] 936-856-4233
  texasnationalgolfclub.com
Texas Star GC, *Euless* .... 18 [S] 817-685-7888
  texasstargolf.com
Texas State Univ San Marcos, *San Marcos* .... 9 [U] 512-245-7593
  campusrecreation.txstate.edu
Texas Sundown Ranch GC, *Sanger* .... 9 [R] 940-458-5979
Texas Womans Univ GC, *Denton* .... 18 [U] 940-898-3163
  twu.edu
The Bandit GC, *New Braunfels* .... 18 [P] 830-609-4665
  banditgolfclub.com
The Battleground at Deer Park, *Deer Park* .... 18 [M] 281-478-4653
  deerparktx.gov
The Bend at Brazoria, *Rosharon* .... 9 [S] 281-431-2954
The Bonham GC, *Bonham* .... 9 [V] 903-583-8815
The Bridges GC, *Gunter* .... 18 [S] 903-696-0022
  bridgestexas.com
The Briggs Ranch GC, *San Antonio* .... 18 [V] 210-670-9400
  briggsranchrealty.com
The Challenge At Cypress Hills, *Waskom* .... 18 [P] 903-938-4941
  thechallengegolfgroup.com
The Challenge At Eagles Bluff, *Bullard* .... 18 [V] 903-825-2999
  eaglesbluff.com
The Challenge At Gladewater, *Gladewater* .... 18 [P] 903-845-4566
  gladewatercc.com
The Challenge At Oak Forest, *Longview* .... 18 [V] 903-297-3448
  thechallengeatof.com
The Champions Course At Weeks Park,
  Wichita Falls .... 18 [M] 940-767-6107
  weeksparkgolf.com
The Cliffs Resort, *Graford* .... 18 [R] 940-779-4520
  thecliffsresort.com
The Club At Cimarron, *Mission* .... 18 [V] 956-581-7408
  clubatcimarron.com
The Club At Comanche Trace, *Kerrville* .... 27 [V] 830-792-6282
  comanchetrace.com
The Club At Concan, *Concan* .... 18 [P] 830-232-4471
  concangolf.com
The Club at Falcon Point, *Katy* .... 18 [V] 281-392-7888
  falconpoint.com
The Club At Runaway Bay, *Runaway Bay* .... 18 [P] 940-575-2225
  runawaybay.com
The Club at Sonterra, *San Antonio* .... 36 [V] 210-496-1560
  clubatsonterra.com
The Club of Cordillera Ranch, *Boerne* .... 18 [V] 830-336-4653
  cordilleraranch.com
The Country Place, *Carrollton* .... 9 [V] 972-416-0660
  thecountryplace.org
The Courses of Clear Creek, *Fort Hood* .... 27 [A] 254-287-4130
  hoodmwr.com/coursesof_cc.htm
The Deerwood Club of Kingwood, *Kingwood* ..... 18 [V] 281-360-1065
  theclubsofkingwood.com
The Dominion CC, *San Antonio* .... 18 [V] 210-698-1146
  the-dominion.com

The Falls Resort & Club, *New Ulm* .... 18 [R] 979-992-3123
  thefallsresort.com
The First Tee Junior Golf-FM Law Pk, *Houston* .... 9 [M] 713-264-2100
  thefirstteehoustonfmlawpark.org
The GC At Castle Hills, *Lewisville* .... 18 [R] 972-899-7400
  castlehillsgolfclub.com
The GC At Champions Circle, *Fort Worth* .... 18 [R] 817-497-2582
  championscirclegolf.com
The GC At Crown Valley, *Weatherford* .... 18 [P] 817-441-2222
  crownvalleygolfclub.com
The GC At Crystal Falls, *Leander* .... 18 [M] 512-259-5855
  crystalfallsgolf.com
The GC At Fossil Creek, *Fort Worth* .... 18 [P] 817-847-1900
  thegolfclubatfossilcreek.com
The GC At Frisco Lakes, *Frisco* .... 18 [P] 972-292-3089
  friscolakesgc.com
The GC At McKinney, *McKinney* .... 18 [V] 972-540-6880
  thegolfclubatmckinney.com
The GC At Star Ranch, *Hutto* .... 18 [P] 512-252-4653
  starranchgolf.com
The GC At the Resort, *Fort Worth* .... 18 [R] 817-750-2178
  resortgolfclub.com
The GC At Twin Creeks, *Allen* .... 18 [P] 972-390-8888
  twincreeksgolfclub.com
The GC of Dallas, *Dallas* .... 18 [V] 214-331-4336
  golfclubdallas.com
The GC of Texas, *San Antonio* .... 18 [R] 210-677-0027
  golfcluboftexas.com
The Hawk GC, *Spring Branch* .... 18 [P] 830-885-7495
  thehawkgolfclub.com
The Lake CC, *Waco* .... 36 [S] 254-756-2161
  texasjuniorgolf.org
The Legends GC on Lake LBJ, *Kingsland* .... 18 [R] 325-388-8888
  legendsgolftx.com
The Links At West Fork, *Conroe* .... 18 [P] 936-441-6193
  westforkgolf.com
The Newport Dunes GC, *Port Aransas* .... 18 [R] 361-749-4653
  newportdunesgolf.com
The Northwood Club, *Dallas* .... 18 [V] 972-934-0544
  northwoodclub.org
The Palms GC At Pleasure Island, *Port Arthur* ..... 18 [P] 409-984-5000
  pleasureislandtx.com
The Patch GC, *Groves* .... 9 [P] 409-963-3763
The Practice Tee Golf Ctr, *Richardson* .... 9 [M] 972-235-6540
  thepracticetee.com
The Quarry GC, *San Antonio* .... 18 [P] 210-824-4500
  quarrygolf.com
The Rawls Course at Texas Tech, *Lubbock* .... 18 [U] 806-742-4653
  texastechgolf.ttu.edu
The Republic GC, *San Antonio* .... 18 [P] 210-359-0000
  republicgolfclub.com
The Retreat, *Cleburne* .... 18 [V] 817-556-2700
  theretreat-texas.com
The Timberlinks At Denton, *Denton* .... 9 [P] 940-380-1318
  timberlinksgolf.com
The Trails of Frisco GC, *Frisco* .... 18 [S] 972-668-4653
  thetrailsoffriscogc.com
The Training Station, *Richmond* .... 9 [P] 281-343-8800
  gotrainingstation.com
The Tribute at The Colony, *The Colony* .... 18 [R] 972-370-5465
  thetributegc.com
The Village GC, *Conroe* .... 27 [M] 936-856-5531
  thevillagegc.com

208   [A] = MILITARY   [M] = MUNICIPAL   [P] = PUBLIC   [R] = RESORT

Golf Yellow Pages, 18th Edition — TEXAS

Course	Location	Holes	Type	Phone
The Westin La Cantera Resort	San Antonio	18	[R]	210-558-4653
lacanteragolfclub.com				
The Woodlands CC - Player Course	The Woodlands	18	[R]	281-863-1490
thewoodlandscc.com				
The Woodlands CC Palmer Course	Spring	27	[V]	281-863-1440
thewoodlandscc.com				
The Woodlands CC Tournament Course	Spring	18	[R]	281-863-1540
thewoodlandscc.com				
The Woods at Jacksonville	Jacksonville	18	[V]	903-589-1759
thechallengeatthewoods.com				
Thorntree CC	Desoto	18	[V]	972-296-7317
thorntreecc.com				
Throckmorton CC	Throckmorton	9	[P]	940-849-3161
Tierra Del Sol	Pharr	18	[M]	956-702-2320
Tierra Santa GC	Weslaco	18	[P]	956-973-1811
tierrasanta.com				
Tierra Verde GC	Arlington	18	[M]	817-478-8500
arlingtongolf.com				
Timarron CC	Southlake	18	[V]	817-481-7529
timarronclub.com				
Timber Creek GC	Friendswood	27	[P]	281-993-1140
timbercreekgolfclub.com				
Timberview GC	Fort Worth	18	[P]	817-478-3601
timberviewgolf.com				
Tin Cup CC	Merkel	18	[P]	325-928-3193
Tomball CC	Tomball	18	[V]	281-351-5102
tomballcountryclub.org				
Tony Butler Muni GC	Harlingen	27	[M]	956-216-5970
myharlingen.us				
Tour 18 GC Dallas	Flower Mound	18	[P]	817-430-2000
tour18-dallas.com				
Tour 18 GC Houston	Humble	18	[P]	281-540-1818
tour18golf.com				
Town East Golf Ctr	Sunnyvale	9	[P]	972-226-8749
TPC Craig Ranch	McKinney	18	[V]	972-747-9005
tpccraigranch.com				
TPC San Antonio	San Antonio	36	[R]	210-491-5806
tpcsanantonio.com				
Traditions Club At Texas A&M	Bryan	18	[V]	979-779-1007
traditionsclub.com				
Treasure Hills GC	Harlingen	18	[P]	956-425-1700
treasurehillsgc.com				
Trophy Club of Dallas	Trophy Club	36	[V]	817-837-1911
trophyclub-dallas.com				
Tropic Star RV Resort GC	Pharr	9	[R]	956-787-5957
Tule Lake GC	Tulia	9	[P]	806-995-3400
Turkey Run	Rising Star	9	[S]	254-643-4602
Turtle Hill GC	Muenster	18	[P]	940-759-4896
playtheturtle.net				
Twin Creeks CC	Cedar Park	18	[V]	512-331-5900
twincreeksclub.com				
Twin Lakes GC	Canton	18	[P]	903-567-1112
twinlakesgolfcourse.com				
Twin Rivers GC	Waco	18	[S]	254-848-7800
twinriversgolfclub.net				
Twin Wells GC	Irving	18	[M]	972-438-4340
twinwellsgc.com				
Underwood G Complex	El Paso	36	[A]	915-562-1273
Univ of Texas GC	Austin	18	[N]	512-266-6464
utgolfclub.com				
Up to Par	Garland	9	[P]	972-530-0585
Uvalde Memorial Park GC	Uvalde	18	[P]	830-278-6155
Vaaler Creek GC	Blanco	18	[S]	830-833-0706
vaalercreekgolfclub.com				
Valley International CC	Brownsville	27	[R]	956-546-5331
Van Zandt CC	Canton	18	[V]	903-567-2336
vanzandtcc.com				
Vaquero Club	Westlake	18	[V]	817-746-6000
vaqueroclub.com				
Victoria CC	Victoria	18	[V]	361-575-6161
victoriacc.com				
Village Exec GC	Weslaco	9	[P]	956-968-6516
Vista Hills CC	El Paso	18	[V]	915-592-6565
vistahillscc.com				
Walden G&CC	Montgomery	18	[V]	936-448-4668
waldengolf.com				
Walden on Lake Houston	Humble	18	[V]	832-445-2115
waldencc.com				
Waller CC Estates	Waller	9	[S]	936-931-3335
Walnut Creek CC	Mansfield	36	[V]	817-473-6111
walnutcreekcc.com				
Ward County GC	Monahans	18	[M]	432-943-5044
WaterChase GC	Fort Worth	18	[P]	817-861-4653
waterchasegc.com				
Waterford Texas	Marble Falls	18	[V]	877-798-8183
waterfordtexas.com				
Waterview GC	Rowlett	18	[M]	972-463-8900
waterview.americangolf.com				
Waterwood National Resort & CC	Huntsville	18	[R]	936-891-5050
waterwoodnational.com				
Waxahachie CC	Waxahachie	18	[S]	972-937-3521
waxahachiecountryclub.com				
Webb Hill CC	Wolfe City	18	[P]	903-496-2221
webbhillcountryclub.com				
Wedgewood GC	Conroe	18	[P]	936-441-4653
wedgewoodgolfcourse.com				
Weimar GC	Weimar	9	[M]	979-725-8624
Wellington CC	Wellington	9	[P]	806-447-5050
West Brazos Golf Ctr	Brazoria	9	[P]	979-798-4653
westbrazosgolfcenter.com				
Westdale Hills GC	Euless	9	[P]	817-267-3304
westdalehillsgolf.com				
Western Texas College GC	Snyder	9	[U]	325-573-9291
wtc.edu				
Weston Lakes CC	Fulshear	18	[V]	281-346-1967
wlakes.com				
WestRidge GC	McKinney	18	[P]	972-346-2212
westridgegolfcourse.com				
Westwood GC	Houston	18	[V]	713-774-2521
wwgolfclub.com				
Westwood Shores CC	Trinity	18	[V]	936-594-9172
Wharton CC	Wharton	9	[V]	979-532-5940
Whispering Pines GC	Trinity	18	[V]	936-594-4980
whisperingpinesgolfclub.com				
White Bluff Resort	Whitney	36	[R]	254-694-0303
whitebluffresort.com				
White Wing GC	Georgetown	18	[P]	512-864-1244
sctxca.org				
Whitestone GC	Benbrook	18	[P]	817-249-9996
whitestonegolf.com				
Wichita Falls CC	Wichita Falls	18	[V]	940-767-1481
wichitafallscc.com				
Wildcat GC	Houston	36	[P]	713-413-3400
wildcatgolfclub.com				

[S] = SEMI-PRIVATE [V] = PRIVATE [U] = UNIVERSITY [N] = UNIVERSITY-PRIVATE

TEXAS

Golf Yellow Pages, 18th Edition

Course	Location	Holes	Type	Phone
Wilderness GC,	Lake Jackson	18	[M]	979-297-4653
thewildernessgc.com				
Wildflower CC,	Temple	18	[V]	254-771-1177
wildflowerclub.com				
Wildhorse GC of Robson Ranch,	Denton	18	[P]	940-246-1001
robson.com/the-preserve/golf				
Wildwood GC,	Village Mills	18	[R]	409-834-2940
wildwoodresortcity.com				
Willow Brook CC,	Tyler	18	[V]	903-592-8229
wbcctyler.com				
Willow Creek GC,	Spring	18	[V]	281-376-4061
willowcreekclub.com				
Willow Creek Golf Ctr,	Abilene	9	[P]	325-691-0909
willowcreekpar3.com				
Willow Fork CC,	Katy	18	[V]	281-579-6611
willowforkclub.com				
Willow Springs GC,	San Antonio	18	[M]	210-226-6721
willowspringsgolfsa.com				
Willow Springs GC,	Haslet	18	[P]	817-439-1318
wsgolf.com				
Wind Creek GC,	Sheppard AFB	18	[A]	940-676-6369
Windcrest GC,	Windcrest	9	[V]	210-655-1421
windcrestgolfclub.com				
Windrose GC,	Spring	18	[P]	281-370-8900
windrosegolfclub.com				
Winkler County GC,	Kermit	9	[P]	432-586-9243
Winters CC,	Winters	9	[P]	325-754-4679
Wolf Point Club (Personal),	Port Lavaca	18	[ ]	713-467-2207
WolfCreek Golf Links,	Colorado City	9	[P]	325-728-5514
Wolfdancer GC,	Lost Pines	18	[R]	512-308-4770
wolfdancergolfclub.com				
Wood Hollow Golf & DR,	Longview	18	[P]	903-663-4653
Woodbridge GC,	Wylie	18	[P]	972-429-5100
wbgolfclub.com				
Woodforest GC At Fish Creek,	Montgomery	27	[P]	936-588-8800
woodforestgolf.com				
Woodhaven CC,	Fort Worth	18	[V]	817-457-5150
woodhavenclub.com				
Woodlake GC,	San Antonio	18	[P]	210-661-4141
woodlakegolfclub.com				
Woodland Hills GC,	Nacogdoches	18	[P]	936-564-2762
woodlandhillsgolfclub.com				
Woodlawn CC,	Sherman	18	[P]	903-893-9657
woodlawncountryclub.com				
World Houston GC,	Houston	18	[P]	281-449-8384
worldhoustongolf.com				
Wright Park Muni GC,	Greenville	9	[P]	903-457-2996
ci.greenville.tx.us				
Yoakum County GC,	Denver City	18	[P]	806-592-2947
Yoakum Muni GC,	Yoakum	9	[P]	361-293-5682
cityofyoakum.org				
Yorktown CC,	Yorktown	9	[P]	361-564-9191
YWCA Hueco Conf & Rec Ctr Golf,	El Paso	9	[S]	915-855-8075
Z Boaz GC,	Fort Worth	18	[M]	817-738-6287
fortworthgolf.org				

UTAH

Course	Location	Holes	Type	Phone
Alpine CC,	Highland	18	[V]	801-322-3971
alpinecountryclub.org				
Bear Lake GC,	Garden City	9	[P]	435-946-8742
bearlake.com				
Ben Lomond GC,	Ogden	18	[P]	801-782-7754
benlomondgolf.com				
Birch Creek GC,	Smithfield	18	[M]	435-563-6825
birchcreekgolf.com				
Bloomington CC,	St George	18	[V]	435-673-4687
bloomingtoncountryclub.com				
Bonneville GC,	Salt Lake City	18	[M]	801-583-9513
slc-golf.com				
Bountiful Ridge GC,	Bountiful	18	[M]	801-298-6040
bountifulutah.gov				
Camperworld Hot Springs,	Garland	9	[P]	435-458-3200
camperworld.com				
Canyon Breeze GC,	Beaver	9	[M]	435-438-2601
beaverutah.net				
Canyon Hills Park GC,	Nephi	9	[M]	435-623-9930
Carbon County GC,	Helper	18	[P]	435-637-2388
carboncountryclub.com				
Cascade Golf Ctr,	Orem	18	[P]	801-225-6677
cascadegolfcenter.com				
Cedar Ridge GC,	Cedar City	18	[M]	435-586-2970
cedarcity.org				
Central Valley GC,	Salt Lake City	9	[P]	801-973-6271
centralvalleygolfcourse.net				
Cherokee Springs Golf & RV Resort,	Hatch	9	[R]	435-619-0391
cherokeespringsresort.com				
Copper GC,	Magna	9	[V]	801-250-6396
Coral Canyon GC,	Washington	18	[P]	435-688-1700
coralcanyongolf.com				
Coral Cliffs GC,	Kanab	9	[P]	435-644-5005
coralcliffsgolfcourse.com				
Cottonwood CC,	Salt Lake City	9	[V]	801-277-2691
cottonwoodcc.com				
Cove View GC,	Richfield	18	[M]	435-896-9987
coveviewgolf.com				
Crane Field GC,	Clinton	18	[P]	801-779-3800
cranefieldgolf.com				
Davis Park GC,	Fruit Heights	18	[M]	801-544-0401
davisparkgolfcourse.com				
Dinaland GC,	Vernal	18	[P]	435-781-1428
uintahrecreation.org				
Dixie Red Hills GC,	St George	9	[M]	435-627-4444
redrockgolftrail.com				
Eagle Lake GC,	Roy	9	[P]	801-825-3467
eaglelake-golf.com				
Eagle Mountain GC,	Brigham City	18	[M]	435-723-3212
eaglemountaingc.com				
Eaglewood GC,	North Salt Lake	18	[M]	801-299-0088
eaglewoodgolf.com				
El Monte GC,	Ogden	9	[P]	801-629-0694
ogdencity.com				
Entrada at Snow Canyon CC,	St George	18	[R]	435-674-7500
golfentrada.com				
Ferron Millsite GC,	Ferron	9	[P]	435-384-2887
Fore Lakes GC,	Murray	18	[P]	801-266-8621
Forest Dale GC,	Salt Lake City	9	[P]	801-483-5420
slc-golf.com				
Fox Hollow GC,	American Fork	18	[M]	801-756-3594
foxhollowutah.com				
Frank Skull GC,	Dugway	9	[A]	435-831-2305
Gladstan GC,	Payson	18	[M]	801-465-5286
gladstangolf.com				
Glen Eagle GC,	Syracuse	18	[P]	801-773-4653
golfgleneagle.com				
Glendale GC,	Salt Lake City	18	[M]	801-974-2403
slc-golf.com				

[A] = MILITARY   [M] = MUNICIPAL   [P] = PUBLIC   [R] = RESORT

UTAH

Course	Location	Holes	Type	Phone
Glenmoor GC	South Jordan	18	[P]	801-280-1742
Glenwild GC & Spa	Park City	18	[V]	435-615-9966

glenwild.com

| Green River GC | Green River | 9 | [M] | 435-564-8882 |

stateparkgolf.utah.gov

| Green Spring CC | Washington | 18 | [M] | 435-673-7888 |

greenspringgolfcourse.com

| Hidden Valley CC | Sandy | 27 | [V] | 801-571-2951 |

hiddenvalley.cc

| Hobble Creek GC | Springville | 18 | [M] | 801-489-6297 |

springville.org

| Homestead GC & Resort | Midway | 18 | [R] | 435-654-1102 |

homesteadresort.com

| Hubbard Memorial GC | Hill AFB | 18 | [A] | 801-777-3272 |

hill.af.mil

| Jeremy G&CC | Park City | 18 | [V] | 801-531-9000 |

thejeremy.com

| Jordan River Par 3 | Salt Lake City | 9 | [M] | 801-533-4527 |

slc-golf.com

| Kokopelli GC | Apple Valley | 18 | [P] | 435-272-4653 |

kokopelliut.com

| Lakeside GC | West Bountiful | 18 | [M] | 801-295-1019 |

lakesidegolfcourse.com

| Logan G&CC | Logan | 18 | [V] | 435-753-6050 |
| Logan River GC | Logan | 18 | [M] | 435-750-0123 |

loganutah.org

| Meadowbrook GC | Taylorsville | 18 | [M] | 801-266-0971 |

slcountygolf.slco.org

| Mick Riley GC | Murray | 18 | [M] | 801-266-8185 |

slcountygolf.slco.org

| Moab GC | Moab | 18 | [M] | 435-259-6488 |

go-utah.com/moabgolf

| Mount Ogden GC | Ogden | 18 | [M] | 801-629-0699 |
| Mountain Dell GC | Salt Lake City | 36 | [M] | 801-582-3812 |

slc-golf.com

| Mountain View GC | West Jordan | 18 | [M] | 801-255-9211 |

slcountygolf.slco.org

| Mulligans GC | Ogden | 9 | [P] | 801-392-4653 |
| Mulligans Golf & Game | South Jordan | 27 | [M] | 801-254-3377 |

mulligans-south.com

| Murray Parkway GC | Murray | 18 | [M] | 801-262-4653 |

murray.utah.gov

| Nibley Park GC | Salt Lake City | 9 | [M] | 801-483-5418 |

slc-golf.com

| Oakridge CC | Farmington | 18 | [V] | 801-295-5531 |

oakridgecc.com

| Ogden G&CC | Ogden | 18 | [V] | 801-621-2063 |

ogdencountryclub.com

| Old Mill GC | Salt Lake City | 18 | [M] | 801-424-1302 |

slcountygolf.slco.org

| Oquirrh Hills GC | Tooele | 18 | [M] | 435-882-4220 |

tooelecity.org

| Outlaw GC at Hideout Canyon | Park City | 18 | [V] | 877-878-0188 |

hideoutcanyon.com

| Palisade GC | Sterling | 18 | [R] | 435-835-4653 |

stateparkgolf.utah.gov

| Paradise Golf Resort | Fillmore | 9 | [P] | 435-743-4439 |

golfparadiseatfillmore.com

| Park City GC | Park City | 18 | [M] | 801-615-5800 |

parkcitygolfclub.org

| Park Meadows CC | Park City | 18 | [P] | 435-649-2460 |

parkmeadowscc.com

| Promontory Club - Dye Canyon Course | Park City | 18 | [V] | 435-333-4218 |

promontoryclub.com

| Promontory Club - Painted Valley Course | Park City | 18 | [V] | 435-333-4218 |

promontoryclub.com

| Red Ledges GC | Heber City | 18 | [V] | 435-657-4054 |

redledges.com

| Remuda GC | Ogden | 18 | [P] | 801-731-7200 |

remudagolf.com

| River Oaks GC | Sandy | 18 | [M] | 801-568-4653 |

sandy.utah.gov

| Riverbend GC | Riverton | 18 | [M] | 801-253-3673 |

slcountygolf.slco.org

| Riverside CC | Provo | 18 | [V] | 801-373-8262 |

riversidecountryclub.org

| Roosevelt Muni GC | Roosevelt | 18 | [M] | 435-722-9644 |

rooseveltcity.net

| Rose Park GC | Salt Lake City | 18 | [M] | 801-596-5030 |

slc-golf.com

| Round Valley GC | Morgan | 18 | [P] | 435-829-3796 |
| Sand Hollow Golf Resort | Hurricane | 27 | [R] | 435-656-4653 |

sandhollowresort.com

| Schneiters Bluff | West Point | 18 | [P] | 801-773-0731 |

schneitersgolf.com

| Schneiters Pebble Brook GC | Sandy | 18 | [P] | 801-566-2181 |
| Schneiters Riverside GC | Ogden | 18 | [P] | 801-399-4636 |

schneitersgolf.com

| Sherwood Hills GC | Wellsville | 9 | [P] | 435-245-6055 |

sherwoodhills.com

| Sky Mountain GC | Hurricane | 18 | [M] | 435-635-7888 |

cityofhurricane.com

| Skyline Mountain Resort & GC | Fairview | 9 | [R] | 435-427-9575 |

skylinemountain.com

| Skyway G&CC | Tremonton | 9 | [P] | 435-257-5706 |
| Soldier Hollow GC | Midway | 36 | [M] | 435-654-7442 |

soldierhollow.com

| South Mountain GC | Draper | 18 | [M] | 801-495-0500 |

slcountygolf.slco.org

| Southgate GC | St George | 18 | [M] | 435-627-4440 |

redrockgolftrail.com

| Spanish Oaks GC | Spanish Fork | 18 | [M] | 801-798-9816 |

spanishfork.org

| St George GC | St George | 18 | [M] | 435-627-4404 |

redrockgolftrail.com

| Stansbury Park GC | Tooele | 18 | [P] | 801-328-1483 |

stansburygolf.com

| Stonebridge GC At Lake Park | West Valley City | 27 | [M] | 801-957-9000 |

golfstonebridgeutah.com

| Sun Hills GC | Layton | 18 | [P] | 801-771-4814 |

sunhillsgolf.com

| Sunbrook GC | St George | 27 | [M] | 435-627-4727 |

redrockgolftrail.com

| Sunriver GC | St George | 18 | [P] | 801-986-0001 |

sunrivergolf.com

| Sunset View GC | Delta | 18 | [M] | 435-864-2508 |

golfsunsetview.com

| Swan Lakes GC | Layton | 9 | [P] | 801-546-1045 |

swanlakesgolf.com

| Talisker GC At Tuhaye | Kamas | 18 | [V] | 435-333-3636 |

taliskerclub.com

| TalonsCove at Saratoga Springs | Saratoga Springs | 18 | [P] | 801-407-3030 |

talonscove.com

| Thanksgiving Point GC | Lehi | 18 | [R] | 801-768-7401 |

thanksgivingpoint.com

| The Barn GC | Ogden | 18 | [P] | 801-782-7320 |
| The Cedar Hills GC | Cedar Hills | 18 | [M] | 801-796-1705 |

cedarhillsgolfclub.com

[S] = SEMI-PRIVATE   [V] = PRIVATE   [U] = UNIVERSITY   [N] = UNIVERSITY-PRIVATE

UTAH

The Country Club, *Salt Lake City* .... 18 [V]   801-487-7569
  saltlakecountryclub.com
The Hideout GC, *Monticello* .... 18 [M]   435-587-2200
  hideoutgolf.com
The Links At Overlake, *Tooele* .... 18 [P]   435-882-8802
  overlakegolf.com
The Links At Sleepy Ridge, *Orem* .... 18 [M]   801-434-4653
  sleepyridgegolf.com
The Ranches GC, *Eagle Mountain* .... 18 [P]   801-789-8100
  theranchesgolfclub.com
The Reserves At East Bay, *Provo* .... 27 [P]   801-373-6262
  eastbaygolf.com
Thunderbird GC, *Orderville* .... 9 [R]   435-648-2188
Univ of Utah GC, *Salt Lake City* .... 9 [U]   801-581-6511
  utah.edu/campusrec
Valderra GC at the Ledges, *St George* .... 18 [P]   435-634-4640
  ledges.com
Valley View GC, *Layton* .... 18 [M]   801-546-1630
  valleyviewutah.com
Victory Ranch GC, *Kamas* .... 18 [V]   435-785-5030
  victoryranchclub.com
Wasatch Mt St Park GC, *Midway* .... 36 [M]   435-654-0532
  stateparkgolf.utah.gov
West Ridge GC, *Salt Lake City* .... 18 [M]   801-966-4653
  golfwestridge.com
Willow Creek CC, *Sandy* .... 18 [V]   801-942-1621
  willowcreekcc.com
Wingpointe GC, *Salt Lake City* .... 18 [M]   801-575-2345
  slc-golf.com
Wolf Creek GC & Resort, *Eden* .... 18 [R]   801-745-3737
  wolfcreekresort.com

VERMONT

Alburg Golf Links, *Alburg* .... 18 [P]   802-796-4248
  alburggolflinks.com
Apple Island Resort GC, *South Hero* .... 9 [R]   802-372-9600
  appleislandresort.com
Arrowhead GC, *Milton* .... 9 [P]   802-893-0234
Bakersfield CC, *Bakersfield* .... 18 [P]   802-933-5100
Barton CC, *Barton* .... 18 [P]   802-525-1126
  bartongolfclub.com
Basin Harbor Club, *Vergennes* .... 18 [R]   802-475-2309
  basinharbor.com
Bellows Falls CC, *Bellows Falls* .... 9 [S]   802-463-9809
Blush Hill CC, *Waterbury* .... 9 [P]   802-244-8974
  blushhillcountryclub.com
Bradford GC, *Bradford* .... 9 [P]   802-222-5207
  bradfordgolfclubinc.com
Brattleboro CC, *Brattleboro* .... 18 [P]   802-257-7380
  brattleborogolf.com
Burlington CC, *Burlington* .... 18 [V]   802-658-3856
  burlingtoncountryclub.org
Catamount Club, *Williston* .... 9 [P]   802-878-7227
  catamountgolf.com
CC of Barre, *Barre* .... 18 [P]   802-476-7658
  ccofbarre.com
CC of Vermont, *Waterbury Center* .... 18 [V]   802-244-1800
  countryclubvt.com
Cedar Knoll CC, *Hinesburg* .... 27 [P]   802-482-3186
  cedarknollgolf.com
Champlain CC, *Swanton* .... 18 [P]   802-527-1187
  champlaincountryclub.com

Copley CC, *Morrisville* .... 9 [P]   802-888-3013
  copleygolfcourse.com
Crown Point CC, *Springfield* .... 18 [P]   802-885-1010
  crownpointcc.com
Dorset Field Club, *Dorset* .... 18 [V]   802-867-4002
  dorsetfieldclub.com
Ekwanok CC, *Manchester* .... 18 [V]   802-362-1774
Enosburg Falls CC, *Enosburg Falls* .... 18 [P]   802-933-2296
  efccvt.com
Essex CC, *Essex Junction* .... 18 [P]   802-879-3232
  essexccvt.com
Farm Resort GC, *Morrisville* .... 9 [R]   802-888-3525
  farmresortgolf.com
Green Mountain National GC, *Killington* .... 18 [M]   802-422-4653
  greenmountainnational.com
Haystack GC, *Wilmington* .... 18 [S]   802-464-8301
  haystackgolf.com
Jay Peak GC, *North Troy* .... 18 [R]   802-327-2184
  jaypeakresort.com
John P Larkin CC, *Windsor* .... 9 [P]   802-674-6491
  clublarkin.com
Killington GC, *Killington* .... 18 [R]   802-422-6700
  killingtongolf.com
Kirby CC, *Concord* .... 9 [S]   802-748-9200
Kwiniaska GC, *Shelburne* .... 18 [P]   802-985-3672
  kwiniaska.com
Lake Morey CC, *Fairlee* .... 18 [P]   802-333-4800
  lakemoreyresort.com
Lake St Catherine CC, *Poultney* .... 18 [S]   802-287-9341
  lsccc.net
Manchester CC, *Manchester Center* .... 18 [V]   802-362-2233
  mccvt.com
Montague GC, *Randolph* .... 18 [P]   802-728-3806
  montaguegolf.com
Montpelier Elks CC, *Montpelier* .... 9 [P]   802-223-7457
Mount Snow GC, *West Dover* .... 18 [R]   802-464-4254
  mountsnow.com
Mountain View CC, *Greensboro* .... 9 [S]   802-533-7477
  mvcc.biz
Mt Anthony CC, *Bennington* .... 18 [P]   802-447-7079
  golfingvermont.com
Neshobe GC, *Brandon* .... 18 [P]   802-247-3611
  neshobe.com
Newport CC, *Newport* .... 18 [S]   802-334-2391
  newportscountryclub.com
Northfield CC, *Northfield* .... 9 [S]   802-485-4515
  northfieldcountryclub.com
Okemo Mountain Resort & GC, *Ludlow* .... 18 [R]   802-228-1396
  okemo.com
Orleans CC, *Orleans* .... 18 [P]   802-754-2333
  orleanscc.com
Points North GC, *Stowe* .... 9 [V]   802-253-7059
Proctor Pittsford CC, *Pittsford* .... 18 [P]   802-483-9379
  proctor-pittsford.com
Prospect Pointe CC, *Bomoseen* .... 9 [S]   802-468-5581
Quechee Club, *Quechee* .... 36 [V]   802-295-9356
  quecheeclub.com
Ralph Myhre GC, *Middlebury* .... 18 [U]   802-443-5125
  ralphmyhregolfcourse.com
Richford CC, *Richford* .... 9 [P]   802-848-3527
Rocky Ridge GC, *St George* .... 18 [P]   802-482-2191
  rockyridge.com

Golf Yellow Pages, 18th Edition — VIRGINIA

Course	Holes	Phone
Rutland CC, *Rutland*	18 [P]	802-773-3254
rutlandcountryclub.com		
Sitzmark Lodge & GC, *Wilmington*	18 [R]	802-464-3384
Spruce Peak at Stowe Mountain, *Stowe*	18 [R]	802-253-3563
sprucepeak.com		
St Johnsbury CC, *St Johnsbury*	18 [P]	802-748-9894
thestjcc.com		
Stamford Valley GC, *Stamford*	9 [P]	802-694-9144
Stonehedge GC, *North Clarendon*	9 [P]	802-773-2666
Stowe CC, *Stowe*	18 [S]	802-253-3000
stowe.com		
Stratton Mountain CC, *Stratton Mountain*	27 [R]	802-297-2200
stratton.com		
Sugarbush GC, *Warren*	18 [R]	802-583-6100
sugarbush.com		
Tater Hill GC, *Chester*	18 [P]	802-875-2517
okemo.com		
The GC At Equinox, *Manchester Village*	18 [R]	802-362-7870
equinoxresort.com		
The Links At Lang Farm, *Essex Junction*	18 [P]	802-878-0298
linksatlangfarm.com		
Vermont National CC, *South Burlington*	18 [S]	802-264-9418
vermontnational.com		
West Bolton GC, *Jericho*	18 [P]	802-434-4321
westboltongolfclub.com		
White River GC, *Rochester*	9 [P]	802-767-4653
whiterivergolf.com		
Wilcox Cove GC, *Grand Isle*	9 [R]	802-372-8343
wilcoxcove.com		
Williston GC, *Williston*	18 [P]	802-878-3747
willistongolfclub.com		
Woodbury GC, *Woodbury*	9 [P]	802-456-1250
woodburygolf.com		
Woodstock CC, *Woodstock*	18 [R]	802-457-6674
woodstockinn.com		

VIRGINIA

Course	Holes	Phone
1757 GC, *Dulles*	9 [P]	703-444-0901
1757golfclub.com		
Aeropines GC, *Virginia Beach*	36 [A]	757-433-2866
cnic.navy.mil/Oceana		
Algonkian Regional Park GC, *Sterling*	18 [M]	703-450-4655
nvrpa.org		
Allegheny CC, *Covington*	9 [P]	540-862-5789
Amelia G&CC, *Amelia Court House*	9 [V]	804-561-2640
Appleland Sports Ctr, *Stephens City*	9 [P]	540-869-8600
Aquia Harbour G&CC, *Stafford*	9 [P]	540-659-4478
Army Navy CC Arlington, *Arlington*	27 [V]	703-521-6800
ancc.org		
Army Navy CC Fairfax, *Fairfax*	27 [V]	703-359-5825
ancc.org		
Ashley Plantation GC, *Daleville*	27 [S]	540-992-4653
ashleyplantation.com		
Auburn Hills GC, *Riner*	18 [S]	540-381-4995
auburnhillsgc.com		
Augustine GC, *Stafford*	18 [S]	540-720-7374
augustinegolf.com		
Ballyhack GC, *Roanoke*	18 [V]	540-427-1395
ballyhackgolfclub.com		
Bassett CC, *Bassett*	9 [V]	276-629-3242
bassettcc.com		
Battlefield GC, *Chesapeake*	18 [P]	757-482-4779
playthebattlefield.com		
Bay Creek GC, *Cape Charles*	36 [R]	757-331-8620
baycreekresort.com		
Bayville GC, *Virginia Beach*	18 [V]	757-460-7936
bayvillegolfclub.com		
Beaver Hills GC, *Martinsville*	18 [P]	276-632-1526
beaverhillsgolf.com		
Bedford CC, *Bedford*	9 [V]	540-586-8407
bedfordcountryclub.com		
Belle Haven CC, *Alexandria*	18 [V]	703-329-5264
bellehavencc.com		
Belmont CC, *Ashburn*	18 [V]	703-723-5334
belmontcc.info		
Belmont GC, *Henrico*	18 [M]	804-501-4653
belmontgolfcourse.com		
Bide A Wee GC, *Portsmouth*	18 [M]	757-393-8600
bideaweegolf.com		
Birdwood GC, *Charlottesville*	18 [U]	434-293-4653
boarsheadinn.com		
Birkdale G&CC, *Chesterfield*	18 [S]	804-739-8800
birkdalegolf.com		
Blacksburg CC, *Blacksburg*	18 [R]	540-552-9164
blacksburgcc.com		
Blacksburg Muni GC, *Blacksburg*	9 [M]	540-961-1137
blacksburg.gov/recreation/golf		
Blue Hills GC, *Roanoke*	18 [P]	540-344-7848
bluehillsgc.com		
Blue Ridge CC, *Galax*	18 [P]	276-236-5637
Blue Ridge Shadows GC, *Front Royal*	18 [R]	571-238-6166
blueridgeshadows.com		
Boonsboro CC, *Lynchburg*	18 [V]	434-384-3411
boonsborocountryclub.com		
Botetourt CC, *Troutville*	18 [P]	540-992-1451
botetourtcc.com		
Bow Creek GC, *Virginia Beach*	18 [M]	757-431-3763
vbgov.com/parks		
Bowling Green CC, *Front Royal*	36 [P]	540-635-2095
bowlinggreencc.net		
Brambleton GC, *Ashburn*	18 [M]	703-327-3403
nvrpa.org		
Brandermill CC, *Midlothian*	18 [V]	804-744-1185
brandermill.cc		
Briery CC, *Keysville*	9 [P]	434-736-8569
Bristow Manor GC, *Bristow*	18 [P]	703-368-3558
bristowmanorgc.com		
Broad Run Golf & Practice Facility, *Bristow*	9 [P]	703-365-2443
broadrungolf.com		
Brookside GC, *Roanoke*	9 [P]	540-366-6059
Browning's GC, *Culpeper*	18 [P]	540-854-4454
Brunswick CC, *Lawrenceville*	9 [V]	434-848-2933
Bryce Resort GC, *Basye*	18 [R]	540-856-2121
bryceresort.com		
Bull Run GC, *Haymarket*	18 [P]	703-753-7777
bullrungolfclub.com		
Burke Lake Golf Ctr, *Fairfax Station*	18 [M]	703-323-1641
fairfaxcounty.gov/parks/golf/burkegolf		
Cahoon Plantation GC, *Chesapeake*	18 [S]	757-436-2775
cahoonplantation.com		
Cameron Hills Golf Links, *King George*	18 [P]	540-775-4653
cameronhills.com		
Cannon Ridge GC, *Fredericksburg*	18 [R]	540-735-8000
golfcannonridge.com		
Captains Cove G&YC, *Greenbackville*	9 [P]	757-824-5478
captscove.com		

[S] = SEMI-PRIVATE   [V] = PRIVATE   [U] = UNIVERSITY   [N] = UNIVERSITY-PRIVATE

VIRGINIA

Golf Yellow Pages, 18th Edition

Castle Rock GC, *Pembroke* .... 18 [P] 540-626-7276
Cavalier G&YC, *Virginia Beach* .... 18 [V] 757-428-6161
  cavaliergyc.com
Caverns CC, *Luray* .... 18 [R] 540-743-7111
  luraycaverns.com
CC of Fairfax, *Fairfax* .... 18 [V] 703-273-3445
  ccfairfax.org
CC of Petersburg, *Petersburg* .... 18 [V] 804-733-4458
  ccofpetersburg.com
CC of Virginia, *Richmond* .... 36 [V] 804-287-1301
  theccv.org
CC of Virginia - Westhampton, *Richmond* ...... 18 [V] 804-288-2891
  theccv.org
Cedar Hills CC, *Jonesville* .... 18 [P] 276-346-1535
Cedar Point CC, *Suffolk* .... 27 [V] 757-238-3554
  cedarpointcountryclub.com
Cedars CC, *Chatham* .... 9 [P] 434-656-8036
Chantilly National G&CC, *Centreville* ...... 18 [V] 703-631-9562
  cngcc.org
Chatmoss CC, *Martinsville* .... 18 [V] 276-638-7648
  chatmosscc.org
Chesapeake GC, *Chesapeake* .... 18 [S] 757-547-1122
  golfhamptonroads.net
Clear Creek GC, *Bristol* .... 18 [M] 276-466-4833
  clearcreekgolfclub.net
Cliff View GC & Inn, *Covington* .... 18 [R] 540-962-2200
  cliffviewinc.com
Cliftondale CC, *Clifton Forge* .... 9 [P] 540-862-2081
Club At Creighton Farms, *Aldie* .... 18 [V] 703-957-4805
  creightonfarms.com
Colonial Heritage GC, *Williamsburg* ..... 18 [P] 757-645-2030
  colonialheritageclub.com
Colonial Hills GC, *Forest* .... 18 [P] 434-525-3954
  colonialhillsgolf.com
Countryside GC, *Roanoke* .... 18 [M] 540-563-0391
  countrysidegolfclub.com
Crewe CC, *Crewe* .... 9 [V] 434-645-7240
Culpeper CC, *Culpeper* .... 18 [V] 434-825-1748
  countryclubofculpeper.com
Cypress Cove CC, *Franklin* .... 18 [V] 757-562-6878
  southamptoncounty.org/cypressgrove.asp
Cypress Creek Golfers Club, *Smithfield* ... 18 [S] 757-365-4774
  cypresscreekgolfersclub.com
Cypress Point CC, *Virginia Beach* .... 18 [P] 757-490-8822
  golfhamptonroads.net
Dan Hall Mountain Resort & CC, *Coeburn* ...... 9 [R] 276-395-2487
  virginiagolf.com/danhall.html
Danville GC, *Danville* .... 18 [V] 434-792-8956
  danvillegolfclub.com
Deer Cove GC, *Williamsburg* .... 18 [A] 757-887-6539
Deerfield GC, *Damascus* .... 9 [P] 276-475-5649
  vacreepertrail.us/deerfield
Dogwood Trace GC, *Petersburg* .... 18 [M] 804-732-5573
  dogwoodtracegolf.com
Dominion Valley CC, *Haymarket* .... 18 [V] 571-261-4101
  dominionvalley.com
Draper Valley GC, *Draper* .... 18 [P] 540-980-4653
  drapervalleygolf.com
Eagle Haven GC, *Norfolk* .... 18 [A] 757-462-8526
Eaglewood GC, *Langley AFB* .... 27 [A] 757-764-4547
  langley.af.mil
Eastern Shore Y&CC, *Melfa* .... 18 [V] 757-787-1525
  esycc.com

Elizabeth Manor G&CC, *Portsmouth* ...... 18 [V] 757-488-6605
  elizabethmanorgolf.com
Emporia CC, *Emporia* .... 18 [V] 434-634-4304
Evergreen CC, *Haymarket* .... 18 [V] 703-754-4125
  evergreencc.org
Fairfax National GC, *Centreville* .... 27 [S] 703-631-9226
  fairfaxnationalgolfclub.com
Falling River CC, *Appomattox* .... 18 [V] 434-352-7037
Farmington CC, *Charlottesville* .... 27 [V] 434-245-0680
  farmingtoncc.com
Farmville Municipal GC, *Farmville* .... 9 [S] 434-392-6656
  golffarmvilleva.com
Fauquier Springs CC, *Warrenton* .... 18 [V] 540-347-4205
  fauquiersprings.com
Fawn Lake CC, *Spotsylvania* .... 18 [V] 540-972-3084
  fawnlakevirginia.com
Fincastle CC, *Bluefield* .... 18 [V] 276-326-1178
  fincastlecountryclub.com
Fords Colony CC At Williamsburg, *Williamsburg* ..54 [R] 757-258-4130
  fordscolony.com
Forest Greens GC, *Triangle* .... 18 [M] 703-221-0123
  forestgreens.com
Forest Park CC, *Martinsville* .... 18 [V] 276-632-1711
  forestparkcountryclub.com
Fort Belvoir GC, *Fort Belvoir* .... 36 [A] 703-806-5878
  belvoirgolf.com
Fort Lee Cardinal GC, *Fort Lee* .... 27 [A] 804-734-2899
  leemwr.com
Four Winds GC, *Rappahannock Academy* .... 18 [S] 804-742-5647
  fourwindsclub.com
Fredericksburg CC, *Fredericksburg* ...... 18 [V] 540-373-4171
  fredclub.org
Front Royal CC, *Front Royal* .... 9 [M] 540-636-9061
  warrencountyva.net
Galax Muni GC, *Galax* .... 9 [M] 276-236-2641
  galaxparks-rec.com
Generals Ridge GC, *Manassas Park* ..... 18 [M] 703-335-0777
  generalsridge.com
Giles CC, *Pearisburg* .... 9 [V] 540-921-1099
  gilescountryclub.com
Glenmore CC, *Keswick* .... 18 [V] 434-817-0502
  glenmoremember.com
Glenrochie CC, *Abingdon* .... 18 [V] 276-628-3572
  glenrochiecc.com
Glenwood GC, *Richmond* .... 18 [P] 804-226-1793
  glenwoodgolfclub.com
Gloucester CC, *Gloucester* .... 9 [P] 804-693-2662
Golden Eagle Executive Course, *Irvington* .... 9 [R] 804-438-5000
  tidesinn.com
Golden Eagle GC, *Irvington* .... 18 [R] 804-438-5000
  tidesinn.com
Golden Horseshoe GC, *Williamsburg* ....45 [R] 757-220-7696
  colonialwilliamsburgresort.com
Goodyear GC, *Danville* .... 18 [V] 434-797-1909
  goodyeargolf.com
Goose Creek GC, *Leesburg* .... 18 [P] 703-729-2500
  goosecreekgolf.com
Gordon Trent GC, *Stuart* .... 18 [P] 276-694-3805
  gordontrent.com
Great Oaks CC, *Floyd* .... 18 [V] 540-745-2189
Greenbrier CC, *Chesapeake* .... 18 [V] 757-547-7375
  greenbrierclub.com
Greendale GC, *Alexandria* .... 18 [M] 703-971-6170
  fairfaxcounty.gov/parks/golf/greendale

[A] = MILITARY   [M] = MUNICIPAL   [P] = PUBLIC   [R] = RESORT

VIRGINIA

Course	Location	Holes	Type	Phone
Greens Folly GC,	South Boston	18	[S]	434-572-4998
greensfolly.com				
Greenway Creek GC,	Glade Spring	18	[P]	276-429-2626
Gypsy Hill GC,	Staunton	18	[M]	540-332-3949
staunton.va.us				
Halifax CC,	Halifax	18	[V]	434-476-2940
Hanging Rock GC,	Salem	18	[P]	540-389-7275
hangingrockgolf.com				
Hanover CC,	Ashland	18	[V]	804-752-6596
hanovercountryclub.com				
Hat Creek GC,	Brookneal	9	[P]	434-376-2292
Hells Point GC,	Virginia Beach	18	[S]	757-721-3400
hellspoint.com				
Heritage Hunt G&CC,	Gainesville	18	[V]	703-743-1000
heritagehuntgolf.com				
Heritage Oaks GC,	Harrisonburg	18	[M]	540-442-6502
heritageoaksgolf.com				
Hermitage CC,	Manakin Sabot	36	[V]	804-784-3811
hermitagecountryclub.com				
Herndon Centennial GC,	Herndon	18	[M]	703-471-5769
herndongolf.com				
Heron Ridge GC,	Virginia Beach	18	[S]	757-426-3800
heronridge.com				
Hidden Creek CC,	Reston	18	[V]	703-437-4222
hiddencreekcc.com				
Hidden Valley CC,	Salem	18	[V]	540-389-8990
hiddenvalleycc.com				
Highland Springs GC,	Highland Springs	18	[P]	804-737-4716
highlandspringsgolfclub.com				
Highlands Golfers Club,	Chesterfield	18	[P]	804-796-4800
highlands-golf.com				
Hilltop GC,	Alexandria	9	[P]	703-719-6504
hilltopgolfclub.com				
Hobbs Hole GC,	Tappahannock	18	[S]	804-443-4500
hobbshole.com				
Holston Hills CC,	Marion	18	[V]	276-783-7484
Honey Bee GC,	Virginia Beach	18	[R]	757-471-2768
honeybeegolf.com				
Horsepasture Par 3,	Ridgeway	9	[P]	276-957-4085
Hunting Hawk GC,	Glen Allen	18	[P]	804-749-1900
huntinghawkgolf.com				
Hunting Hills CC,	Roanoke	18	[V]	540-774-4429
huntinghillscc.com				
Independence GC,	Midlothian	27	[P]	804-594-0261
independencegolfclub.com				
Indian Creek Y&CC,	Kilmarnock	18	[V]	804-435-3130
icycc.com				
Ingleside Resort CC,	Staunton	18	[R]	540-248-7888
International Town & CC,	Fairfax	18	[P]	703-968-7070
internationalcc.com				
Ivy Hill GC,	Forest	18	[P]	434-525-2680
ivyhillgc.com				
Jacksons Chase At Pine Hills,	Middletown	18	[P]	540-635-7814
jacksonschase.com				
James River CC,	Newport News	18	[V]	757-596-3112
jamesrivercountryclub.com				
Jefferson GC,	Falls Church	9	[M]	703-573-0444
fairfaxcounty.gov/parks/golf/jefferson				
Jefferson Lakeside CC,	Richmond	18	[V]	804-266-2382
jeffersonlakeside.com				
Jordan Point GC,	Hopewell	18	[P]	804-458-0141
virginiagolf.com/jordanpoint.html				
Kempsville Greens Muni GC,	Virginia Beach	18	[M]	757-474-8441
vbgov.com/parks				
Kiln Creek G&CC,	Newport News	27	[R]	757-874-2600
kilncreekgolf.com				
Kinderton CC,	Clarksville	18	[P]	434-374-8822
kerrlake.com/kcc				
King Carter GC,	Irvington	18	[P]	804-435-7842
kingcartergolfclub.com				
Kingsmill Resort & GC,	Williamsburg	63	[R]	757-253-3906
kingsmill.com				
Kinloch GC,	Manakin Sabot	18	[V]	804-784-8000
kinlochgolfclub.com				
Lake Bonaventure CC,	St Paul	9	[V]	276-762-7618
Lake Chesdin Golfers Club,	Chesterfield	18	[V]	804-590-0031
clublink.ca/member_about_lakechesdin.html				
Lake Gaston GC,	Gasburg	18	[P]	434-577-2888
playlggc.com				
Lake Monticello GC,	Palmyra	18	[P]	434-589-3075
lakemonticellogolf.org				
Lake of the Woods CC,	Locust Grove	18	[V]	540-972-2230
lowagolf.org				
Lake Ridge Park Golf & Marina,	Woodbridge	9	[M]	703-494-5564
pwcparks.org				
Lake Wright GC,	Norfolk	18	[M]	757-459-2255
golfhamptonroads.net				
Lakeview CC,	Harrisonburg	36	[P]	540-434-8937
lakeviewgolf.net				
Laurel Hill GC,	Lorton	18	[M]	703-493-8849
fairfaxcounty.gov/parks/golf/laurelhill				
Lees Hill GC,	Fredericksburg	18	[S]	540-891-0111
leeshillgc.com				
Lexington G&CC,	Lexington	18	[V]	540-463-3542
lgcc1902.com				
London Downs GC,	Forest	18	[S]	434-525-4653
londondownsgolf.com				
Lonesome Pine CC,	Big Stone Gap	18	[V]	276-523-0739
Longview GC,	Galax	18	[P]	276-238-4653
Longwood GC,	Farmville	9	[U]	434-395-2613
longwood.edu				
Loudoun G&CC,	Purcellville	18	[V]	540-338-7705
loudouncc.com				
Lunenburg CC,	Kenbridge	9	[V]	434-676-8774
Mariners Landing G&CC,	Huddleston	18	[S]	540-297-7888
marinerslandinggolf.com				
Massanutten-Mountain Greens,	McGaheysville	36	[R]	540-289-4941
massresort.com				
Massanutten-Woodstone Meadows,	McGaheysville	36	[R]	540-289-4941
massresort.com				
Mattaponi Springs GC,	Ruther Glen	18	[P]	804-633-7888
mattaponisprings.com				
MCCS Medal of Honor GC,	Quantico	18	[A]	703-784-2424
quantico.usmc-mccs.org				
McIntyre Park GC,	Charlottesville	9	[M]	434-977-4111
virginiagolf.com/mcintirepark.html				
Meadowbrook CC,	Richmond	18	[V]	804-275-9189
meadowbrookccconline.org				
Meadowcreek GC,	Charlottesville	18	[M]	434-977-0615
meadowcreekgolf.org				
Meadows Farms GC,	Locust Grove	27	[P]	540-854-9890
meadowsfarms.com				
Meadows G&CC,	Christiansburg	18	[P]	540-382-3732
meadowsgolfcc.com				
Mecklenburg CC,	Chase City	9	[V]	434-372-4075

[S] = SEMI-PRIVATE [V] = PRIVATE [U] = UNIVERSITY [N] = UNIVERSITY-PRIVATE

VIRGINIA
Golf Yellow Pages, 18th Edition

Mill Quarter Plantation CC, *Powhatan* ....18 [P]   804-598-4221
   millquarter.com
Millwood CC, *Boyce* .... 9 [V]   540-837-1080
Montclair CC, *Dumfries* .... 18 [V]   703-670-3915
   montclaircc.com
Monte Vista GC, *Ewing*..9 [P]   276-861-4014
Mount Vernon CC, *Alexandria* .... 18 [V]   703-780-3565
   mountvernoncc.org
Mountain View GC, *Appomattox*..........................9 [P]   434-352-3970
Nansemond River GC, *Suffolk* ....18 [P]   757-539-4356
   nansemondrivergolfclub.com
Needles Eye GC, *Monterey*.................................. 9 [V]   540-468-2427
Newport News GC At Deer Run, *Newport News*.36 [M]   757-886-7925
   nngolfclub.com
Northampton CC, *Cape Charles* ....9 [S]   757-331-8423
   virginiagolf.com/northampton.html
Nottoway River CC, *Blackstone* .... 9 [V]   434-292-4485
Oak Marr Golf Ctr, *Oakton* ....9 [M]   703-255-5390
   fairfaxcounty.gov/parks/golf/oakmarr
Oasis Sports Park, *Chesterfield* ....9 [P]   804-739-6833
   oasissportspark.com
Ocean View GC, *Norfolk* ....18 [M]   757-480-2094
   oceanviewgc.com
Old Hickory GC, *Woodbridge* ....18 [P]   703-580-9000
   golfoldhickory.com
Old Trail GC, *Crozet*..18 [P]   434-823-8101
   oldtrailgolf.com
Ole Monterey GC, *Roanoke* ....18 [P]   540-563-0400
Ospreys GC at Belmont Bay, *Woodbridge* ....18 [R]   703-497-1384
   ospreysgolf.com
Owls Creek Golf Ctr, *Virginia Beach* ....18 [P]   757-428-2800
   golfhamptonroads.net
Packsaddle Ridge GC, *Keezletown*......................18 [P]   540-269-8188
   packsaddle.net
Par 3 Golf At Sandy Bottom Park, *Bridgewater*.....9 [M]   540-828-3705
Peaks Par 3 GC, *Lynchburg* ....9 [P]   434-528-3458
Penderbrook GC, *Fairfax* ....18 [P]   703-385-3700
   penderbrookgolf.com
Pendleton GC, *Ruther Glen*.................................18 [P]   804-448-4727
   pendletongolfva.com
Pete Dye River Course of Virginia Tech, *Radford*...18 [P]   540-633-6732
   rivercoursegolf.com
Piankatank River GC, *Hartfield*...........................18 [S]   804-776-6516
   piankatankrivergolf.com
Pinecrest GC, *Alexandria* ....9 [M]   703-941-1061
   fairfaxcounty.gov/parks/golf/pinecrest
Pleasant Valley Golfers Club, *Chantilly* ....18 [P]   703-631-7902
   pleasantvalleygc.com
Pohick Bay Regional Park GC, *Lorton* ....18 [M]   703-339-8585
   nvrpa.org
Poplar Forest GC, *Forest* ....9 [P]   434-534-9418
Poplar Grove GC, *Amherst*..................................18 [P]   434-946-9933
   poplargrovegolf.com
Prince George Country Course, *Disputanta* ....18 [P]   804-991-2251
   princegeorgegolfclub.com
Prince William GC, *Nokesville*............................18 [P]   703-754-7111
   princewilliamgolf.com
Princess Anne CC, *Virginia Beach* .... 18 [V]   757-422-3360
   princessannecc.com
Providence GC, *Richmond*..................................18 [P]   804-276-1865
   providencegolfcourse.com
Pulaski CC, *Pulaski*... 18 [V]   540-980-5851
   pulaskicountryclub.com

Queenfield Plantation GC, *Manquin* ....18 [P]   804-769-8838
   queenfieldgolf.com
Quinton Oaks GC, *Callao* ....18 [P]   804-529-5367
   quintonoaks.com
Raspberry Falls Golf & Hunt Club, *Leesburg*.........18 [P]   703-779-2555
   raspberryfalls.com
Red Wing Lake GC, *Virginia Beach*......................18 [M]   757-437-2037
   vbgov.com/parks
Regency At Dominion Valley CC, *Haymarket*...... 18 [V]   571-261-2505
   regencydominionvalley.com
Reston National GC, *Reston* ....18 [P]   703-620-9333
   restonnationalgc.com
Richmond CC, *Richmond*................................... 18 [V]   804-784-5663
   richmondcountryclubinc.com
Richwood GC, *Bluefield*..9 [P]   276-322-4575
   richwoodgolf.com
Ringgold GC, *Ringgold*..27 [P]   434-822-8728
   ringgoldgolfclub.com
River Bend G&CC, *Great Falls* .... 18 [V]   703-759-3030
   rbgcc.org
River Creek Club, *Leesburg*................................ 18 [V]   703-779-8486
   rivercreekclub.com
River Ridge GC, *Bracey*..9 [P]   434-636-3351
   riverridgeassoc.com
Riverfront GC, *Suffolk* ....18 [S]   757-484-2200
   riverfrontgolf.com
Rivers Bend GC, *Chester* ....18 [P]   804-530-1000
   riversbendgolfclub.com
Roanoke CC, *Roanoke* .... 27 [V]   540-343-1330
   roanokecc.com
Robert Trent Jones GC, *Gainesville* .... 18 [V]   703-754-7533
   rtjgc.com
Rock Harbor GC, *Winchester*..............................18 [P]   540-722-7111
   rockharborgolf.com
Royal Virginia GC, *Louisa* ....18 [P]   804-457-2041
   royalvirginiagc.com
Salem GC, *Salem* ....9 [M]   540-387-9802
Salisbury CC, *Midlothian*................................... 27 [V]   804-794-8255
   salisburycountryclub.com
Saltville GC, *Saltville*...9 [P]   276-496-7779
Scenic View GC, *Chilhowie* ....9 [P]   276-646-3535
Scott County Park & GC, *Gate City* ....9 [M]   276-452-2442
   scottcountyva.com/park
Scottos World of Golf, *Waynesboro* .... 9 [V]   540-943-7283
Sewells Point GC, *Norfolk* ....18 [A]   757-444-5572
Shadow Ridge GC, *Amherst*...............................18 [P]   434-946-2008
Shenandoah Crossing, *Gordonsville* ....18 [R]   540-832-9543
Shenandoah Valley GC, *Front Royal*....................27 [P]   540-636-4653
   svgcgolf.com
Shenvalee GC, *New Market*................................27 [R]   540-740-9930
   shenvalee.com
Skyland Lakes GC, *Fancy Gap*.............................18 [P]   276-728-4923
Sleepy Hole, *Suffolk*...18 [M]   757-538-4100
   sleepyholegolfcourse.com
Somerset GC, *Locust Grove*................................18 [R]   540-423-9300
   somersetgc.com
South Hill CC, *La Crosse* .... 9 [V]   434-757-7558
South Riding Golfers Club, *South Riding* ....18 [S]   703-327-3673
   southridinggc.com
South Wales GC, *Jeffersonton*.............................18 [P]   540-937-3250
   virginiagolf.com/southwales.html
Southern Hills G&SwimClub, *Danville*................18 [S]   434-792-9178

[A] = MILITARY   [M] = MUNICIPAL   [P] = PUBLIC   [R] = RESORT

VIRGINIA

Spotswood CC, *Harrisonburg* .... 18 [V]   540-434-4886
  spotswoodcc.com
Spring Creek GC, *Gordonsville* .... 18 [P]   540-832-0744
  springcreekgolfclub.com
Springfield G&CC, *Springfield* .... 18 [V]   703-451-8338
  sgccva.org
Sterling GC, *Sterling* .... 18 [P]   703-430-1400
  sterlinggolfclub.com
Stonehenge G&CC, *Richmond* .... 18 [V]   804-378-7845
  stonehengeclub.com
Stoneleigh GC, *Round Hill* .... 18 [V]   540-338-4653
  stoneleighgolf.com
Stonewall GC, *Gainesville* .... 18 [P]   703-753-5101
  stonewallgolfclub.com
Stumpy Lake GC, *Virginia Beach* .... 18 [M] 757-467-6119
  stumpylakegolf.com
Suffolk GC, *Suffolk* .... 18 [M] 757-539-6298
  suffolkgolfcourse.com
Swannanoa CC, *Afton* .... 18 [P]   540-943-8864
  swannanoa.com
Sycamore Creek GC, *Manakin Sabot* .... 18 [P]   804-784-3544
  sycamorecreekgolfcourse.com
Sycamore Ridge GC, *Goodview* .... 18 [P]   540-297-6490
Tanglewood Shores G&CC, *Bracey* .... 9 [V]   434-636-2254
Tanyard CC, *Louisa* .... 18 [S]   540-967-1889
  tanyardgolf.com
Tazewell County CC, *Pounding Mill* .... 18 [V]   276-988-3593
The Brookwoods GC, *Quinton* .... 18 [P]   804-932-3737
  brookwoodsgolf.com
The Club At Ironwood, *Staunton* .... 18 [V]   540-248-7273
  theclubatironwood.com
The Club At Viniterra, *New Kent* .... 18 [S]   804-932-3888
  theclubatviniterra.com
The Clubs of Olde Mill, *Laurel Fork* .... 18 [R]   276-398-2638
  oldmill.net
The Colonial GC, *Lanexa* .... 18 [P]   757-566-1600
  golfcolonial.com
The Dominion Club at Wyndham, *Glen Allen* ...... 18 [V]   804-360-1200
  tdcva.com
The Federal Club, *Glen Allen* .... 18 [V]   804-798-4996
  thefederalclub.com
The First Tee of Chesterfield, *Richmond* .... 18 [P]   804-275-8050
  thefirstteerichmondchesterfield.org
The Foundry GC, *Powhatan* .... 18 [P]   804-598-3243
  foundrygolfclub.com
The Gauntlet GC, *Fredericksburg* .... 18 [P]   540-752-0963
  golfgauntlet.com
The GC At Brickshire, *Providence Forge* .... 18 [P]   804-966-7888
  brickshiregolf.com
The GC At Lansdowne, *Lansdowne* .... 45 [R]   703-729-4071
  lansdowneresort.com
The Greene Hills Club, *Stanardsville* .... 18 [V]   434-985-7328
  greenehillsclub.com
The Hamptons GC, *Hampton* .... 27 [M] 757-766-9148
  hampton.gov/thehamptons
The Highland Course-Primland Resort,
  Meadows Of Dan .... 18 [R]   276-222-3827
  primland.com
The Hollows GC, *Montpelier* .... 27 [P]   804-883-5381
  thehollows.com
The Homestead Resort, *Hot Springs* .... 54 [R]   540-839-7739
  thehomestead.com
The Kanawha Club, *Manakin Sabot* .... 9 [V]   804-784-3070

The Keswick Club, *Keswick* .... 18 [R]   434-979-3440
  keswick.com
The Lamberts Point GC, *Norfolk* .... 9 [M]   757-489-1677
  lambertspointgolf.com
The Links at City Park, *Portsmouth* .... 9 [M]   757-465-1500
  portsmouthva.gov
The Manor Resort GC, *Farmville* .... 18 [R]   434-392-2244
  themanorresort.com
The Olde Farm GC, *Bristol* .... 18 [V]   276-669-1042
  theoldefarm.com
The Piedmont Club, *Haymarket* .... 18 [V]   703-753-9240
  piedmontclub.com
The Pines GC At Fort Eustis, *Fort Eustis* .... 27 [A]   757-878-2965
  eustismwr.com
The Rivanna Resort & GC, *Palmyra* .... 18 [R]   434-589-3730
  rivannaresort.com
The Signature At West Neck, *Virginia Beach* ...... 18 [P]   757-721-2900
  signatureatwestneck.com
The Tartan Course, *Weems* .... 18 [R]   804-438-6005
  tartangolfclub.com
The Tradition GC At Broad Bay, *Virginia Beach* .... 18 [V]   757-496-9090
  traditionalclubs.com
The Tradition GC At Kiskiack, *Williamsburg* ...... 18 [R]   757-566-2200
  traditionalclubs.com
The Tradition GC At Royal New Kent,
  Providence Forge .... 18 [P]   804-966-7023
  traditionalclubs.com
The Tradition GC At Stonehouse, *Toano* .... 18 [S]   757-566-1138
  traditionalclubs.com
The Tradition GC At The Crossings, *Glen Allen* .... 18 [P]   804-261-0000
  traditionalclubs.com
The Vista Links GC, *Buena Vista* .... 18 [M] 540-261-4653
  thevistalinks.com
The Waterfront CC, *Moneta* .... 18 [V]   540-721-2653
  thewaterfrontcc.com
The Westham GC at Magnolia Green, *Moseley* ...... 9 [S]   804-639-5701
  westhamgolfclub.com
The Woodlands GC, *Hampton* .... 18 [M] 757-727-1195
  hampton.gov/thewoodlands
Trump National GC - Washington, DC,
  Potomac Falls .... 36 [V]   703-444-4801
  trumpnationaldc.com
Tuscarora CC, *Danville* .... 18 [V]   434-724-4191
Twin Lakes GC, *Clifton* .... 36 [M] 703-631-9372
  fairfaxcounty.gov/parks/golf/twinlakes
Two Rivers CC, *Williamsburg* .... 18 [V]   757-258-4610
  governorsland.com
Victoria GC, *Victoria* .... 9 [V]   434-696-3019
Village Green GC, *Callao* .... 9 [P]   804-529-6332
Virginia Beach National GC, *Virginia Beach* .... 18 [S]   757-563-9440
  vbnational.com
Virginia Golf Ctr & Acad, *Clifton* .... 9 [P]   703-830-2400
  virginiagolfcenter.com
Virginia National GC, *Bluemont* .... 18 [P]   540-955-2966
  virginianational.com
Virginia Oaks GC, *Gainesville* .... 18 [P]   703-754-7977
  virginiaoaksgc.com
Virginia Tech GC, *Blacksburg* .... 9 [U]   540-231-6435
  recsports.vt.edu/facilities/VTGolfCourse
Virginian GC, *Bristol* .... 18 [V]   276-645-6950
  thevirginian.com
Washington G&CC, *Arlington* .... 18 [V]   703-558-0564
  washingtongolfcc.com

[S] = SEMI-PRIVATE   [V] = PRIVATE   [U] = UNIVERSITY   [N] = UNIVERSITY-PRIVATE

VIRGINIA — Golf Yellow Pages, 18th Edition

Waters Edge CC, *Penhook* .... 18 [V]   540-576-3343
  thewatersedgecc.com
Waynesboro CC, *Waynesboro* .... 18 [V]   540-942-9340
  waynesborocountryclub.org
West Point CC, *West Point* .... 9 [V]   804-843-3168
Westfields GC, *Clifton* .... 18 [R]   703-631-3300
  westfieldsgolf.com
Westlake G&CC, *Hardy* .... 18 [S]   540-721-4214
  golfthewestlake.com
Westpark GC, *Leesburg* .... 18 [P]   703-777-7023
  westparkgc.com
Westwood CC, *Vienna* .... 18 [V]   703-938-2593
  westwoodcc.com
Wilderness Road GC, *Duffield* .... 9 [P]   276-328-0938
Williamsburg CC, *Williamsburg* .... 18 [V]   757-221-0573
  williamsburgcountryclub.com
Williamsburg National GC, *Williamsburg* .... 36 [S]   757-258-9642
  wngc.com
Willow Creek CC, *Rocky Mount* .... 9 [V]   540-483-0797
Willow Oaks CC, *Richmond* .... 18 [V]   804-272-1455
  willowoakscc.org
Willowbrook CC, *Breaks* .... 9 [V]   276-531-8542
  wbcountryclub.com
Winchester CC, *Winchester* .... 18 [V]   540-662-3821
  winchestercountryclub.net
Windjammer GC of Windmill Point Resort,
  White Stone .... 9 [R]   804-435-1166
Windy Hill Sports Complex, *Midlothian* .... 18 [P]   804-794-0010
  windyhillsports.com
Wintergreen Resort - Devils Knob, *Roseland* ..... 18 [R]   434-325-8250
  wintergreenresort.com
Wintergreen Resort Stoney Creek, *Nellysford* .... 27 [R]   434-325-8250
  wintergreenresort.com
Winton CC, *Amherst* .... 18 [P]   434-946-7336
  wintongolf.com
Wolf Creek G&CC, *Bastian* .... 18 [P]   276-688-4610
  wolfcreekgolfcourse.net
Woodberry Forest GC, *Woodberry Forest* .... 9 [N]   540-672-3787
Wytheville GC, *Wytheville* .... 18 [P]   276-228-2143
YMCA of South Hampton Rds-Junior, *Virginia Beach* 9 [P] 757-563-8990
  thefirstteehr.org

WASHINGTON

Airport Golf Ctr, *Tumwater* .... 9 [P]   360-786-8626
  airportgolfcenter.com
Airway Hills Golf Range & Par 3, *Pullman* .... 9 [P]   509-872-3092
  airwayhills.com
Alderbrook G&YC, *Union* .... 18 [S]   360-898-2560
  alderbrookgolf.com
Allenmore Public GC, *Tacoma* .... 18 [P]   253-627-7211
Alta Lake GC, *Pateros* .... 18 [P]   509-923-2359
  altalakegolf.com
American Lake Veterans GC, *Lakewood* .... 9 [A]   253-583-1058
  alvetsgolfcourse.com
Antler Springs of Chattaroy GC, *Deer Park* .... 18 [P]   509-292-4653
  antlersprings.com
Apple Tree GC, *Yakima* .... 18 [P]   509-966-5877
  appletreeresort.com
Auburn GC, *Auburn* .... 18 [M]   253-833-2350
  auburngolf.org
Avalon GC, *Burlington* .... 27 [P]   360-757-1900
  avalonlinks.com

Bakers Edge GC, *Maple Falls* .... 9 [P]   360-599-2416
Ballinger Lake GC, *Mountlake Terrace* .... 9 [P]   425-697-4653
  ballingerlakegolf.com
Banks Lake GC, *Electric City* .... 18 [P]   509-633-0163
Battle Creek GC, *Marysville* .... 27 [P]   360-659-7931
  battlecreeklinks.com
Bayshore GC, *Shelton* .... 9 [S]   360-426-1271
Beacon Rock GC, *North Bonneville* .... 9 [P]   509-427-5730
  beaconrockgolf.com
Bear Creek CC, *Woodinville* .... 18 [V]   425-883-4770
  bearcreekcc.com
Bear Creek GC, *Winthrop* .... 9 [P]   509-996-2284
  bearcreekgolfcourse.com
Bear Mountain Ranch GC, *Chelan* .... 18 [R]   509-682-8200
  bearmt.com
Bellevue GC, *Bellevue* .... 18 [M]   425-452-7250
  bellevuepgc.com
Bellingham G&CC, *Bellingham* .... 18 [V]   360-733-3450
  bellinghamgcc.com
Belmor Mobile Home Park G&CC, *Federal Way* ... 9 [P]   253-838-0517
Big Bend G&CC, *Wilbur* .... 9 [P]   509-647-5664
  golfwilbur.com
Birch Bay Village GC, *Blaine* .... 9 [V]   360-371-2026
Black Rock Creek GC, *Sunnyside* .... 18 [S]   509-837-5340
  blackrockcreekgolfclub.com
Blue Boy West GC, *Monroe* .... 9 [P]   360-793-2378
  blueboywest.com
Brae Burn G&CC, *Redmond* .... 9 [V]   425-652-1757
Broadmoor GC, *Seattle* .... 18 [V]   206-325-8444
  broadmoorgolfclub.com
Brookdale GC, *Tacoma* .... 18 [P]   253-537-4400
  brookdalegolf.com
Buckskin GC, *Richland* .... 9 [M]   509-942-0888
Camaloch GC, *Camano Island* .... 18 [R]   360-387-3084
  camalochgolf.com
Camas Meadows GC, *Camas* .... 18 [P]   360-833-2000
  camasmeadows.com
Canterwood G&CC, *Gig Harbor* .... 18 [V]   253-851-1745
  canterwood.com
Canyon Lakes GC, *Kennewick* .... 18 [P]   509-582-3736
  canyonlakesgolfcourse.com
Capitol City GC, *Lacey* .... 18 [P]   360-491-5111
  golfcapitolcity.com
Carnation GC, *Carnation* .... 18 [P]   425-333-4151
  carnationgolf.com
Carson Mineral Hot Springs Spa & Golf Resort,
  Carson .... 18 [R]   509-427-5150
  carsonhotspringresort.com
Cascade GC, *North Bend* .... 9 [P]   425-888-0227
  cascadegolfcourse.com
Cedarcrest GC, *Marysville* .... 18 [M]   360-363-8460
  cedarcrestgc.com
Chambers Bay GC, *University Place* .... 18 [M]   253-460-4653
  chambersbaygolf.com
Cherry Hill GC, *Granger* .... 9 [P]   509-854-1800
  cherryhillrecreation.com
Chewelah G&CC, *Chewelah* .... 27 [P]   509-935-6807
  chewelahgolf.com
Christy's Golf Range & Par 3, *Federal Way* .... 9 [P]   253-927-0644
Clarkston CC, *Clarkston* .... 18 [V]   509-758-7911
  clarkstongolfandcountryclub.com
Club Green Meadows, *Vancouver* .... 18 [V]   360-256-1510
  clubgreenmeadows.com

218   [A] = MILITARY   [M] = MUNICIPAL   [P] = PUBLIC   [R] = RESORT

Golf Yellow Pages, 18th Edition — WASHINGTON

Colfax GC, *Colfax* .... 9 [P] 509-397-2122
 colfaxgolf.com
Colockum Ridge GC, *Quincy* .... 18 [R] 509-787-6206
 colockumridgegolf.com
Columbia Park GC & DR, *Kennewick* .... 18 [M] 509-586-2800
Columbia Point GC, *Richland* .... 18 [M] 509-946-0710
 columbiapointgolfcourse.com
Crescent Bar Resort, *Quincy* .... 9 [R] 509-787-1511
 crescentbarresort.com
Crossroads GC, *Bellevue* .... 9 [M] 425-452-4873
Dakota Creek GC, *Custer* .... 18 [P] 360-366-3131
 dakotacreekgolf.com
Deer Meadows GC, *Davenport* .... 18 [P] 509-725-8488
 deermeadows.net
Deer Park GC, *Deer Park* .... 18 [R] 509-276-5912
 deerparkgolf.com
Delphi CC, *Olympia* .... 9 [S] 360-357-6437
 delphigolfcourse.com
Desert Aire GC, *Desert Aire* .... 18 [P] 509-932-4439
 desertairegolf.com
Desert Canyon Golf Resort, *Orondo* .... 18 [R] 509-784-1111
 desertcanyon.com
Desperados Pasture GC, *Rochester* .... 18 [P] 360-273-5774
Discovery Bay GC, *Port Townsend* .... 18 [P] 360-385-0704
 discobaygolf.com
Dominion Meadows GC, *Colville* .... 18 [S] 509-684-5508
 dominionmeadowsgolf.com
Downriver GC, *Spokane* .... 18 [M] 509-327-5269
 spokanegolf.org
Druids Glen GC, *Covington* .... 18 [P] 253-638-1200
 druidsglengolf.com
Eagle Ridge GC, *Spokane* .... 9 [P] 509-443-9751
Eaglemont GC, *Mt Vernon* .... 18 [S] 425-424-0800
 eaglemontgolf.com
Eagles Pride GC At Fort Lewis, *Fort Lewis* ...... 27 [A] 253-967-6522
 fortlewismwr.com
Elk Run GC, *Maple Valley* .... 18 [P] 425-432-8800
 elkrungolf.com
Ellensburg GC, *Ellensburg* .... 9 [S] 509-962-2984
Enumclaw GC, *Enumclaw* .... 18 [M] 360-825-2827
 enumclawgolfcourse.com
Esmeralda GC, *Spokane* .... 18 [M] 509-487-6291
 spokanegolf.org
Everett G&CC, *Everett* .... 18 [V] 425-259-8141
 everettgolfcc.com
Fairway Village G&CC, *Vancouver* .... 9 [S] 360-254-9325
Fairwood G&CC, *Renton* .... 18 [V] 425-226-9700
 fairwood.org
Fircrest GC, *Fircrest* .... 18 [V] 253-564-5792
 fircrestgolf.com
Fisher Park GC, *Yakima* .... 9 [M] 509-575-6075
 ci.yakima.wa.us
Flowing Lake GC, *Snohomish* .... 18 [P] 360-568-2753
Fort Steilacoom GC, *Lakewood* .... 9 [P] 253-588-0613
 lakespanawaygc.com
Foster Golf Links, *Tukwila* .... 18 [M] 206-242-4221
 fostergolflinks.com
Four Seasons Ranch, *Port Angeles* .... 9 [V] 360-457-5211
Gallery GC, *Oak Harbor* .... 18 [A] 360-257-2178
 navylifepnw.com
Gateway GC, *Sedro Woolley* .... 9 [P] 360-855-1661
 ci.sedro-woolley.wa.us

GC At Redmond Ridge, *Redmond* .... 18 [P] 425-836-1510
 redmondridgegolf.com
Gig Harbor GC, *Gig Harbor* .... 9 [V] 253-851-2378
 gigharborgolfclub.com
Glen Acres G&CC, *Seattle* .... 9 [V] 206-244-3786
 glenacresgolf.com
Glendale CC, *Bellevue* .... 18 [V] 425-746-7944
 glendalecc.com
Gleneagle GC, *Arlington* .... 18 [P] 360-435-6713
 gleneaglegolfcourse.net
Gold Mountain GC, *Bremerton* .... 36 [M] 360-415-5432
 goldmt.com
Goldendale CC, *Goldendale* .... 9 [S] 509-773-4705
Golf Green Golf Ctr, *Longview* .... 9 [P] 360-425-0450
Grandview GC, *Custer* .... 18 [P] 360-366-3947
 golfatgrandview.com
Grays Harbor CC, *Aberdeen* .... 9 [V] 360-532-1931
Green Lakes Par 3 GC, *Seattle* .... 9 [M] 206-632-2280
 seattle.gov
Green Mountain GC, *Vancouver* .... 18 [P] 360-833-8463
 golfgreenmountain.com
Hangman Valley GC, *Spokane* .... 18 [M] 509-448-1212
 spokanecounty.org
Harbour Pointe GC, *Mukilteo* .... 18 [P] 425-355-6060
 harbourpointegolf.com
Harrington G&CC, *Harrington* .... 9 [P] 509-253-4308
Hartwood GC, *Brush Prairie* .... 9 [P] 360-896-6041
Hat Island GC, *Everett* .... 9 [V] 360-444-6611
 hatisland.org
High Cedars GC, *Orting* .... 27 [P] 360-893-3171
 highcedars.com
High Valley CC, *Packwood* .... 9 [V] 360-494-8431
Highland GC, *Cosmopolis* .... 18 [P] 360-533-2455
Highlander GC, *East Wenatchee* .... 18 [P] 509-884-4653
 highlandergolfclub.com
Highlander Greens, *Moses Lake* .... 9 [U] 509-766-1228
Highlands GC, *Tacoma* .... 9 [P] 253-759-3622
 highlandsgolf.net
Holmes Harbor GC, *Freeland* .... 18 [P] 360-331-2363
 holmesharbor.com
Homestead G&CC, *Lynden* .... 18 [R] 360-354-1196
 homesteadgolfclub.com
Horn Rapids GC, *Richland* .... 18 [P] 509-375-4714
Horseshoe Lake GC, *Port Orchard* .... 18 [P] 253-857-3326
 hlgolf.com
Husum Hills GC, *White Salmon* .... 9 [P] 509-493-1211
Indian Canyon GC, *Spokane* .... 18 [M] 509-747-5353
 spokanegolf.org
Indian Summer CC, *Olympia* .... 18 [V] 360-923-1075
 indiansummergolf.com
Inglewood GC, *Kenmore* .... 18 [V] 425-488-8800
 inglewoodgolfclub.com
Interbay Golf Center, *Seattle* .... 9 [M] 206-285-2200
 premiergc.com
Ironwood Green GC, *Glenoma* .... 9 [P] 360-498-5425
Island Greens, *Clinton* .... 9 [P] 360-579-6042
 islandgreens.com
Jackson Park GC, *Seattle* .... 27 [M] 206-363-4747
 premiergc.com
Jade Greens GC, *Auburn* .... 9 [P] 253-931-8562
 jadegreens.com
Jefferson Park GC, *Seattle* .... 27 [M] 206-762-4513
 premiergc.com

[S] = SEMI-PRIVATE   [V] = PRIVATE   [U] = UNIVERSITY   [N] = UNIVERSITY-PRIVATE

WASHINGTON — Golf Yellow Pages, 18th Edition

Kahler Glen GC, *Leavenworth* ....18 [R] 509-763-4025
  kahlerglen.com
Kayak Point GC, *Stanwood* ....18 [P] 360-652-9676
  golfkayak.com
Kenwanda GC, *Snohomish* ....18 [P] 360-668-1166
  kenwandagolf.com
Kitsap G&CC, *Bremerton* ....18 [V] 360-373-5101
  kitsapgolfcc.com
Lake Chelan GC, *Chelan* ....18 [R] 509-682-8026
  lakechelangolf.com
Lake Cushman GC, *Hoodsport* ....9 [S] 360-877-5505
  lakecushmangolf.com
Lake Limerick CC, *Shelton* ....9 [R] 360-426-6290
  lakelimerick.com
Lake Padden GC, *Bellingham* ....18 [M] 360-738-7400
  lakepaddengolf.com
Lake Spanaway GC, *Tacoma* ....18 [M] 253-531-3660
  lakespanawaygc.com
Lake View Par 3 GC, *Vancouver* ....18 [P] 360-693-9116
Lake Wilderness GC, *Maple Valley* ....18 [M] 425-432-9405
  lakewildernessgc.com
Lake Woods GC, *Bridgeport* ....9 [M] 509-686-5721
Lakeland Village GC, *Allyn* ....27 [P] 360-275-6100
  lakelandvillagegolf.com
Lakeview G&CC, *Soap Lake* ....18 [V] 509-246-0336
Lamms Links, *Oak Harbor* ....9 [P] 360-675-3412
Leavenworth GC, *Leavenworth* ....18 [S] 509-548-7267
  leavenworthgolf.com
Legion Memorial GC, *Everett* ....18 [M] 425-259-4653
  legionmemorialgolf.com
Lewis River GC, *Woodland* ....18 [R] 360-225-8254
  lewisrivergolf.com
Liberty Lake GC, *Liberty Lake* ....18 [M] 509-255-6233
  spokanecounty.org
Linden G&CC, *Puyallup* ....9 [V] 253-845-2056
  lindengolf.com
Links At Olson Mansion, *Maple Valley* ....9 [P] 425-433-0711
  olsonmansion.com
Lipoma Firs GC, *Puyallup* ....27 [P] 253-841-4396
Longview CC, *Longview* ....18 [P] 360-425-3132
  goodknightgolf.com
Loomis Trail GC, *Blaine* ....18 [P] 360-332-1725
  semiahmoo.com
Lopez Island GC, *Lopez Island* ....9 [P] 360-468-2679
  lopezislandgolfclub.com
Lynnwood Muni GC, *Lynnwood* ....18 [M] 425-672-4653
  ci.lynnwood.wa.us
Ma 8 Golf, *Manson* ....9 [P] 509-687-6338
Madrona Links GC, *Gig Harbor* ....18 [P] 253-851-5193
  madronalinks.com
Manito G&CC, *Spokane* ....18 [V] 509-448-2045
  manitocc.com
Maple Grove Golf, *Randle* ....9 [R] 360-497-2741
  kmresorts.com
Maplewood GC, *Renton* ....18 [M] 425-430-4800
  ci.renton.wa.us
McCormick Woods GC, *Port Orchard* ....18 [P] 360-895-0130
  mccormickwoodsgolf.com
Meadow Park GC, *Tacoma* ....27 [M] 253-473-3033
  meadowparkgolf.com
Meadow Springs CC, *Richland* ....18 [V] 509-627-2321
  meadowspringscc.com

Meadow Wood GC, *Liberty Lake* ....18 [M] 509-255-9539
  meadowwoodgolf.com
Meadowmeer G&CC, *Bainbridge Island* ....9 [S] 206-842-2218
  orgsites.com/wa/meadowmeergc
Meridian Valley CC, *Kent* ....18 [V] 253-631-3133
  meridianvalleycc.com
Mill Creek CC, *Mill Creek* ....18 [V] 425-743-5664
  millcreek.cc
Mint Valley GC, *Longview* ....18 [M] 360-442-5442
  mint-valley.com
Moses Lake G&CC, *Moses Lake* ....18 [V] 509-765-5049
  moseslakegolfclub.com
Mount Adams CC, *Toppenish* ....18 [S] 509-865-4440
  mtadamsgolf.com
Mount Cashmere GC, *Cashmere* ....9 [P] 509-782-1207
Mount Si GC, *Snoqualmie* ....18 [P] 425-391-4926
  mtsigolf.com
New World Golf Ctr, *Bellingham* ....9 [P] 360-398-1362
Newaukum Valley GC, *Chehalis* ....27 [P] 360-748-0461
  golfnvgc.com
Nile Shrine GC, *Mountlake Terrace* ....18 [S] 425-776-5154
  nilegolf.com
North Bellingham GC, *Bellingham* ....18 [P] 360-398-8300
  northbellinghamgolf.com
North Shore GC, *Tacoma* ....18 [S] 253-927-1375
  northshoregc.net
Oakbrook G&CC, *Tacoma* ....18 [R] 253-584-8770
  oakbrookgcc.com
Oaksridge GC, *Elma* ....18 [P] 360-482-3511
Oasis Park Muni GC, *Ephrata* ....9 [P] 509-754-5102
Ocean Shores GC, *Ocean Shores* ....18 [R] 360-289-3357
  oceanshoresgolf.com
Odessa GC, *Odessa* ....9 [P] 509-982-0093
Okanogan Valley GC, *Omak* ....9 [S] 509-826-6937
  okanoganvalleygolf.com
Olympia Country & GC, *Olympia* ....18 [V] 360-866-7121
  olympiacountryclub.com
Orcas Island GC, *Eastsound* ....9 [R] 360-376-4400
  orcasgolf.com
Orchard Hills CC, *Washougal* ....18 [V] 360-835-5444
  orchardhillscc.com
Oroville GC, *Oroville* ....9 [P] 509-476-2390
Othello GC, *Othello* ....9 [P] 509-488-2376
Overlake G&CC, *Medina* ....18 [V] 425-454-5031
  overlakegcc.com
Overlook GC, *Mt Vernon* ....9 [P] 360-422-6444
Pacific Lutheran Univ GC, *Tacoma* ....9 [U] 253-535-7393
  plu.edu
Painted Hills GC, *Spokane* ....18 [P] 509-928-4653
  spokanevalleygolf.com
Palouse Ridge GC, *Pullman* ....18 [U] 509-335-4342
  palouseridge.com
Pasadena Ridge Par 3 GC, *Spokane* ....9 [V] 509-927-0149
  pasadenaridge.com
Pasco Golfland, *Pasco* ....9 [P] 509-544-9291
Pend Oreille G&CC, *Metaline Falls* ....9 [P] 509-446-2301
Peninsula GC, *Port Angeles* ....18 [S] 360-457-6501
  golfinportangeles.com
Peninsula GC, *Long Beach* ....9 [P] 360-642-2828
  peninsulagolfcourse.com
Pheasant Creek GC, *Touchet* ....9 [P] 509-394-4653
  pheasantcreekgolfcourse.com
Pine Acres Par 3 GC, *Spokane* ....9 [P] 509-466-9984

[A] = MILITARY   [M] = MUNICIPAL   [P] = PUBLIC   [R] = RESORT

WASHINGTON

Pine Crest GC, *Vancouver* .... 9 [P] 360-573-2051
pinecrestgc.net
Point Roberts G&CC, *Point Roberts* .... 18 [S] 360-945-4653
pointrobertsgolfcourse.com
Pomeroy GC, *Pomeroy* .... 9 [M] 509-843-1197
Port Townsend GC, *Port Townsend* .... 9 [P] 360-385-4547
porttownsendgolf.com
Potholes GC, *Othello* .... 9 [R] 509-346-9491
potholesgolf.com
Prospector at Suncadia Resort, *Cle Elum* .... 18 [R] 509-649-6401
suncadiaresort.com
Quail Ridge GC, *Clarkston* .... 18 [P] 509-758-8501
golfquailridge.com
Rainier G&CC, *Seattle* .... 18 [V] 206-242-2800
rainiergolfcc.com
Raspberry Ridge GC, *Everson* .... 9 [P] 360-354-3029
raspberryridgegc.com
Resort At Port Ludlow, *Port Ludlow* .... 27 [R] 360-437-0272
portludlowresort.com
Ritzville Muni GC, *Ritzville* .... 9 [M] 509-659-9868
River Ridge GC, *Selah* .... 9 [P] 509-697-8323
Riverbend G Complex, *Kent* .... 27 [M] 253-854-3673
riverbendgolfcomplex.com
Riverside GC, *Chehalis* .... 18 [P] 360-748-8182
playriversidegolf.com
Riviera Community Club, *Anderson Island* .... 9 [V] 253-884-4993
rivieraclub.org
Rock Island GC, *Rock Island* .... 9 [P] 509-884-2806
Rolling Hills GC, *Bremerton* .... 18 [P] 360-479-1212
rhgolfcourse.com
Royal City GC, *Royal City* .... 9 [M] 509-346-2052
royalcitygolf.com
Royal Oaks CC, *Vancouver* .... 18 [V] 360-256-1350
royaloaks.net
Sage Hills Golf Resort, *Warden* .... 18 [R] 509-349-2603
sagehills.com
Sahalee CC, *Sammamish* .... 27 [V] 425-868-8800
sahalee.com
Salish Cliffs GC, *Shelton* .... 18 [R] 800-667-7711
salish-cliffs.com
San Juan G&CC, *Friday Harbor* .... 9 [P] 360-378-2254
sanjuangolfclub.com
Sand Point CC, *Seattle* .... 18 [V] 206-523-4994
sandpointcc.com
Sandy Pointe GC, *Ferndale* .... 9 [V] 360-384-3921
mysandypoint.com
Scott Lake G&CC, *Olympia* .... 9 [P] 360-352-4838
Sea Links GC, *Blaine* .... 9 [P] 360-371-5400
sealinksgolfcourse.com
Seattle GC, *Seattle* .... 18 [V] 206-363-5444
seattlegolfclub.com
Semiahmoo GC, *Blaine* .... 18 [R] 360-371-7005
semiahmoo.com
Shelter Bay GC, *La Conner* .... 9 [V] 360-466-3805
Shuksan GC, *Bellingham* .... 18 [P] 360-398-8888
shuksangolf.com
Similk Beach GC, *Anacortes* .... 18 [P] 360-293-3444
Skagit G&CC, *Burlington* .... 18 [V] 360-757-0530
skagitgolfclub.com
Skamania Lodge GC, *Stevenson* .... 18 [R] 360-427-2540
skamania.com
Skyline GC, *Cathlamet* .... 9 [P] 360-795-8785
skylinegolf.net

SkyRidge GC, *Sequim* .... 9 [P] 360-683-3673
skyridgegolfcourse.com
Snohomish GC, *Snohomish* .... 18 [P] 360-568-2676
snohomishgolfcourse.com
Snoqualmie Falls GC, *Fall City* .... 18 [P] 425-222-5244
snoqualmiefallsgolf.com
Spokane CC, *Spokane* .... 18 [V] 509-466-9813
spokanecountryclub.com
St John G&CC, *St John* .... 9 [P] 509-648-3259
Sudden Valley G&CC, *Bellingham* .... 18 [S] 360-734-6435
suddenvalleygolfcourse.com
Sumner Meadows Golf Links, *Sumner* .... 18 [M] 253-863-8198
golfsumnermeadows.com
Sun Country Golf Resort, *Cle Elum* .... 18 [R] 509-674-2226
golfsuncountry.com
Sun Willows, *Pasco* .... 18 [M] 509-545-3440
sunwillowsgolfcourse.com
Sundance GC, *Nine Mile Falls* .... 18 [P] 509-466-4040
sundancegc.com
SunLand G&CC, *Sequim* .... 18 [S] 360-683-6800
sunlandgolf.com
Sunserra Golf LLC, *Quincy* .... 9 [P] 509-787-4156
sunserra.com
Suntides GC, *Yakima* .... 18 [P] 509-966-9065
suntidesgolf.com
Surfside GC, *Ocean Park* .... 9 [P] 360-665-4148
Tacoma Country & GC, *Lakewood* .... 18 [V] 253-588-0404
golftcgc.com
Tahoma Valley G&CC, *Yelm* .... 18 [P] 360-458-3332
tahomavalley.com
Tall Chief GC, *Fall City* .... 12 [P] 425-222-5911
tallchiefgolfcourse.com
Tam O Shanter G&CC, *Bellevue* .... 9 [V] 425-746-1578
tamoshanter.net
Tanwax Greens GC, *Eatonville* .... 9 [P] 360-832-8400
Tapps Island GC, *Lake Tapps* .... 9 [S] 253-862-7011
tapps-island.org
Tekoa GC, *Tekoa* .... 9 [P] 208-274-3234
The Cedars At Dungeness, *Sequim* .... 18 [P] 360-683-6344
dungenessgolf.com
The Cedars on Salmon Creek, *Brush Prairie* .... 18 [P] 360-687-4233
golfcedars.com
The Classic GC, *Spanaway* .... 18 [P] 253-847-4440
classicgolfclub.net
The Creek at Qualchan, *Spokane* .... 18 [M] 509-448-9317
spokanegolf.org
The Fairways at West Terrace, *Cheney* .... 18 [P] 509-747-8418
golfthefairways.com
The GC At Echo Falls, *Snohomish* .... 18 [P] 360-668-3030
echofallsgolf.com
The GC At Hawks Prairie, *Lacey* .... 36 [P] 360-412-0495
hawksprairiegolf.com
The GC At Newcastle, *Newcastle* .... 36 [P] 425-793-5566
newcastlegolf.com
The Home Course, *Dupont* .... 18 [P] 253-964-0520
thehomecourse.com
The Links At Moses Pointe, *Moses Lake* ..... 18 [R] 509-764-2275
mosespointe.com
The Members Club At Aldarra, *Fall City* ...... 18 [V] 425-222-7828
thememberscluboataldarra.com
The Plateau Club, *Sammamish* .... 18 [V] 425-836-4653
plateauclub.com
The Yakima CC, *Yakima* .... 18 [V] 509-452-2266
yakimacountryclub.com

[S] = SEMI-PRIVATE [V] = PRIVATE [U] = UNIVERSITY [N] = UNIVERSITY-PRIVATE

WASHINGTON

Golf Yellow Pages, 18th Edition

Three Lakes GC, *Malaga*......................18 [P] 509-663-5448
  threelakesgolf.com
Three Rivers GC, *Kelso*........................18 [P] 360-423-4653
  3rivers.us
Touchet Valley GC, *Dayton*....................9 [M] 509-382-4851
TPC Snoqualmie Ridge, *Snoqualmie*....... 18 [V] 425-396-6001
  tpcsr.com
Trailhead At Liberty Lake, *Liberty Lake*......9 [S] 509-928-3484
  libertylakewa.gov/golf
Tri City CC, *Kennewick*..........................18 [S] 509-783-6014
  tccountryclub.com
Tri Mountain GC, *Ridgefield*..................18 [M] 360-887-3004
  trimountaingolf.com
Trophy Lake Golf & Casting, *Port Orchard*...18 [P] 360-874-8337
  trophylakegolf.com
Tumble Creek At Suncadia, *Cle Elum*........ 18 [V] 509-649-6484
  tumblecreek.com
Tumwater Valley Muni GC, *Tumwater*.........18 [M] 360-943-9500
  tumwatervalleygc.com
Twin Lakes G&CC, *Federal Way*................. 18 [V] 253-927-4440
  twinlakesgolf.net
Twin Rivers GC, *Fall City*.......................18 [P] 425-222-7575
  twinriversgolfcourse.com
Tyee Valley GC, *Seatac*..........................18 [P] 206-878-3540
Useless Bay G&CC, *Langley*.................... 18 [V] 360-321-5958
  uselessbaygolf.com
Vashon Island G&CC, *Vashon*...................9 [V] 206-463-9410
  vashoncountryclub.com
Veterans Memorial GC, *Walla Walla*..........18 [M] 509-527-4507
Vic Meyers GC At Sun Lakes, *Coulee City*....... 9 [R] 509-632-5738
  sunlakesparkresort.com
Village Greens GC, *Port Orchard*.............18 [M] 360-871-1222
Walla Walla CC, *Walla Walla*................. 18 [V] 509-525-1562
Walter E Hall GC, *Everett*......................18 [M] 425-353-4653
  walterhallgolf.com
Wandermere GC, *Spokane*....................18 [P] 509-466-8023
  wandermere.com
Washington National GC, *Auburn*...........18 [R] 253-333-5000
  washingtonnationalgolfclub.com
Wayne GC, *Bothell*..............................18 [P] 425-485-6237
Wellington Hills GC, *Woodinville*..............9 [P] 425-485-5589
Wenatchee G&CC, *East Wenatchee*........... 18 [V] 509-884-7105
  wenatcheegolfclub.org
West Richland GC, *West Richland*............18 [P] 509-967-2165
  westrichlandgolf.com
West Seattle GC, *Seattle*......................18 [M] 206-935-5187
  premiergc.com
Westwood West GC, *Yakima*....................9 [P] 509-966-0890
Whidbey G&CC, *Oak Harbor*................... 18 [V] 360-675-4546
  whidbeygolfandcc.com
Whispering Firs GC, *McChord AFB*...........18 [A] 253-982-2124
  62services.com
White Horse GC, *Kingston*.....................18 [S] 360-297-4468
  whitehorsegolf.com
Willapa Harbor GC, *Raymond*..................9 [P] 360-942-2392
  willapaharborgolf.com
Willows Run GC, *Redmond*....................63 [P] 425-883-1200
  willowsrun.com
Wine Valley GC, *Walla Walla*..................18 [P] 509-525-4653
  winevalleygolfclub.com
Wing Point G&CC, *Bainbridge Island*......... 18 [V] 206-842-7933
  wingpointgolf.com

Yakima Elks G&CC, *Selah*....................... 18 [V] 509-697-7177
  yakimaelksgolf.com

WEST VIRGINIA

Alpine Lake Resort, *Terra Alta*................18 [R] 304-789-2481
  alpinelake.com
Apple Valley CC, *Fairmont*.....................9 [P] 304-363-9551
  golfapplevalley.net
Barbour CC, *Philippi*............................9 [S] 304-457-2156
Beaver Creek GC, *Beaver*......................18 [S] 304-763-9116
Bel Meadow CC, *Mt Clare*......................18 [S] 304-623-3701
  belmeadow.com
Berry Hills CC, *Charleston*.................... 18 [V] 304-744-8790
  berryhillscc.com
Big Bend GC, *Tornado*..........................18 [M] 304-722-0400
  kcprc.com
Black Knight CC, *Beckley*......................9 [V] 304-253-2661
  blackknightcc.com
Black Wolf Links, *Gary*..........................9 [M] 304-383-4615
Bluefield Elks Club, *Bluefield*..................9 [P] 304-327-6511
Bridge Haven GC, *Fayetteville*...............18 [P] 304-574-2120
  wvweb.com/bridgehaven
Bridgeport CC, *Bridgeport*.................... 18 [V] 304-842-3111
  bccwv.com
Brooke Hills Park GC, *Wellsburg*..............18 [P] 304-737-1236
  brookehillspark.com
Buckhannon CC, *Buckhannon*..................9 [V] 304-472-2250
Cacapon St Park Resort, *Berkeley Springs*...18 [R] 304-258-1022
  cacaponresort.com
Canaan Valley Resorts GC, *Davis*.............18 [R] 304-866-4121
  canaanresort.com
Capon Springs Resort GC, *Capon Springs*.....9 [R] 304-874-3695
  caponsprings.net
Cato Park GC, *Charleston*......................9 [M] 304-348-6859
  cityofcharleston.org/recreation
Cherry Hill CC, *Richwood*......................9 [P] 304-846-9876
  golfcherryhill.com
Clarksburg CC, *Clarksburg*..................... 18 [V] 304-624-5807
Clear Fork Valley GC, *Oceana*................18 [S] 304-682-6209
Coonskin Park GC, *Charleston*................18 [M] 304-341-8013
  kcprc.com
Cress Creek CC, *Shepherdstown*............. 18 [V] 304-876-3375
  cresscreek.com
Crispin GC, *Wheeling*..........................18 [R] 304-243-4141
  oglebay-resort.com
Deerfield CC, *Weston*...........................9 [P] 304-269-1139
Dunkard Valley GC, *Blacksville*................9 [P] 304-432-8486
  dunkardvalley.com
Edgewood CC, *Sissonville*..................... 18 [V] 304-984-9207
  edgewoodcc.com
Elks GC, *Elkins*....................................9 [P] 304-636-9704
Fairmont Field Club, *Fairmont*.................9 [V] 304-367-0238
Fountain Springs GC, *Peterstown*............18 [P] 304-753-4653
GC of West Virginia, *Waverly*..................18 [S] 304-464-4420
  golfclubwv.com
Glenville CC, *Glenville*..........................9 [P] 304-462-5907
Grand Vue Park GC, *Moundsville*..............18 [P] 304-845-9810
  marshallcountytourism.com
Grandview CC, *Beaver*..........................18 [P] 304-763-2520
Green Hills CC, *Ravenswood*..................18 [S] 304-273-3396
  greenhillsgolfclub.com
Green Hills CC, *Fairmont*...................... 18 [V] 304-287-7439
  greenhillsclub.com

[A] = MILITARY   [M] = MUNICIPAL   [P] = PUBLIC   [R] = RESORT

WEST VIRGINIA

Course	Holes	Type	Phone
Greenbrier Hills GC, *Rainelle*	9	[M]	304-438-9050
Greenbrier Sporting Club, *White Sulphur Springs*	18	[V]	304-647-6114
gbrsc.com			
Guyan G&CC, *Huntington*	18	[V]	304-736-1141
guyangolfandcountryclub.com			
Hawks Nest St Park GC, *Gauley Bridge*	9	[S]	304-632-1361
hawksnestsp.com			
Hidden Valley CC, *Point Pleasant*	9	[S]	304-675-9739
Hide A Way GC, *West Milford*	9	[P]	304-745-4900
wvhideaway.com			
Highland Hills Par-3 GC, *Follansbee*	9	[P]	304-797-7606
Highland Springs GC, *Wellsburg*	18	[P]	304-737-2201
Highlands GC Fisher Mountain, *Franklin*	18	[P]	304-358-2261
highlandsgolfwv.com			
Holly Meadows GC, *Parsons*	9	[M]	304-478-3406
Lake Floyd GC, *Bristol*	9	[P]	304-782-1577
Lakeview CC, *Cool Ridge*	9	[P]	304-787-4031
Lakeview Golf Resort & Spa, *Morgantown*	36	[R]	304-594-2011
lakeviewresort.com			
Lewisburg Elks CC, *Lewisburg*	18	[P]	304-645-3660
lewisburgelkscc.com			
Little Creek CC, *South Charleston*	18	[S]	304-746-4653
littlecreekgolfcourse.com			
Locust Hill GC, *Charles Town*	18	[S]	304-728-7300
locusthillgolf.com			
Logan CC, *Chapmanville*	9	[V]	304-855-9018
Meadow Ponds G&CC, *Cassville*	18	[P]	304-328-5570
meadowponds.com			
Meadowland GC, *Winfield*	9	[P]	304-937-3065
Mill Creek GC, *Burlington*	9	[S]	304-289-3160
Mingo Bottom GC, *Elizabeth*	18	[P]	304-275-3378
mingobottom.com			
Minibel GC, *Vienna*	9	[P]	304-295-7711
minibelpar3.com			
Moundsville CC, *Moundsville*	18	[V]	304-845-2153
Mountain View GC, *Webster Springs*	9	[P]	304-847-5928
mountainview-golf.com			
Mountaineer G&CC, *Morgantown*	18	[P]	304-328-5520
mountaineergolf.com			
Mountaineers Woodview GC, *New Cumberland*	18	[P]	304-387-8260
mtrgaming.com			
Nicholas Memorial GC, *Summersville*	9	[M]	304-872-9850
North Bend GC, *Harrisville*	9	[P]	304-643-2206
Orchard Hills G&CC, *Barboursville*	9	[P]	304-736-8225
Paradise Lake GC, *Morgantown*	9	[P]	304-291-0827
Parkersburg CC, *Vienna*	18	[P]	304-295-4841
Pete Dye GC, *Bridgeport*	18	[P]	304-842-2801
petedye.com			
Pikewood National GC, *Morgantown*	18	[P]	304-864-3085
pikewoodgolfclub.com			
Pipestem GC, *Pipestem*	27	[R]	304-466-1800
pipestemresort.com			
Pleasant Hills GC, *New Manchester*	9	[P]	304-387-0068
Pleasant Valley CC, *Weirton*	18	[V]	304-723-0070
pleasantvalleyccwv.com			
Pocahontas GC, *Marlinton*	9	[P]	304-799-7466
pccgolf.com			
Polish Pines CC, *Keyser*	9	[R]	301-786-4131
Preston CC, *Kingwood*	18	[P]	304-329-2100
prestoncc.info			
Princeton Elks CC, *Princeton*	9	[S]	304-425-3273
Raven GC At Snowshoe Mountain, *Snowshoe*	18	[P]	304-572-6500
snowshoemtn.com			
Riverbend GC At EvUnBreth, *Buckhannon*	9	[P]	304-472-6295
riverbendgolfwv.com			
Riverside GC, *Mason*	18	[S]	304-773-5354
riversidegolfclubwv.com			
Riverview CC, *Madison*	18	[P]	304-369-9835
Riviera CC, *Lesage*	18	[S]	304-736-7778
Roane County CC, *Spencer*	9	[S]	304-927-2899
Salem CC, *Salem*	9	[P]	304-782-3187
Sandy Brae GC, *Clendenin*	18	[P]	304-965-6800
Scarlet Oaks GC, *Poca*	18	[S]	304-755-8079
scarletoaksgolf.com			
Shawnee Regional Park GC, *Independence*	9	[M]	304-341-8030
kcprc.com			
Sistersville CC, *Sistersville*	9	[V]	304-652-3005
Sleepy Hollow G&CC, *Charles Town*	18	[S]	304-725-5210
golfsleepyhollow.com			
Sleepy Hollow GC, *Hurricane*	18	[V]	304-757-9416
sleepyhollowgolfclub.com			
South Hills GC, *Parkersburg*	18	[P]	304-422-8381
southhillsgolf.com			
Speidel GC At Oglebay, *Wheeling*	54	[R]	304-243-4141
oglebay-resort.com			
Spring Valley CC, *Huntington*	18	[V]	304-429-5570
svcountryclub.com			
St Marys GC, *St Marys*	9	[P]	304-684-3557
Stonebridge GC, *Martinsburg*	18	[S]	304-263-4653
stonebridgegolfcoursewv.com			
Stonewall-Arnold Palmer Sig, *Walkersville*	18	[R]	304-269-8885
stonewallresort.com			
Sugarwood GC, *Lavalette*	18	[P]	304-523-6500
sugarwoodgolfclub.com			
Sunny Croft GC, *Clarksburg*	9	[P]	304-624-4421
sunnycroft.org			
The Brier Patch Golf Links, *Beckley*	18	[S]	304-253-4653
The Esquire CC, *Barboursville*	18	[S]	304-736-1476
The Greenbrier Resort, *White Sulphur Springs*	54	[R]	304-536-1110
greenbrier.com			
The Pines CC, *Morgantown*	18	[V]	304-296-3466
thepinescc.com			
The Resort At Glade Springs, *Daniels*	36	[R]	304-763-2000
gladesprings.com			
The Resort At Glade Springs Woodhaven GC,			
Daniels	18	[R]	304-763-3332
gladesprings.com			
The Woods Resort, *Hedgesville*	36	[R]	304-754-7222
thewoods.com			
Triadelphia CC, *Man*	9	[S]	304-583-9030
Tug Valley CC, *Sprigg*	9	[P]	304-235-2106
Twin Falls Resort St Park, *Mullens*	18	[R]	304-294-4044
twinfallsresort.com			
Twin Silos At Lavalette, *Lavalette*	18	[P]	304-525-7405
twinsilosatlavalette.com			
Twisted Gun GC, *Wharncliffe*	18	[P]	304-664-9100
twistedgungc.com			
Tygart Lake Public GC, *Grafton*	18	[P]	304-265-3100
tygartlakegolfcourse.com			
Valley View CC, *White Sulphur Spring*	9	[S]	304-536-1600
valleyview.cc			
Valley View CC, *Moorefield*	18	[P]	304-538-6564
Wheeling CC, *Wheeling*	18	[V]	304-232-2020
wheelingcountryclub.com			
Wheeling Park Exec GC, *Wheeling*	9	[M]	304-243-4181
wheeling-park.com			

[S] = SEMI-PRIVATE [V] = PRIVATE [U] = UNIVERSITY [N] = UNIVERSITY-PRIVATE

WEST VIRGINIA

Golf Yellow Pages, 18th Edition

White Oak CC, *Oak Hill* .... 9 [V] 304-465-5639
Williams CC, *Weirton* .... 18 [V] 304-748-2340
   williams-countryclub.com
Willowwood CC, *Hinton* .... 9 [P] 304-466-3220
   hintonelks.com
Woodbrier GC, *Martinsburg* .... 9 [P] 304-274-9818
Woodridge Plantation GC, *Mineral Wells* .... 18 [S] 304-489-1800
   woodridgeplantation.com
Worthington GC, *Parkersburg* .... 18 [P] 304-428-4297

WISCONSIN

19th Hole Sports Bar & Grill, *St Germain* .... 9 [P] 715-542-4042
   whitetaillodge.com
27 Pines GC, *Sturgeon Bay* .... 9 [P] 920-746-8762
Abbey Springs GC, *Fontana* .... 18 [R] 262-275-6113
   abbeysprings.com
Alaskan GC, *Kewaunee* .... 9 [P] 920-388-3940
Alpine Resort & GC, *Egg Harbor* .... 27 [R] 920-868-3000
   alpineresort.com
Alpine Valley Resort, *Elkhorn* .... 27 [R] 262-642-7374
   alpinevalleyresort.com
Amacoy Resort GC, *Bruce* .... 9 [R] 715-868-6952
American Legion GC, *Wausau* .... 9 [P] 715-675-3663
   wausauamericanlegion.org
Antigo Bass Lake GC, *Deerbrook* .... 18 [S] 715-623-6196
   basslakecc.com
Apostle Highlands GC, *Bayfield* .... 18 [P] 715-779-5960
   golfbayfield.com
Arcadia CC, *Arcadia* .... 9 [P] 608-323-6495
   arcadiacountryclub.com
Argue ment GC, *New Glarus* .... 9 [P] 608-527-6366
   argumentgolf.com
Arrowhead Springs GC, *Richfield* .... 9 [P] 262-628-2298
Auburn Bluff GC, *Campbellsport* .... 9 [P] 920-533-4311
Autumn Ridge GC, *Valders* .... 18 [P] 920-758-3333
   autumnridgegolfcourse.com
Badger Creek GC, *New Holstein* .... 18 [S] 920-898-5760
Badlands GC, *Roberts* .... 18 [P] 715-749-4150
   badlandsgolf.net
Baehmanns Golf Ctr, *Cedarburg* .... 9 [P] 262-377-0768
   golfcedarburg.com
Baraboo CC, *Baraboo* .... 18 [S] 608-356-8195
   baraboocountryclub.com
Barker Lake CC, *Winter* .... 9 [R] 715-266-4152
   haywardlakes.com/barkerlake.htm
Barnyard 9 GC, *Prairie Du Chien* .... 9 [P] 608-326-4941
Barronett Hills GC, *Barronett* .... 9 [P] 715-822-3285
Bass Creek GC, *Janesville* .... 9 [P] 608-876-6631
   golfbasscreek.com
Bay Ridge GC, *Sister Bay* .... 9 [V] 920-854-4085
   bayridgegolf.com
Beaver Dam CC, *Beaver Dam* .... 18 [S] 920-885-4106
   beaverdamcountryclub.com
Beechwood GC, *Porterfield* .... 9 [P] 715-789-2844
   crivitzrecreation.com/beechwood
Big Fish GC, *Hayward* .... 18 [P] 715-934-4770
   bigfishgolf.com
Big Foot CC, *Fontana* .... 18 [V] 262-275-3411
   bigfootcc.org
Big Oaks GC, *Kenosha* .... 27 [P] 262-694-4200
   bigoaksgolf.com
Big Sand Lake GC, *Phelps* .... 9 [R] 715-545-2484
Big Stone G&CC, *Three Lakes* .... 9 [P] 715-546-2880

Birchwood GC, *Kieler* .... 9 [P] 608-748-4743
   birchwoodgolfcourse9.com
Bishops Bay CC, *Middleton* .... 18 [V] 608-232-4201
   bishopsbay.com
Black Bear GC, *Minong* .... 18 [P] 715-466-2314
   blackbeargolf.com
Black Bear Trail GC, *Suring* .... 18 [P] 920-842-4653
   blackbeartrailgolfcourse.com
Black River GC, *Medford* .... 9 [P] 715-748-5520
   blackrivergolf.com
Blackhawk CC, *Madison* .... 18 [V] 608-231-2456
   blackhawkcc.com
Blackhawk GC, *Janesville* .... 9 [M] 608-757-3090
   crown-golf.com
BlackStone Creek GC, *Germantown* .... 18 [P] 262-255-4200
   blackstonecreekgc.com
Blackwolf Run GC, *Kohler* .... 36 [R] 920-457-4446
   destinationkohler.com
Bloomer Memorial GC, *Bloomer* .... 18 [M] 715-568-1743
Blue Mound G&CC, *Wauwatosa* .... 18 [V] 414-258-4870
   bluemoundgcc.com
Bombers GC, *Niagara* .... 9 [P] 715-251-3110
   wildmanranch.com
Bottens Green Acres GC, *Lake Nebagamon* .... 9 [R] 715-374-2567
Branch River CC, *Cato* .... 18 [V] 920-682-5901
   branchrivercc.com
Bridgewood GC, *Neenah* .... 9 [P] 920-722-9819
   bridgewoodgolf.com
Brighton Dale Links, *Kansasville* .... 45 [M] 262-878-1440
   co.kenosha.wi.us/publicworks/golf
Bristol Oaks CC, *Bristol* .... 18 [P] 262-857-2302
   bristoloaks.com
Bristol Ridge GC, *Somerset* .... 18 [P] 715-247-3673
   bristolridgegolfcourse.com
Broadlands GC, *North Prairie* .... 18 [P] 262-392-6320
   broadlandsgolfclub.com
Brookfield Hills GC, *Brookfield* .... 18 [P] 262-782-0885
   brookfieldhillsgolf.com
Brown County GC, *Oneida* .... 18 [M] 920-497-1731
   co.brown.wi.us
Brown Deer Park GC, *Milwaukee* .... 18 [M] 414-352-8080
   countyparks.com/golf
Browns Lake GC, *Burlington* .... 18 [M] 262-763-6065
   hhfairway.com
Bulls Eye CC, *Wisconsin Rapids* .... 18 [V] 715-423-2230
   bullseyecc.com
Butte des Morts CC, *Appleton* .... 18 [V] 920-738-5544
   buttedesmortscc.org
Butternut Hills GC, *Sarona* .... 18 [P] 715-635-8563
   butternuthillsgolf.com
Castle Rock G&CC, *New Lisbon* .... 18 [P] 608-847-4658
   castlerockgolfcourse.com
CC Estates GC, *Fontana* .... 9 [S] 262-275-3705
   countryclubestategolf.com
CC of Beloit, *Beloit* .... 18 [V] 608-364-9000
   ccbeloit.com
Cecilias GC, *Janesville* .... 9 [P] 608-754-8550
   ceciliasgolf.com
Cedar Springs GC, *Manawa* .... 9 [P] 920-596-2905
   cedarspringsgolfcourse.com
Chaska GC, *Greenville* .... 18 [P] 920-757-5757
   chaskagolf.com
Chenequa CC, *Hartland* .... 18 [V] 262-367-1325
   chenequacc.org

224 [A] = MILITARY   [M] = MUNICIPAL   [P] = PUBLIC   [R] = RESORT

Golf Yellow Pages, 18th Edition — WISCONSIN

Course	City	Holes	Type	Phone
Chequamegon Bay GC,	Ashland	18	[S]	715-682-8004
golfashland.com				
Cherokee CC,	Madison	18	[V]	608-249-1000
cherokeecountryclub.net				
Cherry Hills GC,	Sturgeon Bay	18	[P]	920-743-3240
cherryhillsgolf.com				
Chippewa Valley GC,	Menomonie	18	[P]	715-235-9808
cvgolf.com				
Christmas Mountain Village GC,	Wisconsin Dells	27	[P]	608-254-3971
christmasmountainvillage.com				
Clam River GC,	Shell Lake	9	[P]	715-468-2900
Clear Lake GC,	Clear Lake	9	[P]	715-263-2500
Clifton Highlands GC,	Prescott	27	[P]	715-262-5141
cliftonhighlands.com				
Clifton Hollow GC,	River Falls	27	[P]	715-425-9781
cliftonhollow.com				
Club X To C,	Gleason	9	[P]	715-536-1546
clubxtoc.com				
CNC Links,	Newton	9	[P]	920-726-1800
cnclinks.com				
Coachmans Golf Resort,	Edgerton	27	[R]	608-884-8484
coachmans.com				
Coldwater Canyon GC,	Wisconsin Dells	18	[P]	608-254-8489
chulavistaresort.com				
Cole Acres CC,	Cuba City	9	[P]	608-744-2476
Columbus CC,	Columbus	9	[M]	920-623-5880
Couderay Riverside GC,	Radisson	9	[P]	715-945-2593
Coulee Golf Bowl,	Onalaska	9	[P]	608-781-1111
bad link				
Countryside GC,	Kaukauna	18	[P]	920-766-2219
countrysidegolfclubwi.com				
Crane Meadow GC,	Schofield	9	[P]	715-355-1264
Creekview Par Three At Albion,	Edgerton	9	[P]	608-884-2250
creekviewparthree.com				
Crystal Springs GC,	Seymour	18	[P]	920-833-6348
crystalspringsgolf.com				
Cumberland GC,	Cumberland	18	[M]	715-822-4333
cumberlandgolfclub.com				
Currie Park GC,	Milwaukee	18	[P]	414-453-7030
countyparks.com/golf				
Dairymens CC,	Boulder Junction	18	[R]	715-385-2111
dairymensinc.org				
Darlington CC,	Darlington	9	[P]	608-776-3377
darlingtoncc.com				
De Smidts G&CC,	Crivitz	18	[P]	715-854-7939
desmidts.com				
Decatur Lake GC,	Brodhead	18	[P]	608-897-2777
decaturlakegolf.com				
Deer Haven GC,	New Berlin	18	[P]	262-650-0760
deerhavengolfclub.us				
Deer Run GC,	Brillion	9	[P]	920-756-2528
Deer Run GC & Resort,	Washington Island	9	[R]	920-847-2017
deerrunwi.com				
Deer Trak GC,	Oconomowoc	18	[P]	920-474-4444
deertrakgolf.com				
Deer Valley GC,	Barneveld	27	[P]	608-924-3033
deervalleygolf.com				
Delbrook GC,	Delavan	27	[M]	262-728-3966
delbrookgc.com				
Devils Head Resort & Convention Ctr,	Merrimac	36	[R]	608-493-2251
devilsheadresort.com				
Dineen Park GC,	Milwaukee	9	[M]	414-871-4020
countyparks.com				
Dodge Point GC,	Mineral Point	18	[S]	608-987-2814
dodgepointcountryclub.com				
Door Creek GC,	Cottage Grove	27	[P]	608-839-5656
doorcreekgolfcourse.com				
Doyne Park GC,	Milwaukee	9	[M]	414-257-3718
countyparks.com/golf				
Dretzka Park GC,	Milwaukee	18	[M]	414-354-7300
countyparks.com/golf				
Drugans Castle Mound CC,	Holmen	18	[P]	608-526-3225
drugans.com				
Eagle Bluff GC,	Hurley	18	[M]	715-561-3552
eaglebluffgolfclub.com				
Eagle Creek GC,	Hortonville	18	[P]	920-757-1000
eaglecreekgolfclub.net				
Eagle Links GC,	Kaukauna	18	[P]	920-759-0945
Eagle River GC,	Eagle River	18	[M]	715-479-8111
eaglerivergolfcourse.com				
Eagle Springs Golf Resort,	Eagle	9	[R]	262-594-2462
eaglespringsgolfresort.com				
Eastwin Valley Par 3 GC,	Two Rivers	9	[P]	920-793-5997
eastwinvalleygolf.com				
Eau Claire G&CC,	Altoona	18	[V]	715-836-8420
ecgcc.com				
Echo Hills GC,	Turtle Lake	9	[P]	715-986-2662
Edelweiss Chalet CC,	New Glarus	18	[P]	608-527-2315
edelweissccc.com				
Edgewater CC,	Tomahawk	9	[P]	715-453-3320
explorewisconsin.com/edgewatercountryclub				
Edgewater GC,	Grafton	9	[S]	262-377-1230
edgewatergolfclub.com				
Edgewood GC,	Big Bend	36	[S]	262-662-3110
edgewoodgolf.com				
Edgewood GC,	Oconto	9	[P]	920-834-2681
Elks CC,	Manitowoc	9	[V]	920-682-8082
Ellsworth CC,	Ellsworth	9	[P]	715-273-4438
ellsworthcountryclub.com				
Emerald Hills GC,	Two Rivers	9	[P]	920-794-8726
Entwood GC,	Holcombe	9	[S]	715-595-4035
entwoodgolf.com				
Erin Hills GC,	Hartford	18	[P]	262-670-8600
erinhills.com				
Ettrick GC,	Ettrick	9	[P]	608-525-6262
ettrickgolf.com				
Evansville CC,	Evansville	18	[P]	608-882-6524
evansvillegolfclub.com				
Evergreen GC,	Plymouth	9	[M]	920-893-8822
plymouthgov.com				
Evergreen GC,	Elkhorn	27	[S]	262-723-5722
evergreengolf.com				
Fairfield Hills GC,	Baraboo	9	[P]	608-356-5524
fairfieldhillsgolfcourse.com				
Fairways of Woodside,	Sussex	18	[P]	262-246-7042
fairwaysofwoodside.com				
Far Vu GC,	Oshkosh	18	[P]	920-231-2631
farvugolf.com				
Fire Ridge GC,	Grafton	18	[S]	262-375-2252
fireridgegc.com				
Five Flags GC,	Balsam Lake	9	[P]	715-825-2141
Forest Hills GC,	La Crosse	18	[M]	608-779-4653
foresthillsgolf.org				
Forest Point GC,	Gordon	9	[P]	715-376-2322
forestpoint.com				

[S] = SEMI-PRIVATE   [V] = PRIVATE   [U] = UNIVERSITY   [N] = UNIVERSITY-PRIVATE

WISCONSIN
Golf Yellow Pages, 18th Edition

Course	Holes	Type	Phone
Four Seasons Club, *Pembine*	9	[R]	715-324-5244
fourseasonswi.com			
Fox Hills Resort, *Mishicot*	45	[R]	920-755-2831
fox-hills.com			
Fox Hollow GC, *La Crosse*	18	[P]	608-786-4653
foxhollowgolfandbanquets.com			
Fox Lake GC, *Fox Lake*	18	[P]	920-928-2508
foxlakegolfclub.com			
Fox Run GC, *Webster*	18	[P]	715-866-7953
foxrungolf.net			
Fox Valley GC, *Kaukauna*	18	[V]	920-766-1340
foxvalleygolfclub.com			
Foxboro GC, *Oregon*	18	[P]	608-835-7789
foxborogolfclub.com			
Foxfire GC, *Waupaca*	18	[S]	715-256-9000
playfoxfiregolf.com			
Frederic CC, *Frederic*	18	[P]	715-327-8250
fredericgolfcourse.com			
Gateway GC, *Land O Lakes*	9	[P]	715-547-3929
GC at Camelot, *Lomira*	18	[P]	920-269-4949
golfcamelot.com			
Geneva National GC, *Lake Geneva*	54	[S]	262-245-7000
genevanationalresort.com			
George Williams GC, *Williams Bay*	18	[U]	262-245-9507
aurora.edu/gwcampus			
Glacier Wood GC, *Iola*	18	[S]	715-445-3831
glacierwoodiola.com			
Glen Cairn GC, *Ogdensburg*	18	[P]	920-244-7653
Glen Erin GC, *Janesville*	18	[P]	608-741-1100
gleneringolf.com			
Glen Hills GC, *Glenwood City*	9	[P]	715-265-4718
glenhillsgolf.com			
Glenway GC, *Madison*	9	[M]	608-266-4737
cityofmadisongolf.com			
Golden Sands Golf Community, *Cecil*	18	[S]	715-745-2189
goldensandscecil.com			
Grand Geneva Resort, *Lake Geneva*	36	[R]	262-248-8811
grandgeneva.com			
Grand View GC, *Hortonville*	9	[P]	920-779-6421
grandviewgolf.org			
Grant Park GC, *South Milwaukee*	18	[P]	414-762-4646
countyparks.com/golf			
Grantsburg Muni GC, *Grantsburg*	9	[M]	715-463-2300
Green Acres GC, *Pembine*	9	[P]	715-324-5707
Green Bay CC, *Green Bay*	18	[V]	920-339-4653
greenbaycountryclub.com			
Green Lake Campground GC, *Green Lake*	9	[R]	920-294-3543
greenlakecampground.com			
Greenfield Park GC, *Milwaukee*	18	[M]	414-453-1750
countyparks.com/golf			
Greenwood Hills CC, *Wausau*	18	[V]	715-849-1772
greenwoodhillscc.com			
Hackbarth Hills GC, *Janesville*	9	[P]	608-754-1156
Hammond GC, *Hammond*	9	[P]	715-796-2266
hammondgolfclub.com			
Hansen GC, *Milwaukee*	18	[M]	414-453-4454
countyparks.com/golf			
Hartford GC, *Hartford*	18	[P]	262-673-2710
hartfordgolfclubwi.com			
Haskell Noyes Park GC, *Milwaukee*	9	[M]	414-353-4653
countyparks.com/golf			
Hawks Landing GC, *Verona*	18	[S]	608-848-4295
hawkslandinggolfclub.com			
Hawks View GC, *Lake Geneva*	36	[R]	262-348-9900
hawksviewgolfclub.com			
Hawthorne Hills GC, *Saukville*	18	[M]	262-692-2151
Hayward G&TC, *Hayward*	18	[P]	715-634-2760
haywardgolf.com			
Hayward National GC, *Hayward*	18	[P]	715-634-6727
haywardnationalgolf.com			
Hiawatha GC, *Tomah*	18	[P]	608-372-5589
golfhiawatha.com			
Hickory Grove GC, *Fennimore*	9	[P]	608-822-3314
hickorygrovegolfcourse.com			
Hickory Hills CC, *Chilton*	18	[P]	920-849-2912
hhccgolf.com			
Hickory Hills GC, *Eau Claire*	18	[P]	715-878-4543
golfhickoryhills.com			
Hidden Glen At Bentdale Farms, *Cedarburg*	18	[V]	262-387-0100
hiddenglengolfclub.com			
Hidden Greens North, *Solon Springs*	18	[P]	715-378-2300
hiddengreensnorth.com			
Hidden Waters GC, *Waupaca*	9	[P]	715-258-5054
High Cliff GC, *Sherwood*	18	[P]	920-734-1162
highcliffgolf.com			
Highland Ridge GC, *de Pere*	18	[P]	920-337-9986
Hillcrest G&CC, *Altoona*	18	[V]	715-832-2929
hillcrestgolfcc.com			
Hillview GC, *La Crosse*	9	[P]	608-788-2072
Hilly Haven GC, *de Pere*	18	[P]	920-336-6204
hillyhaven.com			
Holiday Lodge Golf Resort, *Tomah*	18	[R]	608-372-9314
holidaylodgegolf.com			
Homestead Supper & C, *Wisconsin Rapids*	9	[P]	715-423-7577
homesteadrapids.com			
Hon E Kor CC, *Kewaskum*	27	[P]	262-626-2520
hon-e-kor.com			
Horseshoe Bay GC, *Egg Harbor*	18	[R]	920-868-4103
horseshoebaygolfclub.net			
Hudson GC, *Hudson*	18	[V]	715-386-6515
hudsongolfclub.com			
Hunters Glen, *Crivitz*	18	[P]	715-854-8008
golfhuntersglen.com			
Idlewild GC, *Sturgeon Bay*	18	[P]	920-743-3334
idlewildgolfclub.com			
Indianhead GC, *Mosinee*	18	[P]	715-693-6066
indianheadgolfcourse.com			
Inshalla CC, *Tomahawk*	18	[P]	715-453-3130
inshallacc.com			
Irish Hills GC & DR, *La Crosse*	9	[P]	608-788-6904
Irish Waters GC, *Kaukauna*	18	[P]	920-788-7444
irishwatersgolf.com			
Ironwood GC, *Sussex*	27	[P]	262-538-9900
ironwoodgolfcourse.com			
Ives Grove Golf Links, *Sturtevant*	27	[M]	262-878-3714
hhfairway.com			
Janesville CC, *Janesville*	18	[V]	608-755-7760
janesvillecc.com			
Johnson Park GC, *Racine*	18	[M]	262-637-2860
racinegolfonline.com			
Kastle Greens GC, *Marion*	18	[P]	715-754-5667
Kenosha CC, *Kenosha*	18	[V]	262-552-8221
kenoshacountryclub.com			
Kenosha Muni GC, *Kenosha*	9	[M]	262-653-4090
kenosha.org			

[A] = MILITARY   [M] = MUNICIPAL   [P] = PUBLIC   [R] = RESORT

Golf Yellow Pages, 18th Edition — WISCONSIN

Kestrel Ridge GC, *Columbus* ....18 [P] 920-623-4653
  kestrelridgegolf.com
Kettle Hills GC, *Richfield* ....45 [P] 262-628-0200
  kettlehills.com
Kettle Moraine GC, *Dousman* ....18 [P] 262-965-6200
  kettlemorainegolf.com
Kilkarney Hills GC, *River Falls* ....18 [P] 715-425-8501
  kilkarneyhills.com
Koshkonong Mounds CC, *Fort Atkinson*...........18 [P] 920-563-2823
  kmccgolf.com
Krooked Kreek GC, *Osceola* ....18 [P] 715-294-3673
  krookedkreek.com
Krueger Haskell GC, *Beloit* ....18 [M] 608-364-2929
  ci.beloit.wi.us
La Crosse CC, *Onalaska* .... 18 [V] 608-781-5837
Lake Arrowhead GC, *Nekoosa* ....36 [P] 715-325-2929
  lakearrowheadgolf.com
Lake Beulah CC, *Mukwonago*..............................27 [P] 262-363-8147
Lake Breeze GC, *Winneconne* ....18 [P] 920-582-7585
  lakebreezegolfclub.com
Lake Forest GC, *Eagle River* .... 9 [R] 715-479-4211
  lakeforestresort.com
Lake Geneva CC, *Lake Geneva* .... 18 [V] 262-248-2373
Lake Hallie GC, *Chippewa Falls*...........................18 [P] 715-861-5442
  lakehalliegolf.com
Lake Lawn Resort, *Delavan*..................................18 [R] 262-728-7950
  lakelawnresort.com
Lake Mills GC, *Lake Mills* ....18 [P] 920-648-5013
  lakemillsgolfclub.com
Lake Park GC, *Milwaukee*....................................18 [M] 414-961-2656
  countyparks.com/golf
Lake Ripley CC, *Cambridge*................................. 18 [V] 608-423-3411
  lakeripleycc.com
Lake Windsor CC, *Windsor* ....27 [P] 608-846-4711
  lakewindsor.com
Lake Wisconsin CC, *Prairie Du Sac* .... 18 [S] 608-643-2405
  lakewisconsincc.com
Lake Wissota GC, *Chippewa Falls*........................18 [P] 715-382-4780
  lakewissotagolf.com
Lakeland Hills GC, *Lodi*.. 9 [P] 608-592-3757
Lakeshore Muni GC, *Oshkosh* ....18 [M] 920-235-6200
  lakeshoregolfcourse.net
Lakeview Golf & Pizza, *Hayward*..........................9 [P] 715-462-3787
Lakewood GC, *Lake Geneva* ....18 [P] 262-249-9710
Lakewoods Forest Ridges GC, *Cable* ....18 [R] 715-794-2698
  lakewoodsresort.com
Lancaster Muni CC, *Lancaster* ....18 [M] 608-723-4266
Lauderdale Lakes GC, *Elkhorn* ....9 [P] 262-742-2454
  lauderdalelakescountryclub.com
Ledgeview GC, *de Pere*.......................................27 [P] 920-336-6077
  ledgeviewgolfcourse.com
Lincoln Park GC, *Milwaukee*.................................9 [M] 414-962-2400
  countyparks.com/golf/golf
Little River CC, *Marinette*.....................................18 [P] 715-735-7234
  littlerivercc.com
Luck GC, *Luck*..18 [M] 715-472-8452
  luckgolfcourse.com
Ludden Lake GC, *Mineral Point* ....9 [P] 608-987-2888
  explorewisconsin.com
Lynndales Golf, *Rice Lake*.....................................9 [P] 715-234-5966
Madeline Island GC, *La Pointe*............................ 18 [S] 715-747-3212
  madelineislandgolf.com
Madison GC, *Milwaukee* ....9 [M] 414-466-1020
  countyparks.com/golf
Maple Bluff CC, *Madison*..................................... 18 [V] 608-249-2000
  maplebluffcc.com
Maple Grove CC, *West Salem* ....18 [P] 608-786-1500
  maplegrovecc.com
Maple Hills GC, *Wittenberg* ....9 [P] 715-253-2448
Maplecrest CC, *Kenosha*..................................... 18 [S] 262-859-2887
Maplewood GC, *Pickerel* ....9 [P] 715-484-4653
  maplewoodgolfcourse.com
Marlinks Golf Farm, *Wautoma* ....18 [P] 920-787-5812
Marshfield CC, *Marshfield*....................................18 [P] 715-384-4409
  golfmcc.com
Mascoutin CC, *Berlin*..27 [S] 920-361-2360
  mascoutingolf.com
Maxwelton Braes Golf Resort, *Baileys Harbor*.....18 [R] 920-839-2321
  maxwelton-braes.com
Mayville GC, *Mayville* ....18 [P] 920-387-2999
  mayvillegolfcourse.com
McCauslin Brook G&CC, *Lakewood*....................18 [P] 715-276-7623
  mccauslinbrook.com
Meadow Links GC, *Manitowoc*...........................18 [P] 920-682-6842
Meadow Springs CC, *Jefferson*............................18 [P] 920-674-2783
Meadowbrook CC, *Racine* .... 18 [V] 262-637-7461
  meadowbrookcc.com
Meadows of Sixmile Creek, *Waunakee* ....18 [P] 608-849-9000
  madisongolf.com
Meadowview GC, *Owen* ....9 [P] 715-229-2355
  meadowviewgolf.net
Mee Kwon Park GC, *Mequon*..............................18 [M] 262-242-1310
  co.ozaukee.wi.us/parks/meekwonpark.htm
Mellen CC, *Mellen*..9 [P] 715-274-7311
  golfmellen.com
Menomonie CC, *Menomonie*................................9 [S] 715-235-3595
  menomoniegolf.com
Mequon CC, *Mequon* .... 27 [V] 262-242-2470
  mequonclub.com
Merrill GC, *Merrill* ....18 [P] 715-536-2529
  merrillgolfclub.com
Merrill Hills CC, *Waukesha* .... 18 [V] 262-548-1103
  merrillhills.com
Mid Vallee GC, *de Pere* ....27 [P] 920-532-6644
  midvallee.com
Millers Glen GC, *Howards Grove*..........................9 [P] 920-565-3674
Milwaukee CC, *River Hills*.................................... 18 [V] 414-362-5200
  themilwaukeecountryclub.com
Minnesuing Acres GC and Conf Center,
  Lake Nebagamon...9 [R] 715-374-2262
  minnesuingacres.com
Minocqua CC, *Minocqua* .... 18 [V] 715-356-5217
  minocquacountryclub.com
Missing Links GC, *Mequon*...................................9 [P] 262-243-5711
  missinglinksmequon.com
Monona GC, *Madison* ....9 [M] 608-266-4736
  cityofmadisongolf.com
Monroe CC, *Monroe* .... 18 [V] 608-325-3159
  monroecountryclub.com
Moor Downs GC, *Waukesha* ....9 [M] 262-548-7821
  waukeshacountyparks.com
Morningstar Golfers Club, *Waukesha*.................18 [P] 262-662-1600
  golfthestar.com
Mound View G&CC, *Friendship*............................9 [P] 608-339-3814
  moundviewgolf.com

[S] = SEMI-PRIVATE [V] = PRIVATE [U] = UNIVERSITY [N] = UNIVERSITY-PRIVATE

WISCONSIN
Golf Yellow Pages, 18th Edition

Course	Holes	Type	Phone
Mr Golfs Ultimate Range, *de Pere*	9	[P]	920-338-9535
mrgolf.net			
Muskego Lakes CC, *Muskego*	18	[S]	414-425-6500
muskegolakes.com			
Mystique Meadows GC, *Stratford*	9	[P]	715-384-2000
mystiquemeadows.com			
Naga Waukee GC, *Pewaukee*	18	[M]	262-367-2153
waukeshacountyparks.com			
Nakoma GC, *Madison*	18	[V]	608-238-3141
nakoma.org			
Neillsville CC, *Neillsville*	9	[P]	715-743-3780
neillsvillecc.com			
Nemadji GC, *Superior*	36	[M]	715-394-0266
nemadjigolf.com			
New Berlin Hills GC, *New Berlin*	18	[M]	262-780-5200
newberlinhills.com			
New Richmond GC, *New Richmond*	27	[S]	715-246-6724
nrgolfclub.com			
Nicolet CC, *Laona*	18	[P]	715-674-4780
nicoletcountryclub.com			
Nine Springs GC, *Madison*	9	[M]	608-271-5877
ninespringsgolfcourse.com			
Nippersink Golf Resort, *Genoa City*	18	[R]	262-279-6311
nippersinkresort.com			
Norsk GC, *Mt Horeb*	9	[P]	608-437-3399
norskgolfclub.com			
North Hills CC, *Menomonee Falls*	18	[V]	262-251-5750
nhccwi.com			
North Shore CC, *Mequon*	27	[V]	262-242-7004
nscountryclub.org			
North Shore GC, *Menasha*	18	[V]	920-734-9631
nsgolfclub.com			
NorthBrook CC, *Luxemburg*	18	[S]	920-845-2383
northbrookcc.com			
Northern Bay Golf Resort & Marina, *Arkdale*	18	[R]	608-339-9891
northernbayresort.com			
Northern Pines GC, *Iron River*	9	[P]	715-372-5260
northernpinesgolf.com			
Northwood GC, *Rhinelander*	18	[P]	715-282-6565
northwoodgolfclub.com			
Norwood Acres, *Lake Nebagamon*	9	[P]	715-374-3210
norwoodacres.com			
Oak Hills GC, *Oak Creek*	9	[P]	414-762-9994
oakhillsgolfwi.com			
Oak Ridge GC, *Milton*	27	[P]	608-868-4353
Oakgreen GC, *Fond Du Lac*	18	[P]	920-922-2273
Oakwood Park GC, *Franklin*	18	[S]	414-281-6700
countyparks.com/golf			
Oconomowoc GC, *Oconomowoc*	18	[V]	262-567-7721
ocongolfclub.org			
Oconto GC, *Oconto*	9	[P]	920-834-3139
Odana Hills GC, *Madison*	18	[M]	608-266-4078
cityofmadisongolf.com			
Ojibwa GC, *Chippewa Falls*	9	[P]	715-723-8823
ojibwagc.com			
Old Hickory GC, *Beaver Dam*	18	[S]	920-887-7179
oldhickorycc.com			
Olde Highlander GC, *Oconomowoc*	18	[R]	262-567-6048
olympiasportscenter.com			
Oneida G&CC, *Green Bay*	18	[V]	920-498-6500
oneidagolfandcountryclub.com			
Oshkosh CC, *Oshkosh*	18	[V]	920-231-1078
oshkoshcc.com			
Osseo Golf & Rec Ctr, *Osseo*	9	[P]	715-597-3215
Ozaukee CC, *Mequon*	18	[V]	262-242-3710
ozaukeecc.com			
Paganica GC, *Oconomowoc*	18	[P]	262-567-0171
paganicagolfcourse.net			
Park Falls CC, *Park Falls*	9	[P]	715-762-4396
parkfallscountryclub.com			
Parkway GC, *Pound*	18	[P]	920-897-3950
Pattison Park GC, *Superior*	9	[P]	715-399-2489
Peninsula St Park GC, *Ephraim*	18	[S]	920-854-5791
peninsulagolf.org			
Petrifying Springs GC, *Kenosha*	18	[M]	262-552-9052
co.kenosha.wi.us/publicworks/golf			
Pheasant Hills GC, *Hammond*	18	[P]	715-796-2500
pheasanthillsgolf.com			
Pine Acres GC, *Abrams*	9	[P]	920-826-7765
pineacresgolfcourse.com			
Pine Crest GC, *Dallas*	9	[S]	715-837-1268
Pine Crest Par 3, *Wisconsin Dells*	9	[P]	608-254-2165
Pine Hills CC, *Sheboygan*	18	[V]	920-458-3536
pinehillscc.com			
Pine Hills GC, *Gresham*	18	[P]	715-787-3778
mohican.com			
Pine Meadow GC, *Eau Claire*	9	[P]	715-832-6011
Pine Trail GC at Saddle Ridge, *Portage*	9	[P]	608-742-7174
saddleridgegolf.com			
Pine Valley GC, *Marathon*	18	[P]	715-443-2848
golfpinevalley.net			
Pinewood CC, *Harshaw*	18	[P]	715-282-5500
pinewoodcc.com			
Pinewood GC, *Menomonie*	9	[P]	715-235-2900
Platteville G&CC, *Platteville*	18	[P]	608-348-4653
plattevillegolf.com			
Pleasant View GC, *Middleton*	36	[M]	608-831-6666
golfpleasantview.com			
Plum Lake GC, *Sayner*	9	[S]	608-542-2598
plumlakegolfclub.com			
Poplar GC, *Poplar*	18	[P]	715-364-2689
poplargolf.com			
Portage CC, *Portage*	18	[S]	608-742-5121
portagecc.net			
Prairie du Chien CC, *Prairie Du Chien*	18	[S]	608-326-6707
pdccountryclub.com			
Prairie Woods GC, *Avalon*	18	[P]	608-883-6500
prairiewoodsgolfcourse.com			
Prentice GC, *Prentice*	9	[M]	715-428-2127
Princeton Valley GC, *Eau Claire*	9	[P]	715-834-3334
princetonvalleygolf.com			
Quail Run Golf Links, *Richland Center*	9	[P]	608-647-3117
Quit Qui Oc GC, *Elkhart Lake*	27	[P]	920-876-2833
quitquioc.com			
Racine CC, *Racine*	18	[V]	262-637-8537
racinecountryclub.com			
Rainbow Springs GC, *Mukwonago*	36	[R]	262-363-4550
rainbowspringsgolf.net			
Raymond Heights Golf Ctr, *Caledonia*	9	[P]	262-835-2020
golfwisconsin.com			
Reedsburg CC, *Reedsburg*	18	[S]	608-524-3134
reedsburgcountryclub.com			
Reid GC, *Appleton*	18	[M]	920-832-5926
appleton.org			
Rhinelander CC, *Rhinelander*	9	[V]	715-365-3201
Rib Mountain GC, *Wausau*	9	[P]	715-845-5570

[A] = MILITARY [M] = MUNICIPAL [P] = PUBLIC [R] = RESORT

WISCONSIN

Course	Location	Holes	Type	Phone
Ridgeway CC,	Neenah	18	[V]	920-722-2979
ridgewaygolf.com				
River Falls GC,	River Falls	18	[S]	715-425-7253
riverfallsgolfclub.com				
River Island GC,	Oconto Falls	9	[P]	920-846-3303
River Run Sparta GC,	Sparta	18	[M]	608-487-1608
spartagolf.com				
Riverdale CC,	Sheboygan	18	[P]	920-458-2561
riverdalecountryclub.com				
RiverEdge GC,	Marshfield	18	[P]	715-676-3900
wisconsin-golfcourse.com				
Rivermoor GC,	Waterford	18	[S]	262-534-2500
rivermoorgolfclub.com				
Rivers Bend GC,	Germantown	9	[P]	262-255-6557
Riverside GC,	Clintonville	18	[S]	715-823-2992
riversidegolfing.com				
Riverside GC,	Janesville	18	[M]	608-757-3080
janesville-golf.com				
Riverview CC,	Appleton	9	[V]	920-734-4741
riverview-cc-appleton.com				
Riverview GC,	Antigo	9	[P]	715-623-2663
Rock River CC,	Waupun	18	[P]	920-324-2621
golfrrcc.com				
Rock River Hills GC,	Horicon	18	[M]	920-485-4990
rockriverhills.com				
Rolling Greens GC,	Durand	9	[S]	715-672-8139
rggolfcourse.com				
Rolling Hills CC,	Oconomowoc	18	[P]	262-567-7833
rollinghillsccw.com				
Rolling Meadows GC,	Fond Du Lac	27	[M]	920-929-3735
rollingmeadowsgolfcourse.com				
Rolling Oaks GC,	Barron	18	[P]	715-537-3409
rollingoaksgolf.net				
Royal Oaks Golf Resort,	Waupaca	9	[R]	715-258-5103
gglbbs.com/royaloak				
Royal Scot CC,	New Franken	18	[P]	920-866-2356
royalscotgolfclub.com				
Royal St Patricks GC,	Wrightstown	18	[P]	920-532-4300
royalstpatricks.com				
Sandalwood GC,	Abrams	18	[P]	920-826-7770
Scenic View GC,	Slinger	18	[P]	262-644-5661
scenicviewcc.com				
Sentryworld Sports Ctr,	Stevens Point	18	[P]	715-345-1600
sentryworld.com				
Serendipity CC,	Viroqua	9	[P]	608-637-7708
Seven Lakes GC,	Reedsville	18	[P]	920-775-4000
sevenlakesgd.com				
Shamrock Heights Golf & Supper Club, New London		18	[S]	920-982-9993
newlondongolf.com				
Shawano Lake GC,	Shawano	18	[P]	715-524-4890
shalagoco.com				
Sheboygan Town & CC,	Sheboygan	27	[P]	920-467-2509
townandcountrygolf.com				
Shepherds Meadow GC,	Poynette	9	[R]	608-635-3837
shepherdsmeadowgolf.com				
Sherwood Forest GC,	Sherwood	9	[P]	920-989-3400
golfsherwoodforest.com				
Shoop Park GC,	Racine	9	[M]	262-681-9714
racinegolfonline.com				
Shorewood GC,	Green Bay	9	[U]	920-465-2118
uwgb.edu/shorewood				
Silver Spring GC,	Menomonee Falls	36	[P]	262-252-4666
silverspringgolf.com				
Sioux Creek GC,	Chetek	9	[P]	715-924-3139
chetek.com/siouxcreek				
Sir Lanserlot GC,	Plymouth	18	[P]	920-892-4834
Siren National GC,	Siren	18	[P]	715-349-8000
sirennational.com				
Skyline GC,	Black River Falls	18	[M]	715-284-2613
golfskyline.com				
Snowflake Ski & Golf,	Westby	9	[S]	608-634-3211
snowflakeskiclub.com				
Songbird Hills GC,	Hartland	18	[P]	262-246-7050
golfsongbird.com				
South Hills CC,	Franksville	18	[P]	262-835-4441
southhillscc.com				
South Hills G&CC,	Fond Du Lac	18	[V]	920-921-3636
southhillsgolfandcountryclub.com				
Spider Lake Golf Resort,	Hayward	9	[R]	715-462-3200
spiderlakegolfresort.com				
Spooner GC,	Spooner	18	[S]	715-635-3580
spoonergolf.com				
Spread Eagle GC,	Florence	9	[P]	715-696-3696
Spring Brook GC,	Wisconsin Dells	9	[P]	608-254-1477
spring-brook.com				
Spring Creek Golf Ctr,	Whitewater	9	[P]	920-563-4499
springcreekgolf.com				
Spring Green GC,	Spring Green	9	[M]	608-588-2335
vi.springgreen.wi.gov				
Spring Valley CC,	Salem	18	[P]	262-862-2626
springvalleyccsalem.com				
Spring Valley GC,	Spring Valley	18	[P]	715-778-5513
springvalleygolf.net				
Spring Valley GC,	Union Center	9	[P]	608-462-8691
golfspringvalley.com				
St Croix National GC,	Somerset	18	[P]	715-247-4200
stcroixnationalgolf.com				
St Croix Valley GC,	St Croix Falls	9	[P]	715-483-3377
St Germain GC,	St Germain	18	[M]	715-542-2614
stgermain-golfclub.com				
St Johns Northwestern GC,	Delafield	9	[U]	262-646-7151
sjnma.org				
Stevens Point CC,	Stevens Point	18	[V]	715-345-8905
stevenspointcountryclub.com				
Stonehedge GC,	Egg Harbor	9	[P]	920-868-2566
Stoneridge GC,	West Bend	18	[S]	262-692-6300
stoneridgegolf.com				
Stoughton GC,	Stoughton	18	[V]	608-873-8464
stoughtoncountryclub.com				
Sun Prairie GC,	Sun Prairie	18	[S]	608-837-6211
golfspgc.com				
Sunset Hills GC & DR,	Sheboygan Falls	9	[P]	920-467-0780
sunsethills-golf.com				
Sunset Par 3,	Oshkosh	9	[P]	920-235-8114
Sunset View Golf & Estates,	Chetek	9	[P]	715-859-6211
chetek.com/sunsetview				
Tagalong GC,	Birchwood	18	[R]	715-354-3397
tagalonggolf.com				
Tahkodah Hills GC,	Cable	9	[P]	715-798-3760
Tahoe Lynx GC,	Mercer	9	[P]	715-476-0050
tahoelynxgolfcourse.com				
Teal Wing GC,	Hayward	18	[R]	715-462-9051
teallake.com/golf.htm				
Tee A Way GC,	Ladysmith	9	[P]	715-532-3766
tee-away.com				
Tee Hi Club,	Medford	9	[P]	715-748-3990

[S] = SEMI-PRIVATE   [V] = PRIVATE   [U] = UNIVERSITY   [N] = UNIVERSITY-PRIVATE

WISCONSIN — Golf Yellow Pages, 18th Edition

Course	Info	Phone
Telemark GC, *Cable*	18 [R]	715-798-3104
telemarkgolfcourse.com		
Thal Acres Links & Lanes, *Westfield*	18 [P]	608-296-2850
thalacres.com		
The Amery GC, *Amery*	18 [M]	715-268-7213
amerygolfclub.com		
The Bog, *Saukville*	18 [P]	262-284-7075
golfthebog.com		
The Bridges GC, *Madison*	18 [P]	608-244-1822
golfthebridges.com		
The Bull At Pinehurst Farms, *Sheboygan Falls*	18 [P]	920-467-1500
golfthebull.com		
The Club At Strawberry Creek, *Bristol*	18 [V]	262-857-8400
strawberrycreekclub.com		
The GC At Cedar Creek, *Onalaska*	18 [V]	715-783-8100
cedarcreekonalaska.com		
The GC of Lawsonia, *Green Lake*	36 [R]	920-294-3320
lawsonia.com		
The House on the Rock Resort & GC, *Spring Green*	27 [R]	608-588-7000
thehouseontherock.com		
The Legend At Bergamont, *Oregon*	18 [S]	608-835-6900
thelegendatbergamont.com		
The Legend At Brandybrook, *Wales*	18 [V]	262-968-9711
thelegendatbrandybrook.com		
The Legend at Bristlecone, *Hartland*	18 [P]	262-367-7880
thelegendclubs.com		
The Oaks GC, *Cottage Grove*	18 [R]	608-837-4774
golftheoaks.com		
The Orchards At Egg Harbor, *Egg Harbor*	18 [R]	920-868-2483
orchardsategharbor.com		
The Preserve At Deer Creek, *New Dublin*	9 [P]	262-784-9779
preserveatdeercreekgolf.com		
The Ridges GC, *Wisconsin Rapids*	18 [P]	715-424-3204
ridgesgolfcourse.com		
The Riverbend GC, *Melrose*	9 [P]	608-488-7291
The Woods Family Course, *Wisconsin Dells*	9 [R]	608-253-4653
wildrockgolfclub.com		
The Woods GC, *Green Bay*	18 [P]	920-468-5729
golfthewoods.com		
Thornberry Creek At Oneida, *Oneida*	18 [P]	920-434-7501
golfthornberry.com		
Thornbrook GC, *Fond du Lac*	9 [P]	920-922-2722
Timber Ridge GC, *Minocqua*	18 [S]	715-356-9212
timberridgegolfclub.com		
Timber Terrace GC, *Chippewa Falls*	9 [P]	715-726-1500
timberterracegolfcourse.com		
Towne CC, *Edgerton*	18 [P]	608-884-4231
Trapp River GC, *Wausau*	18 [P]	715-675-3044
tapprivergolf.com		
Trappers Turn GC, *Wisconsin Dells*	27 [R]	608-253-7000
trappersturn.com		
Trempealeau Mountain GC, *Trempealeau*	18 [P]	608-534-7417
golfthemountain.com		
Tri City GC, *Wisconsin Rapids*	9 [P]	715-423-1380
bullseyecc.com		
Tripoli CC, *Milwaukee*	18 [V]	414-351-7200
tripolicc.org		
Trout Lake GC, *Arbor Vitae*	18 [P]	715-385-2189
troutlakegolf.com		
Troy Burne GC, *Hudson*	18 [P]	715-381-9800
troyburne.com		
Tuckaway CC, *Franklin*	18 [V]	414-425-4280
tuckawaycountryclub.com		
Tumbledown Trails GC, *Verona*	18 [P]	608-833-2301
tumbledowntrails.com		
Turtle Greens GC, *Beloit*	9 [P]	608-676-4334
Turtleback Golf & Conf Ctr, *Rice Lake*	18 [P]	715-234-7641
turtlebackgolf.com		
Tuscumbia G&CC, *Green Lake*	18 [P]	920-294-3382
tuscumbiacc.com		
Twin Lakes CC, *Twin Lakes*	18 [S]	262-877-2500
tlccgolf.com		
Twin Oaks GC, *Denmark*	18 [P]	920-863-2716
Two Oaks North GC, *Wautoma*	18 [P]	920-787-7132
twooaksgolf.com		
Univ Ridge GC, *Verona*	18 [U]	608-845-7700
universityridge.com		
Utica CC, *Oshkosh*	18 [P]	920-233-4446
Valley Golf & Supper Club, *Mondovi*	18 [P]	715-926-4915
thevalleygc.com		
Valley Green GC, *Muskego*	9 [P]	414-425-9985
Vernon Hills GC, *Peshtigo*	18 [P]	715-582-9200
Veterans GC, *Tomah*	9 [A]	608-372-1243
tomah.va.gov		
Viking GC, *Strum*	9 [P]	715-695-3306
Village Greens GC, *Green Bay*	9 [P]	920-434-3939
village.howard.wi.us		
Viroqua Hills GC, *Viroqua*	18 [P]	608-637-7615
viroquahillsgolf.com		
Vitense Golfland, *Madison*	9 [P]	608-271-1411
vitense.com		
Voyager Village CC, *Danbury*	27 [P]	715-259-3911
voyagervillage.com		
Walnut Grove GC, *Cochrane*	18 [P]	608-248-2800
walnutgrovegolf.com		
Walsh Golf Ctr, *La Crosse*	9 [P]	608-781-0838
Wanaki GC, *Menomonee Falls*	18 [M]	262-252-3480
waukeshacountyparks.com		
Wander Springs GC, *Greenleaf*	27 [P]	920-864-4653
wandersprings.com		
Warnimont Par 3 GC, *Cudahy*	18 [M]	414-481-1400
countyparks.com/golf		
Washington County GC, *Hartford*	18 [P]	262-670-6616
golfwcgc.com		
Washington Park GC, *Racine*	9 [M]	262-635-0118
racinegolfonline.com		
Watertown CC, *Watertown*	18 [V]	920-261-1375
watertowncc.com		
Waupaca CC, *Waupaca*	9 [V]	715-258-7271
waupacacc.com		
Wausau CC, *Schofield*	18 [V]	715-359-6164
wausaucountryclub.com		
Wausaukee Club, *Athelstane*	9 [V]	715-856-5211
wausaukeeclub.com		
Waushara CC, *Wautoma*	27 [P]	920-787-4649
wausharacountryclub.com		
Wedgewood GC, *Omro*	9 [P]	920-685-6161
wedgewoodsupperclub.com		
West Bend CC, *West Bend*	18 [V]	262-334-9541
westbendcc.com		
West Bend Lakes, *West Bend*	18 [P]	262-675-9922
westbendlakesgolf.com		
West Brook Hills GC, *Plain*	9 [M]	608-546-2047
plainwi.govoffice2.com		
Western Lakes GC, *Pewaukee*	18 [S]	262-691-0900
westernlakes.com		

[A] = MILITARY   [M] = MUNICIPAL   [P] = PUBLIC   [R] = RESORT

Golf Yellow Pages, 18th Edition — WYOMING

Westhaven GC, *Oshkosh* .... 18 [P] 920-233-4640
  westhavengolfclub.com
Westmoor CC, *Brookfield* .... 18 [V] 262-796-7800
  westmoor.org
Westridge GC, *Neenah* .... 18 [P] 920-725-2050
  golfwgc.com
Westwood GC, *Phillips* .... 9 [P] 715-339-3600
  westwoodsandtrap.com
Weymont Run CC, *Weyauwega* .... 9 [P] 920-867-3412
Whispering Pines GC, *Cadott* .... 18 [P] 715-289-4653
  whisperingpinesgc.net
Whispering Springs GC, *Fond Du Lac* ... 18 [P] 920-921-8053
  whisperingspringsgolf.com
Whistling Straits, *Sheboygan* .... 36 [R] 920-565-6050
  whistlingstraits.com
White Eagle GC, *Hudson* .... 18 [P] 715-549-4653
  whiteeaglegolf.com
White Lake CC, *Montello* .... 18 [R] 608-297-2255
  whitelakegolf.com
White Tail Wilderness, *Webster* .... 9 [P] 715-866-8276
Whitecap Skye GC, *Upson* .... 18 [P] 715-561-2776
  skyegolf.net
Whitehall Public GC, *Whitehall* .... 9 [P] 715-538-4800
Whitetail CC, *Colfax* .... 18 [P] 715-962-3888
  whitetailgolf.com
Whitewater CC, *Whitewater* .... 9 [V] 262-473-3305
  whitewatercountryclub.com
Whitnall Park GC, *Hales Corners* .... 18 [M] 414-425-7931
  countyparks.com/golf
Wild Ridge GC, *Eau Claire* .... 36 [P] 715-834-1766
  wildridgegolf.com
Wild Rock GC at the Wilderness, *Wisconsin Dells* .18 [R] 608-253-4653
  wildrockgolfclub.com
Wildwood GC, *Minocqua* .... 18 [P] 715-356-3477
  wildwoodgolfcourse.info
Wildwood Marshes GC, *Hayward* .... 9 [P] 715-462-3990
  wildwoodmarshes.com
Willow Run GC, *Pewaukee* .... 18 [P] 262-544-8585
  willowrungolf.com
Winagamie GC, *Neenah* .... 27 [P] 920-757-5453
  winagamiegolf.com
Winchester Hill GC, *Larsen* .... 18 [S] 920-836-2476
Windwood Of Watertown, *Watertown* ..... 18 [S] 920-262-0702
  madisongolf.com
Windy Acres GC, *Monroe* .... 9 [P] 608-325-3240
Wisconsin Club, *Milwaukee* .... 18 [V] 414-353-8800
  wisconsinclub.com
Wisconsin River GC, *Stevens Point* .... 18 [P] 715-344-9152
  golftheriver.com
Woodland GC, *Oak Creek* .... 9 [P] 414-762-1101
Woodland Ridge GC, *Crivitz* .... 27 [P] 715-854-7833
  woodlandridgegolfcourse.com
Yahara Hills GC, *Madison* .... 36 [M] 608-838-3126
  cityofmadisongolf.com
Yellow Lake GC, *Danbury* .... 9 [P] 715-866-7107
Yellowstone GC, *Blancharddville* .... 9 [P] 608-543-3664
  yellowstonegolfcourse.com
Zablocki Park GC, *Milwaukee* .... 9 [M] 414-282-6510
  countyparks.com/golf

WYOMING

3 Creek Ranch GC, *Jackson* .... 18 [V] 307-734-7222
  3creekranch-jh.com
A Bar A Ranch GC, *Encampment* .... 9 [R] 307-327-5454
  abararanch.com
Airport GC, *Cheyenne* .... 18 [M] 307-637-6418
  cheyennecity.org
Antelope Hills GC, *Dubois* .... 9 [S] 307-455-2888
  antelopehillsgolfclub.net
Bell Nob GC, *Gillette* .... 18 [M] 307-686-7069
  ccprd.com
Buffalo GC, *Buffalo* .... 18 [M] 307-684-5266
Canyon Valley Resort GC, *Ten Sleep* ...... 9 [R] 307-366-2768
  canyonvalleyresort.com
Casper CC, *Casper* .... 18 [V] 307-265-0767
Casper Muni GC, *Casper* .... 27 [M] 307-233-6620
  casperwy.gov
Cedar Pines GC, *Upton* .... 9 [S] 307-468-2847
Cheyenne CC, *Cheyenne* .... 18 [S] 307-637-2230
  cheyennecountryclub.com
Cottonwood CC, *Torrington* .... 18 [M] 307-532-3868
  city-of-torrington.org/golf_course.htm
Douglas Community GC, *Douglas* .... 18 [M] 307-358-5099
  douglasgolfclub.com
F E Warren AFB GC, *Fe Warren AFB* .... 18 [A] 307-773-3556
  90svs.com
Fossil Island GC, *Kemmerer* .... 9 [S] 307-877-6954
Foster Gulch GC, *Lovell* .... 9 [S] 307-548-2445
Gillette GC, *Gillette* .... 9 [P] 307-682-4774
Glenrock GC, *Glenrock* .... 9 [P] 307-436-5560
Green Hills Muni GC, *Worland* .... 18 [M] 307-347-8972
Hay Creek GC, *Wright* .... 9 [M] 307-464-0747
  wrightwyoming.com
Jackson Hole G&TC, *Jackson* .... 18 [S] 307-733-3111
  jhgtc.com
Jacoby Park GC, *Laramie* .... 18 [P] 307-745-3111
  jacobygc.com
Kendrick GC, *Sheridan* .... 18 [M] 307-674-8148
  city-sheridan-wy.com
Keyhole CC, *Pine Haven* .... 9 [P] 307-756-3775
Lander GC, *Lander* .... 18 [M] 307-332-4653
  landergolfclub.com
Laramie CC, *Laramie* .... 9 [S] 307-745-8490
  thelaramiecountryclub.com
Leaning Rock GC, *Pine Bluffs* .... 9 [M] 307-245-3807
Legion Town & CC, *Thermopolis* .... 9 [S] 307-864-5294
Little America Resort & Golf, *Cheyenne* .... 9 [R] 307-775-8500
  littleamerica.com/cheyenne
Midway GC, *Basin* .... 9 [P] 307-568-2255
Newcastle CC, *Newcastle* .... 9 [S] 307-746-2639
Niobrara CC, *Lusk* .... 9 [M] 307-334-2438
Old Baldy Club, *Saratoga* .... 18 [R] 307-326-5222
  oldbaldyclub.com
Olive Glenn G&CC, *Cody* .... 18 [S] 307-587-5551
  oliveglenngolf.com
Paradise Valley CC, *Casper* .... 18 [V] 307-237-3673
  paradisevalleyccwyo.com
Pine Rock GC, *Meeteetse* .... 9 [P] 307-868-2177
  pinerockgolf.com
Prairie View GC, *Cheyenne* .... 9 [P] 307-637-6420
  cheyennecity.org
Purple Sage Muni GC, *Evanston* .... 18 [M] 307-789-2383
  purplesagegolf.com
Rendezvous Meadows Golf, *Pinedale* ..... 9 [M] 307-367-4252
  pinedaleonline.com/golf.htm

[S] = SEMI-PRIVATE   [V] = PRIVATE   [U] = UNIVERSITY   [N] = UNIVERSITY-PRIVATE

WYOMING

Riverton CC, *Riverton*..................................18 [S] 307-856-4779
   rivertoncountryclub.net
Rochelle Ranch Muni GC, *Rawlins*...............18 [M] 307-324-7121
   rawlinswy.org
Rolling Green GC, *Green River*...................... 9 [V] 307-875-6200
Salt Creek CC, *Midwest*....................................9 [P] 307-437-6511
Saratoga Inn GC, *Saratoga*............................. 9 [R] 307-326-5261
   saratogaresortandspa.com
Sheridan CC, *Sheridan* .... 9 [V] 307-674-8135
   sheridancountryclub.com
Shooting Star of Jackson Hole, *Teton Village*...... 18 [V] 307-739-3270
   shootingstarjh.com
Sinclair GC, *Sinclair*...9 [S] 307-324-7767
Snake River Sporting Club, *Jackson* .... 18 [V] 307-734-7727
   snakeriversportingclub.com
Star Valley Ranch Assoc - Aspen Hills, *Thayne*........9 [S] 307-883-2899
   svrawy.com
Star Valley Ranch Assoc - Cedar Creek, *Thayne*....18 [S] 307-883-2230
   svrawy.com
Star Valley Ranch Resort GC, *Thayne*..................18 [R] 307-883-2448
   starvalleyranchresort.com

Sundance CC, *Sundance*......................................9 [P] 307-283-1191
Targhee Village GC, *Alta* ....9 [P] 208-354-8577
   targheevillage.com
Teton Pines GC, *Jackson*....................................18 [R] 307-733-1733
   tetonpines.com
The GC At Devils Tower, *Hulett* .... 18 [V] 307-467-5773
   devilstowergolf.com
The Powder Horn GC, *Sheridan*..........................27 [P] 307-672-5323
   thepowderhorn.com
The Powell GC, *Powell* ....18 [M] 307-754-7259
   powellgolfclub.com
Three Crowns GC, *Casper* ....18 [P] 307-472-7696
   threecrownsgolfclub.com
Trail Ruts GC, *Guernsey* ....9 [M] 307-836-2255
   golfandcamp.com
Valli Vu GC, *Afton*...9 [M] 307-885-3338
   vallivu.com
Wheatland GC, *Wheatland* ....9 [P] 307-322-3675
White Mountain GC, *Rock Springs*.....................27 [M] 307-352-1415
   rswy.net
Wind River GC, *Riverton*......................................9 [P] 307-856-9606

[A] = MILITARY   [M] = MUNICIPAL   [P] = PUBLIC   [R] = RESORT

Printed in Great Britain
by Amazon.co.uk, Ltd.,
Marston Gate.